HANDBOOK OF AGRICULTURAL ECONOMICS
VOLUME 1A

HANDBOOKS
IN
ECONOMICS

18

Series Editors

KENNETH J. ARROW
MICHAEL D. INTRILIGATOR

ELSEVIER
AMSTERDAM · LONDON · NEW YORK · OXFORD · PARIS · SHANNON · TOKYO

HANDBOOK OF AGRICULTURAL ECONOMICS

VOLUME 1A
AGRICULTURAL PRODUCTION

Edited by

BRUCE L. GARDNER
University of Maryland, College Park

and

GORDON C. RAUSSER
University of California, Berkeley

2001
ELSEVIER
AMSTERDAM · LONDON · NEW YORK · OXFORD · PARIS · SHANNON · TOKYO

ELSEVIER SCIENCE B.V.
Sara Burgerhartstraat 25
P.O. Box 211, 1000 AE Amsterdam, The Netherlands

First edition 2001

Library of Congress Cataloging in Publication Data
A catalog record from the Library of Congress has been applied for.

ISBN: 0-444-82588-6 (set, comprising vols. 1A & 1B)
ISBN: 0-444-50728-0 (vol. 1A)
ISBN: 0-444-50729-9 (vol. 1B)
ISSN: 0169-7218 (Handbooks in Economics Series)

⊗ The paper used in this publication meets the requirements of ANSI/NISO Z39.48-1992 (Permanence of Paper).
Printed in The Netherlands.

INTRODUCTION TO THE SERIES

The aim of the *Handbooks in Economics* series is to produce Handbooks for various branches of economics, each of which is a definitive source, reference, and teaching supplement for use by professional researchers and advanced graduate students. Each Handbook provides self-contained surveys of the current state of a branch of economics in the form of chapters prepared by leading specialists on various aspects of this branch of economics. These surveys summarize not only received results but also newer developments, from recent journal articles and discussion papers. Some original material is also included, but the main goal is to provide comprehensive and accessible surveys. The Handbooks are intended to provide not only useful reference volumes for professional collections but also possible supplementary readings for advanced courses for graduate students in economics.

KENNETH J. ARROW and MICHAEL D. INTRILIGATOR

PUBLISHER'S NOTE

For a complete overview of the Handbooks in Economics Series, please refer to the listing on the last two pages of this volume.

CONTENTS OF THE HANDBOOK

VOLUME 1A

PART 1 – AGRICULTURAL PRODUCTION

INTRODUCTION

The subject matter of agricultural economics has both broadened and deepened in recent years, and the chapters of this Handbook present the most exciting and innovative work being done today. The field originated early in the twentieth century with a focus on farm management and commodity markets, but has since moved far into analysis of issues in food, resources, international trade, and linkages between agriculture and the rest of the economy. In the process agricultural economists have been pioneering users of developments in economic theory and econometrics. Moreover, in the process of intense focus on problems of economic science that are central to agriculture – market expectations, behavior under uncertainty, multimarket relationships for both products and factors, the economics of research and technology adoption, and public goods and property issues associated with issues like nonpoint pollution and innovations in biotechnology – agricultural economists have developed methods of empirical investigation that have been taken up in other fields.

The chapters are organized into five parts, contained in two volumes. Volume 1 contains Part 1, "Agricultural Production", and Part 2, "Marketing, Distribution and Consumers". These two parts include much of the traditional scope of agricultural economics, emphasizing advances in both theory and empirical application of recent years. Volume 2 consists of three parts: "Agriculture, Natural Resources and the Environment", "Agriculture in the Macroeconomy", and "Agricultural and Food Policy". Although agricultural economists have always paid attention to these topics, research devoted to them has increased substantially in scope as well as depth in recent years.

A large-scale effort to review and assess the state of knowledge in agricultural economics was previously undertaken by the American Agricultural Economics Association (AAEA), with publication in four volumes from 1977 to 1992.[1] Those earlier survey volumes have strikingly different subject-matter content from that of the present Handbook, especially considering that they described the same field only 20 years ago. The AAEA volumes have extensive coverage of farm management issues, costs of production in agriculture, and estimates of efficiency of marketing firms. In our judgment little in any fundamental way has been added to our knowledge in these areas, and applications have become routine rather than imaginative research. The largest AAEA volume was devoted entirely to agriculture in economic development. This remains a

---

[1] *A Survey of Economics Literature*, Lee Martin, ed., Minneapolis: University of Minnesota Press. Volume 1, Traditional Field of Agricultural Economics (1977); Volume 2, Quantitative Methods in Agricultural Economics (1977); Volume 3, Economics of Welfare, Rural Development, and Natural Resources (1981); Volume 4, Agriculture in Economic Development (1992).

most important topic, but we cover it in only one complete chapter and parts of several others. This reflects in part the integration of work on developing countries with mainstream applied work. For example, our chapters on production economics, expectations, and risk management also encompass applications to agriculture in developing economies.

That integration points to another gradual but notable change in agricultural economists' research. The AAEA surveys had most of the chapters of one volume devoted to quantitative methods. We do not have any separate methodological chapters. In contrast, we have several chapters with substantial development of economic theory. This reflects an evolution in the research priorities of leading agricultural economists who, following the earlier work of Nerlove on supply and Griliches on technological change, are working at the theoretical frontiers and simultaneously undertaking empirical work – not just purveying new theories to their more "applied" colleagues.

As its title indicates, the AAEA volumes were surveys of literature, and aimed at completeness of coverage within their subject matter. We asked our authors to be selective, to focus on what they saw as the main contributions to the area they covered, and to assess the state of knowledge and what remains to be learned. This approach has left some gaps in our coverage, and has given us some chapters that are perhaps more idiosyncratic than is usual for a survey chapter. In order to pull things together at a higher level of aggregation, we commissioned five "synthesis" chapters, one for each of the five parts of the Handbook. And, to provide our own even broader overview, the editors have written closing syntheses of each volume. Because these syntheses provide capsule summaries of each Handbook chapter, we will not present further description of content here.

Although advances in research in agricultural economics are increasingly being made in many countries, our authors and coverage of applied topics is heavily U.S.-weighted (only six authors work outside of the U.S.: two in Europe, two in Australia, one in Canada, and one in Israel). Of those in the U.S., however, six are economists at the World Bank, an international rather than American institution. Probably in another twenty years or so one will have to become more international to capture the most interesting and exciting developments in the field, but that day has not arrived yet.

Among the many debts we have accrued in the preparation of this Handbook, the most important was Rachael Goodhue. She not only assessed the substance of many chapters, but she persuaded many reviewers and authors alike to complete their assigned responsibilities. Other critical contributors include the dedicated staff who provided support at the University of California, Berkeley, and at the University of Maryland. At Maryland, Liesl Koch served as copy editor and guided the authors' final revisions and preparation of the manuscript with sure judgment and a firm but diplomatic hand, a job best likened to driving a herd of cats. Coordination of correspondence with authors and reviewers was organized and carried out at Berkeley with exemplary efficiency and organizational skill by Jef Samp, Jessica Berkson, and Jennifer Michael, under the direction of Nancy Lewis.

We also want to recognize the comments and suggestions received from 45 reviewers of chapter drafts: Julian Alston, Jock Anderson, Richard Barichello, Eran Beinenbaum, Michael Boehlje, Dan Bromley, Steve Buccola, Allan Buckwell, David Bullock, Michael Caputo, Jean-Paul Chavas, John Connor, Klaus Deininger, Jeffrey Dorfman, Marcel Fafchamps, Gershon Feder, Joe Glauber, Dan Gilligan, Rachael Goodhue, Tom Grennes, Zvi Griliches, Geoff Heal, Eithan Hochman, Matt Holt, Wallace Huffman, D. Gale Johnson, Zvi Lerman, Erik Lichtenberg, Ethan Ligon, Alan Love, Jill McCluskey, Mario Miranda, Arie Oskam, Dick Perrin, Mark Rosegrant, Vern Ruttan, Ed Schuh, Kathleen Segerson, Larry Sjaastad, Spiro Stefanou, Jo Swinnen, Frans van der Zee, Finis Welch, Abner Womack, and Jacob Yaron.

BRUCE GARDNER
GORDON RAUSSER

CONTENTS OF VOLUME 1A

Chapter 2
Uncertainty, Risk Aversion, and Risk Management for Agricultural Producers
GIANCARLO MOSCHINI and DAVID A. HENNESSY

PART 1

AGRICULTURAL PRODUCTION

Chapter 1

PRODUCTION AND SUPPLY

YAIR MUNDLAK

Faculty of Agriculture, The Hebrew University of Jerusalem, Rehovot, Israel

Contents

Handbook of Agricultural Economics, Volume 1, Edited by B. Gardner and G. Rausser

Abstract

The work of more than 50 years aimed at gaining empirical insight into the production structure of agriculture and the related modes of farmers' behavior is reviewed, and orders of magnitude of the various parameters of interest are quoted. The review follows the lines of the evolution of the pertinent research, and it builds on it in forming a general framework for empirical work. This approach broadens the scope of producers' decisions to include the choice of the implemented technology and it also overcomes statistical problems that have accompanied the relevant research for a long time.

JEL classification: Q11

Technology along with the competitive conditions constitute the core of the supply side of the economy. There is hardly a subject in economics that can be discussed with production sitting in the balcony rather than playing center stage. To mention the main favorable subjects in agricultural economics research: product supply, factor demand, technical change, income distribution, the relationships between factor prices and product prices, the competitive position of agriculture, returns to scale, the size distribution of firms, and capital accumulation. The nature of the relationships and the conclusions derived in any particular analysis depend on the order of magnitude of the parameters in question. Hence, whether we want it or not, the empirical analysis of technology and its changes is of cardinal importance, and measurement problems are pertinent even if on the surface it seems that the subject matter is not 'technical'.

In this review, we deal with the various aspects of the analysis. As will become clear, much of the discussion in the literature is methodology driven, not always accompanied by substantive applications. Inasmuch as methodological innovations are desirable, the question is how do they help us to think of, or deal with, specific issues of interest. This is a question that the reader should try to answer for himself, depending on his particular interest. To assist in this endeavor, we summarize here the empirical findings that bear on the main parameters of interest and address some important methodological issues essential to the interpretation of empirical studies and to future research. In many cases, the empirical results display a wide range and thus highlight the need for an appropriate framework for their evaluation. The choice of subjects and the coverage in the discussion are carried out with the purpose of constructing a uniform framework to meet the purpose. This is built on the cumulative experience and contributions provided by numerous studies and on the evolution of the thinking that is so valuable in the reading and the interpretation of the data. To emphasize this aspect, the subjects are introduced largely in an order that highlights this evolution.

There are two fairly distinct periods in the study of agricultural production functions: before and after duality. The changing of the guard was in the early 1970s, although a few studies employing direct estimation continue to appear after 1970. The appearance of duality changed not only the method of estimation but also the questions asked to the extent that there is little continuity in the subjects of interest. This can be accounted for by the fact that much of the work is methodology-driven rather than being an indication that the old questions had been adequately answered or of any explicit agenda.

1. Primal estimates or the Cobb–Douglas culture

1.1. The setting of the agenda

It seems that the empirical work on agricultural production functions originated in a methodological paper by Tintner (1944) and an application by Tintner and Brownlee (1944), which appeared as a short paper in the Notes section of the *Journal of Farm*

Economics and was followed by a full size paper by Heady (1946). This work was influenced by the work of Cobb and Douglas (1928).[1] It thus took about fifteen years to adopt the work of Cobb and Douglas in agricultural economics application.

These studies used data from a random sample of Iowa farms for 1939. The data were classified by area of the state, type, and also size of farm. The inputs included were land, labor, equipment, livestock and feed, and miscellaneous operating expense, a classification that is still applicable today. Interestingly, this early work anticipated some of the more difficult subjects in the empirical work of production functions. Management was recognized as an input, but "[t]he productive agent management has been excluded since there is no satisfactory index of inputs for this factor" [Tintner and Brownlee (1944, p. 566)]. Allusions were also made to the importance of input quality.[2] Heady (1946) expressed similar concerns about the quality issue and the omission of management.[3] Also, based on the criticism of the Cobb–Douglas work that appeared at that time by Reder (1943), Bronfenbrenner (1944), and Marschak and Andrews (1944), Heady (1946) noted that "[t]he functions which have been derived ... are of the inter-firm rather than intrafarm variety ... it can be expected that a multitude of functions exists ... because of the varying combinations of techniques employed and commodities produced" (p. 999). This is a recognition of the problems caused by aggregation over techniques. Similarly, Smith (1945) observed that firms in cross section may employ different techniques, particularly due to fixed plants inherited from the past, and the long-run production functions so derived may represent "mongrels" or hybrids. Aside from the question of input quality, Bronfenbrenner (1944) raised the point that capital and labor are not on the same footing because labor is a flow ("quantity used"), whereas capital is a stock (representing the "available quantity"). This can be interpreted as an early recognition of the conceptual problem of the evaluation of the productivity of durable inputs.

These studies were concerned with the contribution of inputs to output variations and with a comparison of the factor productivity on different farm types and the relationship to their returns. The estimated production elasticities reported by Tintner and Brownlee (1944) for the sample as a whole are: land, 0.34; labor, 0.24; and other assets and variable inputs, 0.41. The sum is 0.99. Heady used a larger sample and a somewhat different classification of inputs to obtain for the sample as a whole: land, 0.23; labor, 0.03; and other assets and variable inputs, 0.59. The sum is 0.85.

---

[1] A regression equation linear in the logarithms "[is] similar to the production function employed by Paul Douglas in his empirical studies" [Tintner and Brownlee (1944, p. 567)]. On the history of the Cobb–Douglas production function, see [Douglas (1976)].

[2] "Using the number of acres in the farms as a measure of inputs of land ignores variations in the quality of land. Measuring inputs of labor in terms of months of labor also ignores variations in the quality and intensity of labor, particularly that of operator and his family" [Tintner and Brownlee (1944, p. 566)].

[3] At the time the issue of management bias was unrecognized, therefore both papers speculated that had management been included, the sum of the elasticities, as a measure of returns to scale, would have increased [Tintner and Brownlee (1944, p. 569), Heady (1946, p. 995)]. However, Heady also indicates that the sum of the elasticities might have decreased due to the introduction of management (Ibid., p. 997).

Several points are of interest. First, these studies were prompted by a methodological innovation introduced by Cobb and Douglas (1928). Yet, their orientation is applicative in nature, and they address substantive issues related to the efficient use of inputs. Second, sampling from the same data source yields different elasticities. The sum of the elasticities of labor and land vary between 0.58 and 0.25 in the two studies respectively. This difference suggests sensitivity of the estimates to output composition and perhaps differences in the physical environment. Third, the sum of the elasticities is smaller than 1.

The approach formulated by the foregoing studies served as a framework for the production function estimation for more than two decades, where attention was focused on the following issues: the contribution of the various factors to the explanation of output variations in the cross section or over time, the production elasticities and their significance, the robustness of the estimates, the role of economies of scale, as judged by the sum of the elasticities, the importance of the quality of inputs, the treatment of management and its relations to the properties of the estimates, the functional forms, and the role of technical change. The data base of these studies varied from observations on individual farms to cross-country comparisons.

The question of efficient use of inputs is the objective of many studies.[4] Lack of robustness of empirical results was raised by Hildebrand (1960) who found that annual cross-section regressions are not robust and any hypothesis can be supported by some results. Lack of robustness is also evident in some other studies that present more than one set of results. Heady and Dillon (1961, Chapter 17) review and summarize 32 studies in various countries based on farm data. The mean elasticities and their coefficient of variation (in parentheses) are: land 0.38 (0.58), labor 0.21 (0.80), and "other services" 0.39 (0.59). In all these studies the sum of all the elasticities is near 1. The magnitude of the coefficient of variation indicates a wide spread in the results among the studies. They compare their results with those obtained in the pioneering cross-country study by Bhattacharjee (1955) and with assumptions made in the literature.[5] All of this indicates an effort to get a definitive substantive solution. But as this target was realized to be elusive, they concluded that "[s]till, the variations shown among the elasticities of Table 17.14 bear witness to the dangers associated with the use of any such global production function" [Heady and Dillon (1961, p. 633)].[6] The discussion is then shifted to the examination of the efficiency of the resource use. For instance, their Table 17.17 presents a ratio of the marginal productivity of labor to its opportunity cost with values varying between 2.84 observed in Taiwan to negative values obtained in dairy farming in Sweden. The median value of this ratio is 0.67. They present similar calculations for land

---

[4] See, for instance, Hopper (1965), Chennareddy (1967), Sahota (1968), and Herdt (1971) for India; Yotopoulos (1967) for Greece; Huang (1971) for Malaya; and Headley (1968) for the US.

[5] Bhattacharjee (1955, regression 4) reports elasticities of 0.36 and 0.3 for land and labor respectively.

[6] Clark (1973) assembles many results of factor shares in an informal framework but with good international coverage. It is very clear that the estimates depend on the economic environment which is a major theme of our discussion.

and capital services, but these are more problematic for conceptual reasons which need not be discussed at this point. To get a view of the diversity of the results, the reader is advised to check some of the country studies based on the primal approach.[7]

In 1944 Marschak and Andrews pointed out that the inputs are endogenous, and therefore Ordinary Least Squares (OLS) estimates of the production function are biased. Their paper extended the scope of the analysis by introducing issues related to the statistical properties of the estimates. Their work and Haavelmo's (1947) work on the consumption function were early examples of the problems of simultaneity in economic analysis and thus revived the question that had been asked by Working (1927) about the meaning of statistical demand equations. That opened up a route of work centered on methodological issues with a life of its own.[8]

The simultaneity problem in the estimation of production functions was overcome by the factor share estimator proposed by Klein (1953) and applied by Wolfson (1958). This estimator is based on the assumption that firms always employ *all* their inputs so as to satisfy the first order conditions for profit maximization given the *current ex post* prices. As such, the factor share estimator is subject to a major conceptual difficulty in that it cannot answer the original question of Cobb and Douglas about the empirical relevance of the competitive conditions because they are imposed in the derivation of the estimator.[9] Although this is seldom explicitly recognized, or acknowledged, all the estimators that use the first order conditions for profit maximization – and to be sure, these include the estimators based on duality as well as on the axioms of revealed preferences – use the very same property and thus are subject to the same limitation.

A different line of attack on the simultaneity problem was taken by Mundlak (1961) and Hoch (1962) through the use of covariance analysis.[10] Applying this method to a sample of family farms in Israel gave lower estimates for the elasticities compared

---

[7] For instance, in addition to the studies mentioned in footnote 5, US: Tintner and Brownlee (1944), Heady (1946), Hildebrand (1960), Griliches (1963a, 1963b, 1964), Kislev (1966), Tweeten and Quance (1969), Kislev and Peterson (1996); India: Lau and Yotopoulos (1972); Israel: Mundlak (1961), Sadan (1968); Mexico: Ulveling and Fletcher (1970); Colombia: Colyer and Jimenez (1971); Taiwan: Yotopoulos, Lau, and Lin (1976), Shih, Hushak, and Rask (1977), Wu (1977); Thailand: Mittelhammer, Young, Tasanasanta, and Donnelly (1980).

[8] The early work on production functions, up to the early 1960s, is surveyed by Walters (1963).

[9] I found the following statement by Clark (1973, fn 8, p. 21) to be interesting: "Douglas told me that when the function was first prepared in the 1920s, he was expecting it to show that wages then actually received by labour were considerably below its true marginal product; and was surprised to find that they were in fact extremely close to the level predicted by the function".

[10] Hoch (1958) examined a solution to the simultaneity problem based on identification through the second moments of the equations disturbances. There is no reference in the literature to an empirical application of this method, perhaps for a good reason because, as indicated by Mundlak and Hoch (1965), it is very sensitive to the specification and in the case of a likely specification error can have an unbounded bias. In another paper, Hoch (1955) suggested the use of covariance analysis. However, the method was not discussed in connection with the simultaneity problem. This is probably the reason that covariance analysis was not mentioned in [Hoch (1958)], which deals head-on with that problem. It is only in [Hoch (1962)] that the covariance analysis is seen as a solution to the simultaneity problem.

to OLS without allowance for firm effect, and their sum declined from roughly 1 to roughly 0.8. Mundlak (1961) interpreted the difference between 1 and the sum of the elasticities as the factor share of management.[11] The method was also used to estimate the managerial capacity and its empirical distribution in [Mundlak (1964a)]. Another substantive result of that study is an elasticity of land near zero. The farms in the sample are very small, and on the surface one would have expected a higher elasticity for land. However, a low elasticity for land is indicative of low profitability of agriculture. This interpretation is supported by the fact that a negligible elasticity for land in Israel was also obtained for a sample of large farms (kibbutzim) in [Sadan (1968)], so the result is unrelated to farm size.

The observations made so far are:

O.1 The estimates are not robust.

O.2 Often, results show a gap between marginal productivity and real factor prices.

O.3 Specifically, there is a difference between estimates based on inter and intrafarm observations.

O.4 Firms use different techniques.

O.5 Input quality is not addressed.

O.6 A lack of clarity on whether to use stock or flow variables.

O.7 Inputs are endogenous, and therefore OLS estimates are inconsistent.

O.8 It is possible to overcome the problem of inconsistency.

O.9 A need to further explore the role and scope of factor-share estimates.

1.2. A simple production model

The initial discussion can be conducted in terms of a single-input Cobb–Douglas production function

$$Y = AX^{\beta} e^{m_0 + u_0}, \tag{1}$$

where m_0 is the firm effect, or management, a firm-specific factor known to the firm but not to the econometrician (private information), and u_0 is a random term whose value is not known at the time the production decisions are made. The conditional expectation of output, given the input, of firm i is[12]

$$Y_i^e \equiv \mathrm{E}(Y|X_i) \cong AX_i^{\beta} e^{m_{0i}}. \tag{2}$$

---

[11] Other sources of farm-specific effects are differences in land quality, micro-climate, and so on. However, the emphasis has been placed on management. The firm effect is observed not only in production functions estimated from farm data; it is also a common phenomenon in cross-section analysis of manufacturing data. Thus, it seems that differences due to farming environment are not the main reason for the firm effects.

[12] Note that $\mathrm{E}(e^{u_0}) \cong (1 + \sigma_{00}^2/2)$; $\sigma_{00}^2 = \mathrm{E}(u_0^2)$. This term is ignored in (2).

At this stage we assume that the price is known, and the firm chooses the input so as to maximize the expected profit:

$$\max_{X_i} \pi^e(X|_{W,P,i}) = PY_i^e - WX_i, \tag{3}$$

where P and W are the product and input prices respectively. The first order condition is met up to the stochastic terms m_1 and u_1

$$\beta A X^{\beta-1} = \frac{W}{P} e^{m_1+u_1}, \tag{4}$$

where m_1 is known to the firm but not to the econometrician, and u_1 is a transitory component. The term m_1 reflects the firm's expectation formation and its utility function. In what follows, we will deal with real prices, so that W is the wage in output units, and P is the product price in input units.

We write Equations (2) and (4) in logarithms, with the variables measured as deviations from their overall mean, and introduce time notations:

$$y_{it} - x_{it}\beta = m_{0i} + u_{0it}, \tag{5}$$

$$y_{it} - x_{it} = w_{it} + m_{1i} + u_{1it} + u_{0it}. \tag{6}$$

When prices are exogenous the reduced form for x (note that $p = -w$) is

$$x_{it} = -c(p_{it} + u_{1it} + m_{1i} - m_{0i}); \quad c = (1-\beta)^{-1}. \tag{7}$$

The four error components are assumed to be IID with the following first two moments:

$$u_{jit} \sim (0, \sigma_{jj}); \quad m_{ji} \sim (\mu_j, \tau_{jj}); \quad j = 0, 1, \tag{8}$$

where $\mu_0 = 0$ and μ_1 is unrestricted. The expected value of all cross products of the error components is zero.[13]

Several of the observations made above are related to the endogeneity of the input. Equation (7) shows that the input is a function of the firm effect, m_{0i}, which is also part of the production function shock, and therefore the input is not exogenous. The bias caused by this dependence contributes to the lack of robustness. Specifically, it contributes to the differences between intra and interfirm estimates (O.3). Also, when biased coefficients are used to test the efficiency of resource use, an erroneous conclusion of an inefficient use of resources (O.2) might be reached even when the firms use resources efficiently, or conversely.

---

[13] Shocks that affect all firms generate time effects that can be treated in the same way as the firm effect. The extension to include time effects is straightforward and need not be reviewed here (see [Mundlak (1963a)]).

Several approaches are offered to overcome the problem of input endogeneity (O.7). When the sample consists of panel data, covariance analysis transforms the variables to deviations from the firm mean, and thereby the firm effect is eliminated from Equation (7). Let the sample average over the time observations be x_i; then Equation (7) is transformed to

$$x_{it} - x_{i.} = -c(p_{it} - p_{i.} + u_{1it} - u_{1i.}),\tag{9}$$

and it is seen that the firm effect has disappeared. The estimator is referred to as a "within" estimator (because it is based on within-firm variations).

An alternative approach is to use the price as an instrumental variable for estimating Equation (5). This is basically the dual approach to estimation, to be discussed below. This estimator is likely to be less efficient than the covariance estimator because it does not use all the pertinent information [Mundlak (1996a)]. This can be seen intuitively from Equation (7). The variability of the input in the sample is generated by four components: p_{it}, u_{1it}, m_{1i}, and m_{0i}. The last term causes the bias and should be eliminated, whereas the other three terms provide the information for the estimation. Hence, the most efficient procedure would be to use the first three components as instrumental variables. However, this cannot be done directly because, of the three variables, only p is observed. The within estimator uses the within-firm variations of p and u_1 as instruments, whereas the dual estimator uses as an instrumental variable the total variations of p but does not utilize the information in u_1. The point is that any variability of input, regardless of whether or not it is consistent with the first order condition for profit maximization, generates points on the production function and therefore helps to trace it, or more technically, helps to identify the production function.

The use of price as an instrument is subject to some limitations. If the sample consists of competitive firms, the between variability of the prices should be nil. If the sample consists of market (rather than micro) data, then the prices are not necessarily exogenous and therefore cannot be used as instrumental variables. In any case, it is possible to combine the two estimators by using the within-input variable and the price as two instrumental variables. Other possible modifications are suggested in [Mundlak (1996a)]. However, all these have not been tried out. The empirical experience is limited to the 'within' and the dual estimators. Some of the results with respect to the 'within' estimator have been mentioned above, whereas the empirical experience with the dual estimator will be discussed below.

The factor-share estimator imposes the first order conditions for profit maximization, in which case the factor share is equal to the production elasticity, β, up to a stochastic term. Using Equation (6) it is easy to see that this estimator is inconsistent.

An important issue in the empirical investigation is whether the function displays constant returns to scale (CRT). If it does, in the case of the single-input function, β is equal to 1, and there is nothing to estimate. Thus the problem is more pertinent to the more realistic case with more than one input. To see this, assume now that there are k inputs. In this case, the model consists of Equation (5) where x and β will be

k-vectors and k-equations of the form of (6) [Cavallo (1976)]. Note that the difference of the first-order conditions for any two inputs, say 1 and 2, is free of m_0 and of u_0

$$x_2 - x_1 = w_2 - w_1 + u_2 - u_1 + m_2 - m_1. \tag{10}$$

Therefore, $x_2 - x_1$ can serve as an instrumental variable. Note that this variable contains all the pertinent information related to the two inputs. There are $k - 1$ such instruments, and there is a need for one more instrument to complete the estimation of the system. The assumption of CRT is a good candidate. In this case, a Cobb–Douglas function where the variables are divided by one of the inputs is free of simultaneous-equations bias.

1.3. Productivity

To understand some of the subsequent literature we turn to another direction of inquiry, that of measuring factor productivity, that was taking place at the same time. The most influential work in agriculture was that of T.W. Schultz (1953). He noted that in the period 1910–1950 agricultural production rose by about 75 percent due to a change in inputs and in technology. The change in inputs was instigated by price change, with labor becoming more expensive and therefore replaced by machines.[14] The importance of inputs is measured by their factor shares: "Land and labor are ... very important in farming, with labor representing 46 percent and agricultural land 24 percent of all inputs used in agriculture in 1910–1914" (p. 100).

He then goes on to discuss the aggregation of inputs and to derive a measure of the overall increase in productivity by comparing the relative changes in output and input. He notices that the results are sensitive to the price weights and the period of analysis. The rise in the annual average productivity for the period as a whole with end of period prices is 1.35 percent, and with beginning of period prices is 0.8 percent.

Where does the technical change come from? Schultz (1953, p. 110) considered three hypotheses:
  (1) Discoveries of new techniques are by-products of scientific curiosity and as such are unpredictable.
  (2) The level of scientific activity reflects cultural and institutional values rather than the value of its fruits, and thus, the development of new techniques is not induced by market conditions.
  (3) Science is supported by society because of its potential material contribution.

There is room for all three, but the gold medal is given to the last one. "Therefore, a new technique is simply a particular kind of input and the economies underlying the

---

[14] "Although new production techniques have been many and important, substitution among inputs is clearly evident and it is consistent with changes that have occurred in the relative prices of inputs ... labor has been withdrawn while other, cheaper inputs have been added" [Schultz (1953, p. 103)]. "United States agriculture has become increasingly dependent on inputs which are acquired from the nonfarm sector" (Ibid., p. 104).

supply and use are in principle the same as that of any other type of input. We do not wish to imply that every human activity entering into the development of new techniques can be explained wholly by considerations of cost and revenue; our belief simply is that a large part of the modern process of technological research from "pure" science to successful practice can be explained by economic analysis" [Schultz (1953, p. 110–111)]. This is the notion of induced innovation. However, "[w]e need also to explain the rate at which farmers adopt new techniques. Clearly, the mere availability of such techniques is no assurance that they will be applied in farming. The process by which farmers take on new techniques, as one would expect, is strongly motivated by economic considerations and yet very little is known about this process" (Ibid., p. 114). Although uncertainty about the new technique is important, Schultz views the new technique as a new input and suggests that the standard economic analysis be applied in the analysis of its adoption. He also recognizes the importance of credit rationing for agricultural markets. This view of technological change is related to the notion of implementation of technology discussed below.

This discussion by Schultz amplifies themes already mentioned above and puts on the agenda new ones, particularly the use of factor shares to measure the relative importance of inputs, the need to differentiate between the change in productivity due to a change in inputs and the change in technology, that the change in inputs takes place in response to changes in factor prices, and that the changes in the quality of inputs has to be taken into account in measuring factor prices. To sum up Schultz's additional observations,

O.10 Part of the change in technology is unpredictable.

O.11 Not all of what is known (in terms of technology) is actually implemented.

These are all key themes for understanding the subsequent work. To assist the discussion on the measurement of productivity, we write the production function as

$$Y(t) = F\big[A_1(t)X_1(t), \ldots, A_k(t)X_k(t), t\big], \tag{11}$$

where the A's are factor-augmenting functions or, not independently, quality indexes. Differentiate the function logarithmically, using a generic notation, $d\ln x/dt = \hat{x}$,

$$\begin{aligned}
\widehat{Y}(t) &= \big[\omega_1(t)\big(\hat{A}_1(t) + \widehat{X}_1(t)\big) + \cdots + \omega_k(t)(\hat{A}_k(t) + \widehat{X}_k(t))\big] + \tau(t) \\
&= [\text{aggregate input}] + \tau(t), \tag{12}
\end{aligned}$$

where the ω's are weights and τ is the relative change in the total factor productivity or the 'residual'. In estimation, the A's should be included as variables in the analysis to avoid specification error.

All productivity measures are based on a comparison of changes in aggregate output with changes in aggregate input. The change in the aggregate input should measure changes in quantity that take place under constant technology. That is, the quality variables should be uncorrelated with the residual $\tau(t)$. If they are correlated, the empirical production function is a locus of points that are generated by more than one function. To illustrate, the work of children in ditch digging is not as productive as that of adults.

Therefore, adjusting the labor input by assigning different coefficients by age or gender will give a more meaningful measure of the labor input. Another example is the measure of fertilizers by their nutrient content. But most of the quality adjustments are of a different nature. A good example is the adjustment of the labor input for education where a measure of schooling multiplies the physical labor input to yield quality-adjusted labor input, measured by the total years of schooling. What is the meaning of this adjustment? If the task is digging ditches, education, at best, should not make a difference. But if there are alternatives to digging by hand, education can make a difference in the profitability of implementing these alternatives. Generalizing, an increase in the level of education, other things equal, is expected to increase the use of more advanced techniques. Thus, in this case technology is not held constant; education is a carrier of a technical change and should be treated as such. We return to this subject when we discuss the results of cross-country estimates of the production function. One implication of this distinction is that the measure of returns to scale should not include the effect of 'quality' variables that represent technology. There is no general agreement on this approach, and for alternatives see, for instance, Griliches and Jorgenson (1966).

The aggregation weights can be based on market values leading to factor shares, as done by Ruttan (1956) and Solow (1957), or by production elasticities derived from empirical production functions. Note that in the case of a Cobb–Douglas production function these elasticities are constant. Otherwise, they vary over the sample as do the factor shares, and the results vary accordingly.

Much of the work on measures of productivity change uses elasticities derived from empirical production functions. Griliches (1963a) deals directly with the effect of input quality on the measurement of productivity and, not independently, on the empirical production function. He argued for the use of the empirical production function to provide the weights for the aggregation of inputs. To this end, he fitted a Cobb–Douglas function to data for the 68 USDA regions in the US in 1949. The emphasis is on the role of education and economies of scale in accounting for productivity changes. He obtained a sum of elasticities of 1.36 from a regression without education and 1.35 with education included. Thus, the education was not the source for the sum of elasticities to exceed 1, which was taken as evidence of economies of scale. This result was incorporated in the analysis of sources of productivity growth, with the assertion that "... changes in output are attributable to changes in the quantities and *qualities* of inputs, and to *economies of scale*, rather than to 'technical change' " (Ibid., p. 332; italics by YM). "This procedure led to an almost complete accounting for the sources of output growth in the United States agriculture during 1940–60 leaving no 'unexplained' residual to be identified with unidentified 'Technical changes' " (Ibid., p. 333). The essence of that discussion is the belief that if the analysis is carried out with care, there should be no unexplained residual left.[15]

---

[15] This view was also repeated in [Griliches (1964)] where the empirical analysis was extended to cover 1954 and 1959. "[I]t is possible to account for all of the observed growth in agricultural output without invoking the unexplained concept of (residual) technical change" (p. 970).

There was some discomfort with the estimates, but nevertheless, those were preferred to factor shares because, relying on Schultz, the agricultural sector was perceived to be in a continuous disequilibrium.[16] As the empirical results show, education is important, the elasticities differ from factor shares, and the sum of elasticities was larger than 1. Therefore, "[t]hese findings, particularly the last two, if accepted, will account for a substantial fraction of the conventionally measured productivity increases" (Ibid., p. 336). In passing, one can question the meaning and the usefulness of the concept of equilibrium used to describe agriculture if it is thought to be in a continuous disequilibrium. Basically, it reflects an application of the concept of static equilibrium to a dynamic process. The two are not the same. We shall return to this below.

Aside from the question of the residual, can the above results be taken as indicative of economies of scale? There are two issues to be considered. First, internal economies of scale is a concept related to the cost structure of a firm and cannot be measured from regional aggregates. There are many farms of different size, and hence there is nothing in the structure of agriculture that suggests economies of scale. The optimal size depends on the technology used and the level of management of the firm. Changes in technology affect the optimal size, but this change in size is the result of the technical change. Second, there is a statistical aspect. Note that the regressions that produce a sum of elasticities larger than 1 are strictly cross-section, and hence they are subject to a bias caused by the correlation between the unobserved regional productivity level and the inputs, similar to the management bias in the analysis based on firm data. This view was taken by Kislev (1966) who analyzed data of 3,000 US districts for 1949 and 1959. To account for the unobserved regional productivity he introduced regional dummies (68 regions), and as a result the sum of elasticities declined from 1.167 to 1.05. Regional dummies do not capture the management effect, so a management bias is still present in these estimates. Very likely this is the reason that the sum of elasticities is still slightly above 1. Kislev and Peterson (1996) reexamine the evidence on economies of scale with reference to empirical results of cross-state estimates of Cobb–Douglas functions for the US[17] The sum of elasticities for each of the years 1978, 1982, and 1987 is 1.3. They do not take it as evidence of increasing returns to scale but rather as an indication of management bias. We return to this subject in the discussion of cross-country studies.

Griliches (1964) also introduces a measure for research and extension as a shifter of the production function, a practice that has been followed in other studies such as the studies based on cross-country data.

---

[16] In the spirit of positive economics, "[t]he most important test of the estimated production functions is not how well it fits the data it was derived from but rather whether and how well it can 'predict' and interpret subsequent behavior" [Griliches (1963a, p. 339)].

[17] The respective results for cross-state regressions for 1978, 1982, and 1987 are: land 0.1, 0.11, 0.13; labor 0.27, 0.27, 0.22; machinery 0.23, 0.27, 0.15; fertilizers and chemicals 0.27, 0.21, 0.27; and other 0.43, 0.43, 0.52.

1.4. The productivity of capital

Durable inputs are entered into the production function and in productivity analysis as stocks. This procedure is sometimes questioned (O.6), and it is suggested that the stock variable should be replaced by a flow that represents the service provided by the stock. This suggestion is based on the assumption that there is a unique variable that represents the service that can be retrieved from the analysis of annual data. Unfortunately, this is not the case. By its very nature, a durable input is purchased if the discounted expected returns from this input over its lifetime cover its cost. Thus, the service from this input is the returns over its lifetime, and this is not easily transferable to a service in a given calendar period, say a year. To sharpen the point, note that the service of a combine in the winter, when there is no harvest, is zero. However, the service for the year is positive. In some years the service is greater than in other years, depending on the area harvested and the yield, and these are affected by stochastic variables. Ex post, the value of these variables is not the same as the expected values. How are the actual values calculated? In a production function analysis, they are determined from the coefficients of the empirical equation. For instance, the coefficient of capital in a Cobb–Douglas function estimates the 'average' elasticity of capital for the sample. This can be used then to compute the marginal productivity of capital for each sample point. In some years, it may be lower than the rental cost, but this does not mean that there was too much capital in that year. The apparent overcapacity is there to provide the service in times of higher demand.

1.5. Productivity and heterogeneous technology

The foregoing discussion provides sufficient empirical evidence to evaluate the most cardinal question related to production: what is the rate, and also the nature, of technical change? Aspects of this question were addressed in one form or another in almost every empirical study of time-series data. Equation (12) characterizes much of the literature which conveys the idea that there is a unique answer to this question, and that if we work hard enough, we will find it or come close to it. Unfortunately, the matter is not that simple.

The available technology is defined as the set of all available techniques, and technical change is a change in this set. An appearance of a new technique implies a change in the available technology. In this sense, the available technology changes continuously; any new scientific publication may represent a change. However, this definition is too broad, and as such its usefulness is limited to serving as a reference point but has no operational value. The available technology contains a subset of techniques which are not implemented and thus are not observed, directly or indirectly. Therefore, there is no metric to measure the stock of the available technology or its change. Any empirical inference about technical change is based on observations and as such, by definition, is restricted to the implemented, rather than the available, technology. This is the domain of the empirical analysis.

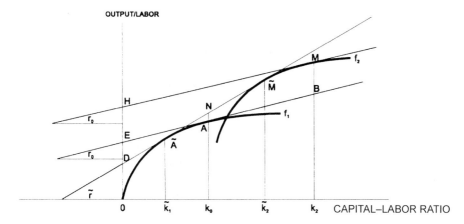

Figure 1. Resource constraint and the choice of technique.

The distinction between the available and implemented technology is not trivial if there is more than one available technique. In this case, the choice of the implemented techniques can affect the calculation of the change in the total factor productivity (TFP). To illustrate the issue, Figure 1 presents two production functions describing, say, traditional (f_1) and modern (f_2) techniques. The horizontal axis measures the input ratio, say capital-labor ratio, and correspondingly, the vertical axis measures the average labor productivity. Initially, only the traditional technique is available, and output is at point A with input ratio k_0. The response to the appearance of the modern technique may take various forms depending on the constraints to its implementation and the market conditions. If the sector is a price taker, production changes from point A to point M with input ratio of k_2. The total change in output, Y_M/Y_A, is decomposed to the input effect, Y_B/Y_A, and the relative change in the TFP, Y_M/Y_B. The point Y_B is obtained by extending the line tangent to the production function at point A to point B with capital-labor ratio k_2. If the supply of capital is initially perfectly inelastic, the input ratio remains at k_0, and resources are allocated to the two techniques to produce the output given by point N. This movement generates a relative change in TFP of Y_N/Y_A. As more capital becomes available, the movement will be along the tangent line from N to $\tilde{M}$. This movement from point N on is explained exclusively by the input change and thus shows no change in the TFP. Consequently, the resulting TFP is different from that obtained in the case of perfectly elastic factor supply. The discussion abstracts from the question of time needed to travel on each path. Actual calculations are done for data collected for calendar time, say a year. The results will differ with the changes in the pace of the yearly movement. However, when the annual results are integrated, the final outcome will depend on the path followed by the economy. Obviously, the path taken under a resource constraint will give a smaller value to the TFP. In this sense, the difference in empirical calculation of the TFP is path-dependent. The reason for the difference between the two results to the same change in the available technology is related to the change in the factor prices, or marginal productivity. The appearance of a new technique which is both capital-intensive and more productive increases the demand for capital. When the capital supply is not perfectly elastic, its price (or its rental rate) will increase so as to internalize all or part, depending on the supply elasticity, of the technical change. Specifically, when capital is initially fixed, the subsequent movement from N to M is fully accounted for by the change in capital availability. Thus, in the first case the contribution of the input is obtained by using the same marginal productivity in the base and new technology, whereas in the second, when the two techniques coexist, the marginal productivity of the scarce resource increases and that of the other resource declines. The resulting change of weights absorbs some of the technical change and assigns it to the inputs.

This is a remarkable result. The technical change might be of considerable magnitude and still may escape the measurement. This is the case where the bias of the technical change is in the direction of a scarce input. This applies not only to physical capital but also to human capital, and specifically to the level of education. It is in this sense that education is a carrier of technology. The literature discusses the slowdown in productivity changes in the US economy during the 1970s. Such a phenomenon is consistent with the process analyzed above where there is a change in technology but it is not captured by the calculation of productivity. The discussion is also related to adjustments in quality done in the calculation of changes in the TFP. The importance of the quality is an outcome of the technical change, and if it is considered as a contribution of the inputs, it takes away from the TFP. Thus attempts to eliminate the residual technical change by such adjustments grossly underestimate the importance of technical change (see for instance [Griliches and Jorgenson (1966)].

The implication of heterogeneous technology for empirical analysis was formulated in [Mundlak (1988, 1993)]. It is outlined in the following section. The approach was applied empirically to time series studies ([Mundlak et al. (1989)], for Argentina; [Coeymans and Mundlak (1993)], for Chile; and [Lachaal and Womack (1998)], for Canada). We will now use this framework to interpret the empirical analysis of cross-country data.

1.6. Heterogeneous technology

Let x be the vector of inputs and $F_h(x)$ be the production function associated with the hth technique, where F_h is concave and twice differentiable, and define the available technology, T, as the collection of all possible techniques, $T = \{F_h(x); h = 1, \ldots, H\}$. Firms choose the implemented techniques subject to their constraints and the environment within which they operate. We distinguish between constrained (k) and unconstrained (v) inputs, $x = (v, k)$, and assume, without a loss of generality, that the constrained inputs have no alternative cost. The optimization problem calls for a choice of the level of inputs to be assigned to technique h so as to maximize profits. To simplify the presentation, we deal with a comparative statics framework and therefore omit a time index for the variables. The Lagrangian equation for this problem is

$$L = \sum_h p_h F_h(v_h, k_h) - \sum_h w v_h - \lambda \left(\sum_h k_h - k_0 \right), \tag{13}$$

subject to $F_h(\cdot) \in T;\ v_h \geqslant 0;\ k_h \geqslant 0$,

where p_h is the price of the product produced by technique h, w is the price vector of the unconstrained inputs, and k_0 is the available stock of the constrained inputs. The solution is characterized by the Kuhn–Tucker necessary conditions. Let $s = (k, p, w, T)$ be the vector of state variables of this problem and write the solution as: $v_h^*(s)$, $k_h^*(s)$, $\lambda^*(s)$. The optimal inputs v_h^*, k_h^* determine the intensity at which the hth technique is implemented, where zero intensity means no implementation. The optimal output of technique h is $y_h^* = F_h(v_h^*, k_h^*)$, and the implemented technology (IT) is defined by $IT(s) = \{F_h(v_h, k_h);\ F_h(v_h^*, k_h^*) \neq 0,\ F_h \in T\}$.

The essence of the analysis is that the implemented technology is endogenous and determined jointly with the level of the unconstrained inputs conditional on the state variables. This result cannot be overemphasized, and it is essential for the interpretation of all the empirical results, regardless of specification. Of particular importance is the interpretation of the aggregate production function which expresses the aggregate of outputs, produced by a set of micro production functions, as a function of aggregate inputs. This function is not uniquely defined because the set of micro functions actually implemented, and over which the aggregation is performed, depends on the state variables and thus is endogenous. A change in the state variables causes a change in the implemented technology and in the use of inputs. It is in this sense that the function is endogenous and as such not identified. It can be identified if there are deviations from the first-order conditions. Given such deviations, we get an empirical function as $F(x, s)$. This function has a second degree approximation which looks like a Cobb–Douglas function, but where the elasticities are functions of the state variables and possibly of the inputs:

$$\ln Y = \Gamma(s) + B(s, x) \ln x + u, \tag{14}$$

where y is the value added per worker, $B(s, x)$ and $\Gamma(s)$ are the slope and intercept of the function respectively, and u is a stochastic term. This expression is given below a more descriptive structure which leads to an approach in its estimation which requires the knowledge of factor shares. The factor shares needed for this approach were not available in the cross-country application reviewed below, and therefore we do not go into it.

Variations in the state variables affect $\Gamma(s)$ and $B(s, x)$ directly as well as indirectly through their effect on inputs:

$$\partial \ln y / \partial s_h = \partial \Gamma(\cdot) / \partial s_h + \ln x \left[\partial B(\cdot) / \partial s_h \right] + B(\cdot)[\partial \ln x / \partial s_h]. \tag{15}$$

The last term shows the output response to a change in inputs under constant technology. The innovation in this formulation lies in the response of the implemented technology to the state variables as shown by the first two terms on the right-hand side. The elasticities have a time index, which is suppressed here, indicating that they vary over the sample points. Because the state variables have a large spread across countries, the coefficients of the Cobb–Douglas function are expected to change accordingly. This is the reason for the lack of robustness in the results.

When the available technology consists of more than one technique, a change in the state variables may cause a change in the composition of techniques in addition to a change of inputs used in a given technique. In this case, the empirical function is a mixture of functions and as such may violate the concavity property of a production function. Consequently, the evaluation of empirical results should deal with the role of the state variables in production in addition to that of the inputs (or their prices in the case of dual functions). Some state variables are included in many of the studies without a reference to an explicit theory.

The state variables can be classified in the following groups: constraints, incentives, available technology, physical environment, and the political environment. There is no clear-cut separability between inputs and state variables. For instance, when capital is a constraint, its coefficient in the production function will reflect not only its productivity in a given technique but also its contribution to output through the change in the composition of the implemented techniques. A similar argument applies to the role of prices in the empirical dual functions. It is conjectured that future progress in the empirical analysis of production will have to deal more explicitly with the role of the state variables within a coherent framework. In this review, we concentrate on the role of inputs and limit our discussion of the state variables to serve this end. As such, it is incomplete but still serves a starting point to stir thinking on the subject.

1.7. Cross-country studies

The considerable spread between countries in agricultural productivity, in resource use, and in the economic and physical environment provides an important source of information for testing our understanding of the factors that determine productivity. The cross-country analysis of Bhattacharjee (1955) had no follow-up until the revival by Hayami (1969, 1970) and Hayami and Ruttan (1970). This revival added important variables that were missing in the original paper, namely measures of some capital components (livestock and machines) and of education.

The underlying assumption of these studies is that all countries use the same production function. But this assumption lacks empirical support. To get an idea of the prevailing heterogeneity, we can compare the elasticities obtained in the earlier cross-country studies (Table 1) with those obtained from country studies listed in footnote 7. For an order of magnitude, we refer to the values Hayami and Ruttan used in their exercise for sources of growth differences between countries: labor 0.4, land 0.1, livestock 0.25, fertilizers 0.15, machinery 0.1, education 0.4, and research and extension 0.15. As to the sum of elasticities, in their analysis for 1960, the estimates were in the range of 0.95–0.98. The exercise attributes about two thirds of the output differences among

Table 1
Estimated production elasticities – cross country

Study	Period	Sample	Labor	Land	All	Comments
Bhattacharjee (1955)	1948–1950	22 countries	.30	.36	1.00	
Hayami (1969)	1960	38 countries	.45[a]	.20[a]	1.00[a]	Elasticities used for productivity measures.
Hayami & Ruttan (1970)	1955, 1960, 1965	38 countries	.40[b]	.10[b]	1.00[b]	Elasticities used for productivity measures.
Nguyen (1979)	1970 1975	40 countries 35 countries	.38 .37	.02 −.03	0.99 0.92	Regression includes education.
Mundlak & Hellinghausen (1982)	1960–1980	58 countries[c]	.46	.16	1.00	Uses principal components method.
Antle (1983)	1965	66 countries	.33	.17	0.92	Includes infrastructure and education.
Kawagoe, Hayami, & Ruttan (1985)	1960, 1970, 1980	43 countries	.45[d]	.10[d]	1.00[d]	Elasticities used for productivity measures.

[a] Range of coefficients: Labor .43–.53, Land .18–.25, Sum 0.96–0.97.
[b] Range of coefficients: Labor .34–.49, Land .06–.12, Sum 0.94–0.98.
[c] Data is pooled for time period.
[d] Range of coefficients: Labor .41–.55, Land .01–.10, Sum 1.01–1.10.

countries to input differences and one third to differences in human capital. Subsequent studies updated and extended the analysis.

Nguyen (1979) updated Hayami and Ruttan results by computing regressions for 1970 and 1975. The results are similar to those obtained by Hayami and Ruttan with two exceptions: the elasticity of machines increased with time,[18] and the elasticity of fertilizers declined and approached zero in 1975. He finds that when education is measured as a sum of primary and secondary education, it is not significant, but secondary education alone is significant. He takes the view that the secondary education has a causal effect on productivity. Alternatively, we can interpret this result as indicative that education is endogenous, and higher productivity increases the demand for education. The adjustment to a changing economic environment is at the margin, and this places the emphasis on secondary education.

Kawagoe and Hayami (1983) and Kawagoe, Hayami, and Ruttan (1985) further update the analysis to include 1980. Like Nguyen they test for a change of coefficients over time and state that the production elasticities of conventional and nonconventional inputs remained largely the same, although some pronounced changes occurred between 1960 and 1980: the elasticity of labor declined from 0.53 to 0.41, machinery increased from 0.04 to 0.12, fertilizer increased from 0.13 to 0.25, and land increased from 0.04

[18] Similar results were obtained by Shumway, Talpaz, and Beattie (1979) for the US.

to 0.08. Thus, there is no evidence of land-saving technical change. It is hard to think of fertilizer share as being as high as 0.25, which is also in direct contrast to the results obtained by Nguyen, in which the fertilizer elasticities were approaching zero.

Another deviation from the earlier results of Hayami and Ruttan is a sum of elastic-ities for developing countries of about 1.3, which they take as evidence of increasing returns to scale. This magnitude affects the growth-accounting exercise because, as in-dicated by Equation (12), an increase in the input weights used for calculating TFP increases the contribution of the aggregate input and reduces the TFP. This explains their conclusion that the cross-country differences in output are mainly due to differ-ences in inputs with a very small role for the residual, under 7 percent and as low as −5.5 percent. This conclusion on negligible change in the TFP is similar to that reached by Griliches (1964). As we argue below, they both are the outcome of biased coefficients which exaggerate the relative importance of the inputs. This interpretation is supported by the results reported by Kislev and Peterson (1996) who computed the Hayami–Ruttan regressions with country dummies, and the sum of elasticities declined from 1.32 to 1.077, with the latter not significantly different from 1.

A search for variables that represent the shift in the productivity level in the context of cross-country studies led Evenson and Kislev (1975) to emphasize research, and Antle (1983) to emphasize infrastructure. The problem with this group of variables is that some of them are unobservable, others are measured in some countries and not in others, and finally, because of multicollinearity, regressions do not support all of the variables that are actually used in the analysis.[19]

An implicit questioning of the assumption of uniform technology is detected in the work of Hayami and Ruttan when they divide the countries into two groups, developed and developing. This would imply that the technology changes with the level of de-velopment. However, this classification is not sufficiently informative because neither group is homogeneous. To introduce the impact of the level of development, it is more informative to include an income variable in the regression. This procedure opens up the door for extending the analysis to allow for heterogeneous technology. Mundlak and Hellinghausen (1982) remove the assumption that all countries *employ* the same production function. Instead, it is assumed that all countries have *access to the same technology* and they differ in the implementation of the technology, in line with O.11. The variables postulated to affect the choice of technology, referred to as state variables, were resource endowment and the physical environment. The resource constraint con-sists of physical and human capital. As no information was available on the individual components of this constraint, it is represented in the study by the per capita total out-put in the country. The results show a great spread in the estimates across countries and

---

[19] As Evenson and Kislev (1975) noted, "... with the inclusion of research variable, the fertilizer variable declines in size and significance, the same being true about the schooling coefficient .... These two variables, together with the technical education variable, served in the original Hayami and Ruttan analysis as proxies for human capital and research. These proxies are effectively replaced by genuine research variable ..." (p. 180). A somewhat similar result was obtained by Antle (1983) with an infrastructure variable.

over time which is accounted for, in part, by differences in the physical and economic environment.

All these results provide clear evidence for the lack of robustness of the empirical results, which is consistent with O.1. One possible way to stabilize the results is to choose a more flexible functional form than the Cobb–Douglas. The major changes that were introduced were the constant elasticity of substitution (CES) function by Arrow et al. (1961) and the translog function by Christensen, Jorgenson, and Lau (1973). The CES function generalized the Cobb–Douglas function by allowing a constant elasticity of substitution to differ from 1. The translog function is an example of a flexible function, a function that allows a second degree approximation to a production function. The few experiments with the CES function in agricultural economics did not prove it to be significantly different from Cobb–Douglas, and therefore it was not widely applied.[20] The situation is different with quadratic functions that have been widely used since the early 1970s, largely in connection with the dual approach, as reviewed below. From the vantage of the present discussion, we note that the main feature of a quadratic production function is to make the marginal productivities, or the production elasticities, depend on the input combination for which these coefficients are calculated. Thus, we can still postulate that all producers (or countries) use the same production function and their production elasticities vary with their choice of inputs.

Alternatively, it is possible that the producers do not use the same production function and the choice of the function is an economic decision. The variability in the state variables that exist in cross-country data offers an opportunity to gain an insight to the determinants of resource productivity. For instance, the available technology, common to all countries, varies over time. On the other hand, capital constraints and the physical environment are country specific. There are three processes which can be studied by decomposing the country-panel data to three orthogonal components to yield the regression[21]

$$y_{it} - y_{..} = (x_{it} - x_{i.} - x_{.t} + x_{..})w(it) + (x_{.t} - x_{..})b(t) + (x_{i.} - x_{..})b(i)$$
$$+ e_{it}, \tag{16}$$

---

[20] Hayami (1970) tried several modifications to the cross-country analysis. He found that a Cobb–Douglas function is not rejected when the maintained hypothesis is a CES function and that Nerlove-type distributed lags as well as serial correlation correction as suggested by Griliches gave "implausible results". Heady and Dillon (1961) discuss various functional forms used in agricultural research, including the quadratic function. Fuss, McFadden, and Mundlak (1978) discuss functional forms used in economic analysis. For an interpretation of the literature on the elasticities of substitution and their relationship to functional forms, see Mundlak (1968).

[21] Regressions that use time and country dummies provide estimates of $w(it)$, those that use only country dummies provide estimates of matrix-weighted averages of $w(it)$ and $b(t)$, those that use only time dummies provide estimates of matrix-weighted averages of $w(it)$ and $b(i)$, whereas regressions without time or country dummies provide estimates of matrix-weighted averages of all three coefficients in Equation (16). It is in this sense that the three sets of coefficients in Equation (16) constitute a canonical set.

Table 2
Cross-country panel

Variable	Within time and country		Between time		Between country	
	Estimate	t-score	Estimate	t-score	Estimate	t-score
Inputs:						
Capital	0.37	6.90	1.03	6.01	0.34	13.13
Land	0.47	3.78			−0.03	−2.82
Labor	0.08		−0.16	−0.16	0.26	13.67
Fertilizer	0.08	1.53	0.14	0.33	0.43	21.91
Technology:						
Schooling	0.09	0.55	−0.28	−0.06	0.02	0.52
Peak yield	0.83	3.80	−0.32	−0.07	0.06	4.19
Development	0.52	3.36	−0.21	−0.33	0.31	2.97
Prices:						
Relative prices	0.04	1.78	0.02	0.09	0.01	1.95
Price variability	−0.03	−0.97	−0.07	−0.26	−0.08	−2.82
Inflation	−0.00	−0.75	0.04	0.71	0.07	4.25
Environmental:						
Potential dry matter					0.16	2.68
Water availability					0.44	7.96

Note: R-square for 777 obs. = .9696, 1970–1990, 37 Countries. Source: Mundlak, Larson, and Butzer (1999).

where y is log output, x is log input (or a vector of inputs), a dot in the subscript indicates an average over the missing index, $w(it)$, $b(t)$, and $b(i)$ are the regression coefficients of the within-country-time (or, simply, within), between-time, and between-country variables respectively.

The between-time process captures the impact of changes over time in the state variables common to all countries such as changes in the available technology (technical change). The between-country process captures the impact of the country-specific variables that take place when the available technology is held constant, but other state variables differ across countries and contribute to the differences in the implemented technology. Finally, the within-country-time process represents the effect of changes in the outputs, inputs, and state variables when the available technology and the country-specific environment are held constant and thus comes closest to a production function representing what we refer to as the core technology.

This approach was used by Mundlak, Larson, and Butzer (1999) in the analysis of a sample of 37 countries for the period 1970–1990. The study differs from other studies in that it uses a new series of agricultural capital and in the state variables that were included. This choice of variables limited the sample to countries which had all the required information. We will concentrate here on the coefficients of the conventional inputs. The results are summarized in Table 2, which presents the estimated elasticities for the three regressions where the dependent variable is the log of agricultural GDP.

A striking result is the relative importance of capital. The capital elasticity is 0.37 for the core technology and 0.34 in the between-country regression. This result is quite robust to various modifications of the model and to the disaggregation of capital. On the other hand, the capital elasticity in the between-time regression is 1.03. This represents the response common to all countries in the sample. It indicates that, on average for the sample, an increase in capital was accompanied with a proportional increase in output. This strong response is consistent with the view that physical capital has been a constraint to agricultural growth. This empirical proposition is well illustrated by McGuirk and Mundlak (1991) in the context of the Green Revolution.

The between-time regression shows that the shift to more productive techniques is associated with a decline in labor. The labor coefficient in the core technology is also relatively low, whereas that of the between-country regression is more in line with the other cross-country studies. The low labor elasticity obtained for the core technology and the between-time regressions is an indication of the labor-saving technical change in agriculture, which is consistent with the slight decline of labor over time. This is not news, but it is emphasized here because it comes out of an integral view of the process which separates between the core technology and the changes that took place over time and between countries. These results highlight the importance of capital in agricultural production, an attribute critical in the understanding of agricultural development and its dependence on the economic environment. This indicates that agricultural technology is cost-capital intensive compared to nonagriculture.[22]

This last conclusion is further reinforced by the magnitude of the land elasticity in the core technology and is at variance with the view that land is not an important factor of production in modern agriculture. This view is based on an incorrect reading of the data where no distinction is made between changes in the technology and the movement along a given production function. The sum of capital and land elasticities is around 0.8 in various formulations, making it clear that agriculture should be more sensitive than nonagriculture to changes in the cost of capital, and less to changes in labor [Mundlak et al. (1989)]. This value of the sum is a bit high compared to the literature. It is possible that a different choice of countries and time periods would lead to somewhat different results. However, a sum of 0.8 for land and capital elasticities leaves room for the conclusion on the importance of capital to remain intact.

The introduction of state variables to account for technology, prices, and physical environment results in a production function that displays constant returns to scale and thus avoids the pitfalls of previous studies and the misguided conclusions that followed. Using the within elasticities from Table 2 and the median growth rates for the sample, we see that aggregate input and total factor productivity residual technical change each accounts for about one half of the total output growth of 3.82 percent per year. This evaluation of the contribution of aggregate input is substantially smaller than the rate

---

[22] We say that a technology is cost-capital intensive with respect to a reference technology if its factor share of capital is larger than that of the reference technology.

reported in the cross-country studies referred to above. These studies use the between-country estimates where the weight of fertilizers is high and that of land is low. The median growth rate of land in the sample was 0.12 percent and that of fertilizers was 3.04. The difference in the elasticities of these two variables accounts for much of the difference in the growth accounting. In addition, the studies that report increasing returns to scale overstate the role of inputs and understate the role of technical change.

1.8. The rate of technical change

As indicated above, all measures of technical change refer to changes in the implemented technology and thus report not only on the advances in knowledge but also on its implementation. Direct measures deal mainly with changes in the TFP and not with its bias. The latter is the subject of the studies based on duality to be discussed below. We summarize some results to give orders of magnitude to the changes in the TFP and its importance.

Ball (1985) calculates total factor productivity growth using constructed Tornqvist-Theil indexes of outputs and inputs for US agriculture for the period 1948–1979 based on data adjusted for quality variations. The inputs are labor, capital, and intermediate inputs, such as energy, agricultural chemicals, feed and seed, and miscellaneous. The result is average annual growth of productivity of 1.75 percent as compared with 1.7 percent obtained from USDA data. Capalbo and Vo (1988) review the evidence on agricultural productivity, and their result for 1950–1982 is TFP of 1.57 as compared to 1.95 as obtained by the USDA for the same period.[23] Ball et al. (1997) present the production accounts for US agriculture for the period 1948–1994 and report growth rates for the period and subperiods, based on Fisher indexes. The average growth rates for the period as a whole are 1.88, −0.07, and 1.94 percent for production (including intermediate products), aggregate input, and TFP, respectively.[24] Note that, because of the decline in the aggregate input, the growth in the TFP is larger than that in production. This result is extremely different from the studies based on cross-state data for the US, which attribute most of the change in output to inputs rather than to productivity. However, it is similar to the 1.9 percent growth result obtained by Mundlak, Larson, and Butzer (1999) for 37 countries for the period 1970–1990 discussed above.

---

[23] The cost shares were:

Year	Labor	Equipment & livestock	Land & structures	Chemicals	Energy	Other
1960	0.24	0.25	0.16	0.04	0.04	0.26
1980	0.11	0.21	0.41	0.06	0.04	0.17

The average annual growth rates were: output 1.76, labor −1.32, family labor −3.09, equipment 2.04, animal capital 0.38, structures and land 0.1, fertilizer 5.01, pesticides 6.07, energy 1.58, other materials 1.2, and all inputs 0.17.

[24] The change in the TFP during 1948–1979 is approximately 1.47 percent – a figure derived from Ball et al.'s (1997) results – which is lower than the figure reported in [Ball (1985)]. The difference is due to the changes in the measurement of the variables.

Jorgenson and Gollop (1992) compare the postwar productivity performance of US agriculture with sectors in the private nonfarm economy using the total price function. Productivity growth explains 82 percent of economic growth in agriculture, but only 13 percent in the private nonfarm economy. The average annual growth rate of TFP growth in agriculture during 1947–1985 was 1.58 percent, nearly four times larger than that of the rest of the economy.

Rosegrant and Evenson (1992) examine total factor productivity growth and its sources in the crops sector in India, using district panel data for the period 1956–1987. They first compute TFP and second explain its variations in terms of variables representing investments in research, extension, human capital, and infrastructure. TFP in the Indian crops sector grew during the period 1957–1985 at an average annual rate of one percent, and this accounted for about one third of total output growth in that sector. The growth rate for the same period was 0.78 in Bangladesh and 1.07 in Pakistan. Research, extension, domestic and foreign inventions, and adoption of modern varieties show statistically significant, positive impacts on TFP. The effect of the proportion of area irrigated on TFP is slightly negative, indicating that irrigation has no additional effects on productivity except through its contribution to total input levels. In any case, this procedure is only adequate if the coefficients estimated in the first stage are independent of the variables that explain the changes in the TFP. This is a strong assumption that needs empirical support, and it is inconsistent with the result reported in [McGuirk and Mundlak (1991)]. The new productive varieties are more intensive in irrigation and fertilizers, which have been scarce resources.

1.9. Primal estimates – summary

The centerpiece in primal estimation is the Cobb–Douglas function. This approach does not impose competitive conditions but instead submits them to empirical testing. Such testing often shows a difference between the factor shares and the estimated production elasticities. This is not an absolute rejection of the prevalence of the competitive conditions but rather a conditional result, based on the model used and the statistical procedure. Still it is indicative that wide gaps may exist.

Tables 1 and 2 present selected summary results of the studies reviewed as well as others with a similar message. It is noted that the elasticity of labor never exceeds 0.5, and in most cases it varies in the range of 0.25 to 0.45. This value is well below the elasticity of labor in nonagriculture.[25] If we consider all nonlabor income as capital income, the result supports the position that agriculture is cost-capital-intensive and therefore is less susceptible to increases in the wage rate than nonagriculture. Also, the labor elasticity declines with time, indicating that the technical change was labor-saving.

---

[25] In most studies on agriculture, output is measured as production, which includes raw materials, whereas production analysis in nonagriculture is conducted in terms of value added. Thus an exact comparison calls for applying the same output concept in both sectors. This was done in [Mundlak et al. (1989)] for Argentina, where it was found that the factor share of labor in agriculture is indeed lower than that in nonagriculture.

In country studies, the elasticity of land varies between zero in some cases to about one third. We interpret this elasticity to be a measure of the competitive position of agriculture. From the point of view of farm income it is meaningful to look at the sum of labor and land elasticities, and this sum is fluctuating around 0.5.

The sum of elasticities of farm inputs (that is, inputs decided on by the farmer, in contrast to public inputs) is used as a measure of economies of scale. In some studies based on cross-sectional data this sum is larger than 1; this was taken by the authors as evidence of increasing returns to scale. We attribute this result to statistical bias.

One justification for estimating production functions is to provide weights for the computation of technical change. However, this approach has not provided any substantive advantage as compared to the use of factor shares, even though they may not be the same as the production elasticities. The reason is that mistakes in specification and interpretation of statistical studies are often greater than the discrepancies between the factor shares and the true production elasticities. An example is the error involved in the finding of increasing returns to scale and its incorporation in the computation of total factor productivity that leads to the elimination of the residual in a comparison of growth over time or productivity differences across countries. It is tempting to speculate that such a procedure was motivated by the belief that all growth can be accounted for and therefore there should be no residual. As we take an opposite view, we do not feel that the loss of explanation involved in the reduction of the sum of elasticities to 1 causes any loss in insight; on the contrary, it directs our attention to search for an understanding of the process.

An important feature common to many of the studies is lack of robustness of the estimates and their dependence on the variables used and the sample coverage. This finding contributed to a search in three directions: 1. *Overcoming the simultaneous-equations bias caused by the endogeneity of the inputs*. As we shall see in the next section, dual estimates that were supposed to solve this problem do not produce more robust results. 2. *Algebraic form of the production function*. Indeed, the Cobb–Douglas function is restrictive, but natural generalizations enlarged, rather than shrank, the range of results. 3. *Allowing for the endogeneity of the implemented technology*. This approach utilizes the variability to improve our insight of the observed productivity differences over time and across countries.

2. The duality culture

Quadratic production functions, by their nature, contain many variables that are correlated, and therefore the estimated parameters suffer from low precision (big confidence regions) to the extent that they often do not make sense. To overcome this problem, the common procedure is to estimate the production function parameters by fitting the factor shares, with or without the constraint of the production function itself. The implicit idea is that the variations observed in the factor shares in the sample can be attributed to differences in input ratios, or said differently, to different locations on the production function. Judging by the trend in the literature, the estimates of such functions, the most popular being the translog function, were not satisfying, and therefore a rescue was sought in the form of profit or cost functions. By this shift, the factor shares become functions of prices rather than of quantities. This shift is somewhat arbitrary in that it is not backed by any justification. We should note that the basic idea of duality is that each point on the production function corresponds uniquely to a vector of price ratios. The converse does not hold in general unless a strong assumption on the nature of the production function is imposed. Once this is imposed, then variations in prices cause, and therefore reflect, variations in quantities. This exhausts their information about technology. Hence, if regressing the shares on quantities was not satisfactory, why should prices do a better job? A plausible possibility is that the price variations cause not only movements along a given production function but also movements across production functions. This possibility is not part of the literature, but it is part of the more general framework of our discussion.

Under duality, the technology is summarized by profit, cost, or revenue functions, referred to as dual functions. The profit function is expressed in terms of factor and product prices, the cost function is expressed in terms of the factor prices and output, and the revenue function is expressed in terms of the product prices and inputs. In time-series analysis, each of these functions includes a measure of changes in technology, usually time trend. Also, the profit or cost functions are allowed to include some fixed inputs and thus are qualified as restricted or short run. Similarly, the revenue or profit functions can be restricted by the inclusion of a constraint on output (that is, a production quota).

Duality theory became a standard subject in economic analysis in the late 1960s.[26] It was adopted for empirical applications with some great hopes, but as with many innovations, the test of time has been less generous. There were several reasons for such hopes. For competitive firms, prices, unlike quantities, are exogenous and therefore when used as explanatory variables do not cause simultaneous-equations bias that is part of life in the primal estimation. This property is indeed valid but with a limited liability. First, it is not automatically applicable to data at the market or industry level. Second, it is unnecessary to estimate a dual function in order to utilize the exogeneity of prices, when this is indeed the case.

More profoundly, the econometric literature was initially motivated by the ease that duality offers to characterize the production structure.[27] Interestingly, this view paves

---

[26] See [McFadden (1978, p. 5) and Jorgenson (1986)] for a brief review of the history of duality.

[27] "An alternative approach to production theory is to start directly from observed economic data–supplies, demands, prices, costs, and profits. The advantage of such an attack is that the theory can be formulated in terms of causal *economic* relationships that are *presumed* [italics by YM] to hold, without intervening constructive steps required on the traditional theory. Because this approach is not bound by computational tractability in the step from production technology to economic observations, the prospect is opened for more satisfactory models of complex production problems" [Fuss and McFadden (1978, p. vii)]. Similarly "[d]emand and supply can be generated as explicit functions of relative prices without imposing the arbitrary constraints on production patterns required in the traditional methodology" [Jorgenson (1986, p. 1843)].

the way to avoid duality rather than to use it. Heuristically speaking, duality means that by following some rules (optimization), one can move from a production function to dual functions (or behavioral functions, namely product supply and factor demand) and return to the original function.[28] Thus knowing the production function, it is possible to move to the behavioral functions and vice versa. This is a simple journey under self-duality when both the technology and the dual functions have closed-form expressions. Examples are the Cobb–Douglas or the CES functions. The problem arises when self-duality does not exist, as is the case with the more complicated functional forms such as the quadratic functions. However, the move to duality in this case shifts the weight from one foot to the other in that it makes the derivation of the behavioral functions direct, but ignores the fact that questions asked about the production function itself require the exact indirect computations that were to be avoided by moving to the dual functions.[29]

For instance, given the profit, or cost, function, what is the marginal productivity of an input, and how is it affected by the input ratios? The answer to the first question is simple because by construction the competitive conditions are imposed, and therefore the marginal productivity is equal to the real factor price. The dependence of the marginal productivity on the other inputs is a question that has only a complicated answer, except when the function is self-dual. The empirical (econometric) literature on duality does not ask these questions. Thus it appears that duality is just a name, and the property is not fully exploited in the sense that the estimated behavioral functions are not used to answer questions related to relationships between inputs and outputs. However, the progress made in the ease of obtaining numerical solutions makes it possible to move from one system to the other; therefore this should cease to be an important consideration. The choice of whether to estimate a primal or a dual function should then be made on the basis of other criteria, such as statistical precision, and as argued in [Mundlak (1996a)] the dual approach to the study of the production structure is generally inferior to the direct approach. In this section we review a sample of the empirical work related to agriculture.[30]

The combination of duality and the use of quadratic functions has extended the analysis to cover topics related to the properties of the production structure and comparative statics that, with some exceptions,[31] had not been part of the agenda of most studies at the time and thereby extended the area of inquiry. Of particular interest is the attempt to fit production systems that are consistent with the assumptions of comparative statics.

---

[28] For a formal discussion, see [Diewert (1974)].

[29] It is therefore not surprising that a recent survey of duality contributions in production economics chooses to devote "[p]rimary attention ... to alternative ways of measuring output supply and input demand functions rather than identifying the production function" [Shumway (1995, p. 179)]. The fact is that there is little to survey on the other subjects.

[30] Shumway (1995) provides references to additional works. The survey by Jorgenson (1986) covers applications in other sectors.

[31] For instance, Mundlak (1964b) uses the second order conditions of optimization to rule out the Cobb–Douglas function as a legitimate multi-product function.

But this is done at the cost of ignoring the subjects covered in the eleven observations made above (with the exception of O.7 and O.8).

To fully describe all the properties of comparative statics, the single-output function with m inputs, or the corresponding dual function, should have at least $(m + 1)(m + 2)/2$ parameters [Hanoch (1975)]. A quadratic function that maintains the symmetry conditions has exactly this many parameters, and as such it is considered flexible in the sense that it can provide a second order approximation to the unknown true production function.[32] But since inputs tend to move together, it is statistically difficult to estimate the function directly with precision, and therefore the procedure has been to fit factor shares to the data. It is in this respect that such procedures are basically an extension of the factor share estimator.

For the dual functions to describe a production system consistent with comparative statics, they have to maintain some properties that can be tested empirically. The less trivial ones are monotonicity and convexity (or concavity, as the case may be). When the estimation is of factor demand or product supply, the monotonicity imposes signs on the first derivatives of the dual functions, whereas convexity imposes conditions on the second derivatives of the dual functions, or more to the point on the sign of the Hessian matrix. If these conditions are not met, the system is inconsistent with profit maximization. Besides these regularity properties, the dual form is used to test various hypotheses about the production structure such as separability, homotheticity, and the form of technical change.

A major shortcoming of the approach is the difficulty in achieving the regularity conditions in empirical analysis.[33] Although duality is a micro theory, many of the studies use macro data. The studies vary in functional forms used, in the type of function used in the estimation, and in the questions asked. We will try to give the flavor of these studies by sampling some that are most oriented to our needs.

---

[32] The parameters in question are first and second order derivatives. Their value is likely to depend on the input and output combination and thus differ with the observations. Consequently, in the event of wide variations in the sample, an approximation by a fixed coefficient function may be erroneous.

[33] In a survey of studies of US agricultural productivity, based mostly on duality, it was observed that "... empirical results and theoretical consistency are sensitive to model specification. ... Many researchers found the translog to be ill-behaved over portions of the data set, that is, monotonicity and curvature properties hold only locally [Caves and Christensen (1980)]. This was also evident in many of the models presented in this chapter. ... not all the econometric models satisfied locally the monotonicity conditions and the curvature conditions" [Capalbo (1988, p. 184)]. And in another review: "The review exposed some of the limitations of existing research. For example, it is not clear what should be done with empirical models that violate theoretical properties" [Capalbo and Vo (1988, p. 124)]. More recently, "... as most students of the existing empirical literature on agricultural supply response systems know, failure to satisfy convexity in estimated profit functions is not unique to this study" [Chambers and Pope (1994, p. 110)]. For additional supportive evidence, see also [Fox and Kivanda (1994) and Shumway (1995)].

This result had been anticipated: "Some expansions, such as the translog function ... can never except in trivial cases satisfy monotonicity or convexity conditions over the entire positive orthant" [Fuss et al. (1978, p. 234)]. This reservation is related to the functional form. However, this is not all: the major difficulty comes from the fact that the implemented technology is not constant over the sample.

Early application of duality to the study of agricultural production was made by Lau and Yotopoulos (1972) and Yotopoulos, Lau, and Lin (1976). They used a Cobb–Douglas profit function. As Cobb–Douglas is a self-dual function, it was a straightforward matter to obtain from the profit function estimates of the production function elasticities and to compare them with direct estimates of the same parameters. This comparison reveals some substantive differences. Unfortunately, such a numerical comparison of the dual and the primal estimates had no follow-up and has practically vanished from empirical analysis.

2.1. Studies based on cost functions

Define the restricted cost function

$$C(w, k, y, t) = \min_{v}\left[wv; \; y = F(v, k, t)\right], \tag{17}$$

where v is a vector of unrestricted (variable) inputs with prices denoted by w, k is a vector of constrained inputs which are assumed to have no alternative cost, y is a vector of outputs, and t is a technology index. By the envelope theorem (Shephard's Lemma)

$$\frac{\partial \ln C(w, k, y, t)}{\partial \ln w_j} \equiv S_j(w, k, y, t). \tag{18}$$

Various restrictions are imposed in empirical analysis; many of the studies assume that all inputs are unrestricted, in which case k is not part of the argument. In what follows, to simplify the notation we will use this assumption unless indicated otherwise. The empirical results depend on the structure imposed on the function. Several properties are of interest:
  Homotheticity:

$$C(w, y, t) = \phi(y)C(w, t); \quad \text{Hence, } S_j(w, y, t) = S_j(w, t). \tag{19}$$

  Neutral technical change:

$$C(w, y, t) = A(t)C(w, y); \quad \text{Hence, } S_j(w, y, t) = S_j(w, y). \tag{20}$$

  Homotheticity and neutrality:

$$S_j(w, y, t) = S_j(w). \tag{21}$$

The cost function is expressed as a quadratic function in the variables or as a monotonic transformation of the variables, most commonly logarithmic, yielding the translog function. The share equations are then linear in the same variables. Unless indicated otherwise, the technology is represented by a time trend. The empirical analysis deals with the estimation of the factor share equation under one of the above restrictions, often not tested empirically. There is no single central issue in these studies: different studies emphasize different topics. The most important ones are related to the behavior of factor shares with respect to changes in factor prices, the trend in the shares (time as an index of technology), and the effect of output when homotheticity is not assumed. Some studies emphasize methodological aspects by testing the properties of the function needed to describe a production system consistent with comparative statics.

Binswanger (1974) estimates a translog homothetic cost function from a cross-state data set for the US for the period 1949–1964. Agriculture is assumed to be a price-taker in all inputs, including land. He compares factor demand elasticities (evaluated at the mean) with those derived under the constraint of Cobb–Douglas. Except for land, the elasticities are near 1. They are close to the Cobb–Douglas-based elasticities for machinery and fertilizer but much lower for land (-0.34 as compared to -0.85). This result can be attributed to the fact that the model assumes a perfectly elastic supply of land, but this is not the case in reality, and the estimates reflect the data that were generated by a fairly inelastic land supply.

The cross-price derivatives of the cost function provide a measure of substitution. It is found that "[t]he best substitutes are land for fertilizer . . . It was a surprise . . . to find that machinery is a better substitute for land than for labor" [Binswanger (1974, p. 384)]. To explain the result, note that in general shocks, and specifically technical shocks, are both land-expanding and land-augmenting [Mundlak (1997)]. Technical change in agriculture caused a decline in the product price and thereby suppressed its expansion effect, so that under the new technology less land was needed to produce the demanded output. The new techniques were more fertilizer-intensive and machine-intensive, resulting in the positive association between machines and fertilizers and the negative association of these two variables with land demand.

The technical change is labor-saving and machine-using; the labor share declined at the average annual rate of 5.5 percent, and that of machines increased at the rate of 2.5 percent. Regional dummies were significantly different from zero. The inclusion of regional dummies qualifies the estimates as within-region estimates. The fact that they are significantly different from zero indicates differences in regional productivity and that the explanatory variables need not be exogenous.

Ray (1982) uses a translog cost function with two outputs, livestock and crops, in estimating the technology of US agriculture in 1939–1977. He imposes Hicks-neutral technical change and finds decreasing returns to scale for aggregate output, indicating that technology is nonhomothetic. The reason for the decreasing returns can be attributed to the fact that not all the inputs are included in the analysis, and thus, the estimates are of a short-run cost function. The average annual rate of the technical change is 1.8 percent. The own demand elasticities are less than 1. The substitution of hired labor for machines is much smaller than that between labor and fertilizers. Also, Ray finds substitution between labor and fertilizer, in contrast to Binswanger (1974), who claims complementarity.

Kako (1978) uses a translog cost function to study rice production in Japan in 1953–1970. Constant returns to scale is imposed, and technical change is measured by time trend with different slopes for three subperiods. The average percentage change in factor use during the period was: labor 2.6, machinery 3.9, fertilizers 4.4; the rice area did not change. Output grew at the rate of 2.7 percent. The input changes are decomposed to output effect, substitution (or price) effect, and technical change. The technical change was dominating for labor, whereas the output effect dominated the changes in fertilizers and machinery. Thus technical change was largely labor saving but had little effect on the other inputs. What picture does this finding portray of rice production? If the rice area did not change, it is not clear what changes in output could prompt an increase in machines. Perhaps part of the answer is related to the calculation of technical change. It is reported that 56 percent of the increase in output is attributed to technical change; thus, indirectly the use of machines is affected by technical change. We can think about these changes in terms of changes in the composition of techniques which became labor-saving and machine- and fertilizer-using. Finally, the fact that land did not change during the period is consistent with the view that land supply is far from being perfectly elastic as implicitly assumed in the formulation. As such, the results are likely to be distorted.

Kuroda (1987) estimates a translog cost function using national averages data for Japan for the period 1952–1982 and concludes that "... the production process of post-war Japanese agriculture was characterized neither by Hicks neutrality nor homotheticity. Biases ... reduced labor relative to other factor inputs ..." (p. 335).

Lopez (1980) used a generalized Leontief cost function to study the structure of production of Canadian agriculture in 1946–1977. The paper emphasizes two subjects, tests for integrability and for homotheticity. A necessary condition for integrability is symmetry of the price coefficients in the derived demand equations. Integrability is not rejected, and it is concluded that there is a production function that can represent Canadian agriculture. The idea is that the cost function can be derived from this production function. This is the idea of duality, but things are not that simple. Below we question the validity of the assumption that market prices used in an analysis of macro data are exogenous and maintain the requirements underlying the derivation of a cost function. If the assumption is violated, the estimated coefficients of the cost function would be biased. Given that the integrability conditions are met, the fitted function may be integrated to an aggregate technology, but this is not the relevant one for Canadian agriculture.[34] By way of analogy, a negatively slopped line fitted to price-quantity data need not represent a demand, or supply, function, and it may be a combination of supply and demand functions.

The factor demand equations include output and time trend. The output coefficients are significantly different from zero, indicating nonhomotheticity. The time coefficients were not significantly different from zero except for labor. This indicates neutral technical change with respect to all inputs except for labor. However, when homotheticity was

---

[34] On this issue see [Mundlak and Volcani (1973)].

imposed, the time coefficients became significantly different from zero, and the signs were consistent with factor-augmenting technical change. This is another illustration of the tradeoff between the inclusion of output and time trend in the equations. We discuss this finding below. The own-factor-demand elasticities are less than 1, cross-elasticities are all positive. Labor is a substitute for all inputs except for land.

Clark and Youngblood (1992) estimate a translog cost function for central Canadian agriculture (Ontario and Quebec) for 1935–1985 using a time-series approach instead of including a time trend as a technical change measure. They concur with Lopez (1980) that technical change is neutral but output is an important variable in the shares of land and fertilizers.

2.2. What is the message?[35]

Factor shares in agriculture have undergone changes over time; particularly, the share of labor declined, that of machinery and purchased inputs increased. How much of these changes can be attributed to economic factors? The studies reviewed above indicate that some of these changes were associated with changes in factor prices. Still, the major part of the changes is attributed to changes in output or reflects the time trend. There is a tradeoff between the role of homotheticity and neutrality of the technical change. When output was included in the equation, it tended to replace the role of the time variable.[36] This result is consistent with the fact that the new techniques are more productive and use different factor ratios than the old techniques.

Two conceptual limitations to the empirical analysis of cost functions may distort the results. First, the cost function is derived for a price-taker agent and as such does not apply to macro data where prices are determined by market supply and demand. The factor demand is derived from the cost function, and therefore it is affected by shocks affecting the cost function. These shocks are thereby translated to the factor prices. In short, factor prices need not be exogenous. This limitation applies to all studies that use market data – rather than firm data – including studies based on profit functions. This is not a trivial point because agriculture cannot be assumed to be a price-taker in the rural labor and capital markets, and definitely not in the land market.

Second, a cost function is derived conditional on output, and this is interpreted erroneously in empirical analysis to mean that output is exogenous. In general, there is no

---

[35] Issues related to the choice of functional form are discussed by Chalfant (1984). He argues that the translog and the Generalized Leontief cost functions are less appropriate for modeling agricultural production since they do not result in negative own-demand elasticities of substitution for all inputs. However, the estimates resulting from the use of the Fourier flexible form also failed to satisfy the negative own elasticities for all of the factors (p. 119). Lopez (1985a) discusses similar issues for profit functions.

[36] This is also consistent with the conclusion of a survey by Capalbo (1988, pp. 184–185): "Nonhomothetic functions performed better than models that maintained neutral technical change or constant returns to scale, or both". Wide variations were obtained in the level and bias of technical change, although all the reported results indicate that the technical change was labor-saving and chemical and equipment-using, whereas the results with respect to land are ambiguous.

reason to believe that the marginal cost, and therefore output, is independent of shocks to the cost function.[37] This problem is not shared by profit functions.

2.3. Studies based on profit functions

The profit function provides a compact form to summarize a multiproduct technology and an efficient way to introduce the properties imposed by theory on this system. This possibility is utilized in the empirical analysis, and thus there is no direct comparison with results obtained from the cost function with a single aggregate output. Also, the profit function facilitates the examination of whether the technology is that of joint production [Chambers and Just (1989)].

The restricted profit function of an individual producer is defined by

$$\pi(p, w, k, T) = \max_{y, v}(py - wv: \ y, x \in T), \tag{22}$$

where y is a vector of outputs; x is a vector of J inputs decomposed to variable, v, and fixed, k, components: $x = (v, k)$ with dimensions (J_v, J_k), $J_v + J_k = J$; T is the available technology set; p is the vector of product prices; and w is the vector of factor prices. It can be decomposed to conform to the decomposition of x. However, where ambiguity does not exist, such a decomposition is not made explicit. By the envelope theorem (Hotelling's Lemma) the product supply and factor demand functions are written:

$$y_i(p, w, k, T) = \frac{\partial \pi}{\partial p_i}, \qquad v_j(p, w, k, T) = -\frac{\partial \pi}{\partial w_j}. \tag{23}$$

The equations in (23) can be expressed also as shares. Like the cost function, the profit function is expressed as a quadratic function of a monotonic transformation of the variables. Then, Equations (23) become linear in the same variables.

Lopez (1984) estimates a Generalized Leontief profit function for Canadian agriculture, using 1971 cross-section data. The Hessian matrix (the matrix of the second partial derivatives of y_i and v_j) evaluated at the sample points has mostly the wrong sign, indicating that the profit function is not everywhere convex. The elasticities are generally low, particularly for supply (0.01 for crops and 0.472 for animal products). There is a gap between the variables used in the analysis and those assumed in the theoretical model. The paper suggests that there is sufficient variability across regions for a meaningful analysis, but this variability is in part spurious, reflecting quality variations; thus it is likely that the results reflect data problems.

Antle (1984) uses a single product translog profit function to estimate input demand and output supply functions for US agriculture for 1910–1978. Technical change is

---

[37] An exception in nonagriculture is the interesting study by Nerlove (1963) of the power-generating plants where the output is demand-driven and as such is exogenous.

represented by time trend and time dummies for subperiods.[38] The findings lead to the acceptance of symmetry, convexity, and structural change in the postwar period and to the rejection of homotheticity, parameter stability, and neutral technical change. Also, he finds differences in the direction of the technology bias between the pre and postwar periods.[39] Scale effects are very important post-war and are not important pre-war. "It shows that changes in factor use were more a function of technical change and a scale change in the postwar period than in the prewar period. Thus, input use in the post-war period was apparently less price responsive over time than in the pre-war period" [Antle (1984, p. 418)]. This conclusion is consistent with the world of heterogeneous technology as discussed above.

The low price elasticities are claimed to be consistent with those reported by Shumway (1983) and Weaver (1983) and as such are considered to be acceptable. This result is also consistent with many other studies of supply response reporting low supply elasticity. In our discussion of the subject at a later stage, the low elasticity is attributed to inelastic factor supply. Antle (1984) also suggests that his results are in line with induced innovations.[40] However, his argumentation indicates that the pace of the technical change was related to the implementation rather than to the pace of changes in the available technology itself.

Shumway and Alexander (1988) fit a system of five outputs and four inputs to US regional data for the period 1951–1982. They had to impose price linear-homogeneity, symmetry, and convexity.[41] It is indicated that the great variability of the results "... clearly document the importance of considering regional differences in predicting the distributional effects of potential changes in economic conditions ..." (p. 160). Technical change was not Hicks-neutral. The own-price-demand elasticities varied from 0 to −1.42, and output elasticities varied from 0.01 to 1.22, with great variations across regions.

Shumway, Saez, and Gottret (1988) estimated a quadratic profit function with five output groups and four input groups for the US for the period 1951–1982. Land and family labor are fixed; time trend represents technology. As in the previous study, symmetry, linear homogeneity, and convexity in prices had to be imposed. Estimates were obtained for regional data under the assumption that regional prices are exogenous, and for national data where the variable-factor prices were endogenized. The regional estimates are aggregated and compared with the national estimates. The output-supply and

---

[38] "Without time dummy variables, very small D-W statistics were obtained, suggesting misspecification" [Antle (1984, p. 417)].

[39] "The prewar is biased toward labor and mechanical technology and against land, whereas the postwar technology is biased against labor and toward machinery and chemicals" [Antle (1984, p. 420)].

[40] "Actual on-farm technology, therefore, lagged behind agricultural research, and estimates of the prewar technology should not be expected to show much evidence of technical change bias toward mechanical or chemical technology" [Antle (1984, p. 420)].

[41] "Convexity of the profit function was not maintained in the model exploration phase" [Shumway and Alexander (1988, p. 155)].

input-demand elasticities are low and become even lower when upward-slopping supply curves for the variable inputs were introduced. The low response is attributed to fixity of land and family labor.

Additional support for the proposition that techniques, outputs, and inputs are determined jointly is obtained from the fact that important properties of a production function are not maintained under aggregation over techniques: "A larger number of US parameters are significant when derived from the regional estimates (53 percent) than when directly estimated (42 percent)" [Shumway et al. (1988, p. 334)].[42] More important, "[s]ymmetry of price parameters in the system of Equations (1) and (2) was not preserved in the national aggregation" (p. 334, footnote 2). The findings also support the proposition that shocks affect land expansion and land augmentation in the same direction: "All five outputs increase as the quantity of real estates services increase . . . . All variable inputs are complements to real estates. Half are complements to family labor, and a third are complements to other variable inputs" (p. 334).

Huffman and Evenson (1989) fit a normalized quadratic restricted profit function with six outputs and three variable inputs to data for US cash grain farms during 1949–1974. They expand on previous duality-based studies by allowing the shares to depend on agricultural research, extension, and farmers' schooling in addition to time. The partial effect of research is in the direction of fertilizer-using and labor- and machine-saving. As research was machine-saving, the observed increased use of machines is attributed to declining prices. There is asymmetry in the explanation of the increased use of machines and the decline in the use of labor. This can be resolved by assuming that the change has been facilitated by a decline in the cost of machines and that the new machines require less labor than the old machines. This explanation is consistent with the heterogeneous technology framework. The effect of extension was small. The shadow value of private crop research is near zero, but it is high for public research. The own-price elasticities at the sample means are: fertilizer -1.2, fuel -0.72, machinery -0.61, labor -0.51, soybean 1.3, wheat 0.97, and feed grains 0.016.

Bouchet, Orden, and Norton (1989) fit a normalized quadratic profit function to data for French agriculture in 1959–1984. This was a period of strong growth, mainly in cereals, a decline in labor, and an increase in labor cost. The analysis differentiates between short- and long-run response. The supply is price responsive, but the elasticities are below 1. "However, the response to price changes are estimated to be inelastic even in the long run when usage of quasi-fixed capital and family labor have fully adjusted to optimal levels" (p. 292). The estimates of the long-run response are obtained under the implicit assumption of perfectly elastic supply of quasi-fixed inputs. When in reality the supply functions were not perfectly elastic, the estimated responses are biased downward.

---

[42] The standard errors for the aggregated coefficients were obtained under the assumption of independence of the regional estimates and as such are an approximation. National shocks affect all regions, and therefore their coefficients are jointly affected and thereby correlated. This may be the reason for the difference in significance levels.

The findings show that both family labor and capital have a strong positive effect on the supply of cereals, milk, and animal products. This result raises two puzzles. First, cereals is not a labor-intensive product, and therefore it is not obvious why it should have a strong positive response to changes in family labor. Second, one would expect an opposite effect of labor and capital. This similarity of effects can be explained by a strong expansion effect that dominates the substitution effect. The expansion effect is prompted by the technical change that accounts for the observed growth. Putting it all together, the observed changes can be accounted for in terms of changes in the composition of techniques.

Ball et al. (1993a) use restricted and unrestricted profit functions to evaluate the consequences of the Common Agricultural Policy (CAP). The main empirical result is that the response elasticities are low but in line with values that appear in the literature using other functional forms and less demanding models. Land and labor are taken as fixed in the evaluation, and this is the reason for obtaining low response elasticities.

2.4. Dual estimates – summary

In summarizing the foregoing findings it has to be kept in mind that the reviewed studies are mostly for the US, Canada, and Japan, so the numerical values may not be fully representative. However, the main developments in the agriculture of these countries are shared by other countries. The post-war period is characterized by a strong technical change in agriculture, both in the level and in the direction of factor use. Yields increased together with improved varieties and the use of chemicals, while labor was replaced by machines. Thus, the results have broad implications, and they facilitate the drawing of important methodological conclusions.

What distinguishes the dual approach from the primal is the appearance of prices in the empirical equation. Hence, in evaluating the performance of this approach we address the following questions:

- What has been the contribution of prices to the empirical equation?
- What additional information is obtained from the dual equations, and how can they be interpreted?
- Are the underlying assumptions of duality met?
- What are the statistical benefits of this approach?
- Where do we go from here?

The dual estimates are obtained by regressing factor shares on prices, time trend, and sometimes output. When the change in the use of inputs is decomposed to price, trend (a proxy for technology), and output effects, it is found that trend and output capture most of the changes, whereas the role of prices is the least important. Thus the contribution of prices to the explanation of inputs or output variations is rather limited.

The price elasticities of factor demand and product supply are usually obtained under the assumption that producers are price-takers in the product and factor markets. On the whole, the own-price elasticities are less than 1. There is no uniformity in the signs of the cross elasticities, but in general, most inputs appear to be substitutes. The strength of the own and cross elasticities reflects in part the fact that in reality factors' supply is not perfectly elastic as the models assume, and therefore the results need not represent the demand-driven substitution as it is thought. This is the case with respect to elasticities related to labor, land, and capital. We further elaborate on this subject below.

With respect to other findings, interestingly, on the whole the studies based on duality do not show increasing returns to scale. Technical change, obtained by including a time trend in regressions of factor shares, is largely labor-saving, capital-using, and fertilizer-using, with the results on land being somewhat ambiguous. This is reflective of the data, which means that whatever was the effect of prices, it was not sufficient to change conclusions that could be drawn from the raw data. This does not give a strong mark to the analysis in that the results are obvious without it.

Duality between technology and prices holds under well-defined conditions that can be tested empirically. In most studies these underlying conditions are not fully met; particularly the concavity of the cost function or the convexity of the profit function is violated. Therefore, the estimated technology is inconsistent with the basic premises of the model. In a way, this is the most disappointing result because duality theory is a very powerful theory, and the question is why it does not come through in the empirical analysis. There may be more than one reason, but probably the most important one is related to the changes in technology.

One of the expected virtues of duality has been related to its solution of the simultaneous-equations bias realized in some primal estimators. However, as indicated above, in general dual estimators are inferior to primal estimators on the grounds of statistical efficiency. Where do we go from here? We return to this question at the end of the paper.

3. Multiproduct production

Most of the primal studies of production use a measure of a single output, value output, even though output consists of more than one product. The outcome is a truncated picture of the technology and limits its usefulness. Estimates based on input data aggregated over products are not sufficiently informative in that they do not provide a simple way to address questions of interest such as: What is the factor productivity in the production of a particular product? Does such productivity depend on the level of output of the other products, and if it does, is it because of overall input constraint or because of technological interdependence? Also, without a complete presentation of the multiproduct production function, it is impossible to derive the supply of the individual products. It is not due to unawareness of the importance of the complete presentation but rather due to lack of data and complexity of specification and estimation. The situation has improved considerably with the appearance of the dual approach. As the foregoing review indicates, many of the empirical studies based on the profit function facilitate the derivation of the behavioral functions, specifically product supply, without having to resort to the primal function.

The data problem is a reflection of the fact that industry statistics for agriculture do not report the inputs by products, except for land and some product-specific inputs such as livestock. This is a convention, and by itself it reveals nothing about the nature of the production process. In principle, micro data collected from farm surveys can alleviate the problem. This is at least the case with respect to inputs which are easy to allocate to the various products, such as feeds or fertilizers, but the allocation of the use of fixed inputs requires more effort, and therefore such data are relatively scarce and do not surface with high frequency in reported studies to clarify some of the underlying issues discussed in this section.

Most farms produce more than one product, and this raises the question of the reason for the diversification. Possible reasons are:

(1) Interdependence in production where the marginal productivity of a factor of production in the production of one product depends on the level of production of another product, for example, wool and mutton, or milk and beef on dairy farms.

(2) Better utilization of some fixed inputs, or alternatively due to production quotas on some outputs, which frees resources to produce other products [Moschini (1988)].

(3) Savings due to vertical integration, where the farm produces intermediate inputs which are consumed on the farm, such as corn and hogs, or hay and livestock. Such integration saves marketing charges in the broad sense (transportation, trade margins, spoilage, etc.).

(4) Risk management.

To sort out the reasons for the diversification of production we need to go beyond the output-aggregate production function.

To put some structure to the discussion, let $T(y, x)$ denote the production set which contains all the feasible combinations of the vectors of outputs (y) and inputs (x). This set is contained in the nonnegative orthant, it is closed, convex, contains free disposals, and the origin. Its efficiency frontier, $t(y, x) = 0$, is unique. Studies with aggregate value output take the form $py = f(x)$, where py is the inner product of p and y. This is a special case of the more general presentation obtained by imposing separability on $t(y, x)$: $t(y, x) = Y(y) - X(x) = 0$ [Mundlak (1964b)]. Hall (1973) shows that this imposition is equivalent to a multiplicative decomposition of the cost function, $C(w, y) = H(y)c(w)$. The general presentation of output by $Y(y)$ has two advantages over the more restricted single aggregate output presentation: First, the function with aggregate value output is not a single-valued function and its parameters depend on the output composition along the expansion path [Mundlak (1963b)], whereas $Y(y)$ can be formulated to overcome this shortcoming. Second, it allows for interdependence in production. An application of this approach to the output aggregation of Israeli agriculture using a multi-stage CES function was made by Mundlak and Razin (1971). The limitation of this type of separability is that it is applicable only when the technology is interdependent, and the derived ratio of output prices is independent of the ratio of factor prices [Hall (1973)]. The latter, to be sure, applies also to the aggregate single-product production function.

Most agricultural production is thought to be carried out by independent techniques for individual products. In this case, the profit or the cost functions will be additive and the supply of product j will be independent of the price of product h [Hall (1973), Lau (1978)]. We can write these functions as follows: $C(w, y) = \sum_j C_j(w, y_j)$, where $C(w, y)$ is the minimum cost of producing the output vector y at factor prices w, and similarly, $C_j(w, y_j)$ is the minimum cost of producing output y_j. A similar result applies for the profit function: $\pi(p, w) = \sum_j \pi_j(p_j, w)$. This additivity constitutes only a sufficient condition for independent production. As Shumway, Pope and Nash (1984) indicated, common constraints imposed on production may produce nonzero cross price coefficients in supply. To show this, we note that the problem under consideration is a special case of the heterogeneous technology discussed above, where the techniques are identified with the products and as such are explicit. Repeating that discussion with more details, the maximization problem is:

$$
L(v_j, k_j, \lambda) = \sum_j p_j F_j(v_j, k_j) - \sum_j w v_j - \lambda \left(\sum_j k_j - k \right);
$$

subject to $F_j(\cdot) \in T$; $v_j \geqslant 0$; $k_j \geqslant 0$.

Let F_{xj} be the vector of marginal productivity of x in the production of product j. The Kuhn–Tucker necessary conditions for a solution are

$$
\begin{aligned}
(p_j F_{vj} - w)v_j &= 0, & p_j F_{vj} - w &\leqslant 0, \\
(p_j F_{kj} - \lambda)k_j &= 0, & pj F_{kj} - \lambda &\leqslant 0, \\
\left(\sum k_j - k \right)\lambda &= 0, & \sum k_j - k &\leqslant 0, \\
v_j &\geqslant 0; \; k_j \geqslant 0; \; \lambda \geqslant 0.
\end{aligned}
$$

Thus, even though $\partial F_{xj}/\partial y_h = 0$, it is possible that $\partial y_j/\partial p_h = \partial y_j/\partial k_j \partial k_j/\partial p_h \neq 0$, because a change in a product price may cause a change of the shadow price of the constraints in the production of that product. Therefore, when the constraints are binding, their allocation among the various products changes and causes a reshuffle of the inputs and outputs. The term joint production encompasses the two cases, interdependence in production and the sharing of constraints. The importance of the latter can be detected empirically by introducing the constraints k to the profit function.

The discussion does not indicate how to allocate the inputs to the various products. This subject is developed by Just, Zilberman, and Hochman (1983) who utilize the first order conditions for profit maximization to extract the input allocation to the individual crops. The method is further developed by Chambers and Just (1989) by introducing a flexible production function and developing a test for joint production. Without going into details, we note that in principle the allocation is determined by the Kuhn–Tucker conditions above to yield $v_j(s)$, $k_j(s)$, and $y(s)$, where $s = (p, w, k, T)$ is the vector of state variables. The two studies apply the method to the same data set and obtain plausible results in spite of the complexity in the calculations.

The essence of the discussion is that diversity in production is not necessarily a result of interdependence in production. Leathers (1991) extends the discussion to extract implications for industrial organization. Dealing with the cost functions and taking the unconstrained cost function as the long-run function, it is implied that in the long run the constraint will not serve as a cause for diversity in production. Note, however, that agricultural production is seasonal, and since the firms are of finite size also in the long run, there is considerable scope for better utilization of resources by diversification. Just recall the old days when farm plans drawn by linear programming yielded combinations of products which utilized best the available resources.

The discussion on industrial organization deals with production at the firm level but, as we see repeatedly in this survey, we should be aware that micro theory is applied to macro data without blinking. Thus, there is another reason for diversification which is more important for the macro data – marketing costs. To put it in perspective, note that all countries produce almost all agricultural products that the physical environment permits. This can be attributed in large part to the fact that domestic production saves the various charges that are involved in international trade. Agriculture is stretched out geographically and this entails high trade costs, particularly in developing countries where the infrastructure leaves much to be desired. Finally, risk management can lead to diversification, but this is well known and need not be elaborated upon here.

4. Nonparametric methods

4.1. Description

Evidently, it is not easy to find a meaningful and robust empirical presentation of technology. The search for culprits has pointed at, among others, the parametric presentation, or functional form, of the production function, and thus the nonparametric presentation surfaced. A somewhat similar problem had been encountered much earlier in the theory of consumer choice, which sought a presentation without having to resort to the unobservable utility (objective) function. In the case of consumer choice, the empirical inference is based on the observed budget constraint, quantities, and prices. In the case of production, we observe the values of the profit (objective) function but do not observe the technology constraint, and the problem is to infer about it from the data. In the context of production, this approach was developed by Afriat (1972), Hanoch and Rothschild (1972), and Varian (1984). Recently, it has been discussed and applied to agriculture in a series of papers: Fawson and Shumway (1988), Chavas and Cox (1988, 1994), Cox and Chavas (1990), Tauer (1995), Featherstone, Moghnieh, and Goodwin (1995), Bar-Shira and Finkelshtain (1999), among others.

In describing the approach, we modify somewhat the notation used above. Let $y = (y_1, \ldots, y_H)$ be a netput vector whose positive components are outputs and the negative components are inputs, and p be the vector of corresponding prices. The profit is the inner product py. It is assumed that y comes from a feasible production set Y that maintains the free disposal property: if $y \in Y$ and $y \geqslant y'$, then $y' \in Y$.

The pivot of the analysis is the assumption that the observed netputs are optimal under the observed prices and the underlying (but unobserved) technology. Thus, if we observe

y^i and p^i, we assume that under p^i there is no netput in the production set that brings higher profit than the observed y^i. More compactly, $p^i y^i \geqslant p^i y$ for all $y \in Y$. If this holds for all the observed netputs, then it is said that the production set Y p-rationalizes the data. Then $p^i y^i \geqslant p^i y^j$ for all $i, j = 1, \ldots, n$, where n is the sample size. Varian (1984) shows that this condition guarantees the existence of a closed, convex, negative monotonic production set and referred to it as the Weak Axiom of Profit Maximization (WAPM). Bar-Shira and Finkelshtain (1999) further extend the analysis.

The underlying assumption is empirical in nature, and its validity can be tested by comparing all possible inner products between the observed netputs and prices [Fawson and Shumway (1988)]. If a netput is chosen, it should be optimal under the price regime prevailing at the time. A situation which is inconsistent with the hypothesis is when a netput is chosen even though it seems to be inferior to another netput under its own price regime: $p^j y^j < p^j y^i$ and $p^i y^j < p^i y^i$. This raises the question of why y^j was chosen in the first place when it was inferior to y^i under p^j. The negative answer is that there was a violation of profit maximization. The positive one is technical change, so that when y^j was chosen, y^i was not feasible. As technology progresses with time, we expect more recent observations to represent more productive technologies than did earlier observations. Consequently, in time series analysis, when $t > 0$, we expect $p^0 y^t - p^0 y^0 > 0$, or equivalently, $L_q = p^0 y^t / p^0 y^0 > 1$ where L_q is the Laspeyres quantity index. If this is not the case, then the conclusion is that this binary comparison is inconsistent with profit maximization.

Fawson and Shumway (1988) apply the test to regional data of US agriculture and find that the majority (typically, 80–90 percent) of the observations would be inconsistent with profit maximization if technical change were not allowed for. Featherstone, Moghnieh, and Goodwin (1995) apply the test to micro data of Kansas farms. The conditions of profit maximization, or of cost minimization, were violated by a large proportion of the observations. The number of violations declined when technical change was allowed for, but was still sizable.

When a particular netput is more profitable than another one under the two pertinent price regimes, it is concluded that it comes from a more productive technology. Based on this concept, Bar-Shira and Finkelshtain (1999) rank the technologies and apply their framework to data on US agriculture. They show that the ranking of the technologies does not always follow the chronological order, namely in some years the rank is lower than that of previous years. As no one suggests that there has been a regression in the technology of US agriculture, this finding can either be attributed to a violation of profit maximization or it may arise from more fundamental difficulties in identifying the technology through prices, an issue on which we elaborate in the discussion below. Bar-Shira and Finkelshtain quantify the technical change by computing the revenue per dollar expenses at constant prices. This is an index of change in the output-input ratio, and it is reminiscent of the early work on productivity at NBER and Schultz's (1953) discussion of productivity in agriculture. This then brings us back to square one. Finally, they examine whether the technical change is biased. Chavas and Cox (1988, 1994) go further in discussing procedures for inferring the nature of the technical change by examining what changes in the components of the netputs should be made in order to induce equality of the profits of the two netputs evaluated in terms of the base prices, or simply to bring the L_q to 1. The procedure is discussed and modified by Chalfant and Zhang (1997).

The literature deals with some more specific topics, such as separability of the technology and returns to scale. Finally, the tests discussed above are deterministic in the sense that they classify the data by those observations that are consistent with the hypothesis and those that are not. This does not take into account the possibility of errors in the data. Statistical tests have been suggested to deal with such errors. We do not cover these topics here, and we now move on to an evaluation of the method and its application.

4.2. Discussion

Under the conditions of WAPM, there exists a production set with the underlying properties needed for the production theory. Therefore, the central issue of the nonparametric analysis is to check for the empirical validity of WAPM. Note that this involves asking the same important question that was initially raised by Cobb and Douglas (1928) on the empirical validity of the competitive conditions and which received attention in the early work on the primal production function. However, as the empirical studies show, the conditions of WAPM are typically not met unless technical change is allowed for; but, to allow for technical change, the assumption that all the observations are optimal is used. At this point the common domain with the work on the primal function vanishes, and the approach becomes more similar to that of the dual function, where the optimality is imposed and not tested. This is to say that the technology is identified by the prices.

Allowing for technical change amounts to making productivity statements based on output and input indexes. It is well known that such measures are subject to the index-number bias caused by the inability to make full allowance for the substitution triggered by changes in relative prices. Thus, the method shares the problems as well as the merits of productivity measures through the use of index numbers.

It is important to note that such measures cannot differentiate between neutral and differential technical change. To show this in a simple setting, assume a cost function $C(w, A, y) = C(w_1/A_1, \ldots, w_m/A_m, y)$ where the A's are the factor-augmenting functions. Without a loss in generality, we will examine the case of a linear homogeneous production function. Also, assume $A_j^t \geq 1$ for all j and t. Let $A_1^t = \min_j\{A_j^t\}$ for all t, recall (19) and (20), and rewrite $C(w, A, y) = ya_1c(aw)$; $a_1 = 1/A_1$, $a_j = A_1/A_j$, $j > 1$. Thus, a_1 can be thought of as the Hicks-Neutral coefficient. Evaluate the technical change as follows, for $t > 0$:

$$\frac{C(w^0, A^0, y^0)/y^0}{C(w^t, A^t, y^t)/y^t} = \frac{a_1^0}{a_1^t} \frac{c(a^0 w^0)}{c(a^t w^t)}.$$

We write more compactly $C(w^t, A^t, y^t) \equiv C(t)$, $c(a^t, w^t) \equiv c(t)$.

We now evaluate this ratio for neutral and for differential technical change. We do it under constant prices, $w^t = w^0 = w$, and for a given output, $y^t = y^0$, so that the technical change is evaluated by the savings in inputs needed to produce a given output. The inputs considered come from the input requirement set: $x^t \in V(y, t)$.

Hicks Neutral Technical Change (HNTC): Let $1 = A_1^0 < A_1^t$, $a_j^t = 1$ for all $j > 1$ and all t, hence $V(y, 0) \subseteq V(y, t)$, $C(t) = wx^t$, $wx^t < wx^0$. Imposing these conditions, we get $c(t) = c(w)$, and

$$\frac{C(0)}{C(t)} = \frac{wx^0}{wx^t} = A_1^t > 1.$$

Thus the rate of factor saving is equal to the rate of the HNTC.

Factor Augmenting Technical Change (FATC): Let $A_1^t = 1$ for all t, $a_j^t \leqslant a_j^0$ for all $j > 1$ and all t, with the inequality in effect for at least one j, hence $y^0 < y^t$ and $V(y, 0) \subseteq V(y, t)$. Impose $y^t = y^0$ and $a_j^0 = 1$, then, $wx^t < wx^0$, and the effect of the technical change under these conditions is

$$\frac{C(0)}{C(t)} = \frac{wx^0}{wx^t} = \frac{c(w)}{c(a^t w)} > 1.$$

This measure is similar to that of HNTC, but it is due to FATC; it is therefore referred to as the Neutral Equivalent of Differential Technical Change (NEDTC) [Mundlak and Razin (1969)]. The conclusion is that the ratio wx^0/wx^t is affected by neutral as well as by differential technical change, and therefore we cannot differentiate between them.

The problems in the application of the nonparametric method are similar to those faced in the applications of duality. The theory is a micro theory, and therefore its application to macro data can distort the results. Prices are not exogenous, the supply of inputs is not perfectly elastic, and in the short run, which may last for some time, there are constraints to the convergence to long-run equilibrium. We return to this topic in the discussion on dynamics below. This raises the question of how to price durable inputs in the analysis, underlining the problem that arises from the fact that the econometrician does not necessarily know the prices, or price expectations, observed by the firm and thus may use the wrong prices. All these may lead to behavior which can be incorrectly interpreted as deviations from profit maximization. To see that this can create a problem, we note that Bar-Shira and Finkelshtain (1999, Figure 8) present a graph of the profits (the product of the netput and its price) in US agriculture for the period 1945–1994. It appears that from 1958 on, with the exceptions of three years, agriculture was operating at a loss, and at times, at a big loss. During this period, output continued to increase. Thus, this suggests that somehow these prices are not the relevant prices.

All these problems occur within the traditional framework of homogeneous technology. If we allow for heterogeneous technology, additional considerations come up. First note that, by definition, the observed netputs represent the implemented technology, and as such the corresponding production sets are conditional on the state variables. As we move from one year to the next (or across farms for that matter), the state variables may change and with them, the implied production sets. Thus, it is possible to get a regression in productivity because of the change in the underlying economic environment, as indeed it is presented in Bar-Shira and Finkelshtain (1999, Figure 9).

5. Supply analysis[43]

5.1. Background

Analytically, the supply function of the competitive firm is the partial derivative of the profit function with respect to the product price. As we have seen above, it is one of the functions estimated in using duality to characterize the production structure. However, it has been considered as an entity by itself. The reason can be attributed to substance and history. The interest in supply analysis in agriculture had begun long before the work on the production function in agriculture and was completely disconnected from it. From its very beginning, supply response analysis was very much concerned with policy issues rather than with the application or development of formal econometric analysis. This is revealed by the titles of some of the early work: "The Farmers' Response to Price" [Bean (1929)], "The Nature of Statistical Supply Curves" [Cassels (1933)], "The Maintenance of Agricultural Production During Depression: The Explanations Reviewed" [Galbraith and Black (1938)], "Can Price Allocate Resources in American Agriculture?" [Brewster and Parsons (1946)]. Some of this discussion was motivated by the fact that agricultural production did not contract during the Great Depression of the thirties when prices of agricultural products declined substantially. The explanation for this was provided by D. Gale Johnson (1950), who indicated that not only product prices decreased in the depression, but factor prices decreased as well. This brings in the cyclical behavior of agriculture.

The central theme, the role of prices in determining output, has not changed much since. However, there are additional aspects high on the public agenda which are related to the ability to increase food supply to meet the growing demand. While the role of prices is related to the behavior under given supply conditions, the growth aspect is related to the shift in these conditions. This is a neat classification, which unfortunately does not apply to the data. Observations are determined by all the forces that affect supply, and it is therefore for the empirical analysis to sort out the role of the various factors.

Empirical supply functions regress output on prices and other variables with the purpose of extracting the output response to price. Most of the studies used aggregate time-series data, but there were some exceptions [Mundlak (1964a)]. On the whole, these studies were formulated within a static framework. As price signals do not come out

---

[43] In part, the discussion is based on [Mundlak (1996b)].

strong and loud in such studies, salvage is sought in using an appropriate price expectation and in a search for variables other than prices to be included in the equation.

The shift of attention to dynamic considerations gained impetus with the introduction of distributed lags to the supply analysis by Nerlove (1956, 1958). Two basic ideas are behind the formulation: adaptive expectations and partial adjustment. They both have a common outcome, a gradual adjustment in response. This is applied to expectation formation whenever a gap exists between the expected and the actual values. Similarly, it is applied to the closure of the gap between the actual output and the long-run desired output. The basic empirical equation that emerges has the form of

$$y_t = bp_t + cy_{t-1} + u_t, \tag{24}$$

where b and $b/(1 - c)$ are the coefficients of short- and long-run supply response respectively. This formulation gave a neat and simple format for supply analysis and was therefore widely adapted. A summary of many studies using this framework is provided by Askari and Cummings (1976).

This efficient form for connecting the price response and the length of run has not provided the needed insight into the structure of agricultural production, nor of the origin and the nature of its dynamics [Mundlak (1966, 1967)]. In what follows we concentrate on approaches that attempt to overcome this limitation. As a background, we summarize the main empirical findings of supply analysis reported in the literature:

O.12. The short-run aggregate agricultural supply elasticity, when estimated directly, falls in the range of 0.1–0.3.

O.13. The estimated elasticities decrease with the level of aggregation. Higher values are obtained for the elasticities of individual products than for the aggregate output.

O.14. Indirect estimation of the supply elasticity, obtained through the estimation of factor demand, resulted in larger values than those obtained by direct estimation.

O.15. In the empirical analysis it was observed that adding a lagged output to a supply equation which relates output to price increases the quality of the fit and often eliminates the existing serial correlation. When measures of capital, or of fixed inputs, are added to the equation, the statistical relevance of the lagged dependent variable is reduced or vanishes. A similar result is obtained when a trend variable is added.

O.16. When the sample was divided to subperiods according to the direction of the price changes, it was found that

(a) The supply elasticity was higher for a period of increasing prices.

(b) When capital is included in the supply function, its coefficient was positive for periods of increasing prices and zero for periods of decreasing prices.

(c) When a distributed lag was used, the rate of adjustment was higher for a period of increasing prices.

O.17. The dependence of the value of the supply elasticity on the length of run reflects a constrained optimization. The severity of the constraints vanishes with time. This view leads to a formulation of a well-defined structure.

The work with duality reviewed above supplements the observations O.12 and O.13 and shows in general higher elasticities for factor demand than for the product supply which is the foundation for O.14.

5.2. Static analysis

The starting point of the analysis is the behavioral functions in Equation (23) above. The strength of the response of output and inputs to changes in prices depends on the relative importance of the restricted inputs. The unrestricted case when all inputs are variables is referred to as the long run and is represented by the following behavioral functions:

$$y^*(p, w, T), \qquad v^*(p, w, T), \qquad k^*(p, w, T). \tag{25}$$

Empirical analyses are based on dated data where some of the inputs are restricted. In this case, the response is given by Equations (23), and as such, the empirical analysis of (23) produces a restricted or short-run response. The relationship between the restricted supply and the unrestricted supply is given by the identity

$$y(p, w, k^*, T) = y^*(p, w, T). \tag{26}$$

By differentiation,

$$\varepsilon_{ii}^u = \varepsilon_{ii}^r + \sum_j \beta_{ij}^* \varepsilon_{ij}, \tag{27}$$

where $\varepsilon_{ii} = \partial \ln y_i / \partial \ln p_i$, ε_{ii}^u and ε_{ii}^r are the unrestricted (long-run) and restricted (short-run) elasticities, respectively, $\beta_{ij}^* = \partial \ln y_i / \partial \ln k_j^*$ is the production elasticity of k_j, the jth component of k, in the production of the ith product, and $\varepsilon_{ji} = \partial \ln k_j^* / \partial \ln p_i$ is the demand elasticity of k_j with respect to p_i. Thus, the long-run elasticity is the sum of the short-run elasticities and of the indirect price effect which measures the price effect on the investment in the restricted factors. The relationships in (27) are obtained under the identity in (26), and as such they are restricted to the long-run equilibrium. The demand for capital and the incorporation of nonequilibrium values in the analysis are discussed below.

It is obvious that the estimation of Equations (27) requires an elaborate statistical analysis, and we have already seen that it is difficult to get robust results. There is however a simple way to approximate meaningfully the supply elasticity. As shown in [Mundlak (1996b)], given the competitive conditions for the unrestricted inputs, the supply elasticity for a price-taker agent is approximately

$$\varepsilon = \frac{\sum_v S_v}{1 - \sum_v S_v}, \tag{28}$$

where S_v is the factor share of the vth variable input. The sum is taken over all the unrestricted inputs; it is an estimate of the scale elasticity of the 'short-run' production function, namely, the part of the function that expresses the output as a function of the unrestricted inputs conditional on the restricted ones. The scale elasticity need not be constant everywhere, as the approximation is defined locally, and thus it depends on the classification of inputs to v and k. What is important for the present discussion is that it can be evaluated in general as the sum of the factor shares of the variable inputs. This framework facilitates the derivation of orders of magnitude of the short-run supply elasticity by using empirical evidence on the elasticities of the agricultural production functions. This can be done at various levels of aggregation. To illustrate, consider the aggregate supply under the simplifying assumption that locally, the factor supply functions facing the industry are perfectly elastic and that there is no redistribution of the restricted factors among the firms in response to price variations in the short run. We assume that land, capital, and often labor are fixed in the short run. These inputs account for approximately 0.8 to 0.9 of total output, implying that the supply elasticity is between 0.11 and 0.25. The lower value is in line with the empirical results as summarized above.

The division between variable and restricted inputs is to some extent arbitrary. Such a dichotomy implies a zero supply elasticity for the restricted inputs and infinite elasticity for the variable inputs. This dichotomy is often assumed in many of the empirical analyses using derivatives of the profit function. It may hold true for the individual firm but not for the industry as a whole. Taking these considerations into account, the analysis is generalized by introducing the factor supply functions. The smaller the factor supply elasticities, the smaller the product supply elasticity [Brandow (1962), and Floyd (1965)]. Extended analytic results are given in [Mundlak (1996b)]. For instance, for a production function homogeneous of degree $\mu \leqslant 1$ in the unrestricted inputs, the supply elasticity is

$$\varepsilon = \mu \left[(1 - \mu) + \sum (\alpha_v / s_v) \right]^{-1}, \tag{29}$$

where $s_v \neq 0$ is the supply elasticity of the vth input, and α_v is the factor share in the total cost of the variable inputs. Equation (29) generalizes Equation (28) in that when the factor supply functions are perfectly elastic for all factors, that is, $s_v = \infty$, the two equations become identical. For a linear homogeneous production function, $\mu = 1$, and Equation (29) reduces to $\varepsilon = (\sum \alpha_v / s_v)^{-1}$ which is a finite number. Thus, a constant returns to scale aggregate production function is compatible with a finite supply function because the sector is not a price-taker in some inputs.

This expression of the supply elasticity in terms of the factor shares provides the insight for the inverse relationship between the length of run and the size of the supply elasticity. The shorter the run, the more restrictions there are on factor adjustment, and therefore, the smaller the supply elasticity. Restrictions on the overall factor supply, such as farmland, do not apply to the allocation of the factor to alternative crops. For this reason, the lower the level of aggregation of the analysis, the larger the supply elasticity (O.13).

Turning to the relationship between factor demand and the supply elasticities (O.14), we note that the price effect on input demand contains substitution and expansion effects. Of these, only the expansion effect contributes to the supply because the substitution effect of all the inputs cancels out. Technically, this is the meaning of the singularity of the Slutsky, or Hessian, matrix. This explains the findings in [Griliches (1959)] and subsequent work where the indirect supply elasticity obtained by using the factor demand elasticities gave larger values than those obtained by direct estimation of the supply function; simply, the substitution effect was not eliminated. The same holds for the estimation of the behavioral functions using the duality framework.

6. Dynamics

Equations in (23) and (25) constitute a recursive system where the long-run values of k are expressed by (25), whereas the short-run values of v and y are determined by (23) conditional on k and prices. It does not specify the time pattern of the changes in k. The analysis is now extended to deal with this subject. The extension is triggered by the fact that k affects output and cost in more than one period.

6.1. The firm's problem

It is postulated that the competitive firm chooses inputs that affect the flow of present and future profits with the objective of maximizing its expected present value. We consider here a simple case where a single output, y, is produced with a durable input, capital, k, and a nondurable, or variable, input, v, that can be hired at the ongoing wage rate, $w(t)$, using a concave and twice differentiable production function, $y = F(k, v, \tau)$, where τ represents technology. The various variables are functions of time, and the income flow at time t is $R_t = F(k_t, v_t, \tau_t) - c(I_t) - w_t v_t - q_t I_t$. Income and factor prices are measured in units of output, q and w are the real price of the investment good (I) and of the variable input, respectively, and $c(I)$ is the real cost of adjustment [Lucas (1967), Gould (1968), Treadway (1969)]. The underlying idea behind the adjustment cost is that the marginal cost of investment increases as a function of the investment rate, and hence if the firm acts too fast this cost will be excessively high. The function is convex in I (or in the ratio I/k). Let r be the interest rate, $\beta = (1+r)^{-1}$ is the discount factor; the optimization problem calls for selecting the time path of inputs $\{v_j, k_j\}$ that maximizes the expected value of the firm at the base period, 0,

$$\max_{k_{j+1}, v_j} \left\{ E_0 \left[\sum_{j=0}^{\infty} \beta^j \left[F_j(k_j, v_j, \tau_j) - w_j v_j - q_j I_j - c(I_j) \right] \right] \right\} \tag{30}$$

subject to $I_j = k_{j+1} - (1 - \delta)k_j$, the initial value k_0, and terminal conditions, where k_j is the capital stock at the beginning of period j, and δ is the depreciation rate. The expectation, E_0, is taken over the future prices and the technology whose distribution is assumed known.[44]

To obtain the first order conditions we first differentiate (30) with respect to the non-durable inputs, v_j, to obtain:

$$ E\left[\frac{\partial F(\cdot)}{\partial v_j} - w_j\right] = 0. \tag{31} $$

By assumption, the input v_j at any time j has no effect on the revenue in subsequent periods, and therefore its level is determined by equating the expected value of the marginal productivity to that of its real price in each period, as shown by Equation (31). Consequently, the optimization problem can be solved in steps. First, determine for each period the optimal level v_j as a function of prices and k_j, and substitute the result in the production function to obtain the function, $F(k_j, s_j)$, where $s_j \equiv (\tau_j, w_j, q_j, r, \delta, c)$ is the vector of the exogenous variables. The second stage consists of solving

$$ \max_{k_{j+1}} \left\{ E_0 \sum_{j=0}^{\infty} \beta^j \left[F_j(k_j, s_j) - c(I_j) - q_j I_j \right] \right\} \tag{32} $$

subject to $I_j = k_{j+1} - (1 - \delta)k_j$.

Label the rate of capital appreciation $\hat{q} \equiv \dot{q}/q$ and $\tilde{q}_j \equiv q_j[r + \delta - (1 - \delta)\hat{q}_j]$, which is the rental cost of capital, or briefly the rental rate, evaluated at time j. It is the product of the initial price of the capital good, q, and the annual "charges" consisting of the discount and depreciation rates, adjusted for the expected capital gain, $\hat{q}$. Similarly, $\tilde{c}_I \equiv c_I(j)[r + \delta - (1 - \delta)\hat{c}_j]$ gives the change in the adjustment cost due to a change of the timing of a unit of investment, *on the optimal path*, from one year to the next. Differentiate (32) with respect to k_{j+1} and rearrange the result to obtain, for the case when an internal solution exists,

$$ E_0\{\beta F_k(j + 1) - [\tilde{c}_I(j) + \tilde{q}_j]\} = 0, \tag{33} $$

where we use the notation $F(k_j, s_j) \equiv F(j)$ and similarly for other functions, and the subscripts k and I indicate the direction of the partial derivatives of the functions in question. Under static expectations, where the present prices are expected to remain constant indefinitely, $E(\hat{q}) = E(\hat{c}) = 0$, and (33) becomes $\{\beta F_k(j+1) - (r+\delta)[c_I(j) + q_j]\} = 0$. In the absence of adjustment cost, this condition reduces to the equality of the marginal productivity of capital and the rental rate [Jorgenson (1967)]. This condition applies to every point on the optimal path. The addition of the adjustment cost affects

---

[44] The terminal condition is $\lim_{j \to \infty} E_0\{\beta^j [F_k(j) - c_I(j) - q_j]k_j\} = 0$.

the rental rate, and thus it affects not only the pace of investment but also the optimal level of capital.

The solution can be expressed in terms of the shadow price of capital defined as the present value of the marginal productivity of capital, net of the adjustment cost, in present and future production: $S_t \equiv \sum_{j=0}^{\infty} h^j F_k(t+j)$, where $h \equiv (1-\delta)\beta < 1$. The system can be solved to yield

$$E_t\{S_t - (q_t + c_I(t))\} = 0. \tag{34}$$

This condition states that investment is carried out to the point where the shadow price of capital generated by the investment is equal to the cost of investment including the cost of adjustment. The marginal productivity depends on the technology and the inputs at the various points in time, and therefore its evaluation requires an assumption that the investment under consideration is the only investment to be made. If other investments are contemplated, the marginal productivity would have to be evaluated conditional on such investments.

6.2. Discussion

The condition in (31) is extremely important for empirical analysis in that it implies that along the optimal path, the use of the inputs which have no effect on the revenue or the cost in subsequent periods is determined by equating the marginal productivities to their real prices in each period. This leads to a recursive system [Mundlak (1967)]. First, we determine for each period the optimal levels of the variable inputs as functions of the exogenous variables, including prices and $k(t)$. Second, we solve for $k(t)$ on the optimal time path:

$$k^*\big[E(q, \hat{q}, \delta, r, c, w, p, T)\big], \tag{35}$$

where we insert p, the product price, explicitly. All the variables in (35) are functions of time. The introduction of the intertemporal optimization results in replacing $k^*(\cdot)$ in (25) with (35), thereby adding exogenous variables as well as uncertainty with respect to the future time path of the exogenous variables. However, the recursive structure remains the same.

6.3. The role of prices and technology

The solution is quite sensitive to changes in the exogenous variables. To gain some insight into the meaning of the solution, we use a Cobb–Douglas production function, $y = A v^a k^b$. The first order condition in (31) provides a solution $v = (a/w)y$ for the nondurable input. This solution is substituted in the production function to yield, with some simplification,

$$Y = \big(Aa^a\big)^{1/(1-a)} w^{-a/(1-a)} k^{b/(1-a)}. \tag{36}$$

The marginal productivity of capital conditional on w is[45]

$$\frac{\partial y}{\partial k}\bigg|_{w} = \frac{b}{1-a}\left(Aa^{a}\right)^{1/(1-a)}w^{-a/(1-a)}k^{(b+a-1)/(1-a)}. \tag{37}$$

This derivative is equated to the rental price of capital to provide a solution for k^*, when such a solution exists.

Equation (36) is the short-run supply function conditional on k. Output declines with w, but as w is the ratio of nominal wage to output price, p, output increases with p. To simplify the discussion without a loss in generality, we continue by ignoring the adjustment cost. The condition in Equation (33) simplifies to

$$E_0\left\{\beta F_k(j+1) - \tilde{q}_j\right\} = 0. \tag{38}$$

The long-run values (starred) are obtained by using Equations (36) and (38) to yield

$$k^* = (b/\tilde{q})y^*, \quad y^* = \left(Aa^a b^b\right)^{\varepsilon}w^{-a\varepsilon}\tilde{q}^{-b\varepsilon}, \quad \varepsilon = 1/(1-a-b). \tag{39}$$

Prices affect the desired capital directly through the rental rate and indirectly through the effect on the optimal output. It is important to differentiate between the direct and the indirect price effect. A change in the wage rate has only an indirect effect on capital with an elasticity $E_{k/w} = -a\varepsilon$. The elasticities of the real rental rate, $E_{k/\tilde{q}}$, are -1, $-b\varepsilon$, and $(a-1)\varepsilon$ for the direct, indirect, and total effect respectively. Similarly, the elasticities of capital with respect to a change in the product price are 1, $(a+b)\varepsilon$, and ε for the direct, indirect, and total effect respectively. Note that the indirect effect $(a+b)\varepsilon$ is considerably stronger than the direct effect. It is useful to illustrate the order of magnitude of the elasticities in question for arbitrary values of the parameters (Table 3). The elasticity of labor is maintained at 0.3 for the three cases, whereas the elasticity of capital varies from 0.6, a highly capital-intensive process, to 0.1. Note that 0.1 is approximately the estimated elasticity of machinery in many studies, whereas a value of 0.3 represents a broader capital aggregate, including structures. The difference $1-a-b$ is the share of fixed factors which vary across cases. In the first case it would be management, whereas in the last case it might also include land. The values in this table provide an insight into the interpretation of the empirical results.

To simplify the discussion, we have abstracted from taxes. To add taxes, they have to be inserted in the income expression in (1), and the prices in the foregoing results would have to be adjusted for taxes [Jorgenson (1963)]. The empirical evaluation of the effect of taxes is done in two steps: first, evaluate the effect of the tax on the time path of the rental rate; and second, determine the response of investment to price. It is the latter that is the focus of the empirical analysis.

---

[45] This derivative is evaluated for v kept at its short-run optimal level, which is different from the derivative conditional on v derived from the production function: $\frac{\partial y}{\partial k}\big|_{v} = b\frac{y}{k}$.

Table 3
Capital-demand elasticities

Prices	$a = 0.3, b = 0.6, \varepsilon = 10$			$a = 0.3, b = 0.3, \varepsilon = 2.5$			$a = 0.3, b = 0.1, \varepsilon = 1.67$		
	D	I	T	D	I	T	D	I	T
W	0	−3	−3	0	−0.75	−0.75	0	−0.5	−0.5
$\tilde{q}$	−1	−6	−7	−1	−0.75	−1.75	−1	−0.17	−1.17
P	1	9	10	1	1.5	2.5	1	0.67	1.67
NTC	0	10	10	0	2.5	2.5	0	1.67	1.67

Legend: D = Direct, I = Indirect, T = Total, W = wage rate, P = product price, $\tilde{q}$ = rental rate, NTC = Neutral technical change.

Neutral technical change is perceived as a change in the multiplicative coefficient (A) of the production function. It affects output and thereby the desired capital level without affecting the capital-output ratio. The demand elasticity with respect to neutral technical change is equal to ε. Capital-using technical change, captured here as an increase in b, generates an increase in capital demand and in the capital-output ratio. The overall effect of such a technical change on output depends on what happens to the degree of the function. When the degree is held constant, an increase in b implies a decline of a, and therefore, without imposing a more detailed structure, the net effect on output is ambiguous.

To summarize, the expected magnitude of the estimated demand elasticities depends strongly on what variables are held constant in the sample, and therefore we can expect a considerable variability in the empirical results.

6.4. Disinvestment

In general, empirical analysis treats positive and negative accumulation symmetrically even though the costs involved are completely different. The cost of acquisition of a new tractor is different from the selling price of a used one. Implications of this additional detail are discussed by Glenn Johnson (1958), Edwards (1959), Johnson and Quance (1972, pp. 185–195), and more recently by Chavas (1994) and Hamermesh and Pfann (1996). To place this detail in perspective, we note that on the whole, agricultural investment is positive for most of the time, and therefore the subject of disinvestment is of secondary importance and does not affect our views on the development of agriculture. Its empirical importance is largely limited to the analysis of cyclical behavior and the analysis based on micro data which include firms with zero or negative investment.

There are several important reasons for the difference between the acquisition and the selling price. First, the service life of the new capital good is longer than that of the used one, and therefore it is more valuable. Conceptually, this aspect can be incorporated into the analysis by disaggregating the capital goods by age and vintage and pricing the different goods accordingly. The optimization problem of the price-taker farmer would then include acquisition prices by age and vintage instead of one price. If an old machine is sold, someone is buying it because it meets his needs. This indicates that there is a market for all types of machines which are actually traded. The extension of the analysis to include this kind of heterogeneity should give qualitatively different results from the one obtained when the farmer is restricted from purchasing the used equipment (who will then buy it?), as the standard model assumes. The interesting question is what the qualitative effect is.

Second, part of the gap between the price of new and used equipment can be attributed to marketing charges and asymmetric information of the pertinent agents. Third, there is the cyclical element. There is a tendency to sell unutilized capacity in bad times when the excess demand for capital goods is declining and with it the price of the used equipment. The cyclical price behavior is likely to differ according to the origin of the capital goods. Used machines are supplied by farmers, and for our purpose they are expected to behave as do capital goods of agricultural origin. Their price is determined endogenously within agriculture and reflects the expected stream of the marginal productivity of capital over its remaining lifetime. To trace the consequences of this extension, it is necessary to work out the market equilibrium for used equipment. This will result in a market clearing price, and used equipment will be employed according to conditions analogous to Equation (34). New machines are of nonagricultural origin, and their supply price reflects the conditions in nonagriculture. Therefore the price may be less sensitive to the cyclical conditions in agriculture as compared to used machines. To sum up, the introduction of a second-hand market adds details to the analysis but not a new theory.

The asymmetry between investment and disinvestment is more pronounced in models with internal adjustment costs. Obviously, a demolition of a building or a slaughter of a cow does not stretch out over time. The symmetry assumption simplifies the formulation, but it is unrealistic. Its restrictive nature goes undetected because much of the empirical work is based on aggregate data. However, there are some exceptions such as Chang and Stefanou (1988) and Lansink and Stefanou (1997).

6.5. Empirical investment analysis

In general, time series of aggregate investment show a positive serial correlation. The determination of the source for this dynamic relation is a key question in investment research. There are two basic approaches. Initially, the dynamics was superimposed on the model, and we therefore refer to it as exogenous dynamics. Alternatively, the dynamics can be developed from the theory, such as in the case of models based on adjustment cost, and it is therefore referred to as endogenous dynamics.

Aside from the pattern of the dynamics, the empirical analysis should reveal the response of k^* to changes in its determinants, where k^* is unobserved and therefore is replaced by the actual capital stock, or changes in it. The actual capital stock by itself is not a well-defined variable, but in this discussion we will ignore the issues involved in the construction of the capital stock.

6.6. Exogenous dynamics

For a variety of reasons, there is a time difference between the date of a firm's decision on a new investment and its completion. The implication is that a decision taken by the firm in a given year may affect investment in future years, or alternatively, the investment in a given year reflects past decisions and, more so, past signals. Such a time distribution of the response was a major justification for the distributed lags analysis, referred to as the flexible accelerator models, introduced by Chenery (1952) and Koyck (1954). In such models, the actual capital stock differs from the desired stock. Koyck's formulation uses geometric weights to express the current capital stock as a weighted average of past values of desired capital. This process can be presented by an adjustment equation

$$k_t - k_{t-1} = \mu(k_t^* - k_{t-1}), \tag{40}$$

where μ, $0 \leqslant \mu \leqslant 1$, is the coefficient of adjustment. Nadiri and Rosen (1969) extended this model to more than one quasi-fixed factor.

The desired capital is unobserved. In the case of a Cobb–Douglas production function, the desired capital stock is proportional to the long-run output, and the latter can replace the first. Introducing this substitution into Equation (40) and simplifying, we can write the following investment function, where I_t is the *net* investment in year t,

$$I_t = \mu\gamma_0 + \mu\gamma y_t^* - \mu k_{t-1} + \text{error}. \tag{41}$$

However, the replacement of k^* by y^* is of little help because the latter is also unobservable. In practice, actual output is used instead in empirical analysis [Jorgenson (1963)]. In so doing, the difference between the short- and the long-run supply is overlooked. The elasticities for long-run response express the response with respect to lasting price and technology changes. Transitory price changes are likely to affect output according to the short-run supply function, but as such should not affect the capital demand. Consequently, the variable used in the analysis measures with error the relevant variable and thereby introduces a downward bias in the estimation [Mundlak (1966)].[46] The problem can be overcome by aggregating the variables over time and thereby reducing to a large extent the effect of the transitory variations [Mundlak (1964a, Chapter 6)].

The underlying assumption in Equation (40) is that the adjustment of the actual stock to changes in the desired stock is gradual, but this is not always the case. Often, there are distinct scale economies in the size of the investment, where the unit cost declines with the size of the project, and the optimal size of the investment unit exceeds the demand or requires more resources than are currently available. Consequently, the firm may delay the investment until it is justified to construct a larger project at a lower unit cost (Ibid.).

---

[46] For more detailed discussion of this subject, see [Mundlak (1964a)].

The phenomenon of lumpy investment at intervals longer than a year is inconsistent with the adjustment cost assumption. However, this is not detected in empirical analysis which uses macro data obtained as aggregates over firms and as such conceal it. Again, with micro data the problem can be overcome by aggregating the variables over time and thereby reducing the importance of the exact timing of the investment (Ibid.). This problem has resurfaced in the context of analysis based on adjustment costs, and we return to it below.

6.7. Endogenous dynamics – the primal approach

There has been a great deal of empirical work based on the Euler equation on nonagricultural data. The equation involves unobservable variables, and to overcome this limitation, alternative approaches have been taken; these are reviewed by Chirinko (1993) and Galeotti (1996). To illustrate the basic issues at stake, we present an empirical version of Equation (33), with the assumption that $c(\cdot) = (c/2)I^2$ so that $c(\cdot)$ does not depend on the capital stock. Let z be the expected gap between the marginal productivity of capital and the rental rate, $z_{t+j} \equiv \mathrm{E}_t\{\beta F_k(t + j + 1) - \tilde{q}_{t+j}\}$. Rearranging Equation (33) subject to the assumption on the adjustment cost, it follows that

$$\mathrm{E}_t(I_{t+j}) - h\,\mathrm{E}_t(I_{t+j+1}) = \frac{1}{c}\,z_{t+j}. \tag{42}$$

An expected decline in the rental rate or an expected increase in the productivity of capital causes an increase in z, and hence the difference between current investment and expected next-year investment increases. This means that at the margin, current investment increases in order to take advantage of the current opportunities.

For the purpose of estimation, F_k is spelled out explicitly in terms of its arguments, and thus the parameters of the production function enter the equation. Similarly, in some applications, the cost of adjustment is formulated so as to depend on some variables, including output. When the marginal productivity of capital and the adjustment costs are written explicitly in terms of their determinants, the empirical equation contains output and prices. The empirical equation is then used to estimate the parameters of the production function, of the adjustment-cost function, and of h. Unlike in the exogenous dynamic models, it is assumed here that the observed capital stock is *always* equal to the optimal one.

There are several problems in using this equation for empirical analysis. First, in this formulation the adjustment-cost parameters are, by assumption, the only source for the dynamics. When in reality the time pattern of investment is affected by other causes, their influence will be captured by the cost of adjustment parameters, and the empirical analysis will give a distorted picture of the dynamics. Second, the Euler equation, (42), provides arbitrage conditions between adjacent periods which have to be met on the *optimal path*. When the observations are located off the path, this condition is inconsistent with the data. If the model is stable, deviations from the optimal path generate a correction toward the path. This correction is not described by the model, but it is empirically important and as such it affects the estimates. This may be the reason for the fact that empirical estimates obtained from the Euler equations do not produce robust results. Third, the Euler equation is not an efficient way to estimate the parameters of the production function. As argued earlier, it is more efficient to estimate the production function directly. Fourth, recall that $h = (1 - \delta)/(1 + r)$, so that h is not a stable parameter and should be treated as a variable. When h is treated like a constant, variations in h are captured by the equation error, and as such the error is not independent of the investment term on the right-hand side of the equation. This causes a bias in the estimate.

6.8. Endogenous dynamics – the dual approach

The dual approach, as developed by McLaren and Cooper (1980) and Epstein (1981), has provided an elegant framework to deal simultaneously with several issues of dynamic adjustment in a practical fashion. It has been applied in agricultural economics research, reviewed below, and it is therefore summarized here.

Following the literature, the presentation is in terms of continuous time, and the cost of adjustment appears as an argument in the production function. A crucial element in this framework is the assumption of static price expectation whereby the present prices and technology are assumed to remain constant indefinitely. Modifications of this assumption are discussed below.

The production function, $F(k, I)$, is expressed in terms of the quasi-fixed factors, k, and the investment, I.[47] The variables are vectors of comparable dimensions. A partial list of the regularity conditions on the production function includes: $F_k(\cdot) > 0$, $F_I(\cdot) < 0$, and $F(\cdot)$ is strongly concave in I. The optimization calls for:

$$J(s) = \max_I \int_0^\infty e^{-rt} \left[F(k, I) - \tilde{q}'k + J_{k'}(I - \delta k) \right] dt \tag{43}$$

subject to $k(0) = k_0$, and the terminal conditions. $J(s)$ is the value function, a prime means transpose, $\tilde{q}$ is the vector of rental rates, $s = (k, \tilde{q}, r, \delta)$ is the vector of exogenous variables, J_k is the vector of multipliers of the constraint $\dot{k} = I - \delta k$, and as such it represents the shadow price of capital. Note that (43) is expressed in terms of the rental rate, unlike the argument of (30), which is expressed in terms of the price of the capital good. Also, under static expectations, $\tilde{q}$ does not contain the capital-appreciation term. This difference in formulation can be of significance in the case of nonstatic expectations. In what follows, unless indicated otherwise, r and δ are assumed to be constant. All the variables are functions of time and, unless needed, the time notation is avoided.

---

[47] Initially, all inputs can be considered to be quasi-fixed, and it is up to the analysis to determine if a particular input is variable. Alternatively, the production function can be the concentrated function in the quasi-fixed variables.

Because the prices and the technology are assumed constant, only their current values matter. This is the major analytic payoff of the assumption of static expectations. Consequently, the problem becomes similar to that of the duality used in the static analysis. The difference between the two models is in the nature of the solution; in the dynamic case, it consists of the time path of the control variables.

Under the regularity conditions on F, the value function J satisfies the Hamilton–Jacobi–Bellman equation [Kamien and Schwartz (1991, p. 261)]:

$$r J(s) = \max_I \{ F(k, I) - \tilde{q}'k + J_k(s)'(I - \delta k) \}. \tag{44}$$

A partial list of the regularity conditions on the value function includes: $(\delta + r) J_k + \tilde{q} - J_{kk} k > 0$ (equivalent to $F_k > 0$), $J_k > 0$ (positive shadow price of capital; follows from the adjustment cost assumption of $F_I < 0$), and a necessary condition that J is convex in prices (because J is a maximum problem).

The behavioral functions are derived by differentiating $J(\cdot)$ with respect to the exogenous variables to yield a generalized Hotelling's Lemma. Specifically, a differentiation with respect to $\tilde{q}$ and rearrangement yields:

$$\dot{k}^* = J_{\tilde{q}k}^{-1} \left(r J_{\tilde{q}}(k, s) + k \right), \tag{45}$$

where we write $J(k, s)$ to remind us that k is an argument of J. Thus, the following holds on the optimal path:

$$r J(s) \equiv F(k, \dot{k}^* + \delta k) - \tilde{q}'k + J_k'(s)\dot{k}^*. \tag{46}$$

The steady state value of k is obtained by setting $\dot{k}^* = 0$ and solving:

$$k^* + r J_{\tilde{q}}(k^*, s) = 0. \tag{47}$$

Given the regularity conditions on $J(\cdot)$, a duality between $F(\cdot)$ and $J(\cdot)$ is established. Let

$$F^*(k, I) = \min_{\tilde{q}} \{ r J(k, \tilde{q}) + \tilde{q}'k - J_k(k, \tilde{q})'(I - \delta k) \}. \tag{48}$$

Heuristically, the duality prevails if J derived from (43) is used in (48) to derive $F^*(\cdot)$, and $F^*(\cdot) = F(\cdot)$. Inversely, if F derived from (48), by using J that maintains the regular conditions on J, is used in (43) to derive J^*, then $J = J^*$. This is the meaning of the duality, but as in the static case, this relation is seldom exploited in empirical work. However, there is a revealed difference in aspiration between the static and dynamic analyses. As discussed above, the empirical duality analysis sprung up as an alternative to the primal approach for estimating production functions. The dynamic analysis is focused on the derivation of the demand for the quasi-fixed factors of production. As such, the interest is in the empirical performance of (44) and (47) and the conditions underlying their derivation.

The empirical implementation requires algebraic formulation of the value function. The quadratic function, in the pertinent variables (or a monotone transformation thereof, such as logarithms or power functions), has been widely used because of its convenience:

$$J(s) = a_0 + \left(a_k' a_{\tilde{q}}' \right) \begin{pmatrix} k \\ \tilde{q} \end{pmatrix} + \frac{1}{2} (k' \tilde{q}') \begin{pmatrix} A_{kk} & A_{k\tilde{q}} \\ A_{\tilde{q}k} & A_{\tilde{q}\tilde{q}} \end{pmatrix} \begin{pmatrix} k \\ \tilde{q} \end{pmatrix}, \tag{49}$$

where a_k, $a_{\tilde{q}}$, k, and $\tilde{q}$ are column vectors, and the A_{ij} are matrices of conforming dimensions. Given (49),

$$J_{\tilde{q}} = a_{\tilde{q}} + A_{\tilde{q}k}k + A_{\tilde{q}\tilde{q}}\tilde{q}; \quad J_{\tilde{q}k} = A_{\tilde{q}k}. \tag{50}$$

Substitute in (47) and impose $k = k^*$:

$$k^* = -r(I + rA_{\tilde{q}K})^{-1}(a_{\tilde{q}} + A_{\tilde{q}\tilde{q}}\tilde{q}), \tag{51}$$

where I is the identity matrix. Substitute (50) in (45) and simplify using (51),

$$\dot{k}^* = M(k - k^*); \quad M \equiv (I + rA_{\tilde{q}k})^{-1}, \tag{52}$$

where M is the adjustment matrix. Note the similarity of Equations (52) and (40). In addition to the fact that (52) is a differential equation and (40) is a difference equation, Equation (52) is a multivariate equation and M is expressed in terms of coefficients of the value function. Otherwise, in empirical applications, the two versions are similar in form, so that the foregoing discussion provides a foundation for the distributed lag formulation. Using a discrete time approximation, the empirical equation can be written as

$$k_t = (I - M)k_{t-1} - Mk_t^*. \tag{53}$$

The adjustment matrix, M, is constant, but under a different specification of the value function it can become a function of some exogenous variables.

6.9. Empirical investment analysis in agriculture

The following review of individual studies is intended to span the space of the empirical parameters, and to convey the cumulative experience which should help us in forming a view of the scope of the various approaches and to learn from their inherent difficulties. This should help in outlining the strategy for future research. Our discussion is limited to the estimation of investment functions and will skip over the important conceptual and practical issues involved in measurements of capital (see for instance: [Griliches (1963c), Ball et al. (1993b), Larson et al. (1999)].

Unlike studies of production or supply functions, there are only a few empirical studies of investment in agriculture using the direct or primal approach. Griliches (1960, 1963c) studied the demand for tractors in the United States in 1921–1957 using a distributed lag framework where the desired stock is determined by the real price of tractors and by the interest rate. The results show the importance of price variables as determinants of investment.

Heady and Tweeten (1963, Chapter 11) analyzed the purchases of all farm machinery in the United States in the period 1926–1959, excluding 1942–1947. They report a garden variety of regressions. The core explanatory variables are machines-to-commodity price ratio, a ratio of equity to liabilities of the farm sector, or alternatively a measure of farm income, a time trend, and in some cases, the lagged value of the dependent variable. They conclude that "... a 1 percent increase in the price of either trucks, tractors or equipment aggregate ... is predicted to increase respective annual purchases 1 percent; stock 0.2 percent in one or two years. In four years the elasticity of machinery purchases Q_i with respect to P_i remains about unity, but with respect to P_R [commodity price − YM] is 2 or more. A sustained 1 percent rise in prices received by farmers is expected to increase stock for these same items 0.2 percent in one or two years, 0.5 percent in four years and more than 2 percent in the long run" (pp. 327–328). The trend variable was robust, and the equity/liability ratio had the right sign and was significant. This can be interpreted as a sign of cyclical behavior, with higher investment in good times.

As in many empirical applications, their equations contain fewer variables than what is called for by the theory. Presumably, the equation should include all prices and a measure of technology. In general, with a short time series the empirical equation does not sustain all the pertinent variables. For instance, in the study of Heady and Tweeten (1963), the inclusion of more prices was not supported by the data. One way to deal with this problem is to collapse the prices and other exogenous variables into one measure, the rate of return. The higher the expected rate of return, the higher the investment demand. The rate of return can be thought of as a proxy for the gap between the expected marginal productivity of capital and the rental rate, labeled as z in Equation (42).

Mundlak (1964a, Chapter 6) used a panel of farm micro data to study investment in farm structures using the accelerator formulation and demonstrated the importance of aggregating the data over time in order to eliminate the noise that exists in annual micro data. This finding is consistent with lumpy investment and is not supportive of the idea of a convex cost of adjustment function that results in a gradual adjustment. As indicated earlier, this may be typical for many investments in agriculture.

The application of firm theory to the estimation of the aggregate industry investment function overlooks the fact that the supply of capital goods is not perfectly elastic. One way to incorporate this element is to estimate the allocation of total investment to the various sectors. This is the approach taken by Mundlak, Cavallo, and Domenech (1989) for Argentina, and Coeymans and Mundlak (1993) for Chile. The differential sectoral profitability is measured by the rate of return. The long-run elasticity with respect to the ratio of sectoral rates of return is roughly 1 in both countries.

6.10. Dynamic factor demand using duality

The empirical application of the static expectations model assumes that every year the firm recalculates its plans conditional on the new information on prices and technology. The model provides an interpretation of the flexible accelerator, and it facilitates a convenient way to estimate the adjustment pattern of the quasi-fixed factors. The empirical inference has substantive and analytic aspects. The first is judged by the economic meaning of the results, regardless of the method used to derive them. The second is more complex. For the theory to be applicable, the empirical results should be consistent with the underlying conditions of the model. For the duality to be of interest, the prices should appear as arguments in the derived factor demand, their coefficients should have the right sign, and the value function should be convex in the prices. That is, in terms of Equation (49), $A_{\bar{q}\bar{q}}$ should be positive definite. In what follows, we summarize findings, pertinent to our discussion, of some leading studies dealing mostly with agriculture. Some of these studies use micro data, while the others use macro data.

There is a similarity in the basic assumptions underlying the static and dynamic dual analysis. Most important is the assumption, often made regardless of the level of aggregation of the data, that the factor supply and the product demand are all perfectly elastic. Other than that, the technology is generally represented by a time trend. The term "capital" is used freely to any aggregate of capital goods. Our foregoing discussion indicates that the demand elasticity for an input depends on its production elasticity or factor share. Thus, we should expect a different demand elasticity for a single item, say machinery, than for an aggregate measure.

Epstein and Denny (1983) applied the Epstein (1981) model to the US manufacturing annual data for the period 1947–1976. This application has had an influence on the studies in agriculture, and we therefore begin by reviewing here some of its pertinent sections. The technology is represented by a cost function, and hence the value function is derived by choosing the investment that minimizes the present value of the time path of the cost of production. Because it is a minimum problem, the value function should be concave in prices, which implies that the matrix analogous to $A_{\bar{q}\bar{q}}$ in (49) should be negative definite. In the estimation, the symmetry in price response was imposed, but the nonnegativity condition is violated. The authors argue that the violation is statistically only marginal. Following this line of thinking, we should note that the origin is also included in the joint confidence region for the price coefficients, which means that the null hypothesis of no price response cannot be rejected. The authors are aware of this problem, but do not accept the outcome because it is inconsistent with the concept of duality underlying the analysis. This raises the question of what do we learn from superimposing a model which is rejected by the data. The cost of this procedure is that we avoid the search for the reasons of the violation of confirming duality with the given sample.

The results show that labor and capital turn out as quasi-fixed. The rate of adjustment is fast for labor, an adjustment coefficient of 0.9, which implies a closure of the gap in a little over a year. On the other hand, the rate for capital is slow, an adjustment coefficient of 0.12, which means that it takes about 8 years to close the gap. The adjustment matrix is not diagonal, implying an interaction in the adjustment of the two factors toward their steady exogenous values. The authors are disturbed by the direction of the interaction. "It implies that a 'deficient' stock of labor reduces the demand for capital" [Epstein and Denny (1983, p. 660)]. This finding is acceptable, however, with the choice of technique approach.

The own price elasticities for capital and labor are negative but small, both in the short run and the long run. The largest numerical value is the long-run elasticity of capital, which varies between −0.25 and −0.18 for the three reported years. Because the technology is represented by a cost function, output is one of the arguments of the factor demand and, as in the studies based on the primal approach, it has a much stronger influence on demand. "With respect to output changes, a different pattern emerges. The short-run labor elasticity is roughly 0.6 and the long-run is roughly 60 percent higher. Most of the changes in labor occur in the short-run. For capital, the short-run response is negligible while the long-run response is large, an output elasticity approximately equal to 1.4" [Epstein and Denny (1983, p. 662)]. This implies that in the long run labor expands at about the same rate as output but capital grows at a faster rate, which is consistent with capital deepening and also with the hypothesis that capital is a carrier of new techniques.

The authors are aware of the fact that the theory is a micro theory, but it is applied to aggregate data. There would be no difference between the micro and macro models if the firms were similar in some sense, and the micro unit would be representative of the firms in the industry. However, the conditions for this, as developed by the authors and which are similar in nature to those of linear aggregation, are stringent. In the case of the cost function, the value function should be linear and additive in k and y. Specifically, this implies no interaction between size of the firm and factor intensity, which is unlikely in the case of heterogeneous technology. The authors estimate the model under these conditions and find that "... the resulting structure failed to satisfy the regularity conditions" [Epstein and Denny (1983, p. 662)]. In passing, it should be indicated that even if the stringent conditions for aggregation were maintained, there would still be the problem of upward-slopping factor supply that would differentiate between the micro and macro studies.

Turning to agriculture, we begin with macro studies of the US agricultural sector or industries thereof. One of the earliest applications of the duality model is the study by Vasavada and Chambers (1986) of the factor demand of US agriculture.[48] The model deals with four input categories: land, labor, machinery, and materials. The results indicate that land, labor, and capital services are quasi-fixed factors, and materials are

---

[48] Lopez (1985b) used the cost of adjustment in studying the dynamics of the Canadian food processing industry.

variable factors. The univariate flexible accelerator hypothesis is rejected; thus the adjustment process of the various factors is interdependent. The results show a long adjustment period for capital (10 years) and labor (9 years), and a short period for land (2 years). This pattern is puzzling, but before going deep into the rationalization of the results, it is noted that the coefficients of the adjustment matrix are mostly nonsignificant. This suggests that the null hypothesis of no adjustment might not be rejected, in which case there is no response to changes in the desired values. Obviously, this is inconsistent with the fact that inputs change every year.

An inspection of the price coefficients indicates that with the exception of materials, the own-price coefficients are not significantly different from zero. Furthermore, "Because all the diagonal elements are not positive, convexity of the value function cannot be accepted" [Vasavada and Chambers (1986, p. 955)].[49]

Luh and Stefanou (1991) estimate factor demand for US agriculture in 1950–1982. Like Vasavada and Chambers (1986), they also obtain a slow convergence to long-run equilibrium values: 0.15 of the gap for capital and 0.11 for labor. Interestingly, unlike Vasavada and Chambers (1986), they find independent convergence of labor and capital. This is consistent with the idea that the equations are strongly influenced by the factor supply.

Taylor and Monson (1985) study the factor demand in the US southeastern states in the period 1949–1981. The quasi-fixed factors are land and farm machinery, which the authors refer to as capital. The variable factors are labor and materials. "Fifteen of the estimated 26 parameters are at least two times their corresponding asymptotic standard errors" (p. 5). The price coefficients have the correct signs, hence monotonicity is maintained. Convexity is largely maintained. It seems though that most of the insignificant coefficients are those of prices, and this weakens the finding on convexity. The price elasticities, both short-run and long-run, are mostly low and fairly distant from 1. The hypotheses of independent rates of adjustment and instantaneous adjustment are rejected. The rate of adjustment was 0.55 for machinery and 0.18 for land, which means that it takes roughly two years to close the gap in machinery and six years to close the gap in land.

Howard and Shumway (1988) study the US dairy industry in the period 1951–1982. The analysis deals with two quasi-fixed inputs: herd size and labor, whereas feeds is a variable input. They use a modified version of the generalized Leontief equation. Their untested justification for the use of a micro model to the study of the industry is basi-

---

[49] Vasavada and Chambers (1986) remark that "... [t]here are no estimated diagonal elements with negative point estimates whose asymptotic confidence intervals do not encompass zero and positive numbers at traditionally reasonable levels of significance. Hence, the divergence from convexity, if it exists, may not be significant" (p. 955). This is not a strong supporting argument. It can be conjectured that if a joint confidence region were constructed for all the diagonal parameters in question, it would contain the origin, implying that the quadratic term in prices can be omitted; this reduces the model to absurdity.

cally the assumption that the technology is invariant to the size of the firm.[50] A similar assumption was tested by Epstein and Denny (1983) and was rejected.

As to the results, "Nearly half of the parameters were significant at the 5 percent level, which was quite robust compared to other estimated dynamic dual models" [Howard and Shumway (1988, p. 842)]. This is hardly a complimentary comment, and it illustrates the difficulties associated with the application of the model. R^2 is high for the inputs but low for the output (0.29).[51] The adjustment rate for cows and labor is 0.09 and 0.4 respectively. This raises a question: When prices change, why would labor respond when the adjustment in herd size is sluggish? It is suggested that "[t]he slow adjustment of cows is consistent with the very inelastic short-run milk supply found in previous studies" [Howard and Shumway (1988, p. 842)]. This now suggests that the capital stock is a function of output, but this is an explanation that the present model intends to replace and as such it is questionable. A different line of reasoning suggests that because the study deals with the industry as a whole, the changes in output reflect expected changes in aggregate demand, and this possibility is not accommodated by the model.

The monotonicity conditions on the value function were held at nearly all observations. However when the convexity was imposed, the model did not converge, and this is an indication of inconsistencies. "All the short-run own price input demand elasticities were negative, but the output own-price elasticity was positive for only fifteen of the thirty-two observations" [Howard and Shumway (1988, p. 844)]. In dynamic models, a sign reversal can happen in the short run, but this would have to come from a sign reversal in some inputs. This is not shown to be the case here. "The short-run, own-price input demand elasticities for cows and labor became more elastic over time. The increasing own-price elasticity for labor was consistent with the increasing proportion of hired to family labor over the period" (Ibid., p. 845). Again, the question of identification comes up. With what we know about the declining number of farm operators in the US (as elsewhere), the question is whether this is not a reflection of changes in labor supply rather than in labor demand.

Next, we review two studies that extend the assumption of the model to allow for a difference in the pace of adjustment between positive and negative investment. Chang and Stefanou (1988) apply the model to a panel data of 173 Pennsylvania dairy farms in 1982–1984. Hired labor and feeds are variable inputs, whereas family labor, herd size (cow), real estate, and equipment are quasi-fixed. Results are reported only for the adjustment coefficients, so that we cannot evaluate the impact of the specification on

---

[50] "The dairy industry consists of many price-taking firms, and theory suggests that in long run competitive equilibrium all such firms operate at the minimum average cost ... it is necessary and sufficient for consistent aggregation across firms that the value function be affine in capital" [Howard and Shumway (1988, p. 840)].

[51] The actual empirical equation is not presented. However, in general, the inputs are regressed on their lagged values and the other variables. When the dependent variable is quasi-fixed, the regression is of a stock variable on its lagged value. Such equations in general show a very good fit. The output is a flow variable, and this may explain its relatively low value.

the price coefficients. It is stated that "... at least half of the parameter estimates are significant at the 10 percent significant level especially those associated with prices of *variable* factors" (p. 149, italics by YM). If this statement suggests low precision of the estimated price coefficients, as in the other studies, the results are better for the adjustment coefficients, where most of the own adjustment coefficients are significant at the 1 percent level. The adjustment of the four quasi-fixed inputs are interdependent. There is a difference in the response when asymmetry is allowed for. "In the symmetric model, the estimated own adjustment coefficient for durable equipment is 0.8072, the highest among four quasi-fixed factors. The adjustment rates for family labor, herd size and real estate are relatively more sluggish. In the asymmetric specification the adjustment of durable equipment also appears to be sluggish. Family labor and herd size follow a similar adjustment pattern in that the contracting adjustment rate is higher than the expanding one... The adjustment rates for real estate and durable equipment are somewhat confusing in terms of their signs and magnitude" (p. 151).

Lansink and Stefanou (1997) extend further the asymmetric model by allowing also for changes in the investment regime. The model is applied to a sample of specialized cash crop farms in Holland, 1971–1992. There are 4,040 observations, 2.4 percent of which reported negative investment, 29.4 percent of which had zero investment, and the remainder of which had positive investment. Quasi-fixed inputs are machinery and rootcrop-specific area. Fixed inputs are the total area of rootcrops and other outputs and labor. There are two outputs, rootcrops and 'others'. Variable inputs include pesticides, fertilizers, and 'others'.

"This model contains 92 parameters, including two parameters related to the expected error terms in Equation (20). The estimated model generated 49 percent of the parameters estimated significant at the critical 5 percent level. Convexity ... is found not to hold" [Lansink and Stefanou (1997, p. 1346)]. It is concluded that the parameter difference between the two regimes is significant for the adjustment parameter of machinery and the parameter relating machinery investment to the quality of labor. Simulation shows response to prices in both the probability of being in a particular regime and in the magnitude.

Finally, "The adjustment rate for machinery is 13 percent a year toward the long-run equilibrium machinery target in the presence of a disinvestment regime and 7 percent a year in the presence of an investment regime" (p. 1349). The rate of disinvestment is in line with conventional rates of depreciation used for machinery, which suggests disinvestment by attrition.

Under the assumption of static expectations, firms recalculate the optimal plan every year conditional on the prevailing prices and technology. But prices are subject to variations and the firms know it, so they must exercise some judgment as to the permanence of a given price regime. This brings up the question of expectations. Luh and Stefanou (1996) replace the assumption of static expectations with "nonstatic expectations", which are introduced by first order autoregressive regressions. The model is applied to US agriculture, using two alternative data sets. The quasi-fixed inputs are capital and labor. The results are not invariant to the data set. The hypotheses of static price expectations are all soundly rejected for one data set but not for the other. Similarly, the test for independent adjustment rejects the null (independence) for one set but not the other. Quasi-fixity is accepted for both sets. As to the rate of adjustment: "While estimated adjustment rates vary, taken together these results suggest that capital and labor take two to three years to adjust to their long-run equilibrium levels. Other adjustment cost models for US agriculture ... report adjustment rates for capital and labor ranging, respectively, from 9 percent to 55 percent and from 7 percent to 40 percent. Our study predicts moderate adjustment speed for capital but much faster labor adjustment compared to other studies" [Luh and Stefanou (1996, pp. 1001–1002)]. Not all the required properties of the value function are met (Table 6). The authors are disturbed by the fact that the results are sensitive to the data sets.

Thijssen (1996) compares static expectations with rational expectations, using panel data of Dutch dairy farms, 1970–1982. The specification is different from the studies reviewed above in that labor and land are treated as exogenous; capital is the only endogenous variable. The results obtained by imposing the constraints of the rational expectations do not make sense and are inconsistent with the theory. The results with static expectations give elasticities of long-run demand for capital of 0.59, −0.45, and −0.13 for the prices of output, capital services, and variable inputs, respectively. However, the coefficients of labor and land are insignificantly different from zero.

The impact of the resource constraint on the demand of the factors that are allowed to vary can be evaluated by comparing the short-run and long-run price elasticities. Output control as a component of agricultural policy introduces another constraint. Fulginiti and Perrin (1993) and Moschini (1988) showed that production quotas on a product reduce the supply elasticities of the nonmanaged products. This can be attributed to the reduction in the scope for substitution. Richards and Jeffrey (1997) use the dynamic duality framework and data for Alberta dairy farms over the period 1975–1991. They attribute the impact to the investment that is tied up in the purchase of production quotas, which may amount to "... half of the total cost of establishing a dairy farm, may cause farmers to face a real capital constraint" (p. 555).

As to the results, monotonicity and symmetry are not rejected, but "... imposing convexity on the full four quasi-fixed inputs model caused the estimation procedure to fail to converge" (Ibid., p. 561). The model was reduced to contain only two quasi-fixed inputs, but "[a]s with the full model, the reduced model does not converge with convexity imposed parametrically. Given these results, further estimation proceeds with two quasi-fixed inputs, dairy cattle and quota licenses, with only symmetry imposed" (Ibid., p. 561). The estimated adjustment coefficients were 0.0995 for quota and 0.1556 for cattle. Obviously, the adjustment of the quotas to their long-run equilibrium is slow, and the question is whether this reflects only the demand side or, as with the studies based on industry data, the slow adjustment reflects the changes in the supply of quotas.

6.11. Discussion

We can now repeat the questions asked in our summary discussion of the static dual approach to the estimation of the production functions. These should be answered at two levels: methodological and substantive. On the methodological level, the answer is simple: The approach provides an efficient and powerful way to discuss and formulate dynamic factor demand. Similar to the static duality framework, this assertion is true regardless of the outcome of the empirical analysis. In this respect, the claim made by some of the authors that the empirical analysis tests the validity of the competitive conditions is not accurate. The most that can be claimed for the empirical analysis is that the conducted tests are of the particular specification. A rejection of a particular specification is not a rejection of the competitive conditions.

The substantive message is more complex. Like in the static case, the essence of the duality framework is the ability to identify the technology by means of prices. It is therefore only natural that we concentrate our attention on the role of prices. The results with the dual dynamic framework are similar, if not more pronounced, to those obtained in the static case in that the convexity in prices of the value function is generally violated. Moreover, the price effect is relatively weak, and the long-run price elasticities and, of course, the short-run elasticities of the factor demands are relatively low. In some cases the whole price matrix is not significantly different from zero. All this suggests that the raison d'être of the duality model is put to question. We return to possible explanations below.

The dynamic dual approach concentrates on the behavioral equations and grossly neglects the inference on the production function itself. This is a good example of the principle of comparative advantage. The dynamic behavior indicates a gradual adjustment to the prevailing, and ever-changing, gaps between the desired long-run values of the quasi-fixed factors and their current values. This result is obtained by the inclusion of lagged values of the dependent stock variable in the empirical equation, as has been the case with the exogenous dynamics. The difference between the two approaches is that the dual dynamic model connects the adjustment coefficients to those of the value function. This can be considered the strength of the approach, but at the same time it also represents its weakness. In essence, this approach attributes the whole dynamics to the internal cost of adjustment. The empirical results show that in most cases the adjustment is sluggish, and in this respect it is also not different from those obtained under (the presumably naive approach of) exogenous dynamics.

There are many investment studies in nonagriculture with cost of adjustment. Often the empirical equation includes output as a variable. In the exogenous dynamics case, output is introduced to the model through the explicit expression of the marginal productivity of capital, and as such, the output coefficient is related to the production function, or through the cost function when the technology is represented by the cost function. On the other hand, in the endogenous dynamics models it is introduced also, and sometimes solely, through the expression for the adjustment cost, and as such it describes a completely different process than that implied from the first case. In summarizing the empirical record in nonagriculture, Chirinko (1993) notes that output performs well in explaining investment and that the performance of prices is rather weak. He also notes a lack of robustness of the results.

Can all these results be rationalized? There are two aspects of the decision to invest in any given year: growth and timing. The growth aspect reflects the long-term view about the prospects of the contemplated investment. The question is when to act. The timing aspect is related to the prevailing price variability which generates opportunities for cost reduction, or capital gains. This possibility is ruled out in a world of static expectations where the current prices are assumed to remain constant indefinitely. This is the reason that the value function can be formulated in terms of the annual capital charges (rental rates) rather than in terms of the total expenditures on the capital goods. It is only under the latter formulation that the expected capital gains constitute a component of the rental rate, as for instance in (32) or (34). The prospects for capital gains introduce cyclical considerations into the model. This also holds true for the interest rate which varies over time and also across individuals, reflecting their financial position. However, the interest rate is taken to be constant, as in the empirical studies reviewed above.

Furthermore there is the problem of price expectations. There are no clear-cut systematic differences in the estimates associated with different assumptions about the nature of the price expectations. It is difficult to conceive that the expectations do not matter, so it must follow that the tried alternatives have something in common, probably an error component. When the price variables are subject to measurement error, their estimated coefficients are likely to be biased downward. This problem is more serious for the capital goods than for the variable inputs because they require price forecasts for the entire lifetime of the project. If this argument is true, the own price elasticities of the variable inputs should have a lower downward bias and also be more precise (have higher t-ratios) than those of the durable inputs. A superficial inspection of the studies reviewed above indicates that this might be the case.

Duality is a micro theory, and therefore the applications with macro data add additional problems. The question of whether the macro function can be considered as that of the representative firm has already been mentioned above. But the test of the conditions for the ideal aggregation that will allow this interpretation deals only with the consequences of aggregation. There is still the problem that the factor supply and product demand are not perfectly elastic as the model assumes. Consequently, there is an identification problem, and the estimated coefficients reflect both supply and demand. This problem is shared also with the static estimates, but the dynamic model has an additional problem in that the pace of the closure of the gap is likely to reflect the pace of the changes in the factor supply or product demand. For instance, in interpreting the studies on US agriculture it is important to note that the movement of labor and capital have taken opposite directions. The decision of labor to leave agriculture is a decision made by households on their employment conditional on the opportunities outside agriculture. As for capital, its supply is not perfectly elastic, and agriculture has to compete with other industries for resources. This is consistent with the study by Lee and Chambers (1986), which tests for the credit constraint in US agriculture in 1947–1980 and concludes that farmers do not face a perfectly elastic supply of funds or credit (p. 865). As such, it is also supportive of the discussion on the choice of technique.

For the micro data, we noted that in many cases the investments are lumpy. A tractor is not purchased gradually, a piece at a time, and similarly for a milking shed. This pattern is masked in the analysis with macro data because the aggregation over firms gives a smooth time path of the investment, but the results do not shed light on the decisions made at the farm level.

Why does output perform better in studies where it appears as a variable? The foregoing discussion suggested some reasons for a revealed weak price response. In addition, as illustrated in the foregoing discussion, a change in price has direct and indirect effects on the desired capital stock, and the indirect effect is considerably larger. Thus, part of the effect of output on the desired capital stock may reflect an indirect effect of price. In addition, changes in output represent not only price effects but also changes in technology. As technology is the engine of growth, it probably plays a key role in explaining actual investment in many cases.

In conclusion, the endogenous dynamics models have two basic limitations. First, they describe a dynamic process in terms of unobserved variables, and thereby lose the main potential of explaining the timing of investment; and second, their only engine for the dynamics is the internal cost of adjustment. There has been no obvious advantage to their performance in empirical analysis nor has there been any particular insight gained by their empirical application.

7. The scope for policy evaluation

In the discussion of duality, the question was raised as to where we go from here. At this stage, it is clear that this question should be addressed within the broader framework that has evolved from the foregoing discussion. The core of the production structure, as outlined above, can be summarized by the following functions:

$$y(v, k, T) \qquad \text{Production function} \qquad (54)$$

$$v(p, w, k, T) \qquad \text{Demand for nondurable inputs} \qquad (55)$$

$$w(v, s(v)) \qquad \text{Supply of nondurable inputs} \qquad (56)$$

$$k^*(s(k^*)) \qquad \text{Capital demand on the optimal path} \qquad (57)$$

$$k(k^*, s(k)) \qquad \text{Actual capital} \qquad (58)$$

$$T(s(T)) \qquad \text{Implemented technology} \qquad (59)$$

where $s(x)$ is the vector of the exogenous variables pertinent to the supply or demand of x, whichever the case may be. Specifically, $s(v)$ are the exogenous variables that affect the supply of the nondurable (variable) inputs, $s(k^*)$ affect the capital demand on the optimal path, $s(k)$ are the variables that determine the dynamics of convergence of the capital stock to the optimal path, and $s(T)$ determine the implemented technology. Some of the exogenous variables were discussed explicitly above, others are discussed in the references or are left in an implicit form. In passing we note that the role of these variables in empirical analysis is still to be more fully unveiled in future research. The system should also include land which is not dealt with explicitly here because we have already covered considerable ground without land. Mechanically, we can think of land as being a component of capital, in which case the supply condition of this component should be carefully specified.[52]

To obtain the dynamics of the supply, substitute the functions (55)–(59) in the production function to obtain

$$y\big[p, w, s(v), s(k^*), s(k), s(T)\big]. \tag{60}$$

Obviously, a function of the form $y(p, w)$ cannot capture all the complexities of Equation (60). The function serves as an approximation whose quality depends on the importance of the missing exogenous variables, which in turn depend on the data base. More generally, this is the problem of estimates based on duality which depend heavily on prices. When dealing with micro data with constant technology, the only relevant issue that will differentiate between the general expression in (60) and $y(p, w)$ is the handling of capital. On the other hand, when dealing with aggregate time-series data, all the exogenous variables may have an important impact.

Can such systems be evaluated empirically? The answer is positive, as has been demonstrated by Cavallo and Mundlak (1982) and Mundlak, Cavallo, and Domenech (1989) for Argentina; Coeymans and Mundlak (1993) for Chile; Lachaal and Womack (1998) for Canada; and at a lower level of aggregation, McGuirk and Mundlak (1991) for the Punjab agriculture under the Green Revolution. These studies show clearly that agriculture responds to prices following endogenous dynamics, of a different form from those discussed above, and that it takes time for the response to reach its full course.

Studying the production structure in all its complexities is both research-intensive and promising. What is the alternative? I will leave it for the reader to formulate his or her own answer. However, in thinking of an answer, we have to keep in mind that more than 70 years have passed since the work of Douglas. During this period, considerable work and ingenuity has been directed to improve the specification and the estimation method, but as we have indicated, there is no simple, robust way to describe reality. In part, the reality has many faces, and in part the researchers have many faces. As in *Rashamon*, we vary in our reports of the same phenomenon.

With this background, we can now address the cardinal question of what effect policy can have on production. Traditionally, the evaluation of the consequences of policy is limited to the examination of resource allocation. The present framework introduces an additional dimension, the determination of the implemented technology. The dependence of the implemented technology on the environment is the key factor to understanding why less-developed countries lag persistently behind the performance of developed countries. The economic environment is affected by policies, sector-specific

---

[52] For a discussion of land, see [Mundlak (1997)].

as well as sector-neutral. The response to changes in the economic environment is not immediate, and it is therefore important to spell out the role of the dynamics of response through resource allocation and the choice of the implemented technology. This is what the above structure does.

7.1. Summary and conclusions

We have reviewed the more important issues concerning empirical production and supply analysis with emphasis on agriculture. In order to confront aspiration with reality, we have deliberately substantiated the main arguments with explicit, and in some cases detailed, references to the reviewed studies.

The literature, spread over 50 years of research, has evolved from analysis of specific issues concerning the production function *per se* to analysis which binds together competitive conditions with the technology. Initially, the incorporation of competitive conditions dealt with static (one period) analysis, and this was extended later on to dynamic analysis. The lack of robust, and often of meaningful, results triggered a search in several directions: better precision in the estimation, an appropriate parametric form of the production function, or avoidance of a parametric presentation altogether, and ultimately the consequences of heterogeneous technology. To some extent, the different approaches have been associated with different questions asked and consequently resulted in different results, which are not always comparable. This complicates the assessment, and consequently the evaluation of a given approach is done by comparing the results with the underlying assumptions and expectations, as well as with the substantive message. This state of affairs is unsatisfying because the essence of duality is that knowing the production function, one can derive the behavioral equations and conversely, but the analysis is seldom carried out that far. Still, the search in the various directions has been essential for the understanding of the process, for marking the boundaries of the empirical analysis, and for developing alternative approaches that might overcome some of the difficulties. This is research.

The primal approach consisted initially of the estimation of a Cobb–Douglas production function using both micro and macro data. The main yield of these studies consists of production elasticities, a check of the prevalence of profit maximization, and a measure of economies of scale. The results have not been robust and have varied with the samples. We have provided some numerical results for the production elasticities which, on the whole, show that labor elasticity in agriculture is smaller than in nonagriculture, indicating that agriculture is more susceptible to changes in the cost of capital and less to changes in the wage rates than nonagriculture. Economies of scale have been detected mainly in strictly cross-sectional studies and are attributed to statistical bias due to the correlation between the unobserved idiosyncratic productivity and the input level, or simply the endogeneity of inputs. The main approaches to overcome this statistical bias have been the use of covariance analysis in panel data and the use of prices as instrumental variables (and more recently a combination of the two). The covariance analysis also provides a measure of the managerial ability – the idiosyncratic productivity – of the various firms (or other observation units such as a country or a region as well as time). This measure is based on the same concept as that of the residual, or the TFP.

The extension of the analysis to production functions with richer parametric presentation offered greater flexibility in fitting the function to data, and bred expectations for more robust results. How do such extensions modify the conclusions drawn from the Cobb–Douglas model with respect to elasticities, profit maximization, and scale economies? In most cases, no comparison of the production elasticities obtained by the different functions is reported. Perhaps additional work would be required, perhaps this question has not come up, but there is also a more profound reason. The more general functions are either nonlinear in the parameters (such as the CES, or some of the quadratic functions) or contain too many parameters which leads to multicollinearity, and therefore are not easy to estimate directly. The situation is simplified considerably when the parameters are estimated from the first order conditions for profit maximization, rather than from the production function itself. This requires the imposition of profit maximization on the model. In many cases, the dependent variables are the factor shares, or a monotone function thereof. This procedure precludes the testing of the profit maximization and of economies of scale. The explanatory variables in these equations are the inputs. Thus, the essence of such extensions is to attribute the differences in the factor shares across observations to the variations in the input ratios, whereas in the Cobb–Douglas case the elasticities are constant. In many cases the variability in the input ratios in the sample is not sufficiently large to induce the observed spread in the factor shares.

Because the parametric enrichment of the specification of the production function generated the need to use the first order conditions for profit maximization in empirical analysis, it thereby eliminated the possibility of testing this hypothesis empirically. This state of affairs generated a potential scope for the nonparametric methods which offers a simple test for profit maximization. One can think of a two-stage analysis: a preliminary test of the hypothesis by nonparametric methods, and if the hypothesis is not rejected, a follow-up with parametric specification that imposes the conditions for profit maximization. Unfortunately, this course of action suffers from the fact that under technical change, the test for profit maximization loses much of its purity. The allowance for technical change implicitly utilizes profit maximization, and thus the analysis loses not only its purity but also much of its usefulness. Having said this, we note that there is a more profound consideration. The question of profit maximization is not a qualitative one that can be answered yes or no. Even if profit maximization is the rule, there are deviations from the first order conditions, and therefore the imposition of these conditions in the estimation may lead to erroneous results. Such deviations from the first order conditions may reflect considerations such as risk, dynamic considerations in the case of the price of durables, or simply a discrepancy in the price perception between the econometrician and the firms.

Given the estimates of the primal function, it is possible to calculate the elasticities of the behavioral functions, product supply and factor demand, and the value of the objective functions, profit, cost, or revenue as the case may be. Duality offers a reverse course of action where the point of departure is the objective function. When the objective function is known, it can be used to derive the production function. In principle, there are several reasons to use duality in empirical analysis. First, it is a powerful theoretical concept. Second, prices are thought to be exogenous and therefore can be used to identify the technology, thereby overcoming the endogeneity of the inputs in the direct estimation of the production function. Third, it may provide a useful presentation of the technology. The first point is valid, but the problem is in its empirical implementation. The second point is valid only for micro data, but even then the method does not utilize all the information available for the identification of the production function, and as such it is not efficient compared to the primal estimates. The third point is valid only when the implemented technology is independent of the prices.

When the objective function is rich in parameters, the dual specification is reduced for empirical analysis by the use of the envelope theorem to yield empirical equations where the dependent variables are inputs, outputs, or factor shares. Those are regressed on the pertinent prices, time trend, and sometimes output. When the change in the use of inputs is decomposed to price, trend (a proxy for technology), and output effects, it is found that trend and output capture most of the change, whereas the role of prices is the least important. Thus the contribution of prices to the explanation of inputs or output variations is rather limited. Duality between technology and prices holds under well-defined conditions that can be tested empirically. In most studies these underlying conditions are not fully met; in particular the concavity of the cost function or the convexity of the profit function is violated. Therefore, the estimated technology is inconsistent with the basic premises of the model.

The price elasticities of factor demand and product supply are usually obtained under the assumption that producers are price takers in the product and factor markets. On the whole, the own-price elasticities are less than one. There is no uniformity in the signs of the cross elasticities, but in general, most inputs appear to be substitutes. The magnitude of the own and cross elasticities reflects in part the fact that in reality factor supplies are not perfectly elastic as the models assume, and therefore the results need not represent demand-driven substitution as is thought. This is the case with respect to elasticities related to labor, land, and capital. We further elaborate on this subject below.

With respect to other findings, interestingly, on the whole the studies based on duality do not show increasing returns to scale. Technical change, obtained by including a time trend in regressions of factor shares, is largely labor-saving, capital-using, and fertilizer-using, with the results for land being somewhat ambiguous.

The interest of agricultural economists in the behavioral functions had long preceded the work on production functions. The work on supply response, which was triggered by policy considerations rather than methodological innovations, is similar in nature to that of the empirical estimation of behavioral functions that emerged from the estimation of the dual functions. The initial work on supply response was in part intuitive; it lacked the duality framework, and basically it had been inspired by the primal approach. Still, it emphasized two related cardinal topics whose importance has not diminished: quasi-fixed factors and dynamics. The root of the importance of these topics is in the fact that static analysis is timeless, whereas data are dated. This requires that behavioral equations will be conditional on the available quantities of quasi-fixed factors, a condition that has been overlooked in many (but not all) of the studies based on duality. Such functions are termed short-run, or restricted, functions. Supply elasticities derived from short-run functions are inversely related to the relative importance of quasi-fixed factors (as measured by their factor shares). The larger is the relative weight of the quasi-fixed factors, the larger is the gap between the short- and long-run supply (or factor demand) elasticities. This gap was well highlighted by distributed lag analysis which introduced dynamics into the empirical analysis. The distributed lags model is a powerful empirical tool because of its simplicity. But when the distributed lags model is applied to the outputs or inputs that are endogenous in the short run, this simplicity is achieved at the cost of ignoring the underlying production structure. The extension of the analysis to the long run requires determining the optimal level of the quasi-fixed factors, and this is done within the framework of multiperiod optimization, an important subject of current research.

Intertemporal optimization determines the optimal time path for durable goods, or simply capital goods. The first-order conditions for optimization using the primal approach sets the marginal productivity of capital equal to the user cost at any point on the optimal path. Endogenous dynamics are generated within the model, mostly by the inclusion of adjustment costs, whereas exogenous dynamics superimpose the dynamics on the model without an explicit expression for the causality. Under the dual approach, as in the static case, the value function is specified parametrically and serves as a starting point for deriving the factor demand. There is a similarity in the basic appearance of the empirical equations of these alternative approaches in that they all express the capital demand in terms of incentives and the existing capital stock.

There are two aspects of the decision to invest in any given year: growth and timing. The growth aspect reflects the long-term view about the prospects of the contemplated investment, and the timing aspect is related to the question of when to act. The expected profitability of investment is affected by changes in technology and prices. Over the long haul, technology changes more than real prices. In fact, in the case of agriculture, investment has taken place in spite of a decline in real prices. Yet, the emphasis in empirical analysis has been to explain investment in terms of prices, while technology is represented by time trend. This is particularly true for studies based on the dual approach. Time trend is not sufficiently reflective of the changes in technology. Thus it might be more promising to measure the incentives in terms of the rate of return on capital, which summarizes the information on technology and prices, rather than in terms of prices.

The dynamic dual approach provides an efficient and powerful way to discuss and formulate dynamic factor demand. However, the results with the dual dynamic framework are similar, if not more pronounced, to those obtained in the static case in that convexity in prices of the value function is generally violated. Moreover, the price effect is relatively weak, and the price elasticities, and especially the short-run elasticities, of the factor demands are relatively low. In some cases the whole price matrix is not significantly different from zero. All this suggests that the *raison d'être* of the duality model is put to question. On the other hand, in studies which, for whatever reason, include output as an explanatory variable, output appears as a very prominent variable. It is suggested that this is due to the fact that output is a good proxy for profitability and may reflect the effect of technical change, as well as prices.

There are several possible reasons for the poor performance of prices. Some of them are due to the fact that duality is a micro theory, and therefore the applications with macro data add additional problems. In addition, there is the problem of long horizon which requires generating expected prices, and technology for that matter, for the entire lifetime of the investment. These have to be generated, and there is considerable scope for error. In addition, in the case of the dual approach, the specification is very parameter-intensive, and this creates imprecision in the estimation of individual coefficients.

The empirical results indicate a gradual and sluggish adjustment to the ever changing gaps between the desired long-run values of the quasi-fixed factors and their current values. This raises a question whether the sluggish response is the outcome of the internal cost of adjustment or alternatively a reflection of the fact that total resources are limited and the economy is facing an upward-slopping factor supply, which may be fairly inelastic.

As we progress with the review, it has become evident that some of the difficulties that have been encountered in the empirical work could be accounted for if we allow for heterogeneous technology. Changes in the available technology and in the economic environment generate opportunities for firms to seize on. The implementation of new available technologies is governed by economic considerations and is affected by the variables used in conventional analysis, such as prices or capital. It is suggested that the scope of this approach should be further investigated as a step in our attempt to come up with a uniform and robust framework that would be applicable to a wide range of economic and physical environments. An important advantage of this framework is that it provides a channel for introducing the direct effect of policy on productivity.

To conclude, in spite of all these difficulties of obtaining a uniform robust model, we know today quite a bit about orders of magnitude of some important parameters.

Acknowledgement

I am indebted to Rita Butzer for comments and for editorial assistance.

References

Afriat, S.N. (1972), "Efficiency estimation of production function", International Economic Review 13(3):568–598.

Antle, J.M. (1983), "Infrastructure and aggregate agricultural productivity: International evidence", Economic Development and Cultural Change 31(3):609–619.

Antle, J.M. (1984), "The structure of US agricultural technology, 1910–78", American Journal of Agricultural Economics 66(4):414–421.

Arrow, K.J., H.B. Chenery, B.S. Minhas and R.M. Solow (1961), "Capital-labor substitution and economic efficiency", Review of Economics & Statistics 43(3):225–250.

Askari, H., and J.T. Cummings (1976), Agricultural Supply Response: A Survey of the Econometric Evidence (Praeger Publishers, New York).

Ball, V.E. (1985), "Output, input and productivity measurement in US agriculture: 1948–79", American Journal of Agricultural Economics 67(3):475–486.

Ball, V.E., J.-C. Bureau, K. Elkin and A. Somwaru (1993a), "Implications of the common agricultural policy reform: An analytical approach", USDA, mimeograph.

Ball, V.E., J.-C. Bureau, J. Butault and H.P. Witzke (1993b), "The stock of capital in European community agriculture", European Review of Agricultural Economics 20:437–450.

Ball, V.E., J.-C. Bureau, R. Nehring and A. Somwaru (1997), "Agricultural productivity revisited", American Journal of Agricultural Economics 79(4):1045–1063.

Bar-Shira, Z., and I. Finkelshtain (1999), "Simple nonparametric tests of technological change: Theory and application to US agriculture", American Journal of Agricultural Economics (forthcoming).

Bean, L.H. (1929), "The farmers' response to price", Journal of Farm Economics 11:368–385.

Bhattacharjee, J.P. (1955), "Resource use and productivity in world agriculture", Journal of Farm Economics 37(1):57–71.

Binswanger, H.P. (1974), "A cost function approach to the measurement of elasticities of factor demand and elasticities of substitution", American Journal of Agricultural Economics 56(2):377–386.

Bouchet, F., D. Orden and G.W. Norton (1989), "Sources of growth in French agriculture", American Journal of Agricultural Economics 71(2):280–293.

Brandow, G.E. (1962), "Demand for factors and supply of output in a perfectly competitive industry", Journal of Farm Economics 44(3):895–899.

Brewster, J.M., and H.L. Parsons (1946), "Can prices allocate resources in American agriculture?", Journal of Farm Economics 28(4):938–960.

Bronfenbrenner, M. (1944), "Production functions: Cobb–Douglas, interfirm, intrafirm", Econometrica 12(1):35–44.

Capalbo, S.M. (1988), "A comparison of econometric models of US agricultural productivity and aggregate technology", in: S.M. Capalbo and J.M. Antle, eds., Agricultural Productivity: Measurement and Explanation (Resources for the Future, Washington, DC) 159–188.

Capalbo, S.M., and T.T. Vo (1988), "A review of the evidence on agricultural productivity and aggregate technology", in: S.M. Capalbo and J.M. Antle, eds., Agricultural Productivity: Measurement and Explanation (Resources for the Future, Washington, DC) 96–137.

Cassels, J.M. (1933), "The nature of statistical supply curves", Journal of Farm Economics 15(2):378–387.

Cavallo, D. (1976), "A note on consistent estimation of a production function with partially transmitted errors", Department of Economics mimeo (Harvard University, Cambridge, MA).

Cavallo, D., and Y. Mundlak (1982), Agriculture and Economic Growth in an Open Economy: The Case of Argentina, Research Report No. 36 (International Food Policy Research Institute, Washington, DC).

Caves, D.W., and L.R. Christensen (1980), "Global properties of flexible functional forms", American Economic Review 70(3):422–432.

Chalfant, J.A. (1984), "Comparison of alternative functional forms with application to agricultural input data", American Journal of Agricultural Economics 66(2):216–220.

Chalfant, J.A., and B. Zhang (1997), "Variations on invariance or some unpleasant nonparametric arithmetic", American Journal of Agricultural Economics 79(4):1164–1176.

Chambers, R.G., and R.E. Just (1989), "Estimating multioutput technologies", American Journal of Agricultural Economics 71(4):980–995.

Chambers, R.G., and R.D. Pope (1994), "A virtually ideal production system: specifying and estimating the VIPS model", American Journal of Agricultural Economics 76(1):105–113.

Chang, C.C., and S.E. Stefanou (1988), "Specification and estimation of asymmetric adjustment rates for quasi-fixed factors of production", Journal of Economic Dynamics and Control 12(1):145–151.

Chavas, J.-P. (1994), "Production and investment decisions under sunk cost and temporal uncertainty", American Journal of Agricultural Economics 76(1):114–127.

Chavas, J.-P., and T.L. Cox (1988), "A nonparametric analysis of agricultural technology", American Journal of Agricultural Economics 70(2):303–310.

Chavas, J.-P., and T.L. Cox (1994), "A primal-dual approach to nonparametric productivity analysis: The case of US agriculture", The Journal of Productivity Analysis 5(4):359–373.

Chavas, J.-P., and T.L. Cox (1992), "A nonparametric analysis of agricultural technology", American Journal of Agricultural Economics 74:583–591.

Chenery, H.B. (1952), "Overcapacity and the acceleration principle", Econometrica 20(1):1–28.

Chennareddy, V. (1967), "Production efficiency in South Indian agriculture", Journal of Farm Economics 49(4):816–820.

Chirinko, R.S. (1993), "Business fixed investment spending: a critical survey of modeling strategies, empirical results, and policy implications", Journal of Economic Literature 31(4):1875–1911.

Christensen, L.R., D.W. Jorgenson and L.J. Lau (1973), "Transcendental logarithmic production frontiers", Review of Economics and Statistics 55(1):28–45.

Clark, C. (1973), The Value of Agricultural Land (Pergamon Press, Oxford).

Clark, J.S., and C.E. Youngblood (1992), "Estimating duality models with biased technical change: A time series approach", American Journal of Agricultural Economics 74(2):353–360.

Cobb, C.W., and P.H. Douglas (1928), "A theory of production", American Economic Review 18(1):139–165.

Coeymans, J.E., and Y. Mundlak (1993), Sectoral Growth in Chile: 1962–82, Research Report No. 95 (International Food Policy Research Institute, Washington, DC).

Colyer, D., and G. Jimenez (1971), "Supervised credit as a tool in agricultural development", American Journal of Agricultural Economics 53(4):639–642.

Cox, T.L., and J.-P. Chavas (1990), "A nonparametric analysis of productivity: The case of US agriculture", European Review of Agricultural Economics 17(4):449–464.

Diewert, W.E. (1974), "Applications of duality theory", in: M. Intrilligator and D.A. Kendrick, eds., Frontiers of Quantitative Economics, Vol. II (North-Holland, Amsterdam).

Douglas, P.H. (1976), "The Cobb–Douglas production function once again: its history. Its testing, and some new empirical values", Journal of Political Economy 84(5):903–916.

Edwards, C. (1959), "Resource fixity and farm organization", Journal of Farm Economics 41(4):747–759.

Epstein, L.G. (1981), "Duality theory and functional forms for dynamic factor demands", Review of Economic Studies 48(1):81–95.

Epstein, L.G., and M.G.S. Denny (1983), "The multivariate flexible accelerator model: its empirical restrictions and an application to US manufacturing", Econometrica 51(3):647–674.

Evenson, R.E., and Y. Kislev (1975), Agricultural Research and Productivity (Yale University Press, New Haven).

Fawson, C., and C.R. Shumway (1988), "A nonparametric investigation of agricultural production behavior for US subregions", American Journal of Agricultural Economics 70(2):311–317.

Featherstone, A.M., G.A. Moghnieh and B.K. Goodwin (1995), "Farm-level nonparametric analysis of cost-minimization and profit-maximization behavior", Agricultural Economics 13(2):109–117.

Floyd, J.E. (1965), "The effects of farm price supports on the returns to land and labor in agriculture", Journal of Political Economy 73(2):148–158.

Fox, G., and L. Kivanda (1994), "Popper or production?", Canadian Journal of Agricultural Economics 42(1):1–13.

Fulginiti, L., and R. Perrin (1993), "The theory and measurement of producer response under quotas", Review of Economic and Statistics 75(1):97–106.

Fuss, M., and D. McFadden (1978), "Flexibility versus efficiency in ex ante plant design", in: M. Fuss and D. McFadden, eds., Production Economics: A Dual Approach to Theory and Applications (North-Holland, Amsterdam) 311–364.

Fuss, M., D. McFadden and Y. Mundlak (1978), "A survey of functional forms in the economic analysis of production", in: M. Fuss and D. McFadden, eds., Production Economics: A Dual Approach to Theory and Applications (North-Holland, Amsterdam) 219–268.

Galbraith, J.K., and J.D. Black (1938), "The maintenance of agricultural production during depression: The explanations reviewed", Journal of Political Economy 46(3):305–323.

Galeotti, M. (1996), "The intertemporal dimension of neoclassical production theory", Journal of Economic Surveys 10(4):421–460.

Gould, J.P. (1968), "Adjustment costs in the theory of investment of the firm", Review of Economic Studies 35(1):47–55.

Griliches, Z. (1959), "The demand for inputs in agriculture and a derived supply elasticity", Journal of Farm Economics 41(2):309–322.

Griliches, Z. (1960), "The demand for a durable input: Farm tractors in the United States, 1921–57", in: A.C. Harberger, ed., The Demand for Durable Goods (The University of Chicago Press, Chicago) 181–207.

Griliches, Z. (1963a), "The sources of measured productivity growth: United States agriculture, 1940–1960", Journal of Political Economy 71(4):331–346.

Griliches, Z. (1963b), "Estimates of the aggregate agricultural production function from cross-sectional data", Journal of Farm Economics 45(2):419–428.

Griliches, Z. (1963c), "Capital stock in investment functions: Some problems of concept and measurement", in: C.F. Christ et al., eds., Measurement in Economics: Studies in Mathematical Economics and Econometrics, in Memory of Yehuda Grunfeld (Stanford University Press, Stanford, CA).

Griliches, Z. (1964), "Research expenditures, education, and the aggregate agricultural production function", American Economic Review 54(6):961–974.

Griliches, Z., and D. Jorgenson (1966), "Sources of measured productivity change: Capital input", American Economic Review 56(2):50–61.

Haavelmo, T. (1947), "Methods of measuring the marginal propensity to consume", Journal of the American Statistical Association 42:105–122.

Hall, R.E. (1973), "The specification of technology with several kinds of output", Journal of Political Economy 81(4):878–892.

Hamermesh, D.S., and G.A. Pfann (1996), "Adjustment costs in factor demand", Journal of Economic Literature 34(3):1264–1292.

Hanoch, G. (1975), "Production and demand models with direct or indirect implicit additivity", Econometrica 43(3):395–419.

Hanoch, G., and M. Rothschild (1972), "Testing the assumptions of production theory: A nonparametric approach", Journal of Political Economics 80:256–75.

Hayami, Y. (1969), "Sources of agricultural productivity gap among selected countries", American Journal of Agricultural Economics 51(3):564–575.

Hayami, Y. (1970), "On the use of the Cobb–Douglas production function on the cross-country analysis of agricultural production", American Journal of Agricultural Economics 52(2):327–329.

Hayami, Y., and V.W. Ruttan (1970), "Agricultural productivity differences among countries", American Economic Review 60(5):895–911.

Headley, J.C. (1968), "Estimating the productivity of agricultural pesticides", American Journal of Agricultural Economics 50(1):13–23.

Heady, E.O. (1946), "Production functions from a random sample of farms", Journal of Farm Economics 28(4):989–1004.

Heady, E.O., and J.L. Dillon (1961), Agricultural Production Functions (Iowa State University Press, Ames).

Heady, E.O., and L.G. Tweeten (1963), Resource Demand and the Structure of the Agricultural Industry (Iowa State University Press, Ames).

Herdt, R.W. (1971), "Resource productivity in Indian agriculture", American Journal of Agricultural Economics 53(3):517–521.

Hildebrand, J.R. (1960), "Some difficulties with empirical results from whole-farm Cobb–Douglas-type production functions", Journal of Farm Economics 42(4):897–904.

Hoch, I. (1955), "Estimation of production function parameters and testing for efficiency", Econometrica 23(3):325–326.

Hoch, I. (1958), "Simultaneous equation bias in the context of the Cobb–Douglas production function", Econometrica 26(4):566–578.

Hoch, I. (1962), "Estimation of production function parameters combining time-series and cross-section data", Econometrica 30(1):34–53.

Hopper, W.D. (1965), "Allocation efficiency in a traditional Indian agriculture", Journal of Farm Economics 47(3):611–624.

Howard, W.H., and C.R. Shumway (1988), "Dynamic adjustment in the US dairy industry", American Journal of Agricultural Economics 70(4):837–847.

Huang, Y. (1971), "Allocation efficiency in a developing agricultural economy in Malaya", American Journal of Agricultural Economics 53(3):514–516.

Huffman, W.E., and R.E. Evenson (1989), "Supply and demand functions for multiproduct US cash grain farms: Biases caused by research and other policies", American Journal of Agricultural Economics 71(3):761–773.

Johnson, D.G. (1950), "The nature of supply function for agricultural products", American Economic Review 40(4):539–564.

Johnson, G.L. (1958), "Supply function-some facts and notions", in: E.O. Heady, H.G. Diesslin, H.R. Jensen, and G.L. Johnson, eds., Agricultural Adjustment Problems in a Growing Economy (The Iowa State College Press, Ames, Iowa) 74–93.

Johnson, G.L., and L. Quance (1972), The Overproduction Trap in US Agriculture (The Johns Hopkins University Press for Resources for the Future, Baltimore, Maryland).

Jorgenson, D.W. (1963), "Capital theory and investment behavior", American Economic Review 53(2):247–259.

Jorgenson, D.W. (1967), "The theory of investment behavior", in: R. Ferber, ed., Determinants of Investment Behavior, (Columbia University Press, National Bureau of Economic Research, New York) 129–155.

Jorgenson, D.W. (1986), "Econometric methods for modeling producer behavior", in: Z. Griliches and M.D. Intriligator, eds., Handbook of Econometrics, Vol. III (North-Holland, Amsterdam) 1841–1915.

Jorgenson, D.W., and F.M. Gollop (1992), "Productivity Growth in US agriculture: A postwar perspective", American Journal of Agricultural Economics 74(3):745–750.

Just, R.E., D. Zilberman and E. Hochman (1983), "Estimation of multicrop production functions", American Journal of Agricultural Economics 65(4):770–780.

Kako, T. (1978), "Decomposition analysis of derived demand for factor inputs: The case of rice production in Japan", American Journal of Agricultural Economics 60(4):628–635.

Kamien, M.I., and N.L. Schwartz (1991), Dynamic Optimization, 2nd edition (North-Holland, Amsterdam).

Kawagoe, T., and Y. Hayami (1983), "The production structure of world agriculture: An intercountry cross-section analysis", The Developing Economies 21:189–206.

Kawagoe, T., Y. Hayami and V.W. Ruttan (1985), "The intercountry agricultural production function and productivity differences among countries", Journal of Development Economics 19:113–132.

Kislev, Y. (1966), "Overestimates of returns to scale in agriculture – a case of synchronized aggregation", Journal of Farm Economics 48(4):967–983.

Kislev, Y., and W. Peterson (1996), "Economies of scale in agriculture: A reexamination of evidence", in: J.M. Antle and D. Sumner, eds., The Economics of Agriculture, Papers in honor of D. Gale Johnson, Vol. 2 (University of Chicago Press, Chicago) 156–170.

Klein, L.R. (1953), A Textbook of Econometrics (Row, Peterson and Co, Evanston, IL).

Koyck, L. (1954), Distributed Lags and Investment Analysis (North-Holland, Amsterdam).

Kuroda, Y. (1987), "The production structure and demand for labor in postwar Japanese agriculture, 1952–82", American Journal of Agricultural Economics 69(2):328–337.

Lachaal, L., and A.W. Womack (1998), "Impacts of trade and macroeconomic linkages on Canadian agriculture", American Journal of Agricultural Economics 80(3):534–542.

Lansink, A.O., and S.E. Stefanou (1997), "Asymmetric adjustment of dynamic factors at the firm level", American Journal of Agricultural Economics 79(4):1340–1351.

Larson, D., R. Butzer, Y. Mundlak and A. Crego (1999), "A cross-country database for sector investment and capital," Working Paper No. 9903 (The Center for Agricultural Economic Research, Rehovot).

Lau, L.J. (1978), "Applications of profit functions", in: M. Fuss and D. McFadden, eds., Production Economics: A Dual Approach to Theory and Applications, Vol. 1 (North-Holland, Amsterdam) 133–216.

Lau, L.J., and P.A. Yotopoulos (1972), "Profit, supply, and factor demand functions", American Journal of Agricultural Economics 54(1):11–18.

Leathers, H.D. (1991), "Allocable fixed inputs as a cause of joint production: A cost function approach", American Journal of Agricultural Economics 73(4):1083–1090.

Lee, H., and R.G. Chambers (1986), "Expenditure constraints and profit maximization in US agriculture", American Journal of Agricultural Economics 68(4):857–865.

Lopez, R.E. (1980), "The structure of production and the derived demand for inputs in Canadian agriculture", American Journal of Agricultural Economics 62(1):38–45.

Lopez, R.E. (1984), "Estimating substitution and expansion effects using a profit function framework", American Journal of Agricultural Economics 66(3):358–367.

Lopez, R.E. (1985a), "Structural implications of a class of flexible functional forms for profit functions", International Economic Review 26(3):593–601.

Lopez, R.E. (1985b), "Supply response and investment in the Canadian food processing industry", American Journal of Agricultural Economics 67(1):40–48.

Lucas, R.E. (1967), "Optimal investment policy and the flexible accelerator", International Economic Review 8:78–85.

Luh, Y.H., and S.E. Stefanou (1991), "Productivity growth in US agriculture under dynamic adjustment", American Journal of Agricultural Economics 73(4):1116–1125.

Luh, Y.H., and S.E. Stefanou (1996), "Estimating dynamic dual models under nonstatic expectations", American Journal of Agricultural Economics 78(4):991–1003.

Marschak, J., and W.H. Andrews, Jr. (1944), "Random simultaneous equations and the theory of production", Econometrica 12(3&4):143–205.

McFadden, D. (1978), "Cost, revenue, and profit functions", in: M. Fuss and D. McFadden, eds., Production Economics: A Dual Approach to Theory and Applications (North-Holland, Amsterdam) 3–109.

McGuirk, A., and Y. Mundlak (1991), Incentives and Constraints in the Transformation of Punjab Agriculture, Research Report No. 87 (International Food Policy Research Institute, Washington, DC).

McLaren, K.R., and R.J. Cooper (1980), "Intertemporal duality: Application to the theory of the firm", Econometrica 48(7):1755–1762.

Mittelhammer, R.C., D.L. Young, D. Tasanasanta and J.T. Donnelly (1980), "Mitigating the effects of multicollinearity using exact and stochastic restrictions: The case of an aggregate agricultural production function in Thailand", American Journal of Agricultural Economics 62:199–210.

Moschini, G. (1988), "A model of production with supply management for the Canadian agricultural sector", American Journal of Agricultural Economics 70(2):318–329.

Mundlak, Y. (1961), "Empirical production function free of management bias", Journal of Farm Economics 43(1):44–56.

Mundlak, Y. (1963a), "Estimation of production and behavioral functions from a combination of cross-section and time-series data", in: C.F. Christ et al., eds., Measurement in Economics: Studies in Mathematical Economics and Econometrics, in Memory of Yehuda Grunfeld (Stanford University Press, Stanford, CA) 138–166.

Mundlak, Y. (1963b), "Specification and estimation of multiproduct production functions", Journal of Farm Economics 45(2):433–443.

Mundlak, Y. (1964a), An Economic Analysis of Established Family Farms in Israel, 1953–1958 (The Falk Project for Economic Research in Israel, Jerusalem).

Mundlak, Y. (1964b), "Transcendental multiproduct production functions", International Economic Review 5(3):273–284.

Mundlak, Y. (1966), "On the microeconomic theory of distributed lags", Review of Economics and Statistics 48(1):51–60.

Mundlak, Y. (1967), "Long-run coefficients and distributed lag analysis: A reformulation", Econometrica 35(2):278–293.

Mundlak, Y. (1968) "Elasticities of substitution and the theory of derived demand", Review of Economic Studies 35:225–236.

Mundlak, Y. (1988), "Endogenous technology and the measurement of productivity", in: S.M. Capalbo and J.M. Antle, eds., Agricultural Productivity: Measurement and Explanation (Resources for the Future, Washington, DC) 316–331.

Mundlak, Y. (1993), "On the empirical aspects of economic growth theory", American Economic Review 83(2):415–420.

Mundlak, Y. (1996a), "Production function estimation: Reviving the primal", Econometrica 64(2):431–438.

Mundlak, Y. (1996b) "On the aggregate agricultural supply", in: J.M. Antle and D. Sumner, eds., The Economics of Agriculture, Papers in honor of D. Gale Johnson, Vol. 2 (University of Chicago Press, Chicago) 101–120.

Mundlak, Y. (1997), "Land expansion, land augmentation, and land saving", Benjamin H. Hibbard Memorial Lecture Series (Department of Agricultural and Applied Economics, University of Wisconsin, Madison, WI).

Mundlak, Y. (2000), Agriculture and economic growth; Theory and Measurement (forthcoming).

Mundlak, Y., D. Cavallo and R. Domenech (1989), Agriculture and Economic Growth in Argentina, 1913–84, Research Report No. 76 (International Food Policy Research Institute, Washington, DC).

Mundlak, Y., and R. Hellinghausen (1982), "The intercountry agricultural production function: Another view", American Journal of Agricultural Economics 64(4):664–672.

Mundlak, Y., and I. Hoch (1965), "Consequences of alternative specifications in estimation of Cobb–Douglas production functions", Econometrica 33(4):814–828.

Mundlak, Y., D. Larson and R. Butzer (1999), "Rethinking within and between regression: The case of agricultural production functions," Annales D'Economie et de Statistique 55–56:475–501.

Mundlak, Y., and A. Razin (1969), "Aggregation, index numbers and the measurement of technical change", Review of Economics and Statistics 51(2):166–175.

Mundlak, Y., and A. Razin (1971), "On multistage multiproduct production functions", American Journal of Agricultural Economics 53(3):491–499.

Mundlak, Y., and Z. Volcani (1973), "The correspondence of efficiency frontier as a generalization of the cost function", International Economic Review 14(1):223–233.

Nadiri, M.I., and S. Rosen (1969), "Interrelated factor demand functions", American Economic Review 59(4):457–471.

Nerlove, M. (1956), "Estimates of the elasticities of supply of selected agricultural commodities", Journal of Farm Economics 38(2):496–509.

Nerlove, M. (1958), "Distributed lags and estimation of long-run supply and demand elasticities: Theoretical considerations", Journal of Farm Economics 40(2):301–313.

Nerlove, M. (1963), "Returns to scale in electricity supply", in: C.F. Christ et al., eds., Measurement in Economics: Studies in Mathematical Economics and Econometrics, in Memory of Yehuda Grunfeld (Stanford University Press, Stanford, CA) 167–200.

Nguyen, D. (1979), "On agricultural productivity differences among countries", American Journal of Agricultural Economics 61(3):565–570.

Ray, S.C. (1982), "A translog cost function analysis of US agriculture, 1939–77", American Journal of Agricultural Economics 64(3):490–498.

Reder, M.W. (1943), "An alternative interpretation of the Cobb–Douglas function", Econometrica 11(3&4):259–264.

Richards, T.J., and S.R. Jeffrey (1997), "The effect of supply management on Herd size in Alberta dairy", American Journal of Agricultural Economics 79(2):555–565.

Rosegrant, M.W., and R.E. Evenson (1992), "Agricultural productivity and sources of growth in South Asia", American Journal of Agricultural Economics 74(3):757–761.

Ruttan, V.W. (1956), "The contribution of technological progress to farm output: 1950–1975", Review of Economics and Statistics 38(1):61–69.

Sadan, E. (1968), "Capital formation and growth in the Israeli cooperative farm", American Journal of Agricultural Economics 50:975–990.

Sahota, G.S. (1968), "Efficiency of resource allocation in Indian agriculture", American Journal of Agricultural Economics 50:584–605.

Schultz, T.W. (1953), Economic Organization of Agriculture (McGraw-Hill, New York).

Shih, J.T., L.J. Hushak and N. Rask (1977), "The validity of the Cobb–Douglas specification in Taiwan's developing agriculture", American Journal of Agricultural Economics 59(3):554–558.

Shumway, C.R. (1983), "Supply, demand, and technology in a multiproduct industry: Texas field crops", American Journal of Agricultural Economics 65(4):748–760.

Shumway, C.R. (1995), "Recent duality contributions in production economics", Journal of Agricultural and Resource Economics 20(1):178–194.

Shumway, C.R., and W.P. Alexander (1988), "Agricultural product supplies and input demands: Regional comparisons", American Journal of Agricultural Economics 70(1):153–161.

Shumway, C.R., R.D. Pope and E. Nash (1984), "Allocatable fixed inputs and jointness in agricultural production: Implications for modeling", American Journal of Agricultural Economics 66(1):72–78.

Shumway, C.R., R.R. Saez and P.E. Gottret (1988), "Multiproduct supply and input demand in US agriculture", American Journal of Agricultural Economics 70(2):330–337.

Shumway, C.R., H. Talpaz and B.R. Beattie (1979), "The factor share approach to production function "estimation": Actual or estimated equilibrium shares?", American Journal of Agricultural Economics 61(3):561–564.

Smith, V.E. (1945), "The statistical production function", Quarterly Journal of Economics 59(4):543–562.

Solow, R.M. (1957), "Technical change and the aggregate production function", Review of Economics and Statistics 39(3):312–320.

Tauer, L.W. (1995), "Do New York dairy farmers maximize profits or minimize costs?", American Journal of Agricultural Economics 77(2):421–429.

Taylor, T.G., and M.J. Monson (1985), "Dynamic factor demands for aggregate southeastern United States agriculture", Southern Journal of Agricultural Economics 17(2):1–9.

Thijssen, G. (1996), "Farmers' investment behavior: An empirical assessment of two specifications of expectations", American Journal of Agricultural Economics 78(1):166–174.

Tintner, G. (1944), "A note on the derivation of production functions from farm records", Econometrica 12:26–34.

Tintner, G., and O.H. Brownlee (1944), "Production functions derived from farm records", Journal of Farm Economics 26(3):566–571 (a correction in JFE Feb. 1953, 35:123).

Treadway, A.B. (1969), "On rational entrepreneurial behavior and the demand for investment", Review of Economic Studies 36(2):227–239.

Tweeten, L.G., and L. Quance (1969), "Positivistic measures of aggregate supply elasticities: Some new approaches", American Economic Review 59(2):175–183.

Ulveling, E.F., and L.B. Fletcher (1970), "A Cobb–Douglas production function with variable returns to scale", American Journal of Agricultural Economics 52(2):322–326.

Varian, H.R. (1984), "The nonparametric approach to production analysis", Econometrica 52(3):579–597.

Vasavada, U., and R.G. Chambers (1986), "Investment in US agriculture", American Journal of Agricultural Economics 68(4):950–960.

Walters, A.A. (1963), "Production and cost functions: An econometric survey", Econometrica 31(1–2):1–66.

Weaver, R.D. (1983), "Multiple input, multiple output production choices and technology in the US wheat region", American Journal of Agricultural Economics 65(1):45–56.

Wolfson, R.J. (1958), "An econometric investigation of regional differentials in American agricultural wages", Econometrica 26(2):225–257.

Working, E.J. (1927), "What do statistical demand curves show?", Quarterly Journal of Economics 41:212–235.

Wu, C.C. (1977), "Education in farm production: The case of Taiwan", American Journal of Agricultural Economics 59(4):699–709.

Yotopoulos, P.A. (1967), Allocative Efficiency in Economic Development (Center of Planning and Economic Research, Athens).

Yotopoulos, P.A., L.J. Lau and W.L. Lin (1976), "Microeconomic output supply and factor demand functions in the agriculture of the province of Taiwan", American Journal of Agricultural Economics 58(2):333–340.

Chapter 2

UNCERTAINTY, RISK AVERSION, AND RISK MANAGEMENT FOR AGRICULTURAL PRODUCERS

GIANCARLO MOSCHINI and DAVID A. HENNESSY

Department of Economics, Iowa State University, Ames, IA

Contents

Handbook of Agricultural Economics, Volume 1, Edited by B. Gardner and G. Rausser
© *2001 Elsevier Science B.V. All rights reserved*

Abstract

Uncertainty and risk are quintessential features of agricultural production. After a brief
overview of the main sources of agricultural risk, we provide an exposition of expected
utility theory and of the notion of risk aversion. This is followed by a basic analysis of
agricultural production decisions under risk, including some comparative statics results
from stylized models. Selected empirical topics are surveyed, with emphasis on risk
analyses as they pertain to production decisions at the farm level. Risk management is
then discussed, and a synthesis of hedging models is presented. We conclude with a detailed review of agricultural insurance, with emphasis on the moral hazard and adverse
selection problems that arise in the context of crop insurance.

JEL classification: Q12

1. Introduction

Because of the complexities of physical and economic systems, the unfolding of most processes that we care about exhibits attributes that cannot be forecast with absolute accuracy. The immediate implication of this *uncertainty* for economic agents is that many possible outcomes are usually associated with any one chosen action. Thus, decision making under uncertainty is characterized by *risk*, because typically not all possible consequences are equally desirable. Although uncertainty and risk are ubiquitous, in agriculture they constitute an essential feature of the production environment and arguably warrant a detailed analysis.

Considerable research has been devoted to exploring questions connected with the effects of uncertainty and risk in agriculture, and these efforts have paralleled related developments in the general economics literature. In this chapter we set out to review a number of these studies, especially as they relate to farm-level production decisions. To economize on our coverage of earlier work, and at the risk of not doing justice to some ground-breaking studies, we can refer to Dillon's (1971) survey as a starting point. In addition to providing an exposition of expected utility (EU) theory, which contributed to rooting subsequent studies in modern economic analysis, that survey provides an exhaustive account of previous studies of uncertainty and risk in agricultural economics. Subsequent useful compendia include Anderson, Dillon and Hardaker (1977), who consider a comprehensive set of applications of decision theory to agricultural production under uncertainty, and Newbery and Stiglitz (1981), who not only provide a thorough study of commodity price stabilization issues, but also analyze a number of problems that are relevant to the understanding of risk in agriculture.

The aforementioned contributions have been accompanied and followed by considerable research that is relevant to our pursuit. As we undertake to provide a critical survey of these studies, we are mindful of the subjective bias and unintended oversights that an exercise such as this inevitably entails, a risk heightened in our case by the encompassing nature of the topic and the sheer volume of the relevant literature. We apologize for errors of omission and commission, and we hope that our review will nonetheless prove useful to the applied researcher.

1.1. Uncertainty and risk in agriculture

Despite the fact that any taxonomy is somewhat arbitrary, it is useful to start by outlining the main sources of uncertainty and risk that are relevant from the point of view of the agricultural producer. First, there is what can be broadly defined as *production uncertainty*: in agriculture the amount and quality of output that will result from a given bundle of inputs are typically not known with certainty, i.e., the production function is stochastic. This uncertainty is due to the fact that uncontrollable elements, such as weather, play a fundamental role in agricultural production. The effects of these uncontrollable factors are heightened by the fact that time itself plays a particularly important role in agricultural production, because long production lags are dictated by the biological processes that underlie the production of crops and the growth of animals. Although there are parallels in other production activities, it is fair to say that production uncertainty is a quintessential feature of agricultural production.

Price uncertainty is also a standard attribute of farming activities. Because of the biological production lags mentioned above, production decisions have to be made far in advance of realizing the final product, so that the market price for the output is typically not known at the time these decisions have to be made. Price uncertainty, of course, is all the more relevant because of the inherent volatility of agricultural markets. Such volatility may be due to demand fluctuations, which are particularly important when a sizable portion of output is destined for the export market. Production uncertainty as discussed earlier, however, also contributes to price uncertainty because price needs to adjust to clear the market. In this process some typical features of agricultural markets (a large number of competitive producers, relatively homogeneous output, and inelastic demand) are responsible for generating considerable price volatility, even for moderate production shocks.

Additional sources of uncertainty are relevant to farming decisions when longer-term economic problems are considered. *Technological uncertainty*, associated with the evolution of production techniques that may make quasi-fixed past investments obsolete, emerges as a marked feature of agricultural production. Clearly, the randomness of new knowledge development affects production technologies in all sectors. What makes it perhaps more relevant to agriculture, however, is the fact that technological innovations here are the product of research and development efforts carried out elsewhere (for instance, by firms supplying inputs to agriculture), such that competitive farmers are captive players in the process. *Policy uncertainty* also plays an important role in agriculture. Again, economic policies have impacts on all sectors through their effects on such things as taxes, interest rates, exchange rates, regulation, provision of public goods, and so on. Yet, because agriculture in many countries is characterized by an intricate system of government interventions, and because the need for changing these policy interventions in recent times has remained strong (witness the recent transformation of key features of the agricultural policy of the United States and the European Union, or the emerging concerns about the environmental impacts of agricultural production), this source of uncertainty creates considerable risk for agricultural investments.

1.2. Modeling issues

Two concepts of paramount importance in economic modeling are *optimization* (the rational behavior of economic agents) and *equilibrium* (the balancing of individual claims in a market setting). The application of both of these concepts raises problematic issues when uncertainty is involved. In particular, to apply the powerful apparatus of optimization to individual choices under uncertainty one needs to determine what exactly is being optimized. Although a universally satisfactory answer to this question is far from obvious, the most widely used idea is that agents exposed to uncertainty and risk maximize expected utility. This paradigm represents the culmination of a research program that dates back to Bernoulli (1738), and rests on some compelling assumptions about individual choice. Most of the applications that we will review rely on the EU model (indeed, often some restricted version of it). Thus, in what follows we will briefly review the EU hypothesis before we proceed with a survey of applications. We should note, however, that despite its normative appeal, the EU framework has recently come under intense scrutiny because of its inability to describe some features of individual behavior under risk, and a number of generalizations of the EU model have been proposed [Machina (1987), Quiggin (1993)].

A modeling strategy that recurs in the applied literature is the distinction between uncertainty and risk attributed to Knight (1921). According to this view, risk arises when the stochastic elements of a decision problem can be characterized in terms of numerical objective probabilities, whereas uncertainty refers to decision settings with random outcomes that lack such objective probabilities. With the widespread acceptance of probabilities as subjective beliefs, Knight's distinction between risk and uncertainty is virtually meaningless and, like other authors [e.g., Hirshleifer and Riley (1992)], we will ignore it here.[1] Thus, the notions of uncertainty and risk are interchangeable in what follows, although, like Robison and Barry (1987), we tend to use the word *uncertainty* mostly to describe the environment in which economics decisions are made, and the word *risk* to characterize the economically relevant implications of uncertainty.

2. Decision making under uncertainty

Economic models of individual choice are necessarily rooted in the assumption of rationality on the part of decision makers. Perhaps the most common and widely understood such model is given by the neoclassical theory of consumer choice under certainty. The primitive assumption is that there is a preference ordering on commodity bundles that satisfies the consistency requirements of completeness and transitivity. These basic rationality postulates, coupled with the assumption of continuity (a hardly avoidable and basically harmless mathematical simplification), allow consumer choices to be characterized in terms of an ordinal utility function, a construct that enhances the analytical power of the assumptions. Choice under uncertainty could be characterized within this elementary setting, given minor modification of the original assumptions. For example, as in Debreu (1959), the standard preference ordering of neoclassical consumption theory could be applied to state-contingent commodity bundles. The analysis can then proceed without reference to the probability of the various states of nature. Whereas such an approach has proven useful for some problems [Arrow (1964), Hirshleifer (1966)], for a number of other cases, including applications typically of interest to agricultural economists, a more specific framework of analysis is desirable. By explicitly recognizing the mutually exclusive nature of alternative random consequences,

---

[1] We should note, however, that in some cases this approach is not totally satisfactory, as illustrated for example by the so-called Ellsberg paradox [Ellsberg (1961)].

one can get a powerful representation of decision making under uncertainty. This leads to the so-called EU model of decision under uncertainty, arguably the most important achievement of modern economic analysis of individual behavior. Although there exist a number of lucid expositions of this model [for a textbook treatment, see Mas-Colell et al. (1995, Chapter 6)], we present (somewhat informally) the main features of EU theory, to set the stage for the review of applications that follows.

2.1. Preferences over lotteries and the expected utility model

Let A represent the set of all possible actions available to decision makers, and let S represent the set of all possible states of nature. The specific action chosen by the agent and the particular state of nature that is realized (with the former choice being made prior to the resolution of uncertainty about the true state of nature) determine the outcomes (consequences) that the agent cares about. In other words, consequences are random variables as given by the function $c : S \times A \to C$, where C is the set of all possible consequences. For example, C could be the set of all possible commodity bundles as in standard consumer theory, in which case $C = \mathbb{R}^n_+$. Alternatively, as in many applications, it is monetary outcomes that are of interest to the decision makers, in which case one can put $C = \mathbb{R}$. Suppose for simplicity that the set C is finite, and that there are N possible consequences. Given an objectively known probability for each state of nature, then choosing a particular action will result in a probability distribution (a lottery, a gamble) over outcomes. Formally, one can define a lottery as a probability list $L \equiv (\ell_1, \ell_2, \ldots, \ell_N)$ such that ℓ_i is the probability (likelihood) that consequence $c_i \in C$ will arise (of course, $\ell_i \in [0, 1]$ and $\sum_i \ell_i = 1$).

In this setting, primitive preferences are represented by a preference relation $\succsim$ defined over the set of all possible lotteries $\mathcal{L}$. Assuming that this relation is rational (complete and transitive) and satisfies a specific continuity assumption, then all lotteries can be ranked by a function $V : L \to \mathbb{R}$ in the sense that, for any two lotteries L and L', we have $L \succsim L' \Leftrightarrow V(L) \geqslant V(L')$. Because the underlying assumption is that the decision maker is concerned only with the ultimate consequences, compound lotteries in this setting are always equivalent to the corresponding reduced lottery. Thus, for example, a gamble that gives lottery L with probability λ and lottery L' with probability $(1 - \lambda)$ is equivalent to a simple lottery whose probabilities are given by the mixture $\lambda L + (1 - \lambda)L''$. So far, the parallel with standard consumer theory is quite close [in particular, for example, $V(L)$ is an ordinal function]. To get the EU model, a further assumption is required at this point, namely the "independence axiom" [Samuelson (1952)]. This condition requires that, if we consider the mixture of each of any two lotteries L and L' with another lottery L'', the preference ordering on the two resulting lotteries is independent of the particular common lottery L''. That is, for any L, L' and L'', and any $\lambda \in (0, 1)$,

$$L \succsim L' \Leftrightarrow \lambda L + (1 - \lambda)L'' \succsim \lambda L' + (1 - \lambda)L''. \tag{2.1}$$

One may note that an equivalent assumption in the standard choice problem of consumer theory would be very restrictive, which is why it is seldom made in that context. Here, however, the independence assumption is quite natural because of a fundamental feature of decision problems under uncertainty: consequences are mutually exclusive.[2]

The independence axiom, coupled with the other standard rational choice assumptions, has the remarkable implication that there exists a utility function defined over consequences, $U : C \to \mathbb{R}$, such that

$$L \succsim L' \Leftrightarrow \sum_{i=1}^{N} \ell_i U(c_i) \geqslant \sum_{i=1}^{N} \ell'_i U(c_i), \tag{2.2}$$

where again, ℓ_i is the probability that consequence c_i will attain under L and ℓ'_i is the probability that consequence c_i will attain under L'. In other words, with the independence axiom, the utility function over lotteries can always be represented as the mathematical expectation of a utility function defined over consequences, that is $V(L) = E[U(c)]$ where $E[\cdot]$ is the mathematical expectation operator. As such, the utility function $V(L)$ is linear in probabilities. The function $U(c)$ is usually referred to as the von Neumann–Morgenstern (vNM) utility function.[3] This vNM utility function $U(c)$ is monotonically increasing and is cardinal in the sense that it is defined up to an increasing linear transformation [that is, if $U(c)$ represents the preference relation $\succsim$, then any $\widehat{U}(c) \equiv \alpha + \beta U(c)$, with $\beta > 0$, provides an equivalent representation of this relation]. When the outcomes of interest are described by continuous random variables with joint cumulative distribution function $F(c)$, the EU model implies that $V(F) = \int U(c)\,dF(c)$. In conclusion, in the EU model the problem of selecting the action that induces the most preferred probability distribution reduces to that of maximizing the expected utility of outcomes.

Versions of the EU model more general than the one just discussed are available. Perhaps the most important is the EU model with subjective probability developed by Savage (1954).[4] In this framework one does not assume that the probabilities of various states of the world are objectively given. Rather, the existence of probabilities for the states of nature and of a vNM utility function for the consequences are both implied by a set of axioms. Prominent among these is the "sure-thing" axiom, roughly equivalent to the independence condition discussed earlier. A crucial element for this approach is that probabilities are inherently subjective, an idea pioneered by de Finetti (1931).

---

[2] Despite its theoretical appeal, the empirical validity of the independence axiom has been questioned, especially in light of the so-called Allais paradox [Allais (1953)].

[3] This convention recognizes these authors' pioneering contribution to the development of the EU model in [von Neumann and Morgenstern (1944)]. But others call $U(\cdot)$ the Bernoulli utility function, in recognition of Daniel Bernoulli's solution of the St. Petersburg paradox [Bernoulli (1738)], which anticipated some of the features of the EU model.

[4] Anscombe and Aumann (1963) provide an easier (albeit somewhat different) set-up within which one can derive Savage's subjective EU model.

2.2. Risk aversion

The EU model allows us to capture in a natural way the notion of risk aversion, which is a fundamental feature of the problem of choice under uncertainty. This notion is made precise when the consequences that matter to the decision maker are monetary outcomes, such that the vNM utility function is defined over wealth, say $U(w)$ where $w \in \mathbb{R}$ is realized wealth. In a very intuitive sense, a decision maker is said to be risk averse if, for every lottery $F(w)$, she will always prefer (at least weakly) the certain amount $E[w]$ to the lottery $F(w)$ itself, i.e., $U[\int w \, dF(w)] \geqslant \int U(w) \, dF(w)$ [Arrow (1965), Pratt (1964)]. But by Jensen's inequality, this condition is equivalent to $U(w)$ being concave. Thus, concavity of the vNM utility function provides the fundamental characterization of risk aversion.

In many applied problems it is of interest to quantify risk aversion. For example, when can we say that an agent a is more risk averse than another agent b? Given the representation of risk aversion in terms of the concavity of $U(\cdot)$, then we can say that agent a is globally more risk averse than agent b if we can find an increasing concave function $g(\cdot)$ such that $U_a = g(U_b)$, where U_i denotes the utility function of agent i ($i = a, b$). An interesting question, in this context, concerns how the degree of risk aversion of a given agent changes with the level of wealth. For this purpose, two measures of risk aversion that have become standard are the Arrow–Pratt coefficient of absolute risk aversion $A(w)$ and the Arrow–Pratt coefficient of relative risk aversion $R(w)$ [Arrow (1965), Pratt (1964)]. Because concavity of $U(w)$ is equivalent to risk aversion, the degree of concavity of $U(w)$, as captured for example by $U''(w)$, is a candidate to measure the degree of risk aversion. But because $U(w)$ is defined only up to an increasing linear transformation, we need to normalize by $U'(w) > 0$ to obtain a measure that is unique for a given preference ordering. Thus, the coefficient of absolute risk aversion is defined as $A(w) \equiv -U''(w)/U'(w)$.[5] As is apparent from its definition, absolute risk aversion is useful for comparing the attitude of an agent towards a given gamble at different levels of wealth. It seems natural to postulate that agents will become less averse to a given gamble as their wealth increases. This is the notion of decreasing absolute risk aversion (DARA), i.e., $A(w)$ is a decreasing function of w [when $A(w)$ is merely nonincreasing in w, the notion is labeled nonincreasing absolute risk aversion (NIARA)]. As we shall see, most comparative statics results of optimal choice under uncertainty rely on this condition.

Sometimes, however, it is interesting to inquire about the attitude of risk-averse decision makers towards gambles that are expressed as a fraction of their wealth. This type of risk preference is captured by the coefficient of relative risk aversion $R(w) \equiv wA(w)$. Unlike the case of absolute risk aversion, there are no compelling *a priori* reasons for

---

[5] Note that $A(w)$ can also be used to compare the risk aversion of two agents. If $A_a(w)$ and $A_b(w)$ are the coefficients derived from the vNM utility functions U_a and U_b, respectively, then agent a is more risk averse than agent b if $A_a(w) \geqslant A_b(w)$ for all w. This characterization is equivalent to that given earlier in terms of U_a being an increasing concave transformation of U_b.

any particular behavior of $R(w)$ with respect to w. An assumption that is sometimes invoked is that of nonincreasing relative risk aversion (NIRRA), implying that an agent should not become more averse to a gamble expressed as a fixed percentage of her wealth as the level of wealth increases.[6]

Of some interest for applied analysis are utility functions for which $A(w)$ and $R(w)$ are constant. The constant absolute risk aversion (CARA) utility function is given by $U(w) = -e^{-\lambda w}$, where λ is the (constant) coefficient of absolute risk aversion. The constant relative risk aversion (CRRA) utility function is given by $U(w) = (w^{1-\rho})/(1-\rho)$ if $\rho \neq 1$, and by $U(w) = \log(w)$ if $\rho = 1$, where ρ is the (constant) coefficient of relative risk aversion.[7]

2.3. Ranking distributions

As discussed, the choice problem under uncertainty can be thought of as a choice among distributions (lotteries), with risk-averse agents preferring distributions that are "less risky". But how can we rank distributions according to their riskiness? Earlier contributions tried to provide such ranking based on a univariate measure of variability, such as the variance or standard deviation [for example, the portfolio theory of Markowitz (1952) and Tobin (1958) relied on a *mean-standard deviation* approach]. But it was soon determined that, for arbitrary distributions, such ranking is always consistent with EU only if the vNM utility function is quadratic. Because of the restrictiveness of this condition, a more general approach has been worked out in what are known as the *stochastic dominance* conditions [Hadar and Russell (1969), Hanoch and Levy (1969), Rothschild and Stiglitz (1970)].

A distribution $F(w)$ is said to *first-order stochastically dominate* (FSD) another distribution $G(w)$ if, for every nondecreasing function $U(\cdot)$, we have

$$\int_{-\infty}^{\infty} U(w)\,dF(w) \geq \int_{-\infty}^{\infty} U(w)\,dG(w). \tag{2.3}$$

It can be shown that under FSD one must have $F(w) \leq G(w)$ for all w, a condition that provides an operational way of implementing FSD. Thus, this condition captures the idea that more is better in the sense that any agents for which w is a "good" should prefer $F(w)$ to $G(w)$. More to the point of choosing between distributions based on their riskiness, $F(w)$ is said to *second-order stochastically dominate* (SSD) another distribution $G(w)$ if the condition in (2.3) holds for every increasing and concave function $U(\cdot)$

---

[6] Arrow (1965) suggests that the value of $R(w)$ should hover around 1 and, if anything, should be increasing in w. His arguments are predicated on the requirement that the utility function be bounded, a condition that allows EU to escape a modified St. Petersburg paradox [Menger (1934)]. The relevance of these boundedness arguments for the behavior of $R(w)$, however, depends on $U(\cdot)$ being defined on the domain $(0, +\infty)$, a requirement that can be safely dropped in most applications.

[7] Note that, whereas CARA utility can be defined on $(-\infty, +\infty)$, CRRA utility is at most defined on $(0, +\infty)$. CARA and CRRA are special cases of the Hyperbolic Absolute Risk Aversion utility function.

[such that any risk averter will prefer $F(w)$ to $G(w)$]. It can be shown that in such a case one has

$$\int_{-\infty}^{w} \left[F(t) - G(t) \right] dt \leqslant 0 \qquad\qquad (2.4)$$

for every w. Thus, (2.4) provides an operational characterization of SSD that can be used to compare distributions. A closely related notion is that of a *mean-preserving spread* [Rothschild and Stiglitz (1970)], which consists of taking probability mass away from a closed interval and allocating it outside that interval so that the mean of the distribution is unchanged. It turns out that, if a distribution function $G(\cdot)$ can be obtained from $F(\cdot)$ by a sequence of such mean-preserving spreads, then $F(\cdot)$ SSD the distribution $G(\cdot)$. Thus, when $F(w)$ and $G(w)$ have the same mean, the notion of a mean-preserving spread is equivalent to that of second-order stochastic dominance.

One should note that FSD and SSD produce only partial ordering of probability distributions. It is quite possible for any two distributions that neither one stochastically dominates the other, so that we cannot know for sure which one would be preferred by a particular risk-averse agent. Still, stochastic dominance and mean-preserving spreads give a precise characterization of what it means to have an increase in risk, and these conditions have proved to be extremely useful in analyzing the economic impact of changes in risk [Rothschild and Stiglitz (1971)].

When the distributions being compared are restricted to belonging to a particular class, it turns out that the validity of ranking distributions based on their mean and standard deviation can be rescued. In particular, if all distributions being compared differ from one another by a location and scale parameter only [i.e., $G(w) = F(\mu + \sigma w)$, where μ and σ are the location and scale parameters, respectively], then, as Meyer (1987) has shown, the mean-standard deviation ordering of distributions is quite general, in the sense that it is equivalent (for this class of distributions) to second-order stochastic dominance ordering.[8] The location-scale condition is restrictive (for example, it requires that an increase in variance occurs if and only if a mean-preserving spread occurs). Nonetheless, this condition applies to a number of interesting economic problems by the very definition of the problems themselves (for example, the theory of the competitive firm under price uncertainty) and also has some expositional value as discussed by Meyer (1987).[9]

3. The agricultural producer under uncertainty and risk aversion

The decision environment of agricultural producers is generally multifaceted and complex. Many distinct sources of risk may exist, and many discretionary actions may be

---

[8] As argued by Sinn (1989), there seem to exist earlier statements of this result.

[9] In any case, it should be clear that this result does not establish equivalence between EU and a linear mean-variance objective function, a criterion used in many agricultural economics applications.

available to the decision maker. Decisions and realizations of randomness may occur at several points in time. Further, actions may influence the distributions of yet-to-be realized random variables, while the realizations of random variables may alter the consequences of subsequent actions. To represent such an intricate network of interactions is analytically very difficult, but insights are possible by focusing on simpler stylized models. Thus, in the analysis that follows we start with an exceedingly simple model, and then gradually increase the complexity of the decision environment that we study. But first, an outline of model specifications that have the most relevance to agricultural decision making under uncertainty is in order.

3.1. Modeling price and production uncertainty

As outlined earlier, the main risks that a typical farmer faces are due to the fact that output prices are not known with certainty when production decisions are made and that the production process contains inherent sources of uncertainty (i.e., the relevant technology is stochastic). It is important, therefore, to understand how these fundamental sources of risk affect production decisions.

To capture the essence of price risk for competitive producers, consider the problem of choosing output q to maximize $E[U(w_0 + \tilde{\pi})]$, where w_0 is the initial wealth and profit $\tilde{\pi}$ is random due to price uncertainty, that is,

$$\tilde{\pi} = \tilde{p}q - C(q, r) - K, \tag{3.1}$$

where $\tilde{p}$ denotes output price, $C(q, r)$ is the (variable) cost function (conditional on the vector of input prices r), and K represents fixed costs.[10] This is essentially the model considered by Sandmo (1971), among others. Note that, because there is no production uncertainty in this model, the technology of production has been conveniently represented by the cost function $C(q, r)$ so that the relevant choice problem can be couched as a single-variable unconstrained maximization problem.

When the production function is stochastic, it is clear that a standard cost function cannot represent the production technology [Pope and Chavas (1994)]. Thus, for the pure production uncertainty case, the production problem is best represented as that of choosing the vector of inputs x to maximize $E[U(w_0 + \tilde{\pi})]$, with random profit given by

$$\tilde{\pi} = pG(x; \tilde{e}) - rx - K, \tag{3.2}$$

where $G(x; \tilde{e})$ represents the stochastic production function by which realized output depends on the vector of inputs x and a vector of random variables $\tilde{e}$. The latter represents factors that are important for production but are typically outside the complete

---

[10] To emphasize and clarify what the source of uncertainty is in any particular model, the overstruck ˜ will often be used to denote a random variable.

control of the farmer (examples include weather conditions, pest infestations, and disease outbreaks). It is clear that, in general, the production uncertainty case is more difficult to handle than the pure price risk case. In particular, it is typically necessary to restrict one's attention to the special case where $\tilde{e}$ is a single random variable. Versions of this model have been studied by Pope and Kramer (1979) and MacMinn and Holtmann (1983), among others.

Because price and production uncertainty are both relevant to agricultural production, it seems that the relevant model should allow for both sources of risk. Essentially, this entails making price p a random variable in (3.2). Joint consideration of price and production risk turns out to be rather difficult. Some results can be obtained, however, if the production risk is multiplicative, an assumption that was systematically used by Newbery and Stiglitz (1981), by Innes (1990), and by Innes and Rausser (1989). Specifically, the production function is written as $\tilde{e}H(x)$, where $\tilde{e}$ is a non-negative random variable (without loss of generality, assume $E[\tilde{e}] = 1$), and so one chooses input vector x to maximize $E[U(w_0 + \tilde{\pi})]$ with random profit given by

$$\tilde{\pi} = \tilde{p}\tilde{e}H(x) - rx - K. \tag{3.3}$$

Obviously, if the analysis is restricted to the consideration of a single random variable $\tilde{\varepsilon} \equiv \tilde{p}\tilde{e}$, it is clear that this model is isomorphic to the pure price risk case. In fact, as noted by a number of authors [Pope and Chavas (1994), Lapan and Moschini (1994), O'Donnell and Woodland (1995)], in this case there exists a standard cost function conditional on expected output, say $C(\overline{q}, r)$ where $\overline{q}$ is expected output,[11] that is dual to the production technology. Hence, the decision problem under joint price and (multiplicative) production risk can also be expressed as a single-variable unconstrained optimization problem because random profit in (3.3) can be equivalently expressed as

$$\tilde{\pi} = \tilde{p}\tilde{e}\overline{q} - C(\overline{q}, r) - K. \tag{3.4}$$

Before proceeding, we may note some restrictive features of the models just outlined. First, the models are static. There are essentially only two dates: the date at which decisions are made and the date at which uncertainty is realized (in particular, all decisions here are made before the resolution of uncertainty). Second, we are considering only one output and, for the time being, we are ignoring the possibility of risk management strategies. Although some of these assumptions will be relaxed later, such simplifications are necessary to get insights into the basic features of the production problem under risk.

In this setting, the basic questions that one may want to ask are:
  (i) How does the existence of uncertainty affect choice?
  (ii) Given uncertainty, how does a change in an exogenous variable affect choice? and

---

[11] Hence, for any given vector x of inputs, $\overline{q} = H(x)$.

(iii) To what extent does the existence of uncertainty alter the nature of the optimization problem faced by the decision maker?

For three of the basic contexts that we have outlined above (pure price risk, pure production risk with only one random variable, and joint price and production risk with multiplicative production risk), the answers to these questions can be characterized in a unified framework.

3.2. Static models under risk neutrality

Section 2 presented some concepts concerning the effects of riskiness on the expected value of a function. The first- and second-derivatives of a function were found to be key in determining how shifts in a stochastic distribution affect the expected value of a function. Although the structure of risk preferences, as expressed by the utility function, is certainly of consequence in determining the effects of risk on choice, risk-neutral decision makers may also be influenced by risk. Consider an expected profit-maximizing producer who faces a profile of profit opportunities $z(a, \beta, \tilde{\varepsilon})$ where a is a vector of choices (actions) at the discretion of the producer, β is a vector of exogenous parameters, and $\tilde{\varepsilon}$ is a single random variable that follows the cumulative distribution function $F(\varepsilon)$. Without loss of generality, let $\varepsilon \in [0, 1]$. The producer's problem is to

$$\underset{a}{\text{Max}} \int_0^1 z(a, \beta, \varepsilon) \, dF(\varepsilon), \tag{3.5}$$

which yields the vector of first-order conditions

$$\int_0^1 z_a(a, \beta, \varepsilon) \, dF(\varepsilon) = 0, \quad \text{where } z_a(\cdot) \equiv \partial z(\cdot)/\partial a.$$

Assuming that the choice vector is a singleton, and given concavity of $z(a, \beta, \tilde{\varepsilon})$ in a, from the concepts of stochastic dominance discussed earlier it is clear that an FSD shift in $\tilde{\varepsilon}$ will increase optimal a if $z_{a\varepsilon}(a, \beta, \varepsilon) \geqslant 0 \ \forall \varepsilon \in [0, 1]$, whereas an SSD shift will increase optimal choice if, for all $\varepsilon \in [0, 1]$, $z_{a\varepsilon}(a, \beta, \varepsilon) \geqslant 0$ and $z_{a\varepsilon\varepsilon}(a, \beta, \varepsilon) \leqslant 0$.

A specification of $z(a, \beta, \tilde{\varepsilon})$ which is of immediate interest is that of pure price risk as given by (3.1), where $a \equiv q$ and where the stochastic output price satisfies $\tilde{p} = \beta_1 + (\tilde{\varepsilon} - \bar{\varepsilon})\beta_2$ (here $\bar{\varepsilon} \equiv \text{E}[\tilde{\varepsilon}]$). One may interpret $\beta_1 + (\tilde{\varepsilon} - \bar{\varepsilon})\beta_2$ as a location and scale family of stochastic output price distributions with mean price equal to $\beta_1 \equiv \bar{p} \geqslant 0$, and the price variation parameter equal to $\beta_2 \geqslant 0$. Then the first-order condition for expected profit maximization is $\bar{p} - C_q(q, r) = 0$, and only the mean of the stochastic price is of relevance in determining optimal choice.

The more general form, where $\tilde{\varepsilon}$ cannot be separated out in this manner, may arise when production is stochastic. Then, even if $z_{a\varepsilon}(\cdot) \geqslant 0$, an increase in $\bar{\varepsilon}$ does not necessarily imply an increase in optimal a. The stochastic shift in $\tilde{\varepsilon}$ must be of the FSD dominating type, and an increase in the mean of $\tilde{\varepsilon}$ is necessary but insufficient for such a shift to occur.

It is also interesting to note that, in this risk-neutral case, an increase in an exogenous variable, say β_i, will increase optimal choice if $z_{a\beta_i}(a, \beta, \varepsilon) \geqslant 0 \; \forall \varepsilon \in [0, 1]$, regardless of the distribution of $\tilde{\varepsilon}$:

$$
\frac{\mathrm{d}a}{\mathrm{d}\beta_i} = -\frac{\int_0^1 z_{a\beta_i}(a, \beta, \varepsilon) \, \mathrm{d}F(\varepsilon)}{\int_0^1 z_{aa}(a, \beta, \varepsilon) \, \mathrm{d}F(\varepsilon)} \geqslant 0. \tag{3.6}
$$

3.3. Static models under risk aversion

Given the payoff $z(a, \beta, \tilde{\varepsilon})$, the objective of a risk-averse producer is written as

$$
\operatorname*{Max}_a \int_0^1 U\big[z(a, \beta, \varepsilon)\big] \, \mathrm{d}F(\varepsilon), \tag{3.7}
$$

where $U(\cdot)$ is increasing and concave, profit $z(\cdot)$ is held to increase in ε, and the objective function is concave in a, i.e., $\Delta \equiv \mathrm{E}\{U_{zz}[\cdot][z_a(\cdot)]^2 + U_z[\cdot]z_{aa}(\cdot)\} < 0$. Aspects of this problem, such as requirements on the nature of the utility function and payoff function and on the nature of the stochastic shift such that a increases, have been considered in some detail by Meyer and Ormiston (1983, 1985) and Eeckhoudt and Hansen (1992), among others. The first-order condition is

$$
\int_0^1 U_z\big[z(a, \beta, \varepsilon)\big] z_a(a, \beta, \varepsilon) \, \mathrm{d}F(\varepsilon) = 0, \tag{3.8}
$$

with parameterized solution at the value $a^* = a[F(\varepsilon), \beta]$.

3.3.1. Introduction of uncertainty

To ascertain how uncertainty affects choice for a risk averter, we will follow Krause (1979) and Katz (1981) and compare the solution under uncertainty with the solution when uncertainty is removed by setting the random element equal to its mean (i.e., setting $\tilde{\varepsilon} = \bar{\varepsilon}$). When uncertainty is removed, risk preferences are irrelevant, and the optimal choice $\hat{a}$ satisfies $z_a(\hat{a}, \beta, \bar{\varepsilon}) = 0$. When uncertainty exists, on the other hand, then the first-order condition can be expressed as

$$
\mathrm{Cov}\big[U_z(\cdot), z_a(\cdot)\big] + \mathrm{E}\big[U_z(\cdot)\big]\mathrm{E}\big[z_a(\cdot)\big] = 0. \tag{3.9}
$$

If $z_{a\varepsilon}(\cdot) \geqslant 0$, then the fact that the expectation of the product of two negatively covarying variates is less than the product of the expectations, together with risk aversion, implies that the covariance term must be negative. Because marginal utility is positive, satisfaction of the first-order condition requires that $\mathrm{E}[z_a(\cdot)] \geqslant 0$ when $z_{a\varepsilon}(\cdot) \geqslant 0$. We wish to compare a^*, the solution under uncertainty, with $\hat{a}$. If $z_{a\varepsilon\varepsilon}(\cdot) \leqslant 0$, then Jensen's inequality implies $\mathrm{E}[z_a(\hat{a}, \beta, \tilde{\varepsilon})] \leqslant 0$. But we know that $\mathrm{E}[z_a(a^*, \beta, \tilde{\varepsilon})] \geqslant 0$

given $z_{a\varepsilon}(\cdot) \geqslant 0$, and it follows that $\mathrm{E}[z_a(a^*, \beta, \tilde{\varepsilon})] - \mathrm{E}[z_a(\hat{a}, \beta, \tilde{\varepsilon})] \geqslant 0$. Because the only difference between the two expectations is the evaluation of a, and because $z_a(\cdot)$ is decreasing in a, then $a^* < \hat{a}$ [Krause (1979)]. The reduction in optimal a arises for two reasons. First, even for a risk-neutral producer, the existence of uncertainty reduces input use because it decreases the expected marginal value of the input, $\mathrm{E}[z_a(\cdot)]$. Second, risk aversion means that the increase in utility associated with an increase in $\tilde{\varepsilon}$ from $\overline{\varepsilon}$ is (in absolute value) lower than the decrease in utility associated with a decrease of the same magnitude in $\tilde{\varepsilon}$ from $\overline{\varepsilon}$. Because $z_{a\varepsilon}(\cdot) \geqslant 0$ (that is, an increase in a renders the payoff function more sensitive to the source of risk), the risk-averse producer will reduce sensitivity by decreasing a.

For an expected utility maximizer with payoff (3.1) (i.e., a competitive producer under price uncertainty only), it is clear that $z_{a\varepsilon}(\cdot) = 1 \geqslant 0$ and $z_{a\varepsilon\varepsilon}(\cdot) = 0 \leqslant 0$, so that the existence of price uncertainty reduces production. For payoff (3.2) (i.e., a competitive producer with stochastic production), $G_{a\varepsilon}(\cdot) \geqslant 0$ and $G_{a\varepsilon\varepsilon}(\cdot) \leqslant 0$ are sufficient conditions to sign the impact of introducing uncertainty. For a detailed analysis of input choice under stochastic production for risk-averse agents see Ramaswami (1992), who established requirements on an input-conditioned distribution function for a risk averter to choose less, or more, than an expected profit maximizer. A parallel analysis of Equation (3.9) shows that when $z_{a\varepsilon}(\cdot) \leqslant 0$ and $z_{a\varepsilon\varepsilon}(\cdot) \geqslant 0$, then risk aversion implies $a^* \geqslant \hat{a}$. The price uncertainty payoff [Equation (3.1)] never conforms to $z_{a\varepsilon}(\cdot) \leqslant 0$, but the production uncertainty model may. Thus, we see that the impact of the existence of uncertainty on optimal choice by a risk averter depends upon second and third cross-derivatives of the payoff function.

3.3.2. Marginal changes in environment

We now look at marginal changes in the decision environment, as represented by an increase in β. Intuitively, we know that the conditions required to identify the effects of these marginal changes are likely to be more stringent than those required to sign the effects of introducing uncertainty. Following Ormiston (1992), we differentiate Equation (3.8) partially with respect to a and β to obtain

$$\frac{\mathrm{d}a^*}{\mathrm{d}\beta} = \frac{1}{\Delta} \int_0^1 A[z] z_\beta(\cdot) U_z[\cdot] z_a(\cdot) \, \mathrm{d}F(\varepsilon) - \frac{1}{\Delta} \int_0^1 U_z[\cdot] z_{a\beta}(\cdot) \, \mathrm{d}F(\varepsilon), \qquad (3.10)$$

where $A[\cdot] = -U_{zz}[\cdot]/U_z[\cdot]$ is the absolute risk-aversion function defined earlier. Now we can partition the effect of β on a in three, which we will call (A) the wealth impact, (B) the insurance impact, and (C) the coupling impact [Hennessy (1998)]. The coupling impact is represented by the expression $-\int_0^1 U_z[\cdot] z_{a\beta}(\cdot) \, \mathrm{d}F(\varepsilon)/\Delta$ in (3.10) and has the sign of $z_{a\beta}(\cdot)$ if this term is uniform in sign. If β acts to increase the marginal effect of a on payoff $z(\cdot)$, then it will increase the producer's disposition to use a. For the price uncertainty case of (3.1) with $\tilde{p} = \beta_1 + (\tilde{\varepsilon} - \overline{\varepsilon})\beta_2$, we have $z_{a\beta_1}(\cdot) = 1$. For the production uncertainty case of (3.2), where p is a nonstochastic shift variable, we have $z_{ap}(\cdot) = G_a(\cdot) > 0$.

Many agricultural support policies are constructed with the specific intent of having or not having a coupling effect. A price subsidy on an exogenous, institutional output or input quantity is decoupled in the sense that $z_{a\beta}(\cdot) = 0$, whereas with a true price subsidy the actual quantity is coupled. As an illustration, a modification of specification (3.1) is

$$z(a, \beta, \tilde{\varepsilon}) = [\beta_1 + (\tilde{\varepsilon} - \bar{\varepsilon})\beta_2]a - C(a, r) - K + \beta_3 G(a^0),$$

where $G(a^0)$ is some exogenous institutional reference production level. Here, $z_{a\beta_1}(\cdot) \geqslant 0$, but $z_{a\beta_3}(\cdot) = 0$. However, $z_{a\beta_2}(\cdot) = \tilde{\varepsilon} - \bar{\varepsilon}$ in this case, and this coupling effect does not have a uniform sign.

Effects (A) and (B) are intertwined in the first term on the right-hand side of (3.10). Let $J(\cdot, \varepsilon) \equiv A[\cdot]z_\beta(\cdot)$, so the expression is $Q \equiv \int_0^1 J(\cdot, \varepsilon)U_z[\cdot]z_a(\cdot)\, \mathrm{d}F(\varepsilon)/\Delta$. Integrating by parts yields

$$Q = \frac{1}{\Delta}\left[J(\cdot, v)\int_0^v U_z[\cdot]z_a(\cdot)\, \mathrm{d}F(\varepsilon) \Big|_{v=0}^{v=1} - \int_0^1 \int_0^v U_z[\cdot]z_a(\cdot)\, \mathrm{d}F(\varepsilon)\frac{\mathrm{d}J(\cdot, v)}{\mathrm{d}v}\, \mathrm{d}v \right],$$

$$= -\frac{1}{\Delta}\int_0^1 \int_0^v U_z[\cdot]z_a(\cdot)\, \mathrm{d}F(\varepsilon)\frac{\mathrm{d}J(\cdot, v)}{\mathrm{d}v}\, \mathrm{d}v, \tag{3.11}$$

where v is used as the dummy variable of integration for the variable ε. To identify effects (A) and (B) note that, if $z_{a\varepsilon}(\cdot) \geqslant 0$, the first-order condition (3.8) implies that the expression $\int_0^v U_z[\cdot]z_a(\cdot)\, \mathrm{d}F(\varepsilon)$ is never positive because of the positivity of marginal utility and because $z_a(\cdot)$ is negative at low ε and increases to be positive at high ε. Therefore, given $\Delta < 0$, Q is positive if $\mathrm{d}J(\cdot, v)/\mathrm{d}v \leqslant 0$. Differentiate to obtain $\mathrm{d}J(\cdot, v)/\mathrm{d}v = z_\beta(\cdot)A_z[\cdot]z_\varepsilon(\cdot) + A[\cdot]z_{\beta\varepsilon}(\cdot)$. The first part of this expression may be called the wealth effect (A) because its negativity depends upon the NIARA property and the sign of $z_\beta(\cdot)$ (recall that $z_\varepsilon(\cdot) \geqslant 0$). All other things equal, if β shifts the distribution of payoffs rightward ($z_\beta(\cdot) \geqslant 0$), as would be the case with a reduction in fixed costs K in payoff specifications (3.1) or (3.2), and if preferences are NIARA ($A_z[\cdot] \leqslant 0$), then a increases. When $\tilde{p} = \beta_1 + (\tilde{\varepsilon} - \bar{\varepsilon})\beta_2$, then $z_{\beta_1}(\cdot) \geqslant 0$ for specification (3.1). Because $z_{a\beta_1}(\cdot) \geqslant 0$, both coupling and wealth effects act to increase optimal a, and this is the Sandmo (1971) result that NIARA is sufficient for a shift in mean price to increase production. Notice that because $z_{\varepsilon\beta_1}(\cdot) = 0$, the second part of $\mathrm{d}J(\cdot)/\mathrm{d}v$ may be ignored. Whereas β_1 has both wealth and coupling effects, it is easy to describe a wealth effect that does not also involve coupling. Setting $z(a, \beta, \tilde{\varepsilon}) = [\beta_1 + (\tilde{\varepsilon} - \bar{\varepsilon})\beta_2]a - C(a, r) - K + \beta_3 G(a_0)$, an increase in β_3 or a decrease in K induces an increase in optimal a under NIARA. Coupling may also occur without wealth effects, although this case is somewhat more difficult to show.

The second part, $A[\cdot]z_{\beta\varepsilon}(\cdot)$, is the insurance effect (B). If the favorable exogenous shift acts to stabilize income, that is if $z_{\beta\varepsilon}(\cdot) \leqslant 0$ or β advances less fortunate states of the environment by more than it advances more fortunate states, then optimal a tends to increase. This would occur in specification (3.2) if $\beta = p$ and $G_{p\varepsilon}(\cdot) \leqslant 0$. In the case of an insurance contract on the source of uncertainty, say $M(\beta, \tilde{\varepsilon})$, the payoff is $pG(a, \tilde{\varepsilon}) - wa - K + M(\beta, \tilde{\varepsilon})$ and the insurance contract decreases risk if $M_{\beta\varepsilon}(\cdot) \leqslant 0$ while $pG_{\varepsilon}(\cdot) + M_{\varepsilon}(\cdot) \geqslant 0$. The similarity of wealth (i.e., risk aversion) and insurance effects has been discussed in detail by Jewitt (1987).

Because of the price uncertainty inherent in agricultural production environments, the effect of an increase in β_2 for the specification (3.1), where $\tilde{p} = \beta_1 + (\tilde{\varepsilon} - \bar{\varepsilon})\beta_2$, is of particular importance. From $z_{\varepsilon\beta_2} = 1$, it can be seen that the β_2 parameter has a negative insurance effect. It has already been concluded, however, that the coupling effect of β_2, that is $z_{a\beta_2}(\cdot)$, does not have a uniform sign. Thus, although it may be intuitive to expect that an increase in β_2 would decrease optimal a, to determine that requires more work in addition to the NIARA assumption [Batra and Ullah (1974), Ishii (1977)]. Since changing the parameter $\beta_2 \geqslant 0$ in this setting does not cover the set of all Rothschild and Stiglitz mean-preserving spreads, the above results do not demonstrate that all mean-preserving spreads of price decrease the optimal choice for the model in (3.1). Whereas Meyer and Ormiston (1989), Ormiston (1992), and Gollier (1995), among others, have made advances toward identifying precisely the set of spreads that act to decrease production for NIARA and various conditions on the payoff function, this problem has not yet been completely solved.[12]

3.3.3. Uncertainty and cost minimization

It is well known that profit maximization is predicated upon satisfaction of the cost minimization assumption. Does cost minimization continue to hold under risk, when the objective is expected utility maximization? It turns out that the answer is yes, provided that "cost minimization" is suitably defined. Consider the competitive firm where the input vector x is chosen to maximize $E[U(w_0 + \tilde{\pi})]$, where $\tilde{\pi} = R(x, \tilde{\varepsilon}) - rx$. Here $R(x, \tilde{\varepsilon})$ is a revenue profile (that can accommodate both price and/or production uncertainty) and $\tilde{\varepsilon}$ denotes the source of revenue uncertainty. Pope and Chavas (1994) show that, if the revenue profile satisfies the restriction $R(x, \tilde{\varepsilon}) = K(\psi(x), \tilde{\varepsilon})$, where $\psi(x)$ is (possibly) vector-valued, then the relevant cost function can be written as $C(q^{\psi}, r)$, where q^{ψ} is the vector of conditioning values corresponding to the functions $\psi(x)$. Hence, technical efficiency is satisfied in the sense that the EU maximizing choice of x is consistent with the cost minimizing means of obtaining some (vector) level of $\psi(x)$. The simplest special case arises with multiplicative production risk, when $R(x, \tilde{\varepsilon}) = H(x)\tilde{\varepsilon}$. As anticipated in Section 3.1, in such a case the cost function is written as $C(\bar{q}, r)$, where $\bar{q}$ is

---

[12] The conclusions drawn thus far are, of course, only relevant for the given context. Noting that peasants in less developed countries often consume a significant fraction of their own production, Finkelshtain and Chalfant (1991) concluded that production and consumption decisions cannot be modeled separately for these agents. Their generalization of the Sandmo model suggests that production may plausibly increase under an increase in price uncertainty.

expected output. Thus, the relevant cost function for this special case is rather standard, with the expected output level playing the role of a deterministic output level under certainty. More generally, however, a vector of conditioning values will be needed. For example, if there is no price risk but the production function has the stochastic form suggested by Just and Pope (1978) (to be discussed further in Section 4.2), then revenue is written as $R = pM(x) + p[V(x)]^{1/2}\tilde{e}$ with $E[\tilde{e}] = 0$. It follows that the EU-consistent cost function here can be written as $C(\overline{q}, \sigma^2, r)$, where $\overline{q}$ is a level of expected output [corresponding to the function $M(x)$] and σ^2 is a level of output variance [corresponding to the function $V(x)$].

That cost minimization always holds for EU maximizers, even when the revenue profile does not satisfy the restriction invoked by Pope and Chavas (1994), is shown by Chambers and Quiggin (1998). Their approach is best illustrated for the production uncertainty case in which the random variable $\tilde{e}$ takes on a finite number (say N) of values. Given the stochastic production function $G(x, \tilde{e})$, then realized output for any given realization of the random variable (e_i, say) is $q_i = G(x, e_i)$. If ℓ_i denotes the probability of e_i occurring, then the producer's EU problem is

$$\text{Max}_{x} \sum_{i=1}^{N} \ell_i U(pG(x, e_i) - rx). \tag{3.12}$$

Now define a cost function $C(q_1, \ldots, q_N, r)$ as

$$C(q_1, q_2, \ldots, q_N, r) \equiv \text{Min}_{x}\{rx: q_i \leqslant G(x, e_i), \ \forall i = 1, 2, \ldots, N\}. \tag{3.13}$$

One may note the formal similarities of $C(q_1, \ldots, q_N, r)$ with a standard multioutput cost function, although the interpretation here is rather different. At any rate, it follows that the producer's EU maximization problem can be equivalently expressed as

$$\text{Max}_{q_1, q_2, \ldots, q_N} \sum_{i=1}^{N} \ell_i U(pq_i - C(q_1, q_2, \ldots, q_N, r)). \tag{3.14}$$

Thus, it is clear that EU maximizers do minimize costs, in some sense.

3.4. Dynamics and flexibility under uncertainty

A consideration of decision making under risk is not complete without discussion of the interactions between risk and time. Although suppressed in the two dates (one period) models discussed above (i.e., action at time 0 and realization at time 1), the fact is that time and uncertainty are intertwined because information sets become more complete as time passes. To illustrate, we consider a simple extension of the price uncertainty case of model (3.1). Specifically, let $a \equiv (x_1, x_2)$ such that $z(a, \beta, \tilde{\varepsilon})$ is of form $\tilde{\varepsilon}R(x_1, x_2) - r_1 x_1 - r_2 x_2$ where $\tilde{\varepsilon}$ represents stochastic output price, and assume that x_1 is chosen before the realization of $\tilde{\varepsilon}$, whereas x_2 is chosen after $\tilde{\varepsilon}$ is observed. Following Hartman (1976), the problem may be posed as

$$\underset{x_1}{\text{Max}} \int_0^1 \underset{x_2}{\text{Max}}\left[\varepsilon R(x_1, x_2) - r_2 x_2\right] dF(\varepsilon) - r_1 x_1. \tag{3.15}$$

Applying backward induction, the second-stage problem is solved first. The first-order condition is $\varepsilon R_{x_2}(x_1, x_2) = r_2$, where x_1 and ε are now predetermined. Assuming strict concavity of $R(\cdot)$ in x_2, the first-order condition is solved to yield $x_2^* = S(x_1, r_2, \varepsilon)$. Given this short-run demand function for x_2, the producer problem reduces to

$$\underset{x_1}{\text{Max}} \int_0^1 \left[\varepsilon R\big(x_1, S(x_1, r_2, \varepsilon)\big) - r_2 S(x_1, r_2, \varepsilon)\right] dF(\varepsilon) - r_1 x_1. \tag{3.16}$$

Defining $L(x_1, r_2, \varepsilon) \equiv \varepsilon R(x_1, S(x_1, r_2, \varepsilon)) - r_2 S(x_1, r_2, \varepsilon)$, the envelope theorem gives the first-order condition for the first-stage problem (choosing x_1) as

$$\int_0^1 L_{x_1}(x_1, r_2, \varepsilon)\, dF(\varepsilon) - r_1 = 0. \tag{3.17}$$

Now, the Rothschild and Stiglitz mean-preserving spread condition implies that optimum x_1 increases with such a spread if $L_{x_1 \varepsilon \varepsilon}(x_1, r_2, \varepsilon) \geq 0$. Setting optimum output as $G^*(x_1, r_2, \varepsilon)$, the envelope theorem can be used to show that this is the same as requiring $G^*_{x_1 \varepsilon}(x_1, r_2, \varepsilon) \geq 0$. Further analysis reveals that this condition is equivalent to the requirement that $\partial[R_{x_1 x_2}(\cdot)/R_{x_2 x_2}(\cdot)]/\partial x_2 \leq 0$. Thus, when ex-post flexibility exists, the effects of uncertainty depend upon relationships between third derivatives of the production technology. In general, although the impact of a mean-preserving spread in ε on the distribution of x_2^* depends upon the sign of $\partial^2 S(\cdot)/\partial \varepsilon^2$, the impact on x_1 is less readily signed and the effect on mean $R(\cdot)$ is yet more difficult to sign. Obviously, the analysis becomes even more involved when decision makers are assumed to be risk averse.

A second set of problems, called real option problems because of structural analogies with financial options, arise from the interactions between time and uncertainty in long-term investment decisions when there are sunk costs or irreversible actions. Consider a decision in 1999 to invest in precision farming education and equipment. At that time it was not yet clear whether the technology was worth adopting. The decision maker may invest early in the hope that the technology will turn out to be profitable. But the investment may turn out to be unprofitable, so there is also an incentive to defer the decision for a year, say, to learn more about the technology in the intervening period. But deferment will mean losing a year of additional profits if the technology turns out to be profitable. Similar sunk cost and information problems may arise in a number of other farm production decisions. Although real option problems such as these can be addressed by rigorous stochastic neoclassical models [e.g., Chavas (1994) or Feinerman et al. (1990)]

or by standard optimal control approaches [Rausser and Hochman (1979)], the more structured contingent claims approach popularized by Dixit and Pindyck (1994) has assumed prominence because it lends itself to empirical and theoretical analysis.

A stylized continuous-time variant of dynamic programming, real option theory connects time and uncertainty by modeling a source of randomness as a stochastic process evolving over time. Some such processes give rise to differential equation relationships between the distribution, time, and the flow of rewards. These relationships can be solved to give a decision-conditioned expected present value, and this expected present value is then optimized over the choice set. The choice set may involve deciding to invest now or to wait, or deciding how much to invest. Marcus and Modest (1984) studied optimal decisions for producers facing price and yield uncertainty and using futures markets, whereas Turvey (1992b) used the approach to study agricultural support policies in Canada. Purvis et al. (1995) adopted the framework to explain Texas dairy industry technology adoption decisions under cost and regulatory uncertainty, and found that the expected rate of return on the proposed investment might have to be double the threshold identified by a nonstochastic analysis for the decision to be attractive. The approach also provides a simple way of studying adjustment costs. For example, Leahy (1993) studied shutdown and startup costs for a competitive firm facing random prices.

4. Selected empirical issues

Our cursory review thus far has focused on analytical methods and theoretical analyses. But considerable empirical research in agricultural economics has been done to test, quantify, and otherwise put to use a number of features of risk models. In this section we will look, in some detail, at a number of contributions that have had a primarily empirical bent.

4.1. Identifying risk preferences

In an early empirical study of agricultural decision making under risk, Lin, Dean and Moore (1974) elicited preferences over hypothetical lotteries from managers of six large California farms. Using quadratic programming methods, they estimated the mean-variance frontier available to the farmer. They then compared the farm plans suggested by the elicited preference structure with plans suggested by the expected profit maximization rule, with plans suggested by lexicographic preference structures, and with the actual implemented plans. They found that, although no stylized preference structure was clearly a superior fit, for each of the six farms the EU framework performed at least as well as the other paradigms. For Nepalese rice farmers, Hamal and Anderson (1982) also used hypothetical lotteries and found evidence in support of DARA. The analysis was less conclusive concerning the slope of relative risk aversion.

Dillon and Scandizzo (1978) modified the approach of Lin, Dean and Moore (1974) by eliciting preferences from a relatively large number of subsistence farmers and sharecroppers in northeastern Brazil. Risk attitudes were imputed from choices between hypothetical lotteries that realistically reflected the farm payoffs faced by these decision makers. Unlike the study by Lin, Dean and Moore, however, the hypothetical decisions were not validated through comparison with actual decisions. The lotteries posed were of two types, those in which the family subsistence requirement was covered but surplus income was at risk, and those in which the subsistence requirement was also at risk. Hypothetical returns were adjusted until certainty equivalence between lottery comparisons was established. The replies were then fitted to three decision criteria: mean-standard deviation, mean-variance, and CARA expected utility objective functions. As expected, both farmers and sharecroppers tended to be more risk averse when subsistence income was at risk. Surprisingly, smallholders tended to be more risk averse than sharecroppers. Dillon and Scandizzo (1978) found less clear evidence about the impact of socioeconomic factors on risk attitudes. Perhaps the most interesting indication was that, even within seemingly homogeneous groups, a wide dispersion of risk preferences appeared to exist.

Taking an econometric approach, Moscardi and de Janvry (1977) estimated a Cobb–Douglas production function for corn with data from small Mexican subsistence farms. Using a safety-first framework, they imputed a measure of risk aversion from the divergence between actual fertilizing decisions and optimal decisions under risk neutrality. They found evidence of considerable risk aversion, and they also suggested that risk attitudes might be functions of socioeconomic variables (such as family size and age of operator) that may evolve over time. Brink and McCarl (1978) also estimated risk attitudes as a residual that rationalizes observed choices relative to "optimal" ones as predicted by a mathematical programming model (relying on a linear mean-standard deviation objective function). Thirty-eight Midwestern crop producers at a Purdue University decision analysis workshop listed their resources and identified their preferred crop acreage allocation plan. The risk parameter giving a plan deemed closest to the announced plan was assumed to represent risk preferences. The analysis concluded that risk aversion seemed to be low. Measuring risk essentially as a residual, however, is an obvious limitation of these studies (because such a procedure ignores other potential reasons for observed decisions to depart from the model's optimal decisions).

Because of the limitations of inferring risk from observed production decisions, and because hypothetical payout surveys can give unstable results, Binswanger (1980) made real payments to peasant farmers in India. Outcomes were determined by tossing a dice, and the amount at risk varied from 0.5 rupees to 500 rupees (negative payout states were not considered). The 500 rupees payout amounted to about 2.3 percent of average household wealth, and corresponded in magnitude to substantial fertilization investments. (It was believed that some households were constrained by capital resources from fertilizing adequately.) Preliminary tests found that individuals tended to treat money gifted to them on the day of the experiment for the purpose of participating in the experiment as if it were their own. Preliminary results also suggested that once lotteries for low gambles had primed individuals to making lottery decisions about real money, then a hypothetical 500 rupees game appeared to give results that were statistically similar to a real 500 rupees game. To conserve financial resources, the hypothetical 500 rupees game was used thereafter.

Capturing risk attitudes by the coefficient of partial risk aversion, it was found that subjects tended to become more risk averse as the size of the gamble increased.[13] Compared with the hypothetical scenario interviewing method, the imputed risk aversion coefficient was less dispersed when real money was involved. This would suggest that the interviewers may have had difficulty taking the interviews as seriously as they would real-world decisions. On the effects of socioeconomic characteristics, Binswanger (1980) found that wealthier, better-educated, and more progressive farmers tended to be less risk averse, as did those who had off-farm salaries. Prior luck in the game also tended to reduce the degree of risk aversion (only the luck regressor, however, had consistently high t statistics across all gamble sizes). Overall, Binswanger interpreted the results as being supportive of the hypothesis that it is resource and infrastructural constraints, such as access to information and credit, that induce caution among peasants rather than the hypothesis of innate conservatism.

In a different analysis of these Indian data, Binswanger (1981) considered the foundations of the EU framework and concluded that decision makers did not integrate possible outcomes from a gamble with pre-existing income, but rather treated them separately in their decision calculus. This conclusion is somewhat at variance with Binswanger's (1980) conclusion from pretest analysis that subjects treated gifted money as their own. The separation of gamble money from pre-existing wealth lends some support to Kahneman and Tversky's (1979) prospect theory approach to decision making. Failure of income integration has serious implications for modeling decisions, but has generally been ignored in the empirical literature. Binswanger also used inferences drawn from safety-first type models to identify inconsistencies with the data, and he concluded that the decision makers did not appear to act in a safety-first manner. Finally, Binswanger identified evidence in the data to support both DARA and decreasing relative risk aversion (DRRA) preferences.

Surveying work on risk preferences and risk management to that time (including work by Binswanger already cited), Young (1979) and Hazell (1982) raised concerns about all approaches. The direct elicitation (interview) method is reliable only to the extent that it captures the preference structure that would be used in real decisions, and evidence suggested that it might not do so. Experimental approaches might be too expensive to implement in developed countries.[14] Approaches based on observed supply and input demand behavior impute risk as the residual component explaining discrepancies between expected profit-maximizing solutions and actual decisions. But discrepancies may be due to other effects, such as imperfect information and heterogeneous resource

---

[13] The coefficient of partial risk aversion is defined as $-\pi U''(\pi + w_0)/U'(\pi + w_0)$, where w_0 is initial wealth and π is profit.

[14] Binswanger estimated that, were he to run his experiments in the United States, it would have cost $150,000 (circa 1978) rather than $2,500.

endowments. To the extent that such research had identified determinants of risk preferences, Young concluded that farmers in developing countries appeared to be more risk averse than those in developed countries, and he observed that this conclusion is consistent with DARA. But because the studies considered did not explicitly control for the availability and use of risk management institutions, which tend to be more widely available in developed countries, developed-country farmers may appear to be less risk averse than they actually are.

Returning to the task of econometrically estimating risk structures, Antle (1987) expressed the optimality conditions for EU maximizing choices in terms of a given individual's absolute risk aversion and downside risk aversion coefficients.[15] The Generalized Method of Moments (GMM) procedure was then applied to identify means, variances, and covariances of risk preference parameters based on data from the International Crops Research Institute for the Semi-Arid Tropics (ICRISAT) pertaining to one of the six Indian villages (Aurepalle) that had been considered by Binswanger (1980, 1981). Antle (1987) found a mean Arrow–Pratt index similar to that reported in Binswanger (1980). Dissatisfied that this approach required some, if only minimal, assumptions concerning the technology available, Antle (1989) developed a method that did not involve joint estimation with technology. Antle's view was that it would be better to estimate risk preference structures separately from technology rather than jointly. His concerns about a joint estimation arose mainly from problems involving the data required for the estimation of technology, and the discontent with alternative econometric approaches to joint estimation. The econometric methods applied again involved GMM estimation on data from the ICRISAT India village study. The means of the Arrow–Pratt and downside risk aversion indices were, as expected, similar to those estimated earlier.

Among other econometric estimations of risk attitudes, Myers (1989) assumed CRRA and joint lognormality of the distributions of output price and producer consumption, and developed a reduced-form rational expectations approach to testing for the aggregate level of relative risk aversion for U.S. producers who store crops. Annual data over the period 1945 to 1983 suggest a coefficient of relative risk aversion between 1.5 and 4.5 for corn and wheat storers, but the estimates for soybeans are implausible. Exploiting technical attributes of CRRA and of constant partial relative risk aversion (CPRRA),[16] Pope (1988) developed implications for optimal choices by individuals expressing such preferences. In Pope and Just (1991), these implications, together with implications for choice under CARA preferences, were tested on state-level Idaho potato acreage data. CARA and CPRRA hypotheses were rejected, but CRRA was not. Chavas and Holt (1990), studying U.S.-level corn and soybean acreage allocation decisions, also used the tests proposed by Pope (1988) and rejected both CRRA and CPRRA. Testing for the impact of wealth, proxied by an index of proprietor equity, on allocation decisions, they found evidence to reject CARA in favor of DARA.

---

[15] This downside risk aversion coefficient is defined as $U'''(\cdot)/U'(\cdot)$. Note that $U'''(\cdot) > 0$ is necessary for DARA. For the related, but distinct, coefficient of absolute prudence $(-U'''(\cdot)/U''(\cdot))$ see Kimball (1990).

[16] This means that $-\pi U''(\pi + w_0)/U'(\pi + w_0)$ is invariant to changes in π for the level of w_0 in question.

4.2. Estimating stochastic structures

As mentioned earlier, production risk is an essential feature of agriculture, and estimation of such stochastic production structures has obvious immediate interest for farm management as well as to address agricultural policy issues. For example, production uncertainty has implications for the implementation of crop insurance. Also, environmental externalities such as water contamination and ecosystem destruction may sometimes be traced back to the use of such agricultural inputs as nitrogen and pesticides; production uncertainty, together with risk aversion, may increase application of these inputs. Existing statistical procedures for studying relationships between stochastic distributions have tended to emphasize stochastically ordered comparisons, such as first- and second-degree dominance, between elements in a set of distributions. But economists, especially agricultural economists, are often interested in conditional relationships. To reconstruct nonparametric stochastic relationships between crop yield and input use would often require volumes of data beyond that usually available to analysts. Further, as the literature on the impacts of stochastic shifts on decisions has shown, the necessary and the sufficient conditions for a stochastic shift to have a determinate impact on the decisions of a meaningful class of decision makers are generally not among the simpler types of stochastic shifts.

The complexity of the decision environment is substantially reduced if one can treat technology as being nonrandom. If one is primarily concerned with price uncertainty, then it might be convenient to assume deterministic production. Thus, one can estimate the distribution of the realized random element without regard to the choices made. In other cases, however, it is not possible to simplify the decision environment in this way. Although random yield – the consequence of interactions between choices and random weather variables – can be measured, it would be more difficult to measure and aggregate in a meaningful manner the various dimensions of weather. In such a case, it is more convenient to estimate the input-conditioned distribution of yield. Although they do not lend themselves to estimating or testing for general production function relations, existing stochastic ordering methods can be useful in testing for the nature of and impacts of exogenous stochastic shifts in, say, the distribution of output price, and for studying discrete decisions such as the adoption of a new technology.

Although studies applying stochastic dominance methods to agricultural problems are numerous [e.g., Williams et al. (1993)], most of these studies compare point estimates of the distributions and do not consider sampling errors. Tolley and Pope (1988) developed a nonparametric permutation test to discern whether a second-order dominance relationship exists. More recently, Anderson (1996) used the nonparametric Pearson goodness-of-fit test on Canadian income distribution data over the years 1973 to 1989 to investigate, with levels of statistical confidence, whether first-, second-, and third-order stochastic dominance shifts occurred as time elapsed.

For input-conditioned output distributions, Just and Pope (1978) accounted for heteroskedasticity by developing a method of estimating a two-moment stochastic production function by three-stage non linear least squares techniques. The function is of the form

$$\tilde{q} = M(x) + \left[V(x)\right]^{1/2}\tilde{\varepsilon}, \tag{4.1}$$

where q is output, $E[\tilde{\varepsilon}] = 0$, $\text{Var}[\tilde{\varepsilon}] = 1$, and x is a vector of input choices. The functions $M(x)$ and $V(x)$ determine the conditional mean and variance of q, respectively, and can be chosen to be sufficiently flexible to meet the needs of the analysis. Just and Pope (1979) applied their method to Day's (1965) corn and oats yield-fertilization data set, and found the results generally, but not totally, supportive of the hypothesis that an increase in fertilization increases the variance of output. Their readily estimable approach has proven to be popular in applied analyses. For example Traxler et al. (1995) used the approach in a study of the yield attributes of different wheat varieties in the Yaqui Valley (Mexico), and found that whereas earlier varietal research appeared to emphasize increasing mean yield, later research appeared biased toward reducing yield variance.

Suggesting that mean and variance may not be sufficient statistics to describe stochastic production, Antle and Goodger (1984) used an approach due to Antle (1983) to estimate an arbitrarily large number of input-conditioned moments for large-scale California milk production. They rejected the statistical hypothesis that input-conditioned mean and variance are sufficient statistics. An interesting simulation finding was that a CARA decision maker facing the estimated technology substantially increased dairy rations relative to a risk-neutral decision maker. This suggests that the marginal risk premium in Ramaswami (1992) may be negative on occasion.

Nelson and Preckel (1989) identified the need for a flexible approach to estimating parametric yield distributions when accommodating skewness is important. Gallagher (1987), among others, has observed negative skewness for crop yields. The Just–Pope approach is insufficiently flexible, whereas the Antle–Goodger method, which is nonparametric, may be inefficient. Finding inspiration in Day's (1965) suggestion that the beta distribution would likely fit most yield distributions quite well, Nelson and Preckel conditioned beta distribution parameters on input choices. The output density function is then

$$f(q \mid x) = \frac{\Gamma(\alpha + \beta)}{\Gamma(\alpha)\Gamma(\beta)} \frac{(q - q^{\min})^{\alpha-1}(q^{\max} - q)^{\beta-1}}{(q^{\max} - q^{\min})^{\alpha+\beta-1}}, \tag{4.2}$$

where $\Gamma(\cdot)$ is the gamma function, output q is supported on the interval $[q^{\min}, q^{\max}]$, and the distribution parameters are conditional on inputs, i.e., $\alpha = \alpha(x)$ and $\beta = \beta(x)$. For field-level corn yields in five Iowa counties over the period 1961 to 1970, Nelson and Preckel set $q^{\min} = 0$, and let both $\alpha(x)$ and $\beta(x)$ be Cobb–Douglas functions of nitrogen, phosphorus, potassium, field slope, and soil clay content. Using a two-stage maximum likelihood method, they found that the marginal effects of nitrogen, phosphorus, and potassium on skewness, variance, and even mean were mixed in sign.

The maximum likelihood approach to estimating parameterized conditional densities has proven to be quite popular. A gamma distribution relationship between applied nitrogen levels and late spring soil nitrate levels has been used in Babcock and Blackmer (1992) to study the effects of information concerning spring soil nitrate levels on subsequent side-dressing and on expected profit; a beta distribution has been applied by Babcock and Hennessy (1996) to study input use in the presence of crop insurance. A different line of inquiry has sought to model the nonnormality of crop yield distributions by estimating transformations of the normal distribution. Taylor (1990) employed a hyperbolic trigonometric transformation to deviations from a linear yield trend estimation on corn, soybean, and wheat crops. Moss and Shonkwiler (1993) and Ramírez (1997) have extended this approach to accommodate stochastic yield trends and multivariate distributions, respectively. But the presumption that yields are not normally distributed has been called into question by Just and Weninger (1999), who criticize a number of features of statistical analyses implemented by previous studies and conclude that the empirical evidence against normality is weak.

Stochastic production has implications for the estimation of dual representations of production technologies. For example, as discussed in Section 2.3.3, when the production function is affected by multiplicative risk and producers maximize expected utility the relevant cost function is $C(\bar{q}, r)$, where $\bar{q}$ is expected output. When the stochastic production function is written more generally as $G(x, \tilde{e})$, the relevant cost function still has the structure $C(\bar{q}, r)$ if producers are risk neutral (they maximize expected profits).[17] Pope and Just (1996) call such a function the "ex ante cost function", and convincingly argue that a number of previous studies have resulted in inconsistent estimates of technological parameters because they have estimated a standard cost function $C(q, r)$ (conditional on realized output q) when in fact they should have been estimating $C(\bar{q}, r)$. Estimation of the ex ante cost function $C(\bar{q}, r)$ is problematic, on the other hand, because it is conditional on expected output $\bar{q}$, which is not observable. The solution proposed by Pope and Just (1996) entails estimating $\bar{q}$ jointly with the structure of the ex ante cost function. The specific procedure that they suggest fails to achieve consistent estimation of technological parameters because it does not address the nonlinear errors-in-variables problem that typically arises in this context [Moschini (1999)]. But by exploiting the full implications of expected profit maximization, Moschini (1999) shows that it is possible to effectively remove the errors-in-variables problem and obtain consistent estimation of the ex ante cost function parameters.

4.3. Joint estimation of preferences and technology

Most research studies considered thus far have sought to identify risk preferences without estimating the source of randomness, or they have sought to estimate the source

---

[17] Of course, in such a case the parameters of the cost function $C(\bar{q}, r)$ may include parameters of the distribution of the random variable $\tilde{e}$.

of randomness without simultaneously estimating the risk preference structure. Those papers that have simultaneously identified risk preferences and the source of randomness [e.g., Moscardi and de Janvry (1977)) or Antle (1987)] have treated either one or both components in a rather elementary manner. Separating the estimation of the two structures is econometrically inefficient to the extent that a joint estimation imposes cross-estimation restrictions and accommodates error correlations. Using a Just–Pope technology with Cobb–Douglas mean and variance functions together with a CARA risk preference structure, cross-equation restrictions and a nonlinear three-stage least squares estimator, Love and Buccola (1991) applied a joint estimation for Iowa corn and soybean production. The data pertained to three of the five counties studied by Nelson and Preckel (1989). Love and Buccola found considerable variation in the estimated coefficient of risk aversion across the three Iowa counties under consideration. Concerning technology, they contrasted their results with a straightforward Just–Pope estimation and with the Nelson and Preckel analysis to find that each estimated similar technology structures.

The Love and Buccola approach is restrictive in the sense that CARA was imposed. Chavas and Holt (1996) developed a joint estimation method that is able to test for CARA or DARA. Applying their estimator to corn and soybean acreage allocation in the United States, and on a data set much the same as that used in their 1990 work, they assumed that the production technology was a quadratic function of allocated acres and that the utility function is $u(\pi_t, t) = \int_L^{\pi_t} \exp(\alpha_0 + \alpha_1 z + \alpha_2 z^2 + \alpha_3 t)\, \mathrm{d}z$, where L is a lower bound on profit realizations, t is time, the α are parameters to be estimated, π_t is profit in year t, and z is a dummy variable of integration. Their analysis found strong statistical evidence for the presence of downside risk aversion and for rejecting CARA in favor of DARA.

Although the approach by Chavas and Holt does generalize the representation of risk preferences, the assumed technology was not flexible in the Just–Pope sense. Further, their specification can say little about the impact of relative risk aversion. Using Saha's (1993) expo-power utility specification, $U[\pi] = -\exp(-\beta\pi^\alpha)$ where α and β are parameters to be estimated, Saha, Shumway and Talpaz (1994) assumed a Just–Pope technology and jointly estimated the system using maximum likelihood methods. Data were for fifteen Kansas wheat farms over the four years 1979 to 1982, and there were two aggregated input indices in the stochastic technology (a capital index and a materials index). The results supported the hypotheses of DARA and increasing relative risk aversion (IRRA). Also, the materials index was found to be risk decreasing, so risk-averse agents may have a tendency to use more fertilizer and pesticides than risk-neutral agents.

Before leaving the issue of risk estimation, a comment is warranted about subsequent use of the estimates. There may be a tendency on the part of modelers engaged in policy simulation to use without qualification risk preference structures that were identified in previous research. Newbery and Stiglitz (1981, p. 73) have shown that caution is warranted in accommodating the particular circumstances of the simulation exercise. One must ensure that the chosen risk preference structure is consistent with reasonable levels of risk premia for the problem at hand. The set of coefficients of absolute risk aversion that give reasonable risk premia vary from problem to problem.

4.4. Econometric estimation of supply models with risk

One of the most widely agreed upon results from the theory of the firm under price uncertainty is that risk affects the optimal output level. Normally, the risk-averse producer is expected to produce less than the risk-neutral producer, ceteris paribus, and the risk-averse producer will adjust output to changing risk conditions (e.g., decrease production as risk increases). Econometric studies of agricultural supply decisions have for a long time tried to accommodate these features of the theory of the firm. There are essentially two reasons for wanting to do so: first, to find out whether the theory is relevant, i.e., to "test" whether there is response to risk in agricultural decisions; second, assuming that the theory is correct and risk aversion is important, accounting for risk response may improve the performance of econometric models for forecasting and/or policy evaluation, including welfare measurement related to risk bearing.

To pursue these two objectives, a prototypical model is to write supply decisions at time t as

$$y_t = \beta_0 + x_t'\beta_1 + \beta_2\mu_t + \beta_3\sigma_t^2 + e_t, \tag{4.3}$$

where y denotes supply, μ denotes the (subjective) conditional expectation of price, σ^2 denotes the (subjective) conditional variance of price, x represents the vector of all other variables affecting decisions, e is a random term, t indexes observations, and $(\beta_0, \beta_1, \beta_2, \beta_3)$ are parameters to be estimated (β_1 is a vector). Clearly, this formulation simplifies theory to the bone by choosing a particular functional form and, more important, by postulating that mean and variance can adequately capture the risk facing producers. Whereas more sophisticated models may be desirable, from an econometric point of view Equation (4.3) is already quite demanding. In particular, the subjective moments of the price distribution μ_t and σ_t^2 are unobserved, and thus to implement Equation (4.3) it is necessary to specify how these expectations are formed.

The specification of expectations for the first moment is a familiar problem in econometric estimation. Solutions that have been proposed range from naive expectations models (where $\mu_t = p_{t-1}$), to adaptive expectations (where μ_t is a geometrically weighted average of all past prices), to rational expectations (where μ_t is the mathematical expectation arrived at from an internally consistent model of price formation, for example). A review of price expectations formation for price levels is outside the scope of this chapter, but we note that, not surprisingly, parallel issues arise in the context of modeling variance. Behrman (1968) allowed for price risk to affect crop supply in a developing country by measuring σ_t^2 as a three-year moving average (but around the unconditional mean of price). Similar ad hoc procedures have been very common in other studies, although often with the improvement of a weighted (as opposed to simple) average of squared deviations from the conditional (as opposed to unconditional) expectation of the price level [e.g., Lin (1977), Traill (1978), Hurt and Garcia (1982), Sengupta and Sfeir (1982), Brorsen et al. (1987), Chavas and Holt (1990, 1996)]. A more ambitious and coherent framework was proposed by Just (1974, 1976), whereby first and second moments of price are modeled to the same degree of flexibility by extending Nerlove's (1958) notion of adaptive expectations to the variance of price. This procedure has been used in other studies, including [Pope and Just (1991), Antonovitz and Green (1990), and Aradhyula and Holt (1990)]. More recently, advances have been made by modeling the time-varying variance within the autoregressive conditional heteroskedasticity (ARCH) framework of [Engle (1982)], as in [Aradhyula and Holt (1989, 1990), Holt and Moschini (1992), and Holt (1993)].

The empirical evidence suggests that risk variables are often significant in explaining agricultural production decisions. The early work by Just (1974), as well as some other studies, has suggested that the size of this supply response to risk may be quite large, but the quantitative dimension of this risk response is more difficult to assess because results are typically not reported in a standardized manner. For example, an interesting question in the context of supply response concerns the size of the likely output contraction due to risk. As model (4.3) suggests, an approximate estimate of this output reduction (in percentage terms) is simply given by the elasticity of supply with respect to the price variance σ_t^2, but this basic statistic often is not reported. As a yardstick, however, we note that for broiler production Aradhyula and Holt (1990) found a long-run price variance elasticity of -0.03, whereas for sow farrowing, the comparable long-run elasticity estimated by Holt and Moschini (1992) was -0.13.

Although such estimates may suggest a fairly sizeable production response to the presence of risk, caution is in order for several reasons. First, as is often the case in applied economic modeling, these empirical results are drawn from models that are based on individual behavior but that are estimated with aggregate data without explicit consideration of aggregation conditions. Second, insofar as producers use appropriate risk management procedures (see Section 5), the conditional variance typically used may not be measuring the relevant risk.[18] Finally, estimating response to conditional variance is inherently difficult. To illustrate this last point, consider the adaptive expectation approach that specifies the (subjective) conditional mean and the conditional variance as follows:

$$\mu_t = \sum_{k=0}^{\infty} \lambda^k (1 - \lambda) p_{t-k-1}, \tag{4.4}$$

$$\sigma_t^2 = \sum_{k=0}^{\infty} \phi^k (1 - \phi) [p_{t-k-1} - \mu_{t-k-1}]^2, \tag{4.5}$$

---

[18] For example, a producer facing price risk and using futures contracts optimally to hedge risk would be exposed only to residual basis risk, and conceivably that is what the variance terms should measure.

where usually $\lambda \in (0, 1)$ and $\phi \in (0, 1)$. These parameterizations are appealing because they make the unobservable variable a function of past realizations (which are, at least in principle, observable) in a very parsimonious way. It is known that the assumption of adaptive expectations for the mean of price is rather restrictive, and it turns out that such an assumption for the variance is even more restrictive.

By definition, if μ_t denotes the agent's conditional expectation of price, then a price-generating equation consistent with the agent's beliefs is $p_t = \mu_t + u_t$, where u_t is a random term with a zero conditional mean. Hence, an equivalent way of saying that the producer's expected price is formed adaptively as in Equation (4.4) is to say that the producer believes that price is generated by

$$p_t = p_{t-1} - \lambda u_{t-1} + u_t \tag{4.6}$$

with $E[u_t \mid P_{t-1}] = 0$, where P_{t-1} denotes the entire price history up to period $t - 1$. Thus, adaptive expectation for the conditional mean of price is equivalent to assuming that the agent believes that price changes follow an invertible first-order moving-average process, a rather restrictive condition.[19]

Given that Equation (4.6) is the relevant price model, the adaptive expectation model for the variance of Equation (4.5) can be rewritten as

$$\sigma_t^2 = \phi \sigma_{t-1}^2 + (1 - \phi) u_{t-1}^2. \tag{4.7}$$

Note that for the model to be internally consistent the agent must believe that the random terms u_t are drawn from a distribution with mean zero and variance σ_t^2. But, as is apparent from (4.7), for most types of distributions (including the normal), σ_t^2 is bound to converge to zero as time passes. Indeed, Equation (4.7) shows that the adaptive expectation model for conditional price variance is a special case of Bollerslev's (1986) generalized ARCH (GARCH) model, specifically what Engle and Bollerslev (1986) called the "integrated" GARCH model. For this model, $\sigma_t^2 \to 0$ almost surely for most common distributions [Nelson (1990)].[20] The fact that these models imply that $\sigma_t^2 \to 0$ leads to the somewhat paradoxical situation of modeling response to risk with models that entail that risk is transitory. As Geweke (1986, p. 59) stated, "... the integrated GARCH model is not typical of anything we see in economic time series".

These undesirable modeling features are avoided if the conditional price variance is modeled by a regular GARCH model, such as the GARCH(1,1) model:

$$\sigma_t^2 = \alpha_0 + \alpha_1 \sigma_{t-1}^2 + \alpha_2 u_{t-1}^2, \tag{4.8}$$

---

[19] See, for example [Pesaran (1987, p. 19)].

[20] Similar problems also apply to other more ad hoc parameterizations, such as that used by Chavas and Holt (1990), where $\sigma_t^2 = \sum_k \alpha_k u_{t-k}^2$ and α_k are predetermined constants satisfying $\sum_k \alpha_k = 1$.

where $\alpha_0 > 0$ bounds the conditional variance away from zero (and thus precludes $\sigma_t^2 \to 0$), and $\alpha_1 + \alpha_2 < 1$ ensures stationarity of the conditional variance process. This class of models, popular in finance studies, has been applied to agricultural supply models by Aradhyula and Holt (1989, 1990), Holt and Moschini (1992), Holt (1993), and others. Whereas this approach offers a coherent framework for modeling production response to risk, the GARCH model makes explicit the relation between conditional and unconditional variance and brings to the fore an important feature of the problem at hand. Namely, models such as (4.3) can identify response to variance only if the latter is time-varying. If, on the other hand, producers perceive variance to be relatively constant, then no response to risk can be estimated. For example, in the logic of the model (4.8), a constant variance would imply that $\alpha_1 = \alpha_2 = 0$, such that the conditional variance is the same as the unconditional variance (α_0, in such a case), and the term $\beta_3\alpha_0$ in Equation (4.3) would then be absorbed by the intercept.

We conclude this section with two observations. First, the assumption that producers perceive a constant conditional variance may not be a bad approximation. Most economic time series do seem to display ARCH properties, but the ability to forecast squared errors is usually very limited even in these models [Pagan and Schwert (1990)], and this is particularly true for the planning horizons typical of agricultural production decisions [Holt and Moschini (1992)]. Thus, in such cases conditional variance does not do much better than unconditional variance for the purpose of measuring the relevant risk; hence, identifying and estimating risk response may be too ambitious an undertaking.[21] But second, the fact that we may have trouble identifying risk response does not mean that production adjustments to risk are not present. Indeed, virtually any supply model that has been estimated without a risk term is consistent with a potentially large risk response insofar as the relevant risk is an unconditional variance that is captured by the intercept.

4.5. Risk and equilibrium in supply and production systems

The models that we have just reviewed introduce a risk variable in a single equation supply model. As mentioned earlier, representing risk in terms of a single variable (say, price variance) may be justified as an approximation to the more general EU model and will be an admissible procedure only under certain restrictive conditions (for example, normality and CARA). Whereas consideration of higher moments has been advocated [Antle and Goodger (1984)], it is arguable that such ambitions may be frustrated in most empirical applications. The single equation nature of these supply models, on the other hand, can only be a partial representation of the more complete production and supply system that may represent the agricultural producer's decision problem. Thus, generalizing risk response models to systems of equations may be desirable, and it has been

---

[21] A related point is that, unlike typical finance applications, agricultural supply models with risk are usually estimated with a small sample of observations.

pursued by Coyle (1992), Chavas and Holt (1990, 1996), and Saha, Shumway and Tal-paz (1994), among others. Consideration of such complete supply systems is common in applied work under assumptions of certainty or risk neutrality, thanks partly to the popularization of flexible functional forms for dual representations of technology (such as profit and cost functions), which greatly simplify the derivation of coherent systems of output supply and input demand equations. Extension of this "dual" approach un-der risk has been explored by Coyle (1992), but because his set-up relies on a linear mean-variance objective function (which, as discussed earlier, is consistent with EU only under restrictive assumptions), it is unclear whether this dual approach is better than the corresponding "primal" approach.

The system approach typically can accommodate such integrability conditions as symmetry, homogeneity, and curvature (say, convexity in prices of the profit function). Interest in these restrictions can arise for at least two reasons. First, this set of testable restrictions may be used to validate the theoretical framework. Second, if testing the the-ory is not an objective, then maintaining these restrictions may be useful in improving the feasibility/efficiency of estimation, as well as improving the usefulness of empirical results for policy and welfare analysis. If one wanted to consider the integrability condi-tions for EU maximizing producers, what would such conditions look like? Pope (1980) pursued this question and showed that the simple symmetry and reciprocity conditions that hold under certainty need not hold under uncertainty. But, as in any optimization problem, some symmetry conditions must exist, and for the case of a producer who maximizes expected utility under price uncertainty, these conditions were characterized by Pope (1980), Chavas and Pope (1985), and Paris (1989). In general the relevant sym-metry conditions will involve wealth effects (and thus will depend on risk attitudes). Re-strictions on preferences, however, can reduce the symmetry and reciprocity conditions of the risk-averse case to those of the certainty case. That will happen, for example, if the utility function is of the CARA type [Pope (1980)]. Alternatively, restrictions on the technology can also reduce the symmetry and reciprocity conditions of the risk-averse case to those of the certainty case. Specifically, if the production function is homoth-etic, then input demands satisfy the symmetry conditions that hold under certainty; and if the production function is linearly homogeneous, then the corresponding reciprocity conditions also hold [Dalal (1990)].

A fundamental restriction of output supply and input demand functions under cer-tainty is that of homogeneity of degree zero in prices. Thus, for example, if all input and output prices are scaled by a constant (for instance, a change of units of measure-ment from dollars to cents), then all real decisions are unaffected, i.e., there is no money illusion. In general the homogeneity property does not seem to hold under price uncer-tainty, as noted by Pope (1978) and Chavas and Pope (1985), unless restrictions are placed on preferences. Because a proportional change in all input and output prices induces a corresponding change in profit, the decisions of a producer with CARA pref-erences are affected by such a proportional change. On the other hand, if the producer holds CRRA preferences, then decisions are not affected by such a proportional change in all prices.[22]

Spelling out such homogeneity conditions is quite useful, and indeed Pope (1988) used homogeneity to derive tests for the structure of risk preferences. But because homogeneity of degree zero of choice functions in prices is typically associated with the absence of money illusion, the conclusion that homogeneity need not hold under uncertainty may seem somewhat puzzling. One way to look at the problem is to recognize that the absolute risk-aversion coefficient is not unit-free; thus, for example, it is meaningless to postulate a particular numerical value for λ independent of the units of measurement of prices. If doubling of all prices were associated with halving of λ, for example, then even under CARA choices would not be affected by such a change. There is, however, a more fundamental way of looking at the homogeneity property. The crucial element here is to recognize that the vNM utility function of money, say $U(\pi)$, is best interpreted as an indirect utility function of consumer demand, such that π creates utility because it is used to purchase consumption goods. Thus, $U(\pi) \equiv V(p^c, \pi)$ where $V(p^c, \pi)$ is the agent's indirect utility function, and p^c denotes the price vector of consumption goods. In analyses of risk models, the vector p^c is subsumed in the functional $U(\cdot)$ under the presumption that these prices are held constant. Because $V(p^c, \pi)$ is homogeneous of degree zero in p^c and π, it follows that, when consumption prices are explicitly considered, the vNM utility function is homogeneous of degree zero in all prices (i.e., consumption prices, output prices, and input prices). Thus, homogeneity (i.e., lack of money illusion) must hold even under uncertainty, when this property is stated in this extended sense.

Storage opportunities introduce dynamics and require a more careful accounting for equilibrium issues as well as for expectation formation when modeling supply. In particular, because negative storage is impossible, nonlinearities are inherent in the equilibrium problem. Using U.S. soybean market data over the period 1960 to 1988, Miranda and Glauber (1993) develop an equilibrium rational expectations model that explicitly represents the behavior of producers, consumers, and storers (both private and public). They find evidence to suggest that both acres supplied and storage activities respond negatively to increased price risk. The storage result suggests that risk management institutions may facilitate efficiency by reducing impediments to intertemporal transactions.

4.6. Programming models with risk

In a number of agricultural economics applications, especially those with a normative focus, risk has been considered within suitably parameterized programming models that

---

[22] For example, if output and input prices are scaled by a constant $k > 0$, then profit changes from π to $k\pi$. If utility is CARA, then $-\exp(\lambda\pi) \neq -\exp(-k\lambda\pi)$, because scaling prices by k is equivalent to changing the constant coefficient of risk aversion. On the other hand, if utility is CRRA, say $U = \log(\pi)$, then scaling profit by k clearly has no effect on choices.

can readily be solved (and simulated) by appropriate computational methods. The classical quadratic programming problem of Freund (1956) maximizes a weighted linear summation of mean and variance subject to resource constraints:

$$\text{Max}_{x} \, \mu(x) - \frac{1}{2}\lambda V(x) \quad \text{such that } G(x) \leqslant 0, \tag{4.9}$$

where $\mu(x)$ and $V(x)$ are mean and variance of returns as a function of choices, $G(x) \leqslant 0$ is a vector of equality and inequality constraints, and λ measures the magnitude of risk aversion. Sharpe (1963), among others, refined the approach into a convenient and economically meaningful single-index model for portfolio choice. Applications of the method in agricultural economics include Lin, Dean and Moore (1974) and Collins and Barry (1986), both of which consider land allocation decisions. Because solving quadratic programming problems was, at one time, computationally difficult, Hazell (1971) linearized the model by replacing variance of reward with the mean of total absolute deviations (MOTAD) in the objective function. Hazell's MOTAD model has been extended in several ways by Tauer (1983), among others, and the general method has been used widely in economic analyses of agricultural and environmental issues [Teague et al. (1995)]. Risk considerations can also be introduced as a constraint, and many such programming problems go under the general rubric of safety-first optimization as studied by Pyle and Turnovsky (1970) and Bigman (1996).[23]

Given the strong relationship between time and uncertainty, risk has a natural role in dynamic optimization problems. The analytical problems associated with identifying the time path of optimal choices often requires numerical solutions for such problems. This is particularly true in agricultural and resource economics, where the necessity to accommodate such technical realities as resource carry-over may preclude stylized approaches such as the real options framework discussed previously. Stochastic dynamic programming is a discrete-time variant of optimal control methods and is robust to accommodating the technical details of the rather specific problems that arise in agricultural and natural resource economics. A standard such problem is

$$\text{Max}_{x_t} \sum_{t=0}^{T} \beta^t E_0\left[\pi(x_t, y_t)\right] \quad \text{such that } y_t = f(y_{t-1}, x_{t-1}, \varepsilon_t), \ y_0 \text{ given,} \tag{4.10}$$

where T may be finite or infinite, β is the per-period discount factor, and $\pi(x_t, y_t)$ is the per-period reward. The goal is to choose, at time 0, a contingently optimal sequence, x_0 through x_T, to maximize the objective function. But the problem is not deterministic because randomness, through the sequence ε_t, enters the carry-over equation, $y_t = f(y_{t-1}, x_{t-1}, \varepsilon_t)$. This means that a re-optimization is required at each point in the time sequence. To initialize the problem, it is necessary that y_0 be known. For

---

[23] Note that safety-first approaches to risk modeling may be difficult to reconcile with the EU framework.

analytical convenience, Markov chain properties are usually assumed for the stochastic elements of the model. Many variants of the above problem can be constructed. For example, time could modify the per-period reward function or the carry-over function. Applications of the approach include capital investment decisions [Burt (1965)] and range stocking rate and productivity enhancement decisions [Karp and Pope (1984)].

4.7. Technology adoption, infrastructure and risk

A class of production decisions where risk is thought to play an important role is that of new technology adoption. Early work in this area, reviewed by Feder, Just and Zilberman (1985), analyzed the relationships among risk, farm size, and technology adoption. More recent studies that consider the possible impact of risk on adoption include Antle and Crissman (1990) and Pitt and Sumodiningrat (1991). The availability of irrigation has been shown to be an important risk factor for technology adoption. It both increases average productivity and reduces variability of output, and often involves community or government actions (thus emphasizing how risk management opportunities may often depend upon local institutional factors). For references to the impacts of risk and irrigation on technology adoption, with special regard to the adoption of high-yielding but flood-susceptible rice in Bangladesh, see Azam (1996), Bera and Kelley (1990), and other research cited therein. This line of research suggests that technologies are often best introduced in packages rather than as stand-alone innovations. Other work on structure includes Rosenzweig and Binswanger (1993), who studied the structural impacts of weather risk in developing countries, and Barrett (1996), who considered the effects of price risk on farm structure and productivity. In the context of hybrid maize adoption, Smale, Just and Leathers (1994) argue that it is very difficult to disentangle the importance of competing explanations for technology adoption, and suggest that previous studies may have overstated the importance of risk aversion.

The introduction of a new technology often requires a substantial capital investment, and so the functioning of credit markets plays a crucial role. For collateral-poor farmers in rural communities of the less developed world, credit is often unattainable through formal channels. For example, Udry (1994) finds that in four northern Nigeria villages more than 95 percent of borrowed funds were obtained from neighbors or relatives. One of the reasons for the importance of informal lending channels is the limited means by which formal credit providers can obtain relevant information concerning the riskiness of projects. As discussed in Ray (1998), less formal sources (such as the landlord, a local grain trader, or the village moneylender) are in a better position to judge risks and to provide credit. But, perhaps due to high default risk or to the systemic nature of risk when all borrowers are from the same village, interest rates are often very high. Bottomley (1975) developed a simple model that relates equilibrium rates to default risk. It has been suggested that moneylender market power may also affect rates but, from a survey of the literature, Ray (1998) concludes that local moneylending markets tend to be quite competitive. However, as Bottomley (1975) pointed out, the true interest rate may often be difficult to ascertain because loans are often tied in with other business dealings such as labor, land lease, and product marketing agreements.

Faced with production and price risks, poorly performing credit markets would seem to imply inadequate investments, perhaps especially in risk-reducing technologies. On the other hand, the limited liability nature of credit may create incentives for borrowers to engage in riskier projects that are also less productive on the average, compared with the projects that would have been chosen if the credit line were not available. Basu (1992) studies the effect of limited liability and project substitution on the structure of land lease contracts.

5. Risk management for agricultural producers

The purpose of risk management is to control the possible adverse consequences of uncertainty that may arise from production decisions. Because of this inherently normative goal, stating the obvious might yet be useful: risk management activities in general do not seek to increase profits per se but rather involve shifting profits from more favorable states of nature to less favorable ones, thus increasing the expected well-being of a risk-averse individual. It should also be clear that production and risk management activities are inherently linked. Most business decisions concerning production have risk implications, and the desirability of most risk management choices can only be stated meaningfully with reference to a specific production context. As for the risk implications of production decisions, a useful classification of inputs can be made following Ehrlich and Becker (1972), who identified "self-insurance" and "self-protection" activities. Self-insurance arises when a decision alters the magnitude of a loss given that the loss occurs. Self-protection takes place when a decision alters the probability that a loss will occur. Of course, agricultural inputs may have both self-insurance and self-protection attributes; for instance, fertilizer may reduce both the probability and conditional magnitude of a crop nutrient deficiency,[24] and livestock buildings can operate in the same way upon weather-related losses. Ehrlich and Becker (1972) use this classification to show that input choices modify the demand for market insurance. Expenditures on market insurance and self-insurance substitute for each other, whereas expenditures on self-protection could actually increase the demand for market insurance.

Abstracting from self-insurance and self-protection effects of production choices, farmers usually have access to a number of other tools that have a more direct risk management role. These include contractual arrangements (e.g., forward sales, insurance contracts) as well as the possibility of diversifying their portfolio by purchasing assets

---

[24] In a comprehensive review of literature on crop yield variability determination, Roumasset et al. (1989) conclude that nitrogen tends to increase variability. For technology adoption, Antle and Crissman (1990) suggest that variability tends to increase initially but decrease again after more is learned about the innovation.

with payoffs correlated with the returns on production activities. Risk management decisions are obviously constrained by the given institutional and market environments, i.e., what tools and programs are actually available to the farmer. Thus, the possible incompleteness of risk markets and the imperfections of capital markets are bound to be crucial to risk management.[25] As will be discussed in this section, existing risk markets, such as contingent price markets and crop insurance, typically do not allow producers to eliminate all risk (for given production choices, it may be impossible to take market positions such that the resulting total payoff is invariant to the state of nature). Whereas this may suggest scope for welfare-increasing government intervention, it also indicates that farmers just may have to bear some residual risk.[26]

In what follows we analyze in some detail contractual relationships that a producer may enter into in order to manage price and quantity risk. In particular, we emphasize price-contingent contracts (forward, futures and options) and crop insurance contracts. Whereas the analysis hopefully will clarify the role of various risk-management tools, we should emphasize that the results of most of the models analyzed below do not translate into direct risk management recommendations. For example, given the endogeneity of many of the risks faced by producers, a discussion of risk management that takes production decisions as given is to some extent artificial, although it may be analytically useful. More generally, one should keep in mind that farmers ultimately likely care about their consumption, itself the result of an intertemporal decision. Risky production and risky prices of course imply a risky farm income, but such income uncertainty may not necessarily translate into consumption risk because borrowing/saving opportunities, as well as income from other assets and/or activities (diversification), may be used to smooth consumption over time. It is nonetheless instructive to consider certain aspects of risk management in stylized models.

5.1. Hedging with price contingent contracts

"Hedging" here refers to the acquisition of contractual positions for the purpose of insuring one's wealth against unwanted changes. As discussed earlier, output price is one of the most important sources of risk for agricultural producers. Several instruments are available to farmers of developed countries to "hedge" this price risk, notably forward contracts and price contingent contracts traded on organized futures exchanges.

---

[25] When capital markets are imperfect, internal funding can be very important for production decisions. For this reason, Froot, Scharfstein, and Stein (1993) argue that one of the main purposes of hedging in a business is to manage cash flow so that profitable investment opportunities that arise might be pursued. The time sequence of cash flows may also be important under the risk of business failure, as discussed by Foster and Rausser (1991).

[26] From a welfare point of view, farmers may not be the main losers from market incompleteness. Myers (1988) showed empirically that the incompleteness may benefit producers when food demand is inelastic and may benefit consumers under other circumstances. Lapan and Moschini (1996) in a partial equilibrium framework, and Innes and Rausser (1989) and Innes (1990) in a general equilibrium framework, identified roles for second-best policy interventions when some risk markets are missing.

5.1.1. Forward contracts and futures contracts

The biological lags that characterize agricultural production mean that inputs have to be committed to production far in advance of harvest output being realized, at a time when output price is not known with certainty. The simplest instrument often available to farmers to deal with this price risk is a "forward contract". With such a contract a farmer and a buyer of the agricultural output agree on terms of delivery (including price) of the output in advance of its realization. For example, a farmer and a buyer can agree that a certain amount of corn will be delivered at a given time during the harvest season at the local elevator for a certain price. It is readily apparent that conditions exist under which such a contract can completely eliminate price risk. To illustrate, let $q =$ output quantity produced, $h =$ output quantity sold by means of a forward contract, $p =$ the output price at the end of the production period, $f_0 =$ the forward price quoted at the beginning of the period, and $\pi =$ the profit at the end of the period. Then the random end-of-period profit of the firm that uses forward contracts is

$$\tilde{\pi} = \tilde{p}q - C(q) + (f_0 - \tilde{p})h, \tag{5.1}$$

where $C(q)$ is a strictly convex cost function (which subsumes the effects of input prices).[27] If the farmer's utility function of profit is written as $U(\pi)$, where $U''(\cdot) < 0 < U'(\cdot)$, the first-order conditions for an optimal interior solution of an EU maximizer require

$$\mathrm{E}\big[U'(\tilde{\pi})\big(\tilde{p} - C'(q)\big)\big] = 0, \tag{5.2}$$
$$\mathrm{E}\big[U'(\tilde{\pi})(f_0 - \tilde{p})\big] = 0, \tag{5.3}$$

from which it is apparent that optimal output q^* must satisfy $C'(q^*) = f_0$. This is the "separation" result derived by Danthine (1978), Holthausen (1979), and Feder, Just and Schmitz (1980). Optimal output depends exclusively on the forward price, which is known with certainty when inputs are committed to production, and hence the production activity is riskless.

The importance of the separation result lies in the fact that the agent's beliefs about the distribution of cash and futures prices, and her degree of risk aversion, are inconsequential for the purpose of making production decisions. The agent's beliefs and her risk attitudes, however, may affect the quantity of output that is sold forward. In particular, from (5.3) it follows that

$$h^* \gtreqless q^* \quad \text{as } \mathrm{E}[\tilde{p}] \lesseqgtr f_0. \tag{5.4}$$

---

[27] Input prices are implicitly compounded to the end of the period using the (constant) market interest rate, so that all monetary variables in (5.1) are commensurable.

Thus, for example, a producer who believes that the forward price is biased downward (i.e., $E[\tilde{p}] > f_0$) has two ways of acting to take advantage of her information (i.e., "speculating"): she could produce more than under an unbiased forward price, while holding constant the amount sold forward; or she could decrease the amount sold forward, while holding output at the level that is optimal when the forward price is unbiased. Either action results in some uncommitted output being available at harvest time that will fetch the (risky) market price. But speculating by varying output has decreasing returns [because $C''(q) > 0$ by assumption], whereas speculating by varying the amount sold forward has constant returns. Hence, speculation here takes place exclusively by varying the amount sold forward. Similarly, changes in risk aversion, and in the riskiness of the price distribution, in this setting affect forward sales but not production decisions.

An extension of the results just discussed considers futures contracts instead of forward contracts. A futures contract is, essentially, a standardized forward contract that is traded on an organized exchange, such as the Chicago Board of Trade or the Chicago Mercantile Exchange [Williams (1986)]. A futures contract typically calls for delivery of a given quantity (say, 5,000 bushels) of a certain grade of a commodity (say, No. 2 yellow corn) at a specified delivery time (say, December of a given year) at a specified location (say, a point on the Mississippi River). Because of these features, the futures price may not be exactly suited to hedge the risk of a given producer. On the other hand, futures markets are quite liquid and hedging by using futures is readily possible for all producers, even when a local buyer offering a forward contract is not available. Using futures contracts, a producer can lock in on a price for future delivery; the problem, of course, is that this precise futures price may not be what the producer needs. Such discrepancies may be due to any one of the three main attributes of an economic good: form, time, and space.[28] Because of that, the local cash price that is relevant for the producer is not the one that is quoted on the futures market, although usually it is highly correlated with it. In addition, one should note that futures entail lumpiness (only 5,000 bu. at a time for most grains, for example) as well as transactions costs. Thus, relative to a forward contract, a futures contract is an imperfect (although possibly effective) risk-reduction instrument, i.e., the producer that uses futures contracts retains "basis risk".[29]

To illustrate hedging under basis risk, let us modify the notation of the previous section by letting f_0 = futures price quoted at the beginning of the period, $\tilde{f}$ = futures

---

[28] For example, the commodity grown by the producer may be of a different kind (or a different grade) than that traded on the exchange; or, the producer may realize the output at a different time than the delivery time of the contract; or, the producer may realize the output at a different location than that called for in the futures contract. Grade differences may be handled by pre-specified premiums or discounts over the futures price; differences in the type of commodity lead to the problem of "cross-hedging" of Anderson and Danthine (1981); see DiPietre and Hayenga (1982) for an application. The imperfect time hedging problem was explicitly addressed by Batlin (1983).

[29] Basis in this context refers to the difference, at the date of sale, between the (local) cash price and futures price.

price at maturity of the futures contract, and h = amount of commodity sold in the futures market. As before, $\tilde{p}$ represents the cash price at harvest time, and thus basis risk means that, typically, $\tilde{p} \neq \tilde{f}$. In general, it is difficult to fully characterize the production and hedging decisions under basis risk. Some results may be obtained, however, by restricting the relationship between cash and futures prices to be linear, as in Benninga et al. (1983):

$$\tilde{p} = \alpha + \beta \tilde{f} + \tilde{\theta}, \tag{5.5}$$

where α and β are known constants, and $\tilde{\theta}$ is a zero-mean random term that is independent of the futures price.[30] The end-of-period profit of the producer can then be represented as

$$\tilde{\pi} = (\alpha + \beta f_0 + \tilde{\theta})q - C(q) + (f_0 - \tilde{f})(h - \beta q). \tag{5.6}$$

Now, if the futures price is unbiased (i.e., if $E[\tilde{f}] = f_0$), it is apparent that, for any given output q, the optimal futures hedge is $h^* = \beta q$.[31] Additional results for this basis risk case are presented in Lapan, Moschini and Hanson (1991). Because in this case random profit reduces to $\tilde{\pi} = (\alpha + \beta f_0 + \tilde{\theta})q - C(q)$, the effective (hedged) price, $\alpha + \beta f_0 + \tilde{\theta}$, is still random. Hence, under risk aversion, production takes place at a point at which marginal cost is lower than the expected price (given optimal hedging), i.e., $C'(q^*) < (\alpha + \beta f_0)$, indicating that a portion of price risk due to the basis cannot be hedged away. Because there is some residual uncertainty concerning the local cash price, the degree of risk aversion also influences optimal output. Specifically, the output level q^* is inversely related to the degree of risk aversion, as in earlier results of models of the competitive firm under price risk [Baron (1970), Sandmo (1971)]. Also, a ceteris paribus increase in nondiversifiable basis uncertainty (a mean-preserving spread of $\tilde{\theta}$) will in general decrease the optimal output level, a sufficient condition being that preferences satisfy DARA [Ishii (1977)].

It is important to realize that with basis risk, even in its special formulation of Equation (5.5), the separation result, discussed earlier for the case of forward contracts, does not apply. Because hedging does not eliminate basis risk, if the agent believes that the futures price is biased then her choice will involve the possibility of investing in two risky assets (production of output and trading in futures). Thus, if the agent believes that the futures price is biased, her optimal speculative response will entail changes in both these risky assets. For the special case of CARA preferences and of a linear basis as

---

[30] Actually, whereas independence is sufficient for our purposes, the slightly weaker assumption that $\tilde{f}$ is conditionally independent of $\tilde{\theta}$ is both necessary and sufficient [Lence (1995)]. Of course, for some distributions (such as the multivariate normal) these two notions of independence are equivalent. Indeed, if $(\tilde{p}, \tilde{f})$ are jointly normally distributed, then the linear basis representation in (5.5) follows.

[31] Hence, the optimal futures hedge ratio h^*/q is equal to $\beta = \text{Cov}(\tilde{p}, \tilde{f})/\text{Var}(\tilde{f})$, the coefficient of the theoretical regression of cash price on futures price, a result that has been used in countless empirical applications.

in (5.5), however, one can still prove a separation result between production and hedging (speculative) decisions. Specifically, in such a case the optimal output level q^* does not depend on the parameters of the producer's subjective distribution of futures prices [Lapan et al. (1991)], although it does depend on the agent's degree of risk aversion and on the parameters α and β, which define the expectation of the cash price (conditional on the futures price).

The results just outlined pertain to a static problem and, more crucially, pertain to a competitive producer who faces only price risk. For most commodities, however, the hedging problem needs to consider the fact that farmers typically are exposed to both price and production uncertainty. An early attempt at allowing both price and production risk was that of McKinnon (1967), who considered the hedging problem of minimizing the variance of profit for a given planned output level. Because of the complications generated by the joint presence of price and production risk, efforts to extend McKinnon's risk-minimization analysis to EU maximization often have relied on the assumption that producers maximize an objective function increasing in the mean and decreasing in the variance of revenue/profit. This approach was followed by Rolfo (1980), Newbery and Stiglitz (1981, Chapter 13), and Anderson and Danthine (1983), among others. In these studies it is shown that the correlation between the random production and random price is crucial for determining the optimal hedging strategy. Because demand considerations suggest the correlation is typically negative, a "natural" hedge is already built into the price system and the optimal strategy is to hedge an amount lower than expected output.

Such a mean-variance approach usually is justified on the grounds that it is e̓ ̓ct for a CARA utility function if wealth/profit is normally distributed. But profit typically is not normally distributed when output is uncertain because it entails the product of two random variables [Newbery (1988)]. Indeed, the need to analyze our hedging problem in a general framework is clearly illustrated by noting that, under production uncertainty, the optimal hedge in general is less than expected output even when output and price are independent [Losq (1982)], a result that cannot be established by mean-variance analysis. Of course, the difficulty is that it is not possible to establish useful general hedging results that hold for arbitrary concave utility functions and arbitrarily jointly distributed random prices and quantities. If one assumes a CARA utility function, however, an exact solution to the hedging problem under production uncertainty may be possible, as illustrated by Bray (1981), Newbery (1988), and Karp (1988).

A model that captures the essence of a typical farmer's planting hedge was presented in Lapan and Moschini (1994), who consider futures hedging for a competitive producer who faces both production (yield) and price risk and whose only available hedging instrument is a futures contract (with basis risk). Following Newbery and Stiglitz (1981), stochastic output is represented in terms of a production function with multiplicative risk, i.e., $\tilde{Q} = \tilde{y}q(x)$, where x denotes the vector of inputs, $\tilde{y}$ is a random variable with mean $\bar{y}$, and $\tilde{Q}$ is random output. As noted earlier, with multiplicative production risk, input choices can still be represented by a standard cost function, say $C(q)$ where q denotes the scale of production.[32] With input prices assumed constant (they are typically known at the time production and hedging decisions are made) and subsumed in the function $C(\cdot)$, realized total profits are[33]

$$\tilde{\pi} = \tilde{p}\tilde{y}q - C(q) + (f_0 - \tilde{f})h. \tag{5.7}$$

Thus, the producer knows f_0 when q and h are chosen, but the realizations of the random variables $\{\tilde{f}, \tilde{p}, \tilde{y}\}$ are not known. The difference between $\tilde{f}$ and $\tilde{p}$ reflects basis risk.

Within this context, and assuming that producers maximize a CARA utility, and that the three random variables $\{\tilde{f}, \tilde{p}, \tilde{y}\}$ are jointly normally distributed, Lapan and Moschini (1994) derive and discuss the exact analytic solution to the optimal hedging problem. In particular, they show that the optimal futures hedge satisfies

$$h^* = \frac{f_0 - \overline{f}}{\lambda S_{11}} + q\left[\overline{y}\frac{S_{12}}{S_{11}} + \overline{p}\frac{S_{13}}{S_{11}}\right]. \tag{5.8}$$

Here S_{ij} are the elements of the matrix $S \equiv [\lambda q B + V^{-1}]^{-1}$, where λ is the coefficient of absolute risk aversion, V is the variance-covariance matrix of the three random variables, and B is an accounting matrix of zeros and ones. Hence, an important result here is that the optimal hedge does depend on the degree of risk aversion, even when the futures price is perceived as unbiased. This insight was not present in earlier mean-variance models of hedging under production uncertainty [e.g., Rolfo (1980), Newbery and Stiglitz (1981)]. For likely parameter values, this risk preference effect may be important and the optimal hedge may differ substantially from the mean-variance one. Furthermore, the optimal hedge under yield uncertainty depends on the conditional forecast of the harvest price ($\overline{p}$) and of the yield term ($\overline{y}$), even when the futures price is perceived as unbiased. Thus, in addition to precluding the separation result, production uncertainty also entails that the optimal hedge is inherently time-varying because conditional forecasts will be revised as harvest approaches.

The empirical application reported by Lapan and Moschini (1994), based on a generalization of Myers and Thompson's (1989) hedge ratio estimation procedure, showed that the optimal hedge is considerably less than the full hedge, and that the amount sold forward declines as risk aversion increases. Of course, CARA, joint normality, and multiplicative production risk are rather restrictive assumptions, but nonetheless this model is useful because it can relax the straitjacket of the mean-variance framework and provide insights into the EU maximizing optimal hedge. Although analytical results based

---

[32] Thus, for any level of inputs, $q = q(x)$. In this setting, q aggregates planted acreage and other inputs, and $\tilde{y}$ reflects random yield.

[33] Of course, simultaneous use of crop insurance contracts (discussed later) would alter the nature of this problem.

on more general assumptions are difficult to obtain, empirically it is easy to consider alternative risk preference structures and stochastic distributions. For example, Lapan and Moschini (1994) solve numerically for the optimal hedge for CRRA preferences and log-normally distributed $\{\tilde{f}, \tilde{p}, \tilde{y}\}$, and find that the conclusions obtained under CARA and normality are reasonably robust.[34]

5.1.2. Options on futures

Among the instruments traded on commodity exchanges, futures contracts arguably have the most direct relevance to risk management for farmers. With the introduction of options on futures for many commodities in the 1980s, however, the possibility of trading put and call options has attracted considerable attention.[35] The use of options as hedging devices when the producer faces only price (and basis) risk (but not production risk) was considered by Lapan, Moschini and Hanson (1991). They emphasize that the inclusion of commodity options in a decision maker's portfolio leads to a violation of the two main conditions for a mean-variance representation of expected utility: (i) options truncate the probability distribution of price (so that the argument of the utility function, profit or wealth, is not normally distributed even if the random price is normal), and (ii) the use of options generally means that the argument of utility is not monotonic in the random attributes. The model essentially entails adding another hedging instrument (options) to the payoff in Equation (5.7). A basic modeling issue here is that, given the presence of futures, one of these basic types of options is redundant (for example, a put can always be constructed using a futures and a call). Hence, for modeling purposes attention can be limited to any two of the three types of assets (futures, puts, and calls). Equivalently, as emphasized by Lapan, Moschini and Hanson (1991), one can consider futures and a combination of puts and calls such as straddles.[36] The use of futures and straddles is fully equivalent to allowing the use of futures and calls (or puts), but it has the analytical advantage of illuminating the interpretation of a number of results because the payoff of a straddle is essentially orthogonal to the payoff of a futures contract.

Lapan, Moschini and Hanson (1991) show that, when the futures price is unbiased (from the producers' own point of view), then options are redundant hedging instruments. The key insight here is that, unlike futures contracts, options allow the construction of payoffs that are nonlinear in the realized futures price. But when futures prices

---

[34] Whereas the discussion here has emphasized price-contingent contracts, some yield futures have traded on the Chicago Board of Trade. Clearly, such contracts are potentially useful for farmers (provided enough liquidity exists). A mean-variance analysis of the hedging problem with both price and yield futures is presented by Vukina, Li, and Holthausen (1996).

[35] A "put" conveys to the buyer the right to sell the underlying futures contract at a given price (the "strike price"). This right can be exercised over a certain period of time (the life of the option), and for this right the buyer must pay a "premium" (the price of the option) to the seller (the underwriter). Similarly, a "call" conveys to the buyer the right to sell the underlying futures at the strike price during the life of the option. See [Cox and Rubinstein (1985)] for more details.

[36] A (short) straddle can be constructed by selling one call and one put at the same strike price (or, because of the redundancy just mentioned, it can be constructed by buying one futures and selling two calls).

and options premiums are perceived as unbiased (such that the only reason to trade these instruments is to hedge the risky cash position), the relevant payoff of the producer is linear in the futures price. Hence, the optimal hedging strategy involves using only futures contracts, which provide a payoff that is linear in the price of interest (the option payoff is uncorrelated with the risk that remains after the optimal futures hedge). If futures prices and/or options premiums are perceived as biased, however, then there is a speculative motive to trade futures and options, and options are typically used along with futures.

In this context it is clear that a hedging role for options is likely when there is a non-linear relation between profit and the futures prices, such as the presence of nonlinear basis risk or the presence of production uncertainty together with price uncertainty. The latter situation is obviously of great interest to farmers, and has been analyzed by Moschini and Lapan (1995). They study the problem of a farmer with end-of-period profit given by

$$\tilde{\pi} = \tilde{p}\tilde{y}q - C(q) + (f_0 - \tilde{f})h + \left(r - |\tilde{f} - k|\right)z, \tag{5.9}$$

where z is a short straddle with strike price k and premium r (note that the payoff of the straddle depends on the absolute value of the difference between realized futures price and strike price). The producer knows f_0, k, and r when q, h, and z are chosen, but the realizations of the random variables $\{\tilde{f}, \tilde{p}, \tilde{y}\}$ are not known. Under the assumption of CARA and normality, Moschini and Lapan (1995) provide analytic solutions for the optimal use of futures and straddles. If futures and options prices are perceived as unbiased, then the optimal hedging strategy entails selling futures and buying straddles. Of course, because of the simultaneous presence of price and production uncertainty, the optimal use of the hedging instruments depends on the agent's degree of risk aversion, and in general the optimal hedge is less than the full hedge. For example, for a representative soybean producer with a local relative risk aversion of $R = 2$, and after translating optimal levels of futures and straddles into futures and puts, the optimal hedge is to sell futures in an amount of about 63 percent of the expected output and to buy puts in an amount of about 15 percent of expected output.

If the producer perceives the futures and straddle prices as being biased, then there is a speculative motive to trade these assets. An interesting result here is that, if the agent perceives only the options price to be biased, then only the straddle position is affected, whereas if only the futures price is perceived as biased, both futures and options positions will be affected.[37] This result is reminiscent of the speculative hedging role of options illustrated by Lapan, Moschini and Hanson (1991, 1993), and in particular, cannot be obtained by using the special mean-variance framework.

---

[37] Thus, options are useful to provide insurance against the risk of speculating on the futures price because the nonlinearity of their payoffs can compensate for the speculation outcome of extreme price realizations. But futures are not useful to hedge the speculative risk induced by the optimal option use under biased option prices.

5.1.3. The time pattern of hedging

The discussion so far has dealt with a simple version of the hedging problem, a one-period (two-dates) model. At the beginning of the period, when the risky cash position is incurred (say, when corn is planted or when feeder cattle are bought and placed in the feedlot), the farmer hedges by trading futures and other derivatives (options). At the end of the period, when the cash position is liquidated (because the crop is harvested or the cattle are sold), the financial positions are closed. But what if the farmer were free to adjust the futures hedge after it is established and before it is closed? Two questions are relevant here. Does the possibility of revising the optimal hedge affect the initial hedging decision? And, if it is optimal to revise the hedge over time, how is the hedge revised? These problems have been addressed, in different contexts, by (among others) Anderson and Danthine (1983), Karp (1988), and Myers and Hanson (1996). It turns out that the answer to these questions depends crucially on, among other things, whether the producer believes that futures prices are biased or unbiased, and whether or not there is production uncertainty in the model.

Because our focus is on risk reduction (hedging), suppose that futures prices are unbiased. Also, consider first the pure price and basis risk case (no production risk), and suppose that there are T periods, with the initial hedge being taken at $t = 0$, and the last hedge being lifted at $t = T$, and that the terminal profit of the producer is

$$\tilde{\pi}_T = \tilde{p}_T q + \sum_{t=1}^{T} (1+i)^{T-t} (\tilde{f}_t - \tilde{f}_{t-1}) h_{t-1} - C(q), \tag{5.10}$$

where i is the per-period interest rate. If the producer maximized the EU of terminal profit, $E[U(\tilde{\pi}_T)]$, then the optimal hedging problem (for any given level of output q) can be solved by backward induction. Suppose first that $i = 0$ and that the linear basis assumption made earlier is rewritten as

$$\tilde{p}_T = \alpha + \beta \tilde{f}_T + \tilde{\theta}_T. \tag{5.11}$$

Then, it is easily shown that the optimal hedge is to sell an amount $h_t^* = \beta q$ for all $t = 0, \ldots, T - 1$. Thus, if futures prices are unbiased, the static optimal hedge solution gives the optimal hedging strategy at any time based upon the conditional moments available at that time. In particular, the myopic hedging rule (i.e., the hedge that does not take into account that later revisions in the hedge positions are possible) is the same as the optimal dynamic hedging strategy [Karp (1988)].

Because profits/losses of the futures position are marked to market in Equation (5.10), if the interest rate is positive then the optimal futures hedge at time t should be adjusted by a factor of $(1 + i)^{T-t}$. This gives a first, albeit trivial, reason for the pure hedge to change as time t moves from 0 to T, as the amount sold forward will increase over time because of this pure discounting effect. As harvest approaches, the agent may revise her expectations about futures (and therefore cash) prices at T. However, there would be no need to adjust the futures position through the growing season due to these changed price expectations, provided the farmer continued to believe that the futures price was unbiased. A second reason to revise the hedge position arises if the moments of the distribution of cash and futures prices (for time T) change over time (as a result of new information), in which case the optimal hedge will be revised as time progresses from t to T, as illustrated by Myers and Hanson (1996). Furthermore, in that situation the ability to revise the futures hedge does affect the initial (at time $t = 0$) hedge position, so that myopic and optimal dynamic hedges differ.

As illustrated by Anderson and Danthine (1983), Karp (1988), and Lapan and Moschini (1994), production uncertainty gives yet another fundamental reason for the optimal hedge to change over time. Because production uncertainty implies that the futures market cannot provide a perfect hedge, the hedge itself depends on the agent's forecast of realized cash price (realized futures price) and realized yield, even when the futures price is unbiased [recall Equation (5.8)]. Clearly, changes in expectations of realized yields (and hence output) will lead to revisions in the futures position. Even if yield forecasts do not change, however, changes in the futures price (and therefore in the expected cash price) will lead to changes in the optimal hedge if the realizations of yields and price are correlated.

A somewhat different dynamic hedging problem arises when the production setting allows for some inputs to be chosen after the uncertainty is resolved, as in the ex-post flexibility models of Hartman (1976) and Epstein (1978). This hedging problem has been studied by Moschini and Lapan (1992), who emphasize that in this model the ex-ante profit of the firm is nonlinear (convex) in the risky price (hence, once again, the mean-variance framework is unlikely to be very useful unless one is willing to assume that the utility function is quadratic). They derive a special case of the separation result for this instance of production flexibility (without basis and production risk, of course), which attains when the shadow price of the quasi-fixed input (the input that is chosen ex-ante) is linear in the output price. This linearity means that the incremental risk due to changes in the quasi-fixed inputs can be fully hedged using futures (because the payoff of the futures position is also linear in price). The nonlinearity of profit in the risky price, however, means that not all income risk can be hedged via futures for the case of production flexibility, and thus there is a pure hedging role for options, over and above that of futures.

5.1.4. Hedging and production decisions

The hedging review so far has emphasized the optimal use of hedging instruments conditional on a given output or a given expected output. An important but distinct question concerns how the availability of these hedging opportunities affects the firms' choice of output. As mentioned earlier, in the special case where basis risk and production risk are absent, the availability of futures contracts allows a separation between production and hedging (speculative) decisions. Specifically, the futures price determines the optimal output level, irrespective of the subjective beliefs of the producer, and any difference between the agent's price expectations and the prevailing futures price only affects the hedging/speculative position. Even in this simple case, however, whether the hedging opportunity increases output depends crucially on whether the futures price is biased or not. If the futures price is perceived as unbiased, then the availability of futures hedging induces the risk-averse firm to expand output.

When we relax the restrictive assumptions that lead to the separation result, and allow for basis and production risk (in addition to futures price risk), in general the planned output of the risk-averse firm will depend on both the futures price and price expectations. The question of how hedging affects the choice of planned output, therefore, is only meaningful in the context of unbiased prices, but even in this context it turns out that general propositions are not possible. Some insights, however, are provided by Moschini and Lapan (1995) for the case of jointly normally distributed random variables and CARA preferences. In particular, they show that if the level of risk aversion is small or if the orthogonal production risk is sufficiently small and the futures price is unbiased, then the availability of futures hedging induces the risk-averse firm to produce a larger output level. Essentially, the ability to hedge effectively changes (increases) the risk-adjusted price the firm perceives for its output. Similarly, it is shown that, if the degree of risk aversion or the level of pure production risk is not too large and futures and option prices are unbiased, then the availability of options (in addition to futures) also causes the firm to increase output.

5.1.5. The value of hedging to farmers

Whereas the foregoing cursory review suggests a potentially important role for futures and option contracts to manage farmers' risk, empirical surveys often find that use of such contracts by farmers is limited.[38] Many explanations for this situation have been offered. From a purely economic point of view, it is clear that existing futures markets do not complete the set of markets in the Arrow–Debreu sense, and thus futures are unlikely to provide a full hedge in a number of production situations. For example, as discussed earlier, consideration of basis and other risks may substantially affect (typically reduce) the optimal futures hedge. Furthermore, even abstracting from basis and other risks, one may note that the time horizon of existing futures is limited (i.e., the most distant delivery date for agricultural futures is often little beyond one year). Thus, producers who hedge optimally their one-period risk are still exposed to some intertemporal price

---

[38] A recent survey [U.S. General Accounting Office (1999)] finds that use of risk management tools by farmers is actually fairly common in the United States. In 1996, 42 percent of the United States' two million farmers used one or more risk management tool, and use of risk management strategies was even more frequent for larger farms. For example, among farmers with annual sales greater than $100,000, 55 percent used forward contracts and 32 percent engaged in hedging with futures and/or options (52 percent of these farmers also purchased crop insurance, a risk management tool discussed below).

risk even after accounting for "rollover" hedging [Gardner (1989), Lapan and Moschini (1996)].

From a more practical viewpoint, certain costs of hedging that are typically neglected in the analysis, such as brokerage fees, initial deposit, and the requirement to mark to market, may deter hedging activities. Lence (1996) argues that such costs may make the net benefits of hedging almost negligible and may help explain why many farmers do not hedge. Also, limited use of futures by farmers may, to a certain extent, result from mistrust and lack of proper education on the working of such instruments, an observation that suggests a clear scope for extension activities. But one should also keep in mind that the futures markets may be indirectly quite important for agricultural risk management even when many farmers do not use futures contracts directly. For example, futures may be routinely used by country elevators to hedge the risk of storing grain, and these elevators may in turn offer forward contracts to farmers.

5.2. Crop insurance

Given the susceptibility of crop yields to weather fluctuations, there is obviously a latent demand for crop insurance. Although crop insurance markets have existed for a long time in some parts of the world (e.g., the United States, Canada, and Sweden), their existence has depended crucially on government support, and these governments often have seen fit to subsidize or even run crop insurance markets. Unsubsidized private insurance markets for agricultural risks have been confined mostly to single-peril insurance contracts. Wright and Hewitt (1990) express the belief that private agricultural insurance markets may fail because the costs of maintaining these markets imply unacceptably low average payouts relative to premiums. Furthermore, they suggest that the perceived demand for crop insurance may be overstated because farmers can use diversification and savings to cushion the impact of a poor harvest on consumption. Although Wright and Hewitt's conjectures are solidly motivated, little has been done to verify the claims empirically. It seems clear, however, that unsubsidized agricultural insurance may not be attractive to farmers because it may be too costly. In particular, the costs of private insurance contracts arise, in part, from information problems that are inherent in these insurance contracts, and it is to these problems that we now turn.

Almost invariably crop insurance markets that have benefited from government intervention, especially for multiple-peril contracts, have been either unexpectedly costly to maintain or unattractive to producers, or both. Consider, for example, the case of the U.S. Federal Crop Insurance Corporation (FCIC), which subsidizes insurance for U.S. crop growers. Below is a table of acreage participation rates and loss ratios for some of the major grain and oilseed crops over the ten-year period 1987 to 1996. The loss ratio is the ratio of indemnities to premium payments, and does not include premium subsidies.[39] When one notes that loss ratios of no more than 0.7 are deemed necessary for

---

[39] In addition to subsidizing premiums, the FCIC also absorbs the administrative costs.

Table 1
FCIC Coverage and Payouts 1987–1996

Crop	U.S. acres planted (millions)	Acres that are FCIC insured (percent)*	Loss ratio*
Wheat	71.0	46.8	1.53
Corn	73.6	38.3	1.22
Soybeans	59.9	35.3	1.06
Sorghum	11.4	37.9	1.37
Barley	8.9	44.0	1.44
Rice	2.9	29.5	2.42

* Averages reported are the annual numbers averaged over 10 years.
  Sources: United States Department of Agriculture (1996) and Federal Crop Insurance Corporation (1997).

unsubsidized insurance to be viable given the administrative costs of running it [Wright (1993)], it is clear that the acreage premia would have to be raised substantially for the program to be self-sustaining. Even so, despite heavy government involvement, the subsidized programs are insufficiently generous to attract even a majority of acres planted to these crops. Indeed, the reported participation rates are artificially high because in 1989 and some subsequent years producers had to sign up to be eligible in the event of ad hoc relief, and in 1995 producers had to sign up in order to be eligible for very attractive target price programs. Knight and Coble (1997) provide a detailed overview of the multiple-peril crop insurance environment since 1980. Given that a good insurance policy should attract decision makers who are willing to lose money on average in order to have a less variable income, it is obvious that the FCIC programs have left much to be desired.

Not the least of the problems that arise in crop insurance markets is the existence of a strong political interest in their perceived success. Although the political aspects of these markets are many and varied, the following provides a flavor. Just as in the United States, government involvement in Canadian crop insurance markets has been both extensive and of questionable success. One of the precursors to crop insurance in Canada was the 1939 (federal) Prairie Farm Assistance Act. In the words of the Minister of Agriculture at the time, and referring to a long-standing federal policy of encouraging the settlement of the Prairie provinces, the act "... is intended to take care of people who were put on land that they should never have been put on. That is our reason for being in this at all, and it is our reason for paying two-thirds or three-quarters of the costs out of the treasury of Canada (Standing Committee on Agriculture and Colonization)". Sigurdson and Sin (1994) provide a description of the political history of Canadian crop insurance policy, and Gardner (1994) gives an overview of the United States crop insurance policy in relation to other agricultural policies.

In the United States, one of the more important political aspects of crop insurance is the unwillingness of the federal government to ignore the pleas for monetary disaster assistance when a crop failure is widespread. Given that farm-level crop failures tend to be strongly positively correlated, this undermines the incentive to purchase crop insurance. Disaster assistance is an example of one economic problem – moral hazard – that afflicts crop insurance markets.

When considering a risk, insurance companies may observe certain parameters of the decision environment such as geographic location, soil type, and yield history. They may also observe certain actions such as input use. It is often infeasible to observe all relevant facts, however, and even if observable it may be impossible to write an insurance contract based upon these observations. When it is impossible or excessively costly to write a contract based upon relevant actions, then moral hazard problems may arise. Similarly, when contracts based upon relevant environmental parameters are infeasible, then adverse selection problems may arise. In the remainder of this section, we delineate the nature of the two major economic incentive problems that impede well-functioning crop insurance contracts, and we discuss possible remedies to these problems.

5.2.1. Moral hazard

A risk-neutral insurer who is contemplating the business of a risk-averse producer will seek to specify a contract payout schedule, net of premium, such that a profit is made on the average and also that the producer finds the contract to be sufficiently attractive to sign. Using a standard principal-agent model, as in Chambers (1989), let R be gross revenue and let $I(R)$ be the net contract payoff schedule (premium minus payout), with $C[I(R)]$ as the cost of administering that payoff schedule. Then, assuming symmetric information, i.e., that the insurer can contract upon observable input choices, the insurer's problem is

$$\operatorname*{Max}_{x,I(R)} \int_a^b \left\{ I(R) - C[I(R)] \right\} \mathrm{d}F(R \mid x) \quad \text{such that}$$

$$\int_a^b U[R - I(R) - rx] \mathrm{d}F(R \mid x) \geqslant \bar{u}, \tag{5.12}$$

where R is supported on $[a, b]$, $\bar{u}$ is the minimum level of expected utility that must be maintained to entice the producer to insure, $F(R \mid x)$ is the revenue distribution function conditional on the input vector x, and r is the input price vector.

Standard analysis, due to Borch (1962), yields the requirement that $I(R)$ satisfy the point-wise condition

$$\frac{1 - C_{I(R)}[I(R)]}{U_\pi[\pi]} = \mu, \tag{5.13}$$

where μ is the Lagrange multiplier for the EU constraint in problem (5.12). Now, if the insurer's cost is invariant to the nature of the schedule, then optimality requires $U_\pi[\pi]$

to be constant, and so for risk-averse producers $I(R)$ must be such that $R - I(R) - rx$ is constant. This is the classical risk-sharing result, namely that the risk-neutral insurer should accept all risk from the risk-averse producer. Under general conditions, this result continues to hold if the insurer is risk averse but contracts upon a large number of independent risks.[40] Because the insurer here assumes all the risk, and given the participation constraint, then $I(R) = R - rx - U^{-1}[\bar{u}]$, and the optimal x is that which maximizes the producer's expected profit.[41]

This set-up is drastically changed, and moral hazard problems arise, when the insurer contracts on a risk-averse producer whose inputs are unobservable (i.e., there is asymmetric information). This is because the insurer has but one instrument, the payoff schedule, to address two goals. To be attractive a contract must mitigate the uncertainty facing insurers, but to make a profit the contract must ensure that producers do not take advantage of the limited control over insurance payoffs that arise from the insurer's inability to observe input use. The insurer's problem when inputs are not observable, but the stochastic technology $F(R \mid x)$ is known, can be stated as

$$\operatorname*{Max}_{I(R)} \int_a^b \{I(R) - C[I(R)]\}\, dF(R \mid x) \quad \text{such that}$$

$$\int_a^b U[R - I(R) - rx]\, dF(R \mid x) \geqslant \bar{u}, \tag{5.14}$$

$$x = \arg\max \int_a^b U[R - I(R) - rx]\, dF(R \mid x).$$

The additional incentive compatibility constraint ensures that the rational insurer endogenizes the input consequences of the payoff schedule posed. For both problems (5.12) and (5.14), in general the participation constraint is binding and the producer achieves utility level $\bar{u}$. Under moral hazard, however, it is not optimal for the risk-neutral principal to assume all risk. Some residual risk must be borne by the (risk-averse) producer and hence, to achieve a given $\bar{u}$, the expected payouts to the producer have to be larger than under symmetric information. Chambers (1989) discusses the welfare loss associated with the incentive constraint as well as the possibility that it might cause crop insurance markets to fail.

The implications of the moral hazard problem are not as clear-cut as intuition might suggest. Being relieved of some of the consequences of low input use, the producer may reduce input intensity. On the other hand, as previously shown, if input use is risk

---

[40] Unfortunately, risks across crop production units usually tend to be more systematic than idiosyncratic in nature.

[41] In the trivial case where inputs are unobservable but the producer is risk neutral, this expected profit-maximizing result may also be achieved by setting the schedule $I(R)$ equal to a constant. In this way, the producer faces all the consequences of the actions taken. But then, of course, the insurance company serves no purpose and will never be able to cover any administrative costs.

increasing then a high-risk environment may cause the producer to use fewer inputs than a lower-risk environment. Thus the existence of insurance may, in mitigating risk, encourage input use. That is, risk sharing and moral hazard effects may oppose each other.

To model econometrically the moral hazard problem, the crop producer contemplating whether to insure may be viewed as having to make two decisions: whether or not to insure, and the choice of input vector. In one of the first econometric analyses of the effects of crop insurance, Horowitz and Lichtenberg (1993) assumed that the decision to insure affects input use but not the other way around. Modeling the insurance decision by Probit analysis and modeling input choice as a linear regression on the insurance decision, among other regressors, they studied corn production decisions in ten Corn Belt states and concluded that the decision to insure increased significantly the use of nitrogen and pesticides. These results are somewhat surprising, so other researchers sought to confirm the conclusions on different data sets and using other methodologies. Smith and Goodwin (1996) estimated a simultaneous equations model of input use and crop insurance purchases for Kansas dryland wheat farmers, and concluded that insurance and input decisions are likely simultaneously determined. Further, their results suggest that insurance reduces the use of agricultural chemicals. Estimating an input-conditioned beta distribution for farm-level Iowa corn production, Babcock and Hennessy (1996) simulated optimal input use under different types and levels of insurance for risk-averse producers and also concluded that insurance would likely decrease input use. Although more empirical investigations are warranted, it would appear that risk sharing through crop insurance reduces input use.

The moral hazard problem was also studied in the West African Sahel region, which is at risk to drought. Following on work by Hazell (1992), among others, Sakurai and Reardon (1997) identified quite strong potential demand for area-level rainfall insurance. Their analysis also raises the concern that moral hazard arising from food aid could undermine the viability of such contracts.

In identifying two types of risk, production risk and land value risk arising from soil depletion, Innes and Ardila (1994) suggest an intertemporal environmental aspect to the incentive problem. For fragile land, a contract tailored to insure against production risk may exacerbate land value deterioration, and so one might not be able to ignore dynamic aspects of moral hazard. This is especially true if the operator does not own the land. Dynamic issues also arise in work by Coble et al. (1997) who find evidence that input reduction by insured producers occurs mainly when a crop loss is most likely, thus exacerbating the magnitude of the loss.

Moral hazard problems may not be confined to input intensity issues. If output is difficult to verify, then false yields may be reported. Such illegal acts raise questions concerning contract design, the structure of legal sanctions, and the nature of detection technologies. Hyde and Vercammen (1997) argue that, whereas it is difficult to motivate the structure of insurance contracts actually offered (i.e., the attributes of monotonicity, convexity, deductibility, and co-insurance) as a response to moral hazard on input use alone, actual contracts can plausibly be an optimal response to moral hazard on both input use and yield verification together.

5.2.2. Adverse selection

When, unlike the producer, the insurer is not completely informed about the nature of the risk being insured, then the insurer faces the problem of adverse selection. Ignoring input choices, let a risk-neutral insurer have categorized three production units owned by different operators and of equal size (say, one acre without loss of generality), A, B, and C, into the same risk cohort. From the information available to it, say common average yield ($\overline{y}$), the insurer can observe no difference among these three acres. In fact, the associated yield distributions differ; suppose all acres realize two outcomes, each with probability $1/2$, but the realizations for acre A are $\{\overline{y} - 10, \overline{y} + 10\}$, those for B are $\{\overline{y} - 20, \overline{y} + 20\}$, and those for C are $\{\overline{y} - 30, \overline{y} + 30\}$. With unit price, if the insurance payout equaled $\text{Max}[\overline{y} - y, 0]$, then the expected payouts for acres A, B, and C would be 5, 10, and 15, respectively. In such a case, assuming full participation, the actuarially fair premium for a contract covering all three risks would be 10/acre. However, if the acre A producer is insufficiently risk averse, then she may conclude that the loss ratio for acre A, at $5/10 = \frac{1}{2}$, is too low and may not insure the acre. If the insurer continues to charge 10/acre when covering only acres B and C, then an average loss of $22\frac{1}{2}$/acre is incurred. On the other hand, if the premium is raised to $12\frac{1}{2}$/acre so that a loss is avoided, then acre B may not be insured. Thus, the market may unravel in stages.

Avoiding adverse selection may require the successful crop insurance program to identify, acquire, and skillfully use data that discriminate among different risks. Although perhaps costly to implement, such data management procedures may be crucial because, unless rates are perceived as being acceptable, the market may collapse. The phenomenon of unravelling suggests that identifying a sufficiently large number of relatively homogeneous risks is a prerequisite for a successful contract. Useful discriminators would appear to include mean yield. Skees and Reed (1986) and Just and Calvin (1993) have found evidence suggesting that yield variance may decrease with increased mean yield, and so, even if the trigger insurance yield increases with mean yield, rates should probably be lower for more productive acres. Goodwin (1994), studying Kansas crops (1981–90), finds the relationship between yield variability and mean yield to be tenuous and suggests that farm yield histories be used to calculate yield variability rather than impute variability from historical mean yield. He also concludes that other factors, such as enterprise size, could be informative in setting premium rates.

The degree of homogeneity required to sustain the contract depends upon, among other things, the degree of risk aversion expressed by producers. The more risk averse the producers, the more tolerant they will be of actuarially unfair rates. In an investigation of adverse selection in contracts on corn production, Goodwin (1993) studied county-level data for the ninety-nine Iowa counties over the period 1985 to 1990 and found the elasticities of acreage insured to expected payoff to be in the range of 0.3–0.7. At the farm level, these elasticities may be higher. Further, he found that counties where the risk of payout is low are quite sensitive to the premium charged, so that an across-the-state (of Iowa) premium increase might not make corn yield insurance more profitable because substantial cancellations by the better risk prospects may occur. He concluded that the best approach to loss ratio reduction may involve fine-tuning the rate setting at the county or farm level.

Adverse selection may be either spatial or temporal in nature. The problem type discussed thus far may be categorized as being spatial in the sense that the factors differentiating risks occur at a given point in time. An alternative form of adverse selection, identified by Luo, Skees and Marchant (1994), may arise when attributes of a given risk vary temporally.[42] Coble et al. (1996) consider the case of adverse selection in crop insurance contracts for Kansas dryland wheat farmers over the years 1987 to 1990. Preseason rainfall was used as an indicator for intertemporal adverse selection whereby an unseasonably low (high) level of rainfall occurring before contract signing would entice marginal risks into (out of) signing, thus increasing the loss ratio if rates do not reflect the implications of the water deficit prevailing at signing. Although finding some evidence of adverse selection, they did not identify any of an intertemporal nature.

There are, of course, many factors other than adverse selection that determine the decision for, and the magnitude of, crop insurance participation. To understand adverse selection it is necessary to isolate its impact by accounting for other determinants of participation. In addition to the aforementioned research, econometric analyses of the determinants of insurance participation have been conducted by Gardner and Kramer (1986), Just and Calvin (1990), and Smith and Baquet (1996), among others. Although the conclusions are somewhat mixed, an overview of results suggests that participation tends to increase with farm size. This may be because of the negative correlation between farm size and the importance of off-farm income, or because of increased borrowing. Also, enterprise specialization tends to increase participation, presumably because of increased risk exposure. Further, and suggestive of adverse selection, higher yield variability land is more likely to be insured. However, estimates by Coble et al. (1996) infer that this is true even if rates account for the increased riskiness.

5.2.3. Further discussion

Though conceptually distinct, the differences between the moral hazard and adverse selection problems often disappear in practice. Noting that both moral hazard and adverse selection are problems of information asymmetry, Quiggin, Karagiannis and Stanton (1993) posed the situation in which a wheat and corn producer contemplating crop insurance has one acre of good land and one acre of bad land. Given the decision to insure wheat but not corn, the planting of wheat on poor quality land might be viewed as moral

---

[42] If the producer is better informed about the temporal evolution of risk, then adverse selection may occur. However, as discussed in [Knight and Coble (1997)], the insurer may be just as informed about the temporal risk as the producer, but may be either unable or unwilling to adjust rates. In such a situation, the problem is not one of adverse selection.

hazard. However, given the decision to plant poor land to wheat, the decision to insure wheat only may be viewed as adverse selection. Thus, it should be no surprise that the potential remedies to each problem are similar.

Due to the informational nature of the main barriers to successful crop insurance markets, the obvious solution is, where feasible, to acquire and use as much information as marginal cost and profit considerations allow. To improve performance by reducing adverse selection, the FCIC changed its approach to rate setting in 1985 to accommodate additional information. Subsequent contracts changed the determination of the insurable yield from an average of past yields observed in a locality to an average of past yields observed on the farm in question. Even so sensible a reform, however, may give rise to incentive problems. As pointed out by Vercammen and van Kooten (1994), producers might manipulate input use in a cyclical manner to build up insurable yield levels before cashing in (in a probabilistic sense) by reducing input use for a few years.

On the other hand, area yield insurance [Halcrow (1949), Miranda (1991), Mahul (1999)], where indemnities are based upon the average yield of a suitably wide area (say, a county), eliminates the moral hazard problem and may reduce or eliminate adverse selection. In addition, just as futures markets permit hedge ratios in excess of one, a producer may take out an arbitrary level of area yield insurance coverage without giving rise to concerns about increased moral hazard. Area yield insurance rates are likely to be lower than farm-specific rates because an area yield index will usually be less variable than yield on a given farm. However, because farm-specific risks are not insured, producers may continue to be subjected to some (possibly substantial) production risk.

Revenue insurance is a recurrently popular concept because it directly addresses the income risk problem facing producers. A further possible advantage is that, in combining price and yield insurance, the approach may mitigate somewhat the incidence of moral hazard and adverse selection. Miranda and Glauber (1991), as well as Babcock and Hennessy (1996), conducted simulation analyses for U.S. crop production, and Turvey (1992a, 1992b) studied the costs and benefits of such a program in Canada. The potential for revenue insurance arises from the fact that, even together, price contingent markets (for a fixed quantity) and yield contingent markets (for a fixed price) are not likely to fully stabilize income. Hennessy, Babcock and Hayes (1997) have shown that this targeting attribute of revenue insurance means that it can increase the welfare impact of a given expenditure on income support relative to various alternatives of price and yield support.

Compulsory insurance has often been proposed to eliminate the political need for continual ex-post interventions. If adverse selection is a major problem in competitive insurance markets, however, then compulsory insurance is unlikely to gain the political support necessary for a long-term solution. More effective re-insurance on the part of crop insurers may facilitate the reduction of market rates, and thus reduce adverse selection, because systemic risk is pervasive in the insurance of crop risks and so pooling is largely ineffective for the insurer [Miranda and Glauber (1997), Duncan and Myers (1997)]. Given the diminishing importance of agriculture in developed economies, the introduction of crop loss risks into a well-diversified portfolio of risks would reduce the high level of systematic risk in crop insurance markets, and so may reduce the risk premia required by crop insurers. But crop insurance differs in many ways from other forms of insurance, and it may prove difficult to entice reinsurers into accepting these contracts. If a permanent solution exists that is politically more acceptable than a laissez-faire market approach, it may involve a package of reforms that is balanced to mitigate the incentive impacts but incurs low budgetary costs. Such a package should also take care not to undermine existing or potentially viable risk markets. Finally, the policy mix must be flexible because the technology and organization of crop production may undergo fundamental changes in the coming years.

6. Conclusion

It is abundantly clear that considerations of uncertainty and risk cannot be escaped when addressing most agricultural economics problems. The demands imposed on economic analysis are complex and wide-ranging, with issues that extend from the pure theory of rational behavior to the practicality of developing risk-management advice. The economics profession at large, and its agricultural economics subset, has responded to this challenge with a wealth of contributions. In this chapter we have emphasized theoretical and applied analyses as they pertain to production decisions at the farm level. The EU model provides the most common approach to characterizing rational decisions under risk, and it has been the framework of choice for most applied work in agricultural economics. Whereas our review has provided only a nutshell exposition of the framework's main features, the careful student will dig deeper into its axiomatic underpinning as a crucial step to appreciating what modeling decisions under risk means. More generally, we can note that a satisfactory model of decision making under risk requires assuming an extended notion of rationality. Agents need to know the entire distribution of risky variables, and need to take into account how this randomness affects the distribution of outcomes over alternative courses of action. Thus, the decision maker's problem is inherently more difficult under uncertainty than under certainty.

Because the notion of rational behavior under risk arguably requires agents to solve a complex problem, it is perhaps useful to distinguish between whether models are meant to provide a *positive theory* (aiming to describe how agents actually make decisions under risk) or a *normative theory* (the purpose of which is to prescribe a rational course of action for the particular risky situation). This distinction is admittedly somewhat artificial, and most models are suitable to either interpretation. Yet being more explicit about whether one's analysis is pursuing a positive or normative exercise is possibly quite important in applied contexts such as those covered in this chapter. Much agricultural risk management work is meant as a normative activity, and this may have implications for the choice of models. For instance, the EU model has been criticized, on positive grounds, for failing to describe accurately how agents actually behave under risk in some situations; such a critique, of course, says nothing about the suitability of the EU model for normative (prescriptive) purposes.

Models of decision making under risk bring to the forefront the fact that decisions will be affected in a crucial way by the agent's preferences, i.e., her attitudes towards risk. Consequently, it is quite important to quantify the degree of agricultural producers' risk aversion, and a number of studies have endeavored to do just that. The conclusions may be summarized as follows: within the EU framework, producers typically display some aversion to risk, and risk preferences probably conform to DARA. But evidence on the magnitude of risk aversion is less conclusive and falls short of providing useful parameters that are critical for normative statements (whether in terms of risk management advice to farmers or in terms of suggesting desirable government policies).

Considerations of risk aversion also raise concerns about a very common attribute of applied studies that have a positive orientation. Namely, whereas theoretical models are meant for individual decision making, empirical models are often implemented with aggregate data. The danger of ignoring the implicit aggregation problem is obviously a general concern that applies to economic models of certainty as well. But the fact that risk attitudes play an important role in models with risk, and given that such preferences are inherently an individual attribute, suggests that agents' heterogeneity is bound to be more important when risk matters. It seems that more can and should be done to tackle aggregation considerations in a satisfactory manner.

The complexities of the decision maker's problem under risk raise additional issues for the applied researcher. Agents' beliefs about the characteristics of uncertainty are obviously crucial in this context. The EU model, by relying on the notion of subjective probabilities, neatly solves the theoretical modeling question. But the applied researcher may need to model explicitly how the agent makes probability assessments (i.e., to model her expectations). Whereas the rational expectation hypothesis provides perhaps the most ambitious answer to this question, it is informationally very demanding when (as is typically the case in risky situations) the entire distribution of the random variables matters. This raises the question of whether rational expectations are legitimate from a theoretical point of view, but also implies that empirical models that wish to implement rational expectations can be computationally quite demanding, even for the simplest model under risk. Indeed, many empirical models reviewed in this chapter appear somewhat oversimplified. The modus operandi seems to be to allow theoretical modeling to be as sophisticated as desired but to keep empirical models as simple as possible. Such oversimplifications naturally beg the question of the relationship of empirical models to the theoretical constructs that are used to interpret results, and raise some concerns about what exactly we can learn from this body of empirical studies.

Notwithstanding the remaining criticisms and concerns that one may have, the studies surveyed in this chapter have addressed an important set of problems. Uncertainty and risk are essential features of many agricultural activities, and have important consequences for the agents involved and for society at large. Although welfare and policy considerations related to risk are discussed elsewhere in this *Handbook*, we should note that the economic implications of the existence of risk and uncertainty are related to the particular institutional setting in which agents operate. Insofar as the set of relevant markets is not complete, then this market incompleteness has the potential of adversely affecting resource allocation, as well as resulting in less than optimal allocation of risk-bearing. Indeed, the incompleteness of risk markets for agricultural producers has often been cited as a motivation for agricultural policies in many developed countries. But arguably neither existing markets nor government policies have solved the farmers' risk exposure problems. Risk continues to have the potential of adversely affecting farmers' welfare, as well as carrying implications for the long-run organization of agricultural production and for the structure of resource ownership in the agricultural sector.

Acknowledgements

We appreciate the comments of many colleagues including Jock Anderson, Keith Coble, Sergio Lence, Mario Miranda, Bob Myers, and the Handbook's editors. This chapter was largely written in 1997, and slightly revised in 1998. We have not attempted to cover work published more recently. Other unhedged errors and omissions are the responsibility of the authors. Journal paper No. J-17995 of the Iowa Agriculture and Home Economics Experiment Station, Ames Iowa. Project No. 3463, supported by Hatch Act and State of Iowa funds.

References

Allais, M. (1953), "Le comportement de l'homme rationnel devant le risque: Critique des postulats et axiomes de l'école américaine", Econometrica 21:503–546.
Anderson, G. (1996), "Nonparametric tests of stochastic dominance in income distributions", Econometrica 64:1183–1193.
Anderson, J.R., J.L. Dillon and B. Hardaker (1977), Agricultural Decision Analysis (Iowa State University Press, Ames, IA).
Anderson, R., and J.-P. Danthine (1981), "Cross-hedging", Journal of Political Economy 89:1182–1196.
Anderson, R., and J.-P. Danthine (1983), "The time pattern of hedging and the volatility of futures prices", Review of Economic Studies 50:249–266.
Anscombe, F., and R. Aumann (1963), "A definition of subjective probability", Annals of Mathematical Statistics 34:199–205.
Antle, J.M. (1983), "Testing the stochastic structure of production: A flexible moment-based approach", Journal of Business and Economic Statistics 1 (3):192–201.
Antle, J.M. (1987), "Econometric estimation of producers' risk attitudes", American Journal of Agricultural Economics 69:509–522.
Antle, J.M. (1989), "Nonstructural risk attitude estimation", American Journal of Agricultural Economics 71:774–784.
Antle, J.M., and C.C. Crissman (1990), "Risk, efficiency, and the adoption of modern crop varieties: Evidence from the Philippines", Economic Development and Cultural Change 38:517–537.
Antle, J.M., and W.J. Goodger (1984), "Measuring stochastic technology: The case of Tulare milk production", American Journal of Agricultural Economics 66:342–350.
Antonovitz, F., and R. Green (1990), "Alternative estimates of fed beef supply response to risk", American Journal of Agricultural Economics 72:475–487.

Aradhyula, S.V., and M.T. Holt (1989), "Risk behavior and rational expectations in the U.S. broiler market", American Journal of Agricultural Economics 71:892–902.

Aradhyula, S.V., and M.T. Holt (1990), "Price risk in supply equations: An application of GARCH time-series models to the U.S. broiler market", Southern Economic Journal 57:230–242.

Arrow, K. (1964), "The role of securities in the optimal allocation of risk bearing", Review of Economic Studies 31:91–96.

Arrow, K. (1965), Aspects of the Theory of Risk-bearing (Yrio Jahnsson Foundation, Helsinki).

Azam, J.-P. (1996), "The impact of floods on the adoption rate of high-yielding rice varieties in Bangladesh", Agricultural Economics 13:179–189.

Babcock, B.A., and A.M. Blackmer (1992), "The value of reducing temporal input nonuniformities", Journal of Agricultural and Resource Economics 17:335–347.

Babcock, B.A., and D.A. Hennessy (1996), "Input demand under yield and revenue insurance", American Journal of Agricultural Economics 78:416–427.

Baron, D.P. (1970), "Price uncertainty, utility, and industry equilibrium in pure competition", International Economic Review 11:463–480.

Barrett, C.B. (1996), "On price risk and the inverse farm size-productivity relationship", Journal of Development Economics 51:193–215.

Basu, K. (1992), "Limited liability and the existence of share tenancy", Journal of Development Economics 38:203–220.

Batlin, C.A. (1983), "Production under price uncertainty with imperfect time hedging opportunities in futures markets", Southern Economic Journal 49:681–692.

Batra, R.N., and A. Ullah (1974), "Competitive firm and the theory of input demand under price uncertainty", Journal of Political Economy 82:537–548.

Behrman, J.R. (1968), Supply Response in Underdeveloped Agriculture: A Case Study of Four Major Crops in Thailand, 1937–63 (North Holland, Amsterdam).

Benninga, S., R. Eldor and I. Zilcha (1983), "Optimal hedging in the futures market under price uncertainty", Economics Letters 13:141–145.

Bera, A.K. and T.G. Kelley (1990), "Adoption of high-yielding rice varieties in Bangladesh", Journal of Development Economics 33:263–285.

Bernoulli, D. (1738), "Specimen theoriae novae de mensura sortis", Commentarii Academiae Scientiarum Imperialis Petropolitanae 5:175–192 (Translation by Sommer, L., 1954, and published in Econometrica 22:23–36).

Bigman, D. (1996), "Safety-first criteria and their measures of risk", American Journal of Agricultural Economics 78:225–235.

Binswanger, H.P. (1980), "Attitudes toward risk: Experimental measurement in rural India", American Journal of Agricultural Economics 62:395–407.

Binswanger, H.P. (1981), "Attitudes toward risk: Theoretical implications of an experiment in rural India", Economic Journal 91:867–890.

Bollerslev, T.P. (1986), "Generalized autoregressive conditional heteroskedasticity", Journal of Econometrics 31:307–327.

Borch, K. (1962), "Equilibrium in a reinsurance market", Econometrica 30:424–444.

Bottomley, A. (1975), "Interest rate development in underdeveloped rural areas", American Journal of Agricultural Economics 57:279–291.

Bray, M. (1981), "Futures trading, rational expectations, and the efficient market hypothesis", Econometrica 49:575–596.

Brink, L., and B.A. McCarl (1978), "The tradeoff between expected return and risk among cornbelt farmers", American Journal of Agricultural Economics 60:259–263.

Brorsen, B.W., J.-P. Chavas and W.R. Grant (1987), "A market equilibrium analysis of the impact of risk on the U.S. rice industry", American Journal of Agricultural Economics 69:731–739.

Burt, O.R. (1965), "Optimal replacement under risk", Journal of Farm Economics 47:324–346.

Chambers, R.G. (1989), "Insurability and moral hazard in agricultural insurance markets", American Journal of Agricultural Economics 71:604–616.

Chambers, R.G., and J. Quiggin (1998), "Cost functions and duality for stochastic technologies", American Journal of Agricultural Economics 80:288–295.

Chavas, J.-P. (1994), "Production and investment decisions under sunk cost and temporal uncertainty", American Journal of Agricultural Economics 76:114–127.

Chavas, J.-P., and M.T. Holt (1990), "Acreage decisions under risk: The case of corn and soybeans", American Journal of Agricultural Economics 72:529–538.

Chavas, J.-P., and M.T. Holt (1996), "Economic behavior under uncertainty: A joint analysis of risk preferences and technology", Review of Economics and Statistics 78:329–335.

Chavas, J.-P., and R. Pope (1985), "Price uncertainty and competitive firm behavior: Testable hypotheses from expected utility maximization", Journal of Economics and Business 37:223–235.

Coble, K.H., T.O. Knight, R.D. Pope and J.R. Williams (1996), "Modeling farm-level crop insurance demand with panel data", American Journal of Agricultural Economics 78:439–447.

Coble, K.H., T.O. Knight, R.D. Pope and J.R. Williams (1997), "An expected indemnity approach to the measurement of moral hazard in crop insurance", American Journal of Agricultural Economics 79:216–226.

Collins, R.A., and P.J. Barry (1986), "Risk analysis with single-index portfolio models: An application to farm planning", American Journal of Agricultural Economics 68:152–161.

Cox, J.C., and M. Rubinstein (1985), Options Markets (Prentice-Hall, Englewood Cliffs, N.J.).

Coyle, B.T. (1992), "Risk aversion and price risk in duality models of production: A linear mean-variance approach", American Journal of Agricultural Economics 74:849–859.

Dalal, A.J. (1990), "Symmetry restrictions in the analysis of the competitive firm under price uncertainty", International Economic Review 31:207–211.

Danthine, J.-P. (1978), "Information, futures prices, and stabilizing speculation", Journal of Economic Theory 17:79–98.

Day, R. (1965), "Probability distributions of field crop yields", Journal of Farm Economics 47:713–741.

Debreu, G. (1959), Theory of Value: An Axiomatic Analysis of General Equilibrium (Yale University Press, New Haven).

de Finetti, B. (1931), "Sul significato soggettivo della probabilità", Fundamenta Mathematicae 17:298–229.

Dillon, J.L. (1971), "An expository review of Bernouillian decision theory in agriculture: Is utility futility?", Review of Marketing and Agricultural Economics 39:3–80.

Dillon, J.L., and P.L. Scandizzo (1978), "Risk attitudes of subsistence farmers in Northeast Brazil: A sampling approach", American Journal of Agricultural Economics 60:425–435.

DiPietre, D.D., and M.L. Hayenga (1982), "Cross-hedging wholesale products using live hogs futures", American Journal of Agricultural Economics 64:747–751.

Dixit, A.K., and R.S. Pindyck (1994), Investment under Uncertainty (Princeton University Press, Princeton).

Duncan, J., and R.J. Myers (1997), Crop insurance under catastrophic risk, Staff Paper 97-10 (Department of Agricultural Economics, Michigan State University).

Eeckhoudt, L., and P. Hansen (1992), "Mean-preserving changes in risk with tail-dominance", Theory and Decision 33:23–39.

Ehrlich, I., and G. Becker (1972), "Market insurance, self-insurance, and self-protection", Journal of Political Economy 80:623–648.

Ellsberg, D. (1961), "Risk, ambiguity, and the savage axioms", Quarterly Journal of Economics 75:643–669.

Engle, R.F. (1982), "Autoregressive conditional heteroskedasticity with estimates of the variance of the United Kingdom inflation", Econometrica 50:987–1007.

Engle, R.F., and T. Bollerslev (1986), "Modelling the persistence of conditional variances", Econometric Reviews 5:1–50.

Epstein, L.G. (1978), "Production flexibility and the behavior of the competitive firm under price uncertainty", Review of Economic Studies 45:251–261.

Feder, G., R.E. Just and A. Schmitz (1980), "Futures markets and the theory of the firm under price uncertainty", Quarterly Journal of Economics 94:317–328.

Feder, G., R.E. Just and D. Zilberman (1985), "Adoption of agricultural innovations in developing countries: A survey", Economic Development and Cultural Change 33:255–298.

Federal Crop Insurance Corporation (1997), Crop insurance actuarial information public access server, World Wide Web site http://www.act.fcic.usda.gov/./actuarial/

Feinerman, E., E.K. Choi and S.R. Johnson (1990), "Uncertainty and split nitrogen application in corn production", American Journal of Agricultural Economics 72:975–984.

Finkelshtain, I., and J.A. Chalfant (1991), "Marketed surplus under risk: Do peasants agree with Sandmo?", American Journal of Agricultural Economics 73:557–567.

Foster, W.E., and G.C. Rausser (1991), "Farm behavior under risk of failure", American Journal of Agricultural Economics 73:276–288.

Freund, R.J. (1956), "Introduction of risk into a programming model", Econometrica 24:253–263.

Froot, K.A., D.S. Scharfstein and J.C. Stein (1993), "Risk management: Coordinating corporate investment and financing policies", Journal of Finance 48:1629–1658.

Gallagher, P.W. (1987), "U.S. soybean yields: Estimation and forecasting with nonsymmetric disturbances", American Journal of Agricultural Economics 69:796–803.

Gardner, B.L. (1989), "Rollover hedging and missing long-term futures markets", American Journal of Agricultural Economics 71:311–325.

Gardner, B.L. (1994), "Crop insurance in U.S. farm policy", in: D.L. Hueth, and W.H. Furtan, eds., Economics of Agricultural Crop Insurance: Theory and Evidence (Kluwer Academic Publishers, Boston) 17–44.

Gardner, B.L., and R.A. Kramer (1986), "Experience with crop insurance programs in the United States", in: P. Hazell, C. Pomareda and A. Valdés, eds., Crop Insurance for Agricultural Development: Issues and Experience (Johns Hopkins Press, Baltimore) 195–222.

Geweke, J. (1986), "Modelling the persistence of conditional variances: Comment", Econometric Reviews 5:57–61.

Gollier, C. (1995), "The comparative statics of changes in risk revisited", Journal of Economic Theory 66:522–535.

Goodwin, B.K. (1993), "An empirical analysis of the demand for crop insurance", American Journal of Agricultural Economics 75:425–434.

Goodwin, B.K. (1994), "Premium rate determination in the Federal crop insurance program: What do averages have to say about risk?", Journal of Agricultural and Resource Economics 19:382–395.

Hadar, J., and W. Russell (1969), "Rules for ordering uncertain prospects", American Economic Review 59:25–34.

Halcrow, H.G. (1949), "Actuarial structures for crop insurance", Journal of Farm Economics 21:418–443.

Hamal, K.B., and J.R. Anderson (1982), "A note on decreasing absolute risk aversion among farmers in Nepal", Australian Journal of Agricultural Economics 26:220–225.

Hanoch, G., and H. Levy (1969), "The efficiency analysis of choices involving risk", Review of Economic Studies 36:335–346.

Hartman, R. (1976), "Factor demand with output price uncertainty", American Economic Review 66:675–681.

Hazell, P.B.R. (1971), "A linear alternative to quadratic and semivariance programming for farm planning under uncertainty", American Journal of Agricultural Economics 53:53–62.

Hazell, P.B.R. (1982), "Applications of risk preference estimates in firm-household and agricultural sector models", American Journal of Agricultural Economics 64:384–390.

Hazell, P.B.R. (1992), "The appropriate role of agricultural insurance in developing countries", Journal of International Development 4:567–582.

Hennessy, D.A. (1998), "The production effects of income support under price uncertainty", American Journal of Agricultural Economics 80:46–57.

Hennessy, D.A., B.A. Babcock and D.J. Hayes (1997), "Budgetary and producer welfare effects of revenue insurance", American Journal of Agricultural Economics 79:1024–1034.

Hirshleifer, J. (1966), "Investment decisions under uncertainty: Applications of the state-preference approach", Quarterly Journal of Economics 80:252–277.

Hirshleifer, J., and J.G. Riley (1992), The Analytics of Uncertainty and Information (Cambridge University Press, Cambridge, U.K.).

Holt, M.T. (1993), "Risk response in the beef marketing channel: A multivariate generalized ARCH-M approach", American Journal of Agricultural Economics 75:559–571.

Holt, M.T., and G. Moschini (1992), "Alternative measures of risk in commodity supply models: An analysis of sow farrowing decisions in the United States", Journal of Agricultural and Resource Economics 17:1–12.

Holthausen, D.M. (1979), "Hedging and the competitive firm under price uncertainty", American Economic Review 69:989–995.

Horowitz, J.K., and E. Lichtenberg (1993), "Insurance, moral hazard, and chemical use in agriculture", American Journal of Agricultural Economics 75:926–935.

Hurt, C.A., and P. Garcia (1982), "The impact of price risk on sow farrowings, 1967–78", American Journal of Agricultural Economics 64:563–568.

Hyde, C.E., and J.A. Vercammen (1997), "Costly yield verification, moral hazard, and crop insurance contract form", Journal of Agricultural Economics 48:393–407.

Innes, R. (1990), "Government target price interventions in economies with incomplete markets", Quarterly Journal of Economics 106:1035–1052.

Innes, R., and S. Ardila (1994), "Agricultural insurance and soil depletion in a simple dynamic model", American Journal of Agricultural Economics 76:371–384.

Innes, R., and G.C. Rausser (1989), "Incomplete markets and government agricultural policy", American Journal of Agricultural Economics 71:915–931.

Ishii, Y. (1977), "On the theory of the competitive firm under price uncertainty: Note", American Economic Review 67:768–769.

Jewitt, I. (1987), "Risk aversion and the choice between risky prospects: The preservation of comparative statics results", Review of Economic Studies 56:14–25.

Just, R.E. (1974), "An investigation of the importance of risk in farmer's decisions", American Journal of Agricultural Economics 56:14–25.

Just, R.E. (1976), "Estimation of a risk response model with some degree of flexibility", Southern Economic Journal 42:675–684.

Just, R.E., and L. Calvin (1990), "An empirical analysis of U.S. participation in crop insurance", Unpublished report to the Federal Crop Insurance Corporation.

Just, R.E., and L. Calvin (1993), "Adverse selection in U.S. crop insurance: The relationship of farm characteristics to premiums", Unpublished manuscript, University of Maryland.

Just, R.E., and R.D. Pope (1978), "Stochastic specifications of production functions and economic implications", Journal of Econometrics 7:67–86.

Just, R.E., and R.D. Pope (1979), "Production function and estimation and related risk considerations", American Journal of Agricultural Economics 61:276–284.

Just, R.E., and Q. Weninger (1999), "Are crop yields normally distributed?", American Journal of Agricultural Economics 81:287–304.

Just, R.E., and D. Zilberman (1983), "Stochastic structure, farm size and technology adoption in developing agriculture", Oxford Economic Papers 35:307–328.

Kahneman, D., and A. Tversky (1979), "Prospect theory: An analysis of decision under risk", Econometrica 47:263–291.

Karp, L.S. (1988), "Dynamic hedging with uncertain production", International Economic Review 29:621–637.

Karp, L.S., and A. Pope (1984), "Range management under uncertainty", American Journal of Agricultural Economics 66:437–446.

Katz, E. (1981), "A note on a comparative statics theorem for choice under risk", Journal of Economic Theory 25:318–319.

Kimball, M.S. (1990). "Precautionary saving in the small and in large", Econometrica 58:53–73.

Knight, F. (1921), Risk, Uncertainty and Profit (Houghton Mifflin, Boston).

Knight, T.O., and K.H. Coble (1997), "Survey of U.S. multiple peril crop insurance literature since 1980", Review of Agricultural Economics 19:128–156.

Krause, M. (1979), "A comparative static theorem for choice under risk", Journal of Economic Theory 21:510–517.

Lapan, H., and G. Moschini (1994), "Futures hedging under price, basis, and production risk", American Journal of Agricultural Economics 76:465–477.

Lapan, H., and G. Moschini (1996), "Optimal price policies and the futures markets", Economics Letters 53:175–182.

Lapan, H., G. Moschini and S. Hanson (1991), "Production, hedging and speculative decisions with options and futures markets", American Journal of Agricultural Economics 72:66–74.

Lapan, H., G. Moschini and S. Hanson (1993), "Production, hedging and speculative decisions with options and futures markets: Reply", American Journal of Agricultural Economics 75:748–750.

Leahy, J.V. (1993), "Investment in competitive equilibrium: The optimality of myopic behavior", Quarterly Journal of Economics 108:1105–1133.

Lence, S.H. (1995), "On the optimal hedge under unbiased futures prices", Economics Letters 47:385–388.

Lence, S.H. (1996), "Relaxing the assumptions of minimum-variance hedge", Journal of Agricultural and Resource Economics 21:39–55.

Lin, W. (1977), "Measuring aggregate supply response under instability", American Journal of Agricultural Economics 59:903–907.

Lin, W., G. Dean and C. Moore (1974), "An empirical test of utility vs. profit maximization in agricultural production", American Journal of Agricultural Economics 56:497–508.

Losq, E. (1982), "Hedging with price and output uncertainty", Economic Letters 10:65–70.

Love, H.A., and S.T. Buccola (1991), "Joint risk preference-technology estimation with a primal system", American Journal of Agricultural Economics 73:765–774.

Luo, H., J.R. Skees and M.A. Marchant (1994), "Weather information and the potential for inter-temporal adverse selection", Review of Agricultural Economics 16:441–451.

Machina, M.J. (1987), "Choice under uncertainty: Problems solved and unsolved", Journal of Economic Perspectives 1:121–154.

MacMinn, R.D., and A.G. Holtmann (1983), "Technological uncertainty and the theory of the firm", Southern Economic Journal 50:120–136.

Mahul, O. (1999), "Optimum area yield crop insurance", American Journal of Agricultural Economics 81.

Marcus, A.J., and D.M. Modest (1984), "Futures markets and production decisions", Journal of Political Economy 92:409–426.

Markowitz, H. (1952), "Portfolio selection", Journal of Finance 7:77–91.

Mas-Colell, A., M.D. Whinston and J.R. Green (1995), Microeconomic Theory (Oxford University Press, Oxford).

McKinnon, R.I. (1967), "Futures markets, buffer stocks, and income instability for primary producers", Journal of Political Economy 75:844–861.

Menger, K. (1934), "Das unsicherheitsmoment in der wertlehre", Zeitschrift für Nationalökonomie. Translation in: M. Shubik, ed., 1967, Essays in Mathematical Economics in Honor of Oskar Morgenstern (Princeton University Press, Princeton).

Meyer, J. (1987), "Two-moment decision models and expected utility maximization", American Economic Review 77:421–430.

Meyer, J., and M.B. Ormiston (1983), "The comparative statics of cumulative distribution function changes for the class of risk averse agents", Journal of Economic Theory 31:153–169.

Meyer, J., and M.B. Ormiston (1985), "Strong increases in risk and their comparative statics", International Economic Review 26:425–437.

Meyer, J., and M.B. Ormiston (1989), "Deterministic transformations of random variables and the comparative statics of uncertainty", Journal of Risk and Uncertainty 2:179–188.

Miranda, M.J. (1991), "Area-yield crop insurance reconsidered", American Journal of Agricultural Economics 73:233–242.

Miranda, M.J., and J.W. Glauber (1991), "Providing crop disaster assistance through a modified deficiency payment program", American Journal of Agricultural Economics 73:1233–1243.

Miranda, M.J., and J.W. Glauber (1993), "Estimation of dynamic nonlinear rational expectations models of primary commodity markets with private and government stockholding", Review of Economics and Statistics 75:463–470.

Miranda, M.J., and J.W. Glauber (1997), "Systemic risk, reinsurance, and the failure of crop insurance markets", American Journal of Agricultural Economics 79:206–215.

Moscardi, E., and A. de Janvry (1977), "Attitudes toward risk among peasants: An econometric approach", American Journal of Agricultural Economics 59:710–716.

Moschini, G. (1999), Production Risk and the Estimation of Ex-ante Cost Functions, Staff Paper # 315 (Department of Economics, Iowa State University). Forthcoming, Journal of Econometrics, 2001.

Moschini, G., and H. Lapan (1992), "Hedging price risk with options and futures for the competitive firm with production flexibility", International Economic Review 33:607–618.

Moschini, G., and H. Lapan (1995), "The hedging role of options and futures under joint price, basis, and production risk", International Economic Review 36:1025–1049.

Moss, C.B., and J.S. Shonkwiler (1993), "Estimating yield distributions with a stochastic trend and nonnormal errors", American Journal of Agricultural Economics 75:1056–1062.

Myers, R.J. (1988), "The value of ideal contingency markets in agriculture", American Journal of Agricultural Economics 70:255–267.

Myers, R.J. (1989), "Econometric testing for risk averse behavior in agriculture", Applied Economics 21:542–552.

Myers, R.J., and S.D. Hanson (1996), "Optimal dynamic hedging in unbiased futures markets", American Journal of Agricultural Economics 78:13–20.

Myers, R.J., and S.R. Thompson (1989), "Generalized optimal hedge ratio estimation", American Journal of Agricultural Economics 71:858–868.

Nelson, D.B. (1990), "Stationarity and persistence in the GARCH(1,1) model", Econometric Theory 6:318–334.

Nelson, C.H., and P.V. Preckel (1989), "The conditional beta distribution as a stochastic production function", American Journal of Agricultural Economics 71:370–378.

Nerlove, M. (1958), The Dynamics of Supply: Estimation of Farmers Response to Price (Johns Hopkins University Press, Baltimore).

Newbery, D.M. (1988), "On the accuracy of the mean-variance approximation for futures markets", Economics Letters 28:63–68.

Newbery, D.M.G., and J.E. Stiglitz (1981), The Theory of Commodity Price Stabilization – A Study in the Economics of Risk (Clarendon Press, Oxford).

O'Donnell, C.J., and A.D. Woodland (1995), "Estimation of Australian wool and lamb production technologies under uncertainty: An error components approach", American Journal of Agricultural Economics 77:552–565.

Ormiston, M.B. (1992), "First and second degree transformations and comparative statics under uncertainty", International Economic Review 33:33–44.

Pagan, A.R., and G.W. Schwert (1990), "Alternative models for conditional stock volatility", Journal of Econometrics 45:267–290.

Paris, Q. (1989), "Broken symmetry, symmetry, and price uncertainty", European Economic Review 33:1227–1239.

Pesaran, M.H. (1987), Limits to Rational Expectations (Blackwell Press, Oxford).

Pitt, M.M., and G. Sumodiningrat (1991), "Risk, schooling and the choice of seed technology in developing countries: A meta-profit function approach", International Economic Review 32:457–473.

Pope, R.D. (1978), "The expected utility hypothesis and demand-supply restrictions", American Journal of Agricultural Economics 60:619–627.

Pope, R.D. (1980), "The generalized envelope theorem and price uncertainty", International Economic Review 21:75–86.

Pope, R.D. (1988), "A new parametric test for the structure of risk preferences", Economics Letters 27:117–121.

Pope, R.D., and J.-P. Chavas (1994), "Cost functions under production uncertainty", American Journal of Agricultural Economics 76:196–204.

Pope, R.D., and R.E. Just (1991), "On testing the structure of risk preferences in agricultural supply analysis", American Journal of Agricultural Economics 73:743–748.

Pope, R.D., and R.E. Just (1996), "Empirical implementation of ex-ante cost functions", Journal of Econometrics 72:231–249.

Pope, R.D., and R.A. Kramer (1979), "Production uncertainty and factor demands for the competitive firm", Southern Economic Journal 46:489–501.

Pratt, J. (1964), "Risk aversion in the small and in the large", Econometrica 32:122–236.

Purvis, A., W.G. Boggess, C.B. Moss and J. Holt (1995), "Technology adoption decisions under irreversibility and uncertainty: An *ex ante* approach", American Journal of Agricultural Economics 77:541–551.

Pyle, D.H., and S.J. Turnovsky (1970), "Safety first and expected utility maximization in mean-standard deviation portfolio analysis", Review of Economics and Statistics 52:75–81.

Quiggin, J. (1993), Generalized Expected Utility Theory – The Rank-Dependent Model (Kluwer Academic Publishers, Boston).

Quiggin, J., G. Karagiannis and J. Stanton (1993), "Crop insurance and crop production: An empirical study of moral hazard and adverse selection", Australian Journal of Agricultural Economics 37:95–113.

Ramaswami, B. (1992), "Production risk and optimal input decisions", American Journal of Agricultural Economics 74:860–869.

Ramírez, O.A. (1997), "Estimation and use of a multivariate parametric model for simulating heteroskedastic, correlated, nonnormal random variables: The case of corn belt corn, soybean, and wheat yields", American Journal of Agricultural Economics 79:191–205.

Rausser, G.C., and E. Hochman (1979), Dynamic Agricultural Systems: Economic Prediction and Control (North-Holland, New York).

Ray, D. (1998), Development Economics (Princeton University Press, Princeton NJ).

Robison, L.J., and P.J. Barry (1987), The Competitive Firm's Response to Risk (MacMillan, New York).

Rolfo, J. (1980), "Optimal hedging under price and quantity uncertainty: The case of a cocoa producer", Journal Political Economy 88:100–116.

Rosenzweig, M.R., and H.P. Binswanger (1993), "Wealth, weather risk and the composition and profitability of agricultural investments", Economic Journal 103:56–78.

Rothschild, M., and J.E. Stiglitz (1970), "Increasing risk: I. A definition", Journal of Economic Theory 2:225–243.

Rothschild, M., and J.E. Stiglitz (1971), "Increasing risk: II. Its economic consequences", Journal of Economic Theory 3:66–84.

Roumasset, J.A., M.W. Rosegrant, U.N. Chakravorty and J.R. Anderson (1989), "Fertilizer and crop yield variability: A review", in: J.R. Anderson, and P.B.R. Hazell, eds., Variability in Grain Yields (Johns Hopkins University Press, Baltimore) 223–233.

Saha, A. (1993), "Expo-power utility: A 'flexible' form for absolute and relative risk aversion", American Journal of Agricultural Economics 75:905–913.

Saha, A., C.R. Shumway and H. Talpaz (1994), "Joint estimation of risk preference structure and technology using expo-power utility", American Journal of Agricultural Economics 76:173–184.

Sakurai, T., and T. Reardon (1997), "Potential demand for drought insurance in Burkina Faso and its determinants", American Journal of Agricultural Economics 79:1193–1207.

Samuelson, P. (1952), "Probability, utility, and the independence axiom", Econometrica 20:670–678.

Sandmo, A. (1971), "On the theory of the competitive firm under price uncertainty", American Economic Review 61:65–73.

Savage, L.J. (1954), The Foundations of Statistics (Wiley, New York).

Sengupta, J.I., and R.E. Sfeir (1982), "Risk in supply response: An econometric application", Applied Economics 14:249–268.

Sharpe, W.F. (1963), "A simplified model for portfolio analysis", Management Science 2:277–293.

Sigurdson, D., and R. Sin (1994), "An aggregate analysis of Canadian crop insurance policy", in: D.L. Hueth, and W.H. Furtan, eds., Economics of Agricultural Crop Insurance: Theory and Evidence (Kluwer Academic Publishers, Boston) 45–72.

Sinn, H.-W. (1989), "Two-moment decision models and expected utility maximization: Comment", American Economic Review 79:601–602.

Skees, J.R., and M.R. Reed (1986), "Rate-making for farm-level crop insurance: Implications for adverse selection", American Journal of Agricultural Economics 68:653–659.

Smale, M., R.E. Just and H.D. Leathers (1994), "Land allocation in HYV adoption models: An investigation of alternative explanations", American Journal of Agricultural Economics 76:535–546.

Smith, V.H., and A. Baquet (1996), "The demand for multiple peril crop insurance: Evidence from Montana wheat farms", American Journal of Agricultural Economics 78:189–201.

Smith, V.H., and B.K. Goodwin (1996), "Crop insurance, moral hazard, and agricultural chemical use", American Journal of Agricultural Economics 78:428–438.

Standing Committee on Agriculture and Colonization (1947), Minutes of the Proceedings and Evidence, (Canadian House of Commons, Ottawa, Canada) June 10.

Tauer, L.W. (1983), "Target MOTAD", American Journal of Agricultural Economics 65:606–610.

Taylor, C.R. (1990), "Two practical procedures for estimating multivariate nonnormal probability density functions", American Journal of Agricultural Economics 72:210–218.

Teague, M.L., D.J. Bernardo and H.P. Mapp (1995), "Farm-level economic analysis incorporating stochastic environmental risk assessment", American Journal of Agricultural Economics 77:8–19.

Tobin, J. (1958), "Liquidity preference as behavior towards risk", Review of Economic Studies 25:65–86.

Tolley, H.D., and R.D. Pope (1988), "Testing for stochastic dominance", American Journal of Agricultural Economics 70:693–700.

Traill, B. (1978), "Risk variables in econometric supply models", Journal of Agricultural Economics 29:53–61.

Traxler, G., J. Falck-Zepeda, R.J.I. Ortiz-Monasterio and K. Sayre (1995), "Production risk and the evolution of varietal technology", American Journal of Agricultural Economics 77:1–7.

Turvey, C.G. (1992a), "An economic analysis of alternative farm revenue insurance policies", Canadian Journal of Agricultural Economics 40:403–426.

Turvey, C.G. (1992b), "Contingent claim pricing models implied by agricultural stabilization and insurance policies", Canadian Journal of Agricultural Economics 40:183–198.

Udry, C. (1994), "Risk and insurance in a rural credit market: An empirical investigation in Northern Nigeria", Review of Economic Studies 61:495–526.

United States Department of Agriculture (1996), Agricultural Statistics (various issues from 1990 to 1996).

United States General Accounting Office (1999), Agriculture in Transition – Farmers' Use of Risk Management Strategies, GAO/RCED-99-90, Washington, D.C.

Vercammen, J., and G.C. van Kooten (1994), "Moral hazard cycles in individual-coverage crop insurance", American Journal of Agricultural Economics 76:250–261.

von Neumann, J., and O. Morgenstern (1944), Theory of Games and Economic Behavior (Princeton University Press, Princeton).

Vukina, T., D. Li and D.M. Holthausen (1996), "Hedging with crop yield futures: a mean-variance analysis", American Journal of Agricultural Economics 78:1015–1025.

Williams, J. (1986), The Economic Functions of Futures Markets (Cambridge University Press, Cambridge, U.K.).

Williams, J.R., G.L. Carriker, G.A. Barnaby and J.K. Harper (1993), "Crop insurance and disaster assistance designs for wheat and grain sorghum", American Journal of Agricultural Economics 75:435–447.

Wright, B.D. (1993), "Public insurance of private risks: Theory and evidence from agriculture", in: M.S. Sniderman, ed., Government Risk Bearing (Kluwer Academic Publishers, Boston).

Wright, B.D., and J.D. Hewitt (1990), All Risk Crop Insurance: Lessons from Theory and Experience (Giannini Foundation, California Agricultural Experiment Station, Berkeley).

Young, D.L. (1979), "Risk preferences of agricultural producers: Their use in extension and research", American Journal of Agricultural Economics 61:1067–1070.

Chapter 3

EXPECTATIONS, INFORMATION AND DYNAMICS

MARC NERLOVE

Department of Agricultural and Resource Economics, University of Maryland, College Park, MD

DAVID A. BESSLER

Department of Agricultural Economics, Texas A & M University, College Station, TX

Contents

Handbook of Agricultural Economics, Volume 1, Edited by B. Gardner and G. Rausser
© 2001 Elsevier Science B.V.   All rights reserved

Abstract

The role of expectations in the empirical analysis of agricultural supply is examined under the assumption of separation of expectations and constraints in dynamic decision making. Extrapolative, adaptive, implicit, rational and quasi-rational, and futures-based models of expectation formation are discussed. Empirical and experimental evidence for and against various models of expectation is summarized.

JEL classification: Q11

"We decide on one particular course of action out of a number of rival courses because this one gives us, as an immediately present experience, the most enjoyment *by anticipation* of its outcome. Future situations and events cannot be experienced and therefore their degree of desirableness cannot be compared: but situations and events can be *imagined*, and the desirableness of these experiences which happen in the imagination can be compared. What gives imagined things a claim to be treated as the equivalents of future things? It is some degree of belief that the imagined things will take actual shape at the dates we assign to them."
G.L.S. Shackle, 1952.

"All production is for the purpose of ultimately satisfying a consumer. Time usually elapses, however – and sometimes much time – between the incurring of costs by the producer (with the consumer in view) and the purchase of the output by the ultimate consumer ... Meanwhile the entrepreneur ... has to form the best expectations he can as to what the consumers will be prepared to pay when he is ready to supply them (directly or indirectly) after the elapse of what may be a lengthy period; and he has no choice but to be guided by these expectations, if he is to produce at all by processes which occupy time ... the behaviour of each individual firm ... will be determined by its *short-term expectations* ... The *actually realised* results ... will only be relevant in so far as they cause a modification of subsequent expectations.
John Maynard Keynes, 1936.

1. Introduction

We consider the role of expectations and new information in agricultural economics, with reference to other work on expectation formation. The chapter is presented in four main parts. In the opening section we describe the structure of the problem of modeling dynamic optimizing behavior under uncertainty. Central to almost all treatments of the subject since the work of Keynes and Hicks in the 1930s is the separation assumption, in which dynamic decision problems are modeled by separating expectation formation from optimizing behavior. Two examples of dynamic models of agricultural supply response are used to illustrate the approach. In the second part, we present the five principal alternative approaches for modeling expectation formation: extrapolative expectations, adaptive expectations, implicit expectations, rational and quasi-rational expectations, and futures markets. In the third part, we consider the evidence on the validity of these five approaches, focusing primarily on rational expectations and the more operational variant, quasi-rational expectations. Evidence from both indirect tests, such as restrictions on parameters in an econometric model, and direct tests, such as tests of unbiasedness and orthogonality of elicited expectations obtained from survey and experiments, is presented. The chapter concludes by offering directions for future research.

2. Expectations and dynamic optimization

2.1. The structure of the problem

If current decisions did not constrain future possibilities, opportunities, or costs, expectations of future events would not be relevant to these decisions. It is precisely because what we do today constrains what we can do tomorrow that the future is relevant to the present.[1] (See [Nerlove (1972)].) Current events influence what we do today both directly and indirectly; directly, because present circumstances affect the desirability or profitability of actions now; indirectly, because events in the present influence our expectations of the future. These two effects may be quite different. What is the relation between dynamic optimization under uncertainty with respect to future opportunities and constraints and how economic agents form their expectations of the future and make decisions and plans?[2]

Hicks (1946) found a solution to the problem of formulating a dynamic theory of the firm under certainty by dating all variables and applying static theory to the expanded set of variables and constraints, although, in the end, he was clearly not happy with this solution [Hicks (1977)]. The Hicksian solution essentially converts the dynamic decision-making problem into a static problem. It fails to reveal the dynamic structure of decisions and constraints and to deal explicitly with uncertainty, the costs of information, or the costs of formulating plans and decisions. In principle, we know how to set the problem up as a dynamic programming problem under uncertainty, in which conditional distributions of future unknown exogenous variables are estimated by using all available information up to the present [Nerlove (1972)]. The problem of costly information is more difficult to incorporate since its value is usually not known until it is acquired, but this problem can be resolved within a Bayesian framework. (See, *inter alia*, [Horvath and Nerlove (1996), Kiefer (1988–89)].) In such a "theoretically correct" formulation, decisions and expectations are not separable; the explanation of behavior proceeds directly from assumptions about agents' priors and the dynamic constraints of their optimization problem to the decisions they take now and in the future in response to future events.[3]

---

[1]   This is also true with respect to future events over which we have no control, such as events after one's death. The imminent end of the world, if known, would certainly change behavior today because constraints current behavior would impose on future options would no longer hold after the end of the world. In this sense, the future matters because of the constraints it would impose on current behavior if there were a future.

[2]   The problem of what constitutes rational behavior in a dynamic context is not so simple; see [McClennen (1990)] for a careful analysis from a philosopher's point of view. Nor is it a trivial matter to make the concepts of information and uncertainty precise. There is a very extensive literature in economics on these matters which has been artfully summarized and integrated in [Hirshleifer and Riley (1992)].

[3]   Notwithstanding, Mundlak (1966, 1967) has suggested that a dynamic theory should be formulated in a manner which takes explicit account of the restrictions implied by the Hicksian extension of static theory. This is an extreme form of the separation assumption, to which we would not subscribe. As Treadway (1967) has shown, the propositions of usual comparative static theory do not generally hold in a dynamic context. But

The theoretically correct formulation of the problem of dynamic decision making under uncertainty does not lend itself to empirical application, nor has it generally been adopted in studies of agricultural supply or other topics investigated by agricultural economists and, more generally, in empirical studies of expectations and plans (see [Nerlove (1983)], and the references cited therein). Instead, a separation between expectations and decisions is made and the effects of changing expectations on behavior is analyzed. "The Hicksian model of dynamic planning under certainty is the basis for a more empirically relevant framework for the analysis of plans and expectations .... The Hicksian assumption of certainty means that information about the future value of a variable is single valued and costless. We continue to regard expectations and plans as single valued but recognize that the economic agent knows that they may turn out to be wrong. As of a particular date, information about the future can be acquired only at a cost, albeit a cost which decreases for a particular future date as that date draws near. Planning and decision making are themselves costly activities. Therefore only what is necessary to plan will be planned, only decisions which cannot be postponed will be made, and only the information about the future necessary to those plans and decisions and only to the accuracy warranted by the cost of error will be gathered. Plans will not always be fulfilled, single-valued expectations will often turn out to be wrong, and both will be continually revised" [Nerlove (1983, p. 1252)]. We refer to the assumption that dynamic decision problems can be analyzed in terms of expectations and the impact of expectations on decisions as the *separation assumption*. It is clearly only an approximation, albeit an empirically and theoretically useful one.

Even when the separation assumption is adopted, there is another serious problem which models of expectation formation and dynamic behavior share with most other models on which econometric analyses are based: they typically assume a representative economic agent whose optimizing decisions are the basis for the analysis. Not only does such an assumption raise the question so ably and concisely discussed by Kirman (1992), but another branch of the literature has emphasized the role of heterogeneity

---

this does not mean that separation of expectations and optimizing behavior is impossible within the context of an appropriately formulated dynamic model [Nerlove (1972)].

The econometric modeling of dynamic decision making processes has recently enjoyed a resurgence of interest; see, for example Kapteyn, Kiefer, and Rust (1995), especially the paper by Miranda and Schnitkey (1995). It is, however, not clear to us whether such econometric "fine-tuning" is really desirable, notwithstanding Nerlove (1972) and more recently Nerlove and Fornari (1997). Carrying forward the research of more than two decades, Hildenbrand (1994), for example, shows that the specification of behavioral relationships at the individual level does not play a dominant role in determining the sort of relationship commonly estimated econometrically. He argues, in the context of cross-section expenditure studies, that certain invariant features of the distribution of household characteristics and attributes are much more important in determining the relationships of interest, and that these can be derived without any need to specify a precise model of microeconomic behavior. We believe that Hildenbrand's conclusions are valid generally and beyond the context of econometric analysis of household expenditure surveys. Many restrictions imposed by microeconomic theory, whether static or dynamic, are of very limited value in improving econometric estimation. Other aspects of the data-generating process are much more important. To attempt to fine-tune the econometrics by imposing such restrictions can lead to results which may be highly misleading.

of expectations in the determination of aggregate outcomes [Nerlove (1983), Frydman and Phelps (1983)]. Such heterogeneity is inconsistent with the representative agent assumption.[4]

2.2. Examples of the separation of expectations and constraints in dynamic decision making

The device of separation of expectations from plans and decisions and the utility of such separation in both theory and empirical analysis may be illustrated by two models of agricultural supply: The first of these examples is the well-known model of agricultural supply response developed by Nerlove (1956a, 1956b, 1958c) for corn, cotton, and wheat in the U.S. The second is a more elaborate model of small ruminant production and supply in Indonesia developed by Nerlove and Soedjana (1996).[5] The importance of the second example is to show that a comparative static analysis is possible in models involving both dynamic optimization and uncertainty, *even though the process of expectation formation is not specified*, as long as the separation assumption is maintained. The representative agent assumption is also common to these examples.

2.2.1. The Nerlove supply model[6]

Stripped to its essentials, this model for an annual crop consists of three equations:

$$A_t - A_{t-1} = \gamma (A_t^* - A_{t-1}), \tag{1}$$

$$P_t^* - P_{t-1}^* = \beta (P_{t-1} - P_{t-1}^*), \tag{2}$$

$$A_t^* = a_0 + a_1 P_t^* + a_2 Z_t + U_t, \tag{3}$$

where A_t is actual area under cultivation in t; P_t, actual price of the crop per unit in t; A_t^*, "desired" or equilibrium area to be under cultivation in t; P_t^*, "expected normal" price in t for subsequent future periods; Z_t, other observed, presumably exogenous, factors; U_t, unobserved, "latent" factors affecting area under cultivation in t; and β and γ are "coefficients of expectation and adjustment", reflecting the responses of expectations to observed prices and observed areas under cultivation to changes in equilibrium areas.

---

[4] See also the discussion of heterogeneity in the determination of aggregate outcomes in the preceding footnote.

[5] The interesting study of Miranda and Schnitkey (1995) does not employ this separation. They assume that the two relevant stochastic variables, revenue less variable cost of milk and the market price of a heifer less the slaughter value of a replace cow, follow a first-order vector autoregression (VAR), known to the dairy farmer, the parameters of which are to be estimated along with the rest of their model. However, such a model could be interpreted in terms of rational or quasi-rational expectations under the separation assumption; see below, Section 3.4.

[6] This discussion is taken from [Nerlove (1979)].

The statistical problems of estimating a model such as (1)–(3), particularly of identifying relevant observed exogenous variables, not subject to expectational lags, and problems due to serially correlated disturbances, are well known. In addition, the use of area cultivated, one input in the production process to represent planned output, the problem of choosing the relevant price or prices, and other issues of specification, such as the inclusion of expected yields, weather conditions, and price and yield variances to take account of elements of risk, have been widely discussed in the literature (see, for example, *inter alia* [Just (1974), Askari and Cummings (1976, 1977)]).

The Nerlove supply response model incorporates dynamic elements in two different ways: First, a distinction is made between a long-run equilibrium position, toward which producers are assumed to be moving, and their current position. The former is determined on the basis of a static theory of optimization, in this case the standard microeconomic theory of the firm and the assumption that the exogenous variables of the problem, in this case mainly prices, are given once and for all. Nerlove (1972, p. 225) called this the assumption of static, or stationary, expectations. The important point is that whatever these expectations are and however they are formed, the concept of a long-run equilibrium solution to the optimization problem is well defined only if it can be assumed that the values of the exogenous variables expected in the future are unchanging; it does not matter if the constant future value of each variable differs from its current value, as indeed it plausibly will. Having a well-defined notion of a long-run equilibrium position then permits us to examine the question of why producers are currently at a position different from that equilibrium. At this point the discussion usually becomes vague; one can argue in various ways (Nerlove, 1972, pp. 228–231), but perhaps the most common approach is through the introduction of adjustment costs. Rarely, however, are models explicitly introducing these costs formulated or the rationale for such costs carefully examined.[7]

The dynamic element in the basic supply response models is introduced at this point without a formal theory by the simple ad hoc assumption that in each period, if we are dealing with discrete time, a fraction of the difference between the current position and the long-run equilibrium is eliminated, i.e., Equation (1) above.

The second way in which dynamic elements are incorporated in the basic supply response model is through a description of expectation formation, e.g., the adaptive expectations generated by Equation (2), in which expected "normal" prices are revised each period in proportion to the difference between last period's observed price and the previous expectation. Above, we argued that static, or stationary, expectations are necessary to make the concept of a long-run equilibrium meaningful; the adaptive expectations model does not violate this principle, since it is not solely next period's price to which P_t^* refers but "normal" price, i.e., an average price expected to prevail in all future periods. Nerlove (1956a, 1956b, 1958c) makes the argument that farmers rationally

---

[7] The literature up to about 1970 is surveyed, and two models of investment behavior incorporating both separable and non-separable adjustment costs are discussed, in [Nerlove (1972, pp. 231–241)]; see also [Nerlove et al. (1979 and 1995, pp. 317–320)].

should respond, not to the best forecast they can make of next period's price, but rather to some average or "normal" level; the argument rests intuitively on the idea that there are costs of adjustment. However, virtually any plausible model one can construct, with costs of rapid adjustment of, say, a durable factor of production, will generally involve response to prices in many future periods, although the weights which attach to the more distant future will usually be less than to the near future. Moreover, unless the optimization problem has a specific form, it will generally be non-optimal to behave as if one were responding to a point estimate of each future value. When the optimization problem is of this specific form, however, we say that there exist certainty equivalents to the uncertain future values of the variables to which response is occurring [Theil (1957), Malinvaud (1969)]. Such certainty equivalents are the conditional expectations of the variables to which they refer; they are minimum-mean-square-error forecasts based on the information available up to the time the forecast is made and taking into account the structure of the system generating the data. Muth (1961) has termed such forecasts "rational expectations". We will discuss rational expectations models of agricultural supply at some length below.

2.2.2. A model of small ruminant production and supply

The dynamics of annual crop supply are particularly simple; their very simplicity may obscure the relation between expectations and dynamic optimizing behavior. Better examples of greater dynamic complexity may be found in the study of perennial crops, such as rubber, coffee, cocoa, palm oil or asparagus, or of livestock. The following model shows that a comparative static analysis is possible in models involving both dynamic optimization and uncertainty, *even though the process of expectation formation is not specified*, as long as the separation assumption is maintained. Nonetheless, it also illustrates the importance of expectations in determining dynamic optimizing behavior.

Small ruminant production and supply presents an ideal case to illustrate the points made above, being neither too simple nor, because of the short gestation and maturation period of the animals, as complex as cattle and many perennial crops. The following development is based on Nerlove and Soedjana (1996), hereinafter N&S, whose primary purpose is to elucidate the role which small ruminants play as a store of value in the context of traditional Indonesian society. In their paper, details of which are not elsewhere published, they make considerable use of neoclassical monetary theory, an aspect of the analysis which we neglect here. Small ruminants in general are referred to as "sheep".

N&S assume that sheep live for two periods. In the first period, they are gestating or prepubescent. In the second period, all the time that they remain in the herd, they reproduce at a rate $\alpha > 1$. At the end of the first period, which is the same as the beginning of the second period, some are sold and do not survive to reproduce. Let

> S_t = the stock of sheep at the beginning of period t;
>
> s_{t+1} = sales at the end of period t or the beginning of period $t+1$.

Then, the stock at the beginning of period $t + 1$ is

$$S_{t+1} = \alpha[S_t - s_{t+1}]. \tag{4}$$

Let

$C(S) =$ the costs of maintaining a herd of size S for one period;

$p_t =$ the price per sheep sold expected in period t;

$p_0 =$ the actual price in the current period, $t = 0$, at the end of which s_0 sheep are sold.

Assume that these expectations are held with certainty, or alternatively, that the structure of the problem is such as to admit of certainty equivalents. Let S_0 be the initial herd size. The costs of maintaining this herd during the first period are sunk costs and must be borne out of revenues generated previously. Current gross revenue at the end of the initial period is p_0s_1, but the costs of maintaining the herd in the following period $C(S_1)$ must be paid from these revenues, so that net revenue in the current period is $R_0 = p_0s_1 - C(S_1)$. In general,

$$R_t = p_ts_{t+1} - C(S_{t+1}), \quad t = 0, 1, \ldots. \tag{5}$$

Along the lines of neoclassical monetary theory, N&S assume that the utility function of the representative farmer is additively separable over time and a homothetically weakly separable function of the stock of sheep and current revenue (which can be taken as a Hicks-composite commodity if the prices of real commodities consumed by the farmer are assumed not to change). That is, we assume that the farmer's consumption decisions are determined by maximizing a "branch" utility function in real commodities given the revenues realized from the sale of sheep at the beginning of each period. Thus, the utility of the farmer in each period is given by

$$u_t = U[\varphi(R_t), S_{t+1}] = U\left[\varphi\left(p_t\left\{S_t - \frac{S_{t+1}}{\alpha}\right\} - C(S_{t+1})\right), S_{t+1}\right]. \tag{6}$$

Given the additive temporal separability of total utility, as is well known [Barro (1974), Barro and Becker (1989), Nerlove and Raut (1997)], total utility can be expressed as

$$TU = \sum_{t=0}^{\infty} \beta^t u_t, \quad \text{where } 0 < \beta < 1. \tag{7}$$

In a perfectly functioning capital market, β would equal the rate of interest at which the farmer could borrow, but in the absence of such a market, as we assume here, β

expresses the farmer's rate of time discount. Assume that the farmer has an infinite horizon as if he expected to live forever.

Assume that φ is chosen so that U_1 (where the subscript denotes a derivative with respect to the argument in question) is normalized to 1, i.e., $\varphi'U_1 = 1$, and that $U_2 \geqslant 0$ and $U_{22} \leqslant 0$ and that the farmer maximizes TU by choosing the sequence of herd sizes $S_1, S_2, \ldots$, given the initial herd size S_0.

Maximizing TU with respect to the sequence S_t, $t = 1, \ldots, \infty$, given S_0, is now in the form solved by Stokey and Lucas (1989, pp. 68–84), who show that it is equivalent to maximizing

$$U\big[\varphi(R_0), S_1\big] + \beta v(S_1, p_1, p_2, \ldots) \tag{8}$$

with respect to S_1, where

$$R_0 = p_0 \left[S_0 - \frac{S_1}{\alpha} \right] - C(S_1)$$

and where v is the maximized value of TU in the next period given the value S_1 of the initial stock in that period, chosen in the initial period, and price expectations in all future periods.

The first-order condition for this problem, recalling that U_1 is normalized to 1, is

$$-\frac{p_0}{\alpha} - C' + U_2 + \beta v' = 0. \tag{9}$$

Define

$$\mu(S_1) = \beta v' + U_2,$$

which is the value of a sheep saved in the current period in terms of future breeding capacity, and therefore addition to future revenues and utility plus the utility of having her in stock next period as a store of value. Rearranging terms, we have

$$\alpha\mu(S_1) - p_0 = \alpha C'. \tag{10}$$

Equation (10) is quite intuitive. It says that at an optimum of the producer, the marginal cost of maintaining an animal in the herd next period must be equal to the value of a sheep saved minus the opportunity cost of not selling her. The coefficient $\alpha > 1$ multiplies both μ and C' to account for the fact that a sheep saved today will become α sheep tomorrow.

The left-hand side of (10) is proportional to marginal cost. Average cost may decline initially for very small herd sizes because of certain fixed costs such as barns, but must rise after a certain size of herd (rather small in semi-subsistence Indonesian agriculture),

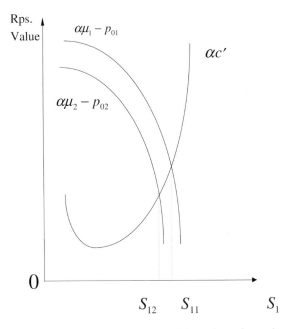

Figure 1. Relationship of the optimal stock of livestock to prices and costs.

and, at some point, begin to rise steeply because of the labor and other resource constraints which the farmer faces. The behavior of the right-hand side is more problematic: $U_{22} \leqslant 0$, so that the second term of μ must be declining with S_1, but if expected future prices of sheep are rising fast enough, v' may not decline with S_1, even if marginal future costs of increasing herd size are rising rapidly. N&S assume that this is not the case.[8] This provides the first illustration of the power of the *separation assumption.*

The solution is graphically depicted in Figure 1.

It is apparent both from Equation (10) and the figure that an increase in the current price of sheep, expectations of future prices unchanged, will lead, *ceteris paribus*, to a decline in the herd size next period, and thus to an increase in sales. But if an increase in the current price is accompanied by an increase in expectations of future prices, causing a rise in μ sufficient to offset the increase in p_0, the current supply of sheep to the market may actually decline. (Of course, this is true irrespective of whether the stock of sheep enters the utility function directly.)

---

[8]   This corresponds to the well-known transversality condition, which is generally assumed in dynamic optimization problems (see [Stokey and Lucas (1989), p. 98)]. If this condition does not hold and if expectations of rapidly rising future prices are not offset by rapidly rising costs of future herd size, μ may rise with S_1, in which case an equilibrium of the producer would still exist in the rising part of the $\alpha C'$ curve, but not in the region of increasing returns to herd size in which $\alpha C'$ is falling.

The rationale for such perverse supply response to price, in general, was cogently argued by Jarvis (1986) and Rosen (1986); Jarvis' empirical verification for Argentine beef cattle relied on ad hoc assumptions about expectation formation; Nerlove and Fornari (1997) provide evidence for the U.S. beef cattle industry of a positive response to current price holding expectations of future prices constant, but a negative response to increases in expected future prices holding current prices constant, using a rational expectations model of price expectation formation. The N&S result, as is the case with Rosen's result, is free of any significant restriction on the nature of expectation formation. If the $\alpha\mu - p_0$ curve cuts the $\alpha C'$ curve in the segment of the latter that is rising extremely rapidly, we would expect to observe hardly any supply response either to current price or to expected future prices.[9]

As the foregoing model illustrates, it is unnecessary to make any specific assumption about the formation of expectations to derive useful results concerning the role of expectations in the determination of dynamic optimizing behavior. Nonetheless, in order to study such behavior econometrically, it is necessary to specify a model of the way in which expectations are formed. To this we now turn.

3. Alternative models of expectation formation[10]

In this section we examine the leading models of expectation formation used in empirical time series analysis of agricultural supply and in other areas of applied economics. The justification for considering models of expectation formation in the context of a model of economic (optimizing) behavior rests in large part on the separation assumption discussed above, to which must be added the assumptions that (1) group behavior can be adequately explained by treating it as the behavior of a single representative and hypothetical decision maker (the representative agent assumption); and (2) the representative decision maker behaves as if responding to single-valued certainty equivalents (the certainty equivalent assumption). The expectations, to which economic agents are assumed to respond, are both subjective and aggregative. They are not necessarily, or even generally, directly observable. The problem in empirical analysis discussed in this

---

[9] Many other results follow from this model. For example, N&S deduce the effects of improved access to financial institutions: Changes in the effectiveness with which local financial institutions serve the semi-subsistence Indonesian farmer will, in the first instance, primarily affect U_2, the direct marginal utility of holding an additional sheep in the herd. Less directly, changes in U_2 will also affect μ, the value of future maximized net revenues from sheep raising. If U_2 is set to zero v', the future value of having a sheep in the herd will fall even if expectations of future prices and costs are unchanged; the term U_2 in μ will be eliminated entirely. Consequently, the entire curve $\alpha\mu - p_0$ will shift downwards relative to the $\alpha C'$ curve. Unless, before the assumed change the curves crossed in the very nearly vertical portion of the $\alpha C'$ curve and still cross there, the optimal herd size will be reduced by better access to financial institutions. This situation is depicted in Figure 1 by the vertical portion of the $\alpha C'$ curve.

[10] This section is adapted from [Nerlove (1958c, Chapter 2), Nerlove (1961), and Nerlove and Fornari (1997)].

section is to construct a hypothesis which relates these expectations to observable variables. In this section we will consider five types of models or approaches to the study of expectation formation within the context of a simple model of supply response: (a) Extrapolative; (b) Adaptive; (c) Implicit; (d) Rational and Quasi-Rational; and (e) Futures Market Based. In the next section, we consider research when data related to expectations are more directly observable, for example from surveys or experiments. One can argue that futures prices, when available, are intermediate between direct and indirect observation of expectations.[11]

3.1. Extrapolative

The classical approach in agricultural supply analysis (at least prior to [Nerlove (1956a, 1956b)] was to suppose that expectational variables could be directly identified with some past actual value of the variable to which the expectation refers. For example, the supply of an agricultural commodity at a future time depends on its price expected at that time. It might be assumed that this expectation is the current value of price, so that supply is simply related to lagged price. An extension of this approach, due to [Goodwin (1947)], is to suppose that expected price in period t is actual price in $t - 1$ plus (or minus) a fraction of the change in price from period $t - 2$ to $t - 1$:

$$p_t^* = p_{t-1} + \alpha(p_{t-1} - p_{t-2}),$$ \hfill (11)

where p_t^* is the price expected in period t. Muth (1961) calls the expectations generated by (11) "extrapolative".

3.2. Adaptive

The origins of adaptive expectations are somewhat obscure. Nerlove (1956a) attributes the idea to Phillip Cagan in his 1956 Ph.D. dissertation on hyper-inflations; but later (1956b, 1958c) says that the idea is essentially Hicks'. Milton Friedman claims he got the idea from Bill Phillips of Phillips Curve fame. After an exhaustive look at empirical studies of expectations that existed before 1956, here's what Nerlove (1958c, pp. 50–53) writes:

> ... the main results of the ... studies examined indicate that there is widespread underestimation of actual changes and that forecasters could generally do a better job at predicting the levels of actual outcomes if they used some simple mechanical device such as a projection of the current value of the variable to be predicted. The question immediately arises as to whether entrepreneurs are really trying to forecast a particular value of an economic variable, or whether, as suggested above

---

[11] However, for storable commodities, cash prices also reflect the same information, so that a futures price is no more and no less an expectation than the current price.

they try to forecast the "normal" *level* of future values of the variable. As indicated above, entrepreneurs' response to a change which they consider only temporary may be very limited. True, entrepreneurs could make greater profits the more accurate their knowledge of the future; but these profits might not be much greater than those they might make if they altered their plans only in response to changes in the expected level of future values of the economic variable under consideration. ... Hence, any model of expectation formation should take account of the fact that these expectations probably do not refer to the immediate and temporary future.

We may take ... a concept of the normal as a starting point in our development of a model of expectation formation. The discussion at this point may most easily be couched in terms of prices and price expectations. If more specific information is not available, it seems reasonable to assume that the "normal" price expected for some future date depends in some way on what prices have been in the past. Expectations of "normal" price are, of course, shaped by a multitude of influences, so that a representation of expected price as a function of past prices may merely be a convenient way to summarize the effects of these many and diverse influences. ...

How should we use past prices to represent expected "normal" price? Each past price represents only a very short-run market phenomenon, an equilibrium of those forces present in the market at the time. ... We observe, however, that entrepreneurs' expectations, if taken as forecasts of the immediate future, predict the levels of actual outcomes in the immediate future less well than would a simple naive model forecast of no change. This fact suggests that entrepreneurs do not regard any particular past price or actual outcome as overwhelmingly indicative of long-run normal conditions. If they did their expectations might do better when considered as forecasts.

Continuing, Nerlove relates the idea to Hicks' definition of the elasticity of expectations:

Hicks may very well have had this notion in mind when he defined "the elasticity of a particular person's expectations of the price of a commodity x as the ratio of the proportional rise in expected future prices of x to the proportional rise in its current price" (1946, p. 205). Hicks, it will be remembered, distinguished two limiting cases: an elasticity of zero, implying no effect of a change in current price upon expected future prices; and an elasticity of one implying that if prices were previously expected to remain constant, i.e., were at their long-run equilibrium level, they will now be expected to remain constant at the level of current price. By allowing for a range of elasticities between the two extremes, Hicks implicitly recognized that a particular past price or outcome may have something, but not everything, to do with people's notion of the "normal".

And then the key concept of *expected normal price*:

Past values of prices, then, affect people's notions of the "normal" level of prices; individual past prices do not exert their influence equally, however: more recent prices are a partial result of forces expected to continue to operate in the future; the more recent the price, the more it is likely to express the operation of forces relevant to "normal" price. An obvious extension of this point of view would be the representation of people's notion of "normal" price by a weighted moving average of past prices in which the weights decline as one goes back in time. Using Hicks' concept of an elasticity of expectation we can go beyond this formulation; indeed, we can derive it.

Hicks' definition of the elasticity of expectation implies that prices have actually been "normal" up until the time when some change occurred. But, of course, we know that conditions are seldom if ever "normal" in the real world; and "normality" itself is a subjective matter. Let P_t^* stand for people's expectation at time t of long-run "normal" price, and let P_t stand for actual price. Hicks' notion may then be expressed by saying that P_t^* is last period's expected "normal" price plus some factor depending on the elasticity of expectation and last year's actual price. We will go further than this and say that the adjustment factor is proportional to the difference between actual and expected "normal" price. Intuitively this seems quite reasonable. Mathematically we may write

$$P_t^* = P_{t-1}^* + \beta[P_{t-1} - P_{t-1}^*], \quad 0 < \beta \leqslant 1, \tag{12}$$

where β is a constant. If β were equal to zero, it is clear that actual prices would have no effect whatsoever on expected "normal" price. On the other hand, if β were equal to one, expected "normal" price would be equal to last year's actual price. The case of $\beta = 1$ thus corresponds to the type of forecasts generated by the naive model discussed above. In what follows we call β the coefficient of expectation [to distinguish it from an *elasticity*]. The hypothesis proposed may be stated in words: each period people revise their notion of "normal" price in proportion to the difference between the then current price and their previous idea of "normal" price.

At this point, Nerlove (1958c, p. 54) shows that the adaptive expectation hypothesis implies a representation of "expected normal price" as a weighted average of past prices with weights which decline geometrically as one goes back in time:

$$P_t^* = H(1-\beta)^t + \sum_{\lambda=0}^{t} \beta(1-\beta)^{t-\lambda} P_{\lambda-1}, \tag{13}$$

where H is a constant the value of which depends upon the initial conditions. Let us assume that an equilibrium situation existed at and prior to time $t = 0$. Let us further assume, without essential loss of generality, that all prices are expressed as deviations from the equilibrium price existing at time $t = 0$. Then H may be taken to be equal to zero and (13) becomes

$$P_t^* = \sum_{\lambda=0}^{t} \beta(1-\beta)^{t-\lambda} P_{\lambda-1}.$$

We have thus expressed people's notion of the normal price as a weighted average of past prices. The weights of past prices are functions of β and they decline as one goes back in time, since β is between zero and one.

Because expected normal prices at $t = 0$ and before are not observable, the geometrically weighted average can represent only an approximation valid for $t = 0$ in the distant past. And, in practice, because annual agricultural prices can be obtained only for short periods, Nerlove (1956a; 1956b, Chapter 8) proposed to approximate these expectations in terms of farmers' past observed behavior: In effect, if last year's supply depends on last year's expectation of normal price, then last year's supply can be used as a "stand-in" for the unobserved variable.[12]

3.3. Implicit expectations

In a remarkable dissertation [Mills (1955)], which was later largely incorporated in [Mills (1962)], Mills develops the idea of what he calls *implicit expectations*. Here is what he later wrote (1962, pp. 37–39):

> The approach ... starts with a recognition that an expectation, in addition to being a function of observable variables, is also the decision maker's estimate or prediction of a variable. As with any other estimate, an expectation has certain statistical properties which, in principle, are discoverable. This is perfectly obvious. What appears to be an innovation is the argument that, on certain assumptions about the statistical properties of the estimate, the economist can estimate both the behavior relation and the expectation itself in an indirect or implicit way. ... the expectational error [is defined] by

> $$x = x^e + u.$$

> In words, u is the decision maker's error in predicting x. Substituting [x^e in the behavioral relation to be inferred, $Y(x^e)$]:

> $$y = Y(x^e) = Y(x - u)$$

---

[12] Eckstein (1985) presents a model of agricultural supply which, under the assumptions made, is observationally equivalent to the Nerlove supply model with adaptive expectations. Further details are given below in connection with our discussion of rational and quasi rational expectations, Section 3.4.

a relation of the error in the variable type, since the observed variable x differs from the true variable x^e by an error of observation u. Virtually all that is known about statistical properties of estimates of such relations is concerned with the case in which the Y function is linear. ... further discussion will be restricted to the case in which the decision rule is linear in x^e, that is,

$$y = Y(x^e) = \alpha + \gamma x^e.$$

Then, ... we obtain

$$y = \alpha a + \gamma x - \gamma u = \alpha + \gamma x - \varepsilon,$$

where $\varepsilon = -\gamma u$. Now [this equation] is a standard statistical specification of a linear structural equation connecting the observable variables y and x, and on certain assumptions concerning the statistical properties of standard least squares techniques will yield good estimates of α and γ.[13] Assume for the moment that these properties ... are present and that we have least squares estimates a and c of a and g from a sample of observations of x and y. We then obtain an estimate $\hat{y}$ of y from the regression equation,

$$\hat{y} = a + cx,$$

[where a and c are supposed to be the OLS estimates of α and γ]. This estimate is subject to a regression error e defined by

$$e = y - \hat{y}$$

the difference between the observed and predicted values of y. Now the regression error is an estimate of the true residual e:

$$e = \mathrm{est}\, e + \mathrm{est}(-\gamma u).$$

Therefore,

$$e/c = \mathrm{est}(-u) = -\hat{u}.$$

From this we obtain an estimate $\hat{x}^e$ of x^e

$$\hat{x}^e = x - e/c = x - \hat{u} = (y - a)/c.$$

---

[13] Note by MN and DB: The problem is that the standard assumptions cannot hold because u is correlated with the *observed value of x by definition*. This problem is resolved by "rational" expectations, discussed in the next subsection.

We refer to $\hat{x}^e$ as the implicit expectation. The basic idea behind this calculation is very simple. The implicit expectations approach makes possible an estimate of the behavior equation without first obtaining an estimate of the independent variable x^e. Once the behavior equation has been estimated, however, the inverse function provides an estimate of the expectation as a function of the observed decision. We refer to $\hat{x}^e$ as the implicit expectation since it is an estimate of the value such that, if this were the true expectation, it would lead to the behavior actually observed.

The bottom line is that implicit expectations amounts to substitution of the observed future value of a variable, the expectations to which economic agents are assumed to react, by its actual value. The approach runs aground because the expectational errors, which now comprise part of the disturbance in the relation to be estimated, are, by their very definition, correlated with those same observed variables. This problem is resolved by the rational expectations hypothesis, in which the expectational variable is assumed to be the conditional expectation of the future value of the variable conditional on all the information available up to the point at which the expectation is formed.

3.4. Rational expectations and quasi-rational expectations

Since the introduction by Muth (1961), the rational expectations hypothesis (REH) has occupied a central position in discussions of what ought to be done that is however incommensurate with its limited application in econometric practice. It is difficult to disagree with the basic tenet of REH that economic agents make purposeful and efficient use of information, just as they do of other scarce resources, in optimizing their decisions.[14] Yet in actual implementation, the general form of the REH is replaced by the implication that anticipated future values of relevant variables are equal to their expectations conditional on all past data and the model itself, which describes the behavior based on those expectations. (Hereinafter, we refer to this form of the REH exclusively.) There are many reasons why this form of the REH may fail: (1) The objective functions being maximized by agents are not quadratic subject to linear stochastic constraints. (2) Agents are learning about both the processes generating exogenous variables and/or about the model characterizing their behavior in aggregate (see [Horvath and Nerlove (1996)]). (3) The econometrician may fail to specify the behavioral model, especially

---

[14] A devastating indictment of self-fulfilling expectations, the theoretical form of rational expectations, from a strictly theoretical point of view is given in a recent paper by Grandmont (1998). Essentially Grandmont argues that the informational requirements of RE lead to the defense that they are the convergent outcome of a fast learning process. In turn, such an argument requires us to consider the question of stability. His analysis shows that when expectations matter a lot and agents are uncertain about the local dynamics of the system of which they are a part, learning generates locally unstable equilibria. That is, RE are incompatible with stability of equilibrium! Since econometric analysis generally presupposes that we observe a sequence of attained equilibria, such instability implies that such observations do not exist. Needless to say, we ignore this point in the remainder of this chapter, but it is something to ponder.

its dynamics, and/or the information available to agents correctly. (For an extensive and general discussion of the limits of RE, see [Pesaran (1987)].)

Quasi-rational expectations (QRE) are a form of rational expectations obtained by neglecting some of the restrictions implied by the REH.[15] Because of their close relation, we deal with both RE and QRE in the present section. Treating them together, rather than RE first and then QRE, makes for a briefer exposition.

To illustrate the ideas involved, consider a model with a single structural equation relating one endogenous variable, y_t, to one exogenous variable, z^*_{t+1}, with a random white noise disturbance, w_t:

$$y_t = a + bz^*_{t+1} + w_t, \tag{14}$$

w_t i.i.d. WN$(0, \sigma^2_w)$. Suppose that z_t follows a simple ARMA model, say AR(1), for simplicity:

$$z_t = \alpha z_{t-1} + v_t, \tag{15}$$

where the v_t are i.i.d. WN$(0, \sigma^2_v)$ independently of w_t. Then if observations on past values of y_t and z_t are the only information available at t, the RE are

$$z^*_{t+1} = E(z_t \mid \Omega_t) = \alpha z_t, \tag{16}$$

where Ω_t is the relevant information set, consisting of past observations on y_t and z_t and other variables, which are, however, according to this model, irrelevant. Thus one should estimate a, b, α, σ^2_w, and σ^2_v jointly:

$$\begin{aligned} y_t &= a + b\alpha z_t + w_t, \\ z_t &= \alpha z_{t-1} + v_t, \end{aligned} \tag{17}$$

subject to the constraint $b\alpha/\alpha = b$ and $\mathrm{cov}(w_t, v_t) = 0$. The resulting estimate $\hat{\alpha}$ provides the basis for calculating the RE z^*_{t+1} from $\hat{\alpha} z_t$. The QRE are obtained by estimating the second equation of (17) and then in the second stage substituting the calculated values of z_{t+1} as $\hat{z}_{t+1}$ from this estimated equation. Since w_t and v_t are assumed to be independent there is no failure of consistency. Moreover, the QRE are not less efficient, because (17) is a recursive system. In a general QRE model we would not restrict z_t to be AR(1), and this would lead only to a loss of efficiency if the model were really correctly specified, not to inconsistent estimates.

---

[15] Nerlove (1967) contains essentially the idea behind quasi-rational expectations, which are further developed in [Carvalho (1972)].

Next, let

$q_t =$ quantity demanded $=$ quantity supplied;

$p_t =$ market price;

$p_t^* =$ price expected to prevail in t on the basis of information in $t-1$ when
    production decisions are made;

$z_{1t} =$ exogenous variable, e.g., income;

$z_{2t} =$ exogenous variable, e.g., weather;

$u_{1t}, u_{2t}, v_{1t}, v_{2t} =$ latent disturbances, white noise, possibly contemporaneously
    correlated with each other;

$w_t =$ latent disturbances, not necessarily white noise, but current value of which
    is not correlated with any variable in Ω_{t-1}.

Assume the following model:

Demand: $\qquad\qquad q_t = \beta_1 p_t + \gamma_1 z_{1t} + u_{1t};$ $\qquad\qquad\qquad$ (18)

Supply: $\qquad\qquad q_t = \beta_2 p_t^* + \gamma_2 z_{2t} + u_{2t};$ $\qquad\qquad\qquad$ (19)

Expectations: $\qquad p_t^* = \mathrm{E}(p_t \mid \Omega_{t-1}) = p_t + w_t;$ $\qquad\qquad$ (20)

Exogenous variables: $\quad z_{1t} = \alpha_1 z_{1t-1} + v_{1t}, \quad z_{2t} = \alpha_2 z_{2t-1} + v_{2t}.$ $\quad$ (21)

To obtain the fully rational expectations (FRE) estimates, equate supply and demand,
replace p_t^* by $\mathrm{E}(p_t \mid \Omega_{t-1})$, and solve for

$$p_t^* = \frac{\gamma_1}{\beta_2 - \beta_1} \mathrm{E}(z_{1t} \mid \Omega_{t-1}) - \frac{\gamma_2}{\beta_2 - \beta_1} \mathrm{E}(z_{2t} \mid \Omega_{t-1}). \qquad (20')$$

Substitute in (19) and replace $\mathrm{E}(z_{it} \mid \Omega_{t-1})$ by $\alpha_i z_{it-1}$:

$$q_t = \frac{\beta_2 \gamma_1 \alpha_1}{\beta_2 - \beta_1} z_{1t-1} - \frac{\beta_2 \gamma_2 \alpha_2}{\beta_2 - \beta_1} z_{2t-1} + \gamma_2 z_{2t} + u_{2t}. \qquad (22)$$

Estimate (18), (21), and (22) by FIML, taking into account all the cross-equation restrictions resulting from the fact that the coefficients in these equations are combinations of
a smaller number of underlying parameters. The FRE of p_t, given information up to
$t-1$, may be calculated from

$$p_t^* = \frac{\hat{\gamma}_1 \hat{\alpha}_1}{\hat{\beta}_2 - \hat{\beta}_1} z_{1t-1} - \frac{\hat{\gamma}_2 \hat{\alpha}_2}{\hat{\beta}_2 - \hat{\beta}_1} z_{2t-1}, \qquad (23)$$

where the "hatted" values are the FIML estimates.

To obtain the strict QRE estimates of (18) and (19) we would simply replace p_t^* by $E(p_t \mid p_{t-1}, p_{t-2}, \ldots)$, as calculated from the best-fitting ARIMA model. If this seems excessively simple, various intermediate possibilities are open as we shall see. How can one justify QRE in this case? The system (18)–(21) determines current values of q_t, p_t, p_t^*, z_{1t}, and z_{2t} as linear combinations of their own past values and of u_{1t}, u_{2t}, w_t, v_{1t}, v_{2t}, and their past values. For example, the result for p_t, where L is the lag operator, can be written

$$(1 - \alpha_1 L)(1 - \alpha_2 L)p_t$$

$$= \frac{(1 - \alpha_2 L)\gamma_1 v_{1t}}{\beta_2 - \beta_1} - \frac{(1 - \alpha_1 L)\gamma_2 v_{2t}}{\beta_2 - \beta_1} + (1 - \alpha_1 L)(1 - \alpha_2 L)\frac{u_{1t}}{\beta_2 - \beta_1}$$

$$- (1 - \alpha_1 L)(1 - \alpha_2 L)\frac{u_{2t}}{\beta_2 - \beta_1} - (1 - \alpha_1 L)(1 - \alpha_2 L)\frac{\beta_2 w_t}{\beta_2 - \beta_1}. \tag{24}$$

There is a similar equation for each of the other variables. If the latent variable w_t were uncorrelated with u_{1t}, u_{2t}, v_{1t}, and v_{2t}, Equation (24) and each of the corresponding equations for the other variables, including the unobserved variable p_t^*, would be a classical unobserved-components (UC) model [Nerlove (1967), Nerlove et al. (1979)], which has a canonical form that is an ARMA or ARIMA model. The UC formulation places additional within-equation restrictions on the coefficients which appear in each. The REH assures us that w_t is uncorrelated with any past values of u_1, u_2, v_1, and v_2, but in general it is not so with respect to contemporaneous values. This means that these UC representations contain additional parameters reflecting these correlations. While these additional parameters generally result in a failure of identification for the usual univariate UC model, they do not do so in this multivariate context because of the strong cross-equation restrictions implied by the REH.

Writing the canonical forms of (24) and the equations corresponding to it for q_t, z_{1t}, and z_{2t}, we arrive at the VARIMA model, which Sargent (1981) has suggested might be an appropriate basis for estimation, suitably restricted, for the FRE model (18)–(21). If one really did want to obtain the FIML estimates of the FRE model, however, it would be better to work within the framework of the structural equations themselves. We would estimate (18), (19), and

$$p_t = p_t^* - w_t = \frac{\gamma_1 \alpha_1}{\beta_2 - \beta_1} z_{1t-1} + \frac{\gamma_2 \alpha_2}{\beta_2 - \beta_1} z_{2t-1} - w_t, \tag{25}$$

subject to all cross-equation restrictions, assuming v_{1t} and v_{2t} to be contemporaneously uncorrelated with u_{2t} and w_t, but allowing the latter pair to be correlated.

An alternative approach to the application of rational expectations models of agricultural supply is developed in Eckstein (1985). Building on earlier work of Muth (1960), in which conditions for the optimality of adaptive expectations were derived (generalized in [Nerlove (1967)], Sargent and Wallace (1973) and Sargent (1976a, 1976b), who present models in which adaptive and rational expectations models are observationally equivalent, Eckstein presents a dynamic rational expectations agricultural supply model which leads to an acreage response equation identical to the one formulated in [Nerlove (1956a, 1956b, 1958c)]. His model "... explicitly specifies the market conditions and costs of production for a given crop. The dynamic supply equation is derived from the farmer optimization problem and the equilibrium movements of the commodity price, production, and land allocation. ... It is shown that this simple rational expectations equilibrium model, which considers dynamic constraints on land allocations through the cost function, can justify the Nerlovian supply equation. ... Further, the two models have the same reduced-form equations such that they are observationally equivalent" [Eckstein (1985, p. 204)]. Of course, as might be expected, the assumptions and model specification required to arrive at this conclusion are stringent and specific: (1) production is proportional to acreage with an additive economy-wide shock; (2) cost of production per acre is a linear function of initial and harvest-time costs, and current and lagged acreage; (3) aggregate demand for the crop is a function of its price (at harvest) and income, which is assumed to evolve over time in accordance to a stationary second-order autoregressive process; and (4) the market for the crop clears. Changing the assumptions to yield a more realistic supply model would result in one not observationally equivalent – which might not be a bad thing.

3.5. *Futures price based models of expectation formation*

Rational expectations models are based on the idea that all information up to the moment at which the expectation is formed is used in the process. In practice, only observations on the past values of variables, either exogenous or endogenous entering the model, are used. A likely candidate for other information, however, in models of agricultural supply, is provided by the futures price, if one exists, for the commodities in question. The problem is that, in the case of storable commodities, it is arguable that futures prices contain no information about the aggregate of market expectations other than the current spot price. Writing in 1947, Johnson put the matter as follows:

> In commodities in which stocks are held in important volume ... the cash price is a futures price to the same extent as the price in the futures market. Because of the existence of stocks (except for a situation noted below), the present price is a consequence of a combination of forces representing the present value of the product and anticipations relative to prospective values. If anticipations are that the price of the product will be higher six months hence, this will be reflected in both cash and futures prices, since the commodity can be stored and held forward. ... In one case it might be assumed that the futures market represents a better estimate of the future prices than the cash market. This case occurs when there are no stocks, other than working stocks to be carried from one production period to the next. In such a case the cash price could go above the futures price for the future closing after the new harvest. Even here the difference is less marked than it

might be supposed because of the length of the production process in utilizing the product and the necessity of holding stocks for this purpose. .... *For the reasons given above, the variation in the cash prices of the storable commodities from year to year, in most cases, represents the whole bundle of anticipations that goes to make the market* ... ([Johnson (1947, p. 83)], italics added)

This is essentially the position for storable commodities articulated earlier by Working (1942):

> For the most part, relations between futures prices, or between spot and futures prices, indicate merely the market appraisal of price changes that are likely to occur in consequence of activated marginal net cost of carrying the commodity, these marginal net costs being potentially either positive or negative.

But this was not the universally accepted view prior to Working. Working quotes a 1924 report from the Federal Trade Commission to make the point:

> ... there is no definite commercial connection between the two prices [spot and future] tending to hold them together, but instead merely a comparison of the present with a future of which the surrounding and determining conditions are not so related to the present conditions that merchants in general have objective data on the basis of which to calculate a connection between them. The future price set becomes a matter of prediction in a sense involving guesswork instead of commercial calculation of probabilities. [Working (1942, p. 40)]

Tomek and Gray (1970) reiterate Working's position:

> The element of expectations is imparted to the whole temporal constellation of price quotations, and the futures prices reflect essentially no prophecy that is not reflected in the cash price and is in that sense already fulfilled. [Tomek and Gray (1970, p. 373)]

Thus there are strong theoretical reasons to suppose that, empirically, futures prices should offer little improvement over the use of current cash prices in the case of storable commodities. Such markets, moreover, frequently fail to exist, particularly in the case of nonstorable commodities. In such cases, even when they do exist they generally depend on a variety of factors extraneous to producers' behavior. (See [Williams (1986)], especially Chapter 5.)

Notwithstanding these arguments, there is a theoretical literature suggesting that futures prices should be an essential driving variable in understanding agricultural supply. Holthausen (1979) and Feder, Just, and Schmitz (1980) show that a producer's utility-maximizing planting decision will equate marginal cost with the futures price for harvest time delivery, even if his own subjective price expectation differs from the futures price.

The empirical evidence regarding the efficacy of including futures prices in empirical analyses of agricultural supply is summarized in the next section.

4. Empirical studies of expectation formation

In this part of the chapter we deal with the evidence for or against various theories of expectation formation. Our emphasis, almost exclusive in the section on indirect evidence, is on the rational expectations hypothesis and its more operational variant, quasi-rational expectations. There are two reasons for such emphasis: First, since the publication of Muth's paper in 1961, the REH has virtually "swept the field". Except for a few experimental studies, most empirical investigations attempt to test or to exploit the REH. Second, as one colleague put it, "what's the alternative?" There is no generally theoretically acceptable hypothesis other than the REH on which one can base the expectational part of an aggregative behavioral model.

4.1. Direct versus indirect tests

Indirect tests of expectations, through restrictions on parameters from an econometric model, will necessarily be joint tests of both the expectation process used by agents and the underlying economic theory. Rejection of rational expectations, for example, when tested within the confines of a model, is a joint test of the underlying behavioral theory and the agent's use of that theory in forming his expectations on future endogenous variables. Pesaran (1987) summarizes this point:

> In the absence of direct observations on expectations, empirical analysis of the expectations formation process can be carried out only indirectly, and conditional on the behaviourial model which embodies the expectational variables. This means that conclusions concerning the expectations formation process will not be invariant to the choice of the underlying behavioral model ... Only when direct observations on expectations are available is it possible to satisfactorily compare and contrast alternative models of expectations formation. [Pesaran (1987, p. 207)]

Direct study of the expectations of individual agents elicits the response from critics that such study is assumption testing and not consistent with the positive economics precepts of Friedman (1953). One might argue, as well, that direct study of expectations is not consistent with Muth's original purposes:

> The only real test [of the REH], however, is whether theories involving rationality explain observed phenomena any better than alternative theories. [Muth (1961, p. 330)]

While this last statement clearly puts Muth (1961) in Friedman's instrumentalist camp, his more recent work suggests that he has broken camp and moved on to direct testing; see [Muth (1985)].

One might counter such objections to direct testing in several ways:

The difference between an assumption and a theorem is arbitrary. In mathematics it is largely a matter of esthetics which is which. In economics, the distinction is based on other considerations, but still basically a matter of esthetics: The central paradigm consists of a number of assumptions on maximizing behavior and equilibrium. The theorems are the result of adding other assumptions to this core. But evidence is evidence where'er we find it. The hierarchical structure of assumptions in economics and our reluctance to modify the core leads to the wrong-headed idea that one can't test assumptions at all.

A better argument is as follows: Indirect tests are clearly joint tests, so if we reject a particular hypothesis it is not clear whether we are rejecting the underlying behavioral theory or the expectational hypothesis in question. Agents may well form expectations rationally or some other specified way, but in an explicit test may misrepresent their behavior in response to those expectations. Direct observations on agent's expectations may allow us to break the joint hypothesis into two parts, one dealing with the formation of expectations, the other with consequent behavior.

Below, we summarize direct tests of expectational hypotheses. Here we continue with a brief summary of the indirect evidence, primarily related to testing models of rational or quasi-rational expectations.

4.2. Indirect tests[16]

In this section, we will focus on indirect testing of rational expectations (RE) and quasi-rational expectations (QRE) models of expectation formation.

There are several complementary approaches for testing RE and QRE models which have been widely discussed in the literature. These may be grouped into four categories: (a) Minimalist or general tests for whether elements of dynamic structure originate in the process of expectation formation. Such tests depend crucially on the correctness of the nonexpectational dynamics. (b) Tests based on solving the model for its so-called "final form" and checking whether the restrictions implied by various models of expectation formation, including RE, are satisfied. Such tests are difficult to carry out in multivariate cases involving more than one expectational variable. We know of only two instances, both univariate. (c) Tests of RE based on the restrictions imposed on the structural form of the model. Finally, in (d), we consider direct tests based on comparing observations of reported expectations with subsequent realizations, either from survey data or from experimental data.

4.2.1. Minimalist tests

The idea of a "minimalist" test is simple: Generally, a model of dynamic decision making under uncertainty will give rise to several related behavioral relationships. If we specify a model of expectation formation independently of the behavior optimized, such expectations will depend on observed information, frequently lagged values of variables appearing in the model. Inserting the expectations in an equation thus gives rise to a

---

[16] This section draws on [Nerlove and Fornari (1997)].

distributed lag (DL) relationship, or expectational distributed lag (EDL). One minimal characteristic shared by all models involving distributed lags of an expectational nature (EDL) is that the variables subject to EDL enter all related behavioral equations with exactly the same DL distribution [Nerlove (1958b)]. If they do not, we would be led to reject expectations as a source of the lagged behavior. In [Nerlove (1958a)], this criterion was the basis for a test of Friedman's permanent income hypothesis (PIH) against the alternative of DL due to habit persistence in a system of consumer demand functions. The PIH was rejected in this case. Closer to home, Orazem and Miranowski (1986) deal with acreage allocation decisions of Iowa farmers, 1952–77, for four crops – corn, soybeans, hay, and oats – accounting for all but a minute portion of harvested acres in Iowa, and clearly reject EDL. If EDL is rejected, indirect tests of any model of expectation formation cannot be carried out in the context of the behavioral model; thus, EDLs are almost always *assumed.*

4.2.2. Tests based on "final form" VAR or VARMA models

Hansen and Sargent (1981) clearly state the need for multivariate RE models to test the restrictions imposed across behavioral equations, as well as between behavioral equations and the stochastic processes generating the exogenous variables of the model. Multivariate RE models can generally be reduced, at least approximately, to multivariate vector autoregression (VAR) or vector autoregressive moving average (VARMA) models embodying very large numbers of restrictions of an extremely complicated sort. In an earlier paper, Hansen and Sargent (1980) suggest basing a test of REH on the restricted vs. the unrestricted VAR. In his study of land allocation in Egypt between cotton and wheat, Eckstein (1984) formulates the problem as a univariate one and tests the implied restrictions, but we know of no similar attempts in a multivariate context. The reason is not only the complexity of the restrictions resulting from the REH but also the failure of identification when the underlying dynamic structure is not pinned down rather precisely (Wallis). Therefore Nerlove (1972), Nerlove, et al. (1979), and Sargent (1981), among others, stress the need for explicit dynamic optimizing models to lay the basis for specifying which anticipated future values matter, and what other leads and lags are involved in the structural behavioral relationships to be estimated.[17]

4.2.3. Tests in a structural context

It is easier to impose a priori structural restrictions in structural than reduced-form estimation. Restrictions which are relatively simple and transparent in structural terms

---

[17] Despairing of being able to do this satisfactorily led Sargent and Sims (1977) to recommend the use of unrestricted VAR models to check consistency with several possible structural models. The model of beef cattle supply formulated in [Nerlove and Fornari (1997)] is based on an explicit model of dynamic optimization which does permit very precise specification of the future values entering each of several behavioral relationships as well as of the other lags involved, and thus, in principle, leads to a satisfactory test of the REH. The problem of complex restriction in the VARMA form leads the authors to formulate a partial test in a structural context.

are extremely complex in terms of the final form equations (approximating VAR or VARMA). Wallis (1980), Hansen and Sargent (1981), and Fair and Taylor (1983, 1990), among others, clearly recognize the need for structural specification and estimation in this context, but only Eckstein (1984) and Goodwin and Sheffrin (1982), the latter only partially, seem to have carried it out, and then only in a univariate context. The results are inconclusive. The problem is that even in the case of univariate structure, restrictions across the behavioral equation and the stochastic equations generating the exogenous variables, anticipated future values of which affect behavior, are extremely difficult to impose, and, indeed, we would argue, highly problematic in any case, due to the difficulty of correctly specifying the structure of the processes generating these variables (see [Nerlove et al. (1979, pp. 201–290)], for general methods of specifying appropriate univariate and multivariate time-series models). QRE circumvents this difficulty by separating the stochastic relations generating the exogenous variables from the structural behavioral relationships, thus permitting cross-behavioral restrictions to be taken into account more easily, and minimizing contamination due to errors in specifying that part of the model determining the exogenous variables, albeit at the cost of full efficiency. But full efficiency is predicated on correct specification and, for this reason, is rarely a high priority in econometric practice. Nerlove and Fornari (1997) carry out such a test. Some of the structural restrictions are accepted, some not; the results are again inconclusive.

4.2.4. Futures-based models of expectation formation

In a pioneering paper, Gardner (1976) suggests using futures prices for all expectations in agricultural markets. Gardner presents evidence that "Futures prices can be valuable as an adjunct to and as a vehicle for evaluating lagged-price, lagged dependent variable models".

Gardner (1976, p. 81) writes:

> ... an alternative approach to estimating supply elasticity ... [is] to exploit the theoretically well-grounded hypothesis that the price of a futures contract for next year's crop reflects the market's estimate of next year's cash prices. Since the appropriate price for supply analysis is the price expected by producers at the time when production decisions are being made, a futures price at this time is a good candidate for a directly observable measure of product price in supply analysis.

> In the context of crop supply, there are several problems to be faced in the use of futures prices. First, "the market's" estimate as given by a futures price reflects the expectations of nonfarm speculators as well as crop producers, and it reflects directly the expectations only of those crop producers who themselves make futures transactions. Second, there is the issue of which futures contract is most appropriate. Third, at what date should the futures price be observed?

> With respect to the first issue, the use of a futures price can be justified by the hypothesis of rational expectations as developed by John Muth. Under rational

expectations, there is no reason for farmers to have different price expectations from futures speculators, nor for farmers who make no futures transactions to have expectations different from those who do. If the price expectations of those out of the futures market differ from the futures price, there is great incentive for them to enter. Thus, those out of the market likely have price expectations similar to the market price of futures.

The second issue should cause no serious problem so long as the futures contract pertains to the new crop. Of course, even old-crop cash prices are influenced by expectations concerning the new crop. But the cash-futures basis changes from year to year and secularly as the cost of storage (which includes interest) changes. The present analysis uses the first futures price after the crop is in.

The third problem is most difficult because it is not clear exactly when the production decision is made. There may not be any preharvest date at which a farmer can be said to have made irrevocably his decision about planned output. Even after the crop is planted, planned output can be revised and actions taken accordingly in fertilization, pest control, and other practices, such as plowing under a crop or using it for forage. However, the main production decisions are the choices of acreage and techniques to follow in planting. This suggests taking as the expected price the futures price in the period immediately preceding the planting season.

The evidence supporting Gardner's suggestion is mixed. Eales et al. (1990) study price expectations for Illinois corn and soybeans market participants (farmers and grain merchandisers). Surveys of individuals are aggregated into groups. The mean response of the groups shows no significant difference from the nearby futures price; whereas some difference was noted in price variance. Tronstad and McNeil (1989) show that sow farrowing response models using futures price as the expected price compare favorably with similar response models using cash prices. Just and Rausser (1981) provide evidence that futures markets offer superior forecasts of subsequent cash prices when compared to forecasts from large-scale econometric models for several U.S. crops (their results on cattle prices, however, offer much weaker, if not conflicting, evidence on the superiority of futures prices relative to the large-scale model's forecasts).

Other evidence conflicts with Gardner's suggestion [Leuthold (1974), Martin and Garcia (1981), Goodwin and Sheffrin (1982)]. Chavas et al. (1983) offer an interesting discussion of their results on corn and soybean acreage supply response, which is not unlike the suggestion offered earlier by Working (1942), Johnson (1947), and Tomek and Gray (1970) (see the discussion above): "... as argued by Gardner, the futures price appears to be a good substitute for the cash price lagged one year in supply analysis. This is the case for corn and soybeans because the two prices are highly correlated and appear to reflect similar market information. As a result, using both futures and cash prices in supply equations may lead to multicollinearity problems, while deleting one of the two appears to make little difference in estimates of supply elasticities" [Chavas et al. (1983, p. 32)].

Antonovitz and Green (1990) study supply response for fed beef, focusing on naive expectations, ARIMA-type expectations, futures price expectations, and fully rational price expectations. They summarize their results: "... empirical evidence does not support any one model in particular, suggesting that expectations are heterogeneous rather than homogeneous" [Antonovitz and Green (1990, p. 473)]. They conclude with the interesting note, based on root-mean-squared error (rmse) measures on fit models: "the highest value (of rmse) was observed for the rational expectations model perhaps adding additional evidence to reject the hypothesis that expectations are formed rationally" [Antonovitz and Green (1990, p. 485)].

The question of how good an indicator the futures price is of the future cash price was addressed for live cattle (a nonstorable commodity) in [Leuthold (1974)]. There he finds that for distant contracts, "The cash price is a more accurate indicator of future cash price conditions than is the futures price". He concludes, "The producer who looks at the futures prices routinely to establish a feeding margin so that he can decide whether or not to purchase and feed cattle may receive false signals and be misled into a costly decision, either a money loss or foregone profits" [Leuthold (1974, p. 276)].

Covey and Bessler (1995) consider the question of predictability of cash prices using the information in current and past futures prices as a problem of cointegration.[18] They find that daily cash and futures prices for a storable commodity, corn, are cointegrated; however, this long-run relation does not offer any out-of-sample forecast improvement relative to that contained in past cash corn prices, a result which agrees with Working's conclusion (1942). On the other hand, they find no cointegrating relation between cash and futures prices for live cattle prices. Further, short-run forecasts (on data not used to test for cointegration) of cash prices of cattle are improved by conditioning on past futures prices of cattle – suggesting that there is (short-run) information relevant to future cash prices in the current futures price, which is not in the current cash price.

There have been several studies contrasting the forecasting ability of the futures market relative to a publicly available alternative forecast. Just and Rausser (1981) find that forecasts of cash prices made by several commercial forecasting companies were generally not superior, in a mean squared error sense, to corresponding futures market prices. Futures on soybean meal and oil are superior forecasts of subsequent cash prices relative to the econometric forecasts, indicating that the futures market did capture some information which was not captured by 1970s-style econometrics. However, this general superiority (of futures market forecasts) does not extend to forecasts of livestock prices: "some of the econometric forecasts seem to be preferable for livestock commodities ..." [Just and Rausser (1981, p. 207)]. Martin and Garcia (1981, p. 214) find "... the performance of the cattle and hog futures as a rational price formation agency is suspect," a result which supports the finding of Bessler and Brandt (1992), who find that

---

[18] Two variables are said to be cointegrated if they each have one or more unit roots (stochastic trend) and if one can find a linear combination of the two which has fewer unit roots (e.g., each has one unit root, and the regression of one on the other has residuals which are stationary). It is usual to interpret such a result in causal terms. See [Stock and Watson (1988) and Hamilton (1994)].

a commodity expert is root mean squared error superior in forecasting cash cattle prices relative to live cattle futures prices, over a fifteen year period – this forecaster's advantage being reduced forecast error variance, with no advantage found due to reduced bias.

The evidence from futures markets is mixed, but two points emerge. First, futures on livestock prices (apparently) do not capture important long-run information for subsequent cash prices. This finding is supported by empirical studies using econometric models [Just and Rausser (1981), Covey and Bessler (1995)] and by studies of expert opinion [Bessler and Brandt (1992)] and of actual lagged cash prices [Leuthold (1974), Martin and Garcia (1981)]. Second, while futures on storable commodities are able to outperform econometric models, it is not clear that they can outperform optimal univariate ARMA or ARIMA model predictors of cash price. Working's initial thoughts on the subject and Johnson's summary appear not to have been seriously challenged by subsequent analysis. The econometric results of Just and Rausser may be more a criticism of 1970s-style econometrics on data characterized by unit roots than an empirical endorsement of futures markets as forecasts of subsequent cash prices, and is indeed supported by some [Covey and Bessler (1995)]. Of course, these results also suggest the possible superiority of futures prices over poorly specified commodity models.

Gardner's results remain to be explained. He finds that supply response models on two storable commodities using futures market prices as proxies for expectations perform as well as a lagged price expectations models. One argument is that subjects do indeed look at the current cash market and make planting decisions based on that variable (as suggested by Schultz and Brownlee (1941–42); see our discussion below); however, Gardner may have misrepresented such expectations by using the average price from the previous year to represent the most recent cash price. This explanation is not inconsistent with the position taken by Working (1942), Johnson (1947), and Tomek and Gray (1970), and is supported by the empirical result of Covey and Bessler (1995) – that no long-run forecast information, in addition to that contained in current cash price, is in the current futures price. The lagged average price over the previous year may not have been optimal, and the futures market (April or May quote for January delivery) may be closer than the lagged average price to an optimal statistical predictor, which farmers may have been using. Of course, the difficulty in assessing expectations indirectly makes all explanations tentative.

4.3. Tests based on direct observation

4.3.1. What can we learn by asking people what they expect?

Below we summarize attempts to study agents' expectations by directly observing them. These works have been both experimental and nonexperimental or observational, for example in surveys or informal interview studies, where no experimental control is imposed in the collection of the data. Here, we offer a brief discussion on the question of what one can hope to learn by asking people what they expect.

Merely asking a person what he expects a variable to be at some future date has met with considerable skepticism from both decision theorists and psychologists. Savage is an early critic of direct interrogation:

> Attempts to define the relative probability of a pair of events in terms of the answers people give to direct interrogation has justifiably met with antipathy from most statistical theorists. In the first place, many doubt that the concept "more probable to me than" is an intuitive one, open to no ambiguity and yet admitting no further analysis. Even if the concept were so completely intuitive, which might justify direct interrogation as a subject worthy of some psychological study, what could such interrogation have to do with the behavior of a person in the face of uncertainty, except of course for his verbal behavior under interrogation? If the state of the mind in question is not capable of manifesting itself in some sort of extra verbal behavior, it is extraneous to our main interest. [Savage (1954, p. 27)]

Evidence supporting criticism of direct interrogation (interrogation without explicit motivation) comes from the work of the experimental psychologists, Siegel and Goldstein (1959). They hypothesized that observed behavior of participants in an experiment in which no financial incentives were provided, which was inconsistent with assumptions of an underlying theory, may have been due to boredom or game-playing by the experimental subjects. Further, such boredom might be overcome by providing subjects financial rewards, which were directly related to the "goodness" of their responses in experimental tests of an underlying theory. Their experiments show differences between subjects' responses who received financial rewards relative to subjects' who received none. The former are closer than the latter to the a priori predicted response. Davis and Holt (1993) summarize their assessment of the Siegel–Goldstein experiment:

> What we may conclude from this experiment is that financial incentives can sometimes eliminate subtle and unintended biases. For this reason, the payment of financial incentives is a critical element in the administration of economics experiments. [Davis and Holt (1993, pp. 88–89)]

Just how one provides an incentive has been a subject of considerable study. One doesn't want the incentive mechanism itself to induce strategic behavior to mask or misrepresent a subject's beliefs. Scoring rules are measures of goodness used to encourage the assessor to be honest in reporting his true beliefs. Since these beliefs exist solely in the assessor's mind, there is no way to determine whether or not this requirement is satisfied. However, by rewarding or penalizing the assessor according to certain scoring rules, one can encourage an assessor to make his stated beliefs correspond to his true beliefs. Scoring rules have been developed for elicitation of probabilistic beliefs and as such provide a natural application to testing rational expectations. In Muth's words, "... the subjective probabilities of the agent are distributed around the objective probability of the data".

Consider a task where an individual must make a probability assessment $[r' = (r_1, r_2, \ldots, r_n)]$ for an event E which consists of n mutually exclusive and collectively exhaustive outcomes $E_1, E_2, \ldots, E_n$. The quadratic rule, $Q(d, r)$, is defined as

$$Q(d, r) = \left[1 - \sum_{I=1}^{n} (r_i - d_i)^2 \right],$$

where $d_j = 1$ if event E_j occurs, and zero if not. $Q(d, r)$ encourages the assessor to set r (his revealed beliefs) equal to his true probabilities (p). So that if a risk-neutral assessor is rewarded according to a quadratic rule, his or her optimal response is to set r (his or her vector of stated or revealed beliefs on events 1 through n) equal to p (his or her true beliefs on outcomes 1 through n). As the range of the quadratic rule, as given above, is $[-1, +1]$ and one may not wish to entertain negative payoffs, the quadratic rule is used in the form

$$Q(d, r)^* = \left[1 - (1/2) \sum_{I=1}^{n} (r_i - d_i)^2 \right]$$

which has the range $[0, 1]$. The quadratic rule has been applied in weather forecasting, where it is labeled the "Brier score" (see [Murphy and Winkler (1970), and Brier (1950)]). De Finetti has suggested the quadratic rule as a motivational device for testing responses in educational psychology [de Finetti (1965)].[19]

One immediate consequence of the scoring rule literature is that rewards should be designed relative to the utility function of the individual subject. This point is given

---

[19] Other proper scoring rules exist, some of which are reviewed in Murphy and Winkler (1970). Perhaps the most interesting of these is the logarithmic (log) rule, defined as

$$L(d, r) = \left[\ln \left(\sum_{I=1}^{n} d_i r_i \right) \right],$$

where d and r are defined as above and ln is the natural logarithmic operation. Shuford, Albert, and Massengill (1966) show that the log scoring rule is the only proper scoring rule which gives payoffs just in terms of the stated probability of the event which actually occurs (notice that the quadratic rule defines payoffs in terms of probabilities assessed to both the event which obtains as well as all other events).

The log rule presents analysts with an interesting "problem" as its range is $[-\infty, 1]$. When the assessed response is $r_j = 0$ and $d_j = 1$, the negative infinity reward is difficult to work with in applied settings. Following Shuford, Albert, and Massengill (1966, p. 137), a truncated log scoring rule is

$$L(r_k, d_k) = \begin{cases} 1 + \ln r_k, & 0.01 < r_k \leqslant 1, \\ -1, & 0 \leqslant r_k \leqslant 0.01. \end{cases}$$

Bessler and Moore (1979) suggest a version of $L(r_k)$, where all payoffs are positive. Of course truncation will potentially induce responses for which $r' \neq p'$, especially in the neighborhood of truncation. Shuford et al. (1966) study the effects of truncation and conclude, "... for extreme values of p_i, some information about [the subject's] degree-of-belief is lost, but from the point of view of applications, the loss of accuracy is insignificant" (1966, p. 137).

consideration in [Murphy and Winkler (1970) and Holt (1986)]. They suggest the direct elicitation of each subject's utility function and design of a scoring rule (motivational device) which yields optimal responses for that particular utility function.[20]

In a more pragmatic vein, Nelson and Bessler (1989), following work first reported in [Nelson (1987)], pre-screen individuals for linear utility (in the range of rewards offered in subsequent probability elicitation experiments). This "pre-screening" allows them to use the familiar quadratic rule (discussed above), but requires them to drop nearly 60 percent of their original subject pool, as the dropped subjects exhibited significant non-linear utility. They provide an empirical test of the quadratic scoring rule when used in comparison to a linear rule: $H(r_k, d_k) = a_0 r_k d_k$; where $d_k = 1$ if event k obtains, and zero otherwise. The rule defined by H is improper and should induce subjects not to reveal probabilities $r' = p'$. In fact, the optimal response, for a risk-neutral subject facing H, is to find a corner point solution, which disguises the single highest probability as a one and all lower probabilities as zeros (see [Nelson and Bessler (1989, pp. 364–365)]. They find that for risk-neutral subjects, "... the scoring rule used (linear or quadratic) had a significant effect (p-value < 0.0001) on the number of zeros used in a forecast when the observations from eight subjects in each treatment over all forty forecast periods were used". The Nelson and Bessler work provides evidence to suggest that the way subjects are paid is an important consideration in assessment studies.[21]

4.3.2. Experimental data

In the concluding section, we discuss the mixed findings from surveys of expectations from both individual decision makers and commodity experts. Here we deal with laboratory studies of expectation formation, in which monetary payoffs can be tied directly to the assessment and subsequent realization and rewards made according to the loss or utility function of the respondent with control for what the subject saw prior to the assessment. Nelson (1987), Nelson and Bessler (1992), Hey (1994), Dwyer, Williams,

---

[20] In this context, scoring rules are viewed as *ex ante* motivational devices, which aid in helping a subject make his stated beliefs correspond with his "true" beliefs. There is a rich parallel literature in which these same rules are used to evaluate the ex post "goodness" of probabilistic forecasts. For discussion of such see [Kling and Bessler (1989)]. Applications can be found in [Diebold and Rudebusch (1989), and Zellner et al. (1991)].

[21] The issue of payoffs is important as one wants the motivational device to be sensitive to responses which deviate from optimal subject response. That is to say, if the payoff rule is flat in the neighborhood of the optimal response, the subject may have little incentive to respond with precision. We may erroneously conclude from an experimental study that agents respond in a suboptimal manner because the reward mechanism is for all practical purposes flat in a sizable neighborhood of the optimal response. Murphy and Winkler (1970) explore this issue with respect to the log scoring rule (which is particularly flat in a neighborhood of the optimal response). Essentially the same issue has been revisited by the experimental economist Harrison (1989, 1992). Harrison (1989, p. 759) argues: "... anomalies observed in the experiments in question may simply reflect the failure of the experiment to meet widely accepted sufficient conditions for a valid controlled experiment ... the result of this failure is simply that the opportunity cost of 'misbehavior' in these experiments is, by any reasonable standard, minuscule".

Battalio, and Mason (1993), Plott and Sunder (1988), and Williams (1987) are included in the list of experimental studies which attempt to isolate expectation formation from the myriad of other confounding influences that plague reliable inference on expectations formation.

Perhaps the most elaborate experimental study of expectations in market data has been that carried out and reported by Williams (1987). Here agents are provided information on their own (induced) limit price, and they have information on all previous prices generated in the marketplace and all accepted and unaccepted price quotations from these previous periods. Further, they know the total number of market participants and can infer the number of buyers and sellers from price signals sent in the market. Subjects were asked to forecast the mean price they expected to occur in recursive trading periods ($t = 2, 3, 4, 5$); actual trading of units at negotiated prices followed in the manner carried out by subjects in period $t = 1$. The induced supply and demand arrays were constructed to be stationary across periods for the explicit purpose of reproducing in the laboratory a "theoretical steady-state" [Williams (1987, p. 4)], thus, providing opportunity for subjects to learn across time. The inducement of limit prices (costs and values) is important as it provides subjects with structural information (their own cost or value structure) about the underlying market, not dissimilar to the market information behind a Muthian rational agent's behavior. Other experimental studies (see below) of rationality provide the subject with historical prices (realizations). This additional bit of information (individual valuations) and the fact that agents act in a market make Williams' study particularly interesting. A $1.00 forecasting-accuracy payment was paid to the subject with the lowest summed absolute forecast error at the end of the experiment. While this inducement is probably not proper (as we are provided no information on the underlying preference structure of the subjects, e.g., we do not know if they were risk neutral or risk averse), Williams suggests that his reward scheme was sufficient for subjects to take the assessment task seriously and he makes no mention that the reward motivated strategic responses that masked "true" expectations [Williams (1987, p. 7)]. Forecasts from 532 observations from this experiment were found to be biased, based on ordinary least squares regression on pooled time series cross section data in the actual price in period t on the individual forecast of that price made at the end of period $t - 1$. Tests on subsamples trading on individual periods (e.g., $t = 2$; $t = 3$; $t = 4$; $t = 5$) showed biased forecasts as well; although trading for experienced subjects (subjects who had participated in double auctions before this round of experiments) in the last period ($t = 5$) were not found to be biased, suggesting perhaps that experience and learning (in a stable environment) may result in rational expectations. Williams concludes his work as follows: " Using price forecast observations obtained from 146 participants in twelve separate experimental double-auction markets, little empirical support is found for strict Muthian rational expectations assumptions. The forecasts are biased estimates of the realized mean price and forecast errors display significant first-order serial correlation" [Williams (1987, p. 16)]. Williams' results are replicated in double auction asset markets in [Smith et al. (1988)].

Earlier, Schmalensee (1976) presented a total of twenty-three subjects with price observations from a nineteenth century British wheat market, and had them submit both point and interval forecasts of five-year averages of the price series. An adaptive expectations model was found to outperform an extrapolative expectations model, with the response speed in the adaptive model tending to fall at turning points. Schmalensee did not study rational expectations.

More recently, Nelson and Bessler (1992) tested quasi-rationality of laboratory subjects, who were pre-screened for linear utility and motivated through payments from a quadratic scoring rule. Subjects were shown forty to sixty earlier realizations from Monte Carlo generated data on one of five univariate processes: an autoregression of order one (AR1), an autoregression of order two (AR2), a random walk (RW), an integrated moving average process of order one (IMA1), and a subset autoregression of order four (AR4). They were then asked to provide recursive probabilistic one-step-ahead forecasts of the next 40 to 60 data points – with actual outcomes and payoff numbers being revealed on a computer screen sequentially throughout the forecasting exercise. The expected value for each forecasted distribution from each subject was taken to be his expectation. Both individual and aggregate performances were judged by three criteria: Are forecast errors significantly different from zero? Are the forecast errors correlated through time? And do forecasts result in significantly larger mean squared errors relative to forecasts from a minimum mean squared error predictor applied to historical realizations (can the human forecasters perform as well as a model, in a mean square error sense, when both see the same historical observations?)? Table 1 is a summary of the performance tests for aggregates for each of the five time series processes.

Interestingly, the AR1 and RW processes are forecasted well under all three tests. If we apply a standard .05 significance level, the aggregate forecasts from these "simple" series appear to be quasi-rational. However, the more complicated series, the AR4 (a subset AR4) and the IMA1 (which is of course a nonlinear model), are not forecasted as well. The forecasts of the AR4 process fail all three tests, and the forecasts of the IMA1 process fail two of the three tests.

Results for individuals offer less support for quasi-rationality. Over the entire 41 sets of forecasts (8 individuals forecasted the AR1 process; 10 forecasted the AR2 process; 8 forecasted the RW process; 9 forecasted the IMA1 process; and 6 forecasted the AR4 process), 30 individuals passed the bias test, 26 passed the white noise residuals test, and

Table 1
Performance of aggregate forecasts in five experiments [Nelson and Bessler (1992)]

	AR1	AR2	RW	IM1	AR4
Bias test p-value	.133	.891	.494	.264	.020
White noise test p-value	.532	.012	.317	.053	.017
MSE test p-value	.128	.145	.092	.004	.010

8 passed the mean squared error test. The Nelson and Bessler (1992) results appear to be consistent with the results from the survey literature [Zarnowitz (1983)]: aggregates are more likely to generate forecasts which pass tests of rationality (quasi-rationality) than are forecasts of individual agents. This finding appears to be consistent with a line of research on forecasting in general, which finds that aggregates or composites of forecasts outperform individual forecasts (models or people) in out-of-sample forecast evaluations; see [Granger (1989)].

Additional experimental work has followed Nelson (1987) in testing expectations formation on univariate processes. Dwyer et al. (1993) ask subjects to provide one-step-ahead forecasts of a univariate random walk: $x_t = x_{t-1} + \varepsilon_t$, where ε_t is distributed normally with mean zero and variance 1.0. Subjects were motivated with financial rewards, which depended upon both their reported forecast and its ultimate realization. There is no mention that the incentive structure was matched to the utility function of respondents, so we are not able to comment on the possibility of subjects reporting expectations that masked their underlying beliefs. They find that expectations are well described as rational expectations, a random walk embedded in an additive error. This study was extended in [Beckman and Downs (1997)] under four alternative levels of noise. Here the error term was uniformly distributed under four alternative treatments: treatment I, $\varepsilon_t \sim u[-5, +5]$; treatment II, $\varepsilon_t \sim u[-10, +10]$; treatment III, $\varepsilon_t \sim u[-15, +15]$; and treatment IV, $\varepsilon_t \sim u[-20, +20]$. Here each subject received all four treatments; each was randomly assigned to one of the 24 different possible orders in which the four treatments could have been presented (order I, II, II, IV was different from order I, III, II, IV, etc.). Payments were not (apparently) matched to the utility function of the subjects, and followed the rule:

$$\text{Payment} = \$11.00 - \sum_{t=1}^{100} |A_t - F_t|,$$

where A_t is the actual value of x_t and F_t is the subject's forecast of x_t in period t. The hypothesis of interest is that under rational expectations, there should be no difference in the rational expectations forecasts across treatments. What they find is (1993, p. 598): "... increasing the variance of a random walk does create a more diffuse set of deviations from theoretically correct behavior. A one percent increase in the standard deviation of the random error generates a 0.9% increase in the standard deviation of the forecast about the rational expectation."

Hey (1994) considers 48 subjects' assessments on three univariate time series. Each assessor is provided monetary motivation, which is a function of the actual realization of the variable to be forecasted and each subject's forecast, such that risk-neutral agents will be motivated to set their forecast equal to their expected value of the random variable. The first two series are univariate autoregressions; while the third series is an autoregression, which exhibits a structural break partway through the forecast period. Tests of rationality are rejected; however, post hoc data analysis seems to suggest a type of extrapolative expectation scheme, which was sensitive to the particular characteristics of the underlying series. Hey concludes:

> So our statistical tests reject the detailed rational expectations hypothesis, though the general flavor of the data support the general notion that the subjects were trying to be rational in a broader sense. It would appear that the subjects had some general model of the Data Generating Process in their minds which they were using in a broadly sensible fashion. More importantly this general model appeared to be series specific; so that subjects had a different "model of the world" for Series 2 than they had for Series 3. [Hey (1994, p. 20)]

Additional work on experimental tests of rationality exists, some of which is reviewed in [Swenson (1997)]. He concludes: " It is safe to conclude from these (and many other) studies that individuals' forecasts of prices almost never satisfy RE (rational expectations) ... " [Swenson (1997, p. 434)].

4.3.3.   Survey and semi-survey data

Most work on expectations data in economics has been nonexperimental, without the use of explicit benefit or motivational devises. A vast literature exists on the analysis of surveys. Several surveys in agriculture were conducted in the pre-Muthian period and, in fact, were cited by Muth as providing support for rational expectations. Heady and Kaldor (1954) studied over one hundred Iowa farmers over a three-year period, 1947–1949. They tested no particular models of price expectations, but their impressions from their surveys are suggestive:

> No attempt was made in this study to test alternative models used by farmers. Nevertheless, certain impressions were gained while interviewing farmers. No single procedure was employed by all farmers. Moreover, the same farmer often used more than one procedure, depending upon the amount of information possessed and upon the degree of confidence attached to it. In December 1947, some producers were using a simple "parallel" model for their long-range forecasts which implied that prices following World War II would decline as they did after World War I. Other farmers were using a model giving explicit recognition to the supply of corn as a price-making variable. For their 1948 and 1949 forecasts the majority was not using simple mechanical models such as the projection of the current price or recent price trend into the next year but was attempting to analyze and predict the more complex price-making forces. A rather common procedure appeared to start the process of devising expected prices from current prices. The current price then was adjusted for the expected effects of important supply-and-demand forces. [Heady and Kaldor (1954, p. 35)]

Earlier, Schultz and Brownlee (1941–42) considered expectations of Iowa farmers on 1940 corn yields and hog prices. In a sample of 200 farmers, Schultz and Brownlee find that expectations on yield were as follows:

... expectations are not marked up by farmers to the level of recent experience. Instead, recent increases in yields in corn in Iowa are discounted about one-half. The other half is looked upon as a real gain, one which farmers anticipate will continue to be forthcoming, a gain which farmers ascribe to improvements in management practices, hybrid corn, and to the reduction in corn acreage which was occasioned by the AAA, and which resulted in the less productive land being taken out of corn. [Schultz and Brownlee (1941–42, p. 496)]

Later, Bessler (1982) argued that similar expectations behavior would characterize optimal expectations for California and Indiana crop yields. He finds that such yields follow a (0, 1, 1) ARIMA process and expectations of such might be described by the "permanent yield hypothesis":

... we can say that for these yield series a notion of permanent yield might be a useful concept ... that is, farmers forming optimal expectations on these yield series might view yield as composed of both permanent and transitory components ... such behavior might be justified if one notes that specific changes in yield might be viewed as permanent in that they reflect basic changes in technology (new crop varieties, pesticides, and herbicides), whereas other changes might reflect year-to-year variability in weather. [Bessler (1982, p. 22)]

Schultz and Brownlee's survey of 97 hog farmers (1941–42) reaches a different conclusion on the process generating hog price expectations. They note that fluctuation in hog prices "are both numerous and irregular. This behavior of prices probably accounts for the strong preference which Iowa farmers show for current prices in formulating their price expectations". They continue:

Iowa farmers in March 1940 were operating on the assumption that hog prices would continue at about the exceedingly low levels which then prevailed. Changes in supplies, the outbreak of the war, and the two and one-half year decline in hog prices apparently had not been instrumental either in further depressing or lifting prices which farmers anticipated for the hogs which were being farrowed at that time. [Schultz and Brownlee (1941–42, pp. 495–496)]

Surveys conducted post-Muth (since 1961) have generally confirmed much of the qualitative findings of Schultz and Brownlee. These efforts included analysis at both the aggregate level and at the micro- (individual agent) level. Here analysts have been interested in whether agents' expectations are unbiased forecasts of the random variable of interest and whether errors from such forecasts are uncorrelated with information available to the forecaster at the time of the forecast. That is to say, interest has focused on (a) whether $E\{\varepsilon_t = (p_t - {}_{t-k}p_t)\} = 0$, where here ε_t is the forecast error based on forecast ${}_{t-k}p_t$ of an individual agent or the aggregate of forecasts of a group of agents on endogenous variable p made at period $t - k$ for realization at period t, p_t is the actual realization of that same endogenous variable at period t, and E is the expectation operator; and (b) $E\{\varepsilon_t \mid \Omega_{t-k}\} = 0$, where Ω_{t-k} is the set of all available information available to agents at time $t - k$. While Schultz and Brownlee did not formulate such a general set of hypotheses (they focused attention on three particular scenarios, one having price (yield) falling, one having price (yield) remaining constant, and one having price (yield) increasing over the next year), they did show quite clearly that for their sample of farmers, and for their particular year, differences were present in the behavior of agents in forming expectations of yields versus prices. In words not used by Schultz and Brownlee we might say expectations on corn yields followed a nonrandom walk process; whereas expectations on hog prices appeared to follow a random walk.

Studies of aggregate expectations include Carlson (1977), Turnovsky (1970), Jacobs and Jones (1980), Zarnowitz (1983), and many others (see [Pesaran (1987)], for a survey through the mid 1980s).

Zarnowitz (1983) found that in forecasting numerous aggregate economic time series, individual experts participating in the quarterly National Bureau of Economic Research and American Statistical Association survey of business conditions perform worse than group average forecast. He finds:

> ... it is difficult for individuals to predict consistently better than the group ... for most people, most of the time, the predictive record is spotty ... a series of group averages has the advantage that it is helped by cancellation of individual errors of opposite sign. [Zarnowitz (1983, p. 17)]

Studies of aggregate expectations in agriculture include Bessler (1980), Ravallion (1985, 1987), Runkle (1991), Garcia and Leuthold (1992), and Colling, Irwin, and Zulauf (1992). Runkle (1991) finds that farmers' reported expectations of sow farrowings are not rational forecasts of sow farrowings, and suggests that such a result may be less due to underlying irrationality and more due to motivation (or lack thereof) in the assessment survey. Runkle (1991, pp. 599–600) writes:

> Although it may be somewhat surprising that farmers announce irrational forecasts of their own future actions, it would be considerably more surprising if market analysts were to announce irrational forecasts of farmers' actions. Because the market analysts, unlike farmers, are paid for the accuracy of the forecasts they report, they have a strong economic incentive to report accurately.

This suggestion follows the earlier suggestion of Keane and Runkle (1990):

> The survey data include only forecasts from professional forecasters, who have an economic incentive to be accurate. Because these professionals report to the survey the same forecasts that they sell on the market, their survey responses provide a reasonably accurate measure of their expectations. [Keane and Runkle (1990, p. 715)]

Keane and Runkle (1990) and Runkle (1991) provide no evidence that "their survey responses provide a reasonably accurate measure of their expectations". Faith in the market to induce reasonably accurate forecasts might lead one to conclude that astrologers are reasonably accurate because they sell their forecasts in the market!

There is related evidence that professionals are no better in assessing the future than nonprofessionals. Stael von Holstein (1970) found meteorologists' assistants outperformed the meteorologists (who were paid for their expertise) in simple probability forecasting – the latter tended to give tight forecasts, while the former gave diffuse distributions.

Earlier in this century H.A. Wallace gave a spirited summary of a not unrelated point of using experts in judging corn yields:

> That the corn judges did not know so very much about the factors which make for yields is indicated by the fact that their scores were correlated with yield to the extent of.2. The difficulty seems to be that they placed too much emphasis on length of ear and possibly also some fancy points, which caused them to neglect placing as much emphasis on sound, healthy kernel characteristics as they should. [Wallace (1923, p. 304)]

Wallace goes on to suggest that "the things which really are in their [the judges'] minds are considerably different from ... [those which they] professed" [Wallace (1923, p. 304)].

Following Nelson and Bessler (1989), discussed above, it is not just a matter of payment – how one is paid is not unrelated to what one says.

Bessler (1980) finds that the means of aggregate subjective probability distributions of farmers on yields of California field crops are not significantly different from the one-step-ahead forecasts of yields from ARIMA representations of historical county-level yield data; however, higher moments of the aggregate subjective distributions do not match their time series representations. These farmers were not paid for their responses.

Ravallion (1987) finds that daily rice price expectations from a sample of twenty-eight Bangladesh traders (Aratdars) fail both tests of unbiasedness and orthogonality. Ravallion offers possible reasons for these rejections:

> All interviews were done in Bangla by a single interpreter under reasonably close supervision, particularly in the early stages. ... Although a good deal of care was exercised in collecting these data, it seems likely that the results overstate the level of agreement amongst the traders. The interview process can act to transmit information between traders. This is produced by the tendency of an interviewer to form expectations of the answers on the basis of previous interviews which are then used as prompts. [Ravallion (1987, p. 132)]

It would appear that this same criticism offered of Ravallion's survey would apply to the results found in [Bessler (1980)] as well. (Much recent experimental work has adopted computer technology to help in collecting expectations and reporting them without introducing the potential bias associated with the use of human interviewers; see [Davis and Holt (1993, p. 23)] for a general discussion of computers in experimental economics.)

Nerlove (1983) suggests that analysis of aggregate expectations is but a first step in a more elaborate program of analysis of expectations:

While the use of aggregates derived from surveys is an important first step in the analysis of expectations and plans, such analysis should be supplemented by studies based on the micro-data themselves for several reasons: First, the micro-data should be consistent with hypotheses regarding the behavior of the aggregates; for example, expectational aggregates could provide unbiased forecasts of realized aggregates, as asserted by the theory of rational expectations, yet forecasts of individual agents could be systematically and persistently biased. Second, some factors affecting deviations between expectations or plans and subsequent realizations may affect all individuals simultaneously yet vary from period to period and some factors may affect individuals; only through analysis of the micro-data can we disentangle those two groups of effects. Finally, individual variation in variables related to expectations, plans, and realizations may be reduced or obscured in aggregate data. [Nerlove (1983, p. 1256)]

The experience from analysis of non-agricultural micro-data supports Nerlove's recommendation to study micro-data directly. Lovell (1986) summarizes his studies with Hirsch:

For 30 percent of the sampled firms, the mean of anticipated sales, two-months horizon, differed from the mean of actual realizations at the 5 percent level of significance. However, the overestimates of the optimistic firms roughly canceled the underestimates of pessimistic firms so that for industry aggregates there is no bias; this offsetting of systematic error partially explains why the aggregates of anticipation data appear to be more accurate than the predictions of individual firms. [Lovell (1986, p. 115)]

Muth (1985) studied expectations and anticipations data from five Pittsburgh-based firms. He finds that "the standard deviation of the forecast of at least three firms is inconsistent with the rational expectations hypothesis: ... [these firms] have standard deviations greater than the standard deviation of the actual. Since the rational forecast specifies $A = F + e$, where $\mathrm{E}(Fe) = 0$, the variance of A must clearly exceed that of F" [Muth (1985, p.13)].[22] Muth's study raises the issue of costs and benefits of rationality directly; in particular he concludes his study as follows: "... that some of the most significant deviations from rationality occur with firms having a small forecast error ... this suggests that the operating benefits from improved forecasts of the type analyzed here are not worth the extra cost" [Muth (1985, p. 28)].

Much of the non-agricultural expectations survey data are based on categorical responses to surveys where, in particular, respondents are asked to respond as follows: increase (+), no change (=), or decrease (−). Early efforts using such data created aggregate balances, where the number or proportion of respondents reporting a "−" are subtracted from the number or proportion reporting a "+". Nerlove (1983) suggests that

---

[22] Here Muth's idea is as follows: A is the actual realization of the variable of interest, F is the firm's forecast of A based on information held at a previous period, and e is an error term.

such categorical data be analyzed as conditional log-linear probability models; however, such models do not recognize the ordering behind typical categorical responses. Accordingly, Nerlove (1988) suggests treating such data as categorical responses from continuous latent variable models, with categories defined as thresholds. These methods are applied, *inter alia,* by Horvath, Nerlove, and Wilson (1992), and Nerlove and Weeks (1992). Nerlove and Schuermann (1995a, 1995b) estimate such a model by simulation maximum likelihood methods.[23] For quarterly surveys of British manufacturing firms and for Swiss firms, they reject both rational expectations and adaptive expectations.

In studies related to agriculture, we also see rejections of rational expectations with micro data. Irwin and Thraen (1994) summarize ten studies in agriculture which test rationality of individual expectations. In seven of these they find rejections of bias or orthogonality conditions (conditions (a) and (b) given above) which are basic to rational expectations. The authors of the survey attempt to explain differences in results by whether survey respondents had "direct monetary incentives to accurately report their expectations." Unfortunately, the evidence is scanty, if it exists at all, that "direct monetary payoffs" were present in any of the assessment tasks described, and further, the linking of the reward or incentive to the actual survey response is at best unclear in any of the cases considered.

4.3.4. Summary of the evidence

The evidence from both surveys and experimental studies can be summarized as follows:
(1) Aggregates of individual expectations are more likely to pass rationality tests than are individual expectations; Zarnowitz (1983), Nelson and Bessler (1992), Williams (1987), Nerlove and Schuermann (1995a, 1995b).
(2) There is considerable heterogeneity in individual expectations; Schultz and Brownlee (1941–42), Nelson and Bessler (1992).
(3) Subjects are able to recognize difference in underlying stochastic processes and adapt their forecasts to accommodate these differences, but not necessarily in an optimal manner; Schultz and Brownlee (1941–42), Hey (1994).

That agents in experimental markets look as if they are trying to build rational components into their forecasts [Hey (1994), Swenson (1997)], but do not do so adequately to pass a rationality test accords with the qualitative findings from Heady and Kaldor's (1954, p. 39) survey: "The current price then was adjusted for the expected effects of important supply-and-demand forces". That agents are not able to pass more stringent tests of rationality was recognized long ago in the psychological literature. Starting with the work of Meehl (1954), psychologists have (almost always) found clinical judgments of numerical variables to be inferior to mechanical (statistical) predictions. That is, when both a clinical judgment and a statistical predication of a criterion variable are available, such as academic success or prisoner parole recidivism, the statistical prediction

---

[23] See [McFadden and Ruud (1994)].

is rarely inferior to the clinical judgment. The twenty cases studied in Meehl's seminal book generated a plethora of additional studies, all reaching similar conclusions – "an apparent superiority for mechanical models ..." [Sawyer (1966, p. 178)].

Our survey of experimental work finds that only for the most simple univariate process (the random walk studied in [Dwyer et al. (1993)] do we find clear evidence of rational expectations. Introduction of complexity, in terms of more complex univariate structures [Nelson and Bessler (1992), and Beckman and Downs (1997)] or market equilibria [Williams (1987)] results in clear rejections of rationality. Perhaps Simon's assessment of human behavior captures what the experimental results are telling us:

> Human behavior ... is not to be accounted for by a handful of invariants. It is certainly not to be accounted for by assuming perfect adaptation to the environment. Its basic mechanisms may be relatively simple, and I believe they are, but that simplicity operates in interaction with extremely complex boundary conditions imposed by the environment and by the very facts of human long-term memory and the capacity of human beings, individually and collectively, to learn. [Simon (1979, p. 510)]

Environmental conditions related to the costs and benefits of responding in a "rational manner" to laboratory questions ought to be a prime point of focus in future laboratory work.

5. Conclusions and directions for further research

We began our discourse on expectations and their role in dynamic optimizing behavior with a statement of the central simplifying assumption which runs through both theoretical and empirical work in this area and one which is adopted in the remainder of our essay. This is the assumption of separation of expectations and optimizing behavior, which goes back at least to the work of Keynes and Hicks in the 1930s. Such separation is a powerful simplification both theoretically and empirically, but we know that it is not theoretically correct. In a "theoretically correct" but essentially useless formulation, decisions and expectations are not separable; the explanation of behavior proceeds directly from assumptions about agents' priors and the dynamic constraints of their optimization problem to the decisions they take now and in the future in response to future events. We do not see any viable alternative over most of the range of problems in dynamic optimizing behavior under uncertainty studied by agricultural and general economists. Yet the state of the results of recent experimental studies of expectations, discussed further below, suggests the need to relax or modify this assumption and to provide a clearer framework of analysis for understanding the relation between how expectations are formed and reported and the uses to which such expectations are put and the rewards of optimizing behavior. The importance of incentives in experimental design suggests that experimental subjects may be better able to say what they will do than what they expect on the basis of the information presented to them.

Two models showing how the separation assumption works in practice were discussed in some detail. The first, oriented toward empirical application to historical time series data, was the old Nerlove supply model. The second, designed not for direct empirical application but rather for the derivation of comparative statics results, was a model of small ruminant production and supply. In this connection, we showed that, provided the separation assumption can be maintained, it is generally unnecessary to know anything about the mechanism by which expectations are formed in order to draw interesting and useful theoretical conclusions, and thus illustrated the power of the assumption. Were the authors of this chapter primarily economic theorists, we might, in view of the many difficulties discussed above in the main body of this chapter, conclude that further research ought to focus on questions of a purely theoretical nature. Unfortunately, most serious, real world, empirical questions do require a component of the model designed to deal with people's responses that includes some specification of the way in which expectations are formed and how they influence behavior.

Next, in Section 2, we turned to the five principal models of expectation formation used in analyses of aggregate time series data: extrapolative; adaptive; implicit; two variants of rational, fully rational and quasi-rational; and futures price based models. Extrapolative and adaptive expectations were used extensively in early studies of agricultural supply and related phenomena. Adaptive expectations models held up well in the sense that they generally yielded intuitively plausible conclusions with respect to the other parameters being estimated, but these models had the unfortunate tendency to confound expectation formation with other dynamic aspects of behavior and, moreover, in practice generally produce highly variable results for the same product supply in different periods or circumstances, which suggests, as argued in [Nerlove (1979)], that we are leaving out far too much in the nonexpectational part of our models. Implicit expectations, which were introduced prior to the formulation of the rational expectations hypothesis, share many of the latter's attractive features but suffer from a fatal flaw, corrected in Muth's 1961 formulation. Futures price based expectations for storable commodities are simply inconsistent with the basic paradigms of economics (utility maximizing agents and equilibrium),[24] and the evidence supporting them is mixed, all the more so for nonstorable commodities.[25] In any case, such models are of limited significance for aggregate time series studies since futures markets do not exist, or have not existed for considerable periods, for those commodities we would like to study. Rational expectations (RE) are the most theoretically attractive model of expectation formation. The model is, however, difficult to apply in practice, and, as shown in Section 3, generally fails to be supported empirically in those few attempts to test the REH. The difficulties of applying the rational expectations model in practice are corrected by

---

[24] Which doesn't, of course, mean that they're wrong, only that in accepting them we'd be forced to discard too much else which has proved useful and valid in the discipline.

[25] Gardner's (1976) results give weak support to the theory that the futures price is an *indicator* of expected future prices, but the evidence he presents is also consistent with misspecification of the underlying supply models.

the simplification of quasi-rational expectations (QRE). QRE are extremely easy to apply to time series data, are less subject to problems related to the specification of the underlying behavioral model, and are asymptotically equivalent to the RE under correct specification. For agricultural economists who continue to analyze aggregate time series data, adoption of RE as a maintained hypothesis and application in the form of QRE would allow a highly desirable concentration on the substance of the behavioral part of the model, and strikes us as the way to go. But, as a tool for research on expectation formation itself, we believe that such studies are a dead end.

The final section of this chapter, Section 3, considers the evidence, both direct and indirect, principally for rational expectations, since this hypothesis is now the leading, if not the sole, contender for our hearts and minds. Apart from the minor difficulty that all expectational models of distributed lags (EDL) fail what we call "minimalist tests", models based on QRE appear to work fairly well for aggregate time series data, in the sense that assuming them gives behavioral results consistent with theory. As we point out, however, the analyses so far undertaken are not really tests of rational expectations but rather of the dynamic optimization model in which they are imbedded. We conclude that further attempts to test RE in an aggregate time series context, while not exactly futile, are not worth the effort.

The unsatisfactory state of affairs with respect to conventional econometric analysis in this area has led to considerable recent research, building on the earlier work of the Iowa State group, which emphasizes direct observation of the expectations themselves, as reported by respondents to survey questionnaires or as predictions in an experimental context. The goal of this research is not only to test models of expectation formation freed from the constraints imposed by the behavioral model in aggregate time series analysis, but also to understand better the way in which expectations are actually formed and how they might influence subsequent behavior, and to refine models of expectation formation in the light of this evidence. It is in this connection, as our discussion of motivation – particularly of the payoff structure to participants in experiments – suggests, that the separation assumption begins to break down. When asked in a survey what they expect with respect to such-and-such, about what and how do respondents answer? On the whole we remain ignorant of respondents' state of mind, and really carefully designed surveys directed to elucidating these matters remain to be carried out. The problem is that most economic surveys are designed for purposes other than understanding people's behavior and, particularly, how they form expectations of the future and respond to those expectations.

Experimental studies are carried out on a far smaller scale than surveys. For this reason, experimental studies of how people predict, which may perhaps be assumed to be indicative of how expectations are formed, have recently been undertaken. Unfortunately, insufficient attention has been paid to the conditions set in the experiments related to the costs and benefits of responding in a "rational manner" to the laboratory questions. Following Simon's dictum on the complexity of "boundary conditions" imposed by the environment, complexity has been added in a haphazard manner. Subjects have not been able to respond in ways consistent with the experimenters' theories.

Perhaps this is because the subjects have been brought into the lab without giving consideration to external validity: Do the experimental results have anything to say about real world agents? Experimentalists have focused instead on internal validity: Were the results valid within the scope of this particular experiment? Little or no motivation, with flat payoff functions (in the neighborhood of the rational expectation response), may have given the impression that laboratory subjects were either bored, irrational, or both. But the real world provides large incentives as payoffs, and those who fail to respond in an acceptable manner are dropped from the experiment – the market does not allow subjects who consistently forecast poorly to stay around very long, especially those who do not begin with large initial endowments.

Our view is that motivation in experiments, particularly related to how subjects predict the future and how they behave in the context of such predictions, needs to be taken more seriously if we're going to make the leap from nice, simple, internally valid results to useful, externally valid results. In this context, the separation assumption, which has been central to virtually all theoretical thinking and empirical study of dynamic optimizing behavior, may need to be discarded or, at the very least, relaxed.

Whereas the problems of internal validity are solvable within the limits of the logic of probability, the problems of external validity are not logically solvable in any neat, conclusive way. Generalization always turns out to involve extrapolation into a realm not represented in one's sample. Campbell and Stanley (1963, p. 17–18) write:

> ... there is a general empirical law we are assuming, along with all scientists. This is the modern version of Mill's assumption as to the lawfulness of nature. In its modern, weak version, this can be stated as the assumption of the "stickiness" of nature: we assume that the closer two events are in time, space and measured value on any or all dimensions, the more they tend to follow the same laws. While complex interactions and curvilinear relationships are expected to confuse attempts at generalization, they are more to be expected the more the experimental situation differs from the setting to which one wants to generalize. Our call for greater external validity will thus be a call for that maximum similarity of experiments to the conditions of application which is compatible with internal validity.

In assessing external validity, we will have to come to terms with the incentive structure built into our experiments. Adding complexity [Nelson and Bessler (1992), Williams (1987), Beckman and Downs (1997), Swenson (1997), Hey (1994)] without a matching incentive structure is almost asking for chaotic results. The direction which additional complexity should take in the laboratory should be dictated by the types of behavioral questions asked in other contexts. We ought to add more complexity in studying behavior of relevance to questions related to the formulation of policy. Keep the experiment simple on all other counts and, if we are serious about testing rationality, make the slope of the payoff function match the real world in the neighborhood of the rational expectations response. But the real issue is not what model to use, but rather how we might best proceed to get answers to the substantive questions with which we are concerned.

Acknowledgements

Nerlove's contribution was supported by the Maryland Agricultural Experiment Station. Bessler's contribution was supported by the Texas Agricultural Experiment Station. We are indebted for helpful suggestions to the editors of this volume, Bruce L. Gardner and Gordon C. Rausser, to an anonymous referee, and to Eliseu Alves, Ray Battalio, Zvi Eckstein, David M. Grether, Wallace E. Huffman, Richard E. Just, Anke Meyer, Robert G. Nelson, and Sarah Teichner, who commented on portions of earlier drafts.

References

Amman, H.M., D. Kendrick and S. Achath (1995), "Solving stochastic optimization models with learning and rational expectations", Economics Letters 48:9–13.

Antonovitz, F., and R. Green (1990), "Alternative estimates of fed beef supply response to risk", American Journal of Agricultural Economics 72:475–487.

Askari, H., and J.T. Cummings (1976), Agricultural Supply Response: A Survey of the Econometric Evidence (Praeger Publishers, New York).

Askari, H., and J.T. Cummings (1977), "Estimating agricultural supply response with the Nerlove model: A survey", International Economic Review 18:257–292.

Barro, R.J. (1974), "Are government bonds net wealth?", Journal of Political Economy 82:1095–1117.

Barro, R.J., and G.S. Becker (1989), "Fertility choice in a model of economic growth", Econometrica 57:481–501.

Beckman, S.R., and D. Downs (1997), "Forecasters as imperfect information processors: Experimental and survey evidence", Journal of Economic Behavior and Organization 32:89–101.

Bessler, D.A. (1980), "Aggregated personalistic beliefs on yields of selected crops estimated using ARIMA processes", American Journal of Agricultural Economics 62:666–674.

Bessler, D.A. (1982), "Adaptive expectations, the exponentially weighted forecast, and optimal statistical predictors: A revisit", Agricultural Economics Research 34:16–23.

Bessler, D.A., and J.A. Brandt (1992), "An analysis of forecasts of livestock prices", Journal of Economic Behavior and Organization 18:249–263.

Bessler, D.A., and C.V. Moore (1979), "Use of probability assessments and scoring rules for agricultural forecasts", Agricultural Economics Research 31:44–47.

Brier, G.W. (1950), "Verification of forecasts expressed in terms of probability", Monthly Weather Review 78:1–3.

Campbell, D., and J.C. Stanley (1963), Experimental and Quasi-Experimental Designs for Research (Houghton Mifflin Company).

Carlson, J. (1977), "A study of price forecasts", Annals of Economic and Social Measurement 6:27–56.

Carvalho, J.L. (1972), Production, investment and expectations: A study of the United States cattle industry, Ph.D. dissertation (Department of Economics, University of Chicago).

Chavas, J.-P., R. Pope and R. Kao (1983), "An analysis of the role of futures prices, cash prices and government programs in acreage response", Western Journal of Agricultural Economics 8:27–33.

Colling, P.L., S.H. Irwin and C.R. Zulauf (1992), "Weak-and strong-form rationality tests of market analysts' expectations of USDA hogs and pigs reports", Review of Agricultural Economics 14:263–270.

Covey, T., and D.A. Bessler (1995), "Asset storability and the information content of intertemporal prices", Journal of Empirical Finance 2:103–115.

Davis, D.D., and C.A. Holt (1993), Experimental Economics (Princeton University Press, Princeton, NJ).

De Finetti, B. (1965), "Methods for discriminating levels of partial knowledge concerning a test item", The British Journal of Mathematical and Statistical Psychology 18:87–123.

Diebold, F.X., and G.D. Rudebusch (1989), "Scoring the leading indicators", Journal of Business 62:369–391.

Dwyer, G.P., A.W. Williams, R.C. Battalio and T.I. Mason (1993), "Tests of rational expectations in a stark setting", The Economic Journal 103:586–601.

Eales, J., B. Engle, R. Hauser and S. Thompson (1990), "Grain price expectations of Illinois farmers and grain merchandisers", American Journal of Agricultural Economics 72:701–708.

Eckstein, Z. (1984), "A rational expectations model of agricultural supply", Journal of Political Economy 92:1–19.

Eckstein, Z. (1985), "The dynamics of agricultural supply: A reconsideration", American Journal of Agricultural Economics 67:204–214.

Fair, R.C., and J.B. Taylor (1983), "Solution and maximum-likelihood estimation of dynamic nonlinear rational expectations models", Econometrica 50:1169–1185.

Fair, R.C., and J.B. Taylor (1990), "Full information estimation and stochastic simulation of models with rational expectations", Journal of Applied Econometrics 5:381–392.

Feder, G., R. Just and A. Schmitz (1980), "Futures markets and the theory of the firm under price uncertainty", Quarterly Journal of Economics 96:317–328.

Fornari, I. (1994), U.S. beef cattle supply: Tests of quasi-rational expectations against fully rational expectations, Unpublished Ph.D. Dissertation (University of Pennsylvania).

Foster, K.A. (1990), A Dynamic model of cattle inventories and supply in the U.S. beef cattle industry, Ph.D. Dissertation (University of California, Davis).

Friedman, M. (1953), "The methodology of positive economics", in: Essays in Positive Economics (The University of Chicago Press, Chicago) 3–43.

Friedman, M. (1957), A Theory of the Consumption Function (Princeton University Press, Princeton).

Frydman, R., and E.S. Phelps (1983), Individual Forecasting and Aggregate Outcomes (Cambridge University Press, New York).

Garcia, P., and R.M. Leuthold (1992), "The effect of market information on corn and soybean markets", in: Proceedings of the 1992 NCR-134 Applied Commodity Price Analysis, Forecasting and Market Risk Management Conference, Chicago, IL, April, pp. 59–74.

Gardner, B.L. (1976), "Futures prices in supply analysis", American Journal of Agricultural Economics 58:81–84.

Goodwin, R.M. (1947), "Dynamical coupling with especial reference to markets having production lags", Econometrica 15:181–204.

Goodwin, T.H., and S.M. Sheffrin (1982), "Testing the rational expectations hypothesis in an agricultural market", Review of Economics and Statistics 64:658–667.

Grandmont, J.-M. (1998), "Expectations formation and stability of large socioeconomic systems", Econometrica 66:741–781.

Granger, C.W.J. (1989), "Combining forecasts – twenty years later", Journal of Forecasting 8:167–173.

Hamilton, J.D. (1994), "Cointegration", in: Time Series Analysis, Ch. 19 (Princeton University Press, Princeton).

Hansen, L.P., and T.J. Sargent (1980), "Formulating and estimating dynamic linear rational expectations models", Journal of Economic Dynamics and Control 2:7–46.

Hansen, L.P., and T.J. Sargent (1981), "Linear rational expectations models for dynamically interrelated variables", in: R.E. Lucas and T.J. Sargent, eds., Rational Expectations and Econometric Practice (University of Minnesota Press, Minneapolis) 127–156.

Hansen, L.P., and T.J. Sargent (1991), "Exact linear rational expectations models: Specification and estimation", in: L.P. Hansen and T.J. Sargent, eds., Rational Expectations Econometrics (Westview Press, Boulder, CO) 45–75.

Harrison, G. (1989), "Theory and misbehavior of first-price auctions: A reply", American Economic Review 79:749–762.

Harrison, G. (1992), "Theory and misbehavior of first-price auctions: Reply", American Economic Review 82:1426–1443.

Heady, E.O., and D.R. Kaldor (1954), "Expectations and errors in forecasting agricultural prices", Journal of Political Economy 62:34–47.

Hey, J. (1994), "Expectations formation: Rational or adaptive or …?" Journal of Economic Behavior and Organization 25:329–349.

Hicks, J.R. (1946), Value and Capital, 2nd edn. (Clarendon Press, Oxford).

Hicks, J.R. (1977), Economic Perspectives Further Essays on Money and Growth (Clarendon Press, Oxford).

Hildenbrand, W. (1994), Market Demand: Theory and Empirical Evidence (Princeton University Press, Princeton).

Hirshleifer, J., and J.G. Riley (1992), The Analytics of Uncertainty and Information (University Press, Cambridge).

Holt, C.A. (1986), "Scoring-rule procedures for eliciting subjective probabilities and utility functions", in: P. Goel and A. Zellner, eds., Bayesian Inference and Decision Techniques: Essays in Honor of Bruno de Finetti (Elsevier Science, New York) 279–290.

Holthausen, D. (1979), "Hedging and the competitive firm under price uncertainty", American Economic Review 69:989–995.

Horvath, B., and M. Nerlove (1996), "Some econometric implications of learning", in: E. Helmstädter, G. Poser and H.J. Ramser, eds., Beiträge zur Angewandten Wirtschaftsforschung (Duncker u. Humblot, Berlin) 319–337.

Horvath, B., M. Nerlove and D. Willson (1992), "A reinterpretation of direct tests of forecast rationality using business survey data", Mimeo (University of Pennsylvania).

Irwin, S.H., and C.S. Thraen (1994), "Rational expectations in agriculture? A review of the issues and the evidence", Review of Agricultural Economics 16:133–158.

Jacobs, R.L., and R.A. Jones (1980), "Price expectations in the United States: 1947–1975", American Economic Review 70:269–276.

Jarvis, L.S. (1986), "Supply response in the cattle industry: The Argentine case", Giannini Foundation Special Report (University of California).

Johnson, D.G. (1947), Forward Prices for Agriculture (The University of Chicago Press, Chicago).

Just, R.E. (1974), "Econometric analysis of production decisions with government intervention: The case of the California field crops", Giannini Foundation Monograph 33.

Just, R., and G. Rausser (1981), "Commodity price forecasting with large-scale econometric models and the futures market", American Journal of Agricultural Economics 63:197–209.

Kapteyn, A., N. Kiefer and J. Rust, eds. (1995), "The microeconometrics of dynamic decision making", Special issue, Journal of Applied Econometrics 10 (supplement).

Keane, M.P., and D.E. Runkle (1990), "Testing the rationality of price forecasts: New evidence from panel data", American Economic Review 80:714–735.

Keynes, J.M. (1936), The General Theory of Employment, Interest and Money (Harcourt, Brace & Co, New York).

Kiefer, N.M. (1988–89), "Optimal collection of information by partially informed agents", Econometric Reviews 7:133–148.

Kirman, A.P. (1992), "What or whom does the representative agent represent?", Journal of Economic Perspectives 6:117–136.

Kling, J., and D.A. Bessler (1989), "Calibration-based predictive distributions: An application of prequential analysis to interest rates, money, prices and output", Journal of Business 62:477–499.

Leuthold, R. (1974), "The price performance on the futures market of a nonstorable commodity", American Journal of Agricultural Economics 56:271–279.

Lovell, M.C. (1986), "Tests of the rational expectations hypothesis", American Economic Review 76:110–124.

Malinvaud, E. (1969), "First order certainty equivalence", Econometrica 37:706–718.

Martin, L., and P. Garcia (1981), "The price forecasting performance of futures markets for live cattle and hogs: A disaggregated analysis", American Journal of Agricultural Economics 63:209–215.

McClennen, E.F. (1990), Rationality and Dynamic Choice: Foundational Explorations (University Press, Cambridge).

McFadden, D., and P.A. Ruud (1994), "Estimation by simulation", Review of Economics and Statistics 76:591–608.

Meehl, P. (1954), Clinical versus Statistical Prediction: A Theoretical Analysis and Review of the Evidence (University of Minnesota Press, Minneapolis).

Mills, E.S. (1955), The theory of inventory decisions, Ph.D. Dissertation (University of Birmingham, England).

Mills, E.S. (1962), Price, Output, and Inventory Policy: A Study in the Economics of the Firm and Industry (John Wiley, New York).

Miranda, M.J., and G.D. Schnitkey (1995), "An empirical model of asset replacement in dairy production", in: Kapteyn et al., eds., op. cit.

Mundlak, Y. (1966), "On the microeconomic theory of distributed lags", Review of Economics and Statistics 48:51–60.

Mundlak, Y. (1967), "Long-run coefficients and distributed lag analysis: A reformulation", Econometrica 35:278–293.

Murphy, A., and R. Winkler (1970), "Scoring rules in probability assessment and evaluation", Acta Psychologica 34:273–286.

Muth, J.F. (1960), "Optimal properties of exponentially weighted forecasts", Journal of the American Statistical Association 55:299–305.

Muth, J.F. (1961), "Rational expectations and the theory of price movements", Econometrica 29:315–335.

Muth, J.F. (1985), "Short-run forecasts of business activity", Paper presented at the joint Pittsburgh Meeting of the Eastern Economic Association-International Society for Inventory Research, March.

Nelson, R.G. (1987), Probability elicitation and the formation of expectations: An experimental approach, Ph.D. Thesis (Texas A&M University).

Nelson, R.G., and D.A. Bessler (1989), "Subjective probabilities elicited under proper and improper scoring rules: A laboratory test of predicted responses", American Journal of Agricultural Economics 71:363–369.

Nelson, R.G., and D.A. Bessler (1992), "Quasi-rational expectations: Experimental evidence", Journal of Forecasting 11(2):141–156.

Nerlove, M. (1955), "The predictive test as a tool for inference: The demand for meat in the United States", Unpublished M.A. Dissertation (The Johns Hopkins University, Baltimore, MD).

Nerlove, M. (1956a), "Estimates of elasticities of supply of selected agricultural commodities", Journal of Farm Economics 38:496–509.

Nerlove, M. (1956b), "Estimates of the elasticities of supply of corn, cotton, and wheat", Ph.D. Dissertation (The Johns Hopkins University, Baltimore, MD).

Nerlove, M. (1958a), "The implications of Friedman's permanent income hypothesis for demand analysis", Agricultural Economics Research 10:1–14.

Nerlove, M. (1958b), Distributed Lags and Demand Analysis, Agricultural Handbook No. 141 (Government Printing Office, Washington, D.C.).

Nerlove, M. (1958c), The Dynamics of Supply: Estimation of Farmers' Response to Price (Johns Hopkins University Press, Baltimore, MD).

Nerlove, M. (1961), "Time-series analysis of the supply of agricultural products", in: E.O. Heady et al., eds., Agricultural Supply Functions: Estimating Techniques and Interpretation (Iowa State University Press, Ames, IA).

Nerlove, M. (1967), "Distributed lags and unobserved components in economic time series", in: W. Fellner et al., eds., Ten Economic Essays in the Tradition of Irving Fisher (John Wiley & Sons, New York).

Nerlove, M. (1972), "Lags in economic behavior", Econometrica 40:221–251.

Nerlove, M. (1979), "The dynamics of supply: Retrospect and prospect", American Journal of Agricultural Economics 61:874–888.

Nerlove, M. (1983), "Expectations, plans and realizations in theory and practice", Econometrica 51:1251–1279.

Nerlove, M. (1988), "Analysis of business-test survey data by means of latent variable models", in: W. Franz, W. Gaab and J. Walters, eds., Theoretische und angewandte Wirtschaftsforschung, Heinz Konig zum 60 (Springer Verlag, Heidelberg).

Nerlove, M., and I. Fornari (1997), "Quasi-rational expectations, an alternative to fully rational expectations: An application to U.S. beef cattle supply", Journal of Econometrics 83:129–161.

Nerlove, M., D.M. Grether and J.L. Carvalho (1979), Analysis of Economic Time Series: A Synthesis (Academic Press, New York) Reprinted with corrections (1995).

Nerlove, M., and L. Raut (1997), "Growth models with endogenous population", in: M.R. Rosenzweig and O. Stark, eds., The Handbook of Population and Family Economics (Elsevier, New York).

Nerlove, M., and T. Schuermann (1995a), "Expectations: Are they rational, adaptive, or naive? An essay in simulation-based inference", in: G.S. Maddala, P.C.B. Phillips and T.N. Srinivasan, eds., Advances in Econometrics and Quantitative Economics (Basil Blackwell, Oxford).

Nerlove, M., and T. Schuermann (1995b), "Businessmen's expectations are neither rational nor adaptive", Unpublished working paper (Department of Agricultural and Resource Economics, University of Maryland).

Nerlove, M., and T.D. Soedjana (1996), "Slametans and sheep: Savings and small ruminants in semi-subsistence agriculture in Indonesia", Unpublished working paper (Department of Agricultural and Resource Economics, University of Maryland).

Nerlove, M., and M. Weeks (1992), "The construction of multivariate probability simulators with an application to the multinomial probit model", Mimeo (University of Pennsylvania).

Nerlove, M., D. Willson and B. Horvath (1992), "A reinterpretation of direct tests of forecast rationality using business survey data", in: K.H. Oppenländer and G. Poser, eds., Business Cycle Analysis by Means of Economic Surveys, Part 1 (Aldershot, Avebury).

Orazem, P., and J. Miranowski (1986), "An indirect test for the specification of expectation regimes", Review of Economics and Statistics 68:603–609.

Pesaran, M.H. (1987), The Limits to Rational Expectations (Basil Blackwell, Oxford).

Plott, C., and S. Sunder (1988), "Rational expectations and the aggregation of diverse information in laboratory security markets", Econometrica 56:1085–1118.

Pierce, D.A. (1975), "Forecasting in dynamic models with stochastic regressors", Journal of Econometrics 3:349–374.

Ravallion, M. (1985), "The informational efficiency of traders' price expectations in a Bangladesh rice market, Oxford Bulletin of Economics and Statistics 47:171–184.

Ravallion, M. (1987), Markets and Famines (Oxford University Press, Oxford).

Rosen, S. (1986), "Dynamic animal economics", American Journal of Agricultural Economics 68:547–557.

Runkle, D.E. (1991), "Are farrowing intentions rational forecasts?", American Journal of Agricultural Economics 73:594–600.

Sargent, T.J. (1973), "Rational expectations, the real rate of interest, and the natural rate of unemployment", in: Brookings Papers on Economic Activity 429–492.

Sargent, T.J. (1976a), "A classical macroeconometric model for the United States", Journal of Political Economy 84:207–237.

Sargent, T.J. (1976b), "The observational equivalence of natural and unnatural rate theories of macroeconomics", Journal of Political Economy 84:631–639.

Sargent, T.J. (1981), "Interpreting economic time series", Journal of Political Economy 89:213–248.

Sargent, T.J., and C.A. Sims (1977), "Business cycle modeling without pretending to have too much a priori information", in: C.A. Sims, ed., New Methods in Business Cycle Research (Federal Reserve Bank, Minneapolis).

Sargent, T.J., and N. Wallace (1973), "Rational expectations and the dynamics of hyperinflation", International Economic Review 14:328–350.

Savage, L. (1954), The Foundations of Statistics (Wiley, New York).

Sawyer, J. (1966), "Measurement and prediction, clinical and statistical", Psychological Bulletin 66:178–200.

Schmalensee, R. (1976), "An experimental study of expectations formation", Econometrica 44:17–41.

Schultz, T.W., and O.H. Brownlee (1941–42), "Two trials to determine expectation models applicable to agriculture", Quarterly Journal of Economics, 55:487–496.

Shackle, G.L.S. (1952), Expectation in Economics, 2nd ed. (University Press, Cambridge).

Shuford, E., A. Albert and H.E. Massengill (1966), "Admissible probability measurement procedures", Psychometrika 31:125–145.

Siegel, S., and D.A. Goldstein (1959), "Decision-making behavior in a two-choice uncertain outcome situation", Journal of Experimental Psychology 57:37–42.

Simon, H.A. (1979), "Rational decision making in business organizations", American Economic Review 69:493–513.

Simon, H. (1997), Models of Bounded Rationality, Vol. III: Empirically Grounded Economic Reason Part 4: Behavioral Economics and Bounded Rationality (The MIT Press, Cambridge, MA) 267–443.

Smith, V., G. Suchanek and A. Williams (1988), "Bubbles, crashes, and endogenous expectations in experimental spot asset markets", Econometrica 56:1119–1151.

Stael von Holstein, C.-A. (1970), Assessment and Evaluation of Subjective Probability Distributions (The Economic Research Institute at the Stockholm School of Economics, Stockholm).

Stock, J.H., and M.W. Watson (1988), "Testing for common trends", Journal of the American Statistical Association, 83:1097–1107.

Stokey, N.L., and R.E. Lucas (1989), Recursive Methods in Economic Dynamics (Harvard University Press, Cambridge).

Swenson, C. (1997), "Rational expectations and tax policy: Experimental market evidence", Journal of Economic Behavior and Organization, 32:433–455.

Theil, H. (1957), "A note on certainty equivalence in dynamic planning", Econometrica 25:346–349.

Treadway, A.B. (1967), "Rational entrepreneurial behavior and the dynamics of investment", Ph.D. Dissertation (The University of Chicago).

Tomek, W.G., and R.W. Gray (1970), "Temporal relationships among prices on commodity futures markets: Their allocative and stabilizing roles", American Journal of Agricultural Economics 52:372–380.

Tronstad, R., and T. McNeil (1989), "Asymmetric price risk: An econometric analysis of aggregate sow farrowings, 1973–86", American Journal of Agricultural Economics 71:630–637.

Turnovsky, S.J. (1970), "Empirical evidence on the formation of price expectations", Journal of the American Association 65:1441–1454.

Wallace, H.A. (1923), "What's on the corn judge's mind?", Journal of the American Society of Agronomy 15:300–304.

Wallis, K.F. (1980), "Econometric implications of the rational expectations hypothesis", Econometrica 48:49–73.

Williams, A. (1987), "The formation of price expectations in experimental markets", Journal of Money, Credit, and Banking 19:1–18.

Williams, J. (1986), The Economic Function of Futures Markets (Cambridge University Press).

Winkler, R. (1983), "Judgements under uncertainty", in: S. Kotz and N. Johnson, eds., Encyclopedia of Statistical Sciences, Vol. 4 (John Wiley and Sons, New York).

Working, H. (1942), "Quotations on commodity futures as price forecasts", Econometrica 10:39–52.

Zarnowitz, V. (1983), "The accuracy of individual and group forecasts from business outlook surveys", National Bureau of Economic Research Working Paper Number 1053.

Zellner, A., A. Hong and C. Min (1991), "Forecasting turning point in international output growth rates using Bayesian exponentially weighted autoregression, time-varying parameter and pooling techniques", Journal of Econometrics 49:275–304.

Chapter 4

THE AGRICULTURAL INNOVATION PROCESS: RESEARCH AND TECHNOLOGY ADOPTION IN A CHANGING AGRICULTURAL SECTOR

DAVID SUNDING and DAVID ZILBERMAN

Department of Agricultural and Resource Economics, University of California at Berkeley, Berkeley, CA

Contents

Handbook of Agricultural Economics, Volume 1, Edited by B. Gardner and G. Rausser

Abstract

The chapter reviews the generation and adoption of new technologies in the agricultural sector. The first section describes models of induced innovation and experimentation, considers the political economy of public investments in agricultural research, and addresses institutions and public policies for managing innovation activity. The second section reviews the economics of technology adoption in agriculture. Threshold models, diffusion models, and the influence of risk, uncertainty, and dynamic factors on adoption are considered. The section also describes the influence of institutions and government interventions on adoption. The third section outlines future research and policy challenges.

Keywords

innovation, diffusion, adoption, technology transfer, intellectual property

JEL classification: Q16

Technological change has been a major factor shaping agriculture in the last 100 years [Schultz (1964), Cochrane (1979)]. A comparison of agricultural production patterns in the United States at the beginning (1920) and end of the century (1995) shows that harvested cropland has declined (from 350 to 320 million acres), the share of the agricultural labor force has decreased substantially (from 26 to 2.6 percent), and the number of people now employed in agriculture has declined (9.5 million in 1920 vs. 3.3 million in 1995); yet agricultural production in 1995 was 3.3 times greater than in 1920 [United States Bureau of the Census (1975, 1980, 1998)]. Internationally, tremendous changes in production patterns have occurred. While world population more than doubled between 1950 and 1998 (from 2.6 to 5.9 billion), grain production per person has increased by about 12 percent, and harvested acreage per person has declined by half [Brown et al. (1999)]. These figures suggest that productivity has increased and agricultural production methods have changed significantly.

There is a large amount of literature investigating changes in productivity,[1] which will not be addressed here. Instead this chapter presents an overview of agricultural economic research on innovations – the basic elements of technological and institutional change. Innovations are defined here as new methods, customs, or devices used to perform new tasks.

The literature on innovation is diverse and has developed its own vocabulary. We will distinguish between two major research lines: research on innovation generation and research on the adoption and use of innovation. Several categories of innovations have been introduced to differentiate policies or modeling. For example, the distinction between innovations that are *embodied* in capital goods or products (such as tractors, fertilizers, and seeds) and those that are *disembodied* (e.g., integrated pest management schemes) is useful for directing public investment in innovation generation. Private parties are less likely to invest in generating disembodied innovations because of the difficulty in selling the final product, so that is an area for public action. Private investment in the generation of embodied innovations requires appropriate institutions for intellectual property rights protection, as we will see below.

The classification of innovations according to form is useful for considering policy questions and understanding the forces behind the generation and adoption of innovations. Categories in this classification include mechanical innovations (tractors and combines), biological innovations (new seed varieties), chemical innovations (fertilizers and pesticides), agronomic innovations (new management practices), biotechnological innovations, and informational innovations that rely mainly on computer technologies. Each of these categories may raise different policy questions. For example, mechanical innovations may negatively affect labor and lead to farm consolidation. Chemical and biotechnological innovations are associated with problems of public acceptance and environmental concerns. We will argue later that economic forces as well as the state of scientific knowledge affect the form of innovations that are generated and adopted in various locations.

---

[1] See Mundlak (1997), Ball et al. (1997), and Antle and McGuckin (1993).

Another categorization of innovation according to form distinguishes between process innovations (e.g., a way to modify a gene in a plant) and product innovations (e.g., a new seed variety). The ownership of rights to a process that is crucial in developing an important product may be a source of significant economic power. We will see how intellectual property rights and regulations affect the evolution of innovation and the distribution of benefits derived from them.

Innovations can also be distinguished by their impacts on economic agents and markets which affect their modeling; these categories include yield-increasing, cost-reducing, quality-enhancing, risk-reducing, environmental-protection increasing, and shelf-life enhancing. Most innovations fall into several of these categories. For example, a new pesticide may increase yield, reduce economic risk, and reduce environmental protection. The analysis of adoption or the impact of risk-reducing innovations may require the incorporation of a risk-aversion consideration in the modeling framework, while investigating the economics of a shelf-life enhancing innovation may require a modeling framework that emphasizes inter-seasonal dynamics.

Three sections on the generation of innovations follow in Section 1. The first introduces results of induced innovation models and the role of economic forces in triggering innovations; the second presents a political-economic framework for government financing of innovations; and the third addresses various institutions and policies for managing innovation activities. Section 2 discusses the adoption of innovations and includes four sections. The first section considers threshold models and models of diffusion as a process of imitation; the second presents adoption under uncertainty; the third addresses dynamic considerations on adoption; and the last two sections deal with the impact of institutional and policy constraints on adoption. Section 3 addresses future directions.

1. Generation of innovation

1.1. Induced innovations

There are several stages in the generation of innovations. These stages are depicted in Figure 1. The first stage is discovery, characterized by the emergence of a concept or results that establish the innovation. A second essential stage is development, where the discovery moves from the laboratory to the field, and is scaled up, commercialized, and integrated with other elements of the production process. In cases of patentable innovations, between the time of discovery and development there may also be a stage where there is registration for a patent. If the innovation is embodied, once it is developed it has to be produced and, finally, marketed. For embodied innovations, the marketing stage consists of education, demonstration, and sales. Only then does adoption occur.

Some may hold the notion that new discoveries are the result of inspiration occurring randomly without a strong link to physical reality. While that may sometimes be the case, Hayami and Ruttan (1985) formalized and empirically verified their theory of

Figure 1.

induced innovations that closely linked the emergence of innovations with economic conditions. They argued that the search for new innovations is an economic activity that is significantly affected by economic conditions. New innovations are more likely to emerge in response to scarcity and economic opportunities. For example, labor shortages will induce labor-saving technologies. Environment-friendly techniques are likely to be linked to the imposition of strict environmental regulation. Drip irrigation and other water-saving technologies are often developed in locations where water constraints are binding, such as Israel and the California desert. Similarly, food shortages or high prices of agricultural commodities will likely lead to the introduction of a new high-yield variety, and perceived changes in consumer preferences may provide the background for new innovations that modify product quality.

The work of Boserup (1965) and Binswanger and McIntire (1987) on the evolution of agricultural systems supports the induced-innovation hypothesis. Early human groups, consisting of a relatively small number of members who could roam large areas of land, were hunters and gatherers. An increase in population led to the evolution of agricultural systems. In tropical regions where population density was still relatively small, farmers relied on slash-and-burn systems. The transition to more intensive farming systems that used crop rotation and fertilization occurred as population density increased even further. The need to overcome diseases and to improve yields led to the development of innovations in pest control and breeding, and the evolution of the agricultural systems we are familiar with. The work of Berck and Perloff (1985) suggests that the same phenomena may occur with seafood. An increased demand for fish and expanded harvesting may lead to the depletion of population and a rise in harvesting costs, and thus trigger economic incentives to develop alternative aquaculture and mariculture for the provision of seafood.

While scarcity and economic opportunities represent potential demand that is, in most cases, necessary for the emergence of new innovations, a potential demand is not sufficient for inducing innovations. In addition to demand, the emergence of new innovations requires technical feasibility and new scientific knowledge that will provide the technical base for the new technology. Thus, in many cases, breakthrough knowledge gives rise to new technologies. Finally, the potential demand and the appropriate knowledge base are integrated with the right institutional setup, and together they provide the background for innovation activities. These ideas can be demonstrated by an overview of some of the major waves of innovations that have affected U.S. agriculture in the last 150 years.

New innovations currently are linked with discoveries of scientists in universities or firms. However, in the past, practitioners were responsible for most breakthroughs. Over the years, the role of research labs in producing new innovations has drastically increased, but field experience is still very important in inspiring innovations. John Deere, who invented the steel plow, was a farmer. This innovation was one of a series of mechanical innovations that were of crucial importance to the westward expansion of U.S. agriculture in the nineteenth century. At the time, the United States had vast tracts of land and a scarcity of people; this situation induced a wide variety of labor-saving innovations such as the thresher, several types of mechanical harvesters, and later the tractor.

Olmstead and Rhode (1993) argue that demand considerations represented by the induced-innovation hypothesis do not provide the sole explanation for the introduction of new technologies. They conclude that during the nineteenth century, when farm machinery (e.g., the reaper) was introduced in the United States, land prices increased relative to labor prices, which seems to contradict the induced-innovation hypothesis. As settlement of the West continued and land became more scarce, land prices may have risen relative to labor, but the cost of labor in America relative to other regions was high, and that provided the demand for mechanical innovations. Olmstead and Rhode (1993) argue that other factors also affected the emergence of these innovations, including the expansion of scientific knowledge in metallurgy and mechanics (e.g., the Bessemer process for the production of steel, and the invention of various types of mechanical engines), the establishment of the input manufacturing industry, and the interactive relationship between farmers and machinery producers.

The infrastructure that was established for the refinement, development, and marketing of the John Deere plow was later used for a generation of other innovations, and the John Deere Company became the world's leading manufacturer of agricultural mechanical equipment. It was able to establish its own research and development (R&D) infrastructure for new mechanical innovations, had enough financial leverage to buy the rights to develop other discoveries, and subsequently took over smaller companies that produced mechanical equipment that complemented its own. This pattern of evolution, where an organization is established to generate fundamental innovations of a certain kind, and then later expands to become a leading industrial manufacturer, is repeated in other situations in and out of agriculture.

It seems that during the settlement period of the nineteenth century, most of the emphasis was on mechanical innovation. Cochrane (1979) noted that yield per acre did not change much during the nineteenth century, but the production of U.S. agriculture expanded drastically as the land base expanded. However, Olmstead and Rhode (1993) suggest that even during that period there was heavy emphasis on biological innovation. Throughout the settlement period, farmers and scientists, who were part of research organizations such as the Agricultural Research Service (ARS) of the United States Department of Agriculture (USDA), and the experiment stations at the land-grant universities in the United States, experimented with new breeds, both domestic and imported, and developed new varieties that were compatible with the agro-climatic conditions of the newly settled regions. These efforts maintained per-acre yields.

Once most of the arable agricultural land of the continental United States was settled, expansion of agricultural production was feasible mostly through increases in yields per acre. The recognition of this reality and the basic breakthroughs in genetics research in the nineteenth century increased support for research institutions in their efforts to generate yield-increasing innovations. Most of the developed countries established agricultural research institutions. After World War II, a network of international research centers was established to provide agricultural innovations for developing countries. The establishment of these institutions reflected the recognition that innovations are products of R&D activities, and that the magnitude of these activities is affected by economic incentives.

Economic models have been constructed to explain patterns of investment in R&D activities and the properties of the emerging innovations. Evenson and Kislev (1976) developed a production function of research outcomes particularly appropriate for crop and animal breeding. In breeding activities, researchers experiment with a large number of varieties to find the one with the highest yield. The outcome of research efforts depends on a number of plots. In their model, the yield per acre of a crop is a random variable that can assume numerous values. Each experiment is a sampling of a value of this random variable and, if experiments are conducted, the experiment with the highest value will be chosen. Let Y_n be yield per acre of the nth experiment and n assumes value from 1 to N. The outcome of n experiments is $Y_N^* = \max\{Y_1, \ldots, Y_N\}$. Y_N^* is the maximum value of the n experiment. Each Y_n can assume the value in the range of $(0, Y_X)$

with probability density $g(Y_n)$ so that $Y_{\max} g(Y_n) \, dY_n = 1$. The outcome of research on N plots Y_N^* is a random variable with the expected value $\mu(N) = E\{\max_{n=1,N} Y_n\}$.

Evenson and Kislev (1976) showed that the expected value of Y_N^* increases with the number of the experiment, i.e., $\mu_N = \partial EY^*/\partial N > 0$, $\mu_{NN} = \partial^2 EY^*/\partial N^2 < 0$. As in Evenson and Kislev, consider the determination of optimal research levels when a policymaker's objective is to maximize net expected gain from research. Assume that the research improves the productivity of growers in a price-taking industry with output price P and acreage L. The new innovation is adopted fully and does not require extra research cost. The optimal research program is determined by solving

$$\max_N PL\big(U(N)\big) - C(N).$$

The first-order condition is

$$PL\mu_N - C_N = 0, \tag{1}$$

where C_N is the cost of the Nth research plot, and $C_N > 0$, $C_{NN} > 0$. Condition (1) implies that the optimal number of experiments is such that the expected value of the marginal experiment, $(PL\mu_N)$, equals the marginal cost of experiments, (C_N). Furthermore, the analysis can show that the research effort increases with the size of the region, $(\partial N/\partial L > 0)$, and the scarcity of the product, $(\partial N^*/\partial P > 0)$. Similarly, lower research costs will lead to more research effort.

The outcome of research leading to innovations is subject to much uncertainty and, in cases where a decision-maker is risk averse, risk considerations will affect whether and to what extent experiments will be undertaken. For simplicity, consider a case where decision-makers maximize a linear combination of mean and variance of profits, and thus the optimization problem is

$$\max_N PL\big[\mu(N) - C(N)\big] - \frac{1}{2}\phi P^2 L^2 \sigma^2(N),$$

where $\sigma^2(N)$ is the variance of Y_N^*, the maximum value of yield of N experiments, and ϕ is a risk-aversion coefficient. The variance of maximum outcome of N experiments declines with N in most cases so that $\sigma_N^2 = \partial \sigma^2(N)/\partial N < 0$. The first-order condition determining N is

$$PL\mu_N - \phi \sigma_N^2 P^2 L^2 - C_N = 0. \tag{2}$$

Under risk aversion, N is determined so that the marginal effect of an increase of N or expected revenues plus the marginal reduction in the cost of risk bearing is equal to the marginal cost of experiments. A comparison of conditions (1) and (2) suggests that the risk-reducing effect of extra experiments will increase the marginal benefit of experiments under risk aversion. Thus, a risk-averse decision-maker who manages a line of research, is likely to carry out more experiments than a risk-neutral decision-maker. Note, however, that expected profits under risk aversion are smaller than under risk neutrality since risk-neutral decision-makers do not have a risk-carrying cost. If experimentation has a significant fixed cost $(C(N) = C_0 + C_1(N))$, there may be situations when risk aversion may prevent carrying out certain lines of research that would be done under risk neutrality. Furthermore, one can expand the model to show that risk considerations may lead risk-averse decision-makers to carry out several substitutable research lines simultaneously in order to diversify and reduce the cost of risk bearing. Thus, uncertainty about the research outcome may deter investment in discovery research, but it may increase and diversify the research efforts once they take place.

There has not been much research on investment in certain lines of research over time. However, the Evenson–Kislev model suggests that there is a decreasing expected marginal gain from experiments. If a certain yield was established after an initial period of experimentation, the model can be expanded to show that the greater the initial yield, the smaller the optimal experiment in the second period. That suggests that the number of experiments carried out in a certain line of research will decline over time, especially once significant success is obtained, or when it is apparent that there are decreasing marginal returns to research. On the other hand, technological change that reduces the cost of innovative efforts may increase experimentation. Indeed, we have witnessed, over time, the tendency to move from one research line to another and, thus, both dynamic and risk considerations tend to diversify innovative efforts.

The Evenson–Kislev model explains optimal investment in one line of research. However, research programs consist of several research lines. The model considers a price-taking firm that produces Y units of output priced at P and also generates its own technology through innovative activities (research and development). There are J parallel lines of innovation, and j is the research line indicator, $j = 1, \ldots, J$. Let V_j be the price of one unit of the jth innovation line and m_j be the number of units used in this line. Innovations affect output through a multiplicative effect to the production function, $g(m_i, \ldots, m_j)$, and by improving input use effectiveness. The producers use I inputs, and i is the input indicator, $i = 1, \ldots, I$. Let the vector of inputs be $m = \{m_i, \ldots, m_j\}$. We distinguish between the actual unit of input i used by the producer, X_i, and the effective input e_i where $e_i = h_i(m)X_i$. Thus, it is assumed that a major effect of the innovation is to increase input use efficiency, and the function $h_i(m)$ denotes the effect of all the lines of input effectiveness. An innovative line j may increase effectiveness of input i, and in this case $\partial h_i/\partial m_j > 0$. Thus, the production function of the producer is

$$Y = g(m)f\left(X_1 h_1(m), X_2 h_2(m), \ldots, X_I h_I(m)\right).$$

For simplicity, assume that, without any investment in innovation, $h_i(m) = 1$, for all i; thus, $Y = f(X_1, \ldots, X_2)$. The producer has to determine optimal allocation of resources among inputs and research lines. In particular, the choice problem is

$$
\max_{X_i, m_i} pg(m) f\left[X_1 h_1(m), X_2 h_2(m), X_3 h_3(m), X_I h_I(m)\right] - \sum_{i=1}^{I} w_i X_i - \sum_{j=1}^{J} v_i m_i,
$$

where w_i is the price of the ith input and v_j is the price of one unit of the jth line of innovation. The first-order condition to determine use of the ith input is

$$
pg(m) \frac{\partial F}{\partial e_i} h_i(w) - w_i = 0 \quad \forall i. \tag{3}
$$

Input i will be chosen at a level where the value of marginal product of input i's effective units, $pg(m) \frac{\partial F}{\partial e_i}$, is equal to the price of input i's effective units, which is $w_i / h_i(m)$. If the innovations have a positive multiplicative effect, $g(m) > 1$, and increase input use efficiency, $h_i(m) > 1$, then the analysis in [Khanna and Zilberman (1997)] suggests that innovations are likely to increase output but may lead to either an increase or decrease in input use. Input use is likely to increase with the introduction of innovations in cases where they lead to substantial increases in output. Modest output effects of innovations are likely to be associated with reduced input use levels.[2]

The optimal effort devoted to innovation line j is determined according to

$$
\frac{\partial g}{\partial m_i} pf(m) + g(m) p \sum_{i=1}^{I} \frac{\partial h_i}{\partial m_j} X_i - v_j = 0 \quad \forall j. \tag{4}
$$

Let the elasticity of the multiplicative effect of innovation with respect to the level of innovation j be denoted by $\varepsilon_{m_j}^g = \frac{\partial g}{\partial m_j} \frac{m_j}{g(m)}$, and let the elasticity of input i's effectiveness coefficient, with respect to the level of innovation j, be $\varepsilon_{m_j}^{h_i} = \frac{\partial h_i}{\partial m_j} \frac{m_j}{h_i}$. Using (3), the first-order condition (4) becomes

$$
PY\left[\varepsilon_{m_j}^g + \sum_{i=1}^{I} S_i \varepsilon_{m_j}^{h_i}\right] - m_j v_j = 0, \tag{5}
$$

where $S_i = w_i X_i / PY$ is the revenue share of input i. Condition (5) states that, under optimal resource allocation, the expenditure share (in total revenue of innovation line j) will be equal to the sum of elasticities of the input effectiveness, with respect to research line j, and the elasticity of the multiplicative output coefficient with respect to this research line. This condition suggests that more resources are likely to be allocated to

---

[2] Khanna and Zilberman (1997) related the impact of technological change on input use to the curvature of the production function. If marginal productivity of e_i declines substantially with an increase in e_i, the output effects are restricted and innovation leads to reduced input use.

research lines with higher productivity effects that mostly impact inputs with higher expenditure shares that have a relatively lower cost.[3]

Risk considerations provide part of the explanation for such diversification, but whether innovations are complements or substitutes may also be a factor. When the tomato harvester was introduced in California, it was accompanied by the introduction of a new, complementary tomato variety [de Janvry et al. (1981)]. McGuirk and Mundlak's (1991) analysis of the introduction of high-yield "green revolution" varieties in the Punjab shows that it was accompanied by the intensification of irrigation and fertilization practices.

The induced innovation hypothesis can be expanded to state that investment in innovative activities is affected by shadow prices implied by government policies and regulation. The tomato harvester was introduced following the end of the Bracero Program, whose termination resulted in reduced availability of cheap immigrant workers for California and Florida growers. Environmental concerns and regulation have led to more intensive research and alternatives for the widespread use of chemical pesticides. For example, they have contributed to the emergence of integrated pest management strategies and have prompted investment in biological control and biotechnology alternatives to chemical pesticides.

Models of induced innovation should be expanded to address the spatial variability of agricultural production. The heterogeneity of agriculture and its vulnerability to random events such as changes in weather and pest infestation led to the development of a network of research stations. A large body of agricultural research has been aimed at adaptive innovations that develop practices and varieties that are appropriate for specific environmental and climatic conditions. The random emergence of new diseases and pests led to the establishment of research on productivity maintenance aimed at generating new innovations in response to adverse outcomes whenever they occurred.

The treatment of the mealybug in the cassava in Africa is a good example of responsive research. Cassava was brought to Africa from South America 300 years ago and became a major subsistence crop. The mealybug, one of the pests of cassava in South America, was introduced to Africa and reduced yields by more than 50 percent in 1983–84; without treatment, the damage could have had a devastating effect on West Africa [Norgaard (1988)]. The International Institute of Tropical Agriculture launched a research program which resulted in the introduction of a biological control in the form of a small wasp, *E lopezi*, that is a natural enemy of the pest in South America. Norgaard estimated the benefit/cost ratio of this research program to be 149 to 1, but his calculation did not take into account the cost of the research that established the methodology of biological control, and the fixed cost associated with maintaining the infrastructure to respond to the problem.

Induced innovation models such as Binswanger's (1974) are useful in linking the evolution of innovations to prices, costs, and technology. However, they ignore some

---

[3] Binswanger (1974) proves these assertions under a very narrow set of conditions.

of the important details that characterize the system leading to agricultural innovations.[4]

Typically, new agricultural technologies are not used by the entities that develop them (e.g., universities and equipment manufacturers). Different types of entities have their distinct decision-making procedures that need to be recognized in a more refined analysis of agricultural innovations. The next subsection will analyze resource allocation for the development of new innovations in the public sector, and that will be followed by a discussion of specific institutions and incentives for innovation activities (patents and intellectual property rights) in the private sector.

Induced innovations by agribusiness apply to innovations beyond the farm gate. In much of the post World War II period, there has been an excess supply of agricultural commodities in world markets. This has led to a period of low profitability in agriculture, requiring government support. While increasing food quantity has become less of a priority, increasing the value added to food products has become a major concern of agriculture and agribusiness in developed nations. Indeed, that has been the essence of many of the innovations related to agriculture in the last 30 years. Agribusiness took advantage of improvements in transportation and weather-controlled technologies that led to innovations in packing, storage, and shipping. These changes expanded the availability as well as the quality of meats, fruits, and vegetables; increased the share of processing and handling in the total food budget; and caused significant changes in the structure of both food marketing industries and agriculture.

It is important to understand the institutional setup that enables these innovations to materialize. While there has not been research in this area, it seems that the availability of numerous sources of funding to finance new ventures (e.g., venture capital, stock markets, mortgage markets, credit lines from buyers) enables the entities that own the rights to new innovations to change the way major food items are produced, marketed, and consumed.

1.2. Political economy of publicly funded innovations

Applied R&D efforts are supported by both the public and private sectors because of the innovations they are likely to spawn. Public R&D efforts are justified by the public-good nature of these activities and the inability of private companies to capture all the benefits resulting from farm innovations.

Studies have found consistently high rates of returns (above 20 percent) to public investment in agricultural research and extension, indicating underinvestment in these activities, see [Alston et al. (1995), Huffman (1998)]. Analysis of patterns of public spending for R&D in agriculture shows that federal monies tend to emphasize research

---

[4] The Binswanger model (1974) is very closely linked to the literature on quantifying sources of productivity in agriculture. For an overview of this important body of literature, which benefited from seminal contributions by Griliches (1957, 1958) and Mundlak, see [Antle and McGuckin (1993)].

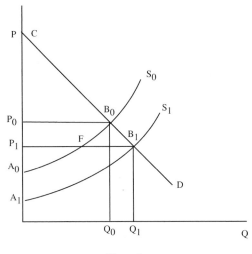

Figure 2.

on commodities that are grown in several states (e.g., wheat, corn, rice), while individual states provide much of the public support for innovation-inducing activities for crops that are specialties of the state (e.g., tomatoes and citrus in Florida, and fruits and vegetables in California). The process of devolution has also applied to public research and, over the years, the federal share in public research has declined relative to the state's share. Increased concern for environmental and resource management issues over time led to an increase in relative shares of public research resources allocated to these issues in agriculture [Huffman and Just (1994)].

Many of the studies evaluating returns to public research in agriculture (including Griliches' 1957 study on hybrid corn that spawned the literature) rely on partial equilibrium analysis, depicted in Figure 2.

The model considers an agricultural industry facing a negatively sloped demand curve D. The initial supply is denoted by S_0, and the initial price and quantity are P_0 and Q_0, respectively. Research, development, and extension activities led to adoption of an innovation that shifts supply to S_1, resulting in price reduction to P_1, and consumption gain Q_1.[5] The social gain from the innovation is equal to the area $A_0 B_0 B_1 A_1$ in Figure 2 denoted by G. If the investment leading to the use of the innovation is denoted by I, the net social gain is $NG = G - I$, and the social rate of return to appropriate research development and extension activities is NG/I.

The social gain from the innovation is divided between consumers and producers. In Figure 2, consumer gain is equal to the area $P_0 B_0 B_1 P_1$. Producer gain is $A_0 F A_1 B_1$

---

[5] Of course, actual computation requires discounting and aggregation, and benefits over time, and may recognize the gradual shift in supply associated with the diffusion process.

because of lower cost and higher sales, but they lose $P_0 B_0 F P_1$ because of lower price. If demand is sufficiently inelastic, producers may actually lose from public research activities and the innovations that they spawn. Obviously, producers may not support research expenditures on innovations that may worsen their well-being, and distributional considerations affect public decisions that lead to technological evolution.[6]

This point was emphasized in Schmitz and Seckler's (1970) study of the impact of the introduction of the tomato harvester in California. They showed that society as a whole gained from the tomato harvester, while farm workers lost from the introduction of this innovation. The controversy surrounding the tomato harvester [de Janvry et al. (1981)] led the University of California to de-emphasize research on mechanical innovations.

De Gorter and Zilberman (1990) introduced a simple model for analyzing political economic considerations associated with determining public expenditures on developing new agricultural technologies. Their analysis considers a supply-enhancing innovation. They consider an industry producing Y units of output. The cost function of the industry is $C(Y, I)$ and depends on output and investment in R&D where the level is I. This cost function is well behaved and an increase in I tends to reduce cost at a decreasing rate $\partial c / \partial I < 0$, and $\partial^2 c / \partial I^2 > 0$ and marginal cost of output $\partial^2 c / \partial I \partial Y < 0$. Let the cost of investment be denoted by r and the price of output by P. The industry is facing a negatively sloped demand curve, $Y = D(P)$. The gross surplus from consumption is denoted by the benefit function $B(Y) = \int_0^Y P(z)\, dz$, where $P(Y)$ is inverse demand.

Social optimum is determined at the levels of Y and I that maximize the net surplus. Thus, the social optimization problem is

$$\max_{Y, I} B(Y) - C(Y, I) - rI,$$

and the first-order optimality conditions are

$$\frac{\partial B}{\partial Y} - \frac{\partial C}{\partial Y} = 0 \Rightarrow P(Y) = \frac{\partial C}{\partial Y}, \tag{6}$$

and

$$-\frac{\partial C}{\partial I} - \gamma = 0. \tag{7}$$

Condition (6) is the market-clearing rule in the output market, where price is equal to marginal cost. Condition (7) states the optimal investment in R&D at a level where

---

[6] Further research is needed to understand to what extent farmers take into consideration the long-term distributional effects of research policy. They may be myopic and support a candidate who favors any research, especially when facing a pest or disease.

the marginal reduction in production cost because of investment in R&D is equal to the cost of investment. The function $-\partial C/\partial I$ reflects a derived demand for supply-shifting investment and, by our assumptions, reducing the price of investment (γ) will increase its equilibrium level. Condition (7) does not likely hold in reality. However, it provides a benchmark with which to assess outcomes under alternative political arrangements.

De Gorter and Zilberman (1990) argued that the political economic system will determine both the level of investment in R&D and the share of the burden of financing it between consumers (taxpayers) and producers. Let Z be the share of public investment in R&D financed by producers. Thus, $Z = 0$ corresponds to the case where R&D is fully financed by taxpayers, and $Z = 1$ where R&D is fully financed by producers. The latter case occurs when producers use marketing orders to raise funds to collectively finance research activities. There are many cases in agriculture where producers compete in the output market but cooperate in technology development or in the political arena [Guttman (1978)].

De Gorter and Zilberman (1990) compare outcomes under alternative arrangements, including the case where producers both determine and finance investment in R&D. In this case, I is the result of a constrained optimization problem, where producer surplus, $PS = P(Y)Y - C(Y, I)$, minus investment cost, rI, is maximized subject to the market-clearing constraint in the output market $P(Y) = \partial C/\partial Y$. When there is internal solution, the first-order optimality condition for I is

$$-\frac{\partial C}{\partial I} - \eta = r,$$

(8)

where

$$\eta = -Y \frac{\partial^2 C}{\partial Y \partial C} \left[1 - \left(\frac{\partial^2 C}{\partial Y^2} \right) \middle/ \left(\frac{\partial P}{\partial I} \right) \right].$$

The optimal solution occurs at a level where the marginal cost saving due to investment minus the term η, which reflects the loss of revenues because of price reduction, is equal to the marginal investment cost, r. The loss of revenues because of a price reduction due to the introduction of a supply-enhancing innovation increases as demand becomes less elastic. A comparison of (8) to (7) suggests that under-investment in agricultural R&D is likely to occur when producers control its level and finance it, and the magnitude of the under-investment increases as demand for the final product becomes less elastic. Below a certain level of demand elasticity, it will be optimal for producers not to invest in R&D at all. If taxpayers (consumers) pay for research but producers determine its level, the optimal investment will occur where the marginal reduction in cost due to the investment is equal to η, the marginal loss in revenue due to price reduction. When the impact of innovation on price is low (demand for final product is highly elastic), producer control may lead to over-investment if producers do not pay for it. However, when $\eta > r$, and expansion of supply leads to significant price reduction, even when taxpayers pay for public agricultural research, producer determination of its level will lead to under-investment.

The public sector has played a major role in funding R&D activities that have led to new agricultural innovations, especially innovations that are disembodied or are embodied but non-shielded. Rausser and Zusman (1991) have argued that choices in political-economic systems are effectively modeled as the outcome of cooperative games among parties. Assume that two groups, consumers/taxpayers and producers, are affected by choices associated with investment in the supply-increasing innovation mentioned above. The political-economic system determines two parameters. The first is the investment in the innovation (I) and the second is the share of the innovation cost financed by consumers. Let this share be denoted as z; thus, the consumer will pay $zc(I)$ for the innovation cost. It is assumed that the investment in the innovation is non-negative ($I \geqslant 0$), but z is unrestricted ($z > 1$ implies that the producers are actually subsidized).

The net effects of the investment and finance of innovations on consumers/taxpayers' welfare and producers' welfare are $\Delta CS(I) - zc(I)$ and $\Delta PS(I) - (1 - z)c(I)$, respectively. The choice of the innovation investment and the sharing coefficients are approximated by the solution to the optimization problem

$$\max_{I,Z} \left(\Delta CS(I) - zc(I)\right)^{\alpha} \left(\Delta PS(I) - (1 - z)c(I)\right)^{1-\alpha}, \tag{9}$$

where α is the consumer weight coefficient, $0 \leqslant \alpha \leqslant 1$. The optimization problem (9) (i) incorporates the objective of the two parties; (ii) leads to outcomes that will not make any of the parties worse off; (iii) reflects the relative power of the parties (when α is close to one, consumers dominate decision-making but the producers have much of the power when $\alpha \rightarrow 0$); and (iv) reflects decreasing marginal valuation of welfare gained by most parties.[7]

After some manipulations, the solutions to this optimization problem are presented by

$$\frac{\Delta CS(I)}{\partial I} + \frac{\partial \Delta PS(1)}{\partial I} = \frac{\partial C}{\partial I}; \tag{10}$$

$$\frac{\alpha_1}{1 - \alpha_1} = \frac{\Delta CS(I) - zc(I)}{\Delta PS(I) - (1 - z)c(I)}. \tag{11}$$

Equation (10) states that innovation investment will be determined when the sum of the marginal increase in consumer and producer surplus is equal to the marginal cost of investment innovation. This rule is equivalent to equating the marginal cost of innovation investment with its marginal impact on market surplus (since $\Delta MS = \Delta PS + \Delta CS$).

---

[7] $\partial PG/\partial I > 0$, $\partial^2 PG/\partial I^2 < 0$, $\partial CS/\partial I > 0$, $\partial^2 CS/\partial I^2 < 0$.

Equation (11) states that the shares of two groups in the total welfare gain are equal to their political weight coefficients. Thus, if α_1 is equal to, say, 0.3 and consumers have 30 percent of the weight in determining the level and distribution of finance of innovation research, then they will receive 30 percent of the benefit. Producers will receive the other 70 percent. Equation (9) suggests that the political weight distribution does not affect the total level of investment in innovation research that is socially optimal, but only affects the distribution of benefits. If farmers have more political gain in determining the outcome because of their intense interest in agricultural policy issues, they will gain much of the benefit from innovation research.

The cooperative game framework is designed to lead to outcomes where both parties benefit from the action they agree upon. Since both demand and supply elasticities for many agricultural commodities are relatively low, producer surplus is likely to decline with expanded innovation research. When these elasticities are sufficiently low, farmers as a group will directly lose from expanded innovation research unless compensated. Thus, in certain situations and for some range of products, positive innovation research is not feasible unless farmers are compensated. This analysis suggests a strong link between public support for innovation research and programs that support farm income. In such situations innovation research leads to a significant direct increase in consumer surplus through increased supplies and a reduction in commodity prices. It will also result in an increase in farmer subsidies by taxpayers. Thus, for a range of commodities with low elasticities of output supply and demand, consumers/taxpayers will finance public research and compensate farmers for their welfare losses. For commodities where demand is quite elastic, say about 2 or 3, and both consumers and producers gain significantly from the fruits of innovation research, both groups will share in financing the research. When demand is very elastic and most of the gain goes to producers, the separate economic frameworks suggest that they are likely to pay for this research significantly, but if their political weight in the decision is quite important (α close to 1), they may benefit immensely from the fruits of the innovation research, but consumers may pay for a greater share of the research.

While this political analysis framework is insightful in that it describes the link between public support for agricultural research and agricultural commodity programs, it may be off the mark in explaining the public investment in innovation research in agriculture, since there is a large array of studies that argues that the rate of return for agricultural research is very high, and thus there is under-investment. One obvious limitation of the model introduced above is that it assumes that the outcomes of research innovation are certain. However, there is significant evidence that returns for research projects are highly skewed. A small number of products may generate most of the benefits, and most projects may have no obvious outcome at all. This risk consideration has to be incorporated explicitly into the analysis determining the level of investment in innovation research. Thus, when consumers consider investment I in innovation research, they are aware that each investment level generates a distribution of outcome, and they will consider the expected consumer surplus gain associated with I. Similarly, producers are aware of the uncertainty involved with innovation research, and they will consider the expected producer surplus associated with each level in assessing the various levels of innovation research.

1.3. Policies and institutions for managing innovation activities

The theory of induced innovations emphasizes the role of general economic conditions in shaping the direction of innovation activities. However, the inducement of innovations also requires specific policies and institutions that provide resources to would-be innovators and enable them to reap the benefits from their innovations.

Patent protection is probably the most obvious incentive to innovation activities. Discoverers of a new patentable technology have the property right for its utilization for a well-defined period of time (17 years in the U.S.). An alternative tool may be a prize for the discoverer of a new technology, and Wright (1983) presents examples where prizes have been used by the government to induce creative solutions to difficult technological problems. A contract, which pays potential innovators for their efforts, is a third avenue in motivating innovative activities. Wright (1983) develops a model to evaluate and compare these three operations. Suppose that the benefits of an innovation are known and equal to B. The search for the innovation is done by n homogeneous units, and the probability of discovery is $P(n)$, with

$$\frac{\partial P}{\partial n} > 0, \qquad \frac{\partial^2 P}{\partial n^2} > 0.$$

The cost of each unit is C. The social optimization problem to determine optimal research effort is

$$\max_{n} P(n)B - nC,$$

and socially optimal u is determined when

$$\frac{\partial P}{\partial N} B = C. \tag{12}$$

The expected marginal benefit of a research unit is equal to its cost. This rule may be used by government agents in determining the number of units to be financed by contracts. On the other hand, under prizes or patents, units will join in the search for the innovation as long as their expected net benefits from the innovation, $P(N)B/N$, are greater than the unit cost C. Thus, optimal N under patents is determined when

$$\frac{P(N)}{N} B = C. \tag{13}$$

Assuming decreasing marginal probability of discovery, average probability of discovery for a research unit is greater than the marginal probability, $P(N)/N > \partial P/\partial N$.

Thus, a comparison of (12) with (13) suggests that there will be over-investment in experimentation under patents and prizes. In essence, under patents and prizes, research units are *ex ante*, sharing a common reward and, as in the classical "Tragedy of the Commons" problem, will lead to overcrowding. Thus, when the award for a discovery is known, contracts may lead to optimal resource allocation.

Another factor that counters the oversupply of research efforts under patent relative to contracts is that the benefits of the innovation under patent may be smaller than under contract. Let B_p be the level of benefits considered for deriving

$$\frac{dL_1^r}{d\overline{L}} = \eta \frac{L_1^r}{\overline{L}} + (r - \eta)R,$$

the research effort under the patent system. B_p is equal to the profits of the monopolist patent owner. Let B_c be the level of benefits considered in determining η_c, the research effort under contract. If η_c is determined by a social welfare maximizing agent, B_c is the sum of consumers' and producers' surplus from the use of the innovation. In this case $B_c > B_N$. Thus, in the case of full information about the benefits and costs, more research will be conducted under contracts if

$$\frac{B_c}{B_p} > \frac{\frac{P(\eta_p)}{\eta_p}}{\frac{\partial P}{\partial n}(\eta_c)}.$$

In many cases, the uncertainty regarding the benefits of an innovation at the discovery and patent stages is very substantial. Commercialization of a patent may require significant investment, and a large percentage of patents are not utilized commercially [Klette and Griliches (1997)]. Commercialization of an innovation requires upscaling and development, registration (in the case of chemical pesticides), marketing, and development of production capacity for products resulting from the patents. Large agribusiness firms have the resources and capacity to engage in commercialization, and they may purchase the right to utilize patents from universities or smaller research and development firms. Commercialization may require significant levels of research that may result in extra patents and trade secrets that strengthen the monopoly power of the commercializing firm. Much of the research in the private sector is dedicated to the commercialization and the refinement of innovations, while universities emphasize discovery and basic research. Thus, Alston, Norton, and Pardey (1995) argue that private-sector and public-sector research spending are not perfect substitutes. Actually, there may be some complementarity between the two. An increase in public sector research leads to patentable discoveries, and when private companies obtain the rights to the patents, they will invest in commercialization research. Private sector companies have recognized the unique capacity of universities to generate innovations, and this has resulted in support for university research in exchange for improved access to obtain rights to the innovations [Rausser (1999)].

1.4. Factors beyond the farm gate

Over the years, product differentiation in agriculture has increased along with an increase in the importance of factors beyond the farm gate and within specialized agribusiness. This evolution is affecting the nature and analysis of agricultural research. Economists have recently addressed how the vertical market structure of agriculture conditions the benefits of agricultural research, and also how farm-level innovation may contribute to changes in the downstream processing sector.

One salient fact about the food-processing sector is that it tends to be concentrated. The problem of oligopsonistic competition in the food processing sector has been addressed by Just and Chern (1980), Wann and Sexton (1992), and Hamilton and Sunding (1997). Two recent papers by Hamilton and Sunding (1998) and Alston, Sexton, and Zhang (1997) point out that the existence of noncompetitive behavior downstream has important implications for the impacts of farm-level technological change.

Consider a situation where the farm sector is competitive and sells its product to a monopsonistic processing sector. Let X denote the level of farm output, R be research expenditures, W be the price paid for the farm output, P be the price of the final good, and f be the processing production function. The monopsonist's problem is then

$$\max_{X} Pf(X) - W(X, R)X. \tag{14}$$

Since the farm sector is competitive, W is simply the marginal cost of producing the raw farm good. It is natural to assume that $\partial W/\partial X > 0$ since supply is positively related to price and $\partial W/\partial R < 0$ since innovation reduces farm costs. Second derivatives of the marginal cost function are more ambiguous. Innovations that increase crop yields may tend to make the farm supply relation more elastic, and in this case, $\partial^2 W/\partial X \partial R < 0$. However, industrialization may result in innovations that limit capacity or increase the share of fixed costs in the farm budget. In this case, $\partial^2 W/\partial X \partial R > 0$ and the farm supply relation becomes less elastic as a result of innovation.

Totally differentiating the solution to (14), it follows that the change in farm output following an exogenous increase in research expenditures is

$$\frac{dX}{dR} = \frac{-\left(P\frac{\partial f}{\partial X} - \frac{\partial^2 W}{\partial X \partial R}X - \frac{\partial W}{\partial R}\right)}{\text{SOC}}.$$

The numerator is of indeterminate sign, while the denominator is the monopsonist's second-order condition, and thus negative. The first and third terms of the numerator are positive and negative, respectively, by the assumptions of positive marginal productivity in the processing sector, and the marginal cost-reducing nature of the innovation. This last effect is commonly termed the "shift" effect of innovation on the farm supply relation. There is also a "pivot" effect to consider, however, which is represented by the second term in the numerator. As pointed out earlier, this term can be either positive or negative depending on the form of the innovation. In fact, if public research makes the

farm supply curve sufficiently inelastic, then a cost-reducing innovation can actually reduce the equilibrium level of farm output. Hamilton and Sunding (1998) make this point
in the context of a more general model of oligopsony in the processing sector. They
point out that an inelastic pivot increases the monopsonist's degree of market power
and increases its ability to depress farm output. If the farm supply relation becomes
sufficiently inelastic following innovation, this effect can override the output-enhancing
effect of cost-reduction. Note further that the "pivot" effect only matters when there is
imperfect competition downstream; the second term in the numerator disappears if the
processing sector is competitive. Thus, in the case of perfect downstream competition,
reduction of the marginal cost of farming is a sufficient condition for the level of farm
output to increase.

The total welfare change from farm research is also affected by downstream market
power. In the simple model above, social welfare is given by the following expression:

$$SW = \int_0^{Y(X(R))} P(Z)\,dZ - \int_0^{X(R)} W(Z, R)\,dZ, \tag{15}$$

where $P(Z)$ is the inverse demand function for the final good. The impact of public
research is then

$$\frac{dSW}{dR} = \left(P\frac{\partial f}{\partial X} - W\right)\frac{dX}{dR} - \int_0^X \frac{\partial W}{\partial R}\,dZ.$$

This expression underscores the importance of downstream market structure. Under
perfect competition, the wedge between the price of the final good and its marginal cost
is zero, and so the first term disappears. In this case, the impact of farm research on
social welfare is determined completely by its impact on the marginal cost of producing
the farm good.[8] When the processing sector is imperfectly competitive, however, some
interesting results emerge. Most importantly, if farm output declines following the cost-
reducing innovation (which can only occur if the farm supply relation becomes more
inelastic), then social welfare can actually decrease. This argument was developed in
Hamilton and Sunding (1998), who describe the final outcome of farm-level innovation
as resulting from two forces: the social welfare improving effect of farm cost reduction
and the welfare effect of changes in market power in the processing industry.

Hamilton and Sunding (1998) show that the common assumption of perfect competition may seriously bias estimates of the productivity of farm-sector research. Social
returns are most likely to be overestimated when innovation reduces the elasticity of
the farm supply curve, and when competition is assumed in place of actual imperfect
competition. Further, Hamilton and Sunding demonstrate that all of the inverse supply
functions commonly used in the literature preclude the possibility that $\partial^2 W/\partial X \partial R > 0$,

---

[8] This point has also been noted recently in Sunding (1996) in the context of environmental regulation.

and thus rule out, *a priori*, the type of effects that result from convergent shifts. More flexible forms and more consideration of imperfect competition are needed to capture the full range of possible outcomes.

The continued development of agribusiness is leading to both physical and intellectual innovation. Feed suppliers, in an effort to expand their market, contributed to the evolution of large-scale industrialized farming. This is especially true in the poultry sector. Until the 1950s, separate production of broilers and chickens for eggs was scarce. The price of chicken meat fluctuated heavily, and that limited producers' entry into the emerging broiler industry. Feed manufacturers provided broiler production contracts with fixed prices for chicken meat, which led to vertical integration and modern industrial methods of poultry production. These firms not only offer output contracts, but they also provide production contracts and contribute to the generation of production technology. Recently, this same phenomenon has occurred in the swine sector, where industrialization has reduced the cost of production.

But agribusiness has spurred the development of another set of quality-enhancing innovations. Again, some of the most important developments have been in the poultry industry. Tyson Foods and other companies have produced a line of poultry products where meats are separated according to different categories, cleaned, and made ready to be cooked. The development of these products was based on the recognition of consumers' willingness to pay to save time in food preparation. In essence, the preparation of poultry products has shifted labor from the household to the factory where it can be performed more efficiently.

In addition to enhancing the value of the final product, the poultry agribusiness giants introduced institutional technological innovations in poultry production [Goodhue (1997)]. Packing of poultry has shifted to rather large production units that have contractual agreements with processors/marketers. The individual production units receive genetic materials and production guidance from the processor/marketer, and their pay is according to the relative quality. This set of innovations in production and marketing has helped reduce the relative price of poultry and increase poultry consumption in the United States and other countries over the last 20 years. Similar institutional and production innovations have occurred in the production of swine, high-value vegetables, and, to some extent, beef. These innovations are major contributors to the process of industrialization of agriculture. While benefiting immensely from technology generated by university research, these changes are the result of private sector efforts and demonstrate the important contributions of practitioners in developing technologies and strategies.

2. Technology adoption

2.1. Adoption and diffusion

There is often a significant interval between the time an innovation is developed and available in the market, and the time it is widely used by producers. Adoption and diffusion are the processes governing the utilization of innovations. Studies of adoption behavior emphasize factors that affect if and when a particular individual will begin using an innovation. Measures of adoption may indicate both the timing and extent of new technology utilization by individuals. Adoption behavior may be depicted by more than one variable. It may be depicted by a discrete choice, whether or not to utilize an innovation, or by a continuous variable that indicates to what extent a divisible innovation is used. For example, one measure of the adoption of a high-yield seed variety by a farmer is a discrete variable denoting if this variety is being used by a farmer at a certain time; another measure is what percent of the farmer's land is planted with this variety.

Diffusion can be interpreted as aggregate adoption. Diffusion studies depict an innovation that penetrates its potential market. As with adoption, there may be several indicators of diffusion of a specific technology. For example, one measure of diffusion may be the percentage of the farming population that adopts new innovations. Another is the land share in total land on which innovations can be utilized. These two indicators of diffusion may well convey a different picture. In developing countries, 25 percent of farmers may own or use a tractor on their land. Yet, on large farms, tractors will be used on about 90 percent of the land. While it is helpful to use the term "adoption" in depicting individual behavior towards a new innovation and "diffusion" in depicting aggregate behavior, in cases of divisible technology, some economists tend to distinguish between intra-firm and inter-firm diffusion. For example, this distinction is especially useful in multi-plant or multi-field operations. Intra-firm studies may investigate the percentage of a farmer's land where drip irrigation is used, while inter-firm studies of diffusion will look at the percentage of land devoted to cotton that is irrigated with drip systems.

2.1.1. The S-shaped diffusion curve

Studies of adoption and diffusion behaviors were undertaken initially by rural sociologists. Rogers (1962) conducted studies on the diffusion of hybrid corn in Iowa and compared diffusion rates of different counties. He and other rural sociologists found that in most counties diffusion was an *S*-shaped function of time. Many of the studies of rural sociologists emphasized the importance of distance in adoption and diffusion behavior. They found that regions that were farther away from a focal point (e.g., major cities in the state) had a lower diffusion rate in most time periods. Thus, there was emphasis on diffusion as a geographic phenomenon.

Statistical studies of diffusion have estimated equations of the form

$$Y_t = K\left[1 + e^{-(a+bt)}\right]^{-1},\tag{16}$$

where Y_t is diffusion at time t (percentage of land for farmers adopting an innovation), K is the long-run upper limit of diffusion, a reflects diffusion at the start of the estimation period, and b is a measure of the pace of diffusion.

With an *S*-shaped diffusion curve, it is useful to recognize that there is an initial period with a relatively low adoption rate but with a high rate of change in adoption.

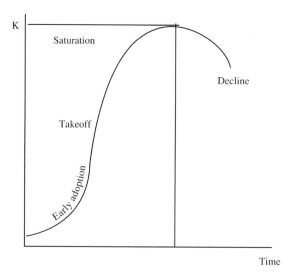

Figure 3.

Figure 3 shows this as a period of introduction of a technology. Following is a takeoff period when the innovation penetrates the potential market to a large extent during a short period of time. During the initial and takeoff periods, the marginal rate of diffusion actually increases, and the diffusion curve is a convex function of time. The takeoff period is followed by a period of saturation where diffusion rates are slow, marginal diffusion declines, and the diffusion reaches a peak. For most innovations, there will also be a period of decline where the innovation is replaced by a new one (Figure 3).

Griliches' (1957) seminal study on adoption of hybrid corn in Iowa's different counties augmented the parameters in (16) with information on rates of profitability, size of farms in different counties, and other factors. The study found that all three parameters of diffusion function (K, a, and b) are largely affected by profitability and other economic variables. In particular, when $\Delta\pi$ denotes the percent differential in probability between the modern and traditional technology, Griliches (1957) found that $\partial a / \partial \Delta\pi$, $\partial K / \partial \Delta\pi$, and $\partial b / \partial \Delta\pi$ are all positive. Griliches' work (1957, 1958) spawned a large body of empirical studies [Feder et al. (1985)]. They confirmed his basic finding that profitability gains positively affect the diffusion process. The use of S-shaped diffusion curves, especially after Griliches (1957) introduced his economic version, has become widespread in several areas. S-shaped diffusion curves have been used widely in marketing to depict diffusion patterns of many products, for example, consumer durables. Diffusion studies have been an important component of the literature on economic development and have been used to quantitatively analyze the processes through which modern practices penetrate markets and replace traditional ones.

2.1.2. Diffusion as a process of imitation

The empirical literature spawned by Griliches (1957, 1958) established stylized facts, and a parallel body of theoretical studies emerged with the goal of explaining its major findings. Formal models used to depict the dynamics of epidemics have been applied by Mansfield (1963) and others to derive the logistic diffusion formula. Mansfield viewed diffusion as a process of imitation wherein contacts with others led to the spread of technology. He considered the case of an industry with identical producers, and for this industry the equation of motion of diffusion is

$$\frac{\partial Y_t}{\partial t} = bY_t\left(1 - \frac{Y_t}{K}\right). \tag{17}$$

Equation (17) states that the marginal diffusion at time t ($\partial Y/\partial t$, the actual adoption occurring at t) is proportional to the product of diffusion level Y_t and the unutilized diffusion potential $(1 - Y_t/K)$ at time t. The proportional coefficient b depends on profitability, firm size, etc. Marginal diffusion is very small at the early stages when $Y_t \to 0$ and as diffusion reaches its limit, $Y_t \to K$. It has an inflection point when it switches from an early time period of increasing marginal diffusion ($\partial^2 Y_t/\partial t^2 > 0$) to a late time period of decreasing marginal diffusion ($\partial^2 Y/\partial t^2 < 0$). For an innovation that will be fully adopted in the long run ($K = 1$),

$$\frac{\partial Y_t}{\partial t} = bY_t(1 - Y_t),$$

the inflection point occurs when the innovation is adopted by 50 percent of producers. Empirical studies found that the inflection point occurs earlier than the simple dynamic model in (17) suggests. Lehvall and Wahlbin (1973) and others expanded the modeling of the technology diffusion processes by incorporating various factors of learning and by separating firms that are internal learners (innovators) from those that are external learners (imitators). This body of literature provides a very sound foundation for estimation of empirical time-series data on aggregate adoption levels. However, it does not rely on an explicit understanding of decision-making by individual firms. This criticism led to the emergence of an alternative model of adoption and diffusion, the threshold model.

2.1.3. The threshold model

Threshold models of technology diffusion assume that producers are heterogeneous and pursue maximizing or satisfying behavior. Suppose that the source of heterogeneity is farm size. Let L denote farm size and $g(L)$ be the density of farm size. Thus, $g(L)\Delta L$ is the number of farms between $L - \Delta L/2$ and $L + \Delta L/2$. The total number of farms is then $N = \int_0^\infty g(L)\,dL$, and the total acreage is $\overline{L} = \int_0^\infty Lg(L)\,dL$.

Suppose that the industry pursued a traditional technology that generated π_0 units of profit per acre. The profit per acre of the modern technology at time t is denoted by $\pi_1(t)$ and the profit differential per acre is $\Delta\pi_t$. It is assumed that an industry operates under full certainty, and adoption of modern technology requires a fixed cost that varies over time and at time t is equal to F_t. Under these assumptions, at time t there will be a cutoff farm size, $L_t^C = F_t/\Delta\pi_t$, upon which adoption occurs. One measure of diffusion at time t is thus

$$Y_t^1 = \frac{\int_{L_t^C}^{\infty} g(L)\,dL}{N}, \tag{18}$$

which is the share of farms adopting at time t. Another measure of diffusion of time t is

$$Y_t^2 = \frac{\int_{L_t^C}^{\infty} Lg(L)\,dL}{\overline{L}}, \tag{19}$$

which is the share of total acres adopting the modern technology at time t.

The diffusion process occurs as the fixed cost of the modern technology declines over time ($\partial F_t/\partial t < 0$) or the variable cost differential between the two technologies increases over time ($\partial \Delta\pi_t/\partial t > 0$). The price of the fixed cost per farm may decrease over time because the new technology is embodied in new indivisible equipment or because it requires an up-front investment in learning. "Learning by doing" may reduce fixed costs through knowledge accumulation. The profit differential often will increase over time because of "learning by using". Namely, farmers will get more yield and save cost with more experience in the use of the new technology.

The shape of the diffusion curve depends on the dynamics of farm size and the shape of farm size distribution. Differentiation of (18) obtains marginal diffusion under the first definition

$$\frac{\partial Y_t^1}{\partial t} = -\frac{g(L_t^C)}{N}\frac{\partial L_t^C}{\partial t}. \tag{20}$$

Marginal diffusion at time t is equal to the percentage of farms adopting technology at this time. It is expressed as $\partial L_t^C/\partial t$ times the density of the farm size distribution at L_t^C, $g(L_t^C)$.

The dynamics of diffusion associated with the threshold model are illustrated in Figure 4. Farm size distribution is assumed to be unimodal. When the new innovation is introduced, only farms with a size greater than L_0^C will adopt. The critical size declines over time and this change triggers more adoption. The marginal adoption between the first and second year is equal to the area $abL_2^C L_1^C$. Figure 4 assumes that the marginal decline in L_t^C is constant because of the density function's unimodality. Marginal diffusion increases during the initial period and then it declines, thus leading to an S-shaped diffusion curve. It is plausible that farm size distribution (and the distribution of other

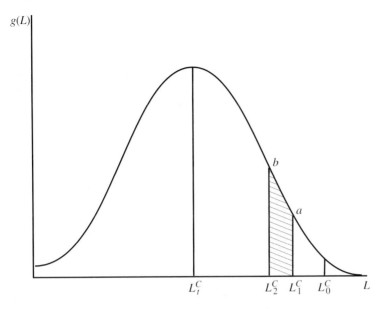

Figure 4.

sources of heterogeneity) will be unimodal and that combined with a continuous decline of L_t^C will lead to S-shaped behavior.[9]

The threshold model was introduced by Paul David (1969) to explain adoption of grain harvesting machinery in the United States in the nineteenth century. He argued that the main source of heterogeneity among farmers was farm size and he derived the minimum farm size required for adoption of various pieces of equipment. Olmstead and Rhode (1993) review historical documents that show that, in many cases, much smaller farms adopted some of the new machinery because farmers cooperated and jointly purchased harvesting equipment. This example demonstrates some of the limitations of the threshold model, especially when heterogeneity results from differences in size.

---

[9] To have an S-shaped behavior, $f^2 Y_t^1 / f t^2 > 0$ for an initial period with $t < \hat{t}$ and $f^2 Y_t^1 / f t^2 < 0$ for $t > \hat{t}$. Differentiation of (20) yields

$$\frac{\partial^2 Y_1^t}{\partial t^2} = -\frac{1}{N} \left[\frac{\partial g(L_t^C)}{\partial L_t^C} \left(\frac{\partial L_t^C}{\partial t} \right)^2 + g\left(L_t^C\right) \frac{\partial^2 L_t^C}{\partial t^2} \right].$$

Assuming unimodal distribution, let L_t^C be associated with the model of $g(L)$. As long as $L_t^C > L_{t^5}^C \, \partial g(L_t^C)/\partial L_t^C < 0$, then $L_t^C < L_{t^5}^C \, \partial g(L_t^C)/\partial L_t^C > 0$. At the early periods, $\partial^2 L_t^C / \partial t^2$ may be small or even negative, but as t increases the marginal decline in L_t^C gets smaller and $\partial^2 L_t^C / \partial t^2$ may be positive. Thus, the change of the sign of both elements of $\partial^2 Y_1^t / \partial t^2$ will contribute to S-shaped behavior.

The threshold model also applies in other cases where heterogeneity results from differences in land quality or human capital. For example, Caswell and Zilberman (1986) argue that modern irrigation technologies augment land quality, and predicted that drip and sprinkler irrigation will be adopted on lands where water-holding capacity is below a certain threshold. They also showed that adoption of these technologies by growers who rely on groundwater will be dependent on well depth. Akerlof's (1976) work on the "rat race" suggests that differences in human capital establish thresholds and result in differences in the adoption of different technologies and practices.

The threshold models shifted empirical emphasis from studies of diffusion to studies of the adoption behavior of individual farmers and a search for sources of heterogeneity. Two empirical approaches have been emphasized in the analysis of monthly cross-sectional data on technological choices and other choices of parameters and characteristics of individual firms. In the more popular approach, the dependent variables denote whether or not certain technologies are used by a farm product or unit at a certain period, and econometric techniques like logit or probit are used to explain discrete technology choices. The dependent variable for the second approach denotes the duration of technologies used by farms. (They answer the question, How many years ago did you adopt a specific technology?) Also, limited variable techniques are used to explain the technology data. Qualitatively, McWilliams and Zilberman (1996) found that the two approaches will provide similar answers, but analysis of duration data will enable a fuller depiction of the dynamics of diffusion.

2.1.4. Geographic considerations

Much of the social science literature on innovation emphasizes the role of distance and geography in technology adoption [Rogers (1962)]. Producers in locations farther away from a regional center are likely to adopt technologies later. This pattern is consistent with the findings of threshold models because initial learning and the establishment of a new technology may entail significant travel and transport costs, and these costs increase with distance.

Diamond's (1999) book on the evolution of human societies emphasizes the role of geography in the adoption of agricultural technologies. China and the Fertile Crescent have been source regions for some of the major crops and animals that have been domesticated by humans. Diamond argues that the use of domestic animals spread quickly throughout Asia and laid the foundation for the growth of the Euro-Asian civilizations that became dominant because most of these societies were at approximately the same geographic latitude, and there were many alternative routes that enabled movement of people across regions. The diffusion of crop and animal systems in Africa and the Americas was more problematic because population movement occurred along longitudinal routes (south to north) and thus, technologies required substantial adjustments to different climatic conditions in different latitudes. Diamond argues that there were other geographic barriers to the diffusion of agricultural technologies. For example, the slow evolution of agricultural societies in Australia and Papua New Guinea is explained by their distance from other societies, which prevented diffusion of practices from else-where.

Geography sets two barriers to adoption: climatic variability and distance. Investment in infrastructure to reduce transportation costs (e.g., roads and telephone lines) is likely to accelerate adoption. One reason for the faster rate of technological adoption in the United States is the emergence of a national media and the drastic reduction in the cost of access that resulted from the establishment of railroads, the interstate highway system, and rural electrification.

Distance is a major obstacle for adoption of technologies in developing countries. The impediment posed by distance is likely to decline with the spread of wireless communication technologies. It is a greater challenge to adopt technologies across different latitudes and varying ecological conditions. The establishment of international research centers that develop production and crop systems for specific conditions is one way to overcome this problem.

2.2. Risk considerations

The adoption of a new technology may expand the amount of risk associated with farming. Operators are uncertain about the properties and performance of a new technology, and these uncertainties interact with the random factors affecting agriculture. The number of risks associated with new technologies gives rise to several modeling approaches, each emphasizing aspects of the problem that are important for different types of innovations. In particular, some models will be appropriate for divisible technologies and others for lumpy ones, and some will explicitly emphasize dynamic aspects while others will be static in nature.

Much of the agricultural adoption literature was developed to explain adoption patterns of high-yield seed varieties (HYV), many of which were introduced as part of the "green revolution". Empirical studies established that these technologies were not fully adopted by farmers in the sense that farmers allocated only part of their land to HYV while continuing to allocate land to traditional technologies. Roumasset (1976) and others argued that risk considerations were crucial in explaining these diversifications, while having higher expected yield also tended to increase risk.

A useful approach to model choices associated with adoption of HYV is to use a static expected utility portfolio model to solve a discrete problem (whether or not to adopt the new technology at all); adoption can also be modeled as a continuous optimization problem in which optimal land shares devoted to new technologies and variable inputs are chosen, see [Just and Zilberman (1988), Feder and O'Mara (1981)].

To present these choices formally, consider a farmer with $\overline{L}$ acres of land, which can be allocated among two technologies. Let i be a technology variable, where $i = 0$ indicates the traditional technology, and $i = 1$ the modern one. Let the indicator variable be $\delta = 0$ when the modern technology is adopted (even if not adopted on all the land), and $\delta_1 = 0$ when the modern technology is not adopted. When $\delta = 0$, L_0 denotes land allocated to traditional technology and L_1 denotes land allocated to the new variety. The fixed cost associated with adoption of the new technology is $\overline{k}$ dollars. Profits per acre under the traditional and modern technologies are π_0 and π_1, respectively, and both are random variables. For convenience, assume that all the land is utilized when the traditional variety is used. Assume that the farmer is risk averse with a convex utility function $U(W)$ where W is wealth after operation and $W = W_0 + \Pi$ when W_0 is the initial wealth level and Π is the farmer's profit.

The optimal resource allocation problem of the farmer is

$$\max_{\substack{\delta=0,1 \\ L_1,L_0}} \text{EU}\Big[W_0 + \delta(\pi_0 L_0 + \pi_1 L_1 - k) + (1-\delta)\pi_0 L\Big] \quad \text{subject to } L_0 + L_1 \leqslant \overline{L}$$

$$\underset{\left\{\begin{array}{c} \text{profits when modern} \\ \text{technology is adopted} \end{array}\right\}}{\uparrow} \qquad\qquad\qquad \underset{\left\{\begin{array}{c} \text{profits when adoption} \\ \text{does not occur} \end{array}\right\}}{\uparrow}.$$

$$\tag{21}$$

Just and Zilberman (1988) considered the case where the profits under both technologies are normally distributed, the expected value of profit per acre under technology i is m_i, the variance of profit per acre of technology i is σ_i^2, and the correlation of the per acre profits of the technologies is ρ. They demonstrated that when the modern technology is adopted ($\delta = 1$) on part of the land, but all of the land is utilized, the optimal land allocation to the modern technology (L_1^*) is approximated by the function $L_1^r(\overline{L})$. Formally,

$$L_1^* = L_1^r(\overline{L}) = \frac{\text{E}(\Delta\pi)}{\phi r(\Delta\pi)} + R\overline{L}, \tag{22}$$

where $\text{E}(\Delta\pi) = m_1 - m_0$ is the difference in expected profits per acre between the modern and traditional technology. $v(\Delta\pi) = v(\pi_1 - \pi_0) = \sigma_0^2 + \sigma_1^2 - 2\rho\sigma_1\sigma_0$ is the variance of the difference of profit per acre of the two technologies. Further,

$$R = \frac{\sigma_0(\sigma_0 - \rho\sigma_1)}{v(\Delta\pi)} = \frac{1}{2} \cdot \frac{\partial v(\Delta\pi)}{\partial\sigma_0} \frac{\sigma_0}{v(\Delta\pi)}$$

is a measure of the responsiveness of $v(\Delta\pi)$ to changes in σ_0, and ϕ is the Arrow-Pratt measure of absolute risk aversion, dependent upon expected wealth.

Numerous adoption studies have addressed the case where the modern technology increased mean yield per acre, $\text{E}(\Delta\pi) > 0$, and had high variance as compared to the traditional technology, $\sigma_1^2 > \sigma_0^2$. These assumptions will be used here. First, consider the case where profits under the traditional technology are not risky, ($\sigma_0^2 = 0$). From condition A, $L_1^* = \text{E}(\Delta\pi)/\phi\sigma_1^2$, adoption does not depend directly on farm size (only indirectly, through the impact of I on risk aversion), and adoption is likely to increase as the expected gain from adoption $\text{E}(\Delta\pi)$ increases and the risk of the modern technologies (σ_1^2) decreases.

When $\sigma_0^2 > 0$ and ϕ is constant, Equation (22) suggests that L_1^r is a linear function of farm size $\overline{L}$. The slope of L_1^r is equal to R, and assuming $\sigma_1^2 > \sigma_0^2$, $R = \sigma_0(\sigma_0 - \rho\sigma_1) - v(\Delta\pi)$ is smaller than one. When the profits of two technologies are highly correlated, $\rho > \sigma_0/\sigma_1$, $R < 0$, $dL_1^R/d\overline{L} < 0$, and acreage of the modern technology declines with farm size. This occurs because the marginal increase with acreage (variance of profits) is larger than the marginal increase of expected profits that slow the growth or even reduce (when $\rho > \sigma_0/\sigma$) the acreage of the modern and more risky technology of larger farms.

Assume now that absolute risk aversion is a function of farm size (a proxy of expected wealth) denoted by $\phi(L)$. In this case, Just and Zilberman showed that the marginal effect of increase on the area of the modern technology is

$$\frac{dL_1^r}{d\overline{L}} = \eta\frac{L_1^r}{L} + (r - \eta)R,$$

where $\eta = -\phi'\overline{L}/\phi$ is the elasticity of absolute risk aversion and is assumed to be between 0 ($\eta = 0$ implies constant absolute risk aversion) and 1 ($\eta = 1$ implies constant relative risk aversion coefficient, $\phi(L) \cdot L = $ constant). In this more general case, L_1^r may be a nonlinear function of $\overline{L}$ and may have a negative slope in cases of high correlation and small η.

Optimal land allocation to the modern technology, L_1^*, is constrained to be between 0 and $\overline{L}$. Thus, it may be different than L_1^r defined in (22). In cases with small η (ϕ does not change much with $\overline{L}$), the increase in risk (variance of profits) with size is much greater than the increase in expected profit with size. When $\overline{L}$ is close to zero, $L_1^R > \overline{L}$ and thus where farm size is below a critical level, $\overline{L}_b$,[10] the modern technology should be fully adopted if it is optimal. From (22) the adoption of the modern technology is optimal if it pays for the extra investment it entails. Thus, farms below another critical size, $\overline{L}_a$, cannot pay for the modern technology and do not adopt it.

Figure 5 depicts some plausible relations between L_1^* and $\overline{L}$. The segment *0abcd* depicts the behavior of L_1^* when $R > 0$ and $\overline{L}_b > \overline{L}_a$. If $\overline{L}_b > \overline{L}_a$ and $R < 0$, L_1^* is depicted by *0abce*. If $\overline{L}_a > \overline{L}_b$, and $R > 0$, L_1^* is depicted by *0gh* and if $\overline{L}_a > \overline{L}_b$ and $R < 0$, L_1^* is depicted by *0gle*. In the last two cases, there is no full adoption of the modern technology.

Feder, Just, and Zilberman (1985) report the results of several studies that show that when adoption occurs, the full share of modern technologies declines with farm size among adopters. These findings are consistent with all the scenarios in Figure 5.

2.3. Mechanisms to address product performance and "fit risk"

Adopters of new technologies, especially if embodied in high capital costs that entail significant irreversible investment, face uncertainty with respect to the performance of

---

[10] At $\overline{L} = \overline{L}_b$, $L_1^r(\overline{L})_b = \overline{L}_b$.

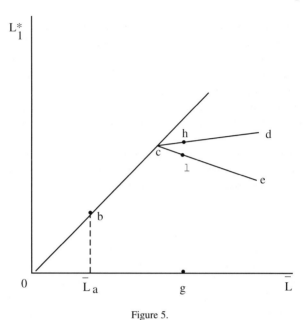

Figure 5.

the product, its reliability, and appropriateness of their operation. When a farmer buys a piece of machinery – be it a combine, harvester, seeder, or cultivator – and it has a breakdown or major malfunction, it may cost a farmer much of his revenues. Conceptually, one may think about several solutions to address some risk, including insurance. The prevailing approach to address such risk is to form a product-backup system. To address the financial risks that are associated with the repair cost of a broken or malfunctioning product, especially in the early life of the product, manufacturers introduced mechanisms such as warranties and established dealerships equipped to repair breakdowns. Thus, the combination of a warranty agreement and a well-functioning technical support system significantly reduces the amount of reliability risk associated with new products.

Significant elements of agribusinesses, such as mechanic shops, are devoted to the repair and maintenance of new capital equipment. The availability and quality of performance of this support will determine the risk farmers face in adoption decisions and, thus, their ability to carry risk. One of the main advantages of large farming operations is their in-house capacity to handle repairs, breakdowns, and maintenance of equipment. That makes them less dependent on local dealers and repair shops, and reduces their risk of having to purchase (in many cases) new products.

The value of the capacity to address problems of product equipment failure swiftly and efficiently is intensified by timing considerations. In many regions, harvesting seasons are short. Leaving a wheat crop unharvested for an extra day or two may expose it to damage due to rain, hail, or pests, thereby decreasing its yield. Market prices of perishable fruits and vegetables are significantly dependent on the timing of harvest;

a one-week delay in harvesting early season fruits or vegetables for shipping can reduce prices by factors of 30 to 40 percent [Parker and Zilberman (1993)]. This timing consideration increases the value of a well-functioning product system. It may provide an explanation for the maintenance of excess capacity to harvest or conduct other vital activities. Of course, the extent to which farmers maintain excess capacity depends on how well the product support system functions. The agricultural community may establish customs and other social and institutional arrangements for mutual help in a crisis situation associated with a breakdown of equipment.

Adoption of new technology entails risk with respect to its appropriateness to the farm and its performance. Results of prior testing by manufacturers represent performance and conditions that may not be exactly similar to those of farmers. New technologies may also require special skills and training. Institutional arrangements to reduce the risk associated with the adoption of new technologies have been introduced. They include product information and demonstration such as educational materials in various media formats as well as hands-on demonstrations. The farmer may go to a dealership to see farm machinery in operation or the equipment may be loaned to the farmer for a supervised and/or unsupervised trial period. For new seed varieties, manufacturers will send farmers samples of seeds for examination. Many farmers will plant small trial plots.

When university researchers are the providers of new seeds, extension plays a major role in demonstration. In the case of new seed varieties and equipment developed by the private sector, extension plays an important role in demonstrating efficacy in local conditions as well as making objective judgments on manufacturers' claims regarding new products.

In addition to various types of extension, the reduction of risk associated with performance and the appropriateness of new technologies is addressed by arrangements such as money-back guarantees. With money-back guarantees, the farmer is given the option to return the product. In this case, obviously the price of the product includes some payment for this option [Heiman et al. (1998)]. However, the money-back guarantee agreement allows farmers longer periods of experimentation with new products. Generally money-back guarantees are not complete and a fraction of the original cost is not returned.

Sometimes renting is used as a mechanism to reduce the risk associated with investment in new products. For example, when sprinkler irrigation was introduced in California, the main distributor of sprinklers in the state was a company called Rain for Rent. This company rented sprinkler equipment to farmers. Over time, the practice of renting sprinkler equipment became much less common and more new sprinkler equipment was purchased. In some cases, farmers use custom services for an initial trial with new technologies, and invest in the equipment only when they feel more secure and certain about its properties.

Many of the marketing strategies, including warranties, money-back guarantees, and demonstrations that are part of businesses throughout the economy, were introduced by agricultural firms including John Deere and International Harvesting. Currently, hundreds of millions of dollars are spent on promotion and education in the use of new products. Unfortunately, not much research has been conducted to understand this aspect of agricultural and technological change in agriculture. It seems, however, that a large body of empirical evidence regarding geographic concentration of new technologies and geographic patterns of technology adoption may be linked to considerations of marketing and product support efforts. New technologies are more likely to be adopted earlier near market centers where dealers and product supports are easily available. Agricultural industries and certain types of technologies may be clustered in certain regions, especially in the earlier life of a new technology, and these regions will generally be located in areas that have technical support and expertise associated with the maintenance and development of the technologies. It seems that considerations of marketing and geographic locations are two areas where more research should be done.

2.4. Dynamic considerations

The outcome of technology adoption is affected by dynamic processes that result in changes in prices of capital goods and input, learning by producers and users of capital goods, etc. Some of these processes have random components and significant uncertainty over time. Some of these dynamic considerations have been introduced to recent microlevel models of adoption behavior.

2.4.1. Optimal timing of technology adoption

The earlier discussion on threshold models recognized that timing of adoption may vary across production units reflecting differences in size, human capital, land quality, etc. The above analysis suggests that, at each moment, decision-makers select technologies with the best-expected net benefits (or expected net present values adjusted by risk). Thus, when a new technology is available decision-makers continuously evaluate whether or not to adopt; when the discounted expected benefits of adoption are greater than the cost, the technology will be adopted. This approach may lead to suboptimal outcomes because decision-makers do not consider the possibility of delaying the technology choice to take advantage of favorable dynamic processes or to enable further learning. These deficiencies have been corrected in recent models.

2.4.2. Learning by using, learning by doing, and adoption of new technologies

Consider a farmer who operates with a traditional technology and is considering adopting a new one that requires a fixed investment. The increase in temporal profit from adoption at time t increases as more experience is gained from the use of this technology. This gain in experience represents learning by doing. Let t_0 be the time of adoption and assume that self-experience is the only source of learning by doing. The increase in operational profits in $t > 0$ is $\Delta\pi(t - t_0)$, $\partial\pi/\partial t > 0$. Let the fixed cost of investment in firm t_0 be denoted by $K(t_0)$. The process of learning by using reduces the manufacturing cost of fixed assets and results in reduction in $K(t_0)$ over time. It is reasonable to assume that the effects of both learning processes decline over time. Thus,

$$\frac{\partial^2 \pi(t - t_0)}{\partial t} < 0, \quad \frac{\partial K(t_0)}{\partial (t_0)} < 0, \quad \frac{\partial^2 K(t_0)}{\partial t^2} > 0.$$

When the farmer disregards the learning processes in determining the time of adoption, adoption will occur when the temporal gain of adoption equals the extra periodical fixed cost. Let r denote discount rate and assume the economic life of the new technology is infinite. At t_0,

$$\Delta\pi(0) = r K(t_0).$$

When the learning processes are taken into account, the marginal reduction in investment cost, because of learning by using, tends to delay adoption, and the marginal benefits from learning by using may accelerate the time of adoption. The optimal conditions that determine t_0 in this more general case are

$$\overset{(+)}{\Delta\Pi(0)} \overset{(-)}{-\ r K(t_0)} \overset{(-)}{+\ \frac{\partial K(t_0)}{\partial t_0}} \overset{(+)}{+\ \int_0^\infty e^{-rt} \frac{\partial \pi(t)}{\partial t}\, dt} = 0.$$

| Extra profit from adoption | Investment cost | Learning by doing effect | Learning by using effect |

In cases where the new technology increases the productivity of an agricultural crop with constant returns to scale,

$$\Delta\Pi(t - t_0) = \Delta\pi(t - t_0) \cdot L,$$

where L is acreage. In this case, both the extra profit from adoption and the learning-by-using effects will increase with farm size and lead larger farms to be early adopters. Higher interest rates will tend to retard adoption because they will increase the investment cost per period and reduce the learning-by-using effect.

2.4.3. Adoption under irreversibility and uncertainty

Adoption sometimes entails irreversible investments with uncertain payoffs. Delay of an adoption decision may enable the producer to obtain more information, reducing overall uncertainty, and increasing expected discounted benefits by avoiding irreversible investment when it is not worthwhile. This observation can be illustrated by the following example that analyzes adoption decisions in a simple, two-period model.

The adoption decision requires an initial investment of $100. The returns from adoption consist of $50 at the initial period, $30 with probability of .5 (low returns case), and \$150 with probability of .5 (high returns case) in the second period. Let r be the discount rate. According to the neoclassical investment theory, adoption should occur at the initial period of the expected net benefit of this decision, and ($ENPV_0$) is positive when

$$ENPV_0 = 50 + \frac{1}{1+r}[0.5 \cdot 30 + 0.5 \cdot 150] - 100 = \frac{90}{1+r} - 50.$$

The standard expected net present value criteria will suggest adoption in the initial period when the discount rate is smaller than 0.8 (since $ENPV_0 > 0$ when $90/(1+r) > 50$ for $r < 0.8$). However, the farmer's set of choices includes an option to wait until the second period and adopt only in the case of high returns. The investment associated with adoption is irreversible, and waiting to observe the returns in the second period enables avoiding investment in the case of low returns. The expected net present value with this approach is

$$ENPV_1 = 0.5 + \frac{(150-100)}{1+r} = \frac{25}{1+r} > 0.$$

When $r = 0.5$, $ENPV_0 = 90/1.5 - 50 = 10$, $ENPV_1 = 25/1.5 = 16\frac{2}{3}$, then the "wait and see" approach is optimal. This approach removes the downside risk of the low-return case in the second period. The value added by waiting and retaining flexibility in light of new information is called "option value" and in this example is defined below as follows:

$$0V = \max[NPV_1 - NPV_0, 0] = \max\left[50 - \frac{65}{1+r}, 0\right].$$

In the case of $r = 0.5$, the option value is 6–2/3 and waiting to see the outcome of the second period is optimal. In the case with $r < 0.3$, the option value is 0 and adoption in the initial period is optimal.

This example is a simple illustration of a more complex, multi-period model of adoption. Suppose a farmer employs two technologies, traditional and modern. The temporal profit from each of the technologies depends on a random variable, S_t. This may be the price of output or input, or it may be the value of a physical variable (climatic condition) that affects profitability. The modern technology usually generates more profits but requires a fixed investment. Let the difference in temporal profit between the two technologies in period t be $\Delta \Pi(S_t) = \Pi_1(S_t) - \Pi_0(S_t)$. Assume that the temporal gain from adoption increases with S_t ($\partial \Delta \Pi/\partial S_t > 0$). Let the cost of the investment in the new technology be denoted by K, and the discount rate be denoted by r. The farmer has to determine when to adopt the modern technology. Let T be the period of adoption. The farmer's optimization problem is

$$
\max_{\substack{T \\ [T=0,1,\dots,\infty]}} \sum_{i=T}^{\infty} \mathrm{E}_{S_t} \left[\frac{\Delta \pi (S_t)}{(1+r)^t} \right] - \frac{K}{(1+r)^T},
$$

where $\mathrm{E}_{S_t}(\cdot)$ denotes expectation with respect to S_t. The nature of the solution depends on the assumption regarding the evolution of the sequence of random variables S_t. For example, suppose $S_t = S_{t-1} + \varepsilon_t$ where all the ε_t's are independently and identically distributed random variables whose means are zero. (If they are normally distributed, S_t is generated by a "random walk" process.) This approach has been very successful in the analysis of options in finance, and Dixit and Pindyck (1994) and McDonald and Siegel (1986) applied it to the analysis of capital investments. They viewed investments with unrestricted timing as "real options" since the decision about when to undertake an investment is equivalent to the decision about when to exercise an option. McDonald and Siegel (1986) considered a continuous time model to determine the time of investment. They assumed that the S evolves according to a Wiener process (which is a differential continuous version of the process described above) and used the Ito calculus to obtain formulas to determine the threshold for adoption, $\overline{S}$. Their analysis suggests that the threshold level of $\overline{S}$ increases as the variance of the temporal random variable ε_t increases.

Their framework was applied by Hasset and Metcalf (1992) to assess adoption of energy conservation in the residential sectors. Thurow, Boggess, and Moss (1997) applied the real option approach to assess how uncertainty and irreversibility considerations will affect adoption of free-stall dairy housing, a technology that increases productivity and reduces pollution. The source of uncertainty in their case is future environmental regulation. Using simulation techniques, they showed that when investment is optimal under the real option approach, expected annual returns are more than twice the expected annual returns associated with adoption under the traditional net present value approach. Thus, the real value approach may lead to a significant delay in adoption of the free-stall housing and occurs when pollution regulations are very stiff.

Olmstead (1998) applied the real value approach to assess adoption of modern irrigation technology when water prices and availability are uncertain. Her simulation suggests that the water price leading to adoption under the real option approach is 133 percent higher than the price that triggers adoption under the standard expected net present value approach. In her simulation, the average delay in adoption associated with the real option approach is longer than 12 years.

There have been significant studies of adoption of irrigation technologies and, while adoption levels seemed to respond significantly to economic incentives, adoption did not occur in many of the circumstances when it was deemed to be optimal using the expected present value criteria. Much of the adoption occurs during drought periods when water prices escalate drastically [Zilberman et al. (1994)]. The option value approach provides a good explanation of the prevalence of adoption during crisis situations.

The analysis of adoption behavior using "real options" models holds much promise and is likely to be expanded. In many cases, not all the adoption investment is "sunk cost". Some of it can be recovered. For example, capital goods may be resold, and added human capital may increase earning opportunities. The delay caused by adoption costs and uncertainties will likely be shorter if these costs are more recoverable, and institutions that reduce irreversibilities (rental of capital equipment, money-back guarantee agreements) are apt to increase and accelerate adoption.

The real option approach provides new insight and is very elegant, but it does not capture important aspects of the dynamics of adoption. It assumes that decision-makers know the distribution of random events that determine profitability when it is more likely that a learning process is going on throughout the adoption process, and adopters adjust their probability estimates as they go along. Furthermore, while adoption requires a fixed initial investment, it also may entail incremental investments, especially when the intensity of use of a new technology changes over time. Thus, a more complete dynamic framework for analyzing adoption should address issues of timing, learning, and sequential investment. Some scholars [Chavas (1993)] have introduced models that incorporate these features, but this research direction requires more conceptual and empirical work.

2.4.4. The Cochrane treadmill

A key issue in the economics of innovation and adoption is to understand the impact of technology change on prices and, in particular, the well-being of the farm population over time. When a supply-increasing innovation is adopted to a significant degree, it will lead to reduction in output prices, especially in agricultural commodities with low elasticity of demand. When it comes to adoption of a new technology, Cochrane (1979) divided the farming population into three subgroups – early adopters, followers, and laggards. The early adopters may be a small fraction of the population, in which case the impact of their adoption decision on aggregate supply and, thus, output prices is relatively small. Therefore, these individuals stand to profit from the innovation.

The followers are the large share of the farm sector who tend to adopt during the take-off stage of the innovation. Their adoption choice will eventually tend to reduce prices, which reduces profits as well. This group of adopters may gain or lose as a result of innovation.

Finally, the laggards (the third group) are the farmers who either adopt at the lag stage of the adoption process or do not adopt at all. These individuals may lose from technological change. If they do not adopt, they produce the same quantity as before, at low prices; and if they adopt, the significant price effect may sweep the gain associated with higher yields. Thus, Cochrane argues that farmers, on the whole, are not likely to gain from the introduction of innovation in agriculture, except for a small group of early adopters. Introduction of new technology may lead to structural change and worsen the lot of some of the small farms. The real gainers from technological change and innovation in agriculture are likely to be consumers, who pay less for their food bill.

Kislev and Schori-Bachrach (1973) developed conceptual and empirical models based on Cochrane's analysis using data from Israel. They show that small subgroups of farmers are the early innovators who adopt the new technologies. When there is a wave of new technologies, these individuals, who have a higher education and other indicators of human capital, will consistently be able to take advantage of technology change and profit. The rest of the farming population does not do as well from technological change.

The Cochrane results are modified in situations where agricultural commodities face perfectly elastic demand, for example, when adopting industry export goods from a small country. In this case, the impact of increased profitability associated with the introduction of a new technology will lead to an increase in land rents which may occur some time after the innovation was introduced. Thus, the early adopters, even if they are farm operators, may be able to make an above-normal profit as a result of their adoption decision, but most of the followers will not gain much from the adoption decision because their higher revenues will be reduced by an increase in rent. Laggards and non-adopters may lose because the higher rent may reduce their profits. Again, landowners will be gainers from the innovations, and not farmers who own no land. Thus, this extension of Cochrane's model reaches the same conclusion-that at least some farmers do not benefit from technological change as much as other agents in the population.

Cochrane's modeling framework was used to argue that, in spite of the high technological change that occurs in agriculture and its dynamic nature, farmers may not be better off and actually some of them may be worse off from innovations. That may justify the "farm problem" that occurred in much of the twentieth century where the well-being of farmers became worse relative to other sectors of the population. Cochrane's basic framework was not introduced formally. Zilberman (1985) introduced the dynamics of the threshold model of adoption that identified conditions under which the quasi-rents of farmers decline over time. His model did not take into account the changes in structure that may be associated with innovation agriculture. When innovations are embodied in technology packages that are both yield-increasing (high-yield varieties) and labor-saving (tractors and other machinery), and agricultural demand is inelastic, then technological change will reduce quasi rent per acre and make operations in the farm sector less appealing to a large segment of the population. Thus the early adopters are likely to accumulate more of the land, increasing their farm size. Over time, structural change will result in a relatively small farm sector, and earnings per farm may actually increase as farms become much bigger. Gardner's (1988) findings show that, in relative terms, the farm population is now as well off or even better off than the nonfarm population, especially in the United States. His findings are consistent with the process of technological change that led to the accumulation of resources by small subgroups of the farm population while the rest migrated to the urban sector where earnings were better. But in addition to the gains from technological change, the adopters may also have benefited from a commodity program that slowed the decline in prices as well as the processes of globalization that makes demand more elastic over time.

A more formal and complete understanding of the distribution and price implications of technological change over time is a challenge for further research on the economics of technology adoption. Stoneman and Ireland (1983) argue that firms producing the components of new technology recognize the dynamics of adoption; they design their production and establish technology component prices accordingly, taking advantage of the monopolistic power. Thus there is a clear linkage between the economics of innovation and adoption that should be investigated further. An understanding of these links is essential for the design of better patent policy and public research strategies.

2.5. Institutional constraints to innovation

While agricultural industries tend to be competitive, the perfectly competitive model does not necessarily apply since farmers may face a significant number of institutional constraints and policies which affect their behavior significantly and result in outcomes that are different from those predicted by the perfectly competitive model. This institutional constraint may be especially important in the area of technological change and adoption. Some of the most important constraints relate to credit as well as tenure relationships, as addressed below. Note that institutional constraints may affect the patterns of adoption of new technologies, but on the other hand, the introduction of new technologies may affect the institutional structure and operation of agricultural industries. We will concentrate on the first problem but will address both.

2.5.1. Credit

Asymmetric information between lenders and borrowers and the uncertain conditions in agriculture and financial markets have led to imperfections in the credit market, most notably credit constraints that affect adoption behavior [Hoff et al. (1993)]. In many cases, farmers use some of their own equity to finance at least part of their investments. In other cases, assets such as land or the crop itself are used as collateral for financing a new technology. The exact formulation of the credit constraint faced by farmers is quite tricky, but it is not unreasonable to approximate as a linear function of acreage. The reason is that, in many cases, land is the major asset of a farming operation.

Just and Zilberman (1983) introduced a credit constraint in their static model of adoption under uncertainty. They assume that investment in the new technology is equal to $k + \alpha L_1$ when α is investment per acre in the modern technology. The constraint on credit per acre is m dollars. Thus, the farm credit constraint is $m\overline{L} \geqslant k + \alpha L_1$. If $m < \alpha_1$, there will be full adoption. However, if $m > \alpha$, the credit constraint will not bind for larger farms. Figure 6 depicts some plausible outcomes for the second case. Consider a case where $R > 0$ and $\overline{L}_a < \overline{L}_b$. Without the credit constraints, optimal allocation of land to the modern technology, as a function of farm size, is depicted by *0abcd* in Figure 6. There may be several scenarios under the credit constraints.

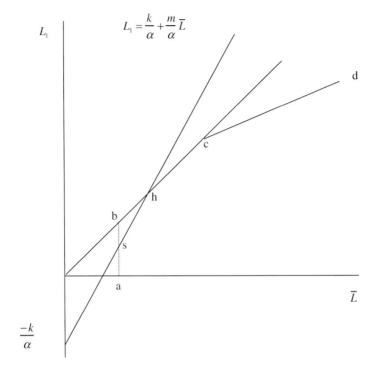

Figure 6.

In terms of Figure 6, when credit is a binding constraint, $L_1 < -\frac{k}{\alpha} + \frac{m}{\alpha}\overline{L}$. Small farms (with sizes in the range $0a$) will be non-adopters. Somewhat larger farms, in the range bh, will be credit-constrained partial adopters. Even larger farms (in the range hc) will specialize in the new technology, and farms of the largest size (corresponding to cd) will be risk diversifiers when m is smaller. Policies to remove credit constraints will be beneficial, especially to smaller farmers, and will enable some to adopt and others to extend their intensity of adoption.

The credit constraints per acre may be affected by the lender's perception of the profitability of agriculture (and farmland prices that reflect the profitability). Initial sub-sidization of credit early in the diffusion process that will enhance adoption will provide evidence that may change (improve in the case of a valuable technology) the lender's perception of the profitability of the industry and the modern technology, and lead to a relaxation of credit constraints. It will thus facilitate further adoption.

The interest rate and other financial charges may be differentiated according to size. Banks may perceive smaller farms to be more risky, so they may need to compensate for the fixed cost of loan processing, etc.[11] If the price of credit is higher for smaller

---

[11] There is significant evidence in the development literature that smaller operators face a higher interest cost.

farms, that extra hurdle will reduce the minimal farm size that is required for new technology adoption and will slow adoption by smaller-sized farms. Thus, advantageous credit conditions may be another reason larger farms adopt new technologies earlier. The reduction of institutions such as the Grameen Bank in Bangladesh and organizations such as the Bank of America in the United States, which in the beginning of the century facilitated loans to smaller operations, may be a crucial element in accelerating the process of technological change in improving adoption.

The financial crisis of the 1980s has led to a realization of the significance of risk associated with emphasizing collateral considerations in loan generation. The value of assets such as land is highly correlated to the profitability of agriculture and, in periods of crises and bankruptcies, land will be less valuable as collateral. That will lead to an increased emphasis on "ability to pay" as a criterion for loan generation. Thus, farmers need to provide sufficient guarantees about the profitability of their investment and their future ability to repay a loan. This may put investment in new technologies at a disadvantage because many of them do not have a sufficient track record that will assure banks of their economic viability. Banks may lack the personnel that are able to correctly assess new technologies and their economic value [Agricultural Issues Center (1994)].

One approach to overcoming this obstacle is by credit subsidies for a new technology, which may be appropriate in situations when investments generate positive externalities. However, an alternative and more prevalent solution is the provision of finance or a loan guarantee by the input manufacturer that leads to a reduction of the financial constraints on farmers. Furthermore, it reduces the fixed cost of adoption since it reduces the cost of searching for a loan. (One of the major implications of restricted availability of credit is the higher cost of finance, even for people who eventually obtain the credit.) Indeed, some of the major automobile and heavy equipment companies have their own subsidiaries or contractual arrangements that provide financing for new purchases of equipment, and seed companies often play an important role in the provision of credit. In many cases farmers may obtain loans for credit provisions through cooperatives or government policies (see chapter on credit).

2.5.2. Tenure

There is a distinct separation between ownership and the operation of agricultural land throughout the world. About 50 percent of the farmland in the United States is operated by individuals who do not own the land, and the financial arrangements between owners and operators vary. In the development literature, there is a significant emphasis on the importance of tenure systems on technology adoption. Most of the literature takes tenure as given and assesses its impact on adoption of technologies. However, this impact depends on the arrangements as well as the nature of the technology. Furthermore, as we will argue later, the introduction of new technologies may result in new tenure relationships.

The simplest relationships are land rent contracts where operators pay a fixed rent to landowners. Several factors will determine how these contracts affect adoption behavior. In the case of short-term contracts, when operators are not secure in maintaining the same land for a long time, the likelihood that they will adopt a technology that requires investment in the physical infrastructure and improvement of the land is very low. In these cases, rental relationships may be a significant deterrent for the adoption of innovations. On the other hand, the fixed-rate rent will not be a major deterrent of adoption if the innovation does not require a significant modification of the physical infrastructure, or if it augments or is dependent upon the human or physical capital of the operator. For example, an operator may purchase a tractor to reduce the cost of his operation. The necessary condition for adoption in this case is that the operator rent a sufficient amount of land every year in order to recapture and repay the investment. Actually, in some cases, the existence of a well-functioning land rental market may accelerate adoption of technologies that require a significant scale of operation. In fact, some farmers may augment the land utilized by them by renting land from others, thus enabling them to adopt large equipment. This was the situation, for example, in California when the cotton harvester was introduced. Therefore, it is useful to distinguish between large operators who use rental agreements to increase the acreage under their control (the rental agreements may facilitate adoption) and small operators without land of their own. For these operators, due to the credit constraints, lack of land may be a deterrent for adoption, even for technologies that do not improve the land and related assets.

2.5.3. Complementary inputs and infrastructure

The introduction of new technologies may increase demand for complementary inputs and when the supply of these inputs is restricted, adoption will be constrained. High-yield "green revolution" varieties require increased water and fertilizer use. McGuirk and Mundlak's (1991) analysis of the adoption of high-yield varieties in the Punjab showed that adoption was constrained by the availability of water and fertilizer. Private investment in the drilling of wells, and private and public investment in the establishment of fertilizer production and supply facilities removed these constraints and contributed to the diffusion of modern wheat and rice varieties in the Punjab. The adoption of high-yield maize varieties in the Punjab was much lower than wheat and rice, mostly because of disease problems. Adoption rates in maize might have been higher if complementary disease-control technologies were available.

Some of the complementary input constraints are eased or eliminated with the appropriate infrastructure. Effective research and extension programs may devise solutions to pest problems thus enabling the adoption of vulnerable varieties. Some of the modeling and analysis of diffusion [Mahajan and Peterson (1985)] suggests that the diffusion rates in regions that are farther from commercial centers are lower. To some extent this reflects barriers for professional support and more limited and costly access to complementary inputs. Improvement in transportation infrastructure may thus be useful for enhancing adoption.

2.6. Adoption and farm policy

Agriculture in developing and developed countries has been subject to government interventions that, in turn, affect technological change. Generally speaking, agricultural policies in developed countries aim to raise and stabilize agricultural incomes and, in some cases, to curtail supplies, while agricultural outputs have been taxed in developing nations. In both cases agricultural inputs have tended to be subsidized.

In recent years, agriculture has been subject to new environmental policies that control and affect the use of certain inputs that may cause pollution. The following is a discussion of the impacts of different policies on technological change.

2.6.1. Price supports

Just, Rausser, and Zilberman (1986) and Just et al. (1988) developed a framework, relying on the model presented in Equation (21), to analyze the impact of agricultural policies on technology adoption for farmers operating under uncertainty. They analyze various policies by tracing their impacts on price distributions of inputs and outputs as well as constraints (i.e., credit) on adoption. Price supports increase the mean of prices received by farmers and reduce their variability by setting lower price bounds. When the new technology has a yield-increasing effect (for example, high-yield variety), and if it is also perceived to have higher risk, price-support policies tend to increase its relative profitability, which leads to an increase in both the extent and intensity of adoption. McGuirk and Mundlak (1991) argue that the introduction of guaranteed markets for Punjabi food grain production by the government procurement policy (which was in essence a price support policy) enhanced the adoption of high-yield wheat and rice varieties in this region.

The mechanism through which price supports impact the adoption behavior of farms of different sizes varies. Smaller farms may increase their adoption because of price supports (their impact on credit) and the reduction in the minimum size required to justify adoption. Larger farms that may be risk diversifiers will increase the share of modern technologies on their land because of the mean effect and the reduction in risk. Price supports may also enhance adoption of mechanical innovations when they increase the relative profitability of operations with a new technology and thus reduce the size threshold required for adoption. Price supports may enhance adoption also through their impact on credit. When the ability to obtain credit depends on expected incomes, price supports will increase adoption when credit is constrained.

2.6.2. Combined output price supports and land diversion policies

In the United States as well as in some European countries, the subsidization of prices has been accompanied by a conditional reduction in acreage. The higher and most secure prices on at least part of the land provide incentives for farmers to adopt yield-increasing varieties. On these lands, they raise the value of property and expected income, which increases their capacity to obtain credit that may enhance the adoption of all types of technologies.

Specific elements of the support program vary over time. In recent years, the base for support has not been the actual yield, but the average base yield that is dependent on the average past performance of either the farmer or the region. The acreage that provides the base for entitlement to the benefits of a diversion program also depends on past performance. According to the specifics of a program, farmers might expand their yield or acreage in order to expand their entitlements in the future. Thus, adoption of high-yielding technologies, or technologies that may be especially beneficial with marginal land, is more likely to occur with price supports/diversion policies.[12] The historical record that provides a base for future program entitlements may, on the other hand, provide disincentives to adopt new crops or to introduce nonprogram crops to certain areas and thus reduce the flexibility of farming. The 1996 Farm Act in the United States makes entitlements that are independent of most farming activities, including choice of crop. However, even under this bill, land that is entitled to income support is somewhat restricted in its choice of crops, and that may retard the adoption and introduction of new crops to some of the major field crop regions of the United States.

Cochrane (1979) argued that the commodity programs in the United States played a major role in the adoption of mechanical and chemical innovations by reducing risk and increasing profitability per acre. The commodity programs as well as the increases in demand and prices during and after World War II led to modernization and structural change in U.S. agriculture. De Gorter and Fisher (1993) used a dynamic model to show that the combination of price supports and land diversion led to intensification of farming in the United States. Lichtenberg's (1989) work demonstrates the importance of economic incentives for the adoption of center-pivot irrigation in Nebraska and other Midwestern states, and suggests that expansion of the irrigated land base in these states benefited from the support programs of the 1970s and 1980s.

2.6.3. Output taxation

Taxation of agricultural outputs, prevalent especially in developing countries, has a disastrous effect on technological change. It reduces the incentive to adopt yield-increasing technologies, increases the scale of operation that justifies financing purchases of new equipment, and depresses the price of agricultural land, thus reducing the ability to borrow. Furthermore, with lower prices, there are incentives to apply intensively modern inputs, which are associated in many cases with the adoption of modern, high-yield varieties in developing countries. The low growth of Argentinian agriculture between 1940 and 1973 is a result of output taxation and other policies that reduced relative prices of agricultural products and slowed investments and technological change in this sector [Cavallo and Mundlak (1982)].

---

[12] The work of Zilberman (1984) provides a rigorous argument on the impact of programs such as deficiency payments and diversion policies on the expansion of acreage and supply.

2.6.4. Trade liberalization and macroeconomic policies

The adoption of innovations is likely to be significantly influenced by policies that affect the general economy. This may include trade and exchange rate policies as well as macroeconomic and credit policies. Macroeconomic policies that lead to high interest rates may reduce adoption because investment in new technologies is more costly. Adoption of mechanical innovations may suffer more significantly with high interest rates, while farmers may switch to technologies that are labor-intensive.

Changes in international trade regimes will affect various regions differently according to their relative advantage. The opening of markets in the United States led to the introduction of high-value varieties in different communities in Central America [Carletto et al. (1996)]. This change in cropping was combined with the establishment of a new infrastructure and the construction of packinghouses and transportation facilities. Thus, when a change in trade rules seems permanent, it may lead to a complete overhaul of the infrastructure, and that may enable adoption of new crops and modernization.

Favorable pricing because of trade barriers enables growers in Europe, Japan, and some parts of the United States to adopt yield-increasing varieties, to invest and develop greenhouse technologies, and to expand the capacity of different technologies, including irrigated agriculture, in situations that would not have warranted it under free trade. The growth and investment in the agricultural sector in both Argentina and Chile suffered during periods when international trade was constrained, and benefited from trade liberalization [Coeymans and Mundlak (1993), Cavallo and Mundlak (1982)].

2.6.5. Environmental policies

A wide array of environmental regulations affects technologies available for agriculture. Pesticide bans provide a strong incentive for the development of alternatives at the manufacturer level and for the adoption of alternative strategies including nonchemical treatment, biological control, etc. On the other hand, the lack of availability of chemicals may retard adoption of high-yield varieties or new crops that are susceptible to a particular pest, especially in cases where nonchemical alternatives are not very effective. The elimination of DBCP (with its unique capacity to treat soil-borne diseases) in the mid-1980s in California led, on the one hand, to the abandonment of some grape acreage and a switch to other crops. At the same time, it enhanced the adoption of drip irrigation that enabled applications of alternatives in other areas.

2.6.6. Input subsidies

There is a wide body of literature [Caswell (1991)] that shows that subsidized water pricing tends to retard the adoption of modern irrigation technologies. However, subsidized input led to the adoption of high-yield varieties and "green revolution" technologies in countries like India. They also increased profitability and thus have an indirect positive impact on adoption through credit effects. Similarly, subsidization of pesticides and fertilizers led to the adoption of high-yield varieties and chemical-intensive technologies in developing and developed countries alike, which is also likely to result in problems of environmental pollution since the environmental side effects of agriculture are often the result of excessive residues. Alternatively, elimination of subsidies and especially taxation of chemical inputs may lead to adoption of more precise application technologies that will reduce residues and actually may increase yield [Khanna and Zilberman (1997)].

2.6.7. Conditional entitlements of environmental programs

Governments have recognized that they can use entitlements to support programs conditional on certain patterns of behavior. Therefore, in recent years there have been attempts to link entitlements to income supports, policies, and other subsidization to certain patterns of environmental behavior. A program like the Environmental Quality Incentives Program (EQIP) in the United States attempts to induce farmers to adopt practices such as low-tillage and soil testing, and to reduce the application of chemicals in exchange for entitlements for some support. In some cases, the benefits of such a program are short-lived and farmers may quit using modern practices once the program benefits disappear. On the other hand, especially when it comes to new, untested technologies, elements of learning-by-doing and experience may improve the profitability of those technologies that have some environmental benefits so that farmers recognize their economic advantages. Thus, the adoption of such technologies may persist in the long run.

3. Future directions

Research on agricultural technology evolves from the technology and the institutions associated with it. At present, agriculture is undergoing a technological revolution as evidenced by the introduction of biotechnology and precision technology. We are also witnessing related processes of industrialization, product differentiation, and increased vertical integration in agriculture [Zilberman et al. (1997)]. These changes raise new issues and introduce new challenges. Several significant changes have been observed thus far from the emergence of biotechnology [Zilberman et al. (1998)].

   With many past technologies, university research identified some of the basic concepts while most of the innovations were done in industries. However, with biotechnology, universities are the source of numerous new discoveries, and technology transfer from universities to industries has triggered the creation of leading products and companies. The unwillingness of private firms to develop university innovations without exclusive rights motivated the establishment of offices of technology transfer that identified buyers who would share the rights to develop university innovations. Each arrangement provides new sources of funding to universities since royalties are divided among universities, researchers, and departments. Thus far, income from technology transfer revenues has paid less than 5 percent of university research budgets. However, in some areas (biology and medicine) it made a difference. Most of the royalties were associated with fewer than 10 innovations [Parker et al. (1998)], reinforcing our existing knowledge that benefits to research tend to concentrate on a small number of critical innovations. Established companies were not willing to buy the rights to develop some of the most radical, yet important, university innovations and biotechnology. Thus, offices of technology transfer, working with venture capitalists, helped to establish new upstart companies, some of which became leading biotechnology firms (e.g., Genentech, Chiron and Amgen). As these companies grew and became successful, some of the major multinationals bought a majority of shares in these companies. Thus, most of the activities in biotechnology have been in medical biotechnology. However, 1996 was the breakthrough year for agricultural biotechnology as millions of acres were planted with pest-resistant varieties of cotton and soybeans. In agricultural biotechnology, we see again the importance of small startups from the collaborations between university researchers and venture capitalists. Most of the startups in agricultural biotechnology have been acquired by giants like Monsanto and DuPont.

The evolution of biotechnology suggests that the university is becoming a major player in industrial development, and it affects the structure and competitiveness of industries. University researchers working with venture capitalists generate new avenues of product development. Sometimes they may force some of the giant companies to change their product development strategy, and may even give up some of their monopolistic power. Other forms of contractual relationships between university researchers and industries are being established. For example, industries support certain lines of research for an exclusive option to purchase the rights for technology. Furthermore, some researchers suddenly find themselves wearing another hat, that of a partner in a technology company, and that may affect the way universities run their patterns of payments and support for researchers. Given these new realities, there is a need for both empirical and conceptual research on innovations and the relationships between public and private research. We need to better understand the existing arrangements of royalties, sharing of royalties within the university, the relationship between publications and patents, and the effect of university research and industrial structure, etc.

With computers, biotechnology, and other new technologies, most of the value is now embodied in specific knowledge. The Cohen–Boyer patent once generated the largest revenues to universities. In this case, companies paid for the right to use a process for genetic manipulation. The key to biotechnology is the process of innovation (which specifies how to conduct specific manipulation) and product innovation (which specifies what type of outcomes can be controlled by which genes). New genetic engineering products will be produced by combining certain procedures and items of knowledge that are protected by certain patent rights. In principle, the developers of new products should pay the royalties to whoever owns the patents. Thus the markets for rights to different types of knowledge will emerge.

A new research agenda is suggested to address the economics of intellectual property rights. In particular, it should address pricing rules for different types of intellectual property rights and the design of biotechnology products given the price structures for different processes and product innovations. An important area of understanding is the pricing of international property rights within complex international systems where protection of intellectual property rights is not always feasible and where there are significant disparities in income.

The research in intellectual property rights will also have implications on the issues of biodiversity and compensation for developing countries for genetic materials that are embodied in their natural resources. Other related issues include the incentives for and integration of research to develop basic foods; the alleviation of starvation in the poorest countries; how new emerging industrial orders in agriculture and biotechnology can provide appropriate technologies to these countries; defining the role of international research institutes and other public entities (e.g., the United Nations and global organizations) in conducting research aimed at the poorest countries; and what type of payment arrangement should exist between research units focused on developing countries and commercial firms in the more developed nations.

Materials and chemicals that were previously produced by chemical procedures may be produced through modified biological organisms. First, biotechnology in agriculture will produce alternative forms of pest control and pest-resistant varieties but, over time, it will produce higher quality food products and new products such as pharmaceuticals and fine chemicals, see [Zilberman et al. (1997)]. With biotechnology the value added of seeds will increase to include some of the rent that was accrued to chemicals. Pesticide manufacturers already have become major players in biotechnology and are taking over seed companies in order to obtain a channel to market their products. Often the owners of the rights to patents try to capture some of the rent through contracting; thus, biotechnology will provide both the incentives to enhance contractual arrangements and vertical integration in agriculture. Some of the recent mergers and acquisitions in agricultural biotechnology can be explained by attempts to obtain rights to intellectual property and access to markets [Rausser et al. (1999)]. Finally, biotechnology causes firms with agricultural characteristics (for example, dairies, livestock operations, and even field crop operations) to produce products in areas that are not traditionally agricultural (pharmaceutical, oils, coloring). As the borderline between agriculture and industry becomes fuzzier, new models replace the competitive models as the major paradigm to assess agriculture.

The new product lines and the new types of industrial organization that may occur with biotechnology will raise environmental concerns and management issues. Biotechnology, thus far, has had a good track record, but it could have a negative potential. The design of the regulatory framework will significantly affect the structure of biotechnology industries and their impact. A more restrictive registration process, for example, may lead to a more concentrated biotechnology. Thus, it will become a research and policy challenge to modify the registration process and to balance the risks and benefits associated with biotechnology through monitoring over time. The optimal design of intellectual property rights agreements in biotechnology will become another issue of major concern. Patent rights that are too broad will lead to concentration in industries. It may stymie competition but may encourage a small number of firms to invest heavily in new products. Biotechnology patent protections that are too narrow may prevent significant investment in a costly research line.

Over the last 30 or 40 years, precision technologies have evolved that adjust input use to variation over space and time and reduce residues. The use of precision technologies is still in its infancy. The development of computer and satellite technology suggests a new, vast potential, but it has had limited use thus far. However, new products are continuously being introduced, and some types of precision technologies will play a major role in the future of agriculture. One challenge in improving precision technology will be to develop the software and management tools that will take advantage of new information. That will present a significant challenge to researchers in farm management. Other issues involve the development of institutions that take advantage of network externalities associated with knowledge and that accumulate and distribute information that is pertinent to farm management. The pricing of knowledge will also become a major issue of research within the context of precision farming.

Another important issue associated with precision farming is the potential for improving environmental quality. The adoption of precision farming may be induced by environmental regulation. The link between environmental regulation, research, development, and the adoption of new products needs to become clearer and provide insight to improve institutions and incentives. Most of the research on technology and innovation thus far has been done within regional bounds, but one of the main challenges of the future is to analyze issues of research and development within an international context. We need to better understand issues of technology transfer and intellectual property rights within nations. In some cases we need to better understand the mechanisms of collaboration between nations to address either global problems or to take advantage of increases in returns to scale. International food research centers and some existing binational research and development arrangements have become very prominent.[13] These types of arrangements may become more important in the future and should be further investigated. Furthermore, the relationship between the private and the public sectors in research and development should be viewed in a global context. A multinational corporation may change the research activities and infrastructure between nations in response to changes in economic conditions, and the activities of such private organizations depend both on national and international public sector policies.

International aspects of research and development are especially important in light of trade agreements such as GATT and NAFTA, and there is very little knowledge on how international trade agreements affect research and development. However, this type of knowledge is crucial because R&D is becoming a key element in the evolution of agricultural industries. An important issue to address, of course, is the development of research infrastructure on global problems, for example, private global climate change. Thus far, this research has been conducted by individual nations without much coordination of finance, finding, and direction. As we recognize our interdependence and

---

[13] For evaluation of the Binational Agricultural Research Development (BARD) fund between Israel and the United States, see [Just et al. (1988)].

the importance of issues such as global management of natural resources, fisheries, and biodiversity, we need to determine what type of mechanism we should use to enhance efficiency and research in knowledge development on a global basis.

In addition to an abundance of new research topics on innovations that should be addressed in the future, there are new research techniques and paradigms that seem very promising for the future. The new evolution in finance examines investments within the context of dynamics, and uncertainty should be further incorporated to assess the economics and management of research. Research activities should be evaluated as part of the management portfolio and financial activities of firms and concerns. The use of financial tools will provide new avenues for pricing research products and international property rights. However, tools, while very useful, have limits of their own. We need to better understand what kinds of processes, in terms of technology and economic and physical forces, give rise to the stochastic processes that are used in financial management. We need to better understand the dynamics of uncertain events and how they affect markets. Research agendas that link general equilibrium modeling with financial tools are an important challenge to economics in general but will be very important in the area of agricultural research and development.

Much of the research has emphasized technical innovations but it may be just as important to understand institutional innovations. What are the reasons for the emergence of institutions such as futures markets, farmer cooperatives, product quality warranties, etc.? To what extent are these institutions induced by economic conditions? How do human capital and political structures affect the emergence of institutions? Zilberman and Heiman (1997) suggest that economic research contributed to the emergence of institutional innovations (e.g., Keynesian macroeconomic policies, emission, etc.). But this topic needs to be studied in-depth which will enable better assessment of investments in social science research. Research on the emergence of institutions will benefit if we have a better understanding of how institutions actually work and the main features that characterize them.

Innovative activities are critically dependent on human capacity to make decisions and learn. The assumption of full rationality that characterizes many economic models is unrealistic. It will be useful to borrow the modeling approach from psychology and other behavioral sciences, and develop models of learning, adoption, and other choices that recognize bounded rationality. Thus far, there is much successful research in other areas, in particular, on uncertainty, and such direction will be very important in the study of innovation and technology.

Technological innovation and institutional change have a profound effect on the evolution of the agricultural sector. The agricultural economic literature on innovation clearly documents that innovations do not occur randomly, but rather that incentives and government policies affect the nature and the rate of innovation and adoption. Both the generation of new technologies and their adoption are affected by intentional public policies (e.g., funding of research and extension activities), unintended policies (e.g., manipulation of commodity prices), and activities of the private sector. One of the challenges of designing technology policies in agriculture is to obtain an optimal mix of public and private efforts. Design of these policies will require improved understanding of the economics of complex processes of innovation, learning, and adoption in a myriad of institutional and technological settings. Economists have made many notable advances through their research on innovation and adoption, but there remains much to be discovered.

References

Agricultural Issues Center (1994), "Financing agriculture in California's new risk environment", in: S.C. Blank, ed., S. Weber, technical ed., Proceedings of a Conference on December 1, 1993 in Sacramento, California (Agricultural Issues Center, University of California, Davis, CA).

Akerlof, G. (1976), "The economics of caste and of the rate race and other woeful tales", Quarterly Journal of Economics 90:591–617.

Alston, J.M., G.W. Norton and P.G. Pardey (1995), Science under Scarcity: Principles and Practice for Agricultural Research Evaluation and Priority Setting (Cornell University Press, Ithaca, NY).

Alston, J., R. Sexton and M. Zhang (1997), "The effects of imperfect competition on the size and distribution of research benefits", American Journal of Agricultural Economics 79(4):1252–1265.

Antle, J.M., and T. McGuckin (1993), "Technological innovation, agricultural productivity, and environmental quality", in: G.A. Carlson, D. Zilberman and J.A. Miranowski, eds., Agricultural and Environmental Resource Economics (Oxford University Press, New York).

Ball, V.E., J.-C. Bureau, R. Nehring and A. Somwaru (1997), "Agricultural productivity revisited", American Journal of Agricultural Economics 79(4):1045–1063.

Berck, P., and J.M. Perloff (1985), "The commons as a natural barrier to entry: Why there are so few fish farms", American Journal of Agricultural Economics 67(2):360–363.

Binswanger, H.P. (1974), "A microeconomic approach to induced innovation", Economic Journal 84(336):940–958.

Binswanger, H.P., and J. McIntire (1987), "Behavioral and material determinants of production relations in land abundant tropical agriculture", Journal of Economic Development and Cultural Change 36(1):73–100.

Boserup, E. (1965), Conditions of Agricultural Growth (Aldine Publishing Company, Chicago).

Brown, L.R., G. Gardner and B. Halweil (1999), "Beyond Malthus. Nineteen dimensions of the population challenge", in: L. Starke, ed., The Worldwatch Environmental Alert Series (W.W. Norton & Company, New York).

Carletto, C., A. de Janvry and E. Sadoulet (1996), "Knowledge, toxicity, and external shocks: The determinants of adoption and abandonment of non-traditional export crops by smallholders in Guatemala", Working paper 791 (Department of Agricultural and Resource Economics, University of California, Berkeley).

Caswell, M. (1991), "Irrigation technology adoption decisions: Empirical evidence", in: A. Dinar and D. Zilberman, eds., The Economics and Management Water and Drainage in Agriculture (Kluwer Academic Publishers, Boston).

Caswell, M.F., and D. Zilberman (1986), "The effects of well depth and land quality on the choice of irrigation technology", American Journal of Agricultural Economics 68(4):798–811.

Cavallo, D., and Y. Mundlak (1982), "Agriculture and economic growth in an open economy: The case of Argentina", Research Report 36 (International Food Policy Research Institute, Washington, DC).

Chavas, J.-P. (1993), "On sustainability and the economics of survival", American Journal of Agricultural Economics 75(1):72–83.

Cochrane, W.W. (1979), The Development of American Agriculture: A Historical Analysis (University of Minnesota Press, Minneapolis).

Coeymans, J.E., and Y. Mundlak (1993), "Sectoral growth in Chile: 1962–82", Research Report 95 (International Food Policy Research Institute, Washington, DC).

David, P.A. (1969), "A contribution to the theory of diffusion", Memorandum no. 71 (Stanford Center for Research in Economic Growth).

de Gorter, H., and E.O. Fisher (1993), "The dynamic effects of agricultural subsidies in the United States", Journal of Agricultural and Resource Economics 18(2):147–159.

de Gorter, H., and D. Zilberman (1990), "On the political economy of public good inputs in agriculture", American Journal of Agricultural Economics 72(1):131–137.

de Janvry, A., P. Leveen and D. Runsten (1981), "The political economy of technological change: Mechanization of tomato harvesting in California", Working paper 177 (Department of Agricultural and Resource Economics, University of California, Berkeley).

Diamond, J. (1999), Guns, Germs and Steel (W.W. Norton and Company, New York).

Dixit, A., and R. Pindyck (1994), Investment Under Uncertainty (Princeton University Press, Princeton).

Evenson, R., and Y. Kislev (1976), "A stochastic model of applied research", Journal of Political Economics 84(2):265–281.

Feder, G., R.E. Just and D. Zilberman (1985), "Adoption of agricultural innovations in developing countries: A survey", Economic Development and Cultural Change 33(2):255–298.

Feder, G., and G.T. O'Mara (1981), "Farm size and the adoption of green revolution technology", Economic Development and Cultural Change 30:59–76.

Gardner, B. (1988), The Economics of Agricultural Policies (Macmillan Publishing Company, New York).

Goodhue, R. (1997), Agricultural complementarities and coordination: Modeling value differentiation and production contracting, Ph.D. Dissertation (Department of Agricultural and Resource Economics, University of California, Berkeley).

Griliches, Z. (1957), "Hybrid corn: An exploration in the economics of technological change", Econometrica 25(4):501–522.

Griliches, Z. (1958), "Research costs and social returns: Hybrid corn and related innovations", Journal of Political Economy 66(5):419–431.

Guttman, J.M. (1978), "Interest groups and the demand for agricultural research", Journal of Political Economy 85(3):467–484.

Hamilton, S.F., and D.L. Sunding (1997), "The effect of farm supply shifts on concentration and market power in the food processing sector", American Journal of Agricultural Economics 79:524–531.

Hamilton, S.F., and D.L. Sunding (1998), "Returns to public investments in agriculture with imperfect downstream competition", American Journal of Agricultural Economics 80(4):830–838.

Hasset, K.A., and G.E. Metcalf (1992), Energy Tax Credits and Residential Conservation Investment (NBER, Cambridge).

Hayami, Y., and V.W. Ruttan (1985), Agricultural Development: An International Perspective (Johns Hopkins University Press, Baltimore).

Heiman, A., J. Zhao and D. Zilberman (1998), "Modeling money-back guarantees as financial options", Mimeograph (Department of Agricultural and Resource Economics, University of California, Berkeley).

Hoff, K., A. Braverman and J. Stiglitz (1993), The Economics of Rural Organization: Theory, Practice and Policy (Oxford University Press, New York, NY).

Huffman, W.E. (1998), "Finance, organization and impacts of U.S. agricultural research: Future prospects", Paper prepared for conference "Knowledge Generation and Transfer: Implications for Agriculture in the 21st Century", University of California, Berkeley, June 18–19, 1998.

Huffman, W.E., and R.E. Just (1994), "Funding, structure, and management of public agricultural research in the United States", American Journal of Agricultural Economics 76(4):744–759.

Just, R., and W. Chern (1980), "Tomatoes, technology, and oligopsony", Bell Journal of Economics 11:584–602.

Just, R.E., G.C. Rausser and D. Zilberman (1986), "Modelling the effects of policy on farmers in developing agriculture", International Journal of Development Planning Literature 1(3):287–300.

Just, R.E., and D. Zilberman (1983), "Stochastic structure, farm size, and technology adoption in developing agriculture", Oxford Economic Papers 35(2):307–328.

Just, R.E., and D. Zilberman (1988), "The effects of agricultural development policies on income distribution and technological change in agriculture", Journal of Development Economics 28:193–216.

Just, R.E., D. Zilberman, D. Parker and M. Phillips (1988), "The economic impacts of BARD research on the U.S.", Report prepared for the Commission to Evaluate BARD, June, 1988.

Khanna, M., and D. Zilberman (1997), "Incentives, precision technology and environmental quality", Ecological Economics 23(1):25–43.

Kislev, Y., and N. Schori-Bachrach (1973), "The process of an innovation cycle", American Journal of Agricultural Economics 55(1):28–37.

Klette, T.J., and Z. Griliches (1997), "Empirical patterns of firm growth and R&D investment: A quality ladder model interpretation", Working paper 5945 (National Bureau of Economic Research, Cambridge, MA).

Lehvall, P., and C. Wahlbin (1973), "A study of some assumptions underlying innovation diffusion functions", Swedish Journal of Economics 75:362–377.

Lichtenberg, E. (1989), "Land quality, irrigation development, and cropping patterns in the northern High Plains", American Journal of Agricultural Economics 71(1):187–194.

Mahajan, V., and R.A. Peterson (1985), Models for Innovation Diffusion (Sage Publications, Beverly Hills, CA).

Mansfield, E. (1963), "The speed of response of firms to new techniques", Quarterly Journal of Economics 77:290–311.

McDonald, R., and D. Siegel (1986), "The value of waiting to invest", Quarterly Journal of Economics 101:707–728.

McGuirk, A., and Y. Mundlak (1991), "Incentives and constraints in the transformation of Punjab agriculture", Research Report 87 (International Food Policy Research Institute, Washington, DC).

McWilliams, B., and D. Zilberman (1996), "Time of technology adoption and learning by doing", Economics of Innovation and New Technology 4:139–154.

Mundlak, Y. (1997), "Agricultural production functions: A critical survey", Working paper (The Center for Agricultural Economic Research, Rehovot, Israel).

Norgaard, R.B. (1988), "The biological control of cassava mealybug in Africa", American Journal of Agricultural Economics 70(2):366–371.

Olmstead, A.L., and P. Rhode (1993), "Induced innovation in American agriculture: A reconsideration", Journal of Political Economy 101(1):100–118.

Olmstead, J. (1998), Emerging markets in water: Investments in institutional and technological change, Ph.D. Dissertation (Department of Agricultural and Resource Economics, University of California, Berkeley).

Parker, D., and D. Zilberman (1993), "Hedonic estimation of quality factors affecting the farm-retail margin", American Journal of Agricultural Economics 75(2):458–466.

Parker, D., D. Zilberman and F. Castillo (1998), "Office of technology transfer: Privatizing university innovations for agriculture", Choices:19–25.

Rausser, G. (1999), "Private/public research: Knowledge assets and future scenarios, Invited fellows address", Annual meeting of the American Agricultural Economics Association, Nashville, TN, August 10, 1999.

Rausser, G., S. Scotchmer and L. Simon (1999), "Intellectual property and market structure in agriculture", Work in progress (Department of Agricultural and Resource Economics, University of California, Berkeley).

Rausser, G., and P. Zusman (1991), Political-Economic Analysis: Explanation and Prescription (Cambridge University Press, New York).

Rogers, E. (1962), Diffusion of Innovations (Free Press of Glencoe, New York).

Roumasset, J.A. (1976), Rice and Risk: Decision-Making among Low-Income Farmers (North-Holland, Amsterdam).

Schmitz, A., and D. Seckler (1970), "Mechanized agriculture and social welfare: The case of the tomato harvester", American Journal of Agricultural Economics 52(4):569–577.

Schultz, T.W. (1964), Transforming Traditional Agriculture (Yale University Press, New Haven, CT).

Stoneman, P., and N. Ireland (1983), "Technological diffusion, expectations and welfare", Oxford Economic Papers 38:283–304.

Sunding, D. (1996), "Measuring the marginal cost of nonuniform environmental regulations", American Journal of Agricultural Economics 78:1098–1107.

Thurow, A.P., W.G. Boggess and C.B. Moss (1997), "An *ex ante* approach to modeling investment in new technology", in: D. Parker and Y. Tsur, eds., Decentralization and Coordination of Water Resource Management (Kluwer Academic Publishers).

United States Bureau of the Census (1975, September), Historical Statistics of the United States. Colonial Times to 1970, Parts 1&2 (United States Department of Commerce, Washington, DC).

United States Bureau of the Census (1980, October), Statistical Abstract of the United States 1980, 101st Edition (United States Department of Commerce, Washington, DC).

United States Bureau of the Census (1998, October)), Statistical Abstract of the United States 1998, 118th Edition (United States Department of Commerce, Washington, DC).

Wann, J., and R. Sexton (1992), "Imperfect competition in multiproduct food industries with application to pear processing", American Journal of Agricultural Economics 74(4):989–990.

Wright, B.D. (1983), "The economics of invention incentives: Patents, prizes, and research contracts", The American Economic Review 73(4):691–707.

Zilberman, D. (1984), "Technological change, government policies, and exhaustible resources in agriculture", American Journal of Agricultural Economics 66(5):634–640.

Zilberman, D. (1985), "Technological change, government policies and exhaustible resources in agriculture", American Journal of Agricultural Economics 66(5):634–640.

Zilberman, D., and A. Heiman (1997), "The value of economic research", American Journal of Agricultural Economics 79(5):1539–1544.

Zilberman, D., D. Sunding, R. Howitt, A. Dinar and N. MacDougall (1994), "Water for California agriculture: Lessons from the drought and new water market reform", Choices:25–28.

Zilberman, D., D. Sunding and M. Khanna (1997), "The changing nature of agricultural markets: Implications for privatization of technology, information transfer, and the role of land-grant research and extension", in: S. Wolf, ed.", Privatization of Information and Agricultural Industrialization (CRC Press, Boca Raton, FL).

Zilberman, D., C. Yarkin and A. Heiman (1998), "Agricultural biotechnology: Economic and international implications", Mimeograph (Department of Agricultural and Resource Economics, University of California, Berkeley).

Chapter 5

STRUCTURAL CHANGE IN AGRICULTURAL PRODUCTION: ECONOMICS, TECHNOLOGY AND POLICY

JEAN-PAUL CHAVAS

Taylor Hall, University of Wisconsin, Madison, WI

Contents

Handbook of Agricultural Economics, Volume 1, Edited by B. Gardner and G. Rausser

Abstract

Over the last few decades, the structure of agricultural production around the world has been changing. An economic analysis of the factors influencing this evolution is presented. Special attention is given to the role of technology and resource mobility. Linkages with changes in market conditions are also evaluated.

Keywords

agricultural production, structure, technology, resource mobility

JEL classification: Q11

1. Introduction

The process of food production has changed significantly over time and over space. Changes have been influenced by the dynamic interactions between improved technologies and increasing human population [Boserup (1965)]. Over the centuries, the production process has evolved from simple forms of food gathering (e.g., hunting and fishing) to complex biotechnologies (e.g., genetic engineering). Hunting and fishing activities remain important sources of food in some parts of the world, and extensive production systems (e.g., pastoralism) still play significant roles in food production where population density is low and/or land productivity is low. However, intensive forms of production are now commonly found around the world. These intensive forms have typically been associated with high population densities, productive land, and rapid technological progress.

The evolving organization and structure of agricultural production remains a subject of considerable interest. Historically, land rights and relations have evolved in response to changing population density, market access, and agrarian policy [Boserup (1965), Binswanger et al. (1993), Binswanger and Deininger (1997)]. At the microeconomic level, various institutional forms can support food production, from territorial rights associated with hunting and fishing, to collective farms (e.g., the Israeli kibbutz), to private farms. Private farms include large commercial farms relying extensively on hired labor as well as family farms relying mostly on family labor. Around the world, the current prevalence of the family farm as a socioeconomic unit of agricultural production (where it is often difficult to distinguish between production unit and household consumption unit) is particularly noteworthy.

The evolution of farm structure is part of a complex evolution of the farm sector and its role in a global economy. The main function of the farm sector is to feed a growing world population. The world population reached 6 billion people in 1999, up from 5 billion people in 1987. Feeding this growing population is a significant challenge, suggesting a strong and increasing demand for food. In this context, it may be surprising to see that the average real price of food has been declining over the last few decades. This has been possible only because of a large increase in food production and remarkable productivity gains. This stresses the importance of technical change in agriculture.

Another notable characteristic of the food sector is the instability of its markets. Part of the instability is due to weather effects, which affect farm production, farm prices, and farm income. Part of the instability is also due to the low price elasticity of demand for food and the perishability of a number of food commodities. An inelastic food demand means that food prices can react sharply to small changes in food supply. This suggests significant risk in anticipating agricultural prices. The instability of agricultural markets and farm income can raise questions about whether market prices always provide appropriate guides to efficient resource allocation in the food sector [e.g., Innes and Rausser (1989), Newbery and Stiglitz (1981)]. This seems particularly relevant in a period of market liberalization, where the role of government in agriculture is declining around the world, with greater emphasis being given to markets and trade.

2. The structure of agricultural production

Since the beginning of the twentieth century, the spread of mechanization, increased land productivity due to technical progress (e.g., the "green revolution"), and rural migrations toward cities have transformed the system of agricultural production around the world. The transformation has taken many forms.

First, migration from rural areas toward urban jobs has been associated with the growth of the industrial and service sector, and with a sharp increase in farm labor productivity due in large part to mechanization. In situations of slow economic development, few urban jobs and a slow growth in the industrial sector have restricted the labor migration flow and reduced the demand for farm mechanization. Alternatively, in situations of rapid economic growth, significant labor migrations have reduced the proportion of the active labor force employed in agriculture. Taking place over several decades, this process has transformed farming into a sector employing only a small portion of the active population. In developed countries, such changes have induced a trend toward mechanization and significant increases in farm size.

The product mix produced by farmers has also changed. In general, farms have evolved toward greater product specialization. In developed countries, this can be seen today through the development of large, specialized animal production units in broiler, dairy or pork production (which contrast with the more traditional mixed crop-animal farms).

Agricultural sectors around the world are increasingly relying on trade and market mechanisms as a means of guiding resource allocation in agriculture. This coincides with a decline of food self-sufficiency motive as a guiding force for the organization and structure of farming, at both the micro level and the national level. As trade for food and fiber developed, the role of agricultural markets has become more important both in developed and developing countries. At the national level, this means less reliance on government programs. At the farm level, economic survival pushes managers toward implementing efficient production systems adapted to local conditions, toward developing marketing skills that can take advantage of market opportunities, and toward risk management strategies that can effectively deal with weather risk and changing market conditions.

Finally, the increasing role of contracts in agriculture is worth emphasizing. For example, the broiler sector has exhibited high growth and significant productivity gains over the last 40 years. It has also been associated with the development of vertical integration, where coordination between different stages of the marketing channel is done mostly through contracts. The use of contracts as a control and coordination mechanism is also commonly found in vegetable production, and increasingly in pork production.

3. Farm structure

3.1. Farm size and returns to scale

Issues related to the structure of agriculture and to the survival of the family farm have long been subjects of interest and controversy [see, e.g., Allanson (1992), Gale (1993), Goetz and Debertin (1996), Hearn et al. (1996), Lianos and Parliarou (1986), Weiss (1998)]. At the center of this debate is the relationship between farm size and economic efficiency: are large farms more efficient than small farms? Is it possible to identify an "optimal" farm size? The nature of returns to scale in production can help shed some light on these issues.

Returns to scale reflects the relationship between average production cost and firm size. Increasing (decreasing) returns to scale corresponds to an average cost (per unit of output)[1] being a decreasing (increasing) function of output. And constant returns to scale means that average cost is unaffected by firm size. Alternatively, finding that larger firms exhibit a lower (higher) average cost identifies the presence of economies (diseconomies) of scale. In crop production, it often appears relevant to consider land as a fixed factor. Then, returns to scale can be alternatively measured in terms of the properties of the average return per unit of land: increasing (constant, decreasing) returns to scale corresponds to the average return per unit of land being an increasing (constant, decreasing) function of farm acreage. In this context, the average return per acre is the Ricardian rent, measuring the return to land after all other factors of production have been remunerated [e.g., see Chavas (1993)].[2]

Under free entry and exit, competitive firms producing under increasing returns to scale implies negative profit, giving incentives for firms to either exit the industry or expand. And competitive firms producing under decreasing returns to scale implies positive profit, providing incentives for new firms to enter the industry. Thus, under perfect resource mobility, industry equilibrium is expected to include only firms producing in the region of constant returns to scale (which exhibits neither increasing nor decreasing returns to scale). This has stimulated much research trying to identify the shape of the average cost function as it relates to farm size. Alternatively, in the absence of perfect resource mobility, power relations can become closely linked to land rights and the structure of agricultural production [e.g., De Janvry (1981), Binswanger et al. (1993), Binswanger and Deininger (1997)]. For example, Binswanger et al. argue that the historical emergence of large farms in many developing countries was based on power relations and economic distortions, where the international competitiveness of these farms was often maintained by subsidies involving significant social costs. Such situations motivated agrarian reforms redistributing land with an attempt to improve both equity and efficiency.

---

[1] In a multi-output framework, the relevant function is the ray-average cost function, i.e., the cost of production per unit of a factor proportionally rescaling all outputs [see Baumol (1982)].

[2] This means that land rent should not be treated as a cost in cost of production studies.

In developing countries, there is debate about the inverse relationship often observed between farm size and productivity [e.g., Rao and Chotigeat (1981), Eswaran and Kotwal (1986), Binswanger et al. (1993)]. The argument is that, compared to large farms, small family farms face lower labor cost because of lower cost of labor supervision. Then, in situations of unequal land distribution, land reform can in principle generate a more egalitarian access to land while increasing farm productivity and efficiency [e.g., by combining "underused" labor from small farms and the landless with "underused" land on very large farms; see Berry and Cline (1979)]. However, small farms may face higher capital cost (e.g., due to credit rationing and capital market imperfections) if large farms have better access to the capital markets. In such a situation, it is possible for the relationship between farm size and productivity to be U-shaped, large farms enjoying a credit cost advantage while small farms enjoy a labor cost advantage [Binswanger et al. (1993)].

In agriculture of developed countries, the empirical evidence suggests that the average cost function has a typical L shape: average cost tends to decline for small farm sizes, and then reach a lower plateau for average to large farm sizes [e.g., Hall and Leveen (1978)]. This suggests three points. First, economies of scale seem to exist for small farms. Second, there is no strong evidence that diseconomies of scale exist for large farms. Third, there is a fairly wide range of farm sizes where average cost is approximately constant [e.g., Kislev and Peterson (1996)]. This has focused some attention on the "minimum efficient" farm size, i.e., the smallest farm size that can capture the benefits of economies of scale. Knowing this minimum efficient size is particularly relevant for the evaluation of the efficiency of farm structure and land reform policy.

One problem is that there is no clear consensus on what the "minimum efficient" farm size is. For example, Hall and Leveen's (1978) analysis suggests that in California this minimum may be around 100 acres of land. But there is also evidence that small farms can be scale-efficient in developed countries [e.g., Garcia et al. (1982)] as well as in developing countries [e.g., Yotopoulos and Lau (1973), Kalirajan (1981)]. For example, Yotopoulos and Lau, and Kalirajan provide evidence that, in India, small farms (fewer than 10 acres) are at least as efficient as large farms. How can we reconcile these apparent inconsistencies?

First, farmers have the option of choosing among different technologies, each one adapted to particular farm sizes. The typical situation is that, for a given technology, average cost tends to decrease with size, up to some capacity beyond which average cost increases. As farm size increases, a switch can take place from one technology to another better adapted to larger sizes (e.g., through capital investment and mechanization), so that the region of decreasing returns to scale is often not observed. Also, the minimum average cost of each technology may be fairly constant across technologies. This implies that the lower-bound envelope of the minimum average cost across technologies (the "long-run average cost" function) is rather flat. This is illustrated by Matulich (1978), in the context of studying the relationship between average cost and herd size in U.S. dairy farms. This suggests that, while increasing returns to scale may well be present for a given technology, the situation of constant returns to scale may be approximately satisfied across technologies for a wide range of farm sizes. This would help explain why there is empirical evidence of increasing returns and constant returns to scale appearing to coexist in agriculture. Also, it helps explain why farm size can vary over such a wide range, both within a country and across countries. This indicates that, as long as farms have access to a technology adapted to their size, there may not be great efficiency gains from changing farm sizes or from land redistribution schemes. The land redistribution programs recently implemented in South Africa or in the former Soviet Union (FSU) have been motivated by both efficiency and equity concerns. This suggests that, provided that they can be implemented without adverse effects on farmers' access to markets or technology, land reform programs can improve wealth equity while maintaining or even enhancing (e.g., due to better incentives under decentralized management in the FSU) agricultural productivity. However, avoiding these adverse effects while redistributing land can be difficult. As a result, the success of land reform policies can vary significantly across countries [e.g., see Lerman (1999), for the recent FSU experience].

Second, the empirical estimation of returns to scale often depends on the measurement of cost. In agriculture, the measurement of the cost of family labor is problematic. Family labor is often valued at its opportunity cost [e.g., Hall and Leveen (1978)]. However, measuring precisely this opportunity cost may be difficult. Also, there are some questions about whether opportunity cost is the appropriate value of family labor. Microeconomic theory suggests that family labor has a "shadow value" which can depend on both its opportunity cost, and on household preferences with respect to time allocation. The latter becomes important when household farm work generates direct utility to the household (in a way similar to leisure in the neoclassical household model). For example, this would happen whenever family members enjoy working on the farm. In this case, the shadow price of family labor is equal to its opportunity cost [e.g., the wage rate in off-farm work), minus the unit value of "enjoying farm work". Note that the neoclassical agricultural household model [e.g., Singh et al. (1986), Benjamin (1992)] implicitly assumes that the shadow value of "enjoying farm work" is zero (farm work then being valued at its opportunity cost). However, there is empirical evidence against the hypothesis that "enjoying farm work" has zero value [see Lopez (1984), for Canadian agriculture]. This is true for "hobby" farms, where agricultural activities are also seen as "leisure" activities. It also seems to characterize a number of part-time farmers. These arguments suggest that, in general, the shadow value of family labor is not always equal to its opportunity cost. This is particularly relevant to the extent that, while many large commercial farms may approximately satisfy the assumptions of the neoclassical agricultural household model, "hobby" farmers and part-time farmers typically have small farms. This suggests that the valuation of family labor may in fact change with farm size: ceteris paribus, the shadow value of labor on some small farms may be lower than on larger farms because of the enjoyment of farm work by "hobby" farmers and some part-time farmers. This also means that the opportunity cost of labor is an upward-biased estimate of the shadow price of family labor on some small farms. In this case, finding high average production cost on small farms may simply reflect this measurement bias (rather than the existence of increasing returns to scale).

Besides technology, many other factors can also influence the choice and efficiency of farm size. They include transaction costs, market imperfections, access to markets, and pecuniary economies. In developing countries, access to markets may vary across farm sizes [e.g., credit rationing is more prevalent on small farms; see Binswanger et al. (1993)]. In general, pecuniary economies are said to exist when larger farms pay lower prices for their inputs (due to lower transaction cost and/or stronger bargaining power), thus lowering their average production cost. And for similar reasons, large farms may receive higher prices for their outputs. Then, pecuniary economies would give larger farms some economic advantage and provide an incentive for increased farm size. When paid by farmers, transaction costs are parts of the cost of production (e.g., monitoring costs, transportation costs, information costs). Also, they can contribute to higher input prices (when paid by farm input suppliers) and lower farm output prices (when paid by food traders and processors). In either case, they tend to reduce farm profitability. Some transaction costs may be higher on large farms (e.g., monitoring cost of hired labor), thus giving some cost advantage to smaller farms [e.g., Eswaran and Kotwal (1986), Binswanger et al. (1993)]. Alternatively, information costs about prices or technology may be higher on smaller farms, thus giving some economic advantage to larger farms and providing incentives to increase farm size. And, as it improves information processing in decision making, higher quality of human capital (e.g., due to education or experience) has been found to be positively related to farm size [Sumner and Leiby (1987)].

Also, tax policy can affect farm size and structure [e.g., Gardner and Pope (1978), Lowenberg and Boehlje (1986)]. Tax policy is often designed to stimulate capital investments (e.g., through investment tax credit or depreciation allowances that reduce taxable income). The associated reduction in taxes and increase in after-tax income is typically greater on capital-intensive farms. To the extent that capital-intensive farms tend to be larger, this means that tax policy can favor larger farms and thus provide an incentive for increasing farm size.

Finally, risk exposure can influence the size and structure of farms. This is relevant since risk markets are typically incomplete in agriculture, implying that most farmers face significant price risk (due to biological lags in the production process) as well as production risk (due to weather effects and pest problems). Being in general risk averse [e.g., Lin et al. (1974), Binswanger (1981), Newbery and Stiglitz (1981), Innes and Rausser (1989), Chavas and Holt (1996)], farmers are made worse off by being exposed to risk. In this context, a risk premium has been used as a measure of the implicit cost of private risk-bearing [Pratt (1964)]. Under some conditions, the average risk premium is expected to increase with farm size [Chavas (1993)]. This suggests that risk exposure gives some economic advantage to smaller farms and provides a disincentive for increasing farm size. Alternatively, larger farms may have access to better risk management strategies that can help reduce their risk exposure. These strategies include diversification strategies and the development of flexible plans that can deal better with unforeseen contingencies (e.g., by investing in forms of capital that have multiple uses). They also include financial and marketing strategies (e.g., hedging, contracts, access to capital and financial markets) that can redistribute risk toward agents who are better informed and/or have a better ability to bear risk. In general, it appears that larger farms are more likely to develop (compared to smaller farms) under conditions of reduced risk exposure and/or more refined risk management schemes.

In addition, there is significant uncertainty about product quality in agriculture. For example, pesticide contamination and biotechnology have raised consumer concerns about food safety. This has stimulated the use of contracts as a way to improve food quality. Also, it has increased the prospects for product differentiation and market segmentation in agricultural markets. For example, some farms have been able to capitalize on the growing demand for "organic" food. By using production techniques that are perceived by consumers to produce higher quality and safer products, they can sell their products at higher prices on differentiated markets. This requires establishing separate marketing channels, often a significant challenge. When feasible, this has allowed some small farms (that are typically more labor-intensive and less capital-intensive) to survive and prosper even while facing relatively high production costs.

Finally, compliance with environmental rules and regulations is increasingly important in agriculture. This is motivated by situations of pollution and externalities where farming has adverse impacts on the environment (e.g., nitrate contamination of groundwater). The associated costs can affect the choice of size and location of production units. These effects depend on the environmental externalities generated, the nature of the regulations, and the abatement technology available. In some cases, large farm operations may increase pollution problems by concentrating the pollutants in a few locations (e.g., as in livestock production). Then, environmental regulations would likely have a greater impact on large production units. This may favor smaller farms. Alternatively, it may be that larger farms have access to better abatement technology, which would improve their ability to manage agricultural externalities.

3.2. Economies of scope and diversification

Farms are typically multi-product firms. Most produce more than one output, either implementing crop rotation practices or using an integrated crop-livestock production system. Yet the extent of farm specialization varies both over time and across space. In general, there is a tendency for commercial farms to be more specialized than subsistence farms, with an overall trend toward increased specialization.

The fact that most farms are multi-product firms suggests that the benefits of diversification are significant in agriculture. These benefits take two forms: the presence of economies of scope reflecting the reduced cost associated with producing multiple outputs, and the risk-reducing effects of diversification.

Economies of scope in agricultural activities appear to be significant [e.g., Fernandez-Cornejo et al. (1992), Chavas and Aliber (1993)]. Crop rotations generate well-known benefits. They allow different crops to better exploit the fertility of the soil. For example, corn planted after soybean benefits from the soybean's ability to fix nitrogen. Also, crop rotations contribute to lowering pest populations, thus reducing the need for pesticides. Finally, integrated crop-livestock systems can involve forage production that helps improve land fertility and reduce soil erosion, while manure can ameliorate soil quality and increase crop yields.

As argued above, risk and risk aversion provide incentives for farmers to reduce their risk exposure. To the extent that different activities are influenced differently by weather conditions or pest problems, diversification can be an effective way of reducing farmers' risk exposure. There is empirical evidence that risk reduction is a significant motivation for farm diversification [e.g., Lin et al. (1974)].

Both economies of scope and the risk benefits associated with farm diversification suggest strong incentives for farms to be multi-product enterprises. But this does not explain the historical trend toward more specialized farms. Such a trend indicates that there are also significant benefits to specialization. Such benefits come mainly from improved productivity. Typically, a task is better performed by a specialist than by a general manager. For example, a veterinarian is expected to better manage animal health problems on a farm than a general farm manager. But specialized management may become profitable only on larger firms. Often, the benefits of specialization can be obtained only beyond some minimal scale of operation. This suggests the existence of an important trade-off between farm size and diversification. As farm size increases, the benefits of specialization and the associated enhanced productivity rise, which can counterbalance the benefits of diversification mentioned above. The net effect is that economies of scope tend to decline with farm size. This is supported by empirical evidence of a negative relationship between economies of scope in agriculture and farm size [e.g., Fernandez-Cornejo et al. (1992), Chavas and Aliber (1993)]. This provides an economic rationale for why larger farms tend to be more specialized than smaller farms, as the former are in a better position to capture the benefits of specialization. It also suggests that the trend toward more specialized farm production systems is in large part motivated by productivity improvements.

3.3. Technology and farm organization

Over the last century, agriculture has undergone two remarkable changes: rapid technological change (both in developing and developed countries), and significant reduction in farm labor (mostly in developed and newly industrialized countries). These two factors are not unrelated. First, technical progress was a necessary condition for the decrease in farm labor: without it, feeding the growing urban population would not have been possible. Second, the evolving labor market has had some feedback effects on the nature of technical change in agriculture.

Over the last few decades, productivity growth has been the principal factor responsible for economic growth of agriculture in developed countries [Capalbo and Antle (1988), Ball (1985), Ball et al. (1997)]. For example, over the last four decades, U.S. agriculture has seen an average increase in output of 1.9 percent a year, and an increase in productivity of 1.9 percent a year [Ball et al. (1997)]. This indicates that technical progress (i.e., significant improvements in land and labor productivity) contributed to most of the increase in farm output. Such remarkable results apply to most developed countries [see, e.g., OECD (1995)]. On average, productivity growth in agriculture has been larger than in many other sectors. For example, Jorgenson and Gollop (1992) found that the growth rate of U.S. agricultural productivity has been four times larger than the corresponding rate in the rest of the economy. This stresses the importance of agricultural technical change in developed countries. However, the extent and nature of agricultural productivity growth in developing countries has been less uniform. Over the last three decades, land productivity and labor productivity have increased significantly in most countries [Pardey et al. (1991), Craig et al. (1997)]. However, sub-Saharan Africa has seen stagnation in its agricultural labor productivity [Craig et al. (1997)].

In developed countries, the twentieth century has seen significant economic growth in the non-farm sector, which increased non-farm employment and raised urban wages. This created some disparity between farm and non-farm income and produced incentives for a large labor migration from farms to urban areas [Schultz (1945)]. It significantly reduced the amount of both family labor and hired labor in agriculture. The decrease in hired labor resulted in the typical farm being a family farm with little or no hired labor. And, given that total farmland has been fairly constant in most developed countries, the decrease in family labor has implied a rise in average farm size over time. This also stimulated the adoption of labor-saving technology in agriculture (e.g., mechanization), yielding large increases in farm labor productivity. It illustrates the existence of feedback effects of resource scarcity on technical change.

More generally, these feedback effects have been associated with the "induced innovation" hypothesis [Binswanger (1974), Hayami and Ruttan (1985)]. This hypothesis states that relative resource scarcity tends to guide technological change toward using additional inputs that are plentiful and inexpensive, while saving on scarce and expensive inputs. This is consistent with labor-saving technological change being stimulated by higher wages. This is also consistent with fertilizer-using technological change found in North American, European, and Asian agriculture in the 1960s and '70s [Binswanger (1974), Hayami and Ruttan (1985)].[3] It involved the development of high-yielding varieties (through genetic selection) of corn, wheat, and rice that were particularly responsive to nitrogen fertilizer. The incentive to develop and adopt these new varieties came in part from technological progress in the nitrogen fertilizer industry, which reduced the market price of nitrogen fertilizer. This combination of low-cost fertilizer with high-yielding varieties contributed to large crop yield improvements in developed agriculture, and to the success of the "green revolution" in developing countries.

Note that the period since the mid-1970s has seen higher prices for energy, fertilizers, and pesticides. There is empirical evidence suggesting that this period also saw some

---

[3] However, note that there is also empirical evidence suggesting some inconsistencies between the induced innovation hypothesis and technical change in agriculture [e.g., Chavas and Cox (1997a)]. This stresses the complexity of the process of technical change.

changes in U.S. agricultural technology toward becoming more "input-saving" for these inputs [Chavas and Cox (1997b)]. Again, being consistent with the induced innovation hypothesis, this illustrates that the nature of technical change appears to be sensitive to relative resource scarcity.

Over the last few decades, some agricultural technologies have been identified as contributing to pollution of the environment (e.g., groundwater pollution by nitrates) and degradation of the ecosystem (e.g., pesticide contamination). New technologies are currently being developed in an attempt to reduce these adverse effects of agriculture. They include the development of nitrogen-fixing corn and pest-resistant varieties. These emerging technologies offer new prospects to improve the current management of the ecosystem.

The process of technical change has been found to have large economic effects both within agriculture and within society [e.g., Griliches (1960), Schmitz and Seckler (1970), Huffman and Evenson (1993), OECD (1995)]. The current use of genetic engineering and biotechnology in both crop and animal production gives good prospects for continuing technical progress in agriculture. Typically, the adoption of a new technology is a slow diffusion process [e.g., Griliches (1957)]. At first, a few early adopters can benefit economically from the increased productivity it generates. Eventually, as a majority of producers adopt it, the new technology contributes to higher farm output and lower food prices. As a result, consumers gain significantly from technical progress. At the same time, the farms that are late adopters typically face difficult economic conditions: high production costs accompanied by lower food prices. This is Cochrane's (1958) "treadmill effect": in the presence of rapid technical progress, any farmer who does not quickly adopt new technology is threatened with declining profit. This puts considerable pressure on farm managers to remain informed about emerging technologies and their adaptation to local agro-climatic conditions. In general, the early adopters are likely to have good managerial skills. This means that technical change would tend to favor good managers. This "management bias" has important implications. For example, if specialization tends to be associated with superior management, then technical change would favor specialized production systems. This indicates that the distribution of the benefits from technical progress can vary greatly across firms within an industry.

Notably, most of the new agricultural technology did not originate from the farm. Rather, it typically came from some combinations of private and public institutions that made significant investments in agricultural research and development (R&D). Historically, the payoff from both private and public R&D investments in agriculture has been high. On average, their estimated rate of return has been in the range of 20 to 30 percent in the U.S. [e.g., Griliches (1960), Hayami and Ruttan (1985), Chavas and Cox (1992, 1997a), Huffman and Evenson (1993)]. For both private and public R&D, there is evidence of significant lags between the timing of investment and its effects on farm productivity, the lag varying between 10 and 30 years. The empirical evidence suggests that private R&D investments appear to generate their returns in the intermediate run (after about 8–15 years), while public R&D investments seem to pay off in the longer run (after 15–25 years) [e.g., Huffman and Evenson (1993), Chavas and Cox

(1992, 1997a)]. This is consistent with the 17-year legal patent protection, and the fact that private research tends to be more "applied". In contrast, public research tends to be more "basic", with longer-term and more uncertain payoff. However, the relative role of public versus private agricultural research is changing. In U.S. agriculture, investments in private research have increased faster than in public research. As a result, the share of public research has declined from 50 percent in 1981 to 45 percent in 1996 [Frisvold et al. (1998)]. This move toward the privatization of agricultural research is observed in many countries around the world [OECD (1995)]. With the current developments in biotechnology, it involves a redefinition of the relationships between private research and public research, as they promise to influence technical progress in agriculture in the twenty-first century.

It is worth emphasizing that the rate of technical progress has varied across industries and across regions. As discussed above, over the last few decades, most countries have exhibited large agricultural productivity growth [e.g., OECD (1995), Pardey et al. (1991), Craig et al. (1997)]. This is the main factor explaining the trend toward lower food prices. However, one significant concern relates to the current situation in Africa. Over the last three decades, sub-Saharan Africa has been in large part bypassed by the "green revolution". And current agricultural R&D investments indicate that it is not likely to benefit greatly from new biotechnology. This suggests that the prospects for large agricultural productivity growth in sub-Saharan Africa are not very good. This creates significant challenges to technology and economic development policies in this part of the world.

As discussed above, part of the increase in farm productivity over the last few decades has been associated with increased specialization. In many developed regions (e.g., Western Europe, U.S.A.), at the beginning of the twentieth century, most farm households were small and greatly diversified. Being strongly motivated by food self-sufficiency motives, they attempted to produce most of the household food consumption needs. This changed with the growth of agricultural markets, which facilitated the development of specialization in agriculture at the farm level, the regional level, as well as the national level. Greater specialization reduced the scope of activities and increased the need for market exchange for each farm and each region. It allowed farm managers to focus their skills on just a few enterprises, thus improving their production control and efficiency. It also allowed farm and food marketing firms to become better organized spatially, thus contributing to lower transportation and marketing costs. As a result, farms and regions evolved toward more specialized production systems that exploited their comparative advantage reflecting local agro-climatic conditions. As they became better integrated in the market economy, they received the benefits from market exchange and trade. This contributed to more efficient and more productive agriculture at the farm, regional, national, as well as world levels. This process is still in progress as regions and nations negotiate politically with each other over the distribution of the benefits from trade.

While the role of agricultural markets has for the most part been increasing over time, vertical coordination in some sectors has come to depend on contracts. This is particularly true for highly perishable products such as vegetables, where product quality and timing of economic decisions are closely linked. In those sectors, contractual relationships between producers and food processors typically exist, which stipulate the quality, quantity, and timing of production [Marion (1986)]. By improving product quality and timeliness, contracts can contribute to improving production and marketing efficiency in the food sector. Contractual relationships have also developed in some animal production. Starting in the 1950s, the broiler industry evolved quickly toward vertical integration. This was associated with production contracts, greater specialization, and rapid productivity gains [Lasley et al. (1988)]. A similar process is underway now in pork production, and to some extent in beef production.

Why is this move toward greater integration taking place in agriculture? At least three contributing factors have been proposed: efficiency gains, productivity gains, and the exercise of market power. First, efficiency gains would be obtained in the presence of economies of scope across the production systems being integrated. But, in his investigation of the U.S. pig sector, Azzam (1998) did not uncover evidence of vertical economies of scope between feeder-pig production and finishing. Second, it is often believed that integration can help stimulate productivity. The rapid productivity gains of the broiler industry under vertical integration is an illustrative example [Lasley et al. (1988)]. Third, the possible role of market power as a motivating force behind integration has generated both interest and concerns [e.g., Marion (1986), Azzam (1996), McCorriston et al. (1998)]. Azzam (1996) found some empirical support for the hypothesis that monopsony provided an (inefficient) incentive that contributed to the backward integration of the U.S. beef slaughter industry into the live cattle market.

In general, farmers approach their input and output markets as price takers. However, they can face marketing firms that are large and in a position to exercise market power. This raises questions about the effects of market concentration on the organization and performance of the food sector [Marion (1986), Huang and Sexton (1996), Cotterill (1997)]. Although a discussion of these issues is beyond the scope of this chapter, it seems appropriate here to mention the role of agricultural cooperatives. Cooperatives can be prevalent in particular sub-sectors (e.g., as in the case of the U.S. dairy sub-sector) [Marion (1986)]. Cooperatives can be interpreted as an institutional response to market imperfections. Often, a cooperative projects its member either forward or backward in a marketing channel. It can therefore accomplish many of the same purposes as vertical integration [Sexton (1986)]. Some of the motivations for cooperative formation include improving product quality and avoiding monopoly or monopsony situations [Marion (1986)]. In this context, cooperatives have an efficiency-enhancing role: they can help improve vertical coordination in the agricultural sector. Alternatively, cooperatives can be used as a means of increasing the bargaining power of farmers facing imperfectly competitive markets. When applied to agricultural marketing, cooperatives can generate significant price enhancements through their exercise of bargaining power. Under strong bargaining power, this would increase members' income, but can also lead to inefficient and non-competitive outcomes. However, under free entry, one may expect such inefficiencies to be unsustainable in the long term, unless some form of supply control is implemented.

4. Entry-exit decisions and resource mobility in agriculture

In our earlier discussion of economies of scale, we assumed free entry and exit, i.e., perfect resource mobility. We now examine the role of imperfect resource mobility in agriculture.

The typical family farm is heavily influenced by the life cycle of the farm household manager. Two phases of this life cycle are particularly important: the beginning of the cycle when a young manager decides to work on a farm; and the end of the cycle when an older manager decides to retire from farming. In between, with a few exceptions,[4] the continuation of the family farm is often not an issue. Thus, some of the most important decisions made by a farm household manager are long-term decisions that are not subject to frequent renegotiation. This suggests rather low mobility of farm labor in the short term. Similarly, land rights typically remain under the control of the same manager over extended periods of time. Finally, at least part of farm capital is usually "specialized", meaning that it has few alternative uses. An example is a milking parlor that cannot be moved easily and has no alternative use but the milking of cows. This indicates that agriculture is a sector characterized by restricted resource mobility, at least in the short run. In other words, the dynamic adjustments of land, capital, and agricultural labor tend to take place over many years [e.g., Schultz (1945), Brandow (1977)].

This reduced resource mobility can be traced in large part to special characteristics of agricultural production. Land and climate are specific to particular locations and cannot be moved. As a result, many agricultural adjustments involve spatial adjustments in other factors of production, in particular farm capital and farm labor. Yet agricultural investments in human and physical capital can also be location-specific. When there are significant costs of moving capital or labor over space, this generates a situation of "asset specificity" which affects the dynamic process of resource allocation in agriculture. This is the issue of "asset fixity" analyzed by Johnson and Quance (1972).

4.1. Capital mobility

A situation of asset fixity can be linked to the existence of sunk investment costs. An investment is sunk if the unit value of investment is higher than the unit value of disinvestment. This happens when the purchase price of capital is larger than its salvage value. For example, the salvage value of a milking parlor is typically close to zero, implying that the investment in a milking parlor is almost entirely sunk. The existence of

---

[4] A notable exception includes situations of foreclosure and bankruptcy, where large debt and severe financial stress can force the farm household manager out of agriculture.

sunk cost can be linked to transaction costs and/or market imperfections. In the case of a milking parlor, the lack of alternative uses and the high cost of moving are the main reason why its salvage value is so low. Sunk costs imply that an investment decision cannot be reversed costlessly. In general, there is an economic incentive for decision makers to avoid facing sunk costs. In situations of risk, this means that sunk costs provide an incentive to avoid reversing any decision, i.e., to keep capital in its current utilization. As analyzed by Dixit (1989), Chavas (1994), and Dixit and Pindyck (1994), this has three implications. First, under sunk costs, there is a zone of "asset fixity" where investments fail to respond to small changes in economic incentives [Johnson and Quance (1972)]. This can be interpreted as a "market failure", where changes in relative prices may not help guide the process of resource allocation at least in the short run. And it can lead to the segmentation of markets [e.g., Shiha and Chavas (1995)]. Second, asset fixity provides a disincentive to exit an activity. In the 1950s and 1960s, this generated a situation where agricultural resources were relatively slow to exit U.S. farming even in the face of persistently low return. Third, asset fixity interacts with uncertainty to provide a disincentive to invest. In other words, sunk costs and risk can create "barriers to entry". Vasavada and Chambers (1986) presented empirical evidence supporting a form of asset fixity and the presence of sluggish adjustments to price changes for labor and capital in U.S. agriculture. And the interaction of sunk costs and uncertainty can adversely affect market participation decisions and thus the functioning of markets [e.g., De Janvry et al. (1991), Goetz (1992)].

Advances in farm technology made capital highly productive and attracted capital into agriculture. In the longer term, capital investments have greatly stimulated labor productivity. High capital requirements have also made entry into farming more difficult. This has generated some concerns about the survival of the family farm [e.g., Gale (1993), Weiss (1998), Goetz and Debertin (1996), Allanson (1992)]. Weiss presents some Austrian evidence supporting an emerging bimodal structure of farm sizes: small part-time farmers and large farms surviving, with mid-size farms decreasing in relative number. The role of off-farm income in sustaining small farms has been documented [e.g., Hearn et al. (1996), Lianos and Parliarou (1986)]. It suggests that, in the absence of off-farm income, many prospective young farmers may find it economically unattractive to support a family on a mid-size farm. Finally, it is often suggested that government policies (e.g., government programs, tax policy) have contributed to increases in farm size [e.g., Lowenberg and Boehlje (1986), Goetz and Debertin (1996)]. There is evidence that the benefits from government farm programs are often not equitably distributed: the majority of the associated income transfers tend to go to large farms and relatively wealthy families [e.g., Sumner (1990)]. However, it is not clear how this affects the return per unit of land between small farms and large farms. Furthermore, distinguishing empirically between the effects of government policies and those of technical progress is difficult. As a result, the exact role of government policies in explaining the trend toward larger farms in developed countries remains somewhat unclear [e.g., Gardner and Pope (1978), Sumner (1990)].

4.2. Labor mobility

Individuals on farms have the option of choosing between farm work and non-farm employment. However, except when located near urban areas, choosing non-farm employment often requires moving to an urban area. As mentioned above, rural migration to cities has been an important aspect of structural change in agriculture through most of this century. Migration decisions depend on the nature of labor demand outside agriculture. For example, during the 1950s and 1960s, expanding industrial production created many urban job opportunities in developed countries. This was also a period when average household income was typically higher in urban areas. This stimulated rural migration. The persistence of this income gap over several decades points to "farm labor specificity". At least two factors contribute to this specificity: (1) investments in farm human capital are partially sunk whenever some farm skills have few alternative uses outside the farm sector; and (2) migration decisions involve significant information and transactions costs that are also sunk. This has generated a rather slow adjustment process in the farm labor market. However, over several decades, this process can still provide massive labor shifts across sectors (as observed in developed and newly industrialized countries).

In developed countries, the last two decades have seen most of the employment growth in the service sector. In the U.S., the income gap between farm versus urban households has been reduced (due in part to a leveling-off or a decline in real wages in urban areas). As a result, the income incentive to migrate from rural to urban areas is currently not as strong as it was in the 1950s or 1960s. This suggests that the decision to become a farmer versus working in the non-farm sector has become more complex over the last two decades. After decades of rural migrations to cities, the remaining active farm population is quite small. The fact that farm production increased in the face of such a sharp reduction in farm labor stresses the large labor productivity gains in agriculture. Given that in developed countries farming currently employs only a few percent of the active population, the prospects for important rural migration are now limited. As a result, there is a new focus on the role of non-agricultural activities in rural areas. Also, the concerns have shifted from exit issues to entry issues in agriculture [e.g., Gale (1993)]. What institutions are training and preparing the farmers of tomorrow? What is being done to reduce some of the adverse effects of risk and asset specificity in agriculture? With the rising importance of human capital, the structure of agriculture is slowly evolving toward units of production, stressing the role of technological and managerial skills.

4.3. Markets and trade

Over the last few decades, there has been a great increase in the role of agricultural markets in resource allocation. The 1980s and 1990s have seen an increased reliance on markets and a decreased role of government in agriculture. Structural adjustment policies advocated in the 1980s by the IMF and the World Bank have enhanced the role of agricultural markets in guiding the allocation of agricultural resources in many developing countries. Following decades of extensive involvement of government in the U.S. farm sector [e.g., Brandow (1977)], the Federal Agricultural Improvement and Reform (FAIR) Act of 1996 has set the stage for less government involvement in U.S. agriculture. And after decades of limited progress, GATT and WTO trade negotiations in the 1990s have contributed to reducing trade barriers in world agriculture.

The increased role of markets has been associated with increased resource mobility, especially for capital and finance. Over the last few decades, the international capital market has become very active, large, and fluid. It has significant implications for economic policy and trade. First, by arbitraging financial returns across countries, the international capital market has restricted the effectiveness of monetary policy conducted by any country. Second, exchange rates are now often more sensitive to international capital flows than they are to changes in the balance of trade. In this context, it is not clear that exchange rates always provide proper signals to evaluate the comparative advantage of production in a particular country. Also, the fluidity in the international capital market means a high volatility in exchange rates, which creates fluctuating import and export prices.

As discussed earlier, agricultural production faces significant price risk and production risk. Also, decrease in government involvement has contributed to increased price uncertainty for farmers. What can be done to reduce some of the adverse effects of sunk costs and risk? Good information about market conditions and superior technological and managerial skills seem crucial. Also, various risk management schemes are available. They can be interpreted as private and public safety nets designed to reduce exposure to downside risk. They include the use of insurance against production uncertainty, and of options and futures contracts to reduce price risk. But problems of asymmetric information (moral hazard and adverse selection) have hampered the development of insurance markets. Hedging using futures markets is an effective way to reduce the short-term effects of price risk. For example, traders commonly hedge on exchange rate futures to eliminate the price risk generated by fluctuating foreign currencies. However, the short maturity of most futures contracts means that their usefulness in managing long-term risk is limited. As a result, the use of futures and options markets cannot eliminate the adverse effects of price risk on long-term investments.

Various government schemes can also help. They include food aid to developing countries, price support programs that reduce the prospect of facing declining prices, government subsidy of insurance premium, and government disaster payments. All contribute to decreasing downside risk and thus reducing the negative effects of sunk costs and uncertainty on investment incentives. Finally, production and marketing contracts can also help when they redistribute risk and possibly mitigate the adverse influence of risk on resource allocation. However, the associated benefits may not be broadly shared since only the contracted parties receive them.

While new technologies are playing a significant role feeding a growing population, they are also raising new questions about food quality. This is illustrated by the current debate about "organic" food and bioengineered crops and livestock. The evaluation of food quality raises difficult issues both domestically and in international trade, espe-cially when consumer perceptions differ from scientific opinions. The problem is that there is no universal evaluation of what constitutes "safe" food. There is a concern that food produced from new technologies may have some long-term adverse effects on hu-man health (or on the environment), effects that are difficult to observe in the short term (e.g., the case of BST technology in the dairy sector). As a result, we are entering a new era where it is increasingly difficult to treat food items as standard products. This creates new opportunities for product differentiation in the food sector. It also gener-ates significant challenges for developing marketing systems that respond effectively to consumer demand.

It seems that we are slowly evolving toward a marketing system of differentiated food products. The role of government is to provide minimum standards of food safety to protect human health against well-documented hazards, and enforce them in both do-mestic and international markets. Beyond that, market niches are developing for "higher quality" products that command some price premium. Even in the absence of strong sci-entific evidence, some consumers are willing to pay a premium for food products they perceive to be "safer". With appropriate information (e.g., labeling), consumers are in a position to choose among products of differing quality based on their own evaluation of relative food safety. Contracts can play an important role in establishing quality and product differentiation (e.g., in the case of "organic" food). They work best when pro-ducers and consumers are in close geographic proximity. This provides new economic opportunities for some farms to develop direct marketing schemes to reach local con-sumers. To the extent that large farms may find it more difficult to differentiate their products, this may give some economic advantage to smaller farms. More generally, product differentiation will require establishing vertically integrated marketing systems providing quality control and appropriate labeling throughout the marketing channel. Developing such systems remains a formidable task, with significant implications for the future organization and structure of the food system.

For international trade, the challenges are even more significant. The temptation is al-ways strong to use food safety concerns to promote protectionism. Trade disputes over food quality will likely become more common. This involves the World Trade Organi-zation (WTO) as well as national courts. WTO deals with global rules of trade between nations, interpreting trade agreements and commitments, and trying to settle trade dis-putes generated by countries' trade policies. And national courts are involved in settling private as well as public trade disputes. In a world of differentiated products, there is a need for institutional innovations to safeguard and improve the efficiency of interna-tional transactions [Casella (1992)]. Traders need to have access to a dispute resolution process acceptable to merchants of different national backgrounds. Judges in national courts are often unfamiliar with the "usage of trade" and the technicalities of specific transactions. This has stimulated international arbitration schemes (e.g., the Interna-tional Chamber of Commerce in Paris). As a result, a body of law is developing through the published deliberations of arbitrators, deliberations taken as precedents in succes-sive decisions. This can facilitate the process toward further international integration.

5. Concluding remarks

Rapid technological progress and expanding trade have been major factors influencing agriculture. National food security policies were common among many nations in the 1950s and 1960s. It meant only limited competition for many farmers around the world and limited benefits from specialization. The current liberalization of agricultural markets throughout the world means that farmers now face stiffer competition and stronger incentives to specialize. This can be difficult for many farmers who face economic and financial hardship. But this also provides new opportunities for farms, regions, and nations to identify their comparative advantage, exploit it to remain competitive, and contribute to increasing world food supply. A key issue is the nature of resource mobility and its variations across farms, regions, and nations. The farms, regions, or nations that face lower resource mobility will likely see depressed farm income. Alternatively, the ones with human capital, technological and managerial skills, and higher resource mobility will prosper. The challenge is to develop private institutions and government policies that can assist in the evolving production structure and adjustment process in agriculture.

Acknowledgement

I would like to thank two anonymous referees for useful comments on an earlier draft of the paper.

References

Allanson, P. (1992), "Farm size structure in England and Wales 1939–89", Journal of Agricultural Economics 43:137–148.

Azzam, A.M. (1996), "Testing the monopsony-inefficiency incentive for backward integration", American Journal of Agricultural Economics 78:585–590.

Azzam, A.M. (1998), "Testing for vertical economies of scope: An example from US pig production", Journal of Agricultural Economics 49:427–433.

Ball, V.E. (1985), "Output, input and productivity measurement in US agriculture, 1948–79", American Journal of Agricultural Economics 61:475–486.

Ball, V.E., J.-C. Bureau, R. Nehring and A. Somwaru (1997), "Agricultural productivity revisited", American Journal of Agricultural Economics 79:1045–1063.

Baumol, W.J., J.C. Panzar and R.D. Willig (1982), Contestable Markets and the Theory of Industry Structure (Harcourt B.J., New York).

Benjamin, D. (1992), "Household composition, labor markets and labor demand: Testing for separation in agricultural household models", Econometrica 60:287–322.

Berry, A., and W. Cline (1979), Agrarian Structure and Productivity in Developing Agriculture (Johns Hopkins University Press, Baltimore).

Binswanger, H.P. (1974), "The measurement of technical change biases with many factors of production", American Economic Review 64:964–976.

Binswanger, H.P. (1981), "Attitudes toward risk: Theoretical implications of an experiment in rural India", Economic Journal 91, 867–890.

Binswanger, H.P., and K. Deininger (1997), "Explaining agricultural and agrarian policies in developing countries", Journal of Economic Literature 35:1958–2005.

Binswanger, H.P., K. Deininger and G. Feder (1993), "Agricultural land relations in the developing world", American Journal of Agricultural Economics 75:1242–1248.

Boserup, E. (1965), The Conditions of Agricultural Growth (Allen and Unwin, London).

Brandow, G.E. (1977), "Policy for commercial agriculture, 1945–71", in: L. Martin, ed., Survey of Agricultural Economics Literature (University of Minnesota Press, Minneapolis).

Capalbo, S.M., and J.M. Antle (1988), Agricultural Productivity: Measurement and Explanation (Resources for the Future, Washington, DC).

Casella, A. (1992), "On market integration and the development of institutions: The case of international commercial arbitrage", European Economic Review 40:583–591.

Chavas, J.-P. (1993), "The Ricardian rent and the allocation of land under uncertainty", European Review of Agricultural Economics 20:451–469.

Chavas, J.-P. (1994), "On production and investment decisions under sunk cost and temporal uncertainty", American Journal of Agricultural Economics 76:114–127.

Chavas, J.-P., and M. Aliber (1993), "An analysis of economic efficiency in agriculture: A nonparametric approach", Journal of Agricultural and Resource Economics 18:1–16.

Chavas, J.-P., and T.L. Cox (1992), "A nonparametric analysis of the influence of research on agricultural productivity", American Journal of Agricultural Economics 74:583–591.

Chavas, J.-P., and T.L. Cox (1997a), "An analysis of the source and nature of technical change: The case of U.S. agriculture", Review of Economics and Statistics 79:482–492.

Chavas, J.-P., and T.L. Cox (1997b), "Production analysis: A nonparametric time series application to U.S. agriculture", Journal of Agricultural Economics 48:330–348.

Chavas, J.-P., and M.T. Holt (1996), "Economic behavior under uncertainty: A joint analysis of risk preferences and technology", Review of Economic and Statistics 78:329–335.

Chavas, J.-P., R.D. Pope and H. Leathers (1988), "Competitive industry equilibrium under uncertainty and free entry", Economic Inquiry 26:331–344.

Cochrane, W.W. (1958), Farm Prices: Myth and Reality (University of Minnesota Press, Minneapolis).

Cotterill, R.W. (1997), "The food distribution system of the future: Convergence toward the US or UK model?", Agribusiness 13:123–135.

Craig, B.J., P.G. Pardey and J. Roseboom (1997), "International productivity patterns: Accounting for input quality, infrastructure and research", American Journal of Agricultural Economics 79:1064–1076.

De Janvry, A. (1981), The Agrarian Question and Reformism in Latin America (Johns Hopkins University Press, Baltimore).

De Janvry, A., M. Fafchamps and E. Sadoulet (1991), "Peasant household behavior with missing markets: Some paradoxes explained", Economic Journal 101:1400–1417.

Dixit, A.K. (1989), "Entry and exit decisions under uncertainty", Journal of Political Economy 97:620–637.

Dixit, A.K., and R.S. Pindyck (1994), Investment under Uncertainty (Princeton University Press, Princeton).

Eswaran, M., and A. Kotwal (1986), "Access to capital and agrarian production organization", Economic Journal 96:482–498.

Fernandez-Cornejo, J., C.M. Gempesaw II, J.G. Elterich and S.E. Stefanou (1992), "Dynamic measures of scope and scale economies: An application to German agriculture", American Journal of Agricultural Economics 74:329–342.

Frisvold, G., K. Fuglie and C. Klotz-Ingram (1998), "Growth of private agricultural research", Choices, Second Quarter.

Gale, H.F. (1993), "Why did the number of young farm entrants decline?", American Journal of Agricultural Economics 75:138–146.

Garcia, R., S.T. Sonka and M.S. Yoo (1982), "Farm size, tenure, and economic efficiency in a sample of Illinois grain farms", American Journal of Agricultural Economics 64:119–123.

Gardner, B.D., and R.D. Pope (1978), "How is scale and structure determined in agriculture?", American Journal of Agricultural Economics 60:295–302.

Goetz, S.J. (1992), "A selectivity model of household food marketing behavior in sub-Saharan Africa", American Journal of Agricultural Economics 74:444–452.

Goetz, S.J., and D.L. Debertin (1996), "Rural population decline in the 1980s: Impacts of farm structure and federal farm programs", American Journal of Agricultural Economics 78:517–529.

Griliches, Z. (1957), "Hybrid corn: An exploration in the economics of technical change", Econometrica 25:501–522.

Griliches, Z. (1960), "Research costs and social returns: Hybrid corn and related innovations", Journal of Political Economy 42:1411–1427.

Hall, B.F., and E.P. Leveen (1978), "Farm size and economic efficiency: The case of California", American Journal of Agricultural Economics 60:589–600.

Hayami, Y., and V.W. Ruttan (1985), Agricultural Development: An International Perspective (Johns Hopkins University Press, Baltimore).

Hearn, D.H., K.T. McNamara and L. Gunter (1996), "Local economic structure and off-farm labour earning of farm operators and spouses", Journal of Agricultural Economics 47:28–36.

Huang, S.-Y., and R.J. Sexton (1996), "Measuring returns to an innovation in an imperfectly competitive market: Application to mechanical harvesting of processing tomatoes in Taiwan", American Journal of Agricultural Economics 78:558–571.

Huffman, W.E., and R.E. Evenson (1993), Science for Agriculture: A Long Term Perspective (Iowa State University Press, Ames, IA).

Innes, R.D., and G.C. Rausser (1989), "Incomplete markets and government agricultural policy", American Journal of Agricultural Policy 71:915–931.

Johnson, G.L., and L.C. Quance (1972), The Overproduction Trap in U.S. Agriculture (Johns Hopkins University Press, Baltimore).

Jorgenson, D.W., and F.M. Gollop (1992), "Productivity growth in U.S. agriculture: A postwar perspective", American Journal of Agricultural Economics 74:745–750.

Kalirajan, K. (1981), "The economic efficiency of farmers growing high-yielding, irrigated rice in India", American Journal of Agricultural Economics 63:566–570.

Kislev, Y., and W. Peterson (1996), "Economies of scale in agriculture: a reexamination of the evidence", in: J.M. Antle and D.A. Sumner, eds., Papers in Honor of D. Gale Johnson (University of Chicago Press, Chicago).

Lasley, F.A., H.B. Jones Jr., E.H. Easterking and L.A. Christensen (1988), "The U.S. broiler industry", ERS Agr. Econ. Rep. No. 591 (USDA, Washington, DC).

Lerman, Z. (1999), "Land reform and farm restructuring: What has been accomplished to date?", American Economic Review 89:271–275.

Lianos, T.P., and D. Parliarou (1986), "Farm size structure in Greek agriculture", European Review of Agricultural Economics 13:233–248.

Lin, W., G.W. Dean and C.V. Moore (1974), "An empirical test of utility vs. profit maximization in agriculture production", American Journal of Agricultural Economics 56:497–508.

Lopez, R.E. (1984), "Estimating labor supply and production decisions of self-employed farm producers", European Economic Review 24:61–82.

Lowenberg, D.J., and M. Boehlje (1986), "The impact of farmland price changes on farm size and financial structure", American Journal of Agricultural Economics 68:838–848.

Marion, B.W. (1986), The Organization and Performance of the U.S. Food System (Lexington Books, Lexington, MA).

Matulich, S.C. (1978), "Efficiencies in large-scale dairying: Incentives for further structural change", American Journal of Agricultural Economics 60:642–646.

McCorriston, S., C.W. Morgan and A.J. Rayner (1998), "Processing technology, market power and price transmission", Journal of Agricultural Economics 49:185–201.

Newbery, D.M.G., and J.E. Stiglitz (1981), The Theory of Commodity Price Stabilization: A Study in the Economics of Risk (Clarendon Press, Oxford).

OECD (1995), Technological Change and Structural Adjustments in OECD Agriculture, Paris.

Pardey, P.G., J. Roseboom and J.R. Anderson (1991), Agricultural Research Policy (Cambridge University Press, New York).

Pratt, J. (1964), "Risk aversion in the small and in the large", Econometrica 32:122–136.

Rao, V., and T. Chotigeat (1981), "The inverse relationship between size of land holding and agricultural productivity", American Journal of Agricultural Economics 63:571–574.

Schmitz, A., and D. Seckler (1970), "Mechanized agriculture and social welfare: The case of the tomato harvester", American Journal of Agricultural Economics 52:569–577.

Schultz, T.W. (1945), Agriculture in an Unstable Economy (McGraw-Hill, New York).

Sexton, R.J. (1986), "The formation of cooperatives: A game-theoretic approach with implications for cooperative finance, decision making and stability", American Journal of Agricultural Economics 68:214–225.

Shiha, A., and J.-P. Chavas (1995), "Capital market segmentation and U.S. farm real estate pricing", American Journal of Agricultural Economics 77:397–407.

Singh, I., L. Squire and J. Strauss (1986), Agricultural Household Models: Extensions, Applications and Policy (Johns Hopkins University Press, Baltimore).

Sumner, D.A. (1990), "Targeting and the distribution of program benefits", in: K. Allen, ed., Agricultural Policy in a New Decade (Resources for the Future, Washington, DC).

Sumner, D.A., and J.D. Leiby (1987), "An econometric analysis of the effects of human capital on size and growth among dairy farms", American Journal of Agricultural Economics 9:465–470.

Strauss, J. (1986), "Does better nutrition raise farm productivity?", Journal of Political Economy 94:297–320.

Vasavada, U., and R.G. Chambers (1986), "Investment in U.S. agriculture", American Journal of Agricultural Economics 68:950–960.

Weiss, C.R. (1998), "Size, growth and survival in the Upper Austrian farm sector", Small Business Economics 10:305–312.

Yotopoulos, P.A., and L.J. Lau (1973), "A test of relative economic efficiency: Some further results", American Economic Review 63:214–223.

Chapter 6

LAND INSTITUTIONS AND LAND MARKETS

KLAUS DEININGER and GERSHON FEDER

World Bank, Washington, DC

Contents

Handbook of Agricultural Economics, Volume 1, Edited by B. Gardner and G. Rausser

Abstract

Assignment of land rights affects equity and efficiency, determining among other things households' ability to generate subsistence and income, their social and economic status, incentives to exert effort and make investments, and access to financial markets and consumption-smoothing mechanisms. The chapter discusses costs and benefits of the transition towards individualized land rights. It reviews how characteristics of the agricultural production process, credit access, portfolio risk, and transaction costs affect functioning of land sales and rental markets. Policy conclusions are drawn concerning the transition from communal to individualized land rights, award of formal titles, improved functioning of land sales and rental markets, and redistributive land reform.

JEL classification: Q15

1. Introduction

In agrarian societies land is not only the main means for generating a livelihood but often also for accumulating wealth and transferring it between generations. The way in which land rights are assigned therefore determines households' ability to produce their subsistence and generate marketable surplus, their social and economic status (and in many cases their collective identity), their incentive to exert non-observable effort and make investments, and in many cases also their ability to access financial markets or to arrange for smoothing of consumption and income.

Given this context, markets to exchange rights to land temporarily or permanently can provide a low-cost means to effect transactions that would bring this factor of production to its most productive use. The institutions governing the functioning of land markets will affect the transaction cost associated with such exchanges, the magnitude and distribution of the benefits generated by them, and the incentives for rational economic agents to undertake efficiency-enhancing transfers and land-improving investments. Furthermore, since land is one of the best collateral assets available, clear property rights and greater ease of their exchange are likely to affect the emergence and efficiency of financial markets. This implies that land markets have an essential role in the broader process of economic development.

In this chapter we first examine the way in which property rights in land evolve in an ideal and undistorted environment. We view the emergence of land rights as an endogenous response to increased scarcity of land and the associated incentives for land-related investment, and then discuss other factors – such as further increases in population density, better access to markets, or the introduction of improved technology to exploit the land – that would lead to increased productivity of agricultural cultivation, as well as endogenous technical change. We note that, historically, there have been few cases where such an uninterrupted evolution has been followed. We then briefly sketch the conditions required for as well as the deviations from this ideal path. With this in mind, we discuss factors affecting the costs and benefits of individualized land rights and examine empirical evidence for their magnitude. The implications of tenure security for investment incentives are highlighted.

Having clarified the concept of property rights in land, we turn to land sales and rental markets. We consider the main factors affecting participation in those markets, in particular characteristics of the agricultural production process, labor supervision cost, credit access, the risk characteristics of an individual's asset portfolio, and the transaction costs associated with market participation. These factors will affect land sales and rental markets differently; in particular, even if owner-operated farms are more productive than wage–labor-operated ones, the sales market will not necessarily shift land to them. This implies that, in environments where financial markets are imperfect, land market operation needs to be considered within a broader perspective focusing on access to other markets and the availability of alternative assets. We note that, in general, land rental markets would be less affected by these problems because renting out does not preclude the landlord from utilizing land as a collateral to access credit which could then be passed on to the tenant in an interlinked contract. Removing obstacles – often government regulations or imperfections in other markets – that prevent smooth functioning of land rental markets and taking measures that enhance potential tenants' endowments and bargaining power can considerably increase both the welfare of the poor and overall efficiency of resource allocation. There are also many instances where sales markets are regulated in a manner which hampers incentives for socially optimal behavior. In addition to reducing tenure insecurity, governments can in these situations improve the efficiency of resource use by avoiding interventions limiting rental and sales markets.

Finally, in a number of countries, a highly unequal land ownership distribution implies inefficient and inequitable resource use which the land sales or rental markets are not able to smoothly transform into a more efficient and equitable allocation. Based on these issues we draw policy conclusions concerning the transition from communal to individualized land rights and the award of titles, steps that might be used to improve the functioning of land sales and rental markets, and the scope for redistributive land reform.

2. Property rights in land

2.1. The emergence of land rights

The process of gradual individualization of property rights in land can be conceived as an induced institutional response to higher shadow prices of land to encourage longer-term investments in land, as in the pioneering analysis by Boserup.[1] At the earliest stages of development, even before the establishment of sedentary agriculture, tribes of hunters and gatherers assert control over certain locations where they collect food and engage in hunting. As population density increases, forest fallow systems, and then communal property right systems emerge. Under these arrangements, the general right to cultivation of a piece of land is an inseparable and in principle inalienable element of tribal membership. Cultivation rights are assigned to individuals on a temporary basis, normally as long as the cleared plot is cultivated. Once cultivation has ended (due to exhaustion of soil fertility), the plot falls back to the lineage and the family either selects a new plot (if land is abundant) or has a plot allocated by the chief of the tribe. The fact that land is held by the community or lineage rather than the individual facilitates periodic redistribution of at least part of the land among community members based on population growth, serving as a social safety net and preventing the emergence of a class of permanently landless individuals. Tenure security in a general sense is very high, i.e., individual members enjoy secure and inheritable general rights to cultivatable land which can be reactivated even after a period of absence.

---

[1] It is well understood that this idealized process has rarely been followed in actual history (Boserup herself devotes more than one chapter to the issue of coercion and the description of feudal systems). It is, nonetheless, useful to illustrate the main underlying factors.

As the relative scarcity of land increases, the pledging or intra-community rental of land emerges. This practice, whereby land that is not used can temporarily be pledged to another family, with the stipulation that it has to be returned upon request, facilitates the productive use of land in case the original owner is unable to undertake cultivation. It is distinctly different from permanent land transactions and is generally not allowed to involve people from outside the community.[2] It also does not uniformly apply to all land – unimproved land lying fallow at any given time continues to be at the free disposal of the community, for example, for grazing by domestic animals owned by any family with cultivation rights. Variations of such communal tenure systems, where parcels are re-allocated from time to time in order to accommodate population growth and grazing land is left for communal use, are common in many parts of the developing world, such as China, large parts of Africa, and Mexico.

What are the factors driving this process of successively increasing precision in the definition of property rights to land? The most frequent explanation is that a virtuous cycle of technical change and investment is set in motion by a combination of increasing population density, technical progress, commercial integration, and reduction of risk. Boserup was the first to point out the fact that, historically, higher population density was the driving force behind an endogenous process of better definition and enforcement of property rights, changing arrangements for the organization of production, and higher levels of investment.

The Boserupian framework of changes in the relative scarcity of land and the associated introduction of labor-saving technology can, for example, explain systematic changes in the strength of women's land rights [Platteau (1996)]. Under land abundance and predominance of shifting cultivation, agriculture tends to be female-dominated, polygyny is widespread, and women enjoy high status as workers as well as child-bearers. Marriage is accompanied by the transfer of bridewealth to the bride's family and, in case of the husband's death, women retain land rights either in their native or in their new village. With increased land scarcity and adoption of the plough, the importance of women in agricultural production tends to decline and bridewealth, as well as other customary safeguards to protect widowed and isolated women, disappears. Instead, women receive, upon marriage, pre-mortem inheritance, which – if it remains the property of the wife – establishes a threat point in intra-household bargaining and provides economic security in the case of divorce or death of the husband.

The diffusion of exogenous technical change and/or expansion of trade generally has an investment-increasing effect similar to the one caused by increased population density. By increasing the stream of incomes that can be derived from a unit of land, technical change and trade expansion increase incentives for better definition of property rights in land. Indeed, establishment of tree crops, and the associated heavy investment

---

[2] Indeed, the distinguishing characteristic of communal tenure systems is not a lack of general tenure security but the fact that property rights are not permanently linked to a specific plot, implying the existence of restrictions on the transferability of land rights (especially to individuals who are not members of the community).

in clearing and leveling of land, was generally undertaken only where institutional innovations had enhanced tenure security adequately so that individuals could be sure to reap the benefits from such investments. Similarly, the transportation revolution caused by the steamship in the late nineteenth century led not only to the incorporation of hitherto unexplored countries and states into global trade but also increased the demand for individualized ownership of land. For example the opening of Thailand to international rice trade through the Bowering treaty of 1826 induced a quantum increase in the demand for rice land in the Thailand plains, and brought about the introduction of a formal land registration system [Feeney (1988)].

Another important factor furthering the evolution of individual property rights to land is the reduction of risk to income and consumption. The three major avenues for this to come about are (i) the development of markets for output, capital, and insurance, (ii) technical progress that allows for diversification, reduction of the covariance of yields, and the probability of crop failure, and (iii) the emergence of access to non-covariate streams of off-farm income. It has long been noted that group ownership of land (or joint communal production) can be viewed as an "insurance policy" to eliminate the threat of permanent asset loss or to reduce vulnerability to idiosyncratic consumption shocks. However, the scope for using communal land ownership to insure against non-idiosyncratic shocks is limited by the weather-induced covariance of agricultural production. Especially when collective production on arable land is required to obtain these benefits,[3] households prefer individual ownership once alternative and less costly mechanisms to insure against covariate risks become available [see Key et al. (1998), for the case of Mexican farming communities].[4]

Because monitoring of effort in agricultural production is difficult and costly, collectives where individuals are not residual claimants to profits are highly inefficient forms of agricultural production [Deininger (1995)]. However, contrary to widespread misconceptions, communal tenure systems are generally *not* based on collective production. Instead, production on arable plots is normally undertaken by individuals who are residual claimants to output, implying that, on arable plots, incentives for effort supply by individual cultivators are likely to be appropriate. Inefficiencies may persist with regard to decisions concerning the use of communal areas such as forests and pasture, or the disincentive to invest, derived from the inability to claim ownership rights to specific plots. In an analysis of Mexican farming communities (ejidos), McCarthy et al. (1998) provide empirical evidence for the existence of collective action problems regarding the use of pasture and forest, but not of individually managed plots.

---

[3] Group ownership has often been prevalent where risk is high and where factors such as remoteness, environmental hazard, or presence of external enemies imply that superior insurance mechanisms are not available [Ellickson (1993)].

[4] The potential usefulness of communal land ownership as a device for consumption-smoothing is inversely related to the incidence of locally covariate climatic shocks. It is thus not surprising that, at comparable levels of population density, communal tenure systems have proven to be more durable in environments where such risks are lower.

Communal resource ownership is often motivated by the ability to provide benefits in the form of easier provision of public goods, arrangements to enhance equity, or the ability to take advantage of synergies that would be difficult to realize under fully individualized ownership. Examples include risk reduction through diversification in highly variable environments [Nugent and Sanchez (1993)], the utilization of economies of scale to break seasonal labor bottlenecks [Mearns (1996)], and investment in community-level infrastructure [Boserup (1965), Dong (1996)].[5] As long as effective means of governance and accountable institutions at the local level are available, these systems can be very effective – especially in situations where there is need for community-level investment. For example, under the medieval open field system, cultivation decisions were made collectively but monitoring-sensitive tasks were carried out on an individual basis. This allowed utilizing economies of scale in fencing, harvesting, shepherding, and risk diversification through strip-cropping without compromising the advantages of individual effort supply [McCloskey (1975, 1991), Townsend (1993), Blarel et al. (1992)].

The usufructuary rights given under communal tenure systems do not impose large losses as long as population density is low and land relatively abundant, payoffs for making long-term investments is low, and definition of individual property rights in land is costly. However, even though individuals have the right to cultivate specific plots (a measure that avoids the efficiency losses due to collective production), the lack of permanent rights that is implied by the periodic redistribution of plots may decrease incentives to make long-term land-related investments under communal arrangements. A similar effect comes through the limitation of land transfers to members of the community and the inability to utilize land as a collateral for credit.

Improved access to markets, infrastructure, and financial intermediation are alternative ways to provide the benefits – in terms of insurance, diversification, and access to funds for investment – associated with communal forms of land ownership. At the same time these exogenous factors increase the costs – in terms of investment disincentives and foregone land transactions with outsiders – associated with traditional land ownership systems. This implies that, with economic development, the relative attractiveness of communal systems will decrease and, at some point, it would be economically rational for a community to allocate permanent and fully tradable ownership rights to individuals [see Wilson and Thompson (1993) for Mexico], completing the transition from a communal to an individualized tenure system.

However, instead of following a smooth evolution along the lines outlined above, the transition to individual property rights historically has in the large majority of cases been affected by exogenous interventions. As population growth increases the relative

---

[5] An interesting case to illustrate this is made by Ellickson (1993) who compares different settlements (Jamestown, Plymouth, Salt Lake City, and the Bermudas) to suggest that, while many frontier settlements started out with group ownership and production to utilize economies of scale in defense and other activities, the length of time during which group ownership is maintained can be related to the riskiness of the environment, the frequency of social interaction, and the hierarchy structure of decision-making.

scarcity of land, one observes a general increase in boundary conflicts and social ten-sion.[6] In the absence of strong and representative community-level institutions, this often leads to appropriation of property rights to the communal resources by power-ful individuals, and abuses of power and land-grabbing by local chiefs and headmen.[7] These phenomena are often seen as a major cause of environmental degradation and increased social tension and inequality that leaves out the poor and vulnerable.

History demonstrates that regions with potential for agricultural or non-agricultural exports were generally characterized by the appropriation of large tracts of land through imperialist, colonial, or other overlords who either replaced local chiefs and elders, or tried to co-opt them to enforce their rule. These changes undermined traditional tenure systems, the associated structures of accountability, and thus the institutional underpin-ning of the organic evolution of such systems [Downs and Reyna (1993), Feder and Noronha (1987)].[8] Furthermore, once they realized that access to labor rather than land was the most limiting factor, overlords generally introduced distortions in other markets to reduce the reservation utility of independent farmers and to assure a supply of labor for export production in mines or for the newly established estates. In addition to re-ducing the reservation utility that cultivators could obtain from independent cultivation, such restrictions have contributed to widespread rural poverty and retarded development of competitive markets in rural areas, often laying the basis for continued rural–urban dualism.

In more recent times, governments have, through implicit and explicit taxation, drained the rural sector of resources that could have fueled a process of increased market integration and technology development, while at the same time higher rates of popu-lation growth vastly increased the need for new technology and better infrastructure [Schiff and Valdés (1995)]. The associated lack of markets and technological opportu-nities has, in a number of cases, contributed to a situation akin to the "involution" that had earlier been diagnosed for Asian systems [Geertz (1968)], with far-reaching im-plications for the structure of resource ownership rights. For example in Rwanda, with very high population density (787 persons per km^2), traditional systems of land allo-cation have become defunct and fail to provide even the most basic services they were designed for [Andre and Platteau (1996)]. As traditional limitations on land sales have been discarded, speculative land purchases by individuals with access to non-covariate

---

[6] Zimmerman and Carter (1996a, 1996b) show that incorporating agent heterogeneity, risk, and subsistence constraints can facilitate a more differentiated assessment of the welfare impact and productivity impact of a given institutional innovation (e.g., the adoption of marketable land rights) on different groups of producers.

[7] For example, despite extremely low levels of population density in Zambia, almost 50 percent of small producers feel that their security of tenure is insufficient and are willing to pay (a mean amount of US $ 40) for getting secure ownership rights [Deininger et al. (1998)]. Low-cost means of increasing tenure security and reducing encroachment from outside through better accountability and issuance of community titles could possibly increase welfare and tenure security.

[8] This was independent of whether the intervention was associated with the elimination of traditional tenure systems in favor of individualized rights to the selected group, as in many parts of Central and Latin America, or the use of local chiefs and dignitaries as intermediaries for the central power, as in African countries.

off-farm income lead to a rapid disequalization of landholdings.[9] While costly land disputes consume productive energy, environmental degradation continues unabated and the return to an idealized notion of "communal property rights" is unlikely to be a feasible option. To judge, however, what alternative arrangements would be feasible, it is necessary to consider in more detail the costs and benefits associated with different tenurial arrangements.

Drawing together the evidence on costs and benefits associated with more secure and fuller property rights arrangements, three conclusions emerge. First, where population density is sufficiently high, increased tenure security – not necessarily equivalent to formal title – has an important impact on increased investment. Second, there is some evidence that a higher degree of transfer rights provides additional incentives for investments and for more efficient use of family labor. Finally, the ability to use land as collateral to increase access to medium- and long-term formal credit markets is of importance if foreclosure is feasible. Studies that compared the financial costs and economic benefits of titling programs suggest that high rates of return are possible but that, unless measures to reduce the transaction costs associated with administering credit to smallholders are undertaken, the benefits associated with titles may not accrue equally to all types of farmers.

2.2. Benefits and costs of individualized property rights

The main benefits from well-defined and secure individual property rights relate to (i) greater incentives for (and lower costs of) long-term resource conservation and the associated increased demand for investment; (ii) improving transferability (temporary or permanent) of land to cultivators who have the resources to make better use of it an issue that depends on the presence of economies of scale and the disincentives to rental; and (iii) the ability to use land as collateral in formal credit markets, a benefit that is more significant where formal title exists and land transactions are actually feasible. These benefits need to be weighed against two main types of costs: the administrative and logistical expense associated with definition of boundaries, enforcement of rights, and resolution of disputes among claimants, and the increased risk of losing a safety net provided by communal control of land.

2.2.1. Benefits from individual land rights

Improved tenure security brought about by individualized land rights will be associated with static and dynamic benefits. Even without having full long-term security of tenure, individual cultivation rights that entitle an individual to residual claimancy of profits

---

[9] It is of interest to note that about 65 percent of sales are classified as distress sales – the incidence of which is not restricted to the lowest landholding group – and an additional 17 percent of lands are sold to cover litigation expenses, often arising from land disputes.

generated on a plot mark the difference between collective and private forms of cultivation. The transition from collective to private cultivation has historically been associated with large increases in productivity, as for example in the case of China [McMillan et al. (1989), Lin (1992), Lin et al. (1994)]. However, equally important benefits from better-defined long-term property rights would come about in an intertemporal setting where higher security of tenure would increase the incentives for long-term investments, the incidence of productivity-enhancing transfers, and the supply of credit to make such investments. These aspects are elaborated upon below.

2.2.2. Tenure security

Conceptually, insecurity associated with the lack of well-defined property rights can be understood as a random probability of loss of future income due to conflicting challenges. Eliminating such a threat through informal institutions (customary tenure) or formal institutions (land titles) will clearly increase the subjective payoff from productivity-enhancing, long-term investments, and thus the owner's willingness to undertake them. While the theoretical expectation is straightforward and easily formalized [see, for example, Feder et al. (1986), Besley (1995)], the critical question, and much empirical debate, has focused on the magnitudes of such effects in different settings.

The analysis of different types of land rights in Africa is complicated by the need to take into account the potential endogeneity of investment [Besley (1995)]. The reason is that there may be certain types of investments – from marking of boundaries to planting of trees and hedges, and building of houses or sheds – that may be undertaken with the primary purpose of establishing implicit property rights to land rather than of increasing productivity [Brasselle et al. (1997)]. Depending on how such actions affect the probability of land loss and whether or not there are community rules to provide (partial) compensation for such investments when a plot reverts to the community, it is easy to construct scenarios where communal tenure systems may increase rather than decrease the amount of land-related investment undertaken [Sjaastad and Bromley (1997)].[10]

The key result from a number of studies that have investigated the investment-enhancing effect of tenure security is that, under formal as well as informal regimes, tenure security – as measured by the extent of rights possessed by the owner – significantly affects farmers' investment decisions. Especially where investments are labor-intensive but involve few cash outlays, the unambiguous conclusion is that higher levels

---

[10] Using comparative statics from a simple model it can be shown that communal as compared to individual tenure is more desirable from the individual's point of view as the discount rate increases; the productivity increase generated by investment is smaller compared to rent; the initial probability of eviction is low; and the probability of recovering investment even after eviction is high. A combination of these factors may cause individuals under indigenous tenure to commit resources to land improvement beyond what would be the case under individual resource ownership.

of tenure security – even if they are not associated with high levels of transferability and are defined only at an informal level – do indeed provide an important incentive for increased investment.[11]

Evidence from one of three study areas in Ghana indicates that greater tenure security at the plot level significantly increases the probability that individuals will plant trees and undertake a wide range of other investments such as draining, irrigating, and mulching [Besley (1995)]. The fact that field-specific rights but not mean household rights can be shown to be significant suggests that plot-level tenure security, rather than credit supply effects accruing to the household as a whole, is likely to be at the root of this relationship between tenure security and investment.

Results from China confirm the importance of tenure security for investment. Comparing plots planted with the same crop within the same household but under different tenure regimes, it is found that farmers tend to apply more manure and labor, and to obtain significantly higher yields, on plots that are privately owned and therefore more secure [Rozelle et al. (1996)]. This is the case even though the possible impact of greater tenure security on crop choice (e.g., shifting to orchards instead of growing maize) is not accounted for. Similarly, Yao (1996) finds that higher levels of tenure security in Chinese villages have a strong and very significant investment-enhancing impact (e.g., application of green manure).[12] Analysis of the impact of higher tenure security through land titling in the Brazilian Amazon yields similar results [Alston et al. (1995, 1996)] and there is considerable amount of more anecdotal evidence on a positive association between availability of title and farm output or investment [see Binswanger et al. (1995) for references].

On the other hand, in Niger, a more land-abundant setting, different degrees of tenure security between plots with full private ownership and plots held under usufruct do not give rise to statistically significant differences in application of manure, a medium-term yield-improving investment [Gavian and Fafchamps (1996)]. In this context, farmers apply significantly lower amounts of manure on rented as compared to owned plots, but there is no significant difference between parcels held under full private ownership and those held under "traditional" usufruct. The conclusion is that apparently tenure security on the latter is high enough for farmers to expect to be able to reap the benefits from their (medium-term) investment. At a more general level, it indicates that, in order to determine whether specific property rights arrangements are conducive to higher levels

---

[11] This does not necessarily imply that actions to increase tenure security are warranted or even needed [Platteau (1996)].

[12] At first glance this would seem to be at variance with the finding by Feder et al. (1992) where, for a similar sample from four Chinese provinces, neither short-term nor long-term tenure security (captured by farmers' perception about the possibility that their land may be reallocated before the expiration of the current 15-year contract) had any perceivable impact on investment. One can reconcile the two findings by noting that Feder et al.'s study considers non-attached investment (machinery, livestock, and construction) which should be made independently of individual plots' tenure security and affected more by access to working capital (which indeed emerged as an important determinant of investment).

of investment, more detailed study is necessary and generalizations are unlikely to be helpful. What is instead required is a more differentiated judgment that takes account of the time horizon of the investment, the opportunity cost of the resources used, and the size and distribution over time of the expected payoff associated with the investment.

2.2.3. Transferability

Land markets tend to be highly localized. As a consequence, the ability to transfer land between users may be of limited importance in early stages of development when there is little heterogeneity of skills across the population and non-agricultural opportunities are limited. However, the importance and value of being able to transfer use or ownership rights to land increase with economic development, specialization, and better development of other markets. In this case, the transfer of land from those who have lower productivity to those who are able to make more productive use of the land improves the overall resource allocation. The demand for such exchanges increases further as the rural economy becomes more integrated geographically, facilitating transactions between individuals who are not members of the same community. Such situations generally involve larger problems of asymmetric information and greater benefits from more formal systems of land ownership recording. If the ability to liquidate investments (through land transfers) increases the incentive to undertake such investments, higher levels of transfer rights, and the greater ability to affect transfers which is entailed in formal land rights systems, will not only improve resource allocation but will also be associated with higher levels of investment and labor use by individual cultivators.

The only data that allow testing of this hypothesis come from China, where one observes variability in systems of transfer rights in different communities [Carter and Yao (1998)]. Results suggest that higher levels of transfer rights increase investment (e.g., application of green manure). In addition, evidence from China indicates that higher levels of transfer rights also induce a better allocation of the household's labor endowments in response to, for example, outside employment opportunities. Households with higher levels of transfer rights apply less labor on their farm and devote more time to more remunerative off-farm activities [Yao (1996)], thereby contributing to equalization of factor ratios within a village and increasing overall efficiency. More indirect support for an important efficiency-increasing (but not investment-enhancing) impact of higher transfer rights is provided by Rozelle et al. (1996), who find that an increase in off-farm opportunities narrowed the difference between labor spent on (transferable) private and (non-transferable) communal plots.[13]

---

[13] Evidence is not uniform: for Ghana, the hypothesis that sales and rental rights do not have a significant impact on investment decisions can not be rejected [Besley (1995)]. This suggests that the prospect of being able to transfer land more easily through sales and rental markets in the future is, in this environment, not an important consideration in individuals' decision to effect land-related investment.

2.2.4. Credit access

In addition to inducing investment, secure land ownership is likely to increase the supply of credit from the formal credit system to undertake such investment. The reason
is that, because of its immobility and virtual indestructibility, land with secure, clearly
defined, and easily transferable ownership rights is an ideal collateral. The provision of
a collateral – facilitated by possession of formal land title – is generally a necessary
condition for participation in formal credit markets for medium- and long-term credit.
In fact, there is evidence of titles facilitating access to informal (but impersonal) credit
markets as well [Siamwalla et al. (1990)]. Existence of well-documented and transferable property rights and of institutional arrangements to facilitate the low-cost transfer
of land is likely to make an important contribution to the development of financial markets.

However, while use of titled land as collateral can, under the condition that foreclosure is feasible, reduce a bank's default risk and thereby enhance credit supply, it
will have little impact on the transaction costs associated with administering credit to
small producers in rural areas. In environments where these costs are high, the improved
creditworthiness brought about by possession of land title may therefore not be enough
to facilitate access to formal credit by small farmers. Unless complementary measures
to reduce transaction costs and ensure access to credit by this group are undertaken
alongside with individualized property rights through titling, the benefits from titling
programs may accrue only to medium and large landowners.

The importance of the credit supply effect associated with provision of land title is
supported by evidence from Feder et al.'s (1986) study in Thailand, where farmers'
opinions and econometric evidence point towards improved credit supply as the main
benefit from titling. Land ownership titles induced higher investment in farming capital
(attached investments and other capital);[14] titled land had significantly higher market
values and higher productivity per unit. In three of the four provinces covered, households' credit supply had been significantly enhanced by the availability of title. By contrast, and in line with the above, title was found to have little impact on either investment
or farm income where formal credit markets were not available [Atwood (1990), Carter
and Wiebe (1990), Migot-Adholla et al. (1991), Pinckney and Kimuyu (1994)].[15]

Additional evidence from a study based on panel data from Paraguay indicates that
titling had a positive income or productivity-enhancing effect through credit market benefits for at least some groups of farmers. Due to a strong impact of formal title on both

[14] Problems of endogeneity and self-selection are circumvented by drawing samples from squatter villages
in areas nominally under public ownership (where titles could not be awarded) and private areas where all
residents already had obtained titles.

[15] Pender and Kerr (1996) show that for India land ownership has little impact on credit supply, a fact that
is attributed to severe non-price rationing. Nonetheless, land values for titled land are on average about 15
percent higher than for untitled land, suggesting that possession of formal title reduces the probability of land
loss for potential buyers.

credit supply and investment demand, the benefits from title are relatively large (about 10 percent of farm income), and significantly higher than the cost of titling. However, the impact of awarding titles was strongly size-differentiated. Estimates indicate that producers with fewer than 20 hectares remained rationed out of the credit market and therefore did not benefit at all from the credit-supply effect of title [Carter and Olinto (1996)].

This differential impact suggests that, in environments where other markets (such as credit markets) entail distortions which put smaller and poorer farmers at a disadvantage, individual property rights on equity, and – in the medium to longer term – on the direction and nature of land transfers between different size classes of producers, could imply greater inequity. Whether, in the presence of heterogeneity in endowments, small producers will benefit from such policies depends critically on the ability to reduce, together with titling, transaction costs and policy-induced distortions that limit access to credit markets.

2.2.5. Costs

The most obvious cost associated with formal definition of property rights in land is the expenditure needed to physically demarcate and delineate plots, to establish and maintain accurate records of land ownership, and to enforce these rights and resolve whatever disputes might arise.[16] These costs are borne by individual land owners in situations (for example, frontier settlement) where public enforcement of property rights is absent and individuals make defensive investments such as guards, fences, and other demarcation devices to demonstrate the legitimacy of their claims to property and to defend such rights against possible intruders [Mueller (1997)]. It has been shown that the privately "optimal" amount of spending by individuals on means of protection will be inefficient from a social point of view [Feder and Feeney (1991), De Meza and Gould (1992)]. Furthermore, the defensive activities undertaken often have little social value and may generate negative externalities, an issue that has been emphasized with respect to the Brazilian Amazon where the need to demonstrate "productive" land use to establish ownership claims has been linked to increased deforestation [Binswanger and Elgin (1988), Southgate et al. (1991)]. Even where they are not associated with externalities, defensive activities that are often undertaken in speculative attempts to secure "ownership" of large tracts of land can lead to complete dissipation of the rents to be had [Allen (1991)].[17]

Given the undesirable impacts of private rights enforcement, public provision – in the form of land records, police, and a judiciary – would therefore be preferable in all

---

[16] Note that the number of disputes is itself endogenous, depending on the type of property rights system chosen.

[17] Spontaneous collective action to limit the dissipation of resource rents associated with individualized defense of property rights has been observed in a number of cases where group sizes were small [Umbeck (1977)].

situations except ones characterized by very low levels of population density [Malik and Schwab (1991)]. This is indeed observed throughout human history. The specific form in which land records are established will still depend on the relative costs and benefits from such an activity – something that depends partially on the technology and infrastructure available for record keeping.[18] At initial stages of human development, assignments of property rights appear to have been handled orally by the community (with community functionaries holding public sessions at the gate, for example).

However, the benefits from keeping written records seem to have been so great that, across a large number of cultures, officially validated land records were among the first documents to appear once a written language was developed. In addition to establishing unambiguous ownership rights, written records allow verification of ownership status of land at low cost, thus reducing the scope for asymmetric information about ownership and quality of land, and making land sales and rentals cheaper to implement. [19] This reduction of transaction costs increases the liquidity of the land market and can bring the number of efficiency-enhancing transactions closer to the optimum, i.e., helping to transfer more land from less productive to more productive individuals.

A second type of social cost associated with fully individualized property rights relates to the fact that, at low levels of development, communal land ownership may perform an important insurance function that would be eliminated by establishing fully individualized property rights in land.[20] Furthermore, it has long been known that in cases where other markets are highly incomplete, land sales markets may not automatically transfer land to more productive users. In such situations, individualization of land rights could be doubly disadvantageous [see Platteau (1996) for references]. On the one hand it could pave the way for the emergence of sales markets that deprive traditional communities of their source of livelihood (often without adequate compensation), thus generating social unrest and violence and eliminating an important form of insurance. On the other hand, where land rights are introduced in such an environment, productivity will not necessarily increase, as availability of land rights could induce concentration

---

[18] Ellickson (1993) notes that historically the establishment of formal land rights is closely related to the emergence and widespread use of written language; in many cultures records of land transactions were among the first texts to be officially recorded.

[19] See, for example, the Indian Arthsastra from the fourth century B.C., as well as references in the Bible relating to the period 600 B.C.

[20] Jodha (1990) provides evidence on the importance of access to the commons as a safety net for the poor. Based on panel data from China, Burgess (1997) finds that the equitable allocation of land use rights under communal tenure has an effect similar to a lump sum transfer that provides insurance against low nutritional outcomes in a way that is more incentive–compatible than an *ex post* redistribution. The fact that land ownership has a more significant impact on improving nutrition than on income can be explained by the fact that, with imperfect rural grain markets, considerable cash outlays would be required to achieve a similar effect through market purchases of grain. The presence of equity benefits from periodic redistribution of land rights in China would be consistent with peasants' strong support for the system of periodic redistribution [Kung (1995)].

of landholdings by a privileged minority of wealthy individuals who – for example by having access to non-covariate sources of income – are in a position to accumulate land for speculative purposes without making productive use of this asset.[21]

Historical evidence indeed suggests that, especially in situations where other markets are not well developed or where policy-induced distortions affect the functioning of land markets, increased transferability of land may deprive the poor of an important social safety net. The importance of the insurance aspect is confirmed by the fact that, even where societies have made the transition to individualized land rights, they have often maintained land-related social safety nets to provide insurance for the poor. One example of a mechanism to do so is to allow continuing uses of communal pastures and forest areas of low productive value as well as a universal right to collect leftovers after the harvest or to graze animals on harvested fields. Another example is the provision for periodic redistribution of at least part of the land available to the community.[22] Such redistribution of cultivation rights could decrease productive efficiency by attenuating incentive to make plot-specific investments. The fact that societies have been willing to incur these efficiency losses suggests that the subjective valuation of the benefits in terms of avoiding widespread landlessness, social destitution, and discontent, has been high. This implies that where land is an important asset for poor and marginal groups, both social and efficiency aspects associated with land rights need to be accounted for in assessing the potential benefits from individualizing land tenure arrangements.

3. Land markets: Functioning and efficiency implications

If there are differences in individuals' skills and endowments of different factors of production, markets should help in optimizing factor proportions employed and thus increase overall efficiency of resource allocation. This section aims to outline the main determinants that would affect participation in the land sales or the land rental market, and based on this to elaborate on links and differences between these two markets, in terms of their impact on equity and efficiency of resource allocation.

The productivity advantage of small farmers who rely predominantly on family labor rather than on less motivated hired workers who have to be supervised would imply that, in the absence of imperfections in other markets, a functioning land market should facilitate efficiency- and equity-enhancing transfers from large to small producers, or from ones with lower management skills to better operators. However, land sales transactions could be efficiency-decreasing if, for example due to policy-induced credit

---

[21] Note that this is historically well-founded, as the many examples in Binswanger et al. (1995) demonstrate.

[22] If incentive structures and enforcement mechanisms to ensure that such provisions are actually implemented at the local level are non-existent, the provision for regular redistribution can actually give way to arbitrary behavior and rent extraction by local leaders. For a theoretical and empirical discussion of these issues, see Turner et al. (1998).

market distortions, large owners' advantage in accessing credit would offset the productivity advantage of owner operators; or if, due to the inability to insure, significant land holdings are not part of poor people's optimal asset portfolio.[23] Thus, before actions to activate the land market are undertaken, careful empirical investigation of the functioning of financial markets and insurance mechanism, and possibly steps to improve their functioning, might be in order.

Even if imperfections in markets for credit and insurance reduce the scope for the land sales market to bring about improved land allocation through land transfers from large to small producers, such allocation should – in a frictionless world – be facilitated through the land rental market. One possibility would be an interlinked contract whereby the landlord uses the credit access provided by land ownership to provide the tenant with working capital as part of the rental contract. High transaction costs – part of them related to government regulation – reduce the extent of land rental transactions in a number of countries. Examining the implication of regulations in more detail would be of importance as removing unjustified interventions is likely to go a long way towards improving resource allocation in agricultural systems characterized by very unequal land distribution. Most rental markets in developing countries involve some form of share tenancy. While this arrangement does not lead to full efficiency, it is a second best solution given risk and imperfect capital markets. The sections below elaborate these points and review relevant evidence.

3.1. Key determinants of land market participation

The shadow price of land for different types of agents is determined by the agricultural production function, the households' inherent managerial ability, and by possible imperfections in labor, credit, and land markets that are common in rural areas. If credit and land rental markets were perfect, the supervision costs associated with the use of hired labor would make smaller farms more productive, and would lead households to lease in or lease out the amount of land required to maintain a uniform ratio of family labor endowment to operated area, irrespective of the land ownership distribution [Feder (1985)]. However, imperfections in other markets may change this, with implications for the functioning of land rental and sales markets. For example, in the presence of credit market imperfections, if supply of working capital depends on the amount of land owned, the optimal size of the operational holding will vary systematically with size of the owned holding even if land rental markets were perfect. While the magnitude (and direction) of this effect would depend on the elasticity of output with respect to effective labor and of labor effort with respect to supervision, it can overwhelm the productivity advantage of family farmers and give rise to a positive relationship between

---

[23] Indeed, there is descriptive evidence indicating that in environments with imperfect credit market access, e.g., in Africa, land sales markets result in an efficiency-reducing transfer of land from small to large producers [Collier (1989)].

owned farm size and productivity. In addition to this, capital and insurance market imperfections may also affect the production activities of poor producers – possibly leading them to pursue less risky but also less productive activities. Below we review the factors which affect the productivity of farmers, and thus determine their demand for land.

3.1.1. Economies of scale

The presence or absence of economies of scale would systematically affect the shadow price of land for different farm-size classes. Possible economies of scale could arise from the presence of indivisible factors of production or cost elements leading to an initial range of farm size where the average cost of production declines with farm size. In cases where other markets function reasonably well, optimal farm sizes tend not to exceed the scale at which family labor is fully occupied (utilizing seasonal hired labor for specific tasks).[24] There are few agricultural activities in which significant economies of scale in the production process exist.[25] Some economies of scale are associated with the processing and marketing of many agricultural products, but this does not have important implications for the unit cost of farming operations as long as competitive markets for outputs and inputs exist. Alternatively, access to such markets is sometimes arranged through cooperatives. Only for a few "plantation crops" such as sugarcane, bananas, or tea could the need for immediate large-scale processing or marketing transmit economies of scale from the processing stage to production. To reap the economies of scale associated with the former, production of these crops is generally organized on a scale that corresponds to the optimum scale of the processing factory.[26]

3.1.2. Labor supervision cost

Constant returns to scale would imply that the size of agricultural operations has little impact on productivity. However, the need to supervise hired labor would confer a productivity advantage on owner-operated farm units. The fundamental reason for this is the presence of agency costs [Jensen and Meckling (1976)], which result from the need to manage wage labor and enforce effort in large-scale operations. The lack of incentives for wage workers to exert effort, and the consequent need to supervise labor or to offer incentive contracts, has received considerable attention in industrial

---

[24] A large number of empirical studies [e.g., Olson-Lanjouw (1995) for India, Feder et al. (1989) and Burgess (1997) for China, Olinto (1995) for Paraguay] are indeed unable to reject the hypothesis of constant returns to scale in agricultural production.

[25] Exceptions are limited to cases of highly specialized machinery, specialized livestock production, or plantation crops where economies of scale are transmitted from the marketing to the production stage.

[26] However, the supervision advantages of owner–operators have in many cases motivated large processors to contract production out to smallholders under outgrower or contract farming schemes, often providing credit in kind as well as technical assistance [Glover (1990)].

organization literature [Jensen and Meckling (1976)], and is recognized to have profound implications for the organization of production and for the optimal size of the firm [Calvo and Wellisz (1978), Eswaran and Kotwal (1985a, 1985b)]. The cost of supervision is particularly large in agricultural production due to spatial dispersion of the production process and the need to constantly adjust to micro-variations of the natural environment. Family members are residual claimants to profits and thus have higher incentives to provide effort than hired labor.[27] They share in farm risk, and can be employed without incurring hiring or search costs. These attributes underlie the general superiority of family farming over large-scale wage operations, manifested empirically in an inverse relationship between farm size and productivity. A large number of studies based on aggregate, or cross-sectional, and panel data have confirmed the existence of the inverse farm-size productivity relationship for all but the smallest farm size classes [Berry and Cline (1979), Carter (1984), Benjamin (1995), Newell et al. (1997), Kutcher and Scandizzo (1981), Olinto (1995), Burgess (1998), Udry (1997)].[28] Thus, unless there are other countervailing forces, one would expect land markets to transfer land from large to small producers. We turn now to a discussion of these countervailing effects.

3.1.3. Credit market access

A reason for observing few land market transfers from large to small producers is that it is difficult for small farmers to obtain credit and insurance.[29] This has two implications. On the one hand, credit market imperfections that increase the shadow price of credit for small producers would reduce small farmers' competitiveness in the land sales market, possibly outweighing the supervision cost advantage they enjoy. Also, if there are individuals with non-agricultural income who value land for other than productive reasons, land prices will exceed the net present value of agricultural profits, making it difficult to acquire land in the sales market with the expectation of paying off the debt from agricultural profits alone without recourse to equity.

Asymmetric information and moral hazard lead generally to quantity rationing in credit markets [Stiglitz and Weiss (1981)]. Formal credit markets can overcome the problem of asymmetric information by utilizing a collateral requirement. However, the costs of and political impediments to foreclosure on smallholders' land are often quite significant. This is part of the generally high transaction costs associated with providing credit to small producers. In informal credit markets, close familiarity and social control

---

[27] Empirical evidence confirms that family labor is more productive than hired labor, and that the intensity of supervision by family members affects the performance of hired labor [Frisvold (1994)].

[28] Bhalla and Roy (1988) and Benjamin (1992) have shown that cross-section analyses [e.g., Berry and Cline (1979), Carter (1984), Newell et al. (1997), Kutcher and Scandizzo (1981)] tend to overestimate the productivity advantage of smaller farms if soil quality is not specifically accounted for.

[29] Due to the covariance of production risks, crop insurance is very difficult to obtain and forward markets to insure against price risk are often unavailable to small producers due to high transaction costs.

is used to select promising clients or projects. This is quite costly as the scope for effective supervision is limited. Furthermore, informal lenders have only limited scope to diversify covariate risks, and they typically do not provide much long-term credit. Interest rates on informal loans are thus high. Thus, both limited availability of credit and high cost of borrowing would prevent those who do not have accumulated savings from acquiring land. [30]

Credit market imperfections can thus offset small farmers' supervision cost advantage. For the case of Sudan, for example, yields for virtually all crops are lower for poor (small) farmers and higher for rich (large) farmers, thus turning the farm-size productivity relationship upside down. Furthermore, the land rental market leads to land transfers from poor and labor-abundant smallholders to rich and relatively labor-scarce households [Kevane (1996)]. The reason is that capital market imperfections combined with reasonably functioning land and labor markets and a technology that is not supervision-intensive make it more attractive for small credit-constrained households to rent out land and work for a wage than to engage in owner-cultivation without capital inputs. By contrast, in panel data from Burkina Faso an inverse farm size-productivity relationship was observed even though a positive presence of correlation between yields and cash inflows from non-agricultural employment suggests the presence of capital market imperfections [Udry (1996)]. The conclusion is that imperfections in land, labor, credit, and insurance markets have to be analyzed together. Efforts at land redistribution that do not simultaneously address credit market imperfections may be costly and ineffective.

3.1.4. Portfolio composition

Small producers' inability to access formal markets for credit and insurance often forces them to adopt costly insurance substitutes, one of which is the adjustment of crop and asset portfolios to a low return-low risk combination.[31] In order to ensure satisfaction of a minimum subsistence requirement during periods of distress, credit-constrained producers could hold a portfolio of less risky but also less productive assets than that of unconstrained producers. In particular, smallholders may demonstrate a lower demand for land than that which would seem to be justified by their potential productive advantage. Zimmerman and Carter (1996b) use parameters from Burkina Faso to show that, starting from an egalitarian distribution of land, production risk together with covariance of land prices leads to successive concentration of land via sales from more productive small producers to relatively less productive large farmers. This illustrates

---

[30] The difficulty of land acquisition through borrowing by would-be smallholders, in spite of their productivity advantage, has been highlighted by Binswanger and Elgin (1988) and Carter and Mesbah (1993). Furthermore, they point out that by exhausting access to credit for land acquisition, the ability to borrow for working capital is eliminated.

[31] Examples are provided by Rosenzweig and Wolpin (1993), Dercon (1996), Dercon and Krishnan (1996), and Rosenzweig and Binswanger (1993).

that improving the functioning of land sales markets will not necessarily lead to better resource allocation if other markets' distortions are not tackled.[32]

3.1.5. Transaction costs

A further factor that might prevent land markets from achieving a first-best allocation is the transaction cost associated specifically with land sales. It has often been observed [see, for example, Balcazar (1990), Carter and Zegarra (1995)] that, especially in countries with a dualistic distribution of land ownership, land *sales* markets are highly segmented in the sense that, despite a considerable frequency of land transactions within farm size groups, land sales across farm-size class-boundaries are virtually absent. One explanation is that transaction costs of subdividing large farms to many smallholders are high. Similarly, the fact that certain costs (e.g., formal registration) associated with land transactions are independent of the size of the purchase creates indivisibilities that would either discourage small land transactions or drive them into informality where such costs are not incurred.

While the discussion of costs associated with land *rentals* in the literature is less extensive, government regulations appear to have reduced the amount of land leasing below what would take place otherwise. Even in countries that avoided the imposition of explicit restrictions on tenancy (which, as discussed below, were associated with significant efficiency losses), the threat of expropriative land reform in many countries implied that renting out land to more productive smaller producers exposed the landlord to a considerable risk of losing ownership rights in the course of land reform. To prevent this from happening, many landlords appear to have evicted tenants altogether, resorting instead to mechanization, cattle ranching, or cultivation using a hired labor force [De Janvry and Sadoulet (1989)]. The implications for land rentals, although they have not been rigorously quantified in any of the cases, appear to have been considerable.

3.2. Land sales markets

The discussion of the previous section implies that non-agricultural uses of land as well as credit market imperfections tend to drive the equilibrium price of land above the capitalized value of the income stream from agricultural profits. This would imply that fully mortgage-based land acquisition by the poor will not be possible. In addition, policy distortions will tend to increase the wedge between the price of land and the capitalized value of the income from agricultural production. Use of land as an inflation hedge, as

---

[32] The fact that study of land markets cannot be divorced from the functioning of other markets has been emphasized by Basu (1986) in a model of "interim" land transactions that explicitly serve as a credit substitute. In this context, the supply of land for sale would increase with the probability of being able to buy back the land, the attractiveness of other (financial) assets as compared to land, and the need for liquidity. Sengupta (1997) draws out the implications of limited liability on contract choice within a more general set of contractual options.

well as credit subsidies and tax advantages that allow the use of agricultural activities as a tax shelter, are examples [Gunjal et al. (1996), Brandao and de Rezende (1992), Just and Miranowski (1989), Feldstein (1980)]. To the degree that such distortions confer disproportionate benefits to larger landholders (as in the case of tax advantages, which are generally of no relevance to the poor), this would further bias the operation of the land sales market against redistributing land to landless or marginal landowning house-holds who could have a productivity advantage as family farmers.

Analysis of land market transactions and offer and asking prices in Paraguay indicates the presence of a large gap between willingness to sell and willingness to pay,[33] signif-icant differences in such prices across farm sizes, and very distinct regional patterns of land market performance depending on whether or not other markets exist and how well they function.[34] A similar conclusion is implied by the observation that the degree to which financial markets were accessible to small producers was (together with the initial distribution of assets and the characteristics of the production system) one of the key factors that determined the response of land accumulation patterns to agro-export booms in Guatemala and Chile [Carter and Barham (1996)].

Exposure to undiversifiable residual risk causes farmers to resort to liquidation of their assets during periods of severe crisis, a phenomenon commonly referred to as dis-tress sales. This implies that the covariance of weather risks for the farming population causes land prices to be low (due to insignificant effective demand and high supply) during bad crop years, with the consequence that individuals who had to sell off land during crises may not be able to repurchase land during subsequent periods of recovery [Bidinger et al. (1991)]. Distress sales have not only played a major role historically in shaping more concentrated land ownership patterns, but are also linked in the literature to the elimination of traditional mechanisms for coping with risk [Kranton and Swamy (1997), Brockett (1990)].[35]

The link between unmitigated production risk and distress sales is highlighted by Cain (1981) who examines the implications of different insurance mechanisms on dis-tress sales and the land ownership distribution between 1960 to 1980 for predominantly agricultural villages in India and Bangladesh. These villages faced very high production risks but were characterized by distinct differences in mechanisms of risk insurance: In Maharashtra, India, an employment guarantee scheme operated throughout the period

---

[33] Willingness to sell was significantly higher than was willingness to pay to purchase land, but the gap decreased with farm size (from 50 percent for the smallest farms, to 20 percent for medium-sized units). This could be an indication of labor market imperfections, i.e., the value given to land as a source for self-employment, in addition to small farmers' unwillingness to be bought out.

[34] In Paraguay, land markets function reasonably well in traditionally settled zones in the country's interior, but not at the frontier where the labor cost advantage of family farms appears to be overshadowed by capital market imperfections [Carter and Zegarra (1996)]. This suggests that the productivity advantage of small farmers would manifest itself in the land purchase market only if land market reform were combined with improved access to capital markets.

[35] Distress sales have been important in China [Shih (1992)], in early Japan [Takekoshi (1967)], in the Indian Punjab [Hamid (1983)], and in Latin America following the abolition of communal tenure [Brockett (1990)].

and attained participation rates of up to 97 percent of all households during disasters. Such schemes were absent after the major flood episodes in Bangladesh. Thus, 60 percent of land sales in Bangladesh were undertaken to obtain food and medicine, undoubtedly due at least in part to the lack of other insurance mechanisms. About 60 percent of the currently landless lost their land since 1960, and the Gini coefficient of landownership distribution increased from 0.6 to almost 0.7. This contrasts sharply with the Indian villages, where land sales to finance consumption expenditures accounted for only 14 percent of sales and were incurred mainly by the rich to meet social obligations. On the other hand, 64 percent of land sales were undertaken in order to generate capital for productive investment (digging of wells, purchase of pump sets, and children's education), and the land sales market actually contributed to a slight equalization of the land-ownership distribution. This suggests that in this case the poor were able not only to avoid distress sales, but were able, through access to cash-generating employment, to acquire some land as rich households liquidated agricultural assets to be able to pursue non-agricultural investment. Survey data on land transactions from India indicate that purchases of land are almost all undertaken by individuals with access to sources of income which are not correlated with agricultural production, and that borrowing to finance agricultural land acquisition is virtually non-existent [Sarap (1990)].

3.3. Land rental markets

As the discussion above illustrates, land sales markets will not necessarily lead to an optimal allocation of land in the presence of credit and insurance market imperfections. However, improved resource allocation can be achieved through land tenancy contracts even when other markets are incomplete. Analysis shows clearly that land rental markets serve an important function in equalizing returns to non-tradable factors of production such as family labor and bullocks [Skoufias (1991)].[36] Given the huge diversity of tenancy arrangements, we need first to explain the wide range of tenancy contracts that is empirically observed in developing countries. This gives rise to the second issue, namely, the implications of these contracts for the efficiency of resource allocation.

Assume a constant returns to scale production function $Q = \theta F(e, h)$, where Q is output, e is effort, h is number of tenants, and θ is a stochastic element. Then the range of contracts can be summarized as follows. The landlord's income is $y = h[(1 - \alpha)Q - \beta]$, and the representative tenant's income is $Y = \alpha Q + \beta$. The fixed rent contract is given by $\{\alpha = 1, \beta < 0\}$, the pure wage contract is represented

---

[36] Land rental transactions to circumvent imperfections in credit markets have been important in West Africa in the past [Robertson (1982)], and continue to be observed in a number of developing countries where credit markets are absent or credit is highly rationed. Usufruct mortgage is still reported to be common in Bangladesh [Cain (1981)], Java [Morooka and Hayami (1989)], and Thailand [Fujimoto (1988)]. In the Philippines, tenancy transactions emerged as a credit substitute in response to limitations on the transferability of land [Nagarajan et al. (1991)].

by $\{\alpha = 0, \beta > 0\}$; and the share contract is given by $\{0 < \alpha < 1\}$, with the sign and magnitude of β a function of the landlord's choice of α and the tenant's reservation utility level [Otsuka et al. (1992)].

Under conditions of certainty and the assumption that tenants' effort can be monitored and enforced, the specific choice of contract type does not matter as all contracts lead to equivalent outcomes [Cheung (1969)]. If the assumption of perfect effort enforceability is dropped, and agents are assumed to be risk neutral, only the fixed rent contract is optimal. The reason is that in all other cases tenants receive only a fraction of their marginal product, something that would induce them to exert less than the optimal amount of effort (where the marginal disutility is equal to the full marginal benefit from this action). Any type of contract other than fixed rent would result in undersupply of effort by the producer (tenant or worker), which would lower total production.

Indeed, fixed-rent tenancy is widespread in all developed countries, such as the U.S. and Canada, where about one-third of the agricultural land is cultivated by tenants. The fact that virtually all of this land is rented under fixed-term contracts suggests that such an arrangement would be a relatively efficient way of achieving optimal operational holding sizes in economies with well-functioning credit, risk, and labor markets. However, where markets for credit and insurance are highly incomplete and where the rural landless class is large, as is the case in most developing countries, adoption of a fixed rent contract where rent is paid up-front (i.e., independent of the output from production) may not be feasible or optimal from the perspective of all parties to the transaction.

In such a situation, two main reasons, risk-sharing and limited tenant wealth, could mitigate against adoption of the fixed rent contract and in favor of a sharecropping contract.[37] Although it would reduce the incentive to exert effort, a share contract provides the possibility of partly insuring a risk-averse tenant against fluctuations in output. Where, in risky environments, a risk-averse tenant faces significant uninsured risk, a share contract may well provide the tenant with higher expected utility and thus be adopted despite the lower aggregate productivity involved. In fact, it can be shown that in this case, the Pareto optimal outcome will always require a trade-off between the risk-reducing properties of the fixed-wage contract, under which the tenant's residual risk is zero, and the incentive effects of the fixed-rent contract, which would result in optimal effort supply but no insurance [Otsuka et al. (1992)]. Given risk aversion and incomplete intertemporal markets, a one-period contract is a second-best solution. Part of this shortcoming can be eliminated by state-contingent side payments in the context of a repeated game.[38]

---

[37] There is a third rationale for adoption of the share contract, namely that imperfect information on tenants' unobservable characteristics, such as ability, causes landlords to use sharecropping contracts as a screening device where the tenants' acceptance of certain types of contracts provides a signal for their productive ability [Newbery and Stiglitz (1979)]. Data from India indicate that landlords observe tenants' ability quite well [Olson-Lanjouw (1995)], suggesting that such signaling may not be the main reason for the adoption of sharecropping.

[38] Sadoulet et al. (1997, 1994) observe that close kinship relations provide sufficient assurance to landlords to provide implicit insurance to their tenants, thereby avoiding the inefficiency of the share contract.

Limited tenant wealth increases the landlord's risk when a fixed-rent contract does not involve a front-end payment. In case of a disaster (such as a bad climatic shock), tenants with insufficient wealth are likely to default on the rent payment, implying that landlords will tend to enter into fixed-rent contracts only with tenants who are wealthy enough to pay the rent under all possible output realizations. If tenants are poor, it will be optimal for the landlord to choose a share, rather than a fixed-rent contract [Shetty (1988)]. In a one-period game this would imply that landlords would rank tenants by wealth, choosing to enter into contracts only with the wealthiest tenants. Empirical evidence reported by Quibria and Rashid (1984) confirms such behavior. By implication, the efficiency of any particular tenancy contract is increasing in tenant wealth, and the overall efficiency of the tenancy market would depend on the initial wealth distribution of potential tenants, generating a direct mapping between the distribution of wealth and economic efficiency [Bardhan et al. (1997)]. In a repeated game, landlords would allow all but the least wealthy tenants to earn positive profits in equilibrium, thus using the threat of contract termination (or eviction) as a device to elicit effort supply.

An extension of this argument is provided by Mookherjee (1997), who shows that in the context of bargaining on the terms of an interlinked tenancy contract between landlord and tenant, the efficiency of the contract – i.e., the amount of effort exerted – will always be higher under operator-ownership of the land than under a tenant-landlord relationship.[39] This would imply that redistribution of land from the landlord to the tenant – or any other measure (e.g., increased off-farm opportunities) that would increase the tenant's reservation utility – would be associated with an increase in aggregate productivity. Still, while such a redistribution could increase the aggregate utility of both parties (thus making compensation of the landlord a theoretical possibility), a voluntary market-based transfer of land from the landlord to the farmer is not feasible. The intuition is simple – since a credit-based land purchase does not enhance the tenants' wealth, the limited liability constraint will still be applicable and the debt overhang incurred by the cultivator to purchase the land will reduce the incentive to apply effort instead of just defaulting on the loan. However, a non-market transfer of land from landlords to farmers could be associated with an increase in overall productivity as well as aggregate welfare.

Insights on the relationship between liquid assets and contractual parameters are provided by Laffont and Matoussi (1995) in a study of Tunisian sharecroppers. Their results suggest that differences in the contracting parties' working capital endowments can account for the coexistence of a variety of contracts, even in the same environment and among parties with similar risk aversion characteristics.[40] The positive relationship

---

[39] The scope for other benefits from a more egalitarian distribution of land ownership that are not directly related to agricultural productivity is illustrated by Banerjee et al. (1997).

[40] If risk were a major factor in choosing the optimal type of contract, one would observe significant variation in crop shares according to the riskiness of the crops grown on particular plots. This, however, is not observed empirically.

between the crop share and the tenant's working capital endowment that would be predicted by theory, even with perfect monitoring of effort, is indeed confirmed by the data. Output is shown to increase significantly with tenants' wealth for all contract types as well as for share contracts, but tenant wealth has no effect if only fixed rent contracts are considered. Similarly, the wealth of the landlord has, as expected, a negative effect on the tenant's share and a positive effect on production under the share contract, but none in other forms of contractual arrangements. Working capital thus appears to be a significant explanation of the type of contract chosen and the production gains achieved on a given plot.

The importance of potential tenants' asset endowment is also emphasized by evidence from India which indicates that, due to wealth constraints, a large number of potential tenants are actually rationed out of the tenancy market [Shaban (1991)]. In this context, both the smallest and the largest landholders rent their land to middle farmers who are neither capital-constrained nor suffering from the disadvantage associated with the need to supervise hired labor. This illustrates that the ability of the land rental market to bring about efficiency-enhancing transfers is constrained by potential tenants' endowment of assets and other means of production.

Thus, while land rental markets improve the allocation of resources in the presence of factor market distortions by bringing land to imperfectly or non-tradable factors of production (experience, family labor, animal power), the gains are constrained by endowments of potential transactors. In addition, there is evidence that fixed transaction costs preclude some poor households that desire only relatively minor adjustments from entering the tenancy market. Similarly, data from India suggest the prevalence of imperfect adjustment whereby, on average, farmers realize only about 75 percent of the desired level of land transactions [Skoufias (1995)]. The latter study also indicates that the adjustment effected by the land rental market is asymmetric for net in-renters and out-renters; consistent with the view that market power depends on relative scarcity of factors, in this environment of land scarcity, it is easier to rent out than to rent in.

What, then, is the magnitude of the productivity effects that are brought about by the operation of land rental markets? To obtain credible estimates of the loss due to the second-best nature of sharecropping, one needs to control for unobserved household specific fixed effects, e.g., by comparing input use, productivity, and investment, between sharecropped and owned (or cash-rented) plots for the same household. Bell (1977) was the first to conduct such an analysis in a static context, finding that farmers indeed exert less effort on tenanted plots. Applying the same methodology, Shaban (1987) found that, on average, tenancy was associated with a 32 percent lower output; but the difference was only 16 percent once adjustments were made for differences in land quality. Inputs of family labor and draft animals were significantly lower on sharecropped plots than on owned parcels. No statistically significant differences in productivity were found between owned plots and plots rented on a fixed-rent basis, confirming that fixed-rent contracts induce higher productivity. Other studies yield results that point in the same direction [Sen (1981)].

The productivity loss entailed in sharecropping can be reduced through close social relationships, as confirmed by Sadoulet et al. (1997). Their study compared the attributes of contracts with kin and non-kin, finding that non-kin sharecroppers use significantly fewer inputs and obtain less output. However, for sharecropping among close kin, there is neither a disincentive effect nor a reduction in output. This suggests that embedding contractual arrangements in a long-term personal relationship offers considerable potential to attenuate the disincentives and productivity losses that are otherwise associated with sharecropping contracts. This evidence is in line with the comprehensive review of the literature by Otsuka et al. (1992), who found a large number of studies about equally split between efficiency and inefficiency of sharecropping contracts. Studies that did not find a disincentive effect of sharecropping were generally conducted in environments where such a contract was embedded in enduring family and patron-client relationships or where effort was easily monitored.

Even within households, imperfections in land and labor markets, together with the inability to commit, may prevent individuals from achieving an optimal allocation of productive factors. For plot-level panel data from Burkina Faso, Udry (1995) finds that reallocation of factors from male- to female-controlled plots within the same household could increase output by 6 percent – less than half of the estimated output loss from imperfect allocation of productive factors at the village level (13 percent), but still significant. One interpretation is that, by "renting" out land to their husband, women would risk losing these rights. In the absence of other assets that could be transferred from the husband to the wife to provide assurance, they fail to do so, despite the productivity increases that doing so might entail.

All this implies that, although they cannot completely eliminate structural impediments and bring about a fully efficient allocation of land in an economy, land rental markets can go a long way in bringing the operational distribution of holdings closer to the optimum. However, in quite a few countries, the extent of land rental markets has been greatly diminished by large landowners' reluctance to engage tenants due to concern for potential challenges to their property rights. Furthermore, rental markets' potential to increase overall welfare was not well understood by governments. Consequently, the static productivity loss entailed in sharecropping tended to induce interventions that have limited the extent of rental transactions, thus causing a larger inefficiency in resource allocation. We turn now to discuss these and other policy issues related to land markets.

4. Policy issues

This section reviews the main policy implications of the earlier discussion, focusing on clarification and adjudication of property rights, ways to improve the functioning of land sales and rental markets, and redistributive land reform. These three steps form a rough sequence, in the sense that it is difficult to improve the functioning land sales or rental markets without clarification of land use and ownership rights, or to conduct non-expropriative land reform in an environment where land markets are absent. This implies that government activity should be focused on eliminating distortions and taking measures to reduce market imperfections rather than on attempting to compensate for imperfections and distortions in other markets.

4.1. Clarification and adjudication of property rights

A coherent system of property rights that guarantees security of tenure to cultivators, facilitates access to land by the poor, and encourages investment to increase sustainability and productivity can be of overriding policy importance in two types of settings. In countries making the transition from communal to more individualized forms of land ownership, it is important to have a flexible, stepwise, and decentralized approach that acknowledges differences in demand for tenure security based on diversity across regions and agro-climatic conditions. This requires a legal framework that permits evolution of land rights towards individualized tenure as the need emerges with commercialization and land scarcity. Second, in situations where land tenure arrangements have been severely disrupted by civil strife and war, collectivist land reform, or land-grabbing of influential individuals (e.g., Bolivia, Honduras, Nicaragua, Cuba, Vietnam, Ethiopia, Uganda, Tanzania, and the former Soviet Union), an approach that adjudicates among overlapping claims and establishes clear ownership rights to land at minimum cost is needed.

The evidence reviewed in preceding sections provides support for the view that secure land rights are necessary for longer-term investment nd the associated productivity increases. Land registration and titling systems are often perceived as an important element in policy seeking to promote tenure security and to facilitate more effective land markets. This is because official documentation provides better protection of an owner's property rights, and eliminates the asymmetric information that curtails land markets transactions. However, experience with titling programs indicates that in sparsely populated areas the cost of introducing formal titling systems may outweigh the benefits and that the administrative infrastructure needed to effectively implement such rights is not available. Similarly, formal documentation is not crucial where customary tenure systems provide sufficient security to facilitate the level of investments and land transactions that are relevant for the prevailing economic environment, and where credit markets are not yet developed to the point where collateral use is necessary.

Past interventions have often underestimated the cost and administrative requirements of providing tenure security through formal title and have given little thought to the scope for alternative means to provide such security. Community-based approaches whereby a whole area is demarcated and internal administration of land rights (including provision of documentation by local authorities) is left to the community may in many cases provide a cheaper alternative to formal titles [Platteau (1996)]. However, the critical precondition for such an approach to work is that consistent implementation of this arrangement is feasible, that decentralized institutions are account-

able and effective, and that the certificates awarded by such authorities are legally recognized, entailing a possibility of converting them into more formal titles at a later
stage.

The 1992 modification of the Mexican Constitution, and similar arrangements in a
number of other countries (e.g., Bolivia, Colombia, Côte d'Ivoire, and Nicaragua), allow indigenous and non-indigenous communities to administer property rights internally. In the case of Mexico this also includes communities' right to decide, subject
to established rules of accountability, on the partial or formal transformation of their
land rights into individual freehold title [Gordillo et al. (1997)]. In principle, such an
arrangement would allow the utilization of informational advantages available at the
community level in tailoring property rights to the specific situation at hand. However,
little is known about the transaction costs incurred and the degree to which outcomes
have been equitable and conducive to improved efficiency. Evaluation of these experiences within a consistent framework would be very desirable and could provide valuable insights to fine-tune the approach and make the experience useful for other countries.

The benefits associated with individuals' ability to use title to gain access to formal
credit have been discussed above. Experience indicates that titling programs are most
effective in areas where tenure insecurity already affects incentives, where there is an
incipient formal credit market where title can be used as a collateral because foreclosure
of collateral is enforceable, and where an effective legal system operates.[41] It is important to include safeguards against the grabbing of land (and in particular of hitherto
common land) by powerful and wealthy individuals, who are typically better informed
on the procedures entailed in more formal systems [Feder and Nishio (1996)].

Past experience also suggests that land titling should be systematic and area-based
rather than "on demand".[42] An area-based program with complete coverage can utilize
economies of scale in measurement, adjudication, and a speedy process for conflict resolution. This would reduce the cost of program implementation. Experience in Thailand,
El Salvador, Peru, and Bolivia, along with other countries, demonstrates that this can be
accomplished by introducing titling in combination with a mechanism for dispute resolution on location (within the community) and a comprehensive publicity campaign.[43]
In contrast, "on demand titling" is not only costly, but is often inequitable. It provides
opportunities for land-grabbing to individuals with good political connections and may
preclude poor smallholders from participation due to the high cost of land registration.

---

[41] The example of Kenya, where banks could not foreclose on the land that had been given to them as
collateral because of social and ethnic factors, illustrates that – even where there is a demand for formal credit
and the use of land as collateral – it is only the ability to effectively foreclose on defaulters that will persuade
banks to accept land as a collateral for loans [Ensminger (1988)].

[42] Given the fixed cost element entailed in "on demand" titling (which is based on individual initiative) and
the lack of economies of scale, this format of titling will tend to be more accessible to the wealthier landowner.

[43] This would be of particular importance in the case of Africa where resistance against titling is fueled more
by the fact that generally individualization of land tenure has been associated with extreme land-grabbing
by powerful individuals – much more than the activation of a land sales market that would disempower
smallholders [Bruce (1988)].

4.2. Improving the functioning of land sales and rental markets

Land taxation. A moderate land tax levied and collected by local governments has been advocated as a contribution to effective decentralization. There are two reasons why a land tax is theoretically attractive. On the one hand, taxation of land is one of the few cases of a lump-sum tax where, using asset rather than production values, the effective tax rate on income decreases with the income generated from the land, thus encouraging more productive resource use. On the other hand, a land tax is one of the few taxes that can provide revenues for the local governments, and that – through the capitalization of local amenities in land values – establishes a direct relationship between tax level and the benefits received by taxpayers [Glaeser (1995)].

Several countries have attempted to implement progressive land taxes, where the tax rate would increase with land area or value, as a means to make land speculation less attractive and to induce large landowners to use their land more intensively, or to break up large estates. Experience with this instrument has not been very positive, as implementation and collection of progressive land taxes have been frustrated by political difficulties and resistance in countries as diverse as Argentina, Bangladesh, Brazil, Colombia, and Jamaica [Strasma et al. (1987), Bird (1974)]. Carter and Mesbah (1993) use simulations to show that a progressive land tax by itself is unlikely to be effective even if it is enforceable. Effectively collecting a uniform land tax may be a more realistic goal. However, if environmental risk is high, introduction of a land tax (which has to be paid even if output is low) may not be desirable for equity reasons, and a mix of land tax and output tax (contingent on realized output) Pareto-dominates either tax in isolation [Hoff (1991)]. To avoid negative equity consequences that might be associated with a land tax, a number of developing countries exempt small producers below a certain size from the need to pay land taxes.

Land sales markets. The fear of the undesirable consequences associated with land market operation in an environment characterized by market imperfections seems to have in the past motivated policymakers to impose restrictions on the operation of such markets. Administrative restrictions on land sales, however, have often been costly to enforce and ineffective in preventing inequitable outcomes.

Administrative restrictions on land sales typically take the forms of limits on tradability of land and ownership ceilings. In many cases beneficiaries of land reform or settlers on state-owned land are not allowed to sell or mortgage their land. This deprives them of access to credit, often in the establishment phase when credit would be most needed. It has been shown that, in the presence of such restrictions, smallholders are forced to resort to less efficient arrangements (e.g., usufruct-mortgaging and the associated use of wage labor contracts) to gain access to credit [Hayami and Otsuka (1993)]. The goal of preventing land owners from selling out in response to temporary shocks would be better served by adequate safety nets, technical assistance, and access to complementary finance. Permanently precluding land reform beneficiaries from rental or sales is likely to reduce efficiency – all over the world such restrictions have resulted in large tracts of land being less than optimally utilized. Allowing for some adjustments in response to differential settler ability may be preferable to the losses imposed by this measure.

Another restriction intended to facilitate the breakup of large farms and the associated sales of land to small producers has been the imposition of land ownership ceilings, often together with land taxes. In addition to being largely ineffective,[44] such restrictions appear to have imposed extra cost on all parties. Landowners often took measures to avoid them, and the bureaucracy had to decide on exceptions to allow for the utilization of economies of scale in plantation crops – a process conducive to red tape and corruption. Even in the most favorable case such ceilings would constitute a temporary second-best measure to allow government to deal with the problem in a more thorough way. In many cases the reason for land concentration is not in a relative inefficiency of small farms but rather imperfections and policy-induced distortions in product and financial markets and the limitations on small farmers' ability to self-insure. If this is the case, it would be more effective for government to focus on the root of the problem, e.g., by designing safety nets and helping improve the functioning of other markets, rather than trying to deal with the symptoms. The interpretation that dis-equalization of land ownership is driven by imperfections in other markets is supported by the fact that in Central Uganda, in an area with good non-farm employment opportunities and well-functioning factor markets, land *sales* markets contributed to a pronounced equalization of land ownership [Baland et al. (1999)].[45] This implies that concerns about potential adverse equity impacts of land sales should be addressed by helping small farmers to compete, taking measures to improve the functioning of financial markets, and providing relief to avoid distress sales in cases of disaster.

Land rental markets.   For a number of reasons, and especially in the presence of other market imperfections that would affect land prices, land rental markets may be more effective than sales markets in moving the distribution of operational holdings closer to the optimum. Rather than recognizing the potential of land rental markets to improve agricultural productivity and augment the welfare of landless poor people, governments have often focused efforts on restricting tenancy markets through bans on share tenancy and limits on cash rental fees.

Such measures had very undesirable equity consequences in Latin America where they resulted in tenant evictions and the resumption of large-scale mechanized farming. Even in India, the country where tenancy reforms are generally believed to have had success, benefits to the poor have been limited. Tenant evictions associated with the threat of tenancy reforms caused the rural poor to lose access to about 30 percent of

---

[44] In India, for example, 35 years of implementing ceilings laws have, in all except three states, led to the distribution of less than one percent of the operated area to the target group [Appu (1996)].

[45] The lack of land rental market transactions in this environment may be attributable to relatively insecure ownership rights, which might lead the landowner to lose the land in case of rental.

the total operated area and, by threatening landowners who lease out with the loss of their land, undermined land access through rental markets [Appu (1996)]. If feasible, the transfer of property rights implicit in such tenancy protections should improve static efficiency, as is confirmed by district-level data from West Bengal. In this case, tenancy laws yielded productivity gains of about 40 percent – slightly larger than the static loss estimated by Shaban [Banerjee et al. (1998)]. However, even in this case tenancy reform required intensive bureaucratic involvement and often created overlapping property rights to the same plot, thereby undermining investment incentives and reducing the scope for land (rental and sales) markets after the reform.

Even in countries where tenancy reform has historically constituted a major policy instrument, there is now growing recognition that there is little scope for further tenancy reform and that, even in those cases where it is possible to implement, it provides at best a temporary measure that has to be complemented by market-based mechanisms in the longer term. Tenancy reform is not an option in countries where large-scale owner-cultivation or wage labor is the predominant mode of cultivation. In all of these cases, the critical issue is to reduce remaining obstacles to land transactions without jeopardizing equity objectives. Land rental markets would appear to provide an ideal instrument to achieve this objective.

4.3. Redistributive land reform

As discussed earlier, unmitigated operation of land markets alone would not necessarily produce an optimal land allocation. In the land sales market, credit constraints would restrict the ability of the poor to acquire land (or any other indivisible asset), a phenomenon that has, in a more general context, been shown to be associated with intergenerational persistence of poverty [Banerjee and Newman (1991)].[46] Transactions in the land rental market are easier to accomplish, but may be associated with a more limited impact on investment and productivity as well as tenant welfare. Efficiency-enhancing rental transactions might not come about either because of high transaction costs (especially in an unclear legal environment) or because of government restrictions that threaten rented properties with expropriation. In situations characterized by pervasive inequality in the ownership distribution of land or assets more generally, government involvement in redistributive land reform, aiming to improve efficiency and equity and at the same time remove impediments to the functioning of factor markets, could be justified.

However, historically the experience with government-initiated land reform policies has been mixed, not only because reforms involving significant asset transfers are politically difficult and could be speedily implemented only where they were imposed by

---

[46] This idea has been formalized in theoretical models where lack of collateral keeps individuals in "poverty traps" unable to undertake indivisible investments which would be highly profitable [Galor and Zeira (1993), Eckstein and Zilcha (1994), Jalan and Ravallion (1997), Fafchamps and Pender (1997)]. In such a situation, a one-off asset distribution could be more effective than continuing redistributive efforts with the associated disincentive effects [Banerjee and Newman (1993)].

an outside power or a revolutionary change of regime.[47] In the case of *landlord estates* where tenants already cultivated the land and all that was required was a reassignment of property rights, land reform was generally easy: The organization of production retained the same family farm system, where beneficiaries already had the skills and implements necessary to cultivate their fields. The administrative requirements associated with this type of land reform were minimal, and considerable efficiency gains have often been realized by improving incentives to work and invest by former tenants.[48] The magnitude of such gains was affected by the difference in (long- and short-term) incentives between the before- and after-reform situation. Productivity gains from such reforms were generally more modest if before the reform (i) security of tenure and incentives to invest had already been high, (ii) cash-rent–rather than share-rent–contracts had prevailed, and (iii) landlords had provided tenants with access to credit inputs, and outputs.[49]

In contrast to the generally successful experience in landlord estates, land reform in *hacienda* systems – i.e., systems where tenants have a small house-plot for subsistence but work most of their time on the landlord's home farm – has been very difficult to accomplish. Thus some have argued that the "game of Latin American Land Reform" has been lost [De Janvry and Sadoulet (1989)]. In the large majority of these systems, large landowners responded to the threat of land reform by either evicting tenants who could have made claims to land ownership under a possible reform program, or converting them into wage laborers. In the case of eviction, landlords reduced reliance on hired workers either by resuming extensive livestock production and ranching or – aided by significant credit subsidies – by embarking on highly mechanized self-cultivation [Binswanger et al. (1995)]. This not only reduced tenant welfare but also depopulated farms and created further difficulties for redistributive land reform. A number of further difficulties of effective land reform in hacienda systems are associated with policy distortions, limitations on the functioning of the land market, and inability to provide the necessary complementary elements for land reform beneficiaries to start successful small farm enterprises.

First, the costs of carrying out land reform were often increased by the continued existence of implicit and explicit policy distortions (e.g., agricultural protection and

---

[47] The marked difference in the success of land reform between Korea, Taiwan, and Japan on the one side, and Nicaragua, Cuba, and Vietnam on the other, suggests that the ability to redistribute large amounts of land is not a sufficient condition for land reform to be successful.

[48] Indeed, since the end of World War II, landlord estates in Bolivia, Eastern India, Ethiopia, Iran, Japan, Korea, and Taiwan have been transferred to tenants in the course of successful land reforms. While evidence on the productivity impact of such reforms is much less than what would be desirable, they have generally been associated with significant increases in output and/or productivity [King (1977), Lieten (1996), Besley and Burgess (1998)].

[49] The degree to which land reform improved productivity and cultivator welfare increased with the profitability of existing investment opportunities [Callison (1983), Koo (1968), King (1977)], the degree to which land ownership enabled the new owners to access markets for credit and insurance that had previously been beyond their reach [Dorner and Thiesenhusen (1990)], and the availability of new technology that could be readily adopted [Otsuka (1991)].

selective credit subsidies) that drove land prices above the capitalized value of agricultural profits and often disproportionately benefited large producers. Such distortions increased the fiscal cost of land reform policies and reduced their sustainability by making it profitable for land reform beneficiaries to sell their newly acquired land back to large farmers. Indeed, despite attempts to limit beneficiary desertion through imposition of legal restrictions and the threat of punishment in case of contravention, there is considerable anecdotal evidence on land sales by reform beneficiaries in Nicaragua, Colombia, and El Salvador. In a recent census of Brazilian land reform settlements, only about 60 percent of recently established land reform beneficiaries were actually found tilling their land.

Second, many countries aimed to implement land reform by eliminating or restricting other forms of (rental and sales) market transactions. This completely eliminated price and other market signals, making it more difficult to select beneficiaries and land, and further increased the costs of land reform implementation. It also tilted the balance in favor of a highly centralized mode of land reform implementation that has, in a number of countries, led to the domination of land reform processes by formidable (and often corrupt) centralized bureaucracies. In addition, and probably most important, this virtually eliminated beneficiaries' access to credit markets, despite the evidence that without access to such markets, it is difficult for them to sustain themselves. In Ireland, for example, a large-scale experiment in "negotiated" land reform early in the twentieth century did not have the expected effect for two reasons. On the one hand it did little to alter the structure of production or to improve tenants' rights. More important, however, it actually *worsened* access to credit, by limiting the ability of new landowners to mortgage land, while at the same time cutting off informal credit they had earlier obtained from the landlord [Guinnane and Miller (1997)].[50]

Third, transforming a large farm into a viable smallholder enterprise requires a change in the pattern of production, subdivision of the farm, and construction of infrastructure. As the productivity advantage of land reform hinges on increased incentives by owner-operators and adoption of labor-intensive crops, attention to complementary investments and awareness by beneficiaries is critical. Generally beneficiaries, even if they are workers of the former farm, are not accustomed to making independent entrepreneurial decisions, implying that training and human capital formation is therefore an essential component of the land reform process. Realizing the productivity benefits from land reform requires shifting the focus from political to productivity- and poverty-related objectives.[51]

---

[50] Severely restricted access to credit, together with insecure property rights, has also led to widespread selling of land by former land reform beneficiaries in Nicaragua – often at prices way below the productive value of the land [Joakin (1996)].

[51] The effect of political motivation on beneficiary selection and the stop-and-go cycle of land reform in response to political crises rather than opportunities for productivity increases and poverty reduction are well documented [Barraclough (1970)]. A model of land reform as a piecemeal strategy by the rich to avoid the imminent threat of revolt – with backtracking as soon as the threat weakens [Horowitz (1993)] – would be consistent with such a view.

Due to these difficulties, and the fact that land reform is a highly politicized topic, many of the land reforms that have been undertaken since the 1960s have not achieved their stated objectives. Evidence on the longer-term impact of land reform on poverty and productivity is more limited than desirable.[52] However, measures of macroeconomic adjustment such as elimination of trade protection and credit subsidies have resulted in a considerable reduction of land prices and the importance of land in a large number of developing countries.

This has led a number of countries (e.g., Brazil, Colombia, South Africa) to begin implementing a new model of "negotiated" land reform that aims to replace a centralist and often expropriative approach with provision of a grant that would enable poor people to acquire land through the market. Key elements of this approach are (i) an emphasis on sustainable poverty reduction through elaboration of integrated farm projects by the poor (which are then supported by a land purchase grant), (ii) decentralized execution and integration into development objectives at the local level with an overarching emphasis on beneficiary training and human capital formation, and (iii) private sector involvement in project development, financing, and implementation. Obviously, mere adoption of a "negotiated" mode is not immunity against the shortcomings that have plagued earlier land reform attempts.[53] Initial evidence from pilot programs that have aimed to integrate land reform into a more comprehensive package of support does, however, suggest that the new approach is perceived to be significantly different from earlier land reform attempts [Deininger (1998)]. To what degree this potential can be realized remains to be seen.

5. Conclusion: Areas for further research

While research on land markets and land institutions has been extensive, there are a number of areas where additional or more conclusive knowledge would be of great value. Below we highlight a number of key areas that merit further study.

5.1. Security of land rights

There is broad agreement in the literature that secure individual land rights will increase incentives to undertake productivity-enhancing land-related investments. If there is scope for agricultural intensification, and these rights can be enforced at low cost,

---

[52] One example of such economic analysis is the study by Scott et al. (1976) for Kenya. While it illustrates that land reform can have a positive social rate of return, it is based on data gathered in the immediate aftermath of the reforms, after which data collection was discontinued.

[53] Due to a lack of poverty targeting, an exclusive focus on land purchases but not complementary investments, and a high (75 percent) level of subsidy, a "negotiated" program of land reform that was carried out in Italy during the period 1948–70 had only a limited impact on poverty reduction and was characterized by relatively high costs [Shearer and Barbero (1993)].

and secondary rights to land by other stakeholders are not eliminated in the process, then establishment of such rights would constitute a clear Pareto improvement. However, in many cases, traditional systems are associated with a wide range of equity benefits, not all of which normally can be preserved in a system characterized by private land ownership. Research aiming to understand not only the existence and magnitude of productivity benefits arising from the transition from traditional to private property rights, but also the types of welfare benefits provided by different forms of communal arrangements, their magnitude, and possible alternative mechanisms to generate similar effects, would be very useful. It could facilitate better identification of the point at which a transition from traditional to individualized tenure arrangements might be socially optimal and allow adoption of mechanisms that would ensure tenure security with minimal social disruption. Evaluation of country cases where innovative ways to make this transition have been explored recently could be a starting point for such an endeavor.

5.2. *Improving the functioning of land markets*

While there has been significant research on the static inefficiency of tenancy contracts, the welfare consequences and the impact of tenancy on farmers' investment behavior have received less attention. Assessment of the welfare aspects of tenancy – i.e., the impact of land ownership as compared to mere usufructuary rights on household well-being – would be of relevance to help policymakers determine specific steps for comprehensive land market development. Such analysis should consider the impact of access to land under different systems on productivity and welfare (e.g., through choice of livelihood strategies, higher or smoother consumption, access to credit, ability to accumulate wealth, etc.).

A large body of literature on land price formation and the relationship between land sales and rental prices for developed countries already exists. However, much less is known on this issue for developing countries, in particular how recent dramatic changes in macroeconomic policy have affected land values and the relationship between land prices and agricultural profits. Elimination of credit subsidies and tax privileges, changes in relative prices of different types of agricultural products, and increased attractiveness of non-land financial assets that have been associated with these policies would have important implications not only for land prices but also for the operation of land (sales and rental) markets. This would also affect the type of economic agents who would be able to use these markets to gain access to land and the type of complementary policies (e.g., in the area of credit) that would affect their ability to do so.

Notwithstanding the fact that markets are an important avenue for individuals to gain access to land, non-market transactions such as inheritance, allocation by village chiefs, and informal rentals among kin continue to have a far-reaching impact on a large part of the population and the structure of land ownership and land use in many parts of the world. A large descriptive literature discusses advantages and disadvantages of non-market mechanisms. However, quantitative evidence on the efficiency and equity impact of non-market transactions and the way in which policies that aim to change decision-makers' incentive affect the extent and modalities of such transactions is still limited. Given that informal systems tend to be characterized by lower transaction costs and can provide land access for the poorest segments of the population who may not be able to utilize land rental and sales markets, better understanding of the potential and shortcomings of non-market mechanisms would be of great interest. There is also little doubt that in situations where, either traditionally or due to male out-migration, a significant part of agricultural production activities is carried out by women, the nature of women's land rights – many of which are defined informally – will have far-reaching implications for agricultural productivity and investment. However, much remains to be learned about the interaction between legal prescriptions, social norms, and intra-household bargaining in determining the nature of women's rights to land, and the scope for specific policy interventions to bring about efficiency increases by strengthening these rights.

Over and above the market imperfections characteristic of rural areas, functioning of land rental and sales markets has in the past often been constrained by government interventions – in many cases with the aim to promote equity or overcome market imperfections. While the effectiveness of such policies was often limited, they generally left an institutional legacy that is difficult to dismantle. Research on the links between land and other markets could do much to identify such "second generation reforms" and to facilitate their implementation in an environment characterized by multiple market imperfections.

5.3. Land redistribution

Compared to the volume of resources that has been spent since the 1960s on land reform programs, the effort invested in monitoring their performance and in assessing their impact on poverty reduction and agricultural productivity has been minuscule. As a consequence, evidence on promising models of land reform in hacienda systems and the long-term impact associated with them is extremely limited. Little or no guidance exists on how to compare the effectiveness of different approaches to land reform in (i) reaching specific target groups, (ii) helping these groups to complement land ownership with other investments and thereby increase agricultural productivity, and (iii) enabling them to convert the one-time transfer of land into a sustained improvement in their livelihood. Such evidence will be critical in assessing whether these new approaches to market-assisted land reform are fiscally, socially, and economically sustainable.

Given the recent emphasis in the theoretical literature on asset ownership as a means for sustainable poverty reduction, it would be of great interest to carefully monitor innovative land reform efforts with a view toward drawing the necessary policy conclusions. Issues to be explored include the volume and price of land (sales and rental) transactions, characteristics of participants, and the productivity change associated with land transactions within and outside a specific land reform program. Complementing this with longitudinal information on changes in welfare of specific beneficiaries and the population at large would provide an opportunity to assess the equity impact of land reform and ultimately compare this type of intervention to other policies aimed at the same goal.

References

Allen, D.W. (1991), "Homesteading and property rights; Or, 'how the west was really won'", Journal of Law and Economic 34:1–23.

Alston, L.J., G.D. Libecap and R. Schneider (1995), "Property rights and the preconditions for markets: The case of the Amazon Frontier", Journal of Institutional and Theoretical Economics 151(1):89–111.

Alston, L.J., G.D. Libecap and R. Schneider (1996), "The determinants and impact of property rights: Land titles on the Brazilian Frontier", Journal of Law, Economics & Organization 12(1):25–61.

Andre, C., and J.-P. Platteau (1996), "Land relations under unbearable stress: Rwanda caught in the Malthusian trap" (Centre de Recherche en Economie du Development (CRED), Namur, Belgium).

Appu, P.S. (1996), Land Reforms in India. A Survey of Policy, Legislation and Implementation (Vikas Publishing House, New Delhi).

Atwood, D.A. (1990), "Land registration in Africa: The impact on agricultural production", World Development 18:659–671.

Auty, R.M. (1997), "Natural resource endowment, the state and development strategy", Journal of International Development 9:651–663.

Baland, J.-M., F. Gaspart, F. Place and J.-P. Platteau (1999), "Poverty, tenure security and access to land in Central Uganda: The role of market and non-market processes", mimeo (CRED Dept. of Economics, University of Namur).

Baland, J.-M., and J.-P. Platteau (1996), Halting Degradation of Natural Resources: Is There a Role for Rural Communities? (Oxford University Press, Clarendon Press).

Baland, J.-M., and J.-P. Platteau (1997a), "Coordination problems in local-level resource management", Journal of Development Economics 53(1):197–210.

Baland, J.-M., and J.-P. Platteau (1997b), "Wealth inequality and efficiency in the commons, Part I: The unregulated case", Oxford Economic Papers 49:451–482.

Baland, J.-M., and J.-P. Platteau (1998), "Wealth inequality and efficiency in the commons, Part II: The regulated case", Oxford Economic Papers 50(1):1–22.

Balcazar, A. (1990), "Tanaño de finca, dinamica tecnologia y rendimientos agricolas", Coyuntura Agropecuaria 7(3):107–125.

Banerjee, A., P. Gertler and M. Ghatak (1998), "Empowerment and efficiency: The economics of agrarian reform", mimeo (Dept. of Economics, Massachusetts Institute of Technology).

Banerjee, A.V., and A.F. Newman (1991), "Risk-bearing and the theory of income distribution", Review of Economic Studies 58:211–235.

Banerjee, A.V., and A.F. Newman (1993), "Occupational choice and the process of development", Journal of Political Economy 101(2):274–298.

Banerjee, A., D. Mookherjee, K. Munshi and D. Ray (1997), "Inequality, control rights and rent seeking a theoretical and empirical analysis of sugar cooperatives in Maharashtra", mimeo (Boston University).

Bardhan, P., S. Bowles and H. Gintis (1997), Wealth Inequality, Wealth Constraints and Economic Performance (University of Massachusetts, Amherst).

Barham, B.L., S. Boucher and M.R. Carter (1996), "Credit constraints, credit unions, and small-scale producers in Guatemala", World Development 24(5):793–806.

Barham, B.L., M.R. Carter and W. Sigelko (1995), "Agro-export production and peasant land access: Examining the dynamic between adoption and accumulation", Journal of Development Economics 46:85–107.

Barraclough, S.L. (1970), "Agricultural policy and land reform", Journal of Political Economy 906–947.

Barrett, C.B. (1996), "On price risk and the inverse farm size – productivity relationship", Journal of Development Economics 51:194–215.

Baruah, S. (1990), "The end of the road in land reform? Limits to redistribution in West Bengal", Development and Change 21:119–146.

Basu, K. (1986), "Market for land: An analysis of interim transactions", Journal of Development Economics 20:163–177.

Bell, C. (1977), "Alternative theories of sharecropping: Some tests using evidence from Northeast India", Journal of Development Studies 13:317–346.

Benjamin, D. (1992), "Household composition, labor markets, and labor demand: Testing for separability in agricultural household models", Econometrica 60:287–322.

Benjamin, D. (1995), "Can unobserved land quality explain the inverse productivity relationship?", Journal of Development Economics 46:51–84.

Berry, R.A., and W.R. Cline (1979), "Agrarian structure and productivity in developing countries" (International Labor Organization, Geneva).

Besley, T. (1995), "Property rights and investment incentives: Theory and evidence from Ghana", Journal of Political Economy 103(5):903–937.

Besley, T., and R. Burgess (1998), "Land reform, poverty reduction, and growth: Evidence from India", mimeo, LSE.

Bhalla, S.S., and P. Roy (1988), "Mis-specification in farm productivity analysis: The role of land quality", Oxford Economic Papers 40:55–73.

Bidinger, P.D., T.S. Walker, B. Sarkar, A.R. Murty and P. Babu (1991), "Consequences of mid-1980s drought: Longitudinal evidence from Mahbubnagar", Economic and Political Weekly 26:A105–A114.

Binswanger, H.P., and K. Deininger (1997), "Explaining agricultural and agrarian policies in developing countries", Journal of Economic Literature 35(4):1958–2005.

Binswanger, H.P., K. Deininger and G. Feder (1995), "Power, distortions, revolt and reform in agricultural land relations", in: J. Behrman and T.N. Srinivasan, eds., Handbook of Development Economics, Vol. III.

Binswanger, H.P., and M. Elgin (1988), "What are the prospects for land reform", in: A. Maunder and A. Valdés, eds., Agriculture and Governments in an Interdependent World, Proceedings of the Twentieth International Conference of Agricultural Economists 1988.

Binswanger, H.P., and M.R. Rosenzweig (1986), "Behavioral and material determinants of production relations in agriculture", Journal of Development Studies 22:503–539.

Bird, R. (1974), Taxing Agricultural Land in Developing Countries (Harvard University Press, Cambridge, MA).

Birdsall, N., and J.L. Londoño (1997), "Asset inequality matters: An assessment of the world bank's approach to poverty reduction", American Economic Review 87(2):32–37.

Blarel, B., P. Hazell, F. Place and J. Quiggin (1992), "The economics of farm fragmentation: Evidence from Ghana and Rwanda", World Bank Economic Review 6:233–254.

Boserup, E. (1965), Conditions of Agricultural Growth: The Economics of Agrarian Change Under Population Pressure (Aldine, New York).

Bowles, S., and H. Gintis (1994), "Escaping the efficiency-equity tradeoff: Productivity enhancing asset re-distributions", in: Macroeconomic Policy after the Conservative Era: Research on Investment, Savings, and Finance (Cambridge University Press, Cambridge).

Brandao, A.S.P., and G.C. de Rezende (1992), "Credit subsidies, inflation and the land market in Brazil: A theoretical and empirical analysis", mimeo (World Bank, Washington).

Brasselle, A.-S., G. Frederic and J.-P. Platteau (1997), "Land tenure security and investment incentives: Some further puzzling evidence from Burkina Faso" (CRED, Namur, Belgium).

Brockett, C.D. (1990), Land, Power, and Poverty. Agrarian Transformation and Political Conflict in Central America (Unwin Hyman, Boston).

Brooks, K., and Z. Lerman (1994), "Land reform and farm restructuring in Russia", World Bank Discussion Paper 233 (Washington, DC).

Bruce, J.W. (1988), "A perspective on indigenous land tenure systems and land concentration", in: R.W. Downs and S.P. Reyna, eds., Land and Society in Contemporary Africa (For University of New Hampshire by University Press of New England, Hanover and London).

Bruce, J.W., and S. Migot-Adholla (1994), Searching for Land Tenure Security in Africa (Kendall Hunt Publishing Company, Dubuque, IA).

Burgess, R. (1998), "Land, welfare and efficiency in Rural China", mimeo (London School of Economics).

Cain, M. (1981), "Risk and insurance: Perspectives on fertility and agrarian change in India and Bangladesh", Population and Development Review 7:435–474.

Callison, C.S. (1983), Land to the Tiller in the Mekong Delta: Economic, Social and Political Land Reform in Four Villages of South Vietnam (University Press of America, Bloomington, IN).

Calvo, G.A., and S. Wellisz (1978), "Supervision, loss of control, and the optimum size of the firm", Journal of Political Economy 86:943–952.

Carter, M.R. (1984), "Identification of the inverse relationship between farm size and productivity: An empirical analysis of peasant agricultural production", Oxford Economic Papers 36:131–145.

Carter, M.R., and B.L. Barham (1996), "Level playing fields and laissez faire: Postliberal development strategy in inegalitarian agrarian economies", World Development 24(0):1–17.

Carter, M.R., and D. Mesbah (1993), "Can land market reform mitigate the exclusionary aspects of rapid agro-export growth?", World Development 21(7):1085–1100.

Carter, M.R., and P. Olinto (1996), "Does land titling activate a productivity–promoting land market? Econometric evidence from rural Paraguay" (University of Wisconsin-Madison).

Carter, M.R., L. Shouying, M. Roth and Y. Yao (1996), "An induced institutional innovation perspective on the evolution of property rights in post-reform rural China", mimeo (University of Wisconsin-Madison).

Carter, M.R., and K.D. Wiebe (1990), "Access to capital and its impact on agrarian structure and productivity in Kenya", American Journal of Agricultural Economics 72:1146–1150.

Carter, M.R., and E. Zegarra (1995), "Reshaping class competitiveness and the trajectory of agrarian growth with well-sequenced policy reform", Agricultural Economics Staff Paper Series No. 379 (University of Wisconsin-Madison).

Cheung, N.S. (1969), The Theory of Share Tenancy (University of Chicago Press, Chicago).

Collier, P. (1989), "Contractual constraints on labour exchange in rural Kenya", International Labour Review 128:745–768.

Cramb, R.A. (1993), "The evolution of property rights to land in Sarawak: An institutionalist perspective", Review of Marketing and Agricultural Economics 61(2):289–300.

De Alessi, L. (1980), "The economics of property rights: A review of the evidence", Research in Law and Economics 2:1–47.

De Janvry, A., and E. Sadoulet (1989), "A study in resistance to institutional change: The lost game of Latin American land reform", World Development 17:1397–1407.

De Meza, D., and J. R. Gould (1992), "The social efficiency of private decisions to enforce property rights", Journal of Political Economy 100:561–580.

Deininger, K. (1995), "Collective agricultural production: A solution for transition economies?", World Development 23(8):1317–1334.

Deininger, K. (1998), "Making negotiated land reform work: Initial experience from Brazil, Colombia, and South Africa", World Development, forthcoming.

Deininger, K., P. Olinto, M. Wamulume and D. Chiwele (1998), "Agricultural sector performance in a post-reform environment: Implications for second-generation reforms in Zambia", mimeo (World Bank, Washington, DC).

Dercon, S. (1996), "Risk, crop choice, and savings: Evidence from Tanzania", Economic Development and Cultural Change 44(3):485–513.

Dercon, S., and P. Krishnan (1996), "Income portfolios in rural Ethiopia and Tanzania: Choices and constraints", The Journal of Development Studies 32(6):850–875.

Dong, X.-Y. (1996), "Two-tier land tenure system and sustained economic growth in post-1978 rural China", World Development 24(5):915–928.

Dorner, P., and W.C. Thiesenhusen (1990), "Selected land reforms in East and Southeast Asia: Their origins and impacts", Asian Pacific Economic Literature 4:69–95.

Downs, R.W., and S.P. Reyna, eds. (1993), Land and Society in Contemporary Africa (For University of New Hampshire by University Press of New England, Hanover and London).

Dujon, V. (1997), "Communal property and land markets: Agricultural development policy in St. Lucia", World Development 25(9):1529–1540.

Eckstein, Z., and I. Zilcha (1994), "The effects of compulsory schooling on growth income distribution and welfare", Journal of Public Economics 54:339–359.

Ellickson, R.C. (1993), "Property in land", Yale Law Journal 102(6):1315–1400.

Ensminger, J. (1997), "Changing property rights: Reconciling formal and informal rights to land in Africa", in: J.N. Drobak and J.V.C. Nye, eds., The Frontiers of the New Institutional Economics (Academic Press, San Diego, Harcourt Brace).

Eswaran, M., and A. Kotwal (1985a), "A theory of two-tier labor markets in agrarian economies", American Economic Review 75:162–177.

Eswaran, M., and A. Kotwal (1985b), "A theory of contractual structure in agriculture", American Economic Review 75:352–367.

Eswaran, M., and A. Kotwal (1986), "Access to capital and agrarian production organization", Economic Journal 96:482–498.

Fafchamps, M., and J. Pender (1997), "Precautionary saving, credit constraints, and irreversible investment: Theory and evidence from semi-arid India", Journal of Business and Economic Statistics 15(2):180–194.

Feder, G. (1985), "The relation between farm size and farm productivity: The role of family labor, supervision, and credit constraints", Journal of Development Economics 18:297–313.

Feder, G., et al. (1989), "Agricultural credit and farm performance in China", Journal of Comparative Economics 13(4):508–526.

Feder, G., and D. Feeney (1991), "Land tenure and property rights: Theory and implications for development policy", World Bank Economic Review 5:135–155.

Feder, G., and A. Nishio (1996), "The benefits of land registration and titling: Economic and social perspectives" (The World Bank).

Feder, G., T. Onchan, Y. Chalamwong and C. Hangladoran (1986), Land Policies and Farm Productivity in Thailand (Johns Hopkins University Press, Baltimore, MD).

Feder, G., and N. Raymond (1987), "Land rights systems and agricultural development in Sub-Saharan Africa agriculture and rural development", Dept. RU Paper 64 (Washington, DC).

Feeney, D. (1988), "The development of property rights in land: A comparative study", in: R.H. Bates, ed., Toward a Political Economy of Development: A Rational Choice Perspective (University of California Press, Berkeley).

Feldstein, M. (1980), "Inflation, portfolio choice, and the prices of land and corporate stock", American Journal of Agricultural Economics 62:910–916.

Foster, A.D., and M.R. Rosenzweig (1996), "Comparative advantage, information and the allocation of workers to tasks: Evidence from an agricultural labor market" (University of Pennsylvania).

Frisvold, G.B. (1994), "Does supervision matter? Some hypothesis tests using Indian farm-level data", Journal of Development Economics 43:217–238.

Fujimoto, A. (1988), "The economics of land tenure and rice production in a double-cropping village in Southern Thailand", Developing Economies 26:189–211.

Galor, O., and J. Zeira (1993), "Income distribution and macroeconomics", Review of Economic Studies 60:35–52.

Gavian, S., and M. Fafchamps (1996), "Land tenure and allocative efficiency in Niger", American Journal of Agricultural Economics 78:460–471.

Geertz, C. (1968), "Agricultural involution: The process of ecological change in Indonesia" (For the Association of Asian Studies by University of California Press, Berkeley).

Glaeser, E.L. (1996), "The incentive effects of property taxes on local governments", Public-Choice 89(1–2):93–111.

Glover, D. (1990), "Contract farming and outgrower schemes in East and Southern Africa", Journal of Agricultural Economics 41:303–315.

Gordillo, G., A. de Janvry and E. Sadoulet (1997), "Mexico's second agrarian reform: Household and community responses. 1990–1994" (La Jolla, Calif. Center for U.S.–Mexican Studies, University of California, San Diego).

Guinnane, T.W., and R.I. Miller (1997), "The limits to land reform: The land acts in Ireland, 1870–1909", Economic Development and Cultural Change 45(3):591–612.

Gunjal, K., S. Williams and R. Romain (1996), "Agricultural credit subsidies and farmland values in Canada", Canadian Journal of Agricultural Economics 44(1):39–52.

Hayami, Y., L.S. Adriano, Y. Quisumbing and M.A.R. Quisumbing (1990), Toward an Alternative Land Reform Paradigm, A Philippine Perspective (Ateneo de Manila University Press, Manila).

Hayami, Y., and K. Otsuka (1993), The Economics of Contract Choice: An Agrarian Perspective (Oxford University Press, Clarendon Press, Oxford, New York).

Hoff, K. (1991), "Land taxes, output taxes, and sharecropping: Was Henry George right?", World Bank Economic Review 5:93–111.

Horowitz, A.W. (1993), "Time paths of land reform: A theoretical model of reform dynamics", The American Economic Review 83(4):1003–1010.

Jalan, J., and M. Ravallion (1997), "Are the poor less well insured? Evidence on vulnerability to income risk in rural China", mimeo (The World Bank).

Jensen, M.C., and W.H. Meckling (1976), "Theory of the firm: Managerial behavior, agency costs, and ownership structure", Journal of Financial Economics 3:305–360.

Joakin, J. (1996), "The impact of structural adjustment and property rights conflicts on Nicaraguan agrarian reform beneficiaries", World Development 24(7):1179–1191.

Jodha, N.S. (1990), "Rural common property resources: Contributions and crisis", Economic and Political Weekly 25:A65–A78.

Just, R.E., and J.A. Miranowski (1989), "U.S. land prices: Trends and determinants", in: A. Maunder and A. Valdés, eds., Agriculture and Governments in an Interdependent World, Proceedings of the Twentieth International Conference of Agricultural Economists 1988.

Kevane, M. (1996), "Agrarian structure and agricultural practice: Typology and application to Western Sudan", American Journal of Agricultural Economics 78(1):236–245.

Kevane, M., and B. Wydick (1998), "Social norms and the time allocation of women's labor in Burkina Faso", mimeo.

Key, N., C. Muñoz-Piña, A. de Janvry and E. Sadoulet (1998), "Social and environmental consequences of the Mexican reforms: Common pool resources in the Ejido sector" (Department of Agricultural and Resource Economics, University of California-Berkeley).

King, R. (1977), Land Reform: A World Survey (G. Bell and Sons, London).

Koo, A.Y.C. (1968), Land Reform and Economic Development: A Case Study of Taiwan (Praeger, New York).

Kranton, R.E., and A.V. Swamy (1997), "The hazards of piecemeal reform: British civil courts and the redit market in colonial India" (World Bank, Washington, DC).

Kung, J.K. (1995), "Equal entitlement versus tenure security under a regime of collective property rights: Peasants' preference for institutions in post-reform Chinese agriculture", Journal of Comparative Economics 21:82–111.

Kutcher, G.P., and P.L. Scandizzo (1981), "The agricultural economy of northeast Brazil" (World Bank, Washington, DC).

Laffont, J.-J., and M.-S. Matoussi (1995), "Moral hazard, financial constraints and sharecropping in El Oulja", Review of Economic Studies 62(3):381–399.

Lastarria-Cornhiel, S. (1997), "Impact of privatization on gender and property rights in Africa", World Development 25(8):1317–1333.

Lieten, G.K. (1996), "Land reforms at centre stage: The evidence on West Bengal", Development and Change 27:111–130.

Lin, J.Y. (1992), "Rural reforms and agricultural growth in China", American Economic Review 82:34–51.

Lin, J.Y., F. Cai and Z. Li (1994), "Why China's economic reforms have been successful: Its implications for other reforming economies" (Peking University and the Chinese Academy of Social Sciences).

Liu, S., and M.R. Carter (1996), "Dimensions and diversity of property rights in rural China: Dilemmas on the road to further reform", World Development 26(10):1789–1806.

Malik, A., and R.M. Schwab (1991), "Optimal investments to establish property rights in land", Journal of Urban Economics 29:295–309.

McCarthy, N., A. de Janvry and E. Sadoulet (1998), "Land allocation under dual individual-collective use in Mexico", Journal of Development Economics 56:239–264.

McCloskey, D.N. (1975), "The persistence of English common fields", in: W. Parker and E. Jones, eds., European Peasants and their Markets (Princeton University Press, Princeton, NJ).

McCloskey, D.N. (1991), "The prudent peasant: New findings on open fields", Journal of Economic History 51(2):343–355.

McMillan, J., J. Whalley and L. Zhu (1989), "The impact of China's economic reforms on agricultural productivity growth", Journal of Political Economy 97:781–807.

Mearns, R. (1996), "Community, collective action and common grazing: The case of post-socialist Mongolia", Journal of Development Studies 32(3):297–339.

Migot-Adholla, S., et al. (1991), "Indigenous land rights systems in Sub-Saharan Africa: A constraint on productivity?", World Bank Economic Review (International) 5:155–175.

Moene, K.O. (1992), "Poverty and landownership", American Economic Review 82:52–64.

Mookherjee, D. (1997), "Informational rents and property rights in land", in: J. Roemer, ed., Property Rights, Incentives & Welfare (Macmillan Press).

Morooka, Y., and Y. Hayami (1989), "Contract choice and enforcement in an agrarian community: Agricultural tenancy in Upland Java", Journal of Development Studies 26(1):28–42.

Mueller, B. (1997), "Property rights and the evolution of a frontier", Land Economics 73(1):42–57.

Nagarajan, G., M.A. Quisumbing and K. Otsuka (1991), "Land pawning in the Philippines: An exploration into the consequences of land reform regulations", Developing Economies 29:125–144.

Newbery, D.M.G., and J.E. Stiglitz (1979), "Sharecropping, risk sharing and the importance of imperfect information", in: J.A. Roumasset et al., eds., Risk, Uncertainty, and Agricultural Development (Agricultural Development Council).

Newell, A., P. Kiran and S. James (1997), "Farm size and the intensity of land use in Gujarat", Oxford Economic Papers 49:307–315.

Nugent, J., and N. Sanchez (1993), "Tribes, chiefs, and transhumance: A comparative institutional analysis", Economic Development and Cultural Change 42(1):87–113.

Olinto, P.V. (1995), "Land quality and the inverse relationship between farm size and productivity: A panel data analysis of Paraguayan farm households" (Department of Agricultural Economics, University of Wisconsin-Madison).

Olson-Lanjouw, J. (1995), "Information and the operation of markets: Tests based on a general equilibrium model of land leasing in India", Economic Growth Center Discussion Paper No. 727 (Yale University).

Otsuka, K. (1991), "Determinants and consequences of land reform implementation in the Philippines", Journal of Development Economics 35:339–355.

Otsuka, K., H. Chuma and Y. Hayami (1992), "Land and labor contracts in agrarian economies: Theories and facts", Journal of Economic Literature 30(4):1965–2018.

Otsuka, K., C. Hiroyuki and Y. Hayami (1993), "Permanent labour and land tenancy contracts in agrarian economies: An integrated analysis", Economica 60(237):57–77.

Pender, J.L. and J.M. Kerr (1996), "The effect of transferable land rights on credit, land investment and use: Evidence from South India", mimeo.

Pinckney, T.C., and P.K. Kimuyu (1994), "Land tenure reform in East Africa: Good, bad or unimportant?", Journal of African Economies 3(1):1–28.

Platteau, J.-P. (1996), "The evolutionary theory of land rights as applied to Sub-Saharan Africa: A critical assessment", Development and Change 27:29–86.

Platteau J.-P. (1999), "Intra-family exclusionary processes in access to land–with special reference to Europe and Sub-Saharan Africa", in: A. de Janvry, E. Sadoulet and J.-P. Platteau, eds., Land Reform Revisited: Access to Land, Rural Poverty, and Public Action (Oxford University Press) forthcoming.

Quibria, M.G., and S. Rashid (1984), "The puzzle of sharecropping: A survey of theories", World Development 12:103–114.

Reid, J.D. (1976), "Sharecropping and agricultural uncertainty", Economic Development and Cultural Change 24:549–576.

Robertson, A.F. (1982), "Abusa: The structural history of an economic contract", Journal of Development Studies 18(4):447–478.

Rosenzweig, M.R., and H.P. Binswanger (1993), "Wealth, weather risk and the composition and profitability of agricultural investments", Economic Journal 103:56–58.

Rosenzweig, M.R., and K.I. Wolpin (1993), "Credit market constraints, consumption smoothing and the accumulation of durable production assets in low-income countries: Investments in bullocks in India", Journal of Political Economy 101:223–244.

Rozelle, S., L. Guo and L. Brandt (1996), "Land tenure, property rights, and productivity in China's agricultural sector" (Food Research Institute, Stanford University).

Sadoulet, E., A. de Janvry and S. Fukui (1997), "The meaning of kinship in sharecropping contracts", American Journal of Agricultural Economics 79:394–406.

Sadoulet, E., S. Fukui and A. de Janvry (1994), "Efficient share tenancy contracts under risk: The case of two rice-growing villages in Thailand", Journal of Development Economics 42:243–269.

Sarap, K. (1990), "Factors affecting small farmers access to institutional credit in rural Orissa, India", Development and Change 21:281–307.

Schiff, M., and A. Valdés (1995), "The plundering of agriculture in developing countries", Finance and Development 32(1):44–47.

Scott, M.F., J.D. MacArthur and D.M.G. Newbery (1976), Project Appraisal in Practice: The Little-Mirrlees Method Applied in Kenya (Heinemann Educational Books, London).

Sen, A.K. (1981), "Market failure and control of labour power: Towards an explanation of structure and change in Indian agriculture, Parts 1 and 2", Cambridge Journal of Economics 5(3):201–228, Part 1; 5(4):327–350, Part 2.

Sengupta, K. (1997), "Limited liability, moral hazard and share tenancy", Journal of Development Economics 52:393–407.

Shaban, R.A. (1987), "Testing between competing models of sharecropping", Journal of Political Economy 95:893–920.

Shaban, R.A. (1991), "Does the land tenancy market equalize holdings?", Working Paper (University of Pennsylvania).

Shearer, E.B., and B. Giuseppe (1993), "Public policy for the promotion of family farms in Italy" (The World Bank).

Shetty, S. (1988), "Limited liability, wealth differences and tenancy contracts in agrarian economics", Journal of Development Economics 29:1–22.

Siamwalla, A. et al. (1990), "The Thai rural credit system: public subsidies, private information, and segmented markets", World Bank Economic Review 4:271–295.

Sjaastad, E., and D. Bromley (1997), "Indigenous land rights in Sub-Saharan Africa: Appropriation, security and investment demand", World Development 25(4):549–562.

Skoufias, E. (1991), "Land tenancy and rural factor market imperfections revisited", Journal of Economic Development 16:37–55.

Skoufias, E. (1995), "Household resources, transaction costs, and adjustment through land tenancy", Land Economics 71(1):42–56.

Southgate, E., R. Sierra, and L. Brown (1991), "The causes of tropical deforestation in Ecuador: A statistical analysis", World Development 19:1145–1151.

Stiglitz, J.E., and A. Weiss (1981), "Credit rationing in markets with imperfect information", American Economic Review 71:393–409.

Strasma, J., J. Alsm, E. Shearer and A. Woldstein (1987), "Impact of agricultural land revenue systems on agricultural land usage", mimeo (Land Tenure Center, Madison, WI).

Townsend, R.M. (1993), The Medieval Village Economy: A Study of the Pareto Mapping in General Equilibrium Models (Princeton University Press, Princeton, NJ).

Townsend, R.M. (1994), "Risk and insurance in village India", Econometrica 62(3):539–591.

Townsend, R.M. (1995), "Consumption insurance: An evaluation of risk-bearing systems in low-income economies", Journal of Economic Perspectives 9(3):83–102.

Turner, M.A., L. Brandt and S. Rozelle (1998), "Property rights formation and the organization of exchange and production in rural China", mimeo.

Udry, C. (1995), "Recent advances in empirical microeconomic research in poor countries" (Northwestern University).

Udry, C. (1996), "Gender, agricultural production, and the theory of the household", Journal of Political Economy 104(5):1010–1046.

Umbeck, J. (1977), "The California gold rush: A study of emerging property rights", Explorations in Economic History 14(3):197–226.

Wilson, P.N., and G.D. Thompson (1993), "Common property and uncertainty: compensating coalitions by Mexico's Pastoral Ejidatarios", Economic Development and Cultural Change 41(2):299–318.

Yao, Y. (1996), "Three essays on the implications of imperfect markets in rural China", Ph.D. (University of Wisconsin).

Zimmerman, F., and M.R. Carter (1996a), "Dynamic portfolio management under risk subsistence constraints in developing countries" (Food Research Institute, Stanford University).

Zimmerman, F., and M.R. Carter (1996b), "Rethinking the demand for institutional innovation: Land rights and markets in the West African Sahel" (Stanford University).

Chapter 7

HUMAN CAPITAL: EDUCATION AND AGRICULTURE

WALLACE E. HUFFMAN

Department of Economics, Iowa State University, Ames, IA

Contents

Handbook of Agricultural Economics, Volume 1, Edited by B. Gardner and G. Rausser

Abstract

This chapter presents a review and synthesis of effects of education in agriculture, summarizes major contributions, and suggests major research gaps in the literature. Although growth in knowledge enables skill acquisition and specialization of labor, which generally raises labor productivity, and technical change, the dominant effect on agriculture has been technical change. A puzzle remains why schooling does not have broader direct impacts in agriculture. Furthermore, as we proxy education or general intellectual achievement by schooling in our empirical research, this has led to biased interpretations of impacts when general intellectual achievement of school graduates changes over time and perhaps in nonlinear ways.

Keywords

education, schooling, agriculture, human capital, impact analysis

JEL classification: Q12

Education is widely considered to be the most important form of human capital [Becker (1993, pp. 1–13)]. A major part of formal education or general intellectual achievement is obtained in elementary and secondary schools and in colleges/universities. Although there are differences in exactly what these institutions teach in different parts of the world, common components are skills, knowledge, and a method of analyzing problems [Schultz (1963, pp. 1–19), Becker (1993, pp. 1–13), Bishop (1989)]. Investments of students' and teachers' time and other inputs are used in the schooling process, and schooling of an individual beyond the permanent literary level, which is generally three to four years of formal schooling, has lifetime impacts on almost all of his or her activities. These are widely accepted to include labor productivity and wage rates, but also include choices of occupation, geographical location, information acquisition, and technology. In agriculture, the returns to schooling seem to increase substantially as a country goes from traditional agriculture to modernizing, which creates a dynamic technical and economic environment requiring information acquisition, technology evaluation, and adjustments to change [Schultz (1964), Schultz (1975), Becker (1993, pp. 1–13)].

The objective of this paper is to present a review and synthesis of the broad effects of education on agriculture and to summarize where major contributions lie and where major gaps exist in the literature. The first section presents a conceptual framework for education's contribution. The second section reviews and synthesizes the empirical evidence which is organized around the topics of (1) choices about where to work, (2) technology adoption and information acquisition, (3) agricultural production, (4) agricultural productivity decomposition, and (5) household income. The third section presents a summary of major contributions and research gaps in the literature.

1. A conceptual framework

1.1. Overview

Growth in knowledge seems to be a major factor causing the long-term rise in labor productivity, real wage rates, and per capita incomes in market economies. First, as the stock of knowledge grows, the opportunities for individuals to invest in specialized knowledge (e.g., schooling, training) that raises their productivity occurs [Becker and Murphy (1993), Jones (1998, pp. 71–87)]. Hence, the returns to labor's specialization arise through workers taking on narrower and more specialized tasks, but to get output produced, this means that a group of workers having different skills must cooperate together. "Team production" within or across firms raises special incentive problems [Gibbons (1998), Becker and Murphy (1993)]. As the degree of specialization of labor and tasks increases, the number of different tasks and specialists that must be coordinated increases. For the continuation of this growth process emphasizing knowledge accumulation and specialization, an economy must find new ways to reduce team-labor coordinating costs. Economies that have high coordination/ transaction costs because of a weak economic exchange system (i.e., absence of private property, weak contracts, suppressed prices and markets) reduce the incentives for workers and firms to special-ize, given any stock of knowledge, and reduce labor productivity and per capita incomes [Williamson (1985)].

Second, as the stock of knowledge grows, the opportunities to produce new technolo-gies that become embodied in new capital goods [e.g., Romer (1990)] and intermediate goods [see Jones (1998, pp. 88–107), Huffman and Evenson (1993)] occur. These in-novations are frequently adopted in manufacturing, agriculture, and other sectors. Con-siderable evidence exists for the United States that unskilled labor and capital services are substitutes in manufacturing, but skilled labor and capital services are complements [see Orazem et al. (1997), Griliches (1969, 1970)]. More generally, capital services and labor become less substitutable as the skills of labor increase, and labor and capital ser-vices eventually become complements, especially for college trained labor. This means that as knowledge and technology advance, the demand for skilled (more highly edu-cated) labor grows relative to the demand for less skilled (less educated) labor, and the potential exists for a rise in the real (and relative) wage of skilled labor.

Production on farms is one of biological processes, but major differences exist be-tween crop and livestock production. The seasonal and spatial nature of crop production places severe constraints on large-scale or specialized units and mechanized production. With plant biological (clocks) processes sequenced by day length and temperature, little opportunity exists to use mechanization to speed up the production processes, even on large farms. Because planting and harvesting for any given crop must occur within a nar-row time window at any location, a major limit to size of specialized enterprises occurs. Crop rotation, or nonspecialized production, has historically been one important method for controlling pest and disease problems in crops and balancing soil nutrient availabil-ity with plant nutrient needs. Chemical and biological control of pests and chemical fertilizer applications are relatively new technological alternatives to crop rotation, and they have facilitated crop specialization.

Because plants occupy fixed land area as they grow, machines suitable for mecha-nization of crop production must be mobile and move across the fields or through plant materials that are fixed in location. Furthermore, machines must be small relative to plot or field sizes. Thus, a special type of mechanization is required for crops. This contrasts with industrial (and livestock) production where the production plant is fixed and materials move through it. The latter type of production permits workers to become specialized in one phase of the total production process and this has aided labor produc-tivity in the industrial sector of developed countries. It is difficult for workers in crop production to be fully employed and to specialize in any phase of production.

Livestock production is relatively free of constraints due to seasonal and spatial at-tributes. It is economically feasible to speed up or slow the rate of production by chang-ing the diet and activity level of animals during the growing and finishing phases. Pro-duction can be organized in sequential phases where all phases from birth to finishing occur on one farm or where different farms specialize in different phases. Advances in animal health products, animal feeding, housing and equipment, and management have made it technically possible to speed up the growing and finishing phases by using large confined animal production systems which greatly increase animal densities and populations. To further reduce disease problems in large animal confined systems, animals of different ages can be segregated and raised apart in "all-in, all-out" systems. With the growing and finishing of animals and birds in a facility in phased groups, livestock production becomes similar to production of industrial goods where workers have the opportunity to specialize in a particular phase of production.

When firms are heterogeneous within a sector or have some specialized resources – e.g., land, climate, knowledge – the potential impact of new technologies will differ across them. It is costly for entrepreneurs to acquire information, evaluate the available technologies, and adopt only the new ones that are expected to make them better off. Considerable evidence exists that schooling of entrepreneurs becomes a valuable skill when the technology is changing, for example when agriculture undergoes a transition from traditional to modernizing [Schultz (1975), Becker (1993), Huffman (1998)].[1]

1.2. Agricultural household models

The behavior of agricultural households has been modeled from different perspectives depending on the central issue researchers are considering. If human capital investment decisions – e.g., how much schooling, informal training, and information to obtain or whether to adopt a new technology – are the central focus, models of multi-period household utility maximization with human capital production or innovation have provided a useful guide to empirical models. If household members have obtained their human capital, e.g., formal education, and the impact of this human capital on other outcomes – e.g., occupational choice, hours of work, purchased input use, wage rates, income – is the central focus, one-period static agricultural household models have provided a useful guide to researchers about which variables are expected to affect behavior or outcomes and how they might be related. In particular, behavioral models provide one useful guide to researchers for deciding which variables should be treated as endogenous, e.g., choices, and which are exogenous or causal variables.

In the following two subsections, two representative agricultural household models are outlined. One is a multi-period dynamic agricultural household model, and the other is a single-period static agricultural household model.

---

[1] Average schooling completion levels of the adult population differ greatly across countries. Barro and Lee (1993) have recently constructed good estimates of schooling completion levels for a set of 125 countries for the period 1960–1985. They report summaries for regional groups of countries. In 1985, sub-Saharan Africa and South Asia had the lowest average schooling completion levels for adults, 2.67 and 2.81 years, respectively. In the Middle East and North Africa, the average schooling completion level was 3.51 years, and in Latin America and the Caribbean the average was 4.47 years. In other regions, the average schooling completion level for adults was higher, 5.19 years for East Asia and the Pacific, 8.88 years for the OECD countries, and 9.17 years for centrally planned economies (excluding China). No similar international data exists on schooling completion of the farm population.

1.2.1. A three-period model with human capital production and investment

Building on the multiperiod household decision model of Ghez and Beeker (1975), the human capital (e.g., education) investment model of Ben-Porath (1967) and Mincer (1974, pp. 14–15), and the one-period agricultural household models of Singh et al. (1986) and Huffman (1991b), a multiperiod agricultural household focused on consumption, human capital production, farm production, and human capital service allocation is presented. To capture the main economic issues in human capital investment decisions and yet to keep the model simple enough that many of its implications are easily interpretable, I assume that the household is risk-neutral and has a three-period planning horizon or lifetime.

In each period, the farm household is assumed to consume human capital services, i.e., leisure, L_{1j}, $j = t, t + 1, t + 2$, and goods X_{1j}, and to have a well-behaved intertemporal utility function:

$$U = U(L_{1t}, X_{1t}, L_{1t+1}, X_{1t+1}, L_{1t+2}, X_{2t+2}). \tag{1}$$

The household faces technology constraints on the production of human capital and farm output. First, the production of the human capital in each period, i.e., the investment, is assumed to use two variable inputs: human capital services L_{2j} from an individual's initial human capital endowment or past human capital investment, a purchased input X_{2j}, and a fixed individual or household-specific genetic or innate ability factor A_2:

$$Z_{2j} = F_2(L_{2j}, X_{2j}, A_2), \quad F_2(0, X_{2j}, A_2) = 0, \quad F_2(L_{2j}, 0, A_2) \geqslant 0. \tag{2}$$

$F_2(\cdot)$ exhibits decreasing returns to scale in L_2 and X_2. Hence, when the input prices of L_{2j} and X_{2j} are fixed to the household, the assumption of decreasing returns implies that marginal cost is rising with added Z_{2j}. For schooling, this assumption reflects the upper limit on mental capacity of an individual to learn in each period.

Second, the production of farm output is assumed to use two variable inputs and one fixed input. The variable inputs are human capital services of household members L_{3j} and purchase inputs X_{3j}, and the fixed input is technology and agro-climatic conditions A_3:

$$Z_{3j} = F_3(L_{3j}, X_{3j}, A_3). \tag{3}$$

The farm production function is assumed to exhibit decreasing return to scale in L_3 and X_3 in the region of an optimal solution, e.g., due to natural limitations placed on the production process by agro-climatic conditions.[2]

---

[2] If an active rental or asset market in farmland does not exist, then farmland is part of A_3.

To facilitate the modeling, human capital investments are assumed to change the quantity of human capital services available, but they do not affect the wage rate per unit of human capital service. Hence, this is a model where human capital investments augment the effective number of units of human time that are available each period rather than raising the wage per unit of actual time worked. The latter approach is the one taken by the hedonic wage literature, e.g., Mincer (1974) and Willis (1986).

The household has an initial human capital endowment K_t^0; human capital is permitted to depreciate over time at a rate δ, $0 \leqslant \delta < 1$, due to obsolescence or wearing out, and the human capital services available to the household in each period are:

$$L_j = \alpha K_j = \alpha \sum_{j=t}^{t+2} [(1-\delta)^{j-t} K_t^0 + \gamma (1-\delta)^{j-t-1} Z_{2j-1}], \tag{4}$$

where α (> 0) is the time invariant rate of conversion of human capital stock to services, and γ equals 1, adjusting human capital investment (a flow) to a stock. The available human capital services are allocated among four activities: leisure L_{1j}, human capital production L_{2j}, farm production L_{3j}, and wage work L_j^w:

$$L_j = L_{1j} + L_{2j} + L_{3j} + L_j^w, \quad L_{2j}, L_{3j}, L_j^w \geqslant 0. \tag{5}$$

Because human capital services allocated in any period j to human capital production, farm productions, and wage work can be zero, a non-negativity constraint is imposed on these choices.

The household faces a multiperiod cash budget constraint:

$$\sum_{j=t}^{t+2} \frac{P_{3j}^* Z_{3j} + W_j L_j^w}{(1+r)^{t-j}} = \sum_{i=1}^{3} \sum_{j=t}^{t+2} \frac{P_{ij} X_{ij} + C_j}{(1+r)^{j-t}}, \tag{6}$$

where P_{3j}^* is the (expected) price of farm output and P_{ij} is the (expected) price of the purchased consumption goods, inputs into human capital production, or inputs into farm production, respectively. The (expected) wage rate per unit of human capital services is W_j; $C_j \geqslant 0$ is any fixed cost associated with the household's production or consumption activities, e.g., on licenses or fees; and r is a fixed discount rate.

If Equation (3) is substituted into Equation (6), then the farm production and multiperiod budget constraints are combined into one constraint:

$$\sum_{j=t}^{t+2} \frac{P_{3j}^* F_3(L_{3j}, X_{3j}, A_3) + W_j L_j^w}{(1+r)^{j-t}} = \sum_{i=1}^{3} \sum_{j=t}^{t+2} \frac{P_{ij} X_{ij} + C_j}{(1+r)^{j-t}}. \tag{7}$$

The household can now be viewed as making multiperiod consumption, human capital production, farm production, and labor supply decisions by maximizing Equation (1) subject to Equations (7), (2), (4), and (5), including nonnegativity constraints. The Kuhn–Tucker first-order conditions are

$$\frac{\partial \Phi}{\partial L_{1j}} = \frac{\partial U}{\partial L_{1j}} - \frac{\lambda_j}{(1+r)^{j-t}} = 0, \quad j = t, t+1, t+2, \tag{8}$$

$$\frac{\partial \Phi}{\partial X_{1j}} = \frac{\partial U}{\partial X_{1j}} - \frac{P_{1j}}{(1+r)^{j-t}} = 0, \tag{9}$$

$$\frac{\partial \Phi}{\partial L_{2t}} = \zeta\left(PV^t_{Z_{2t}} MP^{Z_2}_{L_{2t}} - \lambda_t\right) \leqslant 0, \quad L_{2t} \geqslant 0, \quad L_{2t}\left(PV^t_{Z_{2t}} MP^{Z_2}_{L_{2t}} - \lambda_t\right) = 0, \tag{10}$$

where

$$PV^t_{Z_{2t}} = \frac{P^*_{3t+1}}{(1+r)} \frac{\partial Z_{3t+1}}{\partial L_{3t+1}} \frac{\partial L_{3t+1}}{\partial Z_{2t}} + \frac{P^*_{3t+2}}{(1+r)^2} \frac{\partial Z_{3t+2}}{\partial L_{3t+2}} \frac{\partial L_{3t+2}}{\partial Z_{2t}} + \frac{W_t \alpha}{(1+r)}$$
$$+ \frac{W_{t+1}\alpha(1-\delta)}{(1+r)^2},$$

and

$$MP^{Z_2}_{L_{2t}} = \frac{\partial Z_{2t}}{\partial L_{2t}}, \qquad MP^{Z_2}_{x_{2t}} = \frac{\partial Z_{2t}}{\partial X_{2t}};$$

$$\frac{\partial \Phi}{\partial X_{2t}} = \zeta\left(PV^t_{Z_{2t}} MP^{Z_2}_{X_{2t}} - P_{2t}\right) \leqslant 0, \quad X_{2t} \geqslant 0,$$

$$X_{2t}\left(PV^t_{Z_{2t}} MP^{Z_2}_{X_{2t}} - P_{2t}\right) = 0, \tag{11}$$

$$\frac{\partial \Phi}{\partial L_{2t+1}} = \zeta\left(PV^t_{Z_{2t+1}} MP^{Z_2}_{L_{2t+1}} - \frac{\lambda_{t+1}}{1+r}\right) \leqslant 0, \quad L_{2t+1} \geqslant 0,$$

$$L_{2t+1}\left(PV^t_{Z_{t+1}} MP^{Z_2}_{L_{2t+1}} - \frac{\lambda_{t+1}}{1+r}\right) = 0, \tag{12}$$

where

$$PV^t_{Z_{2t+1}} = \frac{P^*_{3t+2}}{(1+r)^2} \frac{\partial Z_{3t+2}}{\partial L_{3t+2}} \frac{\partial L_{3t+1}}{\partial Z_{2t+1}};$$

$$\frac{\partial \Phi}{\partial X_{2t+1}} = \zeta\left(PV^t_{Z_{2t+1}} MP^{Z_2}_{X_{2t+1}} - \frac{P_{2t+1}}{1+r}\right) \leqslant 0, \quad Z_{2t+1} \geqslant 0,$$

$$X_{2t+1}\left(PV^t_{Z_{2t+1}} MP^{Z_2}_{X_{2t+1}} - \frac{P_{2t+1}}{1+r}\right) = 0, \tag{13}$$

$$\frac{\partial \Phi}{\partial L_{3j}} = \zeta P^*_{3j} MP^{Z_3}_{L_{3j}} - \frac{\lambda_j}{(1+r)^{j-t}} \leqslant 0, \quad L_{3j} \geqslant 0,$$

$$L_{3j}\left(\zeta P^*_{3j} MP^{Z_3}_{L_{3j}} - \frac{\lambda_j}{(1+r)^{j-t}}\right) = 0, \tag{14}$$

$$\frac{\partial \Phi}{\partial X_{3j}} = \zeta P^*_{3j} MP^{Z_3}_{X_{3j}} - \frac{P_{ij}}{(1+r)^{j-t}} = 0, \tag{15}$$

$$\frac{\partial \Phi}{\partial L^w_j} = \frac{(-\lambda_j + W_j)}{(1+r)^{j-t}} \leqslant 0, \quad L^w_j \geqslant 0, \quad L^W_j(-\lambda_j + W_j) = 0, \tag{16}$$

plus Equations (7), (2), (4), and (5), where $\lambda_j/(1+r)^{j-t}$ is the marginal utility of human capital services in period j, and ζ is the marginal utility of discounted cash income.

A little interpretation of the first-order conditions is enlightening. Equations (8) and (9) imply the standard condition for optimal mix of consumption goods in each period. The ratios of the marginal utilities of the two goods should equal the ratio of their respective marginal cost or shadow price, i.e., $MU_{L_{1j}}/MU_{X_{1j}} = \lambda_j/P_{ij}$. Equations (10)–(12), and (13) imply that the production of human capital (investment) in each period occurs at minimum cost, i.e.,

$$\frac{MP_{L_{2t}}}{MP_{X_{2t}}} = \frac{\lambda_t}{P_{2t}}, \quad \frac{MP_{L_{2t+1}}}{MP_{X_{2t+1}}} = \frac{\lambda_{t+t}}{P_{2t+1}}.$$

Equations (14) and (15) imply that the production of farm output is at minimum cost in each period,

$$\frac{MP_{L_{3j}}}{MP_{X_{3j}}} = \frac{\lambda_j}{P_{3j}}.$$

Because of the human capital focus of this chapter, Equations (10) through (14) have special meaning. First, they provide the information about the optimal size of the human capital investment in each period. It is the quantity or rate where the present value of the marginal return from a unit of Z_2 equals the present value of the marginal cost. For period t this implies

$$PV^t_{Z_{2t}} = MC_{Z_{2t}} = \frac{\lambda_t}{MP^{Z_2}_{L_{2t}}} = \frac{P_{2t}}{MP^{Z_2}_{X_{2t}}}.$$

Second, insights about the tendency for investing in skill to weaken or strengthen ties to farming are obtained by examining the present value of the marginal return for Z_2. There are two effects – the change in the present value of the additional farm production that results from allocating part of an incremental unit of human capital services to this activity, and the change in the present value of the additional labor market earnings that results from allocating the remaining part of an increment of human capital services to nonfarm wage work.

The allocation of an increment in human capital services between farm production and off-farm work is quite sensitive to the relative impact of human capital on the marginal product of labor in farm and non-farm work or to the elasticity of demand faced by the individual for human capital services. If the marginal product of human capital services is low, perhaps zero, in farm production but relatively large in nonfarm wage work, and it is optimal to invest in human capital, then an agricultural household will increase the share of employed human capital services allocated to nonfarm wage work. This outcome might be expected in countries where skills are rewarded in the nonfarm labor market but where new technologies for agriculture are being developed slowly. Alternatively, wage rates in the nonfarm labor might be unaffected by skill, e.g., due to the physically demanding nature of the work or institutional factors, but agriculture might be receiving a steady stream of new technologies that require skill to use them effectively. In this scenario, an increment of schooling will not affect an individual's nonfarm wage but will raise his marginal product at farm work. Hence, if an investment in an increment of human capital is optimal, an agricultural household will increase the share of its employed human capital services that is allocated to farm work. In this case, investing in schooling for farm people would not necessarily be expected to cause an exit of schooled individuals from farms to the cities for work.

Third, given the three-period lifetime, a comparison of the present value of the marginal return to an investment in period t and $t+1$ shows that delaying the investment from t to $t+1$ significantly reduces the present value of the marginal return. Hence, it is optimal for agricultural households to make large human capital investments early in an individual's life rather than later. Furthermore, it is never optimal in this model for a household to invest any resources in human capital production in period $t+2$ because there is cost but no return.

Fourth, because the marginal cost of human capital production is increasing, it will frequently be optimal for an agricultural household to spread its human capital investment in an individual over more than one period, even with finite life and associated reduced present value of the marginal return. Spreading the investment over time is a good decision when the cost saving exceeds the reduction in returns due to delaying (see Figure 1). Fifth, if the length of life were to be extended to four periods, e.g., due to better public health measures, this would increase the demand for human capital investment, and other things being equal, increase life-time human capital (e.g., schooling) investment per individual.

At an interior solution, except $L_{2t+2} = X_{2t+2} = 0$, the model implies that human capital services are allocated in t and $t+1$ such that at the margin

$$\frac{MU_{L_{1j}}}{\zeta} = PV_{Z_{2j}^t}MP_{L_{2j}} = P_{3j}^*MP_{L_{3j}}^{Z_3} = W_j.$$

Given the finite planning horizon, the optimal allocation of human capital services in $t+2$ is such that at the margin

$$\frac{MU_{L_{1j}}}{\zeta} = P_{3j}^*MP_{L_{3j}}^{Z_3} = W_j.$$

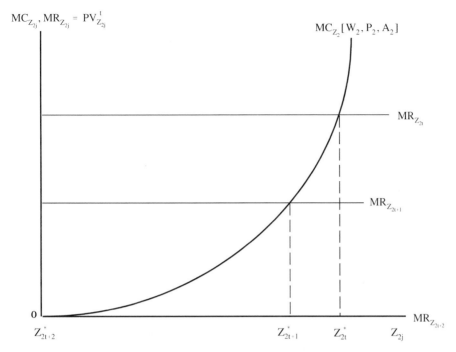

Figure 1. Optimal production of human capital.

In these two scenarios, farm production decisions are separable from household consumption, human capital production, and labor supply decisions, i.e., farm input/output decisions are static profit-maximizing decisions with W_j as the price of L_{3j}. Furthermore, given that life is finite and that investment in human capital early in life increases the total available human capital services available for allocating later in life, a likely scenario in the initial period t is that optimal $L_t^w = L_{3t} = 0$, i.e., none of an individual's human capital services is to farm and nonfarm work, and available human capital services are allocated to consumption and human capital production. In this case, the opportunity cost of human capital services used in human capital production (consumption) is its marginal value in foregone leisure (future labor productivity increases).

As a guide to empirical researchers and research, this model has as endogenous or choice variables in each period the following: the quantity of goods for consumption, leisure, and purchased inputs; inputs for human capital production (investment); human capital services, and purchased inputs; inputs for farm production, human capital services and purchased inputs; and supply of labor (human capital services) to the nonfarm labor market. An upper limit to the set of relevant exogenous variables is the following list:

$$W_t, W_{t+1}, W_{t+2}, P_{1t}, P_{1t+1}, P_{1t+2}, P_{2t}, P_{2t+1}, P_{2t+2}, P_{3t}^*, P_{3t+1}^*, P_{3t+2}^*, P_{3t},$$
$$P_{3t+1}, P_{3t+2}, C_t, C_{t+1}, C_{t+2}, A_2, A_3, \alpha, \delta, \text{ and } r.$$

1.2.2. A one-period static model

Drawing upon the agricultural household models of Singh et al. (1986) and Huffman (1991b, 1996b), the farm household is assumed to make resource allocation decisions for any production cycle by maximizing utility subject to resource and technology constraints. The farm household is assumed to derive utility from a home-produced good Y_1 and from leisure L:

$$U = U(Y_1, L). \tag{17}$$

First, the household faces a technology constraint from the farm-household production or transformation function:

$$F(Y_1, Y_2, Y_3, H, X, A, E) = 0, \quad Y_3 \geqslant 0, \; X \geqslant 0, \tag{18}$$

where Y_1 is output of the home good, and Y_2 and Y_3 are outputs produced for sale. Output Y_3 may or may not be produced, so a non-negativity constraint is imposed. H is hours of farm-household work by members, and X is purchased variable inputs, which might not be used, so a non-negativity constraint is imposed. A is technology and agro-climatic conditions, and E is an education index of household decision makers. The production function permits adopting new inputs (and discarding old ones) and expanding or reducing the number of outputs produced. It also accommodates substitute or complement relationships between variable inputs, and schooling of the decision maker(s) can enhance technical efficiency. For model development, an asymmetric form of the transformation function is used:

$$Y_2 = f(Y_1, Y_3, H, X, A, E), \quad Y_3 \geqslant 0, \; X \geqslant 0. \tag{19}$$

Second, the household faces a human time constraint:

$$T = L + H + H_m, \quad H_m \geqslant 0, \tag{20}$$

where total available time per production cycle T is allocated among leisure L, farm-household work H, and off-farm wage work H_m. A non-negativity constraint is imposed on H_m because it may be zero.

Third, the household faces a cash income constraint:

$$I = P_2 Y_2 + P_3 Y_3 + W_m H_m + V = W_X X, \tag{21}$$

where P_2 and P_3 are the market prices of Y_2 and Y_3, W_m is the market wage rate for off-farm work, V is household nonfarm-nonlabor income net of any fixed costs associated with farm-household production, and W_X is the market price of X. All prices are assumed to be given to households, but the off-farm wage rate depends on human capital E and local economic conditions Φ, i.e., $W_m = W(E, \Phi)$.

If Equation (19) is substituted for Y_2 in Equation (21), then two of the three constraints facing the household are combined:

$$P_2 f(Y_1, Y_3, H, X, A, E) + P_3 Y_3 + W_m H_m + V = W_X X. \tag{22}$$

The household can now be viewed as making consumption, production, and labor supply decisions (i.e., choice set C: Y_1, L, Y_3, H, X, and H_m) by maximizing Equation (17) subject to Equations (22) and (20), including the non-negativity constraints. The Kuhn–Tucker first-order conditions are:

$$\frac{\partial U}{\partial Y_1} = -\lambda_1 P_2 \frac{\partial Y_2}{\partial Y_1}, \tag{23}$$

$$\frac{\partial U}{\partial L} = \lambda_2, \tag{24}$$

$$\lambda_1 \left(P_2 \frac{\partial Y_2}{\partial Y_3} + P_3 \right) \leqslant 0, \quad Y_3 \geqslant 0, \quad Y_3 \left(P_2 \frac{\partial Y_2}{\partial Y_3} + P_3 \right) = 0, \tag{25}$$

$$\lambda_1 P_2 \frac{\partial Y_2}{\partial H} - \lambda_2 = 0, \tag{26}$$

$$\lambda_1 \left(P_2 \frac{\partial Y_2}{\partial X} - W_x \right) \leqslant 0, \quad X \geqslant 0, \quad X \left(P_2 \frac{\partial Y_2}{\partial X} - W_x \right) = 0, \tag{27}$$

$$\lambda_1 W_m - \lambda_2 \leqslant 0, \quad H_m \geqslant 0, \quad H_m (\lambda_1 W_m - \lambda_2) = 0, \tag{28}$$

plus Equations (22) and (20) where λ_1 is the marginal utility of cash income and λ_2 is the marginal utility of human time. With an interior solution, Equations (23), (24), and (28) imply optimal marginal rate of substitution between home goods Y_1 and leisure L of

$$\frac{\partial U / \partial Y_1}{\partial U / \partial L} = -\frac{P_2 \partial Y_2 / \partial Y_1}{W_m},$$

or the ratio of their opportunity costs ($\partial Y_2 / \partial Y_1 < 0$). If production of Y_3 is to occur, the value of the marginal reduction of Y_2 to produce Y_3 must equal the price of Y_3 (i.e., $-P_2 \partial Y_2 / \partial Y_3 = P_3$). At an interior solution, family labor and purchased inputs are to be used such that the value of the marginal product of an input equals its respective price (Equations (26) and (27)).

As a guide to empirical research and researchers, this static model has a slightly different configuration of endogenous and exogenous variables than the three-period model. The endogenous or choice variables are home-produced goods Y_1 and leisure L, production of Y_1, Y_2, and Y_3, purchase of variable inputs X, and hours of on-farm and off-farm work by household members. The upper limit to set of exogenous variables driving these decisions includes P_1, P_2, P_3, W_X, W_m, V, A, and E. In particular, at an interior solution, the farm production decisions can be separated from the household consumption and labor supply decisions. Farm input decisions are then profit-

maximizing decisions where the price of family labor is the off-farm wage. Furthermore, if the household has a "garden" rather than a farm, the agricultural household
model is applicable to most rural and some urban households.

1.3. More about agriculture

Schooling and experience may be productive or unproductive in agriculture depending on economic conditions, but in economies with freely mobile resources, agriculture
must compete with other sectors for skilled (and unskilled) labor. The wage to similarly
skilled labor need not be equal across sectors, but in equilibrium the marginal compensation, including monetary value of nonmonetary attributes of the farm and nonfarm work,
will be equal. Recently the U.S. farm-nonfarm compensating differential has been small
[Huffman (1996a)]. Although agriculture can in some cases compete with the nonfarm
sector on rate of technical change, the opportunities for raising labor productivity in
agriculture through task specialization and coordination or teamwork may be modest
compared to the nonfarm sector, i.e., the skilled individual may face a more inelastic
demand for his services on a farm than in a large nonfarm business. Also, the agricultural sector may in some cases face small market size and high coordination costs that
put it at a disadvantage.

Formal schooling is part skill creation, part local culturalization, and part screening.
The composition differs across countries and through the grade levels within a country.
Skill creation generally receives most of the attention in economics, and skill creation
fits neatly into a human capital framework. Primary schooling, which emphasizes literacy, numeracy, and problem- solving skills for its graduates, creates basic skills that
are generally productive to farm people and provide a foundation for secondary and
higher education. Secondary schooling encompasses a range of skills, sometimes being mainly college preparatory and at the other extreme being quite utilitarian. In the
U.S. before 1890, high schools were primarily college preparatory, located in cities, and
were not teaching skills generally useful to farm people. Starting about 1900, secondary
schools in America were transformed into a new and generally useful institution for the
masses, including farm people [Goldin (1998), Goldin and Katz (1999a, 1999b)]. The
new high schools had a new curriculum centered around English, geometry, algebra,
accounting, and typing, that could serve as a useful terminal degree providing skills for
life's work or as college preparation. These schools were "open", admitting all students
who had completed the requirements of public elementary schools. From 1910 to 1940,
U.S. high school enrollment and graduation rates grew rapidly, especially in the Great
Plains, West, and Midwest where agriculture was relatively important. Higher education
becomes potentially useful to farm people when successful decision making in agriculture requires depth of understanding of science and business or when farm people need
to prepare for an occupation outside of agriculture.

In some agricultural environments, experience rather than schooling may be a more
important form of human capital, while in other environments, schooling has a major
advantage over experience [Schultz (1964), Becker (1993, pp. 1–13), Huffman (1991a,

1985)]. In a static (political, economic, technical) environment, accumulated experience seems to be a better investment than schooling. Information accumulated through experience in farming or working in the household does not depreciate when the environment is unchanging. Work experience is a relatively valuable form of training, e.g., farmers can learn much that is useful for decision making from their own and others' experiences. However, when the political and economic environments are changing in a market economy, or new technologies are regularly becoming available, skills obtained from formal schooling have an advantage over on-the-job training. Most new agricultural technologies are geo-climatic or land-specific, and changing technologies cause rapid depreciation in land-specific human capital. Being able to make good decisions on information acquisition and technology adoption is valuable. Hence, a changing agricultural environment is expected to increase the expected returns to formal schooling and possibly to reduce the opportunity cost of schooling for farm male youth (reduce the expected payoff to farm-specific human capital) [Foster and Rosenzweig (1996)]. These are all arguments for allocative efficiency effects of human capital. Schooling and experience may also enhance the technical efficiency at agricultural production activities, but for enhancing technical efficiency, experience seems likely to be a more important form of human capital in both static and dynamic environments.

For farmers to have access to new technologies, they must have either a successful national research and development (R&D) system or access to international technologies. In all cases, some special attention must be given to adaptive research to meet local agricultural conditions. Farmers in developed countries have access to locally, nationally, and internationally developed technologies, but the technologies available in developed countries are frequently limited to the output of the national public agricultural research system and possibly the international agricultural research centers.

2. Empirical evidence

2.1. Choices about where to work

Worldwide about one-half of the labor force works in agriculture [The World Bank (1997, pp. 220–221)]. A large majority are unpaid farm workers – the farmers who make decisions and work, and other farm family members who work generally without direct compensation – and a minority are hired (nonfarm family) workers. Hired workers are generally of two types: regular full time and seasonal. Seasonal labor demand variation arises largely from the definite seasonal pattern to biological events in plants, which creates unusually large labor demand at planting, weeding, and/or harvest time. The supply of seasonal agricultural labor generally has a local component and a migratory component [see Emerson (1984)].

Over the long term the share of the labor force employed in agriculture has declined dramatically in what are now developed countries, but slowly or not at all in low income or developing countries [Johnson (1997), OECD (1995)]. Decisions on schooling by families and communities are an important factor determining whether individuals work in agriculture or elsewhere. Even in developed countries where farmers are relatively well educated, hired farm workers have significantly less education. For example, in the United States, hired farm workers have about 50 percent as much schooling as farm operators [Huffman (1996b)], and in 1990, 53 percent of seasonal crop workers had less than 8 years of schooling [Gabbard and Mines (1995)]. In this latter group, about 60 percent were foreign born and 40 percent undocumented.[3] This subsection examines the impact of schooling on individuals' choices of where to work in a free society.

Choosing agriculture.   Whether to work in agriculture or in another industry is an important decision worldwide. In India and China, which account for about 40 percent of the world's population, and in other low income countries, about 65 percent of the labor force in 1990 was employed in agriculture. In Western Europe, less than 10 percent of the labor force was employed in agriculture, and in the United States the share was only 3 percent. In noncentrally planned countries, individuals make a choice of an occupation/industry for work.

Orazem and Mattila (1991) have examined occupational choices for U.S. high school graduates. Graduates are assumed to choose the occupation that maximizes their expected lifetime utility, where indirect utility depends primarily on the mean and variance of earnings and income independent of occupational choice. Their model is similar to the three-period conceptual model presented in the previous section, and goes beyond and is superior to the (lifetime) earnings maximization models [e.g., Ben-Porath (1967)]. Schooling is also permitted to produce different amounts of occupation-specific human capital, i.e., schooling is not equally productive across occupations. This occupation-specific human capital is a function of the intensity with which a student invests in school (attendance rate) and school (teacher) quality.

Orazem and Mattila (1991) then use the model to examine the choices of Maryland high school graduates (1951–69) among eight activities: six occupations (including farming, fishing, and mining) and two college options. They found that increasing the mean of the earnings distribution (or reducing the variance) for an occupation/activity i increases the probability that activity i is selected by high school graduates. The quality of secondary schooling is shown to affect graduates' activity choices differentially, suggesting that schooling has an activity-specific and a general training component. In particular, increasing schooling quality reduces the proportion of high school graduates going into farming, fishing, or mining relative to other occupations, or continuing with college. Hence, parameters of occupational-earnings distributions and school quality seem to affect occupational choices of rural youth in free societies, but there is considerable potential here for future research on occupational choice involving agriculture.

---

[3] See Martin et al. (1995) for an extensive review of the use of foreign, including undocumented, workers in U.S. agriculture and an examination of the impacts on U.S. agriculture of the Immigration Reform and Control Act of 1986.

Perloff (1991) has examined wage workers' industrial choice of work (in agriculture versus nonagriculture) and wages by industry for U.S. low-educated nonurban workers. Workers are assumed to choose the industry that gives them the largest total current benefit, i.e., wage adjusted for the monetary value of the (dis)utility of work. The probability of wage-work in agriculture is then a function of individual, family, and regional attributes. Wage equations by industry are then a function of workers' attributes and regional/state location of work.

To focus on the population for which working in agriculture seemed most relevant, Perloff limited his sample to nonurban male wage workers who were age 16 or older, had 9 years or fewer of schooling, and were working 15 or more hours per week. The sample is from the 1988 U.S. Current Population Survey. The results showed that a year of additional schooling increased the probability of working in agriculture for workers having less than 5 years of schooling, but reduced the probability for those having more than 5 years. An additional year of post-schooling experience increased the probability of choosing agriculture only for workers having more than 32 years of experience. A worker being Mexican, non-Mexican Hispanic, or black increased his probability of choosing agriculture.

Using a hedonic wage equation, Perloff found significant differences in the agriculture and nonagriculture wage structures. An additional year of schooling had a (small) positive effect on the wage in agriculture up to 5 years, but no significant effect on the nonagriculture wage. An added year of post-schooling experience had no significant effect on the wage in agriculture but a (small) positive effect on the nonagricultural wage up to 33 years. In agriculture, Mexicans, other Hispanics, and blacks earned significantly more than whites, but in nonagriculture, the blacks earned 15 percent less than whites, and Mexican and other Hispanics had wage rates that were not significantly different from whites' (with the same education and experience). Controlling for demographic differences, the agriculture wage differed significantly across regions and states, but for nonagriculture, no difference across regions and states existed, except in California, where wages were higher. Perloff then fitted a structural participation equation using the predicted agricultural–nonagricultural wage differentials adjusted for selectivity, and found strong positive effects of the agriculture-nonagriculture wage differential on the probability of working in agriculture. He concluded that low-education nonurban male wage workers are quite responsive to the agriculture-nonagriculture wage differential.[4]

Migration.   As economic conditions change in interconnected labor markets, workers in free societies invest in migration to improve their future economic welfare (see the three-period model in the previous section), which tends to reduce or eliminate inter-market wage differences. This complicates the problem of explaining migration because

---

[4] Perloff also concluded that if the supply of undocumented workers to U.S. agriculture was to end, the wage rate in agriculture would rise relatively, and significant positive supply response would arise from low-educated nonurban U.S. workers.

individuals are acting on anticipated wage rate differences rather than the ex post values. Schooling has been hypothesized to play a significant role in these adjustments or reallocations because of its effect on both the costs and returns to migration.

Migratory agricultural workers incur moving costs in exchange for a higher expected wage in a new location. Emerson (1989) examines the earnings structure for migratory and nonmigratory work and the probability of migration for 559 domestic males in a survey of Florida farm workers. A migrant, an individual who has earnings in two or more states during the survey year, is hypothesized to have a different earnings structure for nonmigratory work. He finds that the expected earnings difference between migratory and nonmigratory work increases significantly as the probability of a worker being migratory increases. For these workers, the mean schooling completion level was 6.5 years, and a worker's schooling had a positive but not significantly different from zero (5 percent) effect on being migratory.

Perloff et al. (1998) examine the migratory responsiveness of seasonal agricultural service labor to geographical wage differences using the National Agricultural Workers Surveys 1989–1991. They define migration as a worker traveling at least 75 miles for perishable crop work during a survey year. They test and confirm the hypothesis that workers who have the largest expected gain to migration are the ones who actually migrate for work. In a probit equation explaining the probability of a worker migrating, they find the worker's amount of schooling has no significant effect. However, a worker's U.S. farm labor market experience and a worker being female had significant negative effects on the probability of migration.

Taylor (1986, 1987) examined the decisions of rural Mexican households to allocate adult labor to work in Mexico or to work as undocumented labor in the United States. Mexican households are assumed to employ adults so as to maximize expected (source) household income. If the adult migrates as an undocumented worker, his or her contribution to Mexican source household income is expected remittances net of migration costs, and the probability of successful undocumented migration is assumed to be a function of individual and family attributes. Net remittances and Mexican income from work are each assumed to be a function of individual and source household attributes.

Taylor (1987) fits his model to data for randomly chosen households in a rural Mexican village 2,000 kilometers from the U.S.–Mexican border. In a (reduced-form) equation explaining the probability of undocumented Mexico–U.S. migration, he found that an adult's age has a significantly positive effect up to 36 years for men and 32 years for women, one added year of experience as an undocumented Mexico–U.S. migrant has a significantly positive effect up to 9 years, but an added year of worker schooling has a significantly negative effect. The latter result arises because more educated rural Mexican adults have relatively better labor market opportunities in Mexican cities than in the United States. A Mexican household having a migration kinship network, i.e., family contacts in the United States, has a significantly positive effect on the probability of undocumented Mexico–U.S. migration. The reason put forth in the network reduces the costs to a potential immigrant of crossing the border and finding a job. Hence, Taylor presents evidence which many researchers would find counterintuitive: an individual's schooling reduces rather than increases his or her likelihood to migrate internationally. Migration kinship networks seem to be highly substitutable for educators in understanding Mexico–U.S. migration. Finding collaborative evidence in other parts of the world would seem to be a useful activity.

Taylor (1987) also reports results for fitted income equations, one for Mexico–U.S. migrant remittances and one for income contribution by working in Mexico. He found that a worker's education has a positive and significant effect on his or her Mexican income but no significant effect on remittances to Mexico. U.S. experience as an undocumented migrant has a significantly positive effect on remittances and on Mexican income, but Mexican experience as a migrant in Mexico has a positive effect only on Mexican income. Thus, U.S. work experience seems to produce a type of general human capital, but work experience in Mexico seems to produce country-specific skills.

Taylor (1987) then fits a structural probit to explain Mexican–U.S. undocumented migration. He uses the fitted remittance and Mexican worker income equation, corrected for selection, to estimate for each worker the difference between his or her predicted migrant remittance and predicted Mexican worker income. This difference in income is then shown to contribute positively to the probability of undocumented Mexico–U.S. migration while leaving the effects of a migrant's U.S. experience, migration kinship network, and age largely unchanged from the reduced-form equation.

Barkley (1990) presents economic evidence on the determinants of net migration of labor out of U.S. production agriculture, 1940–1985. This is an especially interesting period because employment in U.S. agriculture declined about 300 percent. He hypothesized and found that labor was responding to a significant decline in the expected payoff to working in agriculture relative to other industries. A higher return to labor in nonfarm work relative to farm work increased the net exit rate from agriculture. Higher real land prices, which raises the wealth position of farm labor that owns land, however, tended to reduce the migration of labor out of agriculture. Government program payments which clearly affect farm income did not affect migration, except perhaps through the land prices or returns to farm labor. Being a farmer creates location-specific information about the land, climate, and input supplies, and Huffman and Feridhanusetyawan (2001) have shown that being self-employed or a farmer causes a significant reduction in the likelihood of an adult male experiencing interstate migration. But formal schooling which creates general skills was shown to have a strong positive effect on the likelihood of migrating.

Huang, Orazem and Wohlgemuth (2001) applied a human capital model, similar to the three-period model, in their examination of the underlying causes of growth and decline in U.S. rural county populations by decade, 1950–90. They examined population growth rates for 306 southern and midwestern counties and tested for human capital and labor market opportunity effects. They found that rural counties that had a higher average adult schooling level at the beginning of a decade had a higher rate of loss of population over the following decade. When a county was farther from a large city, had more concentrated employment by industry, had a larger share of population on farms or share of population who were black, it had a larger rate of population loss over the following decade. Over their study period, schooling yielded higher returns in urban than rural areas. Hence, in rural U.S. counties that invested more in schooling of children, the rate of net export of human capital to other counties was larger. Because of positive, expected geographical spillover effects of rural schooling, a significant part of the cost should be borne by areas that are expected to benefit – e.g., state and federal sources [Olson (1969, 1986)].

In contrast to the human capital approach taken by Huang and Orazem to modeling annual county population growth rates, Goetz and Debertin (1996) rejected a human capital approach. They employed a rather *naive* empirical economic model for explaining rural county population growth rates over 1980–90. It placed all the emphasis on *actual* characteristics of counties at the beginning of the period, e.g., average characteristics of farms, average earnings in farming and other occupations, and total employment across industries, and the net birth rate from 1980 to 1990. The authors argued that individual characteristics, e.g., education and age, are unimportant, and ignored information about the expected commuting distance to work and earning prospects elsewhere. Also, they apparently considered birth rates to be an uneconomic decision. Another deficiency is their use of actual characteristics of counties in 1980 to explain population growth: Individuals presumably use as information for migration decisions anticipated rather than actual characteristics, although past values do represent naive expectations formation.

Off-farm work.   Although farmers or cultivators tend to be tied to the land and to be geographically immobile, off-farm work of farmers is a relatively common international phenomenon. Since the 1950s and 1960s aggregate demand for operator and family farm labor in all of the developed countries has declined [see OECD (1995)], the demand for housework in farm households has generally declined as family sizes have declined and labor-saving household technologies have been adopted [Bryant (1986)], and the real nonfarm wage has generally increased. Faced with needing to make adjustments in labor allocation, farm households in the developed countries have frequently chosen to continue in farming but also to supply labor of some of its members to the nonfarm sector [e.g., see Hallberg et al. (1991)].

Most empirical studies of off-farm work participation of farm household members have used an agricultural household model similar to the static conceptual model presented in the previous section. In this framework, an individual's schooling has been an important determinant of off-farm work participation in middle- and high-income countries. In all the published econometric studies of off-farm work participation of farm operators in the U.S., Canada, and Israel, the operator's schooling has been shown to have a positive and statistically significant effect on his probability of off-farm work (see Table 1). Fewer studies have examined off-farm work decisions of farm wives, but a farm wife's schooling has a positive and significant effect on her probability of off-farm work too [see Huffman and Lange (1989), Gould and Saupe (1989), Tokle and Huffman (1991), Lass and Gempesaw (1992), Kimhi (1994), and Abdulai and Delgado (1999)]. Cross-person schooling effects between spouses are mixed in sign and generally statistical significance. Where wage equations have been part of these econometric

Table 1
Summary of econometric evidence: probability of participation in off-farm work.

Off-farm participation	Location	Dependent data type	Operator's variable	Marginal effect on probability of male operators' off-farm work				
				Operator's schooling	Spouse's schooling	Age	Age^2	Nonfarm asset income
Huffman (1980)	U.S. (Iowa, N.C., Okla.)	1964 census ct. aggre. avg.	Log (odds of off-farm work)	+[a]	+[a]	+	−	+
Sumner (1982)	U.S. (Ill.)	1971 farm level	Probit (1,0)	+	−	+[a]	−[a]	−[a]
Huffman/Lange (1989)	U.S. (Iowa)	1977 farm level	Probit (1,0)	+[a]	−[a]	−	−	−
Jensen/Salant (1985)	U.S. (Miss., Tenn.)	1981 farm level	Probit (1,0)	+[a]	−	+[a]	−[a]	−[a]
Bollman (1979)	Canada	1971 census 1971 census	Probit (1,0)	+[a]	+[a]	−[a]		−[a]
Gould/Saupe (1989)	U.S. (Wis.)	1986 farm level	Probit (1,0)	+	+	+[a]	−[a]	−
Lass, Findeis, and Hallberg (1989)								
Tokle/Huffman (1991)	U.S.	1978–82 household level	Probit (1,0)	+	−[a]	+[a]	+[a]	−[a]
Lass/Gempesaw (1992)	U.S. (Pa.)	1985 farm level	Probit (1,0)	+	+[a]	+[a]	−[a]	−[a]
Kimhi (1994)	Israel (1981 census)	1981 farm level	Probit (1,0)	+[a]	−[a]	+[a]	−[a]	excluded

[a] Computed from a coefficient that is significantly different from zero at 5 percent level.

studies, an individual's schooling always has a positive and significant effect on his or her off-farm wage, and an individual's experience also has been a significant predictor of the wage.

Overall, the review of the literature has shown that the quantity and quality of an individual's schooling affects his or her choice of where to work. In the U.S., higher secondary school quality seems to reduce the likelihood of an individual choosing an occupation in agriculture. For less-educated wage workers, say less than 5 years, added schooling increases the likelihood of working in agriculture. U.S. domestic and undocumented migratory farm workers seem to function relatively well with low levels of schooling. For individuals in developed countries who are farmers and continue farming, additional schooling increases the likelihood that they will participate in off-farm wage work, but not necessarily for those in Green Revolution areas of developing countries. Higher schooling levels are in general associated with a population that is more geographically mobile.

2.2. Technology adoption and information acquisition

The decision to adopt new technologies is an investment decision because significant costs are incurred in obtaining information and learning about the performance characteristics of one or more new technologies and the returns are distributed over time. Furthermore, only a small share of the new technologies that become available will be profitable for any given farmer to adopt. This means that there is a large amount of uncertainty facing farmers, and additional schooling may help them make better adoption decisions and increase farm profitability. Because additional schooling affects the amount of knowledge that a farmer has about how technologies might work and his or her information evaluation skills, additional schooling may affect his or her choice of the type and amount of information to acquire. Hence, a model similar to the three-period model of the previous section provides a useful guide to the empirical literature. Also, see Besley and Case (1993) for examples of particular choice-based empirical models of farmers' technology adoption.

When technology is new and widely profitable, farmers' schooling has been shown to be positively related to the probability of adoption. When a technology has been available for an extended period (e.g., several years) or it is not widely profitable, farmers' schooling is generally unrelated to adoption/use of the technology. Schooling has been shown to affect choice of information channels about new technologies.

Huffman and Mercier (1991) examined the adoption of microcomputers and/or purchased computer services by a 1982–84 sample of Iowa farmers. Farmers' schooling has a positive and statistically significant effect on the probability of adopting a microcomputer, adopting purchased computer services, and adopting both a microcomputer and computer services. As farmers become older, they have fewer years to capture returns from changing, and farmers' age has a negative and significant effect on adopting all combinations of computer technologies. Although arguments can be made for off-farm work releasing credit constraints and giving exposure to computer use and usefulness, a higher probability of off-farm work by these farmers reduces (significantly) the probability of adopting a microcomputer, and tends to reduce adoption of purchased computer services.

Putler and Zilberman (1988) examined computer use by a 1986 sample of (Tulare County) California farmers who had relatively high schooling completion levels. Forty-six percent of these farmers had completed a college bachelor's (4-year) degree, and of them 11 percent had also completed a graduate degree. The authors found that farmers who were college graduates, i.e., individuals who had completed bachelor's and graduate degrees, had higher probabilities of computer adoption than farmers who completed only elementary or high school. However, individuals who completed some college but did not receive at least a four-year degree had adoption probabilities that were similar to individuals who had completed only elementary or high school. Thus, the effective use of a computer in California agriculture seems to require high levels of education. The authors also found that farm size has a positive and significant effect on computer adoption. Farmers' age had a quadratic effect on computer adoption, peaking in the 36–40 age range. The authors' evidence on type of software owned is generally weaker than for computer adoption, but they concluded that it is influenced primarily by the type of farm products produced, the size of the farming operation, ownership of a farm-related business, and education of the farm operator.

Wozniak (1984) examined the adoption of two interrelated cattle feeding technologies – one new and the other mature (available for several years) – for a 1976 sample of Iowa farmers. The new technology was the use of Rumensin which enhances natural microbial activity in rumens, and it became available to farmers about one year before the survey. The mature technology was implanting growth hormones, which is a technology that had been available for several years. Wozniak found that farmers' schooling and frequent contact with agricultural extension information sources had positive and statistically significant effects on the probability of adopting the new technology (Rumensin) but no effect on the probability of adopting the mature technology (implanting). He also found a positive and statistically significant effect of scale/size of the cattle feeding operation on the probability of adopting both feeding technologies. These results suggest that education and extension are important to assessing new innovations and explaining early adoption but not for diffusion or use of mature technologies. Also, the results imply that if an innovation is compatible with current technology, it is more likely to be adopted than if it displaces it.

Rahm and Huffman (1984) examined the adoption of reduced tillage for row crop (corn) seedbed preparation and the efficiency of the adoption decision for a 1976 sample of Iowa farms. Reduced tillage technology refers to seedbed preparation without the aid of a moldboard plow, e.g., chisel plows, field cultivators, primary tillage disks, or no-till planting. Reduced tillage significantly reduces field preparation time and retains crop residue on the soil surface, which has the potential to decrease soil loss from wind and water erosion. It also lowers springtime soil temperatures and decreases evaporation. The profitability of reduced tillage over moldboard plow technology depends on soil characteristics, annual precipitation, cropping system, and other management practices, and it is not profitable for all cropland. The authors found that the probability of a farm operator adopting reduced tillage was not related significantly to his schooling. A large corn enterprise size (acres of corn planted) had a positive and significant effect on a farmer's adoption of reduced tillage, and the cropping system of the farm and soil association of the farmland significantly affected the probability of adoption.

But Rahm and Huffman (1984) also examined the efficiency of a farmer's adoption decision, which is defined as the absolute difference between actual and predicted adoption behavior. Here, farmers who had more education (years of formal schooling) had greater efficiency of reduced tillage adoption. Also, if the farm operator used media sources of information published or marketed by the private sector or if the farm operator or spouse attended short courses, conferences, or meetings at Iowa State University, the efficiency of a reduced tillage adoption was increased. However, a farm operator's active years of experience farming or participation in meetings, field days, or demonstrations sponsored by the extension service did not have a significant effect on the efficiency of reduced tillage adoption.

Soule et al. (1999) have extended the Rahm and Huffman model of adoption of conservation practices. They develop a multiperiod model of the adoption decision, focusing on possible differences that might be associated with different land tenure arrangements, and fit a probit specification of the adoption decision to data from the 1996 Agricultural Resource Management Study survey. They find that if a farm operator has some college education he is more likely to adopt (short-term) conservation tillage practices than if he has less schooling. However, they found no significant effect of the farm operator having some college education on the probability of adopting medium-term practices, e.g., contour farming, strip cropping, establishing grassed waterways.

We turn next to some adoption evidence for developing and transition economies. New high yield wheat and rice varieties became available in the mid-1960s. Foster and Rosenzweig (1996) consider the probability that a sample of Indian farm households had ever adopted high yielding seed varieties by 1971. Schooling completion is low in these households; only 49 percent of households had someone who had completed primary school and 21 percent had someone who had completed secondary schooling. Foster and Rosenzweig found that farm households containing at least one adult who had completed primary schooling were significantly more likely to have adopted the new seeds by 1970–71 than households having no adult who was a primary schooling graduate. Schooling beyond the primary level tended to not significantly affect adoption of high yield varieties (HYV). Households that had more acres of owned land and were located in villages with an agricultural extension program were also more likely to use HYV seeds.

In another study, Foster and Rosenzweig (1995) examined the adoption of high-yielding seed varieties in a national panel sample of Indian rural households pertaining to the crop years 1968–69, 1969–70, and 1970–71. Here they focused on the importance of prior experience with HYV on current rate of use. They found that farmers who had more prior experience with HYV seed had a significantly higher current rate of use of the new seed. They also found that farmers in villages that had more prior experience with HYV also tended to have higher current rates of use of HYV seed.

Their results suggest positive learning-by-doing (or own experience effects) and positive learning-from-neighbors (or experience spillover effects) occur. Because of the fixed-effects specification of their econometric model, farmers' schooling, which does not change over time, does not have an identifiable effect on HYV adoption.

Lin (1991) examined the adoption of high-yielding rice varieties for a 1988 sample of Chinese farmers (Hunan Province). Although China did not have a market economy, a new household-based (rather than collective-based) farming system was introduced to the study area in 1981–82. The average years of formal schooling completed by the household head was 5.5 years, and 93 percent had less than 10 years of schooling. Hybrid rice seeds were released to farmers in 1976, but the price of the seed was set relatively high (10 times conventional seed), although the seeding rate was one-third to one-fourth of conventional rice's seeding rate. Controlling for 16 other variables, Lin found that schooling of the head of the farm household had a positive and significant effect on the probability of adopting middle or late hybrid rice seed. Increasing the land area cultivated by a household also increased the probability of hybrid rice variety adoption. Household head's experience in farming had a positive effect on adoption (at the 10 percent significance level).

Strauss et al. (1991) examined the adoption of cultural practices by upland rice and soybean farmers from survey information collected from 161 central-west Brazilian farms in 1985–86. Both soybeans and upland rice technologies began to be introduced in the region after 1980. The educational distribution of the farmers in the survey is as follows: fewer than 4 years, 56.8 percent; 4–8 years, 29.0 percent; and more than 8 years, 14.2 percent. The authors found that better-educated farmers were more likely to do soil analysis and use fertilizer on both rice and soybean plots, but farmers' education did not significantly affect the probability of using treated soybean seeds, certified rice seeds, or rice blast control. Farmers in areas with more experienced extension agents were more likely to use treated soybean seeds and certified rice seeds, but extension did not have a significant effect on adoption of other practices. Clearly these are a mixed set of results.

Pitt and Sumodiningrat (1991) examined the determinants of rice seed variety choice (HYV vs. traditional variety (TV)) for a 1980 national sample of Indonesian farm households. High-yielding varieties first became available at least a decade earlier. They found that farmers' schooling had a positive but statistically insignificant effect on HYV adoption, holding relative profitability of HYV to traditional varieties constant. Higher expected profitability of HYV and higher quality irrigation for a farm household also had positive and significant effects on the probability of HYV adoption.[5]

Although successful adoption of innovations clearly requires information, few studies have considered the important joint decisions of information acquisition and new

---

[5] See Feder, Just and Zilberman (1985) for a survey of other economic factors affecting adoption of technologies in developing countries. See Birkhaeuser, Evenson and Feder (1991) for a review of impacts of agricultural extension on adoption.

technology adoption. This seems to be a fruitful area for new research. When several information sources exist, early adopters might prefer sources that facilitate faster learning about the innovation. The information channels for early adopters might also be different from those for late adopters.

Wozniak (1993) is an exception in that he examined farmers' joint decisions on information acquisition and technology adoption. He considered the adoption of two technologies – one new (Rumensin) and one mature (implanting) – and four channels of information – one active and one passive information channel for both extension and private sector information providers. In the study, he found that farmers' education significantly increased the probability of adopting new and mature technologies and of acquiring information from extension by talking with extension personnel (passive) and attending demonstrations or meetings (active) about the use of new products or procedures sponsored by extension. Farmers' education did not have a statistically significant effect on acquiring information by talking with private industry personnel or attending demonstrations or meetings on the use of new products or procedures sponsored by private companies. Farmers were more likely to be early adopters if they acquired information actively or passively from private industry information providers than if they acquired information from extension. For both new and mature innovations, positive and significant interaction effects existed between farmers' acquisition of information from public and private sources, i.e., public and private information acquisition seems to be complementary.

In addition, Wozniak (1993) found that scale has a positive and significant effect on adoption of new and mature technologies and on the likelihood of acquiring information from extension actively or passively, but no significant effect on likelihood of acquiring information from private sector firms. Farm operators who had larger off-farm wage income had a lower probability of adopting the new technology and lower probability of talking with private sector information providers. He concluded that off-farm work seems to impact adoption not by easing credit restraints but by reallocating operators' time away from farm-related activities of early technology adoption and gathering technical information.

Klotz et al. (1995) examine California dairy farmers' awareness of recombinant bovine somatotropin (rbST) and its adoption using survey data over a four-year period, 1987–1990. They argue that information acquisition costs per cow decline as the size of a cow herd increases, leading to scale bias to large producers. Empirically they fit a bivariate probit model to explain awareness and adoption of rbST. They find that farmers' schooling has a positive and significant effect on both the probability of awareness and adoption. In addition, they find that as the size of the dairy herd increases, the probability of a farmer's awareness and adoption increases.

Bindlish and Evenson (1997) have undertaken an extensive study of information acquisition and its impacts on agriculture in two poor African countries. They use econometric techniques to examine whether the Training and Visit (T&V) system of extension led to earlier and greater awareness, testing, and adoption of improved farming practices in Burkina Faso and Kenya than would have occurred otherwise. They pay particular attention to the effects of endogenous T&V participation by farmers in their analysis. They found that farmers having more schooling had a high probability of participating as T&V contact farmers or members of contact groups. Holding the probability of T&V participation constant, additional T&V extension had a positive and significant effect on farmers' testing 10 of 12 recommended practices and on adoption of 9 of them. The authors also found positive externalities or spillover effects of T&V participating farmers on the probability that other farmers would test and adopt recommended practices. Farmers having more schooling (and more land) were more likely to learn from other farmers and to test and adopt new technologies.

In Kenya, the findings were less clear-cut. However, T&V extension had a positive effect on the probability of adoption of all recommended practices and a statistically significant effect on most. Higher schooling levels of farmers led to more and earlier awareness and adoption of recommended practices.

Antle and Pingali (1994) considered an interesting pesticide choice and production problem where farmers' education might be expected to matter for acquisition of information and choice of technology. They integrated farm-level survey data with health data collected from the same population of Philippine farmers to measure the impacts of pesticide use on farmers' health and the impact of farmers' health on rice production. They, however, indicate that their sample contained too little variation in farmers' education to find a significant effect on either pesticide use or production. However, an alternative interpretation of their results is that they included "choice variables" as regressors in these equations, e.g., the pesticide use equation contains as regressors the number of pesticide applications and dummy variables for farmers' smoking and drinking, which themselves seem likely to be (partially) determined by farmers' schooling. Welch (1970) and others (see later section) have shown that when the effects of education are channeled through farmers' choices, one cannot expect to hold the "choices" constant in a regression sense and also find a significant effect of education.

Overall, the review of the literature has shown that additional schooling of farmers increases the rate of early adoption of useful agricultural technologies in developed and developing countries. A surprisingly small amount of research, however, has examined farmers' joint decisions on information acquisition and technology adoption, and this is an area for much needed new research. Furthermore, care must be taken in empirical modeling so the models are built on a solid choice-based foundation and permit schooling to affect outcomes.

2.3. Agricultural production

Education of farm labor has the potential for enhancing agricultural production as reflected in gross output/transformation functions (see Equations (3) and (18)) and in value-added or profit functions. These effects are frequently referenced as technical efficiency effects, allocative efficiency effects, or economic efficiency effects of education. When the effects of schooling on production are considered in a gross output-complete input specification, the marginal product of education, a measure of technical efficiency, is limited by the other things that are held constant. A value-added or profit function representation of production accommodates a much broader set of effects that farmers' education may have on production through affecting choices or allocative efficiency – the adoption of new inputs in a profitable manner, the efficient allocation of land (and other quasi-fixed inputs) among alternative uses, the efficient allocation of variable inputs, and the efficient choice of an output mix. The hypothesis is and the empirical evidence has shown that the productivity of farmers' education is enhanced by a wider range of choices. Welch (1970) is generally given credit for delineating these substantive differences.

Some evidence and findings are presented first for developed countries, and second for developing countries. U.S. studies of agricultural production before the 1960s did not focus on farmers' schooling being a potentially important contributor to production, e.g., see Heady and Dillion (1961). Griliches (1963a) presented one of the first studies of the contribution of education to agricultural production. He included an index of the education of farm labor as an input in an aggregate Cobb–Douglas-type production function. The production function was fitted to data for 1949 on aggregate output and inputs for 68 U.S. agricultural regions. Six inputs, including a man-days measure of farm (hired and unpaid family) labor, were included in addition to education. Education per worker was derived from the educational distribution of the rural population and income weighted. Griliches (1963a) found that schooling of farm labor had a positive and statistically significant effect on production and that the coefficient of education was similar in size to the coefficient of farm labor. Griliches (1964) also applied a similar methodology to U.S. state aggregate per farm data for 1949, 1954, and 1959, and obtained similar results for the contribution of education of farm labor to production. His interest in education of workers in agriculture arose primarily from a concern about labor quality and a hypothesis that labor quality was an important input for explaining output.

Huffman (1977, 1981) applied a production function approach to assessing the effects of labor quality in U.S. agriculture, using county data. Huffman (1976a, 1976b) focused on the quantity and quality of farm husband and wife labor allocated to own-farm work. A Cobb–Douglas type production function was fitted to 1964 county data for Iowa, North Carolina, and Oklahoma, where effective labor input was measured as days of work multiplied by a schooling index. The value of the marginal product of husband and wife labor was shown to be larger than the average wage received for off-farm work by farm husbands and wives in these states. However, the implied marginal return in agricultural production to husband's and wife's schooling was generally lower than the average off-farm return to schooling.

Huffman (1981) presented estimates of productivity differences on black- and white-operated farms in the U.S. South (North and South Carolina, Mississippi, and Alabama). Results from fitting a modified Cobb–Douglas production function to 1964 county data showed that the quantity and quality of farmers' education and extension were the primary sources of productivity differences on black- and white-operated farms. The *quantity* differences in schooling and extension on black- and white-operated farms were shown to be *more important* than *quality* difference for explaining black-white farm productivity differences.

Welch (1970) laid the conceptual foundation for broadening the examination of education's contribution to agricultural production, especially allocative effects of farmers' education, but his empirical evidence addressed the issue only indirectly. His model, however, stimulated considerable new research on the topic. Khaldi (1975) and Fane (1975) focused on identifying the contribution of farmers' schooling to allocative efficiency by comparing hypothetical minimum cost of producing realized output to actual cost. For both, hypothetical minimum cost was inferred from an estimated aggregate production function. Khaldi's observations were state average per farm values for all U.S. states for 1964, and Fane used county averages for four Midwestern states for 1959 and 1964. Both studies found that the proportional difference between *actual* cost and *hypothetical* cost declined significantly as the average schooling level of farmers increased (for preferred specifications).

Huffman (1974, 1977) pursued a different route for testing for allocative efficiency effects. He focused on Corn Belt farmers' production of corn and nitrogen fertilizer use in county aggregate average data for 1959 and 1964. This was a period when the price of nitrogen fertilizer fell significantly relative to the price of corn (22–25 percent), and new hybrid seed corn varieties, which could respond well to higher nitrogen fertilizer use, were being developed and marketed by commercial seed corn companies. He found mixed results for the contribution of farmers' schooling to output per acre or technical efficiency. The production function for corn in 1959 and 1964 was shown to be different due to technical change, and schooling's effect was positive and significantly different from zero in Huffman (1974) but not significantly different from zero in Huffman (1977), which used a different set of counties. The next step was to examine changes in nitrogen fertilizer usage. He computed a partial adjustment coefficient showing the actual change in nitrogen fertilizer use as a fraction of the change necessary to reach a hypothetical optimum rate of use, and then related the speed of adjustment to farmers' schooling, extension input, and size. He found a positive and statistically significant relationship between the average education of farmers and the speed of adjustment. Extension and size (of the corn production enterprise) were shown also to be positively related to the speed of adjustment. Hence, both studies found that farmers' schooling increases allocative efficiency.

Huffman and Evenson (1989) examined the effects of farmers' education and other variables on optimal mix of outputs and inputs for multi-output multi-input U.S. cash grain farms. They fitted a system of output supply and input demand equations derived from a profit function to state aggregate per farm data for 42 U.S. states pooled over census years 1949–74. They found that an increase in farmers' schooling biased production decisions on cash grain farms away from fertilizer, labor, and fuel input use, and toward machinery input use; and, with respect to output, toward wheat output and away from soybean and feed grain outputs. Moreover, the relative bias-effects caused by farmers' schooling have been larger among outputs than inputs. They also found that additional agricultural extension biased production decisions in the same direction as farmers' schooling for fertilizer, fuel, and machinery inputs. However, the effects of extension on the other four choices were in the opposite direction from those caused by farmers' schooling.

Some recent agricultural profit function studies, however, have ignored the effects of farmers' education. Weaver (1983) and Shumway (1983) also fitted a system of output supply and input demand functions derived from a profit function to aggregate per farm data for North and South Dakota, 1950–70, and Texas, 1957–79, and omitted education (and extension) from their models. This omission could cause the estimated coefficients of other included variables to be biased and to miss some important effects of education on agriculture. At least the potential effects of farmers' schooling should be carefully examined before deciding that they are insignificant.

Turning to some developing country evidences, Hayami and Ruttan (1985) and Jamison and Lau (1982) summarize much of the early evidence. Few early studies found a positive and statistically significant effect of farmers' schooling on farm output. This seems to have several sources. First, researchers were exploring technical efficiency but not allocative efficiency effects. Second, schooling levels may have been too low to be productive. Third, variance in schooling levels may have been too small. Later studies have had more success.

Pudasaini (1983) chose to examine the effects of education in two regions of Nepal, one undergoing modernization and the other traditional due to its hill country isolation. The average level of schooling was 5 years in the modernizing region and 4.2 years in the traditional region. He fitted yield response, gross sales, and value-added production functions to farm-level data. He found that farmers' schooling had a positive but insignificant effect on crop yields in both regions, but farmers' schooling had a positive and statistically significant effect on the gross sales and value-added for both regions. In the modernizing region, the estimated coefficient of education was 66 percent larger for the value added than the gross sales equation, but in the traditional region, the coefficient of education was only 10 percent larger. The marginal contribution of farmers' schooling to value-added output was about two times larger in the modernizing than in the traditional region. In contrast, he did not find any significant effects of agricultural extension. Hence, this study showed that allocative effects of farmers' education were more important than worker effects, and that allocative effects were quite large in the modernizing region.

Foster and Rosenzweig (1996) used longitudinal Indian rural household data and area- specific information on crop yields and schools to test whether Green Revolution technical change increased the returns to farmers' schooling and whether schooling investments responded to changes in the return to schooling. They argued that the Green Revolution technologies were developed outside of India and imported so the availability of the technologies can be treated as exogenous to rural Indian economic conditions. However, the ability of different regions and households to exploit the new technologies was argued to differ because soils and climates differed regionally and farmers' schooling differed.

Foster and Rosenzweig (1996) used a large sample of households to explain change in farm-level profit, 1969–1970 to 1970–1971. With fixed-effects instrumental-variable estimates, they showed that the profitability of HYV acreage was significantly increased by a farm household member having completed primary schooling (relative to less than primary schooling). The profitability of HYV acreage was also increased significantly by the share of HYV land irrigated. For primary-schooled farm households having 100 percent irrigated HYV acreage, they concluded that farm profit was 39 percent higher (compared to having less than primary schooling and no irrigation). Their results confirmed positive allocative effects of schooling in Indian farming.

Foster and Rosenzweig (1996) then explained the 1971–82 change in household-specific school enrollment rates for children aged 5–14 using a subset of their sample of rural households. They found that primary school enrollment rates were positive and significantly related to the growth of crop yields in the area, but yield growth had a significantly smaller impact on school enrollment for children in nonfarm than farm households. The results suggested that the expected return to primary schooling in India was higher for farm than nonfarm households, and that the difference was associated with the steady change of technologies associated with the Green Revolution.

Subsistence peasant households in the Peruvian Sierra provided Jacoby (1993) with evidence for the contribution of schooling to agriculture for poor Latin American farm households. The sample was from a sizeable survey conducted in 1985-86 from households that reported harvesting some crops and with at least one adult male and female who worked on the family farm during the survey year. The mean schooling of male heads in these households was only 2.9 years. Farm output was defined as the value of crop and livestock production. Jacoby fitted Cobb–Douglas and translog specifications of a farm production function. He found that the head's schooling increased farm output. However, the head's age (as a proxy for experience) did not statistically affect farm output. In these households, work effort (hours of farm work) among adult males and females seemed to respond positively to their productivity, which suggested the opportunity cost of not working was higher for more educated individuals.[6]

Evenson and Mwabu (1997) examined the impact of agricultural extension and farmers' schooling on crop yields of poor African farmers. They pooled 1981–82 and 1990 samples of Kenya farm households. The average level of schooling of these farmers was very low: 47 percent had less than 2.5 years of schooling (only one was a high school graduate). They applied a quantile-regression technique for investigating productivity effects of schooling over the conditional distribution of crop yields. Farmers' schooling (measured qualitatively as greater than or less than 2.5 years) had a positive and significant impact on yields only at the bottom of the yield distribution. Agricultural extension (number of field extension workers per farm) had a generally positive impact on crop yields, but in contrast to schooling, the marginal product was largest at the top end of the yield distribution.

---

[6] Benjamin (1992) presents a rigorous modeling and econometric analysis of Java farm household labor use due to household composition and presence or absence of labor markets.

A few studies have also examined the effect of schooling in non-democratic and emerging market economies, especially for China. The opportunities for schooling to contribute to farm production in China were very limited under the collective farming system but seem to have increased after 1984 with the change to household-responsibility system and opening input markets. Fleisher and Liu (1992) used a large 1987–88 survey of Chinese farm households located in six different geographical regions to test for diseconomies associated with small-scale and multiple plots and effects of schooling and experience of household heads on productivity. Farm output was defined as weighted "rice-equivalence" of "field crops" produced (which excluded largely vegetables and fruits). They fitted a Cobb–Douglas type production function and found positive, but not significantly different from zero effects of schooling and experience of the household head on farm production.

In another study, Yang (1997b) examined effects on production of alternative measures of education in an attempt to strengthen the connections between education and agriculture on small Chinese farms. He chose a value-added measure of farm output so as to capture allocative effects. Although farmers' choices may still be somewhat restricted in China, he hypothesized that the allocative effects would be larger than the worker effects. He considered alternative measures of education that might be expected to affect farm production, including years of schooling of the household head, highest year of schooling completed by any household member, and average schooling of all farm labor. The sample mean values of these variables were 5.6, 7.3, and 6.0 years, respectively. He fitted several different specifications of a Cobb–Douglas type production function. The head's education had a positive but insignificant effect on farm production. Farm workers' education had a positive and significant effect on farm production, but education measured as the highest level completed by *any* farm household member performs *best*. In addition, Yang found that farm workers' experience (post-schooling experience weighted by farm work participation) also had a positive and significant effect on value added. He concluded that the schooling evidence from his sample of small Chinese farms showed allocative effects of education to be more important than worker effects. Furthermore, on these farms, the beneficial effects of schooling were obtained from an individual who frequently did not report any farm work. This seems possible only when farms are small and allocative decisions are relatively simple. The allocative benefits for these small farms were attainable with one well-schooled person per household.

The frontier production and profit function literature also provides evidence of the contribution of farmers' education to increased efficiency. Abdulai and Huffman (1999) showed that schooling of Ghana rice farmers reduces significantly profit inefficiency, which implies enhanced technical and allocation or economic efficiency. The empirical evidence for farmers' education reducing production or technical inefficiency is mixed, e.g., Belbase and Grabowski (1985) and Flinn and Ali (1986) found significant schooling effects but some other studies have found insignificant effects [see Bravo-Ureta and Pinherio (1993)].

Overall, in developing, transition, and developed countries, the review of the literature shows that farmers' schooling has generally greater value through allocative than technical efficiency effects. The positive allocative effects are, however, closely associated with a farming environment where technologies are changing and relative prices are changing. Farmers' schooling has infrequently been shown to increase crop yields or gross farm output because technical-efficiency gains from skills provided by farmers' schooling seem generally to be small. Farmers' schooling has also been shown to change the optimal mix or composition of farm inputs and outputs where production is multi-input and multi-output.

2.4. Total factor productivity decomposition

Productivity statistics, measuring output per unit of input, started in the 1950s showing seemingly costless increases in output. Schultz (1953), Kendrick (1961), and Denison (1962) started to search for underlying sources of productivity for these increases. Their work focused on the general economy and on agriculture where the data were better. Three main classes of methods have been applied in sources of productivity analysis: (1) imputation-accounting methods, (2) statistical meta-production function methods, and (3) statistical productivity decomposition methods (Evenson, this volume). In all of these methods, there is considerable investment in data construction, especially trying to accurately account for quality and quantity of inputs and outputs. Schooling enters primarily at two places: (1) schooling of agricultural labor can reasonably be expected to enhance labor quality or the effective units of labor, and (2) schooling of the farmer or decision maker may more generally increase productivity by enhancing economic efficiency in agriculture.

The best-known early studies of sources of total factor productivity (TFP) change in U.S. agriculture are by Griliches (1963a, 1963b, 1964). In Griliches (1964), an index of education of farm labor was found to have a coefficient in an aggregate production function fitted to state average per farm data for 1949, 1954, and 1959 that was positive and not significantly different from the coefficient for farm labor (person days). This result has frequently been used by other researchers as a justification for constructed quality-adjusted farm labor input measures for TFP measures [e.g., see Ball (1985), Jorgenson and Gollop (1992), Ball et al. (1997)]. When Griliches (1964) then conducted an analysis of differences between unadjusted and adjusted residual agricultural output growth, 1949–59, education of farm labor accounted for about 14 percent of the explained difference.

Huffman and Evenson (1993) assessed research and education's contribution to TFP through statistical decomposition of state agricultural TFP levels. In their TFP measure, farm labor was measured as person-hours of unpaid farm family and hired labor, but no adjustment of education (or experience) was made. They derived TFP measures by state, 1950–82, for a crop sector, livestock sector, and aggregate farm sector. They then used public and private research, farmers' schooling, extension, and government commodity program variables to econometrically explain TFP in an analysis of 42 pooled states, 1950–82. To attain consistency of interpretation they impose some coefficient restrictions across the three productivity equations. They however found that farmers' schooling made a positive and statistically significant contribution to state TFP levels. Their results implied a positive marginal product of farmers' schooling and a relatively large social rate of return (19–40 percent). They concluded that farmers who have more schooling have an advantage in being able to understand scientific advances in the public and private sector, to draw inferences from results and make successful adaptation to their own particular farming operation, and to quickly adapt superior technologies, economic organizations, and management practices.

Huffman and Evenson (1993) also found that farmers' schooling and agricultural extension interact negatively in explaining TFP levels. The marginal product of aggregate crop and livestock extension is positive, and the marginal product is larger in the crop than in the livestock sector. For the livestock sector, the marginal product of extension was negative or zero. The authors, however, obtained evidence that farmers' schooling and extension were substitutes. Over the study period, the average level of farmers' schooling increased by about 4 years, which greatly reduced the marginal product of extension by the end of the period.

In some North American studies of agricultural TFP, authors surprisingly have chosen to ignore the effects of education [see Capalbo and Denny (1986), Antle and Capalbo (1988), and Chavas and Cox (1992)]. It is more common to ignore labor quality adjustments in TFP analyses for developing countries where schooling completion levels are low and data are poor.

Rosegrant and Evenson (1993) are an exception in their TFP research for India and Pakistan. They constructed TFP indexes for the crop sectors for 271 districts in 13 states of India (1956–87) and for 35 districts in 3 states of Pakistan (1955–85) and then conducted a statistical decomposition analysis. The empirical models were similar for the two countries. Average schooling completion levels for farmers in these districts of India and Pakistan were low, perhaps averaging 2 years. They chose to measure farmers' education as the literacy rate. They found that the literacy rate made a positive and statistically significant contribution to crop sector TFP in both countries. In India, agricultural extension (expenditures per farm) also made a positive and significant contribution to TFP.

A few studies have examined the effects of education on agricultural productivity across many countries. Hayami and Ruttan (1970) examined agricultural labor productivity, rather than TFP, differences for 38 developed and developing countries. [See Hayami (1960) for presentation of preliminary results for the same countries.] They assumed that a meta-production function (the envelope of all known and potentially discoverable production activities) exists across countries at a given point in time and over time in a given country. They fitted a Cobb–Douglas type production function to average per farm data. Output was measured as gross (net of feed and seed), and the labor input was measured as the *number* of male workers active in agriculture. In the 1960 data (which seems to be better than for 1955 or 1965), they found a positive and statistically significant effect of the rural literacy rate and of agricultural technical education (graduates from agricultural education facilities at above the secondary level per farm worker) on farm output per worker. They concluded that about one-third of the difference in agricultural labor productivity across the 38 countries was due to differences in human capital (education).

In a related study, Kawagoe, Hayami and Ruttan (1985) expanded the set of countries to 43 (22 less developed) and focused on data for the years 1960, 1970, and 1980. They used the same methodology as Hayami and Ruttan (1970), but the education variables did not perform as well. Positive and significant effects of the literacy rate and agricultural technical education on farm output per worker were obtained from the data pooled across the three years for the less developed countries. For the developed countries, the two education variables did not perform well. This may be due to literacy rates having little variation across developing countries, and to agricultural college graduates frequently taking nonfarm employment rather than working on farms.

Craig et al. (1997) have attempted to push the labor productivity analysis further by expanding the number of countries to 98, making crude adjustments for input quality, and including proxies for rural infrastructure and agricultural research. Conventional agricultural labor is measured as the number of workers, i.e., the economically active agricultural population. No measure of work intensity, i.e., annual hours of work per worker, is included, but they included two labor quality measures, the literacy rate for the population over 15 years of age and life expectancy of the overall population at birth. They fitted a meta-Cobb–Douglas labor productivity equation, including the above adjustments, to the observations on 98 countries pooled over six observations per country (obtained by creating five-year averages from thirty years of annual data). Surprisingly, the coefficient of adult literacy is negative, and sometimes significant, in all reported regression equations. In contrast, the coefficient of life expectancy is positive and significant. The poor performance of literacy seems likely to be due to its very crude measure of schooling, perhaps failing to capture dimensions of schooling that affect production, and no adjustment for intensity of work.

The authors can be criticized for trying to stretch their inferences by including the USSR, Central European countries, and China. From both an economic and econometric perspective this seems highly questionable. First, over the study period, the choice of where and when to work, the range of choices available to farm managers or farmers, the availability of variable inputs, and the incentives to perform were very different in these centrally planned non-market economies than in the market-oriented largely free countries. Little evidence exists that centrally planned economies produced agricultural output at anything like cost-minimizing input combinations. Hence, the methodology applied by Craig et al. (1997) made an unnecessarily heterogeneous sample.

Overall, it seems that some dimension of schooling contributes to TFP or labor productivity, but the current evidence is mixed. In U.S. agricultural productivity data sets, the incorporation of labor quality adjustments has not been uniform. One strand of the literature, started by Griliches and continued by Ball at USDA, emphasizes effective units of labor, which is the product of agricultural labor quantity (days or hours) and an index of labor quality. Another strand of the literature places labor quality effects in the productivity index (residual), and uses an education index, generally for farm operators, to explain TFP levels. When the latter approach has been followed, farmers' schooling has generally had a positive and significant effect on agricultural productivity. In cross-country studies of agricultural labor productivity, it has been difficult to obtain a satisfactory empirical measure of schooling. Consequently, the weak effects of education in cross-country studies seem most likely to be due to data problems rather than to absence of real effects. Although the progress may be slow, this is an area where progress can be made.

2.5. Household income

In the first section, the three-period model has household utility derived from leisure and purchased consumption goods. In that model, household (net) cash income is spent on purchased consumption goods and on purchased inputs for human capital production. Within this model, the optimal life-cycle path of purchased consumption goods will be less concave than net cash income because of the incentive to invest early in human capital and to reduce consumption early and to raise it later in life [Ghez and Becker (1975)]. Furthermore, in both the three-period and single-period models of agricultural household resource allocation, cash income in each period is determined by the household's initial human capital endowment, past net investments in human capital, and current allocation decision for human capital services between leisure and work, farm production decisions, and wage rates and prices. Hence, these models imply that household cash income is *not* an *exogenous variable*, but rather a variable that is the result of current and past decisions of the household, given market wage rates and prices. Hence, household income should not be treated as an exogenous variable in econometric studies of consumption, labor supply, and welfare analyses.

This subsection will focus on the narrower issue of the impacts of education on incomes of agricultural workers and farm households. The impact of schooling on incomes of hired agricultural labor seems to be small in developed countries and insignificant in other countries. Emerson (1989) examined the earnings structure for migratory and nonmigratory work of 559 domestic males in a 1970 survey of Florida farm workers. In fitted annual earnings equations (adjusted for selection), he found a very small positive and significant effect of workers' schooling on earnings (1.4 percent per year for migrants and 1.6 percent per year for nonmigrants, holding weeks worked per year constant). He also found a quadratic effect of workers' experience on earnings. The coefficients for experience were about 50 percent larger for migrants than for nonmigrants. Furthermore, he found that these domestic farm workers sorted or self-selected themselves into migratory and nonmigratory groups in a manner that was consistent with the theory of comparative advantage – i.e., migrants earned more as migrants than they would as nonmigrants, and nonmigrants earned more as nonmigrants than they would as migrants.

Ise and Perloff (1995) employed a hedonic wage equation and static labor supply model to examine the effects of an agricultural worker's legal status on wage earned and hours of work or labor supply. Legal status of a worker was hypothesized to be determined by an individual's demographic attributes. The model was fitted to a random sample of seasonal agricultural service workers from the National Agricultural Workers' Survey. They found that an individual being an English speaker and having more schooling increased the odds of having a preferred legal status. For seasonal agricultural service workers, work experience had a positive and significant effect on the hourly wage in all equations, except for workers having unauthorized status. However, a worker's education did not have a significant effect on the wage. In the labor supply equation for workers having Amnesty or Green Card status, additional schooling reduced significantly weekly hours of work. The authors concluded, not too surprisingly, that agricultural workers who work in the U.S. legally earned substantially more per hour and per week than those having unauthorized status. Thus, investing in obtaining a preferred legal status becomes another form of human capital with highly relevant cost-benefit calculations for potential immigrants and significant effects on workers' incomes.

The attributes of farm work, of farm workers, and employers affect the type of pay system used, e.g., time or piece rate. A piece-rate system is not workable in many circumstances, e.g., due to quality control or no easily defined output, but it is frequently the pay system for harvest labor. A piece-rate system is incentive pay for speedy work, a skill that seems likely to be unrelated to schooling. Rubin and Perloff (1993) examined workers' choice of pay system and hedonic wage equations for both pay systems in a small 1981 sample of harvest workers (in Tulare County, California).[7] The average schooling level for time-pay workers was 4.9 years, and for piece-rate pay workers, 4.1 years. They found that the probability of using/choosing the piece-rate system was strongly related to the age of the workers, where young and older workers who have unproven skills are more likely to choose the piece-rate pay system than are prime age workers, holding the expected pay differential constant. The lowest probability of piece-rate pay occurred for a 34-year old worker. In the hedonic wage equations, adjusted for sample selection, Rubin and Perloff (1993) found that *workers' schooling had a small positive* and statistically significant effect on the *time-rate of pay wage but not on the piece-rate wage*. Experience, proxied by age and age-squared, had a statistically significant effect on the wage rate in both pay systems, and the age at which the peak occurred was about 39 years. The coefficients were, however, larger by a factor of two for the piece-rate than for the time-rate system, suggesting more exaggerated effects of experience for the piece-rate than for the time-rate pay system. Hence, these results suggest that a worker's pay is not related to his or her schooling when the work is piece-rate, but the return is small when it is time-rate of pay.

In a developing country, transportation and communication are relatively expensive, schooling is minimal, and housing in a new location may be difficult to find. Hence,

---

[7] The authors, however, ignored the possibility that employers of agricultural workers are also making a decision about which pay system to offer. This could affect the results [Gibbons (1998)].

workers tend to be less geographically mobile than in the United States, and rural labor markets less integrated. Rosenzweig (1980) used data from a 1970–71 national sample of rural households in India to examine several labor issues, including hedonic wage equations for casual workers employed on a monthly or daily basis. In his sample, mean schooling of male and female landless workers was 1 year and 0.5 year, respectively. The wage equation (adjusted for selection) included individual and local village attributes, and separate equations were fitted for men and women. He found that schooling of males had a small positive (3.9 percent) and statistically significant effect on their wage, but schooling had no significant effect on the female wage. Also, potential experience (as represented by age, and age-squared) had no significant effect on male or female wage rates. Rosenzweig, however, concluded that human capital variables *were not significant predictors of the wage rate for casual labor* in India, and village attributes that affect local labor demand and supply were relatively important.

For farm or landed households, the effects of schooling on income arise primarily from impacts on farm profit or value added and off-farm earnings.[8] In the third subsection, evidence was summarized showing that farmers' schooling increased farm profit in an environment where technology and relative prices are changing. In other agricultural environments where technology and prices are not changing, or where farmers' schooling is below the permanent literacy level, farmers' schooling seems unlikely to have a significant impact on farm profit, value added, or household income.

Huffman (1991b) provides an extensive survey and critique of agricultural household models that have proved useful for examining off-farm labor supply. In U.S. studies of off-farm work, a male farm operator's schooling increases his off-farm wage by 4 to 13 percent [see Sumner (1982), Jensen and Salant (1985), Gould and Saupe (1989), and Huffman and Lange (1989)]. The direct effect of a male operator's education on his off-farm hours, holding his wage constant, has sometimes been significant and positive [e.g., Huffman (1980), Lass and Gempesaw (1992)], and, when only the operator works off-farm, significant and negative [e.g., Jensen and Salant (1985)], and sometimes insignificant [e.g., Sumner (1982), Huffman and Lange (1989)]. Given that the wage elasticity of off-farm hours has been positive [an exception is Lass and Gempesaw (1992)], schooling of farm operators who work off-farm makes a positive contribution to household income in the United States.

The effects of schooling on off-farm income of farm households in developing countries may be different from those in the United States. In a 1970–1971 national sample

---

[8] The seemingly perverse effect of farmers' schooling on cost of milk production from the U.S. Department of Agriculture 1993 Farm Costs and Return Survey (see Short and McBride, 1996) seems most likely due to the way schooling is defined (as dichotomous rather than continuous variable) and the fact that ability or age of farmers is not controlled for. Before 1940, ability and schooling completion among rural youth were not positively correlated. With some selection on who chooses to operate a dairy enterprise, a seemingly positive relationship between schooling and cost should not be taken as evidence that schooling of dairy farmers is unproductive. A negative schooling effect on the cost of milk production does not show up in a study using later data (see El-Osta and Johnson 1998).

of rural households in India, Rosenzweig (1980) found that an individual's schooling and experience were relatively unimportant for explaining wage rates for *casual* labor. In his results for landholding households, schooling had a negative and generally significant effect on off-farm work days of both males and females. The implication was that farm households can better employ members with schooling on the farm than in the casual labor market. In the Philippines, Evenson (1978) found a positive and significant effect of a farm husband's market wage on his hours of wage work and implicitly on household income. For a 1990 sample of Chinese farm households, Yang (1997a) found that an individual's schooling and potential labor market experience have a positive and significant effect on the off-farm wage. He also found that the person in these households who had completed the most schooling was the off-farm work participant. In another study, Yang (1997b) showed that the person having the most schooling in these households also made the allocative decisions on the farm. Hence, schooling for one person in the Chinese farm households has positive effects on household incomes that come from farm and nonfarm effects.

Given that there are several channels through which education can affect farm household income, Huffman (1996a) fitted a reduced-farm household income equation to data for U.S. Current Population Survey married couple farm households, 1978–1982. He used as explanatory variables the following: husband's and wife's education, husband's age and race, family size, local labor market conditions, cost of living and locational amenity variables, and agricultural input and output prices and climate. He found that a husband's and wife's schooling had a significantly positive effect on farm household income. An added year of schooling for husbands increased household income by 1.3 percent, and for wives by about 1 percent.[9]

Overall, the review of the literature has shown that the effects of education on incomes of hired farm workers are mixed. If hired farm workers work piece-rate, schooling doesn't affect their wage but experience may be important if they can acquire skills by specializing in a particular type of work. If they are time-pay wage workers, added schooling may have a small positive impact on their wage. For farm household members in developed and developing countries, the impact of schooling on farm profit or value added is positive when technology is changing rapidly. In developed countries, schooling has been shown to have a positive impact on the off-farm wage and off-farm earnings, but in developing countries the results are mixed, e.g., negative in Indian Green Revolution areas and positive in China. In developed countries, schooling of husbands and wives has a positive effect on farm household (net) income, and in developing countries, the impact is probably positive. Empirical studies, however, have focused infrequently on the effects of education on household or family income.

---

[9] However, a similar model fitted to data for nonmetropolitan nonfarm household income gave estimated coefficients for husbands' and wives' schooling that were about 60 percent larger than for farm households. This model excluded agricultural prices and climate.

3. Summary and research gaps

Economists continue to search for a better understanding of the sources and causes of economic growth and development of regions and nations. Schultz (1988) concluded that a significant set of studies show strong empirical regularities between the educational attainment of a population and their productivity and performance in both market and nonmarket production activities. Furthermore, this chapter has shown that a now sizeable body of empirical evidence on the effects of education in agriculture has accumulated. In particular, the returns to education of farmers increases substantially as a country goes from traditional agriculture to modernizing, which itself becomes a continuing process. First, with modernizing, new technologies are becoming available and the economic environment is changing so that enhanced decision-making skills of farmers (and possibly other family members) are more productive. Second, when the productivity of agriculture increases, the aggregate demand for agricultural labor is reduced and the share of the labor force employed in agriculture declines and in other sectors increases. All currently developed countries have progressed from ones where a very large share of the labor force (over 75 percent) was employed in agriculture [Johnson (1997)], but with modernization of agriculture and economic development the share of the labor force in agriculture is less than 20 percent (and for the United States only 3 percent). There is accumulated empirical evidence that individuals' schooling plays a very important role in occupational choice (increasing the probability in developed countries of working outside of agriculture), migration (more educated individuals have greater geographic mobility out of rural areas), and part-time farming (the probability of off-farm work by those who remain in farming increases), which are all important in reallocating human resources among sectors in a growing and developing country, but could contribute to the remaining rural population having little education.

There is also accumulated evidence that education seems to be a poor private investment. First, in casual rural labor markets of low income countries, schooling (and experience) does not seem to affect wage rates. In urban labor markets of these countries, the returns to education are better. Second, in high income countries, schooling of field workers in fresh fruit and vegetable production has a very low return. Some fresh fruits and vegetables have large income elasticities of demand, and high quality fresh produce is possible only with hand harvesting. Thus, in the United States and some other developed countries, there is growth in the demand for relatively unschooled migratory farm labor to work on a piece-rate pay system. For the United States, this labor is supplied largely by legal and illegal immigrants from Mexico and Central America. Interestingly, the accumulated evidence shows that ethnic migration networks or social capital have been an effective substitute for migrants' own schooling in being successful in the U.S. low-skilled migratory labor market. Furthermore, an assumption that hired farm labor and farm operator (and family) labor are homogeneous in agricultural household models should be carefully scrutinized. In modernizing agriculture, the assumption is almost certainly dubious.

It is useful to think critically about the empirical evidence. Schultz (1988) emphasized that outcomes on educational attainment, occupation, location, labor force participation, and social-economic program participation are never random. This opens the
door to nonrandom selection of comparison groups and potential sample-selection bias
in parameter estimates of econometric models. Techniques have been developed for trying to offset sample selection bias, and they have been applied in many of the studies
reviewed. These techniques are, however, imperfect, and researchers have discovered
that identification problems sometimes arise in implementing selection correction procedures [see Nawata and Nagase (1996) and Heckman (1997)]. The identification problem creates another set of serious parameter biases. Researchers must continue to raise
data quality issues, promote and pursue good experimental designs for new data sets,
and pursue careful analysis where selectivity is likely to be serious.

In our empirical research, we use an individual's years of schooling as proxy for his
or her education, but in the U.S. and in many other countries, the quality of this proxy
has not been constant over time. Education is really general intellectual achievement
(GIA), including developed abilities, e.g., reading, writing, doing mathematics, reasoning, and knowing important facts and principles of science, history, and art [Bishop
(1989)]. These are skills essential for performing many job tasks, the tools for learning new tasks, and the foundations upon which much job-specific knowledge is built.
The production of GIA is multi-factor: school attendance (years completed), quality of
schooling, quantity and quality of out-of-school learning, the general socio-intellectual
environment, innate ability, and other things.

Bishop (1989) summarizes how general intellectual achievement in the U.S. rose
steadily from 1915 to about 1967. For twelfth (and eighth) graders, GIA went into a
decline over 1967–1980, equaling 1.25 grade equivalents and a 2 grade equivalent deviation from trend. Since 1980, GIA of twelfth graders has been increasing again. Thus,
what a year of schooling completed measures has not been constant over time nor does
it have a linear trend. Hence, when individuals included in a survey have graduated from
high school at different times, complex schooling vintage effects may exist, which complicate using years of schooling completed as a proxy for education in cross-sectional
and panel studies, and in interpreting the impact of schooling on social-economic outcomes.

This information does suggest that a better estimate of the impact or return of a year
of schooling can be obtained from U.S. micro-data by including as variables in a regression equation with an individual's years of schooling his or her year of graduation
from high school (or grade school, if he or she is not a high school graduate) and a
dichotomous variable for graduation after 1967. Given the incentive for individuals to
obtain schooling at a young age and to graduate at approximately the same age, at least
in developed countries, and that most surveys do not ask about year of high school (or
elementary school) graduation, we can obtain almost the same information from an individual's age. Including as regressors an individual's age rather than date of graduation
and a dichotomous variable for birth after 1950 contains approximately the same information as the two variables constructed from year of graduation. From the review in

earlier sections, recall that human capital wage, labor supply, and adoption equations generally include an individual's age (and age squared) as regressors to take account of finite life or on-the-job training effects, but production, profit, and cost functions generally do not. Hence, estimates of impacts of schooling from the latter group might be suspect.[10]

The potential for endogenous or stochastic regressor bias in human capital research area is especially high. For example, in some of the off-farm participation and labor supply studies, farm characteristics like size (acres operated) and presence of a dairy enterprise are used as regressors. Our economic models of farm household decision making (for developed countries), however, imply that acres operated, presence of a dairy enterprise, and off-farm work participation are farmers' choices (and not exogenous or randomly assigned). Jointly determined variables are not legitimate regressors, even though they seem to have large explanatory power. Similar types of issues also arise with farmers' information acquisition and technology adoption and with variables to explain migration. The solution seems to be careful economic and econometric modeling of behavior and outcomes and using instrumental variables for regressors that may be stochastic because of endogeneity or serious measurement errors [Green (1997, pp. 435–443)].

Some research gaps or potentially fruitful research directions exist. First, skilled labor and (technologically enhanced) capital services seem to be complements in manufacturing. Agriculture in developed countries is relatively capital-intensive too, but except for farm operators' education, no good evidence exists on whether skilled labor and capital services are substitutes or complements. Also, empirical evidence is missing on the extent to which workers in agriculture are at a disadvantage (or advantage) compared to workers in other sectors for obtaining productivity gains from greater worker specialization, or whether potential productivity gains from specialization differ across crop and livestock enterprises. Some large-scale broiler, swine, cattle feed lot, and dairy operations seem to have production attributes much like manufacturing plants. A key difference between agriculture and other sectors might be differences in opportunities to increase labor productivity through larger investments in skill and specialization of workers. A closely related issue is how new biotechnology and information systems affect the demand for skilled labor in agriculture.

Second, although farmers' schooling and frequently extension have been shown to enhance successful adoption of new technologies in agriculture where heterogeneity of land and climate are important factors, a set of related management decisions has been largely ignored. They are the joint decisions on technology, information acquisition, and risk-bearing methods, and how farmers' schooling affects these choices. In most agricultural societies, a wide range of options exist for technologies, information, and risk-bearing, but models and empirical analyses have generally focused on only one of these outcomes. This limits our ability to learn about successful management strategies

---

[10] See Bishop (1989) for a methodology for constructing vintage of schooling effects in aggregate data.

that farmers use internationally as the technical and institutional environments change. It also limits our ability to learn about potentially important public-private substitution possibilities in providing information and risk-bearing instruments for farmers.

Third, general intellectual achievement of elementary and secondary school students is produced both through schooling and out-of-school activities, so the total decline over 1967 to 1980 in GIA cannot be attributed to a decline in the quality of schooling. Huffman (1998), however, summarizes some of the changes in the organization of U.S. schooling starting in the late 1960s that undoubtedly contributed significantly to the decline in general intellectual achievement of students. He and others have concluded that the last 50 years of schooling research provides a weak knowledge base for guiding schools and school administrators. Too little is known about the successful organization of schooling for efficient production of general intellectual achievement, and new rigorous research is needed.

Fourth, although it is widely accepted that schooling creates new skills that increase workers' productivity in market and nonmarket activities, relatively little empirical research has attempted to identify the effects of adults' schooling on total farm family income net of farm expenses. Farm families in most countries have significant nonfarm income, and cash income is used to purchase consumption goods/inputs, schooling, and health care. Empirical studies have largely focused on individual pieces of a much larger story, e.g., effects on farm gross output, farm profit (value added), off-farm wage rates, or off-farm work hours, but this misses some of the important trade-offs that exist. Although farm income is notorious for large measurement errors and although farm expenses in developed countries generally receive favorable tax treatment, these do not seem serious enough to prevent useful research. Given that governments generally invest in schooling, research, extension, commodity, and credit programs with some intention of increasing farm families' income, it is interesting to ask which of them have been successful. Although Gardner (1992) concluded that there is no empirical evidence in the literature that U.S. government farm program payments have increased net farm income, it is important for future research to estimate and compare the impacts of these government policies on farm family income.

Overall, this chapter has summarized the impacts of education in agriculture for several different environments – e.g., developing country, transition economy, developed country, technically dynamic, and technically static – and concluded that the impacts are positive in some but not all environments. It remains somewhat of a puzzle, however, why schooling in developed countries does not have broader direct impacts in agriculture. One hypothesis is that the dominance of agriculture by biological production processes which are controlled largely by climate and are land surface-area intensive, at least for crop production, greatly limits the potential for raising labor productivity through skill acquisition and specialization of labor that is possible in the non-farm sector. After reviewing the extensive literature cited in this chapter, one should not miss the fact that the dominant effect of education in agriculture of developed countries is to aid and assist farm people with education make the transition to nonfarm work and ultimately to full-time nonfarm occupations. This process has important implications for the composition of the population left behind in agriculture and on the optimal financing of schooling in rural areas.

Acknowledgements

The author is professor of economics and agricultural economics, Iowa State University. Financial support was received from the Iowa Agriculture and Home Economics Experiment Station and the Economics Research Service, USDA. Helpful comments and suggestions were obtained from Gordon Rausser, Bruce Gardner, Peter Orazem, Claudia Goldin, an anonymous reviewer, and others.

References

Abdulai, A., and C.L. Delgado (1999), "Determinants of nonfarm earnings of farm-based husbands and wives in Northern Ghana", American Journal of Agricultural Economics 81(February):117–130.

Abdulai, A., and W.E. Huffman (1999), "Structural adjustment and economic efficiency of rice farmers in Northern Ghana", Economic Development and Cultural Change (forthcoming).

Antle, J.M., and S.M. Capalbo (1988), "An introduction to recent developments in productivity theory and productivity measurement", in: S.M. Capalbo and J.M. Antle, eds., Agricultural Productivity: Measurement and Explanation (Resources for the Future, Washington, DC) 17–95.

Antle, J.M., and P.L. Pingali (1994), "Pesticides, productivity, and farmer health: A Philippine case study", American Journal of Agricultural Economics 76:418–430.

Ball, V.E. (1985), "Output, input, and productivity measurement in U.S. agriculture, 1948–1979", American Journal of Agricultural Economics 67:475–486.

Ball, V.E., J.-C. Bureau, R. Nehring and A. Somwaru (1997), "Agricultural productivity revisited", American Journal of Agricultural Economics 79:1045–1063.

Barkley, A.P. (1990), "The determinants of the migration of labor out of agriculture in the United States, 1940–85", American Journal of Agricultural Economics 72:567–573.

Barro, R., and J.-W. Lee (1993), "International comparisons of educational attainment", Journal of Monetary Economics 32:363–394.

Becker, G.S. (1993), Human Capital, 3rd edn. (The University of Chicago Press, Chicago, IL).

Becker, G.S., and K.M. Murphy (1993), "The division of labor, coordination costs, and knowledge" in: G.S. Becker, Human Capital, 3rd edn (The University of Chicago Press, Chicago, IL) 299–322.

Belbase, K., and R. Grabowski (1985), "Technical efficiency in Nepalese agriculture", Journal of Development Areas 19:515–526.

Benjamin, D. (1992), "Household composition, labor markets, and labor demand: Testing for separation in agricultural household models", Econometrica 60:287–322.

Ben-Porath, Y. (1967), "The production of human capital and the life cycle of earnings", Journal of Political Economy 75:352–365.

Besley, T., and A. Case (1993), "Modeling technology adoption in developing countries", American Economic Review 83:396–402.

Bindlish, V., and R.E. Evenson (1997), "The impact of T&V extension in Africa: The experience on Kenya and Burkina Faso", The World Bank Observer 12:183–201.

Birkhaeuser, D., R.E. Evenson and G. Feder (1991), "The economic impact of agricultural extension: A review", Economic Development and Cultural Change 39:607–650.

Bishop, J. (1989), "Is the test score decline responsible for the productivity growth decline?", American Economic Review 79(February):178–197.

Bollman, R.D. (1979), Off-Farm Work by Farmers, Catalogue No. 99-756 (Statistics Canada, Ottawa, Canada).

Bravo-Ureta, B.E., and R.E. Evenson (1994), "Efficiency in agricultural production: The case of peasant farmers in Eastern Paraguay", Agricultural Economics 10:27–37.

Bravo-Ureta, B.E., and A.E. Pinherio (1993), "Efficiency analysis of developing country agriculture: A review of the frontier function literature", Agricultural and Resource Economics Review 22:88–101.

Bryant, W.K. (1986), "Technical change and the family: An initial foray", in: R. Deacon and W.E. Huffman, eds., Human Resources Research, 1887–1987 (College of Home Economics, Iowa State University) 117–126.

Capalbo, S.M., and M.G.S. Denny (1986), "Testing long-run productivity models for the Canadian and U.S. agricultural sectors", American Journal of Agricultural Economics 68:615–625.

Chavas, J.-P., and T.L. Cox (1992), "A nonparametric analysis of the influence of research on agricultural productivity", American Journal of Agricultural Economics 74:583–591.

Craig, B.J., P.G. Pardey and J. Roseboom (1997), "International productivity patterns: Accounting for input quality, infrastructure, and research", American Journal of Agricultural Economics 79:1064–1076.

Denison, E.F. (1962), The Sources of Economic Growth in the United States and the Alternatives Before Us (Committee for Economic Development, New York, NY).

Dhakal, D., R. Grabowski and K. Belbase (1987), "The effect of education in Nepal's traditional agriculture", Economics of Education Review 6:27–34.

Easter, K.W., M.E. Abel and G. Norton (1977), "Regional differences in agricultural productivity in selected areas of India", American Journal of Agricultural Economics 59:257–265.

El-Osta, H., and J.D. Johnson (1998), "Determinants of financial performance of commercial dairy farms", Technical Bulletin No. 1859, July, USDA, ERS.

Emerson, R.D., ed. (1984), Seasonal Agricultural Labor Markets in the United States (Iowa State University Press, Ames, IA).

Emerson, R.D. (1989), "Migratory labor and agriculture", American Journal of Agricultural Economics 71:617–629.

Evenson, R.E. (1978), "Time allocation in rural Philippine households", American Journal of Agricultural Economics 60:322–330.

Evenson, R.E., and G. Mwabu (1997), "The effects of agricultural extension on farm yields in Kenya" (Economic Growth Center, Yale University).

Fane, G. (1975), "Education and the managerial efficiency of farmers", Review of Economics and Statistics 57:452–461.

Feder, G., R.E. Just and D. Zilberman (1985), "Adoption of agricultural innovations in developing countries: A survey", Economic Development and Cultural Change 33:255–298.

Fleisher, B.M., and Y. Liu (1992), "Economies of scale, plot size, human capital, and productivity in Chinese agriculture", Quarterly Review of Economics and Finance 32:112–123.

Flinn, J.C., and M. Ali (1986), "Technical efficiency in Basmati rice production", Pakistan Journal of Applied Economics 5:63–79.

Foster, A.D., and M.R. Rosenzweig (1995), "Learning by doing and learning from others: Human capital and technical change in agriculture", Journal of Political Economy 103:1176–1209.

Foster, A.D., and M.R. Rosenzweig (1996), "Technical change and human-capital returns and investments: Evidence from the Green Revolution", The American Economic Review 86:931–953.

Gabbard, S.M., and R. Mines (1995), "Farm worker demographics: Pre-IRCA and post-IRCA field workers", in: P.L. Martin et al., eds., Immigration Reform and U.S. Agriculture, Publ. 3358 (University of California, Division of Agriculture and Natural Resources, Oakland, CA) 63–72.

Gardner, B.L. (1992), "Changing economic perspective on the farm problem", Journal of Economic Literature 30:62–101.

Ghez, G.R., and G.S. Becker (1975), The Allocation of Time and Goods over the Life Cycle (Columbia University Press for the National Bureau of Economic Research, New York).

Gibbons, R. (1998), "Incentives in organizations", Journal of Economic Perspective, 12(Fall):115–132.

Goetz, S.J., and D.L. Debertin (1996), "Rural population decline in the 1980s: Impacts of farm structure and federal farm programs", American Journal of Agricultural Economics 78:517–529.

Goldin, C. (1998), "America's graduation from high school: The evolution and spread of secondary schooling in the twentieth century", Journal of Economic History 58(June):345–373.

Goldin, C., and L.F. Katz (1999a), "Education and income in the early 20th century: Evidence from the Prairies, 1915 to 1950" (Harvard University).

Goldin, C., and L.F. Katz (1999b), "Human capital and social capital: The rise of secondary schooling in America, 1910–1940", Journal of Interdisciplinary History 29(Winter):683–723.

Gould, B.W., and W.E. Saupe (1989), "Off-farm labor market entry and exit", American Journal of Agricultural Economics 71:960–969.

Green, W.H. (1997), Econometric Analysis, 3rd edn. (Prentice-Hall, Upper Saddle River, NJ).

Griliches, Z. (1963a), "Estimates of the aggregate agricultural production function from cross sectional data", Journal of Farm Economics 45:419–428.

Griliches, Z. (1963b), "The source of measured productivity growth: United States agriculture, 1940–1960", Journal of Political Economy 71:331–346.

Griliches, Z. (1964), "Research expenditures, education, and the aggregate agricultural production function", American Economic Review 54:961–974.

Griliches, Z. (1969), "Capital-skill complementarity", The Review of Economics and Statistics 51:465–468.

Griliches, Z. (1970), "Notes on the role of education in production functions and growth accounting", in: W.L. Hansen, ed., Education, Income and Human Capital. Studies in Income and Wealth, NBER, Vol. 35 (Columbia University Press, New York, NY).

Hallberg, M.C., J.L. Findeis and D.A. Lass (1991), Multiple Job-Holding Among Farm Families (Iowa State University Press, Ames, IA).

Hayami, Y. (1960), "Sources of agricultural productivity gap among selected countries", American Journal of Agricultural Economics 51:564–575.

Hayami, Y., and V.W. Ruttan (1970), "Agricultural productivity differences among countries", The American Economic Review 60:895–911.

Hayami, Y., and V.W. Ruttan (1985), Agricultural Development: An International Perspective (The Johns Hopkins University Press, Baltimore, MD).

Heady, E.O., and J.L. Dillon (1961), Agricultural Production Functions (Iowa State University Press, Ames, IA).

Heckman, J. (1997), "Instrumental variables: A study of implicit behavioral assumptions used in making program evaluations", Journal of Human Resources 32:441–462.

Huang, T.-L., P.F. Orazem and D. Wohlgemuth (2001), "Rural population growth, 1950–1990: The roles of human capital, industry structure and government policy", American Journal of Agricultural Economics, forthcoming.

Huffman, W.E. (1974), "Decision making: The role of education", American Journal of Agricultural Economics 56:85–97.

Huffman, W.E. (1976a), "Productive value of human time in U.S. agriculture", American Journal of Agricultural Economics 58:672–683.

Huffman, W.E. (1976b), "The value of the productive time of farm wives: Iowa, North Carolina and Oklahoma", American Journal of Agricultural Economics 58:836–841.

Huffman, W.E. (1977), "Allocative efficiency: The role of human capital", Quarterly Journal of Economics 91:59–80.

Huffman, W.E. (1980), "Farm and off-farm work decisions: The role of human capital", Review of Economics and Statistics 62:14–23.

Huffman, W.E. (1981), "Black-white human capital differences: Impact on agricultural productivity in the U.S. south", American Economic Review 71:94–107.

Huffman, W.E. (1985), "Human capital, adaptive ability, and the distributional implications of agricultural policy", American Journal of Agricultural Economics 67:429–434.

Huffman, W.E. (1991a), "Human capital for future economic growth", in: G.L. Johnson and J.T. Bonnen, eds., Social Science Agricultural Agendas and Strategies. Part III (Michigan State University Press, East Lansing, MI) 61–67.

Huffman, W.E. (1991b), "Agricultural household models: Survey and critique", in: M.C. Hallberg, J.L. Findeis and D.L. Lass, eds., Multiple Job-Holding Among Farm Families (Iowa State University Press, Ames, IA) 79–111.

Huffman, W.E. (1996a), "Labor markets, human capital, and the human agent's share of production", in: J.M. Antle and D.A. Sumner, eds., The Economics of Agriculture, Vol. 2, Papers in Honor of D. Gale Johnson (The University of Chicago Press, Chicago, IL) 55–79.

Huffman, W.E. (1996b), "Farm labor: Key conceptual and measurement issues on the route to better farm cost and return estimates", Staff Paper No. 280 (Department of Economics, Iowa State University).

Huffman, W.E. (1998),"Modernizing agriculture: A continuing process", Daedalus 127(Fall):159–186.

Huffman, W.E., and R. Evenson (1989), "Supply and demand functions for multiproduct U.S. cash grain farms: Biases caused by research and other policies", American Journal of Agricultural Economics 71:761–773.

Huffman, W.E., and R. Evenson (1993), Science for Agriculture (Iowa State Press, Ames, IA).

Huffman, W.E., and T. Feridhanusetyawan (2001), "Migration, fixed costs, and location-specific amenities: A hazard rate analysis" (Department of Economics, Iowa State University, Staff Paper No. 340).

Huffman, W.E., and M.D. Lange (1989), "Off-farm work decisions of husbands and wives: Joint decision making", Review of Economic and Statistics 71:471–480.

Huffman, W.E., and S. Mercier (1991), "Joint adoption of micro computer technologies: An analysis of farmers' decision", Review of Economics and Statistics 73:541–546.

Ise, S., and J.M. Perloff (1995), "Legal status and earnings of agricultural workers", American Journal of Agricultural Economics 77:375–386.

Jacoby, H. (1993), "Shadow wages and peasant family labor supply: An econometric application to the Peruvian sierra", Review of Economic Studies 60:903–921.

Jamison, D.T., and L.I. Lau (1982), Farmer Education and Farm Efficiency (Johns Hopkins University Press, Baltimore, MD).

Jensen, H.H., and P. Salant (1985), "The role of fringe benefits in operator off-farm labor supply", American Journal of Agricultural Economics 67:1095–1099.

Johnson, D.G. (1997), "Agriculture and the wealth of nations", Richard T. Ely lecture, American Economic Review 87:1–12.

Jones, C.I. (1998), Introduction to Economic Growth (Norton, New York, NY).

Jorgenson, D.W., and F.M. Gollop (1992), "Productivity growth in U.S. agriculture: A postwar perspective", American Journal of Agricultural Economics 74:745–750.

Kawagoe, T., Y. Hayami and V.W. Ruttan (1985), "The intercountry agricultural production function and productivity differences among countries", Journal of Development Economics 19:113–132.

Kendrick, J.W. (1961), Productivity Trends in the United States (Princeton University Press, Princeton, NJ).

Khaldi, N. (1975), "Education and allocative efficiency in U.S. agriculture", American Journal of Agricultural Economics 57:650–657.

Kimhi, A. (1994), "Quasi maximum likelihood estimation of multivariate probit models: Farm couples' labor participation", American Journal of Agricultural Economics 76:828–835.

Kimhi, A., and M.-J. Lee (1996), "Off farm and work decisions of farm couples: Estimating structural simultaneous equations with ordered categorical dependent variables", American Journal of Agricultural Economics 78:687–698.

Klotz, C., A. Saha and L.J. Butler (1995), "The role of information in technology adoption: The case of rbST in the California Dairy industry", Review of Agricultural Economics 176(Fall/Winter):287–298.

Lass, D.A., J.L. Findeis and M.C. Hallberg (1989), "Off-farm employment decision by Massachusetts farm households", Northeastern Journal of Agricultural and Resource Economics 18:149–159.

Lass, D.A., and C.M. Gempesaw II (1992), "The supply of off-farm labor: A random coefficients approach", American Journal of Agricultural Economics 74:400–411.

Lin, J.Y. (1991), "Education and innovation adoption in agriculture: Evidence from hybrid rice in China", American Journal of Agricultural Economics 73:713–723.

Lin, J.Y. (1995), "Endowments, technology, and factor markets: A natural experiment of induced institutional innovation from China's rural reform", American Journal of Agricultural Economics 77:231–242.

Martin, P.L., W.E. Huffman, R.D. Emerson, J.E. Taylor and R. Rockin, eds. (1995), Immigration Reform and U.S. Agriculture, Publ. 3358 (Division of Agriculture and Natural Resources, University of California, Oakland, CA).

Mincer, J. (1974), Schooling, Experience, and Earnings (Columbia University Press for the National Bureau of Economic Research, New York, NY).

Nawata, K., and N. Nagase (1996), "Estimation of sample selection bias models", Econometric Review 15:387–400.

Newey, W.K., J.L. Powell and J.R. Walker (1990), "Semiparameter estimation of selection models: Some empirical results", American Economic Review 80:324–328.

OECD (1995), Technological Change and Structural Change in OECD Agriculture (OECD, Paris).

Olson, M. (1969), "The principle of fiscal equivalence: The division of responsibilities among different levels of government", American Economic Review 59(May):479–487.

Olson, M. (1986), "Toward a more general theory of government structure", American Economic Review 76(May):120–125.

Orazem, P.F., A. Hallam and E.M. Paterno (1997), "Capital deepening, biased technical change and earnings inequality: A re-examination of the Griliches hypothesis", paper (Department of Economics, Iowa State University).

Orazem, P.F., and J.P. Mattila (1991), "Human capital, uncertain wage distribution, and occupational and educational choice", International Economic Review 32:103–122.

Perloff, J. (1991), "The impact of wage differentials on choosing to work in agriculture", American Journal of Agricultural Economics 73:671–680.

Perloff, J.M., L. Lynch and S. Gabbard (1998), "Migration of seasonal agricultural workers", American Journal of Agricultural Economics 80:154–164.

Pitt, M.M., and G. Sumodiningrat (1991), "Risk, schooling and the choice of seed technology in developing countries: A meta-profit function approach", International Economic Review 32:457–473.

Pudasaini, S.P. (1983), "The effects of education in agriculture: Evidence from Nepal", American Journal of Agricultural Economics 65:509–515.

Putler, D.S., and D. Zilberman (1988), "Computer use in agriculture: Evidence from Tulare County, California", American Journal of Agricultural Economics 70:790–802.

Rahm, M.R., and W.E. Huffman (1984), "The adoption of reduced tillage: The role of human capital and other variables", American Journal of Agricultural Economics 66:405–413.

Romer, P. (1990), "Endogenous technological change", Journal of Political Economics 98:S71–S102.

Rosegrant, M.W., and R.E. Evenson (1993), "Agricultural productivity growth in Pakistan and India: A comparative analysis", The Pakistan Development Review 32:433–451.

Rosenzweig, M. (1980), "Neoclassical theory and the optimizing peasant: An econometric analysis of market family labor in a developing economy", Quarterly Journal of Economics 94(February):31–56.

Rubin, D.K., and J.M. Perloff (1993), "Who works for piece rate and why", American Journal of Agricultural Economics 75:1036–1043.

Schultz, T.P. (1988), "Education investments and returns", in: H. Chenery and T.N. Srinivasau, eds., Handbook of Development Economics, Vol. 1 (North-Holland, Amsterdam, Netherlands) 543–630.

Schultz, T.W. (1953), The Economic Organization of Agriculture (McGraw-Hill, New York, NY).

Schultz, T.W. (1963), The Economic Value of Education (Columbia University Press, New York, NY).

Schultz, T.W. (1964), Transforming Traditional Agriculture (Yale University Press, New Haven, CT). Reprint edition (Arno Press, New York, 1976).

Schultz, T.W. (1975), "The value of the ability to deal with disequilibria", Journal of Economic Literature 13:827–846.

Schultz, T.W. (1978), "On economics and politics of agriculture", in: T.W. Schultz, ed., Distortions of Agricultural Incentives (Indiana University Press, Bloomington, IN).

Short, S.O., and W.D. McBride (1996), "U.S. milk production costs and returns, 1993", Agricultural Information Report No. 732, May, USDA, ERS.

Shumway, C.R. (1983), "Supply, demand, and technology in a multiproduct industry: Texas field crops", American Journal of Agricultural Economics 65:748–760.

Singh, I., L. Squire and J. Strauss (1986), Agricultural Household Models: Extensions, Applications and Policy (Johns Hopkins Press, Baltimore, MD).

Soule, M.J., A. Tegene and K.D. Wiebe (1999), "Land tenure and the adoption of conservation practices", Resource Economics Division, March, USDA, ERS.

Strauss, J., M. Barbosa, S. Teixeira, D. Thomas and R.G. Junior (1991), "Role of education and extension in the adoption of technology: A study of upland rice and soybean farmers in Central-West Brazil", Agricultural Economics 5:341–359.

Sumner, D.A. (1982), "The off-farm labor supply of farmers", American Journal of Agricultural Economics 64:499–509.

Taylor, J.E. (1986), "Differential migration networks, information and risk", in: O. Stark, ed., Migration, Human Capital and Development (JAI Press, Greenwich, CT).

Taylor, J.E. (1987), "Undocumented Mexico–U.S. migration and the returns to households in rural Mexico", American Journal of Agricultural Economics 69:626–638.

Tokle, J.G., and W.E. Huffman (1991), "Local economic conditions and wage labor decisions of farm and rural nonfarm couples", American Journal of Agricultural Economics 73:652–670.

Weaver, R.D. (1983), "Multiple input, multiple output production choices and technology in the U.S. wheat region", American Journal of Agricultural Economics 65:45–46.

Welch, F. (1970), "Education in production", Journal of Political Economy 78:35–59.

Williamson, O. (1985), The Economic Institution of Capitalism (The Free Press, New York, NY).

Willis, R. (1986), "Wage determination: A survey and reinterpretation of human capital earnings functions", in: O. Ashenfelter and R. Layard, eds., Handbook of Labor Economics, Vol. I (North Holland, New York, NY) 525–602.

World Bank (1997), World Development Report, 1997 (Oxford University Press, New York, NY).

World Resources Institute (1992), World Resources, 1992–93 (Oxford University Press, New York, NY).

Wozniak, G.D. (1984), "The adoption of interrelated innovations: A human capital approach", The Review of Economics and Statistics 66:70–79.

Wozniak, G. (1993), "Joint information acquisition and new technology adoption: Later versus early adoption", Review of Economics and Statistics 75:438–445.

Yang, D.T. (1997a), "Education and off-farm work", Economic Development and Cultural Change 45:613–632.

Yang, D.T. (1997b), "Education in production: Measuring labor quality and management", American Journal of Agricultural Economics 79(August):764–772.

Chapter 8

WOMEN'S ROLES IN THE AGRICULTURAL HOUSEHOLD: BARGAINING AND HUMAN CAPITAL INVESTMENTS

T. PAUL SCHULTZ

Yale University, New Haven, CT

Contents

Handbook of Agricultural Economics, Volume 1, Edited by B. Gardner and G. Rausser

Abstract

Three themes are related to women's economic roles in the agricultural household. First the unified family as coordinator of production and consumption over a life cycle. Second the role of separability of production and consumption decisions in the agricultural household that depends on the equivalence of hired and of family labor. Third Nash-bargaining or Pareto efficient collective coordination in the family. Increases in women's human capital affects gender bargaining and is closely related to declines in child mortality, fertility, and population growth, and increases in child "quality" as proxied by child schooling and health status.

JEL classification: Q12

1. Introduction

This chapter takes stock of the methods and empirical findings from economic analyses of women's contribution to social welfare and the determinants of their well-being. To account for women's roles in the agricultural household, economic research has been greatly affected by three steps in the general analysis of the family in the last thirty years. First is the conceptualization of the unified family as a coordinator of the production and consumption of a group of persons over an extended period of the life cycle, with the household production of consumption commodities for family use constrained by the pool of household endowments including time, market prices, and knowledge of home production possibilities [Becker (1965, 1981)]. Second is the role of separability of production and consumption decisions in the agricultural household, which depends on the perfect substitutability of hired and family labor and the adequacy of factor markets [Barnum and Squire (1979); Singh et al. (1986)]. Third is the introduction of individualistic bargaining or collective coordination of the family that preserves the distinct endowments of the individual and the expression of possible differences in personal preferences [McElroy and Horney (1981); Chiappori (1988); Lundberg and Pollak (1993)]. This third innovation has relaxed the unified family model in different ways, and is still being extended and adapted to new problems or forms of game theory and econometrics. It has already been used to guide penetrating empirical studies of the intrahousehold allocation of resources, and much further work is currently underway.

The chapter also explores how gender differentials in various forms of human capital arise, are sustained, and affect social welfare in different cultural regions of the world. Although much of this literature has focused on agricultural households in low income countries, many features of the field are not unique to agriculture, though occasionally issues emerge that are based in the agricultural sciences: effects of crop mix and management for the derived demand for male or female labor, the adoption of new technologies in agriculture, the degradation of the environment due to overused common resources, seasonality, weather as an observable source of risk, etc. One problem area in interpreting existing evidence in this field is the variation in the composition of families, by which I mean both fertility and the extension of nuclear families to absorb other generations and relatives. The consumption, savings, and poverty literatures often mechanically normalize away the variation in household composition, or condition on this composition as though it were an exogenous constraint, when it is widely believed that marriage, fertility, and family extension are choices that respond to the conventional economic variables of prices, sources of income, and personal endowments. The growing numerical importance of female-headed households in many parts of the world, and even the differential survival of existing members of the household, are shown to be responsive to the relative costs and benefits of different family arrangements and compositions.

Changes in women's earning power compared to men's and children's affect what the family specializes in and what other institutions in society, such as firms and government, do. Functions where the family retains a comparative advantage may also be performed with a changing mix of labor and capital in response to the evolution of the wage structure. The secular convergence in productive capacity of men and women is a notable development of this century. This narrowing of the gender gap in labor productivity is closely associated with the narrowing of the difference between male and female adult schooling, and is modified by the improved health and longevity of females compared to males [Schultz (1995a)]. Fertility, mortality, and rural-urban migration determine population growth in the agricultural and nonagricultural sectors, and all of these demographic processes have been shown to respond to the economic productivity of adult males and females, at the household and aggregate levels. Thus, the evolving gender differences in human capital provide the best available explanation for world patterns of demographic transition, interregional migration, and changes in women's participation in the labor force outside of the family [Schultz (1981)]. Yet we have only a poor understanding of what has propelled the advance of women's human capital in different settings throughout the world. Why have women been left at a substantial disadvantage to their male folk in broad parts of South and West Asia and sub-Saharan Africa, and what will be the economic consequences on women's roles, population growth, and economic development?

This chapter is structured as follows. Sections 2 reviews the alternative theoretical approaches to modeling the determinants of individual and family resource allocations and their relevance to the welfare and productivity of women. Section 3 summarizes the empirical evidence on how family allocations respond to changes in the endowments of husband and wife and other features of the family environment. Section 4 examines two attributes of family composition that have received considerable attention: the increased frequency of female-headed households and the gender differentials in child survival that may be related to women's productive roles in society. Section 5 examines the problems of estimating the productivity of women compared with men using either wage functions or production functions, and the general policy implications of the social externalities associated with increasing the schooling of females. Section 6 concludes by reviewing progress made and the challenges that lie ahead in this field.

2. Models of individual and family economic behavior

2.1. Individual consumer demands or expenditure systems

Simple models of consumer demand in a single period generally assume that the consumer receives (exogenously) a disposable income (I) for a reference period such as a year, knows the prices of market goods (P_1, P_2), and then selects a combination of goods (X_1, X_2) to maximize individual utility:

$$U = U(X_1, X_2),$$

(1)

subject to the income constraint:

$$I = P_1 X_1 + P_2 X_2. \tag{2}$$

The decision of how much time to work at a market-determined wage (w) is then incorporated into the consumer's optimization problem by adding leisure (L) to the individual's utility function:

$$U = U(X_1, X_2, L), \tag{3}$$

and a single-period time constraint:

$$T = L + H,$$

where T is assumed to be the total time available for all persons in the reference period and H is the hours worked in the wage market. Market income then becomes the sum of (exogenous) nonearned income (V) and market wage income where the wage is assumed independent of hours worked:

$$I = V + Hw = P_1 X_1 + P_2 X_2. \tag{4}$$

The concept of full income (F) introduced by Becker (1965) is the potential income the individual could obtain by allocating all of his or her time to wage work:

$$F = V + Tw = P_1 X_1 + P_2 X_2 + Lw. \tag{5}$$

The equilibrium conditions from maximizing the utility function (3) with respect to the full income constraint (5) include:

$$MU_L / MU_{X_i} = w/P_i, \quad i = 1, 2. \tag{6}$$

The ratio of the marginal utility of time as leisure to the marginal utility of either good is equal to the ratio of the market wage to the good's price. If, however, the individual spends all of her time in nonmarket activities, called here simply leisure, then the shadow price of leisure (MU_L) presumably exceeds the market wage offer.

   If the commodity or service that enters the utility function of the individual is purchased in the market in the form in which it is consumed, such as bread, the above model may be satisfactory. But if, alternatively, the commodity or service providing the welfare to the individual is produced in the home with market inputs (i_h) and own time (t_h), such as might be expected with health, human capital, or children, home production functions (H) might be assumed to describe these technological and biological possibilities:

$$H = H(i_h, t_h, e), \tag{7}$$

where e is an individual-specific endowment that increases the home output but is not controlled by the individual, and this form of heterogeneity is generally unobserved by the researcher and may affect the productivity of the other inputs and time used in this and other home production processes.

This intermediate layer of home production functions, introduced between market goods and the commodities from which utility is derived, allows the economist to consider substitution possibilities that the home producer may consider in optimizing home production [Becker (1965, 1981)]. The individual or family can now adjust consumer/producer behavior to exogenous changes in market prices, wages, and nonearned income along two dimensions: they can adjust the composition of what they ultimately consume, including leisure, and they can also modify how these home-produced commodities are produced at least cost, through changes in their input factor proportions, as would a market-oriented firm.

Home production functions are more difficult to estimate than production functions that describe technical relationships determining how goods are produced for exchange in the market. This is partly because the output of home production is generally not sold or quantified, and thus the shadow value of such a nontraded commodity may differ across households. For example, the shadow value of a child to one mother may not be the same as to another, because there is no relevant market, and individual preferences (and fecundity) will vary.

In many types of home production, such as the formation of human capital in children, productive endowments of the individual influence input productivity and therefore possibly influence parent allocation of inputs across family members. If these innate endowments are not observed by the researcher, as denoted by e in (7), direct estimation of the marginal productivity of home inputs by regressing H on I and t are likely to yield biased indications of their technological contribution or productivity because the input e is omitted from the estimated home production function. For example, Becker hypothesizes that "ability" of a child increases the private rate of return to schooling a child [Becker (1967, 1981); Becker and Tomes (1979)]. If parents then allocate more schooling to their more able children, the direct association between schooling and productivity of the children would overstate the returns to schooling, other things being equal [Griliches (1977)]. In attempting to estimate the home production function (7), the relationship among observable inputs and outputs will tend to be biased by any correlation between the individual endowment and the observed market and time inputs, which violates the standard estimation assumption that the inputs are independent of the disturbance in the output equation. In household production of children and health human capital, variation in the biological endowments of the couple and children can be of substantial importance. The technical marginal product of inputs can then be seriously misunderstood [Rosenzweig and Schultz (1983); Schultz (1984)]. A parallel problem arises in attempting to estimate the effectiveness of contraception on controlling fertility, when the choice of birth control is informed by the couple's partial knowledge of their fecundity or likelihood of conception given their observed input behavior [Rosenzweig and Schultz (1985, 1989)].

2.2. Multiperson agricultural family and household demands

Issues of allocation and decision-making become more complicated when more than one individual is involved. In reality individuals will differ in their preferences for goods and services and what they can contribute to the welfare of the group. Most of the research on households and the family has been based on the convenient working assumption that families or coresidential groups have identical preferences or one individual dominates the allocation process and consults his, or her, preferences in determining an optimal solution. As a consequence, a stable scheme for the ordering of alternatives is arrived at for the group. In other words, the group is treated as if it were an individual. Because the members of families and households tend to differ in their productive capacities and personalities, as they do in sex and age, households are not likely to be made up of identical individuals. That leaves us with the "dominant dictator" model as the remaining, least implausible, conceptual foundation for the unified family/household decision-making unit. In the next two sections of this paper some alternative approaches for treating the conflicting interests of family members are reviewed and their distinct and testable empirical predictions explored.

These non-unified approaches to household decision-making build on an explicit or implicit bargaining process taking place within the family; they assume either that information is shared symmetrically between cooperative individuals, which then tends to lead to allocations which are Pareto efficient, or that private information is not shared and is hence asymmetrical, with this failure of coordination leading to inefficient allocations across the household members. This is an area of recent methodological progress and an active focus for the new empirical research on family behavior [e.g., Haddad et al. (1997)]. It is accordingly emphasized in this chapter, but two things should be recalled. First the unified household model of Becker (1965, 1981) provided a fruitful general framework to guide research on the division of labor within the family, and the main conclusions drawn in that literature have not yet been called into question by the newer alternative approaches for interpreting family behavior. The exception may prove to be West Africa, where individuals privately manage their own agricultural plots with limited coordination or pooling of resources at the household or family levels [Jones (1983, 1986); Udry (1996)]. Even in this instance, subsequent samples from neighboring regions do not confirm that Burkina families fail the test of Pareto efficiency in their allocation of labor by plot [Akresh (1999)]. Second, documented differences in consumption among persons in the household or family can be interpreted as suboptimal only after researchers specify criteria for optimality [Haddad and Kanbur (1990)], such as calorie distribution between persons within the household. But in this case of calories, for example, the "needs" of individuals may actually be endogenous, to the extent that they vary by the choice of type and amount of work engaged in by individual family members [e.g., Pitt et al. (1990); Higgin and Alderman (1997)] or due to sources of unobserved heterogeneity, such as morbidity and weight. Evidence is only beginning to amass that the error introduced by neglecting intra-household bargaining changes important policy conclusions or alters preferred agricultural development strategies, although the reach of these new approaches to family decision-making is only beginning to be explored [Strauss and Beegle (1996)].

A second significant feature of the agricultural family is the combined functions it performs of producing agricultural output and coordinating consumption and labor supply of its members [Barnum and Squire (1979); Singh et al. (1986)]. It is commonly assumed in such an agricultural model of the family that hired and family labor are identical in production, and that the labor market is perfect in providing the family with both a source of jobs for any excess supply of family workers it may have beyond the profit-maximizing labor demand on its own farm, and a source of hired labor for any shortage of family labor to meet its farm's production requirements. This assumption of separability allows the optimization problem facing the agricultural family to be solved in a two-step process. First, farm outputs and inputs are determined to maximize farm profit. Second, the family maximizes its unified utility to determine how much family labor supply is allocated to farm and off-farm activities, and how much labor is residually hired to satisfy farm labor input requirements [Barnum and Squire (1979); Singh et al. (1986); Pitt and Rosenzweig (1986); Benjamin (1992); Maluccio (1997); DeSilva (1997)]. Without this form of complete and competitive factor market for family and hired labor, the production and consumption decisions would have to be made jointly and they could yield different results from those arrived at by the simpler two-step process. Testing explicitly for this form of separability has not yet produced strong empirical evidence rejecting the simplifying restriction. Risk and uncertainty as well as dynamics in the sequencing of labor and other inputs can complicate separability greatly [Roe and Graham-Tomasi (1986); Skoufias (1993a, 1993b, 1996)], as can other interlinked factor markets, such as those for credit. Specific parameterizations for the profit and family utility functions can be postulated and simulated to trace out the consequences of market failures [de Janvry et al. (1991)]. But these are not, in my view, empirical tests of separability.

Yet it seems likely that there are activities where hired and family labor are not good substitutes, perhaps because of differences in relevant skills and farm-specific management experience, or because incentive and monitoring costs differ in these tasks for family and hired labor. For some special tasks hired labor can be paid according piece rates, as may occur in the case of harvesting, to reduce the cost of monitoring labor. In performing other tasks, family altruism and sharing in final output might provide family labor with better work incentives than can be readily offered hired labor, and then in these tasks family labor would have an efficiency advantage. Even when disaggregated tasks are studied separately by calendar period of the crop cycle, Maluccio finds only a few instances in the Bicol Province of the Philippines where separability is rejected. Pitt and Rosenzweig (1986) and Benjamin (1992) also cannot reject separability among the Indonesian rural families they analyze. One could imagine that in societies in South Asia where it is less common (or socially acceptable) for adult women to work outside of their own family farm, separation would not hold. But in rural India in 1969–1971, families that were relatively short of land and well endowed with female labor did not appear to employ more than the profit-maximizing level of female labor on their own farm. In other words, when both the land and labor markets were modeled jointly, family farms appear to be efficiently allocating their own and hired labor (and land) in a manner that could not be statistically shown to be inefficient due to labor market or family imperfections [Seavy (1987)]. Agricultural production functions estimated at the district level for India suggest that family and hired labor may exhibit different productivity and may deserve to be treated as separate inputs, although this has proven difficult given the extent of gender segregation of agricultural tasks [Deolalikar and Vijverberg (1983); Laufer (1985)]. Where factor markets appear to be least well developed, as in sub-Saharan Africa or parts of South and West Asia, nonseparability in hired-family labor markets is still anticipated by some development economists and these problems are probably more severe for female labor than for male [de Janvry et al. (1991)].

2.3. Intra household allocations and bargaining

The unitary model of household resource allocation is based on the maximization of a single household welfare function subject to a time and resource budget constraint and home production technology, taking as given market prices and wage opportunities. Samuelson (1947, 1956) elaborated on the implausible assumptions required for aggregation of individual preferences to deal with family or household choice in a form that would satisfy the axioms of individual consumer choice. Arrow (1951) went so far to as prove the impossibility of consistently aggregating the preferences of agents for the purposes of systematizing choices made by social units such as the family. Nonetheless, with the palpable importance of the family in coordinating consumption and labor supply behavior, the unitary model of the family [Becker (1965)] has been often used to combine in a single model the process determining household consumer demands and labor supply, allowing for cross effects of the shadow wage rates of all family members to affect all of their labor supply choices [Mincer (1963); Kosters (1966); Heckman (1971); Ashenfelter and Heckman (1974)].

Because the unified model of family behavior does not explicitly deal conceptually with how families aggregate the welfare of individual members to guide its decision-making and to determine the distribution of consumption and welfare among members within the family, the unified model of the family has not shed much light on how individual and family resources affect the welfare of persons *within* the family. This failure to study the intrafamily distribution of welfare cannot be entirely attributed to the lack of a theoretical framework, for reduced-form models can be readily estimated for this purpose. Although it is easy to conceive of "private consumption goods" in the family, it is more difficult to measure empirically forms of "assignable consumption", such that one person's consumption of a good can be readily monitored and would not raise (or lower) the utility of other family members. Human capital, assuming it can be valued and quantified, may be such a private or assignable good, if it has no externalities beyond the economic agent in whom it is invested. With the family ascribed a central role in financing (savings and transfers between possibly altruistic generations) and coordinating human capital investments in children, the allocation of human capital investments among children may provide an empirical window through which to take stock of an important aspect of the personal distribution of welfare within the family [e.g., Thomas (1990, 1994); Strauss and Thomas (1995)].

Schooling and education were the first forms of human capital to be studied across children within a family, and more recently height and weight for age have been analyzed as indicators of long-run nutritional and health status, expected longevity, and productive capacity [Fogel (1994); Strauss and Thomas (1995)]. Becker's (1965, 1981) approach to the gains from marriage emphasizes cumulative returns to individual specialization in time allocation in the household, and imperfect substitution of the labor of one for another family member in either or both market and nonmarket production. The market earnings or income of the individual is not synonymous with the individual's welfare or endowment brought into the family, because earnings reflect the endogenous choice of labor supply that depends on technology and preferences, as well as the endowments and wages of all family members and market-determined exchange prices.

Becker (1981) extends his framework further to deal with the utility of different generations. He continues to assume that a single altruistic decision-maker takes account of the separable welfare of each of his offspring, in the form of subutility functions. Two additional strong assumptions are introduced: that the parent decision-maker maximizes the present discounted value of the family's consumption, and that the parent prefers to equalize the lifetime consumption opportunities across his or her children, despite differences in innate ability and market productivity among children. It is further assumed that this innate source of heterogeneity among children interacts positively with the internal rate of return these children earn from a given human capital investment, and that initial human capital investments yield economic return in excess of market borrowing costs, so all parents want to invest in some human capital for each of their children. Becker and Tomes (1979) elaborate why parents in this framework, guided by efficiency, would invest differentially in the human capital of their children until the returns on these marginal investments fell to the parents' financial cost of borrowing. At that point, further transfers to children from parent would all take the form of nonhuman capital, and thus earn the same market return. These additional nonhuman capital transfers would be allocated to equalize lifetime consumption opportunities across all children, and thus advance the parent's equity goal. This wealth maximization model implies parents *compensate* in their allocation of nonhuman capital transfers (both during their lifetime and in the form of bequest at death) for innate child endowments, whereas they *reinforce* these innate child endowments in their allocation of human capital investments.

If the borrowing costs for parents to invest in their children's human capital vary substantially due to differences in the parents' collateral, only the relatively rich may make the optimal human capital investments in all of their children and still have enough resources left to equalize the consumption opportunities of their offspring through further transfers of nonhuman capital. The rich parents will be able to achieve both efficiency (i.e., wealth maximization) and equity (i.e., equal lifetime consumption for all their children), whereas some poorer parents will presumably have to sacrifice one goal for the other due to their constrained access to credit. Behrman (1997) reviews these and other aspects of Becker's wealth-maximizing parent's solution for intergenerational transfers. The empirical evidence has been mixed on whether parents do actually reinforce innate endowments of their children through their human capital investments. There is also little evidence in the United States, and few studies elsewhere, to suggest that bequests of parents to their children are disproportionately larger for children whose earnings or education are less than the average of siblings. Indeed, the most common pattern is for equal bequests, but this does not address the possibility that parents may make transfers before their death which partially or wholly compensate the child whose lifetime earnings are relatively lower than her siblings.

An alternative specification of the intergenerational family utility function proposed by Behrman, Pollak, and Taubman (BPT) (1982) assumes that human capital and non-human capital transfers to children from the parent are separable in the parent's utility function, and therefore the parents may not treat the two mechanisms for increasing a child's consumption as necessarily equivalent. It is also a goal of the BPT framework to permit parent preferences toward wealth maximization and inequality aversion in children's consumption to vary and these basic preference parameters of parents to be estimated from intergenerational bequest and transfer data.

To make their framework empirically tractable, BPT assume a constant elasticity of substitution functional form for the utility function and a Cobb–Douglas household production function to create the child's human capital. The utility function that aggregates the lifetime earnings capacity (E) of the children is assumed to exhibit a constant elasticity of substitution between children, or in the case of two children:

$$U(E_1, E_2) = \left(\alpha_1 E_1^\rho + \alpha_2 E_2^\rho\right)^{1/\rho}. \tag{8}$$

Equal concern with child 1 and 2's earnings implies $\alpha_1 = \alpha_2$, and $-\infty < \rho < 1$ represents aversion to inequality, where $\rho = -\infty$ implies Rawlesian preference for always increasing the earnings of the less productive child, and $\rho = 1$ implies no inequality aversion or a purely investment strategy in maximizing aggregate family net worth.

The child's lifetime earnings (E) is produced by a Cobb–Douglas production function with the arguments being μ, the child's innate endowment, Y the years of schooling received, and X the resource intensity per year of schooling (or school quality):

$$E_i = \mu_i^\lambda Y_i^\beta X_i^\gamma, \quad i = 1, 2. \tag{9}$$

First order conditions from maximizing utility subject to the production function and budget constraint implies that the relative years of schooling provided two children will be the following function of their relative earnings:

$$Y_1/Y_2 = (\alpha_1/\alpha_2)(E_1/E_2)^\rho. \tag{10}$$

Solving for reduced forms for the relative earnings or schooling of the children, one obtains:

$$Y_1/Y_2 = (\alpha_1/\alpha_2)^{1/(1-\delta\rho)}(\mu_1/\mu_2)^{\lambda\rho/(1-\delta\rho)}, \tag{11}$$

$$E_1/E_2 = (\alpha_1/\alpha_2)^{\delta/(1-\delta\rho)}(\mu_1/\mu_2)^{\lambda/(1-\delta\rho)}, \tag{12}$$

where $\delta = \beta + \gamma$. But the reduced forms are in terms of the endowments of the children which are generally not observed, so data are used to fit the first order condition, where earnings and years of education are observed for the children [Strauss and Beegle (1996)].

This framework is also applied by Behrman (1988) to analyze health investments in nutrition of boys and girls in Indian agriculture [E. Rose (1995)], and extended to consider how the parameters differ between the lean and surplus seasons in agriculture in low income countries [Harriss (1990); Strauss and Beegle (1996)]. One could imagine that parents would demand more equality in the surplus season after the harvest. Other intertemporal variations might be investigated in periods of famine or crisis [Agarwal (1991, 1994)]. Some have found in periods of extreme food scarcity that female child mortality increases more than male mortality, as documented in the famine in China from 1959–61 following the "great leap forward" [Aird (1983)]. Consumption smoothing that shelters human capital accumulation in the form of child health and schooling behavior should also be less constrained by credit for rich parents than poor, if the rich have more collateral [Jacoby (1994)]. Foster (1995) found that during serious floods in Bangladesh in 1988 the landowners were better able to protect their children's nutritional status from the severe shocks of food shortages than were the landless laborers. But differentials by the sex of the child in this form of consumption smoothing behavior did not appear significant [Foster (1996)].

It may not always be the case, however, that increasing wealth leads to a reduction in inequality among children, or more specifically between boys and girls. Studies have suggested that in parts of rural India, Green Revolution gains in agricultural productivity have in some regions led to a reallocation of women's time toward home production in landowning households, as women's participation in off-farm work has diminished, and fertility has remained high [Mukhopadhyay (1994)]. If women realize smaller productive gains from education in home production than in the market, this change in family time allocation could even reduce the incentives for women to receive more education. Although female education has not declined in India, progress in increasing female average levels of schooling has been slower than in most other regions of the low income world [Schultz (1987, 1995a, 1996)].

Some studies do not find a correlation between the education of women and household agricultural productivity or income. For example, an empirical analysis of data of about a thousand rural households in Pakistan collected from 1986 to 1989 included several dozen input and family background variables to estimate crop production functions and household income functions. Household averages for six male and six female human capital variables were included, and female education was insignificantly partially related to both outputs and income. Average female education in the sample is, however, 0.6 years compared with the male mean of 3.7 years. Having already controlled for female health status, test scores, and parent background, it is not surprising that female education is not partially related to crop outputs, livestock income, or nonfarm income [Fafchamps and Quisumbing (1998a)]. More wealthy rural families may withdraw women from agricultural tasks, and employ them in household production for which the outputs are generally not counted in income.[1] Studies of India have also found more educated rural women are not necessarily more likely to work in agriculture, and improvements in household income related to the Green Revolution can even lead landowning households to reduce the labor force participation of their wives [Mukhopadhyay (1994); Unni (1993)]. A national panel study of rural Indian households finds that women with more than a primary education do not work substantially more time in the labor market [Behrman et al. (1997)].

In extensions of the unified household production function approach to estimating reduced-form demands for time allocation, demographic behavior, and demands for market goods, it is not typically possible to recover the basic parameters of the underlying utility function of parents or the technology parameters of the human capital production functions, as in the more restricted BPT framework. Nonetheless, one can assess which factors in the family endowments and constraints affect the gender gaps in human capital formation or intrahousehold inequality in the general neoclassical unified household production model [Rosenzweig and Schultz (1982b); Pitt et al. (1990); E. Rose (1995)]. If innate endowments of children can be measured, then it is also possible to assess whether parents reinforce or compensate for differences in the endowments of their children.

However, the unitary approach maintains the idea that one member dictates and enforces allocations within the family, and that he is a benevolent altruist with sufficient resources to coordinate the behavior of other family members [Becker (1981); Bergstrom (1997)]. While this unified regime may be a reasonable approximation for describing some aspects of family behavior, it would seem more realistic to relax the model, if that modification is not too costly. Conflicting personal preferences for outcomes could affect both the intrahousehold allocation of productive resources and the distribution of consumption that determines personal well-being, as well as affect who finds it in their interest to be in a family versus alone, and the composition of that family.

---

[1] This common pattern in traditional agricultural populations where there are few nonmanual jobs for women in the rural sector can be formally interpreted in terms of the standard family labor supply model in which the husband's cross wage and wealth effects on the woman's market labor supply are negative and outweigh the positive impact of her own wage effect associated with her increased education [Schultz (1981); Alderman and Chishli (1991)]. It is also not uncommon to find that wage rates in casual day labor do not increase notably with the education of the worker, whether male or female. The returns to schooling for a worker in agriculture tend to be realized by a farm manager or farmer, who makes allocative decisions that may be better informed if he or she is better educated [Welch (1970)]. In Africa and Southeast Asia where women do farm on their own, they are noted to reap private income returns to schooling at much the same rate as do men [e.g., Moock (1976)].

2.4. Collective Pareto-efficient and sharing rules households

The collective household models [Chiappori (1988, 1992, 1997)] are in one sense a return to building on individual decision-making models, but they preserve Pareto efficiency for the group which is generally associated with cooperative solutions of a market or bargaining process in which information is shared between the agents, or with situations involving repeated games, where there are private opportunities for learning and hence opportunities to avoid inefficient outcomes.

Browning et al. (1994) show that when the household is Pareto efficient then its objective function can be written as a weighted sum of its member's utilities, or for a two-adult household that would take the following form:

$$
\max \mu U^A\left(X^A, X^B\right) + (1 - \mu)U^B\left(X^A, X^B\right),
$$
$$
\text{subject to } p\left(X^A + X^B\right) = Y,
$$

(13)

where U^i is the utility of family member i, $i = A, B$, X^i is the private consumption of individual i, and μ is the welfare weight of the member A in the household, such that the weights sum to one across member A and B. The sharing rule summarized by μ is itself affected by prices (p) and total household income (Y), and possibly other variables such as the individual's earnings opportunities which could influence the person's reservation utility – that is, the utility she might expect in some alternative family living arrangement.

Demand functions can be expressed conditional on the sharing rule:

$$
X^i = f\left(p, Y, \mu(p, Y)\right),
$$

(14)

and reduced-form demand functions are obtained by substituting out the sharing parameter:

$$
X^i = g(p, Y).
$$

(15)

Browning et al. (1994) show that empirically testable restrictions on $g(\cdot)$ can be obtained that are similar to the matrix of income-compensated responses to prices and wages obtained in the unitary demand model, i.e., Slutsky equations [Strauss and Beegle (1996)]. A two-stage decision process is proposed that restricts the value function to be weakly separable:

$$
W^A\left(U^A\left(U^A\right), U^B\left(X^B\right)\right).
$$

(16)

Egoistic (selfish individual) behavior that assigns no weight to a partner's utility is nested in this formulation. If a specific amount of income, ϕ, is allocated to member

A, and $Y - \phi$ income to B, then each person maximizes their utility function subject to their income constraint, and conditional demand functions can be written as follows:

$$X^i = X(p, \phi). \tag{17}$$

The ratio of the marginal propensity to consume a good with respect to changes in the incomes of the two individual incomes should be the same across all pairs of goods, for example k and j:

$$\frac{\partial X^k / \partial Y^A}{\partial X^k / \partial Y^B} = \frac{\partial X^j / \partial Y^A}{\partial X^j / \partial Y^B}. \tag{18}$$

In the unitary household model this ratio is unity. In the collective model the ratio represents sharing weights that correspond to the individual's relative command over resources or potential income. μ and ϕ are functions of p, Y, tastes and individual income opportunities and assets, as well as what McElroy and Horney (1981) call extra environmental parameters (EEPs) that affect an individual's welfare outside of this family, such as applicable divorce laws [Peters (1986)], welfare policies for single mothers [Schultz (1994b); Lundberg et al. (1997)], extended family support networks [Cox and Jimenez (1990)], and the local ratio of marriageable males to females [Chiappori et al. (1997)] which might alter the reservation utility of being a member of the family. In the unitary model only p, Y, and tastes influence household demands, but in the collective model individual endowments and alternatives (EEPs) can influence demands or explain outcomes dependent on the family bargaining process.

If goods are assignable to either the husband or wife (and are observable), and separate exogenous incomes are attributable to these individuals, then the sharing rule may be derived across estimated household demands. Moreover, the restriction that the sharing rule is constant across pairs of commodities is then testable in estimating the system of demand equations as shown in (18).[2]

The test of the sharing rule's constancy across pairs of commodities reported in the paper by Browning et al. (1994) relies on women's and men's apparel expenditures for a sample of Canadian couples who are purposively selected to both work for wages and have no children. The test relies on earned income of the woman and man to influence the income-sharing parameter ϕ. A wife's clothes are assumed not to influence a husband's utility, and thus satisfy the separability requirements of the utility function, and vice versa. The earnings of the wife must be exogenous and not reflect her labor supply decision, and more specifically, working more time in the labor market may not affect

---

[2] Errors in the measurement of the nonearned income of the individuals, Y^A and Y^B, may differ. But due to the ratio form of Equation (18) used for testing of the constancy of the sharing rule, the attenuation bias introduced by such measurement errors would cancel out across different commodities, k and j, and not affect the estimated ratio or the test of the ratio's constancy across different pairs of commodities. See [Thomas and Chen (1994)].

her requirements for more and more expensive clothes. These are strong assumptions and they lack realism, and the specially selected sample weakens further how one is to interpret the empirical evidence. But the paper illustrates how the collective model can be used to motivate more compelling empirical tests in the future of the cooperative structure of the family.

The framework has been extended to include labor supply by Chiappori (1992), although that requires the observation of the husband's and wife's nonearned income to influence the sharing rule [Fortin and Lacroix (1997)]. If home production is added [Chiappori (1997); Apps and Rees (1996, 1997)], other restrictions are required, such as constant returns to scale of household production and no joint production, just as Becker (1965) assumed originally in his unitary household production model. Marriage matching [Chiappori et al. (1997)] can also be incorporated into the framework, where the sex ratio of marriageable males to females is specified to affect the sharing rule between married couples. The use of the sex ratio to affect marriage gains was first empirically explored by Frieden (1974) employing Becker's (1974) theory, and has subsequently been analyzed by Grossbard and Shechtman (1993). The ratio of marriageable males to females in a suitably defined marriage market (i.e., homogeneous in demographic characteristics and region of residence) should have opposite signed effects on marriage rates of men and women, and presumably displace their reservation utility, and hence affects their bargaining power within marriage [Chiappori et al. (1997)]. If the distributional sharing rule is contracted on entry into marriage, and is thereafter binding, then the sex ratio at the time of the marriage should be the relevant constraint to a household's current sharing rule and resulting demand behavior.

Another way to approach the intra-family allocation process is to prescribe how the surplus in benefits produced by a marriage is distributed between spouses. One specific framework is the symmetric Nash (1953) bargained solution. The two members are assumed to maximize the product of the individual gains from the marriage in excess of their reservation utilities outside of the union:

$$
\max\left[U^A\left(p, Y^A, Y^B, V^A, V^B\right) - U^{RA}\left(p, Y^A, V^A, EPP^A\right)\right]
$$
$$
\times\left[U^B\left(p, Y^A, Y^B, V^A, V^B\right) - U^{RB}\left(p, Y^B, V^B, EPP^B\right)\right] \tag{19}
$$
$$
\text{subject to } Y^A + Y^B + V^A + V^B = Y,
$$

where V^i refers to the nonearned income of individual i, $i = 1, 2$, and EEP^i are parameters that affect the ith individual's reservation utility U^{Ri}. The Nash solution has many attractive features and some disadvantages. The main limitation to the Nash solution is that it focuses on only one, relatively arbitrary, Pareto efficient allocative solution. This solution is also motivated by the concept of a threat point, linked in most discussions to divorce or leaving the union. That extreme irrevocable threat may seem unreasonable for many stable marriages that are not currently near the margin where dissolution would be preferred by either partner. On the other hand, the simplicity of the Nash-bargained setup [Manser and Brown (1980); McElroy and Horney (1981); McElroy

(1990)] opens the door to consideration of conflict within families as an intermediate process affecting observed household behavior. The notion that marriages might operate as a cooperative game with extensive sharing of information is not an unrealistic starting point for analyses of intrahousehold allocations. Many more complex setups which involve repeated games may also lead, in the long run, to solutions which closely resemble Nash-bargained solutions.

The unitary model implies that the distribution of nonearned income between spouses should not affect consumption behavior. Rejecting empirically this implication of resource pooling within the family does not immediately support one over another model of nonunitary family behavior, but it reinforces the search for alternatives to the unitary model, including possibly the Nash-bargained model [Schultz (1990b); Haddad et al. (1997)]. However, it is not satisfactory to examine spousal-specific earnings as a proxy for partner "bargaining power", because earnings depend upon labor supply, which is typically viewed as endogenous to the household's demand system. The shadow wage of the husband and wife might appear preferable, but this measure of the opportunity value of spousal time may also influence home production in the unified family model and reflects the impact of life cycle specialization in market and home production by spouses, and thus is contingent on their endogenous expectations regarding the permanence of the union. Moreover, to exclude, as Browning et al. (1994) have, "couples who were not both working for a wage in the labor force" may in all likelihood introduce sample selection bias. To correct for such a bias and be able to impute the shadow value of time to those who are not currently working for a wage would require the imposition of additional structure in the model, as will be discussed later. Of course, even nonearned income may be related to past savings and accumulation behavior that could differ by market and home production specialization, and thus be endogenous in this setting. However, I know of no systematic empirical evidence of a simultaneity bias between nonearned income and household demand behavior. Indeed, the empirical evidence preponderantly shows that wage labor supply is negatively associated with nonearned income, as would be expected if nonearned income were exogenous in the simple labor supply model.[3]

---

[3] Critics of this empirical approach tend to reject *a priori* the exogeneity of nonearned income, because it could reflect savings which might in turn be related to preferences for labor supply, leading to the expectation that nonearned income would exhibit a positive partial correlation with labor supply, whereas most studies find a negative correlation as expected for an exogenous "income effect". Of course, identification of these models of family bargaining would be more satisfactory if a variable were observed that accounted for a substantial share of the individual variation in nonearned income within and across households, and this variable were theoretically independent of all other individual and family constraints and tastes that might otherwise influence household demand behavior. What is needed are random social experiments that affect the resources of husband and wife independently, but they appear, unfortunately, to be rare. Yet with these refined models in hand, empirical research should proceed to design and measure more satisfactory variables determining the "threat points" of family members, such as inheritances or dowries in certain systems of family property rights.

There is an implicit sense in this literature that the "threat point" in the family bargaining model is the reservation utility the individual could expect to receive outside of the marital union if the union ends or, in other words, if divorce occurs. But Woolley (1988) and Lundberg and Pollak (1993) propose a different interpretation to the marital bargaining process. They introduce an intermediate noncooperative state before divorce is reached which is maintained on the basis of socially sanctioned gender roles and a customary division of labor within the household. For example, women may remain responsible for child care while men maintain responsibility for providing income for the purchase of certain market goods. This noncooperative equilibrium might be adopted before the costs of union dissolution or divorce are incurred. One empirical implication of this "separate spheres" model of marriage bargaining is that changing the recipient of a government's child support payment between the parents is likely to affect the couple's relative bargaining power and thereby influence the household's allocation of consumption, if the parents have different preferences over alternative observed forms of consumption. In the United Kingdom, child payments were redirected in 1990 from fathers to mothers, and expenditures on children's apparel or women's apparel, relative to the expenditures on men's apparel, increased [Lundberg et al. (1997)]. However, relabeling a transfer program may in itself change how it affects consumption patterns. Kooreman (1998) found in the Netherlands when "family assistance" was relabeled a "child payment", it also was associated with an increase in expenditures on children's apparel. But these differential effects of the child payment relative to the effect of other sources of income on children's apparel were the same in female-headed households as in two-parent households, raising doubts about the importance of differences in preferences between mothers and fathers to explain the change in consumption in the U.K.

There remains relatively little strong direct evidence that preferences of mothers and fathers differ with regard to child consumption, holding technology and endowments constant, but many suggestive empirical studies find increments to women's resources are associated with increased child health and well-being [Fuchs (1988); Thomas (1994)]. One straightforward test of the unified family model remains, however, that in a unified family nonlabor income is pooled. Additional restrictive assumptions are required to construct tests to evaluate the Pareto efficiency of intrahousehold allocations. Portraying the family as a noncooperative bargaining unit may be plausible when coresidence ends in divorce and the public-good-character of children is modified by rules of child custody. Before that stage, the challenge remains to show inefficiency due to the "separate spheres" equilibrium. Evidence of family inefficiency emerges from analyses of the allocation of farm production inputs, but not yet clearly from the study of intrahousehold consumption patterns, which depend critically on the observability of private goods [cf. Udry (1996)].

3. Empirical regularities

3.1. How families allocate resources

Evidence has gradually accumulated in the last decade that challenges the strict formulation of the neoclassical unified family demand model [e.g., Becker (1981)]. Models of bargaining that are less restrictive have therefore been developed, as discussed above [Manser and Brown (1980); Haddad et al. (1997)]. First, there is the cooperative Nash-bargained solution (Equation (19)), and then more general cooperative sharing rule models (Equation (13)) that allow partners to choose intrahousehold allocations from among a wider range of Pareto efficient possibilities [Chiappori (1988)]. Noncooperative bargaining models generally presume the existence of asymmetric information, which is reasonable in some cases, such as child support and divorce settlements. They represent a less well defined framework within which to analyze family decision-making, and provide an explanation for outcomes that are not Pareto efficient [Lundberg and Pollak (1993); Jones (1983, 1986); Udry (1996)]. However, few widely accepted empirically testable predictions distinguish between noncooperative schemes, though many extensions of game theory have not yet been adapted to the study of household behavior. The goal here is to describe the initial modeling efforts that have added flexibility to the neoclassical family demand model by dealing with the possibly distinct interests and separate resources of family members. The model may also allow for a partial pooling of resources, rather than the complete pooling as assumed in the unified family demand model. For example, husbands and wives may appear to pool resources and consistently coordinate their use of time only during that period of the life cycle when they have young children at home [Schultz (1981); Lundberg (1988)], or parents may pool resources but other coresidential relatives in the household maintain their own separate finances.

Consider, for example, how the individual supplies labor. It is generally assumed that increases in nonearned income increase the demand for leisure and nonmarket time and reduce time supplied to the labor market. As this framework is adapted to analyze the labor supply behavior of wives and then other family members [Mincer (1963); Kosters (1966); Heckman (1971)], the leisure of each additional family member is added as an argument to the family utility function, but the family's nonearned income is simply pooled. This unified approach to family demands and labor supply consequently assumes that the demand effects of nonearned income would be identical regardless of the individual's status in the family, or that the distribution of the nonearned income by personal source would not affect family coordinated demand and labor supply behavior. Situations may arise where this pooling assumption appears realistic and others where it does not conform to what we think we know about resource pooling of family members or the coordination of family decision-making.

The cooperative Nash-bargained model assumes the couple cooperatively maximizes a product of the individuals' marital gains in their utility compared to their utility available outside of the union as in Equation (19). Unless the utility in the marriage for both partners exceeds their alternatives (i.e., reservation "wages" or U^{Ri}) the union would not be economically viable. This reservation "utility" establishes a "threat point" or lower limit for consumption allocations to each adult within the family. Nonearned income controlled by the husband or the wife is thus expected to raise the "threat point" of that spouse: it leaves the spouse less dependent on marital gains. The bargaining power of the wealthier spouse is thus strengthened, and this potentially changes the distribution of consumption within the family.[4]

Even when there is an observable consensus on who controls physical assets or nonearned income within the family, there remains the problem of specifying "private goods". Leisure is a natural candidate for a normal good whose beneficiary is the specific individual. But in reality the variable observed is often not consumption of leisure but time not counted as work in the market labor force. This time outside of the market labor force may include time in home production, such as household chores and child care. Consequently, it is unclear whether nonmarket time is universally a normal good whose demand increases with income. In other words, does spending more time at home constitute unambiguous evidence of women's increased utility? Counting who is in the market labor force is also subject to some ambiguity, particularly for women where cultural standards of acceptable activities may introduce forms of enumeration bias [Folbre and Abel (1989)]. The margin of uncertainty in the enumeration of women in the labor force is exaggerated in agriculture, for virtually all women on farms do much unpaid work in the production of market as well as nonmarket goods, but surveys and censuses may or may not count such activities as qualifying them as engaged in productive activity or in the "economic" labor force. Durand (1975) discounts much of the reported variation across countries in rates of female participation as unpaid family workers in agriculture as a statistical artifact due to variation in cultural interpretations of women's accepted roles. The definition of workers who are counted in the labor force working in an unpaid capacity in the family can also change within a country over time, creating anomalous shifts in female labor force participation rates, as noted in India between the censuses of 1960 and 1970.

The effect of private nonearned income on forms of consumption other than leisure – such as expenditures on tobacco, alcohol, toys or gender-specific apparel – may be even more ambiguous as a private good, for there is nothing to prevent wealthier women or men from deriving (selfish) satisfaction from varied consumption activities of other members of their household, even if the good appears to be individual-specific and targeted to another individual or demographic group in the household.

Nonearned income (or its sources) might be divided into those elements brought to the marriage or accumulated during the marriage through distinct individual kinship

---

[4] Of course, the bargaining could occur at the outset, when the family is formed, which suggests that members use their initial resource endowments to agree on the weights for individual goals in the "family's utility function". If these resources change unexpectedly, because of a bequest or inheritance or alternative marriage proposition, the "threat points" would shift and a new bargain and agreed-upon family utility function would be adopted as a guide to subsequent intrafamily allocations.

relationships and independent personal activities, the receipt of bequests or inter vivos transfers, or other personal connections. A wife's nonearned income, such as she might have inherited or brought to the marriage as a dowry, might be expected to reduce her market labor supply by a greater amount than would the same amount of nonearned wealth brought to the marriage by her husband [Malathy (1993)]. Conversely, the payment of a bride-price in many areas of sub-Saharan Africa by the groom to the bride's parents may be associated with the bride increasing her supply of time to the family's labor force [Jacoby (1992)].[5] This prediction of the individualistic bargaining model received only modest support from its first empirical test against U.S. household data, probably because most enumerated wealth was in the form of residential housing, for which the ownership was generally reported to be joint or shared equally [Horney and McElroy (1988)]. Subsequent study of the allocation of time of U.S. husbands and wives to housework provided more support for the bargaining or collective approach to household allocation, perhaps because spouse-specific nonearned income was better measured [Carlin (1991)]. Additional studies based on data from Thailand, India, and Brazil unequivocally reject the pooling of nonearned income as it affects family labor supplies, thereby challenging the unified household model [Schultz (1990b); Duraisamy (1992); Thomas (1990)].

In principle, the measurement of nonearned income is intended to capture exogenous differences across persons in their budget constraints that do not also induce a change in money or time prices of various types of consumption or behavior. In practice, nonearned income (rents, dividends, interest, and capital gains) could arise from inheritances that are similar to schooling, in that they are largely financed by parents and extended family and can be viewed as exogenous at the start of adult life. But nonearned income also represents returns on a person's life cycle accumulation of savings, and hence captures in part the person's past behavior. It then becomes, for some purposes, an endogenous choice variable. Hence, it is desirable for survey questionnaires to pursue the source of each individual's current nonearned income, current assets, and the date of receipt of bequests that led to these current assets, and whether they came from the husband's or wife's side of the family. The Rand Malaysian family life survey comes closest to asking these questions, but I know of no analysis of these data from the perspective outlined here [Butz and DaVanzo (1978)]. The Rand Indonesian family life surveys have extended further this line of questioning that should advance research on family bargaining and demand behavior [Rand (1996)].

---

[5] Evidence compiled by Svenberg (1990) indicates that female nutritional status and survival prospects in sub-Saharan Africa are superior overall to male, possibly because women are economically more productive in converting calories into work than men. As a consequence, perhaps, parents are paid bride prices for their daughters and have a stronger incentive to invest in their health. The one region of sub-Saharan Africa where Svedberg's anthropometric indicators of nutrition and mortality do not indicate as strong a bias in favor of females is in Nigeria and perhaps Senegal. Both of these countries contain a significant Islamic element and women's productive roles are more circumscribed in these segments of the population [Caldwell and Caldwell (1987)].

In Thailand women have traditionally participated in the agricultural labor force almost as frequently as men, and agricultural land is often inherited and managed by women. Although marriage among women was nearly universal in the past, divorce and remarriage were not uncommon. In 1981 the nationally representative Socioeconomic Survey collected by the National Statistical Office distinguished between the individual's ownership of nonearned income within families. This large survey thus provides an opportunity to test the resource pooling implications of the unified family demand model. The estimated negative effect of a specified amount of nonearned (from rentals, interest or dividends) income on labor force participation by women aged 25 to 54 is three times larger if this income is owned by the woman compared to the effect of nonearned income owned by her husband. Conversely, a husband aged 25 to 54 reduces his labor force participation three times as much when the family's nonearned income is owned by him rather than by his wife [Schultz (1990b)]. In other societies it may be more difficult to collect meaningful data on the ownership of nonearned income for each individual in a family. For example, in a survey of rural northeast Brazil, few women report nonearned income, though the proportion increases in urban areas, and there it is statistically associated with improvements in indicators of child health and nutritional development, holding constant for the weaker effect of men's nonearned income [Thomas (1990)]. These empirical patterns challenge the validity of the unified family demand model, but they do not tell us which particular bargaining solution or household behavioral model is preferred.

Transfers may also be a useful basis on which to modify the unified family model, and perhaps even distinguish the limits to the layers of the extended (altruistic) family. It may be assumed that transfers, as with nonearned income, serve primarily the interests of the individual who receives them. Transfers may also be reciprocally provided by members of the extended family with the expectation that they are to be used to support particular forms of consumption. For example, a sick child may elicit transfers from kin that are intended to help meet the costs of the child's medical attention or help the family reallocate its time to care for the sick child, though it involves a loss of market income. Whether the distinctive effect of the transfer on consumption patterns or labor supply behavior in the family can be attributed to the individual through whom the transfer is received has not been tested, to my knowledge.

Related issues of altruistic limits to sharing in the extended family are reported in the literature, but few generalizations have emerged. Ainsworth (1996) found in Cote d'Ivoire that foster children are treated equally to biological children in the families into which they were fostered, at least in terms of their time allocation and school attendance. Kochar (1998) examines how the wealth and consumption of a child's household affects the labor supply of their coresidential elderly parents. She finds family ceremonies may function as a "good" that encourages the elderly in the family to work less, compared with consumption of private goods which do not have this disincentive effect on the labor supply behavior of the elderly living with their children. Hayashi (1995) analyzes how the relative income status of the older and younger generation in a Japanese household affects the composition of foods consumed, when the preferences for specific foods are demonstrably different between the younger and older generations. There is much need for further analyses of how the sources of family income affect its allocation, as the family unit is extended from the nuclear unit to the extended kinship system. It is a natural extension to note that in closely knit ethnic groups in many parts of the world, the solidarity of the family and the village provides a consumption-smoothing insurance system against readily monitored individual idiosyncratic risks [Rosenzweig (1988); Townsend (1994); Udry (1994)].

There is some evidence that as women obtain more education and marketable skills, they consume more of their family's resources and are "treated" better. But these patterns do not help to distinguish between the competing intra-family resource allocation models. The unified family demand model emphasizes that the human capital embodied in women affects their value of time and influences the allocation of time and investments within the family [Mincer (1963); Becker (1965)]. Consequently, empirical evidence that time allocations, consumption, and investment patterns within the family respond to differences in male, female, and child wages does not help to discriminate between the unified family demand and bargaining models. But the cooperative Nash-bargained model of household behavior also predicts differential consumption effects of nonearned income depending on who *controls* it. The bargaining framework offers a reasonable way to explain why women may engage in separate jobs from their husbands to enhance their control over the resources they produce. Indeed, this pattern is particularly notable in sub-Saharan Africa and South-East Asia, although women may still work some of their time as an unpaid worker in their family or on their husband's plot of land [Schultz (1990a)].

In parts of Africa, husband and wife cooperate in the joint production of some crops, while other crops or parts of the production process – e.g., marketing – are entirely the responsibility of one sex. The unified model of the family leads to the prediction that the wife allocates her time between the joint crops and her own crops to equalize the value of her marginal product across all activities. The bargaining model, however, allows that she might work more on her own fields, because the value of her marginal product there is more under her control and hence of greater value to her. Jones (1983, 1986) confirmed these predictions of the bargaining model with survey data collected from Yagoua in North Cameroon. Allocative incentives within these Massa families, therefore, may not achieve a strictly efficient use of labor but may advance other individual interests of family members.[6] Udry (1996) has documented a similar pattern in the allocation of family labor between husband and wife controlled agricultural plots

---

[6] In principle there might be a superior Pareto efficient allocation of husband and wife labor that would yield a larger output for both members of the family. But in practice, there are costs in monitoring labor inputs over scattered plots and transaction costs in exchange of inputs and outputs that might be required to provide both persons with the incentives needed to achieve Pareto efficiency. These transaction costs might absorb most of the output gains. Some but not all West African studies have replicated these empirical patterns [e.g., Udry (1996); Doss (1996b, 1997); Smith and Chavas (1997); Akresh (1999)].

in Burkina. The loss in output due to the less-than-Pareto-efficient intrahousehold allocation of the couple's time is estimated by Udry to be about 6 percent, compared with the intra-village level inefficiency of twice this magnitude due to the apparent misallocation of labor across plots of the same crop of different families in the same village. Thus, the bargaining process may interject a modicum of inefficiency in within-family allocation of labor, but it is only about half as large as the within-village inefficiency across households in the allocation of the factors of production [Udry (1996, p. 1040)].

It should also be noted that most production function estimates of the marginal product of women's and men's labor assume that all inputs into the production process are observed and are exogenous. This requires that any omitted inputs are uncorrelated with labor allocations, and the inputs are not allocated on the basis of unobserved factors or shocks, such as management bias or weather, which could affect the productivity of the labor input. If the allocation of these omitted inputs is, however, affected by the assets and empowerment of women and men, then these production inputs must be treated as endogenous and their allocation explained in terms of exogenous factors. Well-defined exogenous market prices for inputs that vary across the sample households might provide one basis for identifying the production function parameters on observed inputs, including those that determine the marginal productivity of male and female labor. For example, in Udry's (1996) analysis of Burkina labor productivity by plot, he notes that male-owned plots receive a disproportionate share of the other variable inputs: manure and child labor. This would suggest that male "power" might contribute to male-owned plots obtaining these additional scarce, but not widely marketed, inputs, and these inputs could complement labor on male-owned plots, explaining the lower productivity of female labor when women work their own plots. Udry is also worried that unmeasured qualities in the plots could favor male-owned plots and account for the greater female productivity on male plots than on their own plots. As noted in many studies comparing the agricultural productivity of women and men, it is extremely difficult to estimate confidently the separate marginal productivity of male and female labor in joint agricultural production without maintaining very strong untested working assumptions [Quisumbing (1996b)].

3.2. Intrahousehold allocation of time

The time allocation of unrelated individuals or groups of individuals combined in a family enterprise may be analyzed by estimating production functions or cost functions, from which the marginal product of different types of labor is inferred. Then when profit and utility are sequentially maximized, the allocation of labor can be attributed to exogenous or quasi-fixed endowments of such factors as land, market prices of inputs and outputs, or the state of nature, e.g., weather. The more common approach to studying time allocation is to start with the demand for leisure within the consumption framework as outlined in Section 2, and then the time worked (or not demanded as leisure) is a function of the wage offered for working, other sources of nonearned income, and relative market prices.

When this consumer demand model is generalized to a unified family of several adults and time allocated to nonmarket production is treated as distinct from leisure, the issue arises whether the time of the husband and the time of the wife in household (non-market) production are substitutes or complements. In Becker's unified model of the family he assumes they are substitutes, and on-the-job training in market work leads to human capital accumulation from work experience. This framework leads to the prediction that gender specialization between market and nonmarket work within the family is likely to occur. Alternatively, if nonmarket time of husband and wife were complements in nonmarket work, it might be expected that some couples would both work in the market and some might even team up to work together in nonmarket production, leading to market and nonmarket specialization across families, rather than within families. Yet to the extent that child care, food preparation, and household chores for the family's own consumption constitute the major nonmarket production activities of the household, Becker's model of specialization within families is intuitively plausible. In the agricultural household model in which the family coordinates its farm production at home, there may be more range for complementarity between spouses. Also during the early and late stages of the nuclear family's life cycle – before childbearing starts and after children leave the parental home – there may be less opportunity for substitution of the spouses' time in nonmarket production, and indeed if nonmarket time of spouses includes leisure they might be complements among the very young and old [Schultz (1981)]. These cross-substitution possibilities between the time of adults in nonmarket activities should be estimated at different periods in the life cycle and not restricted to be constant across all ages, and perhaps be allowed to vary between agricultural and nonagricultural households [e.g., Lundberg (1988)].

An empirically testable implication of the unified demand model is that the income-compensated cross-substitution effects should be symmetric or equal, or specifically those associated with spousal cross-wage effects. This restriction of the unified family demand model implies that, in allocating their labor supplies, husband and wife are in complete agreement as to the value of each other's nonmarket time. It could be imagined, as an alternative hypothesis, that a husband would assign a higher value to his own nonmarket time than does his wife to his nonmarket time. In the case of their valuations of the wife's nonmarket time, the wife might correspondingly value her own time more highly than does her husband. An individualistic bargaining model allows for the possibility that the wife and husband might value some "goods" differently, most naturally their own "leisures". Thus, the strong restriction of the unified family demand model that the income-compensated cross-wage effect of the husband's wage on the demand for the wife's nonmarket time must be equal to the income-compensated effect of the wife's wage on the husband's nonmarket time can be empirically tested. Heckman (1971) tested this statistically with U.S. data and rejected it, although in a subsequent paper this theoretically implied restriction was imposed [Ashenfelter and

Heckman (1974)].[7] But the test is conditional on many other aspects of the demand model, including functional-form approximations [Killingsworth (1983)].

This symmetry property of the family demand model unfortunately is not tested, to my knowledge, in agricultural settings where off-farm wage labor is more common [Huffman (1974, 1976, 1980); Skoufias (1993a); Kimhi and Lee (1996)]. Such analyses might confirm whether women assign a greater value to their off-farm market time than do their husbands, perhaps because women exercise more control of their earnings from off-farm work or because it conveys status (or stigma) depending on the cultural context. To proceed in this direction, information on the nonearned income or individually controlled assets of the farm couple would be required. To evaluate the partial effect of the husband's or wife's nonearned income on family expenditures, the wage rates of both partners and market prices must be held constant. The wage rates and nonearned income determine the full income constraint of the couple, where full income is defined in order to be independent of the family's allocation of time to market work [Becker (1965)].

Shares of income expended on specific items are expected to be more systematically related to the family's permanent or lifetime income than to the family's transitory income. Total expenditures of the family are often viewed as a better measure of permanent or lifetime income than the total of reported current income sources. Total expenditures should, of course, include imputed values for home-produced and consumed goods and services, such as the rental value of owner-occupied housing or home-produced food and apparel. Shares of this family expenditure total spent on specific items, such as food, are then often explained in terms of total expenditures per adult, and relative prices, including the wage rates available to family members or the shadow value of their time if not working for pay in the labor force [Deaton and Muellbauer (1980)]. Methods for dealing with differences in household composition are discussed later in Section 3.3.

To estimate the effect of permanent income on consumption patterns or savings requires a method to distinguish between transitory and permanent income components. One approach is to specify an instrumental variable that is thought to be strongly correlated with the permanent income component, such as education and initial assets or inheritances, but uncorrelated with the transitory income component, due to such factors as weather variation or idiosyncratic shocks to health.[8] This approach to estimation

---

[7] The overall determinant-condition of maximization theory in the family demand model is also rejected by Heckman in the static case (1971: Chapter 2, pp. 32–33). Both the static and "life cycle" estimation approaches pursued by Heckman lead to rejection of the symmetry condition. Ultimately, however, he imposed the restriction to obtain his preferred estimates (Chapter 2, pp. 37–38). One possible explanation for the rejection of the demand system parameter restrictions is the difference in spouse-specific nonearned income effects that may be used to infer individual compensated cross-wage effects.

[8] Alternatively, measures of the deviation in weather from their long-run average can be constructed in a particular agricultural region for unexpected weather shocks and used as an instrumental variable to approximate transitory income in an agricultural household. In this case, the residual household income can approximate the permanent income component [Wolpin (1982); Rosenzweig (1988); Paxson (1992)].

of expenditure-share or savings functions by instrumental variable methods provides a starting point for evaluating whether nonearned income of the husband and wife exert roughly comparable effects on intrahousehold consumption/savings allocations. If the effect of husband nonearned income and wife nonearned income differ to a statistically significant degree (Equation (18)), this finding further weakens the argument for adopting the unified family demand model and strengthens the argument for adopting one of the more individualistic bargaining frameworks [Thomas and Chen (1994)]. Alternatively, total nonearned income may be included as a conditioning variable in the expenditure share or savings functions, and the ratio of wife's to husband's nonearned income is included to test whether nonearned income is pooled within the family. The ratio variable should exert no effect on the expenditure/savings patterns, if the unified family demand model is a valid description of the underlying behavioral process. As in Thailand, this gender-relative nonearned income variable may be expected to increase the allocation of the wife's time to her leisure activities and other female private goods, if a bargaining model is valid and preferences of husband and wife differ in the expected direction for the specific goods being studied.

Investments in children's education and health are expenditures that society may want to encourage. But these expenditure categories are difficult to monetize comprehensively, for that requires imputing a value to the time of each child and parent involved in schoolwork in the home or in health maintenance activities, respectively. Some forms of human capital stocks, however, can be roughly quantified in surveys and assigned as a private good to the individual. In the case of health or nutritional status, "height-for-age" and "weight-for-height" are two anthropometric indicators that are positively correlated with survival and reduced incidence of acute and chronic morbidity, and with wage rates and labor productivity among working adults [Floud et al. (1990); Fogel (1986, 1994); Strauss and Thomas (1995, 1998); Schultz (1995b)]. In the case of education, years of schooling completed is a standard measure of educational investments, although this can be refined by including additional qualitative dimensions of the resource intensity of the years of schooling, such as the hours attending school per year, the training of the teacher, the teacher-student ratio (i.e., inverse of class size), quality of facilities, and books and school supplies [Schultz (1988)].

It has been noted in a number of studies that increments in women's nonearned income and increments in men's nonearned income have a tendency to augment health and educational investments in children, but the effect of women's nonearned income tends to be larger than that of men's. Expenditure shares on food are also often closely related to proxies of women's economic bargaining power in the family, holding permanent income constant [e.g., Thomas (1990, 1994); Hoddinott and Haddad (1995); Doss (1996a, 1997)]. These findings – that enhanced female nonhuman capital increases allocations of family resources on children – are consistent with Fuchs' (1988) psychological hypothesis that mothers exhibit stronger preferences for investments in child welfare than do fathers, or as recently restated that females are less selfish [Eckel and Grossman (1998)]. It is also consistent with the previously noted study that found child support payments paid to mothers rather than to fathers increased child (and female adult) expenditures [Lundberg et al. (1997)]. But assessing longer-term consequences for child well-being of redistributing nonearned income from men to women is complicated by the likely changes such a redistribution scheme might induce in family composition [Schultz (1994b)]. If the comparison group of husband-wife-child units decreases because of an increase in separation, as previously noted in the Seattle Negative Income Experiment in the United States [U.S., DHHS (1983)], attrition bias might arise.

The unified family demand model nonetheless has the appeal of simplicity and widespread applicability, and some useful empirical applications. How much realism should be sacrificed by a theoretical paradigm to gain tractability to a wide range of phenomena is debatable [Becker (1981)]. As the testable restrictions built into the unified family demand model become clearer, and sample surveys elicit more precisely the personal distribution of resource ownership in the family, it is to be expected that future studies will be able to reject this simplified abstraction [Alderman et al. (1995)]. But how much our answers to important policy questions change when we relax the family model and replace it by a bargaining model remains unclear [Strauss and Beegle (1996)]. If one of our goals is to understand the determinants of child welfare, child human capital investments in nutrition and schooling, or women's well-being, then the alternative bargaining or sharing rule models seem to be a useful first step, but it remains to be seen whether these new models will change our interpretation of available data substantially.

For example, in societies where nearly all women marry by age 30 and there is little dissolution of marriage, as was true until the last few decades in Korea, China or Taiwan, the unified model of the family might prove satisfactory. But in much of sub-Saharan Africa and Southeast Asia, where men and women often have different sources of income and distinct responsibilities for the support of family consumption, individual economic interests may be much less submerged in a "unified" family. In the latter regions, the cooperative Nash-bargained model of McElroy and Horney (1981) or the Pareto Cooperative model of Chiappori (1992) appears to be a more attractive framework within which to structure research on family and individual behavior, because it generalizes the unified family demand model and permits the restrictions implied by the unified model to be tested and potentially rejected empirically. These bargaining approaches to the family direct particular attention to who controls what assets and streams of income in the family, and may lead to new insights about how women's status influences the development process, including the timing of the decline in child mortality and fertility that governs the pace of the demographic transition and thereby impacts on the age composition of the population, and potentially on the rates of household savings and investment [Ram and Schultz (1979); Higgins and Williamson (1997)].

3.3. Risk and labor allocation of agricultural households

If farm families are risk averse, greater farm income variability should increase off-farm labor supply. This pattern is observed for a sample of Kansas farm families in 1992 analyzed by Mishra and Goodwin (1997). One might also think that where specialization in managing farm production in the United States devolves predominantly on male family workers, the off-farm labor supply of female adult family members would respond more elastically to farm risk than that of the corresponding male. But the study by Mishra and Goodwin (1997) found the opposite, with the off-farm labor supply of the male farmer increasing more than that of his spouse to the risk associated with farm income, proxied by the coefficient of variation in on-farm earnings for the last ten years.

This approach to intrahousehold coordination of the family members' time allocation across risk-specific occupations tends to assume that the risk associated with the off-farm earnings is not perfectly correlated with the risk associated with the on-farm earnings. There is thus an insurance value to the pooling of the on- and off-farm income risks and a clear justification for following a mixed strategy for the family that combines in this case more than one type of job. It may also be reasonable to assume that the uncertainty of farm earnings is greater than that of off-farm earnings, though I know of few comparisons to document this conjecture [Friedman (1957)].

More generally the family is expected to diversify its mix of crops, its portfolio of income-earning opportunities, so as to trade off a reduction in its aggregate risk against a reduction in the expected value of its total income [Rosenzweig (1988); Jacoby and Skoufias (1992); Kochar (1995); Lilja et al. (1996); Quisumbing (1996a)]. One way that this may occur is when the family coordinates the migration of family members to other occupations or labor markets, and the most common example is by encouraging family members to work outside of the agricultural sector in the urban economy, for which it is plausible to imagine that income risks are not strongly positively correlated with those experienced within the farm. There is also a possibility that the family is not unified and altruistic [Becker (1981)], and that the migrants might engage in strategic behavior with the family at origin [Lucas and Stark (1985)].

Marriages may build dynasties that cement powerful relationships and reduce the risks of its members. Marriage of daughters may be a means to mitigate risk across the extended family. In such an environment the family might encourage daughters to marry husbands who are located in different agri-climatic zones and who would thereby reduce the family aggregate exposure to agricultural production risk, assuming that the daughter's new family and her origin family accept a social obligation to insure each other against some shocks to their earnings. Rosenzweig and Stark (1989) report evidence of this marriage pattern in South Indian ICRISAT villages, where the consumption of farm families is better smoothed from local weather shocks if they have male migrants living outside of the household or daughters married and living in more distant villages. They hypothesize further that as the Green Revolution changes the prevailing agricultural technology, it becomes more costly to monitor whether income variability is due to insured exogenous sources, such as weather, or to endogenous behavior of the family such as effort or choice of more risky new technologies. Then, these traditional risk-reducing insurance strategies of the extended family could become less valuable with more rapid technical change. This might erode the "insurance value" of daughters to farm families in technologically more progressive regions [Rosenzweig (1995)]. Here is another possible explanation for the recently noted trend in India of the value of dowries (i.e., price of marrying a daughter) to increase [cf. Rao (1993)].

3.4. Variation in household composition

Studies of price and income effects on expenditures and savings justify a variety of procedures for standardizing household behavior for differences in the household size and its composition in terms of age and sex [Deaton and Muellbauer (1980); Deaton et al. (1989); Deaton (1997)]. However, these procedures may introduce their own problems as they try to normalize for "consumption needs" implied by household composition. This is because household composition embodies a variety of life cycle choices, including marital status, fertility, and coresidential extension of the family to accommodate other generations and isolated kin, which may also be affected by market prices, income, and preferences. If the form of behavior being modeled, such as savings or time allocation, responds as do fertility and family extension in some manner to price and income conditioning variables, the partial relationship between household composition and economic behavior will not estimate a causal effect or suitable normalization, and controlling directly for this endogenous household composition variable will bias all other estimates of conventional price and income effects.

From this perspective, the researcher could proceed in at least two directions. It is possible to evaluate the effects of prices, etc., within a sample restricted to similar family units, to avoid variation in family composition. Thus, Heckman's (1971) unified model of family labor supply is fit to husband-wife couples who are both wage earners, eliminating the need to deal with (1) nonworking women, for whom the first-order conditions would be different and for whom no wages are observed, or (2) women without husbands, whose labor supply decision-making would be motivated by a somewhat different optimizing framework. For analogous reasons, Browning et al. (1994) restrict their estimation sample to working husbands and wives without children to avoid the effects of variation in household composition on expenditure patterns. However, if the goal is to assess the effect of price and income variables on all women, these selectively drawn samples will tend to yield biased estimates, if as seems likely, the probability of being selected into the sample is correlated with the disturbance in the behavioral equation estimated from the selected sample [Heckman (1979)].[9]

Another strategy is to estimate a reduced-form relationship for the behavior under study, including in the sample all women, which implicitly solves out for intermediate relationships such as the family formation process, the marriage match of spousal characteristics, and the number and characteristics of other "discretionary" members of the household [Lam (1988)]. In this case, we are not able to identify the pathways through which an exogenous variable exerts its total effect, but it is possible to assess the

---

[9] Newman and Gertler (1994) reformulate the rural family's labor supply decision-making problem in order to accommodate in the same estimation framework families with different adult compositions.

1981); Miller (1981, 1997); Martorell et al. (1984); Bardhan (1984); Das Gupta (1987); Klasen (1998)].

Other cultures and regions of the world also exhibit gender differences in child survival that appear to reflect differential investments (neglect) by parents, though they are less well documented, persistent, and perhaps smaller in scale than in India, including the ancient Greeks, Romans, Carthaginians, and Japanese, to name only a few. Historically, fewer females than males survived famines, and this was still evident in China during the great leap forward of 1959–61. The Chinese ratio of male to female registered births today exceeds the conventional range of between 1.03 to 1.06, and increases with higher parities. When the Chinese government in the 1970s adopted a strict population program that sought to enforce a one-child policy, infant and child mortality of females increased markedly, and the growing shortfall in women attracted the attention of demographers [Aird (1983); Zeng (1989)]. Perhaps in response to this development, the Chinese population policy was relaxed somewhat in the rural areas in the 1980s to permit a couple to have a second child, when the first was a girl. With the spread of ultrasound diagnostic equipment that could determine the sex of the fetus, female selective abortion increased the ratio of male to female births, especially at higher parities [Schultz (1997)].

In many equally poor societies gender differences in child nutrition, health status, and survival are smaller or nonexistent, such as in Nicaragua, Brazil, Philippines, Sri Lanka, and Ivory Coast [Blau (1984); Popkin (1980); Senauer et al. (1986, 1988); Thomas et al. (1990); Thomas (1990); Thomas and Strauss (1997); Strauss and Beegle (1996)]. In some regions of sub-Saharan Africa where women take a more active role in the labor force outside of the home than in much of South and West Asia, survival rates for females appear to often exceed those for males, despite low levels of income, high levels of malnutrition, and poor public health services [Sen (1976); Svenberg (1990)]. One interpretation of the available evidence on international patterns of gender differences in child health and survival is that there are marked cultural variations, often related to the relative economic productivity of adult women relative to men. But with increases in wealth, families in most cultural and economic settings appear to exhibit a preference for greater gender equality in nutritional and health investments within the family [Schultz (1995a)].

Periods of acute illness have also been analyzed as economic shocks to the family to assess how consumption smoothing is achieved in periods when there is a marked shortfall in income. Pitt and Rosenzweig (1990) find that when young children are ill, teenage daughters in Indonesian families are particularly likely to retract time from school or the labor market to care for the sick child, rather than teenage sons. Dercon and Krishnan (1997) explore the effects of health shocks on intrahousehold consumption smoothing. They postulate that idiosyncratic shocks to individual health should have no effect on relative interpersonal allocations except for their effect on the household's total budget constraint, if risk is shared in the collective Pareto-efficient or unified models of the family. But instead they find that in poorer households in southern Ethiopia, women bear most of the adjustment burden on the family from adverse health shocks.

Some of their other findings can be reconciled with the bargaining model: they show that the relative position of wives improves when local customary law dictating divorce settlements is more favorable to wives, the household's wealth is greater, and the age gap (proxying productivity or power) between partners is smaller.

The demographic transition is also related in many ways to the improving health and productivity of women. Fertility is commonly observed to be a decreasing function of the productivity of the woman, or opportunity cost of children, often proxied by the education of women [Schultz (1997)]. But declining fertility could also exert a reinforcing feedback effect on a woman's subsequent health and productivity. When the nutritional status of women in Ghana is measured by their body mass index (i.e., weight divided by height squared), and this health status is explained by endogenous inputs of calories, current burden of morbidity, work effort, and parity, it is found that endogenous declines in fertility (parity) are associated with improvement in the nutritional status of women, which in Ghana is strongly related to their wage productivity [Higgin and Alderman (1997); Schultz (1995b)].

There is an analogous pattern across countries in the investments families make in the schooling of girls compared to boys. At low income levels, investments in boy's schooling often exceed that in girl's. As real income per adult increases, public expenditures per child on schools tend to increase as do enrollment rates. But the income-related increase in enrollment rates among girls is significantly larger than it is among boys, particularly at the secondary school level [Schultz (1987, 1996)]. A catching up for girls is evident in both comparisons of different countries with increasing income [King and Hill (1993)] and within countries as income increases [e.g., Chernichovsky (1985); NaRanong (1998); Schultz (1996)]. Equal educational treatment of boys and girls may be a "normal good" within the family, and as income per capita increases, and reproductive goals are freely chosen, a variety of indicators of consumption and investment become more equally distributed between male and female family members.

Investments in the schooling of boys and girls are also influenced by the productive returns schooling imparts, and given gender specialization of work routines [Boserup (1970, 1990)], it would not be surprising for the productive returns to schooling for men and women to differ, at least in the short run, although in the long run one would expect gender specialization in the labor force to diminish as fertility declines and child-rearing occupies a diminishing share of a woman's adult life span. In the Philippines, farm families are observed to invest more in the education of their daughters than of their sons, but to transfer more land to their sons, arriving at a rough economic balance [Quisumbing (1994, 1997)]. Differences in the composition of transfers by parents to their children by gender may help to explain their different propensities to migrate out of agriculture or to adopt new technological innovations. Lanzona (1996) notes that the greater the importance of irrigated land for the family, the greater is the investment in schooling of sons, holding constant for the parent's education and community school infrastructure. One hypothesis for this pattern in the Bicol Province is that the major irrigation projects facilitated the adoption of profitable high-yielding varieties. Where these new agricultural inputs held the most immediate promise, families sacrificed more to educate their sons, preparing them to evaluate and profitably adopt these promising new production possibilities. The education received by daughters prepared them for employment in nonagricultural activities.

The Bicol region of the Philippines has experienced heavy outmigration to regions where per capita incomes are higher. The likelihood of outmigration increases with the earnings of individuals, holding constant for observed determinants of wages, such as education and age. Earnings for both men and women who remain in their parents' home are thus negatively impacted by selection bias, supporting the view that those who stay at home in a backward region are likely to be the less productive workers, controlling for observables [Lanzona (1998)]. Among those males who remain at home, uncorrected wage returns to schooling are about a fifth lower than the returns to schooling that are corrected for sample selection bias of sons who stay at home. Returns to schooling among the selected sample of those men who remain in this poor agricultural region of the Philippines tend to be downward biased by the rapid pace of outmigration, as noted in earlier Latin American studies during the 1970s [Schultz (1988)].

Public policies are limited in their ability to influence the family's final distribution of consumption. The family can usually, if it wants, have the last word on intrahousehold resource allocations. For example, a free school lunch program in Brazil or India may lead to a decrease in the family's supply of food to those children who benefit from the school feeding program. Part of the family's food that would have been supplied to the children in the absence of the program is reallocated within the family to advance the family's own objectives. Evaluation of nutritional intervention programs has tried to assess this redistributional power of the family [Chernichovsky and Zangwill (1988)]. Jacoby (1997) in a study in the Philippines finds that the family may be less effective (or less inclined) than expected in using its redistributional capacity to compensate in home food allocation for food transferred to children through the schools. He found little intrahousehold reallocation of calories in response to the selective feeding program administered through the schools.

To assess what might be the optimal targeting strategy for transferring public resources to particular individuals in the family and to particular uses by that individual requires much information, some of which can be inferred from analyses of household surveys and some from studies of public administration records and variations in pilot programs. First, what is the "leakage" of the transfer to other persons in the household (society) or to other uses? Second, what is the relative social benefit from increasing the consumption of those other beneficiaries (are they also poor relatives or rich middlemen?) and other consumption uses, compared to the primary targets? Third, what administration costs would be incurred to reduce these leakages, and how much? The state could simply contribute to the general pool of family resources, where the location, occupation, and education of household head could be used to target the poor group. Alternatively, the transfer could be invested in the vocational training of specific individuals, or it could provide income-in-kind (i.e., food or health services) to the family, or it could transfer selected consumption goods to specific individuals, such as through a program of school lunches, or even restrict those school food supplements to "inferior" foods that only the poor and malnourished are likely to want to consume. The reduction in leakages and resulting increased "fairness" of the program must be an adequate justification for the mounting costs of administering the targeting [Kanbur et al. (1995)].

Public programs can provide vocational training or access to credit for women, where women are thought to have less than equal access to education and collateral required for borrowing. The expectation is that the resulting gains in women's productivity will provide the private returns for the program, and the gain in women's productivity may have an added impact on intrahousehold consumption patterns favoring women's priorities, such as investments in their children. As noted above, there is an extensive literature suggesting that consumption patterns within families change as the productivity of women increases. Interventions designed to increase women's credit, entrepreneurial capacity, and training for the off-farm labor force are receiving increasing attention by policymakers, but the task of program evaluation is daunting as the simple comparisons are gradually replaced by quasi-experimental manipulations of large databases [e.g., Kennedy and Cogill (1986); Blumberg (1988); Pitt and Khandker (1998)].

4. Marital status, mortality, and health investments

One way that people express their demands for consumption patterns is in the form of the families they create. An increase in many countries in the proportion of households headed by women has been observed recently. This increase in female-headed households can be related to the decline in marriage, the increase in divorce, and a third, somewhat distinct factor, the increase in widowhood, affecting primarily the elderly. The decrease in the prevalence of marriage and the increase in the rate of divorce in many developing and developed countries can be documented over time. There are exceptions, such as Indonesia, where the incidence of divorce appears to have decreased in recent decades; this opposite trend is attributed to the universality of arranged early marriages, which are being slowly modified to allow individuals to exercise greater control over the timing of their marriage and to select their partner. The interpretation of trends in marriage arrangements may also be complicated by increased cohabitation between unmarried couples, which has presumably provided an increasingly accepted substitute for marriage in some settings. In certain regions of Latin America where the average age at civil marriage was relatively late at the start of the twentieth century, consensual marriages were common and may have provided a close substitute for legal marriage for groups with little property to transfer to their children [Nerlove and Schultz (1970)]. The share of women reporting themselves as in consensual unions is again increasing today in some countries of Latin America [Ribero (1999)].

Most empirical evidence of the prevalence of marriage is consistent with the simple economic model of family demands and labor supply [Becker (1974)]. Increased productive opportunities for women in the labor market are associated with delayed age at first marriage and decreased prevalence of currently being married and living with a spouse. The frequency of marriage is linked to changes in the jobs that women take, at least in the industrially developed countries and urban Latin America [Youssef and Hefler (1983); Knodel et al. (1987)]. One explanation for changing marriage patterns is then the increasing productivity of women compared to men in the labor market. According to cross-sectional patterns in family labor supply in industrial or urban economies, increasing the level of male and female wages by the same proportion is generally associated with an increase in women's participation in the labor market, a delay in age at first marriage, and diminished lifetime fertility [Schultz (1981); Layard and Mincer (1985)]. These developments are hypothesized to have reduced the net gains from specialization of husband and wife in market and nonmarket production, respectively, within lifetime marriages [Becker (1981)]. In those societies where women earn nearly as much as men, there are fewer marriages and a larger proportion of households are headed by women.[11] In states within the United States that provided more generous Aid for Families with Dependent Children (AFDC) benefits for mothers without husbands, marriages were less common for women in 1980 and 1990 [Schultz (1994b, 1998)]. Much work remains to elaborate on these regularities and document the other factors that are implicated, such as the ratio of marriageable men to women in the relevant "marriage market" [Chiappori et al. (1997)].

Individual data have also been analyzed to estimate the determinants of age-at-first-marriage among women. More educated women marry later, even in cases where marriage is sufficiently delayed in the overall society to reduce overlapping with school, as in much of Latin America, and East and parts of Southeast Asia [Montgomery and Sulak (1989); Anderson and Hill (1987); King et al. (1986)]. The growing tendency of young, educated women to take paying jobs, financially encourages both them and their parents to delay entry into marriage. Few studies have yet examined how local market demands for female workers affect migration and the timing and duration of marriage for women, but it may be an important part of the story.

Evidence from Thailand suggests that the family bargaining model may help to account for variation in the prevalence of marriage. Demographic and anthropological studies of Thai society document that marriage was until recently nearly universal. About 95 percent of men and women reported themselves as having been married (once) by age 35 [in the 1960 Census cited by Knodel et al. (1987; Table 5.1)]. An informal process of divorce traditionally has also been accepted with frequent remarriage [Smith (1981)]. In the 1981 Socioeconomic Survey of Thailand, 75 and 85 percent of the women and men, respectively, between the ages of 25 and 54 were living in the same household with their spouse. To explain who is currently married, the specialization hypothesis as well as the bargaining model would suggest that marital gains would decrease with an increase in women's predicted wages and increase with an increase in

---

[11] Aggregate data were analyzed, for example, for Chile [DaVanzo (1972)], the U.S. [Frieden (1974); Becker et al. (1977)], and in Puerto Rico [Nerlove and Schultz (1970)]. More recent work on marital status has analyzed individual data [e.g., Boulier and Rosenzweig (1984); Jacoby (1995)].

men's predicted wages, other things equal. This is partly confirmed in Thailand, where the likelihood that a woman age 25 to 54 is currently married and residing with her spouse is lower the greater her predicted market wage opportunities. But Thai men are also less likely to be married if their wages are expected to be higher. The test of the bargaining model is clearer in the case of property income, where these sources of income are not tied to labor supply or the duration of schooling, the shadow price of time, or other market prices which could affect the gains from marriage. If the woman has more property income she is less likely to be living with a husband. On the other hand, the ownership of more property income is associated with a greater proportion of Thai men residing with their wife.[12] But the estimated effect of property income on marriage is nine times larger (and of opposite sign) for women than for men at similar levels of nonearned income [Schultz (1990b)]. Marriage, it would appear, is not a "normal good" for Thai women, although it is for men. According to the bargaining model, property income for women increases their "reservation utility", thereby reducing the proportion of women who find a sufficiently productive (attractive) male to marry.

Other hypotheses could also account for these patterns of marriage and residence in Thailand, and the available survey data do not distinguish perfectly among them. The death of a spouse could increase an individual's wealth through inheritance, and would also shift the individual to the "single" category. About half of the female-headed households in Latin America are widows [Mohan (1986); Rosenhouse (1988)]. Alternatively, women might be more inclined than men, upon divorce, to move back into the household of their parents, other relatives, or children. Marital and residential histories that include the timing of inheritance and transfers are needed to discriminate more adequately among these competing explanations for family formation patterns. Undoubtedly they will differ greatly in different societies, as does the family.

4.1. Households headed by women: Multiple types

Simple comparisons of income of female- and male-headed households are not very informative. Most male-headed households tend to include wives, while customarily few female-headed households include husbands.[13] In some surveys the husband is treated

---

[12] These probit estimates of marriage also include controls for wage rates for the individual, transfer nonearned income (which has a similar sign pattern to property income by sex), age, and urbanization zone in Thailand.

[13] For example, Rosenhouse (1988) illustrates from the 1985 Living Standards Measurement Survey for Peru that 90 percent of the male-headed households currently include wives, while only 5 percent of the female-headed households include husbands. Her data also show that in Peru half of the female household heads are widowed, and they are older than the male heads. These groups are really quite incomparable and not particularly well structured to analyze particular sources of poverty in society. As discussed in the text, there are many possible causes for the increase in female-headed households. The greater longevity of women than men is one possible source. Another source would be the lower frequency of remarriage by women than men. Female household heads also work fewer hours than do male heads, even ignoring the contribution of wives to their households, and the higher average wages received by men than women. Multiple-earner households

as the de jure household head even when he is not recently resident in the household.[14] Which women find themselves in families that are called "male-headed" or in "female-headed" will be influenced by custom, their resources, and other opportunities, as in Thailand. Several studies have found an association between wealth of individuals and decreased frequency of divorce, separation, and death of spouse [Becker et al. (1977); Peters (1986); Grey (1998)]. But the tendency in several parts of the world for the share of households headed by women to increase may be traced to a variety of sources, not all of which imply the same consequences. Improvement in health is associated with a disproportionate fraction of the elderly being female, and older widows have few marriageable males to choose from. This group may not have children to support, and though their consumption, housing, and health needs can represent important issues, these groups also may benefit from accumulating inheritances and private and public old-age support schemes.

Another source of the increase in female-headed households in low income countries is migration, which affects women differently from one region to another depending on their skills and the changes in employment opportunities in the country. In Latin America, migration out of agriculture to the cities was led by women, as it was in Europe and North America. Urban job prospects for women were better than for men, and the ratio of women to men in some metropolitan areas of Latin America was as high as 1.2 in the 1960s [Gregory (1986); Mohan (1986)]. As a result, many urban women did not marry, but they were not necessarily economically disadvantaged compared to those who stayed behind in the countryside. The prospects in Latin America for women to advance from urban jobs as domestic servants – holding constant their education – to ones in industry, commerce, and other services, may even be favorable compared with men. The overall productive status of women relative to men, as well as their survival prospects, is traditionally higher in the cities than in the countryside [Preston and Weed (1976)].

Unlike Latin America, migration flows in Africa were dominated by men, drawn (or driven) to the mines and plantations, domestic services, commerce, state enterprises, and government bureaucracies. Women remained on the land, often continuing to produce

---

are also the rule, not the exception, in Peru. To advance our understanding of the determinants of poverty will require a modeling of the behavioral and biological selection of individuals into households of very different compositions. It is simply difficult to infer anything from the widely reported characteristics of households with male and female heads.

[14] It is easy to fault definitions of "head of household" when there is no consensus on the concept being measured or its use. There is a need to distinguish one individual around which to relate other household members, for the purposes of establishing kinship. There is also the idea of dominant economic provider or family elder whose authority is respected. But in the LSMS in Côte d'Ivoire the customary approach is to count females in the rural sector as belonging to a male-headed household even if the "head" resided in a distant city, more or less permanently. The increasing documentation of short-term seasonal or circulating migration in many low income countries underscores the need to measure household membership according to a variety of rules depending on how the data are to be used. For a list of some of the problems with the current data collection practices, see Rosenhouse (1988).

traditional food crops largely without the aid of modern agricultural inputs or technologies [Boserup (1970); Ember (1983)]. African women initially suffered from lower levels of education than men [Schultz (1987, 1995a); Goldin (1995)], explaining perhaps why men were the first to migrate freely from the rural sector and were more successful in setting themselves up in urban livelihoods [e.g., Caldwell (1968)]. In Africa, therefore, the high proportion of female-headed households (de facto) is not associated with offsetting economic benefits for women. In both Africa and Latin America, however, the divergence of male and female migration streams appears to have contributed to the relative decline in the two-parent household, and to the growth of other social problems.

Women have increased their educational attainment compared to men in most low income countries in recent decades [Schultz (1986, 1995a, 1996)]. Associated with these educational gains, some data also confirm that wage rates and productivity of women have increased relative to that of men. Gains in the market productivity of women compared to men reduces the traditional spheres of specialization by women and men, and erodes the economic advantages of lifetime marriage [Becker (1981)]. It remains difficult, however, to infer how these various developments and the increase in the proportion of female-headed households are causally related [Schultz (1981, 1990a)].

Households headed by women generally report lower per capita income than those headed by men. Market income differences between male- and female-headed households may overstate the gap in welfare unless consideration is given to a broader concept of "full" income which also includes nonmarket production and time allocated to home production and even leisure. Even so, differences in "full" income between male- and female-headed households warrant more study. There may be more children to support per adult in households headed by younger women than in those headed by men [Youssef and Hefler (1983); Barros et al. (1995)]. Changes in family structure can be viewed as the choices of consenting adults, but society may be involved in the impact on third parties – in this case, children dependent primarily on their mothers. If the physical and mental development of children is adversely affected by this shift in family structure, then society may wish to intervene to reverse the trend or to compensate for its adverse consequences on children.

Governments in more developed countries have for a century or longer sought to design a "safety net" to help support female-headed households with dependent children [Palmer et al. (1988)]. The incentives built into most such assistance programs designed for lone mothers and their children have worried social observers, from Malthus (1798) to Murray (1984), for they could encourage women to separate from their husbands or to have births out of wedlock to become eligible for public support. The conditions of work for husbands in the poorhouses of nineteenth century England may have been designed to be onerous in order to reduce the attractiveness of relying on the Poor Laws for support [Besley et al. (1993)]. The United States has also tried to increase the likelihood that a father pays for the support of his children, even if he does not reside with his child's mother, but child support payments in the U.S. elevate relatively few poor children out of poverty [Beller and Graham (1993); Currie (1995)]. Most high income countries today, with the notable exception of the United States, do not condition their child support programs on the marital status of the mother, perhaps so as not to discourage marriage [Palmer et al. (1988)]. In the United States there is little evidence that existing welfare programs are responsible for higher fertility levels, but there are indications across states that welfare programs reduce the prevalence of marriage, at least for white women [Schultz (1994b, 1998)]. Data from other countries suggest that widespread increases in the fraction of female-headed households are not primarily due to transfer programs, but rather are partly a response to the decreasing difference between the labor productivity or wages of men and women.

4.2. Sex differences in survival: Costs and household choice

The composition of the household is primarily a choice of adults responding to their endowments, possibilities for production and exchange, and preferences. In addition the intrahousehold allocations of resources can affect differentially the very survival of family members by sex and age, and thereby modify further household composition.[15] Analysis of these survival patterns sheds light on how the economic productivity and status of adult men and women may affect the costs to parents of rearing boys and girls, and potentially influence the availability of food and medical care for different family members. These survival patterns may also clarify how individual and community resources as well as the production environment of agricultural households can change sex-specific survival rates.

Dowries and brideprices arrived at in the marriage market provide information on differences in adult lifetime productivity of men and women. A dowry makes a daughter more marriageable. Thus, a couple with four girls is required to save more from the same lifetime income to accumulate the two extra dowries they will need to assure their daughters suitable husbands, than a more typical couple who has two daughters and two sons (assuming the typical couple does not share in the dowries their sons receive in marriage). Elaina Rose (1995) and Deolalikar and Rose (1995) have shown that in India the revelation at birth of the sex of a child has an immediate impact on the family's subsequent consumption (and savings) level, just as we would expect from such a lifetime windfall capital loss (or gain). The birth of a girl leads the family to increase its savings, and correspondingly to reduce its consumption, while increasing the husband's market labor supply and reducing his leisure.

In most parts of the world females live longer than males, presumably because given roughly comparable living environments and consumption possibilities, females are less frail than males [Preston and Weed (1976); Verbrugge (1985); Waldron (1986); United

---

[15] Based on ultrasound examination of the fetus or amniocentesis, sex-selective abortion can also permit parents to alter the sex composition of their births. Where there are strong preferences in a society for a particular sex of a child, these technologies are linked to growing imbalances of the sex ratio at birth. The ratio of male to female births tends to increase notably (e.g., from 1.05 to 2 or more) for higher order births today in China and Korea [Zeng et al. (1993); Schultz (1997)] and possibly in other Asian areas [Miller (1998)].

Nations (1982)]. Apparently this survival advantage enjoyed by females has grown wider in many countries in this century [Preston and Weed (1976); Trovato and Lulu (1996)]; in earlier centuries age-specific mortality estimates do not suggest a similar widespread sex imbalance, although there have been suggestive time series variations [Klasen (1998)]. Yet there are well-documented contemporary exceptions, such as in North India where early child mortality still occurs more frequently for girls than boys [Visaria (1971); Miller (1981); Das Gupta (1987)]. This previously noted reversal of the more common gender difference in child mortality in parts of South and West Asia is attributed to different access between boys and girls in otherwise similar families to food, home care, and to medical interventions [Sen (1976); Chen et al. (1981)].

The level of dowries for brides in India is one quantifiable facet of the higher net costs incurred by parents to rear a girl to maturity than a boy, and might explain part of the relative neglect of daughters by parents where dowries are on average relatively large [Miller (1981, 1997)]. Where the local economy's derived demand for labor favors female labor relative to male labor, wages for women relative to men should increase, and labor force participation of women is also likely to rise. In such districts where women are relatively more productive in the market labor force, the net costs of rearing girls compared to boys are lower because the parents might expect to capture some of these productive advantages realized by their daughters working before they marry, and because local dowries required by a groom's family would be lower due to the higher present discounted value of a bride's future wage opportunities.[16] As noted earlier, district- and household-level data for rural India in the 1960s indicate that as conditions favor more women to work outside of their family (i.e., instrumental variable estimates) there are improvements in female relative to male child survival rates [Rosenzweig and Schultz (1982b)]. The greater productivity of females is thus one explanation by the increased investment of families in the health and survival of females.

Sub-Saharan Africa is often contrasted with South Asia, for in both regions women have received a small fraction of the education that men have, and thus women's productivity is substantially lower than men's, on average. But in sub-Saharan Africa women engage in many forms of production, jointly with their husbands and separately on their

---

[16] Other factors have also been linked to the marriage comparative advantage due to specialization and market determination of dowries. When population growth accelerated in many low income countries after the Second World War, due primarily to a decline in child mortality, a predictable shortage of grooms emerged two decades later. Slowly the supply of marriageable-aged women increased relative to the supply of marriageable-aged (older) men. The evolution in the age composition of the population has been attributed a role in the secular increase in dowries in India [Rao (1993)]. The widespread trend of female educational attainments to catch up to that of males [Schultz (1995a)] has also contributed to delaying the age when women are inclined to marry, presumably because marriage and continuation of schooling for the woman are relatively incompatible. These pressures have led not only to a decline in the years of educational attainment gap between men and women in the same age cohort, but also a decline in the age gap between husbands and wives. Both the closure of the education and age gaps between spouses is likely to decrease the gap between the economic productivity of husbands and wives that is an important source of the gains from marriage.

own plots and in their own businesses. This greater parity of women and men in production outside of the home in sub-Saharan Africa is a possible explanation for why sex differences in childhood survival in Africa are more similar to the rest of world than to South and West Asia [United Nations (1982)].

Systems of household demand equations are generally specified as depending on total income and market prices. Household's composition is employed as a deflator for income, to obtain a needs-based welfare measure of household income per "consumer unit", which implies that demands are conditioned on composition and statistically that household composition is uncorrelated with the disturbance in the estimated demand relationship [Deaton et al. (1989)]. As emphasized in Section 3.4, this approach has serious limitations. If there were a valid consumer equivalence scale, and household composition were not affected by its members' choices, e.g., fertility and extension, household income or total expenditures could then be divided by the sum of household members, as weighted by their equivalent consumption scale, to obtain the average welfare level of household members [Gronau (1988)]. With no consensus on an equivalence scale, methods for estimating this scale have been invented. The most common practice is to regress the share of total expenditures for a specific group of goods across survey households on (1) the log of total income, (2) the log of household size, and (3) a series of variables representing the share of household members in each relevant age and sex group [Deaton and Muellbauer (1980); Deaton (1986)]. The coefficients on these age and sex group variables represent the proportionate difference between the income "requirements" of that group and the excluded group, say prime-age males. By considering an expenditure group that does not exhibit unitary income elasticity, such as food, compensating variations in income (expenditure) can be derived as would leave the household's welfare constant while changing its age/sex composition. A "discriminatory bias" within the family in expenditures according to sex can thus be estimated from the difference between the coefficients on male and female age groups [Deaton (1989)].

In rural Kenya, for example, Evenson and Mwabu (1996) found that household educational expenditures were of a similar magnitude regardless of whether children age 7 to 14 in the household were boys or girls, but girls between the ages of 15 and 19 were associated with only half the household educational expenditures as boys in these ages. They conclude that the high cost of continuing into secondary schools was more frequently accommodated by families for boys than for girls, a reality that is confirmed from Kenyan sex-specific school enrollment rates. Their evidence suggested that these poor rural Kenyan families were allocating nearly a fifth of their expenditures to the education of their many children. Because expenditure surveys rarely report who in the family benefits directly from specific expenditures, such as those on education, the analysis of intra-household allocation of resources among members is difficult. Without direct information on which child benefits from educational expenditures, the estimation approach of Evenson and Mwabu provides at least an indirect estimate.

I have considered in this section some of the complex factors behind the growing share of female-headed households evident in many parts of the modern world. Although the precise causes of this trend and its consequences are poorly understood, it is closely associated with societies investing more equally in the human capital of men and women. Where women's human capital relative to that of men is lowest, there is further evidence of differential survival favoring men, just as it is for schooling and training in the labor market. Section 5 surveys the evidence on the private and social returns to investments in women's and men's human capital, to assess whether regional patterns in gender distribution of human capital could be an efficient response to distinctive conditions in these regions, or whether these patterns appear to be inefficient social and private allocations of investment resources that might help to account for secular economic growth trends in these various regions.

5. Investment in women's human capital: Measuring returns

It is widely believed that investments in human capital account for much of the secular growth in economic output per individual worker, per adult in a household, and per capita in an aggregate economy. To summarize the many forms that human capital can take, economists have in recent years considered a growing array of processes, some relatively well understood, for which the production process has been repeatedly represented, quantitatively and statistically. In the case of schooling, the internal rate of return can be derived from streams of direct and opportunity costs set against the later increased market productivity of the person, if he or she survives [Becker (1964)]. But in many other forms of human capital, the biological and behavioral mechanisms determining accumulation are less well understood, and the consequences of these forms of human capital for individual lifetime labor productivity per unit time worked are more uncertain. The internal rates of return to these forms of human capital accumulation other than schooling are therefore not well established, because the investment cost components of the human capital accumulation process are less precisely defined (e.g., what share of the cost of nutrition is attributed to investment and what share to consumption?), and the private and social returns are also more uncertain when the investors in human capital allocate more of their time to nonmarket production activities for which the value of output is difficult to price (e.g., reduced child mortality). Two directions have been followed, estimating wage functions and production functions.

5.1. Estimating wage functions without bias

The literature on human capital returns was first built on evidence of schooling returns to males [Becker (1964)], where the conceptual ambiguities were least serious and the data most satisfactory. For women, and for the many important forms of human capital other than schooling, such as health and migration, more research is needed to deal with the major sources of statistical bias [Schultz (1995a)]. In poor agricultural households, women tend not to work for a wage. Thus, the first and foremost problem is constructing a satisfactory model to explain which women in the agricultural household work off-farm for a wage rate, and this off-farm labor supply decision (selection into the wage earner sample) must be assumed to depend on observed variables that do not theoretically enter into the market wage offer or modify the person's labor productivity as a wage worker [Heckman (1979); Huffman (2000, this volume)]. The natural identifying exclusion restriction to motivate the sample selection correction model of the woman's wage equation is an exogenous source of variation in the woman's nonmarket productivity that would not be relevant to her market productivity or wage rate. One possible source of such variations might be nonlabor income, such as inherited wealth or other nonearned income sources [Schultz (1990b, 1995a)]. These identifiers of the wage participation equation might include attributes of the agricultural household that would either raise the woman's labor productivity in agricultural work within the family enterprise or increase the value of the woman's product in home production and leisure activities, but have no theoretical reason to affect off-farm wages. For modeling the behavior of the agricultural household, land and fixed capital of the farm are often treated as quasi-fixed factors and assumed predetermined for the time allocation decisions of family members. But it is important to stress that it is not appropriate to rely on the number and age of children in the household to determine time allocation, particularly for the wife, for these variables merely reflect fertility decisions of the couple that are likely to be jointly determined with the lifetime plan for the woman's allocation of her time among home, farm, and off-farm production activities. Another factor that could be particularly important in the off-farm labor force participation decision would be the transportation costs associated with the distance between the farm household and non-farm employment opportunities, and the analogous effect of the household's remoteness on the diffusion of information about job opportunities in neighboring areas.

Correcting for possible sample-selection bias in estimating the wage function from wage earners, a number of studies have assessed separately for men and women the wage returns to schooling. A variety of other human capital stocks have also been included in some studies: (1) anthropometric indicators of nutritional status such as adult *height* as a lifetime proxy for the balance of nutrients and the burden of disease experienced in childhood [Fogel (1994); Strauss and Thomas (1995, 1998)]; (2) weight divided by height squared, or the Body Mass Index (*BMI*) as a nonmonotonic proxy for current malnutrition or health status [Fogel (1986)]; (3) current intakes of *calories, proteins,* and *other micro-nutrients* as short-run inputs required for physical and possibly mental labor [Thomas and Strauss (1997)]; (4) duration of acute spells of *disabling illness* (or injury) reported during a retrospective reference period of a month or two weeks [Schultz and Tansel (1997)]; (5) functional limitations in performing Activities of Daily Living (*ADL*) [Strauss et al. (1995)]; (6) subjective categorical assessments of personal health; and finally, (7) migration and the mobility of labor that is associated with workers finding locations where they can be more productive, which tend to increase with development and specialization [Sjaastad (1962); Gisser (1965); Kuznets (1971); Schultz (1982, 1995a)]. Migration and formal education of the worker may also weaken the capacity of the family at origin to determine the lifetime employment opportunities of its children, and consequently migration and education may themselves reduce the importance of apprenticeship vocational training that traditionally occurs within the family.

There has been a long debate on how to get behind the direct correlation between these stocks of human capital and wage productivity to disentangle the causal effect of human capital on wages for a representative member of the population [Griliches (1977)]. The most common concern has been that other factors affecting labor productivity are omitted from the analysis when estimating the effect of human capital on wage rates, and these omitted factors may be correlated with the observed stocks of human capital, and these factors can sometimes be plausibly implicated as a factor determining who receives the observed human capital investments. For example, the "ability" of the individual is expected to raise their productivity, and might reasonably increase also their receipt of schooling (or other human capital inputs). The analogous argument is made that family wealth may permit parents to borrow at lower interest rates to invest in their children's schooling [Becker (1967); Jacoby (1994); NaRanong (1998)], or that family wealth increases the demand for children's education because the child's education is viewed by the parent as a normal consumption good. Family wealth and connections may be used to obtain for children better-paying jobs, or wealthy parents could invest in other unobserved forms of human capital for which the wage returns are misattributed to observed human capital, i.e., education [Lam and Schoeni (1993)].

This omitted-variable bias is compounded by errors-in-measurement bias that arises if the human capital stock variable is itself not reported accurately or measured precisely. Griliches (1977) among others illustrates how efforts to "control for" omitted variable bias that might be expected to otherwise overstate the wage returns to human capital will also augment the errors-in-measurement bias that would understate the wage returns to the poorly measured human capital inputs. The net effect of these often offsetting sources of bias is not obvious, and a proposed solution used increasingly in economics is to specify a suitable instrumental variable that is correlated with the human capital stock. For example, a locality-specific variation in the price of an input to produce that form of capital can serve as an instrumental variable, such as the local school tuition or distance to a school, or in the case of health the price of nutrients or the distance to health care. Of course this local price or program variation must explain a sufficient amount of the variation across a sample of persons in their human capital investments, and it must not be correlated with the unexplained variation in wage rates.

The studies by Angrist and Krueger (1991a, 1991b) of U.S. data illustrate that instrumental variable estimates of the wage return to schooling can be as large or larger than the direct ordinary least squares (OLS) estimates. In many contexts the returns to schooling are not overestimated by OLS methods, and therefore the errors-in-measurement bias might appear to be larger (in a negative direction) than the omitted-variable bias (in the positive direction) [Card (1998)]. The same conclusion can be drawn from studies of wage functions in the West African countries of Ghana and Côte d'Ivoire that simultaneously control for schooling, height, BMI, and migration [Schultz (1995b)]. Although these four proxies for human capital are positively intercorrelated, suggesting that the inclusion of all is likely to reduce the returns estimated individually, each retains much of its own contribution to explaining wage variation. Moreover, the significant effects of schooling on wages are reduced by at most 15 percent by the inclusion of the other nutrition, health, and migration variables. Instrumental variable estimation methods designed to correct for sources of bias in the wage function do not, in this West African case, change statistically the returns to education and migration, but increase markedly those to nutrition and health, as proxied by adult height and BMI.[17] The returns to all four forms of human capital are similar for men and women, even though women have received substantially fewer years of schooling than men in these two countries. There is a growing body of evidence in a variety of countries that rates of return to schooling of men and women in wage employment, when they are corrected for sample selection bias, are of a similar magnitude for both sexes. In countries where women have received substantially less education than men, the returns tend to be higher for women than for men at the secondary and higher educational levels [King and Hill (1993); Schultz (1995a); Mwabu and Schultz (1996)].

Also mounting is evidence collected by economic historians [Floud et al. (1990); Fogel (1994); Steckel and Floud (1997)], epidemiologists [Waterlow et al. (1977); Spurr (1983); Falkner and Tanner (1986); Waterlow (1988)], and development economists [Strauss (1986); Strauss and Thomas (1995, 1998); Knaul (1998); Ribero and Nunez (1998)] that improved nutrition and health are important determinants of stature, labor productivity, and time allocation [Khandker (1987, 1988); Binswanger et al. (1980); Kimhi (1994); Sahn and Alderman (1996)]. Persuasive as these conceptual and empirical studies are, they have not been assembled into the form that one needs to infer the internal wage rate of return to private or social investments in child and adult nutritional status, as they impact on the present value of the individual's lifetime productive capacity. Most investigations find nonlinear relationships between increases in nutritional status and productivity, where economic returns to constant physical increments of nutritional inputs diminish with increasing scale. These nonlinearities imply different groups will benefit by different amounts given comparable increments to their nutrition or anthropometric status, and therefore, if the nutritional and health improvements can be effectively targeted to the poor, they are likely to have larger proportionate effects on lifetime productivity. Simple measures of nutritional status can also be excessive (i.e., BMI above 28 implies obesity) and hence counterproductive in terms of labor productivity, mortality, and morbidity. Nonetheless, the limitations of existing analytical methods and small samples do not provide precise estimates of the counterproductive effects of excessive BMI (or height) in poor countries [Schultz (1995b)]. Public health and disease abatement programs and nutritional intervention schemes must be costed-out and implemented in a random experimental program in order to assess how much they increase nutritional outcomes and adult wage productivity for different target groups [Newman et al. (1994)]. This process should define the circumstances under which the productive payoff to such public investment programs will justify the commitment of public

---

[17] The Hausman specification tests suggest that education should be treated as exogenous, whereas height and BMI appear to be endogenous or measured with error [Schultz (1995b)].

resources. Then it will be possible to compare confidently the private monetary returns to nutrition and health programs using the same metric as with the private wage returns to schooling [Becker (1964); Mincer (1974)].

The impact of human capital on wage productivity does not exhaust the issues involving human capital returns when it comes to comparisons of women and men. First, women tend to allocate more of their time than men to nonmarket production activities, and our assessment of the returns to human capital is primarily based on market wage differentials. The correction for sample selection bias may deal with the unobserved differences between those individuals who work in the market sector and those who do not. But for nonwage workers, labor productivity returns to human capital will remain more difficult to gauge, aggregate, and value [Michael (1982); Haveman and Wolfe (1984)].

Studies that have separated self employed from wage earners have not generally found salient differences in the percentage increase in hourly earnings associated with an additional year of schooling [Chiswick (1976, 1979); Fields and Schultz (1982); Ben-Porath (1986); Strauss and Thomas (1995)]. It would be preferable, however, to analyze the range of employment opportunities faced by a more educated worker, including whether to migrate to the urban sector, and whether to work as self employed or in wage employment. Vijverberg (1995) has been able to do this with a sample from Côte d'Ivoire, and decompose the market returns to education for women and men into that portion that accrues due to each of these reallocations of the time of better-educated workers to the sectors where their labor is more highly rewarded.[18] However, for those workers entirely in nonmarket production or working in an unpaid capacity in a family enterprise, the attribution of human capital returns may still be obscured. Yet at this time there is little evidence on the magnitude of this bias, or even its sign.

---

[18] Another intersectoral allocation of labor occurs between the private and public sectors. Glick and Sahn (1997) evaluate the returns to men and women in Guinea from education, and how it differs between self employment, private wage sector, and public wage sector, and they find public sector jobs provide a larger wage premia for educated workers, particularly for women. Van der Gaag and Vijverberg (1987) also report substantial wage differentials between public and private sector wages in Côte d'Ivoire, but after they control for education and other worker characteristics in a switching regression framework that corrects for the self selection of workers into the sector where they are most productive, the public-private wage gap is eliminated. If the goal is to decompose the total gain from education or another form of human capital into that which arises from migration and from gaining access to particular sectors of employment, a more complicated structural model of the sector allocation of labor is required. But estimates of this structural decomposition will depend critically on additional controversial identifying restrictions, which if they are incorrect could distort any interpretation of the data. Reduced form wage equations based on the entire population within a relatively closed labor market is therefore the best starting point for an analysis of schooling, health, and nutrition returns [Schultz (1988)]. Comparisons of the efficiency of female and male farm operators also found few cases where schooling increased the profit of the farm operator more or less for men or women [Moock (1976); Guyer (1980); Dey (1981); Buvinic et al. (1983); P. Rose (1995); Lilja et al. (1996); Alesina and Djata (1997); Smith and Chavas (1997); Yang (1997)].

5.2. Gender productivity differences from production functions

Production functions are used to summarize the production possibilities confronted in agriculture, and to estimate the marginal products of inputs used in a specific combination [Heady and Dillon (1961)]. But when men and women work jointly in producing agricultural outputs, estimates of the marginal productivity of men relative to women are generally not estimated with much precision [Quisumbing (1996a, 1996b); Jacoby (1992, 1995); Fafchamps and Quisumbing (1998a, 1998b)]. This problem may arise because the allocation of family labor to production is endogenously determined, and therefore affected by productive factors omitted from the production analysis, such as management skills (e in Equation (7)), or affected by the preferences of family members toward work and leisure [Mundlak and Hoch (1965); Singh et al. (1986)]. This problem may be exacerbated because men and women often perform distinctive functions in the natural sequence of agricultural production activities, and thus they are not generally good substitutes for each other within some functions, e.g., men do not often plant rice or women plow. Moreover, the success of one stage in the production process can then augment the relative demand for male and female labor in a later stage. For example, if the plowing and planting labor is approximately predetermined by the plot size and quality, the labor required for harvesting will depend also on how good the weather was up to the harvest, or the extent of pest infestation, etc. [Laufer (1985)]. For example, assume the share of women's labor in the total labor input over the entire season is an increasing function of the size of the harvest, because women are called upon to assist in harvesting only when the crop is plentiful. Under these assumptions, unobserved weather productive effects would be attributed in estimating a normal (OLS) single-stage production function to women's labor productivity, biasing upward production function estimates of women's marginal product. Only when labor and other agricultural inputs are properly endogenized, and the stages of the production process suitably modeled, is it likely that estimates of the production function will become a satisfactory basis for inferring the marginal product of male and female labor. These difficulties are reviewed in Quisumbing (1996b), and reinforce our initial reliance on comparisons of male and female wage rates, even when the proportion of women in the wage labor force is relatively small.

Another dilemma arises in using family farm production data to infer the productivity of labor. How should the education of the men and women in the family labor force or hired labor force be appropriately aggregated? Much of the early evidence of productive returns to schooling in small-scale agriculture in poor countries was based on the schooling of the male head of household [Jamison and Lau (1982)]. It was reasoned that the farm management decisions for which education was decisive fell on the male head of the farming family, and thus his education would be important and his spouse's education would not. Others have debated whether to include the average education of the family labor force, or the highest education of any family worker under the presumption that a younger family member who was not head could, if well educated, solve the production problem and guide the others to follow his or her plan [Yang (1997)]. Jolliffe

(1997) finds evidence in the Ghana Livings Standard Survey of 1988–89 that the highest education or average education of the family labor force performed better than the head's education in empirically accounting for farm profits, total income or nonfarm income. But this conclusion does not resolve our need to jointly assess the economic return to schooling for both the husband and wife.

Finally, agricultural production functions have been used to clarify the adoption of agricultural innovations, the diffusion of new technologies, and the distribution of benefits from this process that accounts for much of the growth in agricultural productivity. The first insight was that the rate of technical change or increase in farm yields was positively related to the amount of extension activity per farmer within a (U.S.) state, and by the educational attainment of farmers in that state. But extension activity and farmer education were found to be substitutes for each other, suggesting that the benefits of extension were concentrated among the least educated farmers who could not otherwise decipher quickly the new technological options that would be most profitable [Welch (1970); Huffman (1974, 1976, 1980); T.W. Schultz (1975)]. Extension activity was therefore a leveling force that promoted greater income equality in the context of a technologically dynamic agricultural sector such as was observed in the United States. These patterns were then replicated in many low income countries [e.g., Moock (1976); Jamison and Moock (1984); Birkhaeuser et al. (1991)]. The conclusion was that there must be a pool of new technology worth extending to farmers and an efficient extension service. Again it was found that the extension activity, in this context, had greater benefits for less educated farmers.

5.3. Agricultural crops, extension, and the environment

It has been argued that the colonial administrators did not look with favor on female farming systems in Africa, and Boserup (1970) has documented the results of this pattern of governance. She argues that agricultural extension systems promoted cash crops to engage the idleness of men who as seen by the Europeans did little work in traditional agricultural systems in Africa. Land rights of ownership and use that were enjoyed traditionally by women were gradually assigned to men. New technologies that were developed and introduced to enhance the productivity of agriculture had the effect of then increasing the productivity of labor in cash crops relative to subsistence food crops. As a consequence, the economic productivity of men relative to women in African agriculture tended to increase. These colonial efforts to promote agriculture tended to be perpetuated by the subsequent independent nations with a continued focus on raising the yields and profitability of cash crops for export. This emphasis on cash crops could most readily be explained by the same motives as occupied the colonial regimes – obtaining a reliable source of government revenue, whether the export crop was coffee, cocoa, or cotton.

The traditional shift from hoe to plow agriculture with economic development often led to a reduction in the burden on women as the mainstay of the workforce in agriculture, although it might eventually have increased the demand for female labor again after irrigation permitted multiple cropping of the land in each year, raising the share of labor required for weeding and transplanting, tasks for which female labor may be more productive than men's [Boserup (1970)]. But in Africa, where draft animals were rare (due partly to the endemic tsetse fly), this displacement of women from the burdens of subsistence agriculture did not proceed as rapidly or as widely as in Asia or Latin America. Nonetheless, the shift in the mix of crops grown in agriculture toward cash crops was often associated with male domination of the new, often more profitable, crops. But there were exceptions as well. Many of the successful cocoa farmers of Ghana were women [Hill (1963); Guyer (1980)]. With their enormous disadvantage in educational attainment compared to men, and their challenged rights to use the land and offer it as collateral for credit, African women have continued nonetheless to dominate the agricultural sector [Evenson and Siegel (1998)].

This process of the introduction of cash crops is well documented in West Africa where irrigation made rice a commercial crop, shifting it from a traditionally female crop to one dominated by males [Dey (1981); Jones (1983); Von Braun and Webb (1989)]. In East Africa coffee also became a cash crop, and one more often produced by males than females. Whatever the causes for this evolution of commercial crops in Africa, the result was that women, who obtained a small fraction of the schooling that men received, often lost control of the new, more profitable crops to men [Murdock and Provost (1973); Ember (1983); Kennedy and Cogill (1986); Smith and Chavas (1997)]. The crops that benefited most from agricultural research and development efforts in Africa, and the gender bias in the extension effort toward male farmers, is attributed by Boserup (1970) to the colonial administrators. I have not encountered alternative explanations for the resulting gender bias in the redistribution of resources. But the differential educational attainment of men and women in Central, East, and West Africa is a significant anomaly that needs to be explained, for it does not prevail in southern Africa. This unequal investment in education placed women in most of sub-Saharan Africa at a great disadvantage in deciphering what was most profitable in the new spectrum of agricultural crops, modern varieties, and inputs.

Birkhaeuser et al. (1991) find the extension systems of Africa are far from uniformly successful, but they have been on average cost-effective. As Boserup (1970) argued, they initially tended to be dominated by male extension agents and were relatively ineffective in transmitting their technologies to female farmers. But these agricultural extension institutions have in some countries changed their practices, and female agents have been hired and trained to reach more effectively female farmers. When the gender bias in contacts or visits between the extension agents and farmers is allowed for, it has been shown that female farmers are as effective as males in increasing their yields in response to new technological inputs. The effects of female extension staff are particularly positive for female farm managers. In Burkina Faso the yields of female farm managers appear to be higher than male farm managers in millets and maize, whereas male managers are higher than female managers in cotton and groundnuts [Evenson and Siegel (1998)]. Modeling the gender of the farmer and the agent appears to be an essential aspect of the process of technology transfer, learning by doing, and diffusion.

Environmental degradation is often seen as an example of market failure in the management of a resource for which social externalities are not taken into account by private decision-makers. Women's specific production tasks in the rural sector are often linked to the negative social externalities of removing forest coverage, depleting the neighborhood's supply of fuelwood, reducing the fertility of commonly held land, and accelerating erosion due to overgrazing of the commons. Because of the gender division of labor in many settings, the costs of environmental degradation may be borne disproportionately by women. For example, women must spend more of their time fetching fuel from greater distances, or they must reduce their livestock herds that depend on the degrading common resources [Meinzen-Dick et al. (1997)]. It is also argued that the intensification of agriculture is related to a decline in women's productive contribution to agriculture [Ember (1983)]. Fertility and population growth depends sensitively on women's educational attainment relative to men's [Schultz (1997)]. Population growth has also been attributed a significant role in India reducing forest cover and increasing degradation of the land [Foster et al. (1998)]. Reducing environmental degradation is yet another possible beneficial social externality attributable to society's investments in women's education and productivity which is likely to reduce fertility and dampen the pressure of population on the environment.

5.4. Externalities of women's human capital

Human capital is complex because it functions as both a consumption and investment good, being valued for itself and for the increased productivity it imparts to the worker. But these consumption benefits of human capital do not alter the rationale for estimating productive returns in the labor market as a lower bound on the full private returns received by the individual or family that would combine observed productive returns and the unobserved consumption returns.

It has also been argued that human capital is the source of social externalities, or benefits, that are not captured by the nuclear or even extended private family who is called on to sacrifice current consumption to invest in human capital. If this were true, then there is a case to allocate public resources to subsidize the socially optimal level of human capital investments, or at least treat these externalities as defraying the current public costs of human capital formation programs in schools, public health programs, family planning, etc. With the exception of investments in public health to reduce social exposure to communicable diseases, there are few well-documented examples of social externalities of human capital. There is little empirical evidence that an economy or labor market functions better in the aggregate because its population is better educated, over and above the private returns to education that are captured by better-educated workers and form the basis of estimates of wage returns. There are no widely accepted estimates of the externalities for economic growth arising from subsidies for the adoption and use of birth control in family planning programs. Although these notions have remained plausible to program advocates, they have been difficult to substantiate empirically in the form of scientifically defended estimates of production functions that quantify social spillovers from private investments in human capital. The exception, however, may be women's education, as alluded to earlier.

It is widely believed that there are social externalities beyond the private family that arise from female schooling, largely because female education impacts a variety of household production processes that synergistically foster the accumulation of human capital in the next generation of children. Women's schooling is associated with a reduction in child mortality among her children, whereas the impact of men's schooling is less substantial [Heller and Drake (1979); Schultz (1980); Cochrane et al. (1980); Mensch et al. (1985); Schultz (1994b, 1995a)]. There need be no market failure here, because a woman's family privately internalizes these gains. But societies also value child health, and thus allocate public resources to public health programs, and in particular preventative child health interventions. Similarly, publicly subsidized schooling occurs due to a consensus that increasing school enrollments yields social benefits that outweigh the public outlays. And a mother's education generally has a larger impact on children's schooling than the father's education [cf. King et al. (1986)].

There is one challenge to this interpretation of the empirical record that needs more study, but because it relies on the roles of unobservable variables, such as preferences of the parents, it is more complicated to describe. Suppose men who prefer to have fewer and better educated children seek wives who are better educated and thus more productive in producing human capital in children. These (unobserved) preferences of men for lower fertility and higher "quality" children would lead them to make the necessary sacrifices in other areas (i.e., reduce their other consumption) to marry better- educated women, or more specifically, better educated women than they would be expected to marry, on average, in the normal functioning of the marriage market. In this case, it becomes ambiguous whether the lower fertility and increased child schooling associated with a mother's schooling is a causal effect of the home productivity of a woman's schooling, the preferences of women for higher quality children, or an incidental outcome of the marriage matching process and men's and women's preferences.

In rural Bangladesh and India empirical evidence has been assembled, conditional on a structural model, that suggests part of the correlation between women's schooling and their children's schooling is due to the marriage matching process and consequently can be more appropriately attributed to men's preferences than to women's differential productivity in schooling their children [Foster (1996); Behrman et al. (1997)]. The Indian study first notes that women's schooling does not contribute to increased agriculture productivity, whereas men's schooling has been linked since the 1960s to the adoption of new agricultural technologies and consequently to increases in rural incomes [Foster and Rosenzweig (1995)]. Women's and men's schooling may also not earn much of a private return in the labor market for casual routine rural wage labor in India. A remaining possible economic reason of rural Indian and Bangladeshi families for sending girls to school in increasing numbers is that the better-educated women are able to increase the schooling (and health) of their children. Men who want better-educated (healthier) children are thus motivated to marry a better-educated woman with increased productivity in producing child human capital. An improved understanding of the joint determination of the marriage market and these home child human capital production processes could affect the magnitude of estimates of the technological productivity of female education on child human capital, and plausibly reduce them in circumstances where women's schooling is privately valued by men mainly for its productive effects on child-rearing.

The final potential externality of schooling relates to fertility, which is widely found to be inversely related to women's schooling [Schultz (1981, 1994a); Cochrane (1979); Cochrane et al. (1980)]. If family planning programs are currently subsidized by the state because a reduction in fertility is thought to impart a social benefit, then increasing the schooling of girls should also be subsidized for it is associated after about a decade with diminished fertility. In this instance, not all societies base their support for family planning on the desirability of reducing fertility; some endorse these programs to improve women's lifetime welfare opportunities and strengthen their reproductive rights. There are also a handful of instances in Africa where the first few years of female education seem to have little effect on a woman's fertility, perhaps because of the low quality of available education, or the counterbalancing effect of schooling on improving reproductive health and avoiding sexually transmitted diseases that induce subfecundity and prevent some women from having the number of births they want. On balance, the evidence suggests that increments to the schooling of men, holding constant the educational attainment of women, are associated in low income countries with increases in fertility, although this pronatal effect of male education seems to diminish as the country develops and child labor becomes less important to family income [Schultz (1994a, 1997)]. The social costs of high fertility and rapid population growth are difficult to scientifically quantify [National Research Council (1986)], but many countries have concluded that their society stands to gain in the long run by slowing rapid population growth, and this conclusion would justify assigning a higher priority to women's education than to men's in these countries.

To conclude this section, if the private market wage returns are of comparable magnitudes for men and women, but the social externalities associated with reduced child mortality, increased child anthropometric capacities, increased child school enrollments, and decreased fertility are all linked more positively to women's schooling than they are to men's schooling, and these outcomes are also positively valued by society, it is efficient for society to invest more in the schooling of women than of men [McGuire and Popkin (1990)]. A deeper understanding of the marriage market may sharpen our insights into these connections, but is unlikely to reverse these basic findings. The magnitude of the subsidy that would be socially optimal will depend on the value society assigns to slowing population growth and transferring resources in the form of human capital to the younger generation. It would also seem clear that where female school enrollments are markedly lower than male, there would be a *prima facie* case for greater subsidies for female education. The only reason to revise this mandate is if market wage returns for female schooling fall substantially below those of male schooling, presumably due to an overproduction of women's human capital given the social institutions prevailing in the labor market. I have not yet found a well-designed empirical study that reports such an overproduction of women's schooling.

5.5. Does women's economic control over household resources create social externalities?

The conclusion of many empirical studies of child development is that increased economic resources in the hands of the mother is generally associated with improvements in birth outcome, survival, infant and child nutrition and health, child physical growth and maturation, earlier entry into school, increased school enrollment for age, and more years of school completed.[19] The first issue in assessing this empirical evidence for supporting the collective approach to the family is whether the increased economic resources of the mother are evaluated appropriately. Clearly, the early studies that relied on the labor market earnings or income of women as their measure of women's control over economic resources were not satisfactory. This initial measure depended directly on the woman's labor supply decision, and if women with more economic resources worked in the market less of their time, as might be accounted for by economic theory, the market earnings of women could be a misleading indicator of the theoretically desired variable.

Economic theory suggests the measure of lifetime "full income" is needed for the woman (and man), both within the existing family configuration and if possible in the alternative or "reservation arrangement" she might choose, e.g., divorce or separation

---

[19] The literature on these issues is enormous and full of complexities that cannot be examined in the scope of this paper. The evidence on female education on child mortality is widely accepted after the Latin American Census samples were cross-tabulated and as World Fertility Surveys become available for a widening sample of low-income countries [e.g., Behm (1976, 1980); Caldwell (1979); Schultz (1980); Cochrane et al. (1980); Rosenzweig and Schultz (1982a, 1982b); Farah and Preston (1982); Mensch et al. (1985); Barrera (1990); Thomas et al. (1990)]. The studies of anthropometric indicators of child health began somewhat later, but also clearly indicated that better education of the mother was correlated with better height and BMI indicators for her children (summarized in [Behrman and Deolalikar (1988, 1989); Behrman and Wolfe (1984, 1989); Strauss and Thomas (1995, 1998)]. Schooling of children as a function of maternal education is also a frequently found pattern, although a few exceptions can be found where father's education is equally strongly and positively related to child schooling, if household income is not controlled [e.g., Rosenzweig and Evenson (1977); Chernichovsky (1985); King et al. (1986); Duraisamy (1988); Duraisamy and Malathy (1991); Malathy (1993); Jacoby (1994); Glewwe and Jacoby (1994, 1995); Lloyd and Blanc (1995); Haveman and Wolfe (1995); Lavy (1996); Tansel (1997); Holmes (1997); Behrman et al. (1997); Behrman (1997); NaRanong (1998); Sipahimalani (1998)]. Not only do these studies differ in how they measure women's control over resources, starting with education and then advancing toward labor market productivity [Kennedy and Cogill (1986); Senauer et al. (1986); Engel (1988); Blumberg (1988); Kennedy and Peters (1992); Haddad and Hoddinott (1994); Thomas (1990, 1994); Thomas and Chen (1994); Hoddinott and Haddad (1995)]. The studies also control in different ways for the endowments of the husband, family income, and family composition. As argued throughout this paper, there are serious analytical problems with most methods for dealing with family composition, and consequently there is continuing search for better methods to explicitly model marriage matching and marital status [e.g., Boulier and Rosenzweig (1984); Schultz (1994b); Foster (1996); Behrman et al. (1995, 1997)].

from the union. The full income is composed of both her potential full-time earnings and her claims on nonearned income. The objective is to estimate from a suitable, sample selection corrected wage function her opportunity wage in the labor force or in the household, if the latter is larger, and that wage would then be weighted by a standard full-time labor supply (i.e., 2000 hours per year), to which returns to nonhuman capital and other nonearned income sources would be added. When the procedure or data for estimating and imputing wages is not satisfactory, the woman's nonearned income component may be examined separately as an exogenous factor conditioning household outcomes, just as the parallel nonearned income variable is included for the man in the household as another resource constraint on the family. Analogously, this nonearned income component of the husband and wife can serve as an instrumental variable for identifying the effect of a constructed full family income variable [cf. Heckman (1971)]. In both the unified family model and the bargaining family model the value of the husband's and wife's time, or shadow wage rates, is expected to modify consumption and investment patterns, because the time of family members enters into the shadow prices of many consumption commodities and investment activities, and thereby modifies family demands, independently of bargaining power or differences in preferences among family members. To reject the unified family model and to support alternatives, such as the family bargaining models, it has been shown that the personal distribution of nonearned income in the family affects the allocation of consumption and human capital investments. Perhaps the most readily interpreted evidence of this form is that an individual's own nonearned (exogenous) income causes a greater reduction in own time allocated to work than does the spouse's nonearned income, holding constant for the family's total nonearned income and the shadow value of the time of both spouses. This empirical regularity strongly suggests that the pooling of family resources is less than perfect.

The simplest comparisons of the effect of women's empowerment on family outcomes may not distinguish between the formal models of family behavior, but they highlight the main policy conclusion that emerges from this literature. How are family outcomes related to women's human capital as initially summarized by her education? To assess this conditional effect, one also wants to control for the value of her husband's education, for the self-selected population of couples, and for the relative supply of potential husbands in the local community marriage market. In most investigations of this design, women's schooling has a greater beneficial effect on child human capital formation and survival than does the husband/male education. Fertility is lower, child mortality is lower, and the children's generation completes more years of schooling, tends to start school earlier, attends more often, etc. [Schultz (1986, 1993, 1994a, 1995a)].

The second problem for constructing comparisons is the family composition. How is one to deal with the self selection of those women who are living with a man, or living on their own, or living with other relatives? How is one to treat the potential earnings or nonearned income of a resident man, if he is not currently married to the woman? All these ambiguities in what constitutes the appropriate test of the bargaining model hypothesis that female nonearned income has a larger positive effect on child development (if she prefers child welfare compared to her mate) than male nonearned income, alerts us to the difficulty of drawing definitive conclusions from the empirical evidence that is currently at hand, and validating a complete version of the bargaining model of the family.

To the extent that society views these outcomes of lower fertility and child mortality and increased schooling of youth as objectives it values investing in, the advancement of women's schooling creates a positive social externality. On the basis of this externality argument, societies may optionally expend public resources promoting the schooling of women. Although gender equity is one powerful reason for supporting such an allocation of resources, the argument here is based on economic efficiency – maximizing total output. The externality argument relies on an *efficiency gain* in terms of women's schooling saving resources from other programs that seek to accomplish the same goals: reduce child mortality, reduce fertility, and increase the schooling of the next generation of youth. One policy intervention with this objective would be fellowships to promote the attendance at school of more girls. The evidence suggests that female enrollments are especially low for poor families in poor countries where credit constraints are a particular disadvantage for girls [e.g., NaRanong (1998)]. Carefully graduated inducements for girls to continue in school might also take the form of subsidized school uniforms for girls, but not necessarily boys.[20] Tax and transfer schemes that encourage higher continuation rates in school for girls should be careful not to prepare women to enter traditionally female-dominated occupational tracks in the school system, for this might "over supply" the labor market with these skills and reduce the wage returns women receive for their years in school relative to men. It is likely that the externality argument for promoting female schooling would be strongest in those societies where the sex imbalance in schooling is currently greatest. Thus the externality argument for publicly subsidizing female schooling more than male schooling would be strongest in many of the countries of South and West Asia and sub-Saharan Africa where child mortality is high, average schooling levels are low, and fertility remains relatively high, sustaining moderate to rapid rates of population growth [Subbarao and Raney (1995); Schultz (1995a)].

Public finance arguments can also justify redirecting human capital toward women in order to recover educational subsidies, broaden the tax base, and reduce tax distortions. If government revenue requirements are fixed and can be met only by taxing market transactions, as seems reasonable, reallocating school enrollments toward women

---

[20] Programs that improve the economic welfare of women may be justified on many accounts, but it should not be assumed that they increase human capital investments in girls. For example, the Grameen Bank in Bangladesh is widely credited with successfully providing micro enterprise credit to groups of poor women. Although these programs were associated with increasing the income of the women in the villages that benefited from the placement of such programs, a study found no evidence that as the incomes of these women rose, their fertility declined, and found that it may have increased compared to pre-program fertility levels. It is possible that credit subsidies for women's enterprises increase the value of children's labor in their enterprises and even weaken their incentives to invest in the schooling of their girls, who are most likely to work alongside their mothers [Pitt and Khandker (1998)].

rather than men should expand the market earned-income tax base and allow the tax rate to decline and distortions of consumption and production decisions to diminish. It is a well-documented empirical regularity that the market labor supply response associated with an increase in own schooling is more positive for women than for men. This regularity may help explain the large increase in female market labor supply in the 20th century, first in the industrially advanced countries, and more recently throughout most other parts of the world, at least in the nonagricultural sector of the economy [Schultz (1981, 1990a)]. One interpretation of this empirical regularity is that this labor supply effect of schooling is due to the uncompensated wage effect caused by education increasing worker productivity. It is widely concluded that the substitution effect of own wage on female labor supply exceeds the income effect of the wage, whereas in the case of male labor supply, the positive substitution effect is more or less offset by the negative income effect, weighted by hours worked in the market, leaving a small uncompensated own wage effect for males of either positive or negative sign [Schultz (1981); Killingsworth (1983)]. Increase a woman's schooling by one year and her market labor supply will tend to increase by more than for a man, perhaps because she has a wider range of home production activities from which she can reallocate her time to work in the market labor force.

In studies of farm families the parallel pattern emerges in high and low income countries. Increases in female schooling are associated with increased labor supply to off-farm labor market activities and often also increased farm labor supply. In the case of men, the general tendency is for male labor supply to off-farm activities to increase but farm labor supply to decrease by approximately the same amount [Huffman (1980); Huffman and Lange (1989); Tokle and Huffman (1991); Kimhi and Lee (1996)]. Thus the tax base of male earnings does not substantially respond to increased male schooling, but the female market earnings will increase with her schooling. Moreover, estimates of family labor supply models suggest that the cross-wage effect of the male wage (schooling) on the female labor supply also tends to be substantial and negative, whereas the effect of female wage (schooling) on male labor supply is rarely estimated to be significant [Killingsworth (1983)]. Consequently, the own female schooling effect on the market earnings tax base is positive, and the cross effect of male schooling is negative, reinforcing the conclusion that the tax base would expand with a redirection of human capital formation from men to women. In other words, a larger fraction of the increased public cost of education is recouped by the public sector through added tax payments when women are educated than when men are educated, increasing the social returns to women's schooling relative to men's.

6. Conclusions and direction for further work

Three decades ago economists were challenged to treat the family as a unified coordinator of both consumption demands and the time allocation of its various members [Becker (1965)]. Two decades ago models of the agricultural household combined the profit-maximizing production problem of the farm with the utility-maximizing problem of the family deciding on time allocation and consumption [Barnum and Squire (1979); Singh et al. (1986)]. This second advance depended on the assumption of separability between the farm production and the family consumption decisions, and it implied that hired and family labor were equivalent and all families had access to well-functioning labor markets to bring their labor demands into balance with their family supplies. Econometric testing of this restrictive assumption has continued in a variety of contexts and it is somewhat surprising that it has not been resoundingly rejected, as yet, based on studies of Indonesia, India, and the Philippines [e.g., Singh et al. (1986); Pitt and Rosenzweig (1986); Seavy (1987); Benjamin (1992); Maluccio (1997); De-Silva (1997)]. This literature has concluded that families with a relative shortage or excess of family labor for a farm's production needs do not exhibit distinctively different own-farm input proportions. Even for family female labor in India, where it might be expected that off-farm labor involves social stigma and monitoring costs, the tests of separability appear to be satisfied [Seavy (1987)]. Although factor markets are undoubtedly imperfect in many settings, econometricians have not built a strong case for rejecting the premises underlying the simplified agricultural household model that treats the production and consumption decisions as approximately separable. Women's roles in the agricultural household have not been central to this separability literature, but from the outset the agricultural household model introduced the idea that women's family labor supply might diminish as farm profits increased due to technical change, increasing the demand for hired labor more than would otherwise be expected from a traditional analysis based on farm production functions [Barnum and Squire (1979); Singh et al. (1986)].

A third generation of research on women, family production, and consumption behavior has developed in the last decade, drawing upon three issues. The first is the relaxation of the theory of the unified altruistic model of the family to deal with family members having different control over individual resources and potentially different preferences for consumption. An objective of this theoretical literature is to take the theory against data, and thus to be able to test the restrictions implied by the theory against household survey data across cultures. The second issue is the growing interest in what determines intrahousehold resource allocations, and the resulting distribution of well-being among members of the household. The third issue is the recognition that families and separate individuals observed in a survey are selected into these production-consumption units according to economic and social matching based on preferences and endowments. Thus, it is not appropriate to treat two-parent families as a random sample of the population to test a family bargaining theory, any more than to assume that wage earners represent the productive potential of all individuals. Little empirical work has integrated these three strands of research, and that is one of the major challenges of the field.

Intergenerational perfect altruism can be rejected in the U.S., to the extent that parent and child living in separate households do not perfectly smooth each other's consumption [Altonji et al. (1992)]. Nonetheless this leaves some margin for "altruism" to express itself over time in the form of transfers and bequests [Cox (1990); Cox et al. (1996); Quisumbing (1994, 1995, 1996a, 1996b)]. The formation and composition of families is changing in ways that can be partly explained by economic models of individual and group cooperative or strategic behavior. Thus, the samples restricted to married or single persons, with or without coresidential children, headed by females or males, with or without elderly dependent parents, are not random with regard to the economic consumption and production choices economists want to understand. A more comprehensive theoretical framework is needed that accounts for how individuals are matched and marriages and separations are determined, and other mechanisms that modify fertility, child survival by sex, home-leaving age for offspring by sex, and whether or not elderly parents enter the home of their child, etc. [e.g., Foster (1996)]. Without such a theory of household formation and composition, answers to many analytical questions cannot be obtained from our data.

A second reason for relaxing the unified family model is the growing interest in intrahousehold resource allocation – who receives what within the household and why? The unified family model provides a framework for answering some questions about the distributional consequences of changing wages for men, women, and children, access to local programs, and market prices as they may modify reduced form outcomes in the family. However, the nonunified or bargaining models of the household provide a more focused framework to assess indicators of individual welfare, such as height, BMI, and schooling, and for indicators of the consequences of individually controlled nonearned resources in the household, such as dowry and inheritances. The bargaining models have justified collecting data on separate sources of nonearned income by husbands and wives, separate assets that they bring to their marriage, personal support networks they maintain in their extended families and communities, and individual access they have to credit based on collateral or personal connections. Although a few social scientists continue to debate how conceptually to measure women's "status" in society, most economists have accepted the idea that the labor productivity of women relative to men, outside of their family, is a critical factor governing changes in the form and functioning of today's families and a factor affecting positively women's status and welfare. Moreover, it is a measure of status and welfare that can be approximately measured in many diverse cultural settings.

Other work in this field seeks to understand the nonhuman capital that women control within a family and can take with them in the event that the family separates. Anthropologists have studied certain forms of social and network capital and may provide economists with guidance into this new murky terrain of modeling and help to measure empirically what is meant by "gender empowerment" or "social capital". Feminists have also been outspoken in their pursuit of deeper social values than those reflected in economic-market-determined prices and wages [Folbre (1994)]. Little progress has been made in response to this challenge, though it deserves more study.

The evolving variety of household allocation models based on cooperative or noncooperative bargaining is growing, and the data used for testing them is improving. It is somewhat early to highlight the empirical regularities that this literature has found or that give them any policy interpretation, but selections have been cited in this chapter. There is frequently a regular relationship between nonearned income or nonhuman capital controlled by women in the family and increased consumption shares of food (incidentally, a sign of poverty according to Engel's law), but there is also a tendency for children to be healthier and better nourished and attending school longer and more consistently, holding constant in one manner or another for the family's overall budget constraint. Even this glimmer of an empirical regularity, which might be interpreted as encouraging policymakers to target resources for child support to the custody of mothers rather than fathers, needs to be carefully examined in controlled experiments before policy lessons are drawn [Newman et al. (1994)]. The full ramifications of such policy interventions need to be studied longitudinally for a considerable period of time during which other behavioral adaptations can be expected to occur. One can imagine providing support to mothers (rather than fathers) would also increase the rate of marital dissolution, and the lifetime welfare of affected children would not necessarily improve, while that of the father might deteriorate. Economists may not yet be able to provide firm answers in this complex area of how society can effectively support particular objectives within the family. The problem merits more study. The field is trying to fashion more relevant theory and collect data that promises to be more useful than what was available to researchers in the past. Applying these new methods and examining these new data to understand the role of women in agricultural (and nonagricultural) families is a basic challenge for economists, one that will keep the profession occupied for some time.

Acknowledgement

I have benefited from the comments on an earlier draft by Ayal Kimhi, Agnes Quisumbing, John Strauss, and three anonymous referees.

References

Agarwal, B. (1991), "Social security and the family: Coping with seasonability and calamity in rural India", in: E. Ahmad, J.D. Drez, J. Hills and A. Sen, eds., Social Security in Developing Countries (Oxford University Press, Oxford).

Agarwal, B. (1994), A Field of One's Own: Gender and Land Rights in South Asia (Cambridge University Press, Cambridge, UK).

Ainsworth, M. (1996), "Economic aspects of child fostering in Cote d'Ivoire", in: T.P. Schultz, ed., Research in Population Economics, Vol. 8 (JAI Press, Greenwich, CT).

Aird, J.S. (1983), "The preliminary results of China's 1982 census", The China Quarterly 96:613–640.

Akresh, R. (1999), "Using regional heterogeneity as a predictor of Pareto inefficient intrahousehold allocations in a west African agricultural setting", processed (Yale University, New Haven CT).

Alderman, H., P.-A. Chiappori, L. Haddad, J. Hoddinott and R. Kanbur (1995), "Unitary versus collective models of the household", World Bank Research Observer 10:1–19.

Alderman, H., and S. Chishli (1991), "Simultaneous determination of household and market-oriented activities of women in rural Pakistan", in: T.P. Schultz, ed., Research in Population Economics, Vol. 7 (JAI Press, Greenwich, CT).

Alesina, A.A., and K.K. Djata (1997), "Relative efficiency of women as farm managers: Profit function analysis in Côte d'Ivoire", Agricultural Economics 16:47–53.

Altonji, J., F. Hayashi and L. Kotlikoff (1992), "Is the extended family altruistically linked?", American Economic Review 82:1177–1198.

Amin, S., and A.R. Pebley (1978), "The impact of a public health intervention on excess female mortality in Punjab, India", Mimeo (Princeton, New Jersey).

Anderson, K.H., and M.A. Hill (1987), "Age at marriage in Malaysia: A hazard model of marriage timing", Journal of Development Economics 26:223–234.

Angrist, J., and A.B. Krueger (1991a), "Does compulsory school attendance affect schooling and earnings", Quarterly Journal of Economics 106:979–1014.

Angrist, J., and A.B. Krueger (1991b), "Estimating the payoff to schooling using the Vietnam-era draft lottery", Industrial Relations Section, Princeton University.

Apps, P., and R. Rees (1996), "Labour supply, household production and intra family welfare distribution", Journal of Public Economics 60:199–220.

Apps, P.F., and R. Rees (1997), "Collective labor supply and household production", Journal of Political Economy 105:178–190.

Arrow, K. (1951), Social Choice and Individual Values (John Wiley and Sons, New York, NY).

Ashenfelter, O., and J.J. Heckman (1974), "The estimation of income and substitution effects in a model of family labor supply", Econometrica 42:73–85.

Bardhan, P.K. (1984), Land, Labor and Rural Poverty: Essays in Development Economics (Columbia University Press, New York).

Barnum, H., and L. Squire (1979), "An econometric application of the theory of the farm household", Journal of Development Economics 6:79–102.

Barrera, A. (1990), "The role of maternal schooling and its interaction with public health programs in child health production", Journal of Development Economics 32:69–91.

Barros, R., L. Fox and R. Mendonca (1995), "Poverty among female-headed households in Brazil", in: T.P. Schultz, ed., Investment in Women's Human Capital (University of Chicago Press, Chicago, IL).

Becker, G.S. (1964), Human Capital (Columbia University Press, New York).

Becker, G.S. (1965), "A theory of the allocation of time", Economic Journal 75:493–517.

Becker, G.S. (1967), "Human capital and the personal distribution of income", Woytinsky Lecture, University of Michigan, Ann Arbor, MI.

Becker, G.S. (1974), "A theory of marriage", in T.W. Schultz, ed., Economics of the Family (University of Chicago Press, Chicago, IL).

Becker, G.S. (1981), A Treatise on the Family (Harvard University Press, Cambridge, MA).

Becker, G.S., E.M. Landes and R.T. Michael (1977), "An economic analysis of marital instability", Journal of Political Economy 85:1141–1187.

Becker, G.S., and N. Tomes (1979), "An equilibrium theory of the distribution of income and intergenerational mortality", Journal of Political Economy 87:1141–1187.

Behm, H. (1976), La Mortalidad en los Primeros Anos de Vida en los Paises de America Latina (CELADE, San Jose, Costa Rica).

Behm, H. (1980), "Socioeconomic determinants of mortality in Latin America", in: Socioeconomic Determinants and Consequences of Mortality (WHO, Geneva).

Behrman, J.R. (1988), "Intrahousehold allocation of nutrients in rural India", Oxford Economic Papers 40:32–54.

Behrman, J.R. (1997), "Intrahousehold distribution in the family", in: M.R. Rosenzweig and O. Stark, eds., Handbook of Population and Family Economics (Elsevier Science, Amsterdam).

Behrman, J., N. Birdsall and A. Deolalikar (1995), "Marriage markets, labor markets and unobserved human capital", Economic Development and Cultural Change 43:585–601.

Behrman, J.R., and A. Deolalikar (1988), "Health and nutrition", in: H. Chenery and T.N. Srinivasan, eds., Handbook on Economic Development, Vol. 1, Chapter 15 (North Holland, Amsterdam).

Behrman, J.R., and A. Deolalikar (1989), "Seasonal demands for nutrient intakes and health status in rural south India", in: D.E. Sahn, ed., Causes and Implications of Seasonal Variability in Household Food Security (Johns Hopkins University Press, Baltimore, MD).

Behrman, J.R., A. Foster and M.R. Rosenzweig (1997), "Women's schooling, home teaching, and economic growth", Journal of Political Economy 107:632–714.

Behrman, J., R. Pollak and P. Taubman (1982), "Parental preferences and provision of progeny", Journal of Political Economy 90:52–73.

Behrman, J.R., and B.L. Wolfe (1984), "More evidence on nutrition demand: Income seems overrated and women's schooling underemphasized", Journal of Development Economics 14:105–128.

Behrman, J.R., and B.L. Wolfe (1989), "Does more schooling make women better nourished and healthier?", Journal of Human Resources 24:644–663.

Beller, A.H., and J.W. Graham (1993), The Economics of Child Support (Yale University Press, New Haven, CT).

Benjamin, D. (1992), "Household composition, labor markets and labor demand", Econometrica 60:287–322.

Ben-Porath, Y. (1986), "Self employment and wage earners in Israel", in: U.O. Schmelz and G. Nathan, eds., Studies in the Population of Israel, Vol. 30 (Hebrew University, Magnes Press, Jerusalem, Israel).

Bergstrom, T.C. (1997), "A survey of theories of the family", in: M.R. Rosenzweig and O. Stark, eds., Handbook of Population and Family Economics (Elsevier Science, Amsterdam).

Besley, T., S. Coate and T. Guinnane (1993), "Understanding the workhouse test: Information and poor relief in nineteenth-century England", Economic Growth Center Discussion Paper No. 702 (Yale University, New Haven, CT).

Binswanger, H.P., R.E. Evenson, C.A. Florencio and B.N.F. White, eds. (1980), Rural Household Studies in Asia (Singapore University Press, Singapore).

Birkhaeuser, D., R. Evenson and G. Feder (1991), "The economic impact of agricultural extension", Economic Development and Cultural Change 39:607–650.

Blau, D. (1984), "A model of child nutrition, fertility and women's time allocation", in: T.P. Schultz and K.I. Wolpin, eds., Research in Population Economics, Vol. 5 (JAI Press, Greenwich, CT).

Blumberg, R.L. (1988), "Income under female versus male control", Journal of Family Issues 9:51–84.

Boserup, E. (1970), Women's Role in Economic Development (St. Martins Press, New York, NY).

Boserup, E. (1990), Economic and Demographic Relationships in Development (Johns Hopkins University Press, Baltimore, MD).

Boulier, B.L., and M.R. Rosenzweig (1984), "Schooling, search, and spouse selection", Journal of Political Economy 94:712–732.

Browning, M., F. Bourguignon, P.-A. Chiappori and V. Lechine (1994), "Income and outcomes: A structural model of intra household allocation", Journal of Political Economy 102:1067–1096.

Butz, W.P., and J. DaVanzo (1978), The Malaysian Family Life Survey: Summary Report, R-2351 (The Rand Corporation, Santa Monica).

Buvinic, M., M. Lycette, W.P. McGreevy, eds. (1983), Women and Poverty in the Third World (Johns Hopkins University Press, Baltimore, MD).

Caldwell, J.C. (1968), "Determinants of rural-urban migration in Ghana", Population Studies 22:361–378.

Caldwell, J.C. (1979), "Education as a factor in mortality decline", Population Studies 33:395–413.

Caldwell, J.C., and P. Caldwell (1987), "The cultural context of high fertility in SubSaharan Africa", Population and Development Review 13:409–437.

Card, D., (1998), "The causal effect of education on earnings", Center For Labor Economics Working Paper No. 2, Berkeley CA. In: O. Ashenfelter and D. Card, eds., Handbook of Labor Economics, Vol. 3A, chap. 30, North Holland, Amsterdam.

Carlin, P.S. (1991), "Intrafamily bargaining and time allocation", in: T.P. Schultz, ed., Research in Population Economics, Vol. 7 (JAI Press, Greenwich, CT).

Chen, L., A. Chowdhury and S. Hoffman (1980), "Anthropometric assessment of energy-protein malnutrition and subsequent risk of mortality during preschool aged children", American Journal of Clinical Nutrition 33:1836–1845.

Chen, L., E. Hug and S. D'Souza (1981), "Sex bias in the family allocation of food and health care in rural Bangladesh", Population and Development Review 7:55–70.

Chernichovsky, D. (1985), "Socioeconomic and demographic aspects of school enrollment and attendance in rural Botswana", Economic Development and Cultural Change 33:319–332.

Chernichovsky, D., and L. Zangwill (1988), "Microeconomic theory of the household and nutrition programs", Population and Human Resources Department Working Paper 82 (The World Bank, Washington, DC).

Chiappori, P.-A. (1988), "Rational household labor supply", Econometrica 56:63–89.

Chiappori, P.-A. (1992), "Collective labor supply and welfare", Journal of Political Economy 100:437–467.

Chiappori, P.-A. (1997), "Introducing household production in collective models of labor supply", Journal of Political Economy 105:191–209.

Chiappori, P.-A., B. Fortin and G. Lacroix (1997), "Household Labor Supply, sharing rule and marriage market", processed (Delta, Paris).

Chiswick, C.U. (1976), "On estimating earnings functions for LDCs", Journal of Development Economics 4:67–78.

Chiswick, C.U. (1979), "The determinants of earnings in Thailand", Research Project No. 671-36 (The World Bank, Washington, DC).

Cochrane, S.H. (1979), Fertility and Education (Johns Hopkins University Press, Baltimore, MD).

Cochrane, S.H., J. Leslie and D.J. O'Hara (1980), "The effects of education on health", The World Bank Staff Working Paper 405 (Washington, DC).

Cox, D. (1990), "Intergenerational transfers and liquidity constraints", Quarterly Journal of Economics 105:187–218.

Cox, D., B.E. Hansen and E. Jimenez (1996), "Are households altruistic?", processed (Boston College).

Cox, D., and E. Jimenez (1990), "Achieving social objectives through private transfers: A review", World Bank Research Observer 5:205–218.

Currie, J. (1995), Welfare and Well Being of Children (Harwood Academic Publishers, Chur Switzerland).

Das Gupta, M. (1987), "Selective discrimination against female children in rural Punjab, India", Population and Development Review 13:77–100.

DaVanzo, J. (1972), Determinants of Family Formation in Chile, 1960 (The Rand Corporation, Santa Monica, CA).

Deaton, A. (1986), "On measuring child costs: With application to poor countries", Journal of Political Economy 94:720–744.

Deaton, A. (1989), "Looking for boy-girl discrimination in household expenditure data", World Bank Economic Review 3:1–15.

Deaton, A. (1997), The Analysis of Household Surveys (Johns Hopkins University Press, Baltimore, MD).

Deaton, A., and J. Muellbauer (1980), Economics and Consumer Behavior (Cambridge University Press, Cambridge, UK).

Deaton, A., J. Ruiz-Castillo and D. Thomas (1989), "The influence of household composition on household expenditure patterns", Journal of Political Economy 97(1):179–200.

de Janvry, A., M. Fafchamps and E. Sadoulet (1991), "Peasant household behavior with missing markets", Economic Journal 101(409):1400–1417.

Deolalikar, A., and E. Rose (1995), "Gender, savings and production in rural India", processed (University of Washington).

Deolalikar, A., and W.P.M. Vijverberg (1983), "The heterogeneity of family and hired labor in agricultural production: A test using district-level data from India", Journal of Economic Development 8:45–69.

Dercon, S., and D. Krishnan (1997), "In sickness and in health: Risk sharing within households in rural Ethiopia", processed (Center for the Study of African Economics, Oxford University).

DeSilva, S. (1997), "Heterogeneity of family and hired labor: Implications on the separation of consumption and production decisions in rural adjustment", processed (Economic Growth Center, Yale University, New Haven, CT).

Dey, J. (1981), "Gambrian women: Unequal partners in rice development projects?", Journal of Development Studies 17:109–122.

Doss, C.R. (1996a), "Intrahousehold resource allocation in an uncertain environment", American Journal of Agricultural Economics 78:1335–1339.

Doss, C.R. (1996b), "Testing among models of intrahousehold resource allocation", World Development 24:1597–1609.

Doss, C.R. (1997), "The effect of women's bargaining power on household health and education outcomes: Evidence from Ghana", processed paper (Williams College, Williamstown, MA).

Duraisamy, P. (1988), "An econometric analysis of fertility, child schooling and labour force participation of women in rural Indian households", Journal of Quantitative Economics 4:293–316.

Duraisamy, P. (1992), "Gender intrafamily allocations of resources and child schooling in south India", Economic Growth Center Discussion Paper No. 667 (New Haven, CT).

Duraisamy, P., and R. Malathy (1991), "Impact of public programs on fertility and gender specific investment in human capital in children in rural India", in: Research in Population Economics, Vol. 7 (JAI Press, Greenwich, CT).

Durand, J.D. (1975), The Labor Force in Economic Development, Princeton (Princeton University Press, NJ).

Eckel, C.C., and P.J. Grossman (1998), "Are women less selfish than men: Evidence from dictator experiments", Economic Journal 108:726–735.

Engel, P.L. (1988), "Intrahousehold allocation of resources: Perspective from psychology", in: B.L. Rogers and N.P. Schlossen, eds., Intrahousehold Resource Allocation (United Nations University Press, Tokyo).

Ember, C.R. (1983), "The relative decline in women's contribution to agriculture with intensification", American Anthropologist 85:285–304.

Evenson, R.E. (1978), "Time allocation in rural Philippine households", American Journal of Agricultural Economics 60(2):322–330.

Evenson, R.E., and G. Mwabu (1996), "Household composition and expenditures on human capital formation in Kenya", in: T.P. Schultz, ed., Research in Population Economics, Vol. 8 (JAI Press, Greenwich, CT) 205–232.

Evenson, R.E., and M. Siegel (1998), "Gender and agricultural extension in Burkina Faso" (forthcoming) Africa Today.

Fafchamps, M., and A.R. Quisumbing (1998a), "Human capital, productivity, and labor allocation in rural Pakistan" (forthcoming) Journal of Human Resources.

Fafchamps, M., and A. Quisumbing (1998b), "Social roles, human capital, and intrahousehold division of labor: Evidence from Pakistan", IFPRI Discussion Paper (Washington, DC).

Falkner, F., and J.M. Tanner, eds. (1986), Human Growth: A Comprehensive Treatise, Vol. 3, 2nd ed. (Plenum Press, New York, NY).

Farah, A.A., and S.H. Preston (1982), "Child mortality differentials in Sudan", Population and Development Review 8:365–383.

Fields, G.S., and T.P. Schultz (1982), "Income generating functions in a low income country: Colombia", Review of Income and Wealth 28(1).

Floud, R., K. Wachter and A. Gregory (1990), Height, Health, and History (Cambridge University Press, Cambridge, UK).

Fogel, R.W. (1986), "Physical growth as a measure of well being of populations", in: F. Falkner and J.M. Tanner, eds., Human Growth, Vol. 3, 2nd ed. (Plenum Press, New York, NY).

Fogel, R.W. (1994), "Economic growth, population theory and physiology", American Economic Review 84:369–395.

Folbre, N. (1994), Who Pays for the Kids? (Routledge, London).

Folbre, N., and M. Abel (1989), "Women's work and women's households: Gender bias in the U.S. census", Social Research 56:545–569.

Fortin, B., and G. Lacroix (1997), "A test of the unitary and collective model of household labour supply", Economic Journal 107:933–955.

Foster, A.D. (1995), "Prices, credit markets and child growth in low income rural areas", Economic Journal 105(430):551–570.

Foster, A. (1996), "Analysis of household behavior when households choose their members", processed (University of Pennsylvania).

Foster, A., and M. Rosenzweig (1995), "Information, learning and wage rates in low income rural areas", in: T. Paul Schultz, ed., Investing in Women's Human Capital (University of Chicago Press, Chicago).

Foster, A.D., and M.R. Rosenzweig (1996), "Technical change and human capital returns and investments: Evidence from the green revolution", American Economic Review 86(4):931–953.

Foster, A.D., M.R. Rosenzweig and J.R. Behrman (1998), "Population growth, income growth and deforestation in a large developing country" (Brown University, Providence RI).

Frieden, A. (1974), "The U.S. marriage market", in: T.W. Schultz, ed., Economics of the Family (University of Chicago Press, Chicago, IL).

Friedman, M. (1957), A Theory of the Consumption Function (Princeton University Press, Princeton, NJ).

Fuchs, V.R. (1988), Women's Quest for Economic Equality (Harvard University Press, Cambridge, MA).

Garg, A., and J. Morduch (1996), "Sibling rivalry, resource constraints, and the health of children: Evidence from Ghana", Development Discussion Paper No. 553 (Harvard Institute for International Development, Cambridge, MA).

Gisser, M., (1965), "Schooling and the farm problem", Econometrica 33(3):582–592.

Glewwe, P., and H. Jacoby (1994), "Student achievement and schooling choice in low income countries: Evidence from Ghana", Journal of Human Resources 29:842–864.

Glewwe, P., and H. Jacoby (1995), "An economic analysis of delayed primary school enrollment and childhood malnutrition in a low income country", Review of Economics and Statistics 77:156–169.

Glick, P., and D. Sahn (1997), "Gender and education impacts on employment and earnings in West Africa", Economic Development and Cultural Change 45:793–823.

Goldin, C. (1995), "The U shaped female labor force function in economic development and economic history", in: T.P. Schultz, ed., Investment in Women's Human Capital (University of Chicago Press, Chicago, IL).

Gregory, P. (1986), The Myth of Market Failure: Employment and the Labor Market in Mexico (Johns Hopkins University Press, Baltimore, MD).

Grey, J.S. (1998), "Divorce-law changes, household bargaining, and married women's labor supply", American Economic Review 88(3):628–642.

Griliches, Z. (1977), "Estimating the returns to schooling", Econometrica 45:1–22.

Gronau, R. (1988), "Consumption, technology and intrafamily distribution of resources", Journal of Political Economy 96:1183–1205.

Grossbard-Shechtman, S. (1993), On the Economics of Marriage (Westview Press, Boulder, CO).

Guyer, J. (1980), "Food, cocoa, and the division of labour by sex in two west African societies", Comparative Studies in Society and History 22:355–373.

Haddad, L., and J. Hoddinott (1994), "Women's income and boy–girl anthropometric status in Côte d'Ivoire", World Development 22:545–553.

Haddad, L., J. Hoddinott and H. Alderman, eds. (1997), Intrahousehold Resource Allocation in Developing Countries (Johns Hopkins University Press, Baltimore, MD).

Haddad, L.J., and R. Kanbur (1990), "How serious is the neglect of intrahousehold inequality?", Economic Journal 100:866–881.

Harriss, B. (1990), "Anti-female discrimination in nutrient sharing", Economic and Political Weekly 30 (January):179.

Haveman, R., and B. Wolfe (1984), "Education and well being: The role of nonmarket effects", Journal of Human Resources 19:377–407.

Haveman, R.H., and B.L. Wolfe (1995), "The determinants of children's attainments", Journal of Economic Literature 33:1829–1878.

Hayashi, F. (1995), "Is the Japanese extended family altruistically linked?", Journal of Political Economy 103(3):661–674.

Heady, E.O., and J.L. Dillon (1961), Agricultural Production Functions (Iowa State University Press, Ames, IA).

Heckman, J.J. (1971), "Three essays on the supply of labor and the demand for goods", unpublished Ph.D. Dissertation (Princeton University).

Heckman, J.J. (1979), "Sample selection bias as a specification error", Econometrica 47:153–161.

Heller, P., and W. Drake (1979), "Malnutrition, child morbidity, and the family decision process", Journal of Development Economics 6:203–235.

Higgin, P., and H. Alderman (1997), "Labor and women's nutrition: The impact of work effort and fertility on nutritional status in Ghana", Journal of Human Resources 32(3):577–595.

Higgins, M., and J. Williamson (1997), "Age structure dynamics in Asia and dependence on foreign capital", Population Development Review 23:261–293.

Hill, P. (1963), The Migrant Cocoa Farmer of Southern Ghana (Cambridge University Press, Cambridge, UK).

Hoddinott, J., and L. Haddad (1995), "Does female income share influence household expenditure", Oxford Bulletin of Economics and Statistics 57:77–96.

Holmes, J. (1997), "Measuring the determinants of school completion in Pakistan: Analysis of censoring and selection", processed (Economic Growth Center, Yale University, New Haven, CT).

Horney, M.J., and M.B. McElroy (1988), "The household allocation problem: Empirical results from a bargaining model", in: T.P. Schultz, ed., Research in Population Economics, Vol. 6 (JAI Press, Greenwich, CT).

Huffman, W.E. (1974), "Decision making "The role of education", American Journal of Agricultural Economics 56(1):85–97.

Huffman, W.E. (1976), "The value of the productive time of farm wives", American Journal of Agricultural Economics 58:836–841.

Huffman, W.E. (1980), "Farm and off-farm work decisions: The role of human capital", Review of Economics and Statistics 62:14–23.

Huffman, W. (2000), "Human capital: Education and agriculture", in: B. Gardner and G. Rausser, eds., Handbook of Agricultural Economics (Elsevier Science, Amsterdam).

Huffman, W.E., and M.D. Lange (1989), "Off-farm work decisions of husbands and wives", Review of Economics and Statistics 71:471–480.

Jacoby, H. (1992), "Productivity of men and women and the sexual division of labor in peasant agriculture in the Peruvian Sierra", Journal of Development Economics 37:265–287.

Jacoby, H. (1994), "Borrowing constraints and progress through school: Evidence from Peru", Review of Economics and Statistics 76:145–158.

Jacoby, H. (1995), "The economics of polygamy in SubSaharan Africa: Female productivity and the demand for wives", Journal of Political Economy 103:938–971.

Jacoby, H. (1997), "Is there an intrahousehold 'Flypaper Effect'?", International Food Policy Research Institute Discussion Paper No. 31 (Washington, DC).

Jacoby, H., and E. Skoufias (1992), "Risk, seasonality, and school attendance: Evidence from rural India", Rochester Center for Economic Research, Working Paper No. 328 (University of Rochester). Review of Econ. Studies, 64:311–335.

Jamison, D.T., and L.I. Lau (1982), Farmer Education and Farm Efficiency (Johns Hopkins University Press, Baltimore, MD).

Jamison, D., and P. Moock (1984), "Farmer education and farm efficiency in Nepal", World Development 12:67–86.

Jolliffe, D. (1997), "Whose education matters in the determination of household income", International Food Policy Research Institute Discussion Paper No. 39 (Washington, DC).

Jones, C.N. (1983), "The mobilization of women's labor for cash crop production", American Journal of Agricultural Economics 65:149–154.

Jones, C.N. (1986), "Intra-household bargaining in response to the introduction of New Crops", in: J.L. Moock, ed., Understanding Africa's Rural Households and Farming Systems (Westview Press, Boulder, CO).

Kanbur, R., M. Keon and M. Thomala (1995), "Labor supply and targeting in poverty programs", in: D. van de Walle and K. Nead, eds., Public Spending and the Poor (Johns Hopkins University Press, Baltimore).

Kennedy, E.T., and B. Cogill (1986), "Income and nutritional effects of the commercialization of agriculture: The case of Kenya", Mimeo (International Food Policy Research Institute, Washington, DC).

Kennedy, E., and P. Peters (1992), "Household food security and child nutrition", World Development 20:1077–1085.

Khandker, S.R. (1987), "Labor market participation of married women in Bangladesh", Review of Economics and Statistics 69:536–541.

Khandker, S.R. (1988), "Determinants of women's time allocation in rural Bangladesh", Economic Development and Cultural Change 37:111–126.

Killingsworth, M. (1983), Labor Supply (Cambridge University Press, Cambridge).

Kimhi, A. (1994), "Quasi maximum likelihood estimation of multinomial probit models: Farm couple's labor participation", American Journal of Agricultural Economics 76:828–835.

Kimhi, A., and M.-J. Lee (1996), "Off-farm work decision of farm couples: Estimating structural simultaneous equations with ordered categorical dependent variables", American Journal of Agricultural Economics 78:687–695.

King, E.M., and M.A. Hill, eds. (1993), Women's Education in Developing Countries (Oxford University Press, New York, NY).

King, E.M., J.R. Peterson, S.M. Adioetomo, L.J. Domingo and S.H. Syed (1986), Change in the Status of Women Across Generations in Asia (The Rand Corporation, Santa Monica, CA).

Klasen, S. (1998), "Marriage, bargaining and intrahousehold resource allocation: Excess female mortality among adults during early German development, 1740–1860", Journal of Economic History 58:432–467.

Knaul, F. (1998), "Linking health, nutrition and wages" (ILO, Geneva, Switzerland, and CIDE, Mexico City).

Kniesner, T.J., M.B. McElroy and S.P. Wilcox (1987), "Family structure, race, and the hazards of young women in poverty", Working Paper No. 86-9 (University of North Carolina, Chapel Hill, NC).

Knodel, J., A. Chamrathrithirong and N. Debavalya (1987), Thailand's Reproductive Revolution (University of Wisconsin Press, Madison, WI).

Kochar, A. (1995), "Explaining household vulnerability to idiosyncratic income shocks", American Economic Review, 85:901–918.

Kochar, A. (1998), "Parental benefits from intergenerational co-residence: Empirical evidence from rural Pakistan", presented at NEUDC Conference, Economic Growth Center (Yale University, New Haven, CT).

Kooreman, P. (1998), "The labeling effect of a child benefit system", processed (University of Groningen, Netherlands).

Kosters, M. (1966), Income and Substitution Effects in a Family Labor Supply Model (The Rand Corporation, Santa Monica, CA).

Kuznets, S. (1971), Economic Growth of Nations (Harvard University Press, Cambridge, MA).

Lam, D. (1988), "Assortative mating with household public goods", Journal of Human Resources 23:462–487.

Lam, D., and R.F. Schoeni (1993), "Effects of family background on earnings and returns to schooling", Journal of Political Economy 101:710–740.

Lanzona, L.A. (1996), "Intergenerational educational mobility in rural Philippines" (Economic Growth Center, Yale University, New Haven, CT).

Lanzona, L.A. (1998), "Migration, self selection, and earnings in the Philippine rural communities", Journal of Development Economics, 56:27–50.

Laufer, L. (1985), "The substitution between male and female labor in rural Indian agricultural production", Discussion Paper 472 (Economic Growth Center, Yale University, New Haven, CT).

Lavy, V. (1996), "School supply constraints and children's educational outcomes in rural Ghana", Journal of Development Economics 51:291–314.

Layard, R., and J. Mincer, eds. (1985), "Trends in women's work, education, and family building", Journal of Labor Economics 3:1 pt. 2.

Lilja, N., J.H. Sanders, C.A. Durham, H. Groote and I. Dembele (1996), "Factors influencing the payments to women in Malian agriculture", American Journal of Agricultural Economics 78:1340–1345.

Lloyd, C.B., and A.K. Blanc (1995), "Children's schooling in SubSaharan Africa: Role of fathers, mothers, and others", processed (Population Council, New York, NY).

Lucas, R.E.B., and O. Stark (1985), "Motivations to remit evidence form Botswana", Journal of Political Economy, 93:901–918.

Lundberg, S. (1988), "Labor supply of husbands and wives: A simultaneous equation approach", Review of Economics and Statistics 70:2.

Lundberg, S., and R. Pollak (1993), "Separate spheres bargaining and the marriage market", Journal of Political Economy 101(6):988–1010.

Lundberg, S.J., R.A. Pollak and T.J. Wales (1997), "Do husbands and wives pool their resources?", Journal of Human Resources 22(2):463–480.

Malathy, R. (1993), "Women's choice of work and fertility in urban Tamil Nadu, India", Economic Growth Center Discussion Paper No. 695 (Yale University, New Haven, CT).

Malthus, T.P. (1798), An Essay on the Principle of Population and a Summary View of the Principle of Population (reprint 1970, Penguin, Baltimore, MD).

Maluccio, J. (1997), "Essays on development: Labor markets in rural Philippines", Ph.D. Dissertation (Yale University, New Haven, CT).

Manser, M., and M. Brown (1980), "Marriage and household decisionmaking: A bargaining analysis", International Economic Review 21:31–44.

Martorell, R., J. Leslie and P. Moock (1984), "Characteristics and determinants of child nutritional status in Nepal", American Journal of Clinical Nutrition 39:74–86.

McElroy, M.B. (1990), "The empirical content of Nash-bargained household behavior", Journal of Human Resources 25:559–583.

McElroy, M.B., and M.J. Horney (1981), "Nash bargained household decisions", International Economic Review 22:333–350.

McGuire, J.S., and B.M. Popkin (1990), "Helping women improve nutrition in the developing world", World Bank Technical Paper 114 (World Bank, Washington, DC).

Meinzen-Dick, R., L.R. Brown, H.S. Feldstein and A.R. Quisumbing (1997), "Gender, property rights, and natural resources", International Food Policy Research Institute Working Paper No. 29 (Washington, DC).

Mensch, B., H. Lentzner and S. Preston (1985), Socioeconomic Differentials in Child Mortality in Developing Countries (United Nations, New York, NY).

Michael, R.T. (1982), "Measuring nonmonetary benefits of education", in: W.W. McMahon and T.G. Geske, eds., Financing Education (University of Illinois Press, Urbana, IL).

Miller, B.D. (1981), The Endangered Sex: Neglect of Female Children in Rural North India (Cornell University Press, Ithaca, NY).

Miller, B.D. (1997), "Social class gender and intrahousehold food allocations in children in South Asia", Social Science and Medicine 44(11):1685–1695.

Miller, B.D. (1998), "Selective abortion of millions of females in Asian populations", in: A. Basu, ed., Abortion in a Changing World (New York, Oxford University Press).

Mincer, J. (1963), "Market prices, opportunity costs and income effects", in: C. Christ et al., eds., Measurement in Economics (Stanford University Press, Stanford, CA).

Mincer, J. (1974), Schooling Experience and Earnings (Columbia University Press, New York, NY).

Mishra, A.K., and B.K. Goodwin (1997), "Farm income variability and the supply of off-farm labor", American Journal of Agricultural Economics 79(3):880–887.

Mohan, R. (1986), Work Wages and Welfare in a Developing Metropolis (Oxford University Press, New York, NY).

Montgomery, M.R., and D.B. Sulak (1989), "Female first marriage in East and Southeast Asia", Journal of Development Economics 30:225–240.

Moock, P.R. (1976), "The efficiency of women as farm managers: Kenya", American Journal of Agricultural Economics (December) 831–835.

Mukhopadhyay, S. (1994), "Adapting household behavior to agricultural technology in West Bengal, India", Economic Development and Cultural Change 43:91–115.

Mundlak, Y., and I. Hoch (1965), "Consequences of alternative specifications in estimation of Cobb–Douglas production functions", Econometrica 33(4):814–828.

Murdock, G.P., and C. Provost (1973), "Factors in the division of labor by sex: A cross cultural analysis", Ethnology 12:203–225.

Murray, C. (1984), Losing Ground (Basic Books, New York).

Mwabu, G., and T.P. Schultz (1996), "Education returns across quantiles of the wage function: Alternative explanations for returns to education by race in South Africa", American Economic Review 86:335–339.

NaRanong, V. (1998), "Gender, credit constraints, and education in rural Thailand", Economic Growth Center Discussion Paper (Yale University, New Haven, CT).

Nash, J.F. (1953), "Two person cooperative games", Econometrica 21:128–140.

National Research Council (1986), Population Growth and Economic Development: Policy Questions (National Academy Press, Washington, DC).

Nerlove, M., and T.P. Schultz (1970), Love and Life Between the Censuses, RM-6322-AID (The Rand Corporation, Santa Monica, CA).

Newman, J.L., and P. Gertler (1994), "Family productivity, labor supply, and welfare in a low income country", Journal of Human Resources 29(4):989–1026.

Newman, J., L. Rawling and P. Gertler (1994), "Using randomized control designs in evaluating social sector programs in developing countries", World Bank Research Observer 9:181–201.

Palmer, J.L., T. Smeeding and B.B. Torrey (1988), The Vulnerable (Urban Institute Press, Washington, DC).

Paxson, C. (1992), "Using weather variability to estimate the response of savings to transitory income in Thailand", American Economic Review 82:15–33.

Peters, H.E. (1986), "Marriage and divorce: Informational constraints and private contracting", American Economic Review 76:437–454.

Pitt, M.M., and S.R. Khandker (1998), "The impact of group-based credit programs on poor households in Bangladesh: Does the gender of participants matter", Journal of Political Economy 106(5):958–996.

Pitt, M., and M. Rosenzweig (1986), "Agricultural prices, food consumption, and the health and productivity of Indonesian farmers", in: I. Singh, L. Squire and J. Strauss, eds., Agricultural Household Models (Johns Hopkins University Press, Baltimore, MD).

Pitt, M., and M. Rosenzweig (1990), "Estimating the intrahousehold incidence of illness: Child health and gender inequality in the allocation of time", International Economic Review 31(4):969–989.

Pitt, M., M.R. Rosenzweig and M.D.N. Hassan (1990), "Productivity, health, and inequality in the intrahousehold distribution of food", American Economic Review 80:1139–1156.

Popkin, B.M. (1980), "Time allocation of the mother and child nutrition", Ecology of Food and Nutrition 9:1–14.

Preston, S., and J.A. Weed (1976), "Causes of death responsible for international and intertemporal variation in sex mortality differentials", World Health Statistics Report.

Quisumbing, A.R. (1994), "Intergenerational transfers in Philippine rice villages", Journal of Development Economics 43:167–195.

Quisumbing, A.R. (1995), "The extended family and intrahousehold allocation", Food Consumption and Nutrition Division, Discussion Paper No. 3 (International Food Policy Research Institute, Washington, DC).

Quisumbing, A.R. (1996a), "Modeling household behavior in developing countries", American Journal of Agricultural Economics 78:1346–1348.

Quisumbing, A.R. (1996b), "Male–female differences in agricultural productivity", World Development 24:1579–1595.

Quisumbing, A.R. (1997), "Better rich, or better there? Grandparent wealth, coresidence and intrahousehold allocation", International Food Policy Research Institute Discussion Paper No. 23 (Washington, DC).

Ram, R., and T.W. Schultz (1979), "Life span health, savings and productivity", Economic Development and Cultural Change 27:399–421.

Rand and Demographic Institute (1996), 1993 Indonesian Family Life Survey, DRU-1195/3-NICHD/AID (Rand, Santa Monica, CA).

Rao, V. (1993), "The rising price of husbands", Journal of Political Economy 101:666–677.

Ribero, R. (1999), "Changing marriage pattern in Colombia", Manuscript (Economic Growth Center, Yale University, New Haven, CT).

Ribero, R., and J. Nunez (1998), "Productivity of household investment in health: The case of Colombia", Draft (Economic Growth Center, Yale University, New Haven, CT).

Roe, T., and T. Graham-Tomasi (1986), "Yield risk in a dynamic model of the agricultural household", in: I. Singh, L. Squire, and J. Strauss, eds., Agricultural Household Models (John Hopkins University Press).

Rose, E. (1995), "Consumption smoothing and excess female mortality in rural India", Economic Research Discussion Paper 95-03 (Seattle, WA). Review of Econ. and Stat. 81:41–49.

Rose, P. (1995), "Female education and adjustment programs", World Development 23:1547–1560.

Rosenhouse, S. (1988), "Identifying the poor: Is headship a useful concept?", Draft (October) (Population Council, New York).

Rosenzweig, M.R. (1988), "Risk, implicit contracts and the family in rural areas of low income countries", Economic Journal 98:1148–1170.

Rosenzweig, M.R. (1995), "Women, insurance capital, and economic development in rural India", in: T.P. Schultz, ed., Investment in Women's Human Capital (University of Chicago Press, Chicago).

Rosenzweig, M.R., and R.E. Evenson (1977), "Fertility, schooling and economic contribution of children in rural India", Econometrica 45:1065–1079.

Rosenzweig, M.R., and T.P. Schultz (1982a), "Child mortality and fertility in Colombia", Health Policy and Education 2:305–348.

Rosenzweig, M.R., and T.P. Schultz (1982b), "Market opportunities, genetic endowments and the intrafamily distribution of resources", American Economic Review 72:803–815.

Rosenzweig, M.R., and T.P. Schultz (1983), "Estimating a household production function: Heterogeneity and the demand for health inputs", Journal of Political Economy 91:723–746.

Rosenzweig, M.R., and T.P. Schultz (1985), "The supply and demand of births, and their life-cycle consequences", American Economic Review 75:992–1015.

Rosenzweig, M.R., and T.P. Schultz (1989), "Schooling, information, and nonmarket activity", International Economic Review 30:457–477.

Rosenzweig, M., and O. Stark (1989), "Consumption smoothing, migration and marriage: Evidence from rural India", Journal of Political Economy 97:905–926.

Sahn, D.E., and H. Alderman (1996), "The effect of food subsidies on labor supply in Sri Lanka", Economic Development and Cultural Change 45(1):125–146.

Samuelson, P.A. (1947), Foundations of Economic Analysis (Harvard University Press, Cambridge, MA).

Samuelson, P.A. (1956), "Social indifference curves", Quarterly Journal of Economics 70:1–22.

Schultz, T.P. (1980), "Interpretation of relations among mortality, economics of the household, and the health environment", in: Socioeconomic Determinants and Consequences of Mortality Differentials (WHO, Geneva).

Schultz, T.P. (1981), Economics of Population (Addison-Wesley, Reading, MA).

Schultz, T.P. (1982), "Lifetime migration within educational strata in Venezuela", Economic Development and Cultural Change 30:559–593.

Schultz, T.P. (1984), "Studying the impact of household economics and community variables on child mortality", Population and Development Review 10 (Suppl.):215–235.

Schultz, T.P. (1986), "Value and allocation of time in high income countries: Implications for fertility", in: Below Replacement Fertility in Industrial Societies (Supplement: Population and Development Review), Vol. 12, 87–107.

Schultz, T.P. (1987), "School expenditures and enrollments, 1960–1980", in: D.G. Johnson and R. Lee, eds., National Academy of Sciences background papers, Population Growth and Economic Development (University of Wisconsin Press, Madison, WI).

Schultz, T.P. (1988), "Educational investment and returns", in: H. Chenery and T.N. Srinivasan, eds., Handbook of Development Economics, Vol. 1 (North Holland, Amsterdam).

Schultz, T.P. (1990a), "Women's changing participation in the labor force", Economic Development and Cultural Change 38:451–488.

Schultz, T.P. (1990b), "Testing the neoclassical model of family labor supply and fertility", Journal of Human Resources 25:599–634.

Schultz, T.P. (1993), "Returns to women's education", in: M.A. Hill and E.M. King, eds., Women's Education in Developing Countries (Oxford University Press, New York, NY).

Schultz, T.P. (1994a), "Human capital, family planning and their effects on population growth", American Economic Review 83:255–260.

Schultz, T.P. (1994b), "Marital status and fertility in the United States", Journal of Human Resources 29:637–669.

Schultz, T.P., ed. (1995a), Investment in Women's Human Capital (University of Chicago Press, Chicago, IL).

Schultz, T.P. (1995b), "Human capital and development", in: G.H. Peters et al., eds., Agricultural Competitiveness, 22nd International Conference of Agricultural Economists (Dartmouth, Aldershot, England).

Schultz, T.P. (1996), "Accounting for public expenditures on education: An international panel study", in: Research in Population Economics, Vol. 8 (JAI Press, Greenwich, CT).

Schultz, T.P. (1997), "The demand for children in low income countries", in: M.R. Rosenzweig and O. Stark, eds., Handbook of Population and Family Economics, Vol. 1A (North Holland, Amsterdam).

Schultz, T.P. (1998), "Eroding the economic foundations of marriage and fertility in the United States", Structural Change and Economic Dynamics 9:391–413.

Schultz, T.P. (1999), "Who heads a household and tests of the lifecycle savings hypothesis", Draft (Economic Growth Center, Yale University, New Haven, CT).

Schultz, T.P., and A. Tansel (1997), "Wage and labor supply effects of illness in Côte d'Ivoire and Ghana: Instrumental variable estimates for days disabled", Journal of Development Economics 53:251–286.

Schultz, T.W. (1975), "The value of the ability to deal with disequilibria", Journal of Economic Literature 13:827–846.

Seavy, D. (1987), "Land leasing and labor hiring in rural India: An empirical study of household factor adjustment", Ph.D. Dissertation (Yale University, New Haven, CT).

Sen, A.K. (1976), "Family and food: Sex bias in poverty", in: Resources, Values and Development (Blackwell, Oxford).

Senauer, B., M. Garcia and E. Jacinto (1988), "Determinants of the intrahousehold allocation of food in the rural Philippines", American Journal of Agricultural Economics 70:170–180.

Senauer, B., D. Sahn and H. Alderman (1986), "The effects of the value of time on food consumption patterns in developing countries: Evidence from Sri Lanka", American Journal of Agricultural Economics 68:920–927.

Singh, I., L. Squire and J. Strauss, eds. (1986), Agricultural Household Models: Extensions, Applications and Policy (Johns Hopkins Press, Baltimore, MD).

Sipahimalani, V. (1998), "Demand for education in the rural Indian household", processed (Yale University, New Haven, CT).

Sjaastad, L. (1962), "The costs and returns of human migration", Journal of Political Economy 70:80–92.

Skoufias, E. (1993a), "Labor market opportunities and intrafamily time allocation in rural households in South Asia", Journal of Development Economics 40:277–310.

Skoufias, E. (1993b), "Seasonal labor utilization in agriculture", American Journal of Agricultural Economics 75:20–32.

Skoufias, E. (1996), "Inter-temporal substitution in labor supply", Journal of Development Economics 51:217–237.

Smith, D.P. (1981), "Marriage dissolution and remarriage in Sri Lanka and Thailand", WFS Scientific Reports No. 7 (International Statistical Institute, Voorburg, Netherlands).

Smith, L.C., and J.-P. Chavas (1997), "Commercialization and the balance of women's dual roles in non-income-pooling west African households", American Journal of Agricultural Economics 79:589–594.

Spurr, G. (1983), "Nutritional status and physical work capacity", Yearbook of Physical Anthropometry 26:1–35.

Steckel, R.H., and R. Floud (1997), Health and Welfare During Industrialization (University of Chicago Press, Chicago, IL).

Strauss, J. (1986), "Does better nutrition raise farm productivity?", Journal of Political Economy 94:297–320.

Strauss, J., and K. Beegle (1996), "Intrahousehold allocations: A review of theories, empirical evidence and policy issues", MSU International Development Working Paper No. 62 (Michigan State University, East Lansing).

Strauss, J., P.J. Gertler, O. Rahman and K. Fox (1995), "Gender and life-cycle differentials in the patterns and determinants of adult health", in: T.P. Schultz, ed., Investment in Women's Human Capital (University of Chicago Press, Chicago, IL).

Strauss, J., and D. Thomas (1995), "Human resources: Empirical modeling of household and family decisions", in: J. Behrman and T.N. Srinivasan, eds., Handbook in Development Economics, Vol. 3A (Elsevier, Amsterdam).

Strauss, J., and D. Thomas (1998), "Health, nutrition and economic development", Journal of Economic Literature 36:766–817.

Subbarao, K., and L. Raney (1995), "Social gains from female education: A cross-national study", Economic Development and Cultural Change 44(1):105–128.

Svenberg, P. (1990), "Undernutrition in SubSaharan Africa: Is there a sex-bias?", Journal of Development Studies 26:469–486.

Tansel, A. (1997), "Schooling attainment, parental education, and gender in Côte d'Ivoire and Ghana", Economic Development and Cultural Change 45:825–856.

Thomas, D. (1990), "Intra household resource allocation: an inferential approach", Journal of Human Resources 25:635–664.

Thomas, D. (1994), "Like father, like son; like mother, like daughter", Journal of Human Resources 29:950–989.

Thomas, D., and C.L. Chen (1994), "Income shares and shares of income: Empirical tests of models of household resource allocation", Working Paper 94-08 (The Rand Corporation, Santa Monica, CA).

Thomas, D., and J. Strauss (1997), "Health and wages: Evidence on men and women in urban Brazil", Journal of Econometrics 77:159–186.

Thomas, D., J. Strauss, and M.H. Henriques (1990), "Child survival, height for age and household characteristics", Journal of Development Economics 33:197–234.

Tokle, J.G., and W.E. Huffman (1991), "Local economic conditions and wage labor decisions of farm and rural nonfarm couples", American Journal of Agricultural Economics, 73:652–670.

Townsend, R.M. (1994), "Risk and insurance in village India", Econometrica 62:539–592.

Trovato, F., and N.M. Lulu (1996), "Narrowing sex differentials in life expectancy in the industrialized world: Early 1970s to early 1990s", Social Biology 43:20–37.

Udry, C. (1994), "Risk and insurance in a rural credit market", Review of Economic Studies 61(3):495–526.

Udry, C. (1996), "Gender, agricultural production, and the theory of the household", Journal of Political Economy 104:1010–1046.

United Nations (1982), "Levels and trends in mortality since 1950", Population Studies No. 74 (United Nations, New York, NY).

Unni, J. (1993), "Labor supply decisions of married women in rural India", Economic Growth Center, Discussion Paper No. 691 (Yale University, New Haven CT).

U.S. Department of Health and Human Services (1983), Final Report of the Seattle-Denver Income Maintenance Experiment, Vol. I, Part V (U.S. Government Printing Office, Washington, DC).

Van der Gaag, J., and W.P.M. Vijverberg (1987), "Wage determinants in Côte d'Ivoire", Living Standard Measurement Survey Working Paper No. 33 (The World Bank, Washington, DC).

Verbrugge, L.M. (1985), "Gender and health: An update on hypotheses and evidence", Journal of Health and Social Behavior 26:156–182.

Vijverberg, W.P.M. (1995), "Educational investments and returns for women and men in Côte d'Ivoire", in: T.P. Schultz, ed., Investment in Women's Human Capital (University of Chicago Press, Chicago, IL).

Visaria, P.M. (1971), The Sex Ratio of the Population of India, 1961. Census of India, Vol. 1, Monograph 10 (Office of Registrar General of India, New Delhi).

Von Braun, J., and P. Webb (1989), "The impact of new crop technology on the agricultural division of labor in a West African setting", Economic Development and Cultural Change 37(3):513–534.

Waldron, I. (1986), "What do we know about sex differences in mortality?", Population Bulletin of the United Nations, No. 18 (United Nations, New York, NY).

Waterlow, J.C., ed. (1988), Linear Growth Retardation in Less Developed Countries, Nestle Nutrition Workshop Series, Vol. 14 (Raven Press, New York, NY).

Waterlow, J., R. Buzina, J. Lane, M. Nichman and J. Tanner (1977), "The presentation and use of height and weight data for comparing the nutritional status of groups of children under the age of ten years", Bulletins of the World Health Organization 55:489–498.

Welch, F. (1970), "The economics of education", Journal of Political Economy 78:35–59.

Wolpin, K.I. (1982), "A new test of the permanent income hypothesis: The impact of weather on the income and consumption of farm households in India", International Economic Review 23:583–594.

Woolley, F. (1988), "A noncooperative model of family decision making", Working Paper TIDI/125 (London School of Economics).

Yang, D.T. (1997), "Education in production: Measuring labor quality and management", American Journal of Agricultural Economics 79:764–772.

Youssef, N., and C. Hefler (1983), "Establishing the conditions of women-headed households in the third world", in: M. Buvinic, M.A. Lycette and W.P. McGreevy, eds., Women and Poverty in the Third World (Johns Hopkins University Press, Baltimore, MD).

Zeng, Yi (1989), "Is the Chinese family planning program tightening up?", Population and Development Review 15:233–237.

Zeng, Yi, Tu Ping, GuBaochang, Xu Yi, Li Bhua and Li Yongping (1993), "Causes and implications of the recent increase in the reported sex ratio at birth in China", Population and Development Review 19:283–302.

Chapter 9

HUMAN CAPITAL: MIGRATION AND RURAL POPULATION CHANGE

J. EDWARD TAYLOR and PHILIP L. MARTIN

Department of Agricultural and Resource Economics, University of California, Davis, CA

Contents

Handbook of Agricultural Economics, Volume 1, Edited by B. Gardner and G. Rausser

Abstract

The movement of labor out of agriculture is a universal concomitant of economic modernization and growth. Traditional migration models overlook many potential interactions between migration and development. Given imperfect markets characterizing most migrant-sending areas, migration and remittances can have far-reaching impacts, both positive and negative, on incomes and production in agricultural households. Linkages through product and factor markets transmit impacts of migration from migrant-sending households to others inside and outside the rural economy. Recent theoretical and empirical studies reveal the complexity of migration determinants and impacts in rural economies, and they point to new arenas for policy intervention.

JEL classification: Q12

The migration of labor – geographically out of rural areas and occupationally out of farm jobs – is one of the most pervasive features of agricultural transformations and economic growth. This is true both historically in developed countries (DCs) and currently in less developed countries (LDCs). Among nations, the share of rural population declines sharply as per capita incomes increase (Figure 1), from 70 to 80 percent in countries with the lowest per capita GNPs to less than 15 percent in the highest-income countries. The share of the national workforce in agriculture plunges even more sharply (Figure 2), from 90 percent or higher in low-income countries to less than 10 percent in high-income countries. Developing countries from Mexico to India have experienced dramatic declines in their rural population shares over the past three decades, despite significantly higher rates of natural population growth in rural than in urban areas.

As internal migration redistributes populations and workforces from rural to urban areas, many countries – including those with the world's most dynamic fruit, vegetable, and horticultural crop production – turn to foreign-born migrants, frequently of rural origin, for labor. In the United States, for example, an estimated 69 percent of the 1996 seasonal agricultural service (SAS) workforce was foreign-born [Mines et al. (1997)], and in California, the nation's largest agricultural producer, more than 90 percent of the SAS workforce was foreign-born. The majority (65 percent) of these migrant farmworkers originated from households in rural Mexico.

The world's great migrations out of rural areas are accelerating, making internal and international migration potentially one of the most important development and policy issues of the twenty-first century. The most populous countries also are among the most rural (Figure 1). The greatest migration potential is in China, where 71 percent of the population is rural and an estimated one-third of the rural labor force of 450 million is either unemployed or underemployed. Despite barriers to labor mobility imposed by China's household registration (hukou bu) system, China currently has more migration than anywhere else, with between 50 and 100 million rural-to-urban migrants [Roberts (1997)]. Meanwhile, in high-income countries, farmers, with their reliance on foreign-born migrant workforces, find themselves at odds with an increasingly restrictionist public and policy stance towards immigration.

The determinants of migration and migrants' impacts, both on migrant-sending areas and on the rural communities that receive them, have been the subject of a prolific and growing literature in agricultural and development economics, a centerpiece of public policy debates, and a source of sharpening controversy and anxiety in migrant "host" countries and communities. The determinants of out-migration from rural areas and the impacts of this migration on rural areas are the focus of this chapter.

Section 1 presents a critical synthesis of theories of the determinants of migration out of rural areas, with a focus throughout on the implications of these theories for empirical analysis of migrant labor supply. It starts out with the (mostly implicit) role of migration in classical, two-sector models, in which the rural sector is characterized as having redundant or surplus labor, then presents neoclassical and expected-income models, human-capital models, and the "new economics of labor migration" (NELM). For the most part, economic theories of migration were developed in the context of

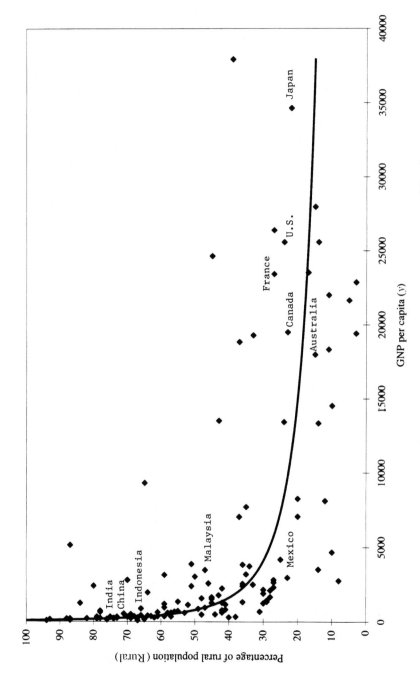

Figure 1. Rural population shares and GNP per capita, 1994. Regression line: Rural $= 395.12y^{-0.31}$ ($R^2 = 0.535$, $N = 127$).

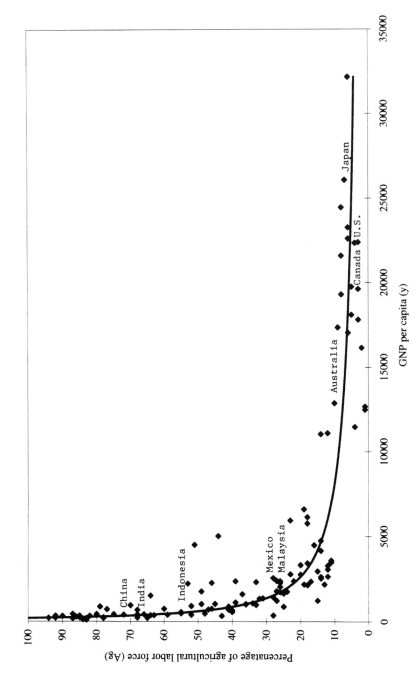

Figure 2. Agricultural labor shares and GNP per capita, 1990. Regression line: $Ag = 2672.9y^{-0.6211}$ ($R^2 = 0.783$, $N = 122$).

developing countries. However, virtually all economic models of rural out-migration and farm labor migration in developed countries are rooted in the migration theories presented here.

Section 2 presents modeling techniques that have been used to test the theories presented above. Section 3 reviews key findings of empirical farm labor migration research and reassesses migration theories based on these findings.

A significant theoretical and empirical literature addresses welfare effects of migration on migrant-sending economies. A nascent literature deals with impacts of migration on rural, migrant-receiving areas, e.g., the many small rural communities throughout the United States that are being transformed by migrants working in agriculture or agricultural processing industries. There is also fledgling research on impacts of rural-to-rural migration within LDCs, with a focus on the environment. Section 4 assesses this rural migration-impacts research, linking it to the migration models and findings presented in Sections 1 through 3. The impacts of migration are intimately tied to migration determinants, including the incentives to migrate and the selectivity of migration.

Most countries do not explicitly attempt to control rural out-migration (China is the significant exception). However, they do hold immigration policy levers, and there are some policy efforts to influence internal migration indirectly, e.g., via interventions in labor markets or by altering the availability of public services for migrants. High-income countries, especially the United States, have a long history of implementing policies aimed at restricting the inflow of foreign-born (mostly unauthorized) farmworkers without creating labor shortages on farms. These policies include fines for employers who knowingly hire unauthorized immigrants, farmworker legalization, restriction of public services to immigrants and their families, and guest worker programs. In many cases, these immigration policy changes have had unintended consequences for farmers and rural communities. Section 5 concludes with a discussion of policy implications of migration research. In particular, what economic justifications, if any, are there for designing policies to influence the supply or demand of migrant labor?

1. Theories of rural out-migration

1.1. The classical two-sector model

Social scientists have studied the movement of labor out of rural areas for a long time. Migration is addressed by Adam Smith in *The Wealth of Nations* (1776). In industrial revolution England, Ravenstein (1885) and Redford (1926) argued that a combination of Malthusian forces, land scarcity, and enclosure – that is, "supply push" variables – drove rural-to-urban migration. Others pointed to "demand-pull" variables, including the rapid development of manufacturing that fed population growth and urban poverty in Manchester during the early nineteenth century [e.g., Engels (1845)]. Johnson (1948) recognized rural out-migration as a solution to surplus labor and low incomes in agriculture.

The modern economics literature on migration often is traced to Lewis' (1954) seminal work on economic development with unlimited supplies of labor. Lewis does not propose an explicit migration model. His contribution is to explain the mechanisms by which an unlimited supply of labor in traditional sectors of less developed countries (LDCs) might be absorbed through capital accumulation and savings in an expanding modern sector. Nevertheless, migration plays an important role in the Lewis model. Ranis and Fei's (1961) formalization and extension of the Lewis model was the precursor to a generation of neoclassical and "neo-neoclassical" two-sector models which dominated the migration literature through the 1980s. Although originally designed to examine the reallocation of labor between rural and urban areas, it is potentially applicable to international migration. A Lewis-type model may offer some insights into rural out-migrations associated with very high wage elasticities, as appears to be the case for internal migration in some less developed countries (LDCs) and possibly also for foreign migrant-labor supply to some developed countries (e.g., Mexican migration to fill US agricultural jobs) – that is, migration that is largely demand-driven.[1]

The Lewis dual economy consists of a "capitalist" sector and a "noncapitalist" sector. Although Lewis did not intend this, in practice the capitalist sector has generally become identified with the urban economy and the noncapitalist sector with agriculture or the rural economy. The capitalist sector hires labor and sells output for a profit, while the noncapitalist (or subsistence) sector does not use reproducible capital and does not hire labor for a profit. Initially, labor is concentrated in the noncapitalist sector. As the capitalist sector expands, it draws labor from the noncapitalist sector. If the capitalist economy is concentrated in the urban economy, labor transfer implies geographic movement, i.e., rural-to-urban migration.

In theory, migration implies an opportunity cost for the rural economy, which loses the product of the individuals who migrate. However, the centerpiece of the Lewis model (and essence of the classical approach) is the assumption that labor is available to the industrial sector in unlimited quantities at a fixed real wage, measured in agricultural goods. In the limiting case, this implies that there is surplus or redundant labor in rural areas, such that the marginal product of rural labor is zero, and labor thus may be withdrawn from rural areas and employed in the urban sector without sacrificing any loss in agricultural output. That is, the opportunity cost or "shadow price" of rural labor to fill urban jobs is zero. (Various institutional arrangements ensure that consumption by members of the farm workforce is roughly equal to the average product of farm output, even if their marginal product is below this average.) Lewis argued that at least a quarter of the agricultural population in India was "surplus to requirements."

More generally, the supply of labor from the subsistence sector is unlimited if the supply of labor is infinitely elastic at the ruling capitalist-sector wage. A zero marginal

---

[1]   In the classical model, migration is demand-driven in the sense that the supply of farm labor to nonfarm jobs is perfectly elastic (i.e., the supply curve is horizontal). Therefore, the movement of workers from farm to nonfarm jobs results solely from outward shifts in the nonfarm labor-demand curve.

product of labor in the noncapitalist sector is not a precondition for this. However, in the Lewis model, earnings at the prevailing capitalist-sector wage must exceed the noncapitalist-sector earnings of individuals willing to migrate, i.e., the average product of labor in the traditional sector. Moreover, any tendency for earnings per head to rise in the noncapitalist sector must be offset by increases in the labor force there (e.g., through population growth, female labor-force participation, or immigration).

A key testable hypothesis of the Lewis model is that rural out-migration is not accompanied by a decrease in agricultural production nor by a rise in either rural or urban wages. The Lewis assumption of general surplus labor in LDCs has been questioned, especially by Schultz (1964). [Also see Jorgenson (1967), and the exchange between Robinson (1969), and Gardner (1970)].

1.2. Neoclassical two-sector models

In Ranis and Fei's (1961) interpretation of the Lewis model, the perfectly elastic labor supply to the capitalist sector ends once the redundant labor in the rural sector disappears and a relative shortage of agricultural goods emerges, turning the terms of trade against the modern or capitalist sector. Through migration, the marginal value products of labor are equated between the two sectors; the Lewis classical world ends and the analysis becomes neoclassical. The dual economies merge into a single economy in which wages are equalized across space. Rural-to-urban migration exerts upward pressure on wages and on the marginal value product of labor in rural areas, while putting downward pressure on urban wages, assuming that wages adjust to ensure that both rural and urban labor markets clear. Empirically, in addition to the convergence of wages across sectors, one should observe an inverse relationship between rural out-migration and farm wages, on one hand, and agricultural production, on the other (other things (including technology) being equal). In addition, assuming full employment of labor in both rural and urban sectors and minimal transactions costs, inter-sectoral wage differentials should be the primary factors driving rural out-migration [Jorgenson (1967), Ranis and Fei (1961)].

Internal and international migration are modeled according to this perfect-markets neoclassical specification in virtually all computable general equilibrium models, both national [e.g., Adelman and Taylor (1991), Levy and Wijnberger (1992)] and international [e.g., the NAFTA models of Robinson et al. (1991)]. In contrast, most microeconomic models of rural out-migration are grounded on Todaro's seminal work, which incorporates labor-market imperfections, including urban unemployment, into a migration model (see the following section).

Despite its popularity for some modeling purposes, wage-driven neoclassical analysis of rural out-migration has largely been discredited for a number of reasons. These reasons include the empirical observation that urban formal-sector wages are "sticky", and migration tends to persist and even accelerate in the face of high and rising urban unemployment in LDCs [Todaro (1969, 1980)]; documented persistent differences in wage rates for comparable agricultural tasks across geographical areas [e.g., Rosenzweig (1978)]; and unskilled urban manufacturing wage rates that have remained 1.5 to

2 times agricultural wages over long periods of time [Squire (1981)], despite significant rural-to-urban migration. Such differences in the returns to homogeneous labor across sectors are not consistent with the predictions of neoclassical migration models. They are evidence of market imperfections – although, significantly (see the new economics of labor migration, below), not necessarily of imperfections in labor markets.

The continuation of migration despite high and increasing urban unemployment is the primary motivation for Todaro's (1969) expected income model of migration in the presence of labor-market imperfections, and imperfections in other markets – including markets for capital and risk – are a focus of the new economics of labor migration.

1.3. The Todaro model

Todaro (1969) proposed a modification of the neoclassical migration model in which each potential rural-to-urban migrant decides whether or not to move to the city based on an expected-income maximization objective. Expected urban income at a given locale is the product of the wage (the sole determinant of migration in the neoclassical models described above), and the probability that a prospective migrant will succeed in obtaining an urban job. Expected rural income is calculated analogously. Individuals are assumed to migrate if their discounted future stream of urban-rural expected income differentials exceeds migration costs; i.e., if

$$\Delta = \int_0^T e^{\delta t} \left[p_u(t) y_u - y_r(t) \right] \mathrm{d}t - c \tag{1}$$

is positive, where $p_u(t)$ is the probability of urban employment at time t, y_u denotes urban earnings given employment, $y_r(t)$ represents expected rural earnings at time t, c is migration costs, and δ is the discount rate. Otherwise, they remain in the rural labor market. Note that this is not a model of risk and uncertainty; in the Todaro specification, individuals are assumed to be risk-neutral. For example, a mean-preserving increase in the variability of urban income leaves the migration propensity unchanged. As a result, utility maximization is tantamount to expected income maximization. The perfect-markets or wage-driven neoclassical model may be viewed as a special case of the Todaro model, in which the probability of employment at migrant destination (and origin) equals one.

The power of the Todaro model is its ability to explain the continuation and, frequently, acceleration of rural-to-urban migration in the face of high and rising urban unemployment. Its salient departure from perfect-markets neoclassical models is that it does not assume the existence of full employment; hence, a higher wage or income in the urban sector than in the rural sector is not a sufficient, or even necessary, condition for migration. In an environment of high unemployment, this wage or income is conditional upon the migrant's success at securing a job. A high (e.g., institutionally set) urban wage coupled with a low probability of obtaining a job at that wage may result in an expected wage that is lower in urban than in rural areas where the conditional wage is low but the likelihood of employment is high. Conversely, high rural unemployment will make a given expected urban wage more conducive to promoting migration. Increases in urban employment (e.g., resulting from government-sponsored jobs programs) may increase urban unemployment rates through migration, and a rise in the urban minimum wage may reduce output in both the urban and rural sectors while increasing urban unemployment [Harris and Todaro (1970)].

Because this is characterized as a dynamic problem, migrants may perceive a low probability of urban employment initially [and queue for urban jobs; see Fields (1975)] but anticipate an increase in this probability over time, e.g., as they broaden their urban contacts. Contacts with family or friends in urban areas prior to migration (i.e., migration networks) may stimulate migration by shortening – or perhaps eliminating – the initial queuing period.

Although originally cast in the context of rural-to-urban migration, the Todaro model is also applicable to international migration [e.g., see Todaro and Maruszko (1987)].

Despite what has proven to be a seminal contribution to understanding determinants and impacts of rural out-migration, the Todaro model makes a number of restrictive assumptions. Some of these have been a focus of considerable subsequent research. They include:
(1) the assumption that urban job allocation follows a simple lottery mechanism;
(2) neglect of the competitive informal sector, which acts as a sponge for surplus labor;
(3) the assumption of a rigid urban-sector wage;
(4) the (perhaps unreasonable) time horizons and discount rates required to equate the present values of expected urban and rural incomes [e.g., see Cole and Sanders (1985, p. 485)]; and
(5) the omission of influences, besides expected income, that shape potential migrants' decisions and also their potential impacts on rural economies [Williamson (1988)].
It has been observed that, in LDCs, while nominal urban wages are typically 50 to 100 percent higher than nominal rural agricultural wages, urban unemployment rates typically are less than 10 percent. Thus, the rate of urban unemployment does not appear to reconcile the urban-rural wage differential; i.e., migration does not appear to equilibrate expected incomes across sectors [Rosenzweig (1988)]. In addition to overstating urban unemployment rates, the Todaro model almost certainly overstates the costs of migration for rural, migrant-sending areas. Neither this nor more traditional neoclassical migration models can explain temporary migration or the substantial flow of income remittances from migrants to their places of origin.

Assumption (5) is arguably the most restrictive and far-reaching of the assumptions and the one upon which much of the most recent research on migration and rural population has focused. It is the focus of the most recent wave of literature on migration determinants and impacts, which has become known as the new economics of labor migration (see below).

1.4. Human capital theory and migration

The essentially macro perspective embodied in both the classical and neoclassical migration models presented earlier leaves unanswered a fundamental question: Why do some individuals migrate while others do not? More critical from a rural welfare point of view, what distinguishes the labor "lost" to migration from that which remains in the rural sector? Differences in wage rates and in the returns to migration may be explained largely by differences in skill-related attributes across workers, including experience and schooling.

As presented above, the classical and neoclassical migration models offer few insights into the question of migrant selectivity. In a Lewis world, when capital accumulation in the modern sector shifts the marginal value product curve outward, increasing the quantity of labor demanded at the prevailing urban wage, some reserve labor from rural areas is assumed to migrate to the modern sector and fill this excess demand. However, we do not know who these migrants are, or what distinguishes them from those who do not migrate. In the demand-driven, classical world of infinite labor supply, urban jobs must be rationed among redundant members of the rural population according to some rule that is left unclear in the Lewis model. Migrants presumably are individuals possessing specific characteristics on the basis of which modern-sector jobs are rationed out. For example, if urban construction jobs in Mexico City or farm jobs in California hire only agile, strong young men, only this demographic group will respond to new labor demands by migrating. Nevertheless, the supply of labor, even for this specific group, is assumed to be infinite at the prevailing wage in a Lewis-type model. In this way, a Lewis demand-driven migration model almost invariably begs the question of migrant selectivity.

The same problem potentially arises in an aggregate, wage-driven neoclassical model and in the Todaro expected-income model. Presumably, the individuals who migrate are those for whom the urban-rural wage (or expected earnings) differential is largest and/or for whom migration costs are lowest.

A well-developed literature addresses the question of migrant selectivity in the neoclassical and Todaro worlds by merging migration theories with human capital theory, arising from the early work of Mincer (1974), Becker (1975), and others. Human capital models of migration represent an effort to provide the migration theories presented above with a micro grounding, permitting tests of a far richer set of migration determinants and impacts.

In the perfect-markets neoclassical version of the human-capital migration model [e.g., Sjaastad (1962)], wages at prospective migrant origins and destinations are assumed to be a function of individuals' skills affecting their productivity in the two sectors. In a Todaro model, human capital characteristics of individuals may influence both their wages and their likelihood of obtaining a job once they migrate. In both types of model, characteristics of individuals may also affect migration costs (and the rate at which future urban-rural earnings differentials are discounted).

The human capital view of migration has the key implication that the types of individuals selected into migration are those for whom, over time, the discounted income (or expected-income) differential between migration and nonmigration is greatest and/or migration costs are lowest. As Todaro (1980) pointed out:

"Migrants typically do not represent a random sample of the overall population. On the contrary, they tend to be disproportionately young, better educated, less risk-averse, and more achievement oriented and to have better personal contacts in destination areas than the general population in the region of out-migration."

Human capital migration theory produces a number of testable hypotheses. First, because this is a dynamic model, the young should be more mobile than the old, inasmuch as they stand to reap returns from migration over a longer period of time. Second, migration between locales should be negatively related to migration costs. This has been interpreted by many researchers as implying a negative association between migration flows and distance. However, considerations besides distance (especially access to information) may make distance less of a deterrent for some individuals (e.g., better-educated individuals or those with "migration networks", contacts with family or friends at prospective migrant destinations). Third, as Rosenzweig (1988) points out, neutral productivity growth in an economy – e.g., equal rates of growth in the rural and urban sectors – will increase migration from low-income (e.g., rural) to high-income (e.g., urban) sectors or areas. Fourth, specific human capital variables that yield a higher return in region A than in region B should be positively associated with migration from B to A. In addition to these predictions, human capital theory implies that income (or, in the Todaro case, expected income) differentials between rural and urban areas are eliminated by migration over time.

1.5. The new economics of migration

Continuing interactions between migrants and rural households suggest that a joint-household model would be more appropriate than an individual-level model of migration decisions. However, a joint-household model has difficulty explaining why the entire family does not move if expected incomes are higher in the urban sector, why higher-income migrants would remit income to lower-income relatives at the place of origin, or why – as has been found in some national studies – migrant remittances, while positively related to migrant earnings in urban areas, are not negatively related to the pre-transfer income of the rural household of origin. One is also left with the puzzle of why geographically extended families are prevalent in LDCs but less so in high-income countries [Rosenzweig (1988)], and the troubling assumption that households can be characterized by a single utility function and budget constraint.

The fundamental view of the new economics of labor migration is presented in Stark (1991) and Stark and Bloom (1985). Rather than being entirely the domain of individuals, migration decisions are viewed as taking place within a larger context – typically the household, which potentially consists of individuals with diverse preferences and differential access to income and is influenced by its social milieu. The perspective that migration decisions are not taken by isolated actors but by larger units of related people, typically households or families, is a trademark of the NELM. So is the contention that people act collectively not only to maximize income, but also to minimize risks and loosen constraints created by a variety of market imperfections, including missing or incomplete capital, insurance, and labor markets. Finally, the effect of income on utility may not be the same for a given actor across socioeconomic settings, which motivates the relative deprivation theory of migration discussed below.

Stark (1982, 1978) argues that an implicit contractual arrangement exists between migrant and household. An LDC farm household wishing to invest in a new technology or make the transition from familial to commercial production lacks access to both credit and income insurance. By placing a family member in a migrant labor market, such a household can create a new financial intermediary in the form of the migrant. Rural households incur the costs of supporting migrants initially. In turn, once migrants become established in their destination labor market, they provide their households with liquidity (in the form of remittances) and with insurance (because of a low correlation between incomes in migrant labor markets and farm production; indeed, the correlation between remittances and farm production may be negative, as when migrants respond to crop failure by increasing the share of earnings they remit). Mutual altruism reinforces this implicit contract, as do inheritance motives (i.e., nonremitting migrants stand to lose their rural inheritance) and migrants' own aversion to risk, which encourages them to uphold their end of the contract in order to be supported by the rural household should they experience an income shock (e.g., unemployment) or other misfortune in the future. Anthropological research [e.g., Fletcher (1997), Rouse (1991)] points to the importance of rural households-of-origin as refuges for migrants who fall ill or suffer other sorts of misfortune (e.g., trouble with the law, substance dependence, etc.) that prevent them from working or residing at the migrant destination for extended periods of time.

Migration, while enabling families to spread their labor across sectors, may promote rural population growth by creating fertility incentives, as well. The role of grown children as migrants adds a new benefit to having children in rural areas; i.e., the future role of migrant children in facilitating production transformation, reducing family income risk, etc. No empirical research has attempted to test this migration-fertility link. However, Rosenzweig and Evenson's (1977) finding that children's wages significantly increased fertility in rural India suggests that a positive effect of migration on children's future earnings would have a similar effect.

NELM motives for migration, together with the post-migration resource transfers they imply, are likely to be of greater importance in less developed countries than in developed economies. The lack of a modern communications infrastructure in LDC rural areas makes information sparse and its acquisition costly. Asset markets that function relatively well in modern economies may be completely lacking in LDCs (futures markets and crop insurance are striking examples, but rural credit markets often are missing or incomplete, as well). Because of this, NELM research on rural out-migration has focused almost exclusively on LDCs.

Stark (1982) expounds migration's role as an intermediate investment that facilitates the transition from familial to commercial production. It performs this role by providing rural households with capital and a means to reduce risk by diversifying income sources. Lacking access to credit and income insurance outside the household, households self-finance new production methods and self-insure against perceived risks to household income by investing in the migration of one or more family members. That is, market imperfections in rural areas – not the distortions in labor markets emphasized by Todaro (1969) – are hypothesized to be a primary motivation for migration.

Stark and Levhari (1982) use a graphical presentation to argue that migration is a means to spread risk, rather than being a manifestation of risk-taking behavior on the part of migrants. Stark and Katz (1986) formalize the argument that rural–urban migration, a labor-market phenomenon, is caused by imperfections in capital markets.

The spectrum of factors influencing migration decisions extends beyond the household. A household's income position vis-à-vis its reference group (e.g., the village) also influences its behavior, including migration. Stark (1984) and Stark and Yitzhaki (1988) present a relative deprivation model of migration, in which the household's objective is to maximize utility which, in turn, is a negative function of relative deprivation, or the bundles of goods of which the household is deprived within its reference group. In this model, a given expected income gain from migration does not have the same effect on the probability of migration for households situated at different points in the rural income distribution, or in communities with different income distributions. From a broader perspective, mean-preserving increases in rural income inequalities, to which migration would be completely immune in a Todaro model, may stimulate migration by increasing relative deprivation. By operationalizing the relative deprivation concept, Stark and Taylor (1989, 1991) test the importance of relative versus absolute income considerations in internal and international migration decisions by rural Mexican households (see Section 3).

Because skill-related attributes of individual family members influence the costs and benefits of migration for households, as well as for individuals, human capital theory has been incorporated into NELM models. However, the household perspective implies critical interactions between individual and household variables, including assets and the human capital of household members other than the migrants. These variables influence the marginal cost of migration for households (including the marginal effect of migration on farm production), as well as the impacts of remittances and the income insurance provided by migrants on the expected utility of the household as a whole.

The NELM perspective leads to significantly broader arenas for potential impacts of migration upon rural economies, for policy interventions to influence migration, and for the potential list of variables influencing migration decisions. A number of key implications of NELM models differ sharply from those of neoclassical migration models. First, contrary to both classical and neoclassical theories, the loss of labor to migration may increase (rather than decrease or, in the case of Lewis, leave unchanged) production in rural economies, by enabling households to overcome credit and risk constraints on production. Second, a positive income (or expected income) differential between urban and rural areas is not a necessary condition for migration. Migration in the presence of a negative urban-rural income differential is consistent with the NELM (provided that the variance of urban incomes and/or income covariance between the two sectors is sufficiently low). Third, the individuals who migrate are not necessarily those whom a traditional human capital model would predict; the impact of an individual's out-migration on the productivity of other family members also matters. Moreover, while constituting a motivation for migration, imperfections in capital and insurance markets also may constrain migration, resulting in the seeming paradox that increases in rural incomes (which enable households to self-finance migration costs and self-insure against migration risks) may promote, rather than impede, migration [e.g., see Schiff (1996)]. Fourth, equal expected income gains from migration across individuals or households does not imply equal propensities to migrate, as predicted by a Todaro model, when risk and/or relative income considerations also influence migration decisions. From a migration policy point of view, the NELM shifts the focus of migration policy from intervention in rural or urban labor markets to intervention in other (most notably, rural capital and risk) markets, in which an underlying motivation for migration is found.

The progression of migration theory from the relatively simple, perfect-markets neo-classical model to NELM models involves both increasing complexity and more generality in how we think about migration determinants and impacts. Just as the wage-driven neoclassical model is a special case of the Todaro model, both may be viewed as special cases of NELM models, in which some or all market constraints that influence migration are nonbinding (e.g., households are risk-neutral or have access to efficient insurance markets), relative income considerations do not affect utility, and the effect of household variables on migration are negligible.

2. The analysis of migration determinants

Each of the migration theories outlined above implies a different objective function underlying migration decisions, a different set of potential variables shaping these decisions, and a distinct set of possible outcomes of migration for the rural economy. The most fundamental distinction concerns the unit of analysis. The classical and neoclassical (including Todaro) models treat migration as the result of an individual decision-making process. The objective function varies, but in all cases the individual is both decision maker and actor. On a micro level, this genre of migration research treats migration as a discrete choice (although potentially it could be represented as a continuous but limited variable, ranging from zero – no migration – to T – the maximum amount of time the individual has available for migration and nonmigration activities). In aggregate-level analyses, which represent the majority of empirical applications, the decisions of individuals are summed up into migration flows across space, and the migration (dependent) variable then becomes continuous.

In contrast to classical and perfect-markets neoclassical models, NELM models consider the family or household as the unit of analysis; family members are assumed to act collectively to maximize expected income and also to loosen constraints associated with missing credit, insurance, and other markets. Because of this, the NELM perspective fits neatly with the literature on agricultural household models, both neoclassical [e.g., Barnum and Squire (1979), Singh et al. (1986)] and in the context of missing or incomplete markets [Strauss (1986), De Janvry et al. (1991)]. Methodologically, the NELM approach, with its focus on risk and market imperfections, requires the use of simultaneous, rather than recursive, farm household models to analyze both the determinants and impacts of rural out-migration. Nash-bargained household models [e.g., McElroy and Horney (1981)] also are potentially useful to analyze the implicit contractual relationship between migrants and family members who do not migrate. The NELM posits a role for variables hitherto ignored in the migration literature – especially relative-income considerations – as influencing household utility and thus migration decisions.

Migration decisions are inherently dynamic, shaped by a future stream of expected costs and benefits (appropriately discounted). Individuals or households may rationally choose to participate in migration even if the short-run expected utility gain from doing so is negative, provided that the discounted future gains are positive and sufficiently large. Few studies explicitly model migration as a dynamic phenomenon [for an exception, using aggregate country data, see Larson and Mundlak (1997)]; usually, the problem is treated as static. The theoretical complexity of introducing dynamics without oversimplifying the objective function or constraint set confronting migration decision makers, together with the paucity of longitudinal data, has discouraged the development of truly dynamic migration models.

At either the individual or household level of analysis, the most general objective considered in the migration-decision literature is to maximize a Von Neuman-type expected utility function of the form

$$EU = E\big[U(W, Z)\big], \tag{2}$$

where W denotes a vector of end-of-period consumption goods, Z is a vector of other variables posited to influence family utility, and E is the expectation operator. The utility function $U(\cdot)$ is defined for an individual in the case of the Todaro or straight neoclassical migration models. In a NELM model, it represents family utility, involving some kind of weighting of utilities of individual family members, including migrants and nonmigrants. In every NELM application to date, it has been assumed that family preferences can be represented by a single utility function, and income is pooled within households to define a single family or household budget constraint, as in a standard agricultural household model.

Expected utility is maximized subject to a set of constraints. In all models these include a budget constraint; in most, the primary or sole influence of migration on individuals or households operates through this constraint. Other constraints include an individual or family time constraint, and, in NELM models, production technologies and market (e.g., subsistence) constraints. In models where end-of-period income is not known but consumption decisions may be altered ex post, the vector of consumption goods in the utility function is often replaced by income or wealth, as in most of the risk and uncertainty literature. Such a simplification is usually not appropriate, however, when one or more markets are missing – for example, when perfect hired-labor substitutes are not available to compensate for family leisure demand, or when the household faces a subsistence constraint resulting from a missing staple market, so that consumption decisions cannot be altered contingent upon income outcomes.

Each of the broad theoretical approaches presented earlier may be considered as a special case of this general expected-utility maximization model. David (1974) takes the individual as the unit of observation, represents utility as a function of wealth alone, and then approximates Equation (1) by its second-order Taylor series expansion around mean wealth. This yields the following expression for (approximate) expected utility of income associated with migration:

$$EU_m \approx U(\overline{W}_m) + 0.5U''E(W_m - \overline{W}_m)^2, \tag{2'}$$

where U'' is the second derivative of utility with respect to wealth (significantly, the numerator in the Arrow–Pratt index of absolute risk aversion). Assuming that the non-income component of end-of-period wealth is known with certainty, the squared term in parentheses can be replaced by the income variance, s^2. Letting EU_r (similarly approximated) denote expected utility of wealth if the individual does not migrate (i.e., remains in the rural sector), migration is observed if $EU_m > EU_r$.

Both the Todaro model and the standard neoclassical migration model can be viewed as special cases of the expected utility-maximization problem just presented. If one assumes that individuals are risk neutral (or, equivalently, that income variance is zero), the decision rule implied by Equation (2) collapses to the familiar Todaro migration rule, in which migration is observed if

$$p_m w_m > E[Y_r], \tag{3}$$

where w_m denotes the urban-sector wage and p_m is the probability that a prospective migrant will obtain a job at this wage.

At full employment, $p_m = 1$, and the migration rule in (3) reduces further to the simple neoclassical rule: Migrate if

$$w_m > w_r, \tag{4}$$

where w_r denotes the rural wage. Both Todaro and neoclassical migration rules usually recognize that there are migration costs and include a term to reflect this.

Expression (4) represents the migration probability equation underlying much of the econometric research on rural out-migration and farm labor migration in both LDCs and high income countries. For example, it is the foundation for Perloff, Lynch and Gabbard's (1998) and Emerson's (1984) studies of seasonal agricultural worker migration in the United States. It is also the starting point for all 12 studies of internal migration in LDCs examined in Yap's (1977) review and a large number of subsequent tests of the Todaro expected-income hypothesis [e.g., Knowles and Anker (1975), House and Rempel (1976), Hay (1974), Schultz (1975), Carvajal and Geithman (1974)].

2.1. NELM models

NELM variants of the general migration model take many forms, depending on the focus of the analysis. In most studies, the underlying objective function is implied rather than explicitly spelled out. A household variant of David's model, in which families allocate individual members' time to migration and nonmigration work in a series of discrete choices, appears in Taylor (1986). Household portfolio models of migration also appear, explicitly or implicitly, in Rosenzweig and Stark (1989), Stark and Katz (1986), and Stark and Levhari (1982).

A fundamental difference between individual and household migration models is that, in the household approach, individual family members' labor time is allocated between migration and nonmigration work so as to maximize household expected utility, which may be a function of both the expected value and variance of end-of-period household wealth (and, in the relative deprivation approach, a function of the incomes of other households, as well). Thus, household variables shaping both the first and higher moments of income – including the human capital characteristics of all family members and family assets – figure prominently in the migration decision, together with the human capital of the prospective migrants themselves. In this approach, as in any portfolio-allocation model, maximizing expected income does not necessarily imply allocating each family member's labor time to the market or activity in which her expected earnings or contributions to household income are highest. Risk also matters.

In an agricultural household model, the opportunity cost of migration is the loss of net income from production resulting from the allocation of a marginal unit of family time to migration. Here, migrant selectivity clearly matters to household welfare: the human capital embodied in migrants is likely to complement other family resources in production. Assuming decreasing returns to labor in farm production, the opportunity cost of migration increases with the amount of family time allocated to migration. However, the loss of highly productive family labor to migration may shift the marginal labor product curve leftward, lowering the opportunity cost of migration for the remaining family members. If, on the other hand, migrants act as financial intermediaries for the household, over time they may promote investments that shift the marginal labor product curve back to the right, discouraging future migration. The interplay of lost labor and investment effects of migration is the focus of some of the empirical NELM research presented in Section 3.

Because maximizing utility of expected income is analogous to maximizing expected income itself (given monotonicity of the utility function), household migration models that do not explicitly address risk are treated as expected income-maximization models. Such is the case in Taylor (1987). A model of household expected-income maximization subject to both labor and liquidity constraints is implied by Lucas' (1987) study of migration to South African mines and Taylor's (1992) and Taylor and Wyatt's (1996) studies of marginal income and distributional effects of migration and remittances in rural Mexico. In these models, migration [or, in Lucas (1987), wage work including migration] appears as a continuous variable – family labor time allocated to migration work. Migration and remittances in turn produce feedback on the rural economy, both negative (through lost labor effects) and positive (through loosening of liquidity constraints on farm investments). These models highlight the importance of rural market imperfections in shaping both the motivations for migration and the impacts of migration on rural economies.

As indicated earlier, treating migration as a (limited) continuous variable is not necessarily outside the domain of individual-choice migration models; even for an individual, migration may be like the incomplete adoption of a new technology (in this case, a labor-market technology), with an individual spending part of the year as a labor migrant and the rest of the year on the farm. Nor must one necessarily take a household-level approach to examine feedback of migration on farm production. An individual farmer may find it optimal to engage in migration for part of the year (or, in a dynamic model, for one or more time periods) in order to obtain liquidity needed to invest in farm production (creating a new future stream of farm income). Such models would represent a new twist on NELM.

In practice, the association of NELM effects with household models of migration is motivated by the observation that families in LDC rural areas typically engage in migration by sending one or more members off as migrants (frequently, sons and daughters of the household head), who then share part of their earnings with the rural household, through remittances. While some family members migrate, others stay on the farm.

This observation raises the question of why migrants remit. Classical or neoclassical models of migration behavior do not explain the remitting of a (frequently large) share of migrant earnings back to the rural place of origin. However, remittances are a cornerstone of the NELM, representing one of the most important mechanisms through which determinants and consequences of migration are linked.

The NELM view that migration entails an implicit contract between migrant and household suggests a venue for collective models of household behavior [e.g., Bourguignon and Chiappori (1992)], including game theoretic approaches, and the role of altruism in shaping both migration and remittance behavior. In a Nash-bargained rural household [e.g., McElroy and Horney (1981)] containing migrants, household utility might be represented by the product of net utility gains deriving from household membership for migrants and other household members. Migrants' utility as nonmembers of the household – that is, the utility they would enjoy by severing their ties with the household – represents the threat point in this game. The more insecure that migrants perceive their future prospects outside the household, the smaller this threat point, the less likely migrants will sever ties with the household, and the more income migrants will remit, other things (including migrant earnings) being equal. While a model of pure altruism would predict a negative association between migrant earnings and rural-household wealth, a game-theoretic model would predict just the opposite, particularly if the migrant stands to inherit all or part of this wealth. In short, the greater the migrants' threat point, the greater the likelihood that migrants sever their ties with their rural households, and the lower remittances are likely to be. The lower the migrants' threat point (i.e., the stronger the relative bargaining position of the nonmigrant family members), the lower the probability of migrants severing ties with their rural households, and the higher remittances are likely to be. This type of game theoretic perspective underlies Lucas and Stark's (1985) analyses of remittance behavior in Botswana (see Section 3), and a Nash-bargained household model appears explicitly in Hoddinott's (1994) study of rural out-migration in western Kenya. Contrast these with the overlapping utility function used by Funkhouser (1995) and the more conventional, homogeneous household-farm models underlying Taylor (1992, 1986), which do not imply a game-theoretic dynamic between migrant and household. A model of reciprocal altruism between generations underlies Tcha's (1996) novel and provocative work on rural-to-urban migration in Korea and the United States.

2.2. *Estimation of migration models*

Techniques used to estimate models of migration have evolved considerably over the last two decades, due as much to the development of new econometric methods as to advances in migration theory. All of the studies covered by Yap's (1977) then-exhaustive review of the migration literature and all but two of the studies referenced in Todaro (1980) used a basic, aggregate migration function of the following form:

$$M_{ij} = f(Y_i, Y_j, U_i, U_j, Z_i, Z_j, d_{ij}, C_{ij}) \tag{5}$$

the variables in which are defined as follows:

M_{ij} Total migration flow from place i to place j (sometimes expressed as a net flow or a share of population at place i)

$Y_i(Y_j)$ Average wage or income level at place i (at place j)

$U_i(U_j)$ Unemployment rate at place i (at place j)

$Z_i(Z_j)$ Degree of urbanization of the population at place i (at place j)

d_{ij} Distance between place i and place j

C_{ij} Friends and relatives of residents of i at destination j (a migration network variable)

Populations at places i and j were often included as explanatory variables, as well.

Studies based on Equation (5) take either of two general forms: symmetrical and asymmetrical. In symmetrical models, explanatory variables appear as differences or ratios between regions; e.g., the income variable is Y_i/Y_j, or $Y_i - Y_j$. This constrains the effect on migration to be the same for changes in origin-region variables as for changes in destination-region variables. Implicitly, this approach appears to make some rather valiant assumptions, including perfect information in labor markets such that migrants are just as responsive to changes in labor markets at distant destinations as in the origin labor markets they presumably know well. In a less restrictive approach, explanatory variables for the two regions are included separately; e.g., both Y_i and Y_j appear as right-hand side variables in the migration regression equation. This permits explanatory variables' effects on migration to be asymmetric between regions. Fields

(1979) tests the sensitivity of findings on interregional migration in Colombia to the use of a symmetric versus an asymmetric model specification.

The aggregate specification above has the advantage of being easily estimated using ordinary least squares and aggregate census data available in many countries. However, it has a number of limitations that seriously limit its usefulness for prediction and for policy analysis [some of these are spelled out in Stark (1982)]. In general, the estimated coefficients of aggregate migration regressions do not represent estimates of the structural relationships implied by micro, human capital models. The exception is when a population is homogeneous, in which case average income measures the income an individual would receive in each region. This assumption usually is untenable; indeed, much of the richness of both the findings and policy implications of recent microeconometric migration research (Section 3) results from the heterogeneity among individuals – both migrants and nonmigrants – within regions. Another complication, which follows directly from Todaro's theoretical model, is that employment rates, while posited to influence migration, are, in turn, affected by migration. Endogeneity bias in the unemployment variables raises serious questions about the validity of most aggregate studies' findings. Very few researchers either consider or attempt to correct for this problem. Notable exceptions include Fields (1979), who resorts to a reduced-form migration equation, and Hunt and Greenwood (1984), who explicitly control for feedback of U.S. interstate migration to local labor markets.

The availability of new, micro data on individuals and households containing information on migration, together with advances in econometric techniques to analyze these data, opened up vastly improved avenues for empirical migration studies. As Stark and Bloom (1985) point out, the econometric techniques that have most profoundly influenced migration research include methods to estimate limited dependent variable models, methods to correct for sample selection bias, and techniques to analyze longitudinal and pseudo-longitudinal data.

At the level of the individual, migration usually entails a discrete, dichotomous or polychotomous choice. At the household level, time allocated to migration is a continuous variable; however, it is censored at zero (and also upward, at the family's total time endowment). Analysis based on the estimation rules presented earlier requires either a reduced-form approach, in which income or expected-income terms are replaced by a vector of exogenous (i.e., human-capital) variables, or else direct estimation of structural income variables. The reduced-form approach has been used in a number of studies utilizing probit or logit estimation techniques [e.g., see Taylor (1986), and Emerson (1984)]. These studies test important hypotheses concerning rural migration behavior. However, they have the drawback that structural income variables do not appear in the estimated migration equation, seriously limiting the usefulness of the model for policy analysis.

Estimation of structural income terms is complicated by the fact that individuals and households select themselves into and out of migration, presumably according to their comparative advantage in these activities. Data on migrant earnings or remittances are censored because they are observed only for those who migrate. Similarly, nonmigrant earnings are generally not available for those who are selected into migration. Because the migration selection process is endogenous, shaped by many of the same character-istics that determine earnings in each regime, average migrant earnings may not reflect what nonmigrants would earn if they migrated, and nonmigrant earnings may be a poor indicator of what migrants would earn if they did not migrate. This sample selectivity problem is identical to selectivity problems frequently encountered in the labor literature [e.g., Lee (1978), Heckman (1974), Willis and Rosen (1979), Dickens and Lang (1985), a useful review of estimation techniques for models involving selectivity is available in Maddala (1983)].

Multinomial logit, probit, tobit, two-stage (Heckman), and various maximum-likelihood techniques for estimating discrete-continuous models, not available or ac-cessible two decades ago, today are widely used to estimate migration-decision models at a micro (individual or household) level. Recent examples include Perloff et al. (1998), Emerson (1989), Taylor (1987, 1992), Stark and Taylor (1989, 1991), Lucas and Stark (1985), and Barham and Boucher (1998).

2.3. Human capital variables in migration models

Human capital variables are incorporated into the analysis of individual migration de-cisions by expressing earnings and expected earnings in (2) through (5) as functions of individuals' socio-demographic characteristics. The models may then be estimated ei-ther in reduced form, by expressing migration probabilities as a function of exogenous individual (and household) characteristics, or else in their structural form, by obtain-ing estimates of relevant income and risk variables and subsequently including these in the migration equation. The second approach is considerably more complicated from a modeling point of view. However, it has the advantage that structural variables shap-ing migration decisions often are of greater analytical and policy interest than are the exogenous variables appearing in the reduced-form equation. The exogenous variables may also appear in the structural equation, making it possible to isolate direct from in-direct (through the income and risk variables) of these variables on migration using the structural approach.

2.4. Data limitations and rural wages

Largely because of data limitations, explicit analysis of the role of uncertainty in shap-ing migration decisions (as in expression (3)) is not found in the literature. At the level of the individual, longitudinal data on migrants' wages and employment at their desti-nation for estimating variances of migrant earnings are generally unavailable. Data on employment and wages in rural areas for individuals across time are also rare. Contem-poraneous income variances may be estimated using cross-sectional data, e.g., by em-ploying the approaches for estimating production risk proposed by Just and Pope (1977), Antle (1983), and others, provided that income outcomes are available for both migrants and nonmigrants and measures are taken to correct for potential sample-selection bias.

The migration decision may then be treated as analogous to the choice of production technique in which returns under alternative technologies are modeled following a Just–Pope specification [Taylor (1986)].

Conceptual difficulties with modeling rural wages further complicate the analysis. Much of the rural workforce, including many prospective migrants, do not receive a wage income, but rather, are involved in some sort of agricultural-household production. In these cases, the rural wage in the models above must be replaced by a "shadow" wage, as in farm-household models with missing labor markets [e.g., De Janvry et al. (1991), Singh et al. (1986)], or by expected earnings imputed from this shadow wage. For an individual, earnings imputed at the shadow wage represent the net income from rural production foregone by migrating out of the rural sector. For a household, it is the net loss in income from rural production suffered as a result of the out-migration of a family member. The observed wage of rural wage earners may not accurately reflect this income loss unless hired and family labor are perfect substitutes. [For a discussion of the substitutability of family and hired labor see Bardhan (1988).] Despite this limitation, the rural wage, multiplied by days worked on the family farm, is generally used as a proxy for the opportunity cost of migration in studies where individuals are the unit of observation. In household models, an approach involving estimation of income functions with and without migration is used, correcting for selectivity of migration [Barham and Boucher (1998), Taylor (1992),Taylor and Wyatt (1996)].

The use of rural wages is not likely to pose a problem in studies of rural labor migration in developed countries, where few labor migrants are engaged in household-farm production prior to migration. For example, in studies of US farm labor migration, observed earnings of migrants and nonmigrants are used [e.g., Perloff et al. (1998), and Emerson (1989)]. Nevertheless, because individuals are not randomly selected into these two groups, these, like studies of rural out-migration in LDCs, must test and correct for potential sample selection bias.

3. Rural out-migration: Empirical evidence and evaluation of migration theories

The empirical literature on determinants of rural out-migration is vast and spans a broad range of disciplines. Few studies, however, offer a basis to reliably test central hypotheses derived from the migration theories presented in Sections 1 and 2, above. Empirical research is hampered by high levels of aggregation, the absence of appropriate controls, a lack of micro data sets containing information on the array of variables required to estimate neoclassical and especially NELM migration models, and unreliable survey designs. Remarkably, information on migration and remittances is absent from nearly all household-farm surveys, making it impossible to estimate even the simplest migration decision model. Given advances in migration theory and in econometric estimation techniques over the past two decades, data limitations currently are the major constraint on empirical migration research. Only in relatively few cases have advances in migration theory informed the collection of new household-farm data. As a result, tests of some of the most important and far-reaching propositions concerning migration and rural economies rest on a rather thin body of empirical literature.

Despite the potential richness of micro-level econometric analysis based on the migration decision rules presented earlier, most applied research has involved the estimation of aggregate migration functions of the general form of Equation (6). Wages and employment rates are included as regressors, but rarely is the Todaro expected-income term (the product of these two variables) included, and in even fewer cases is both a Todaro expected income term and a wage term included as a basis for testing the central hypothesis of a Todaro, versus a traditional neoclassical, model.

Results of econometric analyses of aggregate migration flows from LDC rural areas generally support both neoclassical and Todaro expected-income migration theories. [E.g., see reviews by Yap (1977), and Todaro (1980), Fields (1979), Schultz (1982).] That is, in most cases, differentials in average wages or incomes between regions are significant in explaining migration flows in the expected direction. When differences in unemployment rates, the Todaro proxy for job probability, are also included, they typically have independent explanatory power. In the few studies reporting direct tests of the Todaro expected income hypothesis, i.e., including both an expected wage variable and wages as regressors, the expected wage term comes out to be significant [e.g., see Barnum and Sabot (1975) for Tanzania, Levy and Wadycki (1974) for Venezuela, House and Rempel (1976) for Kenya, and Fields (1979) for Colombia].

During the 1960s, there was an average of one million rural–urban migrants in the United States each year, and migrants and their children were involved in disturbances associated with civil rights protests in major U.S. cities. Many leading agricultural economists set out to examine the determinants and effects of rural–urban migration. The 1960s witnessed an explosion of aggregate-level research on farm labor migration and rural–urban labor market linkages, perhaps best exemplified by the studies in Bishop (1967, p. 6) and in the report to the President's National Advisory Commission on Rural Poverty (1967). The sharp divergence in incomes between the farm and nonfarm sectors was attributed to "the failure of the labor market to transfer sufficient quantities of manpower from farms" [Bishop (1967), p. 6]. This view motivated research aimed at estimating, and designing policies to increase, the elasticity of labor supply from farms to the nonfarm sector, while recognizing social costs associated with rural out-migration, particularly for rural areas.

Schuh (1962), in a pioneering study that anticipated Todaro (1969), found econometric evidence that increases in expected nonfarm income, either through a reduction in unemployment or an increase in wages, resulted in large shifts in farm labor supply to the left. He also found that farm incomes could be raised, although not greatly, by price support programs and that education positively affected farm incomes, both by accelerating migration and by raising the productivity of the labor force remaining in agriculture.

Echoing Lewis while also suggesting impediments to mobility out of agriculture, Jones and Christian (1965, p. 524) argued that "the redundant supply of labor in agriculture ... is perpetuated by a lack of opportunity in alternative occupations. Agricultural labor is 'trapped' in the 'other America' ". Others [e.g., President's National Advisory Commission (1967), also see papers in Heady (1961)] suggested that the rate of rural out-migration may have been excessive. The movement of people out of agriculture potentially creates social costs. Maddox (1960) classifies the costs of rural out-migration into three categories: those falling on the migrants themselves; those borne by the communities from which migrants move; and those affecting the communities to which migrants relocate. Maddox concluded that public action was warranted to offset negative externalities associated with out-migration from rural communities, particularly those related to human capital losses. Johnson (1960) cautions that one cannot say with certainty whether a reduction in farm labor will reduce total farm output; if it is associated with a move toward equilibrium, output may increase, while average earnings per farmworker may rise.

The President's National Advisory Commission on Rural Poverty (1967, p. 524) concluded that "the mass exodus from low income rural areas ... has meant that those left behind are often worse off than before". This conclusion reflects a partial-equilibrium view, i.e., that population decline creates a factor-market disequilibrium, reducing the incomes and welfare of those left behind. It ignores the equally plausible role of migration as an ameliorator of disequilibria (e.g., correcting a state of "too many farmers"). Gardner (1974), based on a two-stage least squares analysis of US census data, found that, during the 1960s, the rate of states' farm population loss was positively associated with the rate of growth of average rural-farm family income, and it had no adverse effect on rural nonfarm incomes. If off-farm migration created disequilibria and transitory income losses, it would appear that "the people left behind" were sufficiently mobile to adjust over the ten-year period covered by Gardner's study.

Carrying Schuh's analysis forward, Barkley (1990) found that economic growth resulting in rising returns to nonfarm relative to farm labor significantly explained the occupational migration of labor out of agriculture between 1940 and 1985. The elasticity of out-migration with respect to the ratio of nonfarm/farm average labor products (a proxy for wages) was estimated at 4.5. In contrast to Schuh (1962), however, controlling for this labor returns variable, Barkley found that urban unemployment did not deter labor migration, and the effect of agricultural policies (government payments to agriculture as a share of farm income) on labor migration from agriculture was insignificant. The decreasing effect of these unemployment and agricultural policy variables that were a focus of U.S. migration research in the 1960s probably reflects both that rural-to-urban migration had largely run its course by the end of the period considered by Barkley (1990), and that the principal source of labor for US agriculture had shifted from domestic to foreign.

Migration elasticities were also key inputs into some research on measuring the economic returns to labor-displacing agricultural research. Because many labor-saving agricultural innovations are developed with public funds at public institutions, the rural–urban migration induced by publicly funded research became an issue in the United States several times during the twentieth century. By releasing labor from agriculture, publicly supported research "saved" inputs. Schultz (1953) pioneered studies of the value of inputs saved as a result of agricultural research, generating very high estimates of the rate of return to public research investments. Input savings of $10 billion in 1950 exceeded the cumulative $7 billion expenditures on agricultural research between 1910 and 1950 (in 1950 dollars).

However, if those displaced from agriculture are not re-employed in the higher wage nonfarm sector, and if the costs of these individuals' persisting unemployment are taken into account, estimated returns to agricultural research can fall sharply. Schmitz and Seckler in 1970 used the value-of-inputs-saved approach to measure the return to research on processed tomato mechanization. Based on the value of the hours of labor saved, they estimated in 1983 that the "gross" return to research expenditures was 929 percent to 1282 percent when the opportunity cost of funds was 6 percent. However, if it is assumed that displaced workers receive compensation equivalent to 50 percent of their previous wages, the return to tomato harvester research falls to between 460 and 814 percent. Richard Day (1967) noted that, if those displaced from agriculture wind up in concentrated poverty in cities, then efforts to speed up the diffusion of labor-saving innovations and to hasten migration may simply transfer rural poverty to urban poverty.

Schmitz and Seckler noted that compensation could be paid to displaced workers who migrated from rural to urban areas, making public investment in labor-saving agricultural research highly desirable nonetheless. However, there was no displacement compensation available for most farmworkers, who were excluded from many of the programs developed in the 1930s to cushion the effects of labor market adjustments, including unemployment insurance. In the late 1970s, when the United Farmworkers Union was at its peak strength, it sued the University of California over publicly funded mechanization research that displaced workers. The suit was settled out of court, but one result was that public funds spent on labor-saving research declined sharply [Martin and Olmstead (1985)].

In LDCs, the preponderance of aggregate studies found that the effects of employment-related variables generally equaled or exceeded those of wage-related variables [Massey et al. (1993, 1994, 1998); Schultz (1982) is one of the few exceptions]. For example, Maldonado (1976) found that differentials in both unemployment and wages significantly explained the volume of migration from Puerto Rico to the mainland United States, but the effect of the unemployment variable dominated that of the wage variable. Massey et al. (1994) re-estimated the Maldonado model, replacing the wage ratio with the ratio of expected wages (wages times employment probabilities). They found that unemployment rates still dominated the expected wage ratio in predicting out-migration to the mainland. Ramos (1992) and Castillo–Freeman and Freeman (1992) argue that displacement resulting from structural changes drives migration more than fluctuations in wages. An alternative explanation for the importance of the employment variable is suggested by Hatton and Williamson's (1992) excellent historical analysis of migration to the United States. They conclude that wage differentials shape the underlying propensity to migrate and drive long-term trends, but unemployment rates determine the timing of migration and thus are more important than wages in explaining year-to-year fluctuations in migration rates. Evidence that employment effects dominate wage-rate effects is also provided by Straubhaar (1986) for migration from southern to northern Europe, and by Walsh (1974) for migration between Ireland and Britain.

The impacts of wage and employment-rate differentials on migration are not invariant across migration type. A body of econometric research on Mexico-to-U.S. migration flows lends support to the expected income migration model in explaining illegal and contracted-labor migration across borders. However, expected-income variables appear less effective at explaining legal migration. Most illegal-migrant and contracted (bracero) flows originate in rural Mexico. Jenkins (1977) modeled bracero and illegal migration (proxied by apprehensions) between Mexico and the United States between 1948 and 1972, finding that the Mexico–U.S. wage differential had a positive effect on both, as predicted by a neoclassical model. The wage effect was particularly strong when total (bracero plus illegal) migration was modeled. Blejer, Johnson, and Prozecanski (1978) extended this research by including legal migrants as well. The explanatory variables included the ratios of Mexico/U.S. unemployment, industrial wages, and agricultural wages. They found that the unemployment ratio was significant and of the expected sign, and most of the explanatory power of this variable came from variation in the Mexican unemployment rate. Controlling for this unemployment effect, relative wages did not significantly affect migration. The model performed considerably better for illegal than for legal immigrants, however. White, Bean and Espenshade (1990) found strong econometric evidence that both unemployment and wage ratios explain illegal Mexico-to-U.S. migration (measured by the log of monthly apprehensions) from 1977 through 1988. In an imaginative econometric analysis of Mexico-to-U.S. migration and trade in winter vegetables, Torok and Huffman (1986) found that both U.S. wages and unemployment rates significantly affected the U.S. demand for illegal immigrant workers (proxied by border apprehensions), while wages in Mexico significantly affected Mexico's supply of such workers.

Only two of the 18 studies reviewed by Todaro (1980) and Yap (1977) use micro-level, rather than aggregate, data. As indicated earlier in this chapter, the major difficulties in estimating micro-econometric models of rural out-migration stem not only from data deficiencies but also from potential problems arising from sample selectivity. The selection of individuals into and out of migration is endogenous, reflecting the comparative advantages of individuals and households in migration and nonmigration work [Taylor (1987), Emerson (1989)]. Econometric techniques are well developed and accessible to correct for such selectivity bias [e.g., see Maddala (1983), and Lee (1978)]. To correct for selectivity bias, typically an inverse-Mills ratio, obtained from a first-stage, reduced-form probit regression, is included in income or earnings equations for migrants and nonmigrants, following Heckman's (1974) two-step estimator. This selectivity-correction procedure, in addition to resolving selectivity bias, also yields insights into the relationship between expected returns from migration and individual or family migration decisions [e.g., see Emerson (1989), and Taylor (1987)] and differences in remittance behavior between migrant populations [Funkhouser (1995)].

Unfortunately, few surveys provide the data on earnings (or household-income contributions) of both migrants and nonmigrants required to implement selectivity-correction

techniques, and as a result, selectivity-corrected, structural models of migration decisions by individuals or households are rare. Notable exceptions are Emerson (1989),
Robinson and Tomes (1982), Falaris (1987), Nakosteen and Zimmer (1980), Perloff et
al. (1998), and Taylor (1987). All of these studies employ a "mover-stayer" human-
capital migration model that controls for sample selection bias when estimating the
economic returns from migrating. In contrast to aggregate migration models, which
generally follow a Todaro specification, micro-econometric studies fall either into the
"neoclassical" or "Todaro" category. For example, the agricultural labor migration studies of Emerson (1989) and Perloff et al. (1998) utilize expected earnings, which are
shaped by both wages and employment, as their income variable, while Robinson and
Tomes (1982) and Falaris (1987) use only wages.

Emerson (1989) provides an excellent example, in the context of U.S. agricultural
labor migration, of how human capital theory, combined with micro data and appropriate econometric techniques for limited dependent variables and selectivity correction,
yields insights not available from aggregate migration models. Employing a mover-
stayer model, he offers micro-level support for the expected income model in a study of
migratory labor and agriculture in the United States (Florida). Emerson first estimates
separate earnings equations for migratory and nonmigratory work, correcting for sample
selection bias. The estimated earnings in the two regimes are then used in a structural
probit regression for migration. The results indicate that workers migrate for seasonal
work in response to an expected wage differential favoring migratory work. Expected
earnings for nonmigrant workers exceed those for migrant workers, and migrants are
found not to have an absolute advantage in migratory work. Nevertheless, Emerson
shows that individuals specialize in the type of work in which they have a comparative
advantage. Because farmworkers' expected earnings are a function of both wages and
employment, Emerson's model falls squarely into the Todaro theoretical framework.

Perloff et al. (1998) follow a similar approach in their econometric study of seasonal
agricultural worker migration in the United States, using data from the National Agricultural Workers Study (NAWS) for 1989 through 1991. A novelty of this study is that
it decomposes expected earnings into wages and employment, making it possible to examine the factors influencing each. Their findings support Emerson's (1989) conclusion
that migration responds to expected earnings differentials across locales; however, the
expected-earnings effect is small: employers must offer large earnings premia to induce
workers to move. Earnings increases from migration are found to be due primarily to
wage differentials, not to hours worked. Forty-eight percent of all seasonal farmworkers
were found to migrate at least 75 miles in a given year.

Robinson and Tomes (1982), like the remaining studies in the above list, do not focus
on rural migration; however, their study of interprovince migration in Canada is one of
the earliest applications of a mover-stayer model to interregional migration, and it is
instructive in illustrating the importance of selectivity effects when estimating returns
from migration. They found that returns to migration were overstated when selectivity
was not taken into account. Individuals who moved from place A to place B earned more
at place B than people who stayed at A would have earned at B. Taking into account

selectivity, individual migration was found to depend significantly on potential wage gains. When selectivity was ignored, however, the wage effect became insignificant. Like most studies, Robinson and Tomes also found that, consistent with information theory, both language and education increased mobility of most groups. However, education reduced the mobility of Quebec francophones. The exclusion of employment variables limits this study's relevance for cases in which unemployment is a consideration at migration origins and/or destinations.

3.1. NELM models

A large and growing body of research offers both circumstantial and direct evidence supporting the NELM view that migration decisions take place within a family or household context and are influenced by families' efforts to overcome poorly functioning or missing risk and credit markets. Most of the NELM literature has been cast in the context of rural-to-urban migration. However, in light of relatively high wages available in developed countries (especially compared with LDC rural areas) and a low correlation between these wages and incomes in migrant-sending areas, international migration potentially represents a particularly effective strategy for minimizing family income risks and overcoming liquidity constraints. The importance of migrant, and especially foreign-migrant, income in the "income portfolios" of migrant-sending households is documented in a diversity of settings [e.g., Massey et al. (1994, 1998), Stark et al. (1986), Oberai and Singh (1980), Knowles and Anker (1981)].

Taylor (1987) tests for the significance of expected household income variables in shaping international (Mexico-to-U.S.) migration from rural Mexico. Using data on contributions to household income by migrants and nonmigrants, a selectivity-corrected structural probit migration model is estimated for a sample of households in Michoacán, traditionally the largest source-region for Mexico-to-U.S. migration. Consistent with both a Todaro expected-income and NELM model, increases in expected income contributions from migration by individual family members are found to significantly and positively explain the allocation of these individuals to migration. However, controlling for this expected-income gain, several other individual and household variables also significantly explained migration, through their effect on migration costs or other NELM considerations. Anticipating Emerson's finding that comparative advantage considerations influence migration, this study found that individuals who migrated to the United States were not above average contributors to rural Mexican household incomes, either as workers in Mexico or as migrants in the United States. However, family members with the highest expected contributions to rural Mexican households as nonmigrants were significantly less likely to migrate to the United States.

Family migration networks, or the presence of contacts at prospective migrant destinations, are consistently found to be among the most important variables driving migration [Greenwood (1971), Nelson (1976), Massey et al. (1987)], particularly to destinations that are associated with high migration costs and risks and a scarcity of information [Taylor (1986)]. In the case of rural Mexico-to-U.S. migration, assistance from family members already in the United States is often instrumental in financing new migration. These family contacts also lowered the psychic costs of living and working abroad and played an important role in providing information.

The NELM also hypothesizes that extra-household variables influence migration decisions. Building upon Taylor (1987), Stark and Taylor (1989) test the hypothesis that, controlling for expected absolute income gains from migration, a household's relative income position within its reference group (village) influences migration incentives. They include a measure of households' initial relative deprivation in a structural probit equation for migration. This variable has a positive and significant impact of the probability that rural Mexican households send migrants to the United States. The relative deprivation hypothesis turns on the stability of reference groups in the face of migration; both the migrant and the rest of the household must continue to view the village as the relevant reference group after migration occurs. This is more likely in the case of international migration, into a distinct cultural, social, and economic milieu, than for internal migration. In a subsequent study, Stark and Taylor (1991) find that relative deprivation significantly raises the probability of international (Mexico-to-U.S.) but not internal migration.

Tests of impacts of risk on migration decisions (and vice-versa) hypothesized by the NELM are scarce, largely because of data availability. Rosenzweig and Stark (1989), using unique longitudinal data from India, test the hypothesis that the "exchange" of individuals between households through marriage reflects efforts by households to mitigate risk and smooth consumption in a context of information costs and spatially covariant risks. They find that (a) marriage cum migration reduces variability in consumption, given the variability of income from crop production; and (b) households exposed to higher income risk are more likely to invest in long-distance migration-marriage arrangements. A unique feature of NELM risk models is the possibility of a positive relationship between distance and migration probabilities. In a Todaro model, distance represents a cost of migration and therefore discourages it.

A less direct test of NELM risk-and-migration hypothesis appears in Lucas and Stark (1985), the first attempt to test NELM predictions of migration and remittances. Using cross-sectional farm household data from Botswana for a drought year, a key implication of the NELM – that migrants function as insurance intermediaries – is explored. Families at greater risk of temporary income loss as a result of the drought are found to receive significantly greater remittances in the drought year. The study rejects a "pure altruism" model of remittance behavior, while finding evidence of an inheritance motive to remit.

Echoing Lucas and Stark, Hoddinott (1994) found evidence from west Kenya that wealthier parents, who can offer a greater (inheritance) reward for remittances, extracted a larger share of migrant earnings through remittances. He also found evidence that the credibility of the parental threat to reduce future bequests had a positive effect on remittances, controlling for migrants' earnings.

The roles of family ties are central to Mincer's (1978) and Borjas' (1990) migration-probability models. Borjas (1990) models migration in the context of "dynastic households", positing the welfare of children as an important variable explaining migration decisions. Building upon these and the dynastic fertility model of Barro and Becker (1986), Tcha (1996) finds compelling evidence that reciprocal altruism between generations significantly affects rural-to-urban migration in Korea and in the United States. If migration decision makers' altruism toward their children is high, the weight attached to their own expected income gains from migration (the Todaro variable) may be low relative to the weight attached to the descendants' incomes. If the descendants' permanent incomes are sufficiently large in urban areas (and with urban schooling), migration may be optimal in the absence of a positive urban-rural expected income differential for the parents, provided that parents' altruism toward their children is high. These studies reflect the NELM's emphasis on intra-familial ties when modeling migration decisions; however, they depart from most NELM research by restricting migration to moves by entire households rather than treating migration as a mechanism to diversify family labor allocations across space.

Lucas (1987), Taylor (1992), Taylor and Wyatt (1996), and Rozelle, Taylor and de-Brauw (see Section 4) offer findings consistent with the NELM hypothesis that families participate in migration in an effort to overcome liquidity constraints on local production.

Rosenzweig (1980) tested the hypothesis that capital market and information constraints restrict labor mobility within rural areas. He found that laborers with land are less mobile than the landless. Balan, Browning and Jelin (1973) and Nabi (1984) find that rural-to-urban migrants from households owning land in rural areas are more likely to be temporary migrants. In these studies, the negative effect of land ownership on mobility (or duration of migration) is attributed to the difficulty of selling land holdings without suffering a capital loss. That is, mobility is reduced because of a capital-market imperfection: part of the capital accumulated by rural residents is not transportable.

3.2. More on the selectivity effects of migration

The findings from studies presented earlier indicate that migrants are selected on key characteristics, including their expected earnings potential as migrants and nonmigrants. Individual human capital and household variables, in turn, affect individuals' and households' incomes with and without migration. Because of this, there is a "derived" selectivity of migration on specific individual and household characteristics, through the differential effects of these characteristics in migrant and nonmigrant labor markets. As human capital theory [Sjaastad (1962)] would predict, migrants tend to be younger than their counterparts who do not migrate. Household variables that influence individuals' income creation as migrants and/or nonmigrants (e.g., family migration networks or landholdings) often are found to significantly affect migration as well. The effects of some human capital variables differ sharply across migrant destinations. For example, education typically promotes rural out-migration, but not to all potential migrant destinations. Individuals significantly take their education to labor markets where they will reap the highest economic return to their schooling. In addition to a derived selectivity, through income, there also appear to be direct effects of schooling, age, and other individual and household variables on migration that are independent of expected income [e.g., Massey et al. (1994, 1998), Taylor (1987)].

There is evidence that migration is selective on extra-household variables, as well. Schultz (1988) and Rosenzweig and Wolpin (1985) found that migration in Colombia is selective of characteristics of regions (i.e., relative prices): households sorted themselves across localities with different relative prices. Selectivity of migration based on extra-household variables (e.g., local income disparities) is also documented by Stark and Taylor's (1989, 1991) studies of relative deprivation and migration, described above.

The selectivity of rural out-migration may differ not only across migrant destinations but over time as well. For example, the Binational Study of Mexico-to-U.S. Migration [United States Commission on Immigration Reform (1997)] found that this migration is not only highly selective, reflecting differences in information and the costs and benefits of migration across individuals and households in Mexico, but also that this selectivity process has changed substantially in response to changing characteristics of migrant labor demand in the United States, migrant labor supply in Mexico, and the networks of contacts with family and friends that link prospective migrants with U.S. labor markets. Labor migrants from rural Mexico, once almost entirely solo men with limited schooling, are increasingly female, married, and better educated than those who stay behind. Key human capital variables like schooling may yield low returns in rural areas compared with urban areas, but there may be little reward for education in some migrant labor markets, e.g., low-skill labor markets abroad in which unauthorized immigrants frequently are concentrated.

Taylor (1986) found that schooling had a positive effect on rural out-migration but a significant negative effect on migration to the United States from a sample of rural-Mexican households in 1983. Taylor (1987) found that, controlling for migration selectivity, the income returns to schooling for rural Mexican households were positive for internal migration but insignificant for Mexico-to-U.S. migration, which usually entailed work as illegal immigrants in low-skill activities. Because of this, schooling was negatively related to household income from international migration. However, using data from a more recent survey that included these same households, Taylor and Yúnez-Naude (2000) find that the schooling effect on Mexico-to-U.S. migration was significant and positive. This change may be attributable to Mexico's economic crisis of the mid-1980s and early 1990s, which dramatically reduced expected earnings for urban workers in Mexico.

Using aggregate data on migration between Puerto Rico and the U.S. mainland, Castillo-Freeman and Freeman (1992) and Ramos (1992) also find evidence of shifting migrant selectivity over time. There, however, migration selection increasingly favored the unemployed and individuals with little schooling, apparently because of an increase in the island's minimum wage that reduced employment in low-wage industries [Castillo-Freeman and Freeman (1992)].

4. Impacts of migration on rural economies

In both classical and neoclassical (including Todaro) migration models, the only avenue through which rural out-migration can impact the rural economy is through labor markets. Migration represents a loss of human resources for rural migrant-sending areas. If there is surplus rural labor, however, this labor loss has zero opportunity cost. In the theoretical world developed by Lewis (1954), where the rural migrant-sending areas are characterized by a surplus of workers and a perfectly elastic labor supply, the loss of human resources through migration does not provoke a production decline, nor does it exert upward pressure on rural wages. The only potential welfare effect of out-migration on the rural economy is an increase in the average product of labor for the non-migrating rural population, assuming that rural households cease to support out-migrants once they leave, and vice-versa.

Graphically, this condition is depicted by a marginal product curve for labor in the rural sector that is no longer positive once the entire work force is employed. In Figure 3, any labor force size in excess of L_1 is "redundant" in the sense that it does not contribute positively to agricultural production. This condition means that an amount of labor equal to $L_T - L_1$ may be withdrawn from the rural workforce without inflicting a production loss. As this labor is withdrawn, the average product of labor – total production divided by the remaining rural workforce – increases [Ranis and Fei (1961)]. Beyond this point, the opportunity cost of emigration for the sending economy becomes positive. Once the

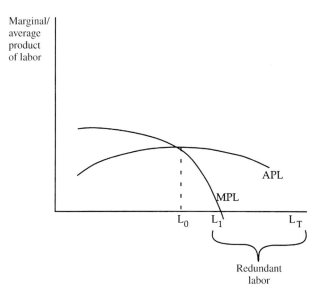

Figure 3. Labor-market impacts of emigration in a Lewis world. An amount of labor equal to $L_T - L_1$ can emigrate without inflicting any production loss on the sending area.

marginal product of rural labor exceeds the urban wage, we leave the classical Lewis world and enter the neoclassical world.

The validity of the Lewis surplus labor hypothesis has been challenged empirically by research showing that, even where surplus-labor conditions prevail most of the year, seasonal bottlenecks may produce a marginal product of labor that is positive [see Gregory (1986), for example]. In this circumstance, the opportunity cost of rural out-migration is not zero, since the loss of workers results in production declines in seasonal activities.

Lewis (1954) actually pays considerable attention to the interaction between rural development and migration. However, the Lewis model (especially its interpretations) has been criticized for implicitly treating the rural sector as a black box from which surplus labor is drawn for use in an expanding modern sector. As such, most treatments of this model offer limited insights into the interactions between migration and rural development.

The Todaro model produces a richer set of rural welfare and policy implications than either its classical or neoclassical predecessors, implicitly shifting migration and unemployment policy focus from the urban to the rural (i.e., labor-supply) sector in two ways. First, a high migration elasticity with respect to urban jobs means that an urban employment-generation project may result in more, not less, urban unemployment. (Considerations of urban or rural unemployment lie outside the realm of the traditional neoclassical migration model.) Because higher urban employment increases the urban expected wage and triggers more migration, policies operating solely on the labor-demand (i.e., urban) side are not likely to significantly reduce urban unemployment. Second, estimates of the shadow price of rural labor to the urban sector are likely to be biased downward if the migration elasticity is ignored. The lost agricultural product of the migrant who secures an urban job does not represent the full opportunity cost of rural out-migration if more than one rural worker is induced to migrate. The opportunity cost for the rural sector also includes the loss of agricultural production of others who migrate but are less fortunate in finding urban employment.

Theoretical economic research on the welfare costs of labor and capital lost to migration focuses principally on international migration. However, the findings of this research are equally relevant to rural out-migration, either to destinations domestic or abroad.

In a perfectly competitive, neoclassical world (without surplus labor or other market imperfections), a worker is paid the marginal value of what he or she produces prior to emigrating. Based on this assumption, early theoreticians argued that emigration should have a neutral effect on the economic welfare of nonmigrants: any decrease in local production attributable to the loss of labor through emigration should equal the wages that workers received prior to emigrating [Grubel and Scott (1966)]. Although local production may decline by an amount equal to the marginal product of the migrant who has departed, the size of the economic pie available to those who do not migrate is exactly the same as before.

Consider an economy characterized by a production function that is homogeneous of degree one, i.e., $y = f(k)$, where y and k are the output-labor and capital-labor ratios, respectively, and $f'(k) > 0$. In this case, outmigration increases k and thus the income per head of those left behind. This basic conclusion does not change when migrants own capital but leave it behind, even if they continue to receive the income generated by their capital. [MacDougal (1960) and Kemp (1964) present a formally identical argument for the case of foreign investment.] The only case in which those left behind may be worse off is when the migrants own a lot of capital and take it with them.

In a Lewis (1954) world of surplus labor, emigration leaves total production unchanged, and the average product of labor for nonmigrants unambiguously increases. However, if migrants take capital with them, the marginal product of labor curve may shift downward, increasing the size of the "redundant" work force and setting the stage for new rounds of rural out-migration. In this scenario, migration may reduce the average product available for nonmigrants.

The migration of migrant-owned capital out of the rural economy is not considered by either Lewis or Todaro. However, both Johnson (1967) and Berry and Soligo (1969) argue that the effect of out-migration on economic welfare in sending areas depends critically on how emigration affects the local capital stock – that is, on how much capital migrants take with them. A loss of capital through migration has two implications. First, the capital supply curve shifts inward, driving up the local rental rate on capital and raising marginal profits. Second, the loss of capital through emigration reduces the productivity of complementary labor inputs. This effect could be illustrated by an inward shift of the labor demand curve, which would reduce the wages of those who stay behind. Berry and Soligo (1969) show that, under general neoclassical assumptions, the out-migration of labor lowers the total income of non-migrants unless (a) emigrants own a disproportionately *large* share of capital and (b) they leave this capital behind when they emigrate. If these conditions hold, emigration increases the capital/labor ratio for those who do not emigrate, thereby raising labor productivity and wages.

The most obvious instance in which conditions (a) and (b) above do not hold is the emigration of human capital, i.e., people with education, skills, entrepreneurial spirit, and a willingness to take risks. By definition, human capital is attached to the migrant and necessarily leaves the rural sector when he or she does. If migrants are positively selected with respect to human capital characteristics, therefore, it will cause a "brain drain" from the rural economy, the effects of which are similar to those of capital flight, lowering the productivity, and hence the wages, of complementary labor in migrant-sending areas.

Thus, two clear lessons relevant to understanding welfare effects of migration on rural areas emerge from early theoretical research on welfare effects of out-migration. First, the effects of labor emigration depend critically on how this migration affects the capital-labor ratio among non-migrants. Second, the distributional effects of emigration are likely to be unequal across socioeconomic groups. Rivera-Batiz (1982), in a seminal piece, explored the theoretical implications of emigration for capital-rich and labor-rich individuals. He showed that if migrants take capital with them, then the real income of capital-rich individuals unambiguously increases, but the effect on labor-rich individuals is unclear. Other studies [Wong (1983), Quibria (1988), Davies and Wooton

(1992)] offer theoretical support to the argument that emigration both is globally beneficial to those who do not migrate and reduces income inequality in migrant-sending areas, provided that it results in an overall increase in the capital-labor ratio within the migrant-sending economy.

4.1. Remittances and welfare

Migration not only produces lost-labor, and possibly also lost-capital, effects on rural economies. It also represents a potentially important source of income and savings, through migrant remittances. Djajic (1986), in an extension of the neoclassical research cited earlier, concludes that nonmigrants benefit from emigration, even if they do not receive any of the remittances themselves, provided that the magnitude of migrants' remittances exceeds a critical threshold roughly equal to the value of the production they would have produced had they stayed behind.

Measuring remittances is difficult because migrants often enter developed countries outside of official channels and repatriate their earnings through informal means. Money may be returned in the form of goods purchased abroad or in the form of cash savings brought back by migrants or visiting family members, what Lozano Ascencio (1993) calls "pocket transfers".

Despite these difficulties, research indicates that migrant remittances, like other types of income transfers, contribute to rural migrant-sending economies in at least three ways: first, they increase income directly, by raising incomes of migrant-sending households; second, they may also raise local incomes indirectly by enabling families to overcome liquidity and risk constraints on local production (the NELM effects described above); and third, they create general-equilibrium effects inside and outside the rural economy.

A number of studies present econometric estimates of remittances in LDCs [e.g., Banerjee (1984), Johnson and Whitelaw (1974), Lucas and Stark (1985), Rempel and Lobdell (1978)]. Unfortunately, few take into consideration the self-selectivity of migration when estimating remittance functions. Exceptions include Hoddinott (1994) and Taylor (1987), which are discussed below.

4.2. NELM impacts

Few researchers have attempted to test the implications of migration for rural incomes and welfare in a NELM framework. The few that do find evidence that migration unleashes an array of indirect effects on rural economies that are largely outside the realm of neoclassical migration models.

Lucas (1987) uses aggregate time-series data on migration to the Union of South Africa from five African sending nations. His econometric analysis finds that the opportunity cost of wage labor, which includes migration, is large: output in migrant-sending households falls as labor is withdrawn from farm production. However, he also finds a positive feedback of migrant remittances on production. Two possible explanations for the second finding are, first, that migrant remittances are invested in production at home, which loosens financial constraints on productivity-enhancing ventures and yields a higher output, and second, that migration diversifies income sources and encourages risk-averse households to undertake unproven, but potentially productive, investments.

Consistent with these predictions, Adams (1991b) finds that rural Egyptian households containing foreign migrants have a higher marginal propensity to invest than do their non-migrant counterparts. Migration thus has a positive effect on investment that is independent of its contribution to total household income. Policy biases against agriculture, however, discourage agricultural investments in favor of land purchases, yielding the remittance-use pattern frequently observed in community studies.

Taylor (1992) estimated the marginal effect of migrant remittances on farm income and asset accumulation using data from households interviewed at two points in time in rural Mexico. Initially (in 1982), the marginal effect of remittances on household income was less than unity – that is, a $1 increase in remittances produced less than a $1 increase in total income within remittance-receiving households – an effect that is consistent with the hypothesis that the marginal product of migrant labor is positive prior to migration.

In a later period (1988), however, the marginal impact of remittances on total income was greater than unity: a $1 increase in remittances brought a $1.85 increase in total household income. This finding is consistent with the view that remittances loosen constraints on local production, once migrants become established abroad. In the Mexican case, Taylor (1992) also found that remittances promoted the accumulation of livestock over time and increased the rate of return to livestock assets (through complementary investments). Moreover, subsequent research using these data showed that, consistent with NELM theory, the marginal income effect of remittances was greatest in the most liquidity-constrained households [Taylor and Wyatt (1996)].

The micro impacts of migration and remittances on agricultural productivity are complex and have been little explored. Rozelle, Taylor and deBrauw (1999), using simultaneous-equation methods and a unique data set from China, found that the loss of labor to migration significantly reduced grain yields, reflecting an absence of on-farm labor markets. However, migrant remittances significantly increased yields, partially offsetting the negative lost-labor effect. Overall, Rozelle et al.'s findings suggest that constraints in the operation of on-farm labor and capital or insurance markets both provide households with a motivation to migrate and distort on-farm operations when labor leaves. Policies alleviating these market constraints could increase production efficiency while reducing the need to send migrants out into the labor force to finance on-farm activities and/or insure against income shocks.

These studies, while offering econometric evidence in support of the new economics of labor migration, also suggest that the relationship between migration and development is not invariant over time or across settings. Over time there appears to be a pattern first of negative and then of positive effects of migration on non-migration income in sending households. Across settings, the extent of the positive effect depends on the profitability of investments in new production activities, which in turn depend on other local conditions.

In Taylor's rural Mexican communities, livestock production proved to be a viable income-generating activity because pastureland was available, transportation links were relatively well developed, and marketing facilities were accessible. Once households were able to overcome the constraint of having limited resources to invest in livestock herds, the potential for economic growth and development was quite large. In other communities, however, profitable investment opportunities in cattle-raising were limited by environmental conditions, market constraints, and government policies that structured the terms of trade against agricultural production.

Thus, government policies represent a vital link between migration and development. Compared with the neoclassical model posited by Todaro and others, the new economics of labor migration developed by Stark and his successors leads to a radically different set of policy prescriptions to reduce emigration. Rather than intervening directly in labor markets, governments that wish to reduce out-migration should attempt to correct failures in local capital and risk markets, thereby offering households credit and insurance alternatives to migration. In the new economic model, imperfect credit and risk markets, not a low equilibrium wage in the labor market, are the fundamental causes of international migration (although credit and risk market imperfections, by restricting growth, may result in a low equilibrium wage).

4.3. General-equilibrium effects

Both rural out-migration and migrant remittances may generate important general-equilibrium effects as well, including feedback on the rural economy. For example, Mexico-to-U.S. migrant remittances in excess of $4 billion annually [United States Commission on Immigration Reform (1987)], most of which flow into Mexico's rural economy, increase rural households' demand for both food and manufactured goods. In this way, they generate demand linkages that may stimulate rural production activities and also incomes and employment in urban areas. Increases in urban incomes, in turn, increase the demand for food and other goods produced in rural areas.

General equilibrium effects of migration and remittances on rural economies can be estimated using economy-wide modeling techniques, which trace how both remittances and the labor lost to migration influence income and production as they work their way through the migrant-sending economy. Unfortunately, with a few exceptions, economy-wide techniques have not been utilized to examine the impacts of out-migration on rural economies. The few that have are from Mexico. They offer evidence at both the national [Taylor et al. (1996)] and village [Taylor and Adelman (1996), Taylor (1996), Adelman et al. (1988)] levels that migrant remittances produce significant multiplier effects on migrant-sending economies; that in the case of international migration, these effects are particularly important for rural areas; and that remittances also tend to have an equalizing effect on the distribution of income among socioeconomic groups.

Kim (1983, 1986) found that between 3 percent and 7 percent of 1976–81 GNP growth in South Korea was attributable, directly or indirectly, to migrant remittances. Ro and Seo (1988) set the figure at a remarkable 33 percent in 1982. Likewise, Hyun (1984) reported that a 10 percent increase in remittances brought a 0.32 percent increase in private consumption, a 0.53 percent increase in fixed investment, a 0.22 percent increased in GDP, and a 0.13 percent increase in prices. Based on his computable general equilibrium (CGE) analysis of Bangladesh, Habib (1985) estimated that the money remitted by Bangladeshi overseas workers in 1983 gave rise to an additional final demand of $351 million, which, in turn, generated 567,000 jobs. Ali (1981) and Mahmud (1989) found that while remittances to Bangladesh were targeted primarily to current consumption, a significant share went to nontraded goods such as land, housing, and education. After estimating employment multipliers, Stahl and Habib (1991) found that each migrant created an average of three jobs through remittances. Taylor et al. (1996) concluded that, in Mexico, remittances flow disproportionately into poor rural and urban households, and they create second-round income linkages that also favor the poor. In other words, many of the benefits of remittances accrue to households other than the ones that receive them, both inside and outside the rural economy; income linkages between migrant and non-migrant households transfer the benefits away from the remittance-receiving household.

Village research by Adelman, Taylor and Vogel (1988) estimated a "remittance multipliere" from international migration equal to 1.78; that is, $1 of international migrant remittances generated $1.78 in additional village income, or 78 cents' worth of second-round effects. The additional income was created by expenditures from remittance-receiving households, which generated demand for locally produced goods and services, bolstering the incomes of others in the village. They also found that remittances created new rural–urban growth linkages by increasing the demand for manufactured goods produced in Mexican cities. Finally, remittances stimulated investments in physical capital and schooling (by $.25 and $.13 per dollar of remittances, respectively) among both migrant and nonmigrant households in the village.

Village CGE studies from Mexico, Java, Kenya, and El Salvador find that migration tends to compete with local production for scarce family resources, raising rural incomes but in some cases producing, in the short run, a "Dutch disease" effect on migrant-sending economies. In the long run, however, remittance-induced investments increase community income. Both the household and regional effects of migration depend, however, on how remittances, and the losses and gains of human resources through out-migration, are distributed across households, on the existence of nontradable consumer and investment goods in the migrant-sending economy, and on production constraints in different households [Taylor and Adelman (1996)].

In general, migration is likely to have the largest positive effect on rural economies when the losses of human and other capital from out-migration are small; when the benefits of migration accrue disproportionately to households that face the greatest initial constraints to local production; and when households that receive remittances have expenditure patterns that produce the largest rural income multipliers.

4.4. Migration, inequality, and rural welfare

A number of researchers have examined the distributional effects of migrant remittances by comparing income distributions with and without remittances [Barham and Boucher (1998), Oberai and Singh (1980), Knowles and Anker (1981)] or by using income-source decompositions of inequality measures [Stark et al. (1986, 1988), Adams (1989, 1991a), Adams and Alderman (1992)]. These studies offer conflicting findings about the effect of remittances on income inequality.

Stark, Taylor and Yitzhaki (1986) provide a theoretical explanation for these conflicting findings. They argue that rural out-migration, like the adoption of a new production technology, initially entails high costs and risks. The costs and risks are likely to be especially high in the case of international migration. Given this fact, pioneer migrants tend to come from households at the upper-middle or top of the sending-area's income distribution [e.g., Portes and Rumbaut (1990), Lipton (1980)], and the income sent home in the form of remittances is therefore likely to widen income inequalities.

This initial unequalizing effect of remittances is dampened or reversed over time as access to migrant labor markets becomes diffused across sending-area households through the growth and elaboration of migrant networks [see Massey et al. (1994)]. Thus, Stark, Taylor and Yitzhaki (1988) found that migrant remittances had an unequalizing effect on the income distribution in a Mexican village that recently had begun to send migrants to the United States, but an equalizing effect on another village that had a long history of participating in Mexico-to-U.S. migration. They then conducted a welfare analysis of remittances using a social welfare function sensitive to both per capita income and inequality. Remittances were shown to increase rural welfare in the case of both villages, although the positive effect of remittances on inequality dampened the welfare effect in the first village.

Taylor (1992) extended this analysis by taking into account the indirect effects of international migration on income and asset accumulation over time. He provides longitudinal evidence in support of the Stark–Taylor–Yitzhaki hypothesis. Lost labor effects tend to dampen the unequalizing effects of remittances in the short run, but the positive indirect effects of migration on household income in poorer families (achieved by loosening capital and risk constraints on local production) make migration more of an income equalizer in the long run.

Over time, the indirect effects of migration on both income and inequality become increasingly important. If the Stark–Taylor–Yitzhaki hypothesis is correct, then we would expect poorer households to have the largest capital and risk constraints on investments in local income-generating activities, and therefore, the largest incentives to place migrants abroad as "financial intermediaries" to facilitate the tasks of risk management and capital acquisition, other things being equal. Initially, however, barriers to international migration in the form of high costs, poor information, and uncertainty discourage poor households from sending their family members to labor abroad.

Stark, Taylor and Yitzhaki (1988) find evidence of such barriers in the Mexican case. As barriers to international migration fall with the expansion of migrant networks, however, the benefits of international migration flow increasingly to the households that are most capital- and risk-constrained (i.e., lower income households). If these households invest in local income-generating activities, then indirect income effects should reinforce the increasingly favorable direct impacts of remittances on sending-area income distributions. This expectation is consistent with Taylor's (1992) and Taylor and Wyatt's (1996) findings from Mexico.

Findings from the relative deprivation migration studies of Stark and Taylor (1989, 1991) indicate that rural income inequality may be a determinant of, as well as influenced by, migration. In a Todaro model, a mean-preserving spread in the rural income distribution does not affect migration, because it leaves the expected income gains from migration unchanged. However, in a relative deprivation model, an increase in rural income inequality that makes some households more relatively deprived creates new incentives for migration by those households. The feedback of migration on relative deprivation may make rural out-migration a self-perpetuating process. As migration creates income gains for some rural households, it makes others (i.e., those not receiving remittance income) more relatively deprived. This, in turn, increases the latter's likelihood of participating in migration in an effort to overcome this relative deprivation in the future.

4.5. Migration's impacts on rural migrant-receiving areas

A large and burgeoning literature addresses the impacts of immigration in developed countries, particularly the United States [for an excellent review, see Borjas (1994)]. However, with very few exceptions, the focus of these studies has been on urban, rather than rural, labor markets. A nascent body of research examines the reshaping of rural economies in the United States through immigration. Interestingly, it echoes many of the themes and findings of research in the 1960s and 1970s on the impacts of rural population change in the United States (see above), but in a context of growing, rather than declining, rural populations. In LDCs, there has been growing interest in rural-to-rural migration and its implications for the environment.

4.6. Impacts of immigration on rural economies in developed countries

Several conceptual models attempt to describe how immigrants affect local populations and economies [Taylor et al. (1997)]. Two models mark the extremes. One argues that the presence of immigrant workers creates economies of scale and multiplier effects. In other words, the arrival of immigrants increases local economic activity and creates or preserves good jobs for local residents. This view characterizes much of the urban-focused research on immigration in the 1980s; for example, see Borjas (1984), DeFritas (1988), Altonji and Card (1991), Bean, Lowell and Taylor, (1988), LaLonde and Topel (1991), Borjas (1990), Grossman (1982), Muller and Espenshade (1985), Winegarden and Khor (1991), Simon, Moore and Sullivan (1993), Card (1990), Butcher and Card (1991), Vroman and Worden (1992), and Fix and Passel (1994). Their findings generally support Piore's (1979) argument that most recent immigrants are concentrated in distinct labor-market segments. According to Piore,

> The jobs (immigrants take) tend to be low-skilled, generally but not always low paying, and to carry or connote inferior social status; they often involve hard or unpleasant working conditions and considerable insecurity; they seldom offer chances of advancement toward better-paying, more attractive job opportunities (p. 17).

Because of this, migrants and native workers tend to be complements, not substitutes, in production. The econometric model these studies employ involves regressing wages and employment (weeks worked) for different native-worker groups on the number of immigrants in local labor markets (SMSAs). Implicitly, this corresponds to a statistical experiment in which immigrants are randomly injected into closed labor markets.

The other extreme view, inspired by neoclassical trade theory, argues that immigrants take over local jobs and freeze low wages into place, competing with at least some groups of workers. It is based on a fundamental critique of the research methods utilized by earlier studies, recognizing that native workers are likely to respond to the arrival of immigrants by moving to less immigrant-impacted labor markets, shifting the labor-supply curve inward and dissipating the impacts of immigration through internal migration. Studies that focus on immigration impacts on local economies, including local rural economies, therefore may mask the macro effect of immigration on wages and employment [Borjas (1994)].

There are reasons to expect a priori that both of these models help characterize the impacts of immigration in rural communities. Taylor, Martin and Fix (1997) found that, in California, the preponderance of new immigrants are low-skilled, capital-poor workers who compete with other low-skilled immigrants for seasonal farm jobs. Most have poverty earnings. They coexist in rural towns with established, usually older immigrant groups who have some access to capital and often specialize in providing farmworkers with services like housing, transportation, food, and job placement. New immigrants create new sources of income (income linkages) for these established residents of farmworker towns, while constituting an inexpensive and flexible source of labor for agricultural employers who typically live outside the towns that house their workforce. The resulting mixture of positive income linkages for some groups and competition for low-wage, seasonal farm jobs among low-skilled immigrants creates a socioeconomic geography of contrast. While California's 12 major agricultural counties had farm sales of over $12 billion in 1993, more than any U.S. state except California itself, an average of 26 percent of all residents of farm towns in these twelve counties lived below the poverty line in 1990. Data from the NAWS indicate that, nationwide, more than 50 percent of all farmworker households had incomes below the poverty line in 1996 [Mines et al. (1997)].

Econometric findings reported in Taylor and Martin (1997) and Taylor, Martin and Fix (1997) point to a circular relationship between farm employment and immigration in 65 rural towns and cities of California. Taylor and Martin (1997); [also see Martin and

Taylor (1999)] estimated a five-equation simultaneous-equation model for immigration, farm employment, migration, poverty, and welfare use. They found evidence of a circular relationship between immigration and farm employment between 1980 and 1990: an additional 100 farm jobs were associated with 143 more immigrants, and an additional 100 immigrants, in turn, were associated with the creation of 36 more farm jobs. Because most farm jobs are seasonal and offer workers below-poverty-level earnings, each additional farm job was associated with $987 in welfare payments in 1990. There was no evidence that poor immigrants were more likely to receive welfare income than poor nonimmigrants in rural California. However, immigration constituted an important link in the farm employment–immigration–poverty–welfare chain. Based on a three-stage least-squares analysis of census tract data, Taylor and Martin (1998) found evidence of a similar "vicious circle" of immigration, poverty, and farm employment in the western United States between 1980 and 1990. It stood in contrast with negative effects of farm employment on poverty and welfare use, both in the West and in the United States as a whole, one decade earlier.

Taylor, Martin and Fix (1997) examine the re-creation of rural poverty through immigration, drawing from an econometric analysis of census data and case studies of rural California communities. They reach three broad conclusions: First, immigration, principally from rural Mexico, is fueling an unprecedented growth in population, poverty, and public service demands in rural California communities. Second, upward mobility of immigrant farmworkers in rural California is the exception rather than the rule. Third, public resources available to integrate newcomers are declining even though the number of immigrants is increasing. In rural areas, federal assistance programs originally created for other purposes have become de facto immigrant assistance programs. This study found no evidence that the poverty impacts of immigration spill over into adjacent communities.

These findings are consistent with those of Gardner (1974) and others who documented a positive relationship between out-migration and rural incomes in earlier periods. Just as rural out-migration appears to have resolved the poverty associated with "too many farmers" between 1940 and 1970, immigration, stimulated by the expansion of low-skill farm jobs, appears to be creating a poverty associated with "too many workers" in the 1980s and 1990s. If history repeats itself, this new rural poverty will stimulate rural-to-urban migration. However, given an elastic supply of low-skilled workers from abroad, it is not clear whether future rural out-migration will alleviate poverty in rural communities.

More research is needed to understand immigration–employment–poverty links in rural areas and design policies to reduce poverty in an era of immigration-driven rural population growth.

4.7. Rural-to-rural migration in LDCs

Nearly all research on internal migration in LDCs addresses rural-to-urban migration, to such an extent that "internal" and "rural-to-urban" are often treated as interchangeable in migration research. Recently, there has been some interest in understanding the magnitude of, and the forces driving, rural-to-rural migration – that is, the redistribution of populations within rural areas. This research is motivated primarily by the environmental ramifications of migration to remote rural areas of those in search of land to continue agricultural livelihoods. The World Bank's 1992 World Development Report notes that migration into new rural environments is an important mechanism by which rural population growth and poverty result in environmental degradation, including deforestation:

> Because they lack resources and technology, land-hungry farmers resort to ...
> moving into tropical forest areas where crop yields on cleared fields usually drop
> sharply after just a few years [The World Bank (1992), p. 7].

Bilsborrow (1992) compares magnitudes of different types of internal migration flows in 14 countries and finds that rural-to-rural migration is the largest in three and exceeds rural-to-urban migration in eleven, despite being almost universally ignored in the literature on internal migration. His research highlights statistical challenges to studying rural-to-rural migration, including questions surrounding the criteria used to classify populations as "rural" versus "urban" in different country settings. Nevertheless, it underlines the potential importance of rural-to-rural migration for some countries, particularly those containing an extensive forest margin or rural frontier, on the one hand, and high rural population densities or inegalitarian land distributions, on the other. Typically, migration to the rural margins is facilitated by public investments in roads to open up new agricultural frontiers [Bilsborrow and Carr (1998)]. Salient examples include migration into the Brazilian and Ecuadorian Amazon, the emergence of new rural plantations in Malaysia and Thailand, agricultural labor migration from southern to northwestern Mexico, and the forced relocation of Javanese in Indonesia.

The same tools used to model rural-to-urban and international migrations and their impacts potentially are useful for studying rural-to-rural migration; however, to date, little formal modeling of rural-to-rural migration has appeared in the economics literature. Understanding the origins of rural-to-rural migration is crucial for determining the causes of, and formulating appropriate policy responses to, migration-induced deforestation in LDCs.

5. Conclusions and policy considerations

The movement of labor out of agriculture is both a quintessential feature of agricultural transformations and a prerequisite for efficient and balanced economic growth. Yet one of the motivations for migration research, particularly for Todaro (1969) and his followers, has been to identify appropriate policy measures to reduce the rate of rural out-migration. The case for government interventions turns on the argument that some market distortions exist and that these distortions result in "too much" rural out-migration as well as in various migration-induced externalities at migrant origins and destinations. Concern over such externalities underlies much of the research on rural out-migration in the United States between 1940 and 1970.

As Romans (1974) [also see discussion in Greenwood (1975)] pointed out, social burdens or benefits from migration can arise from pecuniary externalities (e.g., income redistributive effects of the type discussed by Berry and Soligo (1969) (see Section 4 of this Chapter); impacts of migration on prices and, through them, on the derived demand for labor at migrant origins and destinations; technological externalities (e.g., increasing returns to scale or various external economies associated with migration); and/or market distortions (e.g., effects of migration on the demand for, and revenues to support, public goods and services).

In a neoclassical world of complete and well-functioning markets, there is little or no economic rationale for policies to reduce migration. In Todaro (1969), migration in excess of urban job creation results in high rates of urban unemployment, with obvious welfare costs for urban areas. In addition, because each new urban job stimulates the migration of more than one rural worker, the opportunity cost of urban job creation for the rural economy is larger than would be the case in a context of urban full employment. Todaro's policy prescriptions all focus on interventions in labor markets; i.e., combining urban wage subsidies with physical restrictions on migration, he argues, is necessary to achieve economywide production efficiency (a second-best solution). (Bhagwati and Srinivasan (1974) show that this is actually not correct because a first-best solution is possible using a variety of tax and subsidy schemes, without relying on physical restrictions on migration. They, too, focus on labor-market interventions to reduce unwanted rural-to-urban migration.) The market distortion that results in too much migration in this view is a formal-sector urban wage that is institutionally set above the market-clearing level. This results in urban unemployment and creates the rationale for using an expected-income migration model.

The NELM shifts the focus of migration policy from interventions in labor markets to interventions in other markets, especially those for capital, risk, and information. In this view, market imperfections are the distortions that stimulate migration at levels that would not be optimal in a strictly neoclassical world. There is no reason to assume that disequilibrium in the labor market, reflected in migration, should be addressed by policy interventions in that market. As the Russian proverb cited by Stark (1982) so aptly puts it, "It is not the horse that draws the cart, but the oats".

Unlike in the Todaro approach, however, it is not clear whether there is too much or too little migration in a NELM world. For example, if rural households engage in migration in an effort to reduce their income risk or overcome credit constraints, the result is more migration than would be observed in the presence of perfect rural insurance or capital markets. On the other hand, migration risks, liquidity constraints on financing costly migration, and imperfect information about labor markets at migrant destinations would result in less migration than would be optimal in a world of perfect information and markets. While migration in excess of urban job creation pushes up the shadow wage associated with urban jobs, a positive feedback of migration on rural production reduces this shadow wage [Stark (1982)].

Nevertheless, who migrates matters. Rural market distortions create inefficiencies by discouraging migration by individuals who lack access to information (e.g., because they do not have migration networks, or contacts at migrant destinations) or who are less credit- or risk-constrained. In a first-best world, the individuals who migrate are those whose movement out of the rural sector results in the largest productivity and income gain for the economy as a whole. This is not necessarily the case when rural market imperfections drive migration decisions.

In the light of distortions in rural credit, risk, and information markets, it is clear that migration decisions do not take place in a first-best world in the NELM, as in the Todaro, view. However, adding a new constraint to the general-equilibrium system by physically restricting migration, as Todaro proposes, obviously does not transport us to a second-best world if market distortions outside the labor market drive rural out-migration. Rather than attempt to directly influence rural out-migration, policies should focus on alleviating imperfections in rural markets that encourage "too many" people to leave the rural sector – keeping in mind that leaving does not always mean economically abandoning – and perhaps also on making migration and remittances more conducive to rural development.

In immigrant-receiving rural areas in the United States, the limited evidence available suggests that a continuing influx of foreign workers to fill seasonal jobs may be a double-edged sword. Employers benefit from the presence of low-wage workers, but rural communities bear the costs of providing services and public assistance to impoverished seasonal workers and their families. Immigration policies tend to produce unintended consequences, increasing rather than reducing agriculture's use of immigrant farmworkers and changing the structure of farm labor markets in ways that make immigration and labor laws more difficult to enforce and rural poverty more difficult to extirpate [Thilmany (1996), Martin et al. (1995), Taylor and Thilmany (1993)].

In LDCs, the redistribution of population within rural areas towards extensive forest margins or rural frontiers carries with it potentially far-reaching environmental consequences, including the irreversible loss of biodiversity. Researchers are only beginning to address the negative environmental externalities associated with migration to the rural margins of LDCs. In the meantime, government policies frequently encourage this migration through infrastructure investments and other measures. It is likely that a complex interaction of government policies and market imperfections in migrant-sending areas shapes rural-to-rural migration and that environmental, like economic, outcomes are influenced by the selectivity of this migration.

Because the stakes are high and the potential for policy failures along with market failures considerable, much more research is needed to determine whether, indeed, there is excessive rural migration in LDCs and excessive rural in-migration in high-income countries, and, if so, what the true determinants of this migration and the appropriate roles for government policy are. Disagreements over whether there is too much or too little migration partly reflect a scarcity of solid empirical research documenting alleged market distortions and their influence on migration and its welfare impacts. Until the hypotheses and welfare implications of competing migration models are more thoroughly tested (and appropriate data generated to support such tests), these ambiguities will persist. One thing is certain: regardless of what directions our migration policies and research take, the exodus of population out of the world's rural areas will continue and most likely accelerate in the twenty-first century.

Acknowledgements

Various components of this research were supported by the William and Flora Hewlett Foundation, the Rosenberg Foundation, the Giannini Foundation of Agricultural Economics, the Kellogg Foundation, and by a USDA National Research Initiative grant. We are indebted to Sheila Desai, Mimako Kobayashi, Pauline Griego, and two anonymous referees.

References

Abowd, J., and R. Freeman, eds. (1991), Immigration, Trade, and the Labor Market (University of Chicago Press, Chicago).

Adams, Jr., R.H. (1989), "Worker remittances and inequality in rural Egypt", Economic Development and Cultural Change 38:45–71.

Adams, Jr., R.H. (1991a), "The economic uses and impact of international remittances in rural Egypt", Economic Development and Cultural Change 39:695–722.

Adams, Jr., R.H. (1991b), "The effects of international remittances on poverty, inequality, and development in rural Egypt" (International Food Policy Research Institute, Washington, DC).

Adams, Jr., R.H., and H. Alderman (1992), "Sources of inequality in rural Pakistan: A decomposition analysis", Oxford Bulletin of Economics and Statistics 54(4):591–608.

Adelman, I., and J.E. Taylor (1991), "Multisectoral models and structural adjustment: New evidence from Mexico", Journal of Development Studies (October).

Adelman, I., J.E. Taylor and S. Vogel (1988), "Life in a Mexican village: A SAM perspective", Journal of Development Studies 25:5–24.

Ali, S.A. (1981), "Labor migration from Bangladesh to the Middle East" (The World Bank, Washington, DC).

Altonji, J., and D. Card (1991), "The effects of immigration on the labor market outcomes of less-skilled natives", in: J. Abowd and R. Freeman, eds., Immigration, Trade, and the Labor Market (University of Chicago Press, Chicago).

Antle, J.M. (1983), "Testing the stochastic structure of production: A flexible moment-based approach", Journal of Business and Economic Statistics 1(3):192–201.

Balan, J., H. Browning and E. Jelin (1973), Men in a Developing Society (University of Texas Press, Austin).

Banerjee, B. (1984), "The probability, size, and use of remittances from urban to rural areas in India", Journal of Development Economics 16:293–311.

Bardhan, P. (1988), "Alternative approaches to development economics", in: H. Chenery and T.N. Srinivasan, eds., Handbook of Development Economics, Vol. I (Elsevier Science Publishers, New York).

Barham, B., and S. Boucher (1998), "Migration, remittances, and inequality: Estimating the net effects of migration on income distribution", Journal of Development Economics 55(2):307–331.

Barkley, A.P. (1990), "The determinants of the migration of labor out of agriculture in the United States, 1940–85", American Journal of Agricultural Economics 72(3):567–573.

Barnum, H.N., and R.H. Sabot (1975), "Education, employment probabilities and rural–urban migration in Tanzania", Paper presented at 1975 World Congress Econometric Society.

Barnum, H.N., and L. Squire (1979), "An econometric application of the theory of the farm-household", Journal of Development Economics 6:79–102.

Barro, R., and G. Becker (1986), "Fertility choice in a model of economic growth, unpublished (University of Chicago, Chicago).

Bean, F.D., B.L. Lowell and L.J. Taylor (1988), "Undocumented Mexican immigrants and the earnings of other workers in the United States", Demography 35(1):35–52.

Becker, G.S. (1975), Human Capital, 2nd edn. (Columbia University Press, New York).

Berry, R.A., and R. Soligo (1969), "Some welfare aspects of international migration", Journal of Political Economy 77:778–794.

Bhagwati, J.N., and T.N. Srinivasan (1974), "On reanalyzing the Harris–Todaro model: Policy rankings in the case of sector-specific sticky wages", American Economic Review 64(3):502–508.

Bilsborrow, R.E. (1992), "Rural poverty, migration, and the environment in developing countries: Three case studies", Policy Research Working Paper, World Development Report, WPS 1017 (The World Bank, Washington, DC).

Bilsborrow, R.E., and D.L. Carr (1998), "Population, agricultural land use and the environment in developing countries", Paper presented at the American Agricultural Economics Association Annual Meetings, Salt Lake City, August 3–5.

Bishop, C.E., ed. (1967), Farm Labor in the United States (Columbia University Press, New York).

Blejer, M.I., H.G. Johnson and A.C. Prozecanski (1978), "An analysis of the economic determinants of legal and illegal Mexican migration to the United States", Research in Population Economics 1:217–231.

Borjas, G.J. (1984), "The impact of immigrants on the earnings of the native-born", in: V.M. Briggs and M. Tienda, eds., Immigration: Issues and Policies (Olympus Publishing, Salt Lake City).

Borjas, G.J. (1990), Friends or Strangers: The Impact of Immigrants on the U.S. Economy (Basic Books, New York).

Borjas, G.J. (1994), "The economics of immigration", Journal of Economic Literature XXXII (December):1667–1717.

Borjas, G.J., and R.B. Freeman, eds. (1992), Immigration and the Work Force: Economic Consequences for the United States and Source Areas (University of Chicago Press, Chicago).

Bourguignon, F., and P.-A. Chiappori (1992), "Collective models of household behavior: An introduction", European Economic Review 36:355–364.

Butcher, K.F., and D. Card (1991), "Immigration and wages: Evidence from the 1980s", Economic Impact of Immigration 81(2):292–296.

Card, D. (1990), "The impact of the mariel boatlift on the Miami labor market", Industrial and Labor Relations Review 43(2):245–257.

Carvajal, M.J., and D.T. Geithman (1974), "An economic analysis of migration in Costa Rica", Economic Development and Cultural Change 23(1):105–122.

Castillo-Freeman, A.J., and R.B. Freeman (1992), "When the minimum wage really bites: The effect of the U.S. – level minimum wage on Puerto Rico", in: G.J. Borjas and R.B. Freeman, eds., Immigration and the Work Force: Economic Consequences for the United States and Source Areas (University of Chicago Press, Chicago) 177–212.

Chiappori, P.-A. (1997), "Introducing household production in collective models of labor supply", Journal of Political Economy 105(1):191–209.

Cole, W.E., and R.D. Sanders (1985), "Internal migration and urbanization in the third world", American Economic Review 75:481–493.

David, P.A. (1974), "Fortune, risk, and the microeconomics of migration", in: P.A. Avid and M.W. Reder, eds., Nations and Households in Economic Growth (Academic Press, New York).

Davies, J.B., and I. Wooton (1992), "Income inequality and international migration", Economic Journal 102:789–802.

Day, R. (1967), "The economics of technological change and the demise of the sharecropper", American Economic Review (June):427–449.

DeFritas, G. (1988), "Hispanic immigration and labor market segmentation", Industrial Relations 27(2):195–214.

De Janvry, A., M. Fafchamps and E. Sadoulet (1991), "Peasant household behavior with missing markets: Some paradoxes explained", The Economic Journal 101:1400–1417.

Dickens, W.T., and K. Lang (1985), "A test of dual labor market theory", American Economic Review 75:792–805.

Djajic, S. (1986), "International migration, remittances and welfare in a dependent economy", Journal of Development Economics 21:229–234.

Emerson, R.D. (1984), "Migration in farm labor markets", in: R.D. Emerson, ed., Seasonal Agricultural Labor Markets in the United States (The Iowa State University Press, Ames, IA).

Emerson, R.D. (1989), "Migratory labor and agriculture", American Journal of Agricultural Economics 71(3):617–629.

Engels, F. (1845), The Condition of the Working Class in England, Translated in 1974 from the 1845 edition with introduction by J. Hobsbawm (Panther Press, St. Albans, England).

Falaris, W.M. (1987), "A nested logit migration model with selectivity", International Economic Review 28(2):429–443.

Fields, G. (1975), "Rural–urban migration, urban unemployment and underemployment, and job search activity in LDC's", Journal of Development Economics 2(2):165–188.

Fields, G. (1979), "Lifetime migration in Colombia: Tests of the expected income hypothesis", Population and Development Review 5 (June).

Fix, M., and J.S. Passel (1994), Immigration and Immigrants: Setting the Record Straight (The Urban Institute Press, Washington, DC).

Fletcher, P.L. (1997), "Building from migration: Imported design and everyday use of migrant houses in Mexico", in: B. Orlove, ed., The Allure of the Foreign: Foreign Goods in Post-Colonial Latin America (University of Michigan Press, Ann Arbor).

Funkhouser, E. (1995), "Remittances from international migration: A comparison of El Salvador and Nicaragua", Review of Economics and Statistics LXXVII(1):137–146.

Gardner, B.L. (1970), "Surplus labor in rural Pakistan: Comment", American Journal of Agricultural Economics 52(1):158–159.

Gardner, B.L. (1974), "Farm population decline and the income of rural families", American Journal of Agricultural Economics 56 (August):600–606.

Greenwood, M.J. (1971), "A regression analysis of migration to urban areas of less-developed countries: The case of India", Journal of Regional Science 11:253–262.

Greenwood, M.J. (1975), "Research on internal migration in the United States: A survey", Journal of Economic Literature 13(2):397–433.

Gregory, P. (1986), The Myth of Market Failure: Employment and the Labor Market in Mexico (The Johns Hopkins University Press, Baltimore).

Grossman, J.B. (1982), "The substitutability of natives and immigrants in production", Review of Economics and Statistics 64(4):596–603.

Grubel, H.B., and A.D. Scott (1966), "The international flow of human capital", The American Economic Review 56:268–274.

Habib, A. (1985), "Economic consequences of international migration for sending countries: Review of evidence from Bangladesh", Ph.D. Thesis, University of Newcastle, Australia.

Harris, J.R., and M.P. Todaro (1970), "Migration, unemployment, and development: A two-sector analysis", American Economic Review 60:126–142.

Hatton, T.J., and J.G. Williamson (1992), "International migration and world development: A historical perspective", NBER Working Paper Series on Historical Factors in Long Run Growth No. 41 (National Bureau of Economic Research, Cambridge, MA).

Hay, M.J. (1974), "An economic analysis of rural–urban migration in Tunisia", Ph.D. Dissertation, University of Minnesota.

Heady, E., ed. (1961), Labor Mobility and Population in Agriculture (Iowa State University Press, Ames, IA).

Heckman, J. (1974), "Shadow prices, market wages, and labor supply", Econometrica 42:679–694.

Hoddinott, J. (1994), "A model of migration and remittances applied to Western Kenya", Oxford Economic Papers 46:459–476.

House, W.J., and H. Rempel (1976), "Labour market pressure and wage determination in less developed countries: The case of Kenya", mimeo (Department of Economics, University of Nairobi).

Hunt, G., and M.J. Greenwood (1984), "Migration and interregional employment redistribution in the United States", American Economic Review 74(5):957–969.

Hyun, O.-S. (1984), "A macroeconometric model of Korea: Simulation experiments with a large-scale model for a developing country", Ph.D. Thesis, University of Pennsylvania, Philadelphia.

Jenkins, J.C. (1977), "Push/pull in recent Mexican migration to the U.S.", International Migration Review 11:178–189.

Johnson, D.G. (1948), "Mobility as a field of research", Southern Economic Journal 40:152–161.

Johnson, D.G. (1960), "Output and income effects of reducing the farm labor force", Journal of Farm Economics 42(November):779–796.

Johnson, H.G. (1967), "Some economic aspects of the brain drain", Pakistani Development Review 7:379–411.

Johnson, G.E., and W. Whitelaw (1974), "Urban–rural income transfers in Kenya: An estimated remittances function", Economic Development and Cultural Change 22:473–479.

Jones, L.S., and J.W. Christian (1965), "Some observations on the agricultural labor market", Industrial and Labor Relations Review 18 (4):522–534.

Jorgenson, D.W. (1967), "Testing alternative theories of the development of a dual economy", in: I. Adelman and E. Thorbecke, eds., The Theory and Design of Economic Development (The Johns Hopkins University Press, Baltimore).

Just, R.E., and R.D. Pope (1977), "Stochastic specification of production functions and economic implications", Journal of Econometrics 7(1).

Kemp, M.C. (1964), The Pure Theory of International Trade (Prentice-Hall, Englewood Cliffs).

Kim, S. (1983), "Economic analysis of Korean manpower migration, Sogang University", Journal of Economics and Business, September, 3–16.

Kim, S. (1986), "Labor migration from Korea to the middle east: Its trends and impact on the Korean economy", in: F. Arnold and N.M. Shaw, eds., Asian Labor Migration: Pipeline to the Middle East (Westview Press, Boulder, CO) 163–176.

Knowles, J.C., and R.B. Anker (1975), "Economic determinants of demographic behaviour in Kenya, population and employment", Working Paper No. 28 (International Labour Office, Geneva).

Knowles, J.C., and R.B. Anker (1981), "Analysis of income transfers in a developing country: The case of Kenya", Journal of Development Economics 8:205–226.

LaLonde, R., and R. Topel (1991), "Labor market adjustments to increased immigration", in: J. Abowd and R. Freeman, eds., Immigration, Trade, and the Labor Market (University of Chicago Press, Chicago).

Larson, D., and Y. Mundlak (1997), "On the intersectoral migration of agricultural labor", Economic Development and Cultural Change 45:295–319.

Lee, L.-F. (1978), "Unionism and wage rates: A simultaneous equations model with qualitative and limited dependent variables", International Economic Review 19:415–433.

Levy, M.E., and W.J. Wadycki (1974), "Education and the decision to migrate: An econometric analysis of migration in Venezuela", Econometrica 42(2):377–388.

Levy, S., and S. Wijnberger (1992), "Mexican agriculture in the free trade agreement: Transition problems in economic reform", OECD/Gd(92) 77 Technical Paper No. 63 (Organization for Economic Cooperation and Development, Paris).

Lewis, W.A. (1954), "Economic development with unlimited supplies of labour", Manchester School of Economic and Social Studies 22:139–191.

Lipton, M. (1980), "Migration from rural areas of poor countries: The impact on rural productivity and income distribution", World Development 8:10–20.

Lozano Ascencio, F. (1993), "Bringing it back home: Remittances to Mexico from migrant workers in the United States", Monograph Series, Vol. 37 (Center for U.S.–Mexican Studies, University of California at San Diego).

Lucas, R.E.B. (1987), "Emigration to South Africa's mines", American Economic Review 77:313–330.

Lucas, R.E.B., and O. Stark (1985), "Motivations to remit: Evidence from Botswana", Journal of Political Economy 93:901–918. [Reprinted in Stark (1991).]

MacDougal, G.D.A. (1960), "The benefits and costs of private investment from abroad: A theoretical approach", Economic Record 36:13–35.

Maddala, G.S. (1983), Limited-Dependent and Qualitative Variables in Econometrics (Cambridge University Press, Cambridge).

Maddox, J.G. (1960), "Private and social costs of the movement of people out of agriculture", American Economic Review 50:392–402.

Mahmud, W. (1989), "The impact of overseas labour migration on the Bangladesh economy", in: R. Amjad, ed., To the Gulf and Back: Studies on the Economic Impact of Asian Labour Migration (International Labour Office, Geneva) 55–94.

Maldonado, R. (1976), "Why Puerto Ricans migrated to the United States in 1947–1973", Monthly Labor Review 99(9):7–18.

Martin, P.L., W. Huffman, R. Emerson, J.E. Taylor and R.I. Rochin, eds. (1995), Immigration Reform and U.S. Agriculture (University of California, Division of Agriculture and Natural Resources, Oakland).

Martin, P.L., and A.L. Olmstead (1985), "The agricultural mechanization controversy", Science, 227, 4687 (February):601–606.

Martin, P.L., and J.E. Taylor (1999), "Poverty amid prosperity: Farm employment, immigration, and poverty in California", American Journal of Agricultural Economics 80 (5):1008–1014.

Massey, D.S., R. Alarcón, J. Durand and H. González (1987), Return to Aztlan: The Social Process of International Migration from Western Mexico (University of California Press, Berkeley and Los Angeles).

Massey, D.S., J. Arango, G. Hugo, A. Kouaouci, A. Pellegrino and J.E. Taylor (1993), "Theories of international migration: An integration and appraisal", Population and Development Review 19(3):431–466.

Massey, D.S., J. Arango, G. Hugo, A. Kouaouci, A. Pellegrino and J.E. Taylor (1994), "International migration: The North American case", Population and Development Review 20(4):699–751.

Massey, D.S., J. Arango, G. Hugo, A. Kouaouci, A. Pellegrino and J.E. Taylor (1998), Worlds in Motion: Understanding International Migration at the End of the Millennium (Clarendon Press, Oxford).

Massey, D.S., L.P. Goldring and J. Durand (1994), "Continuities in transnational migration: An analysis of 19 Mexican communities", American Journal of Sociology 99:1492–1533.

McElroy, M.B., and M.J. Horney (1981), "Nash bargained household decisions", International Economic Review 22 (June):333–350.

Mincer, J. (1974), Schooling, Experience, and Earnings (Columbia University Press, New York).

Mincer, J. (1978), "Family migration decisions", Journal of Political Economy 86:749–773.

Mines, R., S. Gabbard and A. Steirman (1997), "A profile of US farmworkers" (U.S. Department of Labor, Washington) (March).

Muller, T., and T.J. Espenshade (1985), The Fourth Wave (The Urban Institute Press, Washington, DC).

Nabi, I. (1984), "Village-end considerations in rural–urban migration", Journal of Development Economics 14:129–145.

Nakosteen, R.A., and M. Zimmer (1980), "Migration and income: The question of self-selection", Southern Economic Journal 46:840–851.

Nelson, J. (1976), "Sojourners versus new urbanites: Causes and consequences of temporary versus permanent cityward migration in developing countries", Economic Development and Cultural Change 24:721–757.

Oberai, A.S., and H.K.M. Singh (1980), "Migration, remittances and rural development: Findings of a case study in the Indian Punjab", International Labor Review 119:229–241.

Perloff, J.M., L. Lynch and S.M. Gabbard (1998), "Migration of seasonal agricultural workers", American Journal of Agricultural Economics 80(1):154–164.

Piore, M.J. (1979), Birds of Passage: Migrant Labor in Industrial Societies (Cambridge University Press, Cambridge).

Portes, A., and R.G. Rumbaut (1990), Immigrant America: A Portrait (University of California Press, Berkeley and Los Angeles).

President's National Advisory Commission on Rural Poverty (1967), The People Left Behind (U.S. Government Printing Office, Washington, DC).

Quibria, M.G. (1988), "A note on international migration, non-traded goods and economic welfare in the source country", Journal of Development Economics 28:377–387.

Ramos, F.A. (1992), "Out-migration and return migration of Puerto Ricans, in immigration and the workforce: Economic consequences for the United States and source areas", in: G.J. Borjas and R.B. Freeman, eds., A NBER Project Report (University of Chicago Press, Chicago and London) 49–66.

Ranis, G., and J.C.H. Fei (1961), "A theory of economic development", The American Economic Review 51:533–565.

Ravenstein, E.G. (1885), "The laws of migration", Journal of the Royal Statistical Society, 48:167–227.

Redford, A. (1968), Labor Migration in England 1800–1850, revised by W.H. Chaloner from the 1926 edition (Augustus Kelley, New York).

Rempel, H., and R. Lobdell (1978), "The role of urban-to-rural remittances in rural development", Journal of Development Studies 14:324–341.

Rivera-Batiz, F.L. (1982), "International migration, non-traded goods and economic welfare in the source country", Journal of Development Economics 11:81–90.

Ro, K.K., and J.K. Seo (1988), "The economic impact of Korea's out-migration", Asian Migrant 1:13–15.

Roberts, K.D. (1997), "China's 'Tidal Wave' of migrant labor: What can we learn from Mexican undocumented migration to the United States?", International Migration Review 31(2):249–293.

Robinson, C., and N. Tomes (1982), "Self-selection and interprovincial migration in Canada", Canadian Journal of Economics 15 (November):474–502.

Robinson, S., M.E. Burfisher, R. Hinojosa-Ojeda and K.E. Thierfelder (1991), "Agricultural policies and migration in a U.S.–Mexico free trade area: A computable general equilibrium analysis", Working Paper No. 617, December (UC Berkeley, Department of Agricultural and Resource Economics).

Robinson, W.C. (1969), " 'Disguised' unemployment once again: East Pakistan, 1951–61", American Journal of Agricultural Economics 51 (August):592–604.

Romans, J.T. (1974), "Benefits and burdens of migration (with specific reference to the brain drain)", Southern Economic Journal 40(3):447–455.

Rosenzweig, M.R. (1978), "Rural wages, labor supply, and land reform: A theoretical and empirical analysis", American Economic Review 68:847–861.

Rosenzweig, M.R. (1980), "Neoclassical theory and optimizing peasant: An econometric analysis of market family labor supply in a developing country", Journal of Econometrics 24 (January–February):181–196.

Rosenzweig, M.R. (1988), "Labor markets in low-income countries", in: H. Chenery and T.N. Srinivasan, eds., Handbook of Development Economics, Vol. I (Elsevier Science Publishers, New York), 714–763.

Rosenzweig, M.R., and R. Evenson (1977), "Fertility, schooling, and the economic contribution of children in rural India: An econometric analysis", Econometrica 45(5):1065–1079.

Rosenzweig, M.R., and O. Stark (1989), "Consumption smoothing, migration and marriage: Evidence from rural India", Journal of Political Economy 97(4):905–926. [Reprinted in Stark (1991).]

Rosenzweig, M.R., and K. Wolpin (1985), "Specific experience, household structure, and integrated transfers: Farm, family land and labor arrangements in developing countries", Quarterly Journal of Economics 100 (Supplement):961–986.

Rouse, R. (1991), "Mexican migration and the social space of postmodernism", Diaspora: A Journal of Transnational Studies 1:8–23.

Rozelle, S., J.E. Taylor and A. de Brauw (1999), "Migration, remittances, and productivity in China", American Economic Review 89(2):287–291.

Schiff, M. (1996), "Trade policy and international migration: substitutes or complements?", in: J.E. Taylor, ed., Development Strategy, Employment, and Migration: Insights from Models (OECD, Paris).

Schmitz, A., and D. Seckler (1970), "Mechanized agriculture and social welfare: The case of the tomato harvester", American Journal of Agricultural Economics 52:569–577.

Schuh, G.E. (1962), "An econometric investigation of the market for hired labor in agriculture", Journal of Farm Economics 44(May):307–321.

Schultz, T.P. (1975), "The determinants of internal migration in Venezuela: An application of the polytomous logistic model", Paper presented at Econometric Society World Congress, Toronto.

Schultz, T.P. (1982), "Lifetime migration within educational strata in Venezuela: Estimates of a logistic model", Economic Development and Cultural Change 30(3):559–593.

Schultz, T.P. (1988), "Heterogeneous preferences and migration: Self-selection, regional prices and programs, and the behavior of migrants in Colombia", Research in Population Economics 6:163–181.

Schultz, T.W. (1953), The Economic Organization of Agriculture (McGraw-Hill, New York).

Schultz, T.W. (1964), Transforming Traditional Agriculture (Yale University Press, New Haven).

Simon, J.L., S. Moore and R. Sullivan (1993), "The effect of immigration on aggregate native unemployment: An across-city estimation", Journal of Labor Research 14(3):299–316.

Singh, I., L. Squire and J. Strauss (1986), "An overview of agricultural household models – The basic model: Theory, empirical results, and policy conclusions", in: I. Singh, L. Squire and J. Strauss, eds., Agricultural Household Models, Extensions, Applications and Policy (The World Bank and the Johns Hopkins University Press, Baltimore) 17–47.

Sjaastad, L.A. (1962), "The costs and returns of human migration", Journal of Political Economy 70 (5):80–93.

Smith, A. (1776), The Wealth of Nations, Edwin Cannan, ed. (Modern Library, New York, 1937).

Squire, L. (1981), Employment Policies in Developing Countries: A Survey of Issues and Evidence (Oxford University Press, Oxford).

Stahl, C., and A. Habib (1991), "Emigration and development in South and Southeast Asia", in: D.G. Papademetriou and P.L. Martin, eds., The Unsettled Relationship: Labor Migration and Economic Development (Greenwood, New York) 163–180.

Stark, O. (1978), Economic-Demographic Interactions in Agricultural Development: The Case of Rural-to-Urban Migration (U.N. Food and Agricultural Organization, Rome).

Stark, O. (1982), "Research on rural-to-urban migration in less developed countries: The confusion frontier and why we should pause to Rethink Afresh", World Development 10:70–73. [Reprinted in Stark (1991).]

Stark, O. (1984), "Rural-to-urban migration in LDCs: A relative deprivation approach", Economic Development and Cultural Change 32(3):475–486. [Reprinted in Stark (1991).]

Stark, O. (1991), The Migration of Labor (Basil Blackwell, Cambridge, MA).

Stark, O., and D. Bloom (1985), "The new economics of labor migration", American Economic Review 75:173–178. [Reprinted in Stark (1991).]

Stark, O., and E. Katz (1986), "Labor migration and risk aversion in less developed countries", Journal of Labor Economics 4(1):134–149. [Reprinted in Stark (1991).]

Stark, O., and D. Levhari (1982), "On migration and risk in LDCs," Economic Development and Cultural Change 31:191–196. [Reprinted in Stark (1991).]

Stark, O., and J.E. Taylor (1989), Relative Deprivation and International Migration, Demography 26:1–14. [Reprinted in Stark (1991).]

Stark, O., and J.E. Taylor (1991), "Migration incentives, migration types: the role of relative deprivation", The Economic Journal 101:1163–1178. [Reprinted in Stark (1991).]

Stark, O., J.E. Taylor and S. Yitzhaki (1986), "Remittances and inequality", The Economic Journal 96:722–740. [Reprinted in Stark (1991).]

Stark, O., J.E. Taylor and S. Yitzhaki (1988), "Migration, remittances in inequality: A sensitivity analysis using the extended Gini index", Journal of Development Economics, 28:309–322. [Reprinted in Stark (1991).]

Stark, O., and S. Yitzhaki (1988), "Labor migration as a response to relative deprivation", Journal of Population Economics 1:57–70. [Reprinted in Stark (1991).]

Straubhaar, T. (1986), "The causes of international labor migrations: a demand-determined approach", International Migration Review 20:835–856.

Strauss, J. (1986), "The theory and comparative statics of agricultural household models: A general approach", in: I. Singh, L. Squire and J. Strauss, eds., Agricultural Household Models (The Johns Hopkins University Press, Baltimore).

Taylor, J.E. (1986), "Differential migration, networks, information and risk", in: O. Stark, ed., Migration Theory, Human Capital and Development (JAI, Greenwich) 147–171.

Taylor, J.E. (1987), "Undocumented Mexico–U.S. migration and the returns to households in rural Mexico", American Journal of Agricultural Economics, 69:626–638.

Taylor, J.E. (1992), "Remittances and inequality reconsidered: Direct, indirect and intertemporal effects", Journal of Policy Modeling 14:187–208.

Taylor, J.E. (1996), "International migration and economic development: A micro economy-wide analysis", in: J.E. Taylor, ed., International Trade, Migration and Development (Organization for Economic Cooperation and Development, Paris).

Taylor, J.E., and I. Adelman (1996), Village Economies: The Design, Estimation and Application of Village-Wide Economic Models (Cambridge University Press, Cambridge).

Taylor, J.E., and P.L. Martin (1997), "The immigrant subsidy in U.S. agriculture: farm employment, poverty, and welfare", Population and Development Review 23(4):855–874.

Taylor, J.E., and P.L. Martin (1998), "Farm employment, immigration, and poverty: The vicious circle" (Department of Agricultural and Resource Economics, University of California, Davis).

Taylor, J.E., P.L. Martin and M. Fix (1997), Poverty Amid Prosperity: Immigration and the Changing Face of Rural California (The Urban Institute Press, Washington, DC).

Taylor, J.E., D.S. Massey, J. Arango, G. Hugo, A. Kouaouci and A. Pellegrino (1996), "International migration and national development", Population Index 62(2):181–212.

Taylor, J.E., and D. Thilmany (1993), "Worker turnover, farm labor contractors and IRCA's impact on the California farm labor market", American Journal of Agricultural Economics, 75 (May):350–360.

Taylor, J.E., and T.J. Wyatt (1996), "The shadow value of migrant remittances, income and inequality in a household-farm economy", Journal of Development Studies 32 (6):899–912.

Taylor, J.E., and A. Yúnez-Naude (2000), "The returns from schooling in a diversified rural economy", American Journal of Agricultural Economics 82(2):287–297.

Tcha, M. (1996), "Altruism and migration: evidence from Korea and the United States", Economic Development and Cultural Change 44:859–878.

Thilmany, D. (1996), "FLC usage among California growers under IRCA: An empirical analysis of farm labor market risk management", American Journal of Agricultural Economics 78(4):946–960.

Todaro, M.P. (1969), "A model of migration and urban unemployment in less-developed countries", The American Economic Review 59:138–148.

Todaro, M.P. (1980), "Internal migration in developing countries: A survey", in: R.A. Easterlin, ed., Population and Economic Change in Developing Countries (University of Chicago Press, London and Chicago) 361–402.

Todaro, M.P., and L.M. Maruszko (1987), "Illegal migration and U.S. immigration reform: A conceptual framework", Population and Development Review 13:101–114.

Torok, S.J., and W.E. Huffman (1986), "U.S.–Mexican trade in winter vegetables and illegal immigration", American Journal of Agricultural Economics 68(2):246–260.

United States Commission on Immigration Reform (1997), "Migration between Mexico and the United States: Binational study", (Editorial y Litografia Regina de Los Angeles, SA, Mexico City).

Vroman, W., and K. Worden (1992), Immigration and State-Level Wage Adjustments in the 1980s (The Urban Institute, Washington, DC).

Walsh, B.M. (1974), "Expectations, information, and human migration: Specifying an econometric model of Irish migration to Britain", Journal of Regional Science 14:107–118.

White, M.J., F.D. Bean and T. Espenshade (1990), "The U.S. 1986 immigration reform and control act and undocumented migration to the United States", Population Research and Policy Review 9:93–116.

Williamson, J.G. (1988), "Migration and urbanization", in: H. Chenery and T.N. Srinivasan, eds., Handbook of Development Economics (Elsevier Science Publishers, New York) 426–446.

Willis, R.J., and S. Rosen (1979), "Education and self-selection", Journal of Political Economy 87:S7–S36.

Winegarden, C.R., and L.B. Khor (1991), "Undocumented immigration and unemployment of U.S. Youth and minority workers: econometric evidence", Review of Economics and Statistics 73(1):105–112.

Wong, K.Y. (1983), "On choosing among trade in goods and international capital and labor mobility (A theoretical analysis)", Journal of International Economics 14:223–250.

The World Bank (1992), World Development Report 1992: Development and the Environment (Oxford University Press, Oxford).

Yap, L. (1977), "The attraction of cities: A review of the migration literature", Journal of Development Economics 4:239–264.

Chapter 10

AGRICULTURAL FINANCE:
CREDIT, CREDIT CONSTRAINTS, AND CONSEQUENCES

PETER J. BARRY

Department of Agricultural and Consumer Economics, University of Illinois, Urbana, IL

LINDON J. ROBISON

Department of Agricultural Economics, Michigan State University, East Lansing, MI

Contents

Handbook of Agricultural Economics, Volume 1, Edited by B. Gardner and G. Rausser

Abstract

The theory and methods used to analyze the market, management, and policy elements of agricultural finance draw substantially on modern finance concepts, but with significant tailoring to the unique characteristics of agricultural sectors throughout the world. Both developed and developing economies are considered in this chapter. Discussed in detail are lender-borrower relationships, financial growth and intertemporal analysis, portfolio theory and financial risk, investment analysis, the financial structure of agriculture, and private and public sector suppliers of financial capital. Other key issues involve the linkages between investment and finance, and the extent of credit rationing in agriculture.

JEL classification: Q14

1. Introduction

Agricultural finance focuses on the acquisition and use of financial capital by the agricultural sectors of both developed and developing economies. Financial capital includes debt, equity, and leased capital, although each of these sources may include numerous forms. Much of the analytical work in agricultural finance has centered on the concept of credit as a firm's borrowing capacity and its utilization in acquiring and managing debt capital. Also receiving considerable attention are the leasing and related payment obligations for farmland and other types of assets, and the management of equity capital. Channels for bringing outside equity capital into agriculture, however, are not well developed. Outside equity has been discouraged from agricultural investment financing in the past by risk and information problems, small farm size, and public policies and preferences.

Agricultural finance includes elements of markets, management, and policy. The market element considers the organization and performance of institutions functioning as financial intermediaries for the agriculture sector, the trading of financial instruments in the financial markets, and potential rationing of credit and other market imperfections. The management element for agricultural firms includes investment analysis, capital structure, performance measurement, financial planning, risk and liquidity management, and establishment of "relationships" with financial intermediaries. These components may be evaluated at the firm level or at the aggregate, sector level. The policy element considers the role of governments in filling gaps and resolving imperfections in the agricultural finance markets and in providing targeted assistance to designated recipients consistent with social goals that are unmet by private sources of financial capital.

Agricultural finance utilizes key concepts of modern finance theory, adapted for application to the unique characteristics of agriculture. For example, the relatively small-scale, non-corporate structure of most farm businesses precludes the issuances, trading, and risk pricing of equity capital shares in public markets. These structural characteristics also result in greater emphasis on reputation and informal information exchanges in the formation of lender-borrower relationships. Consequently, approaches to investment analysis, optimal capital structure, and credit evaluation procedures must accommodate these and other empirical characteristics of agriculture. The unique structural and information characteristics of agricultural sectors have also led to the creation of specialized financial institutions, often publicly authorized, operated, and subsidized.

This chapter identifies and develops key concepts of agricultural finance, by focusing on the market, managerial, and policy elements cited above. The scope of the chapter's analysis includes both developed and developing economies, although most of the applications are drawn from the developed economy setting. Section 2 of this chapter delineates the key financial characteristics of agricultural firms in greater detail. Sections 3 and 4 identify key concepts from modern finance theory and assess their applicability to agricultural finance. Included is insight provided by principal-agent theory, financial contracting, and other elements of organizational economics. Section 5 addresses lender-borrower relationships in agriculture, including the role of social capital as a complement to the traditional relationship concepts. Sections 6 and 7 consider, respectively, firm growth and intertemporal analysis, and the role of risk management in agricultural finance. Section 8 focuses on aggregate investment analysis of the agricultural sector, including farmers' investment behavior, tax policies, and capital structure. Section 9 addresses the relationship among finance, economic growth, and the structure of agriculture. Section 10 focuses on suppliers of financial capital to agriculture, and Section 11 provides a concluding perspective on credit, credit constraints, and their consequences.

2. Financial characteristics of agriculture

Managers of agricultural firms rely heavily on debt capital in combination with their own equity capital to finance their capital base, mechanize and modernize their farming operations, conduct marketing and production plans, and to serve as a valuable source of liquidity in responding to risks. In developing economies, debt capital is also important in smoothing consumption patterns over time. Readily available credit has facilitated many of the significant, long-term changes in the farm sector–increasing commercialization, larger farm sizes, fewer farms, greater specialization, greater capital intensity, adoption of new technology, stronger market coordination, and others [Barry (1995)].

Most farms throughout the world are small in size, not organized as corporations, and have ownership, management, and risk bearing concentrated in the hands of individual farmers and farm families [Barry et al. (1995); Barry (1995)]. Farms in developed economies generally are much larger than their developing economy counterparts. A few farms, especially in developed countries, are large in size, industrialized in operations, and have complex contractual arrangements for ownership, management, labor, and financing. Examples include large-scale cattle feedlots, hog production units, poultry and egg production plants, orchards, and other specialty crop farms.

Despite the small business orientation, agriculture typically is a capital-intensive industry with investments in farmland, buildings, machinery, equipment, and breeding livestock dominating the asset structure of most types of farms. Farm real estate comprises about 70 percent to 80 percent of total assets from year to year for the U.S. farm sector (U.S. Department of Agriculture). Inventories of livestock, machinery, crops, and other non-real-estate farm assets generally make up 10 percent to 15 percent of total assets. The dominance of farm real estate together with the relatively small holdings of financial assets indicates the high capital intensity and low asset liquidity of the sector. High capital intensity and low asset liquidity, in turn, create the demand for longer-term financing and careful matching of repayment obligations with projected cash flows.

The farm sector debt-to-asset ratio typically falls in a relatively low range compared to debt-to-asset ratios in many other economic sectors. The farm sector debt-to-asset ratio in the U.S. increased steadily to reach the 15 percent to 18 percent range in the 1970s and then rose above 20 percent in the mid-1980s, reflecting the decline in farm real estate values that characterized this period. Subsequent reductions in farm debt and recoveries in farmland values in the late 1980s returned the debt-to-asset ratio to the 15 percent to 18 percent range, a range exhibited by other countries with similar characteristics. The farm sector balance sheet for Canada is consistent with the U.S. experience, although debt levels per farm and the aggregate debt-to-asset ratio remained higher than in the U.S. through the end of the 1980s [Freshwater (1989); Barnard and Grimard (1995)]. Similarly, the balance sheet for U.K. agriculture indicates debt-to-asset ratios below 10 percent in the 1970s and in the 10 percent to 18 percent range for the 1980s [Johnson (1990)]. In Australia, the farm sector ratio of long-term debt to total assets was less than 10 percent for 1990–1993 [Buffier and Metternick-Jones (1995)].

These farm sector debt-to-asset ratios are low relative to those in many other economic sectors. For the Australian case, Buffier and Metternick-Jones (1995) report that the long-term debt-to-asset ratio is the lowest for agriculture (10 percent), compared to ten other economic sectors (the three highest ratios are 66 percent for transport, 52 percent for construction, and 50 percent for recreation). Petersen and Rajan (1994) report average institutional debt-to-asset ratios for over 3,400 small non-farm U.S. businesses of 27 percent for corporations and 24 percent for sole proprietorships and partnerships. For large global corporations, selected year-end 1997 ratios of total liabilities to total assets are 87 percent for General Electric Company, 76 percent for IBM, 65 percent for Pepsico, and 50 percent for Amoco Oil Company.[1]

Low debt-to-asset ratios in agriculture, relative to other sectors of the economy, reflect the use of current market values of farm real estate compared with original cost-adjusted book values for depreciable assets in other sectors [Irwin (1968b)]. The lower range for the debt-to-asset ratio, however, is also consistent with the heavy reliance in agriculture on a non-depreciable asset such as farmland in which much of its economic return occurs as capital gains or losses on real estate assets [Melichar (1979); Barry et al. (1995)]. Several studies [Barry and Robison (1986); Ellinger and Barry (1987); Lee and Rask (1976)] have shown that the debt-carrying capacity of non-depreciable assets (for example, land) is considerably lower than that of depreciable assets, under traditional loan repayment arrangements. Lower aggregate debt-to-asset ratios for the farm sector are, therefore, logical to expect.

The dominance of real estate among the farm sector's assets, along with a long-term growth in returns to farm assets (interrupted in the early 1980s) has meant that much of the farm sector's total economic returns has been unrealized capital gains or, on occasion, capital losses.

When subject to financial analysis, the farm sector's financial statements indicate a reasonably solvent industry, but one that experiences chronic liquidity problems and cash flow pressures resulting from relatively low, but volatile, current rates-of-return to farm assets. These characteristics make the farm sector's debt-servicing capacity and creditworthiness vulnerable to downward swings in farm income and land values.

---

[1] The total liabilities for large corporations include contingent and deferred obligations in addition to outstanding debt. They are not, thus, directly comparable to the farm sector ratios, based on farm debt alone.

Non-farm income is also important to the liquidity position and financial well-being of the farm sector. The total annual non-farm income earned by farm operators in the U.S. has exceeded total net farm income since the early 1980s. Most of the non-farm income, however, is earned by large numbers of very small, part-time farms.

The dominance of real estate in the agricultural sector's total assets and farmland's low debt-carrying capacity have fostered an extensive farmland leasing market. The leasing of farmland by farm operators has become a widespread and commonly accepted method of gaining control of land in many countries, one that is especially effective for expanding farm size. In 1992, 43 percent of total farmland in the U.S. was operated by farmers under a rental arrangement with landlords [Economic Research Service (1994)]. The remaining acreage was farmed by an owner-operator. The dominant form of rental arrangement in 1992 was a cash lease (65 percent) in which farmers paid a fixed or flexible amount of cash per acre to the landowner. Share leases and other arrangements constitute the remaining 35 percent of the total acreage under lease. The extent of leasing and share rents differs substantially among regions and states–share leasing is highest, for example, in the high soil productivity areas of the Midwest region of the United States, especially in Illinois (62 percent in 1992).

In general, farmers who lease most of the land they operate can have higher debt-to-asset ratios and experience greater current rates of return to farm assets and equity than those who rely more on ownership. These measurement differences reflect different accounting benchmarks in the profitability and solvency measures for different tenure positions. These financial ratios may also differ substantially among farmers with differences in farm size, age of operator, and major type of enterprise. Reliance on leasing and the resulting higher leverage ratios may also reflect the life cycle of the farm operator. Younger age classes of farmers lease more and tend to have higher leverage ratios.

Agricultural firms face a complex risk environment. Included are risks resulting from lengthy biologically based production, marketing activities, contractual relationships with other parties, changes in asset values, and other related income-generating activities. Farmers also face risks associated with financial leverage and unanticipated changes in interest rates, debt-servicing requirements, and credit availability. Conditions in the general economy, financial markets, government policy, and international markets may all influence the risks faced by farmers. In general, the combined effects of business, financial, and contractual risks are high for most types of farms, thus placing a high value on risk management.

In response to these risks, farmers can employ a broad range of risk management practices [Patrick et al. (1985)]. Besides production and marketing responses to risk, financial responses include holding liquid assets, establishing and maintaining credit reserves, adjusting leverage positions, utilizing insurance, and maintaining flexibility in the frequency of making new capital investments or replacing depreciable assets. Some of the financial responses to risk are directly influenced by public policies, including crop insurance and public credit programs. Finally, a number of studies have shown that rates of return to agricultural assets have low, and in some cases negative, correlations with rates of return on various types of financial and non- farm assets [e.g., Barry (1980);

Arthur et al. (1988); Young and Barry (1987); Gu (1996)]. Thus, the high risks of stand-alone investments in agriculture may be substantially reduced when these investments are added to well-diversified portfolios.

The characteristics of the agricultural sector just described combine to yield a significant and unique setting for the study of agricultural finance. The focus is on a capital-intensive industry in which the dominance of farm real estate has brought liquidity and debt-carrying challenges as well as significant reliance on the leasing of farmland by many farmers. Production units are mostly of smaller scale, although the gap is widening between numerous small, part-time, limited-resource farms and the relatively few but much more economically significant, commercial-scale operations. Business, financial, and contractual risks in agriculture are high, but numerous risk management options are available, especially for larger operations.

These features of the agricultural sectors have been the objects of considerable research in agricultural finance. Numerous farm-level, regional, and sector studies have provided explanations of, or strategies for improving, farm financial structure, firm growth, investment behavior, liquidity and credit management, land valuation and control, leasing arrangements, and risk management. Public policy alternatives for responding to these issues have also been identified and evaluated. Other studies have considered the appropriate structure, regulations, and management of financial institutions providing credit and other financial services to the agricultural sector under the financial characteristics and conditions cited above. Especially important have been evaluations of public credit programs. Subsequent sections of this chapter will consider the approaches and findings of many of these studies in greater detail.

3. Modern finance concepts

Modern finance theory provides a rich perspective on the provision of financial capital by the financial markets and its effects on lender-borrower relationships in agriculture. This perspective is based strongly on the relative information and incentive positions of the parties to a financial contract. It contains elements of agency theory, transactions cost economics, incomplete contracting, property and control rights, and the resulting boundaries of a firm. In this perspective, the firm is viewed, alternatively, as a nexus of contracts [Jensen and Meckling (1976)], a governance structure [Williamson (1996)], or a locus of asset ownership and control [Hart (1988, 1995)], in contrast to the traditional characterization of the firm as a production function [Hart (1988)]. The modern perspective has important implications for evaluating the financial performance of agricultural firms and the financial markets and institutions serving the agricultural sector.

3.1. Agency relationships, adverse selection, and moral hazards

The principal-agent problem is a general one that applies to any contractual, interdependent relationship. Examples in finance are the relationships between a lender (the principal) and a borrower (the agent), stockholders and management, and landlords and tenants. In the lender-borrower case, the lender has entrusted the borrower with the use of loan funds in return for the borrower's promise of a safe and timely return of the funds, plus interest, according to the terms of the loan contract. However, due to the agent's self-interest, informational asymmetries, and uncertain expectations, both contracts and incentive alignments between the principal and agent generally are incomplete. Agency costs attributable to monitoring, bonding, and residual losses then are incurred in structuring, administering, enforcing, and adapting contracts in order to align incentives, resolve informational problems, and respond to uncertainties [Jensen and Meckling (1976); Barry et al. (1992)].

The lender-borrower and landlord-tenant relationships are especially important in agricultural finance. In a credit relationship, two basic concerns of the agricultural lender are (1) whether the borrower/agent is riskier than believed when the loan was originated (an adverse selection problem), and (2) whether the borrower will take on greater risks during the term of the loan than were originally anticipated (a moral hazard problem). These conditions are attributable to asymmetries in both incentives and information between the lender and the farm borrower. The borrower is motivated by profitability and wealth accumulation, because he or she shares directly in the returns (favorable or unfavorable) earned by the loan proceeds. In contrast, the lender is restricted to the fixed returns of the loan funds plus interest, as established in the loan contract, although additional benefits may come from growth over time in a successful borrower's financing needs. Thus, in evaluating a borrower's creditworthiness, the lender emphasizes loan repayability and safety – that is, self-liquidating and asset-generating loans – while the borrower focuses on profitability and wealth.

Asymmetric information is also directly involved in the agency relationship because the lender may lack information about the borrower's goals and actions, as well as about the risks of the projects being financed. Farm borrowers should know more about their productivity, business characteristics, financial position, and repayment intentions than do lenders, and much of financial planning and loan documentation is intended to convey this information from borrowers to lenders. Lenders do specialize in lending and related information processing, and they may have a broader perspective on credit transactions than do borrowers. However, the intentions, abilities, and experiences of individual borrowers are what motivate loan performance.

Adverse incentives for borrowers may also arise because they do not bear the full consequences of their actions. As leverage increases, the consequences of more of the borrower's actions that lead to default are borne by the lender [Stiglitz (1985)]. A borrower, then, has an increasing incentive to take riskier actions and to employ a go-for-broke attitude [Robison et al. (1987); Foster and Rausser (1991)] that increases the cost of financing for the lender and increases the lender's likelihood of becoming an owner of the borrower's assets. The lender, in turn, has an increasing incentive to control the borrower's actions.

These insights from finance theory have helped to guide the research agenda in agricultural finance. Studies have focused closely on the information-intensive, personalized relationships that characterize the arrangements between agricultural lenders and their borrowers, including the lender's procedures for evaluating and monitoring creditworthiness. Rationalizing the specialization of many lenders in financing agriculture is a natural outgrowth of the sector's sources of risk, small business orientation, and capital intensity. Similarly, studies that consider the changing motivations of farmers as debt levels and financial adversities increase have helped to explain tendencies toward go-for-broke behavior, stringency in loan contracts, and intense monitoring arrangements by agricultural lenders. These issues and related studies are further developed below.

3.2. Resolving information and incentive problems

Lenders and borrowers may utilize extensive practices to improve incentive alignments and resolve information problems [Miller et al. (1993)]. Differential loan pricing based on risk-adjusted interest rates is one lender response to the adverse selection problem [Stiglitz and Weiss (1983)]. Credit rationing, institutional adversities, and market failure are possible results of severe credit rationing. Using risk-adjusted interest rates would yield a more dispersed distribution of risky borrowers and lower lending risks on average, thus reducing the adverse selection problems. Adjusting interest rates for risk presumes that sufficient information is available to effectively distinguish among the risk classifications. Thus, information collection, processing, and monitoring by lenders are important contributions to the resolution of agency cost problems before and after the loan contract is established.

Market signaling is another mechanism whereby borrowers and lenders respond to the problems of asymmetric information. Market signaling suggests that one or more of the market participants (the lender or the borrower) convey additional information to other market participants (the borrower or the lender) about the levels of and value placed on creditworthiness. Effective financial accounting systems maintained by creditworthy borrowers provide a distinguishing signal between high and low credit risks, and they provide for monitoring of business performance over time. Because certified or audited accounts are used relatively little in agriculture, lenders must employ their own expertise in distinguishing among farmers' financial performance. Agricultural borrowers may also undertake management practices that distinguish them from their peers and highlight unique skills and levels of productivity. Examples include the use of futures and options contracts to manage risks, producing specialty crops, adopting new production and telecommunication technologies, advanced levels of education, and leadership reputations in local communities.

Extensive financial contracting by lenders involves provisions in a loan contract intended to address potential adverse selection and moral hazard problems [Smith and Warner (1979)]. These non-price methods include collateral requirements, loan repayment upon demand provisions, reporting requirements, performance standards, sales restrictions, constraints on additional borrowing, insurance requirements, default penalties, and foreclosure conditions. Because the contracting costs generally are borne by the borrower, his or her responses tend to reduce asymmetric information problems and align the borrower's actions with the goals of the lender. In addition, the financial market disciplines borrowers through the risk of non-renewal of loans if agency costs are excessive [Stiglitz and Weiss (1983)].

The creation of markets for exchange of financial information is another mechanism for responding to the problems of asymmetric information. Credit-rating companies, for example, specialize in collecting and disseminating information about part of the creditworthiness of agricultural borrowers. Collateral control companies will monitor, control, and validate the status of specific assets (e.g., stored grain, animals in large cattle feedlots) pledged to secure a loan agreement. Field servicing companies, which may include banks or other financial institutions, will service agriculture real estate loans, manage repayments, and monitor loan performance. Written or oral references provided by individuals about others are a commonly used form of market information, and lenders often are willing to exchange at least some information about their customers in order to facilitate the functioning of their respective markets.

If information problems are severe enough, public policies and institutional regulations may be developed to enhance market performance. Such actions might be justified if the market in question serves the public interest and if non-government resolutions to information deficiencies are ineffective. Examples include financial reporting requirements for corporate farms, disclosures of public offerings to financial regulators, truth-in-lending and advertising requirements, and government sponsorship of financial institutions and loan programs.

3.3. Incomplete contracting, property rights, and financial structure

A firm's financial structure can also be examined using the incomplete contracting approach in which the allocation of risk and control among alternative classes of investors is a key focus [Hart (1988); Berglof (1990); Aghion and Bolton (1992)]. Debt and equity are the standard financial instruments, but they are distinguished not only by their relative claims on the firm's assets and earnings, but also by the control rights associated with each type of financial claim – where the residual rights of control (those not designated by the financial contract or by law) are synonymous with ownership. More specifically, the allocations of control and ownership under this approach are state-dependent – under normal conditions, equity holders own and control the firm's assets, although ultimate control is determined by the type of equity (e.g., voting versus non-voting stock, preferred versus common stock, limited versus general partners). Under extreme adversity, however, financial contracts are designed so that ownership and control revert to the debt holders (according to seniority and size of claims). Debt capital, thus, represents a form of contingent ownership of the firm.

Under the property rights approach, the terms of the respective types of financial claims logically must represent more than the need for external funds and the level of compensation for the use of these funds. Unanticipated contingencies raise open questions about who will control the firm under alternative performance conditions and how cases of dispute and financial distress are ultimately resolved. Such contingencies are too numerous and too varied to fully anticipate in a written contract. Thus, contracts are necessarily incomplete in that they do not stipulate the contracting parties' obligations and actions in every eventuality. Incompleteness gives rise to the need to allocate control in situations not covered by the initial contract – that is, the allocation of the residual rights of control.

In effect, the incomplete contracting approach suggests that the parties to the contract must determine at the outset who is best suited to control the firm in various situations and what performance levels will signal the need for a transfer of control. Given this contingent allocation of control, the sharing of return streams is designed to provide the appropriate incentives for the exercise of effort by the parties commensurate with their respective ranges of control [Berglof (1990)]. That is, the party holding residual control rights over a specified range of states should bear the risk and reap the expected returns associated with decisions in these states. This party (the equity holder) will exercise effort commensurate with the anticipated rewards. In less favorable states, however, the rewards to such efforts dissipate, and go-for-broke actions by the equity holder, whose financial claims are substantially diminished, may yield adverse effects that accrue more to the debt holder. Thus, it is logical at this point for the residual rights of control, associated with ownership, to shift to the lender so that he or she can exert appropriate effort to protect the debt claims. It is also logical for the lender to exercise more stringent provisions of financial contracts that increasingly constrain the range of managerial choices available to the equity holder.

3.4. Transaction cost economics

Elements of transaction cost economics also apply to a firm's anticipated financial structure and relationships with suppliers of financial capital. According to Williamson (1996), transaction costs are incurred in drafting, negotiating, governing, safeguarding, and adapting the terms of agreements. The transaction costs are closely related to agency costs, although placing more emphasis on ex-post governance structures versus the ex-ante focus of agency theory and on transaction characteristics versus the characteristics of principals and agents [Williamson (1996)]. The choice of governance structure for coordinating a vertical system and determining the boundaries of firms then focuses on the minimization of transaction costs, based on the characteristics of the transactions and the work efforts of the respective parties.

Within this transaction cost framework, Williamson (1996) suggests that the degree to which assets are specialized to various activities is an important determinant of a firm's financial structure. In his view, investments with low asset specificity are more suitable for debt financing because of their easier redeployment (or re-marketability). Re-marketability is a preferred attribute of assets pledged as collateral to secure a loan. In contrast, equity financing is more likely for relationship-specific assets. Re-marketability of such assets is lower and the returns to specialized assets are more vulnerable to opportunistic rent-seeking by other contracting parties. Thus, Williamson (1996) asserts that a firm's use of debt relative to equity capital is inversely related

to the degrees of specificity of assets owned or controlled by the firm. These transaction cost concepts match well with the tendency for highly specialized agricultural
assets (e.g., buildings, confinement production technologies, irrigation systems) to have
higher equity capital requirements than is the case for more marketable machines, livestock, commodities, and perhaps even farmland.

3.5. Free cash flow concept

Jensen's (1986) free cash flow concept also has applicability to agricultural finance.
The free cash flow concept suggests that managers (agents) of firms with excess cash
flows and abundant financial assets may exercise managerial laxness, devote insufficient attention to detail, squander resources in non-business uses, and otherwise engage
in self-serving behavior that is counter to the objectives of principals. The general effects of such opportunistic behavior are a diminution in the firm's financial performance
and increased vulnerability to mergers, acquisitions, or other losses of business independence. A possible solution to these maladies is the creation of leverage-induced,
external financial obligations that will stimulate increased efforts by agents to satisfy
these obligations, and thus bring closer alignment with the goals of principals.

The free cash flow concept is much more general than Jensen's (1986) application
to corporate control and finance. It applies to many types of agency relationships in
which obligations may lead to stronger incentive compatibility between principals and
agents. In an agricultural setting, the concept suggests that farmers could be induced to
exert greater effort on behalf of lenders and landlords as their obligations to these principals increase. Along these lines, Nasr, Barry, and Ellinger (1998) utilized farm-level
data to test the free cash flow hypothesis and found a positive statistical relationship
between a farm's technical efficiency and its ratio of current debt to total assets. This
result suggests that greater reliance by farmers on current debt to finance their operations is consistent with the hypothesis that they will work harder to meet these financial
obligations.

4. Liquidity preference theory

A major implication of the principal-agent problem in credit relationships is that the
preferences of the lender, as expressed by the interest rate and non-interest rate terms
of the loan contract, may influence the rate of firm growth, risk management practices,
resource allocations, and enterprise choices of the borrower. The influences of interest rate and non-interest rate terms of loans were observed in agricultural finance by
Baker (1968) in the 1960s and tested in a number of empirical studies. Baker's study of
principal-agent problems predated by nearly 10 years the landmark principal-agent and
agency cost work in finance by Jensen and Meckling in the late 1970s. Baker's approach
was motivated by liquidity and incentive alignment issues, however, while Jensen and
Meckling emphasized information and incentive issues.

Baker recognized that optimal resource allocation and enterprise choices of agricultural borrowers would change to reflect lenders' preferences, as manifested in differential financing costs. Baker's conceptual approach was to acknowledge the traditional production economics relationship in which a firm's optimal combination of resources is achieved when the marginal rate of resource substitution equals the inverse of the price ratio. When borrowing is considered as a means of financing inputs, the economic equilibrium is modified to incorporate the financing cost that includes both interest costs and the value (liquidity premium) of borrowing capacity or credit surrendered in the transaction. Given the discrepancy between the preferences of the lender and of the borrower, as reflected by varying loan limits and potentially erroneous borrower expectations of lender behavior, optimal resource allocation can be influenced. This influence can take place whether or not borrowing occurs, through changes in the size and composition of the credit reserve, given its liquidity value to the borrower.

Subsequent empirical work focused on both the liquidity premium concept and the interest rate and non-interest rate responses of agricultural lenders to the managerial actions and business characteristics of farm borrowers. In 1971, Barry and Baker developed a modeling approach for estimating the levels of liquidity premiums that agricultural borrowers with different levels of risk aversion would associate with credit reserves. Related studies by Vandeputte and Baker (1970) and Baker and Bhargava (1974) provided more general specifications of functional relationships between liquidity premiums and sizes of reserves for both cash and multiple sources of credit. Chhikara (1986) then showed how liquidity premiums associated with cash and credit reserves could be derived from the expected utility model, and Barry and Robison (1987) and Gwinn, Barry, and Ellinger (1992) showed how debt capacity and liquidity are related to different levels of risk aversion, thus combining elements of external and internal credit rationing.

Accompanying these studies of how agricultural producers value various sources of liquidity was a companion set of studies that evaluated the credit responses of lenders to numerous strategies in borrowing, debt management, and risk management. Included were measures of credit responses associated with a farmer's choice of lender; sequence and source of borrowing and repayment; financing instrument; asset structure; enterprise mix of farming operations; and degrees of vertical coordination [Baker (1968); Baker and Hopkin (1969); Barry and Baker (1977); Sonka et al. (1980); Barry et al. (1981); Barry et al. (1997)]. Empirical measures were developed for lender responses to many such strategies and situations. The effects of these strategies and situations on farm business performance often are evaluated using mathematical programming or simulation models in which the credit components are based on the lender responses.

Observational techniques used in these studies for estimating lenders' credit responses are based on simulated borrowing requests in which a sample of lenders respond through a survey (mail, personal, or workshop-administered) to case loan requests for representative farms. The case loan typically involves a fully documented loan request over an array of purposes and terms, set high enough to anticipate the lender's rejection and designed for deletion of individual items (usually capital items) until loan approval is obtained. The result is an estimate of the firm's total credit, conditioned by the particular set of circumstances surrounding the loan request. The objective of the approach is a set of functional relationships between the credit responses and the characteristics of the loan situation that would hold as reliable predictors of lender response over a wide range of loan conditions.

Two examples of the simulated loan request approach to measuring lender credit responses are studies by Barry and Willmann (1976) and Pflueger and Barry (1986). Barry and Willmann focused on the relationship between credit availability and forward contracting of commodity sales by farmers as a risk management tool. Using a simulated borrowing approach to evaluate the responses of a sample of lenders to alternative levels of forward contracting by crop farmers, they found that the most preferred levels of contracting generated about 17 percent more total credit and about 53 percent more operating credit than the least preferred levels. When these credit responses were evaluated in a multi-period risk programming model, the risk efficient growth plans included contracting due to both the favorable effects on credit and the lower price risks. The model results indicated contracting even for farmers with little or no risk aversion, and even though expected profits were higher for the non-contract sales, reflecting the misalignment of incentives between the borrower and the lender.

Pflueger and Barry (1986) considered how a sample of non-real-estate lenders would respond to a farmer's use of crop insurance as a risk management tool. The results of the survey, also based on simulated loan requests, indicated a positive credit response by about 60 percent of the lenders, with little changes in interest rates and loan maturities. A stochastic, multi-period simulation model was used to evaluate the effects of the lenders' credit responses and the use of crop insurance on the farm's profitability, solvency, liquidity, and survivability. The simulation results, which modeled an early 1980s farm situation already experiencing financial stress, indicated that crop insurance and the credit responses improved farm survival and liquidity, but additional borrowing occurred to sustain the firm under adverse profit conditions. Thus, reductions in the representative farm's business risk were largely offset by increases in financial risk (see Section 7.2 below).

5. Relationships in agricultural finance

Relationships may involve two important characteristics: information and sympathy. Relationships may arise from close and continued exchanges between two economic agents including suppliers and users of financial capital. Some of the information acquired in these exchanges may involve economic data relating to cash flows, debt obligations, assets, and investment plans. Other kinds of data acquired may include the preferences, values, and character traits shared by the parties to the exchange.

For the most part, financial relationships have been examined in the presence of incomplete information and agents motivated by self-interest [Petersen and Rajan (1994, 1995)]. Most recently, the influence of relationships that include both information and sympathy has been examined using the newly developed social capital paradigm

[Schmid and Robison (1995)]. Social capital represents a different approach to the principal-agent analysis in which sympathy redefines externalities.

An externality is created when one agent creates an outcome for another agent without permission from the affected agent. When social capital exists, what otherwise might be considered an externality is internalized with favorable economic outcomes. Transactions and monitoring costs are reduced because relationships reduce the incentive for exploitive behavior that produces negative externalities, and increase the incentive to meet contracted obligations. Social capital may help explain why family businesses rich in social capital appear to dominate other types of business organizations. To illustrate, family businesses account for 75 percent of Oregon's small companies [Nelton (1990)], and 75 percent of U.S. companies are family-owned or controlled [Calonius (1990)].

In agricultural finance, the key issues and research initiatives have responded to these questions: How have the major attributes of relationships changed over time, and how do relationships respond to changes in market competition? What is the nature of the relationships between agricultural borrowers and their lenders? In what ways do farmers' investments, financial performance, risk management, and other business practices influence the cost, availability, and other terms of financial capital? How is credit scoring applicable to financial relationships in agriculture? How do agricultural lenders manage credit risks? How do relationships between lenders, borrowers, and other parties influence leasing, agribusiness lending, and other business practices? These questions are addressed in the following sections.

5.1. Relationship concepts

Relationships develop through interactions between parties over time and/or across multiple financial products and services. Relationships directly involve the generation of reliable and accurate information about the parties to a financing transaction, the use of such information in evaluating and monitoring creditworthiness, and the impacts information has on the reduction of agency costs and on the resolution of adverse selection and moral hazard problems. The anticipated results of effective relationships are improved availability of financial capital and reduced costs of financing transactions. Increases in competition, however, may work against the benefits of relationships and result in less favorable access to financial markets for newer firms or financially stressed firms.

5.2. Evolving nature of relationships

The nature of relationships has changed over time as financial markets were deregulated, financial market conditions became more volatile, and financial institutions evolved from primarily commercial banks and other depository institutions to broader financial services companies. Hodgman (1961) introduced the customer relationship concept in banking by showing the importance of customers' demand deposits as a source of a bank's capacity to lend and invest, and the resulting importance of a bank's relationship to loan customers who hold demand deposits. Wood (1975) extended Hodgman's customer-deposit relationship to multi-periods by showing how a liberal lending policy may induce increases in future deposits that can, in turn, be loaned or invested. Wood also added the customer loan relationship which suggests that a bank's current lending policy influences its future loan demands. Barry (1978) applied these deposit relationship concepts to estimate the rate of loan-deposit feedback in rural banking at a time when banks were still subject to stringent regulations on deposit rates, ranges of products and services, and geographic scope of operations. His results showed a relatively high rate of loan-deposit feedback that contributed to the bank's profitability of bringing non-local sources of funds into local lending markets.

Sharpe (1990) considered asymmetric information as a determinant of customer relationships attributable to a bank's monopoly power over its established, higher-performing borrowers who become "informationally captured" by the bank. The adverse efficiency consequences of this informational imperfection are reduced by implicit contracts arising from the institution's efforts to create a reputation as a reliable lender. The terms of such contracts depend on the institution's degree of informational advantage, reputational perceptions, and other determinants of customer profitability. Sharpe contrasts his ex-post, information-driven relationship theory to an alternative justification suggested by Wachter and Williamson (1978), based on the existence of ex-ante, relationship-specific capital investment created by the pre-loan evaluation.

More recently, Petersen and Rajan (1994, 1995) considered the interactions between lenders, borrowers, and financial market performance. Their 1994 article uses data from a national survey of small, non-farm businesses to determine that information-based relationships may have significant, positive effects on credit availability, and less significant reductions in credit costs. Their 1995 article uses the same database to test the interactions between lending competition and the availability and cost of credit for young or financially stressed borrowers, both of whom were found to benefit from stronger relationships in more concentrated markets. Less competitive markets may better enable lenders to grant short-run concessions to disadvantaged firms, while adjusting financing terms in more favorable times to share in the future surplus of the borrowing firm.

Barry, Ellinger, and Moss (1997) applied the Petersen and Rajan concepts to evaluate the influence of the competitiveness of agricultural lending markets on lender-borrower relationships. Their findings clearly indicate an inverse relationship between competition and borrower loyalty, which serves as a proxy for the lender-borrower relationship. Bankers in more competitive farm real estate and non-real-estate lending markets tend to have less loyal customers, irrespective of other institutional and market characteristics. Nonetheless, evidence [Barry and Ellinger (1997)] still suggests that rural financial markets are more concentrated and less competitive than their urban counterparts. Agricultural and rural business lending, thus, represents niche markets for many local lenders in which specialization is conducive to relationship-building, targeted skills in financial analysis, and the types of informational advantages cited by Sharpe (1990).

Turvey and Weersink (1997) extend the analysis of the lender-borrower relationship to provide empirical evidence about loan demand/contract curves for agricultural loans. Using explicit linkages to credit-scoring models in estimating loan demand parameters, they find evidence of backward-bending loan demand curves, reflecting the properties of asymmetric incentives and information in agricultural lending. These results, in turn, suggest some degree of credit rationing in agricultural lending.

5.3. Credit evaluation procedures

Previous studies of credit relationships in agriculture have shown that the responses of lenders to the business characteristics, managerial actions, and other agency costs of financing agricultural firms influence the cost, availability, and other terms of financial capital, including the magnitude and composition of liquid credit reserves (see the section on liquidity preference, Section 4 of this chapter). In turn, these cost effects may influence the optimal financial structure (leverage) and financial performance of farm businesses as well as the composition of their assets, risk management practices, and other income-generating activities. These studies do not, however, directly consider the agricultural lender's processes of credit evaluation, including the relative importance of the major variables affecting creditworthiness.

In contrast, a growing set of studies (e.g., Lufburrow et al. (1984); Dunn and Frey (1976); Hardy and Weed (1980); Fischer and Moore (1987); Stover et al. (1985); Miller and LaDue (1989); Turvey (1991); Turvey and Brown (1990); Miller et al. (1994); Novak and LaDue (1994); Chhikara (1989); Splett et al. (1994); and Aguilera-Alfred and Gonzalez-Vega (1993)] have focused on the credit evaluation process, including the development and validation of various types of credit-scoring models, and on predicting financial stress and bankruptcy problems of farmers [Shepard and Collins (1982); Franks (1998)]. Agricultural lenders themselves have accelerated the development and use of more formal methods of credit evaluation [Miller et al. (1993)], in light of growing concerns about loan quality, increased competition in agricultural lending, efforts to control lending costs, and improvements in data quality and loan information systems. These lender-based models have many similarities to one another, although model comparisons indicate a large degree of disparity in model design and use across lenders [Ellinger et al. (1992)].

Credit-scoring and risk-rating models provide systematic, comprehensive ways in which to assess the borrower's financial data and, along with the lender's judgment and other relevant information, reach a valid assessment of the borrower's creditworthiness. The basic steps in model development are to (1) identify key variables that best distinguish among borrowers' creditworthiness, (2) choose appropriate measures for these variables, (3) weight the variables according to their relative importance to the lender, (4) score each loan as a weighted average of the respective variables, and (5) assign the credit scores to the appropriate class [Barry et al. (1995)].

Considerable attention has focused on appropriate statistical methods for evaluating credit-scoring models [Turvey and Brown (1990)]. Moreover, evidence suggests that statistically based models and judgment-based models developed by lenders can yield similar credit evaluations [Splett et al. (1994)]. Recent models have moved beyond estimating the ability to replicate subjective loan classifications by lenders, to concentrate on the borrower's actual loan performance as the validation criterion [Miller and

LaDue (1989); Miller et al. (1994); Turvey (1991)]. Financial planning models of farm businesses have also endogenized farm investment decisions, credit evaluations, and loan pricing based on the credit-scoring procedures of agricultural lenders [e.g., Barry and Ellinger (1989)]. Less is currently known, however, about whether credit-scoring models should be tailored to the structural and/or demographic characteristics of farm borrowers, or whether a single model can effectively do the job.

5.4. Managing borrowers' credit risks

Lenders' management of an individual borrower's credit risks depends significantly on the size and structural characteristics of the borrower's business, and on the characteristics of the financial institution. Larger, industrialized agricultural production units generally seek financing from larger lending institutions, and tend to be treated like other large commercial borrowers. Financial reporting, specialized collateral control, telecommunications, and automated information systems play important roles in lender-borrower relationships for these larger operations. On the other hand, small, part-time farm operations in developed economies are increasingly treated as consumer borrowers, where loan acceptance is determined by credit- scoring, and loan transactions occur with credit cards. Interest rates to small borrowers are higher than on commercial or agricultural loans, and contact between borrower and lender is minimal.

In contrast, informal finance provided to small farms in developing countries by money lenders or peer monitoring in group borrowing relies heavily on personal observations and individual monitoring [Carter (1988); Hoff and Stiglitz (1990)]. The informal closeness of relationships between money lenders, for example, and their borrowers contributes to the resolution of asymmetric information problems, perhaps more effectively than the financial contracting and monitoring arrangements employed in larger-scale commercial finance. Similarly, extended family linkages, which provide opportunities for lending to smooth consumption in developing economies, also reflect the resolution of informational problems.

Between the small farms and the industrialized units are the commercial scale family farms. Their small business scale, geographic remoteness, informal accounting practices, and relatively high business and financial risks create intensive information needs to allow lenders to successfully manage credit risks. Frequent monitoring, periodic farm and office visits, reputations, specialized and experienced loan officers, and a localized community orientation of many agricultural lenders have long characterized key elements of credit risk management for commercial-scale family farms.

Lenders are placing greater reliance on risk-adjusted interest rates to distinguish among borrowers with different credit risks [Miller et al. (1993)]. Differential collateral requirements are also a significant non-price response to credit risk. Timeliness of loan payments and periodic financial reports are relied on heavily to monitor business performance. According to Miller et al. (1993), information about past financial performance is the dominant signal agricultural borrowers can provide to distinguish their credit risks. Projected financial performance, collateral offered, borrower experience, production efficiency, and risk management ability have medium to high importance. Borrower education and reputation in the community have lesser importance.

5.5. Real estate leasing arrangements

Farmers' use of share rent or cash rent leasing is a major financing mechanism for controlling the use of farmland. Despite the high capital investment tied up in the leased land, many leasing contracts have involved informal arrangements in which leases are oral rather than written and/or the contract terms are annual or three to five years in length, despite the long-lived nature of farmland. Even with annual, oral leases, however, it is common to observe long-term relationships between the landlord and the farm operator.

In applying information and transactions costs concepts to leasing arrangements, Allen and Lueck (1992) tested and confirmed that reputation and common law may explain the high incidence of use of short-term and often oral contracts in the leasing of farmland. The information conveyed by reputation and experience has been sufficient to solidify the landlord-tenant relationship in many instances, and transform a short-term legal arrangement into a longer-term financial relationship.

5.6. Agribusiness and trade financing

Agribusiness or trade financing of farmers is a long-standing practice that is especially significant for many operating inputs and for farm machinery. In many countries, the local merchant served as a credit source long before the presence of specialized financial institutions. The modern-day trade firm can compete effectively in the financial markets because it may operate a branch or dealer system efficiently over widely diverse geographic areas, have cost-effective access through the parent company to national financial markets for loan funds, experience low delivery costs, and rely on consistently applied credit evaluation procedures and scoring models. Offering credit or leasing arrangements complements the trade firm's merchandising activities.

Trade firms also develop important, yet different customer relationships with farmers than do specialized lenders [Sherrick and Lubben (1994)]. The trade firm's customer relationship primarily involves the merchandising activity, but it may yield extensive information about a farmer's management ability, business practices, and financial performance. This customer information, in turn, contributes importantly to the evaluation of creditworthiness and, thus, augments the trade firm's management of the credit risk.

5.7. The role of social capital

Agricultural finance is also related to social capital. The traditional economic model is based on individual utility maximization, assuming that individuals are self-motivated. Actions that appear to contradict a preference-based model are often explained away by the emergence of new tastes. For example, gifts to charity that reduce one's own wealth might be explained in a way consistent with self-serving preferences by identifying a taste for philanthropy. Concern for the environment has been described as motivated by the taste for diversity.

While few, if any, would disagree that behavior often may be explained by self-interest, much of human behavior seems inconsistent with selfishness. Social capital emphasizes that an individual's well-being is altered by changes in the well-being of others with whom a relationship exists. Moreover, when one person's accomplishments are the object of another person's caring, he/she has access to advantages (disadvantages) not available to those who lack the vicarious caring. One definition that recognizes the social capital content of caring follows:

> Social capital is the sympathy (antipathy) one person has toward another person, idealized self, or object. The sympathetic (antipathetic) person is said to supply social capital while the person or object of sympathy (antipathy) is said to possess social capital. The persons or objects of social capital may expect benefits (harm), advantages (disadvantages), and preferential (discriminatory) treatment from the providers of social capital. Social capital may be culturally dependent, environmentally influenced, and responsive to a wide range of stimuli including the perceived social capital claimed by others. [Robison and Siles (1997, p. 10)]

Other definitions of social capital include (1) the social obligations or "connections" which are convertible into economic capital under certain conditions [Bourdieu (1986)]; (2) a resource of individuals that emerges from their social ties [Coleman (1988)]; (3) mutually beneficial activities that promote and reinforce a sense of the common good; (4) the ability to create and sustain voluntary associations [Putnam (1995)]; (5) trust [Fukuyama (1995)]; (6) the expectations for action within a collectivity that affect the economic goals and goal-seeking behavior of its members, even if these expectations are not oriented toward the economic sphere [Portes (1995)]; and (7) friends, colleagues, and more general contacts through whom you received opportunities to use other forms of capital [Burt (1992)].

Several applications to agricultural finance are suggested by social capital theory. Social capital changes the relationship between a principal and his or her agent. If the principal has social capital with his agent, as in the case of a landlord and tenant who are related or are close friends, the tenant might act in the interest of the landlord without the need for special contracts to alter incentives or monitoring costs to prevent cheating. As a result, one might expect to find a preference for landlords to lease to close friends and family. Supporting this conclusion was Gwilliams (1993), who pointed out that 81 percent of the participants in share leases were close friends or family, and 89 percent of those entering into cash leases were close friends or family.

Various studies have concluded that social capital alters the terms of trade compared to arm's-length transactions. To examine the extent to which social capital (relationships) influence lenders' loan approval decisions, a mail survey was conducted of bankers in Michigan, U.S.A. [Siles et al. (1994)]. The study concluded that social capital is not likely to change significantly the probability of a very good loan or a very bad loan being approved or disapproved. However, for those loans in between, social capital can increase the probability of loan approval by as much as 60 percent in the U.S. These findings are especially applicable to agricultural finance in light of the important roles played by small, community-oriented banks and the information-intensive nature of lender-borrower relationships in agricultural lending.

Social capital may also influence savers. A survey of 1,000 people 18 years or older, drawn randomly from Michigan zip code areas with populations of 10,000 or less, was conducted in 1992 to find the effect of social capital on one's choice of bank [Hanson et al. (1996)]. The survey results found that a friendly relationship with the bank and its personnel increases the likelihood that customers will stay with their financial institution; an unfriendly relationship results in a large decrease in the probability that the financial institution will retain the customer's business in the future. The survey results suggest that having a friendly relationship with the bank customer increases the interest rate on certificates of deposit that would entice the customer to switch institutions by 74 basis points over the cases when the relationship with the bank customer is unfriendly. Again, the community orientation of smaller banks in rural markets makes social capital considerations important in these markets.

An individual's social capital may lead him or her to develop attachment value towards objects such as farmland, occupations, and ideas. As a result of one's social capital, a farmer may take financial actions to preserve his or her ownership of farmland or make investments in assets to gain the approval of peers that appear to be irrational when considered against the profit-maximizing motive.

One important dimension of social capital involves transaction costs. Because social capital increases the value of trade between social capital-endowed trading partners, trade between these partners is more likely to occur than between the estranged and strangers. Therefore, in economies with high transaction costs associated with limited information and enforcement ability, trading between the social-capital-endowed will be more prevalent. This tendency is especially true in financial markets. Adams (1992) reports that despite tens of billions of dollars committed to establishing sustainable agricultural credit programs in developing countries, there are few successes. They have failed largely because of loan recovery problems, chronic dependency on outside funds, and excessive transaction costs.

In contrast to the formal credit system, Adams (1992) cites informal finance systems in Bolivia and the Philippines that recovered most of their loans while formal lenders were awash in default. The informal finance systems in these countries mobilized and allocated large amounts of voluntary savings while banks had trouble attracting deposits.

The apparent difference between the formal and informal financial systems was relationships. Adams and Canavesi (1992) report that 90 percent of the *pasanakus* (an informal finance organization in Bolivia) were composed largely of friends or fellow workers (p. 316). Esguerra and Meyer (1992) provide similar evidence from the Philippines. And Graham (1992) reports from Niger that loans from family, friends, and relatives constituted a majority of the informal finance activity.

In general, social capital has the capacity to internalize consequences that otherwise might be considered externalities. In light of social capital's ability to internalize externalities, a policy other than one based on an individual's self-interests may be important to consider.

6. Financial growth and intertemporal analysis

The smaller scale, concentrated ownership, and capital intensity of agriculture has placed considerable emphasis on the financial management function of farm businesses. Research and analysis in financial management has a rich and lengthy history, especially in focusing on the financial dimensions of firm growth in agriculture. Key questions and issues have considered static versus dynamic analysis, optimal investment and firm growth patterns, financial leveraging and capital structure, optimization versus simulation models, life cycle consumption and financing plans, and the relationships among a farm's financial, production, and marketing components in influencing its performance over time. Underlying these application areas are the concepts of firm growth.

6.1. Growth concepts

A study of the growth process for agricultural firms requires a shift away from perceiving the firm in a static environment to a dynamic setting [Dorfman (1969); Boussard (1971); Barry (1977)]. For a firm, dynamics deals with deriving an optimal time path from its state in any period to a terminal state – if, in fact, a desired terminal state can be defined. The path is optimal with respect to the firm's objectives. The time path implies the sequential nature of decision making in that decisions in the respective time periods depend on preceding events and on expectations of succeeding events.

Some firm growth and investment studies [Schnitkey et al. (1989); Collins and Karp (1993); Boussard (1971)] have formally cast their empirical analysis in a dynamic setting, although the extent of empirical detail achievable in dynamic analysis is limited. Most studies, however, have been willing to trade off the intertemporal precision of dynamic analysis to allow a more extensive focus on the empirical characteristics of the problem under study. For the most part, a static or comparative static framework is utilized in the following discussion.

The core of the firm growth process is acquiring the control of additional resources that generate returns in excess of their costs and, thereby, add to the value of the firm. In turn, reinvested earnings also add to wealth and increase future income-generating capacity. The relationship between financial structure and firm performance can be expressed in a simple conceptual model, developed first under conditions of certainty and timelessness [Barry (1994)]. In this linear profitability model, a farm's rate of return on equity capital is a weighted average of the difference between the return on assets and the cost of debt, where the weights are the ratios of assets to equity and debt to equity, respectively, and the profit measure is net of withdrawals for taxation and family consumption [Barry et al. (1995)].

The model clearly shows some of the key alternatives for influencing the rate of return on equity capital. That is, the net return on equity will increase as the rate of return on assets is higher, and the rates of interest, taxation, and consumption are lower. Those effects grow stronger as financial leverage increases. That is, an increase in the rate of return on assets by one unit will increase the rate of return on equity by the product of the net rate of savings times the asset-to-equity ratio. Similarly, the effect on the rate of return to equity of a change in the cost of debt is to decrease the rate of return on equity by the product of the net rate of savings times the debt-to-equity ratio. Finally, the effect of a change in leverage on profitability, with the return on assets and the cost of debt held constant, is to increase the rate of return on equity by the product of the net rate of savings times the difference between the rate of return on assets and the cost of debt.

6.2. Empirical modeling

The firm growth concepts cited above have been operationalized in a large number of deterministic firm-level models employed over the years to study the effects of alternative financial strategies and constraints on capital accumulation and growth in income-generating capacity for agricultural firms [Barry (1977)]. These micro-level, intertemporal models of farm firms generally utilize either optimization [Ellinger et al. (1983); Featherstone et al. (1988)] or simulation as the conceptual framework.

Simulation [Mapp and Helmers (1984)] offers considerable flexibility for expressing relationships among variables, handling unique characteristics of decision situations, and for specifying performance measures (e.g., financial ratios) that are widely used in financial analysis. Generally, the decision process in simulation is formulated by the model builder and will vary from model to model. An objective function does not inherently guide the decision process as it does in mathematical programming.

In contrast, the optimization approach involving mathematical (i.e., linear, quadratic, etc.) programming offers the opportunity to observe financial performance, investment patterns, financing activities, and consumption effects that arise from the firm's efforts to push against its resource limits and operating requirements in order to maximize the stipulated objectives. Constrained optimization offers a clear framework in which to present and describe important relationships among variables, resource limits, interperiod transfers, and their data implications. Shortcomings of mathematical programming include the linearity conditions, inability to handle financial ratios, validity of the specified objectives, and reduced flexibility in model specifications relative to simulation.

Both modeling approaches have allowed analysts to identify and evaluate the effects of alternative growth strategies and to better understand how such key attributes as management ability, risk, resource costs, financial position, and reinvestment rates affect the firm growth process. Some models have emphasized the financial components of firm growth, while others focus on production or market considerations. A strong attribute of firm growth models is their ability to link the financial, production, and market components of agricultural businesses, and account for important interactions among these business functions, both over time and under conditions of uncertainty.

6.3. Objective functions

The objective function in optimization models can represent those objects of a decision maker's goals judged relevant to the situation being analyzed. Because managers of agricultural firms may exhibit a wide range of managerial objectives, a variety of objective functions have been evaluated in deterministic growth models. One commonly used approach is to maximize the net worth of the firm at the end of the planning horizon. This formulation is analogous to a comprehensive future value, capital budgeting problem in which the effects of compounding are represented by reinvestment opportunities for each year's earnings among the various investment and production activities in following periods. Other commonly used formulations of objective functions in farm-level multi-period optimization have included (1) maximization of the firm's future net worth plus the sum of annual consumption expenditures, (2) maximization of the present value of annual consumption expenditures plus ending net worth, and (3) maximization of the present value of annual net income [Cocks and Carter (1968); Boehlje and White (1969); Irwin (1968a); Martin and Plaxico (1967); Patrick and Eisgruber (1968); and Barry (1977)].

6.4. Time attitudes and life cycle models

More recent studies by Phimister (1995a, 1995b), Langemeier and Patrick (1993), Lifran (1994), and Barry, Robison, and Nartea (1996) have addressed intertemporal firm-level analysis in the context of life cycle planning and performance models of farm businesses, where production and consumption are linked through the close household-farm relationships that characterize family farming in most countries. Under this approach, intertemporal analysis is expressed as the maximization of the utility of multi-period consumption, constrained by the present value of wealth (and the related consumption opportunities) and the available investment alternatives, including both productive investments and lending and borrowing in a perfect or imperfect financial market.

Time attitudes are explicitly considered by introducing a time attitude function, $w(t)$. This function weights the utility of alternative consumption levels in period t, and identifies the separate roles of the investor's time attitude and the utility of consumption (i.e., tastes) at a specific time.

The time-weighted utility function is

$$\text{Max}\, U = \sum_{t=1}^{T} v(c_t) w(t), \tag{1}$$

where $w(t)$ is the time weight and $v(c_t)$ is the utility of consumption at time t. Under dynamic conditions where time is expressed as distance to the future, Strotz (1956) argued that the function $w(t)$ must take the form $1/(1+n)^t$, where n is a constant in order for individuals to make consistent consumption choices over time (i.e., where actual equals planned consumption). Subsequently, Barry, Robison, and Nartea (1996) generalized Strotz's analysis to allow changes in time attitudes, under a calendar date concept of time, in which the time attitude function $w(t)$ has the form

$$w(t) = \frac{1}{\prod_{t=1}^{T}[1+n(i)]}. \qquad (2)$$

Expression (2) allows changes in the values of time attitudes over time while retaining equality between planned and actual consumption as time passes, as long as no new information would lead to rational changes in the timing of consumption plans. The merits of the time weighted function in (1) are the clear distinction between the time attitude and the utility of consumption at specific points in time, and the theoretical distinction between optimal investment and financing decisions under perfect financial market conditions. At the same time, however, this approach complicates empirical analysis because it requires explicit and accurate information about the investor's time-specific utility functions and about their time attitude function. The complexity is compounded when risk attitudes are considered along with time attitudes. Maximizing terminal net worth is a much easier, although less theoretically satisfying, approach for the close household-farm relationships that characterize the agricultural sectors of many countries.

Phimister (1995a, 1995b) used the life cycle model to address the important policy question of whether the level and form of borrowing constraints influence the ability of farm households to consume, invest, and grow over time. His findings (1995a) indicate that a life cycle model without borrowing restrictions was rejected by data for Dutch dairy farms, although the statistical results for selected financial variables representing lenders' non-price credit responses were inconclusive. Additional results by Phimister (1995b) based on a farm-level optimization model suggest that the form of the borrowing constraint may have an important effect on intertemporal performance.

Phimister employed the time-weighted utility function in his analysis, although a constant time attitude was implied. In reference to Phimister's approach, Barry, Robison, and Nartea (1996) observed that changes over time in farmers' behavioral attributes could affect consumption and financing decisions. In particular, plausible changes in time attitudes (and risk attitudes) could lead to an "internal" constraint on borrowing that yields effects resembling those of lender-induced external borrowing constraints. Allowing the model to accommodate intertemporal changes in time attitudes would address this possibility.

6.5. *Dynamic analysis*

Most of the deterministic firm growth analyses have represented static situations, without explicitly accounting for the passage of time. The static models can accommodate considerable empirical detail, but they do not reflect potentially important dynamic relationships among major variables (e.g., prices of land and other state variables). Thus, static models may overstate or understate the true profit and growth potential for the business situations being modeled. The degree of difference could be sizeable relative to a comparably specified dynamic analysis.

Schnitkey, Taylor, and Barry (1989) examined farmland investment returns using dynamic programming. Consideration was given to optimal purchase and sale decisions for farmland under dynamic linkages between farmland returns and farmland prices, and the effects of these dynamic factors on a farm's financial structure. Comparisons between the decisions obtained from the dynamic programming model and a static capital budgeting model (i.e., net present value) indicated a clear tendency for over-responsive transactions by the static model, resulting in a larger range of investment/disinvestment decisions relative to the dynamic model results.

A similar approach to stochastic dynamic programming was employed by Novak and Schnitkey (1994) who explored how bankruptcy risks may influence farm financial performance. The key insight, enabled by the dynamic properties of their analysis, was that explicit consideration of bankruptcy risks tended to moderate farm investment behavior especially when financial conditions are less favorable. The related reductions in probabilities of bankruptcy and increases in expected terminal wealth were not surprising, but the dynamic specifications yielded the more plausible results.

Dynamic analysis appears especially appropriate in investment situations where lengthy time periods are involved and where the absence of extensive empirical detail is not a major concern. In the latter cases, the static approaches to intertemporal analysis may prove more effective to use, perhaps in combination with key elements of the dynamic models.

6.6. *Life cycle and intergenerational effects*

The close household-business relationship of most agricultural production units results in a strong relationship between the life cycle of the business and the life cycle of the manager. Financial performance, efficiency attainment, and other business characteristics may significantly reflect whether a firm is becoming established, growing, consolidating, or engaged in transferring its resources to new owners [Barry et al. (1995)]. In many cases, the establishment and transfer stages of agricultural firms' life cycles are tied to each other through family relationships [Guinnane (1992); Rosenzweig and Wolpin (1985)]. Optimal timing of a farm's transfer from parent to child then becomes an important issue [Kimhi (1994)].

Estate management is a long-term process that encompasses all of the stages of the life cycle [Boehlje and Eisgruber (1972)]. Included are all of the activities that go into building an estate, generating retirement income, planning an equitable distribution of property among heirs, and minimizing the cost of transferring assets. When substantial holdings of real estate are included in farm estates, the effects of a country's estate and inheritance taxes, liquidation expenses, and other transfer costs may be high. Farm estates generally have low liquidity and limited capacity for generating easily the funds needed to pay such costs, without selling the farm. Tax concessions for qualifying farm estates often occur. In addition, various estate planning strategies have been studied and utilized in order to facilitate the estate transfer process. Such strategies include the form of property ownership, and the use of wills and gifts [Boehlje and Eisgruber (1972)], life insurance [Tauer (1985)], reverse mortgages [Gibson and Barry (1994)], trusts, and others [Harl (1992); Looney and Uchtmann (1994); Thomas and Boehlje (1983)].

7. Portfolio theory and financial analysis

Risk considerations have long played important roles in agricultural finance. Included among the questions addressed are: How does a farm's financial structure influence its overall risk position? How are business and financial risks related to one another? How risky are agricultural investments compared to non-agricultural investments? Do agricultural policies increase or decrease financial risks in agriculture? Do risk attitudes matter? How effective are farmers' financial responses to risk compared to other methods of risk management? These questions have frequently been addressed using portfolio theory, as summarized in the following discussion.

7.1. Portfolio model

Portfolio theory based on mean-variance analysis has received extensive use in agricultural finance, especially in delineating the properties of business risk and financial risk for agricultural firms [Robison and Barry (1977); Barry (1994); Barry and Robison (1987); Robison and Brake (1979)]. Recent theoretical support for the mean-variance criterion has also encouraged its use [Meyer (1987); Meyer and Rasche (1992)]. Portfolio theory includes financial activities by introducing a risk-free asset that can be combined with portfolios of risky assets.[2] Positive and negative holdings of the risk-free asset represent lending and borrowing, respectively, at the risk-free interest rate. Combining the risk-free asset with the efficient portfolios of risky assets enlarges the risk efficient set, makes it more risk efficient, and under normality, yields the stochastic separation property in which the investment decision in risky assets is independent of the financing decision involving the desired combination of the risky assets and the risk-free asset. Movement along the risk-efficient set clearly indicates the risk-return trade-off associated with different levels of financial leverage.

[2] See Barry and Robison (1987), Pinches (1992), or other financial management and investment textbooks for a standard treatment of portfolio theory.

7.2. Business and financial risks

For financial analysis, it is helpful to distinguish between the effects of business risk and financial risk on the agricultural investor's total risk. Business risk arises from the variability of returns to risky assets. It is independent of the financial structure of the portfolio. Financial risk arises from the composition and terms of the financial claims on assets. Any fixed obligation financing, as in borrowing and leasing, is considered a form of financial leveraging.

Business and financial risks in portfolio theory can be modeled in an additive or multiplicative way [Gabriel and Baker (1980); Barry (1983); Collins (1985)]. Following the multiplicative approach and maintaining the assumption of a deterministic interest rate, it can be shown [Barry (1983); Barry and Robison (1987)] that total risk (*TR*), business risk (*BR*), and financial risk (*FR*) are expressed as

$$TR = (BR)(FR) \tag{3}$$

or as

$$\frac{\sigma_e}{\bar{r}_e} = \left(\frac{\sigma_a}{\bar{r}_a} \right) \left(\frac{(\bar{r}_a)(A/E)}{(\bar{r}_a)(A/E) - (i)(D/E)} \right), \tag{4}$$

where $\bar{r}_e$ and σ_e are the expected rate of return to equity and its standard deviation, respectively, $\bar{r}_a$ and σ_a are the expected return and standard deviation of risky assets, i is the cost of debt, and A/E and D/E are the respective ratios of assets and debt-to-equity.

From (4), total risk, expressed as a coefficient of variation ($\sigma_e/\bar{r}_e$) for returns to equity, is the product of business risk and financial risk. In turn, business risk is expressed as the coefficient of variation for returns on risky assets, $\sigma_a/\bar{r}_a$. And financial risk is represented by a flow measure of financial leverage in the investor's portfolio. That is, the second term to the right of the equal sign in (4) relates the returns on risky assets in the numerator to the returns on equity in the denominator. This flow measure of leverage is analogous to a stock measure expressed by the asset-to-equity ratio. As leverage increases, so does the measure of financial risk in (4), thus magnifying total risk while *BR* remains constant.

Equation (4) can be evaluated in terms of possible adjustments in *BR*, *FR*, or both as changes occur in one or more of the model's parameters [Barry and Robison (1987)]. If, for example, the investor's risk attitude were expressed as a constant level of *TR*, then an increase in *BR* may be offset by a decrease in *FR*, or vice versa. The specific form and magnitude of the portfolio adjustments will vary with the structural and operating characteristics of farm businesses, with the risk attitude of the investor, and with the possible responses of lenders and other financial claimants.

Featherstone et al. (1988) employ a similar approach to risk balancing in exploring the relationship between farmers' leverage positions and the reductions in business risk attributable to participation in government stabilization programs for agricultural commodities. They demonstrate that farm policies could result in an increase in financial leverage that offsets the policy-induced reductions in business risks, thus increasing total risk when the opposite effect is the intended policy goal. Ahrendsen, Collender and Dixon (1994) also tested financial structure issues for dairy farms using the risk-balancing concept and could not confirm the concept's ability to explain financial structure, although matters of data quality, variable formulations, cost/size relationships, and others were cited as areas needing further study.

7.3. Risk and financial structure

Under conditions of risk, an investor's objective function is modified to directly account for sources and magnitudes of risk, and the investor's attitudes toward risk. The risk attitude may then become an important variable influencing portfolio decisions, including the investor's preferred relationship between debt and equity capital–that is, optimal financial structure. Barry, Baker, and Sanint (1981) and Barry and Robison (1987) illustrate this effect analytically by expressing the investor's objective function in terms of expected utility maximization, utilizing the mean-variance approach and deriving the optimal financial structure.

Under a deterministic interest rate condition, the Barry, Baker, and Sanint result for optimal debt (D) is

$$D = \frac{\bar{r}_a - i - 2\lambda \sigma_a^2 E}{2\lambda \sigma_a^2}, \tag{5}$$

where λ is the level of risk aversion, $\bar{r}_a$ and σ_a^2 are the expected return to and variance of risky assets, i is the cost of debt, and E is equity capital. Rearranging (5) algebraically will give the optimal debt-to-equity ratio. The optimal financial structure under risk-free borrowing, thus, depends upon the risk attitude as well as on the financial data [see Collins (1985), and Featherstone et al. (1988), for an alternative yet identical portrayal of optimal financial structure].

When the borrowing cost is stochastic (σ_i^2) and correlated (covariance σ_{ai}) with the return on risky assets, Barry, Baker, and Sanint (1981) show that optimal debt is

$$D = \frac{\bar{r}_a - \bar{i} - 2\lambda E(\sigma_a^2 - \sigma_{ai})}{2\lambda(\sigma_a^2 + \sigma_i^2 - \sigma_{ai})}. \tag{6}$$

In both (5) and (6), the optimal financial structure is inversely related to changes in the risk attitude. That is, greater levels of debt are associated with lower levels of risk aversion while other factors remain constant. [See Leatham and Baker (1988), for an empirical analysis, using discrete stochastic programming of a farmer's choice between fixed and adjustable interest rate loans under alternative risk specifications.]

Barry, Baker, and Sanint (1981) use this analytical framework to show how unanticipated variations in the cost and availability of credit combine with other financial and business risks to determine total risks. Consideration of stochastic costs and availability of credit generally lead to lower leverage by farmers, although in selected circumstances high correlations between borrowing costs and assets returns could warrant greater leverage. Their empirical evidence works against this response, however, by showing a strongly positive relationship between credit availability and level of farm income, implying a negative relationship between borrowing costs and levels of income. Moreover, a tendency for capital credit to be more volatile than operating credit suggests that the financing capacity for firm growth is more unstable than financing capacity for annual operations.

Gwinn, Barry, and Ellinger (1992) consider the optimal financial structure of cash grain farms under conditions of risk and for various levels of risk aversion by farmers, as motivated by the debt and equity relationship derived in Equations (5) and (6). They developed a multi-period risk programming model that contained a wide range of investment and financing alternatives, credit specifications, family consumption, and tax relationships. The objective function yielded a risk-return trade-off between the expected value of the farm's terminal net worth and variance-covariance measures on terminal asset and liability values and on annual gross margins of production and sale activities.

The risk programming results were validated by comparisons with performance data for farm businesses from the Illinois Farm Business Farm Management Association. The results indicated substantial differences in financial structure, farm size, and liquidity over a wide range of risk aversion levels. The risk-neutral solution had the largest farm size, the highest financial leverage, the least asset diversity, the fastest rate of financial growth, and the greatest total risk. Increases in risk aversion yielded slower growth, smaller farm sizes, lower financial leverage, larger liquidity, and greater diversity in resource control over ownership and leasing of farmland. Thus, a range of optimal financial structures for family-oriented cash grain farms is plausible to expect, based on differences in levels of risk aversion among farmers.

In studying the theories of capital structure for proprietary firms, Collins and Karp (1993, 1995) draw comparisons between the static, risk-averse expected utility approach [Barry et al. (1981); Collins (1985)] and their stochastic, risk-neutral optimal control approach. Different assumptions about risk attitudes, risk concepts (variability vs. ruin), planning horizons, functional forms, and other decision attributes, together with data deficiencies, hamper the comparisons. The ability to handle multi-period horizons is a strength of the dynamic approach, while accounting for possible changes over time in risk attitudes is a strength of the other. The insights offered by these comparisons are interesting, although the principal contributions to date likely involve identifying the range of variables influencing capital structure, rather than the validity of any particular modeling approach.

8. Aggregate investment analysis

In contrast to the micro-level orientation of much of the financial management work of the past, a substantial literature has addressed aggregate or sector-level financial analysis. Answers have been sought to questions such as: What determines farmers' investment behavior? Are farm investments reversible? How are the investment and capital structure of agriculture related to each other? Do financing terms, credit policies, and taxation affect the aggregate structure of the farm sector? Answers to these questions generally involve micro-foundations, although the possible relationships may be tested econometrically with the use of aggregate data.

8.1. Investment analysis concepts

Consider, first, the determination of farmers' investment behavior. A micro-foundation to this question might express a farmer's investment decision in terms of the net present value model:

$$NPV = -V_0 + \sum_{n=1}^{N} \frac{R_0(1-t)(1+g_p)^n}{(1+i)^n} + \frac{V_N - (V_N - V_0)(t)}{(1+i)^N}, \qquad (7)$$

where

$$i = (i_d)(1-t)(D/A) + (i_e)(E/A) \qquad (8)$$

and

$$V_N = V_0(1+g_v)^N. \qquad (9)$$

Variable V_0 is the asset's initial investment requirement; V_N is the asset's terminal value, reflecting growth or decline at periodic rate g_V; t is the income tax rate; R_0 is the base level of net cash flow per period; g_v is a growth rate (positive, negative or zero) for net cash flows; and i is the weighted after-tax cost of capital, where i_d and i_e are the costs of debt and equity, respectively, and D/A and E/A are the respective ratios of debt and equity to assets.

Investment profitability, thus, depends on the magnitude of discounted returns, including the after-tax terminal value of the assets, compared to the asset's initial investment requirements, using the weighted average cost of financial capital as the discount rate. A positive (negative) net present value signifies profitability (unprofitability) relative to the cost of financial capital. The internal rate of return (IRR), an alternative investment criterion, is the discount rate that yields a net present value of zero [Barry et al. (1995)]. Profitability, then, is based on a comparison of the IRR to the weighted average cost of financial capital.

Comparative statics indicate that investment profitability is inversely related to the initial asset price (investment requirement) and to the cost of capital, and positively related to the level of net cash flows and the growth rates of cash flows and the terminal value. Changes in tax rates have an ambiguous relationship to investment profitability, depending on the nature of the tax (e.g., ordinary income vs. capital gains) and how taxation jointly affects the asset returns and the cost of capital [Robison and Barry (1996)].

The net present value concept is extended when, as is frequently the case, investments are irreversible and/or postponable [Pindyck (1991); Ross (1995)]. Irreversibility occurs when investments result in sunk costs for industry or firm-specific assets or for situations when the lemons problem, government regulations, and institutional arrangements hamper asset redeployability. Postponability gives the prospective investor the opportunity to wait for new information about prices, costs, technology, legal issues, and other market conditions before he or she commits resources to the investment.

The benefits of new information from waiting could enhance investment profitability, but the waiting process incurs costs as well. Included in the costs are foregone returns from making the investment earlier, possible increases in investment expenditures, and adverse profit effects resulting from comparable investments by competitors.

The valuation issues associated with postponing an investment resemble an option valuation problem. In this case, the value added to a net present value model by postponing the investment decision is equal to the value of an options contract for the right to purchase the investment in the future. When a firm makes an irreversible investment, it exercises or nullifies the option to make this investment at a later time. The lost option value is a potentially important opportunity cost that is part of the investment cost.

The present value of the investment's net cash flows must now exceed the initial expenditures by an amount equal to the value of keeping the investment option open [Pindyck (1991)]. In this sense, a project may not only compete with other possible projects, but it competes with itself delayed in time [Ross (1995)]. Option values, thus, represent the maximum price that could be paid to guarantee the right to purchase the investment at its investment cost (exercise price) at a designated time in the future.

Most of the aggregate investment analysis in agricultural finance is consistent with the general specification of the net present value model. Numerous studies have sought to measure and test the relative importance of the respective variables, and the speed with which capital adjustments occur. Similarly, asset replacement models, which represent a special case of investment analysis, have sought to determine optimal holding periods for depreciable assets, based on the key variables affecting profitability [Perrin (1972); Robison and Barry (1996)]. More recent studies have employed the information and incentive arguments of modern finance theory to focus on the linkage between investment and financing [Hubbard (1998)].

8.2. Early investment and tax policy studies

Studies investigating the aggregate demand for one or more farm assets begin to appear in the late 1950s. Cromarty (1959), Griliches (1960), Heady and Tweeten (1963), Fox

(1966), and Rayner and Cowling (1968) all utilized a partial stock-adjustment approach incorporating lag terms which permitted adjustment over time to an optimal stock level. Positive but small coefficients for the lag term were consistently obtained.

Similar behavioral assumptions pertaining to investments were made in these studies: Farmers sought to maximize profits and, thus, achieve a desired level of investment and related service flows. A commonly used variable was the ratio of machinery prices to commodity prices, which was a consistently important explanation of investment behavior. Griliches (1960) was the only one of the above studies to conclude that interest rates significantly explained investment, perhaps reflecting the relatively low and stable interest rates during these times. Rayner and Cowling (1968) found that the farm wage rate relative to tractor prices was a significant explanatory variable for machinery investments in Great Britain. They attributed this finding to structure of the labor force, farm size, and agricultural policy in Great Britain relative to the United States. These studies were completed during the same period of time, and each employed ordinary least squares regression. They achieved similar results, which remained unchallenged for a considerable period of time.

Early work in this area also considered how various forms of market imperfections influenced investment and disinvestment in the agricultural sector. G.L. Johnson (1956), Edwards (1959), G.L. Johnson and Quance (1972), and D.G. Johnson (1950) addressed the concept of asset fixity in agriculture based on the relationship between an asset's marginal productive value to a firm and the spread between the asset's acquisition cost and its salvage value in the marketplace. The wider the spreads between acquisition cost and salvage value, the greater the fixity of assets and the more sluggish are resource adjustments in response to changing market signals. These concepts and the related empirical studies helped to explain the seemingly slow adjustments of resources in agriculture and the tendency for an apparent overinvestment in the sector.

8.3. Investment, capital structure, and taxation

In 1981, Penson, Romain, and Hughes developed an econometric approach to investment analysis that reflected the joint effects of capital structure, taxation, and capacity depreciation patterns on the implicit rental price of durable capital. The capital structure formulation directly reflected the combined use of debt and equity capital employed by farmers when they finance purchases of durable inputs. Their estimating equation related net investment to variables depicting the ratio of farm output to the implicit rental price of capital, the desired capital stock, and lagged net investment.

The findings by Penson, Romain, and Hughes (1981) indicate statistical significance and correct signs for each of the major variables, thus providing good explanations for annual net investment in tractors. In particular, their results are supportive of the engineering-data capacity depreciation patterns for delineating net investment from gross investment and replacement expenditures [see Ball and Witzke (1993), for a recent application]. The conventional geometric decay pattern did the poorest job among those tested of explaining the real annual net investment in farm tractors. The elasticities, computed at the mean, between net investment and the output to capital cost ratio were 2.64 for the engineering data pattern, 2.53 for a one hoss shay pattern, 4.33 for straight line, and 6.59 for geometric decay, suggesting a substantial over-estimate of farmers' investment responses to changes in prices, interest rates, taxes, and other relevant variables under the geometric decay pattern.

Dynamic specifications of investment behavior account for the effects of asset adjustment costs on movements from one capital stock equilibrium to another. The relative fixity of inputs causes such adjustments to take time. The accelerator concept becomes important to the process by which net investment closes the gap between desired and actual levels of capital stock. Under dynamic conditions, the agricultural firm's long-run dynamic problem is to choose time paths for variable inputs and quasi fixed inputs that maximize the present value of net earnings. Especially important to aggregate investment analysis are the difference equations and functional forms for the profit and cost of adjustment functions.

Using the dynamic investment framework, LeBlanc and Hrubovcak and colleagues undertook a series of studies beginning in the 1980s that included examining the effects of interest rates and tax policies on investment in agriculture. Their 1985 study focused on the relationship between agricultural machinery investments, interest rates, and several other important variables. They report three general conclusions from their analysis. First, changes in interest rates had a minor direct effect on the optimal level of agricultural machinery. The response of the optimal capital stock to changes in the interest rate is highly inelastic, less than −0.01 in 1978. Second, interest rates do affect investment by altering the rate of adjustment to new levels of optimal capital stock–higher rates delay investments, and vice versa. Third, the ratio of machinery price to output price is a more important determinant of the adjustment rate than is the real interest rate.

Subsequent studies focused on the investment implications of tax policy using a broader concept of rental rates of capital than interest rates alone. The investment equations in the 1986 study by LeBlanc and Hrubovcak are functions of variable input and output prices, technological change, rental rates of capital, and lagged capital stock. The rental rate is a function of asset price, capacity depreciation, tax variables, the discount rate (weighted average costs of debt and equity capital), and the rate of inflation. Tax policies affect investment by altering the implicit rental price of capital.

Results for their 1986 base model indicate significant inverse relationships between investment and the rental price of capital, dynamically stable adjustment rates, and plausible values for other key variables affecting investments. Specific tax policy effects focused on the impacts of investment tax credit, interest deductibility, and other tax changes during the 1954–1978 period. The results of the tax analysis indicated that nearly 20 percent of net investment in agricultural equipment during the 1956–1978 period was attributed to tax policy, with the investment tax credit and liberalized depreciation allowance having the largest and smallest effects, respectively.

An extension of the tax policy effects by LeBlanc et al. (1992) utilized a similar conceptual framework together with a stochastic coefficient econometric methodology to estimate how the Tax Reform Act of 1986 altered the cost of capital and net investment in agriculture. Their base model results indicated that land price, rental rates of capital, energy price, and lagged capital stock were the most important determinants of net investment, and wages and chemical prices were the least important. The provisions of the 1986 Act were estimated to substantially increase (12.7 percent overall) rental prices of capital, and thus decrease the optimal long-run capital stock in the agricultural sector by an estimated $4 billion or nearly a 25 percent reduction from prior law. These results provide clear evidence of the importance of tax policy on the capital position of agriculture.

Weersink and Tauer (1989) contrast the dynamic optimization approach to estimation of investment functions with a traditional approach in which ad hoc adjustments (e.g., finite distributed lags) are imposed on the time structure of investment. Their traditional model, applied to dairy farms, included variables for capacity utilization, cattle inventories, costs of capital, farm size, external debt, farm income, time, and operator age. All of the variables except size and age were statistically significant. Both the dynamic and traditional models tracked the actual expenditures of dairy farmers reasonably well, although the traditional model was judged to perform better. Both models suggested a significant delay between changes in the determinants of desired capital stock and the actual investment expenditure.

An alternative data-generating approach to machinery investment analysis by Gustafson, Barry, and Sonka (1989) utilized experimental and simulation procedures with a panel of cash grain farmers to test the effectiveness of the approach and to observe the effects on investment expenditures of selected structural, performance, and environmental conditions. While limited in generality due to the small size of the farmer panel, the results show investment levels statistically related to the tenure and leverage position of farm operator, the economic conditions they face, and the age of existing machinery. Alternative public policies of lower commodity price supports, tax reforms, and reductions in interest rates influence the timing of purchases, but do not alter total investment levels.

Elhorst (1993) makes a special effort in his traditional approach to farm investment analysis to utilize farm-level data in the Netherlands and to tailor the econometric approach to differences in investment frequencies among farmers. His "infrequency purchase model" yielded a substantial improvement in estimation results, but still left unexplained substantial portions of the farmers' investments. Elhorst speculates that a greater emphasis on the linkages between investment and financing might be promising to consider.

8.4. Investment and financing relationships

Asymmetric information concepts have also played an important, recent role in analyzing investment behavior in the agricultural sector. Under this approach, credit rationing triggered by asymmetric information, as demonstrated by Stiglitz and Weiss (1981), may serve as a constraint on business investment. Testing whether financial variables become significant in empirically estimated investment equations, when investment is known to be profitable or unprofitable, provides evidence of financial constraints attributable to asymmetric information [Fazzari et al. (1988); Hubbard (1998)].

Jensen, Lawson, and Langemeier (1993) build upon the earlier study of Weersink and Tauer (1989) by using farm-level data to estimate a composite model of agricultural investment that includes variables suggested by the accelerator, neo-classical, and asymmetric information models. Their internal finance variables included real net farm income, interest commitments, real total depreciation, and real off-farm income. Their results indicate that the addition of the internal cash flow variables significantly improved the explanatory power of their agricultural investment model, and that investment was more responsive to the internal cash flow variables than to either the accelerator or neo-classical variables.

Hubbard and Kashyap (1992) also applied asymmetric information concepts to the agricultural sector in exploring the relationship between investment in agricultural equipment and internal finance represented by farmers' net worth positions. A key factor for many models, in which asymmetric information is important, is that the cost of external finance varies inversely with the level of "inside finance". Thus, lenders may become more willing to lend when farmers' net worth improves, and adverse incentive problems should be less important at sufficiently high levels of net worth. The empirical results obtained by Hubbard and Kashyap clearly indicate that the standard perfect-capital-market approach fails to adequately explain investment, due to systematic correlations between the unexplained component of investment and movements in farmers' net worth positions. The correlation is strongest during periods of low net worth. Extending the model to accommodate net worth improves the explanation of farmers' investments, although the effects are significantly more important during deflationary periods than during boom times.

Several studies have considered whether credit rationing affects production levels in the agricultural sector, under asymmetric information concepts. Calomiris, Hubbard, and Stock (1986) evaluated the relationships between state-level farm output and farmers' collateral positions, debt-servicing burdens, and bank failures. They find strong evidence that disruptions in agricultural credit markets can have real effects on farm output, especially through deteriorating collateral positions and institutional failures.

Belongia and Gilbert (1990) use a model of credit rationing to determine whether farmers receive more of their credit from federal agencies when the aggregate supply of credit declines, and whether credit availability is strongly related to the level of farm output. Their empirical results for the 1947–1986 period are consistent with non-price credit rationing from private sector lenders, by showing a higher proportion of government-sponsored lending to agriculture as the growth rate of total agricultural credit declines. The government-sponsored credit, thus, fills the gap when private sector rationing increases. However, further empirical work suggested that government-sponsored non-real-estate credit is not significantly related to agricultural output. The authors suggest that these results fail to indicate an important role of subsidized credit in facilitating agricultural production, and question whether farmers divert such credit to higher- valued opportunities. Belongia and Gilbert (1990) do not, however, consider the credit effects on farmers' financial performance.

In a developing economy setting, Feder et al. (1990) considered the extent to which production credit programs for farm households in China stimulate production or are used for other purposes. Their results indicate that a significant proportion of the short-term credit provided by rural credit cooperatives as "production credit" may actually be utilized for consumption and investment, especially in light of the absence of informal lenders and of medium- and long-term credit for the households in their study. The likely output effect, thus, will be smaller than anticipated. These results clearly highlight the fungibility of credit problem in institutional development lending and its adverse implications for building borrower and lender discipline in credit programs.

8.5. Investment, sunk costs, and risk

Sunk costs, irreversibilities, and risk may interact to influence the likelihood of investment and disinvestment, the mobility of resources, and potential over- or under-investment in agriculture. Following G. Johnson's early work, Tweeten and Quance (1969), Houck (1977), and Traill, Colman, and Young (1978) tested for irreversible supply and demand equations, generally based on separate equations for periods of increasing and decreasing investments. More recently, Vasavada and Chambers (1986) used an asset adjustment cost model to determine that agricultural investments have high degrees of irreversibility. Nelson, Braden, and Roh (1989) also tested for asymmetries in investment and disinvestment periods, finding some evidence that periods of disinvestment are more persistent than periods of investment.

The dynamic properties of sunk costs, irreversibilities, and asset fixity have also received increasing attention in economics research. Part of the focus has been on understanding how these factors influence the role of competitive markets in achieving an efficient allocation of resources [Chavas (1994); Hsu and Chang (1990)]. Also important are the influences on technology adoption, productivity growth, and the structure of agriculture [e.g., Saha et al. (1994); Purvis et al. (1995)].

The adverse effects of sunk costs have important implications for public policies, institutional innovations, and firm-level decision making. Barham and Chavas (forthcoming), for example, illustrate how sunk costs and risk may lead to such response strategies as investments in human capital, public infrastructure, information dissemination, insurance, and other risk management strategies. The intended effects of such actions are to improve resource mobilization, encourage investments and disinvestments, stimulate trade, enhance productivity, and add to welfare outcomes.

9. Finance, economic growth, and the structure of agriculture

Theory and empirical evidence indicate that the sophistication of financial systems and an economy's growth and development are strongly related to one another [Levine (1997); Gertler and Rose (1996)]. Levine argues that the development of financial markets and institutions is a critical and inextricable part of the growth process. In the absence of financial markets, the effects of high information and transaction costs (including the costs of acquiring information, enforcing contracts, and exchanging goods and financial claims) would tend to immobilize savings, stifle risk-taking, constrain investment decisions, hamper technological innovations, and dampen rates of economic growth. High-return, technologically intensive projects generally require long-run commitments of capital, but savers are reluctant to concentrate their funds for lengthy periods in risky investments where good information is lacking. Financial markets, with their liquidity, diversity, and information-providing roles, enable the mobilization and channeling of these savings to their highest payoff uses.

The financial intermediary, thus, provides the service of identifying and monitoring the most promising firms, managers, and prospective investments. The result is a heightened pace of economic growth and development. Levine (1997) cites "... a growing body of empirical analyses, including firm-level studies, individual country studies, and broad cross-country comparisons that demonstrate a positive link between the functioning of the financial system and long-run economic growth" (p. 720). A linkage, however, does not necessarily imply causation.

Is credit a causal factor or a facilitating factor in the structural change and economic growth of agricultural sectors? Agricultural finance clearly is linked to changes in farm structure [Gustafson and Barry (1993); Lins and Barry (1980)]. Past practices in farm lending, which have included more liberal lending in favorable times and more conservative lending in less favorable times, have strongly influenced the size, profitability, and well-being of family farms. Gains in agricultural productivity, the mechanization and modernization of farming operations, more orderly marketing of farm commodities, and liquidity management have benefited considerably from ready availability of agricultural credit.

These benefits of credit in particular, and financial services more generally, are considered to be accommodating, rather than causal, in that the financial capital responds to underlying economic incentives. Availability of credit may often be a necessary condition for capital investments. It is not, however, a sufficient condition. Profit incentives are needed as well. Thus, readily available credit likely has facilitated, but not necessarily caused, many of the changes occurring in agriculture – fewer and larger farms, greater specialization, adoption of new technology, greater capital intensity, and stronger market coordination. Moreover, as the prospects for economic development increase, financial market development becomes more essential. In turn, the enhanced capabilities of financial markets also become predictors of future rates of growth, capital accumulation, and technological change. In this perspective, as observed by Levine, financial markets are endogenous to economic growth and development. They evolve over time, and are essential to economic growth.

Sometimes, however, swings in credit conditions can magnify changes in the financial well-being of agricultural producers. In the U.S., for example, the boom times of the late 1970s were fueled by readily available, low-cost credit, only to be met by the credit management and loan repayment problems of the early 1980s, and the significant stresses faced by many financial institutions, especially those that specialized in agricultural lending.

Credit policies may also have conflicting effects. The historic institutional developments in agricultural finance (i.e., creation of government-sponsored agricultural lenders, direct government loan programs, laws targeted to agricultural loans) have assisted many countries to maintain a pluralistic, smaller-scale, family-oriented, largely non-corporate farming structure. Concurrently, however, credit policies intended to sustain this pluralistic structure of agriculture can also slow resource adjustment, build excess production capacity, create excessive debt, and counter the effects of new technologies and market focuses in agriculture [Lee and Gabriel (1980)]. Emergency or disaster-related public credit can have the effect of substituting for income, thus perpetuating adverse incentives by borrowers. Weak monitoring and enforcement problems in public credit can create moral hazards by both agricultural borrowers and their lenders in seeking to continue use of the public safety net. These actions go well beyond the intended roles of credit markets and undermine their integrity and soundness (see the discussion about public credit in Section 10 of this chapter).

10. Suppliers of financial capital

10.1. Introduction

Suppliers of financial capital include savers with investable funds and financial intermediaries who specialize in the transmission of funds from savers through financial markets to those with need for external sources of funds. The financial institution performs the intermediation process more efficiently and safely than would individual savers and investors, while still earning an acceptable rate of return on the institution's equity capital. Efficient collection and processing of information about the creditworthiness of borrowers, loan performance, and financial market conditions are major services provided by financial intermediaries. Diversity in their holdings of assets and liabilities reduces credit risk, interest rate risk, and liquidity risk, and helps to reconcile liquidity differences between savers and investors. Thus, economic theories of the firm and of markets, along with the informational concepts of modern finance theory, apply to financial intermediaries, similar to their applications to other types of organizations. In the cases of market gaps or major market imperfections, public loan programs or publicly sponsored institutions may emerge as important participants in the intermediation process. This section of the chapter addresses the application of these financial market concepts to agricultural finance.

10.2. Financing the agricultural sector

The historically strong reliance by farmers on debt capital to operate their farms, capitalize their asset bases, and respond to liquidity pressures requires a responsive, modern

financial market. Ideally, agricultural borrowers would prefer a financial market that offers competitive interest rates; ready, low-cost access to credit; reliable availability of
financial capital through all phases of the business cycle; versatile uses of funds; credit
terms tailored to the characteristics of the activities being financed; and effective access to financially related products and services. The financing of agriculture, however,
presents special challenges to the financial markets.

As indicated in Section 2, farms typically are capital-intensive, geographically dispersed, limited in scale and scope, and characterized by lengthy production periods.
They are subject to significant business risks and to cyclical swings in economic conditions, often resulting in liquidity problems at specialized lending institutions serving
agriculture. Imbalances in needs for and availability of local market funds require reliable access to non-local sources of funds. However, non-local funding is challenged because relationships between agricultural borrowers and their lenders typically are characterized by strong reliance on reputations, personal familiarity, and social closeness.
Skills in farmers' financial management and the quality of their financial information
also are more limited in agricultural lending. In light of these characteristics, the availability of competitively priced, dependable credit for agricultural borrowers has long
been an important policy issue, and public credit programs often play significant roles
in enhancing market development and ensuring credit availability.

10.3. Types of agricultural lenders

Most countries have several types of financial intermediaries and other entities that provide loans and financial services to the agricultural sector. Included are [Barry et al.
(1995)]:

- A commercial banking system that relies heavily on deposits as a source of loanable
funds.
- Specialized agricultural lending institutions, with corporate or cooperative organiza-
tions, that depend primarily on financial market sources of funds.
- Government programs at the federal, provincial, and/or state levels that rely on finan-
cial markets or taxation for sources of funds.
- Credit unions composed of members with a common bond.
- Farm-related trade or agribusiness firms.
- Intermediaries that perform important fiduciary or trust functions, such as insurance
firms, pension funds, and trust companies.
- Individuals such as family members, sellers of farmland, neighbors individually or in
groups, and money lenders in the case of developing countries.
- Originators who channel loans into well-diversified loan pools funded by asset-
backed securities.

These sources of financial capital differ in their organizational structures, operational
characteristics, degrees of specialization, sources of funds, relative importance, and relationship to the public sector. They each participate, with varying degrees, in providing
the basic services of financial intermediation: (1) origination of loans, (2) funding of

loans, (3) risk bearing, (4) provision of liquidity, and (5) monitoring, payment collection, and other servicing of loans. Each of these services generates a source of profits to the intermediary and, as financial markets develop and become more competitive, different financial institutions may tend to specialize in the provision of one or more of these services.

10.4. Regulation of financial markets

Public involvement in financial markets is inherently extensive and changes in form as the financial markets of countries experience greater maturity and development. Even the most sophisticated financial markets experience strong public regulation. The need for such regulation is attributed to several factors. Included are the intangible nature of financial assets (promises to repay for debt and ownership titles for equity); the significant importance of information generation, transmission, and processing in the intermediation process; aggregate monetary stability; and safety and soundness for investors in securities issued by government-sponsored institutions. As a result, considerable confidence, trust, and stability are required among market participants in order for financial markets to develop and function effectively. The resulting regulatory environment is intended to safeguard savers and investors, foster competition, respond to market imperfections, facilitate effective monetary policy, and achieve other specific social goals.

Governmental regulation of financial markets may take many forms:
- Restraints on geographic expansion of financial institutions, as with branching and holding company regulations.
- Mandatory specialization in some services (e.g., farm, student, or housing loans; transaction accounts).
- Portfolio diversification through reserve and capital requirements, legal lending limits, and asset allocations.
- Public reporting and examination requirements.
- Special borrowing privileges.
- Fair trade practices.
- Public programs for credit and insurance.
- Laws affecting the design, security, negotiability, and trade of financial instruments.

The extent of regulation varies substantially among types of financial institutions and credit sources. Examples include complete public sponsorship in the case of government loan programs; chartering of government-sponsored, yet privately owned agricultural credit institutions; and comprehensive regulatory oversight of depository institutions and insurance protection for depositors. In contrast, agricultural lending by agribusinesses and trade firms, individuals, and money lenders is largely unregulated, except for the discipline provided by the marketplace. This regulatory mosaic contributes to the effective operation of heterogeneous financial markets, but can also create periodic imbalances in credit markets that raise concerns by market participants about "leveling the regulatory playing field".

10.5. Evolution of financial markets

Financial markets have experienced lengthy, accelerating transition. Innovations in information processing and electronic communications technologies have allowed the breaking-down of geographic barriers, and have led to substantial integration between national and international financial markets. Globalization is common in the trading of many types of financial assets, in the financing of international trade, and in sourcing various types of funds. Deregulation of interest rates and of the range of products and services financial institutions may offer has led to the emergence of broadly based, highly competitive financial services companies, offering a combination of transactions, credit, savings, investments, insurance, counseling, and related services to their customers. At the same time, specialized service providers can still fill well-defined market niches, often through partnering arrangements with other financial services companies.

Securitization is becoming widespread in the financing of residential housing, automobiles, accounts receivable, commercial properties, and other types of assets. In the U.S., the Federal Agricultural Mortgage Corporation (Farmer Mac) provides securitization services for farm real estate loans. Packaging loans into pools, adding credit enhancements, and selling asset-backed securities to investors have proven effective in the reallocation, and management, of credit risks and interest rate risks from financial institutions to financial market investors. The creation and trading of derivative securities in financial risk management is in the vanguard of financial innovations, although subject to strong demands for trader expertise in order for derivative markets to function safely and effectively.

Financial reforms have played an important role in the evolution of financial markets. These reforms have been widespread in recent decades, motivated in part by ideological factors, technological developments, and changing financial market conditions. The reform process usually involves a set of actions taken to ease portfolio controls, target credit to selected borrowers, and limit government intervention in the determination of interest rates [Caprio et al. (1996)]. Relying more on market forces has been viewed as a promising way to enhance the intermediation process and improve the allocation of resources. The evidence [Caprio et al. (1996); Herring and Litan (1995)] suggests that the reform process can be successfully managed, although the timing and degree of success are strongly influenced by a country's financial condition, the sequence of reforms, and the linkages between the country's financial and non-financial sectors.

Reforms have opened domestic financial markets to greater international influences. Integration among markets is especially strong in the wholesaling of funds and financial services [Herring and Litan (1995)]. Integration is less complete, however, in retail markets, including agricultural finance, in which smaller firms and individuals primarily patronize financial service providers in their own locality, region, or country. Interacting with local personnel remains a strong customer preference in agricultural finance, although new telecommunications and transport technologies are making inroads on these preferences.

10.6. Implications for agricultural lending

This evolutionary financial market environment has not excluded the financing of agriculture. Large-scale commercial lenders (including money center and regional banks, and large specialized agricultural lending systems) are meeting the credit and financial services needs of larger, industrialized agricultural production units that have varying types of contractual arrangements with food companies and other agribusiness firms. These industrialized units neither need nor use subsidized credit programs, except perhaps when younger, inexperienced agricultural families become contract growers in integrated poultry, livestock, or dairy operations.

Commercial-scale family farms also tend to be financed by commercial banks and specialized agricultural lenders, perhaps with government sponsorship and/or financing assistance. These credit sources have either acquired, or have access to, the modern financial market technology, although their approach to agricultural lending is gravitating away from the information-intensive, traditional-relationship style toward a price-driven style typical of commercial lending in other sectors. In response, agricultural borrowers must upgrade their skills in financial and risk management, accounting, and financial reporting, consistent with those of other commercial borrowers, in order to compete effectively for loan funds.

Small, part-time, or limited-resource farms remain large in numbers, but relatively small in terms of economic contributions. In developed countries, small farms often rely heavily on non-farm employment as sources of income. In developing countries, small farms often operate at subsistence levels. The financing needs of small farms in developed countries are increasingly treated as consumer-type loans by commercial lenders, with credit-scoring and higher interest rates used to offset the high servicing costs of small loans. Small farmers rely heavily on targeted, public credit programs with concessionary lending terms to meet their financing needs. Individuals, money lenders, trade firms, and other local sources are other credit sources for small farms. For this type of borrower, public credit serves the multiple purposes of facilitating resource adjustments, providing liquidity in times of adversity, and assisting in meeting the creditworthiness requirements of commercial lenders.

10.7. Agricultural finance markets and institutions

Professional studies in agricultural finance have coincided closely with the transition in financial markets cited above. Included are aggregate projections of capital and credit needs in agriculture [Hughes and Penson (1981)], financial market analyses, policy studies, and structural change of financial institutions. Impacts of regulatory changes on the availability, cost, and other financing terms for agricultural borrowers have received considerable attention [e.g., Barry (1981)]. The results of optimization models, simulation, and econometric analyses of financial institutions have highlighted the combined effects of interest rate deregulation and financial stress of agricultural borrowers on the performance and management strategies of different types of financial institutions [Barry (1981); Barnard and Barry (1985); Barry and Lee (1983); Pederson (1992); Robison and Barry (1977)].

During the stress times of the 1980s in the U.S., some institutional responses to risk (e.g., floating interest rates, larger risk premiums in loan rates) had the unintended effects of transmitting credit risk and interest rate risk to healthy agricultural borrowers, thus widening and deepening the adversities. Other strategies (broader loan diversification, expanded geographic markets, gap and duration gap management, insurance) have enhanced the risk-bearing capacities of financial institutions, and have led to more efficient management of credit, interest rate, and liquidity risks [Ellinger and Barry (1989); Barry et al. (1995, 1996)]. Differential loan pricing based on competitive types of loans, borrowers' credit risks, loan sizes, costs of funds, and degrees of financial stress is also an effective element of asset-liability management by financial institutions [Barry (1995); Barry and Calvert (1983); Schmiesing et al. (1985); Bottomley (1975); Lee and Baker (1984)]. These pricing strategies respond to the adverse selection and moral hazard problems of agricultural lending, and are often tied to the growing use of credit-scoring techniques.

Designing flexible repayment programs through variable amortization, debt reserves, graduated payments, shared appreciation loans, and other mechanisms, similar to the flexibility provided by share rent obligations in farm real estate leasing, formalizes the role of financial institutions and credit reserves in accommodating random fluctuations in the financial conditions of agricultural borrowers [Lee and Baker (1984); Rahman and Barry (1981); Khoju et al. (1993); Ellinger et al. (1983); Buffier and Metternick-Jones (1995)]. Lenders, however, have largely refrained from designing loan contracts with these elements of flexibility, preferring instead to implement flexibility when needed through loan extensions, refinancing, deferred payments, workouts, and other means of forbearance.

Impacts of geographic liberalization on the costs and availability of agricultural loans and on institutional performance have been substantially addressed. Restructuring of the Farm Credit System in the U.S., for example, has expanded risk-carrying capacities of system institutions, modestly enhanced operating efficiencies, and altered the management of intra-system agency costs [Barry and Barnard (1985); Lee and Irwin (1996); Collender (1996); Barry et al. (1993)]. Bank structure has been a significant variable in explaining differences in changing market shares [Wilson and Barkley (1988)] and relative lending capacities [Barry and Pepper (1985)] of commercial banks across states in the U.S., as evidenced by studies of bank mergers and acquisitions [Neff and Ellinger (1996)]. Affiliation with multi-bank holding companies was found to significantly reduce the ratio of agricultural loans to total loans for the rural subsidiaries of large bank-holding companies [Belongia and Gilbert (1988)]. The subsidiaries of large bank- holding companies have greater opportunities to diversify risk by lending to businesses in a variety of industries, thus reducing the supply of agricultural credit through commercial banks. An offsetting factor, when statewide branching is permitted, was observed by Laderman, Schmidt, and Zimmerman (1991), who found that rural banks hold higher non-agricultural loan portfolio shares and urban banks hold higher agricultural loan portfolio shares. These more recent studies of the local market effects of structural change in banking are consistent with the mixture of effects found by earlier studies [Board of Governors of the Federal Reserve System (1977); Barry (1995)].

Long-term farm real estate lending by depository institutions can be especially problematic to their risk positions. Reliance on relatively short term sources of funds to finance longer-term loans increases institutional vulnerability to interest rate risks and hampers the availability of fixed-rate long-term loans to agricultural borrowers [Barry and Ellinger (1997)]. The longer-term funding sources available to government-sponsored agricultural lenders, through sales of bonds in financial markets, allow reductions in their vulnerability to interest rate risk, to offset in part the relatively high concentrations of credit risk in these lenders' agricultural loan portfolios. Important policy issues remain concerning the access to longer-term sources of funds by depository institutions and other localized agricultural lenders.

10.8. Public credit policies

Agricultural credit markets are especially vulnerable to the benefits and costs of public intervention. Public credit programs are intended to either correct a market imperfection, fill a gap in the workings of credit markets, or achieve a public purpose through the re-allocation of resources or redistribution of income in the economy [Barry (1995); Bosworth et al. (1987)]. In the U.S., for example, the cooperative Farm Credit System was created beginning in 1916, primarily to fill a gap in farm real estate lending; the Federal Agricultural Mortgage Corporation was created in 1987 to improve the workings of farm real estate lending through the provision of a secondary market for these loans; and the Farm Services Agency (formerly the Farmers Home Administration) was created in the 1940s to provide direct loans to young farmers and other potentially viable farmers who could not qualify for commercial credit. Finally, commodity credit programs were developed as a part of the U.S. government's farm price support and income stabilization policies, and subsidized export credit (loan guarantee) programs [Yang and Wilson (1996)] are intended to enhance the competitive position of U.S. farm products in international markets.

Credit programs that aim to correct market imperfections need not require much, if any, subsidization; they are considered the more successful government programs in credit markets [Bosworth et al. (1987)]. In contrast, efforts to achieve public purposes do involve subsidization, with significant questions raised about the form, magnitude, length, measurability, and recipients of the subsidies. The Federal Credit Reform Act of 1980 in the U.S., for example, fundamentally changed the budgetary treatment of direct loans and loan guarantees. The Act has required explicit measurement of the costs and subsidy elements of federal credit programs. To illustrate, the estimated 1995 subsidy rates for the federal government's Farm Services Agency loans were 13.03 percent for direct loans and 2.49 percent for guaranteed loans [Barry (1995)]. Earlier estimates of subsidy rates were in the range of 7.1 percent to 10.0 percent for Farm Service Agency loans and 0.0 percent to 0.5 percent for Farm Credit System loans [Hughes and Osborne (1987)].

In agricultural development lending, the adverse effects of government intervention have been extensively analyzed [Adams (1971); Adams and Graham (1981); Buttari (1995); Adams and Fichett (1992); Adams and Von Pischke (1992); Von Pischke (1991)]. Among the effects of government intervention are limited assistance to farmers, high default rates, high public costs, non-viable commercial lenders, regressive income effects, weak mobilization of savings, and disincentives to commercial lenders who must comply with subsidy requirements. Interest rate subsidies are especially problematic, creating excess demand for loans and unintended structural consequences [Meyer (1990)]. Even then, however, removals of interventions and regulations can yield high adjustment costs and further unintended structural consequences [Anderson (1990)].

Credit subsidies also create adverse incentives for borrowers who view loans as a gift or grant, and for lenders who become lax in screening loan applicants and monitoring loan performance. Little respect is gained for the obligation to repay and for the integrity of public credit programs [LaDue (1990)]. High delinquency and default rates typically characterize concessionary credit programs in both developed and developing countries [Karmajou and Baker (1980)]. These programs are especially vulnerable to the political hazards of public credit programs, as discussed below.

Key conclusions about government intervention, summarized by Buttari (1995), are that agricultural and rural borrowers need reasonable access to financial services from viable lenders, rather than subsidized credit, and that public policy should be directed to this end. Financial sustainability for both borrowers and lenders is the plausible policy goal. Such a goal will contribute to overall economic growth, to the benefit of both borrowers and lenders. Nonetheless, subsidized credit programs remain widespread and play important roles in international lending programs.

Major questions also concern the appropriateness of credit programs relative to other mechanisms for providing the subsidy [Barry (1995)]. Credit programs have weaknesses in transmitting subsidies because the loan funds may be used for unintended purposes, the borrowers may have had access to credit from other sources, the subsidy benefits may accrue to private lenders rather than to borrowers, and favorable terms of credit may be capitalized into the value of the assets being financed [Lee and Gabriel (1980); Stam (1995); Shalit and Schmitz (1982, 1984)]. Moreover, using credit markets to transmit subsidies undermines the integrity of inherently fragile financial markets. A financial market's primary function is to facilitate financial intermediation by adjusting the liquidity and risk positions of savers and investors. Extensive government regulation contributes to market effectiveness by fostering confidence, trust, and discipline among market participants. Adding a subsidy, however, is counterproductive to market effectiveness. Thus, the larger the subsidy needed to achieve the public purpose, the less the assistance should be channeled through public credit programs.

Among the forms of public credit, the emphasis in the U.S. has clearly shifted away from direct public loans toward publicly guaranteed loans by commercial lenders. As shown above, loan guarantees provide lower subsidies than direct loans, especially since direct loans are seldom priced to cover the government's full cost of funding, administering, and risk-bearing. Pricing for risk through fees and premiums is more explicit with a loan guarantee. Loan guarantees also displace fewer financial market resources, offer greater liquidity for loan sales by institutions, and provide greater use of private lender's knowledge and experience for loan origination, servicing, and management. Coupled with guarantees, time limitations on borrowers' use of guarantee programs also help to reduce moral hazard behavior and encourage timely graduation of borrowers to commercial sources of credit [Barry (1995)].

Credit programs are also vulnerable to political incentives. From a policymaker's perspective, credit programs are a popular, politically expedient policy instrument (Barry (1994, 1995); Hughes et al. (1986)]. They are relatively easy and cost effective to administer, as long as program demands are not growing too fast. While the administrative and risk-bearing costs often are difficult to measure and obscure to taxpayers, the programs are highly visible to a politician's constituents. They can be targeted to specific groups, quickly developed for responding to ad hoc crises, and do not directly influence commodity and input markets, although the secondary effects on asset values, incomes, and risk can be significant. Moreover, credit programs give the impression of financial soundness because loan repayment with interest is intended, although seldom is loan performance totally consistent with this intention.

10.9. Financial stress in agriculture

Periodic episodes of widespread financial stress in agriculture provide insightful case studies about the implications and effectiveness of public credit interventions intended to mitigate the effects of adversity. Evidence from the Depression era of the 1930s, for example, clearly indicates the costly, longer-run effects of debt moratoria and related policies [Rucker (1990); Rucker and Alston (1987); Alston (1984)]. Faced with foreclosure moratoria, commercial lenders tend to curtail future credit availability because they fear that a recurrence of future moratoria could exacerbate repayment problems.

The 1980s in the U.S., Canada, Australia, and other countries was another time of severe financial adversity for many farmers and their lenders [Harl (1990); Peoples et al. (1992)]. High debt loads (accumulated during the favorable times of the 1970s), volatile interest rates, and sharp declines in farm income and land values fueled farmers' financial problems. Farm bankruptcies and farm sales under stress increased substantially and the financial conditions of agricultural lenders deteriorated significantly [Barry and Lee (1983)].

As the crisis times widened and deepened, policy responses in the U.S. also became extensive [Pederson et al. (1987)]. Special bankruptcy laws for farmers were enacted [Dixon et al. (1995); Harl (1992)]. Public credit programs at federal and state levels emphasized debt restructuring, principal and interest buy-downs, and concessionary interest rates. Foreclosure moratoria on government loans were temporarily in effect. Lender bail-outs occurred, and major restructuring of the Farm Credit System was initiated [Lee and Irwin (1996)].

Public support was essential to the financial recovery of many agricultural borrowers and their lenders. The effects are demonstrated vividly by the loan loss experiences of the primary U.S. farm lenders. Between 1980 and 1997, the farm loan losses of commercial banks and the Farm Credit System totaled $4.57 billion and $3.82 billion, respectively, with most of these losses occurring from 1984 to 1988 [Economic Research Service (1998)]. In contrast, the last-resort lending program of the U.S. government experienced loan losses of $20.18 billion, spread widely over the 14-year time period. Without the government support, the losses of farmers, input suppliers, and commercial lenders would have been much greater.

The problems of the 1980s also brought positive, longer-run improvements in lending programs, and further demonstrated the capacity of financial markets to absorb major increases in credit risk by spreading the adverse effects over numerous market participants. Included among the improvements in lending programs were the adoption of more conservative lending practices, greater emphasis on risk management, better financial accounting by agricultural firms, risk-based loan pricing systems, and more formal methods of credit evaluation. The U.S. Farm Credit System was subject to stronger government regulations, institutional restructuring, creation of an insurance program for bond holders, and establishment of several new risk- monitoring and loss-sharing arrangements [Collender and Erickson (1996)]. Public credit programs also shifted away from direct lending to guarantees of loans made by participating commercial lenders, and established more stringent conditions for borrower eligibility. For the most part, these improvements responded directly to the information and incentive problems leading to the high costs of adverse selection and moral hazards in credit relationships between agricultural borrowers and their lenders.

11. Concluding comments

The theory and methods of analysis employed in studies of agricultural finance draw substantially on modern finance concepts, but with significant tailoring to the unique financial characteristics of the agricultural sectors of the world. Farms typically are capital-intensive, geographically dispersed, limited in scale and scope, and characterized by lengthy production periods. They are subject to significant business risks and to cyclical swings in economic conditions. Some are very large in size with complex organizations and financing arrangements. Many others are extremely small and barely subsist. Close relationships to family households predominate, and outside equity capital seldom is employed.

In light of these characteristics, financial management studies at both firm and aggregate levels have given substantial attention to issues associated with firm growth, investment analysis, financial structure, risk and liquidity management, performance measurement, and the role of "relationships" between borrowers and lenders. Other market-related studies have responded to the emergence of specialized agricultural lenders and lending programs targeted to the unique informational and monitoring requirements for financing farm businesses. Designing financing programs commensurate with the risky cash flow patterns of farm businesses, especially patterns attributed to farm real estate and other depreciable assets, has been especially challenging.

Evaluations of public credit programs are prominent as well. Government ownership, sponsorship, or back-up support (i.e., guaranteed or insured loans) has enabled many lenders to cope with the risks of specialized lending. Many government loan programs also provide targeted assistance to young, small, or disadvantaged farmers to help them gain financial viability. Studies have consistently shown, however, that attempts to convey significant subsidies through financial markets are largely ineffective.

Does financing matter in farmers' investment, financial, and business planning? The evidence clearly supports a positive answer to this question. Farmers' use of debt capital is widespread. Moreover, lenders will adjust the cost, availability, and other terms of the debt capital in response to a host of risk characteristics, business practices, and performance results of agricultural producers. These adjustments may often reflect the effects of differing incentives between the lender and borrower, as well as the problems of adverse selection and moral hazard attributable to asymmetric information. The localized, personal nature of lender-borrower relationships in agricultural finance suggests, however, that farm borrowers learn about lenders' preferences rather quickly and can choose whether to adjust their business practices accordingly.

Does external credit rationing occur in agricultural finance? Under normal economic conditions, there is little evidence of widespread, chronic credit rationing in developed countries. Cases where credit is rationed generally involve borrowers with weak creditworthiness. The availability of both specialized and non-specialized agricultural lenders, together with financial reforms that let interest rates respond freely to market conditions, help to ensure the ready availability of loan funds to creditworthy borrowers. In times of financial stress, credit may become more constraining as borrowers' creditworthiness weakens, but such risk responses by lenders can logically be expected. Credit rationing by commercial lenders may be greater in developing countries in which both lenders and borrowers have questionable viability. The small size and subsistence nature of many farms in these settings hamper their development of creditworthiness.

Rather than external rationing, internal rationing of credit is more likely the case. Under internal rationing, farmers' credit decisions reflect their own risk attitudes, time preferences, and other aspects of behavior. Even then, however, lenders still determine and influence the total borrowing capacity of farm businesses, regardless of whether this capacity is used fully, partially, or not at all in actual borrowings. Thus, lenders may ration total borrowing capacity and credit reserves, but not necessarily the portion that is borrowed.

References

Adams, D.W. (1971), "Agricultural credit in Latin America: A critical review of external funding policy", American Journal of Agricultural Economics 53:163–172.

Adams, D.W. (1992), "Taking a fresh look at informal finance", in: D.W. Adams and D.A. Fitchett, eds., Informal Finance in Low-Income Countries (Westview Press, Boulder, CO).

Adams, D.W., and M.L. Canavesi (1992), "Rotating savings and credit associations in Bolivia", in: D.W. Adams and D.A. Fitchett, eds., Informal Finance in Low Income Countries (Westview Press, Boulder, CO).

Adams, D.W., and D.A. Fichett, eds. (1992), Informal Finance in Low-Income Countries (Westview Press, Boulder).

Adams, D.W., and D. Graham (1981), "A critique of traditional agricultural credit projects", Journal of Development Economics 8:347–366.

Adams, D.W., and J.D. Von Pischke (1992), "Micro enterprise credit programs: Deja vu", Paper prepared for SAID (Agricultural Finance Program, Ohio State University, Columbus, Ohio, USA).

Aghion, P., and P. Bolton (1992), "An incomplete contracts approach to financial contracting", Quarterly Journal of Economics 89:488–500.

Aguilera-Alfred, N., and C. Gonzalez-Vega (1993), "A multinominal logit-analysis of loan targeting and repayment at the agricultural development bank of the Dominican Republic", Agricultural Finance Review 53:55–64.

Ahrendsen, B.L., R.N. Collender and B.L. Dixon (1994), "An empirical analysis of optimal farm capital structure decisions", Agricultural Finance Review 54:108–119.

Allen, D.W., and D. Lueck (1992), "The 'Back Forty' on a handshake: Specific assets, reputation, and the structure of farmland contracts", Journal of Law, Economics, and Organization 8:366–376.

Alston, L.J. (1984), "Farm foreclosure moratorium legislation", American Economic Review 74:445–457.

Anderson, J. (1990), "Rural credit and the mix between permanent and temporary wage labor contracts in Pernamburo, Brazil", American Journal of Agricultural Economics 72:1139–1145.

Arthur, L., C. Carter and F. Abizadeh (1988), "Arbitrage pricing, capital asset pricing, and agricultural assets", American Journal of Agricultural Economics 70:359–365.

Baker, C.B. (1968), "Credit in the production organization of the firm", American Journal of Agricultural Economics 49:507–521.

Baker, C.B., and V. Bhargava (1974), "Financing small farm developments in India", Australian Journal of Agricultural Economics 18:101–118.

Baker, C.B., and J.A. Hopkin (1969), "Concepts of finance for a capital-using agriculture", American Journal of Agricultural Economics 51:1055–1065.

Ball, V.E., and H.P. Witzke (1993), "The stock of capital in European community agriculture", European Review of Agricultural Economics 20:437–450.

Barham, B.L., and J.-P. Chavas (1998), "Sunk costs and resource mobility: Implications for economic and policy analysis", Agricultural Economics (forthcoming).

Barnard, F.L., and P.J. Barry (1985), "Interest rate deregulation and agricultural banking: A risk programming analysis", Agricultural Finance Review 45:100–112.

Barnard, C.H., and J. Grimard (1995), "Financial structure of Canadian and U.S. farms, 1989–1991", Canadian Journal of Agricultural Economics 43:79–90.

Barry, P.J. (1977), "Theory and methods in firm growth research, economic growth of the agricultural firm", Tech. Bull. 86 (College of Agriculture Research Center, Washington State University).

Barry, P.J. (1978), "Rural banks and farm loan participations", American Journal of Agricultural Economics 60:214–224.

Barry, P.J. (1980), "Capital asset pricing and farm real estate", American Journal of Agricultural Economics 62:41–46.

Barry, P.J. (1981), "Impacts of regulatory change on financial markets for agriculture", American Journal of Agricultural Economics 63:905–912.

Barry, P.J. (1983), "Financing growth and adjustment of farm firms under risk and inflation", in: K.L. Baum, ed., Modeling Farm Decisions for Policy Analysis (Westview Press, Boulder, CO).

Barry, P.J., ed. (1984), Risk Management in Agriculture (Iowa State University Press, Ames, IA).

Barry, P.J. (1985), "Needed changes in farmers home administration lending programs", American Journal of Agricultural Economics 67:341–344.

Barry, P.J. (1994), "Financial management of family farms: Modeling and empirical research", in: Family Economics and Agricultural Household Models (Elsevier, New York).

Barry, P.J. (1995), The Effects of Credit Policies on U.S. Agriculture (The AEI Press, Washington, D.C.).

Barry, P.J. (1996), "Fund availability at rural banks", Paper presented to annual meeting of regional research project NC-207 (Center for Farm and Rural Business Finance, University of Illinois).

Barry, P.J., and C.B. Baker (1971), "Reservation prices on credit use: A measure of response to uncertainty", American Journal of Agricultural Economics 53:222–227.

Barry, P.J., and C.B. Baker (1977), "Management of financial structure: Firm level", Agricultural Finance Review 37:50–63.

Barry, P.J., C.B. Baker and L.R. Sanint (1981), "Farmers' credit risks and liquidity management", American Journal of Agricultural Economics 63:216–227.

Barry, P.J., and F.L. Barnard (1985), "Interaction effects on rural financial intermediaries of financial stress and deregulation", American Journal of Agricultural Economics 67:1191–1195.

Barry, P.J., J.R. Brake and D.K. Banner (1993), "Agency relationships in the farm credit system: The role of the farm credit banks", Agribusiness: An International Journal 9:233–246.

Barry, P.J., and J.D. Calvert (1983), "Loan pricing and profitability analysis by agricultural banks", Agricultural Finance Review 43:21–29.

Barry, P.J., and P.N. Ellinger (1989), "Credit scoring, loan pricing and farm business performance", Western Journal of Agricultural Economics 14:45–55.

Barry, P.J., and P.N. Ellinger (1997), "Liquidity and competition in rural credit markets" (Federal Reserve Bank of Kansas City, Financing rural America, Kansas City, MO).

Barry, P.J., P.N. Ellinger, J.A. Hopkin and C.B. Baker (1995), Financial Management in Agriculture, 5th edn. (The Interstate Printers and Publishers, Danville, IL).

Barry, P.J., P.N. Ellinger and L.M. Moss (1997), "Lending relationships, customer loyalty, and competition in agricultural banking", Agricultural Finance Review 57:17–28.

Barry, P.J., and W.F. Lee (1983), "Financial stress in agriculture: Implications for agricultural lenders", American Journal of Agricultural Economics 65:945–952.

Barry, P.J., and H.A. Pepper (1985), "Impacts of holding company affiliation on loan/deposit relationships in agricultural banking", North Central Journal of Agricultural Economics 7:65–74.

Barry, P.J., and L.J. Robison (1986), "Economic versus accounting rates of return on farm land", Land Economics 62:388–401.

Barry, P.J., and L.J. Robison (1987), "Portfolio theory and financial structure: An application of equilibrium analysis", Agricultural Finance Review 47:142–151.

Barry, P.J., L.J. Robison and G. Nartea (1996), "Changing time attitudes in intertemporal analysis", American Journal of Agricultural Economics 78:972–981.

Barry, P.J., S.T. Sonka and K. Lajili (1992), "Vertical coordination, financial structure, and the changing theory of the firm", American Journal of Agricultural Economics 74:1219–1225.

Barry, P.J., B. Roberts, M. Boehlje and T. Baker (1997), "Financing capacities of independent versus contract hog production", Journal of Agricultural Lending 10:8–14.

Barry, P.J., B.J. Sherrick, D.A. Lins, D. Banner, B. Dixon and J.R. Brake (1996), "Farm credit system insurance risk simulation model", Agricultural Finance Review 56:68–84.

Barry, P.J., and D.R. Willmann (1976), "A risk programming analysis of forward contracting with credit constraints", American Journal of Agricultural Economics 58:62–70.

Barzel, Y. (1997), Economic Analysis of Property Rights, 2nd edn. (Cambridge University Press, New York).

Belongia, M., and A. Gilbert (1988), "The effects of affiliation with large bank holding companies on commercial bank lending to agriculture", American Journal of Agricultural Economics 70:69–78.

Belongia, M., and A. Gilbert (1990), "The effects of federal credit programs on farm output", American Journal of Agricultural Economics 72:769–773.

Berglof, E. (1990), "Capital structure as a mechanism of control: A comparison of financial systems", in: M. Aoki, B. Gustafson and O. Williamson, eds., The Firm as A Nexus of Treaties (Sage Publications, London).

Board of Governors of the Federal Reserve System (1977), Improved fund availability at rural banks (Washington, DC).

Boehlje, M.D., and L. Eisgruber (1972), "Strategies for the creation and transfer of the farm estate", American Journal of Agricultural Economics 54:461–472.

Boehlje, M.D., and T.K. White (1969), "A production-investment decision model of farm firm growth", American Journal of Agricultural Economics 51:546–564.

Bosworth, B., A. Carron and E. Rhyne (1987), The Economics of Federal Credit Programs (Brookings Institutions, Washington, D.C.).

Bottomley, A. (1975), "Interest rate determination in underdeveloped rural areas", American Journal of Agricultural Economics 57:279–291.

Bourdieu, P. (1986), "The forms of capital", in: J.G. Richardson, ed., Handbook of Theory and Research for the Sociology of Education (Greenwood Press, New York) 241–258.

Boussard, J.M. (1971), "Time Horizons, objective function, and uncertainty in a multiperiod model of firm growth", American Journal of Agricultural Economics 53:467–477.

Brake, J.R., and P.J. Barry (1971), "Flow of funds for the farm sector: Comment", American Journal of Agricultural Economics 53:665–667.

Buffier, B.D., and M.A. Metternick-Jones (1995), "Income equalization deposits: Enhancing farm viability", Review of Marketing and Agricultural Economics 63:191–199.

Burt, R.S. (1992), Structural Holes: The Social Structure of Competition (Harvard University Press, Cambridge).

Buttari, P.J. (1995), "Subsidized credit programs: Theory, record, and alternatives", SAID Evaluation Study No. 75 (U.S. Agency for International Development, Washington, D.C.).

Calomiris, C.W., R.G. Hubbard and J.H. Stock (1986), "The farm debt crisis and public policy", Brookings Papers on Economic Activity 2:441–478.

Calonius, E. (1990), Blood and money, Newsweek Special Edition, The 21st Century Family, Winter/Spring, p. 82. (Source of numbers used in the article: Family Business Magazine "Buchholz and Crane's Corporate Bloodlines".)

Caprio, G., I. Atiyas and J.A. Hanson (1996), Financial Reform: Theory and Practice (Cambridge University Press, New York).

Carter, M.R. (1988), "Equilibrium credit rationing of small farm agriculture", Journal of Development Economics 28:83–103.

Chambers, R., and U. Vasavada (1983), "Testing asset fixity for U.S. agriculture", American Journal of Agricultural Economics 65:761–769.

Chavas, J.-P. (1994), "On sunk costs and the economics of investments", American Journal of Agricultural Economics 76:114–127.

Chhikara, R.K. (1986), "Liquidity management hypothesis: Theoretical foundations, empirical tests and applications", Ph.D. Thesis (University of Illinois, Urbana-Champaign, Illinois).

Chhikara, R. (1989), "The state of the art in credit evaluation", American Journal of Agricultural Economics 71:1138–1144.

Cocks, K.D., and H.O. Carter (1968), "Micro goal functions and economic planning", American Journal of Agricultural Economics 50(2):400–411.

Coleman, J.S. (1988), "Social capital in the creation of human capital", American Journal of Sociology Supplement 94:S95–S120.

Collender, R. (1996), "Can federal action improve efficiency in the market for farm loans?", Agr. Info. Bull. 724-01 (Economic Research Service, U.S. Department of Agriculture, Washington, D.C.).

Collender, R.N., and A. Erickson (1996), "Farm credit system safety and soundness", Agricultural Information Bulletin No. 722 (Economic Research Service, U.S. Department of Agriculture, Washington, D.C.).

Collins, R.A. (1985), "Expected utility, debt-equity structure, and risk balancing", American Journal of Agricultural Economics 67:627–629.

Collins, R.A., and L.S. Karp (1993), "Lifetime leverage choice for proprietary farmers in a dynamic stochastic environment", Journal of Agricultural and Resource Economics 18:225–138.

Collins, R.A., and L.S. Karp (1995), "Static vs. dynamic models of proprietary capital structure: Discussion and preliminary empirical evidence", Agricultural Finance Review 55:1–9.

Cromarty, W.A. (1959), "The farm demand for tractors, machinery, and trucks", Journal of Farm Economics 41:323–331.

Dixon, B.L., E.M. Flynn and J.A. Flaccus (1995), "The chapter 12 experience in the U.S.: Regional comparisons and analysis of filing, discharge, and failure rates", Agricultural Finance Review 55:38–53.

Dorfman, R. (1969), "An economic interpretation of optimal control theory", American Economic Review 59:817–831.

Dunn, D., and T. Frey (1976), "Discriminant analysis of loans for cash grain farmers", Agricultural Finance Review 36:60–66.

Economic Research Service (1994), U.S. Department of Agriculture, AREI Updates, Farmland Tenure (Washington, D.C.) Number 7.

Economic Research Service (1998), U.S. Department of Agriculture, Annual Series, Agricultural Finance, Situation and Outlook (Washington, D.C.).

Edwards, C. (1959), "Resource fixity and farm organization", American Journal of Agricultural Economics 41:747–759.

Elhorst, J. (1993), "The evaluations of investment equations at the farm level", European Review of Agricultural Economics 20:167–182.

Ellinger, P.N., and P.J. Barry (1987), "The effects of tenure position on farm profitability and solvency: An application to Illinois farms", Agricultural Finance Review 47:106–118.

Ellinger, P.N., and P.J. Barry (1989), "Interest rate risk exposure of agricultural banks: A gap analysis", Agricultural Finance Review 49:9–21.

Ellinger, P.N., P.J. Barry and D.A. Lins (1983), "Farm financial performance under graduated payment mortgages", North Central Journal of Agricultural Economics 5:47–53.

Ellinger, P.N., N.S. Splett and P.J. Barry (1992), "Conency of credit evaluations at agricultural banks", Agribusiness: An International Journal 8:517–536.

Esguerra, F., and R.L. Meyer (1992), "Collateral substitutes in rural informal financial markets in the Philippines", in: D.W. Adams and D.A. Fitchett, eds., Informal Finance in Low Income Countries (Westview Press, Boulder, CO).

Fazzari, S.M., R.G. Hubbard and B. Petersen (1988), "Financing constraints and corporate investment", Brookings Papers on Economic Activity 4:141–195.

Featherstone, A.M., C.B. Moss, T.G. Baker and P.V. Preckel (1988), "The theoretical effects of farm policies on optimal leverage and the probability of equity losses", American Journal of Agricultural Economics 70:572–579.

Feder, G., L. Law, J. Lin and X. Luo (1990), "The relationship between credit and productivity in Chinese agriculture: A microeconomic model of disequilibrium", American Journal of Agricultural Economics 76:1151–1157.

Fischer, M., and K. Moore (1987), "An improved scoring function for the St. Paul bank for cooperatives", in: Financing Agriculture in a Changing Environment: Macro, Market, Policy and Management Issues (Southern Illinois University, Carbondale, IL).

Foster, W.E., and G.C. Rausser (May 1991), "Farmer behavior under risk of failure", American Journal of Agricultural Economics 73:276–288.

Fox, K.A. (1966), "Demand for farm tractors in the united states – A regression analysis", Agricultural Economics Report, 103 (United States Department of Agriculture, Washington, DC).

Franks, J.R. (1998), "Predicting financial stress in farm businesses", European Review of Agricultural Economics 25:30–52.

Freshwater, D. (1989), "Canadian agricultural finance in the 1980s and 1990s", Canadian Journal of Agricultural Economics 37:1–27.

Freund, R.J. (1956), "Introduction of risk into a risk programming model", Econometrica 24:253–263.

Fukuyama, F. (1995), Trust: The Social Virtues and the Creation of Prosperity (The Free Press, New York).

Gabriel, S.C., and C.B. Baker (1980), "Concepts of business and financial risk", American Journal of Agricultural Economics 62:560–564.

Gertler, M., and A. Rose (1996), "Finance, public policy, and growth", in: G. Caprio, I., Atiyas and J.C. Hanson, eds., Financial Reform: Theory and Experiences (Cambridge University Press, New York).

Gibson, S., and P. Barry (1994), "Estate planning and the reverse mortgage", Journal of the American Society of Farm Managers and Rural Appraisers 58:13–22.

Giraro, J.A., W.G. Tomek and T.D. Mount (1974), "The effect of income instability on farmers' consumption and investment", Review of Economics and Statistics 56:141–150.

Graham, D.H. (1992), "Informal rural finance in Niger: Lessons for building formal institutions", Chapter 6, in: D.W. Adams and D.A. Fitchett, eds., Informal Finance in Low Income Countries (Westview Press, Boulder, CO).

Griliches, Z. (1960), "The demand for a durable input: Farm tractors in the United States, 1921–57", in: A.C. Harberger, ed., The Demand for Durable Goods (University of Chicago Press, Chicago).

Grossman, S., and O. Hart (1986), "The costs and benefits of ownership: A theory of vertical and lateral integration", Journal of Political Economy 94:691–719.

Gu, D. (1996), "Capital asset pricing and agricultural assets in England and Wales", Journal of Agricultural Economics 47:99–108.

Guinnane, T.W. (1992), "Intergeneration transfers, emigration, and the rural Irish household system", Explorations in Economic History 29:456–476.

Gustafson, C.R., and P.J. Barry (1993), "Structural implications of agricultural finance", in: A. Hallam, ed., Size, Structure and the Changing Face of American Agriculture (Westview Press, Boulder, CO) 383–411.

Gustafson, C., P.J. Barry and S.T. Sonka (1989), "Machinery investment decisions: A simulated analysis for cash grain farms", Western Journal of Agricultural Economics 13:244–253.

Gwilliams, K. (1993), "Farmland leasing and contract choice in Michigan: The influence of social distance", Ph.D. Thesis (Michigan State University).

Gwinn, A.S., P.J. Barry and P.N. Ellinger (1992), "Farm financial structure under uncertainty: An application to grain farms", Agricultural Finance Review 52:43–56.

Hanson, S.D., L.J. Robison and M.E. Siles (1996), "Impacts of relationships on customer retention in the banking industry", Agribusiness: An International Journal 12:27–36.

Hardy, W., and J.B. Weed (1980), "Objective evaluation of agricultural lending", Southern Journal of Agricultural Economics 12:159–164.

Harl, N.E. (1990), The Farm Debt Crisis of the 1980s (Iowa State University Press, Ames, Iowa).

Harl, N. (1992), Agricultural Law: Estate, Tax, and Business Planning (Matthew Bender and Company, New York).

Harl, N.E. (1992), "Chapter 12 bankruptcy: A review and evaluation", Agricultural Finance Review 52:1–11.

Hart, O. (1988), "Incomplete contracts and the theory of the firm", Journal of Law, Economics, and Organization 4:119–139.

Hart, O. (1995), Firms, Contracts, and Financial Structure (Oxford University Press, New York).

Heady, E.O., and L.G. Tweeten (1963), Resource Demand and Structure of the Ag Industry (Iowa State University Press, Ames).

Herendeen, J.B., and W. Grisley (1988), "A dynamic q model of investment, financing, and asset pricing", Southern Economics Journal 55:360–373.

Herring, P.J., and R.E. Litan (1995), Financial Regulation in the Global Economy (The Brookings Institution, Washington, D.C.).

Hochman, E., and G.S. Rausser (1997), "Firm growth policies under different pollution abatement, production, and financial structure", Economic Growth of the Agricultural Firm, Technical Bulletin 86 (College of Agriculture Research Center, Washington State University).

Hodgman, D.R. (1961), "Commercial bank loan and investment policy" (Bureau of Economic and Business Research, University of Illinois).

Hoff, K., and J. Stiglitz (1990), "Introduction: Imperfect information and rural credit markets: Puzzles and policy perspectives", The World Bank Economic Review 4:235–250.

Houck, J. (1977), "An approach to specifying and estimating an irreversible function", American Journal of Agricultural Economics 59:570–572.

Hsu, S., and C. Chang (1990), "An adjustment cost rationalization of asset fixity theory", American Journal of Agricultural Economics 72:298–308.

Hubbard, R.G. (1998), "Capital-market imperfections and investment", Journal of Economic Literature 36:193–225.

Hubbard, R.G., and A.K. Kashyap (1992), "Internal net worth and the investment process: An application to U.S. agriculture", Journal of Political Economy 100:506–534.

Hughes, D., and N. Osborne (1987), "Measuring federal farm credit subsidies", Agricultural Finance Review 47:125–134.

Hughes, D.W., and J.B. Penson (1981), "An overview of farm sector capital and credit needs", Agricultural Finance Review 41:1–19.

Hughes, D.W., S.C. Gabriel, P.J. Barry and M.D. Boehlje (1986), Financing the Agricultural Sector: Future Challenges and Policy Alternatives (Westview Press, Boulder, CO).

Hughes, D., J. Penson, J. Richardson and D. Chen (1987), "Policy responses to financial stress", Agricultural Finance Review 47(Special Issue):100–113.

Irwin, G.D. (1968a), "A comparative review of some firm growth models", Agricultural Economics Research 20:82–100.

Irwin, G.D. (1968b), "Three myths about the balance sheet: The changing financial structure of farming", American Journal of Agricultural Economics 50:1596–1599.

Jensen, M.C. (1986), "Agency costs of free cash flow, corporate finance, and takeovers", American Economic Review 76:323–329.

Jensen, M., and W. Meckling (1976), "Theory of the firm: Managerial behavior, agency costs, and ownership structure", Journal of Finance Economics 3:305–360.

Jensen, F.E., J.S. Lawson and L.N. Langemeier (1993), "Agricultural investment and internal cash flow variables", Review of Agricultural Economics 15:295–306.

Johnson, C. (1990), "Farmland as a business asset", Journal of Agricultural Economics 41:135–148.

Johnson, D.G. (1950), "The nature of the supply function for agriculture", American Economic Review 40:539–564.

Johnson, G.L. (1956), "Supply functions – some facts and notions", in: E.O. Heady, et al., eds., Agricultural Adjustment Problems in a Growing Economy (Iowa State University Press, Ames).

Johnson, G.L., and L. Quance (1972), The Overproduction Trap in U.S. Agriculture (John Hopkins University Press, Baltimore).

Johnson, J., M. Morehart and K. Erickson (1987), "The financial condition of the agricultural sector", Agricultural Finance Review 47(Special Issue):1–18.

Karmajou, F., and C.B. Baker (1980), "Reforming Cameroon's government credit program: Effects on liquidity management by small farm borrowers", American Journal of Agricultural Economics 62:709–718.

Khoju, M.R., C.H. Nelson and P.J. Barry (1993), "Debt service reserve fund as a response to repayment risk", Review of Agricultural Economics 15:217–232.

Kimhi, A. (1994), "Optimal timing of farm transferal from parent to child", American Journal of Agricultural Economics 76:228–236.

Laderman, E., R. Schmidt and G. Zimmerman (1991), "Location, branching, and bank portfolio diversification: The case of agricultural lending", Economic Review, Federal Reserve Bank of San Francisco, 24–37.

LaDue, E. (1990), "Moral hazard in federal farm lending", American Journal of Agricultural Economics 72:774–779.

Langemeier, M.R., and G.F. Patrick (1993), "Farm consumption and liquidity constraints", American Journal of Agricultural Economics 75:479–484.

Leatham, D.J., and T.G. Baker (1988), "Farmers choice of fixed and adjustable interest rate loans", American Journal of Agricultural Economics 70:803–812.

LeBlanc, M., and J.A. Hrubovcak (1985), "The effects of tax policy on aggregate agricultural investment", Agricultural Economics Research 37:12–20.

LeBlanc, M., and J. Hrubovcak (1986), "The effects of interest rates on agricultural machinery investment", American Journal of Agricultural Economics 68:767–777.

LeBlanc, M., J. Hrubovcak, R. Durst, and R. Conway (1992), "Farm machinery investment and the tax reform act of 1986", Journal of Agricultural and Resource Economics 17:66–79.

Lee, H., and R.G. Chambers (1986), "Expenditure constraints and profit maximization in U.S. agriculture", American Journal of Agricultural Economics 68:857–865.

Lee, J., and S. Gabriel (1980), "Public policy toward agricultural credit, future sources of funds for agricultural banks" (Federal Reserve Bank of Kansas City, Kansas City).

Lee, W., and C.B. Baker (1984), "Agricultural risks and lender behavior", in: P.J. Barry, ed., Risk Management in Agriculture (Iowa State University Press, Ames, Iowa).

Lee, W., and G. Irwin (1996), "Restructuring the farm credit system: A progress report", Agricultural Finance Review 56:1–21.

Lee, W., and N. Rask (1976), "Inflation and crop profitability: How much can farmers pay for land?", American Journal of Agricultural Economics 58:984–990.

Levine, R. (1997), "Financial development and economic growth: Views and agenda", Journal of Economic Literature 35:688–726.

Lifran, R. (1994), "Credit constraints in a life-cycle model with self-employment: Empirical evidence for finance", in: F. Caillavet, H. Guyomard and R. Lifran, eds., Agricultural Household Modeling and Family Economics (Elsevier Science, Amsterdam).

Lins, D.A., and P.J. Barry (1980), "Availability of financial capital as a factor of structural change in the U.S. farm production sector, farm structure Committee on Agriculture, United States Senate (U.S. Government Printing Office, Washington, D.C.).

Lins, D.A., and P.J. Barry (1984), "Agency status of the farm credit system", American Journal of Agricultural Economics 66:601–606.

Looney, J., and D.L. Uchtmann (1994), Agricultural Law: Principles and Cases (McGraw-Hill, New York).

Lufburrow, J., P.J. Barry and B.L. Dixon (1984), "Credit scoring for farm loan pricing", Agricultural Finance Review 44:8–14.

Mapp, H., and G. Helmers (1984), "Methods of risk analysis for farm firms", in: P.J. Barry, ed., Risk Management in Agriculture (Iowa State University Press, Ames, Iowa).

Martin, J.R., and J.S. Plaxico (1967), "Polyperiod analysis of capital accumulation of farms in the rolling plains of Oklahoma and Texas", USDA Technical Bulletin 1381.

Melichar, E. (1979), "Capital gains vs. current income in the farming sector", American Journal of Agricultural Economics 61:1082–1092.

Melichar, E.O. (1984), "A financial perspective on agriculture", Federal Reserve Bulletin 70:1–13.

Meyer, J. (1987), "Two moment decision models and expected utility maximization", American Economic Review 77:421–430.

Meyer, J., and R.H. Rasche (1992), "Sufficient conditions for expected utility to imply mean-standard deviation rankings: Empirical evidence concerning the location and scale condition", The Economic Journal 102:91–106.

Meyer, R.L. (1990), "Analyzing the farm-level impact of agricultural credit: Discussion", American Journal of Agricultural Economics 72:1158–1160.

Miller, L.H., and E.L. LaDue (1989), "Credit assessment models for farm borrowers: A logit analysis", Agricultural Finance Review 49:22–36.

Miller, L., P. Barry, C. DeVuyst, D. Lins and B. Sherrick (1994), "Farmer mac credit risk and capital adequacy", Agricultural Finance Review 54:66–79.

Miller, L.H., P.J. Ellinger, P.N. Barry and K. Lajili (1993), "Price and non-price management of agricultural credit risk", Agricultural Finance Review 53:28–41.

Moss, L., P.J. Barry and P.N. Ellinger (1997), "The competitive environment for agricultural bankers in the U.S", Agribusiness: An International Journal 13:431–444.

Nasr, R., P.J. Barry and P.N. Ellinger (1998), "Financial structure and efficiency of grain farms", Agricultural Finance Review 58:33–48.

Neff, D.L., and P.N. Ellinger (1996), "Participants in rural bank consolidations", American Journal of Agricultural Economics 78:721–727.

Nelson, C.H., J.B. Braden and J. Roh (1989), "Asset fixity and investment asymmetry in agriculture", American Journal of Agricultural Economics 71:970–979.

Nelton, S. (1990), "We could use a few good numbers", Nation's Business, p. 53.

Novak, F.S., and G.D. Schnitkey (1994), "The effects of including bankruptcy on dynamic investment decisions", Journal of Agricultural and Resource Economics 19:255–266.

Novak, M., and E. LaDue (1994), "An analysis of multiperiod agricultural credit evaluation models for New York dairy farms", Agricultural Finance Review 54:55–65.

Patrick, G.F., and L.M. Eisgruber (1968), "The impact of managerial ability and capital structure on growth of the farm firm", American Journal of Agricultural Economics 50:491–507.

Patrick, G.F., P.N. Wilson, P.J. Barry, W.G. Boggess and D.L. Young (1985), "Risk perceptions and management responses: Producer-generated hypotheses for risk modeling", Southern Journal of Agricultural Economics 17:231–238.

Pederson, G.D. (1992), "Agricultural bank portfolio adjustments to risk", American Journal of Agricultural Economics 74:672–681.

Pederson, G., M. Boehlje, D. Doye and R. Jolly (1987), "Resolving financial stress in agriculture by altering loan terms: Impacts on farmers and lenders", Agricultural Finance Review 43:123–137.

Penson, J.B. (1987), "Evaluating financial trends in agriculture", Agricultural Finance Review 47:14–20.

Penson, J.B., R.F.J. Romain and D.W. Hughes (1981), "Net investment in farm tractors: An econometric analysis", American Journal of Agricultural Economics 63:629–635.

Peoples, K., D. Freshwater, G. Hanson, P. Prentice and E. Thor (1992), Anatomy of an American Agricultural Credit Crisis (Rowman and Littlefield Publishers, Lanham, MD).

Perrin, R. (1972), "Asset replacement principles", American Journal of Agricultural Economics 54:60–67.

Petersen, M., and R. Rajan (1994), "The benefits of lending relationships: Evidence from small business data", Journal of Finance 45:3–37.

Petersen, M., and R. Rajan (1995), "The effects of credit market competition on lending relationships", The Quarterly Journal of Economics 110:407–443.

Pflueger, B.W., and P.J. Barry (1986), "Crop insurance and credit: A farm level simulation analysis", Agricultural Finance Review 46:1–14.

Phimister, E. (1995a), "Farm consumption behavior in the presence of uncertainty and restrictions on credit", American Journal of Agricultural Economics 77:952–959.

Phimister, E. (1995b), "The impact of borrowing constraints on farm households: A life cycle approach", European Review of Agricultural Economics 22:61–86.

Pinches, G.E. (1992), Essentials of Financial Management (Harper Collins Publishers, New York).

Pindyck, R.S. (1991), "Irreversibility, uncertainty, and investment", Journal of Economic Literature 29:1110–1148.

Portes, A. (1995), "Economic sociology and the sociology of immigration: A conceptual overview", The Economic Sociology of Immigration: Essays on Networks, Ethnicity and Entrepreneurship (Russell Sage Foundation, New York).

Purvis, A., W.G. Boggess, C.B. Moss and J. Holt (1995), "Technology adoption under irreversibility and uncertainty", American Journal of Agricultural Economics 77:541–551.

Putnam, R.D. (1995), "Bowling alone: America's declining social capital", Journal of Democracy 6:65–78.

Rahman, M.L., and P.J. Barry (1981), "Financial control and variable amortization under uncertainty: An application to Texas rice farms", Southern Journal of Agricultural Economics 13:99–104.

Rayner, A.J., and K. Cowling (1968), "Demand for farm tractors in the United States and the United Kingdom", American Journal of Agricultural Economics 50:896–912.

Robison, L.J., and P.J. Barry (1977), "Portfolio adjustments: An application to rural banking", American Journal of Agricultural Economics 59:311–320.

Robison, L.J., and P.J. Barry (1996), Present Value Models and Investment Analysis (Michigan State University Press, East Lansing, MI, USA).

Robison, L.J., and J.R. Brake (1979), "Application of portfolio theory to farmer and lender behavior", American Journal of Agricultural Economics 61:158–164.

Robison, L.J., and S.D. Hanson (1997), "Analyzing firm response to risk using mean-variance models", in: R.B.M. Huirne, J.B. Hardaker and A.A. Dijkhuizen, eds., Risk Management Strategies in Agriculture: State of the Art and Future Perspectives (Backhuys Publishers, The Netherlands).

Robison, L.J., and A.A. Schmid (1996), "Can Agriculture prosper without increased social capital?", in: H.W. Ayer, ed., The Best of Choices, 1986–1996 (American Agricultural Economics Association, Ames, Iowa).

Robison, P.J., and M.E. Siles (1997), "Social capital and household income distributions in the United States: 1980, 1990", Department of Agricultural Economics Report No. 595 and the Julian Zamora Research Institute Research Report No. 18 (Michigan State University, East Lansing, Michigan).

Robison, L.J., P.J. Barry and W.G. Burghardt (1987), "Borrowing behavior under financial stress by the proprietary firm: A theoretical analysis", Western Journal of Agricultural Economics 12:144–151.

Rosenzweig, M.R., and K.I. Wolpin (1985), "Specific experience, household structure, and intergenerational transfers: Farm family land and labor arrangements in developing countries", Quarterly Journal of Economics 100:961–987.

Ross, S.A. (1995), "Uses, abuses, and alternatives to the net present value rule", Financial Management 24:96–102.

Rucker, R. (1990), "The effects of state farm relief legislation on private lenders and borrowers: The experience of the 1930s", American Journal of Agricultural Economics 76:24–34.

Rucker, R., and L. Alston (1987), "Farm failures and government intervention: A case study of the 1930s", American Economic Review 77:724–730.

Saha, A., H.A. Love and R. Schwart (1994), "Adoption of emerging technologies under output uncertainty", American Journal of Agricultural Economics 76:836–846.

Schmid, A.A., and L.J. Robison (1995), "Applications of social capital theory", Journal of Agricultural and Applied Economics 27:59–66.

Schmiesing, B., M. Edelman, C. Swanson and D. Kolner (1985), "Differential pricing of agricultural loans by commercial banks", Western Journal of Agricultural Economics 10:192–204.

Schnitkey, G.D., C.R. Taylor and P.J. Barry (1989), "Evaluating farmland investments considering dynamic stochastic returns and farmland prices", Western Journal of Agricultural Economics 14:143–156.

Scott, J.T., and E.O. Heady (1967), "Regional demand for farm buildings in the United States", Journal of Farm Economics 49:184–198.

Shalit, H., and A. Schmitz (1982), "Farmland accumulation and prices", American Journal of Agricultural Economics 64:710–719.

Shalit, H., and A. Schmitz (1984), "Farmland price behavior and credit allocation", Western Journal of Agricultural Economics 9:303–313.

Sharpe, S.A. (1990), "Asymmetric information, bank lending, and implicit contracts: A stylized model of customer relationships", Journal of Finance 45:1069–1087.

Shepard, L., and R. Collins (1982), "Farm bankruptcy 1910–1978", American Journal of Agricultural Economics 62:609–615.

Sherrick, B., and R. Lubben (1994), "Economic motivations for vendor financing", Agricultural Finance Review 54:120–131.

Siles, M., S.D. Hanson and L.J. Robison (1994), "Socio-economics and the probability of loan approval", Review of Agricultural Economics 16:405–414.

Smith, C.W. (1987), "Agency costs", in: J. Eatwell, M. Milgate and P. Newman, eds., The New Palgrave, a Dictionary of Economics (Macmillan Press, London).

Smith, C., and J. Warner (1979), "On financial contracting: An analysis of bond covenants", Journal of Financial Economics 7:117–161.

Sonka, S., B.L. Dixon and B.L. Jones (1980), "Impact of farm financial structure on the credit reserve of the farm business", American Journal of Agricultural Economics 62:565–570.

Splett, N., P. Barry, B. Dixon and P. Ellinger (1994), "A joint experience and statistical approach to credit scoring", Agricultural Finance Review 54:39–135.

Stam, J. (1995), "Credit as a factor influencing farmland values", Staff Paper No. 9504 (Economic Research Service, U.S. Department of Agriculture).

Stensland, J., and G. Pederson (1997), "The benefits and costs of fee-income generation in small banks", Agricultural Finance Review 57:1–16.

Stiglitz, J.E. (1985), "Credit markets and the control of capital", Journal of Money, Credit, and Banking 17:133–152.

Stiglitz, J.E., and A. Weiss (1981), "Credit rationing in markets with imperfect information", American Economic Review 71:393–411.

Stiglitz, J.E., and A. Weiss (1983), "Incentive effects of terminations: Applications to credit and labor markets", American Economic Review 73:912–927.

Stover, R., R. Teas and R. Gardner (1985), "Agricultural lending decisions: A multiattribute analysis", American Journal of Agricultural Economics 67:513–520.

Strotz, R.H. (1956), "Myopia and inconsistency in dynamic utility maximization", Review of Economic Studies 23:165–180.

Tauer, L. (1985), "Use of life insurance to fund the farm purchase from heirs", American Journal of Agricultural Economics 67:60–69.

Thomas, K.. and M. Boehlje (1983), "Farm estate and transfer planning: A management perspective", North Central Regional Extension Publication No. 193 (University of Minnesota, USA).

Traill, B., D. Colman and T. Young (1978), "Estimating irreversible supply elasticities: Some new approaches", American Journal of Agricultural Economics 60:528–531.

Turvey, C.G. (1991), "Credit scoring for agricultural loans: A review with applications", Agricultural Finance Review 51:43–54.

Turvey, C.G., and R. Brown (1990), "Credit scoring for a federal lending institution: The case of Canada's farm credit corporation", Agricultural Finance Review 50:47–57.

Turvey, C.G., and A. Weersink (1997), "Credit risk and the demand for agricultural loans", Canadian Journal of Agricultural Economics 45:201–217.

Tweeten, L., and L. Quance (1969), "Positive measures of aggregate supply elasticities: Some new approaches", American Journal of Agricultural Economics 51:342–352.

Vandeputte, J.M., and C.B. Baker (1970), "Specifying the allocation of income between taxes, consumption, and savings in linear programming models", American Journal of Agricultural Economics 52:521–528.

Vasavada, U., and R.G. Chambers (1986), "Investment in U.S. agriculture", American Journal of Agricultural Economics 68:950–960.

Von Pischke, J.D. (1991), "Finance at the frontier: Debt capacity and the role of credit in the private economy" (The World Bank, Washington, D.C.).

Wachter, M.L., and B. Williamson (1978), "Obligational markets and the mechanics of inflation", Bell Journal of Economics 9:549–571.

Weersink, A.J., and L.W. Tauer (1989), "Comparative analysis of investment models for New York dairy farms", American Journal of Agricultural Economics 71:136–145.

Williamson, O.E. (1996), The Mechanisms of Governance (The Free Press, New York).

Wilson, P. and D. Barkley (1988), "Commercial banks market shares: Structural factors influencing their decline in the agricultural sector", Agricultural Finance Review 48:49–59.

Wood, J.H. (1975), Commercial Bank Loan and Investment Behavior (John Wiley & Sons, New York).

Yang, S.R., and W. Wilson (1996), "Credit allocation decisions of wheat exporting countries", Canadian Journal of Agricultural Economics 44:53–65.

Young, R.P., and P.J. Barry (1987), "Holding financial assets as a risk response: A portfolio analysis of Illinois cash grain farms", North Central Journal of Agricultural Economics 9(1).

Chapter 11

ECONOMIC IMPACTS OF AGRICULTURAL RESEARCH AND EXTENSION

ROBERT E. EVENSON

Economic Growth Center, New Haven, CT

Contents

Handbook of Agricultural Economics, Volume 1, Edited by B. Gardner and G. Rausser

Abstract

Agricultural research and extension programs have been built in most of the world's economies. A substantial number of economic impact studies evaluating the contributions of research and extension programs to increased farm productivity and farm incomes and to consumer welfare have been undertaken in recent years. This chapter reviews these studies using estimated rates of return on investment to index economic impacts. In almost all categories of studies, median (social) estimated rates of return are high, (often exceeding 40 percent) but the range of estimates was also high. The chapter concludes that most of the estimates were consistent with actual economic growth experiences.

JEL classification: Q16

1. Introduction

Agricultural research is conducted both by private sector firms supplying inputs to farm producers and by public sector experiment stations, universities, and other research organizations. In the United States, agricultural research has been treated as a public sector responsibility for much of the nation's history. The U.S. Patent Office, one of the oldest government agencies in the U.S., recognizing that intellectual property right (patent) incentives were not available to stimulate the development of improved plants and animals in the nineteenth century, initiated programs to search for and import seeds and breeding animals from abroad.[1] After the establishment of the United States Department of Agriculture (USDA) and the Land Grant Colleges in 1862, the Hatch Act in 1878 provided for financial support for the State Agricultural Experiment Station system (SAES). Agricultural research in the public sector today is conducted in both USDA and SAES organizations and to a limited extent in general universities. Agricultural extension is also conducted by private sector firms and by public sector extension programs. Formal extension program development occurred somewhat later in the U.S. than was the case for research.[2]

The development of agricultural research and extension programs in the U.S. occurred at roughly the same time that similar programs were being developed in Europe. By the beginning of the twentieth century, most of today's developed countries had agricultural research systems in place. By the middle of the twentieth century many of today's developing countries had agricultural research and extension systems as well.[3] The perceived success of both research and extension programs in the first half of the twentieth century led to the judgment that these programs should be central components in the large-scale economic development programs ushered in after World War II.

Today, a complex system of international agricultural research centers (IARCs), national agricultural research programs (NARs), and sub-national or regional programs has been built covering most of the globe. Similarly, extension programs have been developed in most countries. These programs are under various forms of review and evaluation, as is appropriate given their perceived importance as public sector investments. Some of these evaluations are administrative or financial, others are informal "peer" reviews and ratings. Some reviews are economic impact evaluations, and these are the concern of this paper.

Economic impact evaluations differ from other evaluations in that they measure economic benefits produced by a program and associate these benefits with the economic

---

[1] Huffman and Evenson (1993) discuss the development of the U.S. research and extension system and the early role of the patent office.

[2] The Capper–Volstead Act of 1914 provided for formal extension services, but as with research programs, official government sanction and support for these programs came only after state and private experiments with precursor programs were deemed to be successful.

[3] See Boyce and Evenson (1975), Judd, Boyce, and Evenson (1986), and Pardey and Roseboom (1989) for international reviews of investment in research and extension.

costs of the program. This means computing a benefit/cost ratio and/or other associated economic calculation, such as the present value of benefits net of costs, or internal rates of return to investment.[4] Many evaluations, such as the "monitoring and evaluation" activities associated with World Bank research and extension projects, provide indicators of benefits (such as the number of beneficiaries) or of project outputs (farmers visited, experiments completed, etc.), but do not calculate actual value measures of benefits and costs. These evaluations are important and useful, but are not economic impact evaluations as defined here.

Economic impact evaluations are intended to measure whether a project or program actually had (or is expected to have) an economic impact and to associate impacts with project or program costs. They do not measure whether the project or program was designed optimally or managed and executed optimally. Many extension and research projects and programs have had significant economic impacts even though they were not as productive as they might have been.[5] Project/program design and execution issues are informed by economic impact studies, but also require other types of evaluation. Economic evaluations, however, address basic investment and resource allocation issues that other evaluations do not address.

Economic impact evaluations can be classified into *ex ante* evaluations (undertaken before the project or program is initiated) and *ex post* evaluations (undertaken after the project is initiated, sometimes after it is completed). In practice, *ex ante* project evaluations are used by international aid agencies and to some degree by national agencies to guide investments at the project level. These evaluations are seldom reported in published form. They are also seldom compared with subsequent *ex post* evaluations.[6]

The organization of this chapter is as follows: in Section 2 a brief review of institutional and analytic models of extension and research impacts is presented. Some of these models have implications for the empirical specifications surveyed in later sections. Section 3 reviews *ex post* studies of extension impacts. A number of these studies were based on farm-level observations, and methodological issues associated with these

---

[4] Many of these evaluations also undertake growth accounting. In addition to the literature reviewed here, a "gray" literature exists. Alston et al. (1998b) report a meta-analysis of rates of return that includes more of the gray literature than reviewed here. Unfortunately, a comparison of studies covered cannot be made as the authors treat their references as "data" and state that data from the International Food Policy Research Institute (IFPRI) studies will not be released until after publication of the report. This chapter has benefited greatly from an earlier review by Reuben Echeverría (1990).

[5] Economic impact studies are often downgraded as measures of investment effectiveness because they do not directly address project/program efficiency. The recent World Bank Operations Evaluation Department (OED) Review of Agricultural Extension and Research [Purcell and Anderson (1997)] reflects this perspective. It is critical of returns to research studies because they do not address project effectiveness. Given the World Bank's use of *ex ante* project evaluation methods (stressing economic impact indicators) the OED perspective on economic impact studies is puzzling.

[6] *Ex ante* economic calculations can be found in project reports of the World Bank and the regional development banks (the Asian Development Bank and the Inter-American Development Bank). As noted, however, few *ex ante–ex post* studies have been undertaken.

studies are addressed. Section 4 reviews *ex post* studies of applied agricultural research impacts. Section 5 reviews studies of R&D spillovers (to the agricultural sector from private sector research and development R&D) and "germplasmic" spillovers from pre-invention science. Section 6 reviews *ex ante* studies. The concluding section addresses the "credibility" of the estimates and consistency of estimated rates of return with actual growth experience.[7]

2. Institutional, analytic, and methodology issues (for *ex post* studies)

Extension programs seek two general objectives. The first is to provide technical education services to farmers through demonstrations, lectures, contact farmers, and other media. The second is to function in an interactive fashion with the suppliers of new technology, by providing demand feedback to technology suppliers and technical information to farmers to enable them to better evaluate potentially useful new technology and ultimately to adopt (and adapt) new technology in their production systems.

Applied agricultural research programs in both the public and private sectors seek to invent new technology for specific client or market groups. The market for agricultural inventions is highly differentiated because the actual economic value of inventions is sensitive to soil, climate, price, infrastructure, and institutional settings. Models of invention typically specify a distribution of potential inventions whose parameters are determined by the stock of past inventions and invention methods or techniques (i.e., the technology of technology production). This feature of invention calls for specifying two types of spillovers: (1) invention-to-invention spillovers (which are often spatial), and (2) science (or pre-invention science)-to-invention spillovers.

The studies reviewed here are empirical and most entail direct statistical estimation of coefficients for variables that measure the economic impacts of extension, applied research, or pre-invention science "services". All require some form of production framework. In this section alternative production frameworks are first briefly reviewed. Then a simple characterization of technological infrastructure is presented and related to extension and research programs. A more formal model of research and extension interactions is then presented. Finally, methodological issues associated with the specification of research and extension variables are discussed.

---

[7] There appears to be considerable skepticism regarding estimated rates of return [Ruttan (1998)]. They are widely perceived to be overestimated. This is true even though the economic impacts for other projects such as rural credit programs, rural development programs, and rural infrastructure programs (roads, etc.) are typically less thoroughly documented or are apparently relatively low. A recent paper [Alston et al. (1998a)] reporting low rates of return proclaims that appropriate time lag estimation techniques result in low returns to research and extension. Serious flaws in this paper are noted later in this review (footnote 20), but the fact that it has attracted attention attests to skepticism. This issue of skepticism is revisited in the growth accounting section of the paper where it is shown that most high rates of return to research and extension are consistent with growth experience.

2.1. Production frameworks

The starting point of economic impact studies is a productivity-technology specification. Consider the general specification of a "meta-transformation function":

$$G(Y, X, F, C, E, T, I, S) = 0, \tag{1}$$

where

Y is a vector of outputs,

X is a vector of variable factors,

F is a vector of fixed factors,

C is a vector of climate factors,

E is a vector of edaphic or soil quality factors,

T is a vector of technology (inventions),

I is a vector of market infrastructure,

S is a vector of farmer skills.

There are several empirical options to identify economic impacts of a change in T (extension and research services) based on this expression. All entail meaningfully defining measures or proxies for T (as well as measuring Y, X, F, C, E, I, and S accurately).

The empirical options are:

(a) To convert (1) to an aggregate "meta-production function" (MPF) by aggregating commodities into a single output measure:

$$Y_A = F(X, F, C, E, T, I, S) \tag{2}$$

and estimating (2) with farm-level or aggregated cross-section and/or time series data.

(b) To derive the output supply-factor demand system from the maximized profits function (or minimized cost function) via the Shephard–Hotelling lemma and estimate the profit function and/or its derivative output supply and factor demand functions. (This is the cost (CF) or profits (PF) production structure.)

$$\pi^* = \pi(P_y, P_x, C, E, T, I, S),$$

$$\partial \pi^*/\partial P_y = Y^* = Y(P_y, P_x, C, E, T, I, S),$$

$$\partial \pi^*/\partial P_x = X^* = X(P_y, P_x, C, E, T, I, S). \tag{3}$$

(c) To derive "residual" total factor productivity (TFP) indexes from (1) and utilize a TFP decomposition specification (the PD production structure):

$$Y/X = \text{TFP} = T(C, E, T, I, S). \tag{4}$$

(d) To derive partial factor productivity (PFP) indexes from (1) and utilize a PFP decomposition specification (the PD(Y) production structure):

$$\text{PFP}(Y/Ha, Y/L \text{ etc.}) = P(C, E, T, I, S). \tag{5}$$

Each of these options has been pursued in the studies reviewed in this paper. Methods for estimation or measuring the relationship between T, the technology variables, and the economic variables, have included direct statistical estimation of (2), (3), (4), or (5), and non-statistical use of experimental and other evidence. The options themselves have different implications and interpretations as well as having functional form implications for estimation.

The aggregate production function structure is often estimated with farm data. It requires that variable inputs, X, be treated as exogenous to the decision maker. It is typically argued in these studies that observed X vectors are profit-maximizing vectors and that these are functions of exogenous prices and fixed factors (as in (3)). This is a strong assumption in many settings. (From (2) one can compute the partial effect of T on Y, i.e., $\partial Y/\partial T$, holding X constant, but one cannot compute the total effect of T on Y ($\partial X/\partial T$ cannot be computed).)

One of the problems with any statistical method is that one must have meaningful variation in the T variables to identify their effects. This often means resorting to data with broad geographic or time series dimensions. Such data are sometimes poorly suited to estimating production parameters. The TFP decomposition specification often has an advantage in these situations because production parameters are implicit in the TFP computations based on prices. With reasonable price data, TFP indexes can be computed over time and in some situations over cross-sections.[8] This may allow better estimates of T effects on productivity, $\partial(Y/X)/\partial T$.

The richest specification is the duality-based specification, (3). It has the advantage that independent variables are exogenous and it allows estimates of T impacts on all endogenous variables in the system.[9]

The partial productivity framework suffers from the obvious fact that these measures are affected by other factors not included in the denominator. Nonetheless, given widely available yield and area data, some useful studies can be undertaken in this framework.

---

[8] Approximations to a Divisia index (Tornqvist/Theil) are generally regarded to be the appropriate TFP calculation method. Some growth accounting adjustments to inputs can affect the estimates of T parameters in (4). For example, adjustments for capital stock quality may effectively remove some of the contributions of research from the TFP measure. Many studies adjust for labor quality using schooling data. This, of course, eliminates the possibility for estimating schooling effects in (4), but it may improve prospects for estimating T effects because schooling S can be dropped from (4).

[9] This specification is also the most demanding of data.

2.2. *Technological infrastructure and institutions*

Agricultural extension and research programs contribute to economic growth in an interactive way. The contribution of each depends on the developmental stage of the economy. Both are subject to diminishing returns. To aid in clarifying these points, consider Figure 1. Here, five different stages or levels of technology infrastructure are considered. For each, a set of yield levels is depicted for a typical crop. These yield levels should be considered to be standardized for fertilizer, water, labor, and other factor levels.

Four yield levels are depicted. The first is the actual yield (A) realized on the average farmer's fields. The second is the "best practice" yield (BP) which can be realized using the best available technology. It is possible that some farmers obtain best practice yields but the average farmer does not. The third yield level is the "research potential" (RP) yield, i.e., it is the hypothetical best practice yield that would be expected to be attained as a result of a successful applied research program directed toward this crop. The fourth

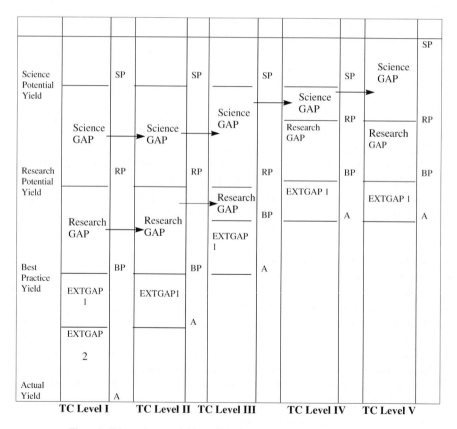

Figure 1. Schematic crop yields (and GAPs) by technological capacity level.

is the "science potential" (SP) yield. This is also a hypothetical yield. It is the research potential yield attainable if new scientific discoveries (e.g., in biotechnology) are made and utilized in an applied research program.

Associated with these yields we can define three "gaps". The "extension gap" is the difference between best practice (BP) and average (A) yields. Extension programs are designed to close this gap. The "research gap" is the difference between research potential (RP) yields and best practice (BP) yields. Applied research programs, if successful, will close this gap (and will thus open up the extension gap). Similarly, a "science gap" exists between science potential (SP) and research potential (RP) yields.

Consider technology infrastructure stage I. This is a stage where little extension, research or science is being undertaken. Farmer schooling levels are low, markets are poor and infrastructure lacking.[10] The extension gap is large in this stage and thus there is considerable scope for a high payoff to extension, even if there are few effective research programs that are raising best practice yields. After extension programs have achieved a transition to stage II, the extension gap will have been reduced to some fraction of its original size (EXTGAP 1). The gains from reducing the original gap (EXTGAP 2) may be quite large and they are "permanent" in the sense that they are long-term gains that could not have been produced by other programs (at least not in a short time period).

Once an economy achieves stage II, it has exploited EXTGAP 2. There is further scope for extension contributions but they are not what they were in stage I (EXTGAP 1). In fact, the economy now becomes dependent on the closing of the research gap to open up the extension gap. As the economy is transformed from stage II to stage III a direct link between research and extension is forged. Extension programs now become responsible for extending relatively newly developed technology to farmers.

When pre-invention science becomes more effective, the research potential yield (RP) is raised and with active research and extension programs the economy may move into stage IV. Further progress, i.e., to stage V and beyond, depends on effective pre-invention science, research and extension programming.

Consider the situation in Africa and Asia. It appears that much of Africa has not made the transition yet to stage II and there is limited evidence that it has achieved a transition to stage III where research systems are producing significant flows of new technology suited to farmers in most regions. This is in contrast to the situation in both South and Southeast Asia where by the mid-1960s many economies were already in stage II and where "green revolution" technology in rice, wheat, corn, and other crops has enabled them to make the transition to stage III. Today, in some Asian countries, there are prospects for moving to stage IV.

It is possible that spill-ins from abroad can raise best practice yields before economies have made the transition to stage II. Most research gains, however, have been realized in economies that have already achieved stage II market, infrastructure, and skill levels. In some cases this has been induced by the development (often in international centers) of

---

[10] Many countries in sub-Saharan Africa fit this description.

genetic resources and methods that increase the RP yield levels. In Africa these RP yield levels for some countries may be quite low because of limited genetic resources and difficult disease and insect problems, so that the research gap is actually quite small. If this is the case, "stimulus from above" in the form of improvements in science (closing of the science gap) may be required to achieve better research performance.

2.3. Formal models

The economics literature includes models of technology diffusion, of invention, and of growth. In practice, these literatures are not well integrated. Technology diffusion (adoption) models typically consider technology to have already been produced and address the mechanisms of diffusion – usually employing a logistic or sigmoid functional form. Models of invention do integrate research and extension activities and are probably most useful for providing structure for the activities discussed in an informal way in Figure 1. The "new endogenous growth" literature has some insights to offer as regards R&D and invention but does not effectively integrate the invention model perspective into formal growth models.[11]

As noted earlier, extension programs are designed to (a) provide general technical adult education services and (b) to facilitate the evaluation and adoption of recently developed technology. The technology diffusion literature specifies a logistic form for the adoption of technology:

$$T_i^* = 1/\big(1 - \exp(a + bt + c\text{EXT})\big). \tag{6}$$

This functional form is relevant to adoption studies (the second function of extension) but not necessarily to studies where the first function of extension is important.[12]

Invention models can be combined with diffusion specifications, but typically are not. Consider an invention discovery model based on a simple random search model. For a given distribution of potential inventions the probability of making an invention for the n th draw from any distribution is $1/n$. A new invention must have a higher quality index (e.g., the yield of a plant variety) than previously discovered inventions. The expected cumulative number of inventions from n experiments (or draws) in a given distribution is:

$$\mathrm{E}(I)n = \sum_{\ell=1}^{n} \frac{1}{i} \approx G + \ln(n). \tag{7}$$

---

[11] The models of Romer (1986, 1990) provide a serious treatment of invention but do not effectively address spillovers.

[12] This is usually estimated by taking logarithms [Feder et al. (1985)].

This expression for research discoveries was first derived by Evenson and Kislev (1975) for an exponential distribution of potential inventions. Kortum (1994) generalized this expression for any search distribution.[13]

Expression (7) relates inventions (I) to research (n). Empirical work relating research to productivity requires the further step of relating inventions to productivity. Kortum (1994) derives the standard relationship between research and productivity used in industrial studies

$$\ln(\text{TFP}) = \lambda \ln(\text{RESS}), \tag{8}$$

where RESS is the cumulated research stock (net of depreciation).[14]

Since empirical studies are undertaken using data where extension services are not constant and where the underlying parameters of applied invention search are also not constant, the empirical specification should be extended to include extension variables and pre-invention research variables.

Extension has two effects on productivity. Most importantly, it speeds up the rate of adoption of inventions by farmers. This role is subject to diminishing returns in a manner similar to invention, calling for a $\ln(\text{EXT})$ term. However, extension can influence inventions as well. It can facilitate inventions by conveying farmer evaluation signals to inventors more rapidly. It can also help inventors to identify unpromising search avenues, and this changes the parameters of the underlying invention search distribution. This argues for a $\ln(\text{EXT}) \times \ln(\text{RESS})$ term.

$$\ln(\text{TFP}) = a + b\ln(\text{RESS}) + c\ln(\text{EXT}) + d\ln(\text{RESS})\ln(\text{EXT}). \tag{9}$$

Pre-invention science is designed to change the parameters of the underlying search distribution as well. These discoveries may shift the mean of the underlying search distribution leading to an added term for pre-invention science.

$$\ln(\text{TFP}) = a + b\ln(\text{RESS}) + c\ln(\text{EXT}) + d\ln(\text{RESS})\ln(\text{EXT}) + e\ln(\text{PRINV}). \tag{10}$$

Pre-invention science may also shift the variance of the underlying distribution as well, calling for an added interaction term in TFP decomposition specifications.

$$\begin{aligned}\ln(\text{TFP}) = {}& a + b\ln(\text{RESS}) + c\ln(\text{EXT}) + d\ln(\text{RESS})\ln(\text{EXT}) \\ & + e\ln(\text{PRINV}) + f\ln(\text{PRINV})\ln(\text{RESS}).\end{aligned} \tag{11}$$

---

[13] This semi-logarithmic approximation is accurate when n is large.

[14] Evenson and Kislev (1975) utilized an exponential distribution of potential inventions. They showed that the logarithmic approximation held for this distribution as well.

Few of the studies reviewed below were motivated by the model described here. It does, however, have some functional form implications, and while they were generally not imposed or even recognized in reported studies, the interpretative insights of the model will be useful in discussing the findings of the studies.[15]

2.4. Specifying research and extension variables in empirical studies

Most of the studies reviewed in subsequent sections utilized a statistical specification of one of the production frameworks discussed above. This requires the development of research and extension variables that are appropriate to the unit of observation. These variables are conceptually similar to capital stock variables that measure capital service flows to the unit of observation. The observation may be a farm or an aggregate of farms. Production or productivity may be measured in level form or in rate-of-change form. The observation is typically for a given location and period.

Research and extension service flow variables then need to consider time weight, spatial weight, and deflator issues.

2.4.1. Time weights

Research and extension programs have economic impacts that typically last for more than one period. Accordingly, the services provided by these programs to a given location in a given period may be based on research and extension activities undertaken in prior periods.

Figures 2a and 2b depict alternative extension and research "time shapes". Consider the extension weights (Figure 2a). Two cases for the effects of extension activity in time t_0 on technology adoption patterns are depicted. In case 1, applicable to advanced technology infrastructure levels (see Figure 1), good substitutes for extension activities exist. Accordingly, productive technology will eventually be fully adopted in the absence of the extension program. The technology will be adopted earlier, given the presence of an extension program.

In case 2, applicable to low levels of technological infrastructure (e.g., stage 1, Figure 1), good substitutes for extension programs do not exist. In this case, productive technology may not be fully adopted in the absence of extension programs. Extension then has both a speeding-up effect and a level effect.[16]

The "time-shape" weights associated with these two extension cases will depend on the production framework used. If the dependent variable is the level of production or of partial productivity, the time weights are as depicted in panels 1.1 and 2.1. For case 1,

---

[15] Note that this model is not a simple "linear model of science" where PRINV recharges the invention pool and inventions determine the productivity of extension. Extension and research have "upstream" effects. However, the idea of exhaustion of invention pools, or of attempting to invent when the pool has not really been created, is relevant to research policy making.

[16] The level effect can be seen as exploiting EXTGAP 2.

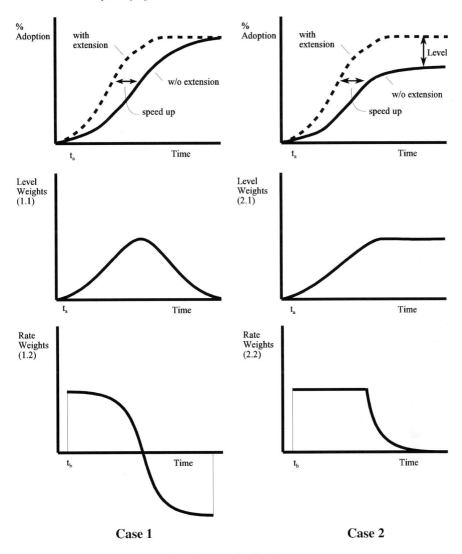

Figure 2a. Extension time shapes.

extension activity conducted prior to period $t - t_a$ is not relevant to the observation. For case 2 all prior extension may be relevant.

When the dependent variable is a rate of change as in a first difference or a change in a TFP index, the time weights are as depicted in panels 1.2 and 2.1. Note that in panel 1.2 there are negative weights for extension in some prior periods. This illustrates the fact that when extension has merely a speeding-up effect it does not actually have a net

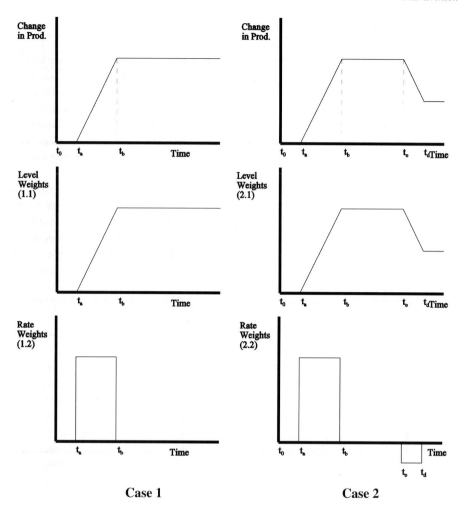

Figure 2b. Research time shapes.

effect on the growth in production or productivity. For case 2 it does have an effect on the level of production and on growth.

Many of the studies reviewed here utilized a total factor productivity (TFP) decomposition framework where production data were first used to compute a TFP index. Then in a second stage this TFP measure is regressed on research and extension variables. Often the TFP measure is set at some level (1 or 100) in the base period (t_b) and then annual changes are "cumulated" in future periods. For this case the time shape weights are as depicted in panels 1.2 and 2.2 for the period $t_{b+1} - t_b$ and cumulated for subsequent periods. This produces a time shape similar to the shape depicted in panels 1.1 and 1.2 except that there is a cut-off in past activities associated with the date t_b.[17]

Research service time shape weights are also depicted for two cases (Figure 2b). In case 1 research activity in t_0 has future impacts that are depicted in three segments:[18]

segment *a* from t_0 to t_a in which no impact is realized

segment *b* for t_a to t_b in which a rising impact is realized

segment *c* from t_0 to ∞ in which the effect is constant

In case 1, research service impacts (in the form of inventions adopted) do not "depreciate". They may become obsolete (i.e., replaced by improved inventions), but the improved inventions "build on" the inventions they displace. Thus the original inventions "live on" as part of the inventions that displace them.

In research case 2 real depreciation of inventions takes place as depicted in the segment d. This may be due to such factors as pest and pathogen responses to host plant resistance breeding improvements, or to incomplete "building on". After some point (segment *e*) research activity at t_0 will be "buried" in future productivity levels.[19] This is reflected in the time weight panels 1.1 and 2.2. As with extension, when the production structure is in rate of change form, the time shapes are quite different (panels 1.2 and 2.2). When cumulated TFP measures are used there is a cut-off on early research that is buried (segment c in case 1 or e in case 2) before t_b, the beginning date of the TFP series. It is not appropriate to include this research (or extension) in the estimation.

Strategies for estimating time weights include:
(a) "free form" estimates obtained by including a number of lagged research and/or extension variables;
(b) "segment length" estimates obtained by constructing alternative lengths of the segments depicted in Figures 2a and 2b and undertaking an iterative search over segment lengths to minimize mean square error (a form of non-linear least squares estimation [Evenson (1968)]);
(c) "distributed lag" estimates obtained by imposing a functional form on the time shape – such as a Nerlovian exponentially declining structure as a quadratic or other form.

---

[17] That is, activities that affected only the base period and prior periods are inappropriate in the specifications because they only affect the constant term.

[18] Note that these segments are not arbitrary. Research programs do not produce immediate impacts. Their contributions rise to a peak after several periods. Utilizing a distributed lag specification that does not recognize this logic can give very misleading estimates of the lag structure.

[19] The contribution is buried in the sense that its contribution is no longer affecting current inventions or improvements even though the original invention may have been quite important.

Free form lag estimates are generally not very satisfactory because with high multicollinearity between lagged research variables, coefficients tend to oscillate between positive and negative values and only make sense when smoothed.

Distributed lag estimates can impose very strong structure on time shapes, especially when improper or redundant (buried) lagged research is included in rate of change specifications.[20]

The segment length method, while crude, does allow flexibility in segment lengths while imposing reasonable shape weights for segments. (It is plausible that some form of non-parametric estimates would be an improvement.)[21]

2.4.2. Location spill-ins – spatial weights

Research and extension services have locational spill-overs. A geographic unit of observation is likely to receive services (spill-in) from activities located outside its geographic boundaries. These must be considered in developing research and extension variables.

Extension variables are perhaps easiest to deal with. Most extension services have a multi-level structure. Field staff are typically assigned to a region and to a set of client farms. Supervisory staff and subject matter specialists are typically assigned to cover more than one field staff unit. Field staff services from one region typically do not flow or "spill in" to other regions. However, subject matter specialist services probably do. This problem for extension is generally dealt with in the context of defining "extension services supplied" variables (see Section 3).[22]

For research variables the problem of spatial weights is more serious, especially as many research studies utilize repeated cross-section observations. These observations

---

[20] If buried research activities are included in a free form estimation specification they are essentially redundant variables. If they are included in a distributed lag specification with a polynomial or other form they can have a significant effect on time weight estimates. A recent paper by Alston et al. (1998a) claims that when "appropriate" estimation techniques are used, rates of return to research and extension are actually quite low. Their specification amalgamates research and extension time weights and includes buried activities in activities that do not contribute to TFP growth after 1950. Their free form estimates of lag weights show high rates of return. Imposing a polynomial specification with the buried activities down-weights more recent lags. This results in a substantial downward bias in rate of return estimates.

[21] The segment length method entails systematically searching for the segment length combination that minimizes means square error.

[22] Fixed effects estimations where spatial dummy variables are incorporated into the specification can have important effects on spill-in. For example, in two recent World Bank studies of Training and Visit (T&V) extension in Kenya, fixed effects in the form of district dummy variables altered the results. In the original study Evenson and Bindlish (1993) argued that using district dummy variables would essentially eliminate most of the relevant cross-section variations for the farms in the seven-district study. District dummies do not allow for "between district" variation. If there are substantial within-district spillovers from the subject-matter specialist and supervisory structure of the T&V system, within-district variation in staffing levels will capture little of the real differences in extension service. In later work Gautam and Anderson (1998) show that including district dummy variables does eliminate much of the correlation between extension services and farm productivity.

must be appropriately matched with the locations where applied research is conducted. Most large national research systems are organized by political region (e.g., the state system in the U.S.) and thus each research center can often be associated with a region. However, units of observation in one region (state) may benefit from research done in another region even when they are not the clients of the other region. They may benefit in two ways:

(1) Farmers may directly adopt inventions made in and for the other region, and
(2) Researchers in the region may experience enhanced research productivity because of inventions made in the other region. (See (11) and (12) where b could
be changed by inventions made in the other regions.)

Spatial spill-in has been handled in three ways in the studies reviewed. Many studies have either ignored the issue or implicitly argued that spill-ins are roughly offset by spill-outs. A number of studies have utilized geo-climate region data to specify spillovers. A small number have defined spill-over barrier measures and used these to specify spillovers.

The geo-climate region methodology is similar to the segment length estimation for time weights. Evenson (1969), Welch and Evenson (1989), and Huffman and Evenson (1993) utilized geo-climate region and sub-region data to define the research stocks for a unit of observation i as:

$$R_i = \sum_j S_{ij} R_j,$$ (15)

where the spatial weights (S_{ij}) measured the relative importance of the neighboring research locations to region i. Searches over S_{ij} weights have also been combined with searches over time segment weights.[23]

The use of spillover barrier indexes in a few studies suggests that these are a convenient means for estimating spatial weights over a number of locations. The spillover barrier between two locations i and j is defined as:

$$SPB_{ij} = 1 - C_{ij}/C_{ii},$$ (16)

where C_{ii} is the minimum cost of producing the good in location i using the best (cost-minimizing) technology available to location i, and C_{ij} is the minimum cost of producing the good in region i when producers are constrained to use location j's minimum cost technology.

Crop yield trial data, where a common set of cultivars are planted in different locations, enable one to actually measure SPB_{ij} by comparing yields in location i of the

---

[23] This procedure is used in [Huffman and Evenson (1993)].

highest yielding cultivar in location i with the yield in location i of location j's highest yielding cultivar.[24] The actual spill-in variable can then be estimated as:

$$R_j = \sum_j (\text{SPB}_{ij})^\alpha R_j, \tag{17}$$

where α can be estimated by non-linear techniques.[25]

2.4.3. Deflators

Deflators are needed for extension service variables for two purposes:
    (1) To put financial data (expenditures) into constant currency units, and
    (2) To account for farm contact heterogeneity.
    The typical extension deflator is the number of farms or of areas served (see Section 3).
    Deflators for research variables are also required to put financial data into constant currency units and to correct for diversity not captured by spillover measures (see Section 4).

3. Studies of agricultural extension impacts

Studies of agricultural extension impacts can be grouped into three categories:
    A. Studies based on farm-level (cross-section) observations where extension services vary by observation but where it is presumed that research services do not vary by observation (Tables 1 and 2).
    B. Studies based on aggregated farm production data (e.g., a district, country or state) usually in a cross-section framework, where both extension and applied research services are specified to vary by observation (and where research variables are included along with extension variables) (Table 3).
    C. Studies based on aggregated farm data (usually repeated cross-section) where for reasons of data availability a variable measuring the combined services of research and extension is constructed (Table 4).
    In this part, studies of the first two categories are reviewed. Discussion of the studies using a combined research-extension variable is deferred to Section 4 where research variables are discussed in more depth.
    Cross-section studies based on farm-level observations where research services can be considered to be constant over observations and where extension services vary should

---

[24] Evenson (1992) developed SPB indexes using international yield trial data for rice and applied them to spillover estimates in India. Da Cruz and Evenson (1997) used similar procedures for Brazil.

[25] An alternative way to scale the SPB weights is $\text{SPB}_{ij}^{\alpha-\gamma}$. This can also be estimated with non-linear techniques.

Table 1
Extension economic impact studies: Statistical methods: Farm as unit of observation; farm specific extension variables

Study	Country	Period of study	Production structure	Extension variable	IRR	Comments
Lever (1970)	Botswana	1969	MPF	Years extension available	nc	Low stat. significance
Harken (1973)	Japan	1972	MPF	Use of media by farms	nc	Path analysis
Moock (1973)	Kenya	1972	PD(Y)	Extension contact factor	nc	Factor analysis
Patrick and Kehrberg (1973)	Brazil	1972	MPF	Extension contacts	42–100+	
Hopcraft (1974)	Kenya	1973	MPF	Extension visits	nc	Demonstrations, visits (maize)
Hopcraft (1974)	Kenya	1973	MPF	Training courses, demonstration	nc	
Moock (1976)	Kenya	1974	PD(Y)	Index of contacts, visits, courses	nc	Significant for low schooling (maize)
Pachico and Ashby (1976)	Brazil	1974	MPF	Extension contacts	nc	n.s. (rice)
Cotlear (1986)	Peru	1975	MPF	Extension contact dummy	nc	Potatoes
Halim (1976)	Philippines	1975	MPF	Extension contacts prior years	nc	(rice)
Capule (1977)	Philippines	1975	MPF	Hours by farmer in extension contacts	nc	
Jamison and Lau (1982)	Malaysia	1980	MPF	Exposure to adult education courses	nc	n.s. (rice)
Pudasaini (1983)	Nepal	1982	MPF	Extension contacts	nc	n.s. (rice, maize)
Jamison and Moock (1984)	Nepal	1982	MPF	Dummy – recent contact	nc	n.s. (rice)
Perraton et al. (1985)	Malawi	1984	PD(Y)	Extension visits to farmers	nc	(maize)

Table 2
Extension economic impact studies: Statistical methods: Farm as unit of observation; extension supply variables

Study	Country	Period of study	Production structure	Extension variable	IRR	Comments
Hong (1975)	Korea	CS(895)	MPF	Extension spending in region	nc	(rice)
Jamison and Lau (1982)	Thailand	CS(184)	MPF	Extension available to village	nc	(non-chemical uses)
Jamison and Moock (1984)	Nepal	CS	MPF	Proportion of village farmers contacted	nc	(wheat)
Feder et al. (1985)	India	1984	PD(Y)	Dummy – extension type service	Low to high	(rice)
Feder et al. (1985)	India	1984	MPF	T&V management experiment	15+	T&V advantage
Cotlear (1986)	Peru	1985	MPF	Proportion hh's in village center	nc	S.S. in tradition region (potatoes)
Chou and Lau (1987)	Thailand	1985	MPF	Dummy: extension service to village	nc	n.s.
Deaton and Benjamin (1988)	Cote d'Ivoire	1986	PD(Y)	Dummy: extension agent available	nc	n.s.
Evenson (1988)	Paraguay	1988	PD(Y)	Hours Extension/Hectare	75–90	S.S. major crops
Evenson and Bravo-Ureta (1994)	Paraguay	1989	ED	Hours Extension/Hectare	nc	Coffee, casava, corn frontier methods
Evenson and Bindlish (1993)	Kenya	1990–91	MPF	Extension/Staff/Farm	100+	timing estimated
Evenson and Bindlish (1993)	Kenya	1982	MPF	Extension/Staff/Farm	88	Pre T&V
Evenson et al. (1995)	Burkina Faso	1991	MPF	Extension/Staff/Farm	91	T&V extension

Table 3
Extension economic impact studies: Statistical methods: Aggregate farms as unit of observation

Study	Country	Period of data	Production structure	Extension variable	IRR
Evenson and Jha (1973)	India	1953–57 CS	PD	Maturity rating district	14
Mohan and Evenson (1975)	India	1955–71 CS	PD	Presence of IADP	15
Huffman (1974)	USA	1959–74 CS	MPF	Extension staff/farm	16
Huffman (1976)	USA	1964 CS	MPF	Staff days/farm	110
Evenson (1979)	USA	1971 CSxTS	PD	Expenditures/region	100+
Huffman (1981)	USA	1979 CS	MPF	Extension days/county	110
Pray and Ahmed (1991)	Bangladesh	1951–61 CSxTS	MPF	Expenditure/district	nc
		1977–86 CSxTS	MPF		nc
Norton & Paczkowski (1993)	USA (Va)		MPF		52
Evenson (1992)	Indonesia	1971–89	PD	Expenditure/farm	92
Librero and Perez (1987)	Philippines	1956–83 CSxTS	MPF	Expenditure/province	nc
Setboonsarng and Evenson (1991)	Thailand	1953–71 CS-TS	PD(Y)	Expenditure/farm	nc
da Cruz et al. (1982)	Brazil	1970–75–80 CS-TS	PD	Expenditure/farm	nc
Evenson (1987)	Latin America	1960–82 CSxTS	PD(Y)	Ext.Ex/geo-climate region	0–80+
	Africa	1960–82 CSxTS	PD(Y)	Ext.Ex/geo-climate region	34–80+
	Asia	1960–82 CSxTS	PD(Y)	Ext.Ex/geo-climate region	80+
Evenson & McKinsey (1991)	India	1956–83 CSxTS	PD(Y)	Expenditure/farm	
	India	1956–83 CSxTS	PD(Y)	Wheat	82
	India	1956–83 CSxTS	PD(Y)	Rice	215
	India	1956–83 CSxTS	PD(Y)	Jowar	167
	India	1956–83 CSxTS	PD(Y)	Bajra	201
	India	1956–83 CSxTS	PD(Y)	Maize	56
	India	1956–83 CSxTS	PD(Y)	All	176
Evenson (1994)	USA	1950–72 CSxTS states	PD	Expenditure/state	Crops 101
	USA	1950–72 CSxTS states	PD	Expenditure/state	Livestock 89
	USA	1950–72 CSxTS states	PD	Expenditure/state	All 82
Evenson and Avila (1996)	Brazil	1970 1970–85 CSxTS	PD	Predicted extension contacts	Crops 33 Livestock 23 Aggregate 19
Evenson and Quizon (1991)	Philippines	1948–84	PD	Expenditure/farm	Positive (low)
Norton and Paczkowski (1993)	USA (Va)	1993	MPF		37

Table 4
Economic impact studies combining extension and public research

Study	Country	Period of analysis	Commodity	Production structure	IRR
Elias (1971)	Argentina	1943–63	Sugarcane	MPF	33–49
del Rey (1975)	Argentina	1943–63	Sugarcane	MPF	35–41
Pray (1978)	Punjab (India)	1906–56	Aggregate	MPF	34–44
	Punjab (Pakistan)	1948–63	Aggregate	MPF	23–37
Avila (1981)	Brazil	1959–78	Rice	MPF	83–119
White and Havlicek (1982)	USA	1943–77	Aggregate	MPF	7–36
Lu et al. (1979)	USA	1939–72	Aggregate	MPF	25
Zentner (1982)	Canada	1946–79	Wheat		30–39
Evenson (1979)	USA	1948–71	Aggregate	MPF	110
Nagy (1983)	Pakistan	1967–81	Maize	MPF	19
	Pakistan	1967–81	Wheat	MPF	58
Feijoo (1984)	Argentina	1950–80	Aggregate	MPF	41
da Silva (1984)	Brazil (Sao Paulo)	1970–80	Aggregate	MPF	60–102
Ayers (1985)	Brazil	1955–83	Soybeans	MPF	23–53
Nagy (1985)	Pakistan	1959–79	Aggregate	MPF	64
Khan and Akbari (1986)	Pakistan	1955–81	Aggregate	MPF	36
Norton et al. (1987)	Peru	1981–87	Aggregate		17–38
Scobie and Eveleens (1987)	New Zealand	1926–84	Aggregate	PD(Y)	30
Harvey (1988)	U.K.	1988	Aggregate		38–44
Setboonsarng and Evenson (1991)	Thailand	1991	Rice	MPF	40
Sterns and Bernsten (1994)	Cameroon	1979–91	Row pea	PD(Y)	3
	Cameroon	1979–91	Sorghum	PD(Y)	0
Howard et al. (1993)	Zambia	1978–91	Maize	PD(Y)	84–87
Kupfuma (1994)	Zimbabwe	1932–40	Maize	PD(Y)	43.5
Mudhara et al. (1995)	Zimbabwe	1970–95	Cotton	PD(Y)	47

offer a good "with/without" experimental design setting in which to measure economic impacts. In cases where panel data for the same farms over time can be utilized, a "before/after" design element is added. A before/after comparison might be made when extension programs were first introduced. However, the only panel farm-level data studies surveyed here of the before/after type attempted to measure the qualitative effect of a change in the design and management of extension from the traditional design to the Training and Visit (T&V) management implemented in World Bank funded extension projects in India [Feder et al. (1985)] in the early 1980s and in Kenya [Evenson and Bindlish (1993)] and Burkina Faso [Evenson et al. (1995)] in the late 1980s.[26]

---

[26] In one sense, the best opportunity to achieve a before/after statistical design is at the time when extension programs are first introduced. The effect of a change in design as in the case of T&V management is difficult to measure.

Tables 1 and 2 report summaries of the farm observation studies. All studies reported estimated coefficients for an extension variable. The production structure used most frequently was the aggregate meta production function although several used productivity (yield) decomposition. Most studies reported statistical significance. Only a few studies actually calculated an internal rate of return (IRR), the measure of impact used to compare studies in this review.

The studies summarized in Table 1 utilized a farm-level or farm-specific extension variable. This was typically an index of extension-staff—farm contact either in visits to the farm by extension staff or in farmer visits to extension meetings or demonstrations. Birkhaeuser et al. (1991), among others, have noted that this variable is subject to endogeneity bias. This is because at least some of the contacts are farmer-initiated. If one observes that more efficient farms have more extension contact, one cannot conclude that extension contact caused the efficiency difference. It may simply reflect the demand for information by the more efficient farmers.

A second form of endogeneity bias in farm-specific extension variables may be due to extension staff selectivity (i.e., the staff contact the best farmers more frequently). The remedy for this problem is to use a statistical procedure to deal with it (instrumental variables or 2SLS, 3SLS in a structural model). Only four of the studies covered in Table 1 utilized this remedy. These four studies did find statistically significant extension impacts, but taken as a group, Table 1 studies do not provide overwhelming evidence for large extension contributions. Many of these studies were early (pioneering) studies, however, that contributed insights to later studies.

The extension studies summarized in Table 2 addressed the endogeneity problem with the extension variable by creating variables measuring "extension services supplied". For some studies this variable took the form of a dummy variable indicating whether a community had extension services supplied to it. For others it was a measure of services supplied per farm or per unit of land area for a defined extension region. These variables were not farm-specific, but were assigned to each farm observation in the extension region.

The extension services variables, as noted, were typically deflated by the number of farms.[27] In addition time weights in some studies were estimated using the segment length method. The India, Burkina Faso, and Kenya studies all concluded that there were significant level segments (see Figure 2, case 2) and that the extension programs were probably mining EXTGAP 2 (see Figure 1). These three studies were of extension systems in countries with relatively low technology infrastructure levels.

---

[27] The "fixed effects" estimation issue is important here. Suppose there are district and sub-district extension programs. One can develop sub-district staff farm variables. District fixed effects will remove all between-district variation. Yet there may be important and real differences in the district programs because of spatial spillovers over sub-district programs. District fixed effects will remove them. [See Evenson and Bindlish (1993) and Gautam and Anderson (1998)].

Several of the studies in Table 2 (including the T&V extension studies) report relatively high rates of return to investment. These rates of return were based on the time weights, deflators, and estimated coefficients.[28]

Table 3 summarizes studies that were based on aggregated data. In some cases [Huffman (1974); Huffman (1981); da Cruz et al. (1982)] the data were district, municipal or state averages compiled from Census of Agriculture data. In other cases production and input data from different sources reported for the district and state level were utilized. One study was international. All of these studies included both research and extension variables and in some cases schooling variables as well (research variable estimates from these studies are summarized in Section 4).

Several of the studies summarized in Table 3 were for a single cross-section, but most were for pooled cross-section-time-series data (or repeated cross-sections). The option of a farm-specific extension variable was not available to these studies and most used a staff or expenditure per farm or area ratio. Several imposed time weights. Several estimated time weights using the segment technique noted above.

Most of the studies summarized in Table 3 reported rate of return calculations. These, of course, are marginal rates of return since they are based on coefficients estimated for the extension variable (sometimes interacted with other variables). The rate of return was typically calculated by simulating a one dollar increase in extension expenditure in time t, then calculating the change in the extension variable in subsequent periods from this investment utilizing the time weights. The estimated coefficient for the extension variable then enables one to construct the "benefits stream" associated with the investment (multiplying by the units affected), and the IRR is calculated from this.

When these estimated rates of return are considered along with the Table 1 and 2 estimates, the general picture suggests a broad range of economic impacts ranging from negligible impacts to very high impacts. Table 4 summarizes studies where the technology variable was based on combined extension and research data. These estimated rates of return range from modest to very high. They will be discussed further in the next section.

4. Studies of applied agricultural research (public sector)

The studies reviewed in this section can be categorized into two groups. The first group of studies adopted a "project evaluation" approach and these report "average" IRRs (see Table 5).[29] The second group adopted a statistical estimation approach utilizing one of the production structures described above. This entailed the construction of a

---

[28] The time weights are important in calculating rates of return to investment. The benefits stream from a given investment depend on these weights. The procedure for computing the benefits stream is to simulate the productivity gains from an expenditure increase in time t for future periods.

[29] Other reviewers describe these studies as using an "economic surplus" methodology. This is not very satisfactory since all studies calculate benefits in terms of economic surplus.

Table 5
Economic impact studies: Public sector. Agricultural research: Project evaluation methods

Study	Country	Commodity	Period	IRR%
Griliches (1958)	USA	Hybrid corn	1940–1955	35–40
Griliches (1958)	USA	Hybrid sorghum	1940–1957	20
Grossfield and Heath (1966)	U.K.	Potato harvester	1950–1967	High NPV computed
Peterson (1967)	USA	Poultry	1915–1960	21–25
Evenson (1969)	South Africa	Sugarcane	1945–1962	40
Barletta (1970)	Mexico	Wheat	1943–1963	90
Barletta (1970)	Mexico	Maize	1943–1963	35
Ayer (1970)	Brazil	Cotton	1924–1967	77+
Schmitz and Seckler (1970)	USA	Tomato harvester	1958–1969	37–46
Ayer and Schuh (1972)	Brazil	Cotton	1924–1967	77–110
Hines (1972)	Peru	Maize	1954–1967	35–40
Monteiro (1975)	Brazil	Cocoa	1923–1975	16–18
	Brazil	Cocoa	1958–1974	60–79
	Brazil	Cocoa	1958–1985	61–79
Fonseca (1976)	Brazil	Coffee	1933–1995	23–25
Hayami and Akino (1977)	Japan	Rice	1915–1950	25–27
Hayami and Akino (1977)	Japan	Rice	1930–1961	73–75
Hertford et al. (1977)	Colombia	Soybeans	1960–1971	79–96
	Colombia	Wheat	1953–1973	11–12
	Colombia	Cotton	1953–1972	None
Pee (1977)	Malaysia	Rubber	1932–1973	24
Peterson and Fitzharris (1977)	USA	Aggregate	1937–1942	50
	USA	Aggregate	1947–1952	51
	USA	Aggregate	1957–1962	49
	USA	Aggregate	1957–1972	34
Wennergren and Whitaker (1977)	Bolivia	Sheep	1966–1975	44
	Bolivia	Wheat	1966–1975	−48
Pray (1978)	Punjab (British India)	Research and extension	1906–1956	34–44
	Punjab (Pakistan)	Research and extension	1948–1963	23–37
Scobie and Posada (1978)	Bolivia	Rice	1957–1964	79–96
Kislev and Hoffman (1978)	Israel	Wheat	1954–1973	125–150
		Dry farming		94–113
		Field crops		13–16
Pray (1980)	Bangladesh	Wheat and rice	1961–1977	30–35
Moricochi (1980)	Brazil	Citrus	1933–1985	78–27
Avila (1981)	Brazil	Rice	1957–1964	79–96
Nagy (1983)	Pakistan	Wheat	1967–1981	58
	Pakistan	Maize	1967–1981	19
da Cruz et al. (1982)	Brazil	Aggregate	1974–1996	22–30
da Cruz and Avila (1983)	Brazil	Aggregate	1977–1982	20
Martinez and Sain (1983)	Panama	Maize	1979–1982	188
Bengston (1984)	USA	Forestry (Particleboard)	1975–2000	19–22

Table 5
Continued

Study	Country	Commodity	Period	IRR%
Feijòo (1984)	Argentina	Aggregate	1950–80	41
Monares (1984)	Rwanda	Potato seed	1978–85	40
Pinazza et al. (1984)	Brazil, Sao Paulo	Sugarcane	1972–82	35
Roessing (1984)	Brazil (CNPS)	Soybeans	1975–82	45–62
Norton and Paczkowski (1993)	USA (Va)	Aggregate	1949–79	58
Bare and Loveless (1985)	USA	Forestry	–	9–12
Bengston (1984)	USA	Forestry	–	35–40
Brinkman and Prentice (1985)	Canada – Ontario	Aggregate	1950	66
Herruzo (1985)	Spain	Rice	1941–80	15–18
Muchnik (1985)	Latin America	Rice	1968–90	17–44
Ulrich et al. (1985)	Canada	Malting barley	1951–88	31–75
Unnevehr (1986)	SE Asia	Rice quality	1983–84	29–61
Brunner and Strauss (1986)	USA	Forestry		73
Chang (1986)	USA	Forestry, pine		nc B/C = 16/1
Haygreen et al. (1986)	USA	Forestry	1972–81	14–36
Newman (1986)	USA	Forestry		0–7
Westgate (1986)	USA	Forestry	1969–2000	37–111
Haque et al. (1987)	Canada	Eggs	1968–84	106–123
Harvey (1988)	U.K.	Agricultural research and extension	Present	−37.5
Beck (1988)	U.K.	Horticultural crop protection	1979–2001	50
Ernstberger (1989)	Brazil	Rice		66–78
Hust et al. (1988)	Canada	Swine	1968–84	45
Luz Barbosa et al. (1988)	Brazil	Aggregate	1974–97	40
Zachariah et al. (1988)	Canada	Broilers	1968–84	8–4
Power and Russell (1988)	U.K.	Poultry feeding research	1980	Benefit cost rate of 10
World Bank (1988)	Burkina Faso Cote d'Ivoire and Togo	Cotton		11–41
Zachariah et al. (1988)	Uruguay	Rice	1965–85	52
Fox et al. (1989)	Canada	Dairy	1968–84	97
Schwartz et al. (1989)	Senegal	Cowpeas	1981–87	60–80
Bojanic and Echeverría (1990)	Bolivia (CIAT)	Soybeans	1974–89	63–80
Norton et al. (1992)	Tunisia	Seed potato	1976–85	81
Mazzueato (1992)	Kenya	Maize	1978	58
Norton and Paczkowski (1993)	USA (Va)	Aggregate	1949–89	58
Ewell (1992)	East Africa	Aggregate	1978–91	91
Schwartz et al. (1993)	Senegal	Cowpea	1980–85	31–92

Table 5
Continued

Study	Country	Commodity	Period	IRR%
Mazzueato and Ly (1994)	Niger	Cowpea, millot and sorghum	1975–91	0
Laker-Ojok (1994)	Uganda	Sunflower, cowpea, Soybean	1985–91	0
Boughton and Henry de Frahan (1994)	Mali	Maize	1969–91	135
Sanders (1994)	Ghana	Maize	1968–92	74
	Cameroon	Sorghum	1980–92	2
Smale and Heisey (1994)	Malawi	Maize	1957–92	4–64
Ahmed et al. (1995)	Sudan	Sorghum	1979–92	53–97
Seck et al. (1995)	Senegal	Cotton	1985–93	34–37
Ouédraego et al. (1995)	Burkina Faso	Aggregate	1988–94	7
Seidi (1996)	Guinea Bissau	Rice	1986–94	26

research services variable(s) and the direct estimation of a coefficient(s) for this variable. Economic impacts in the form of (marginal) IRRs were computed and reported in the studies of this group (see Table 6).

4.1. The project evaluation (economic surplus) studies

The term project evaluation is used here to refer to the use of methods relying on evidence from different sources to measure economic impact.

All methods should, in principle, address locational and timing dimensions. For project evaluation studies these dimensions are generally inherent in the project setup. One of the first and most important studies of this type was the hybrid corn study by Griliches (1958). Griliches did not treat the development of a single variety of hybrid corn or even the set of varieties released in Iowa as the project being evaluated. He recognized that the project encompassed the pre-invention science (PS) entailed in inventing a method of inventing (i.e., the hybridization methodology) and covered applied agricultural research (plant breeding) in both public and private R&D programs.

Griliches also recognized spillover barriers. The pattern of adoption of hybrid corn varieties varied by state because of high degrees of locational specificity of hybrid corn varieties. Alabama did not adopt hybrid corn varieties until applied hybrid corn breeding programs were developed in Alabama, targeting varieties to the soil and climate conditions in Alabama.

The Griliches study set forth the basics of the measurement of benefits. Hybrid corn varieties, when adopted, reduce marginal and average costs, and shift the supply curve to the right (which in competition is the summation of the marginal costs of farmers above the minimum point on the average variable cost curves). Economic benefits are the

Table 6
Economic impact studies: Public sector agricultural research: Statistical methods

Study	Country	Commodity	Period	Prod. structure	IRR
Tang (1963)	Japan	Aggregate	1880–58	MPF	35
Griliches (1964)	USA	Aggregate	1949–59	MPF	25–40
Latimer (1964)	USA	Aggregate	1949–59	MPF	n.s.
Peterson (1967)	USA	Poultry	1915–60	MPF	21–25
Evenson (1968)	USA	Aggregate	1949–59	MPF,T	47
Barletta (1970)	Mexico	All crops	1943–63	PD	45–93
Elias (1971)	Argentina	Sugarcane	1943–63		33–49
Duncan (1972)	Australia	Pastures	1948–69	MPF	58–68
Evenson and Jha (1973)	India	Aggregate	1953–71	PD	40
Cline (1975)	USA	Aggregate	1939–48	MPF	41–50
del Rey (1975)	Argentina	Sugarcane	1943–64	MPF	35–41
Bredahl and Peterson (1976)	USA	Aggregate	1937–42	MPF	56
	USA	Aggregate	1947–57	MPF	51
	USA	Aggregate	1957–62	MPF	49
	USA	Aggregate	1967–72	MPF	34
Kahlon et al. (1977)	India	Aggregate	1960–73	MPF	63
	India	Aggregate	1956–73	MPF	14–64
Lu et al. (1979)	USA	Aggregate	1938–72	MPF	24–31
Evenson and Flores (1978)	Asia (all)	Rice	1950–65	PP(Y)	32–39
	Asia (NARs)	Rice	1966–75	PP(Y)	73–78
	Asia (IRRI)	Rice	1966–75	PP(Y)	74–102
Flores et al. (1978)	Philippines	Rice	1966–75	PP(Y)	75
	Tropical Asia	Rice	1966–75	PP(Y)	46–71
Nagy and Furtan (1978)	Canada	Rapeseed	1960–75	MPF	90–110
Kislev and Hoffman (1978)	Israel	Wheat	1954–73	MPF	125–150
	Israel	Dry farming	1954–73	MPF	94–113
	Israel	Field Crop	1954–73	MPF	13–16
Evenson (1979)	USA	Aggregate	1868–1926	PD,T,G	65
	USA	Aggregate	1927–50	PP,T,G	95
	USA – South	Aggregate	1948–71	PD,T,G	130
	USA – North	Aggregate	1948–71	PD,T,G	93
	USA – West	Aggregate	1948–71	PD,T,G	95
Knutson and Tweeten (1979)	USA	Aggregate	1949–72	MPF (Alt)	28–47
Lu et al. (1979)	USA	Aggregate	1939–72	MPF	23–30
White et al. (1978)	USA	Aggregate	1929–77	MPF	28–37
Davis (1979)	USA	Aggregate	1949–59	MPF	66–100
Davis and Peterson (1981)	USA	Aggregate	1949	MPF	100
	USA	Aggregate	1954	MPF	79
	USA	Aggregate	1959	MPF	66
	USA	Aggregate	1964, 1969, 1974	MPF	37
Hasting (1981)	Australia	Aggregate	1946–68	MPF	nc (ss)
Norton (1981)	USA	Cash grains	1969–74	MPF	31–44
	USA	Poultry	1969–74	MPF	30–56
	USA	Dairy	1969–74	MPF	27–33
	USA	Livestock	1969–74	MPF	56–66

Table 6
Continued

Study	Country	Commodity	Period	Prod. structure	IRR
Otto and Havlicek (1981)	USA	Corn	1967–79	MPF	152–212
	USA	Wheat	1967–79	MPF	79–148
	USA	Soybeans	1967–79	MPF	188
Sundquist et al. (1981)	USA	Corn	1977	PP(Y)	115
	USA	Wheat	1977	PD(Y)	97
	USA	Soybeans	1977	PD(Y)	118
Welch and Evenson (1989)	USA	Aggregate	1969	MPF	55
Abidogun (1982)	Nigeria	Cocoa	1980		42
Evenson (1982)	Brazil	Aggregate	1966–74 (est)	MPF	69
White and Havlicek (1982)	USA	Aggregate	1943–77	MPF	7–36
Smith et al. (1983)	USA	Dairy	1978	MPF	25
	USA	Poultry	1978	MPF	61
	USA	Beef, swine, sheep	1978	MPF	22
Feijoo (1984)	Argentina	Aggregate	1950–80	MPF	41
Makau (1984)	Kenya	Wheat	1922–80	PD(Y)	33
Salmon (1984)	Indonesia	Rice	1965–77	PD(Y)	133
da Silva (1984)	Brazil (Sao Paulo)	Aggregate	1970–80	MPF	60–102
Doyle and Ridout (1985)	U.K.	Aggregate	1966–80	MPF	30
Nagy (1985)	Pakistan	Aggregate	1959–79	MPF	64
Ulrich et al. (1985)	Canada	Malting barley		PD(Y)	51
Boyle (1986)	Ireland	Aggregate	1963–83	MPF	26
Braha and Tweeten (1986)	USA	Aggregate	1959–82	MPF	47
Fox (1986)	USA	Livestock	1944–83	MPF	150
	USA	Crops	1944–83	MPF	180
Khan and Akbari (1986)	Pakistan	Aggregate	1955–81	MPF	36
Wise (1986)	U.K.	Aggregate	1986	MPF	8–15
Evenson (1987)	India	Aggregate	1959–75	PD,T,G	100
Librero and Perez (1987)	Philippines	Maize	1956–83	MPF	27–48
Librero and Perez (1987)	Philippines	Sugarcane	1956–83	MPF	51–71
Scobie and Eveleens (1987)	New Zealand	Aggregate	1976–84	MPF	30
Seldon (1987)	USA	Forestry (products)	1950–80	MPF	163+
Seldon and Newman (1987)	USA	Forestry (products)	1950–86	MPF	236+
Sumelius (1987)	Finland	Aggregate	1950–84	MPF	25–76
Tung and Strain [see Echeverría (1990)]	Canada	Aggregate	1961–80	MPF	high
Librero et al. (1988)	Philippines	Mango	1956–83	PD(Y)	85–107
Russel and Thirtle [see Echeverría (1990)]	U.K.	Rapeseed	1976–85	PD(Y)	BC = 327
Thirtle and Bottomley (1988)	U.K.	Aggregate	1950–81	MPF	70
Evenson (1989)	USA	Aggregate	1950–82	MPF,T,G	43
Evenson (1989)	USA	Crops	1950–82	MPF,T,G	45
Evenson (1989)	USA	Livestock	1950–82	MPF,T,G	11

Table 6
Continued

Study	Country	Commodity	Period	Prod. structure	IRR
Ribeiro (1982)	India	Pearl millet	1987		57
Evenson and McKinsey (1991)	India	Rice	1954–84	MPF,T,G	65
Librero and Emlano (1990)	Philippines	Poultry	1948–81	MPF	154
Pray and Ahmed (1991)	Pakistan	Aggregate	1948–81	MPF	100
Byerlee (1991)	Pakistan	Wheat	1965–88	PD	15–20
Karanjan (1990)	Kenya	Maize	1955–88	PD	40–60
Karanjan (1990)	Kenya	Wheat	1955–88	PD	68
Nagy (1991)	Pakistan	Maize	1967–81	PD	19
	Pakistan	Wheat	1967–81	PD	58
Azam et al. (1991)	Pakistan	Applied research	1956–85	PD,T	58
	Pakistan	Commodity research	1956–85	PD,T	88
	Pakistan	Wheat	1956–85	PD,T	76
	Pakistan	Rice	1956–85	PD,T	84–89
	Pakistan	Maize	1956–85	PD,T	46
	Pakistan	Bajra	1956–85	PD,T	44
	Pakistan	Jowar	1956–85	PD,T	52
	Pakistan	Cotton	1956–85	PD,T	102
Azam et al. (1991)	Pakistan	Sugarcane	1956–85	PD,T	ns
Evenson and McKinsey (1991)	India	Aggregate	1958–83	PD,T,G	65
	India	Wheat	1958–83	PD(Y),T,G	50
	India	Rice	1958–83	PD(Y),T,G	155
	India	Maize	1958–83	PD(Y),T,G	94
	India	Bajra	1958–83	PD(Y),T,G	107
	India	All cereals	1958–83	PD(Y),T,G	218
Dey and Evenson (1991)	Bangladesh	All crops	1973–89	PD	143
	Bangladesh	Rice	1973–89	PD(Y),T	165
	Bangladesh	Wheat	1973–89	PD(Y),T	85
	Bangladesh	Jute	1973–89	PD(Y),T	48
	Bangladesh	Potato	1973–89	PD(Y),T	129
	Bangladesh	Sugarcane	1973–89	PD(Y),T	94
	Bangladesh	Pulses	1973–89	PD(Y),T	25
	Bangladesh	Oilseeds	1973–89	PD(Y),T	57
Iqbal (1991)	Pakistan – Punjab	Rice	1971–88	MPF	42–72
	Pakistan – Sind	Rice	1971–88	MPF	50
	Pakistan – NWFD	Rice	1971–88	MPF	36–11
	Pakistan – Punjab	Cotton	1971–88	MPF	95–102
	Pakistan – Sind	Cotton	1971–88	MPF	49–51
Setboonsarng and Evenson (1991)	Thailand	Rice	1967–80	MPF	40
Evenson and Quizon (1991)	Philippines	Aggregate	1948–84	PF	70
	Philippines	National	1948–84	PF	50
	Philippines	Regional	1948–84	PF	100
Evenson (1992)	India	Aggregate	1959–75	MPF,T,G	72
Kumar and Mruthyunjaya (1992)	India	Cattle	1969–85	MPF	29

Table 6
Continued

Study	Country	Commodity	Period	Prod. structure	IRR
Evenson (1991)	USA	Applied – crop	1950–85	PD	45
	USA	Applied – livestock	1950–85	PD	11
Evenson (1992)	Indonesia	All crops	1971–89	PD,T	212
	Indonesia	Rice	1971–89	PD,T	285
	Indonesia	Maize	1971–89	PD,T	145
	Indonesia	Soybeans	1972–89	PD,T	184
	Indonesia	Mung beans	1971–89	PD,T	158
	Indonesia	Cassava	1971–89	PD,T	ns
	Indonesia	Groundnut	1971–89	PD,T	110
Fan and Pardey (1992)	China	All crops	1965–89	MFP	20
Rosegrant and Evenson (1993)	India	Public research	1956–87	PD,T,G	67
Evenson and Gollin (1996)	IRRI	Rice germplasm	1965–90	PD,T,G	100+
Huffman and Evenson (1993)	USA	Applied – crop	1950–85	PD,T,G	47
	USA	Applied – livestock	1950–85	PD,T,G	45
Evenson et al. (1994)	Indonesia	upland rice	1979–92	PD(Y),T,G	100+
	Indonesia	Irrigated rice	1979–82	PD(Y),T,G	100+
	Indonesia	Maize	1979–82	PD(Y),T,G	100+
	Indonesia	Soybeans	1979–82	PD(Y),T,G	10
	Indonesia	Cassava	1979–82	PD(Y),T,G	0
	Indonesia	Groundnut	1979–82	PD(Y),T,G	10
	Indonesia	Sweet potato	1979–82	PD(Y),T,G	100+
	Indonesia	Mung bean	1979–82	PD(Y),T,G	40
Evenson et al. (1994)	Indonesia	Cabbage	1979–82	PP(Y),T,G	100+
	Indonesia	Potato	1979–82	PP(Y),T,G	100
	Indonesia	Garlic	1979–82	PD(Y),T,G	100+
	Indonesia	Mustard	1979–82	PD(Y),T,G	100+
	Indonesia	Onion	1979–82	PD(Y),T,G	100+
	Indonesia	Shallot	1979–82	PD(Y),T,G	100+
	Indonesia	Rubber	1979–82	PD(Y),T,G	100+
	Indonesia	Oil palm	1979–82	PD(Y),T,G	100+
	Indonesia	Coffee	1979–82	PD(Y),T,G	20–100
	Indonesia	Tea	1979–82	PD(Y),T,G	60–100
	Indonesia	Sugar	1979–82	PD(Y),T,G	50–100
	Indonesia	Orange	1979–82	PD(Y),T,G	80
	Indonesia	Banana	1979–82	PD(Y),T,G	100+
	Indonesia	Papaya	1979–82	PD(Y),T,G	100+
	Indonesia	Mango	1979–82	PD(Y),T,G	0
	Indonesia	Pineapple	1979–82	PD(Y),T,G	100+
	Indonesia	Durian	1979–82	PD(Y),T,G	0
	Indonesia	Meat	1979–82	PD(Y),T,G	0
	Indonesia	Milk	1979–82	PD(Y),T,G	100+
	Indonesia	Eggs	1979–82	PD(Y),T,G	0

Table 6
Continued

Study	Country	Commodity	Period	Prod. structure	IRR
Evenson and Avila (1996)	Brazil	State research			
	Brazil	Soybeans	1979–92	PD(Y),T,G	40
	Brazil	Maize	1979–92	PD(Y),T,G	62
	Brazil	Beans	1979–92	PD(Y),T,G	54
	Brazil	Rice	1979–92	PD(Y),T,G	46
	Brazil	Wheat	1979–92	PD(Y),T,G	42
	Brazil	Federal research			
	Brazil	Soybean	1979–92	PD(Y),T,G	40
	Brazil	Maize	1979–92	PD(Y),T,G	58
	Brazil	Beans	1979–92	PD(Y),T,G	0
	Brazil	Rice	1979–92	PD(Y),T,G	37
	Brazil	Wheat	1979–92	PD(Y),T,G	40
Alston et al. (1998a)	USA	Aggregate		MPF,T	17–31
Chavas and Cox (1992)	USA	Aggregate		MPF	28
Townsend and van Zyl (1997)	South Africa	Wine grapes		MFP	40
Gopinath and Roe (1996)	USA	Aggregate		CF	37
Thirtle et al. (1997)	United Kingdom	Wheat			20+
Townsend et al. (1997)	South Africa	Maize			28–39
Traxler and Byerlee (1992)	Mexico	Crop mgmt			16–23
Makki et al. (1996)	USA	Aggregate	1930–1990		27
Makki and Tweeten (1993)	USA	Aggregate	1930–1990		93
Oehmke (1996)	USA	Aggregate	Pre–1930		neg
	USA	Aggregate	1930–1990		11.6
Morris et al. (1994)	Nepal	Wheat	1960–1990		84
Traxler and Pingali (1996)	India	Wheat			
Yee (1992)	USA	Aggregate	1931–85	MPF	49–58
Norton et al. (1992)	USA	Aggregate	1987	MPF	30
	USA	Cash grains	1987	MPF	31
	USA	Vegetables	1987	MPF	19
	USA	Fruits	1987	MPF	33
	USA	Other field crops	1987	MPF	34
	USA	Dairy	1987	MPF	95
	USA	Poultry	1987	MPF	46
	USA	Other livestock	1987	MPF	55
Khatri et al. (1995)	South Africa	Aggregate			44
Makana and Oehmke (1996)	Kenya	Wheat		PD(Y)	0–12
Akgunkov et al. (1996)	Kenya	Wheat	1921–90		14–30
Isinika (1995)	Tanzania	Aggregate	1972–92		33

change in consumer's and producer's surpluses and are measured by the area under the demand curve between the original supply curve and the shifted supply curve. Griliches noted that this area is well approximated by the change in average variable costs times the original quantity produced. (The elasticity of demand is crucial to the division of economic surplus between consumers and producers, but only affects the size of the small triangle for measurement of economic surplus.)[30]

Griliches (1958) used farm experimental data in a with-without design to measure the average variable cost shift associated with hybrid varieties.[31] With information on adoption rates and the size of the shift, a benefit stream from 1900 to 1957 was created. A cost stream (including both public sector and private firm costs) was also estimated. Griliches (1958) then performed the standard investment calculations to compute the present value of benefits and costs in 1957:

$$PVB_{57} = \sum_{t=1900}^{1957} b_t (1.05)^{t-1900}, \tag{18}$$

$$PVC_{57} = \sum_{t=1900}^{1957} c_t (1.05)^{t-1900}. \tag{19}$$

Griliches then computed the following ratio:

$$\frac{PVB_{57} \times .05 + b_{57}}{PVC_{57} \times .05 + c_{57}}. \tag{20}$$

This procedure converted the cumulated present values to flows, and under the assumption that 1957 benefits (b_{57}) and costs (c_{57}) would continue indefinitely, this ratio was interpreted as a "dollars benefit per dollar cost" ratio. The ratio (approximately 7) was sometimes interpreted as a 700 percent rate of return on investment. Griliches himself later noted that it should be interpreted as a modified benefit-cost ratio, not as a rate of return [Griliches (1998)]. He also computed the internal rate of return for the program (the rate of discount at which $PVB_{57} = PVC_{57}$) to be approximately 44 percent.

The Griliches study established the basic project evaluation methods for subsequent studies where project outcomes were measurable (e.g., adoption of hybrid corn varieties). These included:

(a) carefully defining the project's locational and timing dimensions;
(b) measuring project costs;
(c) measuring project outputs (adoption of hybrid corn varieties);

---

[30] There is little evidence that supply curve shifts have a convergence pattern. There is some evidence [see Evenson and Huffman (1993)] for technology-induced increases in farm size. This would be consistent with divergent supply curve shifts. Huffman and Evenson (1993) note that different magnitudes of shifts for farms of different sizes (e.g., large farms realize shifts, while small farms do not) do not produce non-parallel supply curve shifts.

[31] This shift was estimated to be 28 percent. Many non-economists contend that new technology must have a significant cost advantage (e.g., doubling) before it is adopted. Most careful studies show that this is not the case.

(d) estimating the economic impact of project outputs (i.e., on farm production, costs, and supply);

(e) converting economic impact estimates to project benefit estimates;

(f) performing economic calculations for PVB/PVC, PVB-PVC, and the internal rate of return where PVB = PVC.

Many of the studies summarized in Table 5 actually used statistical evidence. Some are based on time-series data only. Others used repeated cross-section data. The studies in Table 5 are distinguished from those in Table 6 in that they did not generally explicitly address the question of defining a research services variable. Most of the commodity studies summarized in Table 5, while based on partial factor productivity measures (yield changes), did attempt to correct for the "partial" bias by utilizing other input, quantity, and price data.

The 60-plus studies summarized in Table 5 covered a broad range of commodities in a broad range of countries. Almost all report high to very high internal rates of return. (Many studies reported a range of IRRs as noted in Table 5.)

4.2. Studies based on research variable coefficient estimates

In Table 6 a summary of roughly 120 studies utilizing research variable coefficient estimates is made. Some of these are also included in Table 3, where extension IRRs are reported. All of these studies are based on aggregate data. A few are based on cross-section data only. A larger number are based on time-series data. Most are based on repeated cross-section data. As with Table 5, a broad range of countries and commodities are studied, and as with Table 5, most IRRs are in the high to very high range.

The studies summarized in Table 4, where research and extension expenditure data are amalgamated into a single variable, are comparable to some of the studies summarized in Table 6. As noted in the discussion of time shapes and of spatial weights and deflators, the amalgamated variables present very difficult weighting problems. For the most part, the studies summarized in Table 4 were based on crude time lags and deflators as were many of the studies summarized in Table 6. They are probably best interpreted as research studies rather than extension studies.

Relatively few of the studies summarized in Table 6 actually estimated time weights (noted as T). Relatively few incorporated geographic spill-in specificators (noted by G). Most undertook some form of deflation (sometimes via dummy variables).

Several of the studies summarized in Table 6 also included pre-invention science and industrial R&D spill-in variables (these are summarized in Section 5).

Virtually all studies summarized in Tables 4 and 6 reported statistical significance for coefficient estimates of the research variable utilized. The rates of return calculated from these coefficients and the time weights cover a broad range.

As will be noted in the summary, there is a difference between evaluations of aggregate research programs and commodity research programs, with most of the very high IRRs being reported for the commodity programs. It will also be noted that the studies of applied agricultural research using project evaluation methods report fewer very high IRRs than do the studies using statistical methods.

Approximately half of the 200-plus IRRs reported in Table 6 utilized the meta production function structure. Approximately one-quarter used TFP decomposition and one-quarter used a yield decomposition structure. (Very few used the duality format in spite of its obvious richness.)

Many studies report a range of IRRs; only a few of these are average IRRs because most use statistical procedures to estimate impacts.

5. Studies of industrial R&D spill-in and pre-invention science spill-in

Surveys of research expenditure in recent years have identified considerable industrial R&D directed toward products sold to and used in the agricultural sector. Agricultural machinery and agricultural chemicals are obvious cases where industrial R&D is directed toward the improvement of agricultural inputs. Johnson and Evenson (1999) report estimates of patented inventions manufactured in a number of industries that are used in the agricultural sector.

Early studies argued that if the product improvements resulting from this R&D were priced to reflect the full value of the improvement, agricultural productivity would be unaffected by industrial R&D. Recent studies conclude, however, that when new industrial products first come on the market they are priced to only partially capture the real value of the improvement (most new models of equipment are better buys than the equipment that they replace). This produces a spill-in impact.

Table 7 summarizes several studies incorporating industrial R&D variables. As will be noted in the summary, the social (private plus spillover) rate of return to this industrial R&D is roughly equal to the social rate of return to public agricultural research.

Another type of spill-in that is recognized in few studies is the "recharge" spill-in from pre-invention science. Many of the studies summarized in Tables 4, 5, and 6

Table 7
Economic impact studies: Private sector R&D spill-in

Study	Country/region	Period of study	Productive structure	IRR
Rosegrant and Evenson (1993)	India	1956–87	PD	Dom 50+ For 50+
Huffman and Evenson (1993)	USA	1950–85	PD	Crops 41
Ulrich et al. (1985)	Canada		PD	Malting barley 35
Gopinath and Roe (1996)	USA	1991	CF	Food processing 7.2 Farm machinery 1.6 Total social 46.2
Evenson (1991)	USA	1950–85	PD	Crop 45–71 Livestock 81–89
Evenson and Avila (1996)	Brazil	1970–75–80–85	PD	nc

Table 8
Economic impact studies: Pre-invention science

Study	Country	Period of study	Production structure	EMIRR
Evenson (1979)	USA	1927–50	PD	110
		1946–71	PD	45
Huffman and Evenson (1993)	USA	1950–85	PD	Crop 57
				Livestock 83
				Aggregate 64
Evenson et al. (1999)	India	1954–87	PD	Domestic
				Foreign
Evenson and Flores (1978)	Int. (IRRI)	1966–75	PD	74–100
Evenson (1991)	USA	1950–85	PD	Crops 40–59
				Livestock 54–83
Azam et al. (1991)	Pakistan	1966–68	PD,T	39

actually covered a wide range of research program activities including many pre-invention science activities. The studies summarized in Table 8 specifically identified pre-invention expenditures and activities. It may be noted that these studies report relatively high rates of return.

6. *Ex ante* studies

Research and extension programs in either public or private sector organizations require both design and resource allocation decisions. The project evaluation framework has been applied to many research and extension investment decisions. The World Bank and other lending or granting agencies require what is in effect *ex ante* impact evaluation studies as an integral part of the lending process. Yet it is probably fair to say that *ex ante* studies of research and extension lack credibility in these agencies.

Part of the problem with credibility is inherent in the high degree of uncertainty in extension and especially in research projects. As noted in an earlier section, research is subject to considerable uncertainty, including uncertainty as to the parameters of the search pool in which inventions are sought. Some of this uncertainty is associated with the fact that many of the important international and national agencies have not undertaken the *ex ante–ex post* evaluations required to establish credibility in *ex ante* (and in *ex post*) studies. It is of some interest to note that very few of the *ex post* studies reviewed have been completed by staff of the lending agencies or of national programs.[32]

---

[32] The World Bank's OED study of agricultural research and extension [Purcell and Anderson (1997)] did call for higher standards of *ex ante* evaluation of extension projects (and of research projects as well) but

The *ex ante* methodology as it has evolved since the early work of Fishel (1971) is based on the simple investment calculation:

$$PVB_0 = \sum_{t=0}^{\infty} (b/u)_t U_t / (1+\pi)^t,$$

$$PVC_0 = \sum_{t=0}^{\infty} C_t / (1+\pi)^t. \tag{21}$$

For a given research problem area (RPA) and a given research technique (RT) the *ex ante* analyst typically must specify the key design elements of the project and its magnitude. Thus PVC_0 is often specified initially (e.g., this could be a project seeking host plant drought tolerance through conventional breeding techniques, the project would specify the strategies, the pre-breeding activity, number of years, etc.).

Benefits can be separated into benefits per unit per year $(b/u)_t$ and units per year, U_t. At least one of these terms must be obtained by subjective probability estimation (SPE) by scientists with specialized knowledge (e.g., plant breeders with breeding experience and knowledge of genetic sources for drought tolerance). The "units" measure may also require estimation, but typically from different sources. One of the principles of *ex ante* analysis is that the best sources of information be consulted for each component.

Typically, the estimate $(b/u)_t$ has both a timing and a level effect. Since many projects are part of a sequence, it is often the case that the "achievement" estimate is stated in terms of potential achievement and achievement to date. This clarifies what is meant by remaining achievement. Then years-to-achievement estimates can be obtained associated with the potential achievement. In order to allow the source to express uncertainty about the estimate, the analyst can ask for a range of probabilities of achievement or, as in a recent rice research study, years to 25 percent achievement and years to 75 percent achievement [Evenson et al. (1996)].

Table 9 summarizes *ex ante* studies reported in various publications. Some of these studies are pure *ex ante* studies. Others are combined *ex ante–ex post* studies.

Interestingly, as noted in the next section, the rates of return computed for *ex ante* studies have less variability than those for *ex post* studies. They also have a lower mean and median.

---

did not attempt the *ex post–ex ante* comparisons required to give credibility to *ex ante* studies. It chose to stress informal *ex post* ratings of projects and was critical of existing *ex post* economic impact studies. The OED study was primarily concerned with the management and design issues associated with extension. It reached the conclusion that the Bank's T&V management focus was not the most effective management style for extension, although it is difficult to find the basis for this conclusion in the report. The *ex post* studies (see Tables 1 and 2) which concluded that T&V-managed extension programs did have an economic impact, but were less conclusive as to whether the T&V management style was more productive than alternatives, were criticized in the report.

Table 9
Ex ante economic impact studies of agricultural research programs

Study	Country/region	Period of study	Commodity	*Ex ante* IRR
Monteiro (1975)	Brazil	1923–1985	Cocoa	19–20
Fonseca (1976)	Brazil	1933–1995	Coffee	23–27
Easter and Norton (1977)	USA		Maize	
		1982–2000	Crop protection	B/C 137:1
		1985–2000	Production efficiency	B/C 118:1
	USA		Soybeans	
		1982–2000	Crop protection	45:1
		1985–2000	Production efficiency	40:1
Eddleman (1977)	USA	1978–1985	Aggregate	28
			Maize	32
			Soybeans	31
			Wheat	46
			Beef cattle and forage	16
			Swine	52
			Dairy	38
Moricochi (1980)	Brazil (Sao Paulo)	1933–1985	Citrus	18–28
Araji (1981)	USA	1978–2000	Integrated pest management	0–191
da Cruz et al. (1982)	Brazil	1974–1981	Physical capital	53
	Brazil	1974–1992	Total investment	22–43
Ribeiro (1982)	Brazil (M. Gerais)	1974–1994	Aggregate	69
			Cotton	48
			Soybeans	36
da Cruz et al. (1982)	Brazil (EMBRAPA)	1974–1996	Human capital	22–30
da Cruz and Avila (1983)	Brazil (EMBRAPA)	1977–1991	Aggregate	38
Ambrosi and da Cruz (1984)	Brazil (EMBRAPA-CNPT)	1974–1990	Wheat	59–74
Avila et al. (1984)	Brazil (South Central)	1974–1996	Aggregate	38
Bengston (1984)	USA	1975–2000	Forestry (structural particleboard)	19–22
Ulrich et al. (1985)	Canada		Canola	51
Muchnik (1985)	Latin America	1968–1990	Rice	17–44
Martinez and Norton (1986)	USA		Broilers	100+
			Eggs	
Westgate (1986)	USA	1969–2000	Forestry (timber, containerized seedlings)	37–111
Norton et al. (1987)	Peru (INIPA)	1981–2000	Aggregate	17–38
			Rice	17–44
			Maize	10–31
			Wheat	18–36

Table 9
Continued

Study	Country/ region	Period of study	Commodity	*Ex ante* IRR
			Potatoes	22–42
			Beans	14–24
Valdivia (1997)	Indonesia		Small ruminant research	19–25
Norgaard (1988)	Africa	1977–2003	Cassava	B/C 149:1
Henry de Frahan et al. (1989)	Mali	1990–2010	Aggregate	1–25
Karanja (1990)	Kenya	1955–1988	Maize	40–60
Schwartz and Oehmke (1990)	Senegal	1981–2005	cowpea	63
Seré and Jarvis (1998)	Latin America	1987–2037	Pastures	15–20
MacMillan et al. (1991)	Zimbabwe	1991–1996	Maize	B/C 1.35:1
Henry de Frahan et al. (1989)	Mali		Farming-systems research (FSR)	1
Sterns et al. (1993)	West Africa	1981–2017	Training	22–31
Laker-Ojok (1994)	Uganda	1985–2006	Maize	27–58
			Sunflower	10–66
			Soybean	0–20
Morris et al. (1994)	Nepal		Wheat varieties	49
Smale et al. (1998)	Mexico		Bread wheat disease resistance	40
Sterns and Bernsten (1994)	Cameroon	1979–1998	Cowpea	15
			Sorghum	1
Mazzueato and Ly (1994)	Niger	1975–2011	Millet, sorghum, and cowpea	2–10
Bertelsen and Ouédraego (N.d.)	Burkina Faso	1990–2003	Zaï	53
Fisher et al. (1995)	Senegal	1995–2004	Rice	66–83
Tre (1995)	Sierra Leone	1976–2010	Rice	18–21
Anandajayasekeram and Martella (1995)	Zimbabwe	1980–1999	Sorghum	22
	Namibia	1988–1999	Millet	11
Byerlee and Traxler (1995)	International	1970–1990	Wheat varieties	37–48
Mudhara et al. (1995)	Zimbabwe	1970–1995	Cotton	47
Kuyvenhoven et al. (1996)	Mali		Rock phosphate	43–271
Aghib and Lowenberg-DeBoer (N.d.)	10 countries	1985–2009	Sorghum	58
Chisi et al. (1997)	Zambia	1983–2005	Sorghum	12–19
Valdivia (1997)	Indonesia		Small ruminant research	19–25
Norgaard (1988)	Africa	1977–2003	Cassava	149:1
Schwartz and Oehmke (1990)	Senegal	1981–2005	Cowpea	63
MacMillan et al. (1991)	Zimbabwe	1991–1996	Maize	1.35:1
Henry de Frahan et al. (1989)	Mali		Farming-systems research	1
Sterns et al. (1993)	West Africa	1981–2017	Training	22–31
Laker-Ojok (1994)	Uganda	1985–2006	Maize	27–58
			Sunflower	10–66
			Soybean	0–20

Table 9
Continued

Study	Country/ region	Period of study	Commodity	*Ex ante* IRR
Sterns and Bernsten (1994)	Cameroon	1979–1996	Cowpea	15
			Sorghum	1
Mazzueato and Ly (1994)	Niger	1975–2011	Millet, sorghum, and cowpea	2–10
Bertelsen and Ouédraego (N.d.)	Burkina Faso	1990–2003	Zaï	53
Fisher et al. (1995)	Senegal	1995–2004	Rice	66–83
Tre (1995)	Sierra Leone	1976–2010	Rice	18–21
Anandajayasekeram and	Zimbabwe	1980–1999	Sorghum	22
Martella (1995)	Namibia	1988–1999	Millet	11
Kuyvenhoven et al. (1996)	Mali		Rock phosphate	43–27
Aghib and Lowenberg-DeBoer (N.d.)	10 countries	1985–2009	Sorghum	58
Chisi et al. (1997)	Zambia	1983–2005	Sorghum	12–19

7. Assessing the IRR evidence

The IRR evidence summarized in Tables 1–7 covers many studies, commodities, and regions. The studies, however, cannot be regarded as a truly representative sample of economic impact studies of research and extension programs because of "selectivity" bias. This bias takes two forms. First, highly successful programs are more likely to be evaluated. Second, "unsuccessful" evaluations, i.e., evaluations showing no impact, are less likely to be published than evaluations showing impact. There are, however, two factors that suggest that this bias may not be so serious as to render comparative assessments of this evidence to be of little value or relevance. The first is that one can compare the studies covering aggregate programs with studies of specific (successful) commodity programs. The aggregate programs include both successful and unsuccessful programs. The second is that the evidence is based on a substantial part of the world's agricultural research and extension programs.

With the appropriate caveats regarding selectivity, it will be useful to assess the IRR evidence by making comparisons between programs, regions, and periods. It will also be useful to assess the IRR evidence against the model discussed in Part II and against the arithmetic of growth. As noted earlier in this review, many reviewers of development experience suggest that most of the IRRs summarized here are overestimated.[33]

---

[33] This perception is often accompanied by a perception that significant economic growth can be obtained with few resources. TFP methods often create the impression that some growth is a residual "manna from heaven". In practice most TFP decomposition studies show that growth is not available "for nothing". But they also show that when technology infrastructure levels are adequate, small investments in growth production can have very high returns.

Table 10

Growth rate consistency comparisons. Annual growth rates in TFP required to support one percent
of product investment

Time weights	IRR (percent)			
	20	40	60	100
1. Extension (1, 1, 1 0 –)	.39 (SR)	.45 (SR)	.50 (SR)	.57 (SR)
2. Extension (1, 1, .1 .5 –)	.39 (SR)	.45 (SR)	.50 (SR)	.57 (SR)
	.1 (LR)	.2 (LR)	.3 (LR)	.5 (LR)
3. Research (0, .2, .4, .6, .8, 1 –)	.31	.76	1.40	2.80
4. Research (0, .1, .2, .3, .4, .5, .6, .8, .9 1 –)	.42	.87	2.22	5.02

Turning first to the overestimation issue. Are the high IRRs reported inconsistent with actual growth experience? Table 10 reports the growth rate implications for two extension program time weight schemes and two research program time weight schemes for IRRs of 20, 40, 60, and 100 percent.

Consider the first extension time weight program where the effect of extension is simply to speed up adoption three years earlier than it would have occurred in the absence of the program. In the short run, i.e., in the first years after introducing the program, growth rates will be higher. But this will not produce a higher long-run rate of TFP growth.

Now consider the research programs where the contribution of the research program does not depreciate. The two weight sets represent the range of weights for most of the studies reviewed. Weight set 3 is a rapid research effect with the weights rising to the full effect in the sixth year after an investment of one percent of the value of production. A continuous program of investment of one percent of product each year must then produce TFP growth of .31 for an IRR of 20, .76 for an IRR of 40, 1.4 percent for an IRR of 60, and 2.8 percent for an IRR of 100. Weight set 4 is for a slower impact where the full effect of the program is realized in the eleventh year after investment. The growth rates required for these weights are higher. The second extension case is one where one-half of the extension contribution is permanent as in the cases where the technology infrastructure level is TI(1). The long-run growth implications of this are as noted.

IRRs for both extension and research studies are summarized in Table 11. Distributions of IRRs for a number of study categories are presented. Two features characterize virtually every category. The first is that mean and median IRRs are high. Seventy-four percent of the extension IRRs and 82 percent of the research IRRs exceed 20 percent. The second feature of the IRRs is that the range of estimates is broad. Every category (except for private sector R&D spillovers) includes studies reporting both low IRRs and high IRRs. Interestingly the category showing the narrowest range of IRRs is the *ex ante* study category.

Given the breadth of the range of IRRs in each category, it is difficult to draw strong conclusions regarding differences in means between categories. It can be noted, how-

Table 11
IRR estimates summary

	Number of IRRs reported	Percent distribution						Approx. median IRR
		0–20	21–40	41–60	61–0	81–100	100+	
Extension								
Farm observations	16	.56	0	.06	.06	.25	.06	18
Aggregate observations	29	.24	.14	.07	0	.27	.27	80
Combined research and extension	36	.14	.42	.28	.03	.08	.16	37
By region								
OECD	19	.11	.31	.16	0	.11	.16	50
Asia	21	.24	.19	.19	.14	.09	.14	47
Latin America	23	.13	.26	.34	.08	.08	.09	46
Africa	10	.40	.30	.20	.10	0	0	27
All extension	81	.26	.23	.16	.03	.19	.13	41
Applied research								
Project evaluation	121	.25	.31	.14	.18	.06	.07	40
Statistical	254	.14	.20	.23	.12	.10	.20	50
Aggregate programs	126	.16	.27	.29	.10	.09	.09	45
Commodity programs								
Wheat	30	.30	.13	.17	.10	.13	.17	51
Rice	48	.08	.23	.19	.27	.08	.14	60
Maize	25	.12	.28	.12	.16	.08	.24	56
Other cereals	27	.26	.15	.30	.11	.07	.11	47
Fruits and vegetables	34	.18	.18	.09	.15	.09	.32	67
All crops	207	.19	.19	.14	.16	.10	.21	58
Forest products	13	.23	.31	.68	.16	0	.23	37
Livestock	32	.21	.31	.25	.09	.03	.09	36
By region								
OECD	146	.15	.35	.21	.10	.07	.11	40
Asia	120	.08	.18	.21	.15	.11	.26	67
Latin America	80	.15	.29	.29	.15	.07	.06	47
Africa	44	.27	.27	.18	.11	.11	.05	37
All applied research	375	.18	.23	.20	.14	.08	.16	49
Pre-invention science	12	0	.17	.33	.17	.17	.17	60
Private sector R&D	11	.18	.09	.45	.09	.18	0	50
Ex ante research	87	.32	.34	.21	.06	.01	.06	42

ever, that the categories with the greatest proportions exceeding 40 percent are pre-invention science, private sector R&D, rice research, and fruits and vegetables research. Research studies have higher proportions exceeding 40 percent (59 percent) than is the case for extension studies (51 percent). Studies of commodity research programs have a higher proportion exceeding 40 percent (62 percent) than studies of aggregate research programs (57 percent).

Regional distributions vary with studies of both research and extension in Africa and have lower proportions exceeding 40 percent than in other regions. Asian research IRRs are especially high.

Actually, as noted above, some of the very high IRRs are "suspect" in that they could be inconsistent with actual economic growth experience. It is of interest to note that the proportion of very high (exceeding 80 percent) IRRs is highest for statistical commodity research studies where spending ratios are lowest (and where one may well be understating real research expenditure as well). Typically, for commodity programs even in developed countries, research/commodity value ratios are well below one percent. This is particularly true in Asia where the highest proportion of very high IRRs is reported.

The relatively high proportion of very high IRRs for extension may appear suspect, but as noted above, this is probably not inconsistent with growth experience. The high proportion of very high IRRs for pre-invention science is also consistent with growth experience because spending ratios are low.

Studies of industrial R&D indicate that the private IRRs captured by firms are generally similar to IRRs for other investments made by the firm [Mairesse and Mohnen (1995)]. These studies also show considerable spill-overs and indicate that the social rate of return is considerably higher than the private rate of return. The rate of return measured in the studies reviewed here is essentially the difference between the social and private IRR. Given that the public sector IRRs are actually social IRRs and reflect spillovers, the studies reviewed here suggest that the social IRRs for industrial R&D are also high and may well be of the same order of magnitude as public sector social IRRs.

It does not appear that there is a time trend in the IRRs reported. Studies for later periods show IRRs similar to studies of earlier periods.

While this review has not considered the few studies of determinants of investment in public sector agricultural research, it may be noted that the expansion of agricultural research and extension programs in the post World War II era of economic development has been heavily aid-driven. The training of agricultural scientists, especially in the 1950s, 1960s, and 1970s, was funded by international agencies and undertaken in leading agricultural universities in developed countries. Many NARs received grants and loans from international agencies. In recent years, international support has been declining. Some national programs have developed national support bases and these will continue to function. Others have not and are vulnerable to downsizing without international support.

The evidence for economic impacts of research and extension programs is probably more complete and comprehensive than the evidence for many other development programs (e.g., agricultural credit programs). While the range of IRR estimates is wide, the great majority of the IRR estimates indicate a high social rate of return to the investments made. Those high rates of return were realized in many NARs and IARCs and extension programs. These programs were not uniform in terms of design efficiency, scientist skills or management. Most, perhaps all, of these programs could have been improved. The broad scope of the evidence for high payoff suggests considerable international spillovers (and some studies measured this). Many research and extension programs are poorly managed and often resource-constrained. Many fail to produce proper statistical analyses of field trials. The evidence reviewed here is not inconsistent with this. But it does support the original vision of development economists. Research and extension programs have afforded high payoff investment opportunities.

Acknowledgments

Constructive comments from Reuben Echeverría, Bruce Gardner, Wallace Huffman, Jock Anderson, Terry Roe, Yoav Kislev and Vernon Ruttan are acknowledged.

References

Abidogun, A. (1982), "Cocoa research in Nigeria: An ex-post investment analysis", Nigerian Journal of Economic and Social Studies 21–35.

Aghib, A., and J. Lowenberg-DeBoer (N.d.), "The regional impact of collaborative research and extension programs: The case of striga resistant sorghum varieties developed by INTSORMIL", Mimeo (Purdue University).

Ahmed, M.M., W.A. Masters and J.H. Sanders (1995), "Returns to research in economies with policy distortions: Hybrid sorghum in Sudan", Agricultural Economics 12:183–192.

Akgunkov, S., D. Makanda, J. Oehmke, R. Myers and Y. Choe (1996), "A dynamic analysis of Kenya wheat research and rate of return", in: Proceedings of the Conference on Global Agricultural Science Policy in the 21st Century, Melbourne.

Alston, J., B. Craig and P. Pardey (1998a), "Dynamics in the creation and depreciation of knowledge, and the returns to research", EPTD Discussion Paper No. 35 (International Food Policy Research Institute, Washington, D.C.).

Alston, J.M., M.C. Marra, P.G. Pardey, and T.J. Wyatt (1998b), "Research returns redux: A meta-analysis of the returns to agricultural R&D", EPTD Discussion Paper No. 38, Environment and Production Technology Division (International Food Policy Research Institute, Washington, D.C.).

Alston, J.M., and R.J. Venner (1998), "The effects of the U.S. plant variety protection act on wheat genetic improvement", paper presented at the symposium on "Intellectual Property Rights and Agricultural Research Impact", sponsored by NC208 and the CIMMYT Economics Program – El Batan, Mexico, March 5–7, 1998.

Ambrosi, I., and E.R. da Cruz (1984), "Taxas de retorno dos recursos aplicados em pesquisa no Centro Nacional de Pesquisa de Trigo", Passo Fundo (EMBRAPA, Brazil).

Anandajayasekeram, P., and D.R. Martella (1995), "Institutionalization of impact assessment: SACCAR's experience in Southern Africa", paper presented at USAID Collaborative Workshop on Agricultural Technology Development and Transfer in Sub-Saharan Africa, Harare, Zimbabwe, January 24–27, 1995.

Araji, A.A. (1981), "The economic impact of investment in integrated pest management", in: G.W. Norton, W.L. Fishel, A.A. Paulsen and W.B. Sundquist, eds., Evaluation of Agricultural Research, Miscellaneous Publication 8-1981 (Minnesota Agricultural Experiment Station, University of Minnesota).

Avila, A.F.D. (1981), "Evaluation de la recherché agronomique au Brésil: Le ces de la rechereche de l'IRGA ou Rio Grande do Sul", Ph.D. Dissertation (Fac. de Droitet des Sci. Econ., Montpellier).

Avila, A.F.D., J.E.A. Andrade, L.J.M. Irias and T.R. Quirino (1983), "Formacao do capital humano e retorno dos investimentos em telnamento na EMBRAPA", EMBRAPA-DDM Documentos 4, EMBRAPA-DRH Documentos 5 (EMBRAPA-DID, Brazil).

Avila, A.F.D., L.J. Irias and R.F.V. Veloso (1984), "Avaliação dos impactos socioeconómicos do Projeto PRO-CENSUL I-EMBRAPA/BID", Documentos 16 (EMBRAPA-DEP, Brasilia).

Aw-Hassan, A., E. Ghanem, A.A. Ali, M. Mansour and M.B. Solh (1995), "Economic returns from improved wheat technology in upper Egypt", ICARDA Social Science Papers – 1 (International Center for Agricultural Research in the Dry Areas).

Ayer, H.W. (1970), "The costs, returns and effects of agricultural research in Sao Paulo, Brazil", Ph.D. Dissertation (Purdue University).

Ayer, H.W., and G.E. Schuh (1972), "Social rates of return and other aspects of agricultural research: The case of cotton research in Sao Paulo, Brazil", American Journal of Agricultural Economics 54:557–569.

Ayers, C.H.S. (1985), "The contribution of agricultural research to soybean productivity in Brazil", Ph.D. Dissertation (University of Minnesota).

Azam, Q.T., E.A. Bloom and R.E. Evenson (1991), "Agricultural research productivity in Pakistan", Economic Growth Center Discussion Paper No. 644 (Economic Growth Center, Yale University, New Haven, CO).

Bare, B.B., and R. Loveless (1985), "A case history of the regional forest nutrition project: Investments, results, and applications", report submitted to the USDA Forest Service, North Central Forest Experiment Station (University of Washington).

Barletta, N.A. (1970), "Costs and social benefits of agricultural research in Mexico", Ph.D. Dissertation (University of Chicago).

Beck, H. (1988), "Costs and benefits of an agricultural research institute", Agricultural Economics Society Conference, Manchester.

Bengston, D.N. (1984), "Economic impacts of structural particleboard research", Forest Science 30(3):685–697.

Bertelsen, M., and S. Ouédraego (N.d.), "The value of research on indigenous knowledge: Preliminary evidence from the case of zai in Burkina Faso", Mimeo (Purdue University).

Birkhaeuser, D., R.E. Evenson and G. Feder (1991), "The economic impact of agricultural extension: A review", Economic Development and Cultural Change 39(3):607–650.

Bojanic, A., and G. Echeverría (1990), "Refornos a la inversión en investigación agricola en Bolivia: El caso de la soja", Documento de frabajo (ISNAR, The Hague).

Boughton, D., and B. Henry de Frahan (1994), "Agricultural research impact assessment: The case of maize technology adoption in Southern Mali", International Development Working Paper No. 41 (Michigan State University, East Lansing, Michigan).

Boyce, J.K., and R.E. Evenson (1975), Agricultural Research Extension Programs (Agricultural Development Council, Inc., New York).

Boyle, G.E. (1986), "An exploratory assessment of the returns to agricultural research in Ireland, 1963–1983", Irish Journal of Agricultural Economics and Rural Sociology 11:57–71.

Braha, H., and L. Tweeten (1986), "Evaluating past and prospective future payoffs from public investments to increase agricultural productivity", Technical Bulletin T-165 (Agricultural Experiment Station, Oklahoma State University).

Bredahl, M., and W. Peterson (1976), "The productivity and allocation of research: U.S. agricultural experiment stations", American Journal of Agricultural Economics 58:684–692.

Brinkman, G.L., and B.E. Prentice (1985), "Returns to a provincial economy from investment in agricultural research: The case of Ontario in economics of agricultural research in Canada", K.K. Klein and W.H. Furtan, eds. (The University of Calgary Press, Calgary).

Brunner, A.D., and J.K. Strauss (1986), "The social returns to public R&D in the U.S. wood preserving industry (1950–1980)", Draft (Duke University).

Byerlee, D. (1991), "Adaptation and adoption of seed-fertilizer technology: Beyond the green revolution", paper presented at the Conference on Mechanisms of Socio-Economic Change in Rural Areas, Canberra, Australia.

Byerlee, D., and G. Traxler (1995), "National and international wheat improvement research in the post-green revolution period: Evolution and impacts", American Journal of Agricultural Economics 77:268–278.

Capule, C.A. (1977), "Education, extension and national status in Laguna Rice Household", M.A. Thesis (University of the Philippines).

Chang, S.U. (1986), "The economics of optimal stand growth and yield information gathering", report submitted to the USDA Forest Service (North Central Experiment Station, University of Kentucky).

Chavas, J.-P., and T.L. Cox (1992), "A nonparametric analysis of the influence of research on agricultural productivity", American Journal of Agricultural Economics 74:583–591.

Chisi, M., P. Anandajayasekeram, D. Martella, M. Ahmed and M. Mwape (1997), Impact Assessment of Sorghum Research in Zambia (SACCAR, Botswana).

Chou, E.C., and L.J. Lau (1987), "Farmer ability and farm productivity: A study of households in the Chiangmai Valley, Thailand 1972–1978", World Bank Discussion Paper, Education and Training Series, EDT Report 62 (World Bank, Washington, D.C.).

Cline, P.L. (1975), "Sources of productivity change in United States agriculture", Ph.D. Dissertation (Oklahoma State University).

Cotlear, D. (1986), "Farmer education and farm efficiency in Peru: The role of schooling, extension services and migration", World Bank Discussion Paper, Education and Training Series, Report No. EDT 49 (The World Bank).

da Cruz, E.R., and A.F.D. Avila (1983), "Reforno dos investimentos da EMBRAPA no area de abrangencia do BIRD 1", Brasilia, EMBRAPA-DDM (EMBRAPA-DEP Documentos, 19).

da Cruz, E.R., and R.E. Evenson (1997), "Technological spillovers in southern cone agriculture", Economia Aplicada 1(4):709–730.

da Cruz, E.R., V. Palma and A.F.D. Avila (1982), "Taxas de retorno dos investimentos da EMBRAPA: Investimentos totals e capital fisico", Brasilia, EMBRAPA-DID (EMBRAPA-DDM, Documentos, 1).

da Silva, G.L.S.P. (1984), "Contribucao s pesquisa e da extensao rural para a produtividade agricola: Observacoes no Caso de Sa Paulo", in: Congresso Brasileiro de Economia e Sociologia Rural, Anais 22, V.2. Brasilia, D.F. SOBER.

Davis, J.S. (1979), "Stability of the research production coefficient for U.S. agriculture", Ph.D. Dissertation (University of Minnesota).

Davis, J.S., and W. Peterson (1981), "The declining productivity of agricultural research", in: G.W. Norton, W.L. Fishel, A.A. Paulsen and W.B. Sundquist, eds., Evaluation of Agricultural Research, Miscellaneous Publication 8-1981 (Minnesota Agricultural Experiment Station, University of Minnesota).

Deaton, A., and D. Benjamin (1988), "The living standards survey and price policy reform: A study of cocoa and coffee production in Cote d'Ivoire", Living Standards Measurement Study, Working Paper No. 44 (The World Bank).

del Rey, E.C. (1975), "Rentabildad de la estaciòn experimental agricola de Tucumòn", 1943–64, Xa Reuniòn Anual de la Asociaciòn Argentina de Economia Politico, Tomo 1, Mar del Plata, Argentina.

Dey, M.M., and R.E. Evenson (1991), "The economic impact of rice research in Bangladesh" (Bangladesh Rice Research Institute, Gazipur, Bangladesh; International Rice Research Institute, Los Banos, Philippines; and Bangladesh Agricultural Research Council, Dhaka, Bangladesh).

Doyle, C.J., and M.S. Ridout (1985), "The impact of scientific research on UK agricultural productivity", Research Policy 14:109–116.

Duncan, R.C. (1972). "Evaluating returns to research in pasture improvement", Australian Journal of Agricultural Economics 16:153–168.

Easter, K.W., and G.W. Norton (1977), "Potential returns from increased research budgets for the Land-Grant universities", Agricultural Economics Research 29(4):127–133.

Echeverría, R.G. (1990), "Assessing the impact of agricultural research", in: Methods for Diagnosing Research System Constraints and Assessing the Impact of Agricultural Research, Vol. II: Assessing the Impact of Agricultural Research (ISNAR, The Hague).

Eddleman, B.R. (1977), "Impacts of reduced federal expenditures for agricultural research and education", IR-6 Information Report 60.

Elias, V.J. (1971), " Investigaciòn y desarroilo econòmico", Documento de trafajo de investigaciòn y desarrollo No. 7 (Universidad Nacional de Tucumò, Argentina).

Ernstberger, J. (1989), "Wohlfahrtseffekte der Entwicklung und Einfuhrung neuer Relssorten in Brasillen", Ph.D. Dissertation (Technische Universität München).

Evenson, R.E. (1968), "The contribution of agricultural research and extension to agricultural production", Ph.D. Dissertation (University of Chicago).

Evenson, R.E. (1969), "International Transmission of Technology in Sugarcane Production" (Economic Growth Center, Yale University, New Haven).

Evenson, R.E. (1979), "Agricultural research, extension and productivity change in U.S. agriculture: A historical decomposition analysis", Agricultural Research and Extension Evaluation Symposium, May 21–23, 1979, Moscow, Idaho.

Evenson, R.E. (1982), "Observations on Brazilian agricultural research and productivity", Revista de Economia Rural 20:368–401.

Evenson, R.E. (1987), "The international agricultural research centers: their impact on spending for national agricultural research and extension", CGIAR Study Paper No. 22 (The World Bank, Washington, D.C.).

Evenson, R.E. (1988), "Estimated economic consequences of PIDAP I and PIDAP II programs for crop production", unpublished (Yale University, Economic Growth Center).

Evenson, R.E. (1989), "Productivity decomposition in Brazilian agriculture", unpublished manuscript (Economic Growth Center, Yale University, New Haven, CT).

Evenson, R.E. (1991), "Research and extension in agricultural development", Forum Valuazione 2 (November).

Evenson, R.E. (1992), " Notes on the measurement of the economic consequences of agricultural research investments", in: D.R. Lee, S.K. and N. Uphoff, eds., Assessing the Impact of International Agricultural Research for Sustainable Development, Proceedings from a Symposium at Cornell University (CHFAD, Ithaca, New York).

Evenson, R.E. (1994), "Analyzing the transfer of agricultural technology", in: J.R. Anderson, ed., Agricultural Technology: Policy Issues for the International Community (CAB International, Wallingford, U.K.).

Evenson, R.E., E. Abdurachman, B. Hutabarat and A.C. Tubagus (1994), "Economic impacts of agricultural research in Indonesia", Study Report.

Evenson, R.E., and A.F. Avila (1996), "Productivity change and technology transfer in the Brazilian grain sector", Revista de Economia Rural.

Evenson, R.E., Q.T. Azam and E. Bloom (1991), Agricultural Research Productivity in Pakistan (Pakistan Agricultural Research Council, Islamabad).

Evenson, R.E., and V. Bindlish (1993), "Evaluation of the performance of T&V extension in Kenya", World Bank Agricultural and Rural Development Series #7 (World Bank).

Evenson, R.E., and V. Bindlish (1997), "The impact of T&V extension in Africa: The experience of Kenya and Burkina Faso" (World Bank Observer).

Evenson, R.E., V. Bindlish and M. Gbetibouo (1995), "Evaluation of T&V extension in Burkina Faso", World Bank Technical Paper Number 226 (African Technical Department Series).

Evenson, R.E., and B. Bravo-Ureta (1994), "Efficiency in agricultural production: The case of peasant farmers in eastern Paraguay", Agricultural Economics 10(1).

Evenson, R.E., and C. David (1993), Adjustment and Technology: The Case of Rice (OECD).

Evenson, R.E., and P. Flores (1978), Economic Consequences of New Rice Technology in Asia (International Rice Research Institute, Los Banos, Laguna, Philippines).

Evenson, R.E., and D. Gollin (1996), "Genetic resources, international organizations, and rice varietal improvement", Economic Development and Cultural Change 45(3):471–500.

Evenson, R.E., R. Herdt and M. Hossain (1996), Rice Research in Asia: Progress and Priorities (CAB International, Wallingford, U.K.).

Evenson, R.E., and W. Huffman (1993), "The effects of R&D on farm size, specialization and productivity", in: S.R. Johnson and S.A. Martin, eds., Industrial Policy for Agriculture in the Global Economy, Chapter 3 (Iowa State University Press, Ames, Iowa).

Evenson, R.E., and D. Jha (1973), "The contribution of agricultural research systems to agricultural production in India", Indian Journal of Agricultural Economics 28(4):212–230.

Evenson, R.E., and Y. Kislev (1975), Agricultural Research and Productivity (Yale University Press, New Haven, CT).

Evenson, R.E., and J. McKinsey (1991), "Research, extension, infrastructure and productivity change in Indian agriculture", in: R.E. Evenson and C.E. Pray, eds., Research and Productivity in Asian Agriculture (Cornell University Press, Ithaca, N.Y.).

Evenson, R.E., and C.E. Pray (1991), Research and Productivity in Asian Agriculture (Cornell University Press).

Evenson, R.E., C.E. Pray and M.W. Rosegrant (1999), Agricultural Research and Productivity Growth in India, Research Report 109 (International Food Policy Research Institute).

Evenson, R.E., and J. Quizon (1991), "Technology, infrastructure, output supply, and factor demand in Philippine agriculture", in: Research and Productivity in Asian Agriculture (Cornell University Press, Ithaca, NY).

Evenson, R.E., and M. Rosegrant (1993), "Agricultural productivity growth in Pakistan and India: A comparative analysis", The Pakistan Development Review 32(4).

Ewell, P. (1992), "The PRAPACE network: CIPNARS collaboration for sustainable agricultural production in Africa", papers presented at the Symposium on the Impact of Technology on Agricultural Transformation in Sub-Sahara Africa, Washington, D.C.

Fan, S., and P.G. Pardey (1992), Agricultural Research in China: Its Institutional Development and Impact (International Service for National Agricultural Research, The Hague, Netherlands).

Feder, G., R. Slade and L. Lau (1985), "The impact of agricultural extension: The training and visit system in Haryana", World Bank Staff Working Paper No. 756 (The World Bank).

Feijòo, V.M. (1984), "La rentabilldad de la inversiòn en investigaciòn agricola", XIX a Reuniòn Anual de la Asociacion Argentina de Economia Politica, Tomo 1 (Misiones, Argentina).

Fishel, W.L., ed. (1971), Resource Allocation in Agricultural Research (University of Minnesota Press, Minneapolis, MN).

Fisher, M.G., A. Fall and M. Sidibé (1995), "The impact of rice research in the Senegal river valley", Mimeo (ISRA/BAME, Dakar, Senegal).

Flores, P., R.E. Evenson and Y. Hayami (1978), "Social returns to rice research in the Philippines: Domestic benefits and foreign spillover", Economic Development and Cultural Change 26:591–607.

Fonseca, M.A.S. (1976), "Reforno social a los investimentos em pesquisa na cultiura do cafe", Master's Thesis (ESALCQ, Piracicaba, Brasil).

Fox, G. (1986), "Underinvestment, myopia and commodity bias: A test of three propositions of inefficiency in the U.S. agricultural research system" (University of Guelph, Department of Agricultural Economics and Business, Ontario).

Fox, G., R. Roberts and G.L. Brinkman (1989), "The return to Canadian federal dairy cattle research – 1968 to 1984", Working Paper 39/20 (University of Guelph, Department of Agriculture and Business).

Fuglie, K., N. Ballenger, K. Day, C. Klotz, M. Ollinger, J. Reilly, U. Vasavada and J. Yee (1996), "Agricultural research and development: Public and private investments under alternative markets and institutions", Agricultural Economic Report No. 735 (Natural Resources and Environment Division, Economic Research Service, U.S. Department of Agriculture).

Gautam, M., and J.R. Anderson (1998), "Reconsidering the evidence on the returns to T&V extension in Kenya" (Operations Evaluations Department, World Bank).

Gopinath, M., and T.L. Roe (1996), "R&D spillovers: Evidence from U.S. food processing, farm machinery and agriculture", Bulletin No. 96-2 (Economic Development Center, Department of Applied Economics, University of Minnesota, St. Paul, Minnesota).

Griliches, Z. (1958), "Research costs and social returns: Hybrid corn and related innovations", Journal of Political Economy 66:419–431.

Griliches, Z. (1964), "Research expenditures, education and the aggregate agricultural production function", American Economic Review 54:961–974.

Griliches, Z. (1998), Technology, Education and Productivity (Basil Blackwell, Oxford, UK) Chapter 14, 227–243.

Grossfield, K., and J.B. Heath (1966), "The benefit and cost of government support for research and development: A case study", Economic Journal 76:537–549.

Halim, A. (1976), "Schooling and extension and income producing Philippine households" (Bangladesh Agricultural University, Department of Agricultural Extension and Teachers Training).

Haque, A.K.E., G. Fox and G.L. Brinkman (1987), "The rate of return to egg research in Canada – 1968 to 1984", Working Paper 87/10 (Department of Agricultural Economics and Business, University of Guelph).

Harken, B.R. (1973), "The contribution of schooling to agricultural modernization: An empirical analysis", in: P. Foster and J.R. Sheffield, eds., Education and Rural Development (Evans Brothers Ltd.).

Harvey, A. (1988), "Research priorities in agriculture", Journal of Agricultural Economics 39:81–97.

Hasting, T. (1981), "The impact of scientific research on Australian rural productivity", Australian Journal of Agricultural Economics 25(1):48–59.

Hayami, Y., and N. Akino (1977), "Organization and productivity of agricultural research systems in Japan", in: T.M. Arndt, D.G. Dalrymple, and V.W. Ruttan, eds., Resource Allocation and Productivity in National and International Agricultural Research (University of Minnesota Press, Minneapolis).

Haygreen, J., H. Gregerson, I. Holland and R. Stone (1986), "The economic impact of timber utilization research", Forest Products Journal 36(2):12–20.

Henry de Frahan, B., D. Youssouf, S. Traore and M.B. Diarra (1989), "Feasibility study for the expansion of the farming systems research division in the fifth region of Mali" (Ministere de l'Agriculture and Michigan State University, Bamako).

Herruzo, A.C. (1985), "Returns to agricultural research: Rice breeding in Spain", European Review of Agricultural Economics 12:265–282.

Hertford, R., J. Ardila, A. Rocha and G. Trujillo (1977), "Productivity of agricultural research in Colombia", in: T.M. Arndt, D.G. Dalrymple and V.W. Ruttan, eds., Resource Allocation and Productivity in National and International Agricultural Research (University of Minnesota Press, Minneapolis).

Hines, J. (1972), "The utilization of research for development: Two case studies in rural modernization and agriculture in Peru", Ph.D. Dissertation (Princeton University).

Hong, K.Y. (1975), "An estimated economic contribution of schooling and extension in Korean agriculture", Ph.D. Dissertation (University of the Philippines, Los Banos).

Hopcraft, P.N. (1974), "Human resources and technical skills in agricultural development: An economic evaluation of education investments in Kenya's small farm sector", Ph.D. Dissertation (Stanford University).

Howard, J., G. Chitalu and S. Kalonge (1993), "The impact of investments in maize research and dissemination in Zambia. Part I: Main report", International Development Working Paper No. 39/1 (Michigan State University, East Lansing, Michigan).

Huffman, W.E. (1974), "Decision making: The role of education", American Journal of Agricultural Economics 56:672–683.

Huffman, W.E. (1976), "The productive value of human time in U.S. agriculture", American Journal of Agricultural Economics 58(4):672–683.

Huffman, W.E. (1981), "Black-white human capital differences: Impact on agricultural productivity in the U.S. south", American Economic Review 71(1):94–107.

Huffman, W., and R.E. Evenson (1989), "Supply and demand functions for multi-product U.S. cash grain farms", American Journal of Agricultural Economics 71(3):761–773.

Huffman, W.E., and R.E. Evenson (1993), "Science for agriculture: A longterm perspective" (Iowa State University Press, Ames).

Hust, M., G. Fox and G. Brinkman (1988), "The return to Canadian federal swine research – 1968 to 1984", Working Paper 88/4 (Department of Agricultural Economics and Business, University of Guelph).

Iqbal, M. (1991), "The rate of returns to investment in agricultural research: The case of rice and cotton in Pakistan", Dissertation (Ohio State University).

Isinika, A.C. (1995), "Assessing the effect of agricultural research expenditures on agricultural productivity in Tanzania", Ph.D. Dissertation (University of Kentucky, Lexington, Kentucky).

Jamison, D., and L.I. Lau (1982), Farmer Education and Farm Efficiency, World Bank Research Publication (Johns Hopkins University Press, Baltimore).

Jamison, D., and P.R. Moock (1984), "Farmer education and farm efficiency in Nepal: The role of schooling, extension services and cognitive skills", World Development 12(1):67–86.

Johnson, D.K., and R.E. Evenson (1999), "R&D spillovers to agriculture: Measurement and application", Contemporary Economic Policy 17(4):432-456.

Judd, M.A., J.K. Boyce and R.E. Evenson (1986), "Investing in agricultural supply: The determinants of agricultural research and extension", Economic Development and Cultural Change 35(1):77–113.

Kahlon, A.S., H.K. Bal, P.N. Saxena and D. Jha (1977), "Returns to investment in research in India", in: T.M. Arndt, D.G. Dalrymple and V.W. Ruttan, eds., Resource Allocation and Productivity in National and International Agricultural Research (University of Minnesota Press, Minneapolis).

Karanja, D.D. (1990), "The rate of return to maize research in Kenya: 1955–88", M.S. Thesis (Department of Agricultural Economics, Michigan State University, East Lansing, Michigan).

Khan, M.H., and A.H. Akbari (1986), "Impact on agricultural research and extension on crop productivity in Pakistan: A production function approach", World Development 14:757–762.

Khatri, Y.J. (1994), "Technical change and the returns to research in UK agriculture, 1953–1990", Ph.D. Dissertation (Department of Agricultural Economics and Management, University of Reading, England).

Khatri, Y., and C. Thirtle (1996), "Supply and demand functions for UK agriculture: Biases of technical change and the returns to public R&D", Journal of Agricultural Economics 47 (3):338–354.

Khatri, Y., C. Thirtle and J. van Zyl (1995), "South African agricultural competitiveness: A profit function approach to the effects of policy and technology", in: G.H. Peters and D. Hedley, eds., Agricultural Competitiveness: Market Forces and Policy Choice, Proceedings of the 22nd International Conference of Agricultural Economists, Harare, Zimbabwe.

Kim, J.I., and L.J. Lau (1994), "The sources of economic growth in the east Asian newly industrialized countries", Journal of Japanese and International Economics 235–271.

Kislev, Y., and M. Hoffman (1978), "Research and productivity in wheat in Israel", Journal of Development Studies 14(2):165–181.

Knutson, M., and L.G. Tweeten (1979), "Toward an optimal rate of growth in agricultural production research and extension", American Journal of Agricultural Economics 61:70–76.

Kortum, S. (1994), "A model of research, patenting, and productivity growth", Institute for Economic Development, Discussion Paper Series 37 (February) (Boston University).

Kumar, P., and Mruthyunjaya (1992), "Measurement and analysis of total factor productivity growth in wheat", Indian Journal of Agricultural Economics 47 (7):451–458.

Kupfuma, B. (1994), "The payoffs to hybrid maize research in Zimbabwe: An economic and institutional analysis", M.S. Thesis (Department of Agricultural Economics, Michigan State University, East Lansing, Michigan).

Kuyvenhoven, A., J.A. Becht and R. Ruben (1996), "Public investment for soil improvement in West Africa: Economic criteria for phosphate rock use to enhance soil fertility management", Mimeo, Public Goods and Services Project, Wageningen Agricultural University (Wageningen, The Netherlands).

Laker-Ojok, R. (1994), "The rate of return to agricultural research in Uganda: The case of oilseeds and maize", International Development Working Paper No. 42 (Michigan State University, East Lansing, Michigan).

Latimer, R. (1964), "Some economic aspects of agricultural research and extension in the U.S.", Ph.D. Dissertation (Purdue University).

Lever, B.G. (1970), Agricultural Extension in Botswana, Development Study No. 7 (University of Reading, Department of Agricultural Economics).

Librero, A.R., and N. Emlano (1990), Estimating Returns to Research Investment in Poultry in the Philippines (PCARRD, Los Banos, Laguna).

Librero, A.R., N.E. Emlano and M.B. Ocampo (1988), Estimating Returns to Research Investment in Mango in the Philippines (PCARRD, Los Banos, Laguna).

Librero, A., and M. Perez (1987), "Estimating returns to research investment in corn in the Philippines" (Socio-Economic Research Department, Philippine Council for Agriculture, Forestry, Natural Resources Research and Development, Los Banos).

Lu, Y.C., P. Cline and L. Quance (1979), "Prospects for productivity growth in U.S. agriculture", Agricultural Economics Report No. 435 (USDA-ESCS, Washington, D.C.).

Luz Barbosa, M.K.T., E. Rodrigues da Cruz and A.F.D. Avila (1988), "Beneficios sociates y econòmicos de la Investigaciòn de EMBRAPA: Una reevaluaciòn", paper presented at Seminario Latinoamericano y del Caribe Sobre Mecanismos de Evaluaciòn en Instituclones de Investigaciòn Agraria, Palpa, Colombia.

Macmillan, J., G. Mudimuk, J. MacRobert, L. Rugube, E. Guveya, L. Mutemeri and K. Chanakanyuka (1991), "Ex ante B/C analysis of small farm maize research demonstrations, Zimbabwe", Working Paper (Department of Agricultural Economics and Extension, University of Zimbabwe).

Mairesse, J., and P. Mohnen (1995), "Research and development and productivity – A survey of the econometric literature", Preliminary Version of paper (April).

Makana, D.W., and J.F. Oehmke (1996), "The history of and returns to Kenya wheat research" (Department of Agricultural Economics, Michigan State University, East Lansing, Michigan).

Makau, B.F. (1984), "Measurement of economic returns to wheat research in Kenya", unpublished M.A. Thesis (University of Nairobi, Kenya).

Makki, S.S., and L.G. Tweeten (1993), "Impact of research, extension, commodity programs, and prices on agricultural productivity", paper presented at the 1993 meetings of the American Agricultural Economics Association, Orlando, Florida.

Makki, S.S., L.G. Tweeten and C.S. Thraen (1996), "Returns to agricultural research: Are we assessing right?", contributed paper proceedings from the Conference on Global Agricultural Science Policy for the Twenty-First Century, August 26–28, Melbourne, Australia, pp. 89–114.

Marsden, J.S., G.E. Martin, D.J. Parham, T.J. Ridsdill Smith and B.G. Johnston (1980), Returns on Australian Agricultural Research, The joint Industries Assistance Commission – CSIRO benefit-cost study of the CSIRO Division of Entomology.

Martinez, J.C., and C. Sain (1983), "The economic return to institutional innovations in national agricultural research: On-farm research in IDIAP Panama", CIMMYT Economics Program Working Paper 04/83 (CIMMYT, Mexico D.F.).

Martinez, S., and G.W. Norton (1986), "Evaluating privately funded public research: An example with poultry and eggs", Southern Journal of Agricultural Economics (July) 129–140.

Masters, W.A., T. Bedingar and J.F. Oehmke (1996), "The impact of agricultural research in Africa: Aggregate and case study evidence", Mimeo (Department of Agricultural Economics, Purdue University, West Lafayette, Indiana).

Mazzueato, V. (1992), "Non-research policy effects on the rate of return to maize research in Kenya: 1955–88", M.S. Thesis (Department of Agricultural Economics, Michigan State University, East Lansing, Michigan).

Mazzueato, V., and S. Ly (1994), "An economic analysis of research and technology transfer of millet, sorghum and cowpeas in Niger" (ISNAR/East Lansing, The Hague, Netherlands; Michigan State University, Michigan).

Mohan, R., and R.E. Evenson (1975), "The intensive agricultural districts program in India: A new evaluation", Journal of Development Studies 11:135–154.

Monares, A. (1984), "Building an effective potato country program: The case of Rwanda", CIP Social Science Department Working Paper 1984-3 (Lima, Peru).

Monteiro, A. (1975), "Avaliacao economica da pesquisa agricola: O casu do cacau no Brasil", Master's Thesis (Vicosa, UFV).

Moock, P.R. (1973), "Managerial ability in small farm production: An analysis of maize yields in the vihiga division of Kenya", Ph.D. Dissertation (Columbia University).

Moock, P.R. (1976), "The efficiency of women as farm managers: Kenya", American Journal of Agricultural Economics 58(5):831–835.

Moricochi, F. (1980), Pesquisa e assistencia tecnica no cltricultura: Custos e refornos sociates, Master's Thesis (ESALQ, Piracicaba, Brasil).

Morris, M.L., H.J. Dubin and T. Pokhrel (1992), "Returns to wheat research in Nepal", Economics, Working Paper 92-04 (CIMMYT).

Morris, M.L., H.J. Dubin and T. Pokhrel (1994), "Returns to wheat breeding research in Nepal", Agricultural Economics 10:269–282.

Muchnik, E. (1985), As cited by Scobie and Eveleens (1987, p. 57).

Mudhara, M., P. Anandajayasekeeram, B. Kupfuma and E. Mazhangara (1995), Impact Assessment of Cotton Research and Enabling Environment in Zimbabwe, 1970–1995 (SACCAR, Botswana).

Nagy, J.G. (1983), "Estimating the yield advantage of high yielding wheat and maize: The use of Pakistani on-farm yield constraints data", The Pakistan Development Review 93.

Nagy, J.G. (1985), "The overall rate of return to agricultural research and extension investments in Pakistan", Pakistan Journal of Applied Economics 4(1):17–28.

Nagy, J.G. (1991), "Returns from agricultural research and extension in wheat and maize in Pakistan", in: R.E. Evenson and C.E. Pray, eds., Research and Productivity in Asian Agriculture (Cornell University Press, Ithaca, N.Y.).

Nagy, J.G., and W.H. Furtan (1978), "Economic costs and returns for crop development research: The case of rapeseed breeding in Canada", Canadian Journal of Agricultural Economics 26:1–14.

Newman, D.H. (1986), "An econometric analysis of aggregate gains from technical change in southern softwood forestry", Ph.D. Dissertation (Duke University).

Norgaard, R.B. (1988), "The biological control of cassava mealybug in Africa", American Journal of Agricultural Economics 70(2):366–371.

Norton, G.W. (1981), "The productivity and allocation of research: U.S. agricultural experiment stations, revisited", in: G.W. Norton, W.L. Fishel, A.A. Paulsen and W.B. Sundquist, eds., Evaluation of Agricultural Research, Miscellaneous Publication 8-1981 (Minnesota Agricultural Experiment Station, University of Minnesota).

Norton, G.W., J.D. Coffey and E. Berrier Frye (1984), "Estimating returns to agricultural research, extension, and teaching at the state level", Southern Journal of Agricultural Economics (July) 121–128.

Norton, G.W., V. Ganoza and C. Pomareda (1987), "Potential benefits to agricultural research and extension in Peru", American Journal of Agricultural Economics 69:274–257.

Norton, G.W., J. Ortiz and P.G. Pardey (1992), "The impact of foreign assistance on agricultural growth", Economic Development and Cultural Change 40(4):775–786.

Norton, G.W., and R. Paczkowski (1993), "Reaping the return on agricultural research and education in Virginia", Information Series 93-3 (College of Agriculture and Life Sciences, Virginia Polytechnic Institute and State University, Blacksburg, Virginia).

Oehmke, J.F. (1996), "The maturation of the U.S. agricultural research system and its impacts on productivity", Staff Paper #96-85 (Department of Agricultural Economics, Michigan State University, East Lansing, Michigan).

Oehmke, J.F., L. Daniels, J. Howard, M. Maredia and R. Bernsten (1991), "The impact of agricultural research: A review of the ex-post assessment literature with implications for Africa", Mimeo (Department of Agricultural Economics, Michigan State University, East Lansing, Michigan).

Oehmke, J.F., and W.A. Masters (1997), "The impacts of and returns to African agricultural research", Mimeo (Department of Agricultural Economics, Michigan State University, East Lansing, Michigan).

Otto and J. Havlicek, Jr. (1981), "As cited in Evenson, R.E. 1980. Human capital and agricultural productivity change", Draft (Yale University).

Ouedraego, S., and L. Illy (1996), "Evaluation de l'impact economique des cordons pierreux: Cas du plateau central au Burkina Faso", Mimeo (INERA, Ougadougou, Burkina Faso).

Ouedraego, S., L. Illy and F. Lompo (1995), "Evaluation de l'impact economique de la recherche et la vulgarisation agricole: Cas du maïs dans l'ouest du Burkina Faso", Mimeo (INERA, Ougadougou, Burkina Faso).

Pachico, D.H., and J.A. Ashby (1976), "Investments in human capital and farm productivity: Some evidence from Brazil", Study prepared for Cornell University.

Pardey, P.G., and J. Roseboom (1989), ISNAR Agricultural Research Indicator Series: A Global Data Base on National Agricultural Research Systems (Cambridge University Press, New York).

Patrick, G.F., and E.W. Kehrberg (1973), "Costs and returns of education in five agricultural areas of Eastern Brazil", American Journal of Agricultural Economics 55:145–154.

Pee, T.Y. (1977), "Social returns from rubber research on peninsular Malaysia", Ph.D. Dissertation (Michigan State University).

Perraton, H.D., D. Jamison and F. Orivel (1985), "Mass media for agricultural extension in Malawi", Basis Education and Agricultural Extension, World Bank Staff Working Papers, No. 564 (Washington, D.C.).

Peterson, W.L. (1967), "Returns to poultry research in the United States", Journal of Farm Economics 49:656–669.

Peterson, W.L., and J.C. Fitzharris (1977), "The organization and productivity of the federal state research system in the United States", in: T.M. Arndt, D.G. Dalrymple and V.W. Ruttan, eds., Resource Allocation and Productivity in National and International Agricultural Research (University of Minnesota Press, Minneapolis).

Pinazza, A.H., A.C. Gemente and S. Matsuoka (1984), Reforno social dos recursos aplicados em pesquisa canavielra: O caso da varledade NA56-79, Congresso Brasileiro de Economia a Sociologic Rural, Salvador, BA, Anals, SOBER (21).

Power, A.P., and N.P. Russell (1988), "Economic evaluation of scientific research: A case study of the rate of return to poultry layer feeding system research", Government Economic Service Working Paper No. 101, London.

Pray, C.E. (1978), "The economics of agricultural research in British Punjab and Pakistani Punjab, 1905–75", Ph.D. Dissertation (University of Pennsylvania).

Pray, C.E. (1980), "The economics of agricultural research in Bangladesh", Bangladesh Journal of Agricultural Economics 2:1–36.

Pray, C.E., and Z. Ahmed (1991), "Research and agricultural productivity growth in Bangladesh", in: R.E. Evenson and C.E. Pray, eds., Research and Productivity in Asian Agriculture (Cornell University Press, Ithaca).

Pudasaini, S.P. (1983), "The effects of education in agriculture: Evidence from Nepal", American Journal of Agricultural Economics 65(3):509–515.

Purcell, D.L., and J.R. Anderson (1997), Agricultural Extension and Research (The World Bank, Washington, D.C.).

Ribeiro, J.L. (1982), "Retorno a Investimentos em Pesquisa Agropecuaria", Inf. Agropec. 8:39–44.

Roessing, A.C. (1984), "Taxa interna de retorno dos investimentos em pesquisa de soja", Documento 6 (EMBRAPA-CNPS, Brasilia, D.F.).

Romer, P. (1986), "Increasing returns and long-run growth", Journal of Political Economy 94:1002–1037.

Romer, P. (1990), "Endogenous technical change", Journal of Political Economy 98(5):S71–S102.

Rosegrant, M., and R.E. Evenson (1993), "Agricultural productivity growth in Pakistan and India: A comparative analysis", The Pakistan Development Review 32(4):433–438.

Ruttan, V.W. (1998), "International agricultural research: Four papers", Staff Paper Series P98-4 (Department of Applied Economics, University of Minnesota).

Salmon, D. (1984), "An evaluation of investment in agricultural research in Indonesia, 1965–1977", Ph.D. Dissertation (University of Minnesota).

Sanders, J.H. (1994), "Economic impact of the commodity research networks of SAFGRA", in: J.H. Sanders, T. Bezuneh and A.C. Schroeder, eds., Impact Assessment of the SAFGRAD Commodity Networks (US-AID/Africa Bureau, Washington, D.C.).

Schmitz, A., and D. Seckler (1970), "Mechanized agriculture and social welfare: The case of the tomato harvester", American Journal of Agricultural Economics 52:569–577.

Schwartz, L.A., and J.F. Oehmke (1990), "Applying a benefit/cost approach or rate of return analysis to specific CRSP projects", paper presented at the CRSP Conference, Michigan State University, East Lansing, Michigan, Mimeo (Department of Agricultural Economics, Michigan State University).

Schwartz, L., J.A. Sterns and J.F. Oehmke (1993), "Economic returns to cowpea research, extension and input distribution in Senegal", Agricultural Economics 8:161–171.

Schwartz, L.A., J.A. Sterns, J.F. Oehmke, and R.D. Freed (1989), "Impact study of the bean/cowpea collaborative research support program (CRSP) for Senegal", Draft (Department of Agricultural Economics, Michigan State University).

Scobie, G.M., and W.M. Eveleens (1987), "The return to investment in agricultural research in New Zealand: 1926–27 to 1983–84", MAF Economics Research Report 1/87 (Ruakura Agriculture Centre, Hamilton, New Zealand).

Scobie, G.M., and R.T. Posada (1978), "The impact of technical change on income distribution: The case of rice in Colombia", American Journal of Agricultural Economics 60:85–92.

Seck, P.A., M. Sidibé and A.M. Béye (1995), "Impact social de la recherche et du transfer du technologies sur le coton au Senegal", Mimeo.

Seidi, S. (1996), "An economic analysis of rice research, extension, and seed production in Guinea-Bissau: Preliminary evidence from the case of swamp mangrove rice", preliminary report to Rice Economics Task Force of West African Rice Development Association, Bissau, Guinea-Bissau.

Seldon, B.J. (1987), "A nonresidual estimation of welfare gains from research: The case of public R&D in a forest product industry", Southern Economic Journal 54:64–80.

Seldon, B.J., and D.H. Newman (1987), "Marginal productivity of public research in the softwood plywood industry: A dual approach", Forest Science.

Sere, C., and L.S. Jarvis (1998), "The betting line of beef: Ex ante estimates of improved pasture research benefits for the Latin American tropics", paper presented at ISNAR/Rutgers Agricultural Technology Management Workshop, 6–8 July, New Jersey.

Setboonsarng, S., and R.E. Evenson (1991), "Technology, infrastructure, output supply and factor demand in Thailand's agriculture", in: R.E. Evenson and C. Pray, eds., Research Productivity and Income in Asian Agriculture (Cornell University Press, Ithaca).

Smale, M., and P. Heisey (1994), "Maize research in Malawi revisited: An emerging success story", Journal of International Development.

Smale, M., R.P. Singh, K. Sayre, P. Pingali, S. Rajaram and H.J. Dubin (1998), "Estimating the economic impact of breeding nonspecific resistance to leaf rust in modern bread wheat", Plant Disease.

Smith, B., G.W. Norton and J. Havlicek, Jr. (1983), "Impacts of public research expenditures on agricultural value-added in the U.S. and the northeast", Journal of the Northeastern Agricultural Economics Council 12:109–114.

Sterns, J.A., and R. Bernsten (1994), "Assessing the impact of cowpea and sorghum research and extension: Lessons learned in Northern Cameroon", International Development Working Paper No. 43 (Michigan State University, East Lansing, Michigan).

Sterns, J., J. Oehmke and L. Schwartz (1993), "Returns to education: The impacts of MSU training on West African scientists", Agricultural Economics Report No. 567 (Department of Agricultural Economics, Michigan State University, East Lansing, Michigan).

Sumelius, J. (1987), "The return to investment in agricultural research in Finland 1950–1984", Journal of Agricultural Science in Finland 59:257–353.

Sundquist, W.B., C. Cheng and G.W. Norton (1981), "Measuring returns to research expenditures for corn, wheat, and soybeans", in: G.W. Norton, W.L. Fishel, A.A. Paulsen and W.B. Sundquist, eds., Evaluation of Agricultural Research, Miscellaneous Publication 8-1981 (Minnesota Agricultural Experiment Station, University of Minnesota).

Tang, A. (1963), "Research and education in Japanese agricultural development", Economic Studies Quarterly 13:27–41.

Thirtle, C. (1996), "Producer funding of R&D: Productivity and returns to R&D in British sugar, 1954–93", 1996/1 (Department of Agricultural Economics and Management, University of Reading).

Thirtle, C., and P. Bottomley (1988), "Is publicly funded agricultural research excessive?" Journal of Agricultural Economics 31:27–41 and 91–99.

Thirtle, C., and P. Bottomley (1989), "The rate of return to public sector agricultural R&D in the UK, 1965–80", Applied Economics 21:381–400.

Thirtle, C., P. Bottomley, P. Palladino and D. Shimmelpfennig (1997), "The rise and fall of public sector plant breeding in the UK: A recursive model of basic and applied research, and diffusion", contributed paper for the IAAE Conference, Sacramento, August.

Thirtle, C., D. Hadley and R. Townsend (1995), "Policy-induced innovation in Sub-Saharan African agriculture", Development Policy Review 13(4):323–347.

Thirtle, C., J. Piesse and V. Smith (1997), "An economic approach to the structure, historical development and reform of agricultural R&D in the United Kingdom" (Centre for Agricultural Strategy, University of Reading).

Thirtle, C., R. Townsend, J. Amadi, A. Lusigi and J. van Zyl (1999), "The economic impact of agricultural research council expenditures", forthcoming in Agrekon.

Thirtle, C., and J. van Zyl (1994), "Returns to research and extension in South African commercial agriculture, 1947–91", South African Journal of Agricultural Extension 1–7.

Townsend, R., and J. van Zyl (1997), "The returns to research in wine grapes in South Africa", a report to the ARC.

Townsend, R., J. van Zyl and C. Thirtle (1997), "Assessing the benefits of research expenditures on maize production in South Africa", submitted to Agrekon (July).

Traxler, G., and D. Byerlee (1992), "Economic returns to crop management research in a post-green revolution setting", American Journal of Agricultural Economics 74(3):573–582.

Traxler, G., and P.L. Pingali (1996), "International coordination of research roles in plant genetic resource conservation and use", CIMMYT.

Tre, J.-P. (1995), "The rates of return to mangrove rice research in West Africa", unpublished M.S. Thesis (Purdue University, West Lafayette, Indiana).

Ulrich, A., W.H. Furtan and A. Schmitz (1985), "Public and private returns from joint venture research in agriculture: The case of malting barley", in: K. Klein and W. Furtan, eds., Economics of Agricultural Research in Canada (University of Calgary Press, Calgary).

Unnevehr, L.J. (1986), "Consumer demand for rice grain quality and returns to research for quality improvement in Southeast Asia", American Journal of Agricultural Economics 68:634–641.

Valdivia, C. (1997), "Returns to investments in small ruminant research in Indonesia: The small ruminant collaborative research support program (SR-CRSP) in West Java", Agricultural Economics Working Paper No. 1997-5 (Department of Agricultural Economics, University of Missouri-Columbia, Columbia, Missouri).

Welch, F., and R.E. Evenson (1989), "The impact and pervasiveness of crop and livestock improvement research in U.S. agriculture", Economic Growth Center (Yale University, New Haven, Connecticut).

Wennergren, E.B., and M.D. Whitaker (1977), "Social returns to U.S. technical assistance in Bolivian agriculture: The case of sheep and wheat", American Journal of Agricultural Economics 59:565–569.

Westgate, R.A. (1986), "Benefits and costs of containerized forest tree seedling research in the United States", in: D.P. Burns, ed., Evaluation and Planning of Forestry Research, General Technical Report NE-GTR-111 (USDA Forest Service, Northeastern Forest Experiment Station, Broomall, PA).

White, J.F., and J. Havlicek, Jr. (1982), "Optimal expenditures for agricultural research and extension: Implications on underfunding", American Journal of Agricultural Economics 64(1):47–54.

White, J.F., J. Havlicek, Jr. and D. Otto (1978), "Fifty years of technical change in American agriculture", International Conference of Agricultural Economists, Banff, Alberta, Canada, September 3–12, 1979.

Wise, W.S. (1986), "The calculation rates of return on agricultural research from production functions", Journal of Agricultural Economics 37(2):151–161.

Wise, W.S., and E. Fell (1980), "Supply shifts and the size of research benefits: Comment", American Journal of Agricultural Economics 62(4):838–840.

World Bank (1988), "Cotton development programs in Burkina Faso, Cote d'Ivoire, and Togo", A World Bank Operations Evaluation Study (Washington, D.C., The World Bank).

Yee, J. (1992), "Assessing rates of return to public and private agricultural research", Journal of Agricultural Economics Research 44(1):35–41.

Zachariah, O.E.R., G. Fox and G.L. Brinkman (1988), "The returns to broiler research in Canada – 1968 to 1984", Working Paper 88/3 (Department of Agriculture Economics and Business, University of Guelph).

Zentner, R.P. (1982), "An economic evaluation of public wheat research expenditures in Canada", Ph.D. Dissertation (University of Minnesota).

Chapter 12

THE AGRICULTURAL PRODUCER: THEORY AND STATISTICAL MEASUREMENT

RICHARD E. JUST

Agricultural and Resource Economics, University of Maryland, College Park, MD

RULON D. POPE

Department of Economics, Brigham Young University, Provo, UT

Contents

Handbook of Agricultural Economics, Volume 1, Edited by B. Gardner and G. Rausser

JEL classification: Q11

1. Introduction

Agricultural production economics grew out of the study of farm management. Farm management grew out of the study of agronomy and horticulture. Early courses in farm management particularly at Cornell were largely empirically based and sought to develop the underlying economic principles through replication of experiments [Jensen (1977)]. "As marginal analysis reached a climax with Alfred Marshall, agricultural economics was just beginning to emerge as a discipline in land-grant colleges" [Johnson (1955), p. 206]. During the 1920s and 1930s, production economics began to emerge as an integrated field that analyzed farm management and production issues from farming to and including marketing of agricultural products. As in other fields of economics, the unifying paradigms for this emerging discipline were marginal economic analysis, comparative advantage, and competition [Jensen (1977)]. That agricultural production and farm management economics embraced these central economic paradigms of the time was indisputable and as such it could properly be viewed as a subdiscipline of economics. Because the issues and problems were agricultural, most agricultural economists to this day reside in colleges of agriculture throughout the world.

The marriage of economic paradigms to farm management and production economic issues is widely viewed as successful. Agricultural economists working with other agricultural scientists have enlightened many both as to normative and positive economic choices. However, many agricultural economists particularly of older vintages likely identify more with agricultural sciences and less with economics compared to younger vintages who tend to identify more with economics as the parent discipline [Pope and Hallam (1986)].

How and why does agricultural production economics differ from the application of economic principles to other production activities in the economy? Clearly, the goods and services studied are different and that alone may justify a separate field of study. However, in a deeper sense, is the current or proper methodology for studying agricultural production different than for studying, say, manufacturing? A basic question that must be addressed in a volume such as this is, "Why is the study of agricultural economics different than the study of the economics of any other sector?" and in particular, "What are the distinguishing features of agricultural production economics?"

In this chapter, we emphasize the production issues that differentiate agriculture from manufacturing. We begin in the following section by identifying a number of unique features of agricultural production – features not necessarily unique in their existence but unique by their combination and predominance in agriculture. While some mathematical characterizations in this section facilitate understanding, they are merely illustrative with formal analysis delayed to later sections. The purpose of Section 2 is to raise issues and questions related to the unique features of agriculture that are addressed in subsequent sections. The general conclusion is that agricultural production is heavily structured because of spatial, temporal, and stochastic issues. Section 3 develops a set of economic principles that are needed to address a sector dominated by such features. Some examples are used to illustrate the points with no attempt to achieve generality.

The general conclusion is that serious errors can be made if structural issues are ignored in analysis. Section 4 then develops some fundamental theoretical considerations needed to address the principles identified in Section 3 with generality at least in a short-run context. This backdrop is used to discuss the extent to which agricultural production economics, as depicted by the previous chapters in this Handbook, has addressed these needs. The implications of these results are that (i) reduced-form approaches that initiate empirical work from an arbitrary specification of the production possibilities frontier cannot determine many important characteristics of technology, (ii) approaches that under-represent structure are not useful for policy analysis because they embed policy assumptions, (iii) both early primal applications and standard current applications of duality have tended to focus on reduced-form representations, (iv) both dual and primal approaches should be expanded to consider a qualifying degree of structure, and (v) examination of structure is limited by data availability. In Section 5 we consider other needed generalizations that come into play in moving beyond the short run and the extent of related empirical progress thus far. This leads to a critical evaluation of the state of data for agricultural production analysis, a call for action to improve the scope of data, and a conclusion that the current state of agricultural production analysis is heavily limited by data availability.

2. Uniqueness of agricultural technology

Perhaps the most important reason for studying agricultural production separately is the uniqueness of agricultural technology associated with its biological nature and exposure to widely varying and unpredictable elements of nature. This section discusses some of the main features that differentiate agricultural production: (i) lags and intertemporal complexity with limited observability caused by biological processes, (ii) uncertainty in biological processes related to weather and pests, (iii) multiple outputs with cyclical flexibility in the output mix related to growing seasons, (iv) technological change with fragmented and mixed adoption associated with both physical and biological capital adjustment, and (v) atomistic heterogeneity in major characteristics such as soil productivity, climate, infrastructure, environmental sensitivity, farmer abilities, etc. While some limited parallels can be found with some of these features in other sectors, the combination and extent found in agriculture have critical implications for the ability to represent them empirically. They dramatically affect all other aspects of the agricultural sector including domestic markets, international trade, finance, environmental concerns, and policy issues. For example, unanticipated national crop failures cause dramatic swings in world markets and trade as in the commodity boom of the 1970s [Chambers and Just (1981)], and the spatial correlations of production practices with environmental characteristics dramatically influence environmental quality and response to policies [Just and Antle (1990)].

    During the first half century of agricultural economics study, many agricultural production economists cooperated with the biological and soil science disciplines to integrate representations of biological and chemical processes and better represent the intricacies of relevant biological and physical relationships. As in engineering economics, there was a substantive interest in understanding and describing technology in cooperation with other disciplines. This interdisciplinary communication described technology in primal form. Some of the earliest production studies used agronomic data to estimate fertilizer response functions and optimal fertilization rates [Day (1965)]. Over time, a greater understanding of the science of input interactions has been accumulated to allow further economic insights into basic production problems [Berck and Helfand (1990); Paris (1992)]. As agricultural economics has evolved, dual methods have become prominent because of their simplicity, convenience, and power [Binswanger (1974)]. These methods have been widely applied but the applications typically lack the biological and dynamic detail that often accompanies other optimization or econometric models [Bryant et al. (1993); Woodward (1996); Burt (1993); Foster and Burt (1992)]. As a result, questions arise about whether agricultural production economists are now in a poorer position than earlier to assess plausibility of estimates and add cumulatively to a store of stylized facts regarded by the profession to describe agricultural technology. For example, Mundlak's review (2001) of the early production function literature emphasizes elasticity estimates and portrays the cumulative characterization of both production and supply-demand elasticities from that literature. Though no such similar review is available for recent literature, estimates of simple concepts such as elasticities are *remarkably* disparate even when similar methods (e.g., duality) and data are used [Shumway and Lim (1993), Table 3]. In this state of affairs, one must question whether agricultural production economists are approaching or losing track of the goal of better understanding and measuring behavior.

2.1. Sequential biological stages, temporal allocation, and limited observability

Agriculture in much of the world thrives with little division or specialization of labor [Allen and Lueck (1998)] because of (i) the sequential nature of production stages, (ii) non-overlapping annual growing seasons imposed by weather conditions, (iii) long time lags from application of variable inputs to harvest of finished outputs, (iv) relative unobservability of the state of production during this lag, and (v) moral hazard associated with using hired labor in certain stages of production where monitoring the effect on output is difficult.[1] Typically, a single person or family decides what to produce given the current capital stock and available services, and then applies variable inputs stage-by-stage through sequential production stages to produce the final product. A stage-wise delineation of the production process is possible in many cases because a relatively small number of sequential rather than concurrent operations are required. Such a production structure is typically imposed by the biological nature of agricultural

---

[1] For example, harvest labor for fruits and vegetables may be easy to monitor when wages are paid at a piece rate for the amount harvested. However, labor required to seed a crop may be harder to monitor because errors in application rates are largely unobserved until much later when crop stands are apparent or final production is realized.

production. By comparison, manufacturing with a small number of sequential rather than concurrent operations is hard to imagine and likely inefficient because assembly lines are precluded.

For some annual non-irrigated crops, few inputs are applied during the five to nine months between the time of planting and harvesting. For other annual crops, inputs such as pesticides may be applied for preventative reasons before or at planting as well as for prescriptive purposes after planting. A simplifying characteristic of crop production is that application of most inputs involves a costly trip over a field. Thus, most inputs cannot be economically applied continuously (irrigation and inputs applied through irrigation water are exceptions), but rather the timing of input applications is a crucial production decision because of weather.

Because input responses are weather-dependent and harvests are seasonal, production and revenue depend on the timing of input applications. Thus, an m-stage technically efficient input-output relationship might be described by the smooth function,

$$y = f\big(f_1\big(x^1, t_1\big), \ldots, f_m\big(x^m, t_m\big)\big), \tag{1}$$

where x^i is the variable input vector at time t_i and x^m is harvest inputs applied at harvest time t_m. Note that both the quantity of each x^i and the associated time of application t_i are decision variables. In other words, timing as well as quantities are input choices. The chosen harvest date may not correspond to maximum possible production not only due to time preferences and interest rate incentives but because of labor and machinery scheduling problems, weather, and uncertainty of crop maturity. Because of lags, each x^i is relevant to final output, $\partial f/\partial x^i = (\partial f/\partial f_i)(\partial f_i/\partial x^i) \neq 0$.

In one of only a few studies that have treated timing of operations as decision variables, Just and Candler (1985) demonstrate that agricultural production functions tend to be concave in the timing of both planting and harvesting operations so a unique timing exists that is technically efficient. Antle, Capalbo, and Crissman (1994) similarly investigate optimal timing and suggest an efficiency dimension of input timing. Interestingly, optimal timing in the context of the whole farm operation may not be technically efficient when the availability of resources such as labor or machinery services is constrained. That is, available labor and machinery may not be sufficient to harvest all plots at the same time if they should all mature at the same time.[2]

Also unlike manufacturing where the quality of a continuous or intermediate-stage output is observable, the implications of the current state of a crop for final production are highly subjective at each stage of the growing cycle. In most manufacturing processes, the time it takes to create a finished product, $t_m - t_1$, is relatively short. Additionally, intermediate productivity is more observable compared to agriculture, e.g., how far an item has moved on an assembly line or how well an intermediate step of assembly has been accomplished. Thus, continuous monitoring of input productivity and

---

[2] One could define technical efficiency to include any non-price constraints but this seems at variance with typical technologically based definitions.

making related adjustments at each stage of the production process is more effective. In other words, technical efficiency is best achieved by examining carefully each stage's output as it occurs or by testing to reach conclusions about the technical efficiency of individual production stages.

In contrast, the long delay from input application to observed productivity tends to confound the observed effects of inputs applied in multiple stages of agricultural production processes. As a result, one cannot easily infer from output which stage is inefficient. Moreover, the effects of inputs observed on other farms may not apply because of differing soil and climatic features. The focus of management is thus more on following recommended guidelines, experimentation to adapt recommended guidelines to specific farm or plot circumstances, and monitoring exogenous and uncontrollable inputs such as weather and pests in order to formulate counter measures.

To better represent intraseasonal unobservability, suppose the representation of the production process assuming technical efficiency in the intermediate states of production follows[3]

$$y = f^* \left(f_1 \left(x^1, y_0 \right), \ldots, f_m \left(x^m, y_{m-1} \right) \right), \tag{2}$$

where the timings of input applications are implicit decision variables suppressed for simplicity. That is, efficient management at stage i involves maximizing the intermediate output, y_i, where the technology set at stage i is represented by $y_i \leqslant f_i(x^i, y_{i-1})$ and y_0 represents initial conditions [Antle and Hatchett (1986)].[4] One way of conceptualizing the difference between agricultural and manufacturing production in this framework is that the intermediate outputs in agriculture, the y_i's, are largely unobservable. In many manufacturing contexts, the separate stage production functions are readily observed, estimated, and applied separately for management purposes. Thus, efficient farming is directed toward learning well the stage technology through acquiring information available from beyond the farm (such as guidelines from technology developers and universities), experimentation, monitoring uncontrollable inputs, and estimating optimal adjustments accordingly.

This recursively separable structure of production whereby inputs x_i in stage t_i are separable from inputs x^j in stage t_j $(j > i)$ has important implications for agricultural production analysis. For example, labor and capital services applied during pre-planting cultivation will be separable from labor and capital services applied to post-planting herbicide application. This property allows experiment station or extension scientists or scientists from input supply firms to make recommendations on specific input choices that are clear and relevant to farmers assuming that the state variable from the previous

---

[3] For convenience, we use the expression in (2) to represent a production process of the form

$$y = f_n(x_n, f_{n-1}(x_{n-1}, f_{n-2}(x_{n-2}, \ldots, f_1(x_1, y_0) \ldots))).$$

[4] This yields a variant of recursive separability [Blackorby et al. (1978)].

stage is typical (the case of experiment station guidelines) or monitored (the case of professional pesticide applicators).

Timing of operations has been largely ignored in agricultural production economics. Rather, public agricultural production data are recorded on an annual basis. Accordingly, the timing of input applications as well as the intermediate outputs are unobserved. To utilize such data, the firm is typically presumed to solve:

$$y = f^0(x, y_0) = \max_{\{x^i\}} \left\{ f^* \left(f_1(x^1, y_0), \ldots, f_m(x^m, y_{m-1}) \right) \middle| \sum_i x^i = x \right\}. \qquad (3)$$

Initial conditions are typically ignored because data are unavailable in which case the estimated technology corresponds to $y = f^0(x)$. In this approach, the aggregate input vector x is treated as the decision variable in the related profit maximization problem (possibly some elements of x are treated as fixed or quasi-fixed inputs).

Interestingly, the assumptions implicit in (3) for input aggregation tend to be inadequate as a representation of family farming, the predominant form of agricultural production. The reason is that some inputs such as family labor and fixed-capital service flows present recurring input constraints through the growing season rather than across the entire production season. As a result, the shadow price (or opportunity cost) of resources can vary considerably through the growing season. For example, farm machinery is typically idle or underutilized through much of the year but is used heavily during several weeks. A grain farmer's most expensive piece of equipment may be a combine that is used only 3 or 4 weeks of the year. Tractors may be used to capacity only at planting or cultivation time of the few dominant crops grown on a farm. In spite of low average use rates, farmers find ownership advantageous because all farmers in an area tend to need the same machinery services at the same time due to local climate and soil conditions that tend to dictate crop timing. Capital services may be hired to relax such constraints in some cases, but custom machinery service markets do not operate in many cases because demands are too seasonal. The implication is that available service flows from such equipment are constrained by fixed investments but the shadow prices caused by such constraints may vary widely through a crop season. For example, the shadow price of the service of a combine may be almost comparable to or even higher than custom hiring rates in the peak use season, but yet much lower in a secondary harvesting season where excess capacity is available. These possibilities explain why farmers choose to hold stocks of expensive machinery even though average use is light.

Likewise, family labor may have distinct advantages over hired labor for specific functions because of moral hazard. That is, additional labor may be hired for such needs as harvesting where productivity is easily monitored and rewarded by piece rates, but moral hazard problems may make hired labor a poor alternative for other types of labor needs such as seeding. Indeed, the superiority of using family labor for carrying out certain functions is an important explanation for survival and predominance of the family farm [Allen and Lueck (1998)]. As a result, family labor within the conventional production model (which typically does not consider moral hazard) can be reasonably treated as a recurring constraint through the growing season that is far more limiting at some times than at others. Thus, the shadow price of family labor may vary widely through the growing season. The widely varying nature of implicit prices of farmer-controlled resources across labor periods (stages of production) has been well-recognized in programming models used to represent agricultural technology [McCarl et al. (1977); Kutcher and Scandizzo (1981); Keplinger et al. (1998)].[5]

If the implicit shadow prices of recurring farmer-controlled inputs vary widely from stage to stage, then the implicit formulation in Equation (3) may be inadequate. Mundlak (2001) emphasizes the need for this generalization in his discussion regarding the representation of capital inputs as stocks versus flows. To emphasize this difference, let x^i represent a vector of purchased variable inputs in stage t_i, and let z^i represent a vector of uses of farmer-controlled inputs such as family labor and capital services in stage t_i. Also, let k be a vector of maximum uses or availability of services made possible by the fixed stock of farmer-controlled resources in each stage.[6] Then technology can be represented by

$$
\begin{aligned}
y &= f^0(x, y_0 \mid k) \\
&= \max_{\{x^i, k^i\}} \left\{ f^*\big(f_1(x^1, y_0, z^1), \ldots, f_m(x^m, y_{m-1}, z^m) \big) \,\Big|\, \sum_i x^i = x; z^i \leqslant k \right\}.
\end{aligned}
\tag{4}
$$

This formulation makes clear that varying implicit prices of fixed farmer-controlled inputs is likely. In some periods, the optimal choice may be $z^i = k$ with a high implicit price while in others it is some $z^i < k$ with a zero implicit price.

---

[5] Mathematical programming models of agricultural decisions have largely given way to econometric models of decisions as indicated by a review of the literature. Several reasons are as follows. First, there is a great desire for statistical inference whereas inference with inequality constraints is a daunting task [Amemiya (1985); Diewert and Wales (1987)]. Second, in traditional practice, programming approaches have typically used subjective and ad hoc approaches to calibrate models, which some regard as falling short of scientific standards. Third, a primary purpose of production economics has become development of aggregate models of behavior with which to undertake policy analysis. Aggregate programming models tend to generate supplies and demands with large and irregular steps that are regarded as implausible. To the extent firm-level heterogeneity can be handled by smooth econometric models, programming models are less useful. However, recent developments in data envelopment analysis and Bayesian applications have spawned greater interest in merging programming and econometric methods [Fried et al. (1993); Chavas and Cox (1988); Paris and Howitt (1998)]. We note also that modern computer technology is rapidly making possible the boot-strapping of statistical properties of programming models with realistic components such as intermittently binding inequality constraints [Vanker (1996)]. For the purposes of this chapter, we consider primarily the econometric approach to empirical work. However, the principles apply to programming models as well and may be ultimately implemented by some merger of programming and econometric methods.

[6] For simplicity, we assume that farmer-controlled resources and thus maximum uses are constant across production stages in the same growing season. If this is not the case, then time subscripts must be added to the limits of use.

These considerations raise questions about how explicitly models must depict the stage-wise production problem and what types of data are needed to do so. For example, if capital service input data are not available by stages, then Equation (4) suggests that capital input data must measure the state of the capital stock (which determines the maximum possible flow of capital services in each stage) rather than the aggregate flow of capital services over the entire growing season. Modeling the stage-wise choices of capital service flows given these stocks may greatly improve understanding of production decisions if data are available for analysis. But if data are unavailable, how can models represent these implicit production choices sufficiently?

2.2. Flexibility in the output mix and spatial allocation

In principle, all firms conceptually choose among producing and marketing multiple final outputs because, at least in principle at the capital investment stage, they decide what to produce. However, much of agriculture throughout the world involves actually producing multiple products simultaneously. While measures of diversification are beginning to decline in many areas, particularly in the post-war period in the United States and most notably for livestock firms [White and Irwin (1972)], crop farming remains highly diversified. An important factor in choosing an agricultural output mix is spatial allocation of inputs among plots. This aspect of agricultural production makes agriculture an interesting case for study of scope economies and the effect of scale on scope economies [Chavas (2001)].

Many multiple-product manufacturing settings involve products that are produced in fixed or limited proportions determined by fixed plant and equipment or physical properties of production processes such as chemical reactions. In others, multiple products result from abruptly switching an entire plant from the manufacturing of one product to another (where simultaneous production of several outputs is not feasible or economical). In agriculture, a few production processes lead to related joint products with limited flexibility such as meat in combination with hides or cotton in combination with cottonseed. However, farmers often have great flexibility in switching among annual crops from season to season and in allocating land, machinery services, and family labor among crops in the same season. Flexible capital leads to large elasticities of product transformation (and, hence, large supply elasticities) because farmers can readily change their relative output mix from one crop season to the next. Much of this flexibility occurs because allocated inputs have similar marginal revenue product schedules in the production of several crops.[7] For example, land and land preparation machinery have similar marginal values in production of corn and soybeans in the corn belt or in production of wheat and sorghum in the southern Great Plains. This is why other considerations are sufficient to cause farms to rotate plots of land and diversify production among such crops.

---

[7] Flexibility also implies that capital has relatively large marginal products in various states of nature as well.

Marshallian joint production is generally presumed to be a reasonable explanation for many economies of scope and the implied optimality of multi-product farms. Baumol, Panzar and Willig (1988) define inputs for such processes as public inputs because they can be costlessly redirected from one industry to another. Clearly some purchased capital such as buildings or tractors may have some of these characteristics when congestion effects are not present. Some aspects of management skill and information have these properties. Clearly weather is a classic public input [Pope (1976)]. However, the timing and nature of demands on private inputs (or public inputs with congestion effects) can also promote diversification.

For example, when several crops compete for the same farmer-controlled resources, constraints on allocation of these resources can play an important role in determining diversification of the product mix. Farmers must generally allocate farmer-controlled resources consisting of land, management ability, machinery services, and family labor among plots of land. Because these inputs must be allocated spatially among plots, and plots are generally planted to distinct crops (or distinct crop mixes in some developing agriculture), these allocations usually amount to allocations among crops as well. Producing multiple outputs, which have different peak input-use seasons according to their varied stages of production, thus provides a way of more fully utilizing farmer-controlled resources and allowing more off-farm labor possibilities. For example, by producing several crops with different growing seasons, or by producing both crops and livestock which have different seasonality requirements, a farmer may be able to use smaller-scale, less expensive machinery and more fully utilize available family labor and management ability than if the entire farm had to be covered with the same operation at one time. Such considerations can be so important that, when coupled with price incentives, they lead to diversification when specialization otherwise occurs [Pope (1976); Pope and Prescott (1980); Baker and McCarl (1982)].

Interestingly, most agricultural production scientists focus on the rate of application of inputs or input services to a particular plot on which a particular crop is grown. For example, extension specialists recommend different rates of fertilizer application for different crops and soil conditions. Pesticides are often regulated with specified application rates per acre under legal licensing requirements. In this context, the representations in (1)–(4) may apply where y is a vector of outputs and x^i is a vector which distinguishes not only type of input but location (plot and thus crop) of application. With non-jointness of all inputs, Equation (4) becomes

$$y^j = f_j^*\big(f_{1j}\big(x^{1j}, y_0^j, z^{1j}\big), \ldots, f_{mj}\big(x^{mj}, y_{m-1}^j, z^{mj}\big)\big), \quad j = 1, \ldots,$$

$$\text{subject to} \sum_j z^{ij} \leqslant k, \quad i = 1, \ldots, m, \tag{5}$$

where $y^j = y_m^j$ is the quantity produced of output j, x^{ij} is a vector of purchased variable inputs allocated to output j in stage i, and z^{ij} is a vector of uses of farmer-controlled resources allocated to output j in stage i. That is, uses of farmer-controlled resources across all production activities must satisfy availability constraints jointly. Note for convenience and to represent availability constraints appropriately in (5), the first subscript of x is assumed to represent a common timing choice across all production activities so that $t_{ij} = t_i$ is the timing choice for operations in stage i of production for all outputs.[8] Also, note more generally that each y^j could represent a vector of outputs with j indexing additively separable production activities in which case (5) does not imply nonjointness of inputs.

The framework of (5) reflects the notion of allocated fixed inputs introduced by Shumway, Pope, and Nash (1984) and investigated by Just, Zilberman, and Hochman (1983), Leathers (1991), and Just et al. (1990). This literature recognizes that inputs such as land are typically measured and must generally be allocated to the production of specific crops (or crop mixes). While the nonjointness assumptions of these papers may be debatable, the need for farmers to allocate at least some purchased variable inputs and at least some farmer-controlled resources among plots is clear.

Public data typically report inputs and outputs for a region but generally do not give allocations of inputs to crops, plots, or production activities as does farm-level accounting and management data. As a result, problems of estimation of multi-output production relationships in agriculture typically have been simplified to eliminate the allocation problem. As in the case where temporal allocation of inputs is unobserved, elimination of spatial allocation variables presumably assumes implicitly that inputs are allocated among plots to achieve efficiency given that inputs have identical prices across plots. Thus, the firm is treated as solving an allocation problem of the form

$$
\begin{aligned}
y^1 &= f(x, k, y^2, y^3, \dots) \\
&= \max \left\{ y^1 \mid y^j = f_j^* \left(f_{1j}(x^{1j}, z^{1j}), \dots, f_{mj}(x^{mj}, z^{mj}) \right), \ j = 1, \dots; \right. \\
&\qquad \left. \sum_j z^{ij} \leqslant k, \ i = 1, \dots, m; \ \sum_i \sum_j x^{ij} \leqslant x \right\}
\end{aligned}
$$

in the typical case where initial conditions are ignored. These practices raise questions regarding how explicitly allocation decisions must be represented in production models and how much understanding of the production problem can be gained by representing allocations explicitly. Can greater econometric efficiency be gained thereby? What data are required?

2.3. Fragmented technology adoption and embodied technology

Much has been written about technical change and technology adoption in agriculture [see the reviews by Sunding and Zilberman (2001) and by Evenson (2001)]. Such phenomena explain both the successes and failures of the "green revolution" and explain

---

[8] This represents no loss in generality because the input vector may be zero for some production activities in some production stages.

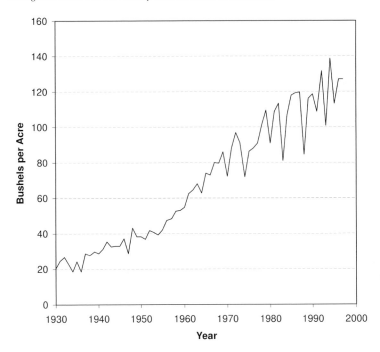

Figure 1. U.S. corn yield growth.

the dramatic growth in agricultural productivity in the twentieth century. More currently, they have much to say about potential agricultural responses to environmental problems, food safety, genetically modified organisms, and the induced innovation that is likely to occur as a result [Sunding and Zilberman (2001); Chavas (2001)]. The dramatic growth in productivity due to technology is illustrated in Figure 1 by the sixfold increase in average U.S. corn yields since 1930. Figure 2 illustrates how much higher the rate of growth in productivity per worker has been in agriculture compared to manufacturing and business.[9] Much of the growth in productivity in developing agriculture has come in the form of higher-yielding seeds, fertilizer use, tube wells for irrigation, and replacement of traditional crops by modern crops. A major explanation in developed agriculture lies in the development of larger-scale machinery, improved crop varieties and livestock breeds, and new inputs such as pesticides and growth hormones. In each case, the technology is embodied in either variable production inputs or in the capital stock.

[9]   To construct Figure 2, U.S. Bureau of Labor Statistics indexes for productivity per hour in manufacturing and business are used. The productivity per worker index for agriculture is constructed from U.S. Economic Research Service data by dividing the index of total farm output by the index of farm labor input (see the 1999 Economic Report of the President). All indexes are then adjusted to 100 in 1949. Because the number of hours in the work week in manufacturing and business has been falling, a fair comparison would imply an even greater divergence in growth of output per worker.

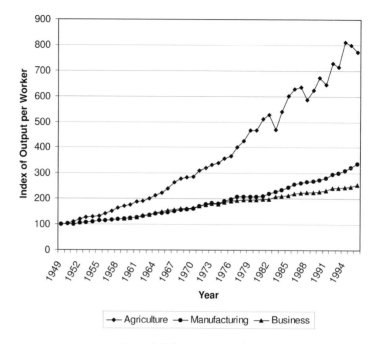

Figure 2. U.S. output per worker.

One of the core features of modern production processes is that production decisions often lag years behind capital decisions. For example, in automobile production, the cycle time from product design to production often takes at least two years. However, once the plant and equipment are in place, the application of inputs typically yields a finished output with very little lag. For example, the typical auto assembly plant produces a car every few minutes and the complete cycle time including pre-assembly of important components is measured in days. For mature industrial processes, this process evolves largely into "quality control".

Some aspects of agricultural production resemble the manufacturing paradigm. For example, producing tree crops and vineyards requires considerable time to put the capital stock in place (e.g., mature trees and vines). Similarly, livestock production involves considerable time to grow mature breeding animals (for gestation, birth, weaning, etc.). These biologically induced lags introduce some interesting and lengthy nonlinear dynamics into the production process [Chavas and Holt (1991, 1993)]. However, a unique aspect of agriculture (compared to manufacturing) is that once the physical capital (perennial crop stands and breeding herds in addition to machinery and buildings) are in place, the lag from the application of variable inputs to the finished output is relatively long.

Another largely unique feature of agricultural production – particularly annual crop production – is that the technology choice is described by a lengthy list of piecemeal decisions that must be made with each new growing season on each plot of land [Sunding and Zilberman (2001); Feder et al. (1985)]. For example, each time a crop is planted a producer can choose to grow a different crop, use a different seed variety, apply fertilizer, use herbicides, apply insecticides, or employ plant growth regulators. A typical grower may choose among 3 to 5 economical crops for the area, each crop may have from 3 to 5 prominent crop varieties with different levels of resistance to unforeseen weather and crop disease conditions, and the farmer may face from 3 to 5 attractive alternative choices each for fertilizers, herbicides, insecticides (if needed), etc. A farmer can choose to use low tillage methods or a variety of tilling operations to control weeds and conserve moisture. Some of these choices are influenced by the stock of equipment (variety and size). The stock of equipment is typically adjusted in piecemeal fashion because most tractors can accept a wide variety of equipment (although the size of equipment is constrained by the size of tractor). The variety of equipment on hand can constrain either the feasible or economical crop set. The size of equipment as well as family labor availability can constrain the amount of land that can be economically allocated to a particular crop/technology combination.

To complicate farmers' choices further, new technology is constantly being developed. New seed varieties and new pesticides are being developed every year and in some cases have dramatic effects on yields.[10] These effects explain the dramatic increase in crop yields as illustrated for corn in Figure 1. A typical problem, however, is that new technologies are unproven and are thus viewed as more risky. Farmers may delay adoption and observe responses obtained by neighbors or allocate small test plots to new technologies. For characterizations of technology to be consistent with such behavior, these uncertainties and options must be represented. Furthermore, technology embodied in machinery or perennial crops is largely fixed by vintage of the capital stock. Some farmers may adopt technologies on a small scale and then increasingly with learning by doing [Foster and Rosenzweig (1995)]. As a result of the complex nature of the technology choice and lags in adoption, a large number of technologies are employed concurrently by different farmers and on different plots by the same farmer [Feder et al. (1985)]. These phenomena complicate drawing inferences from agricultural production data that has been aggregated across heterogeneous farms as discussed further in the section on heterogeneity below. How explicitly does the distribution of technology need to be represented in production models? How much does the distribution of technology depend on the capital distribution? What data on technologies can improve production modeling and how?

2.4. Uncertainty: The role of weather and pests in biological processes

One way agricultural production differs from most manufacturing production is in the magnitude of the impact of uncontrollable factors – many of which are highly stochastic and unpredictable. The dominance of uncertainty in agricultural production is one

---

[10] The term 'pesticide' is a generic term that includes insecticides, herbicides, fungicides, rodenticides, and crop growth regulators.

reason the study of production under risk has flourished in agricultural economics [Moschini and Hennessy (2001)]. The highly unpredictable nature of agricultural production is illustrated by the yearly national-level corn yields depicted in Figure 1. Furthermore, the data in Figure 1 understate variability because averaging at the national level washes out variation among individual farms. Empirical evidence suggests that variability at the farm level is from 2 to 10 times greater than indicated by aggregate time series data [Just and Weninger (1999)]. The most important uncontrollable factors are weather, pests, and unpredictable biological processes, all of which vary from farm to farm. Weather and pests can cause either localized or widespread crop failures or shortfalls through hail storms, high winds, drought, crop disease, insects, and weed infestations.

Production variability translates also into relatively larger price variability in agriculture as well. The difference in price variability among sectors is highlighted by U.S. producer price indexes at the finished goods and consumer foods level. The variance of annual percentage changes in prices over 1989–1998 was 37.7 for crude consumer foods compared to 4.7 for finished consumer goods, 2.1 for finished capital equipment, 3.8 for processed consumer foods (which represents primarily non-food inputs of processing and packaging), and 5.7 for finished consumer goods excluding foods.

To illustrate the extent of uncontrollable random variation at the state level, the coefficients of variation (CVs) for corn and wheat yields in the United States in Table 1 suggest that farmers on average can have only about a 68 percent probability that production will be in an interval equal to 30 percent of expectations (as implied by normality when CVs average about .15). Furthermore, these coefficients of variation are considerably higher in some states (ranging from .04 to about .25 for both crops). The lower coefficients of variation occur mostly in states where expensive irrigation technology is used to compensate for low and irregular rainfall. Furthermore, it should be noted that much of the variation experienced by individual farmers is washed out by the statewide aggregate data summarized in Table 1 so that the statistics in Table 1 represent a significant underestimate of the effect of uncontrollable factors at the farm level.

Weather and pests are continuous inputs that affect crop growth throughout the entire growing season. Characterizing technically efficient decisions on the basis of ex post random draws of output is difficult because the impact of any vector of inputs x^i on output $(\partial y / \partial x^i)$ is obscured by previous weather occurrences embodied in a largely unobserved state of the crop at time t_i and future weather occurrences embodied in the ultimate observed production, y. Drawing on the well-known literature under uncertainty, (x_i', G') is technically inefficient in an ex ante sense in stage t_i if $G(y_i \mid x^i, y_{i-1}) < G'(y_i \mid x^{i'}, y_{i-1})$ for all y_i where G and G' are cumulative distribution functions associated with y_i and $x_i' \geqslant x_i$. This relationship, however, merely represents first-degree stochastic dominance. First-degree stochastic dominance holds for a particular distribution (for a particular input vector) if it yields the largest output for every state of nature. A similar notion can be developed using conventional input distance measures [Färe (1996)]. If first-degree stochastic dominance fails, higher orders of dominance may provide potentially useful comparisons [Eeckhoudt and Gollier (1992)].

Table 1
Coefficients of variation and average yields for U.S. corn and wheat, 1988–97

State	Coefficient of variation		Mean yield	
	Corn	Wheat	Corn	Wheat
Alabama	0.23	0.19	75.2	38.1
Arizona	0.06	0.04	164.5	91.1
Arkansas	0.13	0.22	112.3	43.5
California	0.04	0.06	161.5	77.4
Colorado	0.11	0.10	143.0	33.0
Delaware	0.19	0.15	107.8	55.7
Florida	0.14	0.17	75.4	34.7
Georgia	0.19	0.16	89.6	40.8
Idaho	0.07	0.07	133.5	72.9
Illinois	0.19	0.19	124.3	49.5
Indiana	0.17	0.15	121.9	52.0
Iowa	0.20	0.18	122.3	38.4
Kansas	0.09	0.19	133.7	33.9
Kentucky	0.17	0.19	107.7	49.5
Louisiana	0.13	0.21	106.8	33.9
Maryland	0.22	0.14	104.2	54.6
Michigan	0.14	0.17	106.6	50.3
Minnesota	0.21	0.25	114.6	35.5
Mississippi	0.18	0.24	85.7	37.3
Missouri	0.18	0.16	107.0	43.0
Montana	0.16	0.21	114.7	30.4
Nebraska	0.10	0.12	126.4	34.5
Nevada		0.11		81.7
New Jersey	0.16	0.14	106.2	47.1
New Mexico	0.06	0.22	161.0	27.1
New York	0.10	0.10	101.5	50.7
North Carolina	0.14	0.13	87.7	44.6
North Dakota	0.23	0.25	78.0	29.1
Ohio	0.16	0.13	117.7	53.6
Oklahoma	0.13	0.18	120.1	28.0
Oregon	0.09	0.11	160.9	62.7
Pennsylvania	0.19	0.11	100.6	48.5
South Carolina	0.26	0.17	76.2	41.8
South Dakota	0.21	0.21	81.1	29.3
Tennessee	0.18	0.18	101.2	42.7
Texas	0.12	0.14	112.3	28.3
Utah	0.09	0.14	129.6	41.7
Virginia	0.20	0.13	97.7	54.5
Washington	0.04	0.13	182.0	57.2
West Virginia	0.17	0.09	93.1	47.8
Wisconsin	0.19	0.16	110.9	48.1
Wyoming	0.15	0.15	111.8	27.8
Average	0.15	0.16	111.2	45.8

One of the pressing issues in the measurement of efficiency across firms is that firms may have access to the same technology but may not have access to identical distributions of weather, i.e., identical distributions of outputs given inputs. To denote dependence on local random weather, the production response can be represented by

$$y = f(x^1, \ldots, x^m, k, \varepsilon),$$ (6)

where k represents all relevant capital inputs, ε is a vector of weather occurrences on a particular plot or farm, and the choice of timing of inputs is suppressed for convenience.

Adding intermediate temporal detail, a more informative representation is

$$y = \left\{ f^*\left(f_1(x^1, y_0, z^1, \varepsilon^1), \ldots, f_m(x^m, y_{m-1}, z^m, \varepsilon^m)\right) \mid z^i \leqslant k \right\},$$ (7)

where ε^i represents local weather events occurring during stage t_i of the production process. The possibility for weather events to cause significant variation in final or stage output is large. Weather can cause certain operations (stages) to be largely ineffective or consume excessive resources unless choices of timing are altered. For example, trying to cultivate a field that is too wet can cause tillage to be ineffective or consume excessive labor. Or trying to plant a crop before adequate rain can result in an inadequate stand of seedlings. The associated consequences for output can be dramatic. For example, delaying planting of corn in Iowa beyond the average optimum of May 1 to May 20 implies more than a 10 percent decline in yields [Burger (1998)]. Weather can also reduce plant growth with excessive heat or inadequate rain or destroy crops at any stage through hail storms.

An important result following from the lags in (7) is that realized output may not be monotonically increasing in input variables. For example, bad weather (pest infestations) can reduce yields while motivating managers to use more labor (pesticides). Thus, a regression of output y_{t_n} on some total input vector $x = \sum_i x^i$ may suggest a negative association for some variables even though $\partial E_i(y_{t_n})/\partial x^i$ is positive, where E_i is the expectation of y_{t_n} taken at time t_i (using information available at time t_i). This has led some economists to model particular inputs as controlling the damage to normal growth [Feder (1979)].

Considerable early efforts were made to determine the relationship between yields and weather [Doll (1967); McQuigg and Doll (1961); de Janvry (1972)]. These studies try to use weather and ex post measurements of yields to model the conditional distributional of yields given controlled inputs. Voluminous data compiled by the U.S. National Weather Service include hourly temperature, wind, and precipitation data at a large number of weather stations in the United States. Because the data is so voluminous and detailed, suitable aggregator functions are needed but have not been developed. Alternatively, recent work has been content to consider a Taylor's series approximation of (6) at, say, $E_n(\varepsilon) = 0$ and estimate functions such as $y = \tilde{f}(x, y_0, k) + \tilde{g}(x, y_0, k)\varepsilon$ where y_0 is typically not measured. This leads to a function in terms of controllable inputs plus a heteroscedastic error [Just and Pope (1978, 1979); Antle (1983)]. More formally, a first-order Taylor series approximation of (7) is

$$y = \{ f^*\big(f_1(x^1, y_0, z^1, 0), \ldots, f_m(x^m, y_{m-1}, z^m, 0) \big) \\ + f_\varepsilon^*\big(f_1(x^1, y_0, z^1, 0), \ldots, f_m(x^m, y_{m-1}, z^m, 0) \big) \varepsilon \mid z^i \leqslant k \}, \tag{8}$$

where subscripts of f^* represent differentiation, transposition is ignored for simplicity, and ε is a vector composed of $\varepsilon^1, \ldots, \varepsilon^m$. The key marginal effect of x^i on the variance (mean-preserving spread) of y is thus

$$\partial \operatorname{var}(y)/\partial x^i = 2 f_\varepsilon^*(\cdot) f_{\varepsilon x^i}^*(\cdot) \mathrm{E}_m(\varepsilon^2) \tag{9}$$

and has signs determined by elements of $f_\varepsilon^*(\cdot) f_{\varepsilon x^i}^*(\cdot)$.

While the structure of (8) appears quite complex for empirical purposes, considerable common structure between the first and second right-hand terms can be exploited for efficiency purposes. For example, the same separable structure is preserved in both the mean and the shock portion of production because it is generated by the same recursive structure of the production stages. Thus, if seeds are separable from labor and machinery in mean wheat production, the same should also be true for the variance. As suggested by Antle's (1983) work, the framework in (8) and (9) can also be expanded in a straightforward way to consider higher moments of the output distribution. The more recent work of Chambers and Quiggin (1998) can also be considered as a generalization of this characterization of production because it characterizes stochastic production by the production set in every state of nature [see Moschini and Hennessy (2001) in this Handbook for a brief explanation].[11]

More importantly, Equations (8) and (9) highlight a central issue in decision making when mean-variance decision models are appropriate; namely, that an input may contribute to the mean differently than it contributes to variance. Indeed, the contributions may be opposite in sign. An input in which (9) is negative (positive) is typically called risk reducing (increasing), following Just and Pope (1978, 1979). Another related possibility is to classify inputs based upon the marginal effect of risk aversion on use [Loehman and Nelson (92)]. A large body of research has developed on risk-reducing marketing, production, and financial strategies. Further examples of empirical research measuring the stochastic characteristics of inputs are found in Love and Buccola (1991); Regev et al. (1997); Horowitz and Lichtenberg (1993); and Nelson and Preckel (1989). However, for the most part, these studies have explored possibilities on a piecemeal basis and have not produced a coherent and widely used framework for agricultural production analysis. Many questions remain. How explicitly do stochastic elements of production have to be represented? Does the source of stochasticity make a difference? How can the micro-level stochastic production problem be represented adequately with available data?

---

[11] Assuming technical efficiency, characterizing all the moments of output is equivalent to characterizing efficient production in every state of nature because of the uniqueness of moment-generating functions.

2.5. Interseasonal complexity of biological and physical processes

A host of longer-run (inter-year) issues also complicate matters [Nerlove and Bessler (2001)]. Like manufacturing, these involve evolutions of the capital stock represented in k from one production period to the next and how these affect technology. The state of the capital stock is affected by how heavily it has been used in previous periods (which determines the likelihood of time-consuming breakdowns and costly repairs) as well as by net investment. However, an important consideration in agriculture is that initial crop-year soil conditions and pest infestations/resistances and perennial crop states in y_0 are dependent on previous cropping choices, fertilizer and pesticide applications, and soil tillage. The state of the machinery capital stock may be largely observable through inventory records and by inspecting wear, while the state of soil and pest conditions is largely unobservable except through extensive (and in some cases impractical) testing.[12]

In this context, both y_0 and k are affected by decisions in earlier growing seasons. Regarding t now as spanning growing seasons, output is Markovian through both y_0 and k. This phenomenon is manifest by crop rotation practices where weed or insect cycles are broken by switching a given plot among crops on a regular basis. The need for such rotation is typically realized on the basis of previously observed infestations that occur otherwise, rather than direct indications of carry-over soil or pest conditions. Rotation actions are often undertaken on a preventative basis because once a serious problem occurs it affects an entire growing season before corrections can be made. Thus, a careful delineation of intertemporal production possibilities implies consideration of inter- and intra-year effects. Implied models contain non-linear dynamics with accompanying instability [Chavas and Holt (1991, 1993)].

The static or short-run generic description of technology in Sections 2.1–2.4 is consistent with this depiction of inter-cycle production because the choices made in a previous growing season are fixed in the current growing season. However, this simplification in theoretical modeling does not imply that initial conditions in y_0 can be ignored in empirical work as most production studies have done. Empirical work documenting the importance of inter-cycle production phenomena through carry-over conditions has been limited. See, e.g., Chambers and Lichtenberg (1995) for a rare study of interseasonal investment in soil capital.

The forward impacts of input choice are essential to many agricultural economic problems. For some inputs a positive future effect is clear, $\partial y_{i+j}/\partial x^i > 0$, $j > 0$, while for others it is negative. For example, fertilizer has both initial and future positive effects (ignoring externalities) due to the carryover of nutrients in the soil [Woodward (1996)]. However, many pesticides have negative dynamic effects by inducing pest resistance [Hueth and Regev (1974); Clark and Carlson (1990)]. In addition, interpreting

---

[12] Often limited spot testing of soil is used as a basis for prescribing fertilizer needs but the results give only a crude estimate of the inventory of soil conditions. The extent of weed seed carry-over and gestating insect infestations are impractical to assess.

the y_i's as outputs in a given year, it is clear that nitrogen fixation of legumes and other crop rotational issues have positive marginal dynamic effects on future outputs. Seemingly, micro-studies of crop choice must consider these effects if they influence observed farmer choices. Finally, capital decisions have important interyear effects [Vasavada and Chambers (1986); Vasavada and Ball (1988); Morrison and Siegel (1998)].

While many advances have been made in conceptual representation of these interseasonal issues of production, many questions are not well understood. Data for investigating these issues empirically has been lacking, particularly for crop production, and accordingly few empirical studies have been undertaken. While livestock production has been examined with more dynamic detail, models have been conceptually less elegant and, thus, of less interest. Accordingly, little is known about interseasonal behavioral preferences, particularly where risk issues are important.

2.6. Atomistic heterogeneity and aggregation

While the concepts of production theory generally are developed at the individual firm level, much of the empirical work in agricultural production is done at the aggregate level of a state or nation. Use of aggregate data has occurred because few firm-level data sets have been developed and access to them is limited or conditional.[13] Thus, the discussion of agricultural production analysis cannot be complete without considering the problem of aggregation.

Agriculture is atomistic with respect to most products. That is, the number of firms is large and each is individually unimportant at aggregate levels. Nevertheless, farms differ in many ways. The wide distribution of technology employed simultaneously across farms suggests one dimension of this problem. Another dimension is the wide variation in climate and soil quality across farms. Differences in soil quality have been highlighted historically by U.S. Natural Resources Conservation Service (formerly U.S. Soil Conservation Service) classifications of soil and land characteristics but are increasingly highlighted by precision farming techniques, localized incentives for environmental preservation and conservation practices, and location-specific environmental policy. The implications of variation in climate and soil for crop production and variability are depicted by the variation of both average yields and coefficients of variation of major crops among states in the United States as illustrated in Table 1. These variations explain much of the dramatic difference in crop mixes chosen by farmers from one location to another.

---

[13] There are exceptions such as the Agricultural Resource Management Study (formerly the Farm Cost and Returns Survey) data compiled by the U.S. Economic Research Service and the Kansas State University Farm Management Survey data in developed agriculture, and the ICRISAT Household Survey data and various other World Bank surveys in developing agriculture. However, access to such farm-level surveys tends to be limited to those with in-house affiliations, willingness to analyze the data in-house, or willingness to collaborate, and thus such data has been explored only to a limited extent.

Another dimension of heterogeneity imposed by geographic differences in climate and soil quality is the heterogeneity in prices induced thereby. As a result, land rents, the opportunity cost of labor and the price of services do not follow the law of one price. A considerable amount of output price variation also occurs due to differences in climate-induced product quality and timing of production [Pope and Chambers (1989); Chambers and Pope (1991)].

Though many inputs have similar marginal products across farms as well as space and enterprises, others such as chemicals, purchased services, and some machinery are highly and increasingly specialized. Some pesticides have primarily pre-emergent uses and others have primarily post-emergent uses. Most pesticides are used primarily on only a few crops and thus differ across farms. Aerial spraying equipment is primarily used for post-emergent applications while ground operations are primarily used for pre-emergent application. Aggregating such pesticide uses or machinery services over farms as well as time and space can be problematic. As technology turns more toward genetically engineered seeds, such as Roundup-ready soybeans which introduce dependence on specific pesticides, the allocation of a given total input quantity to enterprises to achieve technical efficiency may be trivial on individual farms but underrepresented by aggregates.

To represent heterogeneity, let $G(\varepsilon, k \mid \theta)$ represent the distribution across all farms of characteristics such as weather and pests, capital and technology, management ability, and other policy and input constraints imposed on farms by external conditions. Then following the representation in (7), aggregate production response is described by

$$y = \int \left\{ f^* \left(f_1(x^1, y_0, z^1, \varepsilon^1), \ldots, f_m(x^m, y_{m-1}, z^m, \varepsilon^m) \right) \mid z^i \leqslant k \right\} \mathrm{d}G(\varepsilon, k \mid \theta).$$
(10)

In this framework, standard regularity conditions fail at the aggregate level even under profit maximization but distribution-sensitive aggregation such as in (10) can preserve practical versions of regularity conditions [Just and Pope (1999)]. These results raise questions about how specifically and explicitly stochastic sources of variation must be represented in production models. Of course, related considerations of heterogeneity in prices, expectations, and risk preferences are necessary to derive supplies and demands from representations of the production technology.

2.7. Implications of the unique features of agricultural production

The discussion in Sections 2.1–2.6 emphasizes a number of unique features of agricultural production that require specific attention. Time lags and stages imposed on the production process by biological characteristics of production suggest that one should appropriately represent the allocation of inputs over time within a crop season. Flexibility of crop mixes and specificity of inputs by crop (or location) highlight the importance of representing allocations over these dimensions. The role of farmer-owned resources such as land and labor, and their allocation, may imply significant economic constraints that, in turn, complicate the aggregation of capital service flows and family labor over time. How appropriate is production modeling when based only on data aggregated across these dimensions? How limited are the sets of issues that can be investigated?

Though empirical economic practices must of necessity work with aggregates at some level, we believe that agricultural economists have often been cavalier about temporal and spatial (biological) structure and heterogeneity in agriculture. This has led to inappropriate grouping of inputs and outputs over space and time. Spatial dimensions of input groupings may be particularly important in agriculture because inputs must be tailored to the heterogeneity of farm resources, which differ substantially by climate and land quality (location). For example, ignoring these circumstances may lead economists to conclude that too much land is used by a large farm with heterogeneous land quality in comparison to a "best practice" when in reality economists are not using "best practice" methods of aggregation. Such practices have implications for measuring technical or other inefficiencies as well as for measuring behavior. Similarly, time dimensions of input groupings may be more important in agriculture because production lags tend to be longer and thus encounter more price heterogeneity.

At a minimum, the conclusions that are being drawn must be carefully and fully qualified given these possibilities. One purpose of this chapter is to identify the extent of needed qualifications. In some cases, existing data allows more careful consideration of aggregation issues. For example, inventories of land qualities and of land allocations can be used to enhance economic understanding. However, data are rarely collected on intraseasonal input choices nor is it generally reported on spatial allocations. Thus, for issues that require data on intraseasonal or spatial choice, limitations of current data imply that there is a clear tension between the description of agriculture in Sections 2.1–2.6 and available data. Perhaps more importantly, these issues raise concern about whether approaches that require the specification of technology, either explicitly or implicitly, can correctly reflect technology when temporal and spatial aggregates are used.

The next few sections of this paper investigate conceptual and theoretical implications of the issues raised thus far regarding temporal (Section 2.1) and spatial (Section 2.2) allocation of inputs, the potential differences among generic inputs represented by embodied technology (Section 2.3), and the stochastic nature of production (Section 2.4). The nature of constraints imposed on service flows by farmer-owned resources is considered explicitly. A set of principles is developed in Section 3 that address these issues in agricultural production analysis. Then fundamental theoretical results are developed to apply these principles in Section 4. In Sections 3 and 4, we provide a critique of current approaches to agricultural production analysis, identify the limitations imposed by data availability, and suggest appropriate qualifications that must be attached to agricultural production studies given data limitations. In some cases, these qualifications invalidate many empirical findings to date. We suggest this is one reason for the poor performance of duality models noted by Mundlak (2001) and that some of these problems arise from trying to apply the concepts of production economics without sufficient attention to the unique features of agriculture discussed in this section.

Following Sections 3 and 4, we address in Section 5 the extent of generalizations that have been achieved in agricultural production analysis regarding the other unique features of agriculture identified above (Sections 2.5–2.6) and related issues. Relatively less emphasis is placed on these issues in this chapter because they are emphasized heavily by Sunding and Zilberman (2001) and Nerlove and Bessler (2001). However, we suggest implications of the principles of this paper that are applicable and which call for more structural and detailed analysis, empirical investigation in the context of a broader maintained model, and more adequate representation of heterogeneity as data allows.

3. Principles of agricultural technology representation

Before proceeding to consider appropriate principles for agricultural production analysis, introduction of some conventional concepts and definitions is useful to facilitate discussion. Following the seminal work of Nobel laureate Gerard Debreu, we define an economic good not only physically but also temporally and spatially [Debreu (1959, pp. 28–32)]. In other words, date and location in addition to physical identification of a commodity are essential. Debreu emphasizes that this distinction "should always be kept in mind" in his comprehensive mathematical representation of economic phenomena (p. 32). Thus, fertilizer applied to a particular wheat field at planting time is considered distinct from post-emergent fertilizer applied to the same wheat field at a later date and from fertilizer applied in planting a barley field or another wheat field even if on the same date and farm. Debreu also emphasizes with a long list of examples that the physical identification of goods must be complete. As an example, he emphasizes that land must be described completely by the nature of the soil and subsoil characteristics, crop residues, etc. (p. 30). These considerations have important implications for the analysis of agricultural production because of the unique features of agricultural production involving long time lags in the production process, wide variation in prices and local weather conditions, and great heterogeneity both among and within farms.

In contrast to Debreu's clear conceptual definitions, we note that carrying the distinction of space and time and even many of the attributes of physical identification has been largely dropped from empirical agricultural production studies. For example, it is not unusual to represent output as a single aggregate commodity, a two-dimensional measure with crop and livestock aggregates, or a short vector consisting of the aggregate production of several crops. Inputs often consist of four to six aggregate annual input quantities such as land, fertilizer, pesticides, seeds, labor, and machinery services. The role of weather and pests is usually swept under the guise of an ad hoc homoscedastic error term. Examples of such studies include many widely referenced studies of U.S. agriculture over the past two decades and virtually all of the production studies referenced in the survey by Shumway (1995). Thus, the specifications in (1)–(10) are rarely employed empirically in agriculture.

For better or worse, agricultural production studies have increasingly relied upon readily available data to illustrate advances in technical methods of analysis. Readily available data, however, tends to consist of highly aggregated public data in which temporal detail (within a growing season) and spatial detail (among plots, farms, or land used to produce specific crops) is lost. As economists have become more heavily focused on policy-related applications, the aggregate level of analysis has taken on elevated importance. By comparison, as economists have focused relatively less on supporting the management of firms, emphasis on analyses of individual firm data has decreased. In consequence, as production economists have become more focused on aggregate responses and aggregate productivity, technology has tended to be described by a production possibilities frontier (PPF) where both inputs and outputs have been stripped of their temporal and spatial dimensions.

Our purpose is to consider the validity and implications of such practices and illustrate the need for development of data sets that allow the underlying hypotheses to be tested. Results demonstrate that the failure of modern agricultural production analysis, and of typical implementations of duality theory in particular, may be due to such practices. We note also, however, that potentially necessary generalizations can be made in a variety of frameworks including dual models, but such generalizations are likely to require better firm-level data than has hitherto been available.

3.1. A general framework for production analysis

To facilitate formal analysis, we define a general notation that applies through the remainder of this chapter. Following the distinctions emphasized by Debreu, available technology for production is represented by $W \in \Im(k, \varepsilon)$ where

> $W \in R^n$ is a netput vector of inputs (if negative) and outputs (if positive);
>
> $\Im$ is the feasible short-run production set;
>
> $k \in R_+^{n_k}$ is a vector of firm-controlled resources;
>
> $\varepsilon \in R_+^{n_\varepsilon}$ is a vector of uncontrolled inputs that describes the state of nature;

both W and k are defined with temporal, spatial, and physical detail; firm-controlled resources in k include family attributes and capital (land, buildings, and machinery) that determine recurring availability of family labor and capital service flows with temporal, spatial, and physical detail; and uncontrolled inputs include weather and pest infestations, also with temporal, spatial, and physical detail. Revisions in the capital stock through investment may change the amount of recurring capital service flows, for example, following a putty-clay framework, but need not be considered in the short-run case of Sections 3 and 4. Because firm-controlled resources are available in fixed amounts depending on capital stocks and family composition, the service flows from them must be allocated either temporally or spatially across competing production activities. These are called allocated fixed factors following the terminology of Shumway, Pope, and Nash (1984).

Typically, the netput vector is partitioned into inputs and outputs. Following Section 2.1, we further distinguish purchased variable inputs from allocated fixed factors so that $W = (Y, -X, -Z)$ where

$Y \in R_+^{n_y}$ is a vector of output quantities,

$X \in R_+^{n_x}$ is a vector of purchased variable input quantities, and

$Z \in R_+^{n_z}$ is a vector of allocations of allocated fixed factors,

where $n = n_y + n_x + n_z$. Thus, allocations of recurring capital service flows and family labor appear in Z. Netputs if negative represent net inputs which impose costs or deplete firm-controlled resources, and if positive represent net outputs which generate revenue. Thus, the partitioning of netputs into inputs and outputs is regarded as a local convenience and may not apply globally. For example, some goods may be purchased as inputs in some circumstances and produced as outputs in others, and some capital services may be provided fully by firm-owned machinery in some circumstances and purchased by means of commercial contracting in others.

We argue that temporal, spatial, and physical distinctions should not be dropped until doing so can be demonstrated to be appropriate. The purpose of Section 3 is to demonstrate some of the problems encountered by doing so while Section 4 presents a more general disaggregated analysis. Interestingly, temporal and spatial distinctions are commonplace in the agricultural marketing literature although largely ignored in the agricultural production literature. To investigate the importance of temporal and spatial detail, the input and output vectors require further partitioning following

$$Y \equiv \{y^1, \ldots, y^m\}, \quad y \equiv \sum_{i=1}^{m} y^i,$$

$$X \equiv \{x^1, \ldots, x^m\}, \quad x \equiv \sum_{i=1}^{m} x^i,$$

$$Z \equiv \{z^1, \ldots, z^m\}, \quad z \equiv \sum_{i=1}^{m} z^i,$$

where $i = 1, \ldots, m$ indexes time and/or location and y, x, and z represent aggregate vectors of outputs, purchased variable inputs, and allocated fixed factors, respectively, which include only physical detail. For example, each x^i may specify quantities of specific seeds, fertilizers, and pesticides to apply as inputs at a time and/or location indexed by i and y^i may give quantities of specific types of outputs that occur at a time and/or location indexed by i. Interesting questions arise in considering aggregation over time and/or space. For example, one may consider when the feasible production set can be adequately represented by $w \equiv (y, -x, -z) \in \Im_{-m}$ where $\Im_{-m}$ represents a feasibility set devoid of temporal and/or spatial detail.

For purposes of facilitating discussion of practical implications of technical efficiency, corresponding price vectors are also defined. Let P be a price vector corresponding to output vector Y and let R be a price vector corresponding to input vector X. Then short-run profits can be represented by $\pi = PY - RX$. Suppose also that price vectors are partitioned temporally and/or spatially as in the case of Y and X so that short-run profits are equivalently expressed as $\pi = \sum_{i=1}^{m} (p^i y^i - r^i x^i)$. Finally, if and only if $p = p^i$ and $r = r^i$ for $i = 1, \ldots, m$ can profits be generally expressed with temporal and/or spatial aggregation as $\pi = py - rx$.

Agricultural economics has long-standing traditions of pursuing production analysis using both set theoretic models (often represented by normative mathematical programming models) and smooth econometric representations of either average or frontier technologies. For example, the production set is commonly represented by the transformation function F where $\Im = \{W \mid F(W) \leqslant 0\}$ in the general netput case or $\Im = \{(Y, -X, -Z) \mid Y \leqslant f(X, Z)\}$ in the partitioned case with explicit inputs and outputs.[14] For smooth econometric representations, equality in the transformation relationship defines the boundary or frontier of the production set, i.e., $F(W) = 0$ or $Y = f(X, Z)$ are the boundaries of production sets defined by $F(W) \leqslant 0$ or $Y \leqslant f(X, Z)$, respectively. Representations of average technologies follow $Y = f(X, Z) + \varepsilon$ where ε represents random or uncontrolled inputs and $E(\varepsilon) = 0$ is used to represent average efficiency conditions. Such models are popular in general agricultural production problems. Alternatively, one-sided error term models such as $Y = f(X, Z) + \varepsilon$ where $\varepsilon \leqslant 0$ have been used where efficiency is of primary interest, in which case all deviations denote random deviations from the case of efficient production, $Y = f(X, Z)$ [see Fried et al. (1993)].[15] In these various models, the technology is described by measures such as production elasticities, scale and scope economies, factor substitution, productivity and

---

[14] In cases with only one output where F is a scalar function, the existence of the function f follows from continuity of F by the implicit function theorem based on the classification of W into Y, X, and Z. As argued below, however, in some cases consideration of a vector-valued f function is appropriate for representing multiple outputs.

[15] Of the smaller programming-based literature in agricultural production economics, data envelopment analysis (DEA) is becoming prominent. The strength of DEA is that it imposes less structure on the form of production and follows the language of leading graduate micro-theory texts [e.g., Varian (1992)]. Its current weakness seems to be that it is not easily used to address the breadth of questions usually considered by agricultural production economists and it generally assumes that all variation in observed production relationships is due to technical inefficiency rather than random, unmeasured, or uncontrollable factors (the same assumption typically applies also to econometric models with one-sided error terms).

Until recently, another weakness was that procedures for statistical inference were not available [Vanker (1996)]. While statistical inference in data envelopment analysis (DEA) models is not yet fully developed, DEA is likely to become fully integrated with econometric methods eventually. In this chapter, our discussion tends to focus on smooth functional representations of production, possibly including cases such as Leontief fixed-proportions production in practice. Thus, we build upon the simple generic representation above to draw implications directly for typical econometric practices. However, we note that the principles and results implied by the unique features of agriculture have applicability for other approaches to modeling agricultural production.

technical change bias, distance functions, separability, and (non)jointness, which we hereafter call "standard characteristics".[16]

3.2. Traditional concepts of efficiency

Traditionally, the frontier of the production set has been used as a representation of technical efficiency. Samuelson (1967), for example, defined aggregate technology by the PPF denoted by $F(y, x) = 0$ where y and x are aggregate vectors of outputs and inputs, respectively (the service flow vector, z, is temporarily dropped for convenience and congruence). Samuelson's PPF was determined by various separate technologies for each individual output denoted by $y_i = f_i(x^i)$ where y_i is an element of y, and x^i is a nonnegative vector of factor allocations to production activity i. The PPF is thus a smooth function determined by aggregation of individual production functions [Samuelson (1967, pp. 230–231)], e.g.,

$$F(y, x) \equiv y_1 - f^*(y_{-1}, x),$$
$$f^*(y_{-1}, x) \equiv \max \left\{ y_1 \mid y_i = f_i(x^i), \ i = 1, \ldots, n_y; x = \sum_{i=1}^{n_y} x^i \right\}, \tag{11}$$

where x is the aggregate input vector that determines the PPF, and y_{-1} is a vector containing all elements of y other than y_1, i.e., $y = (y_1, y_{-1})$. Thus, Samuelson did not maintain the industry (or production activity) distinction when referring to F in (11). For example, where i indexes production activities by time or location, the technology representation in (11) does not retain temporal or spatial detail, respectively.

Following Samuelson, the early literature on production efficiency was based largely on a comparison of actual production to the PPF [e.g., Farrell (1957)]. These boundary points may or may not be technically efficient. For example, the efficient set is at best a subset of the boundary consisting of all $W \in \Im$ such that there is no distinct $W' \in \Im$

---

[16] Typical assumptions employed to make these technology representations meaningful include (suppressing the arguments of $\Im$ for convenience): (1) $\Im$ is nonempty, i.e., there exists at least one $W \in \Im$; (2) $\Im$ is convex in W, i.e., if $W, W' \in \Im$ then $\lambda W + (1 - \lambda)W' \in \Im$ where $\lambda \in [0, 1]$; (3) $\Im$ is closed, i.e., if $W^k \in \Im$ such that $W^k \to W$ then $W \in \Im$; (4) inaction, i.e., $\mathbf{0} \in \Im$; (5) free disposal or monotonicity, i.e., $W - R_+^n \subset \Im$ if $W \in \Im$, which implies that if X can produce Y then $X' \geqslant X$ can produce at least Y; (6) additivity, i.e., if $W, W' \in \Im$ then $W + W' \in \Im$; and some subset of (7a) nonincreasing returns to scale, i.e., if $W \in \Im$ then $\lambda W \in \Im$ where $\lambda \in [0, 1]$; (7b) nondecreasing returns to scale, i.e., if $W \in \Im$ then $\lambda W \in \Im$ where $\lambda \geqslant 1$; and (7c) constant returns to scale, i.e., if $W \in \Im$ then $\lambda W \in \Im$ where $\lambda \geqslant 0$. As an example of a subset of the latter three, decreasing returns to scale occurs when (7a) but not (7c) holds. It is important to note that various combinations of these assumptions have distinct implications. For example, additivity plus constant returns to scale implies that $\Im$ is a convex cone. Also, adding setup costs to any one of the other properties may yield a very different property. For example, setup costs with inaction introduces nonconvexities into W. Note also that items (6) and (7) can be rewritten using a production transformation function as: (6′) if $F(W) \leqslant 0$ and $F(W') \leqslant 0$ then $F(W + W') \leqslant 0$; (7a′) if $F(W) \leqslant 0$ and $\lambda \in [0, 1]$ then $F(\lambda W) \leqslant 0$; (7b′) if $F(W) \leqslant 0$ and $\lambda \geqslant 1$ then $F(\lambda W) \leqslant 0$; and (7c′) if $F(W) \leqslant 0$ and $\lambda \geqslant 0$ then $F(\lambda W) \leqslant 0$.

with $W' \geqslant W$. This conceptualization of production has carried through to the modern production literature with slight generalization and now seems to permeate most empirical production analyses of both the data envelopment analysis and conventional econometric approaches. That is, with these implicit Samuelsonian foundations, the modern production literature has evolved toward representation of production in terms of aggregates of allocations of inputs over time and location. For example, a typical empirical model in agricultural production has aggregate output (either for a commodity group or for total agricultural output) depending on aggregate annual inputs such as fertilizer and pesticides rather than allocations of those inputs to specific locations (e.g., to land in specific crops) and stages of production [e.g., Shumway (1983)].

For example, Diewert (1974) gives a commonly cited definition of the PPF, sometimes called the transformation function, as $y_1 \equiv f^*(y_{-1}, x)$ where (when it exists)

$$f^*(y_{-1}, x) \equiv \max\{y_1 \mid (y_1, y_{-1}, x) \in \Im\}. \tag{12}$$

The dual input distance function is

$$D_I(y, x) \equiv \max\{\alpha \mid x/\alpha \in \upsilon(y)\},$$

where $\upsilon(y)$ is the set of all inputs x that will produce at least y, e.g.,

$$\upsilon(y) = \{x \mid f^*(y_{-1}, x) \geqslant y_1\} = \{x \mid (y, x) \in \Im\}.$$

A corresponding dual representation of the PPF is thus given by $D_I(y, x) = 1$. Because Diewert explicitly used the language that f^* and D_I characterize the production possibilities set and because he immediately applied f^* and D_I to international trade, it seems clear that he considered the components of x and y in $\Im$ as neither spatially nor industry specific following the tradition of Samuelson.[17]

The elimination of spatial and temporal distinction is especially apparent in the celebrated paper by Lau (1978). Lau's functional representation of efficient production is based on the input requirement function. Suppose that a primary input such as labor is denoted separately by λ and that the associated input requirement function is $\lambda = \omega^*(y, x_{-1})$ where x_{-1} represents all other inputs such that the full input vector is $x = (\lambda, x_{-1})$. Clearly, λ and x_{-1} represent total use of the respective inputs because Lau's definition of nonjointness states that production is nonjoint in inputs if there exist individual production functions, $\lambda_i = \omega_i^*(y_i, x_{-1}^i)$, such that

$$\omega^*(y, x_{-1}) = \min\left\{\sum_i \omega_i^*(y_i, x_{-1}^i) \mid x_{-1} = \sum_i x_{-1}^i\right\}, \tag{13}$$

[17] Of course, Diewert's (1982) notation could be used to define a PPF in higher dimensions that include both spatial and temporal distinctions. However, this is not what he did nor has this been the practice in modern production applications to date. Our purpose is to explore the implications of following one practice or the other.

where $x_i = (\lambda_i, x_{-1}^i)$. Thus, each element of x is clearly a sum over industry (or individual production activity) uses.

Lau's definition suggests another way to obtain the PPF from an underlying optimization model under nonjointness – that is, by minimizing the use of one input subject to technology constraints for all outputs and endowment constraints for all other inputs. Clearly, when ω^* and ω_i^* are continuous and monotonic in y and y_i, the relationships $\lambda = v^*(y, x_{-1})$ and $\lambda_i = v_i^*(y_i, x_{-1}^i)$ are equivalent to $F(y, x) = 0$ and $y_1 = f^*(y_{-1}, x)$ in (11), respectively, by the implicit function theorem. Hence, societal (or firm) level efficiency is characterized equivalently by an input requirement function ω^* defined over total uses of other inputs. Again, spatial, temporal, and physical detail in x is omitted in the definition ω^*.

The concept of efficiency to this point has been discussed without regard to prices of either inputs or outputs. A central tenet of this section, however, is that prices are critically important if the leading concepts of production efficiency are to have practical meaning. Otherwise, the efficiency concepts that correspond to aggregation of inputs or outputs may not be consistent with economic optimization of either costs or profits.

Consider first the possibility of functional aggregation in (1) such that inputs can be simply aggregated additively following the approach used for most agricultural data. In such a case,

$$y = f\left(f_1\left(x^1, t_1\right), \ldots, f_m(x^m, t_m)\right) = \tilde{f}\left(x^1 + \cdots + x^m\right). \tag{14}$$

Such additivity (a special case of strong separability) implies that the marginal product of an input in stage i is equal to the marginal product of an input in stage j. Hence, a mean-preserving spread in the distribution of an input across stages will have no impact on output. This assumption implies that generic inputs applied across stages are perfect substitutes, which seems unreasonable in virtually all agricultural production. Thus, such a rationalization for adding generic inputs is summarily rejected.[18] Perhaps more general forms of functional aggregation following Blackorby, Primont, and Russell (1978) are appropriate, but additivity seems unreasonable.

By far, the most common reason to presume that technology can be written with the sum of inputs is based upon efficient allocation across outputs. This explanation commonly proceeds by assuming positive use of each x_i in each stage in (3). Efficiency implies that annual aggregate inputs are allocated among production stages to equate marginal products and rates of technical substitution across stages. Thus, optimization results in the efficient description of technology in terms of the aggregate or added inputs. However, this conclusion crucially hinges on a notion similar to Hick's composite commodity theorem [Hicks (1956)].

---

[18] However, some inputs are apparently perfect substitutes or near perfect substitutes within a stage. For example, two brands of fertilizers with the same chemical content may be perfect substitutes.

Samuelson (1967, p. 231) made clear the assumption that all inputs had to have the same factor prices across industries in his development of the PPF. Under such conditions, efficiency concepts can serve as the first stage of a two-stage optimization process. To this end, if x enters as a sum in the PPF definition, it must enter as the same sum in the calculation of costs. For example, in the Lau problem, if and only if the wage rate is the same for all industries is (13) equivalent to minimizing the cost of an input subject to technology and the endowments of other inputs (e.g., by multiplying both ω^* and ω_i^* by the same wage rate) which then, in turn, is consistent with profit maximization if all input allocations aggregated in x have the same prices.

3.3. Instructive examples of within-firm aggregation

Several examples can illustrate the implicit problem of within-firm aggregation across commodities and allocations in agricultural data. Consider the case with two outputs, y_1 and y_2, distinguished over time or space with corresponding prices p_1 and p_2; and two inputs, x_1 and x_2, distinguished by time or space with corresponding prices r_1 and r_2.

3.3.1. Case 1: Price homogeneity allows additive aggregation independent of prices

Suppose technology follows $y_i = f_i(x_i)$, $i = 1, 2$, so the profit maximization problem is

$$\pi = \max_{x_1, x_2}\{p_1 f_1(x_1) + p_2 f_2(x_2) - r_1 x_1 - r_2 x_2\}.$$

If $p_1 = p_2 = p$ and $r_1 = r_2 = r$, then inputs and outputs can be aggregated additively with $x = x_1 + x_2$ and $y = y_1 + y_2$ so the problem can be represented as

$$\begin{aligned}
\pi &= \max_{x_1, x_2}\{p[f_1(x_1) + f_2(x_2)] - r(x_1 + x_2)\} \\
&= \max_{x}\{pf(x) - rx\} \\
&= \pi^*(p, r),
\end{aligned}$$

where the aggregate technology $f(x)$ is defined independent of prices by an implicit maximization,

$$f(x) = \max_{x_1, x_2}\{f_1(x_1) + f_2(x_2) \mid x = x_1 + x_2\}. \tag{15}$$

The maximization in (15) requires equating the marginal products across input uses. In many instances, economists (and statisticians who produce the data they use) aggregate inputs or outputs simply by adding them as in Equation (14). As noted earlier, such practices are typical in conceptual descriptions of aggregate technical efficiency. In empirical work, perhaps the most common examples of simple adding across space are generic inputs like fertilizer, water or land. On the other hand, capital service or labor categories are often summed across time [Shumway (1983, 1988)]. As noted by this case, the ability to do so properly hinges on the equality of prices.

3.3.2. Case 2: Price heterogeneity requires index aggregation

Reality requires consideration of the case where prices are not equal. For example, land typically has heterogeneous quality. Even hard red No. 2 winter wheat prices differ by location and time. Suppose prices are not identical, $p_1 \neq p_2$ and $r_1 \neq r_2$, but other assumptions follow Case 1. In this case, quantity aggregation requires use of price weights. Assuming the existence of index numbers consistent with Fisher's weak factor reversal property [Fisher (1922)], the profit maximization problem can be represented as

$$\pi = \max_{x_1, x_2} \{ p_1 f_1(x_1) + p_2 f_2(x_2) - r_1 x_1 - r_2 x_2 \}$$

$$= \max_x \{ p f(x) - r x \} \tag{16}$$

$$= \pi^*(p, r), \tag{17}$$

where p is an index of output prices, r is an index of input prices, aggregate quantities are defined with index weights such that $x = x_1^* + x_2^*$ and $y = y_1^* + y_2^*$ where

$$y_1^* = (p_1/p) y_1, \qquad y_2^* = (p_2/p) y_2,$$

$$x_1^* = (r_1/r) x_1, \qquad x_2^* = (r_2/r) x_2, \tag{18}$$

and the aggregate technology is represented by $f(x)$ as defined by an implicit maximization,

$$f(x) = \max_{x_1^*, x_2^*} \{ (p_1/p) f_1(r x_1^*/r_1) + (p_2/p) f_2(r x_2^*/r_2) \mid x = x_1^* + x_2^* \}. \tag{19}$$

In this case, price-weighted marginal products are equated across input uses. Thus, the problem is represented accurately with aggregates but the definitions of the aggregates depend crucially on the price weights. Dependence on the price weights means that an estimate of the technology in (16) or (19) or the profit function in (17) under one price regime may not serve well to forecast the response to a different (possibly unobserved) price regime, i.e., where the corresponding $y = f(x)$ is not known or observed. For example, a very different distribution of prices among the outputs (inputs) could lead to the same price index p (r) as in (17) but a very different $f(x)$.

Examples abound where aggregates are not simply summed but are formed as price-weighted aggregates. Examples are index numbers in Divisia, Paasche or Laspeyres form. Often, Fisher's weak factor reversal property is used so that a quantity (price) index can be implicitly calculated from a price (quantity) index. The important point is explicit recognition that aggregation involves heterogeneous prices and products. Index numbers that are exact for particular technologies have been explored by Diewert (1976), who coined the phrase "superlative indexes" for those that correspond to homogeneous second-order flexible technical forms.

The development of these indexes is typically based upon cost minimization assuming all prices and quantities are positive. When inputs and outputs are positive and separable from one another, index procedures may exist that are exact for both aggregators of inputs (in the production function) and outputs (in the input requirements function). Clearly, the more aggregate the data, the less likely is observation of a zero production. These indexes are clearly useful to represent aggregate output or inputs or even to aggregate a portion of each. However, they do not generally specify technology in a form that can be used to illuminate allocative technical efficiency. Also, exact indexes are not robust with respect to behavioral preferences. Profit maximization is a crucial assumption. For example, risk aversion where inputs affect risk is sufficient to cause failure.

Currently, publicly reported agricultural data at county, state, regional, and national levels of aggregation contain many Laspeyres aggregations [Shumway (1988)] that are exact only for Leontief or linear technology [Diewert (1976)]. Some data particularly at state or lower levels of aggregation are constructed using simple summation aggregators such as a simple average [Pope and Chambers (1989); Chambers and Pope (1991)]. Neither is exact under flexible functional form technology. In recent years, some public data aggregated with Tornqvist–Theil indexes across groups of inputs or outputs has appeared. This approach is exact for homogeneous translog technology [Ball (1985); Ball et al. (1997); Ball et al. (1999)]. However, this and other index approaches are limited by the fact that data on many of the groups that go into these calculations are constructed with simple summations.

In lieu of using public aggregate data, some studies investigate agricultural production using one of the few farm-level data sets that have been collected (e.g., the Kansas State University farm accounting data). Farm-level data is scarce and, in most cases, access is limited. Moreover, from the standpoint of the discussion in this section, farm-level data is typically derived from expenditure and receipt information in accounting records. Expenditures and receipts are typically aggregated additively over input categories, time, and/or spatially separated production activities. Because no indexing of prices is used, the implicit assumptions necessarily correspond to Case 1.

3.3.3. Case 3: Price homogeneity with short-term fixities or corner solutions

Unfortunately, convenient rationalizations that accompany exact index numbers or simple sums in the production possibilities frontier fail when fixed or corner solutions arise. Suppose prices are identical across time or space as in Case 1 but that at least one of the production activities is constrained by short-term fixities. Where the inputs and outputs represent temporal heterogeneity, the fixities could represent family labor or capital service flow constraints that vary by time period. Where the different inputs and outputs represent spatial heterogeneity, the fixities could represent land allocation constraints imposed by government policy (acreage set asides, diversion requirements, environmental restrictions such as pesticide use near surface water, etc.). Suppose technology follows $y_i = f_i(x_i, z_i)$, $i = 1, 2$, where z_i represents, say, the amount of land allocated to production activity i. Suppose further that allocation of a fixed input quantity, z, between the two production activities is limited by a restriction, $z_1 \leqslant z_1^*$, that turns out to be binding. If $p_1 = p_2 = p$ and $r_1 = r_2 = r$, then the profit maximization problem is

$$\pi = \max_{x_1, x_2} \{ p[f_1(x_1, z_1) + f_2(x_2, z_2)] - r(x_1 + x_2) \mid z_1 = z_1^*, z = z_1 + z_2 \}.$$

In this case, the inputs and outputs can be aggregated additively with $x = x_1 + x_2$ and $y = y_1 + y_2$ as in Case 1 but the problem requires a more complicated representation:

$$\begin{aligned} \pi &= \max_{x_1, x_2} \{ p[f_1(x_1, z_1^*) + f_2(x_2, z - z_1^*)] - r(x_1 + x_2) \} \\ &= \max_x \{ p f(x, z_1^*, z) - rx \} \qquad\qquad (20) \\ &= \pi^*(p, r, z_1^*, z). \qquad\qquad (21) \end{aligned}$$

Here the aggregate technology, $f(x, z_1^*, z)$, can be defined independent of prices but not independent of the short-term fixities,

$$f(x, z_1^*, z) = \max_{x_1, x_2} \{ f_1(x_1, z_1^*) + f_2(x_2, z - z_1^*) \mid x = x_1 + x_2 \}.$$

The latter implicit maximization requires equating the marginal products of x across input uses but the marginal products depend on how fixities affect land allocation. If factors affecting these fixities (z_1^* or z) vary over observations (time or space) used to estimate the production problem, then the specification and estimation of (20) or (21) is not as simple and elegant as standard methodologies imply. Specifically, estimation of (20) and (21) is not generally valid unless the disaggregated allocation of land is considered explicitly. This implies that the state-level practice of simply adding acreage for the estimation of crop technologies is problematic unless land is homogeneous. The constrained problem becomes particularly complicated if such constraints are intermittently binding across observations that represent different land qualities or are intermittently imposed across time or space by government policy.

    As noted in Section 2.1, agricultural production economics has compiled substantial conceptual and empirical support for treating capital and family labor service flows as constrained at crucial times during the growing season. Thus, in certain stages of production in (2), labor or capital service constraints may be binding. These will likely have different shadow values because constraints will be binding in some periods and not others. Any attempt to represent efficiency in terms of total availability or total use of a service is inappropriate.

3.3.4. Case 4: The case of corner solutions with ex post adjustment

Now suppose that a random state of nature is introduced to which the producer can respond, e.g., by applying pesticides if a pest infestation is observed. Suppose production follows $y_i = f_i(x_i, z_i, \varepsilon_i) = z_i^{\alpha_i}[\beta_i + (1 - \beta_i)(1 - e^{-x_i})]^{\varepsilon_i}$ where ε_i is a random state of nature equal to zero or one depending on whether a pest infestation occurs, $\alpha_i > 0$, $0 < \beta_i < 1$. Thus, if $\varepsilon_i = 0$, then production is $y_i = z_i^{\alpha_i}$. If $\varepsilon_i = 1$, then a portion of the crop is lost resulting in (i) production $y_i = \beta_i z_i^{\alpha_i}$ if no pesticide is applied or (ii) production asymptotically approaching the case of no pest infestation as large amounts of pesticides are applied. Suppose land allocation must be determined prior to realization of the state of nature and must satisfy the binding land constraint, $z_1 + z_2 = z$. Then the profit maximization problem is represented by

$$
\pi = \max_{z_1, z_2} \left\{ \mathrm{E} \left[\max_{x_1, x_2} \left\{ \sum_i p_i z_i^{\alpha_i} \left[\beta_i + (1 - \beta_i)(1 - e^{-x_i}) \right]^{\varepsilon_i} \right. \right. \right.
$$

$$
\left. \left. \left. - \sum_i r_i x_i \right\} \right] \,\middle|\, z_1 + z_2 = z \right\}
$$

$$
= \max_x \left\{ p f(z, x, \varepsilon_1, \varepsilon_2) - rx \right\} \tag{22}
$$

$$
= \pi^*(z, p, r, \varepsilon_1, \varepsilon_2), \tag{23}
$$

where E is an ex ante expectation, p and r are price indexes for outputs and inputs, respectively, and aggregate quantities are again defined with index weights so that $x = x_1^* + x_2^*$ and $y = y_1^* + y_2^*$ following (18). For this problem, the aggregate technology must be defined by the implicit maximization,

$$
f(x, \varepsilon_1, \varepsilon_2) = \max_{x_1^*, x_2^*} \left\{ \sum_i (p_i/p)(z_i^*)^{\alpha_i} \left[\beta_i + (1 - \beta_i)\left(1 - e^{-rx_i^*/r_i}\right) \right]^{\varepsilon_i} \,\middle|\, x = x_1^* + x_2^* \right\}, \tag{24}
$$

where

$$
(z_1^*, z_2^* \mid x) = \operatorname*{argmax}_{z_1, z_2} \mathrm{E} \left[\max_{x_1^*, x_2^*} \left\{ \sum_i (p_i/p) z_i^{\alpha_i} \left[\beta_i + (1 - \beta_i) \right. \right. \right.
$$

$$
\left. \left. \left. \times \left(1 - e^{-rx_i^*/r_i}\right) \right]^{\varepsilon_i} \,\middle|\, x = x_1^* + x_2^* \right\} \right].
$$

For this problem, the price-weighted marginal products that are equated across input uses are dependent on the states of nature. For example, for (22), (23) or (24) to correctly reflect technology, they must be conditioned on disaggregated states of nature.

These cases make clear that simple index procedures may not be empirically appropriate when corner solutions, fixities, price heterogeneity or ex post adjustments are present.[19] The essential point relevant to representation of production technologies in terms of aggregate inputs and outputs is that either (i) prices (or shadow prices) of those goods that are aggregated additively must be homogeneous or (ii) aggregation must follow index forms appropriate to the (unknown) technology. In the latter case, production choices must not be constrained by fixities and cannot involve ex post adjustment to states of nature. Otherwise, disaggregated data is required to represent efficiency, i.e., production possibilities frontiers expressed solely in terms of simple aggregates are not well defined.

Some important principles implied by the above cases are as follows:

PRINCIPLE 1. *Each unconstrained input aggregation in the efficiency concept should be composed of allocations that have identical prices if fixities or ex post adjustments affect those allocations.*

PRINCIPLE 2. *Each output aggregation in the efficiency concept should be composed of output quantities that have identical prices if fixities or ex post adjustments affect their production.*

It is tempting to state each of these principles in a form that requires identical prices generally. Indeed, the basic concept of technology is typically stated in terms of sets or functions defined over inputs and outputs alone (not depending on prices). Clearly, Case 1 illustrates what is required to represent such technologies. However, Case 2 and the exact aggregation literature clearly show that prices can be appropriately used to aggregate inputs or outputs when, for example, the fixities and ex post adjustments of Cases 3 and 4 are not present. In these cases, theorems are required to rationalize procedures for aggregation using prices as illustrated by the influential work of Diewert (1976). However, these theorems for aggregation via price indexes require knowledge of the functional form of technology, the class of behavior, and all prices that provide behavioral incentives. A number of circumstances limit the practical usefulness of these results. For example, markets for risk are generally believed to be incomplete in agriculture so that necessary prices may not exist. An example can illustrate these index problems when production is random.

3.3.5. Case 5: Dependence of exact indexes on behavior and technology

Suppose technology is quadratic and random of the form

$$y = f(x)\varepsilon = (xAx)\varepsilon, \quad E(\varepsilon) = 1,$$

---

[19] Differences in marginal returns due to failure to adjust to identical prices was recognized as a significant problem in published productivity indexes by Griliches (1963) who attempted to estimate the difference in marginal returns among input allocations and to correct index number measurements accordingly.

(where transposition is suppressed for convenience) and that the firm is an expected utility maximizer solving

$$\max_{x} \mathrm{E}\big[U(w_0 + pf(x)\varepsilon - rx)\big],$$

where all prices are certain, p is output price, r is a vector of input prices, U is utility, E denotes expectation, and w_0 is certain initial wealth. The first-order conditions (assumed sufficient) are

$$pf_x(x) - r - R_x(p, r, w_0) = 0,$$

where R_x is the marginal risk premium. Following the quadratic lemma of Diewert (1976), the difference in output from some base period is given by

$$\mathrm{E}(y) - \mathrm{E}(y_0) = .5[f_x(x) + f_x(x_0)](x - x_0), \tag{25}$$

where x_0 is the base period vector of inputs and y_0 is the corresponding output. Inserting the first-order conditions from expected utility maximization into (25) gives

$$\mathrm{E}(y) - \mathrm{E}(y_0) = .5\big[(r + R_x)/p + (r_0 + R_{x_0})/p_0\big](x - x_0).$$

Assuming that inputs are normalized so that $\mathrm{E}(y_0)$ is a known constant, expected output is known only if the two marginal risk premiums are known. Under risk neutrality, R_x and R_{x_0} are zero and (changes in) output is (are) simply represented by

$$\mathrm{E}(y) - \mathrm{E}(y_0) = .5(r/p + r_0/p_0)(x - x_0),$$

which is a simple index of observed relative input prices and inputs. This result illustrates that knowledge of the proper behavioral model is required for use of index numbers and all dual methods that infer the form of technology using them. Of further interest is that restricting the form of technology can lead to a standard index number. For example, consider homogeneous quadratic production, $y = f(x) = (xAx)^{.5} + (xBx)^{.25}\varepsilon$, $\mathrm{E}(\varepsilon) = 0$ where A and B are parameter matrices. Given constant absolute risk aversion and normality, $p(xAx)^{.5} - .5\lambda p^2\sigma^2(xBx)^{.5}$ is obtained as Fisher's (1922) ideal price index, which is the geometric mean of the Paasche and Laspeyres price indexes where σ^2 is the variance of ε and λ is the absolute risk aversion coefficient. Here the index is standard but its meaning is not. The index recovers expected revenue reduced by the risk premium.

Even when exact index forms are known, it must be recognized that many prices may not be known to firms when inputs are applied or when outputs are planned, implying again that behavior may well not follow optimization of cost, revenue, or profit functions based on index numbers. That is, explicit technological parameters may be eliminated using first-order conditions for optimization. Risk preferences, moments of the distribution of prices and even technological parameters in the marginal risk premium may remain. These also will vitiate the convenience of index number aggregation. The simple fact is that prescription or prediction for unobserved price scenarios (such as are necessary in ex ante policy analyses) cannot be usefully addressed with the exact index number approach. Although one might initially think that these problems refer only to outputs, Case 4 makes clear that input prices in a dynamic world can be subject to many of the same concerns as output price uncertainty.[20]

Principles 1 and 2 must be enlarged when they apply to aggregation of service flows from farmer-owned resources. Suppose the farm production problem is described by

$$
\begin{aligned}
F(y, x, k) &\equiv y_1 - f^*(y_{-1}, x, k), \\
f^*(y_{-1}, x, k) &\equiv \max\{y_1 \mid y = f(x, z^1, \dots, z^m), \ z^i \leqslant k, \ i = 1, \dots, m\}.
\end{aligned}
\tag{26}
$$

Here i indexes time. Use of recurring allocated fixed factors must meet availability constraints. These may be limiting in some time periods and slack in others. An obvious question is when can this problem be represented by time-aggregated service flows in the form

$$
y_1 = f^{**}(y_{-1}, x, z),
\tag{27}
$$

[20] To highlight the severity of this problem, we note that almost all agricultural production studies combine pesticides into one variable. This is problematic because (i) at least some pesticides are applied after commencement of the growing season when some random conditions are already observed (as in Case 4), (ii) many pesticides have highly specific uses, and (iii) individual pesticide prices may not be highly correlated because of the role of patents and market concentration. To illustrate the specificity of uses, grasses on corn lands are typically controlled by Eradicane or Sutan at the pre-planting stage, by Lasso, Dual, or Prowl in other pre-emergent applications, and by Beacon or Accent in post-emergent applications. In contrast, grasses on soybean lands are typically controlled by Treflan or Prowl at pre-planting, by Lasso or Dual in pre-emergent applications, and by a number of additional herbicides in post-emergent applications. Broadleaf weeds on corn lands, on the other hand, are typically controlled by Atrazine at pre-planting, by Atrazine or Bladex in pre-emergent applications, and by Banvel, 2,4-D, Buctril, Permit, or Exceed in post-emergent applications. To illustrate the magnitude of unrelated price movements among leading pesticides, note that newly patented pesticides come onto the market almost every year while patents on others expire, leading to generic competition. Either can cause the price of a specific pesticide competing in a specific use to decline by as much as 20–50 percent while other pesticide prices are rising. Examples include a 43 percent decline in glyphosate price due to patent expiration while the price of atrazine increased 25 percent in response to a dramatic reduction in the number of selling firms during 1989–1992. Such dramatic differences in price variation are not the exception. For example, generic entry following patent expiration caused a price decline of 20 percent for atrazine, 26 percent for diuron, 40 percent for simazine, and 25 percent for trifluralin (not simultaneously) while the pesticide price index and prices for leading pesticides such as Lasso and Lorsban were rising [United States Senate (1987)]. Such examples are likely to increase in importance because of the increasing predominance of pesticide-dependent no-till technologies and because of genetic engineering which is creating niche products such as Roundup-ready soybeans that introduce dependence on specific products. To illustrate this trend, note that pesticides now account for 17–21 percent of the variable costs of corn production and 30–35 percent of the variable costs of soybean production in most areas of the United States [Economic Research Service (1999a and 1999b)]. Thus, serious concern may be warranted when crop- or location-specific variation in pesticide prices is aggregated or swept under the guise of an error term.

where $z = \sum_{i=1}^{m} z^i$? The answer is that the behavior of a profit-maximizing farmer can be represented generally with such a production function only when the shadow prices of service flows are constant over time. The reasons are that (i) profit-maximizing service flows in each time period will have different marginal productivities corresponding to the different shadow prices and (ii) the constraints are typically binding only intermittently. Once aggregated, the differences in shadow prices are lost.[21] A simple example can illustrate.

3.3.6. Case 6: Aggregation of service flows

Let output be additive in the stage outputs with output price equal to 1 where the first stage output is given by $z_1 - .5z_1^2$ and the second stage output is $3z_2 - .5z_2^2$. The first stage has marginal product $1 - z_1$ and the second stage has marginal product $3 - z_2$. Where $k = 2$ the optimal solution is

$$z_1^* = 1, \quad \lambda_1^* = 0, \quad z_2^* = 2, \quad \text{and} \quad \lambda_2^* = 1$$

with output 4.5 where λ_i^* represents the shadow value of the service flow constraint in time period i. One cannot maximize profit or output subject to an aggregate service flow availability constraint, $z = 4$, or an aggregate service flow use constraint, $z = 3$, because the different magnitudes of multipliers in different time periods cause different marginal products. In both cases in this example, the use constraint in the second time period would be violated. However, if the shadow prices and total shadow value of available service flows are observed, one could correctly maximize profit or output subject to $v = \lambda_1^* z_1 + \lambda_2^* z_2$ where v is the total shadow value of available service flows ($v = 2$ in the example above). The problem here is that both the optimal shadow prices and the total shadow value of available service flows depend on parameters of the problem that are likely to vary among observations used for estimation both across stages of production and across farms.

The principle implied by this discussion of shadow prices is as follows.

PRINCIPLE 3.   *For inputs or outputs that are constrained, each output and input aggregation in the efficiency concept should be composed of those allocations that have identical shadow prices. For service flows that are constrained, if shadow prices of service flows are not observed intraseasonally and used for weighted aggregation, each service flow aggregation in the efficiency concept should be composed of service flows*

---

[21] The assumption implicit in the allocated fixed input constraint is a "use it or lose it" concept, e.g., if operator labor is not used this time period it does not add to operator labor available for next period. While this assumption applies quite well to labor and land, some types of machinery if used less may have more machinery life available for future time periods. In such cases, the recurring fixity constraint would apply because of fixed machinery capacity but some further user costs would need to be considered among variable costs to reflect how much of a machine's life is exhausted with use.

*that have identical shadow prices. Alternatively, the efficiency concept should be based
on intraseasonal service flow constraint levels as in* (4) *rather than actual service
flows.*

As Case 6 implies, it is not the total seasonal flow or stock that is relevant. It is the
maximal capacity service flow in each period (which for notational convenience we have
assumed is identical in each period). This capacity is what enters (4). The representation
of technical efficiency will not be smooth in maximal service flow capacities represented
in k because constraints bind in some seasons and do not bind in others.

The implications of not following this principle are difficult to determine because
shadow prices are not readily observable. Furthermore, shadow prices typically depend
on market prices and behavioral objectives. Thus, aggregating service flows makes the
description of technology dependent on prices, policy and behavior. In other words,
the associated efficiency concept is not generally a technical efficiency concept when
aggregate service flow data are used.

We note that agricultural production analysis has been increasingly turning toward
representing aggregate production relationships in terms of aggregate service flows.
That is, agricultural production is increasingly being modeled using capital service
flows as variable inputs as in (27) rather than with capital investments as fixed inputs as
in (26). This movement has both motivated and been motivated by the development of
public agricultural production data as measurements of capital service flows rather than
capital stocks [Ball (1985); Ball et al. (1999)]. Thus, the prevailing direction of emphasis both in agricultural production analysis and data generation appears to be leading
away from a valid representation as in (26) and toward a representation as in (27), the
underlying assumptions of which are inapplicable according to Principle 3 except in a
narrow and unlikely set of circumstances.

The principles of this section highlight the critical nature of heterogeneity due to spatial or temporal price variation in agricultural production. As discussed in Section 2,
some major price variations over typical spatial and temporal aggregations of both inputs and outputs appear to be relatively large and thus render those aggregates of questionable value for testing technical efficiency of production or for simply representing
the standard characteristics of technology.

These examples and principles lead to a set of conditions that are sufficient for simple
aggregate representations of technology dependent on observed data.

3.3.7. The aggregation qualification condition

A. Simple input or output aggregation devoid of prices requires:
   1. Functional separability [Blackorby et al. (1978)], or
   2. Equality of prices and marginal conditions across all aggregated quantities. If
      ex post adjustments under uncertainty apply, then all aggregated quantities must
      also be adjusted according to the same ex post information.

B. Conventional input or output aggregation using prices and observable production data requires the cases for which index forms yield exact cost or revenue optimization in terms of aggregates, e.g, as in the quadratic approximation lemma of Diewert (1976). These aggregations must not be over variables affected other than as aggregates by intertemporal or activity-specific policy constraints or ex post adjustments under uncertainty and must not depend on preferences. Such aggregations are not useful when disaggregated prices are unobserved.

3.4. The production possibilities frontier as a representation of technology

Consider next the typical practice of representing multi-output technologies by their PPFs. With the development and application of tractable flexible forms using dual methods, a number of studies based upon the PPF of multiproduct firms have ensued [e.g., Antle (1984); Ball (1988); Shumway (1983); Weaver (1983)]. That is, in virtually all multi-output empirical applications of duality, allocations of inputs are ignored [Chambers and Just (1989) is an exception]. For empirical purposes (when smoothness is imposed), efficient technology is characterized implicitly by a single-equation representation of the product transformation function involving only aggregate inputs and aggregate outputs. These studies examine issues for which the measurement of $F(y, x)$ is beneficial, including measurement of total factor demands and product supplies, various forms of separability, productivity and technical change, and the standard characteristics of the PPF.[22]

However, examination of an economic sector or firm as a whole by means of the PPF using $F(y, x)$ or its dual profit function cannot answer a number of interesting questions that have policy or management relevance. To illustrate, suppose production is truly nonjoint so that the existence and notion of an underlying technology is clear – the f_i's in Samuelson's case in (11) or the ω_i^*'s in Lau's definition in (13). Total profit, π, is the sum of industry (or production activity) profits where each industry (or production activity) profit, π_i, depends only on the corresponding output price, p_i, and input price vector r,

$$\pi(p, r) = \sum_i \pi_i(p_i, r),\tag{28}$$

where p is the output price vector. The dual to the left side of (28) is the PPF or transformation function, $F(y, x) = y_1 - f^*(y_{-1}, x)$, while the dual to an element of the sum on the right-hand side of (28) is the industry production function, $y_i = f_i(x^i)$.

Note that any structure found to be present in π or F says almost nothing about the structure of any π_i or f_i. For example, separability of π in some partition of r does not

---

[22] For these purposes, however, one must attach a *ceteris paribus* qualification as demonstrated in the following section. That is, changes in policy or behavior can alter the apparent PPF.

imply separability of π_i in that partition nor vice versa. In other words, learning about the structure of $F(y, x)$ either directly or implicitly through $\pi(p, r)$ reveals little about the structure of any $f_i(x^i)$.

PRINCIPLE 4. *The structure of a production possibilities frontier, which is the level at which production technology is represented in most modern production studies, does not reveal the structure of any distinct underlying (industry- or production-activity-specific) technologies.*

3.5. An illustration of the technical content of a production frontier

The point of Principle 4 can be illustrated with an example including two competitive industries (or production activities). Using an underlying technology that is nonjoint and symmetrically separable in inputs from outputs, the PPF exhibits separability in inputs from outputs when the partial production elasticities in both sectors are equal. Thus, a test for separability of the PPF may be only a test about the relationship of production elasticities rather than separability of the underlying technology.

Consider a production technology with two outputs and two allocated inputs, one variable and one fixed, following Cobb–Douglas technology,

$$y_1 = ax_1^{\alpha_1} z_1^{\alpha_2}, \qquad y_2 = bx_2^{\beta_1} z_2^{\beta_2}, \tag{29}$$

where x_1 and x_2 are amounts of the variable input allocated to the respective production activities and z_1 and z_2 are amounts of the fixed input allocated to the respective production activities. The aggregate amounts of the two inputs are thus $x = x_1 + x_2$ and $z = z_1 + z_2$, respectively. Suppose the latter must satisfy the allocated fixed input constraint, $z = k$. These relationships can be considered as constraints on the technology in any behavioral optimization or substituted into (29) to represent technology by

$$y_1 = ax_1^{\alpha_1} z_1^{\alpha_2}, \tag{30}$$

$$y_2 = b(x - x_1)^{\beta_1} (k - z_1)^{\beta_2}, \tag{31}$$

where $X = (x_1, x_2)$ and $Z = (z_1, z_2)$. To maximize profits, $\pi = p_1 y_1 + p_2 y_2 - rx$, subject to the constraints, the first-order conditions corresponding to (29) are

$$\alpha_1 p_1 ax_1^{\alpha_1 - 1} z_1^{\alpha_2} - \beta_1 p_2 b(x - x_1)^{\beta_1 - 1} (k - z_1)^{\beta_2} = 0, \tag{32}$$

$$\alpha_2 p_1 ax_1^{\alpha_1} z_1^{\alpha_2 - 1} \beta_2 p_2 b(x - x_1)^{\beta_1} (k - z_1)^{\beta_2 - 1} = 0, \tag{33}$$

$$\beta_1 p_2 b(x - x_1)^{\beta_1 - 1} (k - z_1)^{\beta_2} - r = 0. \tag{34}$$

Combining (30)–(34) and solving out prices obtains the relationship corresponding to (11) or (12).

Another representation of technology is to solve two of these relationships for prices, e.g., p_1 and p_2, after normalizing the other, e.g., setting $w = 1$, to obtain three remaining relationships devoid of prices. One such representation includes (30), (31) and

$$\frac{\beta_1(k - z_1)}{\alpha_1 z_1} = \frac{\beta_2(x - x_1)}{\alpha_2 x_1}, \tag{35}$$

which follows from combining (32) and (33). To obtain (11) or (12) from (30), (31), and (35), one can solve (35) for z_1. This result can be substituted into (30) which can then be solved for x_1. Then both of these results can be substituted into (31) to obtain an equation in y_1, y_2, x, and k.

Even though this step is possible in principle, an explicit solution cannot be found in practice without constraining the parameter space. Since an example suffices, let $\alpha_1 = \alpha_2$. Then solving (35) for z_1 obtains

$$z_1 = \frac{\beta_1 \alpha_2 x_1 k}{\alpha_1 \beta_2 (x - x_1) + \beta_1 \alpha_2 x_1} \tag{36}$$

and solving (30) for x_1 obtains

$$x_1 = (y_1/a)^{1/\alpha_1}/z_1. \tag{37}$$

Solving (36) and (37) simultaneously yields

$$z_1 = \frac{2y_1^\gamma}{cx}\left[1 + \sqrt{1 + ckxy_1^{-\gamma}}\right], \qquad x_1 = \frac{cxa^{-\gamma}}{2}\left[1 + \sqrt{1 + ckxy_1^{-\gamma}}\right]^{-1},$$

where $\gamma = 1/\alpha_1$, $c = 4\beta_2 a^{1/\alpha_1}/(\beta_2 - \beta_1)$. The negative root is ruled out by positivity constraints. Substituting these results into (31) obtains

$$y_2 = b\left\{x - \frac{cxa^{-\gamma}}{2}\left[1 + \sqrt{1 + ckxy_1^{-\gamma}}\right]^{-1}\right\}^{\beta_1}$$
$$\times \left\{k - \frac{2y_1^\gamma}{cx}\left[1 + \sqrt{1 + ckxy_1^{-\gamma}}\right]\right\}^{\beta_2}. \tag{38}$$

The relationship in (38) illustrates the problem with implicit representation of technology. While the underlying technology in (29) is separable in both inputs and outputs, and nonjoint in inputs, the implicit representation of technology by (38) satisfies none of these properties except in special circumstances.[23] For example, if one further assumes $\beta_1 = \beta_2$, then (38) reduces to

$$(y_1/a)^{1/(2\alpha)} + (y_2/b)^{1/(2\beta)} = (xk)^{1/2}$$

---

[23] Shumway, Pope, and Nash (1984) have previously shown that the presence of allocated fixed inputs can induce an apparent jointness even though the underlying technology is nonjoint. This result is somewhat more

which satisfies separability in both inputs and outputs. Thus, a test for separability in (38) may simply test whether parameters have particular relationships even though the underlying technology satisfies separability regardless.

This misleading conclusion occurs because additional information must be imposed together with technology to obtain (38) from (29). This additional information may be viewed as relatively harmless. For example, the assumption of profit maximization is not needed to obtain (38) from (29). Simple Pareto efficiency is enough or, equivalently, following Chambers (1988, p. 261) one can simply assume inputs and outputs are chosen to maximize, say, y_1 given y_2 and x subject to (30) and (31). Nevertheless, the implied relationship in (38) obscures the underlying technology and makes detection of its standard characteristics misleading and impossible. This example thus verifies Principle 4.

3.6. Prescription versus description

Ignoring or subsuming allocations has led to an ever larger division of interests and methods between farm management economists and production economists. Farm management economists have concentrated on strategies and prescriptions for input allocation across production stages and production activities (which they call enterprises) such that both technical and price efficiency is maintained. Production economists, on the other hand, have tended to assume efficient allocation implicitly in order to concentrate on properties of the multi-output efficiency frontier. An excellent example of this approach is the creation and subsequent analysis of aggregate agricultural productivity by Ball (1985) and Ball et al. (1999). Production economists, while often allowing for technical inefficiencies, typically have had little to say about the allocations of a given input over the growing season or across production activities. While this practice by production economists is due in part to data limitations, the data limitations are at least partially endogenous. Those designing data set construction and reporting have chosen to ignore allocations.

The most fundamental definition of economics involves the allocation of productive resources to the satisfaction of competing wants. In the study of production, application of this practice involves determining the optimal allocation of aggregate inputs to various industries or production activities in addition to simply determining the optimal aggregate. Historically, one of the important motivations for studying agricultural production economics was indeed prescriptive – to improve farm management and help farmers make better decisions. More recently, efforts have been devoted to helping regional and national policymakers formulate better policies. We note, however, that the

---

general because all that is changed in this example if both inputs are variable inputs allocated to separate production activities is that k is replaced by z in (38). The additional first-order condition is used in solving for the additional price of the second variable input. Thus, presence of allocated fixed inputs is not crucial in these results. Rather, ignoring allocations, whether of fixed or variable inputs, is the cause of incorrectly reflecting the properties of technology.

PPF is often inadequate in a prescriptive sense when inputs and outputs are aggregated. For example, it does little good for a water economist to determine the optimal capacity of a water system under rationing if no guidance is available for allocation of rations among jurisdictions or farms. Similarly, it does little good for a farmer to know the profit-maximizing aggregate use of fertilizer if no information is available on how to allocate it among crops of different productivities or plots of different soil capacities. Optimal benefits are generally unattainable without proper allocation.

The same principle applies to allocation of aggregate inputs over time. In the framework of Equation (3), knowledge of f^0 does not reveal the nature of the stage production functions nor do deviations from the frontier in f^0 reveal where inefficiencies occur in allocations.[24] Agricultural economists typically measure or estimate f^0 rather than f^*. Knowledge of f^0 is sufficient to address many interesting questions if it is well defined, but the existence, meaning, and appropriate measurement of f^0 hinges crucially on an implicit assumption of constant input prices within aggregates or lack of corner solutions throughout the stages. During growing seasons with high interest rates and varying input prices, f^0 may not be well defined.

This discussion implies an additional principle broadly derived from Principles 1–4 and put in context as follows.

PRINCIPLE 5. *Descriptions of technology expressed only with aggregates over time and location are not conducive to prescription for farm management and they limit meaningful analysis of policy controls.*

In summary, the conventional PPF that subsumes allocative efficiency is not the object of interest in many economic analyses. In practice, knowing what is good may be of little help without knowing how to get there. Conventional analysis of the PPF leaves out direct information on most allocation decisions. It cannot be used to uncover the structure of any underlying sub-technologies. Furthermore, the conventional PPF is not robust in the presence of various policies, behavioral preferences, and environments. When complexities of behavior or environment are introduced, one must proceed from a more basic notion of production efficiency to determine if the usual concept and calculation of allocative efficiency is appropriate or should be amended. Knowledge of any underlying sub-technologies is essential in this process. Hence, knowledge of the sub-technologies is always relevant but knowledge of the PPF may not be relevant. Moreover, the PPF may not be well defined because dependence on policies and behaviors may not be specified but yet affect empirical observations. The above discussion motivates the need to explore alternative concepts of technical and production efficiency which may be useful in distinguishing underlying technologies from the conventional PPF.

---

[24] Of course being on a production function is not sufficient for allocative technical efficiency.

3.7. Eliminating behavior and policy from representations of technology

Principles 4 and 5 are important because some inquiries are required at the level of a single production activity or of a single input to a single production activity that are not sensible at the aggregate PPF level. For example, inquiries regarding technical efficiency need to be sensitive to the extent of price variation across time, space, and production activities in order to have practical implications for overall firm efficiency or social efficiency. When an environmental agency considers prohibiting use of a single pesticide on a group of crops (perhaps the most common type of economic benefit analysis used by an environmental protection agency), a PPF that aggregates use of all pesticides across all crops will be of little use for analyzing the implications. On a more technical level with respect to the properties of production, homotheticity is essentially about the scaling of inputs and/or outputs leaving ratios unchanged. Examination of homotheticity of agricultural technology, for example, using a regional PPF seems to have little policy (or "what if") relevance due to the fixity of land. Nonjointness as implied by $\partial y_i / \partial p_j = 0$ ($j \neq i$) is likely not present in the PPF due to land fixities even when technologies for individual production activities are nonjoint [Shumway et al. (1984)].

From a practical standpoint, the primary intent of many policies is to alter specific input allocations. For example, acreage controls in agriculture (allotments, set asides, and base acreages) apply to the use of a specific input (land) in a specific production activity (crop). Also, pesticide use standards apply at the crop- and sometimes location-specific levels. For example, EPA registrations allow a pesticide to be used only on crops that appear on its registration label. Other EPA requirements limit how close to surface water certain pesticides can be applied. With respect to outputs, government policy instruments such as target and support prices cause the same crop to be sold at more than one price in the same season (not all of a farmer's crop may qualify for the higher subsidized price). Turning to more recent crop and revenue insurance policies, the alteration of effective prices by indemnity payments is crop-specific in some cases and farm-wide in others. In each of these cases, the focus on a PPF following the modern practices of production economics effectively eliminates the relevant policy consideration by aggregating over decisions that are treated distinctly by policies.

Similar considerations apply to behavioral preferences that treat different production activities differently. While much of the modern production literature is based on profit maximization following standard dual approaches, one of the unique features of agriculture is risky production. If some production activities involve more risk than others, then risk averse farmers will tend to allocate fewer inputs to more risky activities, i.e., expected marginal productivities of inputs will be higher among more risky activities. With either a change in behavior (e.g., an increase in risk aversion with operator age) or an enhancement in policies such as crop insurance or government disaster assistance that mitigate risk, the differences in marginal productivities among production activities of different risks could change. Descriptions of technology that do not reflect individual production activities but only aggregate production possibilities cannot be used to analyze such policies or phenomena. Furthermore, analyses of technical efficiency based on revealed preference data affected by such policies is of questionable import when the effects of such policies are ignored.

Probably the most important reason to explore the underlying technology rather than the PPF has to do with robustness. Unless coupled with estimation of disaggregated production technologies, the observable PPF is policy- and behavior-dependent. For example, data envelopment analysis would tend to identify the production efficiency of the least risk averse farmer or the farmer least affected by policy parameters as "the" PPF. Alternatively, if the basic underlying technologies and preferences are estimated conditional on the specific policies affecting them, then a host of alternative policies can be evaluated, including those that address a specific type of behavior (e.g., like crop insurance addresses risk aversion). Pope and Just (1996) demonstrate that even production uncertainty with risk neutrality has fundamental implications for conceptualization and estimation of the cost function. Risk aversion is critical in evaluating, for example, changes in crop insurance. A conventional PPF (not conditioned on policy or behavior) may be clearly irrelevant for such analyses. It may serve only to indicate a potential that can never be reached or that is irrelevant in practice and, if so, will hold no useful information of social benefit.

Although there might be broad conceptual agreement that the PPF represents technology parameters and technical efficiency, distinguishing between a PPF conditioned on policy and one that is purely technological may be very difficult. They may appear observationally equivalent. For example, the constraint in Case 3 above could represent heterogeneity of land quality or an acreage policy control. In the former case it would be a part of technology while in the latter it would not. If policy controls are mingled with technology then a shift in the PPF has an uncertain source and estimates of the PPF are not useful for policy analysis. Productivity could increase due to either a technical change or a policy change such as elimination of the control. Principle 6 summarizes the advantages of a representation of efficiency that depends solely on technological relationships.

PRINCIPLE 6. *A useful concept of production efficiency for policy and management purposes corresponds to the first stage of a two-stage characterization of the producers optimization problem where the first stage fully reflects technical possibilities and the second stage includes all impacts of policies and behavior on decisions.*

3.8. An example with production errors

The point of Principle 6 can be illustrated by a simple one-input, two-output example using multiplicatively random nonjoint production functions. Let $y_1 = f_1(x_1)\varepsilon_1$, $E(\varepsilon_1) = 1$, and $y_2 = f_2(x_2)\varepsilon_2$, $E(\varepsilon_2) = 1$, where each f_i is strictly increasing. The PPF can be written as

$$y_2 = f_2\big(x - f_1^{-1}(y_1/\varepsilon_1)\big)\varepsilon_2,$$

where $x = x_1 + x_2$. Assuming prices are certain, if uncertainty is ignored in the second stage then the firm is assumed to produce on the PPF described by

$$-\partial y_2/\partial y_1 = f_{x_2}/f_{x_1} = p_1/p_2, \tag{39}$$

$$y_2 = f_2\left(x - f_1^{-1}(y_1)\right). \tag{40}$$

However, because y_1 and y_2 are random, (39) and (40) are not consistent with expected utility maximization. A risk neutral firm will produce where

$$-\partial E(y_2)/\partial E(y_1) = f_{x_2}/f_{x_1} = p_1/p_2,$$

$$y_2 = f_2\left(x - f_1^{-1}(y_1/\varepsilon_1)\right), \tag{41}$$

because y_1/ε_1 is $E(y_1)$ given x_1. Given the nonlinear transformation of y_1 in (40), $E(y_2)$ is not equal on average to the right-hand side of (41). Thus, ignoring uncertainty is inconsistent with two-stage expected utility maximization.

In general, to build a PPF in the Samuelsonian fashion consistent with expected utility maximization under price and production risk, one must identify all of the relevant moments of wealth that enter expected utility and develop a two-stage maximization approach consistent with the overall expected utility maximization problem. For example, if input prices are certain and equal as in the typical generic input case, and ε_1 and ε_2 are independent and have two parameter distributions, then

$$E[U(w)] = U^*(m_{11}, m_{12}, m_{21}, m_{22}, w_0, r),$$

for some function U^* where m_{ij} is the ith moment of revenue for good j ($i, j = 1, 2$), w_0 is additive initial certain wealth, r is the generic input price, U is utility, and w is wealth (assuming cross-moments are zero). An appropriate two-stage procedure is defined by

$$\max_{m_{12}, m_{22}, m_{21}, x} \quad \max_{m_{11}|m_{12}, m_{22}, m_{21}, x} \quad E[U(w)], \tag{42}$$

where x is total input use. If production is nonjoint and described by

$$y_1 = f_1(x_1) + h_1(x_1)\varepsilon_1, \quad E(\varepsilon_1) = 0,$$
$$y_2 = f_2(x_2) + h_2(x_2)\varepsilon_2, \quad E(\varepsilon_2) = 0,$$

and output prices are certain, then $m_{1j} = p_j f_j(x_j)$ and $m_{2j} = p_j^2 h_j(x_j)^2 E(\varepsilon_j^2)$. Thus, h_1, f_2, h_2, and x can be effectively constrained in the first stage of (42).

In summary, the appropriate PPF concept for risk neutrality must be based on expected production but, more generally, the PPF must be tailored to the way risk enters production and the extent of risk aversion. This implies that an empirically useful PPF is necessarily dependent upon behavior and the environment.

4. Fundamentals of modeling agricultural production

This section builds upon the principles of Section 3 to suggest needed advances in models of agricultural production. Some of these advances may be feasible with present limitations while application of others is constrained by data availability. Finally, the meaning of existing empirical work when more general specifications apply is discussed. Traditionally, multi-output technologies were represented either by single-equation forms such as $F(y, x) = 0$, e.g., Klein (1947), or by individual production functions for each output where all inputs are allocated among individual outputs such as in (11), e.g., Pfouts (1961). Regarding these two cases as extremes, we suggest an intermediate premise based on the assertion that multi-output production problems typically exhibit at least one of the following properties: (i) some input(s) must be allocated among production processes or points of application in the production process either temporally or spatially,[25] (ii) some output(s) are produced by more than one production process or at more than one location or time in the production process, and/or (iii) some output(s) are produced as by-products so that their production is related in some way to the production of one or more other outputs.

As an example of (i), land in farms must be allocated among crops or (in developing agriculture) among crop mixes; automobile factory assembly lines are allocated among makes or models of cars; and chemical production plants are allocated among primary chemical processes. As an example of (ii), corn production on a farm is diffused among locations while the output of most manufacturing processes is diffused over time. As an example of (iii), many chemical production processes produce both a primary and one or more secondary chemicals; cotton ginning produces both cotton and cottonseed; and soybean crushing produces both soy oil and soy meal. In some activities, the producer may be able to influence the mix of outputs by adjusting the application of inputs (e.g., the choice of seed variety affects the oil content of soybeans) but, in others, the outputs may be constrained to fixed physical relationships (e.g., chemical reactions). While these examples are sufficient to verify validity of the premise, the discussion in Section 2 suggests that these features of agriculture are widespread and dominant.

This section explores the implications of this premise for technology representation. Results show that typical indirect or single-equation representations in such circumstances can, at best, provide reduced-form "as if" representations of technology that facilitate characterization of supply and demand in perfectly competitive markets but cannot identify the technology itself. At worst, such representations of technology are not

---

[25] Typically, some inputs are allocated to distinct production processes while others apply jointly. Knudsen (1973) argues that full nonjointness in inputs is unlikely because it assumes away technological reasons for the observed existence of multi-output firms. For example, training for management or automated control equipment in a multi-output plant or multi-production-process firm may simultaneously enhance production of all outputs. However, Leathers (1991) shows that a sufficient reason for existence of multi-output firms is short-run fixity of allocated factors.

well defined and are useless for investigation of a host of policy, management, and market structure issues in an imperfect world where credit constraints apply, contingency markets are missing, etc. The true underlying technology may provide more flexibility (the typical effect of unrepresented input allocations) or less flexibility (the typical effect of unrepresented by-product relationships). To develop these results requires a substantial development of conceptual groundwork to permit sorting out behavior from technology and to identify the meaning of various functions of aggregate variables. For this purpose, we place the technical detail in an Appendix but describe results in the following sections.

4.1. Structural concepts and efficiency of production

To facilitate clarity of discussion for the case where a firm's technology is possibly composed of several sub-technologies, several alternative concepts of efficiency must be defined. Sub-technologies are defined as production activities where, more generally than in specifications such as (11), each production activity can have more than one output thus allowing input jointness within sub-technologies. When the technology of a firm is composed of sub-technologies, we will say that the technology has *structure*. Typically, this structure can be exploited to understand the implications of alternative policies and preferences.

Suppose the production set $\Im$ can be described by sub-technologies $(y^i, x^i) \in \Im_i(z^i, \varepsilon)$ where y^i and x^i are subvectors of $Y \equiv \{y^1, \ldots, y^m\}$ and $X \equiv \{x^1, \ldots, x^m\}$, $\Im_i(z^i, \varepsilon)$ represents all possible combinations of y^i and x^i regardless of values taken by other elements of Y and X, and aggregate outputs and inputs satisfy $y \equiv \sum_i y^i$ and $x \equiv \sum_i x^i$, respectively. This structure is sufficient to explore some possible implications of technologies where an important step in choosing the output mix is spatial allocation of inputs among plots as in Section 2.2. The different sub-technologies may represent various crop production activities on different plots. For example, one sub-technology may produce wheat and another soybeans by single cropping techniques and another might produce both wheat and soybeans at different times by double cropping. Clearly, the same principles apply to temporal allocation among time periods as in Section 2.1.[26]

---

[26] For added generality, this framework can easily add dependence of each sub-technology on outputs of lower sub-technologies. For example, the dependence of each successive stage of production on the intermediate outputs of the previous stage can be represented by

$$\{(Y, X) \in \Im(k, \varepsilon)\} \equiv \left\{ (y^1, \ldots, y^m, x^1, \ldots, x^m) \mid (y^i, x^i) \in \Im_i(z^i, \varepsilon, y^{i-1}), \ i = 1, \ldots, m, \right.$$

$$\left. \sum_s z_t^s \leqslant k, \ t = 1, \ldots, T \right\}.$$

Note that a suitable definition of y^{i-1} can permit dependence of each stage on all y^{i-j} for $j > 1$ as typical

For simplicity of presentation, this notation does not represent explicitly the possible presence of public inputs that cause jointness across sub-technologies, i.e., inputs that jointly affect multiple sub-technologies simultaneously. For example, the production set of each sub-technology might be described more completely by $(y^i, x^i) \in \Im_i(x^0, z^i, \varepsilon)$ where x^0 is a vector of public inputs and the detailed use of variable inputs is described by

$$X = \{x^0, x^1, \ldots, x^m\}.$$

For purposes of this chapter, such public inputs may be present but are suppressed from notation to focus on the implications of allocations that are required for production decision implementation.

For notational simplicity, aggregations of the spatial and temporal allocation detail in Y and X vectors are represented by $y = AY$ and $x = BX$, respectively, where A and B are full row rank matrices of ones and zeros. The vectors y and x maintain only physical distinction of outputs and inputs. Because each sub-technology may potentially produce only one or a few physical outputs using some subset of physical inputs, this notation can be suitably collapsed to eliminate identically zero elements of Y and X and related columns of A and B.

In addition to descriptions of sub-technologies, the available technology set is assumed also to be constrained by availability of allocated fixed factors such as machinery services and operator labor. For example, if sub-technologies are indexed strictly by location, then the constraints on allocated fixed factors follow $\sum_i z^i \leqslant k$ as in the case where a farmer's tractor services or labor must be allocated across plots so as not to exceed availability. If sub-technologies are indexed strictly by time and represent the stages of production, then these constraints follow $z^i \leqslant k$, $i = 1, \ldots, m$, as in the case where tractor services or operator labor are available with recurrence in each successive time period. Where $Z = \{z^1, \ldots, z^m\}$ represents the allocation of fixed factors to m sub-technologies with both spatial and/or temporal detail, the constraints on allocated fixed factors may be represented generally and compactly by $CZ \leqslant K$, where C is a matrix of ones and zeros with full row rank, and K is a vector that duplicates k for each time period (or modifies it as appropriate if capacities differ by time period) and is thus a function of k. For example, the first several rows of $CZ \leqslant K$ may constrain the total allocation of labor and machinery services in time period 1 by k, the next several rows may do the same for time period 2, and so on.[27] With this framework, one way of

---

in Markovian frameworks. We forgo the generality of this representation for simplicity of exposition but note the importance of this generality for empirical applications following Section 2.1.

[27] As for purchased variable inputs, the presence of any public fixed factor inputs is suppressed from the explicit notation for simplicity of presentation. For example, each sub-technology production set might be described more completely by $(y^i, x^i) \in \Im_i(x^0, z^0, z^i, \varepsilon)$ where both x^0 and z^0 are vectors of public inputs and the detailed use of fixed factors is represented by $Z = \{z^0, z^1, \ldots, z^m\}$.

describing the technology is[28]

$$\left\{ (y, x) \in \Im_{-i}(k, \varepsilon) \right\}$$
$$\equiv \left\{ (y, x) \mid (y^i, x^i) \in \Im_i(z^i, \varepsilon), \ y = AY, \ x = BX, \ CZ \leqslant K \right\}, \tag{43}$$

where $\Im_{-i}(k, \varepsilon)$ represents the set of potential choices of aggregate output and input vectors, i.e., total amounts of physical outputs and inputs after aggregation over time and space.

We refer to descriptions of technology as on the left-hand side of (43) as reduced-form representations because the underlying structure on the right-hand side is solved out of the problem. Structured technologies can be represented by reduced-form production sets devoid of temporal and/or spatial detail as on the left-hand side of (43), but without the right-hand side structural detail the implications of policy instruments that impose limitations on specific y^i's, x^i's, or z^i's cannot be considered nor can preferences that value specific y^i's, x^i's, or z^i's such as peak operator labor. Furthermore, the specific production plan that attains any distinct $(y, x) \in \Im_{-i}(k, \varepsilon)$ is not apparent without the right-hand side detail in Y, X, and Z.

Alternatively, the technology can be represented completely by

$$\{(Y, X, Z) \in \Im(k, \varepsilon)\}$$
$$\equiv \left\{ (y^1, \ldots, y^m, x^1, \ldots, x^m, z^1, \ldots, z^m) \mid (y^i, x^i) \in \Im_i(z^i, \varepsilon), CZ \leqslant K \right\}, \tag{44}$$

where the selection of an element of the technology set prescribes the production plan completely. Also, the elements of the technology set excluded by any particular policy that limits inputs or outputs at specific times or locations can be clearly imposed on (44) but not on the left-hand side of (43).

We submit that the differences in (43) and (44) are fundamentally important. Clearly, if (43) is appropriate, then it substantially reduces the dimension of the efficient choice set. This is a welcome convenience for the study of some issues. However, serious errors can occur from use of (43) when the Aggregation Qualification Condition fails. We note that virtually all empirical applications of duality to agricultural production use the reduced-form representation on the left-hand side of (43) rather than the structural representation of (44). If the efficiency standards of (43) are inappropriate, the state of the empirical agricultural production literature must be seriously questioned. These

---

[28] While more general descriptions of technology structure with nonlinear relationships in place of A, B, and C are easily possible, such generalizations needlessly complicate the points made below without adding insight. We leave extension to these obvious cases to the reader. It should also be noted that the left-hand side of (43) is defined by k rather than $z = \sum_i z^i$ because the right-hand side of (43) embeds the determination of the z^i's and because the use of allocated fixed factors cannot be freely reallocated among the alternative time periods represented in $CZ \leqslant K$.

differences are best illuminated by defining several concepts of technical efficiency. We begin with the strongest technical efficiency concept imposed by (43). Corresponding formal definitions are given in the Appendix.

Reduced-form technical efficiency corresponds to operating on the efficient frontier of $\Im_{-i}$ defined by (43), which under continuity and monotonicity can be represented as a production possibilities frontier, $F^*(y, x, k, \varepsilon) = 0$.[29]

Note that reduced-form efficiency is the typical concept of production efficiency and is defined in terms of aggregate inputs and outputs. An example is given by (11) for the case where allocated fixed inputs are not present (or are ignored) and production is conjoint. Several weaker concepts of output-oriented technical allocative efficiency can be defined depending on which allocations are considered: (i) allocation of purchased variable inputs, (ii) allocation of allocated fixed inputs, and/or (iii) allocation of production among sub-technologies. Each holds one vector of allocations fixed while optimizing another:

Fixed factor technical allocative efficiency holds for a production plan (Y, X, Z) if no other production plan (Y', X, Z') achieves more of at least one output with no less of others $(Y' \nleq Y)$ without using more allocated fixed factors $(CZ' \leqslant CZ)$.[30]

Variable input technical allocative efficiency holds for a production plan (Y, X, Z) if no other production plan (Y', X', Z) achieves more of one output and no less of others $(Y' \nleq Y)$ without using more purchased variable inputs $(BX' \leqslant BX)$.

Output technical allocative efficiency holds for a production plan (Y, X, Z) if no other production plan (Y', X', Z') achieves more of one aggregate output and no less of other aggregate outputs $(AY' \nleq AY)$ without using more purchased variable inputs $(BX' \leqslant BX)$ or more allocated fixed factors $(CZ' \leqslant CZ)$.

In these definitions, technical allocative efficiency is differentiated from standard concepts of allocative efficiency that depend on prices and correspond to operating at tangencies of price lines with physical trade-off possibilities, e.g., the tangency of the output price line with the PPF. These concepts of technical allocative efficiency are weaker

---

[29] Following Chambers (1988, p. 261), the PPF is defined by $F^*(y, x, k, \varepsilon) = y_1 - f^*(y_{-1}, x, k, \varepsilon) = 0$ where $y = (y_1, y_{-1})$ and $y_1 = f^*(y_{-1}, x, k, \varepsilon) = \max\{y_1 \mid (y, x) \in \Im_{-i}(k, \varepsilon)\}$. The term "efficient frontier" in this context refers to the upper right-hand frontier of the set of possible aggregate outputs and purchased variable inputs, $(y, -x)$.

[30] Consistent with Principle 3, it should be noted in the definition of fixed factor technical allocative efficiency that $z = \sum_i z^{i'} \leqslant z = \sum_i z^i$, which does not include temporal detail, is not an appropriate condition in place of $CZ' \leqslant CZ$, which imposes allocated fixed factor constraints by time period. The reason is that allocated fixed inputs cannot be freely reallocated among time periods as might be the case for purchased variable inputs. The implication is that data on aggregate flows of machinery services are not appropriate for modeling production if decisions are made in a reality of intraseasonal constraints on machinery service flows.

and merely correspond to operating on the physical trade-off frontier. The reason for using these weaker definitions is to identify a measure of technical efficiency that is sufficiently independent of prices, policy, and behavior for various circumstances.

To verify that these concepts of technical allocative efficiency are weaker than reduced-form efficiency, consider a somewhat stronger concept of fixed factor technical allocative efficiency:

Feasible fixed factor technical allocative efficiency holds for a production plan (Y, X, Z) if no other production plan (Y', X, Z') achieves more of at least one output with no less of others $(Y' \nleq Y)$ given feasibility of allocated fixed factors $(CZ', CZ \leq K)$.

Reduced-form efficiency is obtained by combining this stronger concept of feasible fixed factor technical allocative efficiency with variable input and output technical allocative efficiency. Thus, all of the above technical allocative efficiency concepts are implied by reduced-form efficiency.

The potential inappropriateness of reduced-form technical efficiency can thus be studied by considering potential inappropriateness of the technical allocative efficiency concepts. Each of the various forms of technical allocative efficiency (which are implied by corresponding standard concepts of price-based allocative efficiency) may be inconsistent (i) with plausible preferences, (ii) with restrictions imposed by government policies, and (iii) even with profit maximization in absence of policy restrictions. In particular, if the allocated fixed inputs, variable inputs, or outputs that are aggregated over time and space by physical characteristics do not satisfy the Aggregation Qualification Condition, then the respective technical allocative efficiency concept is inappropriate. This condition implies that aggregation is not appropriate in cases where (i) generic input prices are heterogeneous over space and time and disaggregated prices are unobserved, (ii) allocation-specific government policy controls apply, (iii) allocation-specific ex post adjustments respond to unanticipated conditions, or (iv) behavioral criteria more general than profit maximization have allocation-specific considerations (such as risk aversion with allocation-specific risk effects of inputs).

These failures occur because technical allocative efficiency employs a standard of minimizing physical aggregates of fixed allocated resources and/or variable inputs, and/or maximizing physical aggregates of outputs under the assumption of equal marginal productivities and possibly also equal marginal risk effects. If these standards are inappropriate due to, say, spatial or temporal price variation, then the assumption of equal marginal productivities is typically not satisfied. If profit maximization fails due to risk aversion, then the assumption of equal marginal risk effects may not be satisfied. When the Aggregation Qualification Condition is not satisfied, a weaker concept of technical efficiency can be satisfactory.

Feasible disaggregated input-output efficiency corresponds to operating on the efficient frontier of $\Im$ where $\Im$ is defined by (44).

Feasible disaggregated input-output efficiency implies operating on the upper right-hand frontier of the set of possible disaggregated outputs and purchased variable inputs, $(Y, -X)$, given feasible allocations of fixed factors. It is likely the strongest concept of technical efficiency devoid of policy or behavioral content among those above. Similarly, feasible disaggregated input-output efficiency is also likely the strongest concept of efficiency clearly independent of (typically unobserved) spatial and/or temporal price distributions among those above.

If the producer has preferences over leisure as well as profit (and thus, implicitly, over operator labor), then feasible disaggregated input-output efficiency is also inappropriate because the producer may choose a level of operator labor inside the associated fixed allocated input constraint. In this case, fixed factor technical allocative efficiency, which does not require exhausting constraints, may hold while feasible fixed factor technical allocative efficiency fails. For this case, the following weaker concepts of sub-technology and structural technical efficiency are appropriate. If the Aggregation Qualification Condition fails for allocated fixed factors, then these may be the strongest appropriate concepts of technical efficiency.

Sub-technology efficiency corresponds to operating on the efficient frontier of $\Im_i$, which under continuity and monotonicity can be represented as $F_i(y^i, x^i, z^i, \varepsilon) = 0$.[31]

Structural technical efficiency corresponds to operating on the efficient boundary of all sub-technologies simultaneously which under continuity and monotonicity can be represented as

$$
F(Y, X, Z, \varepsilon) \underset{m}{\equiv} \begin{bmatrix} F_1(y^1, x^1, z^1, \varepsilon) \\ \vdots \\ F_m(y^m, x^m, z^m, \varepsilon) \end{bmatrix} \underset{m}{=} 0. \tag{45}
$$

Note that, to avoid confusion, a subscript is added to these equalities to denote vector dimensionality of the equalities.

Intuitively, sub-technology efficiency is appropriate for any objective function that is monotonically increasing in the elements of y^i, a highly plausible condition. The same can be said for the more expansive concept of structural technical efficiency. Note that feasible input-output technical efficiency is obtained by adding feasible fixed factor technical allocative efficiency to structural technical efficiency. While this stronger concept of technical efficiency appears highly plausible because production plans that violate fixed production resource constraints are not feasible, the example above where the producer has preferences with respect to use of particular fixed resource service flows such as operator labor gives an example where it is not.

---

[31] Specifically, define $F_i(y^i, x^i, z^i, \varepsilon) = y_i^i - f_i(y_{-i}^i, x^i, z^i, \varepsilon)$ where y_{-i}^i is the y^i vector with y_i^i deleted and $y_i^i = f_i(y_{-i}^i, x^i, z^i, \varepsilon) = \max\{y_i^i \mid (y^i, x^i) \in \Im_i(z^i, \varepsilon)\}$. The term "efficient frontier" in this context refers to the upper right-hand frontier of the set of possible $(y_i, -x_i)$.

Some important points evident from this discussion are as follows (see Appendix Section A.1 for sketches of proofs).

PROPOSITION 1. *Preferences, policies, and spatial and/or temporal price variation can affect allocation under technologies with structure, which renders typical concepts of technical allocative efficiency (and thus standard concepts of price-based allocative efficiency) inapplicable.*

PROPOSITION 2. *For technologies with structure (technologies composed of sub-technologies), reduced-form technical efficiency, i.e., operating on the aggregate production possibilities frontier, is not necessarily consistent with profit maximization.*

PROPOSITION 3. *If there is at least one allocated fixed (variable) input and the output(s) of at least two sub-technologies are strictly monotonic in that input, then structural technical efficiency is not equivalent to output technical allocative efficiency nor fixed factor (variable input) technical allocative efficiency.*

4.2. The purpose of characterizing production efficiency

Presumably, the major objective of characterizing production efficiency is to decompose the producer's problem usefully into technical, behavioral, and policy components. Without this decomposition, microeconomic models of supply and demand cannot predict or analyze the effects of changes in technology and/or policy. According to the Aggregation Qualification Condition, decomposition whereby the first stage is strictly technical may be correctly accomplished only under particular circumstances. Suppose that Aggregation Qualification Condition A.2 holds prior to imposing any constraints and that all functionals of the decision variables subject to distinct policy controls or behavioral preferences are retained as decision variables in the second stage (Principle 6). For example, if (i) the producer is a profit maximizer, (ii) government policy controls are fully expressed by $(y, x) \in G$, and (iii) prices are identical among sub-technologies ($p = p_i, r = r_i$ for $i = 1, \ldots, m$), then the first stage defined by (43) is devoid of policy and behavioral content and is sufficient to reflect the full generality of the remaining decisions in a second-stage problem of the form $\pi = \max_{y,x}\{py - rx \mid (y, x) \in G \cap \Im_{-i}(k, \varepsilon)\}$.

By comparison, if either a full expression of government policy controls requires $(Y, X) \in G$ or prices (market or shadow) are not identical among sub-technologies, then the first stage must retain the detail of (44). In the case of profit maximization, the corresponding second stage is then of the form $\pi = \max_{Y,X}\{PY - RX \mid (Y, X, Z) \in G \cap \Im(k, \varepsilon)\}$. For example, policy might constrain the use of a particular input such as a fertilizer, pesticide, or tillage practice differently depending on the proximity of an individual plot to surface water resources. Similar conclusions apply to aggregations over time and space as well as over sub-technologies.

If behavioral alternatives to profit maximization are admitted, then additional generalities must be preserved by the first stage. For example, under risk aversion some functional must be included describing how risk is fully determined by second-stage decisions. If this functional is affected differently according to which sub-technology an input is applied (e.g., if fertilizer affects risk on a corn field differently than it affects risk on a wheat field), then distinction in the input vector must be carried to the second stage if behavioral content is to be avoided in the first stage.

Alternatively, suppose the production problem is decomposed so that the first stage is not purely technical but also admits policy constraints or behavioral preferences. For example, where the first-stage decision set G_{-i} is defined by

$$\left\{ (y, x) \in G_{-i}(k, \varepsilon) \right\}$$
$$\equiv \left\{ (y, x) \mid (y^i, x^i) \in G \cap \mathfrak{I}_i(z^i, \varepsilon), \ y = AY, \ x = BX, \ CZ \leqslant K \right\},$$

the description of technology carried to the second stage by $(y, x) \in G_{-i}(k, \varepsilon)$ clearly carries policy content. If so, then determination of whether (y, x) choices are on the frontier of $G_{-i}(k, \varepsilon)$ has little to say about technical efficiency. Policy-constrained behavior may be technically inefficient. Further, statistical tests about the structure of $G_{-i}(k, \varepsilon)$ have little to say about the structural properties of technology. Decisions may be on the frontier of $G_{-i}(k, \varepsilon)$ but yet be technically inefficient. Finally, accurate estimation of the second stage decision equations for this problem will be of little value for analyzing the effects of changes in policies that affect G_{-i}. The parameters of such equations will be dependent on the policies that determine $G_{-i}(k, \varepsilon)$ and thus inappropriate for analyzing alternative policies following the Lucas critique. The important point of this discussion is summarized by the following proposition (see Appendix Section A.2 for a sketch of the proof).

PROPOSITION 4. *If the (first-stage) description of technology depends on policy or behavior, then statistical tests regarding efficiency and structural characteristics do not necessarily apply to technology nor are estimated (second-stage) models useful for policy analysis.*

Proposition 4 points out a problem that applies to many agricultural production studies in the literature to date because of crop- and/or spatial- and/or time-specific policy instruments associated with commercial agricultural and environmental policy. Of course, for estimation, sufficient variation in policy instruments and variables affecting preferences must be observed to facilitate identification and distinction of technical relationships from policy- or preference-induced relationships. In other words, the problem is not whether inputs or outputs are aggregated but that the dimensions and configuration of A, B, and C are likely wrong in most empirical studies. "Wrong" in this context means that either the Aggregation Qualification Condition is violated or that observed data are inadequate for identification because of excessive detail. With limited data, distinction may not be possible.

These considerations motivate the definition of criteria for technical allocative efficiency that satisfy policy- and behavior-independence where feasible aggregation is undertaken to conserve degrees of freedom for estimation. That is, aggregation of Y, X, and Z is appropriate within groups that have common prices and that enter the policy and preference calculus as aggregates. Suppose the technology choice is summarized by $(y^*, x^*, z^*) = H \cdot (Y, X, Z) \in R_+^{n*}$ where $n^* < n$ and H is a full row rank aggregator matrix of ones and zeros similar to A, B, and C. If H preserves distinction for all input and output quantities that have distinct prices, distinct policy controls, distinct ex post adjustment possibilities, or distinct behavioral preferences and implications, then the full flexibility of the technology for responding to price, policy, and behavioral concerns is preserved by the first stage of a production problem that satisfies

$$\{(y^*, x^*, z^*) \in \Im^*(k, \varepsilon)\}$$
$$\equiv \{H \cdot (y^1, \ldots, y^m, x^1, \ldots, x^m, z^1, \ldots, z^m) \mid (y^i, x^i) \in \Im_i(z^i, \varepsilon), CZ \leqslant K\}. \tag{46}$$

Two additional definitions facilitate this distinction.

An aggregation (y^*, x^*, z^*) *is policy- and behavior-relevant* if it satisfies the Aggregation Qualification Condition. The efficient frontier of $\Im^*$ defined in (46) thus provides a standard of technical allocative efficiency independent of policy and behavior.

An aggregation (y^*, x^*, z^*) *is policy- or behavior-dependent* if it does not satisfy the Aggregation Qualification Condition. The efficient frontier of $\Im^*$ defined in (46) thus does not provide a standard of technical allocative efficiency independent of policy and behavior.[32]

Aside from the extreme assumptions of functional separability, the Aggregation Qualification Condition implies distinction must be preserved for all input and output quantities that have distinct prices, distinct ex post adjustments, distinct policy controls, distinct ex post adjustment possibilities, and distinct behavioral preferences and implications. According to Proposition 4, this concept of policy- and behavior-relevance must be satisfied in order to investigate technical efficiency or properties of the technology in a meaningful and relevant way.

For the remainder of this paper, we emphasize that imposing efficiency concepts in the definition of the technology is inappropriate whenever it is incongruent with policy- and behavior-relevance. For example equating marginal rates of technical substitution or marginal value products across allocated fixed factors such as land is inappropriate if (i) agricultural policy restrictions impose crop-specific acreage limitations, (ii) environmental policy imposes land-use restrictions or acreage-specific conservation measures,

---

[32] Note that policy- and behavior-relevance is the opposite of policy- and behavior-dependence. A representation is policy- and behavior-relevant if it applies regardless of the particular policy or behavior in effect.

(iii) the farmer has crop-specific preferences, or (iv) the farmer values leisure and different crops have different returns to operator labor. In each of these cases, policy- or behavior-related considerations cause implicit prices to vary across allocation variables. Similarly, if allocation-specific prices of variable inputs are unobserved then similar marginal conditions may be inappropriate for variable input allocations. Because some aggregation is required for practical and tractable representation of most production problems, we assume from this point forward that the disaggregated description of the production problem includes all aggregation that is policy- and behavior-relevant. That is, the notation of (44) will be assumed to represent a policy- and behavior-relevant description of the production problem as in (46) where asterisks are dropped for convenience.[33]

4.3. Functional representation of technology

A common practice in production economics has been to switch readily from set theoretic notation to smooth functional representation of technology for econometric purposes upon assuming continuity and monotonicity. Technologies with structure can be analyzed somewhat more generally using the dual set theoretical framework developed by Chambers, Chung, and Färe (1996). Related empirical applications are possible along the lines of Chambers and Just (1989). However, the bulk of our presentation uses functional notation to facilitate accessibility for the broader agricultural economics profession and to relate better to common empirical practices. In practice, the switch to a functional representation is typically made arbitrarily with little regard for the structure of production.

From its earliest consideration in economics, multi-output efficiency has been characterized by single-equation multi-output production functions of the form

$$F(Y, X) = 0. \tag{47}$$

Samuelson (1967) argued that such forms are very general and can be derived from a host of underlying production functions and optimal conditions. Some have taken these arguments to mean that (47) can contain a host of distinct functions and conditions of the form, $F_i(Y, X) = 0, i = 1, \ldots, m$, which are imposed simultaneously by, say,

$$F(Y, X) \equiv \sum_{i=1}^{m} [F_i(Y, X)]^2 = 0 \tag{48}$$

---

[33] Accordingly, the policy- and behavior-relevant description of a sub-technology corresponds to

$$\left\{ (y^{i*}, x^{i*}) \in \mathfrak{I}_i^*(z^{i*}, \boldsymbol{\varepsilon}) \right\} \equiv \left\{ \boldsymbol{H} \cdot (0, \ldots, 0, y^i, 0, \ldots, 0, x^i, 0, \ldots, 0, z^i, 0, \ldots, 0) \mid (y^i, x^i) \in \mathfrak{I}_i(z^i, \boldsymbol{\varepsilon}) \right\}$$

and the physical sums of allocations are represented by $c^* z^* = CZ$ where $z^* = (z^{1*}, \ldots, z^{n_z *})$.

[Mittelhammer et al. (1981)].[34] If so, then a simple direct specification that completely determines n_y outputs from n_x inputs following n_y distinct scalar relationships,

$$y_i = f_i(X), \quad i = 1, \ldots, n_y, \tag{49}$$

can be represented by (48) where $F_i(Y, X) = y_i - f_i(X)$, $i = 1, \ldots, n_y$. For practical purposes, however, the representation in (48) is not useful because it yields $\partial F/\partial Y = 0$ and $\partial F/\partial X = 0$ whenever $F(Y, X) = 0$. Such single-equation forms are not consistent with many standard manipulations of production problems and, in particular, violate the standard convexity assumption of duality (see Appendix, Section A.3, for details).

PROPOSITION 5. *Single-equation implicit production functions cannot represent technologies with structure in ways that lend themselves to standard assumptions of duality or other standard manipulations of production problems using Lagrangians, Kuhn–Tucker conditions, or the implicit function theorem.*

To represent technologies with structure, ambiguity about how many functional conditions are imposed by the technology must be resolved. In spite of the potential generality of (47), common single-equation specifications of technology render representations such as (48) and (49) inapplicable. For example, Klein's (1947) multi-product generalization of the Cobb–Douglas production function,

$$F(Y, X) = y_1 y_2^\delta - A x_1^{\alpha_1} x_2^{\alpha_2},$$

or, indeed, any single-equation form that is separable in inputs and outputs,

$$F(Y, X) = h(Y) - g(X) = 0,$$

cannot represent structures such as (48) and (49). Alternatively, the structure in either (48) or (49) is represented unambiguously by (45) without requiring $\partial F/\partial Y = 0$ and $\partial F/\partial X = 0$ when $F(Y, X) = 0$. As a result, the standard assumptions and manipulations identified in Proposition 5 are not excluded. Thus, the form in (45) is used below.

To see that similar implications apply in the dual approach, consider the special input nonjointness case of (49) where $y_i = f_i(x^i)$, $i = 1, \ldots, n_y$. With the dual approach of

---

[34] Samuelson (1967) is somewhat ambiguous on this point. Clearly, Samuelson interprets (11) as giving the maximum amount of any one output given amounts of all inputs and all other outputs. In other words, (11) characterizes the production possibilities frontier associated with a given input vector X. This interpretation alone, however, does not identify whether more than one condition may be required to reflect, say, a technology where 2 outputs follow a particular by-product relationship in addition to a typical implicit production possibilities frontier relationship. We note also that Samuelson also uses standard Lagrangian techniques which, as shown below, are not applicable for representations such as (11) that combine multiple conditions.

Chambers, Chung, and Färe (1996), which is sufficiently general to handle technologies with structure, the input distance function becomes[35]

$$D_I(y, x) = \max\left\{ \min_i \{ D_I^i(y_i, x^i) \} \mid \sum_i x^i = x, y = (y_1, \ldots, y_{n_y}) \right\},$$

where $D_I^i(y_i, x_i)$ is the input distance function associated with sub-technology i. Each of the sub-technology distance functions corresponds to one of the production relationships in Lau's (1978) development illustrated in Equation (13). The left-hand side distance function cannot reflect the structural characteristics of the multiple sub-technology distance functions on the right-hand side. Thus, multiple functions are required to fully represent multiple sub-technology structure in dual as well as primal approaches.

4.4. Structural versus reduced-form representation of technology

A typical view that has followed from the duality emphasis on PPFs has been that the input vector determines the output possibilities set rather than a specific output vector [e.g., Chambers (1988)]. Indeed, this view is appropriate as a reduced-form representation where allocations of aggregate inputs both spatially and temporally as well as among production activities represent a corresponding structural determination of the output mix. The contrast between these reduced-form and structural concepts of technology are analogues of reduced form and structure in econometric models. Each has its appeal. However, unlike econometric models, the just-identified case occurs here only when technologies have trivial structure (i.e., either there are no sub-technologies or the sub-technologies have mutually exclusive sets of inputs and outputs). Otherwise, if technical inefficiency is measured in the reduced form in (43), one cannot identify whether the sub-technologies are inefficient, or whether the inefficiency comes from allocative inefficiency, or whether the Aggregation Qualification Condition is violated.

At the basic level of management decision making, the manager must control decisions that determine which mix of outputs is produced (for given magnitudes of uncontrollable factors). Otherwise, the typical tangency conditions of price lines with production possibilities frontiers cannot be attained by deliberate choice, in which case the

---

[35] To see this result, let the input requirement set for each sub-technology be represented by $v_i(y_i) = \{x^i \mid (y_i, x^i) \in \Im_i\}$ in which case the overall input requirement set is $v(y) = \sum_i v_i(y_i)$. The input distance function is

$$D_I(y, x) = \max\left\{ \alpha > 0 \mid x/\alpha \in \sum_i v_i(y_i) \right\}$$

$$= \max\left\{ \alpha > 0 \mid x^i/\alpha \in v_i(y_i), \ i = 1, \ldots, n_y; \ \sum_i x_i = x \right\}.$$

Since α can only be feasible if $x^i/\alpha \in v_i(y_i)$, $i = 1, \ldots, n_y$, it must satisfy $\alpha \leqslant D_I^i(y_i, x^i)$, $i = 1, \ldots, n_y$, where $D_I(y, x) = \max\{\min_i \{D_I^i(y_i, x^i)\} \mid \sum_i x^i = x, y = (y_1, \ldots, y_{n_y})\}$.

bulk of multi-output production theory is inapplicable. Thus, given convexity of sub-technology production sets (quasi-concavity of the associated production functions), no generality is lost by assuming that input decisions for the underlying sub-technologies determine the output vector with structural technical efficiency uniquely for given magnitudes of uncontrollable factors. This determination is made by the allocation of inputs both spatially and temporally among sub-technologies as in the following axiom.

The Fundamental Axiom of Multi-output Production: For given magnitudes of uncontrollable factors, the complete vector of input decisions uniquely determines the technically efficient vector of outputs.

The complete vector of decisions includes all spatial and temporal allocations of both purchased variable inputs and allocated fixed factors including allocations of recurring service flows from firm-owned resources (as well as any non-allocated fixed factors not represented explicitly here). From a practical standpoint, this axiom simply implies that a farmer can determine the production mix of, say, corn and soybeans (subject to uncontrolled exogenous and random forces such as weather, pest infestations, illness, variations in work quality, and errors in applying decisions) by making all available input decisions including allocations of land, fertilizer, pesticides, labor, machinery services, etc., both spatially and temporally. This axiom, in effect, simply divides all forces affecting production into two groups – controlled and uncontrolled – and assumes that these two groups of forces determine production uniquely. In other words, once all production decisions are made and uncontrolled forces act, the producer is not left with an *ex post* ability to adjust the output mix.

As realistic and innocuous as this axiom seems, it has been the focus of an implicit ongoing debate [compare the PPF-based duality literature to Mittelhammer et al. (1981); Just et al. (1983); Shumway et al. (1984)]. Adopting this Fundamental Axiom, however, immediately leads away from the PPF and toward sub-technology characterizations of technology. The basic points are that (i) PPFs represent a reduced-form summary of the implications of a more basic representation of technology involving spatial and temporal allocations of inputs among sub-technologies, whereas (ii) the structures of sub-technologies have potential implications for production analysis and related policy analysis.

The Fundamental Axiom permits the use of sub-technology representations to examine implications. An immediate implication of the Fundamental Axiom is that sub-technology efficiency under continuity and monotonicity can be represented by

$$y^i \underset{k_i}{=} f_i(x^i, z^i, \varepsilon), \tag{50}$$

where f_i is a multivariate function determining the complete vector of output quantities and k_i is the number of outputs that are not identically zero in sub-technology i. Thus, if $F_i(y^i, x^i, z^i, \varepsilon)$ in (45) includes multiple implicit relationships along the lines of (48) then the representation in (50) is assumed to make these relationships explicit yielding non-trivial derivatives for purposes of standard manipulations of production problems. Thus, whereas $F_i(y^i, x^i, z^i, \varepsilon)$ in (45) represents a sub-technology by its reduced-form PPF, Equation (50) represents the structure of a sub-technology explicitly with the multiple equations of a vector valued function where appropriate. In turn, structural technical efficiency is represented by[36]

$$
Y \underset{\sum_i k_i}{\equiv} \begin{bmatrix} y^1 \\ \vdots \\ y^m \end{bmatrix} \underset{\sum_i k_i}{=} \begin{bmatrix} f_1(x^1, z^1, \varepsilon) \\ \vdots \\ f_m(x^m, z^m, \varepsilon) \end{bmatrix} \underset{\sum_i k_i}{\equiv} f(X, Z, \varepsilon), \tag{51}
$$

which specifies the complete vector of output quantities of the firm. The number of non-identically-zero outputs in Y is thus $\sum_i k_i$. For example, the simple Samuelsonian case of (11) where each sub-technology produces a unique single output yields $k_i = 1$ for all i, which is the case of full input nonjointness.[37] In addition, fixed allocated inputs must obey $CZ \leqslant K$ so that feasible disaggregated input-output efficiency is given by

$$
Y \in \left\{ f(X, Z, \varepsilon) \mid CZ \leqslant K; \not\exists Z' \ni f(X, Z', \varepsilon) \not\leqslant f(X, Z, \varepsilon) \ \& \ CZ' \leqslant K \right\}.
$$

A brief example can illustrate the richness of (51). Suppose a farm has two sub-technologies: one for production of wheat and one for cow-calf production. The wheat sub-technology may produce both grain and straw (both are outputs of harvesting). The cow-calf operation produces both bull calves and heifer calves. The farmer faces decisions of how much labor to allocate to each of the two sub-technologies but each sub-technology has two outputs. Thus, each $f_i(x^i, z^i, \varepsilon)$ is two-dimensional whereas Y is four-dimensional.

The characterization of technology by (50) and (51) employs possibly numerous equations to describe a firm's technology compared to the more traditional single equation reduced-form description of a PPF as in (47). The purpose of the next several sections is to show that the multitude of equations in (50) and (51) have much to say about the structure and properties of technology that can only be uncovered by examining sub-technologies. Furthermore, typical econometric efficiency considerations suggest advantages to estimation of as much of this structure as data availability permits. By comparison, single-equation reduced-form PPF estimation of (47) or duality based supply-demand estimation based on a PPF characterization of the production set suffers from econometric inefficiency [Mundlak (1996)].[38]

---

[36] Again, the reader should bear in mind the possible presence of public inputs, which are suppressed for notational convenience. For example, each $f_i(x^i, z^i, \varepsilon)$ in (50) and (51) might be described more completely by $f_i(x^0, z^0, x^i, z^i, \varepsilon)$ where x^0 and z^0 are public variable and fixed inputs, respectively.

[37] Note that from this point forward Y is assumed to include only outputs that are not identically zero. Thus, $n_y = \sum_i k_i$ where the dimensions of the y^i's are not all the same. Nevertheless, $y = AY$ is assumed to represent aggregation by physical attributes across time, space, and sub-technologies.

[38] The underlying econometric principle has been developed by, for example, Dhrymes (1973), who showed that more efficient estimates of reduced forms are obtained by estimating the underlying structure.

To examine the structural representation of technology for empirical purposes, how-ever, requires careful specification of allocation decisions, by-product relationships, and related concepts of controllability and rank of technologies. These issues are discussed in detail in Appendix Section A.4 but are outlined intuitively here to facilitate remaining discussion. While relatively little may be known regarding specific functional forms, the dimensions of allocations, by-product relationships, controllability and rank can typi-cally be determined quite well on the basis of actual farming practices and information available from production scientists. For example, purchased inputs for crop production must typically be allocated among plots and time (i.e., among specific trips over specific plots with specific farm equipment). When one crop is grown at a time as in developed agriculture, a major decision is how much land to allocate to each crop in each growing season as well as how much seed, fertilizer, and pesticides to apply per unit of land on each crop or plot and when to apply it. These simple observations determine much about the structure of production and the dimension of the producer's decision vector. Addi-tionally, some products like cotton and cottonseed or bull calves and heifer calves are produced in tandem. Cottonseed is not produced as a by-product of wheat production nor is cottonseed produced independent of cotton. These relationships, in effect, reduce the producer's flexibility in choosing the decision vector in substantive ways.

With this background, we say a sub-vector of decisions is locally controllable if the producer is free to vary any part of the vector by a small amount in any direction. The existence of by-product relationships reduces the producer's controllability in choosing output mixes. Assuming continuity and monotonicity and partitioning the Y vector as $Y = (\widetilde{Y}, \widehat{Y})$ where $\widehat{Y} \in R_{+}^{n_b}$, the outputs in $\widehat{Y}$ are called by-products of $\widetilde{Y}$ under tech-nology $\Im$ if there exists a non-trivial relationship $\widehat{Y} = g(\widetilde{Y}, \varepsilon)$ that uniquely determines $\widehat{Y}$. For example, in the case of a wheat sub-technology, if grain and straw are produced in fixed proportions aside from uncontrolled forces, then either output may be consid-ered a by-product of the other. If, on the other hand, the choice of inputs determines the mix of grain and straw output, then the two equations describing their production differ substantively (in rank) and neither output is a by-product of the other. In the fixed proportions case, straw is typically considered the by-product because of its lower value, but this designation is price-dependent and not appropriate in a pure description of technology.

Although this partitioning of the output vector is not unique, results in the Appendix show that the dimension of controllability is determined uniquely by the rank of the technology, i.e., $n_a = \text{rank}(f_X, f_Z)$ where subscripts of f denote differentiation, $n_y = n_a + n_b$, and $\widetilde{Y} \in R_{+}^{n_a}$. The useful purpose of defining the rank of a technology is to determine how many equations are required to represent it empirically and, in turn, what the dimension is of the investigation required to determine production efficiency. This information is also necessary to determine econometric efficiency (how many equations are required to represent structure fully). This framework gives a constructive way to test for the existence of by-products. For example, nonparametric estimates of f can be used to test for the rank of (f_X, f_Z) following Cragg and Donald (1997).

A similar issue of controllability applies to inputs. For example, constraints imposed on allocated fixed inputs by fixed resources of the firm limit the producer's flexibility in making input choices because they must satisfy $CZ \leqslant K$. Because the individual constraints contained therein may or may not be locally binding, suppose that $\widetilde{C}$ and $\widetilde{K}$ represent subsets of the rows of C and K, respectively, corresponding to locally binding constraints. Then $\widetilde{C}Z = \widetilde{K}$ summarizes all locally binding constraints on allocated fixed inputs. Assuming without loss of generality that C includes no redundant restrictions, $\widetilde{C}$ has rank n_c so that $\underset{n_c}{\widetilde{C}Z} = \widetilde{K}$ can be solved uniquely for $\underset{n_c}{\widehat{Z}} = h(\widetilde{Z}, K)$ where Z is partitioned as $Z = (\widetilde{Z}, \widehat{Z})$, $\widetilde{Z} \in R_+^{n_z - n_c}$, and $\widehat{Z} \in R_+^{n_c}$. Obviously, an arbitrary fixed input allocation vector is not fully controllable unless no fixed inputs are limiting. That is, even though there are n_z allocated fixed input decisions, only $n_f = n_z - n_c$ of them are freely controllable.

The presence of allocated fixed input constraints explains why the responses of seemingly independent production activities may appear dependent.[39] That is, input constraints across production activities can induce jointness between them even when the production activities are fully nonjoint [Shumway et al. (1984)]. This is true whether the constraints result from allocated fixed inputs or other sources such as policy parameters imposed on a firm (such as water use restraints, acreage controls or pesticide standards). For this reason, statistical testing for restrictions on the input space appears advisable. For example, nonparametric tests can be used to determine controllability of inputs. Alternatively, such tests can be based upon the existence of a non-trivial h function by regressing $\widehat{Z}$ on $\widetilde{Z}$ for hypothesized partitions of Z.

With this background, a standard form for the structure of technology is useful.

A canonical form for the local structure of multi-output technologies consists of[40]
(i) the controllable production technology,

$$\underset{n_a}{\widetilde{Y}} = \tilde{f}(X, Z, \varepsilon),$$ (52)

(ii) the byproduct relationships,

$$\underset{n_b}{\widehat{Y}} = g(\widetilde{Y}, \varepsilon),$$ (53)

---

[39] In other words, a producer's decisions result in a specific vector of output quantities – a production possibilities surface. Even if aggregate inputs produce a production possibilities surface (as in some dual developments), an additional decision must be made to determine a particular point on the production possibilities surface if the standard multi-output profit maximization theory is appropriate.

[40] Note that Equations (52) and (53) are jointly equivalent to Equation (51) in the sense that either can be solved for the other. Equations (52) and (53) correspond to a representation that solves the x^i's and z^i's out of as many individual equations of (51) as possible. Note, however, that $n_z \geqslant m$ because each sub-technology must have at least one substantive production relationship.

and (iii) the binding input restrictions,

$$\widehat{\underset{n_c}{Z}} = h(\widetilde{Z}, K),$$ (54)

where $\widetilde{Y}$ and $\widetilde{Z}$ are locally controllable, $Z = (\widetilde{Z}, \widehat{Z})$, and the Jacobians of $\widetilde{f}$, g, and h have full row rank.

Appendix Section A.4 derives the following proposition.

PROPOSITION 6. *Every technology that satisfies*
    (i) *the Fundamental Axiom of Multi-output Production,*
    (ii) *continuity, and*
   (iii) *differentiability*
can be characterized locally in canonical form.

This characterization of technology is convenient for applying the various measures of efficiency defined above. For example, each of the individual equations in the controllable technology corresponds to sub-technology efficiency. The equations in the controllable technology plus the by-product relationships correspond to structural technical efficiency. Combining the controllable technology with by-product relationships and input restrictions corresponds to feasible disaggregated input-output efficiency. This description of technology is thus policy- and behavior-relevant.

Before turning to applications of this framework, we consider one remaining generality of the controllable technology. Some inputs may be allocated so that a distinct portion is applied to each production activity, i.e., is allocated to a specific time and location within that activity. However, other distinct input applications may have positive marginal products in more than one output equation as in the case of a public input. This gives rise to joint output relationships that may connect some output equations in the controllable technology. Appropriate modeling of such relationships is essential for proper investigation of issues such as diversification. Indeed, such modeling is essential for understanding issues of scope and scale (to the extent that economies of scope depend on scale). Chavas (2001) mentions several examples of processes that determine economies of scope such as nitrogen fixation, pest control, and crop-livestock interactions. As explained above, single-equation representations cannot convey useful understanding of such multi-dimensional interaction. Economies of scope and diversification may depend on many factors including public inputs as well as binding input restrictions and by-product relationships [even under profit maximization as in Pope (1976)] in addition to typical risk aversion explanations. We submit that the approach of description versus technical detail in Chavas' review is indicative of (i) the poor state of understanding of these issues and (ii) the lack of true explanation provided by PPF approaches.

4.5. The problem with unobservable decision variables

A typical problem for empirical analysis of production is that some variables are not observed. For example, a typical case in aggregate agricultural production is where temporal and spatial allocations of purchased variable inputs within growing seasons are not observed. This lack of data availability seems to motivate the focus on PPFs in typical production studies. As noted above, however, such approaches as typically practiced have not led to policy- and behavior-relevant representations of technology.

Here we investigate the feasible approach to estimation and identification of policy- and behavior-relevant technology when some decisions are not observed. An appropriate approach in this case is to solve unobserved variables out of the system in (52)–(54). We argue that this is the only feasible approach if the resulting representation of technology is to be policy- and behavior-relevant, i.e., truly a representation of nothing more than technology.[41]

Consider, for example, the case where an individual output is not observed. Then the corresponding individual equation in (52) or (53), which explains that output, is not observable and must be dropped from any estimable system. Alternatively, suppose an individual input variable is not observed. If the input appears among the binding constraints, then one of the binding constraints can be solved for that input variable; that result can then be used to substitute for the unobserved variable in (52). If a constraint with known coefficients is solved, such as a simple aggregation constraint for an allocated fixed input, then values of the variable can be calculated from the others to substitute into (52). When a constraint that has unknown coefficients is solved for an unobserved input variable, then an estimable form must be substituted for the unobserved variable in (52). This process may complicate estimation of (52) because numerous parameters may appear in individual equations after substitution thus requiring more observations for identification. But estimation is possible in principle and no justifiable alternative is apparent.

If additional input variables are unobserved, remaining input constraints can be used one-by-one if the unobserved variables appear among the remaining input constraints. Otherwise, one of the remaining equations in (52) must be solved for the unobserved input variable. Such a relationship may include an unobservable error term and add to the stochastic complications of estimation of remaining relationships. But again, estimation is possible in principle with sufficient numbers of observations.

Continuing inductively with this approach which is applicable under the assumptions of the Implicit Function Theorem obtains the following proposition.

---

[41] We remind the reader that all policy- and behavior-relevant aggregations are assumed to be included in the problem representation at this point as in (46). If further policy- and behavior-relevant aggregation is possible, then simple Pareto efficiency among those allocations may yield additional policy- and behavior-relevant structural equations.

PROPOSITION 7. *Aside from by-product relationships, which do not characterize the effects of inputs, the maximum number of non-redundant observable equations that can characterize purely technological relationships is equal to the number of observable controllable outputs (n_a) plus the number of purely technological binding input constraints (n_c) minus the number of unobservable decision variables (if non-negative).*

An immediate implication is as follows.

COROLLARY 1. *Aside from by-product relationships, if the number of observable controllable outputs plus the number of purely technological binding input constraints minus the number of unobservable decision variables is non-positive, then no purely technological relationship is estimable. Any estimable relationship between outputs and decision variables must embody non-technical relationships imposed on the observed data, for example, by behavioral and policy criteria.*

4.6. The typical agricultural production problem

In typical agricultural production problems involving multiple outputs, farmers choose not only a production possibilities set, but choose a production point in that set. In typical dual representations, the choice of a production possibilities set is made by choosing an aggregate input vector. The concept of efficiency based on profit maximization is used to restrict choices to the frontier of the production possibilities set. Then the choice of a point on the frontier is represented implicitly by the choice of an output vector. Outputs, however, are *ex post* observations of the production problem and thus do not characterize the actual process of production or decision making. Choice of an output vector implicitly involves determining other choices relating to how the aggregate input vector is used. These implicit choices typically involve allocation of aggregate inputs over production activities, i.e., over space and time. For example, in examples of basic economic principles with two production processes using the same input, the production possibilities frontier depends on the aggregate amount of input available, and the choice of a point on the frontier is determined by how much of the aggregate input is allocated to one production process versus the other.

With the allocation of fixed inputs discussed by Shumway, Pope, and Nash (1984), farmers must determine how much land to allocate to each crop or how many tractor hours and hours of labor to allocate to each plot, etc. Variable inputs must also be allocated among production activities (plots) and times of application to choose a point on the production possibilities frontier [Just et al. (1983)]. For example, farmers must generally determine how much fertilizer, pesticides, and labor to apply to each crop and plot as well as how much of each variable input to use in the aggregate. We do not contend that all inputs must be allocated but argue that at least some allocation decisions are required to determine the mix of outputs in most agricultural production problems. Such decisions must be considered part of the detailed X and Z vectors that determine outputs.

Allocations of both fixed and variable inputs are typically treated as unobserved in common applications of duality. For example, a common specification of the profit function in multi-output production problems is

$$\max_{y,x}\left\{ py - rx \mid (y,x) \in \Im_{-i}(k,\varepsilon) \right\}$$

where p is an output price vector taken to apply to the entire growing season, r is an input price vector taken to apply uniformly to the entire aggregate of input quantities used, x represents choice of aggregate input quantities without regard to temporal or spatial allocations, and $\Im_{-i}$ represents possible choices of aggregate inputs and aggregate outputs with available technology and fixed inputs [e.g., Shumway (1983); Ball and Chambers (1982); Weaver (1983)]. This specification yields maximum profit as a function of p, r, k, and ε if Aggregation Qualification Condition A.2 holds.

Alternatively, the production framework in (52)–(54) reveals all detailed allocations and decisions that demonstrate how outputs are determined *ex ante* (aside from uncontrollable factors). Clearly, if variable or fixed allocation decisions must be made and allocations are ignored as in a typical dual framework, then the allocations must either be considered unobservable or the econometric efficiency that can be attained with full structural estimation is lost. We note, however, that there is nothing about the modern dual approach that prevents this more detailed empirical investigation. For example, Chambers and Just (1989) use a dual approach to investigate allocations of an observed allocated fixed factor. Similar techniques can also be used to investigate price differences among allocated quantities where they apply following the general theoretical framework of Chambers, Chung, and Färe (1996).

Undoubtedly, some of the elegance and simplicity of the typical reduced form (dual or primal) approach is lost by considering a full structure for production technology as in (52)–(54). However, unobserved or ignored allocations of inputs have dramatic implications for estimation of technology as the following proposition demonstrates (see the Appendix for the proof).

PROPOSITION 8.   *If* (i) *two or more inputs (whether variable or fixed) must be allocated among sub-technologies,* (ii) *the allocations are unobserved or ignored in estimation, and* (iii) *the number of controllable outputs is less than the number of allocated inputs times the number of sub-technologies, then no purely technological relationship other than by-product relationships is estimable. In particular, no purely technological relationship is estimable in the input nonjointness case of* (11).

The conditions of Proposition 8 appear to be broadly applicable and cast doubt on the ability to estimate purely technological relationships from aggregate data. Furthermore, a much stronger result applies if physical inputs must be allocated over space and time within sub-technologies. Proposition 8 focuses only on allocations of inputs over sub-technologies. The problem is that many allocations of inputs over crops as well as space and time are generally not recorded in aggregate data. For example, aggregate public data are generally not available on the allocation among crops (or plots) of variable inputs such as labor or of allocated fixed inputs such as tractor hours. We note, however, that allocation of land among crops is usually available and has not been exploited by typical dual production studies. Thus, the failure to utilize allocation data cannot be blamed entirely on data unavailability.

While we note that allocation data for land among crops is generally available and unutilized (and was a prominent subject of study prior to the duality revolution), the principle of Proposition 8 also suggests that specific assumptions may be required for its use. For example, suppose that land allocations are observed but that other allocations are unobserved as in the following corollary to Proposition 8 (see the Appendix for a proof).

COROLLARY 2. *If* (i) *three or more inputs* (*whether variable or fixed*) *must be allocated among sub-technologies,* (ii) *only the allocations of one input are observed and used in estimation, and* (iii) *the number of controllable outputs is less than the number of observed allocated inputs times the number of sub-technologies, then no purely technological relationship other than by-product relationships is estimable. In particular, no purely technological relationship is estimable in the input nonjointness case of* (11).

The implication of Corollary 2 is that if only land allocations are observed and at least two other input allocations are unobserved, then purely technological relationships are generally unobservable unless specific restrictions are imposed on the technology. For example, one could assume that other allocated inputs are applied in fixed proportions with land. Since such assumptions must be imposed to observe technology, it follows that hypotheses such as fixed input proportions among allocated inputs cannot be rejected with observable data under the conditions of Corollary 2.

In Mundlak's (2001) review (this Handbook), he characterizes the modern dual approach as having not delivered its promised benefits in the empirical analysis of production. We agree but argue that the criticism should not be of the potential of the dual approach but of the failure to pursue understanding of the structure of production. It is simply the *typical practice* of duality (the focus on the PPF alone) that has been limiting. We argue that this practice is, at least in part, a self-imposed limitation of the profession. But it is also, in part, a result of public data limitations. With proper consideration, some hypotheses that have been entertained in the literature may not be testable with available data.

4.7. Estimable relationships among inputs and outputs

To examine additional implications of the criticism in Section 4.6, the production problem can be further characterized by determination of the decision vectors X and Z according to some behavioral criterion given available technology.

A *behavioral criterion* is a rule sufficient to determine production decisions in X and Z uniquely given the full description of technology in (52)–(54).

For example, in the case of profit maximization (ignoring uncontrollable factors for purposes of illustration), the problem is

$$\max_{Y,X,Z}\left\{PY - RX \mid \widetilde{Y} = \underset{n_a}{\tilde{f}}(X, Z, \varepsilon), \ \widehat{Y} = \underset{n_b}{g}(\widetilde{Y}, \varepsilon), \ \widehat{Z} = \underset{n_c}{h}(\widetilde{Z}, K)\right\}. \tag{55}$$

After substitution of the constraints and assuming well-behaved technology, this problem generates a set of $n_o = n_x + n_f$ first-order conditions for optimization of the form

$$\underset{n_o}{\zeta}(X, \widetilde{Z}, P, R, K, \varepsilon) = 0. \tag{56}$$

These n_o relationships together with the n_c binding constraints in (54) uniquely determine X and Z. The remaining $n_a + n_b$ relationships in (52) and (53), in turn, determine Y following the Fundamental Axiom of Multi-output Production. This framework clearly differentiates the relationships defining technology in (52)–(54), which appear as constraints in (55), and the behavioral relationships in (56).

Alternatively, if all allocations of input and output quantities have identical prices over space and time in the production cycle (the typical assumption), the decision problem can be represented by[42]

$$\max_{y,x}\left\{py - rx \mid y = \underset{n_y^*}{Af}(X, \widetilde{Z}, h(\widetilde{Z}, K), \varepsilon), \ x = \underset{n_x^*}{BK}\right\}, \tag{57}$$

where $y \in R_+^{n_y^*}$, $x \in R_+^{n_x^*}$. Several points are important in comparing this problem to typical analysis of aggregate production problems. First, the decision variables in this problem, after substituting constraints, are not simply y and x but rather X and $\widetilde{Z}$. Thus, the number of first-order conditions is $n_x + n_f$. In this set of first-order conditions, the price of one input or output can be arbitrarily normalized (set to 1) because of homogeneity of supplies and demands in prices, which follows from (57). Then, in principle, $n_y^* + n_x^* - 1$ of the $n_x + n_f$ first-order conditions can be solved for the non-normalized prices and substituted into the remaining first-order conditions obtaining $n_o^* = n_x + n_f - n_y^* - n_x^* + 1$ relationships expressed solely in terms of y, X, and $\widetilde{Z}$, say,

$$\underset{n_o^*}{\zeta}(y, X, \widetilde{Z}, K, \varepsilon) = 0. \tag{58}$$

Typically, the number of relationships in (58) is large when there are allocations because n_x^* represents the number of aggregate variable inputs whereas n_x represents the number of variable factor allocation variables summed over all variable inputs and, similarly, n_y^*

---

[42] Note that $y = \underset{n_y^*}{Af}(X, Z, \varepsilon) = A \cdot (\widetilde{Y}, \widehat{Y})$ where $\widetilde{Y} = \underset{n_a}{\tilde{f}}(X, Z, \varepsilon)$ and $\widehat{Y} = \underset{n_b}{g}(\widetilde{Y}, \varepsilon)$. Also note that $Z = (\widetilde{Z}, \widehat{Z}) = (\widetilde{Z}, h(\widetilde{Z}, K))$.

represents the number of aggregate outputs whereas n_f represents the number of fixed factor allocation variables summed over all production activities.

Note, however, that the relationships in (58) cannot be purely technological relationships even though they include only input and output quantities because they are derived from first-order conditions based on the behavioral criterion. Clearly, these relationships include more information than reflected in the pure statement of technology, $\underset{n_y^*}{y} = A f(X, \widetilde{Z}, h(\widetilde{Z}, K), \varepsilon)$ because the rank of first-order conditions leading to (58) is $n_x + n_f - n_y^* - n_x^* + 1$ (if they can be solved uniquely for all decisions) whereas the reduced-form statement of technology in (57) has at most rank n_y^*.

From these results, estimation and hypothesis testing based on first-order conditions, including all dual methodology, does not necessarily reveal information about technology. For example, apparent nonjointness or apparent nonseparability suggested by estimates of any subset of these relationships may simply reflect an interaction among variables induced by the maintained behavioral hypothesis (see the example of Section 3.4). These results are summarized by Proposition 9 (see the Appendix for a proof).

PROPOSITION 9. *Under the conditions of Proposition 8, no hypotheses about the structure of technology are testable. All observable relationships of inputs and outputs are policy- or behavior-dependent.*

All hypothesis tests on the structure of agricultural technology relating to jointness and separability of which we are aware are made in problems where the presence of two or more inputs with unobserved allocations cannot be ruled out. On the basis of Proposition 9, the associated conclusions are invalid.

4.8. The "technology" estimated with standard dual applications

In standard dual applications assuming differentiability, technology is implicitly represented by a scalar PPF relationship of the form derived in (44), $F(y, x, k, \varepsilon) = 0$, i.e., one involving only aggregate inputs and outputs [e.g., Shumway (1983); Ball and Chambers (1982); Weaver (1983)]. From the $n_a + n_b + n_c$ relationships describing technology and firm-controlled resource constraints in (52)–(54) and the $n_o = n_x + n_f$ first-order conditions in (56), exactly one such relationship involving only aggregate inputs and outputs is observable in general. To find this relationship starting from (55), one must aggregate not only the outputs as in (57) but also eliminate all the allocations. In other words, after obtaining (57), the $n_o^* = n_x + n_f - n_y^* - n_x^* + 1$ relationships among all input decisions and outputs that are devoid of prices can be used together with $\underset{n_y^*}{y} = A f(X, \widetilde{Z}, h(\widetilde{Z}, K), \varepsilon)$ and $\underset{n_x^*}{x} = B X$ to solve for all $n_x + n_f$ allocations, which are then substituted into a remaining single condition.

The resulting single condition is of the form $F^*(y, x, k, \varepsilon) = 0$ and is regarded as characterizing the production possibilities frontier. However, under the conditions of

Propositions 7, 8, and 9, this relationship may be determined at least partially by the behavioral criterion. For example, if one of the inputs is an allocated fixed input or involves allocation of a variable input that does not have the same price across all locations or times, then any single-equation representation of technology using only aggregate variables will be policy- or behavior-dependent.

An interesting question is whether knowledge of this frontier can reveal information about the structure of technology for which it is commonly used to test. In general, the answer is no. At best (when the Aggregation Qualification Condition holds), it can only answer very limited questions about the reduced-form structure. The illustrative example of Section 3.4 demonstrates clearly the difference between structure and reduced form.

4.9. Congruent modeling of econometric errors and inefficiencies

Thus far, we have largely ignored uncertainty issues related to agricultural production. In reality, agricultural production is highly subject to random forces such as weather and pests. The presence of such forces in worldwide agricultural production causes prices also to be random and unpredictable – particularly because of long lags between commencement of production and realization of output. Adding unanticipated stochastic variation in production reveals further problems with typical practices.

To illustrate, note that the profits in (55) after substituting constraints can be represented by $P f(X, \widetilde{Z}, K, \varepsilon) - RX$ where

$$
\begin{aligned}
f(X, \widetilde{Z}, K, \varepsilon) &= \left[\widetilde{f}(X, \widetilde{Z}, h(\widetilde{Z}, K), \varepsilon), g(\widetilde{f}(X, \widetilde{Z}, h(\widetilde{Z}, K), \varepsilon), \varepsilon) \right] \\
&= \left\{ (\widetilde{Y}, \widehat{Y}) \mid \widetilde{Y} = \widetilde{f}(X, Z, \varepsilon), \widehat{Y} = g(\widetilde{Y}, \varepsilon), \widehat{Z} = h(\widetilde{Z}, K) \right\}.
\end{aligned}
\tag{59}
$$

Prices and production disturbances are assumed to be random at the time decisions are made and, for simplicity in this section, the behavioral criterion is assumed to be expected profit maximization. The expected profit function and resulting demands and allocations are

$$
\pi(I, K) = \max_{X, \widetilde{Z}} \left\{ E_I[P f(X, \widetilde{Z}, K, \varepsilon) - RX] \right\},
$$

$$
\left[X^*(I, K), \widetilde{Z}^*(I, K) \right] = \operatorname*{argmax}_{X, \widetilde{Z}} \left\{ E_I[P f(X, \widetilde{Z}, K, \varepsilon) - RX] \right\},
$$

respectively, where I represents information (e.g., a subjective distribution) upon which the producer's expectations of P, R, and ε are based.

Assuming mean expected prices are included among I, differentiation of the profit function with respect to them obtains demands, $X = X^*(I, K)$, by the envelope theorem consistent with Hotelling's lemma.[43] Chambers and Just (1989) demonstrate how

---

[43] Depending on the stage of production in a dynamic representation, some of the random disturbances may have already been realized in which case I can include some actual values of some elements of ε.

the allocation equation specifications, $\widetilde{Z} = \widetilde{Z}^*(I, K)$, can also be derived consistent with sub-technology profit function specifications. Because prices and output are random, however, simple differentiation of the profit function does not generally obtain consistent output supply specifications following Hotelling's lemma. Rather, substituting input demands and allocations into (59) yields the actual output supplies,

$$Y = Y^*(I, K, \varepsilon) = f(X^*, \widetilde{Z}^*, K, \varepsilon),$$

which have expectation $E_I(Y) = \overline{Y}^*(I, K) = E_I[f(X^*, \widetilde{Z}^*, K, \varepsilon)]$. This specification generally differs from the derivative of the profit function with respect to mean output prices because of correlation among output prices and quantities, and nonlinearities of output in the production disturbance.

Two often-overlooked problems arise in subjecting this framework to estimation. First, the need to treat allocations differently than variable input demands is typically ignored assuming their prices can be represented implicitly as constants across space and time. Since this practice was criticized above, we abstract from the case with allocations for the remainder of this section because most readers are more familiar with notation that ignores allocations.

The second typically-overlooked problem relates to stochastic specification for estimation. Because input demands are derived by maximizing expected profits rather than actual profits, random variation is removed, leaving the resulting specification devoid of the random disturbances necessary for econometric purposes. The typical practice has been to append arbitrarily an econometric disturbance vector, say δ, to the vector of demand equations so the estimated specifications follow $X = X^*(I, K) + \delta$. Alternatively, the profit function has been treated as a deterministic problem in mean prices, say $\overline{P} = E(P)$ and $\overline{R} = E(R)$, so that application of Hotelling's lemma obtains

$$\overline{\pi}(\overline{P}, \overline{R}, K) = \max_X \{\overline{P} f(X, K, \varepsilon) - \overline{R}X \mid \varepsilon = 0\},$$
$$Y = \overline{Y}^*(\overline{P}, \overline{R}, K) = \partial\overline{\pi}(\overline{P}, \overline{R}, K)/\partial\overline{P},$$
$$X = \overline{X}^*(\overline{P}, \overline{R}, K) = -\partial\overline{\pi}(\overline{P}, \overline{R}, K)/\partial\overline{R}.$$

This approach leaves each specification lacking an econometric disturbance for purposes of estimation. Typical practice has been to simply append disturbances to each relationship obtaining an estimation system of the form

$$Y = \overline{Y}^*(\overline{P}, \overline{R}, K) + \nu, \qquad X = \overline{X}^*(\overline{P}, \overline{R}, K) + \delta, \tag{60}$$

where ν and δ are vector-valued disturbances with zero expectations, e.g., $\varepsilon = (\nu, \delta)$.

A major problem with arbitrarily appending disturbances to a profit-function-based system is suggested by McElroy (1987) who initiated work on congruent specifications of input and output disturbances in the context of cost function estimation. The problem is that after arbitrarily appending disturbances to supply and demand specifications as in

(60), they no longer integrate back to the same underlying profit function.[44] In the spirit of McElroy, the profit function that yields via Hotelling's lemma both random supplies and factor demands as in (60) is of the form

$$\overline{\pi}(\overline{P}, \overline{R}, K) = \max_{X}\left\{\overline{P}[f(X, K) + v] - \overline{R}(X + \delta)\right\}. \tag{61}$$

The remaining problem with McElroy's approach is that disturbances are arbitrarily inserted to satisfy a particular theoretical convenience rather than to correspond to how random forces actually affect decision makers. In particular, the specification in (61) imposes additive errors in the production relationship and thus cannot admit risk-reducing or risk-increasing effects of inputs [Just and Pope (1978)]. Also, if the demand disturbances in (60) represent errors in optimization, then the specification in (61) is inappropriate because it has profits monotonically decreasing in errors, i.e., the decision maker is better off making large negative errors thus contradicting the concept of optimization.

To explore this problem further, an assessment of potential sources of error is instructive. Typically errors in agricultural production systems can be expected to arise from errors in decision making by farmers, random variation in uncontrolled forces such as weather that affect the production process, and errors in variables (measurement errors in data).[45] In each of these cases, the role of disturbances may be different. Yet typical a priori information hardly allows exclusion of one or the other.

The errors-in-optimization (EIO) case.   To illustrate, if disturbances represent errors in decision making, then optimization errors can be simply appended to the profit-maximizing input levels as in the demand system in (60). In this case, however, the supply specification in (60) is no longer appropriate because the errors in input levels affect output following $Y = f(X^* + \delta, K, v)$, which surely differs from the $Y = f(X^*, K, v)$ that generates the supply system in (60).[46]

---

[44] While all the discussion here is in terms of profit functions for simplicity, as illustrated by McElroy's work the same principles apply to cost and revenue function estimation as well.

[45] Another source of error in modeling is econometrician error. Perhaps these errors dominate all others but we refrain from a substantive discussion because (i) a major goal of this entire chapter is to improve econometric modeling, and (ii) the effects of modeling errors are dependent on the particular type of econometrician error and thus present too many alternatives to discuss here. For example, one possible econometrician error is made by assuming disturbances follow EIO (EIV) when EIV (EIO) applies. Another typical example is when, following the practice of modern duality theory, the econometrician specifies a profit function with little thought about the underlying technology because the profit function is not estimated but only used instrumentally to specify demands and supplies. Thus, the factor demands are obtained up to a random error but the profit function depends on this error because the supply or production depends on actual inputs. This is also an econometrician error.

[46] This result showing failure of Hotelling's lemma when input errors are transmitted to production functions is developed formally by Pope and Just (2000a).

The errors-in-variables (EIV) case.   Suppose the disturbances represent errors in variables. For example, let v represent additive errors in measurement for Y and let δ represent additive errors in measurement for X, which are thus not part of the disturbances in ε that affect the true production problem. Then the specification in (60) is appropriate for the case where prices are nonstochastic. However, the profit function does not then follow (61) because the errors in v and δ are not errors that actually affect decision makers and actual outcomes.

The errors-in-uncontrolled-conditions (EIU) case.   If disturbances represent errors in uncontrolled conditions affecting the production process that are not observed until after decision making, then the representation of ε as an argument of f above is appropriate. In this case, the errors possibly interact with other input choices to alter production responses and marginal risk effects of inputs. For this problem, practical wisdom implies that the researcher is not free to choose an arbitrary representation (or point of insertion) of an ad hoc disturbance because the role of the disturbance is a substantive part of the economic problem. For this problem, a first-order Taylor series approximation of Y about $\varepsilon = 0$ yields a Just–Pope production function, $Y = f(X, K, 0) + f_\varepsilon(X, K, 0)\varepsilon$, which provides a minimal yet tractable level of flexibility in the production specification.

Considering these three sources of error begs a discussion of which are most likely to be manifest in agricultural data. Based on the discussion in Section 2.4, it seems that the highly unpredictable effects of weather and pests inherent in the EIU case are most important to admit unless variables that reflect weather and pest conditions are included as measured variables rather than disturbances. While the other two sources of error seem less essential, they cannot be ruled out. Thus, the most conservative approach is to consider all three simultaneously. For example, one might start with a specification for $\pi(I, K) = \max_X\{E_I[P f(X, K, \varepsilon) - RX]\}$ and derive a specification for $X^*(I, K) = \arg\max_X\{E_I[P f(X, K, \varepsilon) - RX]\}$, which explicitly recognizes the potential randomness of prices. Then the supplies and demands might be estimated following

$$X = X^*(I, K) + \delta + \zeta, \qquad Y = f(X^* + \delta, K, \varepsilon) + v, \tag{62}$$

where δ represents errors in optimization (which enter through the decisions and thus affect outputs through the technology that describes output responses to inputs), ζ represents errors in measurement of inputs that do not affect observed outputs, ε represents uncontrolled inputs such as weather, and v represents errors in measurement of outputs.

Misspecification of the role of disturbances in production problems can cause considerable misinterpretation of data and empirical results. For example, Pope and Just (1996) developed what appears to be the first approach for consistent estimation of ex ante cost functions in the EIO case of stochastic production. Moschini (forthcoming) later showed that a different estimator was required for consistent estimation in the EIV case.[47] The contrast of these two papers and the bias and inconsistency resulting from using the wrong estimator demonstrates the importance of focusing carefully on the source of errors in production problems.

Moreover, these results underscore the need to develop robust estimation methods that can address a more general model such as in (62) for the case where the correct disturbance specification is not known a priori. Then statistical inference can be used to determine the correct error specification. In such an effort, Pope and Just (2000b) employ a specification similar to (62) by combining $\delta + \zeta$ into a single disturbance, say ξ, and then including $\lambda \xi$ as the embedded disturbance in place of δ in the production function. Their estimate of λ using aggregate U.S. agricultural data is .919 with a standard error of .322 implying that the pure EIV case is soundly rejected. The EIO case is not rejected even at the .001 level.

The results in this section are derived for the case where all decisions are made ex ante and all uncertainty is then resolved to determine final production and profit. More realistically, decision makers make some decisions, then observe some resolution of uncertainty. Then further decisions are made and further uncertainty is resolved, and so on until the end of a production cycle. Many of the principles in this section can be developed for this more complex and realistic case but space does not allow development here.

Based on the points in this section, we suggest that agricultural production economists have been far too cavalier about inserting disturbances in econometric specifications to facilitate estimation. The form in which disturbances enter has dramatic effects on estimated technology and on the statistical properties of estimators. The form in which disturbances enter can ultimately be answered by statistical inference. Until such answers are forthcoming and accepted, agricultural production estimation should seek for robust specifications or at least specifications consistent with accepted wisdom regarding the nature of agricultural production.

5. Other generalizations and empirical progress

Thus far, we have focused on the static production problem to demonstrate some fundamental principles and show how the structural implications and usefulness of agricultural production analyses depend on specification. In reality, the agricultural production problem is more complex. This section considers briefly several important additional frontiers of generalization: (i) dynamic interseasonal considerations related to physical and biological processes and investment, (ii) market uncertainties and characterization of information regarding them, (iii) implications of imposing behavioral criteria in agricultural production analyses, and (iv) changing technology with atomistic heterogeneity of adoption.

---

[47] Moschini (forthcoming) shows that the Pope and Just (1996) estimator is inconsistent in his EIV case. But Moschini's estimator is inconsistent for EIO cases covered by Pope and Just's estimator under risk aversion [Pope and Just (1998)]. The properties of Moschini's estimator clearly depend on risk neutrality.

5.1. Investment, asset fixity, biological growth, and fertility carryover

In general, agriculture presents a complicated problem of modeling production over time because of partial fixity and limited flexibility of physical production capital, the dynamic nature of biological capital (e.g., perennial plants and animals), accumulations of pest populations and resistance, and evolution of soil fertility and erosion. For example, machinery and buildings may be highly subject to asset fixity considerations [Chavas (2001)] but yet some assets may be highly flexible in application to production of a variety of crops. For example, for the most part the same machinery is used to cultivate wheat, sorghum, barley, oats, rice and most other small grains. Other types of equipment such as hay balers, milking equipment, and tomato harvesters may be highly output specific. Because of the dramatic role that physical capital plays in agricultural production, understanding investment in machinery, buildings, and land is likely the most important step to understanding agricultural production in a time series context. Specifically, lags and dynamic processes appear to be at the heart of understanding large-animal livestock and perennial crop production problems. Similarly, as Evenson (2001) states, lags and dynamic processes are also at the heart of understanding such broad policy questions as the economic aspects of R&D. Indeed, they are at the heart of understanding agricultural productivity.

Because new machinery can often be purchased with little delay, is highly lumpy (many farms have a single combine or high-horsepower tractor), and embodies unique technologies (as in the case of the tomato harvester and related color-sorting equipment), machinery investment may fit the putty-clay model well [Johansen (1972)] and require sophisticated discrete-continuous modeling of physical capital investment [see Just and Zilberman (1983) for a primitive such model]. For example, the problem of machinery replacement appears to be one of comparing the cost of new equipment less salvage value of old equipment (along with the higher productivity of new embodied technology) to the cost of continuing operations with old equipment given its higher repair costs and down time. Similar principles apply to constructing new buildings. The obstacle to analyzing these problems is that available data typically do not report machinery or building vintages (ages). Thus, for example, neither the relative technological improvements embodied in new machinery nor the salvage value of old equipment can be considered adequately in explaining machinery investment. Nor can repair costs be explained adequately by the machinery age distribution because it is unobservable.

Alternatively, development of biological capital (e.g., breeding stock, perennial stands of trees, or fertility content of soil) is constrained by biological and physical laws of nature and may require long lags for biological growth and adjustment. This is why such problems are typically modeled with difference equations that describe the number of animals or (acres of) plants that survive from one time period or age cohort to the next [see, e.g., Nerlove and Bessler (2001)]. With respect to these investments, costs and supply response may follow the traditional model of short- versus long-run cost curves [Viner (1931)]. Thus, knowledge of biological growth functions from the agricultural sciences may greatly improve empirical modeling of agricultural production and allow economists to focus estimation on features of the problem about which economic knowledge is weak (behavior and expectations).

To date, however, relatively little research has been devoted to understanding many of these longer-term problems of agricultural production. Several studies have examined asset fixity in agriculture both theoretically and empirically [e.g., Johnson (1956); Johnson and Quance (1972); Chambers and Vasavada (1983)]. Competing conceptual models with putty-putty, putty-clay, and clay-clay properties have been proposed [e.g., Johansen (1972); Fuss (1977)]. But little recent work has focused on fundamental empirical representations for some important classes of outputs. For example, the work of French, King, and Minami (1985) is essentially the last substantive work on perennial crops. Again, perhaps the major obstacle is lack of data regarding the age distribution of perennial crops. We note also that perennial crops and large-animal capital stocks have hardly been addressed with the modern tools of duality, in part because some of the elegance of duality is lost in doing so. For example, embedding a known biological process in a more complex production problem essentially requires a primal representation of part of the process.

Perhaps agricultural production economists occupied with simple dual approaches have been reluctant to tackle such problems. We suggest that more work is needed to enhance models for perennial crop and large-animal livestock production by combining known aspects of the age distribution evolution of biological capital with the advances in representations of the short-run production problem, dual or otherwise. For example, the canonical form of the short-run production problem remains as in (52)–(54) after adding τ subscripts to each variable to denote crop season (e.g., year). What must be added is the state equation,

$$\boldsymbol{K}_\tau = \kappa(\boldsymbol{K}_{\tau-1}, \boldsymbol{X}_{\tau-1}, \boldsymbol{Z}_{\tau-1}, \boldsymbol{\varepsilon}_{\tau-1}), \tag{63}$$

which describes buildings and machinery (by age and wear attributes), livestock and perennials (by age, size and health attributes), pest populations (by accumulated resistance attributes), soil quality (by accumulated fertility attributes, which depend on previous crop use and inputs), and accumulated debt and credit limitations (which depend on previous decisions to defer or accelerate repayment).[48]

A dual quasi-profit function may represent the short-run production problem if the state equation adequately represents interseasonal aspects of the problem. Such a representation of the production problem would not be complete, however, without adding a representation of how behavioral criteria determine implicit and explicit investment decisions, conservation behavior, crop rotation decisions, etc. (see Section 5.3). That is, behavioral criteria must be supplemented with long-term objective criteria that depend on $\boldsymbol{K}_\tau$; and the behavioral relationships in (56) must be supplemented accordingly

---

[48] While we consider only one lag in defining the state equation, as in any Markov process individual elements of the $\boldsymbol{K}$ vector can represent individual vintages of arbitrary age for any capital stock variable. Thus, the complete age distribution of various capital assets can be included.

with preferences that relate to choices in the stock equation. While the state equation in (63) may be complex, in some cases substantial knowledge of biological growth functions from the agricultural sciences can greatly improve empirical modeling and allow economists to focus estimation on features of the problem about which economic knowledge is weak (behavior and expectations).

5.2. Expectations formation and information acquisition

Representing production problems with price and output risk requires modeling both producer information (expectations) and producer behavior. A variety of approaches to modeling expectations have been used to model short-run (annual) production under uncertainty with some success [see the review by Nerlove and Bessler (2001)]. However, the problem of modeling expectations is more difficult in longer-term dynamic problems because (i) expectations are, in general, not directly observable, (ii) different producers may follow different approaches to forming expectations, and (iii) individual producers may switch among different information bases (or expectations mechanisms) depending on circumstances.

Modeling aggregate behavior is particularly difficult when producers' expectations are neither directly observable nor identical. The problem is that no data are typically available to explain even indirectly how expectations may be distributed among producers. However, Nerlove (1983) presents evidence of considerable heterogeneity in individual expectations. So, in many cases, the present state of knowledge simply does not reveal how vulnerable agricultural production analysis is to this problem.

Just and Rausser (1983) further suggest that rationality with costly information implies endogeneity of the operative expectation mechanism at the individual level. For example, some decision makers may find rational expectations require too much costly information in periods of stability compared to, say, naive expectations, but yet are worth the cost in periods of instability. Nerlove and Bessler (2001) also suggest that separation of expectations and optimizing behavior is not theoretically correct. Rather, the formation of expectations depends on the use to which expectations are put.

These considerations imply that agricultural economists are far from unraveling the role of expectations and the process of expectations formation particularly in heavily dynamic problems. The hope of doing so with aggregate data and current limitations on availability of firm-specific data appears dim [Nerlove (1983)]. Nevertheless, the role of information is becoming of increasing interest in this "age of information". More efforts are focusing on understanding individual information demand and vendor choice [Salin et al. (1998); Wolf et al. (forthcoming)]. We predict an increasing importance of these efforts in both aggregate and broad farm-specific models of agricultural production. For example, suppose the profits in (55) are represented using (59). Then the information choice problem might be represented as

$$\max_{I,X,\widetilde{Z}} \mathrm{E}_I \left[\boldsymbol{P} f(\boldsymbol{X}, \widetilde{\boldsymbol{Z}}, \boldsymbol{K}, \boldsymbol{\varepsilon}) - \boldsymbol{R}\boldsymbol{X} - c_I(\boldsymbol{I}) \mid \boldsymbol{I} \in \boldsymbol{\Phi} \right],$$

where I represents a choice among various available sets of information in Φ, information is acquired with cost $c_I(I)$, and E_I represents a subjective assessment of expectations over P, R, and ε given information vector I. The concept here is one of forming an expectation for the benefits of each information set when the actual information set is unknown and perhaps untried. In forming subjective assessments of the benefits of various information choices, a variety of experimentation and learning-by-doing possibilities arise akin to the problem of learning about new technologies in the technology adoption problem [see Sunding and Zilberman (2001)]. Clearly, much remains to be done to address these issues.

5.3. Imposed versus revealed behavioral criteria

Much of the traditional body of economic theory and empirical modeling, whether by input share equations, duality, or non-parametric estimators, implicitly imposes competitive profit maximization [see Mundlak (2001)]. This behavioral assumption apparently has been quite robust in the general economics literature for problems where certainty approximates reality in short-run production problems. Because of the importance of uncertainty in agriculture, however, this robustness may not apply. Most studies in agricultural economics that recognize this possibility have modeled agricultural production assuming either expected profit maximization or expected maximization of von Neuman–Morgenstern utility under risk aversion. Very little statistical testing against more general maintained behavioral hypotheses has been done, although a few studies have attempted to measure properties of risk aversion (absolute risk aversion, relative risk aversion, and partial risk aversion) and determine whether such measures are constant, increasing or decreasing. For example, Pope and Just (1991), Chavas and Holt (1996), and Bar-Shira, Just and Zilberman (1997) have attempted to determine the structure of risk preferences from actual production data, and Binswanger (1980, 1981) has attempted to determine the structure of risk preferences from revealed preferences for manipulated lotteries.

Outside of the expected utility hypothesis (which has expected profit maximization as a special case), however, few alternative behavioral hypotheses have been considered empirically. However, numerous studies have criticized the expected utility hypothesis on positive grounds because it fails to describe observed behavior [Kahneman and Tversky (1979); Moschini and Hennessy (2001); Chambers and Quiggin (1998)]. One approach is to introduce a different weighting of outcomes in different states following the generalized expected utility approach [Quiggin (1982); Machina (1987)]. While alternatives have been proposed, little comprehensive empirical evidence has been generated in direct comparative support of alternatives. Most recently Buschena and Zilberman (2000) have shown that generalized expected utility models lose much of their predictive dominance over expected utility when a heteroscedastic error structure is used. While the expected utility model has been criticized because it is informationally demanding [Moschini and Hennessy (2001)], generalized approaches tend to be even more informationally demanding at least when many states of nature are considered. An approach that reduces information demands on both decision makers and researchers is to rely on rules of thumb and recommendations of agricultural extension specialists. Just et al. (1990) show for Israeli agricultural data that such behavioral hypotheses tend to better fit observed behavior than the expected utility hypothesis.

Still other generalizations of behavior are appealing. Some of these are suggested by the multiple-goal programming models of farm management [e.g., Candler and Boehlje (1971); de Koning et al. (1995)]. For example, in a business where family labor appears to be a qualitatively different input for some tasks because of moral hazard considerations, farmers may prefer to trade off profit for labor depending on the amount of family labor needed to maximize (expected) profit. Thus, the utility function may have more arguments than profit that must be considered to explain behavior. Similarly, because of complex dynamics caused by biological production relationships, some farmers may prefer to trade off present profits for future wealth or long-term financial security. The large number of alternative objective criteria considered by Barry and Robison (2001) are evidence of such considerations. In recent decades, hobby farming has also become more important in which case farmers may have preferences for specific outputs (e.g., horses) or inputs (e.g., picturesque white fences).

With the possibility of such concerns in farmer preferences, we suggest that agricultural economists have been cavalier regarding behavioral criteria in most standard production studies. Forging ahead with the convenience and intuitive appeal of the profit maximization hypothesis in agricultural production analysis may be subject, at least for some problems, to the McCloskey (1998) criticism of searching under a lamppost for a lost wallet merely because the light is brighter there.

Evenson (2001) states that models of diffusion based on revealed preferences depend on properly sorting out technology, behavior, and expectations from one another. Barry and Robison (2001) emphasize the need for the study of agricultural production to support policy analysis by correctly sorting out (i) the role of constraints such as collateral limits or other credit rationing, (ii) the role of policy in altering behavior, (iii) the role of risk and risk preferences, and (iv) the role of intertemporal behavior. The central points of this paper further demonstrate that sorting out the properties and structure of production depends on sorting out technology from behavior. When behavioral criteria are imposed rather than determined empirically, models may be far from robust and results may fall far short of sorting out this crucial distinction. Moreover, imposing a false behavioral criterion may cause results to suggest a false representation of technology [Alston and Chalfant (1991); Smale et al. (1994)].

To suggest a framework in which observed data rather than assumptions are used to uncover behavioral criteria, recall the canonical representation of the production problem in (52)–(54). From a representation of technology that is complete and yet devoid of behavioral content, the description of the production problem (possibly an econometric system representing it) is properly closed by adding the behavioral relationships (and policy constraints) that determine choices given the technology. However, rather than assuming fixed and known relationships for this purpose, the relationships representing behavior can be made a matter of inference. Models that estimate a risk aversion coefficient (or risk preference structure) take a step in this direction but allow only one (or a few) estimated parameter(s).

Specifically, under the Fundamental Axiom of Multi-output Production, the full production system is closed by supplementing the purely technical equations in (52)–(54) with behavioral relationships such as (56). Under (expected) profit maximization, the researcher assumes that no additional unknown parameters appear in these behavioral equations, e.g., in the case of an interior solution,

$$\frac{\partial}{\partial(X, \widetilde{Z})} E\left[P f\left(X, \widetilde{Z}, K, \varepsilon\right) - RX \right] = 0, \tag{64}$$

where E is the producer's expectation with respect to P, R, and ε and f is defined as in (59). With von Neuman–Morgenstern expected utility maximization, the researcher assumes only one or a few unknown parameters are introduced in a utility function U so that the behavioral relationships in (56) follow

$$\frac{\partial}{\partial(X, \widetilde{Z})} E\left[U\left(P f(X, \widetilde{Z}, K, \varepsilon) - RX \right) \right] = 0.$$

Strangely, the production literature (as represented by the typical duality approach) has tended over the past few decades toward introducing greater parametric flexibility into (52)–(54), e.g., second-order flexible forms, while imposing total inflexibility in (56). In principle, the behavioral equations can be made a matter of inference by estimating a general and perhaps flexible form for them and then testing for expected profit or expected utility maximization in the context of a broader maintained behavioral hypothesis. For example, suppose U is specified as a second-order flexible form in profit, family labor, creditworthiness, and ending wealth. In this context, wealth differs realistically from initial wealth plus profit by including the productive value of physical capital and soil fertility that have distinctly lower salvage or liquidation values. Then the behavioral relationships in (56) may follow

$$\frac{\partial}{\partial(X, \widetilde{Z})} E\left[U\left(P f(X, \widetilde{Z}, K, \varepsilon) - RX, z_{i'}, \omega(K), \eta(K) \right) \right] = 0, \tag{65}$$

where $z_{i'}$ represents total family labor, $\omega(K)$ represents ending wealth as a function of stocks and assets (asset prices are suppressed for convenience), and $\eta(K)$ represents creditworthiness as a function of stocks in K (i.e., asset quantities and accumulated debts). In this case, the complete representation of the problem, which closes the system, includes (52)–(54) and (63) in addition to (65). This approach allows inferences about preferences regarding the difficult practical question of how much profit family farms choose to use for consumption versus reinvestment in the operation (as opposed to simply imposing, say, either maximization of the discounted value of profits or maximization of terminal wealth).

Although space in this Handbook is inadequate for presenting a detailed example of this approach, we suggest that balance in the flexibility of technical and behavioral modeling is needed. In the longer-term planning horizons considered by Barry and Robison (2001) for agricultural finance problems, simulation approaches are often found preferable to optimization. One reason is that little has been determined empirically about (i) the importance of current income and consumption versus net worth, (ii) how farmers trade off short-run returns and riskiness with long-run security, and (iii) how asset fixity versus flexibility are used as tools for accomplishing these trade-offs. By estimating the complete production system with flexible behavioral approaches such as in (65), data can begin to sort out empirical applicability of the variety of simulation criteria identified by Barry and Robison. Also, in this context, the need to consider simultaneity in the combined production system as discussed by Mundlak (2001) becomes clear as does the need to use estimation methods that correct for it.

As an additional consideration, dynamic optimization under uncertainty typically assumes additive temporal separability of utility in order to treat dynamic problems of uncertainty [Nerlove and Bessler (2001)]. Better formal modeling depends on understanding the dynamic aspects of risk preferences and how short-term risk trades off with long-term risk given agricultural producers' preferences. Additive temporal separability of utility and risk preferences may not apply. In reality, a farmer may prefer an income stream with low or negative serial correlation rather than high positive serial correlation given the same overall risk because some types of capital investment, debt payment or consumption can be postponed without great difficulty if they can be made up in the near future. On the other hand, postponing such items for many years can cause reduced production, business failure or severe loss in welfare. No satisfactory approach for addressing such problems has yet been proposed.

To date, only the simplest of models have been developed that permit mid-course corrections as specific risks are resolved. As the review by Moschini and Hennessy (2001) shows, even a two-period model that permits one ex post choice has outcomes that depend on third derivatives of production technology. While statistical significance might be obtained in estimating a third derivative of the production technology in a single production study, the variety of results typically obtained by fitting even second-order flexible specifications leaves a great deal open to question. As suggested by Mundlak (2001), the profession has barely, if at all, come to agreement on many elasticities of production, which are determined by first derivatives. Duality has permitted flexibility in estimation of second derivatives but little agreement has been reached on characterizing second derivatives. The profession has hardly crossed the threshold of trying to identify third derivatives. Admitting needed interaction in estimation of technology and preferences and pursuing it with more balance may make clear why models estimated to date do not forecast as well as statistics of fit suggest they should.

5.4. Technology adoption and technical progress

In addition to dynamic intertemporal relationships, expectations, and behavioral criteria, modeling technology adoption is also a complicated and complex problem [Sunding and Zilberman (2001); Feder et al. (1985)]. Some technology is embodied in physical capital such as machinery and irrigation so adoption depends on long-term financing opportunities. Some is embodied in variable inputs such as seeds, fertilizer, and pesticides so short-run financing is critical. Depending on how well known and locally applicable is the performance of a technology, adoption can depend heavily on subjective risk, experience, and the extent of rents on technology included in input prices. Some technology is adopted through improved breeding methods and is thus relatively costless but requires years of implementation through succeeding production cycles to realize benefits. Other technology can be implemented only after acquiring costly information or acquiring skills of learning by doing, in which case limited experimentation is a prudent way to proceed [see Foster and Rosenzweig (1995)].

In each of these cases, adoption depends on different factors and constraints that affect an individual farm's production. The role of these factors and the extent to which they apply at the individual level is crucial to understanding the aggregate rate of adoption and agricultural productivity growth. Similarly, each of these cases enters differently through behavioral criteria, production constraints, and modifications of production functions. Again, sorting out technology from behavior from external constraints on the firm is crucial. Because of the complexity of factors potentially affecting technology adoption, space in this overview is not adequate for a critical evaluation of the technology adoption literature beyond the principles already developed throughout this chapter. However, we underscore that technology adoption is a highly heterogeneous problem because of heterogeneous physical capital and differing abilities to take advantage of individual technologies among farms, heterogeneous abilities to learn and thus make new technologies work quickly when information is limited, heterogeneous access to information based on education and other factors, heterogeneous credit constraints that limit financial ability to adopt, etc. The role of experimentation and heterogeneity in technology adoption underscores the importance of considering allocation variables, risk preferences, appropriate long-term as well as short-term preferences, etc. All of these issues fall squarely among the topics addressed in this chapter. For example, because much new technology is embodied in inputs that are subject to financial constraints, the associated principles in Section 4 are relevant. Because much new technology is embodied in capital investment with long-term implications and uncertainties, the principles of Sections 5.1–5.3 are relevant. Accordingly, we suggest many remaining avenues to improving understanding of technology adoption.

6. Heterogeneity and data limitations

As much of this essay has concluded, perhaps the most significant obstacle to further progress in agricultural production analysis is lack of better and more detailed data. Mundlak, Moschini and Hennessy (2001), Nerlove and Bessler (2001), Sunding and Zilberman (2001), and Barry and Robison (2001) (all in this Handbook) each emphasize the problem of trying to learn about micro-level behavior from aggregate data and/or modeling aggregate behavior when individual firms are heterogeneous. As pointed out by Moschini and Hennessy, these problems are difficult under certainty but are more difficult under uncertainty. Considering the other surveys in this part of the Handbook, Deininger and Feder (2001) emphasize heterogeneity of farms associated with soil fertility, soil degradation, liquidity, and transactions costs. Huffman (2001) underscores heterogeneity in human capital and education. Schultz (2001) highlights differences in sex, age, and quality of labor among households and household members, and the associated off-farm labor opportunities. Evenson (2001) also emphasizes soil factors, farmer skills, climatic factors, and infrastructure. Given this heavy recognition of heterogeneity, we finally turn to considerations of heterogeneity and a related call for action.

6.1. Heterogeneity and aggregation across firms

In this section, we examine some remaining issues of heterogeneity and suggest that failure to consider heterogeneity across firms causes errors in aggregation so that estimated forms not only misrepresent technology but fail to support the assumptions used to recover technology from estimated structures.[49] Typically, statistical tests have rejected the standard regularity conditions of homogeneity, monotonicity, symmetry, and convexity of profit functions. Since these regularity conditions are typically used to integrate estimated supplies and demands back to the profit function for purposes of inferring properties of technology, such statistical results call into question the associated inferences regarding technology.[50] In this section, we show that exact aggregation across firms fails when heterogeneity among firms is not represented adequately, which explains one source of failure of the standard regularity conditions. The problem is due to over-summarizing micro-level behavior in publicly reported aggregate data.

Consider the disaggregated static profit maximization problem $\pi = \max_{Y,X} \{ PY - RX \mid (Y, X, Z) \in \Im(k, \varepsilon) \}$ with resulting vector-valued firm-level supplies $y_i = y(p, r, k_i)$ and demands $x_i = x(p, r, k_i)$ where an i subscript is now added to index firms. For simplicity of notation, let supplies and demands be combined into a netput vector, $w_i = w(p, r, k_i) = (y_i, -x_i)$, let elements of w_i be denoted by w_{ij} where j indexes netputs, and let the netput price vector corresponding to w_i be denoted by $q = (p, r)$. Thus, netput functions are denoted compactly by $w_i = w(q, k_i) = w_i(q)$. With standard assumptions on technology, profit maximization, and differentiability, individual firm netputs satisfy the four standard regularity conditions of homogeneity, $w_{ij}(\lambda q) = w_{ij}(q)$, $\lambda > 0$; monotonicity, $\partial w_{ij}/\partial q_j \geq 0$; symmetry, $\partial w_{ij}/\partial q_{j'} =$

---

[49] This section draws on Just and Pope (1999) where further results and detail are found.

[50] As shown elsewhere in this chapter, standard approaches for aggregation within the firm fail if behavioral preferences follow various alternatives to profit maximization (as discussed in Section 5.3) or firms face various types of constraints such as policy constraints and imperfect capital market constraints (Section 3.3). Just and Pope (1999) show further that the standard regularity conditions generally fail at the firm level when these conditions are present.

$\partial w_{ij'}/\partial q_j$; and convexity, $\{\partial w_{ij}/\partial q_{j'}\} \geqslant 0$, i.e., positive semidefiniteness of the matrix of cross partials.

Defining aggregate netputs across firms as $\overline{w} = \sum_i w_i$, it follows immediately that the four standard regularity conditions must hold at the aggregate level if they hold at the firm level:

$$\overline{w}_j(\lambda q) = \sum_i w_{ij}(\lambda q) = \sum_i w_{ij}(q) = \overline{w}_j(q);$$

$$\partial \overline{w}_j/\partial q_j = \sum_i \partial w_{ij}/\partial q_j \geqslant 0;$$

$$\partial \overline{w}_j/\partial q_{j'} = \sum_i \partial w_{ij}/\partial q_{j'} = \sum_i \partial w_{ij'}/\partial q_j = \partial \overline{w}_{j'}/\partial q_j;$$

$$\{\partial \overline{w}_j/\partial q_{j'}\} = \left\{\sum_i \partial w_{ij}/\partial q_{j'}\right\} = \sum_i \{\partial w_{ij}/\partial q_{j'}\} \geqslant 0.$$

Thus, exact aggregation preserves the four standard properties but requires knowledge of all micro variables and functions. The implication is that statistical failure of the regularity conditions must be due to either bias in aggregation of factors and characteristics or failure of the regularity conditions at the firm level. Indeed, the regularity conditions can fail at the firm level because of inapplicability of profit maximization, inappropriate (within-season) temporal aggregation, discrete start-up/shut-down decisions, imperfect capital markets (resource constraints), or errors in measurement [Just and Pope (1999)]. These reasons for failure of standard theory at the firm level have been largely explored in earlier sections. Here we focus on reasons for theoretical failure at the aggregate level assuming regularity conditions hold at the firm level. Results show how aggregation bias and failure of aggregate regularity conditions occur because of the typical approach to representing both price and non-price heterogeneity.

Non-price heterogeneity occurs because of differences among firms in physical capital, technology (including farmer ability and soil productivity), information, and constraints (possibly due to government policy). If such factors are constant across firms, then their effects can be captured in constant parameters. However, investment and technology tend to change over time and differ among firms. Government restrictions change from one policy regime to another and depend on individual farm characteristics such as planting and yield histories or proximity to water resources. These differences cause firms to respond differently to changes in prices.

Suppose k_i represents all short-run fixed factors such as physical capital stock and embodied technologies, family labor constraints, debt constraints, and other attributes of the farm and farmer that explain differences in productivity and profits among individual producers after accounting for variable input choices and allocations of fixed factors. If each firm faces the same price vector, an accurate aggregate netput specification is $\overline{w}_j(q, k_1, \ldots, k_\eta) = \sum_i w_j(q, k_i)$ where η is the total number of firms. However, estimation of an aggregate equation of the form $\overline{w}_j(q, k_1, \ldots, k_\eta)$ is likely impractical both because complete firm-specific data is typically not available and because too many parameters require estimation (without considerable simplification).

A feasible approach is to model the distribution of non-price factors. Where $G(k)$ represents the joint distribution of such factors among firms, an accurate specification of aggregate netputs is $\overline{w}_j(q, G) = \int \eta w_j(q, k) \, dG(k)$. If this distribution has a parameter vector, say θ, then aggregate netputs follow

$$\overline{w}_j(q, \theta) = \int \eta w_j(q, k) \, dG(k \mid \theta). \tag{66}$$

From this result, exact aggregation and the standard regularity conditions are preserved if aggregation considers the full distribution of characteristics among firms. While a full distribution would require complete sampling of all firms, if θ is a sufficiently short parameter vector it can be estimated from a random sample of k. Thus, (66) facilitates tractable empirical representation under heterogeneity. Aggregation is then exact aside from errors in estimating θ so that regularity conditions are preserved. For example, if G can be represented by, say, a two-parameter distribution such as a log-normal, then the two parameters can be usefully estimated from survey data over a limited random sample of firms.

Alternatively, aggregate demand is typically estimated in the form $\overline{w}_j(q, \overline{k})$ where $\overline{k}$ is a vector of non-price indexes. A relevant question is whether some choice of $\overline{k}$ can achieve exact aggregation, $\overline{w}_j(q, \overline{k}) = \sum_i w(q, k_i)$, where $\overline{k}(k_1, \ldots, k_\eta)$ is an aggregate index vector of firm characteristics. Such macro indexes typically consist only of sums or means (e.g., total or per capita physical capital). Unfortunately, neither exact aggregation nor the standard regularity conditions are preserved when all moments in θ other than the first are ignored (assuming θ contains two or more parameters). Following (66), other moments corresponding to each of the moments in θ are generally needed for exact aggregation.

This result implies that aggregate netput specifications based on distribution-insensitive indexes cannot, in general, represent the aggregate marginal effects of either price or non-price factors. Aggregate netput specifications based only on total, per capita, or average characteristics cannot represent aggregate marginal effects because aggregate marginal effects depend on how increments in aggregate characteristics are allocated among firms. Similarly, incomplete models depending only on single-moment indexes cannot represent the aggregate marginal effects of prices because marginal price effects depend on the distribution of non-price factors among firms. For example, consider the case where shut-down conditions vary among firms because of differences in characteristics. In such a case, both aggregation and standard regularity conditions fail [see Just and Pope (1999)].

In reality, some of the factors that differentiate farms and farmers such as management ability or soil fertility may be hard to observe. However, other public data on farm characteristics is routinely collected. For example, data on physical capital are compiled by sampling individual farms. Typically, public data report only means or totals for such data collection efforts. Additionally reporting, say, the standard deviation and skewness would be relatively costless. The full data set would be useful but is usually not made available because of right-to-privacy restrictions. However, the major cost is in conducting the survey – a cost that must be incurred whether one or many moments of the distribution are reported – so a more complete reporting of the distribution appears feasible with minor costs of reporting. The results here suggest that models of production and estimates of supplies and demands could possibly be improved substantially as a result.

While the above discussion considers one-dimensional differences among firms, in reality firms differ in multiple ways. Note, however, that $G(\mathbf{k})$ represents the joint distribution of all characteristics among farms including capital structure and technology, information, constraints, farmer abilities, and farm fertility. Thus, the right-hand side of (66) considers cross-characteristic relationships among firms, e.g., between factors such as capital and family labor availability. Therefore, the result in (66) further implies that aggregate netput specifications may depend on correlations among characteristics. By implication, correlation-insensitive indexes of non-price factors cannot, in general, represent the aggregate marginal effects of either price or non-price factors [see Just and Pope (1999) for details].

These results imply that expanded data reporting efforts should focus not only on own-moments of characteristic distributions among firms, but also on cross-moments. For example, if $G(\mathbf{k})$ follows a multivariate log normal distribution, then the mean and covariance matrix of characteristics across firms would be sufficient to facilitate exact aggregation following (66). Unfortunately, much agricultural data is reported in a way that does not reflect correlations of characteristics. This is particularly true of the relationship of productivity characteristics to environmental characteristics because these two sets of characteristics tend to be collected by independent surveys and even by independent government agencies [Just and Antle (1990); Antle and Just (1992)]. For roughly the same data collection costs, correlations could be estimated if data were indexed by farms, and efforts were made to include the same farms in samples. Apparently, more exact aggregation is possible with little additional data collection cost if data reporting efforts are sensitive to these possibilities. If so, more congruence of theory and empirical results seems likely.

A similar additional generalization permits consideration of price heterogeneity. Regardless of competition, firms may face different prices because of transportation costs, volume discounts, and seasonality.[51] Where individual netputs follow $w_j(\mathbf{q}_i, \mathbf{k}_i)$, an

---

[51] The potential magnitude of this problem is illustrated by spatial variations of output prices due to geographic variation in seasonality of crop production. For example, because of typical weather patterns, the wheat harvest in the U.S. typically starts in Texas in May and continues gradually northward to North Dakota in September. If wheat prices vary throughout the year, then southern farmers are not responding to the same price signals as northern farmers. A dramatic example of wide price variation in a single crop season was caused by the Soviet grain deals in the 1970s. As the Soviet Union bought more and more grain in 1972, wheat prices increased from $1.56 per bushel in Texas to $1.70, $1.68, $1.74, $1.81, and $1.90 in Oklahoma,

accurate aggregate netput specification is $\overline{w}_j(\boldsymbol{q}_1, \ldots, \boldsymbol{q}_\eta, \boldsymbol{k}_1, \ldots, \boldsymbol{k}_\eta) = \sum_i w_j(\boldsymbol{q}_i, \boldsymbol{k}_i)$. While complete data on heterogeneity of both prices and characteristics among farms is typically not available, a tractable approach is again available if a joint distribution of prices and characteristics among firms can be estimated. Where $G(\boldsymbol{q}, \boldsymbol{k})$ represents this joint distribution, an accurate specification of aggregate netputs is $\overline{w}_j(G) = \int \eta w_j(\boldsymbol{q}, \boldsymbol{k}) \, \mathrm{d}G(\boldsymbol{q}, \boldsymbol{k})$. If this distribution is parameterized by a vector $\boldsymbol{\theta}$ that can be estimated for each aggregate observation, then aggregate netputs can be represented as $\overline{w}_j(\boldsymbol{\theta}) = \int \eta w_j(\boldsymbol{q}, \boldsymbol{k}) \, \mathrm{d}G(\boldsymbol{q}, \boldsymbol{k} \mid \boldsymbol{\theta})$, which facilitates accurate aggregation to the extent that $\boldsymbol{\theta}$ is accurately estimated. With this approach, aggregate netputs preserve homogeneity in mean and spread parameters of the price distribution; and monotonicity, symmetry and convexity are preserved in mean prices [see Just and Pope (1999)]. For other results on aggregation with price heterogeneity, see Pope and Chambers (1989).

In lieu of this approach, most aggregate specifications attempt to represent netputs as functions of aggregate price indexes, $\overline{\boldsymbol{q}}(\boldsymbol{q}_1, \ldots, \boldsymbol{q}_\eta)$, as well as indexes of characteristics, $\overline{\boldsymbol{k}}(\boldsymbol{k}_1, \ldots, \boldsymbol{k}_\eta)$. The related problem is whether the standard linear aggregation condition, $\boldsymbol{w}(\overline{\boldsymbol{q}}, \overline{\boldsymbol{k}}) = \sum_i \boldsymbol{w}_i(\boldsymbol{q}_i, \boldsymbol{k}_i)$, holds. Such aggregate indexes typically include only average prices or characteristics and include only one index for each price and each characteristic that differentiates individual firms. Again, more accurate aggregation is possible and standard properties are more likely to hold if the indexes used to represent prices as well as characteristics reflect all of the moments in $\boldsymbol{\theta}$ needed to differentiate the distribution of prices and characteristics among aggregate observations used for estimation. Again, because price data are collected at a disaggregated level, at least some measures of dispersion could easily be reported in addition to the simple or weighted averages now reported with no additional data collection costs and small additional reporting costs.

Finally, we suggest the potential for heterogeneity of information. While a non-trivial role of information can be posed under certainty, many interesting information problems in agriculture arise under uncertainty. Agricultural producers must make decisions affecting output before uncertain output prices are known. Producers likely have different expectations for both prices and technology performance. Such heterogeneity can have important implications even under risk neutrality as demonstrated by Pope and Just (1996, 1998).

Suppose the firm maximizes expected profit as in (64). Then the resulting expected netput vector of the firm can be represented by $\boldsymbol{w}(\boldsymbol{q}, \boldsymbol{k}_i, \boldsymbol{I}_i)$ where $\boldsymbol{I}_i$ denotes the information by which farmer i formulates expectations regarding production responses and uncontrolled production effects (disturbances). Assuming farmers' expectations are unbiased, an accurate specification for expected aggregate netput j is

Kansas, Nebraska, South Dakota, and North Dakota, respectively, as the harvest moved north. In 1973, prices increased from $3.04 in Texas to $3.56, $3.75, $3.80, $4.24, and $4.82 in Oklahoma, Kansas, Nebraska, South Dakota, and North Dakota, respectively [Economic Research Service (various years)]. Aggregating inputs and outputs across these farmers based only on the national average price, one would thus expect such volatile price years to appear technically inefficient falsely even if all individual farmers are fully efficient [Chambers and Pope (1991)].

$\overline{w}_j(\boldsymbol{\theta}) = \int \eta E_I[w_j(\boldsymbol{q}, \boldsymbol{k}, \boldsymbol{I})] \, dG(\boldsymbol{q}, \boldsymbol{k}, \boldsymbol{I} \mid \boldsymbol{\theta})$ where $\overline{w}_j$ now represents an expected aggregate netput and G represents a joint distribution of prices $\boldsymbol{q}$, characteristics $\boldsymbol{k}$, and information $\boldsymbol{I}$ over all farmers. Thus, similar conclusions follow as for other cases of heterogeneity.

Characterizing the distribution of information among producers, however, is a daunting task. Only recently has work such as Wolf, Just, and Zilberman (forthcoming) attempted to characterize sources and choices of information by individual firms. However, no systematic and recurring efforts have been developed to compile such data for use in comprehensive production studies. Other studies [e.g., Just (1974)] have attempted to describe producer information by including regression functions explaining moments of subjective price or yield distributions. To date, however, these approaches have been implemented only at the aggregate level and thus introduce potential aggregation problems in information. Perhaps if other firm-level information were sufficiently complete, differences in information among firms could be inferred with these approaches. In either case, it seems that information heterogeneity is a source of aggregation bias that will be difficult to overcome empirically without more complete firm-level data.

This section demonstrates several generalizations whereby congruence of theory and empirical work can be (better) achieved by better data and aggregation. In each case, empirical implementation is constrained by current data availability. The most promising step to improving aggregation appears to be generalizing data reporting to include at least second own- and cross-moments of producer characteristics. Then aggregate supply/demand specifications can be based on at least two-parameter distributions of characteristics among firms. Seemingly, reporting independent distributional data for capital, prices, government controls, and many determinants of technology (e.g., land quality) is possible with little additional public expense. On the other hand, characterization of some factors such as farmer ability and information at the firm level will likely be more difficult.

6.2. Data limitations: a call for action

That existing data seriously limits agricultural production research may be surprising given that Leontief (1971, p. 5), while president of the American Economics Association, pronounced agricultural economic data to be a model which other economic subdisciplines could/should emulate: "Official agricultural statistics are more complete, reliable, and systematic than those pertaining to any other major sector of our economy". The part of this statement that now seems implausible is related to the word "complete". Though agricultural economists' appetite for data is probably insatiable, a brief evaluation of the sources of agricultural production data is worthwhile in assessing whether Leontief's 1971 evaluation is accurate today.

Secondary aggregate data for both crops and livestock are abundant. For example, data on crops include acres planted and harvested, inventories, trade, storage, disappearance, and price. Though there are differences in quality and availability, such data are generally available throughout the world. They are summarized annually in the U.S. Department of Agriculture's publication, Agricultural Statistics, and are available for most countries from the FAO. A second source of aggregate U.S. data is the *Census of Agriculture*, which is published at roughly five-year intervals. Additionally, county and state data on individual commodities and crop and livestock aggregates are widely available therein. However, individual farm data are not released by public sources because of right-to-privacy concerns.

As previous sections have shown repeatedly, aggregate data is a poor substitute for disaggregated data for understanding agricultural production. This is particularly true for problems where allocations within firms over time (production stages) and space (plots) are important but unrecorded, and for problems where variation among firms is crucial (e.g., where risk and heterogeneity of characteristics are important). For example, Just and Weninger (1999) show that farm-level yield variances are from two to ten times greater than reflected by aggregate data so that most of the risk faced by individual farmers is averaged out of aggregate data, and the structure of risk facing farmers is often significantly mischaracterized. Theoretical models suggest that response to risk is unlikely to be measured effectively with secondary aggregate data because it (i) tends to obfuscate individual responses and risk and (ii) offers very poor measurement of wealth on which risk aversion likely depends. In addition, conceptual studies are finding that representation of heterogeneity is of crucial structural importance for policy analysis, particularly when environmental concerns are important, because both actual and contemplated controls depend on localized land characteristics [e.g., Hochman and Zilberman (1978); Just and Antle (1990); Antle and Just (1992)]. Yet the vast majority of agricultural production studies are done using aggregate data without apology. The primary reason is lack of adequate firm-level data.

At the firm level, the "Agricultural Resource Management Study" (formerly "The Farm Cost and Returns Survey") conducted by the U.S. Department of Agriculture's Economic Research Service contains extensive data on individual farms, but these are not available for use outside of the agency as a public use sample. Furthermore, these surveys are limited in scope because of governmental sampling exposure concerns. Lacking are microeconomic data that will allow a more thorough understanding of farm behavior. As discussed throughout this chapter, needed data must be capable of representing considerable heterogeneity. Yet the very identifying data that could permit merging of these observations with the extensive data base on land quality compiled by the U.S. Natural Resources Conservation Service (formerly the U.S. Soil Conservation Service) is typically restricted. As well, for many issues, the data needs to include intertemporal continuity. To avoid excessive survey exposure, observations are typically drawn on different farms from year to year so no information is available to track investment and productive asset replacement over time. In absence of obtaining such data, a reliable analysis of productive asset acquisition and replacement is difficult and doubtful. Panel data is necessary to do a careful and comprehensive analysis of agricultural investment behavior.

In the U.S., some state land grant institutions have developed farm-level data sets across both time and farms by offering farm-level accounting and management assistance (e.g., Kansas State University). However, since participation is farmer-selected these samples are not random. Furthermore, these data are typically not publicly available and the data are not organized around a broad set of recurring economic issues. For example, such data typically record only external transactions of the farms whereas some additional recording of internal decisions (e.g., allocations of variable inputs) and characteristics (e.g., soil quality) could greatly enhance the value of the data. Yet in spite of these limitations, judging by publications in the leading agricultural economic journals, these samples are heavily used by those who have access to them. Such studies try to understand a variety of behaviors ranging from consumption and wealth accumulation to risk response [e.g., Jensen et al. (1993); Saha et al. (1994)].

Perhaps the best approximation of a comprehensive panel data base for agricultural production is the ICRISAT household data base, which represents primitive developing agriculture. With these data, many aspects of developing agriculture have been investigated and considerable additive debate has emerged accordingly. Developed agriculture, however, is considerably more complex because of scale heterogeneity, policy variability, complex finance and investment, greater scope of inputs and outputs, etc. Furthermore, understanding policy, markets and prices in all countries depends heavily on understanding agricultural production in the major developed countries because of their domination of world trade.

We propose that a significant and complete data base for developed agricultural production needs to be developed as an investment by/for the agricultural economics profession, and that access to such data should be made freely available to all in order to facilitate debate. Debate could be additive because researchers would be forced to compare their maintained hypotheses when working with the same data. Such a data set would allow students to hone their research skills more comprehensively and allow the leading contributions of the profession to add cumulatively to a set of commonly held stylized facts. From these, additional knowledge would spring. Such a data base could facilitate investigation of many issues identified by this study as blocked by data unavailability. By comparison, the current proliferation of studies with uncommon data bases and incongruent maintained hypotheses has led to endless speculative explanations of differences in results with little comprehensive comparison [Alston and Chalfant (1991); Smale et al. (1994).

Such a data base could serve much like public labor data have served the labor economics discipline to facilitate debate and development of a set of stylized facts for the discipline and its policy analysis efforts.[52] Labor economics is a field of economics that

---

[52] An example of the usefulness of stylized facts is given for the marketing arm of the agricultural economics discipline by the focus and debate about elasticities of supply and demand during the 1950s and 1960s. Prior to the flexibility fad in supply and demand estimation, empirical production and marketing studies were heavily judged and criticized on the basis of accepted wisdom regarding supply and demand elasticities and whether they added to the profession's knowledge of them.

has aggressively developed a useful set of microeconomic data. These data include the public use samples of the Census and Current Population Survey (CPS). The CPS is a monthly survey of approximately 60,000 households in all 50 states. Approximately one in 1600 households are surveyed. These data are extensive regarding wages, labor force participation, and socio-demographic data. Other panel-type data are found in the "Panel Study of Income Dynamics" (PSID), the National Longitudinal Survey (NLS and NLS Y2), the High School and Beyond Survey, and many special purpose instruments as well. In comparison, the dearth of microeconomic agricultural data makes understanding agricultural production, a seemingly more complex problem, very difficult.

Any effort to create a broad and complete public panel of agricultural production data will likely require more resources than state land-grant efforts could/should devote. Furthermore, state-level development is likely not to lead to the public access that is needed to facilitate a broad professional and cumulative debate. Because the benefits of such data would be broadly applicable, such an effort seems to be merited at the national or even international level. However, because of excessive survey exposure and right-to-privacy restrictions applied to government surveys, a non-governmental organization may be a more effective means of developing such a data set.

If these possibilities are pursued, the agricultural economics profession can once again lead the general economics discipline as an example of empirical excellence. Many of the issues raised throughout this chapter regarding the structure of technology and preferences can be addressed under assumptions much more consistent with practical agricultural knowledge. And many of the thorny generalizations (representation of investment, information acquisition, and the role of disturbances) yet needed to represent the agricultural production problem meaningfully and comprehensively can then be addressed sensibly.

7. Conclusions

Economists have a primary responsibility to discover behavioral relationships. In practice, this has led to use of methodologies that require minimal or no resources for understanding the underlying structure of technology. Ironically, the effort to represent technologies with maximal flexibility has resulted in empirical approaches that exhaust the identifying potential of available data in capturing that flexibility. Little or no identifying potential remains for discovering behavior.

Presumably, all production economists agree that understanding the essential elements of technology is important to economic thought and measurement. Indeed, the concepts and measurement of productive and technical efficiency and the creation and adoption of technology all seem to be undergoing a considerable rebirth of interest in recent years. A fundamental question in these pursuits is, "What elements of technology should economists consider essential?" That no consensus exists is evident by perusing the *American Journal of Agricultural Economics*, the *Journal of Productivity Analysis*, and the *International Journal of Production Economics*. We have argued that agricultural technology is fundamentally different than for most industrial production and that potentially large gains may come from understanding more of the structure that underlies aggregate reduced-form concepts of production technology. Questions regarding economies of scale and scope, prescriptions for farm management, adoption of technology, productivity and technical change, input demand, output supply, outsourcing [Coase (1937)] and the structure of the firm are only properly understood in the context of technology descriptions that include dynamics, risk, technical structure, input allocation, and constraints associated with policy controls and firm-owned resources. If technology, behavior, and policy instruments are confounded in specification and estimation, then models are not useful for investigating the effects of changes in policy, technologies or industry structure.

As an example, one of the most important issues for future policy is the rapid evolution in the nature of the farm firm. Many farms, particularly those in the livestock sector, increasingly resemble the large-scale specialized manufacturing model. Many farms (e.g., those involved in contract farming) resemble component suppliers to manufacturers. Some (e.g., in the poultry industry) specialize as proprietors of technology. These developments likely have explanation in the framework proposed by Coase (1937). Careful representation and analysis of structured technology in the presence of information asymmetries appear to be crucial to understanding why some services are purchased, why others are produced within the farm, and yet others are produced by the operator or owner of the farm [Allen and Lueck (1998)].

If the agricultural economics profession lacks either relevant theory or evidence, it is a profession without science. Improved congruence of theory and evidence is needed to (i) enable researchers to better understand behavior, (ii) provide better support for policymakers, and (iii) facilitate greater appreciation of classroom theory by students. Some of the most basic theoretical properties of production theory – for example, monotonicity, homogeneity, convexity, and symmetry – are rejected by a predominance of empirical work [Shumway (1995)]. Rejection could be due to flawed theory, flawed empirical analysis, or flawed data. We have suggested several possibilities of theoretical failure beginning in Section 3, several possible failures of empirical practices beginning in Section 4.4, and some major shortcomings of available data in Section 6. Likely some combination of these explanations accounts for the poor performance of agricultural production models noted by Mundlak (2001). Without further research – some of which may not be possible with present data – the extent of failure caused by each is almost impossible to determine. Thus, enhancement of data seems to be a first priority.

We noted in our introduction that there is an increasing gulf between farm management economists on one hand and (agricultural) production economists on the other. Economists are accustomed to arguing for the benefits of division of labor. However, we have argued that much of this gulf is due to cavalier empirical treatment by agricultural production economists of the structure of technology, behavioral preferences of producers, and the constraints and policies they face. Our point of departure is the Fundamental Axiom of Multi-output Production. If this axiom is taken seriously, then methods used by production economists and the data required for analysis are fundamentally different.

The results of this paper underscore the need to develop farm-level data and data on input allocations. One of the greatest problems is inappropriate aggregation and inappropriate representation of heterogeneity imposed by present data availability. Public data are mostly aggregate data describing only the first moment of the underlying distribution among farms. Furthermore, data rarely record allocations of inputs except for land. Even most farm-level survey data such as the Agricultural Resource Management Study (formerly the Farm Costs and Returns Survey) carried out by the Economic Research Service do not record input use by crop or application rates. A few private services (e.g., Doane Marketing Research, Inc.) provide data on pesticide use or application rates by crop but this information is rarely if ever used in the journals of the agricultural economics profession in part because of the expense and in part because the data cannot be provided to others as required by some journal policies.

Lack of data on allocations has tended to cause agricultural production analysis to use aggregate implicit representations of technology. Conceptually, we have demonstrated that implicit representation of technology can lead to deceiving conclusions when some producer decisions are unobserved (most particularly, allocations). Hypothesis tests of technology structure using standard dual and implicit representations of technology are shown to be invalid for typical cases. Under-representing the dimensions of the producer's decision problem can cause inappropriate conclusions. If a producer does not simply decide how much fertilizer to use, but must decide how much fertilizer to use on corn and how much to use on wheat, or how much to use at planting and how much to use during the growing period, then these considerations must be taken into account in specifying the technology before solving out the unobserved variables to reach estimable forms. Allocations as well as aggregate use must be considered in testing for technology structure.

While policy- and behavior-relevant aggregations are appropriate in representing technology, the typical practice has been to ignore allocations and characterize technology with purely aggregate variables. While the set notation of duality lends itself to a high level of generality in theory, the typical step to empirical representation has ignored that potential by assuming technology is neatly described by a single equation devoid of allocations. Standard implicit or explicit specifications of scalar product transformation functions of the form $F(Y, X) = 0$ do not permit generality with respect to the rank of the relationship between X and Y.[53] Implicit representation is particularly distorting if some producer decisions are unobserved. That is, when some unobserved variables are solved out of the structural representation before computing the reduced form, the apparent structure of the observable production possibilities frontier may not reflect characteristics of the underlying technology. However, implicit representation is

---

[53] That is, all common scalar specifications of $F(Y, X) = 0$ imply a Jacobian for the transformation from X to Y of rank 1.

an important problem even if all producer decisions are observed and included in the scalar implicit representation of technology. If such generality is not admitted, then implicit forms arbitrarily exclude the potential nonjointness of, say, (45) for which they are used to test. Alternatively, explicit representations such as (11) can be estimated and used to determine the rank of the relationship between X and Y.

More importantly, single-equation and indirect representations of multi-output production can under-represent the dimensionality of the decision problem. Most often, inputs are represented only by aggregate variables that under-represent the dimensionality of the production technology (and the associated decision problem) when inputs must be allocated in some way over space, time, or production activities. As a result, estimates are policy- or behavior-dependent implying that "technology" models are unstable across observations where policy differs (as is typical in time series data) or behavior differs (as is likely in cross section data). In fact, if there are two or more unobserved allocated inputs, then no purely technological relationship is likely observable. With the present state of data, this may be a major constraint to any meaningful analysis of technical efficiency. Also, if decisions are changing frequently because of changes in policy instruments, then time series data and typical dual (PPF) approaches may offer little hope for estimating a stable "technology."

Dual methods, while not inherently tied to this problem, have led to flexible but indirect representations of technology in practice because flexible forms are not self dual [McFadden (1978); Blackorby et al. (1978)]. Because these approaches start from a PPF representation of technology, most estimates of production technologies in the literature likely include behavioral criteria, are contaminated by policy heterogeneity either across firms or time, and are not pure estimates of technology. Associated hypothesis tests about technology are therefore invalid and actually represent joint tests about technology, policy, and behavioral criteria. For example, rejection of a hypothesis of, say, technical change could, in fact, imply rejection of the profit maximization assumption on which standard duality is based.

Because a large part of the empirical agricultural production literature is based on a PPF approach (e.g., the typical PPF dual approach), the limits of usefulness of PPFs need to be recognized. A PPF permits (i) estimation of total factor demands and supplies and (ii) measurement of industry rents, but even these are valid only if the Aggregation Qualification Condition is met. By comparison, estimates of the PPF alone do not permit (i) examination of nonjointness, homotheticity, or separability of the technology, (ii) prescription of decisions, (iii) analysis of effects of changes in policy instruments, or (iv) explanation of how technical change affects decisions. The reason is that PPFs, because they do not represent allocations, may be policy- or behavior-dependent. In any case, tests of nonjointness, homotheticity, and separability on the frontier do not determine similar properties of the underlying technology.

More seriously, under-representing technological dimensionality may induce structural characteristics such as jointness and non-separability on the aggregate variables when similar characteristics do not apply to underlying technology. These possibilities invalidate some tests and limit the usefulness of almost all tests of technology structure to date for multi-output production problems. These results also offer a likely explanation for why empirical methodologies have not delivered according to their conceptual promises [see Mundlak's (2001) criticism]. That is, if the technology description implicitly includes policy and behavioral criteria, then it is not surprising that empirical estimates are not stable and are inappropriately interpreting observed empirical relationships as implausible relationships in the data. Seemingly the practice noted by Moschini and Hennessy (2001) of sophisticated theoretical modeling with simplistic empirical modeling has led to few recognized empirical regularities. Given the potential invalidating implications of ignored realities, we fear that the current state of empirical knowledge of agricultural production sums up to little more than an empty box.

Appendix. Describing technology independent of policy and behavior

This appendix gives a brief formal treatment of some of the points in Sections 4.1–4.4 using the notation introduced in Sections 3.1 and 4.1. The overall technology is assumed to have a structure composed of sub-technologies $(y^i, x^i) \in \Im_i(z^i, \varepsilon)$ that yield aggregate output $y = AY$ using aggregate purchased inputs $x = BX$ given fixed allocated resource constraints $CZ \leqslant K$, i.e.,

$$\{(y, x) \in \Im_{-i}(k, \varepsilon)\} \equiv \{(y, x) \mid (Y, X) \in \cup_i \Im_i(z^i, \varepsilon), y = AY, x = BX, CZ \leqslant K\},$$

(A.1)

which is equivalent to (43). Under continuity and monotonicity, the upper right-hand (efficient) boundary of feasible $(y, -x)$ associated with $\Im_{-i}$ is described by

$$F(y, x, k, \varepsilon) \equiv y_1 - f(y_{-1}, x, k, \varepsilon) = 0,$$
$$y_1 = f(y_{-1}, x, k, \varepsilon) \equiv \max\{y_1 \mid (y, x) \in \Im_{-i}(k, \varepsilon)\},$$

(A.2)

where $y = (y_1, y_{-1})$. To identify the specific production plan necessary to attain any distinct $(y, x) \in \Im_{-i}$, the spatially and temporally detailed vectors $X = (x^1, \ldots, x^m)$, $Z = (z^1, \ldots, z^m)$, and $Y = (y^1, \ldots, y^m)$ not included in (A.2) must be determined. Also, to facilitate determination of the implications of policy instruments that impose limitations on specific x^i's or y^i's, such as $(Y, X) \in G$, the representation in (A.2) does not suffice. Alternatively, this technology can be represented with spatial and temporal detail,

$$\{(Y, X, Z) \in \Im(k, \varepsilon)\} \equiv \{(Y, X) \in \cup_i \Im_i(z^i, \varepsilon)\} \cap \{Z \mid CZ \leqslant K\},$$

(A.3)

which is equivalent to (44). To represent spatially and temporally detailed technology in functional form under continuity and monotonicity, the upper right-hand (efficient) boundaries of feasible $(y^i, -x^i)$ associated with $\Im_i$ are described by

$$F_i\left(y^i, x^i, z^i, \varepsilon\right) \equiv y_1^i - f_i\left(y_{-1}^i, x^i, z^i, \varepsilon\right) = 0,$$
$$y_1^i = f_i\left(y_{-1}^i, x^i, z^i, \varepsilon\right) \equiv \max\left\{y_1^i \mid \left(y^i, x^i\right) \in \Im_i\left(z^i, \varepsilon\right)\right\}, \tag{A.4}$$

where $y^i = (y_1^i, y_{-1}^i)$. The combination of these conditions across all sub-technologies is represented by (45).

A.1. Alternative concepts of efficiency

The alternative concepts of technical efficiency in Section 4.1 are defined formally by

DEFINITION A.1.

(E1) $(y^i, x^i) \in \Im_i(z^i, \varepsilon)$ is sub-technology efficient if there does not exist $(y^{i\prime}, x^i) \in \Im_i(z^i, \varepsilon)$ such that $y^{i\prime} \not< y^i$. With continuity and monotonicity, this condition reduces equivalently to (A.4).

(E2) (Y, X) satisfies structural technical efficiency for a given (Z, ε) if there does not exist $(y^{i\prime}, x^i) \in \Im_i(z^i, \varepsilon)$ such that $y^{i\prime} \not< y^i$ for any sub-technology. With continuity and monotonicity, this condition reduces to (45).

(E3) (Y, X, Z) satisfies fixed factor technical allocative efficiency if there does not exist an alternative allocation Z' such that $(Y', X, Z') \in \Im(k, \varepsilon)$, $CZ' \leqslant CZ$, and $Y' \not< Y$.[54]

(E4) (Y, X, Z) satisfies variable input technical allocative efficiency if there does not exist an alternative allocation X' such that $(Y', X', Z) \in \Im(k, \varepsilon)$, $BX' \leqslant BX$, and $Y' \not< Y$.

(E5) (Y, X, Z) satisfies output technical allocative efficiency if there does not exist an alternative allocation among sub-technologies such that $(Y', X', Z') \in \Im(k, \varepsilon)$, $BX' \leqslant BX$, $CZ' \leqslant CZ$, and $AY' \not< AY$.

(E6) $(y, x) \in \Im_{-i}(k, \varepsilon)$ is technically efficient in a reduced-form sense if there does not exist an alternative allocation of the aggregate input vector x that will produce an aggregate output vector $y' \in \Im_{-i}(k, \varepsilon)$ such that $y' \not< y$. This condition corresponds to the efficient boundary of (A.1) which reduces equivalently to (A.2).

(E7) (Y, X, Z) satisfies feasible disaggregated input-output efficiency if in addition to (E2) there does not exist an alternative allocation Z' such that $(Y', X, Z') \in \Im(k, \varepsilon)$, $CZ' \leqslant K$, and $Y' \not< Y$. This condition corresponds to the efficient boundary of (A.3) and includes (E3).

Because Propositions 1–3 state negative results, they can be proved by examples. For purposes of brevity, proofs of propositions are only outlined.

---

[54] The relationship $Y' \not< Y$ means $Y' \geqslant Y$ with strict inequality in at least one element.

PROOF OF PROPOSITION 1. Consider the full profit-maximization problem with temporal and spatial price detail in $P = (p^1, \ldots, p^m)$ and $R = (r^1, \ldots, r^m)$ ignoring for the moment inability to forecast ε,

$$\pi = \max_{Y,X}\{PY - RX \mid (Y, X, Z) \in \Im(k, \varepsilon)\}. \tag{A.5}$$

Considering aggregation over sub-technologies, the corresponding profit maximization problem,

$$\pi = \max_{y,x}\{py - rx \mid (y, x) \in \Im_{-i}(k, \varepsilon)\},$$

is clearly not an aggregate of the solution to problem (A.5) when $p \neq p_i$ and $r \neq r_i$ for $i = 1, \ldots, m$. Accordingly, (E4) and (E5) may be inconsistent with standard profit maximization behavior. Similarly, imposing a policy or behavioral constraint on a specific element of the X or Z vector as in $(Y, X) \in G$ renders (E4) or (E3) inapplicable, respectively.   □

PROOF OF PROPOSITION 2. See the proof of Proposition 1 and note that (E4) and (E5) are required by profit maximization of (A.1).   □

PROOF OF PROPOSITION 3. This proof follows by noting that (45) has no condition equating marginal productivities of allocated fixed factors and, conversely, equating marginal productivities of allocated fixed factors does not necessarily satisfy (45).   □

As noted in Section 3.4, the problems in Propositions 1–3 may be encountered in aggregating inputs or outputs spatially and/or temporally over allocations that are not subject to the same prices, shadow prices, policy constraints, or preference relationships (see the Aggregation Qualification Condition).

A.2. Two-stage representation of the producer's problem

This section illustrates the issue concerning policy and/or behavioral content in the first-stage of a two-stage decomposition of a production problem. Suppose, for example, that policy and/or behavioral considerations impose only one constraint on the first input in the first sub-technology represented by $h(x_1^1) \leqslant \alpha$. Adding this constraint to (A.1) obtains

$$\{(y, x, x_1^1) \in \Im_{-i}(k, \varepsilon)\}$$
$$= \{(y, x, x_1^1) \mid h(x_1^1) \leqslant \alpha, (y^i, x^i) \in \Im_i(z^i, \varepsilon), y = AY, x = BX, CZ \leqslant K\}.$$

Under continuity and monotonicity, (A.2) thus becomes

$$F(y, x, k, \varepsilon, \alpha) = y_1 - f(y_{-1}, x, k, \varepsilon, \alpha) = 0, \tag{A.2'}$$

$$y_1 = f(\mathbf{y}_{-1}, \mathbf{x}, \mathbf{k}, \boldsymbol{\varepsilon}, \alpha) = \max\{y_1 \mid h(x_1^1) \leqslant \alpha, (\mathbf{y}, \mathbf{x}) \in \mathfrak{I}_{-i}(\mathbf{k}, \boldsymbol{\varepsilon})\}.$$

This form is not dependent on the specific policy or behavioral constraint. That is, the constrained level α can be imposed, adjusted, or dropped in the second-stage problem. However, the form in (A.2′) is substantially different than that in (A.2). Indeed, the domain is a different space.

An alternative way to proceed is to define F with the constraint in place,

$$y_1 = f(\mathbf{y}_{-1}, \mathbf{x}, \mathbf{k}, \boldsymbol{\varepsilon}) = \max\{y_1 \mid h(x_1^1) \leqslant \alpha, (\mathbf{y}, \mathbf{x}) \in \mathfrak{I}_{-i}(\mathbf{k}, \boldsymbol{\varepsilon})\}, \qquad \text{(A.2″)}$$

with F defined as in (A.2). However, if this is done, the frontier is clearly policy- or behavior-dependent. The resulting PPF corresponding to (A.2′) will depend not only on the existence of a policy affecting x_1^1 as in (A.2″) but also on the policy level, α. Likewise, the profit function dual to F will also depend on α. Thus, the true PPF will be policy-dependent and what may appear as technical change or inefficiency in the PPF associated with (A.2″) may be due to changes in policy. Similarly, if the PPF from the first stage is based on (A.2″), then second-stage analyses cannot consider changes in policy or behavior associated with α.

PROOF OF PROPOSITION 4. Because Proposition 4 is stated in negative form, the above example suffices as a proof. □

Using the partial aggregation definitions associated with (46), the definitions of technical allocative efficiency can be generalized and divided into policy- and behavior-relevant and policy- or behavior-dependent categories under Aggregation Qualification Condition A.2.

DEFINITION A.1′.
(E3′) $(\mathbf{y}^*, \mathbf{x}^*, \mathbf{z}^*)$ satisfies fixed factor technical allocative efficiency for a given $\boldsymbol{\varepsilon}$ if there does not exist an alternative allocation $\mathbf{z}^{*\prime}$ such that $(\mathbf{y}^{*\prime}, \mathbf{x}^*, \mathbf{z}^{*\prime}) \in \mathfrak{I}^*(\mathbf{k}, \boldsymbol{\varepsilon})$ in (46) and $\mathbf{y}^{*\prime} \not\leqslant \mathbf{y}$.
(E4′) $(\mathbf{y}^*, \mathbf{x}^*, \mathbf{z}^*)$ satisfies variable input technical allocative efficiency for a given $\boldsymbol{\varepsilon}$ if there does not exist an alternative allocation $\mathbf{x}^{*\prime}$ such that $(\mathbf{y}^{*\prime}, \mathbf{x}^{*\prime}, \mathbf{z}^*) \in \mathfrak{I}^*(\mathbf{k}, \boldsymbol{\varepsilon})$, $\mathbf{x}^{*\prime} \in C(\mathbf{x}^*)$, and $\mathbf{y}^{*\prime} \not\leqslant \mathbf{y}$ where $C(\mathbf{x}^*)$ defines the set of possible purchased variable input allocations with a given vector of aggregate purchases, i.e., $C(\mathbf{x}^*) = \{\mathbf{x}^{*\prime} \mid (\mathbf{y}^{*\prime}, \mathbf{x}^{*\prime}, \mathbf{z}^*) = H(\mathbf{Y}', \mathbf{X}', \mathbf{Z}), \mathbf{B}\mathbf{X}' \leqslant \mathbf{B}\mathbf{X}\}$.
(E5′) $(\mathbf{y}^*, \mathbf{x}^*, \mathbf{z}^*)$ satisfies output technical allocative efficiency for a given $\boldsymbol{\varepsilon}$ if there does not exist an alternative allocation among sub-technologies $\mathbf{y}^{*\prime}$ such that $(\mathbf{y}^{*\prime}, \mathbf{x}^{*\prime}, \mathbf{z}^{*\prime}) \in \mathfrak{I}^*(\mathbf{k}, \boldsymbol{\varepsilon})$, $\mathbf{x}^{*\prime} \in C(\mathbf{x}^*)$, and $\mathbf{y}^{*\prime} \in Y(\mathbf{y}^*)$ where $Y(\mathbf{y}^*)$ defines the set of outputs that correspond to a dominant aggregate output vector, i.e., $Y = \{\mathbf{y}^{*\prime} \mid (\mathbf{y}^{*\prime}, \mathbf{x}^{*\prime}, \mathbf{z}^*) = H(\mathbf{Y}', \mathbf{X}', \mathbf{Z}), \mathbf{A}\mathbf{Y}' \not\leqslant \mathbf{A}\mathbf{Y}\}$.
(E8) $(\mathbf{y}^*, \mathbf{x}^*, \mathbf{z}^*)$ is policy- and behavior-relevant if it satisfies the Aggregation Qualification Conditions, i.e., preserves distinction for all input and output

quantities that have distinct prices, distinct policy controls, distinct ex post adjustment possibilities or distinct behavioral preferences and implications so that (46) preserves full generality of policy and behavioral issues to the second stage.

(E9) (y^*, x^*, z^*) is policy- or behavior-dependent if it does not satisfy the Aggregation Qualification Condition, i.e., does not preserve distinction for all input and output quantities that have distinct prices, distinct policy controls, distinct ex post adjustment possibilities or distinct behavioral preferences and implications, in which case (46) does not preserve the full generality of policy and behavioral issues to the second stage.

Using these definitions jointly one can define, for example, technologies that satisfy various concepts of technical allocative efficiency and are also policy- and behavior-relevant. We submit that policy- and behavior-relevance as defined by (E8) must be a prerequisite requirement for investigating technical efficiency following (E3′), (E4′) or (E5′). Otherwise, tests of technical efficiency are actually confounded tests of policy and behavior that are not meaningful for investigating properties of technology.

A.3. Implicit representation of technical efficiency by scalar functions

All specific single-equation multi-output production functions in the literature of which we are aware satisfy $\partial F/\partial Y \neq 0$ and $\partial F/\partial X \neq 0$ whenever $F(Y, X) = 0$. By comparison, a form such as

$$F(Y, X) \equiv \sum_{i=1}^{m} \left[F_i(Y, X) \right]^{2\nu}, \tag{A.6}$$

where ν is a positive integer can impose multiple constraints of the form $F_i(Y, X) = 0$ but yields $\partial F/\partial Y = 0$ and $\partial F/\partial X = 0$ whenever $F(Y, X) = 0$. Mittelhammer, Matulich, and Bushaw (1981) have shown that such forms do not lend themselves to Lagrangians, Kuhn–Tucker conditions, nor the implicit function theorem. To illustrate, the profit maximization problem $\max_{Y, X} \{ PY - RX \mid F(Y, X) = 0 \}$ can be expressed as the Lagrangian $\mathcal{L} = PY - RX + \lambda F(Y, X)$ for which first-order conditions cannot be solved when $\partial F/\partial Y = 0$ and $\partial F/\partial X = 0$ at $F(Y, X) = 0$.[55]

Two approaches to implicit representation are possible: (i) require non-zero derivatives of F with respect to all relevant inputs and outputs when $F(Y, X) = 0$, or (ii) develop methods to deal with zero derivatives. The first approach facilitates standard mathematical manipulations, but obtains a model that can neither reflect input allocations nor

---

[55] More technically, the Jacobian of the constraint does not have full rank when $F(Y, X)$ has all zero derivatives so the first-order conditions of the Lagrangian are not necessary. For Kuhn–Tucker problems, constraint qualification fails.

impose by-product relationships. By the implicit function theorem, $F(Y, X) = 0$ yields a function such as $y_i = f_i(y_1, \ldots, y_{i-1}, y_{i+1}, \ldots, y_{n_y}, X)$ where all partial derivatives are non-zero. Thus, any input change (even though it may represent an allocation of a distinct input to production of a distinct output) can be transformed into a change in any other output (rather than the output to which it is allocated). Similarly, any transformation between distinct outputs (possibly between a primary output and a by-product that, in reality, can be produced only in fixed proportions) is allowed.

Alternatively, one can argue that assuming non-zero derivatives for F is very restrictive. By comparison, the representation in (A.6) clearly has all zero derivatives and yet implies[56]

$$F(Y, X) \underset{m}{\equiv} \begin{bmatrix} F_1(Y, X) \\ \vdots \\ F_m(Y, X) \end{bmatrix} \underset{m}{=} 0. \tag{A.7}$$

Conversely, one can always transform (A.7) into (A.6) but, interestingly, the Implicit Function Theorem (which is only sufficient, not necessary) can apply in (A.7) even if not in (A.6).

An interesting question is, can the product transformation functions implied by standard profit and cost function specifications admit forms such as (A.7)? The answer is no. A standard axiom of duality is convexity of the feasible technology set $\Im$ which is defined as the set of all feasible combinations of (Y, X). Diewert has shown for the single-output case that if $\Im$ is convex then the corresponding product transformation function, $F(Y, X)$, is a convex function. However, $F(Y, X)$ in (A.6) is not necessarily convex even in the single-output case.[57] Furthermore, a form such as (A.6) is not monotonic in Y and X. Thus, disposability does not correspond to an inequality in (A.6) and the producible output set cannot be defined as $\{Y \mid F(Y, X) \leqslant 0\}$ as in the multi-output development of Chambers (1988). Moreover, all dual developments that derive production functions and product transformation functions do so by implicitly imposing a technical efficiency criterion leading to the convex hull of the technology

---

[56] Mittelhammer, Matulich, and Bushaw (1981) argue that vector-valued implicit functions are required to represent multi-output technology because single-valued functions with non-zero derivatives are restrictive. The result in (26) shows that the vector-valued representation they propose can be derived directly from a single-valued representation if zero derivatives are allowed. In either case, what really matters is the rank of the technological relationship (defined below) rather than the number of equalities used to describe it. Even if expressed in a vector-valued implicit form, one must still verify full rank of the system and make sure no equation discarded in getting to full rank is of a form such as (11) that embodies further restrictions implicitly. (Note that Mittelhammer, Matulich, and Bushaw apparently allow zero derivatives of individual scalar-valued functions contained in vector-valued representations.)

[57] To illustrate where x and y are scalar, let $F(y, x) = [y - f(x)]^2$ where $f(x)$ is concave and let $y_1 = f(x_1)$, $y_2 = f(x_2)$, $y_0 = \theta y_1 + (1 - \theta)y_2$, and $x_0 = \theta x_1 + (1 - \theta)x_2$. Then $F(y_0, x_0) = \{\theta y_1 + (1 - \theta)y_2 - f[\theta x_1 + (1 - \theta)x_2]\}^2 > 0 = \theta F(y_1, x_1) + (1 - \theta)F(y_2, x_2)$. Thus, $F(y, x)$ is concave. Convexity is obtained, for example, if $F(y, x) = y - f(x)$.

set [e.g., Diewert (1974, 1982)]. Additionally, while not a serious problem for single-output problems, imposing both structural technical efficiency and technical allocative efficiency for multi-output production problems limits the rank of the resulting technology representation to unity so that structure (related to sub-technologies) cannot be represented (see Sections 4.6 and 4.7 for further details).[58]

PROOF OF PROPOSITION 5. Proposition 5 follows from the discussion of this section and results in Mittelhammer, Matulich, and Bushaw (1981).   □

A.4. Controllability and rank of structural technology representations

To represent structure of technologies meaningfully, possible redundancies in (50) and (51) must be considered. For example, under continuity, the Jacobian of f_i may not be of full rank, e.g., one of the outputs of the sub-technology may be some function of another as in the case where $y_1^i = g(y_2^i)$, $g' > 0$. In this case, $\text{rank}\{\partial(y_1^i, y_2^i)/\partial X; \partial(y_1^i, y_2^i)/\partial Z\} = 1$. Thus, the decision maker is not able to control the second output independently of the first. Such relationships represent the case of by-products. Similarly, constraints on allocated fixed inputs reduce the dimension of the input space when constraints are binding. Thus, it is helpful to consider the following definitions:

DEFINITION A.2. Let $\widetilde{Y} \in R_+^{n_a}$ be a subset of outputs in $Y \in R_+^{n_y}$ and let $N(\widetilde{Y}) \subset R_+^{n_a}$ denote a neighborhood of $\widetilde{Y}$. The mix of outputs $\widetilde{Y}$ is locally controllable in $R_+^{n_a}$ if $N(\widetilde{Y}) \subseteq \Im$.

If $n_a = 1$, then this neighborhood would correspond to an open set on the real line. If $n_a \geqslant 2$, then N corresponds to an open ball in multi-dimensional space. When controllability is not met, the producer does not have the flexibility to attain all output mixes in $N(\widetilde{Y})$.

DEFINITION A.3. Let $\widehat{Y} \in R_+^{n_b}$ be a subset of outputs in $Y \in R_+^{n_y}$. The outputs in $\widehat{Y}$ are by-products of $\widetilde{Y}$ under technology $\Im$ if there exists a non-trivial relationship in $\Im$ such that only one $\widehat{Y}$ exists for each $\widetilde{Y}$ given uncontrollable factors, i.e., $\widehat{Y} = g(\widetilde{Y}, \varepsilon)$.

The existence of by-product relationships reduces the producer's flexibility in choosing output mixes. The remaining flexibility after taking these relationships into account is described by the rank of a technology.

---

[58] If the PPF is defined conventionally by $F^*(y, x, k, \varepsilon) \equiv y_1 - f^*(y_{-1}, x, k, \varepsilon)$ where $y = (y_1, y_{-1})$ and $y_1 = f^*(y_{-1}, x, k, \varepsilon) \equiv \max\{y_1 \mid (y, x) \in \Im_{-i}(k, \varepsilon)\}$ and if no fixed factors are allocated, then the same function is obtained as in (A.2) upon imposing technical allocative efficiency with respect to inputs and outputs.

DEFINITION A.4. The rank of a technology is the dimension of the largest locally controllable mix of outputs.

To proceed, suppose that the relationships in (50) and (51) are continuous and differentiable.

LEMMA A.1. *Under continuity and differentiability, the rank of a technology*

$$Y_{m \cdot n_y} = f(X, Z, \varepsilon)$$

is given by rank(f_X, f_Z).

PROOF OF LEMMA A.1. Let $W = (X, Z)$ and rank$(f_X, f_Z) = $ rank$(f_W) = \rho$. Then there exists a nonsingular $\rho \times \rho$ Jacobian f_W^* as a submatrix of f_W after appropriate reordering of Y and W. Corresponding to f_W^* are equations $Y^* = f^*(W^*, W^{**})$ which together with $Y^{**} = f^{**}(W^*, W^{**})$ represent a partitioning of $Y = f(W)$ where $W = (W^*, W^{**})$ is a corresponding partitioning of W. By the Implicit Function Theorem, the equation $Y^*_\rho = f^*(W^*, W^{**})$ has a solution where W^* are the active or endogenous variables. Let W_0^*, W_0^{**}, Y_0^* be such a solution. By the Implicit Function Theorem, there is an open ball $\mathcal{B}(Y_0^*)$ such that $Y^* = \{f^*(W^*, W^{**}) \mid W^{**} = W_0^{**}\}$ is a one-to-one transformation for all $Y_0^* \in \mathcal{B}(Y_0^*)$ and W^* near W_0^*. Hence, Y^* of dimension ρ is locally controllable. $\qquad\square$

LEMMA A.2. *Where the rank of a technology is n_a and $\widetilde{Y}$ is a locally controllable vector of outputs in $R_+^{n_a}$, the complete output vector can be partitioned into $Y = (\widetilde{Y}, \widehat{Y})$ where the choice of $\widetilde{Y}$ determines the other outputs in $\widehat{Y} \in R_+^{n_b}$ and $n_b = n_y - n_a$, i.e., the number of by-products in a multi-output technology is equal to the number of outputs minus the rank of the technology.*

PROOF OF LEMMA A.2. Consider the production relations in (51) and assume rank$(f_X, f_Z) = n_a$. By the Inverse Function Theorem and Definition A.2, $\widetilde{Y}$ can be found as a function of (X, Z) for a given ε, say $\widetilde{Y} = \tilde{f}(X, Z, \varepsilon)$. This relationship is simply a subset consisting of n_a of the individual equations contained in (51). Using Definition A.3, $\widehat{Y}_{n_b} = g(\tilde{f}(X, Z, \varepsilon))$, where $n_b = \sum_i k_i - n_a$. $\qquad\square$

From the proof of Lemma A.2, the gradient of f only spans an n_a-dimensional space. In particular, the Jacobian of $\widehat{Y}$ is $g_{\widetilde{Y}} \cdot (\tilde{f}_X, \tilde{f}_Z)$ which is a linear transformation of the Jacobian of $\widetilde{Y}$ given by $(\tilde{f}_X, \tilde{f}_Z)$, which itself has only rank n_a. Next consider input controllability.

DEFINITION A.5. Let $\widetilde{\mathbf{Z}} \in R_+^{n_f}$ be a subset of inputs included in $\mathbf{Z} \in R_+^{n_z}$ and let $N(\widetilde{\mathbf{Z}}) \subset R_+^{n_f}$ denote a neighborhood of $\widetilde{\mathbf{Z}}$. The mix of inputs $\widetilde{\mathbf{Z}}$ is locally controllable in $R_+^{n_f}$ if $N(\widetilde{\mathbf{Z}}) \subseteq \Im$. A subset of inputs is locally restricted if it is not locally controllable.

Even though there are n_z allocated fixed input decisions, only $n_f = n_z - n_c$ of them are freely controllable. Generalizing to the possibility of nonlinear constraints, let $\widehat{\mathbf{Z}} = h(\widetilde{\mathbf{Z}}, \mathbf{K})$ represent the set of allocated fixed inputs determined by the choice of $\underset{n_c}{}$ $\widetilde{\mathbf{Z}}$ given $\mathbf{K}$. Under continuity and differentiability, a parsimonious nonlinear representation of the binding (non-redundant) constraints will have a Jacobian of full rank.

LEMMA A.3. *Let the vector of all constrained inputs be denoted by* $\mathbf{Z} \in R_+^{n_z}$ *and let all locally binding input constraints in* $\Im$ *be summarized by* $\underset{n_c}{\widehat{\mathbf{Z}}} = h(\widetilde{\mathbf{Z}}, \mathbf{K})$ *with full rank Jacobian,* $h_{\widetilde{Z}}$. *Then the input vector can be partitioned into* $\mathbf{Z} = (\widetilde{\mathbf{Z}}, \widehat{\mathbf{Z}})$ *where* $\widetilde{\mathbf{Z}} \in R_+^{n_z - n_c}$ *is locally controllable and the choice of* $\widetilde{\mathbf{Z}}$ *determines the other inputs in* $\widehat{\mathbf{Z}} \in R_+^{n_c}$.

PROOF OF LEMMA A.3. The proof is omitted because it is similar to Lemma A.1. □

Note that this lemma is worded generally so as to apply to all forms of constraints whether associated with firm-owned resources, policy instruments, behavior, or market rationing and whether applicable to allocated fixed inputs or purchased variable inputs.

PROOF OF PROPOSITION 6. The proof of Proposition 6 follows the Fundamental Axiom, which permits technology to be represented as in (51), and from Lemmas A.1–A.3 under continuity and differentiability. □

PROOF OF PROPOSITION 7. This proof is omitted for brevity since it is sketched clearly in the text. □

PROOF OF PROPOSITION 8. If n_c fixed inputs must be allocated among m sub-technologies, then at least $n_c(m-1)$ allocation variables are unobserved. From Proposition 7, the maximum number of non-redundant observable controllable equations is thus $n_a + n_c - n_c(m-1)$. This number is greater than zero only if $n_a \geqslant n_c m$. In the case of nonjointness, $m = n_y = n_a$ in which case this condition reduces directly to $n_c \leqslant 1$. In the case where some variable input allocations are unobserved but their aggregates are observed, a similar proof applies where (i) $x = \mathbf{B}X$ is used to substitute into (52)–(54), (ii) the number of such variable inputs is added to n_c, and (iii) the associated number of unobserved allocations are considered in the calculation. For allocated fixed inputs without binding restrictions, note that m rather than $m - 1$ allocation variables are unobserved so even more variables are unobserved. □

PROOF OF COROLLARY 2. Since n_c fixed inputs must be allocated among m sub-technologies, then at least $(n_c - 1)(m - 1)$ allocation variables are unobserved. From

Proposition 7, the maximum number of non-redundant observable controllable equations is thus $n_a + n_c - (n_c - 1)(m - 1)$. This number is greater than zero only if $n_a + m - 1 \geqslant n_c m$. If $n_a < (n_c - 1)m$, then $n_a + m - 1 < n_c m - 1$. Other assertions follow as in the proof of Proposition 8. $\qquad\square$

PROOF OF PROPOSITION 9. Under the conditions of Proposition 8, no purely technological relationship among inputs and outputs is estimable. All estimable relationships of y and x obtained from solving the production problem with conditions (51) and (58) must embody policy or behavioral criteria. Thus, hypothesis tests on the relationship of input and output variables cannot test the structure of technology alone, but rather test the relationship of variables induced by a combination of behavioral criteria and technology. $\qquad\square$

References

Allen, D.W., and D.L. Lueck (1998), "The nature of the farm", Journal of Law and Economics 41: 343–386.

Alston, J.M., and J.A. Chalfant (1991), "Unstable models from incorrect forms", American Journal of Agricultural Economics 73:1171–1181.

Amemiya, T. (1985), Advanced Econometrics (Harvard University Press, Cambridge).

Antle, J.M. (1983), "Testing the stochastic structure of production: A flexible moment-based approach", Journal of Business and Economic Statistics 1:192–201.

Antle, J. (1984), "The structure of U.S. agricultural technology", American Journal of Agricultural Economics 66:414–421.

Antle, J.M., S.M. Capalbo and C.C. Crissman (1994), "Econometric production models with endogenous input timing: An application to Ecuadorian potato production", Journal of Agricultural And Resource Economics 19:1–18.

Antle, J., and S. Hatchett (1986), "Dynamic input decisions in econometric production models", American Journal of Agricultural Economics 68:939–949.

Antle, J.M., and R.E. Just (1992), "Conceptual and empirical foundations for agricultural-environmental policy analysis", Journal of Environmental Quality 21:307–316.

Baker, T.G., and B.A. McCarl (1982), "Representing farm resource availability over time in linear programs: A case study", North Central Journal of Agricultural Economics 4:59–68.

Ball, V.E. (1985), "Output, input, and productivity measurement in U.S. agriculture, 1948–79", American Journal of Agricultural Economics 67:425–436.

Ball, V.E. (1988), "Modeling supply response in a multiproduct framework", American Journal of Agricultural Economics 70:813–825.

Ball, V.E., J.-C. Bureau, R. Nehring and A. Somwaru (1997), "Agricultural productivity revisited", American Journal of Agricultural Economics 79:1045–1063.

Ball, V.E., and R.G. Chambers (1982), "An economic analysis of technology in the meat products industry", American Journal of Agricultural Economics 64:699–709.

Ball, V.E., F. Gollop, A. Kelly and G. Swinand (1999), "Patterns of productivity growth in the U.S. farm sector: Linking state and aggregate models", American Journal of Agricultural Economics 81:164–179.

Barry, P.J., and L.J. Robison (2001), "Agricultural finance: Credit, credit constraints, and consequences", in: B. Gardner and G. Rausser, eds., Handbook of Agricultural Economics, Vol. 1 (Elsevier, Amsterdam) 513–571.

Bar-Shira, Z., R.E. Just and D. Zilberman (1997), "Estimation of farmers' risk attitude: An econometric approach", Agricultural Economics 17:211–222.

Baumol, W.J., J.C. Panzar and R.D. Willig (1988), Contestable Markets and the Theory of Industry Structure, Revised Edition (Harcourt Brace Jovanovich, San Diego).

Berck, P., and G. Helfand (1990), "Reconciling the Von Liebig and differentiable crop production functions", American Journal of Agricultural Economics 72:985–996.

Binswanger, H.P. (1974), "The measurement of technological change biases with many factors of production", American Economic Review 64:964–976.

Binswanger, H.P. (1980), "Attitudes toward risk: Experimental measurement in rural India", American Journal of Agricultural Economics 62:395–407.

Binswanger, H.P. (1981), "Attitudes toward risk: Theoretical implications of an experiment in rural India", Economic Journal 91:867–890.

Blackorby, C., D. Primont and R.R. Russell (1978), Duality, Separability and Functional Structure (North-Holland, New York).

Bryant, K.J., J.W. Mjelde and R.D. Lacewell (1993), "An intraseasonal dynamic optimization model to allocate irrigation water between crops", American Journal of Agricultural Economics 75:1021–1029.

Burger, B. (1998), "Delayed corn planting – what are your options?", Novartis Seeds, http://www.nk.com/nkwired/1998/05_04_delay.html.

Burt, O. (1993), "Decision rules for the dynamic animal feeding problem", American Journal of Agricultural Economics 75:190–202.

Buschena, D., and D. Zilberman (2000), "Generalized expected utility, heteroscedastic error, and path dependence in risky choice", Journal of Risk and Uncertainty 20:67–88.

Candler, W., and M. Boehlje (1971), "The use of linear programming in capital budgeting with multiple goals", American Journal of Agricultural Economics 53:325–330.

Chambers, R.G. (1988), Applied Production Analysis (Cambridge, New York).

Chambers, R.G., Y. Chung and R. Färe (1996), "Benefit and distance functions", Journal of Economic Theory 70:407–419.

Chambers, R.G., and R.E. Just (1981), "Effects of exchange rate changes on U.S. agriculture: A dynamic analysis", American Journal of Agricultural Economics 63:32–46.

Chambers, R.G., and R.E. Just (1989), "Estimating multioutput technologies", American Journal of Agricultural Economics 71:980–995.

Chambers, R.G., and E. Lichtenberg (1995), "The Economics of sustainable agriculture in the Mid-Atlantic", Department of Agricultural and Resource Economics (University of Maryland, College Park).

Chambers, R.G., and R. Pope (1991), "Testing for consistent aggregation", American Journal of Agricultural Economics 73:808–818.

Chambers, R.G., and J. Quiggin (1998), "Cost functions for stochastic technologies", American Journal of Agricultural Economics 80:288–295.

Chambers, R.G., and U. Vasavada (1983), "Testing asset fixity for U.S. agriculture", American Journal of Agricultural Economics 65:761–769.

Chavas, J.-P. (2001), "Structural change in agricultural production: Economics, technology and policy", in: B. Gardner and G. Rausser, eds., Handbook of Agricultural Economics, Vol. 1 (Elsevier, Amsterdam) 263–285.

Chavas, J.-P., and T.L. Cox (1988), "A nonparametric analysis of agricultural technology", American Journal of Agricultural Economics 70:303–310.

Chavas, J.-P. and M.T. Holt (1991), "On non-linear dynamics: The case of the pork cycle", American Journal of Agricultural Economics 73:819–828.

Chavas, J.-P., and M.T. Holt (1993), "Market instability and nonlinear dynamics", American Journal of Agricultural Economics 75:113–120.

Chavas, J.-P. and M.T. Holt (1996), "Economic behavior under uncertainty: A joint analysis of risk preferences and technology", Review of Economics and Statistics 78:329–335.

Clark, J.S., and G.A. Carlson (1990), "Testing for common versus private property: The case of pesticide resistance", Journal of Environmental Economics and Management 19:45–60.

Coase, R. (1937), "On the nature of the firm", Economica 4:386–405.

Cragg, J.G., and S.G. Donald (1997), "Inferring the rank of a matrix", Journal of Econometrics 76:223–250.

Day, R.H. (1965), "Probability distributions of field crop yields", Journal of Farm Economics 47:713–741.

de Janvry, A. (1972), "Optimal Levels of fertilization under risk: The potential for corn and wheat fertilization under alternative price policies in Argentina", American Journal of Agricultural Economics 54:1–10.

de Koning G.H.J., H. Van Keulen, R. Rabbinge and H. Hanssen (1995), "Determination of input and output coefficients of cropping systems in the European Community", Agricultural Systems 48:485–502.

Debreu, G. (1959), Theory of Value (Wiley, New York).

Deininger, K., and G. Feder (2001), "Land institutions and land markets", in: B. Gardner and G. Rausser, eds., Handbook of Agricultural Economics, Vol. 1 (Elsevier, Amsterdam) 287–331.

Diewert, W.E. (1974), "Applications of duality theory", in: M.D. Intrilligator and D.A. Kendrick, eds., Frontiers of Quantitative Economics, Vol. II (North-Holland, Amsterdam) 106–199.

Diewert, W.E. (1976), "Exact and superlative index numbers", Journal of Econometrics 4:115–145.

Diewert, W.E. (1982), "Duality approaches to microeconomic theory", in: K. Arrow and M. Intrilligator, eds., Handbook of Mathematical Economics, Vol. 2 (North-Holland, Amsterdam).

Diewert, W.E., and T.J. Wales (1987), "Flexible functional forms and global curvature conditions", Econometrica 55:43–68.

Dhrymes, P.J. (1973), "Restricted and unrestricted reduced forms: Asymptotic distribution and relative efficiency", Econometrica 41:119–134.

Doll, J. (1967), "An analytical technique for estimating weather indexes from meteorological measurement", American Journal of Agricultural Economics 49:79–88.

Eeckhoudt, L., and C. Gollier (1992), Risk: Evaluation, Management and Sharing (Harvester Wheatsheaf, New York).

Economic Research Service (1999a), Corn Costs and Returns: 1997–98 Costs of Production from the Agricultural Resource Management Study (U.S. Government Printing Office, Washington D.C.).

Economic Research Service (1999b), Soybean Costs and Returns: 1997–98 Costs of Production from the Agricultural Resource Management Study (U.S. Government Printing Office, Washington D.C.).

Economic Research Service (various years), Wheat Yearbook (U.S. Government Printing Office, Washington D.C.).

Evenson, R.E. (2001), "Economic impacts of agricultural research and extension", in: B. Gardner and G. Rausser, eds., Handbook of Agricultural Economics, Vol. 1 (Elsevier, Amsterdam) 573–628.

Färe, R. (1996), "The opportunity cost of duality", Journal of Productivity Analysis 7:213–224.

Farrell, M.J. (1957), "The measurement of productive efficiency", Journal of the Royal Statistical Society, Series A, General 120:253–281.

Feder, G. (1979), "Pesticides, information, and pest management under uncertainty", American Journal of Agricultural Economics 61:97–103.

Feder, G., R.E. Just and D. Zilberman (1985), "Adoption of agricultural innovations in developing countries: A survey", Economic Development and Cultural Change 33:255–298.

Fisher, I. (1922), The Making of Index Numbers (Houghton Mifflin, Boston).

Foster, A.D., and M.R. Rosenzweig (1995), "Learning by doing and learning from others: Human capital and technical change in agriculture", Journal of Political Economy 103:1176–1209.

Foster, K.A., and O.R. Burt (1992), "A dynamic model of investment in the U.S. beef-cattle industry", Journal of Business and Economic Statistics 10:419–426.

French, B., G. King and D. Minami (1985), "Planting removal relationships for perennial crops: An application to cling peaches", American Journal of Agricultural Economics 67:215–223.

Fried, H.O., C.A.K. Lovell and S.S. Schmidt (1993), The Measurement of Productive Efficiency: Techniques and Applications (Oxford University Press, Oxford).

Fuss, M.A. (1977), "The structure of technology over time: A model for testing the putty-clay hypothesis", Econometrica 45:1797–1821.

Griliches, Z. (1963), "The sources of measured productivity growth: U.S. agriculture, 1940–1960", Journal of Political Economy 71:309–322.

Hicks, J.R. (1956), A Revision of Demand Theory (Oxford University Press, London).

Hochman, E., and D. Zilberman (1978), "Examination of environmental policies using production and pollution microparameter distributions", Econometrica 46:739–760.

Horowitz, J.K., and E. Lichtenberg (1993), "Insurance, moral hazard, and chemical use in agriculture", American Journal of Agricultural Economics 75:926–935.

Hueth, D., and U. Regev (1974), "Optimal agricultural pest management with increasing pest resistance", American Journal Agricultural Economics 56:543–552.

Huffman, W.E. (2001), "Human capital: Education and agriculture", in: B. Gardner and G. Rausser, eds., Handbook of Agricultural Economics, Vol. 1 (Elsevier, Amsterdam) 333–381.

Jensen, H. (1977), "Farm management and production economics, 1946–70", in: Lee Martin, ed., A Survey of Agricultural Economics Literature (University of Minneapolis Press, Minneapolis).

Jensen, F.E., J.S. Lawson and L.N. Langemeier (1993), "Agricultural investment and internal cash flow variables", Review of Agricultural Economics 15:295–306.

Johansen, L. (1972), "Production functions: An integration of micro and macro, short-run and long-run aspects" (North-Holland, Amsterdam).

Johnson, G.L. (1955), "Results from production economics analysis", Journal of Farm Economics 37:206–222.

Johnson, G.L. (1956), "Supply functions – some facts and notions", in: E. Heady et al., eds, Agricultural Adjustment Problems in a Growing Economy (Iowa State University, Ames).

Johnson, G.L., and L.C. Quance (1972), The Overproduction Trap in U.S. Agriculture (Johns Hopkins University Press, Baltimore).

Just, R.E. (1974), "An Investigation of the importance of risk in farmers' decisions", American Journal of Agricultural Economics 56:14–25.

Just, R.E., and J.M. Antle (1990), "Interactions between agricultural and environmental policies: A conceptual framework", American Economic Review 80:197–202.

Just, R.E., and W. Candler (1985), "Production functions and rationality of mixed cropping: The Nigerian case", European Review of Agricultural Economics 12:207–231.

Just, R.E., and R.D. Pope (1978), "Stochastic specification of production functions and economic implications", Journal of Econometrics 7:67–86.

Just, R.E., and R.D. Pope (1979), "Production function estimation and related risk considerations", American Journal Agricultural Economics 61:276–283.

Just, R.E., and R.D. Pope (1999), "Implications of heterogeneity for theory and practice in production economics", American Journal of Agricultural Economics 81:711–718.

Just, R.E., and G.C. Rausser (1983), "Applied commodity price analysis, forecasting, and market risk management", NCR-134 Conference (Des Moines, IA).

Just, R.E., and Q. Weninger (1999), "Are crop yields normally distributed?", American Journal of Agricultural Economics 81:287–304.

Just, R.E., and D. Zilberman (1983), "Stochastic structure, farm size, and technology adoption in developing agriculture", Oxford Economic Papers 35:307–328.

Just, R.E., D. Zilberman and E. Hochman (1983), "Estimation of multicrop production functions", American Journal Agricultural Economics 65:770–780.

Just, R.E., D. Zilberman, E. Hochman and Z. Bar-Shira (1990), "Input allocation in multicrop systems", American Journal Agricultural Economics 72:200–209.

Kahneman, D., and A. Tversky (1979), "Prospect theory: An analysis of decision under risk", Econometrica 47:263–291.

Keplinger, K.O., B.A. McCarl, M.E. Chowdhury and R.D. Lacewell (1998), "Economic and hydrologic implications of implementing a dry year option for the Edwards aquifer", Journal of Agricultural and Resource Economics 23:191–205.

Klein, L.R. (1947), "The use of cross-section data in econometrics with application to a study of production of railroad services in the united states" (National Bureau of Economic Research, Washington D.C.).

Knudsen, N. (1973), Production and Cost Models of a Multi Product Firm (Odense University Press, Odense, Denmark).

Kutcher, G.P., and P. Scandizzo (1981), The Agricultural Economy of Northeast Brazil (Johns Hopkins Press, Baltimore).

Lau, L.J. (1978), "Applications of profit functions", in: M. Fuss and D. McFadden, eds., Production Economics: A Dual Approach to Theory and Applications (North-Holland, Amsterdam) 133–216.

Leathers, H. (1991), "Allocatable fixed inputs as a cause of joint production: A cost function approach", American Journal of Agricultural Economics 73:1083–1090.

Leontief, W. (1971), "Theoretical assumptions and nonobserved facts", American Economic Review 41:1–7.

Loehman, E., and C. Nelson (1992), "Optimal risk management, risk aversion, and production function properties", Journal of Agricultural and Resource Economics 17:219–231.

Love, H.A., and S. Buccola (1991), "Joint risk preference-technology estimation with a primal system", American Journal of Agricultural Economics 73:763–773.

Machina, M.J. (1987), "Choice under uncertainty: Problems solved and unsolved", Journal of Economic Perspectives 1:121–154.

McCarl, B.A., W.V. Candler, D.H. Doster and P.R. Robbins (1977), "Experiences with farmer oriented linear programming for crop planning", Canadian Journal of Agricultural Economics 25:17–30.

McCloskey, D. (1998), The Rhetoric of Economics, 2nd edn. (University of Wisconsin Press, Madison).

McElroy, M. (1987), "Additive general error models for production, cost, and derived demand or share systems", Journal of Political Economy 95:737–757.

McFadden, D. (1978), "Cost, revenue and profit functions", in: M. Fuss and D. McFadden, eds., Production Economics: A Dual Approach to Theory and Applications (North-Holland, Amsterdam).

McQuigg, J.D., and J.P. Doll (1961), "Economic analysis involving random weather inputs,", Journal of Farm Economics 43:909–20.

Mittelhammer, R.C., S.C. Matulich and D. Bushaw (1981), "On implicit forms of multiproduct-multifactor production functions", American Journal of Agricultural Economics 63:164–168.

Morrison, C.J., and D. Siegel (1998), "Knowledge capital and cost structure in U.S. food and fiber industries", American Journal of Agricultural Economics 80:30–45.

Moschini, G. (forthcoming), "Production risk and the estimation of ex-ante cost functions", Journal of Econometrics.

Moschini, G., and D.A. Hennessy (2001), "Uncertainty, risk aversion, and risk management for agricultural producers", in: B. Gardner and G. Rausser, eds., Handbook of Agricultural Economics, Vol. 1 (Elsevier, Amsterdam) 87–153.

Mundlak, Y. (1996), "Production function estimation: Reviving the primal", Econometrica 64:431–438.

Mundlak, Y. (2001), "Production and supply", in: B. Gardner and G. Rausser, eds., Handbook of Agricultural Economics, Vol. 1 (Elsevier, Amsterdam) 3–85.

Nelson, C.H., and P. Preckel (1989), "The conditional beta distribution as a stochastic production function", American Journal of Agricultural Economics 71:370–378.

Nerlove, M. (1983), "Expectations, plans and realizations in theory and practice", Econometrica 51:1251–1279.

Nerlove, M., and D.A. Bessler (2001), "Expectations, information and dynamics", in: B. Gardner and G. Rausser, eds., Handbook of Agricultural Economics, Vol. 1 (Elsevier, Amsterdam) 155–206.

Pfouts, R.W. (1961), "The theory of cost and production in the multiproduct firm", Econometrica 39:650–668.

Paris, Q. (1992), "The von Liebig hypothesis", American Journal of Agricultural Economics 74:1019–1028.

Paris, Q., and R. Howitt (1998), "An analysis of ill-posed production problems using maximum entropy", American Journal of Agricultural Economics 80:124–138.

Pope, R. (1976), "An analysis of factors affecting farm diversification: With special reference to San Joaquin Valley crop farms", Unpublished Ph.D. Dissertation (University of California, Berkeley).

Pope, R., and R. Chambers (1989), "Price aggregation when price-taking firms' prices vary", Review of Economic Studies 56:297–310.

Pope, R., and A. Hallam (1986), "A confusion of agricultural economists? A profession interest survey and essay", American Journal of Agricultural Economics 68:572–594.

Pope, R.D., and R.E. Just (1991), "On testing the structure of risk preferences in agricultural supply analysis", American Journal of Agricultural Economics 73:743–748.

Pope, R.D., and R.E. Just (1996), "Empirical implementation of ex ante cost functions", Journal of Econometrics 25:231–249.

Pope, R.D., and R.E. Just (1998), "Cost function estimation under risk aversion", American Journal of Agricultural Economics 80:296–302.

Pope, R.D., and R.E. Just (2000a), "Random profits with duality", Working paper (Brigham Young University and University of Maryland).

Pope, R.D., and R.E. Just (2000b), "Distinguishing errors in measurement from errors in optimization", Working paper (Brigham Young University and University of Maryland).

Pope, R., and R. Prescott (1980), "Diversification in relation to farm size and other socioeconomic characteristics", American Journal of Agricultural Economics 62:554–559.

Quiggin, J. (1982), "A theory of anticipated utility", Journal of Economic Behavior and Organization 3:323–343.

Regev, U., N. Gotsch and P. Rieder (1997), "Are fungicides, nitrogen, and plant growth regulators risk-reducing? Empirical evidence from Swiss wheat production", Journal of Agricultural Economics 48:167–178.

Samuelson, P.A. (1967), Foundations of Economic Analysis (Atheneum, New York).

Saha, A., C.R. Shumway and H. Talpaz (1994), "Joint estimation of risk preference structure and technology using expo-power utility", American Journal of Agricultural Economics 76:173–184.

Salin, V., A. Thurow, K. Smith and N. Elmer (1998), "Exploring the market for agricultural economics information: Views of private sector analysis", Review of Agricultural Economics 20:114–124.

Schultz, T.P. (2001), "Women's roles in the agricultural household: Bargaining and human capital investments", in: B. Gardner and G. Rausser, eds., Handbook of Agricultural Economics, Vol. 1 (Elsevier, Amsterdam) 383–456.

Shumway, C.R. (1983), "Supply, demand, and technology in a multi-product industry: Texas field crops", American Journal of Agricultural Economics 65:748–760.

Shumway, C.R. (1988), "The statistical base for agricultural productivity research: A review and critique", in: S.M. Capalbo and J.M. Antle, eds., Agricultural Productivity Measurement and Explanation (Resources for the Future, Washington, D.C.) 138–156.

Shumway, C.R. (1995), "Recent duality contributions in production economics", Journal of Agricultural and Resource Economics 20:178–194.

Shumway, C.R., and H. Lim (1993), "Functional form and U.S. agricultural production elasticities", Journal of Agricultural and Resource Economics 18:330–337.

Shumway, C.R., R.D. Pope and E.K. Nash (1984), "Allocatable fixed inputs and jointness in agricultural production: Implications for economic modeling", American Journal of Agricultural Economics 66:72–78.

Smale, M., R.E. Just and H.D. Leathers (1994), "Land allocation in hyv adoption models: An investigation of alternative explanations", American Journal of Agricultural Economics 76:535–546.

Sunding, D., and D. Zilberman (2001), "The agricultural innovation process: Research and technology adoption in a changing agricultural sector", in: B. Gardner and G. Rausser, eds., Handbook of Agricultural Economics, Vol. 1 (Elsevier, Amsterdam) 207–261.

United States Senate (1987), Hearings before the Committee on Agriculture, Nutrition, and Forestry, Federal Insecticide, Fungicide, and Rodenticide Act, 100th Congress, First Session, S. 1516, Part II, April 29, May 20, and July 30, p. 188–189.

Vanker, R.D. (1996), "Hypothesis tests using data envelopment analysis", Journal of Productivity Analysis 7:139–160.

Varian, H. (1992), Microeconomic Analysis, 3rd edn. (W.W. Norton and Co., New York).

Vasavada, U., and V.E. Ball (1988), "A dynamic investment model within a multi-commodity framework", Agricultural Economics 2:123–137.

Vasavada, U., and R.G. Chambers (1986), "Investment in agriculture", American Journal of Agricultural Economics 68:939–949.

Viner, J. (1931), "Cost curves and supply curves", Zeitschrift für Nationalökonomie and Statistik 3:23–46.

Weaver, R. (1983), "Multiple input, multiple output production choices and technology in the U.S. wheat region", American Journal of Agricultural Economics 65:45–56.

White, T., and G. Irwin (1972), "Farm size and specialization", in: G. Ball and E. Heady, eds., Size, Structure and Future of Farms (Iowa State University Press, Ames).

Wolf, S., D.R. Just and D. Zilberman (forthcoming), "Between data and decisions: The organization of agricultural economic information systems", Research Policy.

Woodward, S. (1996), "A dynamic nutrient carryover model for pastoral soils and its application to optimising fertiliser allocation to several blocks with a cost constraint", Review of Marketing and Agricultural Economics 64:75–85.

AUTHOR INDEX

n indicates citation in footnote.

SUBJECT INDEX

HANDBOOKS IN ECONOMICS

1. HANDBOOK OF MATHEMATICAL ECONOMICS (in 4 volumes)
   Volumes 1, 2 and 3 edited by Kenneth J. Arrow and Michael D. Intriligator
   Volume 4 edited by Werner Hildenbrand and Hugo Sonnenschein

2. HANDBOOK OF ECONOMETRICS (in 6 volumes)
   Volumes 1, 2 and 3 edited by Zvi Griliches and Michael D. Intriligator
   Volume 4 edited by Robert F. Engle and Daniel L. McFadden
   Volume 5 edited by James J. Heckman and Edward Leamer
   Volume 6 is in preparation (editors James J. Heckman and Edward Leamer)

3. HANDBOOK OF INTERNATIONAL ECONOMICS (in 3 volumes)
   Volumes 1 and 2 edited by Ronald W. Jones and Peter B. Kenen
   Volume 3 edited by Gene M. Grossman and Kenneth Rogoff

4. HANDBOOK OF PUBLIC ECONOMICS (in 4 volumes)
   Volumes 1 and 2 edited by Alan J. Auerbach and Martin Feldstein
   2 volumes in preparation (editors Alan J. Auerbach and Martin Feldstein)

5. HANDBOOK OF LABOR ECONOMICS (in 5 volumes)
   Volumes 1 and 2 edited by Orley C. Ashenfelter and Richard Layard
   Volumes 3A, 3B and 3C edited by Orley C. Ashenfelter and David Card

6. HANDBOOK OF NATURAL RESOURCE AND ENERGY ECONOMICS
   (in 3 volumes). Edited by Allen V. Kneese and James L. Sweeney

7. HANDBOOK OF REGIONAL AND URBAN ECONOMICS (in 3 volumes)
   Volume 1 edited by Peter Nijkamp
   Volume 2 edited by Edwin S. Mills
   Volume 3 edited by Paul C. Cheshire and Edwin S. Mills

8. HANDBOOK OF MONETARY ECONOMICS (in 2 volumes)
   Edited by Benjamin Friedman and Frank Hahn

9. HANDBOOK OF DEVELOPMENT ECONOMICS (in 4 volumes)
   Volumes 1 and 2 edited by Hollis B. Chenery and T.N. Srinivasan
   Volumes 3A and 3B edited by Jere Behrman and T.N. Srinivasan

10. HANDBOOK OF INDUSTRIAL ORGANIZATION (in 3 volumes)
    Volumes 1 and 2 edited by Richard Schmalensee and Robert R. Willig
    Volume 3 is in preparation (editors Mark Armstrong and Robert H. Porter)

11. HANDBOOK OF GAME THEORY with Economic Applications (in 3 volumes)
    Volumes 1 and 2 edited by Robert J. Aumann and Sergiu Hart
    Volume 3 is in preparation (editors Robert J. Aumann and Sergiu Hart)

12. HANDBOOK OF DEFENSE ECONOMICS (in 1 volume)
    Edited by Keith Hartley and Todd Sandler

13. HANDBOOK OF COMPUTATIONAL ECONOMICS (in 1 volume)
    Edited by Hans M. Amman, David A. Kendrick and John Rust

14. HANDBOOK OF POPULATION AND FAMILY ECONOMICS (in 2 volumes)
    Edited by Mark R. Rosenzweig and Oded Stark

15. HANDBOOK OF MACROECONOMICS (in 3 volumes)
    Edited by John B. Taylor and Michael Woodford

16. HANDBOOK OF INCOME DISTRIBUTION (in 1 volume)
    Edited by Anthony B. Atkinson and François Bourguignon

17. HANDBOOK OF HEALTH ECONOMICS (in 2 volumes)
    Edited by Anthony J. Culyer and Joseph P. Newhouse

18. HANDBOOK OF AGRICULTURAL ECONOMICS (in 3 volumes)
    Volumes 1A and 1B edited by Bruce L. Gardner and Gordon C. Rausser
    Volume 2 is in preparation (editors Bruce L. Gardner and Gordon C. Rausser)

FORTHCOMING TITLES

HANDBOOK OF SOCIAL CHOICE AND WELFARE ECONOMICS
Editors Kenneth J. Arrow, Amartya K. Sen and Kotaro Suzumura

HANDBOOK OF RESULTS IN EXPERIMENTAL ECONOMICS
Editors Charles Plott and Vernon L. Smith

HANDBOOK OF ENVIRONMENTAL ECONOMICS
Editors Karl-Goran Mäler and Jeff Vincent

HANDBOOK OF THE ECONOMICS OF FINANCE
Editors George M. Constantinides, Milton Harris and René M. Stulz

HANDBOOK ON THE ECONOMICS OF GIVING, RECIPROCITY AND ALTRUISM
Editors Serge-Christophe Kolm and Jean Mercier Ythier

HANDBOOK ON THE ECONOMICS OF ART AND CULTURE
Editors Victor Ginsburgh and David Throsby

HANDBOOK ON ECONOMIC GROWTH
Editors Philippe Aghion and Steven N. Durlauf

All published volumes available

HANDBOOKS IN ECONOMICS

1. HANDBOOK OF MATHEMATICAL ECONOMICS (in 4 volumes)
   Volumes 1, 2 and 3 edited by Kenneth J. Arrow and Michael D. Intriligator
   Volume 4 edited by Werner Hildenbrand and Hugo Sonnenschein

2. HANDBOOK OF ECONOMETRICS (in 6 volumes)
   Volumes 1, 2 and 3 edited by Zvi Griliches and Michael D. Intriligator
   Volume 4 edited by Robert F. Engle and Daniel L. McFadden
   Volume 5 edited by James J. Heckman and Edward Leamer
   Volume 6 is in preparation (editors James J. Heckman and Edward Leamer)

3. HANDBOOK OF INTERNATIONAL ECONOMICS (in 3 volumes)
   Volumes 1 and 2 edited by Ronald W. Jones and Peter B. Kenen
   Volume 3 edited by Gene M. Grossman and Kenneth Rogoff

4. HANDBOOK OF PUBLIC ECONOMICS (in 4 volumes)
   Volumes 1 and 2 edited by Alan J. Auerbach and Martin Feldstein
   2 volumes in preparation (editors Alan J. Auerbach and Martin Feldstein)

5. HANDBOOK OF LABOR ECONOMICS (in 5 volumes)
   Volumes 1 and 2 edited by Orley C. Ashenfelter and Richard Layard
   Volumes 3A, 3B and 3C edited by Orley C. Ashenfelter and David Card

6. HANDBOOK OF NATURAL RESOURCE AND ENERGY ECONOMICS
   (in 3 volumes). Edited by Allen V. Kneese and James L. Sweeney

7. HANDBOOK OF REGIONAL AND URBAN ECONOMICS (in 3 volumes)
   Volume 1 edited by Peter Nijkamp
   Volume 2 edited by Edwin S. Mills
   Volume 3 edited by Paul C. Cheshire and Edwin S. Mills

8. HANDBOOK OF MONETARY ECONOMICS (in 2 volumes)
   Edited by Benjamin Friedman and Frank Hahn

9. HANDBOOK OF DEVELOPMENT ECONOMICS (in 4 volumes)
   Volumes 1 and 2 edited by Hollis B. Chenery and T.N. Srinivasan
   Volumes 3A and 3B edited by Jere Behrman and T.N. Srinivasan

10. HANDBOOK OF INDUSTRIAL ORGANIZATION (in 3 volumes)
    Volumes 1 and 2 edited by Richard Schmalensee and Robert R. Willig
    Volume 3 is in preparation (editors Mark Armstrong and Robert H. Porter)

FORTHCOMING TITLES

All published volumes available